W9-AAC-983
McGraw-Hill Ryerson

Higher Learning. Forward Thinking.™

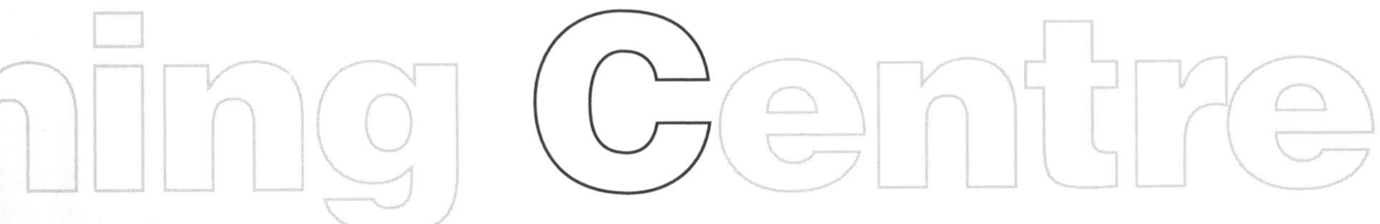
ning Centre

For the Student

Quiz Questions

Do you understand the material? You'll know after taking an Online Quiz! Try the Multiple Choice and True/False questions for each chapter. They're auto-graded with feedback and the option to send results directly to faculty.

Web Links

This section references various Web sites, including all company Web sites linked from the text.

Internet Resources and Questions

Go online to learn how companies use the Internet in their day-to-day activities. Answer questions based on current organization Web sites and strategies.

Microsoft® PowerPoint® Presentations

View and download presentations created for each chapter. Great for pre-class preparation and post-class review.

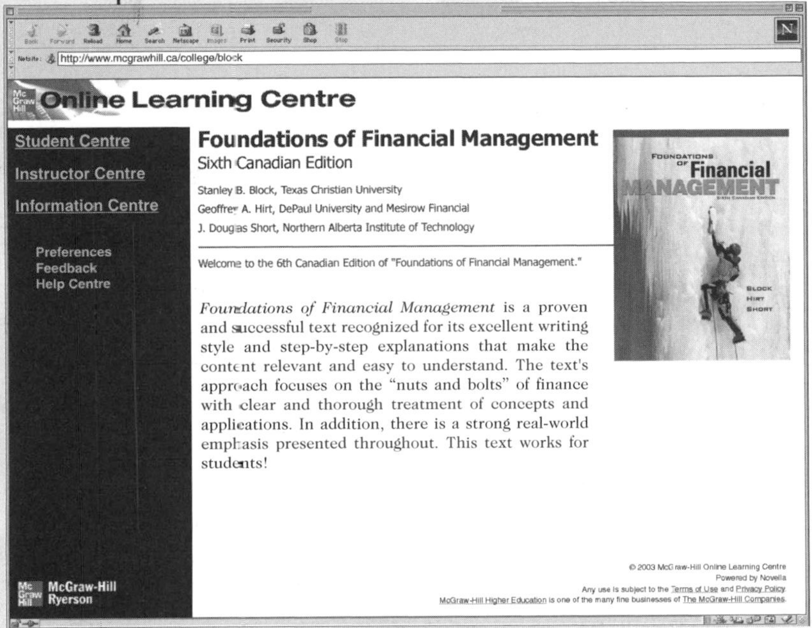
http://www.mcgrawhill.ca/college/block
Online Learning Centre
Student Centre
Instructor Centre
Information Centre
Preferences
Feedback
Help Centre
Foundations of Financial Management
Sixth Canadian Edition
Stanley B. Block, Texas Christian University
Geoffrey A. Hirt, DePaul University and Mesirow Financial
J. Douglas Short, Northern Alberta Institute of Technology
Welcome to the 6th Canadian Edition of "Foundations of Financial Management."
Foundations of Financial Management is a proven and successful text recognized for its excellent writing style and step-by-step explanations that make the content relevant and easy to understand. The text's approach focuses on the "nuts and bolts" of finance with clear and thorough treatment of concepts and applications. In addition, there is a strong real-world emphasis presented throughout. This text works for students!
Financial Management
Block Hirt Short
McGraw-Hill Ryerson

Your Internet companion to the most exciting educational tools on the Web!

The Online Learning Centre can be found at:
www.mcgrawhill.ca/college/block

Foundations of Financial Management

Sixth Canadian Edition

Stanley B. Block
Texas Christian University

Geoffrey A. Hirt
DePaul University and Mesirow Financial

J. Douglas Short
Northern Alberta Institute of Technology

Toronto Montréal Boston Burr Ridge, IL Dubuque, IA Madison, WI
New York San Francisco St. Louis Bangkok Bogotá Caracas Kuala Lumpur Lisbon London
Madrid Mexico City Milan New Delhi Santiago Seoul Singapore Sydney Taipei

McGraw-Hill
Ryerson Limited

A Subsidiary of The ***McGraw-Hill*** *Companies*

FOUNDATIONS OF FINANCIAL MANAGEMENT
Sixth Canadian Edition

ISBN: 0-07-089762-X

3 4 5 6 7 8 9 10 TCP 0 9 8 7 6 5 4

Printed and bound in Canada

Vice President and Editorial Director: *Pat Ferrier*
Senior Sponsoring Editor: *Lynn Fisher*
Developmental Editor: *Maria Chu*
Marketing Manager: *Kelly Smyth*
Supervising Editor: *Anne Macdonald*
Copy Editor: *Karen Hunter*
Production Coordinator: *Madeleine Harrington*
Composition: *GAC Indy Graphics*
Cover Design: *Greg Devitt*
Cover Image Credit: *Kenneth Redding/Imagebank*
Printer: *Transcontinental Printing Group*

National Library of Canada Cataloguing in Publication Data

Block, Stanley B.
Foundations of financial management/Stanley B. Block, Geoffrey A. Hirt, J. Douglas Short.—6th Canadian ed.

Includes bibliographical references and index.
ISBN 0-07-089762-X

1. Corporations—Finance. I. Hirt, Geoffrey A II. Short, J. Douglas III. Title.

HG4026.B56 2002 658.15 C2002-901989-3

To all the diamonds,
that mean everything to me . . .

And to
Baby, Ramlogan, and Paul

J.D.F.S.

Brief Contents

Contents

15 Investment Underwriting: Public and Private Placement 534

16 Long-Term Debt and Lease Financing 560

17 Common and Preferred Stock Financing 608

Preface

Students new to financial management often perceive the finance discipline in the same light as the task before the climber on the cover of this text. Daunting! But rest assured that the climber persevered and made it to the top of the ice wall. You too can find finance a fulfilling challenge by using this text that strives to make the climb as comfortable as possible. ***Foundations of Financial Management*** **is committed to making finance accessible to you.**

In this sixth edition we have made content and presentation revisions to make this text an even better tool for providing you with the skills and confidence you'll need to be an effective financial manager. Concepts are explained in as clear a manner as possible, with numerous "Finance in Action" boxes highlighting real world examples and employing Internet resources to reinforce and illustrate these concepts. The extensive and varied problem material examines these concepts in more detail. In the sixth edition, as always, we remain strongly committed to presenting the concepts of finance in an enlightening, interesting, and exciting manner. This text continues to work for you the student.

Reinforcing Prerequisite Knowledge

Employers of business graduates report that the most successful analysts, planners, and executives have both ability and confidence in their financial skills. We couldn't agree more. One of the best ways to increase your ability in financial planning is to integrate knowledge from prerequisite courses. Therefore, this text is designed to build on students' knowledge from basic courses in accounting and economics, with some statistics. By applying the tools learned in these courses, you can develop a conceptual and analytical understanding of financial management.

For some of you, time has passed since you've completed your accounting courses. Therefore, included in Chapter 2, is a thorough review of accounting principles, finance terminology, and financial statements. With a working knowledge of Chapter 2, you will have a more complete understanding of financial statements, the impact of your decisions on financial statements, and how financial statements can serve you in making effective financial decisions. Furthermore, as you are about to begin your career you will be much better prepared when called on to apply financial concepts.

Module Format Adds Flexibility

Foundations of Financial Management covers virtually every possible topic taught in a financial management course. However it is almost impossible to cover every topic included in this text, within one course. Therefore this book has been carefully crafted to ensure a flexibility that accommodates different course syllabuses and a variety of teaching approaches. We have encouraged instructors to use a format with the text that they find works best for them and for you. After using this text, you may find yourself referring back to those topics that time did not permit you to cover or perhaps to reexamine some of the concepts that you are exploring once again.

Financial management's three basic concerns are the management of working capital, the effective allocation of capital by means of the capital budgeting decision, and the raising of long-term capital with an appropriate capital structure. These topics are covered in Parts 3, 4, and 5 of the text. The introduction to financial management in Part 1 and financial analysis and planning in Part 2 precede these central parts. A broader perspective on finance is addressed in Part 6 of the text.

New Features and Improvements

Integration When applicable we have tried to tie concepts together across chapters. For example:

- The dynamic role of the financial markets in allocating capital, assessing risks, and determining returns is highlighted when appropriate. Examples are found in Chapters 1, 3, 10, 11, and 14.
- The expanded internationalization of the financial markets is a consistent theme, with specific references to the euro, the devaluation of Argentina's peso, and deflation in Japan, found in Chapter 21. Other international examples can be found in Chapters 1, 8, 13, 14, 17, and 19.
- Cost/benefit analysis to emphasize increased value is highlighted in Chapters 7, 12, and 16.
- Leverage in Chapter 5 is connected to the income statement of Chapter 2 and the risks of increased debt in Chapter 16.
- The cash flow cycle of Chapter 6 is tied into the ratio formulas of Chapter 3.

More worked examples Key illustrations are added for hedging (Chapter 6), cash management (Chapter 7), the dividend capitalization model (Chapter 10), and the costs of flotation spread and dilution (Chapter 15).

Simplification If concepts can be simplified it is an improvement. Some examples include:

- The formulas in Chapter 8.
- Deletion of the graphical presentation of time value relationships from Chapter 9.

- Use of the spread as a percentage for flotation cost adjustments in the cost of capital calculation in Chapter 11.
- Deletion of considerable share for share discussion and illustration from Chapter 20.

Tighter focus When appropriate we have tried for a clearer focus in some material. This is evident in:

- **Chapter 1: The Goals and Functions of Financial Management** with a focus on valuation as a role for finance.
- **Chapter 3: Financial Analysis** with a clarified and more user friendly Du Pont method. It also expands on the number of asset utilization ratios.
- **Chapter 14: Capital Markets** with more focused illustrations and an update of the changing financial marketplace.
- **Chapter 19: Derivatives, Convertibles, and Warrants** updates the accounting treatment of warrants.
- **Chapter 21: International Financial Management** includes a discussion of the euro.

Real World Examples Recent "big" names in the news are used for illustrations. These include:

- Nortel in Chapter 3 (big write-offs), Chapter 7 (vendor financing), and Chapter 10 (valuation).
- Enron in Chapter 14 discussing its impact on market efficiency and the fairness of the markets.
- September 11th in Chapter 1 for its impact on financial markets and in Chapter 13 for its influence on risk.

Finance in Action Boxes A popular feature of the text, these now include questions that often require the use of an Internet site and sometimes a stock symbol to find appropriate information related to the chapter material. For example, see Chapter 1, page 18 and Chapter 7, page 227.

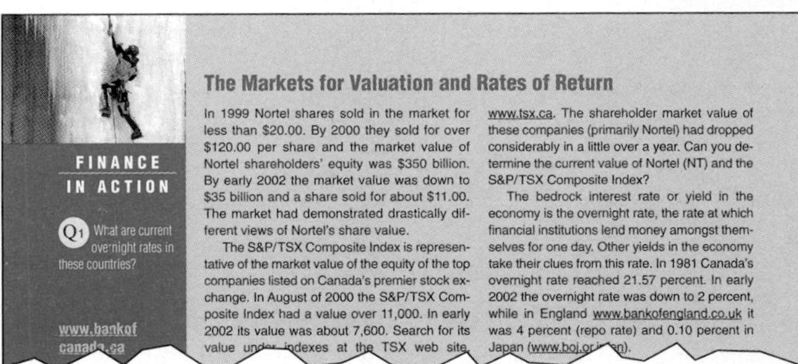

FINANCE IN ACTION

Q1 What are current overnight rates in these countries?

www.bankofcanada.ca

The Markets for Valuation and Rates of Return

In 1999 Nortel shares sold in the market for less than $20.00. By 2000 they sold for over $120.00 per share and the market value of Nortel shareholders' equity was $350 billion. By early 2002 the market value was down to $35 billion and a share sold for about $11.00. The market had demonstrated drastically different views of Nortel's share value.

The S&P/TSX Composite Index is representative of the market value of the equity of the top companies listed on Canada's premier stock exchange. In August of 2000 the S&P/TSX Composite Index had a value over 11,000. In early 2002 its value was about 7,600. Search for its value un[illegible] indexes at the TSX web site www.tsx.ca. The shareholder market value of these companies (primarily Nortel) had dropped considerably in a little over a year. Can you determine the current value of Nortel (NT) and the S&P/TSX Composite Index?

The bedrock interest rate or yield in the economy is the overnight rate, the rate at which financial institutions lend money amongst themselves for one day. Other yields in the economy take their clues from this rate. In 1981 Canada's overnight rate reached 21.57 percent. In early 2002 the overnight rate was down to 2 percent, while in England www.bankofengland.co.uk it was 4 percent (repo rate) and 0.10 percent in Japan (www.boj.or[illegible]).

Small Business Icons Small business references and examples are highlighted throughout the text with an icon.

Calculator Icons Have been added to this edition of the text to highlight where a financial calculator can be used.

Pedagogy

To provide guidance and insights throughout the text, we've made use of a number of proven pedagogical aids, including:

- **Learning Objectives** At the beginning of each chapter learning objectives will help focus your learning as you proceed through the material. The summary of each chapter responds to each of these objectives.

LEARNING | OBJECTIVES

1 Calculate 13 financial ratios that measure profitability, asset utilization, liquidity, and debt utilization.

2 Assess a company's source of profitability using the DuPont system of analysis.

3 Examine the ratios in comparison to industry averages.

4 Examine the ratios and company performance by means of trend analysis.

5 Identify sources of distortion in reported income.

- **Calculators** When the use of a calculator is illustrated a calculator icon appears in the margin. Appendix E demonstrates the use of the three most commonly used business calculators, with the illustrations in the text tending to conform to the Sharp calculator. Chapter 9 demonstrates the use of a calculator with time lines, and the use of tables (as an option). The formulas for present value analysis, which are the basis for calculators, tables, or computers, have been included. Answers computed with the calculator will be more accurate, as compared to the tables, due to the rounding of the table factors. A financial calculator tutorial using the TI BAII Plus can be found on the Online Learning Centre for the text at **www.mcgrawhill.ca/college/block**.
- **"Finance in Action" Boxes** These popular boxes address topics related to the chapter subject matter and deal with the difficulties and opportunities in the financial markets. This edition adds questions appropriate to the topic, often requiring Internet searches for background information. Rewarding discussions of current and historical financial events, issues and practices can begin with this material. Most Finance in Action boxes include at least one web site (URL) relevant to the discussion, which will allow for updating the events outlined in the box. Furthermore, when Canadian companies are discussed their stock market ticker "symbol" is included in the Finance in Action box, as several web sites use this symbol to access information on the company.

End-of-Chapter Material

Practice makes perfect. Each chapter concludes with review and problem materials to help students review and apply what they've learned throughout the chapter. Well over 90 percent of the problems are new or revised from the Fifth Edition.

Summary

1. Financial forecasting allows the financial manager to anticipate events before they occur, particularly the need for raising funds externally. Growth itself may call for additional sources of financing because profit is often inadequate to cover the net buildup in receivables, inventory, and other asset accounts.
2. We develop pro forma financial statements from an overall corporate systems viewpoint. Today computerized spreadsheets greatly facilitate this process. The time perspective is usually six months to a year in the future. In developing a pro forma income statement, we begin by making sales projections; then, we construct a production plan. Finally, we consider all other expenses.

- **Summary** Each chapter ends with a Summary that ties the material back to the specific chapter objectives presented at the beginning of the chapter.

- **Review of Formulas** At the end of every chapter that includes formulas, a list of all formulas used in that chapter is provided for easy reviewing purposes. The formulas from all chapters are included on the tear out perforated **card** that comes with the text.

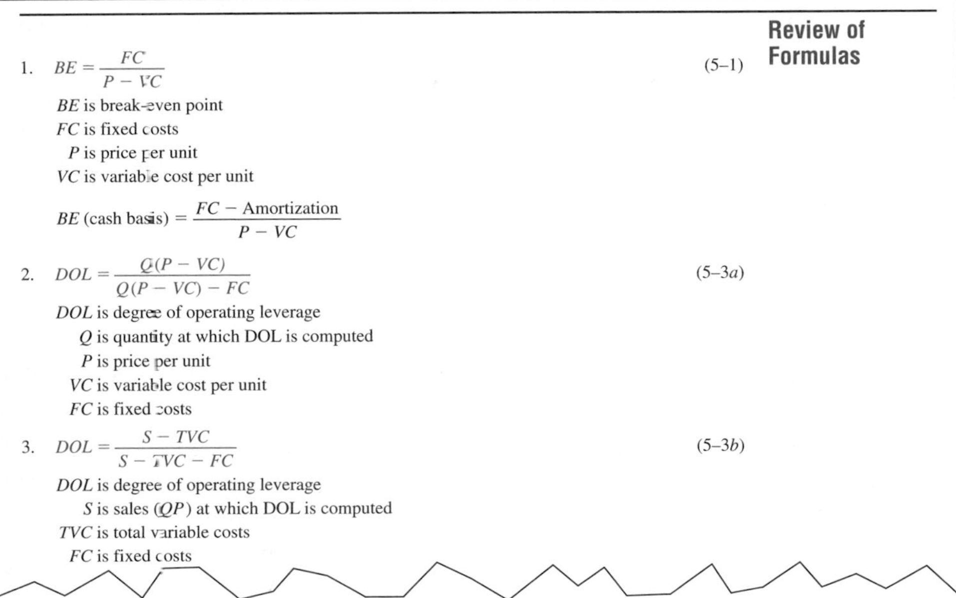

Review of Formulas

1. $BE = \frac{FC}{P - VC}$ (5–1)

   BE is break-even point
   FC is fixed costs
   P is price per unit
   VC is variable cost per unit

   $BE \text{ (cash basis)} = \frac{FC - \text{Amortization}}{P - VC}$

2. $DOL = \frac{Q(P - VC)}{Q(P - VC) - FC}$ (5–3*a*)

   DOL is degree of operating leverage
   Q is quantity at which DOL is computed
   P is price per unit
   VC is variable cost per unit
   FC is fixed costs

3. $DOL = \frac{S - TVC}{S - TVC - FC}$ (5–3*b*)

   DOL is degree of operating leverage
   S is sales (*QP*) at which DOL is computed
   TVC is total variable costs
   FC is fixed costs

- **List of Terms** Similarly, you can use the list of key terms provided at the end of each chapter to test your comprehension and retention. Page numbers are provided and the term is also defined in the glossary.

List of Terms

leverage (concept in general) 134
operating leverage 135
fixed costs 136
variable costs 136
contribution margin 137
break-even analysis 141
degree of operating leverage (DOL) 141
nonlinear break-even analysis 144
financial leverage 145
degree of financial leverage (DFL) 147
EBIT/EPS indifference point 149
leveraged buyout 150
combined leverage 151
degree of combined leverage (DCL) 152

- **Internet Resources and Questions** Each chapter has a section that identifies several Internet sites that provide up-to-date information on many of the topics covered in the chapter. The questions that follow encourage you to explore these web sites and to learn about the financial information that is available on the web. Furthermore the questions expand upon the financial concepts and terms discussed in the chapter. Your familiarity with these web sites will expand your skills and your knowledge base, in financial management.

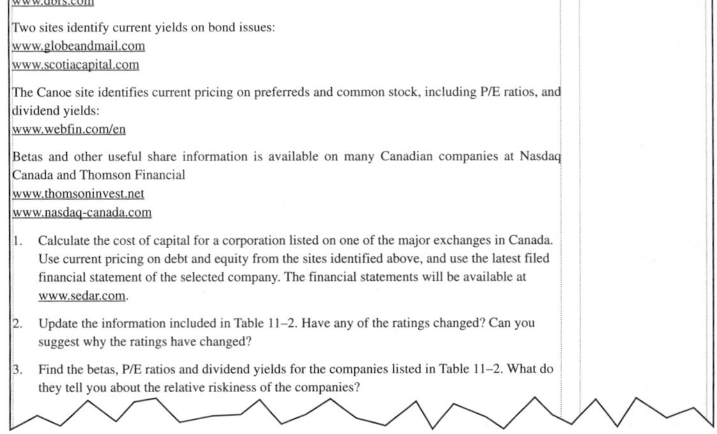

INTERNET RESOURCES AND QUESTIONS

Two Canadian sites rate and grade debt. The ratings determine the spread corporations pay above Government of Canada securities:
www.standardandpoors.com/canada
www.dbrs.com

Two sites identify current yields on bond issues:
www.globeandmail.com
www.scotiacapital.com

The Canoe site identifies current pricing on preferreds and common stock, including P/E ratios, and dividend yields:
www.webfin.com/en

Betas and other useful share information is available on many Canadian companies at Nasdaq Canada and Thomson Financial
www.thomsoninvest.net
www.nasdaq-canada.com

1. Calculate the cost of capital for a corporation listed on one of the major exchanges in Canada. Use current pricing on debt and equity from the sites identified above, and use the latest filed financial statement of the selected company. The financial statements will be available at www.sedar.com.
2. Update the information included in Table 11–2. Have any of the ratings changed? Can you suggest why the ratings have changed?
3. Find the betas, P/E ratios and dividend yields for the companies listed in Table 11–2. What do they tell you about the relative riskiness of the companies?

- **Discussion Questions and Problems** The material in the text is supported by approximately 300 questions and over 500 problems in this sixth edition, to reinforce and test your understanding of the chapter. The problems are a very important part of the text and have been written with care to be consistent with the chapter material. The problems for this edition have been revised, while maintaining the extensive variety and the range of difficulty from previous editions.
- **Comprehensive Problems** Several chapters have Comprehensive Problems that integrate and require the application of several financial concepts into one problem. Some of these comprehensive problems cover several concepts from one or more chapters. For example, see Chapter 3, page 95, Chapter 9, page 316, and Chapter 12, page 460.

Supplemental Material for Students

The Student's Online Learning Centre

The OLC at www.mcgrawhill.ca/college/block includes online study material including Quiz Questions, CBC Video Cases, Web Links, Internet Resources and Questions, Excel Templates (FAST), Learning Objectives, Key Terms and Searchable Glossary, Finance Around the World and more!

Study Guide and Workbook 007-089763-8

This valuable resource, by Dwight C. Anderson and J. Douglas Short provides chapter summaries, and additional problems and multiple-choice questions with solutions to help you better understand financial concepts and to prepare for exams. Ask for it at your bookstore!

Financial Analysis Spreadsheet Templates (FAST)

These templates included with each textbook are designed to help you solve problems using Excel. Several end-of-chapter problems in the text are linked to this software and are indicated with an icon.

Instructional Support

The Instructor's Online Learning Centre

The OLC at www.mcgrawhill.ca/college/block includes a password-protected web site for Instructors. The site offers downloadable supplements and PageOut, the McGraw-Hill Ryerson course web site development centre.

Instructor's CD-ROM

This CD-ROM contains all of the necessary Instructor Supplements, including:

- *Instructor's Manual* Written by the author, this manual integrates the graphs, tables, PowerPoint slides, and problems into a lecture format. Each chapter opens with a brief overview of the chapter and a review of the key learning objectives. The chapter is then outlined in an annotated format to facilitate its use as an in-class reference guide by the instructor. The manual includes *detailed solutions to all problems and questions* at the end of the chapters. The solutions are presented in large type to facilitate their reproduction as transparencies for use in the classroom.

- *Microsoft® PowerPoint® Slide Presentations,* prepared by Terry Fegarty, Seneca College. The PowerPoint package contains relevant tables, figures, and illustrations from the text material that you can customize for your lecture.
- *Computerized Test Bank Software* Prepared by the authors, the test bank includes 1,500 multiple-choice and true-false questions written by the authors according to the revisions of the sixth edition. Additionally there are quiz problems and 10 question matching quizzes, geared to test the student's knowledge of the terms at the end of the chapter. The test bank is available in the Diploma software program. This software includes an easy-to-use menu system that allows quick access to all the powerful features available. The Keyword Search option lets you browse through the question bank for problems containing a specific word or phrase. Questions can be added, deleted or modified.

CBC Video cases, accompanying the text is a series of video segments drawn from CBC broadcasts. These videos have been chosen to visually aid students in tying real-world finance issues to the text, and to illuminate key ideas and concepts presented in the text. A set of instructor notes accompanies the segments available at the Instructor Online Learning Centre. The video segments are available in a VHS format for use in class and through video-streaming on the Online Learning Centre accessible by both instructors and students.

PageOut Visit www.mhhe.com/pageout to create a web page for your course using our resources. PageOut is the McGraw-Hill Ryerson web site development centre. This web-page-generation software is free to adopters and is designed to help faculty create an online course, complete with assignments, quizzes, links to relevant web sites, lecture notes, and more in a matter of minutes.

In addition, content cartridges are also available for course management systems, such as *WebCT* and *Blackboard.*

Acknowledgements

I am indebted to those individuals who have been the source of many improvements in this text through their thoughtful and insightful reviews. I was very impressed by the time and wonderful effort given in those comprehensive reviews. Thank you for the source of stimulation, and I hope I've been able to address most of the concerns you raised and that I have also been able to more effectively present the material, for the benefit of our students. As always I've tried to balance competing visions and still provide the material we need to make our individual styles work in the classroom, and now to some extent in e-space. These individuals include:

Cecile Ashman, Algonquin College
Denny Dombrower, Centennial College
Terry Fegarty, Seneca College
Brian Hobson, Georgian College

Gene Karlik, Red River Community College
Paula McLean, University of Prince Edward Island
Verity Rae, Southern Alberta Institute of Technology
Gabriela Schneider, Grant MacEwan Community College
Zhen Wang, Laurentian University
Erick Wickham, Centennial College
Alison Wiseman, Fanshawe College

A special thank you must be given to Terry Zinger, Laurentian University and Ric Leduc, Fanshawe College for their vigilant efforts as the Technical Reviewers for the text and solutions. Their keen eye and attention to detail has contributed greatly to the quality of the final product.

And this year I was most fortunate to visit some new colleagues at Centennial and Seneca Colleges. I thank them very much for their thoughts and their time. It was a terrific experience and I hope that I have been able to incorporate successfully just a few of their ideas. I look forward to visiting with other instructors in finance in the future.

Special thanks go to two individuals who over several editions have always been there to help find an answer. Robert Short guides me through the capital markets. Mark Woltersdorf simplifies the Income Tax Act and tax practices for my understanding.

The people at RBC Dominion Securities in Toronto have provided invaluable insights into current practices and financial innovations.

For this sixth edition I had wonderful help from Erin Short in the preparation and review of FAST Excel spreadsheets. In addition, Gabriela Schneider made an effective contribution to the presentation of several FAST worksheets.

There are many individuals who contributed in innumerable ways to earlier editions and their efforts live on in this edition. Thank you to H. Allan Conway for his groundwork in preparing the first Canadian edition of this text. I would like to express my gratitude to Stanley B. Block and Geoffrey A. Hirt for the work and care that they continue to put into the U.S. editions of the text. I also appreciate the latitude that they have allowed in adapting the book for the Canadian environment and student.

To my editor Lynn Fisher, my thanks for her commitment to a text focused on the student. Lynn Fisher's efforts to keep me on course were appreciated. Lynn persevered with my personal peccadilloes and I believe we have come up with an even better text with this sixth edition.

To my developmental editor a sincere thanks. Maria Chu juggled with great skill my cut and pastes, e-files, courier deliveries, and phone calls in putting together a workable manuscript.

I would also like to thank Anne Macdonald and Karen Hunter for their terrific attention to detail on the manuscript.

To the marketing representatives a special thanks for doing such a great job of keeping in touch with the current and future users of this text. Call anytime!

Finally, a thanks to my students. I find finance fascinating because it changes everyday and it reflects the future. It is like you.

J. Douglas Short

PART | ONE

INTRODUCTION

CHAPTER 1

The Goals and Functions of Financial Management

Finance is a dynamic, rigorous discipline built on the foundations of accounting and economics. The focus of finance is on increasing value, as measured by market share price, and this theme is played out daily in the world's financial markets. The financial manager performs many functions to enhance value for the shareholder.

CHAPTER | ONE

1 The Goals and Functions of Financial Management

LEARNING | OBJECTIVES

1 Identify how finance builds on the disciplines of accounting and economics.

2 Discuss the analytical decision-making nature of finance within a risk-return framework.

3 Describe the primary goal of finance as the maximization of shareholder wealth as measured by share price.

4 Identify possible conflicting goals of finance such as social goals or management interests.

5 Outline the activities of financial managers that are primarily based on the raising and investing of funds in an efficient manner.

6 Identify the role of financial markets in allocating capital, determining value, and establishing yields.

Today the performance of the financial manager is critical for the firm's success. There is constant change in factors, which are crucial to the firm, such as interest rates, exchange rates, commodity prices, technology, and consumer optimism or pessimism toward the future. These changes immediately affect the firm's cash flows and impact the value of the firm. In today's highly competitive markets, these economic changes put pressure on the firm and on the financial officers to maintain financial viability.

The financial markets value the assets of the firm based on the most productive use of those assets within the context of current market conditions. Financial management is concerned with the determination of value, and to enhance the firm's value, the financial manager must have an astute awareness of the tools of financial management and the sophistication of today's financial markets. As financial markets become more international, the chief financial officer must also manage the global financial affairs of the firm. The board of directors and the president look to the finance department to provide a precious resource—capital—and to manage that resource in an efficient and profitable fashion.

The Field of Finance

Finance is focused on raising capital for the firm, which is then invested to create and to add value. Finance has developed rigorous decision-oriented analysis models. As the field of finance is closely linked to economics and accounting, financial managers need to be familiar with and understand the relationships amongst these disciplines.

Bank of Canada
www.bankofcanada.ca/en/

Economics provides a structure for decision making in such areas as risk analysis, pricing theory through supply and demand relationships, comparative return analysis, and many other important areas. Economics also provides a broad picture of the economic environment in which corporations must continually make decisions. A financial manager must understand the institutional structure that defines the roles of the Bank of Canada and our financial institutions; the banks, investment dealers, trusts, insurance companies, and other financial organizations. Their collective activities affect the cost and supply of capital available to the firm. Knowledge of the markets in which value is determined and where capital formation occurs is important.

Economic variables, such as gross domestic product, industrial production, disposable income, unemployment, inflation, interest rates, and taxes (to name a few), must fit into the financial manager's decision model and be applied correctly. These terms will be presented throughout the text and are integrated into the financial process.

Accounting is sometimes said to be the language of finance because it provides financial data through income statements, balance sheets, and the statement of cash flows. The financial manager must know how to interpret and use these statements in allocating the firm's financial resources to generate the best return possible in the long run. Finance links economic theory with the numbers of accounting, and all corporate managers—whether in the area of production, sales, research, marketing, management, or long-run strategic planning—must know what it means to assess the financial performance of the firm.

Many students approaching the field of finance for the first time might wonder what career opportunities exist. For those who develop the right skills, financial positions include banker, corporate treasurer, stockbroker, financial analyst, portfolio manager, investment banker, financial consultant, and personal financial planner. As you progress through the text, you will become familiar with many of these roles in the financing and decision-making processes. A financial manager in the firm may be responsible for decisions ranging from where to locate a new plant to raising funds via a public share issue. Sometimes the task is simply to figure out how to get the highest return on a million dollars of temporarily idle cash between 5:00 p.m. one afternoon and 8:00 a.m. the next morning. For the small business operator these roles are often undertaken by one person. Nevertheless, it is important for that individual to have knowledge of accounting and economics to assist them in financial decision making. Finance focuses on creating value and these disciplines will help to focus the small businessperson on that goal.

Evolution of Finance as a Field of Study

To appreciate finance as a field of study, a historical perspective on its development over the last century is instructive.

Finance began primarily as a descriptive discipline identifying the instruments and institutions involved in the financing of a firm. Stock exchanges appeared in the 1870s in Toronto and Montreal to facilitate the raising of capital, so descriptions of the functions, procedures, and products of these exchanges naturally followed. Financial instruments such as stocks and bonds were defined, as were the institutions of the financial

FINANCE IN ACTION

Q1 Do Nortel's financial statements reflect its financial performance?

www.nortelnetworks.com
Symbol: NT

www.tsx.ca

www.bigcharts.com
(ca: S&P/TSX Composite Index)

The Foundations

Accounting provides the financial analyst with useful information. Information from the financial statements of the firm can illuminate asset values, although market values often differ from those recorded on the balance sheet. At Nortel there has been a considerable divergence between the book and market value of equity over the last few years. Nevertheless, to the astute financial analyst the financial statements can give clues as to underlying value and if differences are justified.

Nortel shareholders' equity (billions)

	Book Value	Market Value
2000	$29	$350
2001	5	35

In 2001 Nortel revenues fell considerably and its value of assets declined in response to their declining ability to generate cash flow which determines value. Under generally accepted accounting principles (GAAP) Nortel had a loss of U.S.$27.3 billion recognizing the decrease in asset values, but its pro forma earnings reported a loss of only U.S.$4.5 billion based on ongoing operations.

Economics, another building block of finance, provides us with useful theories in order to understand value formation. When the terrorist attacks of September 11, 2001 shook people's confidence in the American economy, the financial markets declined in value reflecting the expectation that many firms would not be able to produce the same returns in a suddenly more uncertain world. Furthermore, the closure of the financial markets caused supply and demand problems. Treasury bills were in short supply as the certificates to close transactions were buried at ground zero. The U.S. Treasury sold extra treasury bills, although the monies weren't needed, to help maintain an orderly market.

Accounting and economics provide indispensable tools to understand how value is determined in financial markets.

When you examine Nortel's financial statements do you find a significant difference between GAAP income and pro forma income? Compare the book value of equity to the market value of equity (available at the TSX site).

The impact of September 11, 2001 on the economy and the financial markets can be seen in the performance of the S&P/TSX Composite Index. Examine how the index has performed since September 11, 2001 at www.bigcharts.com (ca: S&P/TSX Composite Index).

Toronto Stock Exchange
www.tsx.ca

system such as investment dealers, brokers, and securities regulators. An era of conservatism arose during the Depression of the 1930s, with descriptions focused on concerns such as preservation of capital, maintenance of liquidity, reorganization of financially troubled corporations, and the bankruptcy process. Company failures, together with the questionable treatment of outside investors' interests by insiders, led to the development of securities regulations. A by-product of these regulations was the development of published data related to corporate performance, laying the groundwork for later analytical techniques that would use this data and other corporate information.

In the mid-1950s, however, the emphasis in corporate finance shifted away from description to an analytical, decision-oriented approach. The focus was the allocation of **financial capital** (money) for the purchase of **real capital** (plant and equipment) and the creation of value.

Capital budgeting analysis[1] developed to evaluate the long-run decisions that might commit the firm to expensive strategies, technologies, and real capital. Sophisticated techniques assisted the financial manager in an objective decision-making process to allocate the firm's scarce resources among competing managers and proposals. These competing investment proposals would have their expected earnings and cash flows valued on the basis of acceptable rates of return, which would have to at least exceed those obtainable in the financial markets. Using the financial markets to suggest acceptable rates of return eventually lead to the study of how well the markets

[1] A starting point was Joel Dean, *Capital Budgeting* (New York: Columbia University Press, 1951).

reflected intrinsic value and how well they processed information. This study is referred to as **market efficiency.**

Enthusiasm for sophisticated analysis spread to other decision-making issues such as cash and inventory management. The emphasis of finance shifted from that of the outsider looking in to that of the corporate manager making important day-to-day decisions affecting the short- and long-term well-being of the firm. **Capital structure theory,** the study of the relative importance of debt and equity in influencing the firm's value, also began to receive analytical investigation. Also, the foundations were laid for financial theories of risk-return relationships in valuing assets and of risk reduction through diversified portfolio management. In later years, financial models were constructed to value options that assisted in the development of the huge derivatives markets of today. Several Nobel Prizes have been awarded in recent years to acknowledge the significant contributions to the finance discipline of this early work.

Financial theories since the 1950s have migrated from academia to the boardrooms, as managers have employed the quantitative techniques of decision analysis under varying economic conditions. Managers have focused on risk-return trade-offs, capital structure, and the interrelationship between them when implementing strategies. Sometimes these strategies have been successful, and other times, the managers have had to make adjustments due to changes in the economy, new ideas, or new competition. Firms that at one time pursued diversification strategies to reduce risks, based on earlier theories, refocused on their core businesses by the late 1990s. Diversification, effective at the investor level, was questioned at the corporate level. Meanwhile the derivatives market, built on financial theories over the last twenty years, has become huge in size as firms use it to reduce the risks faced from changes in interest rates, exchange rates, and commodity prices.

Increasingly vigorous international competitiveness and rapid changes in the technologies that define product markets and production processes have forced a sharpened focus on the financial objectives of the firm. The use of analytical decision making has been emphasized in large and small business. Financial theories are as applicable to the small business as to the large corporation, although the analysis may not be as in-depth. The small-business owner will be better prepared to adapt to the rigours of the changing marketplace if he or she is knowledgeable about the theories and techniques of decision analysis.

Today e-commerce presents more efficient ways to interact with customers—the business to consumer model (B2C)—and with suppliers—the business to business model (B2B). In the B2C model, credit and debit cards provide instantaneous cash flow. In the B2B model, orders can be placed, inventory managed, and bids to supply product can be accepted on-line. The B2B model can help companies lower their cost of managing inventory, accounts receivable, and cash. As the pace of business increases analytical decision making must occur effectively and quickly using well-founded techniques.

Goals of Financial Management

An area of financial research that has received more attention in the last decade is **agency theory.** This theory examines the relationship between the owners of the firm and the managers of the firm. In privately owned firms, management and the owners are usually the same people. Management operates the firm to satisfy its own goals,

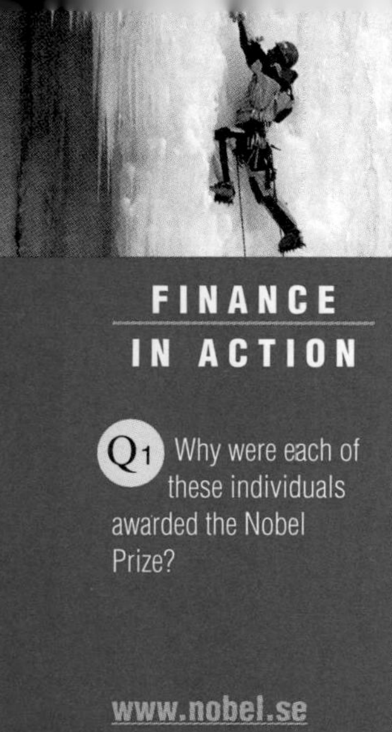

FINANCE IN ACTION

Q1 Why were each of these individuals awarded the Nobel Prize?

www.nobel.se

Nobel Prize Winners for Finance (Economics)

During the last couple of decades several individuals have been awarded the Nobel Prize in economics for their body of work in the discipline of finance. These gentlemen have had a significant impact on financial theory, financial management of firms, and the techniques used to determine value in today's financial markets. Financial managers, analysts, and investors employ techniques derived from the models developed by these Nobel laureates on capital structure, dividend policy, portfolio management, risk-return relationships, the reduction of risk through the use of derivatives, and how financial markets incorporate information into share values.

The Nobel laureates are:

- Franco Modigliani 1985
- Harry Markowitz 1990
- Merton Miller 1990
- William Sharpe 1990
- Robert Merton 1997
- Myron Scholes 1997
- Joseph Stiglitz 2001

Brief descriptions of the men, their theories, and the impact on the discipline of finance, in theory and in practice, can be viewed at the Nobel web site. Search for each laureate by name.

needs, financial requirements, and the like. However as a company moves from private to public ownership, management in an agency position should be making decisions in the best interests of all shareholders. However, diversified ownership interests may result in conflicts between managers and shareholders that can affect the financial decisions of the firm. Furthermore, with increased levels of corporate restructuring, mergers and acquisitions, agency theory has become more important in assessing whether management is achieving shareholder goals in the long run.

Today **institutional investors** such as pension funds and mutual funds own a large percentage of major Canadian companies, and they have more to say about the way publicly owned corporations are managed. As a group, institutional investors have the ability to vote large blocks of shares for the election of a board of directors, who is supposed to run a company in an efficient, competitive manner. The threat of investors being able to replace poorly performing boards of directors makes institutional investors quite influential. Since these institutions represent individual workers and investors, they have a responsibility to see that the firm is managed in an efficient and ethical way.

Despite the different interests at play in formulating a company strategy, all interests are probably best served by creating as much value in the firm as possible. We may be tempted to suggest that the most important goal for financial management is "to earn the highest possible profit for the firm." This seems to be reinforced by income statements where the bottom line is earnings. Under this criterion each decision would be evaluated on the basis of its overall contribution to the firm's earnings. While this seems to be a desirable approach, there are some serious drawbacks to selecting profit maximization as the primary goal of the firm. We will find that the maximization of profits alone may not increase the value of the firm. Our focus is on value.

First, a change in profit may also represent a change in risk. For example, a conservative firm that earned $1.25 per share may become a less desirable investment as its earnings per share increase to $1.50 per share if it has taken on more risk to achieve the increase in earnings. The firm may have incurred more debts or invested in projects that have cyclical earnings. Shareholders of the firm may consider the increase in risk insufficient for the increased earnings.

A second possible drawback to the goal of maximizing profit is that it fails to take into account the timing of benefits. For example, if we could choose between the following two alternatives, we might be indifferent if our emphasis were solely on maximizing earnings.

	Earnings per Share		
	Period One	Period Two	Total
Alternative A	$1.50	$2.00	$3.50
Alternative B	2.00	1.50	3.50

Both investments would provide $3.50 in total earnings, but Alternative B is clearly superior because the larger benefits occur earlier. We could reinvest the difference in earnings for Alternative B for an extra period.

Finally, the goal of maximizing profit suffers from the almost impossible task of accurately measuring the key variable-profit. As you will observe throughout the text, there are different economic and accounting definitions of profit, each of which is open to its own set of interpretations. Furthermore, new complications related to changing prices and international currency transactions add to the ambiguity. Constantly improving methods of financial reporting offer some hope, although there will always be the need for intelligent interpretation of financial facts.

A Valuation Approach

While there is no question that profits are important, the key issue is how to use them in setting a goal for the firm. The ultimate measure of performance is not what is earned, but how the investor values the earnings. In making an analysis of the firm, the investor also considers the risk inherent in the firm's operation. The risk will include the time pattern over which the firm's earnings increase or decrease, the quality and reliability of reported earnings, and many other factors. The investor tries to judge the future earning power of the firm. In this context, current and past profitability may be important guideposts.

The financial manager, in turn, must be sensitive to all of these considerations. He or she must question the impact of each decision on the firm's overall valuation. If a decision maintains or increases the firm's overall value, it is acceptable from a financial viewpoint; otherwise, it should be rejected. This is the one basic principle upon which everything in this text is predicated.

The key model of finance is the present value model that determines the value of assets based on their future "expected" cash flows. Expected implies that there is uncertainty as to the amount and the timing of these cash flows. Therefore, valuation must occur with a consideration given to the risk of the future expected cash flows. Risk will influence the value of assets and the return that investors receive and expect from their investments. A risk-return model is needed to supply an appropriate discount rate to value cash flows in the present value model. We look to the financial markets to assist us in this determination. These resources for valuation models are explored throughout this text.

FINANCE IN ACTION

Decisions for Value

Q1 Was the new company, EnCana, formed?

www.pancanadianenergy.com
Symbol: PCE

www.aec.ca
Symbol: AEC

www.tsx.ca

Working capital, the current assets and liabilities of the firm, must be managed efficiently to create value. With the disruption of airline travel after the September 11, 2001 terrorist attacks, many firms had to reassess their inventory holdings. At Dell they prided themselves on holding only 4 days of inventory and shipping a customized product to the customer almost instantaneously. With the disruption of airline traffic, on which Dell relies heavily, parts became scarce and Dell was unable to fulfill their customer commitments. Larger inventories here would cost Dell money but lost business also has its cost. Investment dealers found it difficult to supply treasury bills as collateral for short-term loans because their inventory of bills was buried at ground zero in Manhattan. This resulted in difficulties in the management of working capital.

In early 2002 PanCanadian and Alberta Energy agreed to merge creating the world's largest independent oil and gas company, EnCana. By merging the two companies, premiums of over 20 percent above current share price were avoided. In 2001 American companies paid these premiums to acquire Gulf Canada, Anderson Exploration, Westcoast Energy and others for over $5 billion each. It was expected that EnCana would annually produce $250 million in operational savings and $250 million in savings from capital projects. Mergers, takeovers, and company expansion are capital budgeting decisions and require an appropriate assessment of risk to determine an appropriate rate of return on these investments. We examine this appropriate rate of return as the cost of capital.

In 1999 Trans Canada Pipelines (TCPL) decreased its dividend unexpectedly and its share price declined significantly. Management was attempting to increase internal cash flow to reduce its debt and improve earnings. By 2001 as investors saw the improved results at TCPL, the share price increased about 90 percent to $19.00. In 2001 when Telus reduced its dividend for similar reasons, the market increased its share price after the announcement. It was expected and welcomed by investors. Back in 1987 Inco, one of the world's largest nickel producers had so much cash it didn't know what to do with it. A U.S.$10 per share dividend was paid and share prices were bid up. Decisions to alter the relationship between debt and equity in the firm are referred to as capital structure decisions.

These are some of the decisions taken by corporations as they attempt to create value for the shareholders. By going to the TSX web site you can see how the share prices of these companies have performed since these decisions were made.

Maximizing Shareholder Wealth

The broad goal of the firm can be brought into focus if we say the financial manager's goal is **shareholder wealth maximization** through achieving the highest possible value (that is, share price) for the firm. This is not a simple task. The financial manager cannot directly control the firm's stock price; he or she can only act in a way that is consistent with the desires of the shareholders in general. Since stock prices are affected by investors' future expectations as well as by the general economic environment, much of what affects stock prices is beyond management's direct control. Even firms with good earnings and favourable financial trends do not always perform well in a declining stock market over the short term.

This goal is more complete than the maximization of profits. Share price reflects investor attitudes to future expected earnings and cash flows and to the risk inherent in those cash flows. Furthermore, the valuation of share price occurs in the marketplace, the result of many complex factors and the actions of market participants. Share price is a value that investors collectively are prepared to pay, whereas earnings are a paper entry prepared by management and their accountants. Earnings may or may not correspond to current values, for many reasons, including accruals and amortization of capital expenditures and can differ, sometimes dramatically, from actual cash flows.

Shareholder Power

Canadian investors tend to be somewhat passive shareholders, trusting the current management of the company to set its own agenda. This may not serve the small investors best interests. Pension plans and mutual funds that conduct much of the investing for the Canadian public and control huge sums of capital have been reluctant to take an active role in the management of the companies in which they hold shares. However, in 2001 the Canadian Business Corporations Act changed allowing a challenge to management without a formal proxy circular. This will make for easier and direct communication amongst shareholders. Groups like the Ontario Teachers Pension Fund have shown a greater willingness to question earnings reports and the excessive stock options given to management.

It doesn't happen very often in Canada, but occasionally shareholders stage a "revolt" and change the management and directors at Canadian corporations. In 1999 shareholders of SPAR Aerospace Ltd. (maker of the Canadarm for the space shuttle), unhappy with the firm's performance installed a new board of directors, paid out $125 million of share capital to shareholders with a special dividend, and amended the shareholders' rights plan, making a takeover easier. In 2001 this led to the sale of SPAR to an American company.

FINANCE IN ACTION

Q1 Is the share price performance of SPAR up since 1999?

www.spar.ca

www.tsx.ca

The concern is not so much with daily fluctuations in share value as with long-term wealth maximization. This can be a difficult task in light of changing investor expectations. In the 1950s and 1960s, investors emphasized maintaining rapid rates of earnings growth. In the 1970s and 1980s investors became more conservative, putting a premium on lower risk and, at times, high current dividend payments. In the 1990s investors focused on globally competitive firms.

By the late 1990s the focus was on high-tech Internet companies. Many of these companies had dreams, but very little revenue and no earnings. Nevertheless, their shares sold at very high prices and some proclaimed the end to old valuation models. Towards late 2000 and throughout 2001, the old valuation models based on earnings and cash flow regained adherents as share prices for many high-tech companies plunged over 90 percent in value.

Management and Shareholder Wealth

In line with the earlier discussion of agency theory, one might ask, "Does modern corporate management actually follow the goal of maximizing shareholder wealth as we have defined it?" In many large corporations stock ownership is diffused and fragmented, so management, with a relatively small ownership position, often controls policy. Under these circumstances management may be more interested in maintaining its own tenure and protecting "private spheres of influence" than in maximizing shareholder wealth. For example, suppose the management of a corporation receives a tender offer to merge the corporation into a second firm. While this offer might be attractive to shareholders, it might be unpleasant to present management that may lose their jobs.

Management has its own interests to look after in operating the firm. Often the management compensation package does not spur management to act in the best interests of shareholders as it emphasizes short-term results over long-term wealth building. Management may also perceive the risk of investment decisions in a manner different from shareholders, leading to different points of view as to the best decision regarding the investment of the firm's resources. The manager of today is considered more of an arbitrator among the different stakeholders in the firm. Those stakeholders can include shareholders, employees, unions, environmentalists, consumer groups, Canada Customs and Revenue, government regulatory bodies, and customers.

Although the model of the modern capitalistic society is that company management is free of direct shareholder involvement, the general Canadian situation is strikingly different. As Table 1–1 shows, only 32 of the 100 largest companies in Canada have widely diffused stock ownership. Many are subsidiaries of U.S. or other foreign multinational companies. A striking number are controlled directly by a family, such as the Desmarais through Power Corporation, or an individual, such as Gerald Schwartz through Onex Corporation. Thus, in general, Canadian managers are very quickly reminded if they are not acting in the best interests of the controlling group of shareholders. In cases where a corporate parent company is widely held, the top managers in the parent company have discretionary decision-making power, but the decisions of the managers of the controlled Canadian company are monitored very closely. Because so many familiar companies are actually subsidiaries of foreign multinationals, Tables 1–2 and 1–3 provide more information regarding the ownership structure of Canadian industry. Market capitalization refers to the company's value of its common shares outstanding and ties in with the firm goal to maximize this value.

Onex Corporation
www.onexcorp.com
Power Corporation
www.powercorp.ca

TABLE 1–1
Ownership of Canada's 100 largest companies*

Widely held	32
Family or individually controlled	24
United States controlled	18
Other foreign country controlled	7
Government controlled	12
Other controlled	7

*As determined by revenues.
Source: National Post Business, *The Financial Post 500,* June 2002.

Patterns of ownership are changing in Canada. Through pension funds, insurance companies, and mutual funds, the average Canadian is participating indirectly in share ownership on a growing scale. Hundreds of billions of dollars are invested by Canadians in mutual funds, of which almost half are invested in common shares. Furthermore, pension fund managers are taking a more active role in the corporations in which they have an investment. Trusteed pension plans, the largest financial intermediary besides banks, have over one-third of their funds invested in common stock. While the pension funds continue to grow, the tightly held ownership of corporate Canada is under stress. There is some evidence of Canadian firms having wider share ownership.

Even in cases where shares are widely held, there are still reasons management should act to maximize shareholders' wealth. First, in most cases, "enlightened management" is aware that the only way to maintain its position over the long run is to be sensitive to shareholder concerns. Poor stock price performance relative to other companies often leads to takeovers and proxy fights for control. Second, members of top management often have sufficient stock option incentives to motivate them to achieve market value maximization for their own benefit. Third, powerful institutional investors are making management more responsive to shareholders.

TABLE 1–2
Largest widely held Canadian corporations

Rank by Sales	Company	Sales (billions)	Market Capitalization	Business
1	Nortel	$45.0	$40.2	Hardware technology
5	C.I.B.C.	23.1	19.9	Banking
7	Royal Bank	22.8	33.1	Banking
10	TransCanada Pipelines	21.2	9.4	Energy transportation
11	Toronto Dominion Bank	20.1	25.6	Banking
12	Bank of Nova Scotia	19.0	24.5	Banking
13	Bank of Montreal	18.6	16.8	Banking
14	BCE	18.1	28.5	Telecommunications
17	Sun Life Financial	16.2	15.7	Insurance
22	Alcan	13.6	17.8	Metals

Compiled from data in National Post Business, *The Financial Post 500*, June 2002 and www.tsx.ca

TABLE 1–3
Largest controlled Canadian corporations

Rank by Sales	Company	Sales (billions)	Market Cap.	Major Shareholder	Location	Percent Held
2	General Motors of Canada	$42.0	—	General Motors	United States	100%
3	Ford Motor Co. of Canada	24.6	—	Ford Motor	United States	100
4	Onex	24.5	$ 3.6	Gerald Schwartz	Canada	67
6	Seagram	23.1	—	Vivendi	France	100
8	George Weston	22.3	13.6	Weston family	Canada	62
9	DaimlerChrysler	21.9	—	DaimlerChrysler	Germany	100
15	Power Corp.	16.9	7.3	Paul Desmarais	Canada	65
16	Imperial Oil	16.6	16.7	Exxon-Mobil	United States	70
19	Bombardier	16.1	5.0	Bombardier family	Canada	62
20	Magna	15.6	8.1	Stronach family	Canada	58

Compiled from data in National Post Business, *The Financial Post 500*, June 2002 and www.tsx.ca

Social Responsibility and Ethical Behaviour

Is our goal of shareholder wealth maximization consistent with a concern for social responsibility for the firm? We believe that in most instances the answer is yes. By adopting policies that maximize values in the market, the firm can attract capital, provide employment, and offer benefits to its host community. This is the basic strength of the private enterprise system. Only successful business firms have the wherewithal to support the fund drives for fine arts organizations, universities, and so forth that are becoming so prevalent as governments reduce spending in these areas.

Nevertheless, certain socially desirable actions, such as installing pollution control equipment, establishing equitable hiring practices, and setting fair pricing standards, may at times be inconsistent with earning the highest possible profit or achieving

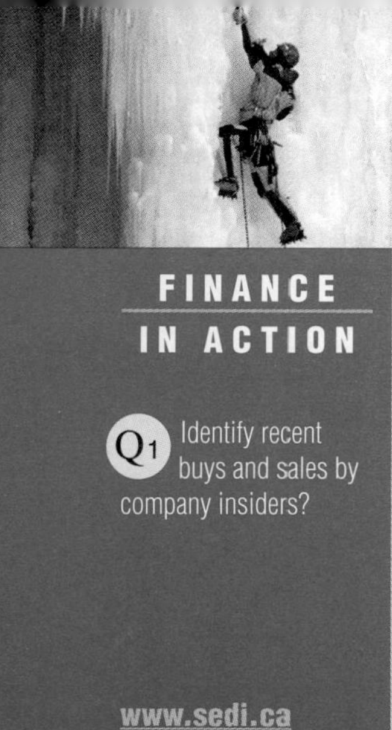

FINANCE IN ACTION

Q1 Identify recent buys and sales by company insiders?

www.sedi.ca

Inside Moves

Andrew Rankin was a senior manager in the mergers and acquisitions section of RBC Dominion Securities. In 2001 he was accused of engaging in insider trading by providing a high school friend with advance notice of company takeovers. Trading took place in offshore accounts and apparently resulted in gains totaling $1.7 million between 1999 and 2001 on takeovers such as Moffat by Shaw and Irwin Toy by Livigroup. A full investigation by the securities commission was initiated.

The Ontario Securities Commission does thorough investigations on about 40 insider trading cases per year. These cases are uncovered by a computer program that identifies spikes in trading activity on publicly traded companies that differ from ordinary trading patterns. The same procedures alerted officials of the Eurex derivatives exchange and European Union to "unusual transactions" in the airline, tourist, and insurance companies shortly before the terrorist attacks on America in September 2001. Advance knowledge of the attacks could have been used by terrorist groups to profit from the tragedy.

Insiders are required by the securities commissions to report their trading activities to SEDI (System for electronic disclosure by insiders). These trades are made public over the web. Some suggest that by tracking this disclosed information an investor can outperform the market.

maximum valuation in the market. For example, pollution control projects frequently offer a negative return on investment. Does this mean firms should not exercise social responsibility in regard to pollution control? The answer is no—but certain cost-increasing activities may have to be mandatory rather than voluntary, at least initially, to ensure that the burden falls equally over all business firms.

Regularly, we hear of unethical and illegal financial practices, on Bay and Wall Streets, by corporate financial "deal makers." **Insider trading** has been one of the most widely publicized issues in recent years. Insider trading occurs when someone has information that is not available to the public and then uses this information to profit from trading in a company's common stock. This practice is illegal and is protected against by the various securities commissions across Canada. Sometimes the insider is a company manager; other times it is the company's lawyer, investment dealer, or even the printer of the company's financial statement. Anyone who has knowledge before public dissemination of that information stands to benefit from either good news or bad news.

Such activities as insider trading serve no beneficial economic or financial purpose, and it could be argued that they have a negative impact on shareholders interests. Illegal security trading destroys confidence in securities markets and makes it more difficult to achieve shareholder wealth maximization.

Functions of Financial Management

Having examined the goals and objectives of financial management, let us turn our attention to the functions it must perform. It is the responsibility of financial management to allocate funds to current and capital assets, to obtain the best mix of financing alternatives, and to develop an appropriate dividend policy within the context of the firm's objectives. These functions are performed on a day-to-day basis as well as through infrequent approaches to the capital markets to acquire new funds. The daily activities of financial management, as outlined in Figure 1–1, require careful monitoring of the cash position of the firm. These duties consume most of the financial

FIGURE 1–1
Functions of the financial manager

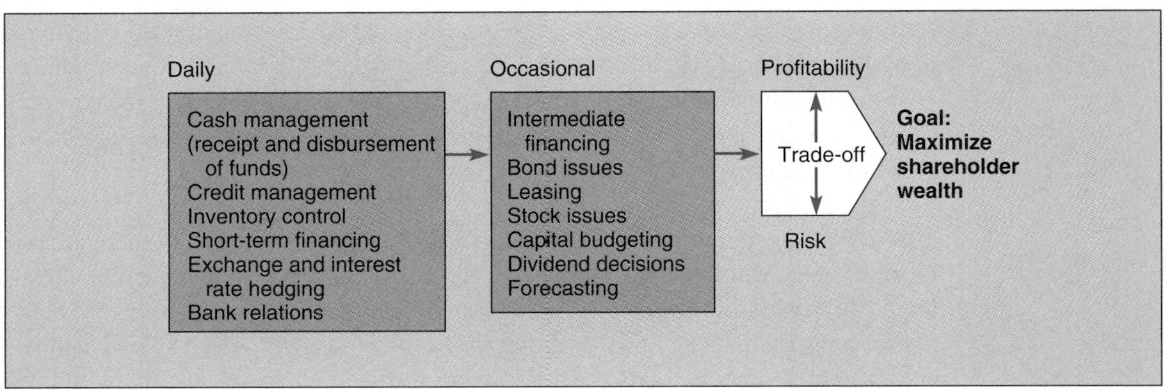

manager's time. Less routine functions of a longer-term nature often require extensive analysis, as these functions sometimes suggest decisions of strategic importance and large capital investment.

As indicated in Figure 1–1, all of these functions are carried out with the awareness of the need to maintain the proper balance among the profitability and risk components of the firm's situation. The appropriate risk-return trade-off must be determined to maximize the market value of the firm for its shareholders. The risk-return decision influences not only the operational side of the business (capital versus labour or Product A versus Product B), but also the financing mix (stocks versus bonds versus retained earnings).

The tasks of the financial manager are being reshaped by increased domestic and international competition, by advances in information technology and management techniques, and by innovations in the types of financial markets and products. The functions of the financial manager are often organized into several positions. A chief financial officer usually takes responsibility for long-term financing and investment; the controller looks after informational flows related to planning, control, and external reporting; and the treasurer looks after external relations, particularly as they apply to daily cash management. A large firm often has many individuals who report to these positions and specialize in the duties required of the functions outlined in Figure 1–1.

Forms of Organization

The finance function may be carried out within a number of different forms of organization. Of primary interest are the sole proprietorship, the partnership, and the corporation.

Sole Proprietorship The **sole proprietorship** represents single-person ownership and offers the advantages of simplicity of decision making and low organizational and operating costs. Most small businesses with one to ten employees are sole proprietorships. The major drawback of the sole proprietorship is that there is unlimited liability to the owner. In settlement of the firm's debts, he or she can lose not only the capital invested in the business, but also personal assets. This drawback can be serious, as few lenders are willing to advance funds to a small business without a personal liability commitment from the owner.

The profits or losses of a sole proprietorship are taxed as though they belong to the individual owner. Thus, if a sole proprietorship makes $25,000, the owner claims the profits in his or her tax return. (In the corporate form of organization, the corporation first pays a tax on profits, and then the owners of the corporation pay a tax on any profit distributed.)

Partnership A **partnership** is similar to a sole proprietorship except there are two or more owners. Multiple ownership makes it possible to raise more capital and to share ownership responsibilities. Most partnerships are formed through an agreement between the participants, known as the *partnership agreement*, which specifies the ownership interest, the methods for distributing profits, and the means for withdrawing from the partnership. For taxing purposes partnership profits or losses are allocated directly to the partners, and there is no double taxation as in the corporate form.

Like the sole proprietorship, the partnership arrangement carries unlimited liability for the owners. While the partnership offers the advantage of *sharing* possible losses, it presents the problem of owners with unequal wealth having to absorb losses. If three people form a partnership with a $10,000 contribution each and the business loses $100,000, one wealthy partner may have to bear a disproportionate share of the losses if the other two partners do not have sufficient personal assets. This form of partnership where all partners assume unlimited liability for the obligations is known as a **general partnership.**

To circumvent this shared unlimited liability feature, a special form of partnership, called a **limited partnership,** can be utilized. Under this arrangement one or more partners are designated general partners and have unlimited liability for the debts of the firm; other partners are designated limited partners and are liable only for their initial contribution. The limited partners are normally prohibited from being active in the management of the firm. You may have heard of limited partnerships in real estate syndications in which a number of limited partners are doctors, lawyers, and chartered accountants with one general partner who is a real estate professional. Not all financial institutions will extend funds to a limited partnership.

Corporation In terms of revenue and profits produced, the **corporation** is by far the most important form of economic unit. The corporation is unique—it is a legal entity unto itself. Thus, the corporation may sue or be sued, engage in contracts, and acquire property.

A corporation is generally incorporated federally or in a single province with registration in all other provinces in which it conducts business. Although the incorporating procedure varies from province to province, two documents are central to the incorporating procedure, a *company charter* and the *company by-laws*. The charter contains the organization's founding principles and is relatively unalterable. The by-laws contain details of company policies and procedures and can be changed by vote of the board of directors and shareholders.

Technically, a corporation is owned by shareholders who enjoy the privilege of limited liability, meaning their liability exposure is generally no greater than their initial investment. However, in the case of small corporations with little in the way of collateral, bankers will generally not lend money to the corporation without a personal guarantee from the owner-manager or a principal shareholder. A corporation also has a continual life and is not dependent on the life span of any one shareholder for maintaining its legal existence.

Bell Canada Enterprises
www.bce.ca

A key feature of the corporation is the easy divisibility of the ownership interest through the issuance of shares of stock. While it would be nearly impossible to have more than 50 or 100 partners in most businesses, a corporation may have thousands of shareholders. For example, as of the end of 2000, Bell Canada Enterprises, probably the most widely held Canadian company, had almost 185,000 registered common shareholders. The shareholders' interests are ultimately managed by the corporation's board of directors. The board of directors, who generally include key management personnel as well as outside directors not permanently employed by it, serve in a stewardship capacity and may be liable for the mismanagement of the firm or for the misappropriation of funds. The average annual director's fee is over $30,000, although some large companies pay over $70,000 a year.

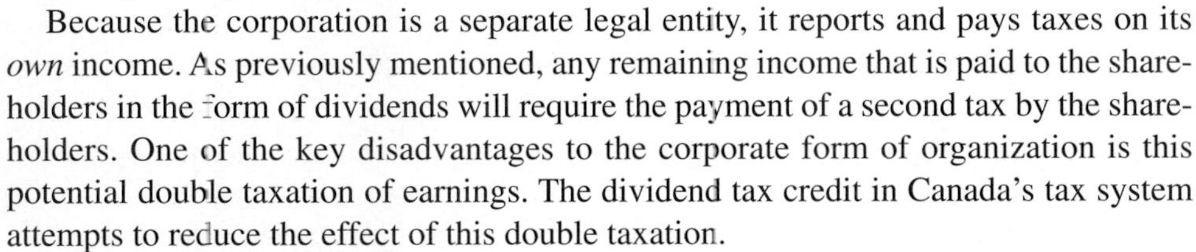

Because the corporation is a separate legal entity, it reports and pays taxes on its *own* income. As previously mentioned, any remaining income that is paid to the shareholders in the form of dividends will require the payment of a second tax by the shareholders. One of the key disadvantages to the corporate form of organization is this potential double taxation of earnings. The dividend tax credit in Canada's tax system attempts to reduce the effect of this double taxation.

Because of the all-pervasive impact of the corporation on our economy and because most growing businesses eventually become corporations, the effects of many decisions in this text are considered from the corporate viewpoint.

The Role of the Financial Markets

The impact of managerial efforts and ethical (or unethical) behaviour on the value of the company is decided daily through price changes in the financial markets. But what are the financial markets? **Financial markets** are the meeting place for people, corporations, and institutions that either need money or have money to lend or invest. In a broad context, the financial markets exist as a vast global network of individuals and financial institutions that may be lenders, borrowers, or owners of public companies. Governments also participate in the financial markets primarily as borrowers of funds for public activities; their markets are referred to as **public financial markets.** Corporations such as Bombardier, Nortel, and CN Rail, on the other hand, raise funds in the **corporate financial markets.** Today we increasingly see the sale of government assets through share issues. In 2002 we expect HydroOne to be the largest share issue in Canadian history at about $5 billion.

HydroOne
www.HydroOne.com

Structure and Functions of the Financial Markets

Financial markets can be broken into many distinct parts. Some divisions, such as domestic and international markets or corporate and government markets, are self-explanatory. Others, such as money and capital markets, need some explanation. **Money markets** refer to those markets dealing with short-term securities that have a life of one year or less. Securities in these markets can include Treasury bills offered by the federal or provincial government, commercial paper sold by corporations to finance

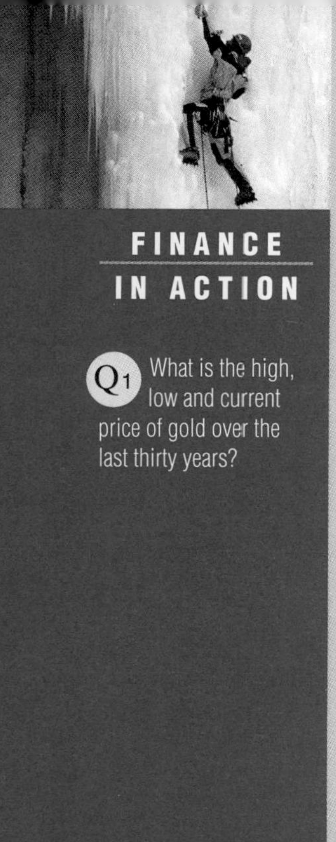

FINANCE IN ACTION

The Pricing Mechanism of Financial Markets

In the late 1990s we saw a tremendous increase in value of Internet stocks. Capital was being reallocated to those companies that appeared to be at the forefront of a new age. The reallocation was by way of the pricing mechanism of the financial markets. As prices rose more capital flowed to the "new age" companies. Internet companies had little in the way of tangible or hard assets. Their value flowed from their ability to manipulate and supply information, which suggested that in the future they would be able to generate large cash flows for shareholders. Then their market values tumbled and the "old" economy companies saw their prices rise.

Gold traditionally has been a hard asset. It has been used to conduct business transactions, as a store of wealth and due to its scarcity it has been used to back the major currencies of the world. Gold that sold for U.S.$850 per ounce in 1980, sold for U.S.$278 per ounce in 2002. Most major currencies have gone off the gold standard and many countries have begun to sell their gold reserves. In an age where capital can be transferred instantaneously around the globe and where many governments have learned to effectively manage their economies with low rates of inflation, gold has lost its significance as a store of wealth and as a reserve currency. Falling gold prices suggest the financial markets no longer value gold as highly as before and are reallocating capital elsewhere.

Where will the pricing mechanism of the financial markets allocate capital resources next?

There are several noteworthy financial markets:

Equity (stock)	Derivative
TSX www.tsx.ca	ME www.me.org
Nikkei www.nni.nikkei.co.jp	CBOE www.cboe.com
NASDAQ www.nasdaq.com	CME www.cme.com
LSE www.londonstockexchange.com	LIFFE www.liffe.com

Q1 What is the high, low and current price of gold over the last thirty years?

www.kitco.com

their daily operations, or certificates of deposit with maturities of less than one year sold by banks. Examples of money market securities are presented more fully in Chapter 7.

The **capital markets** are generally defined as those markets in which securities have a life of more than one year. While capital markets are long-term markets as opposed to short-term money markets, it is often common to break down the capital markets into intermediate markets (one to ten years) and long-term markets (greater than ten years). The capital markets include securities such as common stock, preferred stock, and corporate and government bonds. The capital markets are fully presented in Chapter 14.

Allocation of Capital

Corporations rely on the financial markets to provide funds for short-term operations and for new plant and equipment. A firm may go to the markets and raise new financial capital by either borrowing money through a debt offering of corporate bonds or short-term notes or by selling ownership in the company through an issue of common stock. When a corporation uses the financial markets to raise new funds, the sale of securities is said to be made in the **primary market** by way of a new issue. After the securities are sold to the public (institutions and individuals), they are traded in the **secondary market** between investors. In the secondary market, prices are continually changing, as investors buy and sell securities based on their expectations of the corporation's prospects. Also in the secondary market, financial managers are given feedback about their firm's performance. The markets determine value and allocate capital to its most profitable uses. The present value calculations of Chapters 9 and 10 value financial assets in much the same way as properly functioning markets.

How does the market allocate capital to the thousands of firms that are continually in need of money? Let us assume that you graduate from college as a finance major and are hired to manage money for a wealthy family like the Bronfmans. You are given $250 million to manage, and you can choose to invest the money anywhere in the world. For example, you could buy common stock in Bombardier, the Canadian transportation manufacturer, in Nestlé, the Swiss food company, or in Telefonos DeMexico, the Mexican telephone company; you could choose to lend money to the Canadian or Japanese government by purchasing their bonds; or you could lend money to Petro-Canada. Of course, these are only some of the endless choices you would have.

How do you decide to allocate the $250 million? You will try to maximize your return and minimize your risk. Some investors will choose a risk level that meets their objective and maximizes return for that given level of risk. By seeking this risk-return objective, you will bid up the prices of securities that seem underpriced and have potential for high returns, and you will avoid securities of equal risk that seem overpriced in your judgement. Since all market participants play the same risk-return game, the financial markets become the playing field and price movements become the winning or losing score. With companies of equal risk, those with expectations for high return will have higher common stock prices relative to those companies with poor expectations. Since the prices in the market reflect the combined judgement of all the players in the market, securities price movements provide feedback to corporate managers and let them know whether the market thinks they are winning or losing the competition.

Those companies that perform well and are rewarded by the market with high-priced securities have an easier time raising new funds in the money and capital markets than their competitors. They are also able to raise funds at a lower cost. Go back to that $250 million you are managing. If Petro-Canada wants to borrow money from you at 10 percent and Talisman Energy is willing to pay 9 percent but is also riskier, to which company will you choose to lend money? If you choose Petro-Canada you are on your way to understanding finance. The competition between the two firms for your funds will eventually cause Talisman either to offer higher returns than Petro-Canada or to go without funds. In this way, the money and capital markets allocate funds to the highest quality companies at the lowest cost and to the lowest quality companies at the highest cost. In other words, there is a penalty for firms that fail to perform up to competitive standards.

Petro-Canada
www.petro-canada.ca
Talisman Energy
www.talisman-energy.com

Reliance on Debt

A reality in contemporary finance is the raising of debt in the capital markets to fund the expansion of firms and of government programs. Too much debt can erode a firm's or government's ability to generate sufficient cash flow to comfortably cover its interest expenses. The use of debt is not a short-term, cyclical phenomenon; rather, it appears to be a steady evolution that has occurred in good times as well as bad.

Governments, and in particular the federal government, have been heavy borrowers in the capital markets. The federal **fiscal deficit** represents the difference between the revenues and expenses of the government of Canada. Annual deficits of over $30 to $40 billion persisted into the 1990s despite higher taxes. Deficits accumulate to become total debt. The accumulated debt of the federal government and the provinces exceeded $800 billion by 1996, when the federal debt topped out at $570 billion. By

FINANCE IN ACTION

The Markets for Valuation and Rates of Return

Q1 What are current overnight rates in these countries?

www.bankofcanada.ca

In 1999 Nortel shares sold in the market for less than $20.00. By 2000 they sold for over $120.00 per share and the market value of Nortel shareholders' equity was $350 billion. By early 2002 the market value was down to $35 billion and a share sold for about $11.00. The market had demonstrated drastically different views of Nortel's share value.

The S&P/TSX Composite Index is representative of the market value of the equity of the top companies listed on Canada's premier stock exchange. In August of 2000 the S&P/TSX Composite Index had a value over 11,000. In early 2002 its value was about 7,600. Search for its value under indexes at the TSX web site, www.tsx.ca. The shareholder market value of these companies (primarily Nortel) had dropped considerably in a little over a year. Can you determine the current value of Nortel (NT) and the S&P/TSX Composite Index?

The bedrock interest rate or yield in the economy is the overnight rate, the rate at which financial institutions lend money amongst themselves for one day. Other yields in the economy take their clues from this rate. In 1981 Canada's overnight rate reached 21.57 percent. In early 2002 the overnight rate was down to 2 percent, while in England www.bankofengland.co.uk it was 4 percent (repo rate) and 0.10 percent in Japan (www.boj.or.jp/en).

the late 1990s, the federal government was generating surpluses. However, debt and deficit reduction has forced cutbacks in the services offered by governments and in some cases the sale of public corporations to help reduce the debts.

The government's demand for funding has put direct upward pressure on interest rates. Recently, however, investors have found a decreased supply of government securities in which to invest their excess funds. Additionally, foreign capital is important in providing funds for corporate and government borrowings. This means that Canada has to have attractive interest rates and a stable currency (as foreign investors are concerned about foreign exchange risk). Thus, protection of the foreign exchange value of the Canadian dollar, and a declared resolve to stem inflationary pressures, are driving forces behind the Bank of Canada's interest rate policy.

Interest Rates

Interest rates are a key factor in the financial markets, as they determine the rates of return required on investments and this in turn helps establish the allocation of capital. Interest rates have been volatile in recent history. Short-term interest rates surpassed the 20 percent mark in the 1980s before beginning a sharp decline. By 2001 the prime rate was down to 4 percent, a forty-year low.

Statistics Canada Monthly CPI Report www.statcan.ca/english/Subjects/Cpi/cpi-en.htm

These movements are portrayed in Figure 1–2 along with the annual rate of inflation as measured by the changes in the consumer price index (CPI). Note that in all years except 1974 and 1975, the average **prime rate** exceeded the average rate of inflation. Also note that the difference between the prime rate and the inflation rate was very small between 1972 and 1978. After inflation began to subside in 1983, the spread between the rates widened considerably. This unprecedented situation was largely the result of the Bank of Canada's fears of increased inflation and its policy aimed at squeezing inflation down.

The low interest rates of the 1990s acted to spur the stock and bond markets to record levels. The spread between the prime rate and the CPI remained high. Lower interest rates result in investors placing higher values on the promised or expected pay-

FIGURE 1–2
Prime rate versus percent change in the CPI

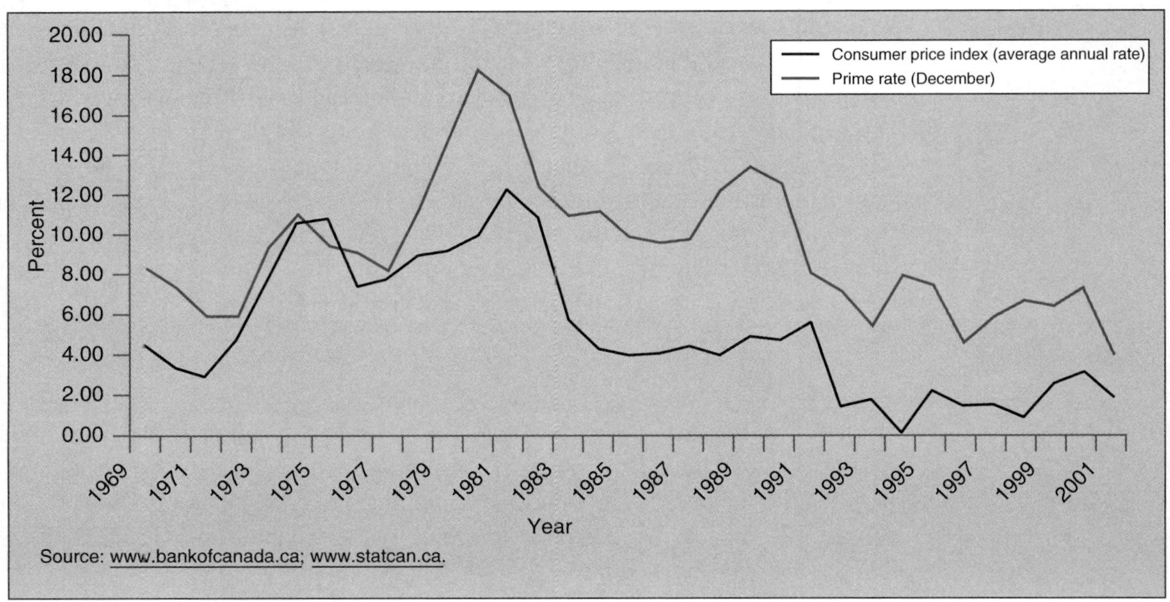

Source: www.bankofcanada.ca; www.statcan.ca.

ments from corporate securities. Furthermore, lower rates result in cheaper financing for new capital projects of the firm.

A major determinant of interest rates is the rate of **inflation.** By 1993, inflation was reduced to an annualized rate of about 2 percent. Inflation rates and related interest rates had not been this low in 30 years. Double-digit inflation had seemed the norm in the late 1970s and early 1980s, although more recent inflation rates are closer to long-term historical norms. The inflation-induced profits of the late 1960s and 1970s are somewhat in the past, but the student should not ignore the lessons of inflated phantom profits and undervalued assets of those past decades. The benefits, drawbacks, and implications of **disinflation** (a slowing of price increases) will be explored in Chapter 3 on financial analysis.

Internationalization of the Financial Markets

Trade between countries is a growing trend that is likely to continue. Global companies are becoming more common, and international brand names such as Sony, Bombardier, Coca-Cola, Nokia, and Mercedes Benz are known the world over. McDonald's food is eaten throughout the world, and McDonald's raises funds on most major international money and capital markets. The growth of the global company has led to the growth of global fund raising, as companies search for the cheapest sources of funds wherever possible.

Financial managers, adjusting to the changing economic environment, should also consider the war on terrorism, the creation of the free trade zone and the Euro of the European Common Market, the North American Free Trade Agreement (NAFTA), and the emergence of the industrial nations of the Far East in addition to Japan. In 1998 the collapsing economies of the Far East had a quick impact on the North American markets. Resource prices dropped over 20 percent in less than a year, which had a dramatic impact on many Canadian companies and the value of our dollar.

We live in a world where international events impact the economies of all industrial countries and where capital moves from country to country faster than was ever thought possible. Computers interact in a vast international financial network, and markets are more vulnerable to changing investor sentiment than they have been in the past. The corporate financial manager has an increasing number of external impacts to consider. Future financial managers will need to have the sophistication to understand international capital flows, computerized electronic funds transfer systems, foreign currency hedging strategies, and many other factors. The following chapters should help you learn how corporations manage these challenges.

Format of the Text

The material in this text is covered under six major parts. You progress from the development of basic analytical skills in accounting and finance to the utilization of decision-making techniques in working capital management, capital budgeting, long-term financing, and other related areas. A length of 21 chapters should make the text appropriate for one-semester coverage.

You are given a thorough grounding in financial theory in a highly palatable and comprehensive fashion—with careful attention to definitions, symbols, and formulas. The intent is, above all, that you develop a thorough understanding of the basic concepts in finance.

Parts

1. *Introduction* This section examines the goals and objectives of financial management. The emphasis on decision making and risk management is stressed, with an update of significant events influencing the study of finance.
2. *Financial Analysis and Planning* You are first given the opportunity to review the basic principles of accounting as they relate to finance (financial statements and funds flow). This review material in Chapter 2 is optional; you may judge whether you need this review before progressing through the section.

   Additional material in this part includes a thorough study of ratio analysis, budget construction techniques, and development of comprehensive pro forma statements. The effect of heavy fixed commitments, in the form of either debt or plant and equipment, is examined in a discussion of leverage.
3. *Working Capital Management* The techniques for managing the short-term assets of the firm and the associated liabilities are examined. The material is introduced in the context of risk-return analysis. The financial manager must constantly choose between liquid, low-return assets (perhaps marketable securities) and more profitable, less liquid assets (such as inventory). Sources of short-term financing are also considered.
4. *The Capital Budgeting Process* The decision on capital outlays is among the most significant a firm will have to make. In terms of study procedure, we attempt to carefully develop "time-value-of-money" calculations; we then proceed to the valuation of bonds and stocks, emphasizing present-value techniques. The valuation chapter develops the traditional dividend valuation model and examines bond price sensitivity in response to discount rates and

inflation. An appendix presents the supernormal dividend growth model, or what is sometimes called the two-stage dividend model. After careful grounding in valuation practice and theory, we examine the cost of capital and capital structure. The text then moves to the actual capital budgeting decision, using previously learned material and employing the concept of marginal analysis. The concluding chapter in this part covers risk-return analysis in capital budgeting with a brief exposure to portfolio theory and a consideration of market value maximization.

5. *Long-Term Financing* You are introduced to Canadian financial markets as they relate to corporate financial management. You consider the sources and uses of funds in the capital markets, with coverage given to warrants and convertibles as well as the more conventional methods of financing. Derivative instruments are also explored. The guiding role of the investment dealer in the distribution of securities is also analyzed. Furthermore, you are encouraged to think of leasing as a form of debt.
6. *Expanding the Perspective of Corporate Finance* A chapter on corporate mergers considers external growth strategy and serves as an integrative tool to bring together such topics as profit management, capital budgeting, portfolio considerations, and valuation concepts. A second chapter on international financial management describes the growth of the international financial markets, the rise of multinational business, and the effects on corporate financial management. The issues discussed in these two chapters highlight corporate diversification and risk-reduction attempts prevalent in the 1980s, 1990s, and today.

Summary*

1. Finance builds on the analytical techniques for decision making from economics and calls on the financial data produced from accounting statements. Finance links these two disciplines.
2. With the development of sophisticated analytical techniques for financial management, its focus has broadened to include not only adequate returns, but also returns in the context of the risk assumed by the firm.
3. The primary goal of the firm is the maximization of the shareholder wealth as measured by share price. This is a more satisfactory goal than profit maximization because it incorporates the risk and timing of cash flows and because share value is objectively determined in the marketplace. Furthermore, this goal best helps to explain decisions made by corporations.
4. The management of corporations may not always act in the best interest of the shareholders. Management has other demands, including its own interests. Agency theory studies the conflicts between shareholders and management and the measures adopted to control the conflicts. The pursuit of socially or ethically acceptable goals may come at the expense of shareholders' wealth.
5. Financial managers are involved in raising funds for the firm and in investing those funds in the most efficient way. The activities of the financial manager include working capital management, capital budgeting, and capital structure financing decisions.
6. The financial markets allocate capital to its best use if they operate freely and properly. The markets determine value, a key variable in decision making. The markets also establish appropriate rates of return or yields for investments.

*Each **chapter summary** is keyed to the **learning objectives** at the beginning of the chapter.

www.mcgrawhill.ca/college/block

List of Terms

financial capital 4
real capital 4
capital budgeting analysis 4
market efficiency 5
capital structure theory 5
agency theory 5
institutional investors 6
shareholder wealth maximization 8
insider trading 12
sole proprietorship 13
general partnership 14
limited partnership 14
corporation 14
financial markets 15
public financial markets 15
corporate financial markets 15
money markets 15
capital markets 16
primary market 16
secondary market 16
fiscal deficit 17
prime rate 18
inflation 19
disinflation 19

Discussion Questions

1. What was the first area of study to generate newfound enthusiasm for decision-related analysis in finance?
2. If shares of both a high-tech startup company and the Royal Bank promised cash flow of $2.00 per share over the next year, for which shares would you be prepared to pay the higher price? Why?
3. What is meant by the goal of maximization of shareholder wealth? Why is profit maximization, by itself, an inappropriate goal?
4. What issue does agency theory examine? Why has it become more important in recent times?
5. Why are institutional investors important in today's financial markets?
6. When does insider trading occur? What government agency is responsible for protecting against the unethical practice of insider trading?
7. The government has passed regulations over the years that require pollution controls, development restrictions, hiring equity, and pay equity. Can a firm still achieve the maximization of shareholder wealth?
8. The senior management of corporations has often received large compensation even after the firms have suffered significant losses. Are senior managers paid too much?
9. Suggest two forms of daily functions and two forms of occasional functions that the financial manager performs.
10. Contrast the liability provisions for a sole proprietorship, a partnership, a limited partnership, and a corporation.
11. Why is the corporate form of organization best suited to a large organization?
12. In terms of the life of securities offered, what is the difference between money and capital markets?
13. What is the difference between a primary and a secondary market?
14. What impact do government debt loads have on the financial markets?

www.mcgrawhill.ca/college/block

INTERNET RESOURCES AND QUESTIONS

The Nobel Web site has a brief description of the work of the winners of the Nobel Prize in economics: www.nobel.se

The federal government's finances are available from the finance department: www.fin.gc.ca

The Bank of Canada has statistics on interest rates and the CPI: www.bankofcanada.ca

1. Select one of the Nobel laureate professors in finance and briefly describe his contribution to the field of finance.
2. What is the current federal government's deficit and accumulated debt?
3. What is the current prime interest rate and CPI?

Selected References

Byrd, John, Robert Parrine, and Gunnar Pritsch. "Stockholder-Manager Conflicts and Firm Value." *Financial Analysts* Journal 54 (May–June 1998), pp. 14–30.

Cooper, Dan, and Glenn Petry. "Corporate Performance and Adherence to Stockholder Wealth-Maximizing Principles." *Financial Management* 23 (Spring 1994), pp. 71–78.

Gilbert, Erika, and Alan Reichert. "The Practice of Financial Management among Large United States Corporations." *Financial Practice and Education* 5 (Summer–Spring 1995), pp. 16–23.

Gup, Benton E. "The Five Most Important Finance Concepts: A Summary." *Financial Practice and Education* 4 (Fall–Winter 1994), pp. 106–109.

Hirt, Geoffrey A. "Integrating Financial Theory and Practice with Institutional-Descriptive Finance." *Journal of Financial Education* 13 (Fall 1984), pp. 19–27.

Jensen, Michael C. "The Eclipse of the Public Corporation." *Harvard Business Review* 67 (September–October 1989), pp. 61–74.

"Corporate Control and the Politics of Finance." *Journal of Applied Corporate Finance* 4 (Summer 1991), pp. 13–33.

Kahn, Charles, and Andrew Winton. "Ownership Structure, Speculation, and Shareholder Intervention." *Journal of Finance* 53 (April 1998), pp. 99–129.

Kose, John, Larry H. P. Lang, and Jeffrey Netter. "The Voluntary Restructuring of Large Firms in Response to Performance Decline." *Journal of Finance* 47 (July 1992), pp. 891–917.

May, Don O. "Do Managerial Motives Influence Firm Risk-Return Strategies?" *Journal of Finance* 50 (September 1995), pp. 1291–1308.

Mehran, Hamid. "Executive Compensation Structure, Ownership and Firm Performance." *Journal of Financial Economics* 38 (June 1995), pp. 163–81.

Tutano, Peter. "Agency Costs of Corporate Risk Management." *Financial Management* 27 (Spring 1998), pp. 67–77.

PART | TWO

FINANCIAL ANALYSIS AND PLANNING

Understanding and utilizing financial statements for the analysis of the firm's performance, for comprehending the dynamics revealed within the balance sheet, and for forecasting the future financial situation of the firm are key skills required of the financial manager.

CHAPTER | TWO

2 Review of Accounting

LEARNING | OBJECTIVES

1 Demonstrate a reasonable ability to prepare the three basic financial statements.

2 Identify the limitations of the income statement as a measure of a firm's profitability.

3 Identify the limitations of the balance sheet as a measure of a firm's financial position.

4 Explain the importance of cash flows as identified in the statement of cash flows.

5 Outline the impact of corporate tax considerations on aftertax cash flow.

6 Identify the different forms of investment income and the different taxes payable on this income.

7 Explain the concept of tax savings.

The language of finance flows logically from accounting. To be adequately prepared to study the concepts of finance, it is necessary to comprehend the material drawn from the accounting area. Although our focus in finance is decision making that seeks to produce value today from future expected cash flows, it is important to understand where a firm has been and where it is at the present time. Financial statements help us to understand this.

Much of the early frustration suffered by students who have difficulty with finance can be overcome if such concepts as retained earnings, shareholders' equity, amortization, and historical/replacement cost accounting are brought into focus.

This chapter examines the three basic types of financial statements—the income statement, the balance sheet, and the statement of cash flows—with particular attention paid to the interrelationships among these three measurement devices. The requirements and the suggestions for the format of these statements are detailed in the handbook of the Canadian Institute of Chartered Accountants (CICA). The ***CICA Handbook*** sets the requirements for the financial statements prepared by chartered accountants.

From these statements we may be able to estimate the future direction of the firm and better understand the basis of value. Furthermore, we can examine the differences between cash flow and income. As special preparation for the financial manager, we also briefly examine income tax considerations affecting financial decisions.

Income Statement

The **income statement** is the major device for measuring the profitability of a firm over a time period. Finance uses analytical decision making with focus on the future. It examines the past patterns from income statements to aid in predicting the timing, the uncertainty, and the amount of future cash flows. Therefore it is important to understand the relationships and interactions between income statement, balance sheet, and cash flow items. An example of the income statement is presented in Table 2–1 for the Kramer Corporation.

TABLE 2–1
Income Statement

KRAMER CORPORATION
Income Statement
For the Year Ended December 31, 2002

1. Sales	$2,000,000
2. Cost of goods sold	1,500,000
3. Gross profits	500,000
4. Selling and administrative expense	220,000
5. Amortization expense	50,000
6. Operating profit (EBIT)*	230,000
7. Interest expense	20,000
8. Earnings before taxes (EBT)	210,000
9. Taxes	99,500
10. Earnings aftertaxes (EAT)	110,500
11. Preferred stock dividends	10,500
12. Earnings available to common shareholders	$ 100,000
13. Shares outstanding	100,000
14. Earnings per share	$1.00

*Earnings before interest and taxes.

Note that the income statement covers a defined time period, whether it be one month, three months, or a year. The statement is presented in a stair-step, or progressive, fashion so that we can examine the profit or loss after each type of expense item is deducted.

We start with sales and deduct cost of goods sold to arrive at **gross profit.** The $500,000 thus represents the difference between the amount for which we bought or manufactured our goods and the sales price. Our profit (or loss) purely from operations of $230,000, or **operating profit** is determined after subtracting selling and administrative expense and amortization.[1] Amortization can be a significant expense derived from the capital assets developed by the firm and identified on the balance sheet. It is possible for a company to enjoy a high gross profit margin (25 to 50 percent) but a relatively low operating profit because of heavy expenses incurred in marketing the product and managing the company.

[1]Amortization was not treated as part of cost of goods sold in this instance, but rather as a separate expense. Depending on the circumstances, all or part of amortization may be treated as cost of goods sold. Amortization as recommended in the *CICA Handbook*, Section 3060.33 recognizes the declining value of a capital asset over its life. Depreciation or depletion are other acceptable terms for amortization.

Having obtained operating profit (essentially a measure of how efficient management is in generating revenues and controlling expenses), we now adjust for revenues and expenses not related to operational matters. In this case we pay $20,000 in interest and arrive at earnings before taxes of $210,000. The interest expense is derived from the financing policies of the firm or its leverage and its impact is explored in Chapter 5. Our tax payments are $99,500 calculated as a percentage of $210,000. This results in aftertax income of $110,500.

This income because of accrual accounting and the matching principle of revenues and expenses is not the same as the cash flow of the firm. It is representative of a longer run view of the firm, but the financial manager's attention to cash flow will enable the firm to survive in the short term. That is why the cash flow statement, examined later in this chapter, is an appropriate complement to the income statement. A $10,500 dividend has been paid to the preferred shareholders, leaving $100,000 in earnings are available to the common shareholders (item 12).

Return to Capital

We should note the return on capital to the three primary sources provided by investors.

Bondholders	$20,000 in interest (item 7)
Preferred shareholders	$10,500 in dividends (item 11)
Common shareholders	$100,000 of earnings available (item 12)

The $100,000 of earnings (profit) may be paid out to the common shareholders in the form of dividends or retained in the company for subsequent reinvestment. The reinvested funds, identified on the balance sheet, theoretically belong to the common shareholders. Remember that retained earnings do not represent cash. It is hoped that these funds will provide future earnings and dividends appropriate to the risk assumed by investing these earnings in accounts receivable, inventories, capital or other assets. In the case of the Kramer Corporation, we have assumed that $50,000 in dividends was paid out to the common shareholders, with the balance retained in the corporation for their benefit.

A short supplement to the income statement, a statement of retained earnings (Table 2–2), usually indicates the disposition of earnings.[2] We see that $50,000 has been added to previously accumulated earnings of $250,000 to arrive at $300,000.

TABLE 2–2
Statement of Retained Earnings

Statement of Retained Earnings
For the Year Ended December 31, 2002

Retained earnings, balance, January 1, 2002	$250,000
Add: Earnings available to common shareholders, 2002	100,000
Deduct: Cash dividends declared in 2002	50,000
Retained earnings, balance, December 31, 2002	300,000

[2]The statement may also indicate any adjustments to previously reported incomes as well as any restrictions on cash dividends.

Valuation Basics from the Income Statement

The goal of the firm was identified in Chapter 1 as the maximization of shareholder value. This value is easy to measure immediately, based on today's market share price. However shareholders, investors, and analysts will be interested in attempting to forecast future value. Over time these future values will determine shareholders' return on their capital.

Shareholders' claim on earnings is a fundamental measure of value. Common shareholders are sensitive to the number of shares outstanding, with more shares resulting in lower earnings available to each shareholder. Therefore to gauge shareholder returns we compute **earnings per share.**

$$\text{Earnings per share (e.p.s.)} = \frac{\text{Earnings available to common shareholders}}{\text{Number of shares outstanding}} \quad (2\text{–}1)$$

As indicated in item 13 of Table 2–1,

$$e.p.s. = \frac{\$100{,}000}{100{,}000 \text{ shares}} = \$1.00$$

A corollary to this is that before any new shares are issued, the financial manager must be sure that the capital raised by issuing the new shares will eventually generate sufficient earnings to avoid reducing earnings per share. The past trends and forecasts of earnings per share is a closely watched financial ratio. Market share prices react immediately to announced earnings particularly if they are different than the consensus of investors.

Shareholders will also be interested in what percentage of earnings is paid out immediately as dividends and this is referred to as the **payout ratio.**

$$\text{Payout ratio} = \frac{\text{Dividend per share}}{\text{Earnings per share}} \quad (2\text{–}2)$$

With $50,000 paid out by Kramer to 100,000 shareholders or dividends per share of $0.50,

$$Payout\ ratio = \frac{\$0.50}{\$1.00} = 0.50 \text{ or } 50\%$$

Growth in earnings is important for the survival of small businesses requiring increasing amounts of capital. Small businesses are often forced to rely on reinvested earnings to fund expansion as their access to the capital market and banking system is restricted. If these sources of external capital are prepared to lend or invest in the small firm they will carefully study the progress made by the firm in earnings growth. Furthermore any valuation of the firm's shares, which are not publicly traded, will focus on earnings.

Shareholders' interest in earnings per share will influence the price they are prepared to pay for shares of the firm. A relationship between earnings per share and current market value is the **price-earnings ratio (P/E ratio).**

$$\text{P/E ratio} = \frac{\text{Market share price}}{\text{Earnings per share}} \quad (2\text{–}3)$$

If the market value per share for Kramer Corporation were $12.00, the price-earnings ratio would be;

$$P/E\ ratio = \frac{\$12.00}{\$1.00} = 12$$

The price-earnings ratio is influenced by the earnings and the sales growth of the firm, the risk (or volatility in performance), the debt-equity structure of the firm, the dividend payment policy, the quality of management, and a number of other factors. Because companies have various levels of earnings per share, price-earnings ratios allow us to compare the relative market value of many companies based on $1.00 of earnings per share.

The P/E ratio indicates expectations as to a company's future performance. Firms expected to provide greater than average returns often have P/E ratios higher than the market average P/E ratio. Investors' expectations as to future returns change over time. This can trigger substantial changes in a company's P/E ratio as indicated in Table 2–3.

TABLE 2–3
Price-earnings ratios for selected companies

		P/E Ratio				
Corporation	**Industry**	**Dec. 1981**	**Sept. 1992**	**Nov. 1995**	**Mar. 1999**	**Sept. 2001**
Abitibi	Forest products	3.7	—	21.1	—	9.3
BCE	Telecommunications	7.8	11.2	14.9	24.8	17.4
Bank of Montreal	Banking	3.9	8.8	8.6	13.8	11.0
Loblaw	Grocery chain	6.2	18.5	18.1	41.8	27.8
Molson	Brewery	9.1	13.5	22.2	6.4	21.3
Open Text	Tech. Software				443.8	43.5
PanCanadian	Petroleum	10.3	143.4	23.3	29.2	7.0
TSE 300	Index	8.6	110.2	13.2	24.55	−81.9

*No P/E ratios are reported on negative earnings. TSE 300 the exception due to huge losses at Nortel and JDS.

Price-earnings ratios, although usually consolidating a great deal of information about a company, can also be confusing. When a firm's earnings are dropping rapidly, perhaps even approaching zero, the decline in its stock price may be more gradual. This process can give rise to the appearance of an increasing P/E ratio under adversity. This happens occasionally in cyclical industries such as Canada's resource-based companies.

EnCana
www.encana.com
Open Text Corporation
www.opentext.com

In 1992 many shares were trading at high P/E ratios due to depressed earnings. PanCanadian was at a ratio well above 100, a reflection of the poor earnings in the petroleum industry. As earnings improved, P/E ratios became more reasonable and by 2001 with record earnings in the oil patch PanCanadian's P/E ratio had dropped considerably on expectations of subdued growth due to expected declines in oil and gas prices. In the late 1990s P/E ratios were high by historical standards due to very low interest rates and good economic growth prospects. Open Text a company in the high-tech business traded at a huge P/E ratio based on future expected earnings not its current meager earnings. By 2001, expectations for future Open Text earnings had declined considerably.

Shareholders may place a higher value on income received from dividends, as compared to future expected earnings that may result from reinvested earnings. Therefore dividends often form the basis of the valuation of the firm's performance. The yield in immediate returns via dividends is the **dividend yield.**

$$\text{Dividend yield} = \frac{\text{Dividends per share}}{\text{Market share price}} \tag{2–4}$$

For Kramer Corporation this is,

$$\textit{Dividend yield} = \frac{\$0.50}{\$12.00} = .0417 \text{ or } 4.17\%$$

Limitations of the Income Statement

A financial analyst examines the income statement with knowledge of how earnings or profits are defined. While the accountant records past events, the financial analyst builds models and suggests values based on the future. Like the economist, the analyst views past events as somewhat irrelevant for valuation purposes. It is the timing of cash flows in the future that is relevant for valuation. The accountant imposes a specific time period on the income statement, requiring accruals that don't necessarily reflect the timing of cash flows or changes in a corporation's value. The accountant and economist, or financial analyst, would likely have different numbers to reflect a company's profits.

The economist defines income as the change in real worth that occurs between the beginning and the end of a specified time period. To the economist, an increase in the value of a firm's land as a result of a new airport being built on an adjacent property is an increase in the real worth of the firm. It therefore represents income. Similarly, the elimination of a competitor might also increase the firm's real worth and, therefore, result in income in an economic sense. The accountant does not ordinarily employ such a broad definition of income. Accounting values are established primarily by actual transactions, and income that is gained or lost during a given period is a function of verifiable transactions. While the potential sales price of a company's property may go from $10 million to $20 million as a result of new developments in the area, its shareholders may perceive only a much smaller gain from operations, as reported in the accounting statements.

Also, as will be pointed out in Chapter 3, there is some flexibility in the reporting of transactions. This means similar events may result in differing measurements of income at the end of the period. The choices accountants make in accounting policies and methods used for value determination should be clearly indicated in the notes to financial statements. The intent of this section is not to criticize the accounting profession, for it is certainly among the best-organized, best-trained, and best-paid professions, but to alert students to the fact that some judgement is involved in financial reporting. Therefore, consumers of financial statements must also be prepared to exercise judgement, look at the footnotes, and sometimes read between the lines. Because finance focuses on cash flows and their timing, one must be careful not to equate income and cash flow.

FINANCE IN ACTION

Q1 Identify the 3rd quarter differences in GAAP and adjusted earnings at Celestica?

Q2 What is the mandate of the Ontario Securities Commission?

www.celestica.com

Symbol: CLS

www.osc.gov.on.ca

Apparently Earnings are Flexible

In June of 1999 the head of the Ontario Securities Commission expressed concern with the "quality" of earnings being reported by publicly traded companies. He suggested that in an effort to meet earnings targets, accountants had resorted to stretching accounting standards beyond their reasonable limits. There is pressure on companies to meet earnings targets and share prices often decline when the target is not met. It is important that we realize that professional accounting bodies allow some latitude in the preparation of financial statements and that the auditors that prepare the statements rely to a significant extent on the discretion of company management. The Securities Commission in each province has the power to force public companies to clarify or reissue financial statements. Under "Hot Topics" the OSC at its web site identifies current concerns in accounting practice.

Corporations have also taken to the issuance of pro forma earnings statements, which are more broadly subject to management interpretation. These statements "adjust" generally accepted accounting principles (GAAP) by excluding such items as goodwill amortization, stock based compensation, expenses related to cost-cutting measures, and other non-cash charges. For example in the 3rd quarter of 2001 Celestica reported GAAP earnings of $32 million and adjusted earnings of $245 million. Corporations argue that these adjustments to earnings better reflect their ongoing operations because the identified charges are not related to their core business. Some believe these adjusted statements mislead investors, while some suggest that the additional information has a distinct advantage. What do you think?

Balance Sheet

The **balance sheet** indicates what the firm owns and how these assets are financed in the form of liabilities or ownership interest. While the income statement purports to show the profitability of the firm, the balance sheet delineates the firm's holdings and obligations. Together, these statements are intended to answer two questions: How much did the firm make or lose, and what is a measure of its worth? Examination of the balance sheet also reveals the firm's ability to accept opportunities and to deal with difficulties. A balance sheet for the Kramer Corporation is presented in Table 2–4.

Note that the balance sheet is a picture of the firm at a point in time—in this—case December 31, 2002. It does not purport to represent the result of transactions for a specific month, quarter, or year, but rather it is a cumulative chronicle of all transactions that have affected the corporation since its inception. In contrast, the income statement measures results only over a short, quantifiable period. Good income statement results usually produce healthy balance sheets. Generally, balance sheet items are stated on an original cost basis rather than at present worth.

Interpretation of Balance Sheet Items

Asset accounts are listed in order of liquidity. **Liquidity** is a measure of how quickly an asset can be converted to cash. The first category of current assets covers items that may be converted to cash within one year (or within the normal operating cycle of the firm). A few items are worthy of mention. *Marketable securities* are temporary investments of excess cash. The value shown in the account is the lower of cost or current market value. *Accounts receivable* include an allowance for bad debts (based on historical evidence) to determine their anticipated collection value. *Inventory* may be in the form of raw material, goods in process, or finished goods, while *prepaid expenses* represent future expense items that have already been paid, such as insurance premiums or rent.

TABLE 2–4
Balance Sheet

KRAMER CORPORATION
Balance Sheet (Statement of Financial Position)
December 31, 2002

Assets		
Current assets:		
Cash		$ 40,000
Marketable securities		10,000
Accounts receivable	$ 220,000	
Less: Allowance for bad debts	20,000	200,000
Inventory		180,000
Prepaid expenses		20,000
Total current assets		450,000
Other assets:		
Investments		50,000
Capital assets		
Plant and equipment, original cost	$1,100,000	
Less: Accumulated amortization	600,000	
Net plant and equipment		500,000
Total assets		$1,000,000
Liabilities and Shareholders' Equity		
Current liabilities:		
Accounts payable		$ 80,000
Notes payable (bank indebtedness)		100,000
Accrued expenses		30,000
Total current liabilities		210,000
Long-term liabilities:		
Bonds payable, 2012		90,000
Total liabilities		300,000
Shareholders' equity:		
Preferred stock, 500 shares		50,000
Common stock, 100,000 shares		350,000
Retained earnings		300,000
Total shareholders' equity		700,000
Total liabilities and shareholders' equity		$1,000,000

With liquidity and cash flow being important considerations, the financial manager must carefully monitor changes in the current assets, as significant increases can quickly tie up cash resources. This will likely require planning arrangements to finance the increases. Chapters 6 to 8 explore these working capital demands.

Investments, unlike marketable securities, represent a longer-term commitment of funds (at least one year). They may include stocks, bonds, or investments in other corporations. Frequently, the account will contain stock in companies that the firm is acquiring.

Plant and equipment is carried at original cost minus accumulated amortization. Accumulated amortization is not to be confused with the amortization expense item indicated in the income statement in Table 2–1 on page 27. Accumulated amortization is the sum of all past and present amortization charges on currently owned assets, while amortization expense is the current year's charge. If we subtract accumulated amortization from the original value, the balance ($500,000) tells us how much of the original cost has not been expensed in the form of amortization.

Total assets are financed through either liabilities or shareholders' equity. Liabilities represent financial obligations of the firm and move from current liabilities (due within one year) to longer-term obligations, such as bonds payable in 2012.

Among the short-term obligations, *accounts payable* represent amounts owed on open account to suppliers, while *notes payable* are generally short-term signed obligations to the banker or other creditors. An *accrued expense* is generated when a financial service has been provided or an obligation incurred and payment has not yet occurred. We may owe workers additional wages for services provided or the government taxes on earned income.

In the balance sheet presented in Table 2–4 on page 33, we see the $1 million in total assets of the Kramer Corporation was financed by $300,000 in debt and $700,000 in the form of shareholders' equity. **Shareholders' equity** represents the total contribution and ownership interest of preferred and common shareholders.

The *preferred stock* investment position is $50,000, based on 500 shares. In the case of *common stock*, 100,000 shares have been issued for $350,000.[3] We can assume that the 100,000 shares were originally sold at $3.50 each.

Finally, there is $300,000 in *retained earnings*. This value, previously determined in the statement of retained earnings (Table 2–2), represents the firm's cumulative earnings since inception minus dividends and any other adjustments.

Valuation Basics from the Balance Sheet

Shareholders' equity minus the preferred stock component represents the **net worth** or **book value** of the firm. If you take everything that the firm owns and subtract the debt and preferred stock obligation, the remainder belongs to the common shareholder and represents net worth.[4] In the case of the Kramer Corporation, we show:

Total assets	$1,000,000
Total liabilities	300,000
Shareholders' equity	700,000
Preferred stock obligation	50,000
Net worth assigned to common	$ 650,000
Common shares outstanding	100,000
Net worth, or book value, per share	$ 6.50

[3]In most current Canadian circumstances, new common stock and preferred stock is issued on a no par value basis. However, some corporate balance sheets still reflect the historical split between the par value of shares on issue and the premium, termed contributed surplus, paid by investors above that par value.

[4]An additional discussion of preferred stock is presented in Chapter 17. Preferred stock represents neither a debt claim nor an ownership interest in the firm. It is a hybrid, or intermediate, security.

The original investment in the firm by shareholders was $350,000 and $300,000 of earnings have since been reinvested in the firm. Together these totals also represent the net worth of $650,000.

Because the concept of net worth (book value) is based on historical asset costs (Assets − Liabilities − Preferred stock), net worth may bear little relationship to value currently put on shareholders' equity by investors or the marketplace via share price. This will occur because the assets held by the firm have increased in value but this increased value is not yet recognized by the financial statements. Analysts often calculate the relationship between **market value per share** and historical **book value per share.**

$$\frac{\text{Market value}}{\text{Book value}} = \frac{\text{MV}}{\text{BV}} = \frac{\text{Market value per share}}{\text{Book value per share}} \qquad (2\text{–}5)$$

For Kramer Corporation with a market value of $12.00;

$$\frac{MV}{BV} = \frac{\$12.00}{\$6.50} = 1.85 \textit{ times}$$

In examining this ratio we have to ask ourselves why market value has moved away from book value and is this justified. A higher ratio suggests that the assets have achieved synergies beyond their original cost and are expected to generate increasing returns by way of cash flows in the future. A lower ratio may suggest the opposite. Kramer ratio appears reasonable.

In Table 2–5 we look at disparities between market value and book value for a number of publicly traded companies in 2001, as identified by the ratio in the last column. Besides asset valuation, a number of other factors may explain the wide differences, including industry outlook, growth prospects, quality of management, and risk-return expectations. Open Text is a technology company with a lot of human capital, which doesn't show up on the balance sheet, and is a firm with good growth potential. Stelco is in the declining steel business with huge investment in tangible capital assets and a product subject to unrelenting competition with poor growth prospects.

TABLE 2–5
Comparison of market value to book value per share, September 2001

Corporation	Market Value per Share	Book Value per Share	Ratio of Market Value to Book Value
Abitibi	$12.08	$ 8.08	1.50
Bank of Montreal	41.50	20.44	2.03
BCE	38.20	20.32	1.88
Inco	25.55	26.27	0.97
Loblaw	52.15	11.84	4.40
Molson	25.50	13.30	1.92
PanCanadian	47.80	18.60	2.57
Open Text	36.10	5.65	6.39
Rogers Comm.	24.00	11.13	2.16
Stelco	3.58	8.49	0.42

Source: Company financial reports (accessible through the TSX web site www.tsx.ca).

Limitations of the Balance Sheet

Lest we attribute too much significance to the balance sheet, we need to examine some of the concepts underlying its construction. Most of the values on the balance sheet are stated on a **historical or original cost basis.** This may be particularly troublesome in the case of plant and equipment and inventory, which may now be worth two or three times the original cost or—from a negative viewpoint—may require many times the original cost for replacement. Choice of accounting policies, which should be disclosed in the financial notes will also influence the values recorded on the balance sheet. Furthermore, we must consider those items such as contingent liabilities that are omitted from the balance sheet or those items such as intangibles that are included. It is often difficult to determine their impact on economic value. Contingent liabilities should be disclosed in footnotes, alerting us to their possible impact on the balance sheet.

The accounting profession has been grappling with the valuation problem for decades, and many attempts to move toward more market-based orientation for financial statements have been made. Discussion was particularly intense when attempting to capture the effects of inflation. In January 1983, the Canadian Institute of Chartered Accountants (CICA) recommended that large companies disclose inflation-adjusted data to supplement the traditional historical cost data. The accounting profession recommended the use of the **current cost method** (sometimes referred to as replacement cost). This method required assets to be revalued at their current costs. There was a significant noncompliance on this issue because of the costs and complexities in preparing these statements. Furthermore, with inflation reduced to less than 2 percent annually for most of the 1990s, as illustrated in Figure 1–2 on page 11, it was not as pressing an issue.

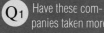

FINANCE IN ACTION

Q1 Have these companies taken more write offs?

Q2 Have their share prices improved lately?

www.jdsuniphase.com

www.nortelnetworks.com

Symbols: JDU, NT

Where did all the assets go?

In 2001 JDS Uniphase Corporation, a leader in the manufacture of fibre optic components, declared a loss of U.S.$50.6 billion for the year. Nortel Networks Corporation an Internet and communications leader lost U.S.$19.2 billion in the second quarter of 2001. Both companies explained that most of their loss was attributable to the write-off of goodwill. For JDS this goodwill write-off was U.S.$41.2 billion and for Nortel U.S.$12.3 billion. Goodwill is the difference between the price paid for the acquisition of another company and the fair value of its tangible assets.

These two companies had gone on a spending spree in the late 1990s acquiring numerous companies in the technology sector not for cash, but by issuing additional stock. Nortel had made 18 acquisitions with, at the time, U.S.$33 billion of its own stock. By 2001 these acquisitions were no longer worth their purchase price and the goodwill on the books of JDS and Nortel wasn't worth much either. Each reduced the value of their goodwill by taking monumental losses on their income statements, resulting in a significant reduction in the book value of their equity. However these were noncash charges to the financial statements.

The values had dropped so drastically because the market for the products of these companies dried up. In some product lines, revenues dropped over 90 percent. Assets are only as valuable as the cash flows they generate. Interestingly the market had already devalued the price of the company shares significantly, long before the accounting statements reflected the change in value. The current share prices of these companies can be found at: www.tsx.ca.

There has also been evidence that the financial statements that were adjusted to more fully reflect current values did not impact significantly on the valuation perspective of investors. The investors had already reflected inflation's impact on company values by raising or lowering market share prices. Investors required only sufficient information from statements on which to base their valuations, but whether it was historical or current value based did not seem to matter. Efficient markets, as discussed in Chapter 14, appear to be indifferent to the way in which financial information is displayed.

Statement of Cash Flows

In financial reporting, the accounting profession requires a third financial statement specifically aimed at supplementing the information provided by the balance sheet and the income statement. In 1998 the **statement of cash flows** replaced the statement of changes in financial position (SCFP) for reporting the cash effects of all changes between a beginning and ending balance sheet for a time period. The change was made by the CICA to meet International Accounting Standards and FASB in the United States. With a global economy the standardization of accounting information worldwide is a desired goal.

International Accounting Standards Committee
www.iasc.org.uk
Financial Accounting Standards Board
accounting.rutgers.edu/raw/fasb

The income statement provides information on the measurement of revenues and expenses over a time period, while the balance sheet shows valuations for assets, liabilities, and shareholders' equity at a point in time. These two statements do not provide adequate information on the amount and timing of cash flowing into and out of the business. Accrual accounting attempts to match revenues and expenses even if the cash flows related to these items occur at quite different times. Therefore, for many internal and external users of a firm's financial information, **cash flow** information is critical. For the small business cash flow statements are particularly important, as cash flow is more relevant to the firm's short-term survival than its reported income. One is likely to be concerned about the quality, timing, and amount of earnings and, hence, the firm's ability to acquire assets and to meet its obligations. Historical cash flows are often useful in estimating future cash flows.

In 1974 the CICA defined the content of a funds flow statement to include the financing and investing activities of the enterprise as well as those operating activities that affected cash or working capital. Since 1985, the CICA has required firms to report the changes in cash and cash equivalents (rather than working capital) resulting from the activities of the firm during a given period. Movements between cash and cash equivalents are not reported. Financing and investing activities that do use cash or equivalents, such as buying a business for shares or by assuming debts should not be included in the cash flow statement.

Cash equivalents are highly liquid investments (usually with maturities of less than three months) less any bank overdrafts. They should have little risk of change in value because they are held to meet short-term commitments. Equity investments are therefore excluded. The *CICA Handbook* suggests the firm disclose its policy distinguishing between cash equivalents and investments. Cash and cash equivalents that have their use restricted due to requirements set by banks or are subject to foreign currency exchange controls should also be disclosed.

By examining the statement of cash flows, analysts can monitor the relative build-up in short-term and long-term assets. Furthermore, they can examine the means of financing used to support any growth in the firm's asset base. They can then judge the appropriateness and the future implications of the financing used.

The statement of cash flows translates income statement and balance sheet data into cash flow information. A corporation that has $1 million in accrual-based accounting profits can determine whether it can actually afford to pay a cash dividend to shareholders, buy new equipment, or undertake new projects. In the very competitive corporate environment of today exacting cash flow analysis is essential for a firm's survival.

Developing an Actual Statement

We use the information previously provided for the Kramer Corporation to illustrate how the statement of cash flows is developed.

But first, let's identify the three primary sections of the statement of cash flows. These sections are:

1. Operating activities.
2. Investing activities.
3. Financing activities.

After each of these sections is completed, the results are added together to compute the net increase or decrease in cash and cash equivalents for the corporation. An example of the process is shown in Figure 2–1. Let's begin with cash flows from operating activities.

FIGURE 2–1

Illustration of concepts behind the statement of cash flows

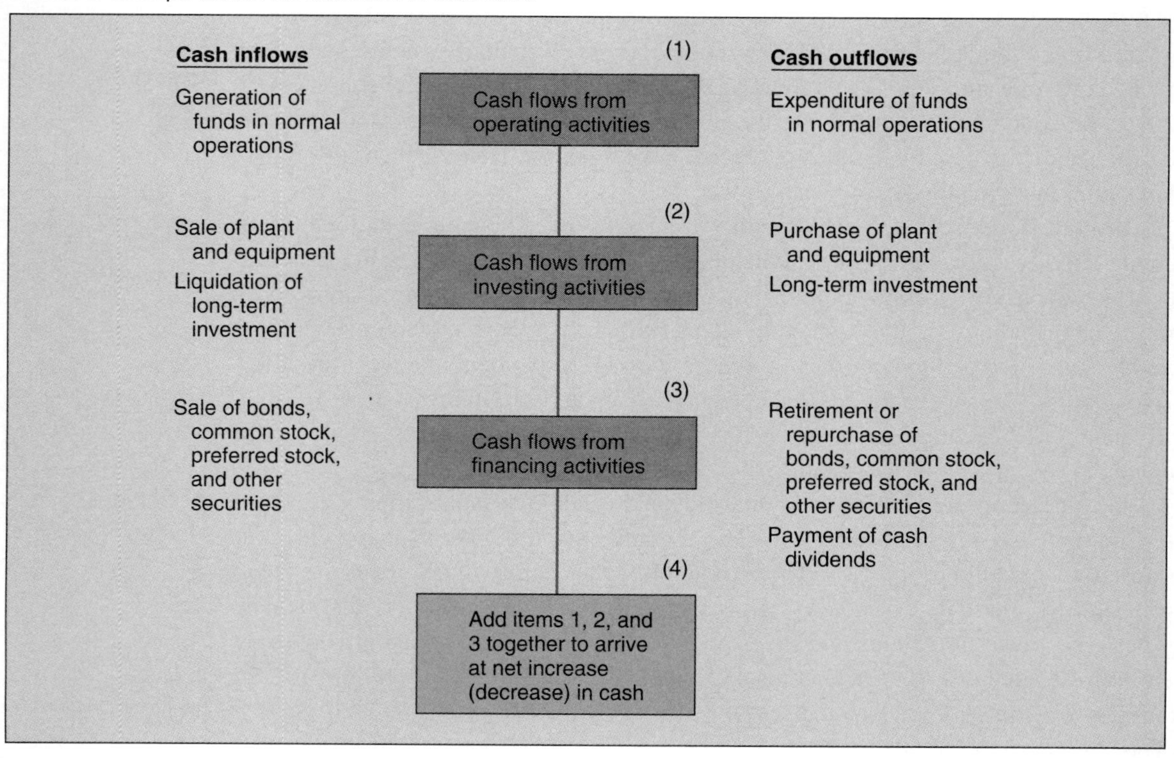

Determining Cash Flows from Operating Activities

Basically, we are going to translate *income from operations* from an accrual to a cash basis. There are two ways to accomplish this objective. First, the firm may use a *direct method,* in which every item on the income statement is adjusted from accrual accounting to cash accounting. This is a tedious process that requires the adjustment of all sales to cash sales, all purchases adjusted to cash purchases, and so on. A June 1998 statement in the *CICA Handbook* encourages the use of the direct method. However, a more popular method is the *indirect method,* in which net income represents the starting point and then adjustments are made to convert net income to cash flows from operations.[5] This is the method we will use here. Regardless of whether the direct or indirect method is used, the same final answer is derived.

We follow these procedures to compute cash flows from operating activities using the indirect method.[6]

- Start with net income.
- Recognize that noncash deductions in computing net income should be added back to net income to *increase* the cash balance. These include such items as amortization, deferred income taxes, restructuring charges, and foreign exchange losses. This produces cash flow from operations.
- Next identify changes in noncash working capital.
- Recognize that increases in current assets are a use of funds and *reduce* the cash balance (indirectly)—as an example, the firm spends more funds on inventory.
- Recognize that decreases in current assets are a source of funds and *increase* the cash balance (indirectly)—that is, the firm reduces funds tied up in inventory.
- Recognize that increases in current liabilities are a source of funds and *increase* the cash balance (indirectly)—that is, the firm gets more funds from creditors.
- Recognize that decreases in current liabilities are a use of funds and *decrease* the cash balance (indirectly)—that is, the firm pays off creditors.

These steps are illustrated in Figure 2–2 on page 40.

We follow these procedures for the Kramer Corporation, drawing primarily on material from Table 2–1 (the previously presented income statement) and from Table 2–6 (on page 41) (which shows balance sheet data for the most recent two years). A quick look at the changes in assets on the balance sheets from one year to the next tells us of increased demands for cash resources.

The analysis is presented in Table 2–7 on page 42. We begin with net income (earnings aftertaxes) of $110,500 and add back amortization of $50,000. We then show that increases in current assets (accounts receivable and inventory) reduce funds and that decreases in current assets (prepaid expenses) increase funds. Also, we show increases in current liabilities (accounts payable) as an addition to funds and decreases in current liabilities (accrued expenses) as a reduction of funds.

---

[5]The indirect method is similar to procedures used to construct the old sources and uses of funds statement.

[6]In addition to the items mentioned, we may need to recognize the gains or losses on the sale of operating and nonoperating assets. We exclude these for ease of analysis.

FIGURE 2–2

Steps in computing cash provided by operating activities using the Indirect method

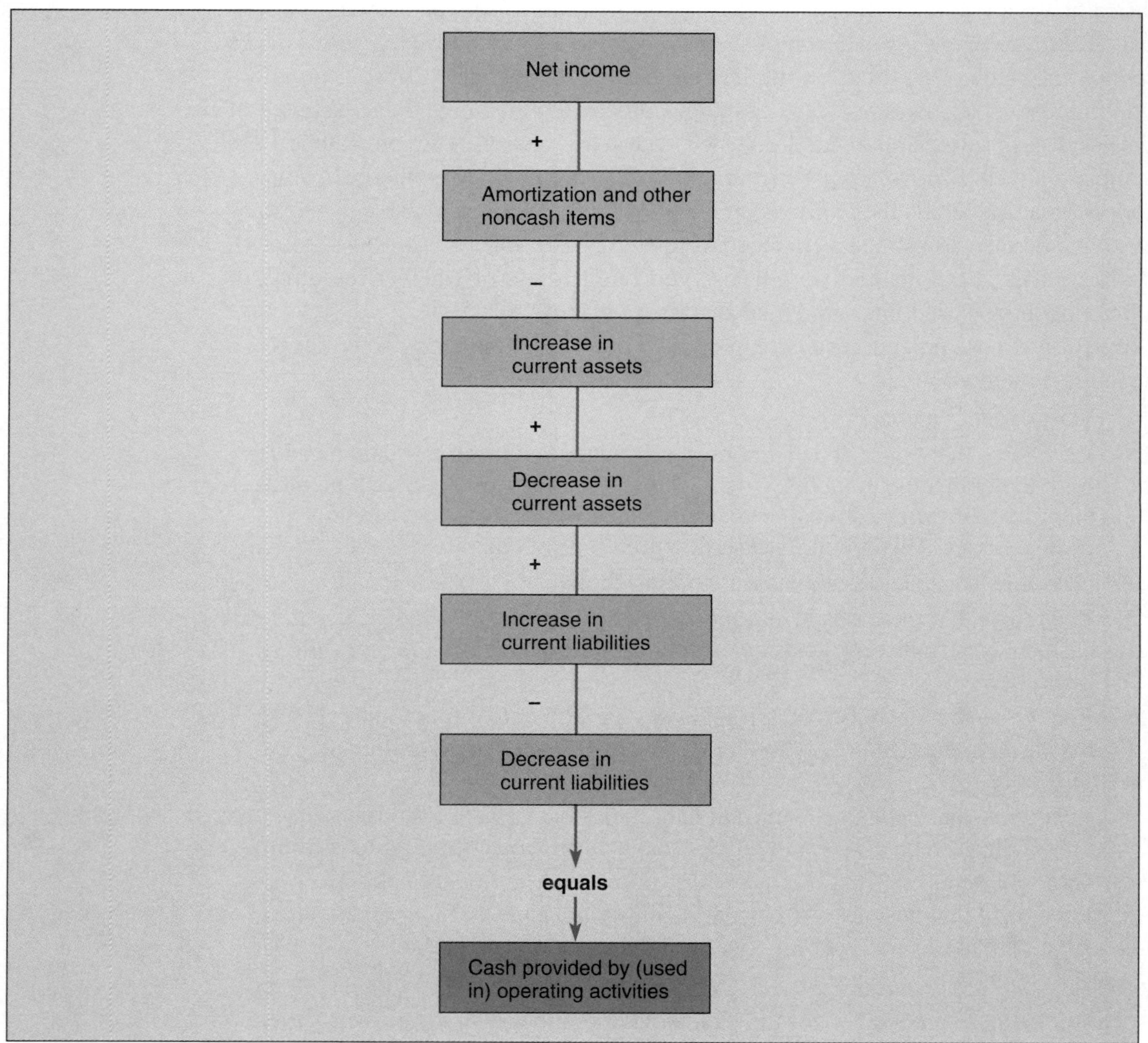

We see in Table 2–7, on page 42, that the firm generated $150,500 in cash flows from operating activities. This figure is $40,000 larger than the net income figure reported to shareholders ($150,500 − $110,500). You can also envision that a firm with little amortization and a massive buildup of inventory might show lower cash flow than reported net income. Once cash flows from operating activities are determined, management has a better feel for what can be allocated to investing or financing needs such as paying cash dividends.

Determining Cash Flows from Investing Activities

The second section in the statement of cash flows relates to long-term investment activities in other issuers' securities or, more importantly, in plant and equipment.

TABLE 2–6
Comparative Balance Sheets

KRAMER CORPORATION
Comparative Balance Sheets

	Dec. 31 2002	Dec. 31 2001
Assets		
Current assets:		
Cash	$ 40,000	$ 30,000
Marketable securities	10,000	10,000
Accounts receivable (net)	200,000	170,000
Inventory	180,000	160,000
Prepaid expenses	20,000	30,000
Total current assets	450,000	400,000
Investments (long-term)	50,000	20,000
Plant and equipment	1,100,000	1,000,000
Less: Accumulated amortization	600,000	550,000
Net plant and equipment	500,000	450,000
Total assets	$1,000,000	$ 870,000
Liabilities and Shareholders' Equity		
Current liabilities:		
Accounts payable	$ 80,000	$ 45,000
Notes payable	100,000	100,000
Accrued expenses	30,000	35,000
Total current liabilities	210,000	180,000
Long-term liabilities:		
Bonds payable, 2012	90,000	40,000
Total liabilities	300,000	220,000
Shareholders equity:		
Preferred stock	50,000	50,000
Common stock	350,000	350,000
Retained earnings	300,000	250,000
Total shareholders' equity	700,000	650,000
Total liabilities and shareholders' equity	$1,000,000	$870,000

Increasing investments represent a *use* of funds, and decreasing investments represent a *source* of funds.

Examining Table 2–6 for the Kramer Corporation, we show the cash flow information in Table 2–8 on page 42.

Determining Cash Flows from Financing Activities

In the third section of the statement of cash flows, we show the effects of financing activities on the corporation. Financing activities apply to the sale or retirement of bonds, common stock, preferred stock, and other corporate securities. Also, the payment of cash dividends is considered a financing activity. The sale of the firm's securities

TABLE 2–7
Cash flows from operating activities

Operating Activities		
Net income (earnings aftertaxes) (Table 2–1)		$110,500
Add items not requiring an outlay of cash:		
Amortization (Table 2–1)	$ 50,000	
Cash flow from operations		160,500
Changes in noncash working capital:		
Increase in accounts receivable (Table 2–6)	(30,000)	
Increase in inventory (Table 2–6)	(20,000)	
Decrease in prepaid expenses (Table 2–6)	10,000	
Increase in accounts payable (Table 2–6)	35,000	
Decrease in accrued expenses (Table 2–6)	(5,000)	
Net change in noncash working capital		(10,000)
Cash provided by (used in) operating activities		$150,500

TABLE 2–8
Cash flows from investing activities

Investing Activities	
Increase in investments (long-term securities) (Table 2–6)	($ 30,000)
Increase in plant and equipment (Table 2–6)	(100,000)
Cash used in investing activities	($130,000)

TABLE 2–9
Cash flows from financing activities

Financing Activities	
Increase in bonds payable (Table 2–6)	$50,000
Preferred stock dividends paid (Table 2–1)	(10,500)
Common stock dividends paid (Table 2–2)	(50,000)
Cash used in financing activities	($10,500)

represents a *source* of funds, and the retirement or repurchase of such securities represents a *use* of funds.

Using the data from Tables 2–1, 2–2, and 2–6, the financing activities of the Kramer Corporation are shown in Table 2–9.

Combining the Three Sections of the Statement

We now combine the three sections of the statement of cash flows. This statement of cash flows reveals information not readily available from the other two statements.

As it reveals the patterns of cash flows in the firm, the information from this statement is valuable information to bankers, creditors, and investors who focus on dividends. These groups are particularly concerned with the liquidity of the firm and its ability to generate cash flow. Highly profitable firms have been known to go bankrupt because of the firm's inability to generate the cash needed to meet its obligations. The

Earnings and Cash Flow: The Difference at Cominco Ltd.

FINANCE IN ACTION

Cominco Ltd. is one of the world's largest producers of zinc and lead concentrates, with interests from Canada's high arctic to Chile in South America. As an integrated natural resource company, its activities include mineral exploration, mining, smelting, and refining. Gold, silver, copper, and cadmium are other metal products of note. Sales in 2000 topped $1.8 billion with net earnings of $170 million. Cominco's net earnings are sensitive to change in commodity prices and the U.S. dollar. A U.S. $0.01 change in the per pound zinc price will change net earnings by $11 million, and a U.S. $0.01 change in the Canadian dollar will change net earnings by $7 million. In 2001 Cominco merged with Teck to become TeckCominco.

To remain competitive in these world markets, Cominco must continually reinvest in modern equipment. These capital investments are funded by borrowing in the capital markets and also from funds generated from Cominco's operations. The accompanying table shows that although earnings were volatile throughout the 1990s, capital expenditures remained strong. An important observation is the significant difference between cash flow from operations and earnings. The most significant contributor to the difference is amortization (or depreciation) charges, which, of course, are related to previous and current capital expenditures. It was this cash flow that partially funded the capital investments. In finance our focus is primarily on cash flow.

	Earnings	Cash Flow from Operations	Capital Expenditures
2000	$170	$412	$189
1999	159	281	95
1998	(23)	109	161
1997	(74)	291	265
1996	152	184	310
1995	104	266	182
1994	132	143	172
1993	(113)	(39)	190
1992	(30)	99	142
1991	(41)	42	142
1990	55	186	238

Note: Figures in millions, available with the latest financial statements.

Q1 Is TeckCominco continuing this substantial investment? Update this table.

www.teckcominco.com

Symbol: TEK.A

statement of cash flows also reveals information on the firm's management of, and requirements for, financing and investment.

We see in Table 2–10 on page 44, that Kramer Corporation created excess funds from operating activities that were utilized heavily in investing activities and somewhat in financing activities. As a result, there is a $10,000 increase in the cash balance, and this can also be reconciled with the increase in the cash balance of $10,000 from $30,000 to $40,000, as indicated in Table 2–6.

Operating activities place cash demands on working capital with current asset buildup and increases in current liabilities. Chapters 6 to 8 examine these demands. Investing activities are examined through the capital budgeting process of Chapter 12. The longer-term capital requirements of financing activities are considered in Chapters 16 to 18 covering bonds, preferred and common shares.

One might also further analyze how the buildups in various accounts were financed. For example, if there is a substantial increase in inventory or accounts receivable, is there an associated buildup in accounts payable and short-term bank loans? If not, the firm may have to use long-term financing to carry part of the short-term needs. An

TABLE 2–10
Statement of cash flows

KRAMER CORPORATION
Statement of Cash Flows
For the Year Ended December 31, 2002

Operating Activities		
Net income (earnings aftertaxes)		$110,500
Add items not requiring an outlay of cash:		
Amortization	$ 50,000	
Cash flow from operations		160,500
Changes in noncash working capital:		
Increase in accounts receivable	(30,000)	
Increase in inventory	(20,000)	
Decrease in prepaid expenses	10,000	
Increase in accounts payable	35,000	
Decrease in accrued expenses	(5,000)	
Net change in noncash working capital		(10,000)
Cash provided by (used in) operating activities		$150,500
Investing Activities		
Increase in investments (long-term securities)	($ 30,000)	
Increase in plant and equipment	(100,000)	
Cash used in investing activities		($130,000)
Financing Activities		
Increase in bonds payable	$ 50,000	
Preferred stock dividends paid	(10,500)	
Common stock dividends paid	(50,000)	
Cash used in financing activities		($ 10,500)
Net increase (decrease) in *cash during the year		$ 10,000
*Cash, beginning of year		30,000
***Cash, end of year**		$ 40,000

*This would include cash equivalents if there were any.

even more important question might be: How are increases in long-term assets being financed? Most desirably, there should be adequate long-term financing and profits to carry these needs. If not, then short-term funds (trade credit and bank loans) may be utilized to carry long-term needs. This is a potentially high-risk situation, in that short-term sources of funds may dry up while long-term needs continue to demand funding. In the problems at the back of this chapter, you will have an opportunity to further consider these points.

Amortization and Cash Flow

One of the most confusing items for finance students is whether amortization is a source of funds to the corporation. In Table 2–7, we added amortization to net income in determining the cash flow from operations. The reason we added back amortization was not because amortization was a source of new funds, but rather, because we had

TABLE 2–11
Comparison of accounting and cash flows

	Year 1	
	(1) Accounting Flows	(2) Cash Flows
Earnings before amortization and taxes (EBAT)	$1,000	$1,000
Amortization	100	100
Earnings before taxes (EBT)	900	900
Taxes	400	400
Earnings aftertaxes (EAT)	$ 500	500
Purchase of equipment		−500
Amortization charged without cash outlay		+100
Cash flow		$ 100
	Year 2	
Earnings before amortization and taxes (EBAT)	$1,000	$1,000
Amortization	100	100
Earnings before taxes	900	900
Taxes	400	400
Earnings aftertaxes (EAT)	$ 500	500
Amortization charged without cash outlay		+100
Cash flow		$ 600

subtracted this noncash deduction in arriving at net income and have to add it back to determine the actual cash flow effect of operations.

Amortization represents an attempt to allocate the initial cost of an asset over its useful life. In essence, we attempt to match the annual expense of plant and equipment ownership against the revenues being produced. Nevertheless, the charging of amortization is purely an accounting entry and does not directly involve the movement of funds. To go from accounting flows to cash flows in Table 2–7, we restored the noncash deduction of $50,000 for amortization that was subtracted in Table 2–1, the income statement.

Let us examine a very simple case involving amortization. Assume we purchase a machine for $500 with a five-year life and we pay for it in cash. Our amortization schedule calls for equal amortization of $100 per year for five years. Assume further that our firm has $1,000 in earnings before amortization and taxes and the tax obligation is $400. Note the difference between accounting flows and cash flows for the first two years in Table 2–11.

Since we took $500 out of cash flow originally (column 2), we do not wish to take it out again. Thus, we add back $100 in amortization each year to "wash out" the subtraction in the income statement.

Free Cash Flow

A term that has received increasingly greater attention is **free cash flow** (FCF). This is actually a by-product of the previously discussed statement of cash flows. Free cash flow is equal to:

Cash flow from operating activities

Minus: Capital expenditures (required to maintain the productive capacity of the firm)

Minus: Dividends (needed to maintain the necessary payout on common stock and to cover any preferred stock obligation).

The concept of free cash flow forces the stock analyst or banker not only to consider how much cash is generated from operating activities, but also to subtract out the necessary capital expenditures on plant and equipment to maintain normal activities. Similarly, dividend payments to shareholders must be subtracted out, as these dividends must generally be paid to keep shareholders satisfied.

The balance, free cash flow, is then available for *special financial activities*. In the last decade, special financing activities have often been synonymous with leveraged buyouts, in which a firm borrows money to buy its stock and take itself private with the hope of restructuring its balance sheet and perhaps going public again in a few years at a higher price than it paid. Leveraged buyouts are discussed more fully in Chapter 15. The analyst or banker normally looks at *free cash flow* to determine whether there are sufficient excess funds to pay back the loan associated with the leveraged buyout.

Income Tax Considerations

After expenses are deducted from revenues, the firm usually is required to pay income taxes on the remaining income. Besides reducing income, cash flows available to the firm will be reduced. Virtually every financial decision is influenced by federal and provincial income tax considerations because of the impact on cash flows. While the intent of this section is not to review the rules, regulations, and nuances of the Income Tax Act, we briefly examine tax rates and note that they will influence corporate financial decisions by reducing income and cash flows. The primary orientation is toward the principles governing corporate tax decisions, though many of the same principles apply to a sole proprietorship or partnership.

We also examine personal tax considerations to identify how various investment returns are taxed differently under the Income Tax Act. This is of interest from a corporate point of view because investors prefer the investment returns that receive the most favourable tax treatment.

Later chapters refer to the specific nature of income tax effects on cash flows under 2001 tax rules. This is especially notable in Chapter 12, where the nature of tax-allowable amortization (known as capital cost allowance) is explored in detail and related to the capital budgeting decision. The Income Tax Act sets rules by which capital expenditure can be deducted from income over several years. The annual expense, known as capital cost allowance in the Income Tax Act, may differ (and usually does) from how the firm amortizes a capital expenditure for accounting purposes. For cash flow effects we are concerned only with what is permissible under the Income Tax Act.

Given the complexity and ever-changing nature of the Canadian tax environment, an individual is well advised to get current tax advice from a tax expert where tax implications may be important.

To a large extent, finance is decision oriented. It is the incremental changes in the firm that come under analysis. When a firm undertakes an investment it wants to know the rate of tax that will be applied to the income that comes from that investment. An investor will also like to know how much the tax bite will be on any returns they receive from an investment. Therefore, as investment analysts we are concerned with the **marginal tax rate,** which is the rate of tax on the last dollar of cash flow or income earned.

Corporate Tax Rates

Canada Customs and Revenue Agency
www.ccra-adrc.gc.ca

Corporate federal and provincial tax rates are continually changing, both in accordance with government's need for revenue and their policies for promoting certain industries. In this section we use rates in force as of late 2001, knowing these will be changed in subsequent budgets by the government of the day. Recently the general trend in tax rates has been slightly downward.

The federal corporate tax rate attempts to be in line with competing international jurisdictions. Currently there is a general corporate rate of 27 percent, set to decrease to 21 percent by 2004. This federal rate has been reduced by 10 percent to allow the provinces to levy their own taxes on corporate income. Table 2–12 outlines the tax rates after combining the federal and provincial rates, including a federal surtax of 4 percent. Small business and manufacturing income are generally accorded reduced tax rates. Corporations should also be aware that some provinces have tax holidays (usually for CCPCs and designated industries), capital taxes on large corporations and payroll taxes. These we will leave to a tax course.

TABLE 2–12
Combined federal and provincial corporate income tax rates, 2001

	Other Corporations		(CCPC) Small Canadian-Controlled Active Business Income (in 000's)	
	Mfg.	Non-mfg.	<$200	$200–300
British Columbia	38.62%	44.62%	17.62%	38.62%
Alberta	35.62	41.62	18.12	26.62
Saskatchewan	32.12	45.12	20.11	32.12/39.12
Manitoba	39.12	45.12	19.12	39.12
Ontario	33.87	41.74	19.49	28.49/40.57
Québec	31.16	37.16	22.16	31.16
New Brunswick	38.12	44.12	17.12	26.12
Nova Scotia	38.12	44.12	18.12	38.12
Prince Edward Island	29.62	44.12	20.62	29.62/38.12
Newfoundland	27.12	42.12	18.12	27.12/36.12
Yukon	24.62	43.12	15.62	24.62/37.12
N.W.T./Nunavut	36.12	42.12	15.62/19.12	36.12

The general working definition of a small business in Canada is a firm that employs less than 100 persons, but small market share and ownership concentration also serve to define a small business. For tax purposes, the first $200,000 of active business income earned per year by a Canadian-controlled private corporation (CCPC) gets a 16 percent deduction of federal tax payable. Income from $200,000 and $300,000 is also subject to reduced rates. These reductions aim to encourage small businesses. Active income is interpreted to exclude personal services corporations and specified investment businesses. Manufacturing and processing industries receive a 7 percentage point

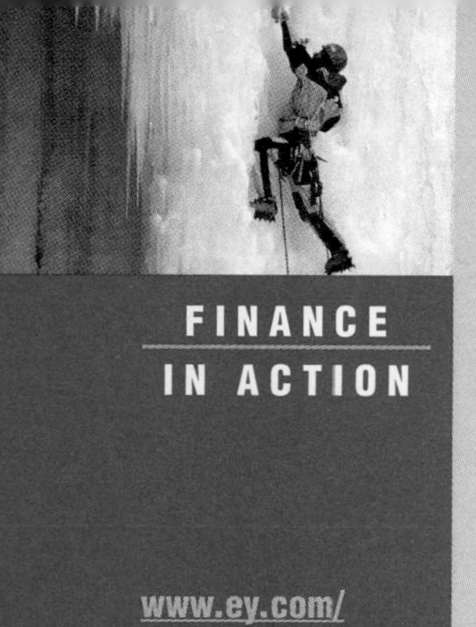

FINANCE IN ACTION

International Tax Rates

In the global economy of the 21st century, corporate investments are driven by the cash flows that can be generated for shareholders. The cash flow that can be made available to shareholders is after taxes are paid. Capital is mobile in today's world and corporations will seek out competitive environments for any major investment. Tax rates are a major consideration in any final investment decision.

Tax rates in different countries are often hard to compare because of the way taxes are calculated and because in some jurisdictions income is often determined differently. With those reservations the following rates are examples of corporate tax rates.

Canada	42–45%
Hong Kong	16
Ireland	20
Japan	41
United Kingdom	30
United States	35

Check out international tax rates in the Worldwide Corporate Tax Guide of Ernst and Young.

www.ey.com/passport

deduction from the federal rate. A small manufacturing business is taxed federally at the same rate as other small businesses. These considerations are included in the marginal tax rates of Table 2–12.

Effective Tax Rate Examples

Let us look at three examples of calculating tax payable for a business year ending December 31, 2001. Active business income is determined by reducing income by allowable expenses, including capital cost allowance.

1. Nonmanufacturing company Canadian-controlled private corporation operating in Ontario:		
Active business income		$100,000
Combined federal and provincial tax rate	19.49%	
Total tax payable		19,490
2. Manufacturing company Canadian-controlled private corporation operating in Nova Scotia:		
Active business income		$100,000
Combined federal and provincial tax rate	18.12%	
Total tax payable		18,120
3. Manufacturing company foreign-controlled operating in British Columbia:		
Active business income		$100,000
Combined federal and provincial tax rate	38.62%	
Total tax payable		38,620

Personal Taxes

Individuals, as of 2001, are taxed by the federal government at rates of 16, 22, 26, and 29 percent of taxable income. These rates are applied progressively as higher amounts of taxable income are reported by the individual. Provincial tax payable, as of 2001, is also calculated on taxable income (which is sometimes defined differently) with the percentage varying between 6.2 and 25 percent across provinces and territories. Furthermore, various surtaxes are payable in some provinces on higher income. For investment purposes, the taxpayer makes decisions based on the marginal tax rate, the tax that will be paid on the last dollar of income received. It is aftertax income that counts.

The Income Tax Act distinguishes between income received as interest (bonds), dividends (shares), or capital gains (increase in an investment's value) and taxes each at different rates. This is of interest to corporations, as it may be a minor influence on the way they raise monies from investors. Investors will prefer one form of income over another, all other things being equal. Table 2–13 shows the top marginal tax rates in each province on incomes in excess of $100,000 and the rate on incomes between $31,000 and $50,000 for each type of investment income.

TABLE 2–13
Combined federal and provincial personal income tax rates, 2001

	Interest		Dividends		Capital Gains	
	Top		Top		Top	
British Columbia	45.70%	32.50%	33.08%	16.58%	22.85%	16.25%
Alberta	39.00	32.00	24.08	15.33	19.50	16.00
Saskatchewan	45.00	35.50	29.58	17.71	22.50	17.75
Manitoba	46.40	38.20	33.83	23.58	23.20	19.10
Ontario	46.41	31.22	31.34	15.94	23.20	15.61
Quèbec	48.72	39.62	33.44	22.07	24.36	19.81
New Brunswick	46.84	36.82	32.38	19.86	23.42	18.41
Nova Scotia	47.34	36.95	31.92	19.90	23.67	18.48
Prince Edward Island	47.37	35.80	31.96	18.46	23.69	17.90
Newfoundland	48.64	38.16	31.87	19.78	24.32	19.08
Yukon	43.01	32.12	29.04	15.82	21.50	16.06
N.W.T./Nunavut	42.05	31.90	28.40	15.71	21.03	15.95

• The 2nd rate is applied to marginal income between $31,000 and $50,000

Dividends for income tax purposes are increased or grossed-up and have a tax credit available as an attempt to overcome double taxation. This occurs because the individual pays both personal tax and corporate tax as a shareholder. Capital gains are tax free on personal residences. Only 50 percent of a capital gain is taxable. The special treatment of capital gains is an attempt to encourage capital formation. With this cursory look at personal taxation, the student should be aware that different forms of income received from the corporation are taxed differently.

Cost of a Tax-Deductible Expense

The businessperson often states that a tax-deductible item, such as interest on business loans, travel expenditures, or salaries, costs substantially less than the amount expended, on an aftertax basis. To investigate how this process works, let us examine the tax statements of two corporations—the first pays $100,000 in interest, and the second has no interest expense. An average tax rate of 40 percent is used for each computation.

	Corporation A	Corporation B
Earnings before interest and taxes	$400,000	$400,000
Interest	100,000	0
Earnings before taxes (taxable income)	300,000	400,000
Taxes (40%)	120,000	160,000
Earnings aftertaxes	$180,000	$240,000

Difference in earnings aftertaxes—$60,000

Although Corporation A paid $100,000 more in interest than Corporation B, its earnings after taxes are only $60,000 less than those of Corporation B. Thus, we say the $100,000 in interest costs the firm only $60,000 in aftertax earnings. The aftertax cost of a tax-deductible expense can be computed as the actual expense times one minus the tax rate. In this case, we show $100,000 (1 − Tax rate), or $100,000 × 0.60 = $60,000. The reasoning in this instance is that the $100,000 is deducted from earnings before determining taxable income, thus saving us $40,000 in taxes and costing only $60,000 on a net basis. The **tax savings** or **tax shield** is computed by multiplying the expense times the tax rate: ($100,000 × 0.40 = $40,000).

Because a dividend on common stock is not tax deductible, we say it cost us 100 percent of the amount paid. From a purely corporate cash flow viewpoint, the firm would be indifferent between paying $100,000 in interest and $60,000 in dividends.

Amortization (Capital Cost Allowance) as a Tax Shield

Amortization often leads to confusion. It is often the major noncash expense of the income statement, and yet our focus in finance is on actual cash flows. Confusion also arises because, in Canada, amortization that is allowable for tax purposes is referred to as *capital cost allowance.* We explore capital cost allowance in more depth in Chapter 12.

Corporations often produce a different income statement for tax purposes, the major difference being the amortization charge. Let us examine a situation in which the accounting amortization charge and the capital cost allowance are the same. We will examine Corporations A and B again, this time with an eye toward amortization rather than interest. Corporation A charges off $100,000 in amortization (capital cost allowance), while Corporation B charges off none.

	Corporation A	Corporation B
Earnings before amortization and taxes	$400,000	$400,000
Amortization (capital cost allowance)	100,000	0
Earnings before taxes	300,000	400,000
Taxes (40%)	120,000	160,000
Earnings aftertaxes	180,000	240,000
+ Amortization charged without cash outlay	100,000	0
Cash flow	$280,000	$240,000
Difference—$40,000		

We compute earnings aftertaxes and then add back amortization to get cash flow. The difference between $280,000 and $240,000 indicates that Corporation A enjoys $40,000 more in cash flow. The reason is that amortization allowable for tax purposes shielded $100,000 from taxation in Corporation A and saved $40,000 in taxes, which eventually showed up in cash flow. Though amortization is not a new source of funds, capital cost allowance (CCA) does provide tax shield benefits that can be measured as CCA times the tax rate, or in this case $100,000 × 0.40 = $40,000. A more comprehensive discussion of amortization's effect on cash flow is presented in Chapter 12 as part of the long-term capital budgeting decision.

Summary

1. The financial manager must be thoroughly familiar with the language of accounting in order to administer the financial affairs of the firm and to prepare an income statement, balance sheet, and statement of cash flows.
2. The income statement provides a measure of the firm's profitability over a specified time period. Earnings per share represent residual income available to the common shareholder that may either be paid out in the form of dividends or reinvested to generate future profits and dividends. A limitation of the income statement is that it reports income and expenses primarily on a transaction basis and thus may not recognize certain important economic changes as they occur.
3. The balance sheet is a snapshot of the financial position of the firm at a point in time, with the shareholders' equity section purporting to represent ownership interest. Because the balance sheet is presented on a historical cost basis, it may not represent the true value of the firm.
4. The cash flow statement, usually called the statement of cash flows, reflects the flows of cash between reporting dates. Through this statement we get a rough picture of operating cash flows and the nature of the firm's investment and financing activities.
5. The corporate tax structure and the tax implications of interest, location, type of business, and amortization affect finance decisions. The aftertax cost and cash flow implications of these items are important throughout the text and are examined in more detail as warranted.
6. The aftertax cash flow to the individual varies depending on whether investment income is in the form of interest, dividends, or capital gain. (Highest to lowest marginal tax rate.)
7. A tax savings is the reduction of taxes otherwise payable as a result of an allowable deduction of an expense from taxable income.

Review of Formulas

1. $$\text{Earnings per share (e.p.s.)} = \frac{\text{Earnings available to common shareholders}}{\text{Number of shares outstanding}} \quad (2\text{–}1)$$

2. $$\text{Payout ratio} = \frac{\text{Dividend per share}}{\text{Earnings per share}} \quad (2\text{–}2)$$

3. $$\text{P/E ratio} = \frac{\text{Market share price}}{\text{Earnings per share}} \quad (2\text{–}3)$$

4. $$\text{Dividend yield} = \frac{\text{Dividends per share}}{\text{Market share price}} \quad (2\text{–}4)$$

5. $$\frac{\text{Market value}}{\text{Book value}} = \frac{\text{MV}}{\text{BV}} = \frac{\text{Market value per share}}{\text{Book value per share}} \quad (2\text{–}5)$$

List of Terms

Discussion Questions

1. Discuss some financial variables that affect the price-earnings ratio.
2. What is the difference between book value per share of common stock and market value per share? Why does this disparity occur?
3. Explain how amortization generates actual cash flows for the company.
4. What is the difference between accumulated amortization and amortization expense? How are they related?
5. Comment on why inflation may restrict the usefulness of the balance sheet as normally presented.
6. Explain why the statement of cash flows provides useful information that goes beyond income statement and balance sheet data.
7. What are the three primary sections of the statement of cash flows? In which section would the payment of a cash dividend be shown?
8. How can we use a statement of cash flows to analyze how a firm's assets were financed?
9. What is free cash flow? Why is it important to leveraged buyouts?
10. Why is interest expense said to cost the firm substantially less than the actual expense, while dividends cost it 100 percent of the outlay?

INTERNET RESOURCES AND QUESTIONS

For current individual and corporate tax rates:	www.kpmg.ca/tax/ www.pwcglobal.com/ca (search tax facts)
The International Accounting Standards Committee:	www.iasc.org.uk
The Canadian Institute of Chartered Accountants:	www.cica.ca
Canada Customs and Revenue Agency:	www.ccra-adrc.gc.ca

1. What is the CICA and what does it do?
2. The CICA identifies current trends in accounting and reporting? What are some of the emerging issues in accounting?
3. What is the International Accounting Standards Committee and what are its objectives?
4. IAS financial statements are accepted by many stock exchanges around the world. Are these statements accepted by Canadian exchanges?

Problems

1. Given the following information, prepare, in good form, an income statement for Dental Drilling Company. Use a corporate tax rate of 22 percent to calculate taxes.

Selling and administrative expense	$ 50,000
Amortization expense	80,000
Sales	400,000
Interest expense	30,000
Cost of goods sold	150,000

2. Prepare in good form an income statement for 4U Cards Ltd. Take your calculations all the way down to computing earnings per share.

Sales	$800,000
Shares outstanding	100,000
Cost of goods sold	300,000
Interest expense	20,000
Selling and administrative expense	40,000
Amortization expense	30,000
Preferred stock dividends	80,000
Taxes	110,000

3. Frantic Fast Foods had earnings aftertaxes of $390,000 in the year 2001 with 300,000 shares outstanding. On January 1, 2002, the firm issued 25,000 new shares. Because of the proceeds from these new shares and other operating improvements, earnings aftertaxes increased by 20 percent.
   a. Compute earnings per share of the year 2001.
   b. Compute earnings per share of the year 2002.
4. The Censored Book Company sold 1,200 finance textbooks to Arctic College for $60.00 each in 2002. These books cost $42 to produce. In addition, Censored Books spent $2,000 (selling expense) to persuade the college to buy its books. Censored Books borrowed $30,000 on January 1, 2002, on which it paid 10 percent interest. Both interest and principal were paid on December 31, 2002. Censored Books' tax rate is 30 percent. Amortization expense for the year was $4,000.

   Did Censored Books make a profit in 2002? Verify your answer with an income statement presented in good form.
5. Lemon Auto Wholesalers had sales of $700,000 in 2002, and cost of goods sold represented 70 percent of sales. Selling and administrative expenses were 12 percent of sales. Amortization expense was $10,000, and interest expense for the year was $8,000. The firm's tax rate is 30 percent.
   a. Compute earnings aftertaxes.
   b. Assume the firm hires Ms. Fender, an efficiency expert, as a consultant. She suggests that by increasing selling and administrative expenses to 14 percent of sales, sales can be increased to $750,000. The extra sales effort will also reduce cost of goods sold to 66 percent of sales (there will be a larger makeup in prices as a result of more aggressive selling). Amortization expense will remain at $10,000. However, more automobiles will have to be carried in inventory to satisfy customers, and interest expense will go up to $15,000. The firm's tax rate will remain at 30 percent. Compute revised earnings aftertaxes based on Ms. Fender's suggestions for Lemon Auto Wholesalers. Will her ideas increase or decrease profitability?
6. Arrange the following income statement items so they are in the proper order of an income statement:

Taxes	Earnings aftertaxes
Shares outstanding	Earnings available to common shareholders
Gross profit	Cost of goods sold
Interest expense	Earnings per share
Amortization expense	Earnings before taxes
Preferred stock dividends	Selling and administrative expense
Sales	Operating profit

7. Betty Ford Company has an operating profit of $200,000. Interest expense for the year was $10,000; preferred dividends paid were $18,750; and common dividends paid were $30,000. The tax was $61,250. The Betty Ford Company has 20,000 shares of common stock outstanding.
   a. Calculate the earnings per share and the common dividends per share for the Betty Ford Company.
   b. What was the increase in retained earnings for the year?
   c. If Betty Ford's share price is $26.40 what is its price-earnings ratio (P/E)?
8. Johnson Alarm Systems had $800,000 of retained earnings on December 31, 2002. The company paid dividends of $60,000 in 2002 and had retained earnings of $640,000 on December 31, 2001.
   a. How much did Johnson earn during 2002?
   b. What would earnings per share be if 50,000 shares of common stock are outstanding?
   c. If Johnson's share price is $13.20 what is its price-earnings ratio (P/E)?
9. Classify the following balance sheet items as current or noncurrent:

Common stock	Investments
Accounts payable	Marketable securities
Preferred stock	Accounts receivable
Prepaid expenses	Plant and equipment
Bonds payable	Accrued wages payable
Inventory	Retained earnings

10. Arrange the following items in proper balance sheet presentation:

Accumulated amortization	$300,000
Retained earnings	96,000
Cash	10,000
Bonds payable	136,000
Accounts receivable	48,000
Plant and equipment—original cost	680,000
Accounts payable	35,000
Allowance for bad debts	6,000
Common stock, 100,000 shares outstanding	188,000
Inventory	66,000
Preferred stock, 1,000 shares outstanding	50,000
Marketable securities	20,000
Investments	20,000
Notes payable	33,000

www.mcgrawhill.ca/college/block

11. Landers Nursery and Garden Stores has current assets of $220,000 and capital assets of $170,000. Current liabilities are $80,000 and long term liabilities are $140,000. There is $40,000 in preferred stock outstanding and the firm has issued 25,000 shares of common stock. Compute book value (net worth) per share.

12. The Holtzman Corporation has assets of $400,000, current liabilities of $50,000, and long-term liabilities of $100,000. There is $40,000 in preferred stock outstanding; 20,000 shares of common stock have been issued.

    a. Compute book value (net worth) per share.

    b. If there is $22,000 in earnings available to common shareholders and Holtzman's stock has a P/E ratio of 15 times earnings per share, what is the current price of the stock?

    c. What is the ratio of market value per share to book value per share?

13. Bradley Gypsum Company has assets of $1.9 million, current liabilities of $700,000, and long-term liabilities of $580,000. There is $170,000 in preferred stock outstanding; 30,000 shares of common stock have been issued.

    a. Compute book value (net worth) per share.

    b. If there is $42,000 in earnings available to common shareholders and Bradley's stock has a P/E of 15 times earnings per share, what is the current price of the stock?

    c. What is the ratio of market value per share to book value per share?

14. In the previous problem what is the P/E ratio if the firm sells at two times book value per share?

15. Fill in the blank spaces with categories 1 through 7:

    1. Balance sheet (BS).
    2. Income statement (IS).
    3. Current assets (CA).
    4. Capital assets (Cap A).
    5. Current liabilities (CL).
    6. Long-term liabilities (LL).
    7. Shareholders' equity (SE).

Indicate Whether Item Is on Balance Sheet (BS) or Income Statement (IS)	If on Balance Sheet, Designate Which Category	Item
________	________	Retained earnings
________	________	Income tax expense
________	________	Accounts receivable
________	________	Common stock
________	________	Bonds payable, maturity 2012
________	________	Notes payable (six months)
________	________	Net income
________	________	Selling and administrative expenses
________	________	Inventories
________	________	Accrued expenses
________	________	Cash
________	________	Plant and equipment

______	______	Sales
______	______	Operating expenses
______	______	Marketable securities
______	______	Accounts payable
______	______	Interest expense
______	______	Income tax payable

16. Identify whether each of the following items increases or decreases cash flow:

Increase in inventory	Dividend payment
Decrease in prepaid expenses	Increase in short-term notes payable
Decrease in accounts receivable	Amortization expense
Increase in cash	Decrease in accounts payable
Decrease in inventory	Increase in long-term investments

17. The Rogers Corporation has a gross profit of $880,000 and $360,000 in amortization expense. The Evans Corporation has $880,000 in gross profit, with $60,000 in amortization expense. Selling and administrative expense is $120,000 for each company. Given that the tax rate is 40 percent, compute the cash flow for both companies. Explain the difference in cash flow between the two firms.

18. Prepare a statement of cash flows for the Solitude Corporation.

Balance Sheets

	December 31, 2002	December 31, 2001
Assets		
Cash	$ 77,490	$ 29,520
Accounts receivable	59,040	66,420
Inventory	154,980	132,840
Equipment	136,530	110,700
Less: accumulated amortization	33,210	22,140
Net equipment	103,320	88,560
Total assets	$394,830	$317,340
Liabilities and Equity		
Accounts payable	$ 62,730	$ 36,900
Taxes payable	7,380	14,760
Common stock	243,540	221,400
Retained earnings	81,180	44,280
Total liabilities and equity	$394,830	$317,340

During 2002, the following occurred:

1. Net income was $73,800.
2. Equipment was purchased for cash, and no equipment was sold.
3. Shares were sold for cash.
4. Dividends were declared and paid.

19. Prepare a statement of cash flows for the Waif Corporation.

Balance Sheets

	December 31, 2002	December 31, 2001
Assets		
Cash	$ 54,500	$ 17,400
Accounts receivable	64,800	52,200
Inventory	142,200	149,300
Land	60,000	87,000
Plant anc equipment	206,000	158,000
Less: Accum. amortization	55,000	33,000
Net plant and equipment	151,000	125,000
Total assets	$472,500	$430,900
Liabilities and Equity		
Accounts payable	$ 27,000	$ 37,000
Bonds payable	118,000	158,000
Common stock	170,000	130,000
Retained earnings	157,500	105,900
Total liabilities and shareholders' equity	$472,500	$430,900

During 2001, the following occurred:

1. Net income was $91,000.
2. Bonds were retired by issuing new common stock.
3. No equipment was sold.
4. Cash dividends were paid.

20. Prepare a statement of cash flows for the Crosby Corporation.

CROSBY CORPORATION
Income Statement
Year ended December 31, 2002

Sales	$2,200,000
Cost of goods sold	1,300,000
Gross profits	900,000
Selling and administrative expense	420,000
Amortization expense	150,000
Operating income	330,000
Interest expense	90,000
Earnings before taxes	240,000
Taxes	80,000
Earnings aftertaxes	160,000
Preferred stock dividends	10,000
Earnings available to common shareholders	$ 150,000
Shares outstanding	120,000
Earnings per share	$1.25

Statement of Retained Earnings
For the Year Ended December 31, 2002

Retained earnings, balance, January 1, 2002	$500,000
Add: Earnings available to common shareholders, 2002	150,000
Deduct: Cash dividends declared and paid in 2002	50,000
Retained earnings, balance, December 31, 2002	$600,000

Comparative Balance Sheets

	Dec. 31, 2002	Dec. 31, 2001
Assets		
Current assets:		
Cash	$ 100,000	$ 70,000
Accounts receivable (net)	350,000	300,000
Inventory	430,000	410,000
Prepaid expenses	30,000	50,000
Total current assets	910,000	830,000
Investments (long-term securities)	70,000	80,000
Plant and equipment	2,400,000	2,000,000
Less: Accumulated amortization	1,150,000	1,000,000
Net plant and equipment	1,250,000	1,000,000
Total assets	$2,230,000	$1,910,000
Liabilities and Shareholders' Equity		
Current liabilities:		
Accounts payable	$ 440,000	$ 250,000
Notes payable	400,000	400,000
Accrued expenses	50,000	70,000
Total current liabilities	890,000	720,000
Long-term liabilities:		
Bonds payable, 2013	120,000	70,000
Total liabilities	1,010,000	790,000
Shareholders' equity:		
Preferred stock	90,000	90,000
Common stock	530,000	530,000
Retained earnings	600,000	500,000
Total shareholders' equity	1,220,000	1,120,000
Total liabilities and shareholders' equity	$2,230,000	$1,910,000

The following questions apply to the Crosby Corporation, as presented in Problem 20.

21. Describe the general relationship between net income and net cash flows from operating activities for the firm.
22. Has the buildup in plant and equipment been financed in a satisfactory manner? Briefly discuss.

23. Compute the book value per common share for 2001 and 2002 for the Crosby Corporation.
24. If the market value of a share of common stock is 2.4 times book value for 2002, what is the firm's P/E ratio for 2002?
25. Prepare a statement of cash flows for the Winfield Corporation for 2002.

WINFIELD CORPORATION
Balance Sheets

	December 31, 2002	December 31, 2001
Assets		
Current Assets:		
Cash	$ 1,750	$ 1,400
Accounts receivable	7,875	5,425
Inventory	33,250	28,000
Prepaid expenses	1,225	1,050
Total current assets	44,100	35,875
Investments (long-term)	17,500	21,000
Capital assets:		
Land	15,750	7,000
Buildings	100,000	100,000
Less: accumulated amortization	61,500	58,000
Net buildings	38,500	42,000
Equipment	36,750	28,000
Less: accumulated amortization	10,500	7,000
Net equipment	26,250	21,000
Total assets	$142,100	$126,875
Liabilities and Shareholders' Equity		
Current liabilities:		
Accounts payable	$ 15,750	$ 17,500
Notes payable	8,750	6,125
Accrued expenses	9,275	7,350
Interest payable	1,225	1,400
Total current liabilities	35,000	32,375
Long-term liabilities:		
Bonds payable, 2014	43,750	38,500
Total liabilities	78,750	70,875
Shareholders' equity:		
Common stock	24,500	24,500
Retained earnings	38,850	31,500
Total shareholders' equity	63,350	56,000
Total liabilities and shareholders' equity	$142,100	$126,875

WINFIELD CORPORATION
Income Statement
Year Ended December 31, 2002

Sales	$210,000
Cost of goods sold	87,500
Gross profits	122,500
Selling and administrative expense	95,900
Amortization expense	10,500
Operating income	16,100
Interest expense	3,500
Other income and losses:	
Gain on sale of investment	5,250
Dividend income	1,575
Loss on sale of equipment	1,050
Net other income and losses	5,775
Earnings before taxes	18,375
Income taxes	4,375
Net income	$ 14,000

During 2002, the following occurred:

a. From the long-term investments, a dividend of $1,575 was received. Shares originally costing $3,500 were sold for $8,750 from the investment account.

b. Land was purchased for $8,750. Purchase was completed with a note payable of $8,750, with interest and principal due in 12 months.

c. New equipment was purchased for $15,750 cash. Old equipment originally costing $7,000 with accumulated amortization of $3,500 was sold for $2,450.

d. Notes payable at $6,125 were paid.

e. Bonds were sold at par for $5,250.

f. A dividend of $6,650 was paid.

g. The 2002 amortization expense was $3,500 for buildings and $7,000 for equipment.

26. For December 31, 2001, the balance sheet of the Dominion Pines Corporation is as follows:

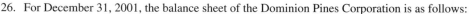

Balance Sheet

Current Assets		Liabilities	
Cash	$ 15,000	Accounts payable	$20,000
Accounts receivable	22,500	Notes payable	30,000
Inventory	37,500	Bonds payable	75,000
Prepaid expenses	18,000		
Capital Assets		**Shareholders' Equity**	
Plant and equipment	$375,000	Common stock	$150,000
Less: Accumulated amortization	75,000	Retained earnings	118,000
Net plant and equipment	300,000		
Total assets	$393,000	Total liabilities and shareholders' equity	$393,000

Sales for 2002 were $330,000, with cost of goods sold being 60 percent of sales. Amortization expense was 10 percent of plant and equipment (gross) at the beginning of the year. Interest expense for the bonds payable was 12 percent, while interest on the notes payable was 10 percent. These are based on December 31, 2001, balances. Selling and administrative expenses were $33,000, and the tax rate averaged 20 percent. During 2002, the cash balance and prepaid expense balance were unchanged. Accounts receivable and inventory each increased by 20 percent, and accounts payable increased by 30 percent. A new machine was purchased on December 31, 2002, at a cost of $60,000. A cash dividend of $6,100 was paid to common shareholders at the end of 2002. Also, notes payable increased by $10,000 and bonds payable decreased by $15,000. The common stock account did not change.

a. Prepare an income statement for 2002.

b. Prepare a balance sheet as of December 31, 2002.

c. Prepare a statement of cash flows for the year ending December 31, 2002.

27. Bobbie's Coffee Beans Ltd., located in downtown Kelowna, B.C., has the following taxable income for 2001 and 2002.

2001	$ 52,000
2002	124,000

a. Compute the total tax obligation for Bobbie's Coffee Beans each year.

b. Compute the average tax rate for each year.

28. Coastal Pipeline Corp. anticipates cash flows from operating activities of $8 million in 2003. It will need to spend $1.5 million on capital investments in order to remain competitive within the industry. Common share dividends are projected at $0.6 million and preferred dividends at $0.25 million.

a. What is the firm's projected free cash flow for the year 2003?

b. What does the concept of free cash flow represent?

29. Given the following information, prepare, in good form, an income statement for the Luba Corporation. Use the corporate tax rates in Chapter 2 to calculate taxes. Luba is a manufacturer in Manitoba.

Selling and administrative expense	$ 77,000
Amortization expense	66,000
Sales	533,000
Interest expense	28,000
Cost of goods sold	226,000

30. For Luba Corporation, what is the tax savings due to amortization expense?

31. R. E. Forms Ltd. had taxable income of $75,000 from an active business in 2001. Calculate its tax payable if it operates in Alberta as compared to operating in Ontario.

32. J. B. Wands has $14,000 to invest. He lives in Saskatchewan and has other income of $40,000 for the year. A current bond issue is paying 6 percent, while a popular share issue offers a 5 percent dividend return.

a. Calculate the better return on an aftertax basis. What is the aftertax yield?

b. What other factors should be considered?

33. Billie Fruit lives in the Yukon and her income fluctuates from year to year ranging from over $100,000 to about $35,000. She has two investments of $20,000 each in shares and both achieving a return of 7 percent, one by dividend and the other by capital gain.

a. Calculate the better return on an aftertax basis if this is a high income year. What is the aftertax yield?

b. Calculate the better return on an aftertax basis if this is a low income year. What is the aftertax yield?

34. Banff Corporation has determined that its average bondholder has a marginal tax rate of 39 percent. Jasper's corporate tax rate is 40 percent. A current bond issue would require a 7 percent yield. Considering the tax savings to the firm and the taxes to be paid by the individual bondholder, what are the overall tax consequences of this issue from the government's perspective?

Selected References

Barber, Brad M., and John D. Lyon. "Firm Size, Book-to-Market Ratio, and Security Returns: A Holdout Sample of Financial Firms." *Journal of Finance* 52 (June 1997), pp. 875–83.

Brennan, Michael J. "A Perspective on Accounting and Stock Prices." *Journal of Applied Corporate Finance* 8 (Spring 1995), pp. 43–52.

Bukics, Rose Marie, Marge O'Reilly-Allen, and Chris Schnitter. "Accounting for Differences." *Financial Executive* 16 (March–April 2000), pp. 36–38.

Canadian Institute of Chartered Accountants. *CICA Handbook.* Toronto: CICA, 2000.

Dharan, Bala G., and Briance Mascarenhas. "Determinants of Accounting Change: An Industry Analysis of Depreciation Change." *Journal of Accounting, Auditing & Finance* 7 (Winter 1992), pp. 1–21.

Duelke, Dean W. "The Importance of Accrual Profits." *Journal of Lending and Credit Risk Management* 82 (February 2000), pp. 82–87.

Enzweiler, Albert J. "Improving the Financial Accounting Process." *Management Accounting* 76 (February 1995), pp. 40–43.

Lamont, Owen. "Cash Flow and Investment Evidence from Internal Capital Markets." *Journal of Finance* 52 (March 1997), pp. 83–109.

Petree, Thomas R., George J. Gregory, and Randall J. Vitray. "Evaluating Deferred Tax Assets." *Journal of Accountancy* 179 (March 1995), pp. 71–77.

Ward, Terry. "Using Information from Cash Flow Statements to Predict Insolvency." *Journal of Commercial Lending* 77 (March 1995), pp. 29–36.

Weber, Joseph. "FASB Grows New Fangs." *Business Week* (July 3, 2000), pp. 132–33.

CHAPTER | THREE

Financial Analysis

3

LEARNING | OBJECTIVES

1 Calculate 13 financial ratios that measure profitability, asset utilization, liquidity, and debt utilization.

2 Assess a company's source of profitability using the DuPont system of analysis.

3 Examine the ratios in comparison to industry averages.

4 Examine the ratios and company performance by means of trend analysis.

5 Identify sources of distortion in reported income.

In Chapter 2, we examined the basic assumptions of accounting and the various components that make up the financial statements of the firm. We now use this fundamental material as a springboard into financial analysis to evaluate the financial performance of the firm. From gaining an understanding of the firm's financial performance we are better able to value the firm.

We examine the firm's performance in light of industry norms and past trends. In dissecting the financial statements, we learn how the various components influence each other and add or subtract from the firm's value. Later we explore the distortions that may exist in cost-based financial statements. Future financial managers, and the student, can begin to appreciate the impact of rising prices (or, at times, declining prices) on the various financial ratios.

Terms such as net income to sales, return on investment, and inventory turnover take on much greater meaning when they are evaluated through the eyes of a financial manager who does more than merely pick out the top or bottom line of an income statement. The examples in the chapter are designed from the viewpoint of a financial manager (with only minor attention to accounting theory).

Ratio Analysis

Ratios are used in much of our daily life. We buy cars based on gas consumption of litres per 100 kilometres; we evaluate purchases on percentage discounts, and hockey players by shooting percentages and save percentages. These are all ratios constructed to judge comparative performance. Financial ratios serve a similar purpose, but you must determine what is being measured in order to construct a ratio and to understand the significance of the resultant number.

Financial ratios are used to weigh and evaluate the operating performance of the firm. While an absolute value such as earnings of $50,000 or accounts receivable of $100,000 may appear satisfactory, its acceptability can be measured only in relation to other values. For this reason, financial managers emphasize ratio analysis.

For example, are earnings of $50,000 actually good? If we earned $50,000 on $500,000 of sales (10 percent profit margin ratio), that might be quite satisfactory; whereas earnings of $50,000 on $5 million could be disappointing (a meagre 1 percent return). After we have computed the appropriate ratio, we must compare our results to those achieved by similar firms in our industry, as well as to our own past performance record. Even then, this number-crunching process is not fully adequate, and we are forced to supplement our financial findings with an evaluation of company management, physical facilities, and numerous other factors.

Ultimately, we hope to establish a link with valuation. We often use ratios of past financial performance to determine our expectations regarding the firm's future success. The ratios may help us to get a fix on the current value of such items as receivables, inventories, capital assets, debts, equity, and the firm based on those future expectations.

Ratios for Comparative Purposes

Comparative ratios are available from many sources, usually for a fee, but many university and public libraries subscribe to financial services that produce ratios. These include;

Dun & Bradstreet Corporation www.dnb.com

Dun & Bradstreet: data on 800 different lines of business. "Industry Norms and Key Business Ratios".

Robert Morris: data on over 100,000 commercial borrowers, 400 categories.

Financial Post: DATAGROUP, www.financialpost.com for demos on 900 publicly traded companies, industry reports for 23 sectors

Statistics Canada: ratios for major industry groups in "Financial Performance Indicators for Canadian Business". Also available at Regional Reference Centres.

Industry associations: for example the Canadian Association of Broadcasters.

Classification System

The ratios classified in this text chapter represent the most commonly used categories and ratios, but others can also be constructed. In Chapter 2 we identified five valuation ratios commonly used in the investment industry. These complement the ratios discussed in this chapter. We will separate 13 significant ratios into four primary categories.

A. Profitability ratios.
   1. Profit margin.
   2. Return on assets (investment).
   3. Return on equity (common shareholders).
B. Asset utilization ratios.
   4a. Receivable turnover.
   4b. Average collection period (days sales outstanding).
   5a. Inventory turnover.
   5b. Inventory holding period.
   6a. Accounts payable turnover
   6b. Accounts payable period
   7. Capital asset turnover.
   8. Total asset turnover.
C. Liquidity ratios.
   9. Current ratio.
   10. Quick ratio.
D. Debt utilization ratios.
   11. Debt to total assets.
   12. Times interest earned.
   13. Fixed charge coverage.

Grouping A, the **profitability ratios,** allow us to measure the ability of the firm to earn an adequate return on sales, total assets, and shareholders' invested capital. Many of the problems related to profitability can be explained by the firm's ability to effectively employ its resources. An adequate sales level is usually important to the proper use of resources. Profitability ratios are most important to equity investors because success in generating profits usually translates into sound share price performance.

The next category is the **asset utilization ratios.** Under this heading, we measure the speed at which the firm is turning over accounts receivable, inventory, and longer-term assets. In other words, asset utilization ratios measure how many times per year a company sells its inventory or collects its entire accounts receivable. For long-term assets, the utilization ratio tells us how productive the capital assets are in generating sales. The effective utilization of assets is the responsibility of management.

In Category C, the **liquidity ratios,** the primary emphasis moves to the firm's ability to pay off short-term obligations as they come due. Short-term obligations to creditors and bankers are of primary concern in the continuing day-to-day operation of the firm. Lack of liquidity places strain on all of the firm's operations. Therefore, bankers focus on the firm's ability to generate timely cash flows.

In Category D, **debt utilization ratios,** the overall debt position of the firm is evaluated in light of its asset base and earning power. It is the debt holder that is primarily concerned with the security behind the debt obligations and should look closely at the overall debt position.

The users of financial statements attach different degrees of importance to the four categories of ratios. To the potential investor or security analyst, the critical consideration is profitability, with secondary consideration given to such matters as liquidity and debt utilization. For the banker or trade creditor, the emphasis shifts to the firm's current ability to meet debt obligations. The bondholder, in turn, may be primarily influenced by debt to total assets—while also eyeing the profitability of the firm in terms of its ability to cover debt obligations. Of course, the shrewd analyst and financial manager look at all the ratios, but with different degrees of attention.

The Analysis

Definitions alone carry little meaning in analyzing or dissecting the financial performance of a company. For this reason we apply our four categories of ratios to a hypothetical firm, the Saxton Company, as presented in Table 3–1. The use of ratio analysis is rather like solving a mystery. We are looking for ratios that appear out of line in comparison to certain standards. One must be aware, however, that no one value is correct. When we have identified a ratio that appears out of line, we may or may not have a clue that should provoke a number of questions: Is the ratio hinting at problems or very good performance? Is the ratio's calculation distorted by easily explained factors? Furthermore, how does one assess a combination of ratios that give conflicting signals? Ratio analysis suggests questions that need to be answered to come to grips with the efficiency and the viability of the firm under analysis.

A. Profitability Ratios We first look at the profitability ratios. In the table on page 68, the appropriate ratio is computed for the Saxton Company and is then compared to representative industry data. Profitability ratios attempt to gauge the efficiency or performance of the firm by relating income earned to an investment base.

The Saxton Company shows a lower return on the sales dollar (5 percent) than the industry average of 6.5 percent. This is the profit margin and reflects a firm's pricing policies and its ability to control costs. The profit margin varies among firms based on their competitive strategy and product mix.

The return on assets (ROA) (investment) of 12.5 percent exceeds the industry norm of 10 percent. This ratio measures the firm's overall efficiency in the use of capital. The creditors, bondholders, and shareholders all expect that an adequate return will be achieved on their investment. One should be careful in interpreting this ratio because the income figure can be distorted by financial decisions (interest costs and dividends) and because the total assets figure is based on historical valuation, which may not reflect recent developments.

The third profitability ratio is the return on equity (ROE) or ownership capital. This measure is closely followed by investment analysts because it represents a return to the owners of the firm, although it does have a number of deficiencies related to an earlier discussion of the goal of the firm and its measurement by share price performance.

When we examine ROA and ROE it is appropriate to compare these returns to other investments of similar risk to determine if the returns are adequate. For example if the firm's ROE is 5 percent while comparable equity investments earn 10 percent the firm is underperforming. These rates of return can often be determined from the yields currently available in the financial markets.

Return on equity suffers from its focus on past results. Often a firm must make decisions that require the sacrifice of earnings today for the future benefit of the firm. Although these prudent decisions will likely be reflected in the pricing of a firm's shares in an efficient market, its current earnings and return on equity ratio will probably

TABLE 3–1
Financial statements for ratio analysis

SAXTON COMPANY
Income Statement
For the Year 2002

Sales (all on credit)	$4,000,000
Cost of goods sold	3,000,000
Gross profit	1,000,000
Selling and administrative expense*	450,000
Operating profit	550,000
Interest expense	50,000
Extraordinary loss	100,000
Net income before taxes	400,000
Taxes (50%)	200,000
Net income	$ 200,000

*Includes $50,000 in lease payments.

Balance Sheet
As of December 31, 2002

Assets

Cash	$ 30,000
Marketable securities	50,000
Accounts receivable	350,000
Inventory	370,000
Total current assets	800,000
Net plant and equipment	800,000
Total assets	$1,600,000

Liabilities and Shareholders' Equity

Accounts payable	$ 50,000
Notes payable	250,000
Total current liabilities	300,000
Long-term liabilities	300,000
Total liabilities	600,000
Common stock	400,000
Retained earnings	600,000
Total liabilities and shareholders' equity	$1,600,000

suffer. Furthermore, return on equity does not give one an appreciation of the risk involved in producing the earnings results. The firm may increase its risk by excessive borrowing or by its involvement in business lines that have less certain results.

Finally, the calculation of this ratio relies on book value and does not examine return based on the actual market value investment. This concern is probably more relevant to investors. Measurement tools such as earnings yield (earnings/market price) or its inverse P/E ratio overcome our concern with investment value, but they do little to address our concerns with future results or the risk inherent in a firm's operations.

Nevertheless, return on shareholders' equity is a closely watched ratio and indicates a firm's performance. For the Saxton Company, return on equity is 20 percent, versus an industry norm of 15 percent. Thus, the owners of Saxton Company appear more amply rewarded than are the other shareholders in the industry.

A. Profitability ratios—

	Saxton Company	Industry Average
3–1. Profit margin $= \frac{\text{Net income}}{\text{Sales}}$	$\frac{\$200{,}000}{\$4{,}000{,}000} = 5\%$	6.5%
3–2. Return on assets (ROA) (investment) =		
a. $\frac{\text{Net income}}{\text{Total assets}}$	$\frac{\$200{,}000}{\$1{,}600{,}000} = 12.5\%$	10%
b. $\frac{\text{Net income}}{\text{Sales}} \times \frac{\text{Sales}}{\text{Total assets}}$	$5\% \times 2.5 = 12.5\%$	$6.5\% \times 1.5 = 10\%$
3–3. Return on equity (ROE) =		
a. $\frac{\text{Net income}}{\text{Shareholders' equity}}$	$\frac{\$200{,}000}{\$1{,}000{,}000} = 20\%$	15%
b. Equity multiplier $= \frac{\text{Total assets}}{\text{Equity}}$	$\frac{\$1{,}600{,}000}{\$1{,}000{,}000} = 1.6$	$\frac{1}{0.6667} = 1.5$
c. ROA × Equity multiplier	$0.125 \times 1.60 = 20\%$	$0.10 \times 1.50 = 15\%$

When examining profitability we might also calculate the gross profit margin, which is gross profit divided by sales. Generally, this ratio is an attempt to identify the relationship between variable costs and sales by factoring out fixed costs. A company with high fixed costs will suffer large declines in overall profitability if its sales decline. For the Saxton Company, the gross profit margin is 25 percent (1,000,000/4,000,000).

Finally, as a general statement in computing all the profitability ratios, the analyst must be sensitive to the age of the assets. Plant and equipment purchased 15 years ago may be carried on the books far below its replacement value in an inflationary economy. A 20 percent return on assets purchased in the late 1950s or early 1960s may be inferior to a 15 percent return on newly purchased assets.

DuPont Analysis

DuPont
www.dupont.com

The DuPont system causes the analyst to examine the sources of a company's profitability. The DuPont company was a forerunner in stressing that satisfactory return on assets may be achieved through high profit margins or a rapid turnover of assets, or a combination of both. Under the DuPont system of analysis, the use of debt may also be important. Figure 3–1 illustrates the key points in the DuPont system of analysis.

Since the profit margin is an income statement ratio, a high profit margin indicates good cost control, whereas a high asset turnover ratio demonstrates efficient use of the assets on the balance sheet. Different industries have different operating and financial structures. For example, in the heavy capital goods industry, the emphasis is on a high profit margin with a low asset turnover; in food retailing, the profit margin is low, and the key to satisfactory returns on total assets is a rapid turnover of assets.

FIGURE 3–1
DuPont analysis

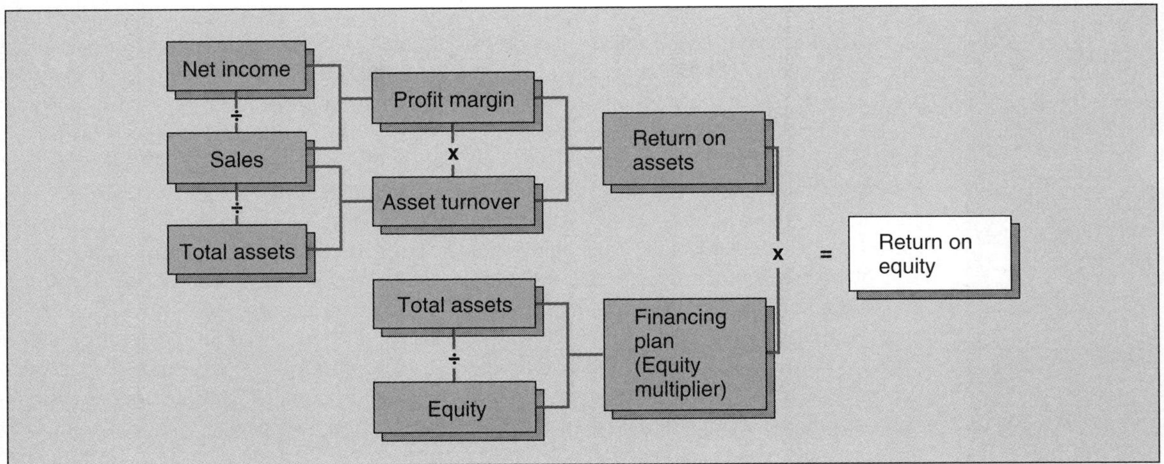

For the Saxton Company, it is noteworthy that the return on assets is higher than the industry, while its return on sales is lower. This has been achieved by a more rapid turnover of assets. Formula 3–2*b* shows sales to total assets is 2.5 for the Saxton Company and only 1.5 for the industry. Thus, Saxton generates more sales on its asset base than the industry on average. This can be beneficial, as it shows a more efficient operation, but it may also suggest overuse of the assets. This could be the result of underinvestment in the firm.

Return on total assets as described through the two components of profit margin and asset turnover is part of the **DuPont system of financial analysis.**

$$\text{Return on assets (ROA) (investment)} = \text{Profit margin} \times \text{Asset turnover}$$

A high return on equity may be the result of one or two factors; a high return on total assets or a generous utilization of debt, or a combination thereof. This can be seen through Formula 3–3*c*, which represents a modified or second version of the DuPont formula.

$$\text{ROE} = \text{ROA} \times \text{Equity multiplier}$$

Note that return on assets, is taken from Formula 3–2, which represents the initial version of the DuPont formula (Return on assets = Net income/Sales × Sales/Total assets). Return on assets is then increased or levered by the amount of debt to equity in the capital structure. Return to shareholders (ROE) is greater than the return on assets (ROA) by the equity multiplier.

$$\text{Equity multiplier} = \frac{\text{Total assets}}{\text{Equity}}$$

The use of debt, in relation to equity, has magnified the return to shareholders. Leverage is explored in more detail in Chapter 5.

In the case of the Saxton Company, the modified version of the DuPont formula shows:

FINANCE IN ACTION

Q1 Has the return on equity changed for each firm since late 2000?

www.cpr.ca
Symbol: CP

www.cpships.com
Symbol: TEU

www.fairmonthotels.com
Symbol: FHR

www.fording.ca
Symbol: FDG

www.pancanadian.ca
Symbol: PCE

Applying DuPont Analysis at Canadian Pacific

In 2001 one of the great holding companies of Canada was split into five separate companies. This type of split is sometimes referred to as "unlocking the asset value" of a vast conglomerate. The time in which firms pursued diversification as a corporate strategy has passed and today companies are more prepared to focus on a core business. They want to "stick to their knitting." Canadian Pacific was synonymous with Canada and was often considered the means by which a global investor could buy a piece of Canada. It was the company formed to help build Canada in the early days of Confederation.

It is worthwhile to examine the profit margins, asset turnovers, and debt structures for each of the major divisions at year-end 2000, before the split. The divisions each had significant differences. CP Rail and PanCanadian had similar profit margins and debt structures, but PanCanadian achieved a higher return on equity because of its higher turnover of sales to assets. Fairmont Hotels and Resorts had a much lower profit margin than CP Rail, but was able to achieve a similar return on equity by turning over sales quicker. CP Ships which had a higher return on assets than CP Rail had a lower return on equity because of a lower debt usage in its capital structure and thus a lower equity multiplier. The use of debt is referred to as financial leverage and its benefits and drawbacks are explored in Chapter 5. Fording, Canada's largest coal exporter, with a low profit margin and limited use of debt had meager returns on equity.

	Profit Margin	×	Asset Turnover	=	Return on Assets	×	Equity Multiplier	=	Return on Equity
CP Rail	14.56%		.4150		6.04%		2.473		14.94%
CP Ships	4.92		1.5132		7.44		1.590		11.83
Fairmont Hotels	5.81		.9890		5.75		2.482		14.27
Fording	3.86		.9009		3.48		1.894		6.59
PanCanadian Energy	14.40		.7982		11.49		2.244		25.79

The DuPont method provides insight into the components of profitability within the divisions of Canadian Pacific before it was split into five separate companies. The DuPont method may also highlight weaknesses and opportunities at the newly independent companies.

As these companies go their separate ways it will be interesting to see if and how they reshape themselves to achieve profitability for the shareholders. The latest financial statements of these companies, analyzed by means of the DuPont method, will show if there has been a change in how they achieve return on equity.

$$\text{Equity multiplier} = \frac{\text{Total assets}}{\text{Equity}} = \frac{\$1{,}600{,}000}{\$1{,}000{,}000} = 1.6$$

$$\text{ROE} = \text{ROA} \times \text{Equity multiplier} = 0.125 \times 1.60 = 20\%$$

Actually, the return on assets of 12.5 percent is higher than the industry average of 10 percent, and the equity multiplier of 1.6 is higher than the industry norm of 1.5. Both ROA and leverage contribute to a higher return on equity than the industry average (20 percent versus 15 percent). Note that if the firm had a 50 percent debt-to-assets ratio, return on equity would be 25 percent.[1]

$$\text{Equity multiplier} = \frac{\text{Total assets}}{\text{Equity}} = \frac{\$1{,}600{,}000}{\$800{,}000} = 2.0$$

$$\text{ROE} = \text{ROA} \times \text{Equity multiplier} = 0.125 \times 2.0 = 25\%$$

[1]The return would be slightly less than 25 percent because of increased financing costs with higher debt.

This does not necessarily mean debt is a positive influence, only that it can be used to boost return on equity. The ultimate goal for the firm is to achieve maximum valuation for its securities in the marketplace, and this goal may or may not be advanced by using debt to increase return on equity. Because debt represents increased risk, a lower valuation of higher earnings is possible.[2] Every situation must be evaluated individually.

B. Asset Utilization Ratios The second category of ratios relates to asset utilization and the ratios in this category may explain why one firm can turn over its assets more rapidly than another. Notice that all of these ratios relate the balance sheet (assets) to the income statement (sales). The Saxton Company's rapid turnover of assets is explained in these formulas.

Generally a firm will desire higher turnover ratios that indicate that the assets are being used efficiently to generate sales. If the turnover ratios slow down the firm might be concerned that inventories might become obsolete or that accounts receivable may turn to bad debts. On the other hand, too rapid turnover of assets may indicate a lack of capital to fund assets, leading to undo wear on capital assets, inventory stock-outs and/or credit policies that inhibit sales because they are too strict.

When calculating ratios using the income statement, a flow concept, and the balance sheet representing the stock position of the firm at a point in time, distortions may occur because of fluctuations in the firm's level of activity. Sometimes the ratios are calculated based on an average of balance sheet positions between two points in an attempt to overcome these distortions. The ratios shown below have not made this adjustment.

Saxton collects its receivables faster than does the industry. This is shown by the receivables turnover of 11.4 times versus 10 times for the industry and, in daily terms, by the average collection period of 32 days, which is 4 days faster than the industry norm. The average collection period suggests how long, on the average, customers' accounts stay on the books. Average daily credit sales are $10,959 ($4,000,000/365). Receivable turnover of 11.4 times (365 days) per year, has a reciprocal of 32 days sales outstanding (365/11.4). A quick collection period for accounts receivable is important; it demonstrates efficient management and has a positive influence on cash flow. However, one must be careful that the collection policies do not hamper credit sales.

B. Asset utilization ratios—

		Saxton Company	Industry Average
3–4a.	Receivables turnover = $\frac{\text{Sales (credit)}}{\text{Receivables}}$	$\frac{\$4{,}000{,}000}{\$350{,}000} = 11.4$	10.0 times
3–4b.	Average collection period = $\frac{\text{Accounts receivable}}{\text{Average daily credit sales}}$	$\frac{\$350{,}000}{\$10{,}959} = 32$	36 days
3–5a.	Inventory turnover = $\frac{\text{Cost of goods sold}}{\text{Inventory}}$	$\frac{\$3{,}000{,}000}{\$370{,}000} = 8.1$	7.0 times

[2]Further discussions of this point are presented in Chapters 5 and 10.

		Saxton Company	Industry Average
3–5b.	Inventory holding period = $\frac{\text{Inventory/}}{\text{Average daily COGS}}$	$\frac{\$370,000}{\$8,219} = 45$	52 days
3–6a.	Accounts payable turnover = $\frac{\text{Cost of goods sold}}{\text{Account payable}}$	$\frac{\$3,000,000}{\$50,000} = 60.0$	12.0 times
3–6b.	Accounts payables period = $\frac{\text{Accounts payable}}{\text{Average daily purchases (COGS)}}$	$\frac{\$50,000}{\$8,219} = 6$	30 days
3–7.	Capital asset turnover = $\frac{\text{Sales}}{\text{Capital assets}}$	$\frac{\$4,000,000}{\$800,000} = 5.0$	5.4 times
3–8.	Total asset turnover = $\frac{\text{Sales}}{\text{Total assets}}$	$\frac{\$4,000,000}{\$1,600,000} = 2.5$	1.5 times

*Formulas 3–4b can also be solved by receivables/sales × 365, formula 3–5b by inventory/COGS × 365, and formula 3–6b by payables/COGS × 365.

In addition, the firm turns over its inventory 8.1 times per year as contrasted with an industry average of 7 times.[3] Inventory turns of 8.1 times over 365 days per year, has a reciprocal or inventory holding period of 45 days (365/8.1) versus the industry average of 52 days. This tells us that Saxton generates more sales per dollar of inventory than the average company in the industry, and we can assume the firm uses very efficient inventory-ordering and cost-control methods. Although high inventory turns are generally good, they may be evidence of underinvestment in assets and may result in stock-outs, which have a high opportunity cost.

The accounts payable turnover of 60 is well above the industry average of 12 times. Payable turns of 60 times over 365 days per year, has a reciprocal or accounts payable period of 6 days (365/60) versus the industry average of 30 days. This ratio can be distorted if we must use COGS rather than purchases on credit. Nevertheless in the case of Saxton they appear to not being taking full advantage of trade credit as compared to the industry which is taking a lot longer to pay creditors. If Saxton used trade credit more effectively by shortening its turnover of payables it could significantly reduce short term borrowing and resultant interest costs by the firm. This concept is explored more fully in Chapter 7. Small businesses, which have a tough time arranging borrowing from banks, must effectively balance their credit position between current assets and liabilities. This can be done by watching collection, holding and payable periods. If Saxton is collecting from its customers in slightly over 30 days it might expect to be paying its suppliers in a similar period of time.

The firm maintains a slightly lower ratio of sales to capital assets (plant and equipment) than does the industry (5 versus 5.4). This is a relatively minor consideration in

[3]Turnover is sometimes shown as sales divided by inventory, when cost of goods sold information can not be obtained.

view of the rapid movement of inventory and accounts receivable. Finally, the rapid turnover of total assets is again indicated (2.5 versus 1.5). We again raise our concerns that an appropriate amount of capital is deployed in the firm and that reinvestment is occurring at proper intervals.

C. Liquidity Ratios After considering profitability and asset utilization, the analyst needs to examine the liquidity of the firm. The Saxton Company's liquidity ratios fare well in comparison with the industry. Today, with more sophisticated means of managing current assets, one does not want to see ratios that are too high, as this would be evidence of inefficient management. Management is expected to be on top of maturing short-term liabilities and to be able to satisfy them without overly large precautionary balances of current assets. The quick (or acid test) ratio, by excluding inventories, focuses on current assets that can be converted to cash in the fastest time.

The asset utilization ratios, if they are weakening will usually cause cash flow problems for the firm as the assets are not turning to cash as quickly as expected. This weakening of asset efficiencies will eventually show up in deteriorating liquidity ratios.

Further analysis might call for a cash budget to determine if Saxton can meet each maturing obligation as it comes due. In Chapter 4 we will develop cash forecasts. For the small business, cash budgets will be crucial to stay in operation and will be carefully scrutinized by any lender. Many profitable firms have failed because they have run out of cash. Liquidity allows the small business to remain flexible and able to meet short term obligations because bank loans and capital markets are difficult, if not impossible, to access.

C. Liquidity ratios—

		Saxton Company	Industry Average
3–9.	Current ratio = $\frac{\text{Current assets}}{\text{Current liabilities}}$	$\frac{\$800{,}000}{\$300{,}000} = 2.67$	2.1
3–10.	Quick ratio = $\frac{\text{Current assets} - \text{Inventory}}{\text{Current liabilities}}$	$\frac{\$430{,}000}{\$300{,}000} = 1.43$	1.0

D. Debt Utilization Ratios The last grouping of ratios, debt utilization, allows the analyst to measure the prudence of the debt management policies of the firm. Debt utilization, referred to as leverage is explored in Chapter 5 under risk and return considerations with the potential impact on the performance of the firm.

Debt to total assets of 37.5 percent is slightly above the industry average of 33 percent, but well within the prudent range of 50 percent or less. One way to benefit from an inflationary economy is through the use of heavy long-term debt, enabling longstanding obligations to be repaid in dollars reduced in value with the passage of time. Another common variation of debt to assets is the debt/equity ratio. For Saxton this would be 60 percent ($600,000/$1,000,000). Often this ratio is calculated only with long-term debt obligations (including their current portion). Whatever method is used it is important to remain consistent when examining the ratio trends over time.

D. Debt utilization ratios—

		Saxton Company	Industry Average
3–11.	Debt to total assets =		
	$\frac{\text{Total debt}}{\text{Total assets}}$	$\frac{\$600{,}000}{\$1{,}600{,}000} = 37.5\%$	33%
3–12.	Times interest earned =		
	$\frac{\text{Income before interest and taxes}}{\text{Interest}}$	$\frac{\$550{,}000}{\$50{,}000} = 11$	7 times
3–13.	Fixed charge coverage =		
	$\frac{\text{Income before fixed charges and taxes}}{\text{Fixed charges}}$	$\frac{\$600{,}000}{\$100{,}000} = 6$	5.5 times

Ratios for times interest earned and fixed charge coverage show that the Saxton Company debt is being well managed compared to the debt management of other firms in the industry. Times interest earned indicates the number of times that our income before interest and taxes covers the interest obligation (Formula 3–12). The higher the ratio, the stronger is the interest-paying ability of the firm. The figure for income before interest and taxes in the ratio is the equivalent of the operating profit figure presented in Table 3–1 on page 67.

Fixed charge coverage measures the firm's ability to meet all fixed obligations rather than interest payments alone, on the assumption that failure to meet any financial obligation will endanger the position of the firm. In the present case the Saxton Company has lease obligations of $50,000 and $50,000 in interest expenses. Thus, the total fixed charge financial obligation is $100,000. We also need to know the income before all fixed charge obligations. In this case we take income before interest and taxes (operating profit) and add back the $50,000 in lease payments.

Income before interest and taxes	$550,000
Lease payments	50,000
Income before fixed charges and taxes	$600,000

The fixed charges are safely covered 6 times, exceeding the industry norm of 5.5 times. The various ratios are summarized in Table 3–2. The conclusions reached in comparing the Saxton Company to industry averages are generally valid, though exceptions may exist.

In summary, the Saxton Company more than compensates for a lower return on the sales dollar by a rapid turnover of assets, principally inventory and receivables, and a wise use of debt. The student should be able to use these 13 measures to evaluate the financial performance of any firm.

TABLE 3–2
Ratio analysis

	Saxton Company	Industry Average	Conclusion
A. Profitability			
1. Profit margin	5.0%	6.5%	Below average
2. Return on assets	12.5%	10.0%	Above average due to high turnover
3. Return on equity	20.0%	15.0%	Good due to ratios 2 and 11
B. Asset Utilization			
4a. Receivable turnover	11.4	10.0	Good
4b. Average collection period	32	36	Good
5a. Inventory turnover	8.1	7.0	Good
5b. Inventory holding period	45	52	Good
6a. Accounts payables turnover	60.0	12.0	Poor
6b. Accounts payable period	6	30	Poor
7. Capital asset turnover	5.0	5.4	Below average
8. Total asset turnover	2.5	1.5	Good
C. Liquidity			
9. Current ratio	2.67	2.1	Good
10. Quick ratio	1.43	1.0	Good
D. Debt Utilization			
11. Debt to total assets	37.5%	33.0%	Slightly more debt
12. Times interest earned	11	7	Good
13. Fixed charge coverage	6	5.5	Good

Interpretation of Ratios by Trend Analysis

In our examination of ratios, we have compared Saxton Company's results only to the industry average during a particular year in an attempt to identify possible problems. However, one might ask if a comparison to industry averages is appropriate. Would it be more appropriate to compare with the industry leader? How comparable is this company's business to the industry? Furthermore, is a look at a company at a point in time sufficient, or do trends that develop over time tell a more complete story?

Over the course of the business cycle, sales and profitability may expand and contract, and ratio analysis for any one year may not present an accurate picture of the firm. Therefore, we look at **trend analysis** of performance over a number of years. However, without industry comparisons, even trend analysis may not present a complete picture. For example, in Figure 3–2 on the next page, we see that the profit margin for the Saxton Company has improved, while asset turnover has declined. This by itself may look good for the profit margin and bad for asset turnover. However, when compared to industry trends, we see the firm's profit margin is still below the industry average. On asset turnover, Saxton has improved in relation to the industry even though it is in a downward trend. Similar data could be generated for the other ratios.

By analyzing companies in the same industry, one company can compare its performance to its competitors. In comparing the Bank of Montreal and the Royal Bank

FIGURE 3–2
Trend analysis

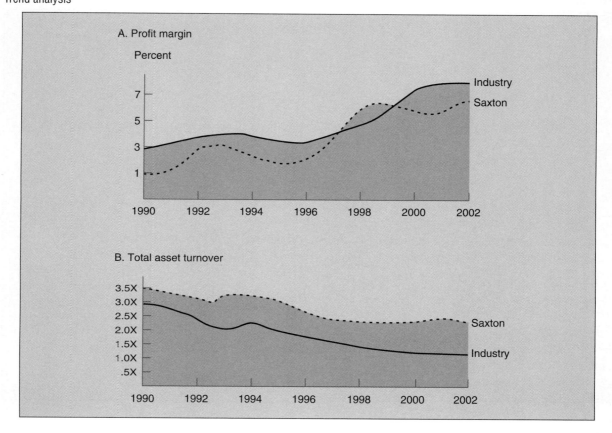

of Canada, we assume that the goal of management is to become the best, not just to match the average performance for the industry. Using return on assets and return on equity as selected ratios, Table 3–3 compares these two companies. Notice the very low return on assets which is a characteristic of the highly leveraged banking industry. Leverage will be further explored in Chapter 5. Despite low returns on assets the shareholders enjoyed healthy returns on equity.

Bank of Montreal
www.bmo.com
Royal Bank of Canada
www.rbc.com

After the recessionary period of 1992–93 the Royal Bank has consistently outperformed the Bank of Montreal. The better return on assets has translated into better returns on shareholders' equity. The market has been willing to pay a higher current share price for each dollar of profitability. In other words, the price/earnings multiple of the Royal Bank has been higher than that of the Bank of Montreal over the last several years.

Another technique for the examination of company trends is to prepare common-size financial statements. This method expresses the items on the balance sheet as a percentage of total assets and presents the items on the income statement as a percentage of total sales. This is demonstrated for the Saxton Company in Table 3–4 on page 78. With the statements expressed in this manner, we can examine financial statement items that are changing relative to other items. As a certain item becomes more or less significant on the balance sheet or income statement, we want to determine if this is a healthy trend. When the lines of the income statement are expressed as a percentage of revenues, the firm can focus on its cost structure identifying areas for improvement.

TABLE 3–3
Trend analysis of competitors

	Bank of Montreal		Royal Bank	
Year	Return on Assets	Return on Equity	Return on Assets	Return on Equity
1992	0.61	14.1	0.08	<0.3>
1993	0.63	14.1	0.21	2.4
1994	0.68	14.9	0.70	16.8
1995	0.68	15.4	0.69	16.6
1996	0.74	17.0	0.70	17.6
1997	0.66	17.1	0.70	19.3
1998	0.59	15.2	0.70	18.4
1999	0.61	14.1	0.65	15.6
2000	0.79	18.0	0.81	19.8
2001	0.60	13.8	0.74	16.4

Source: Annual reports. www.bmo.com Symbol:BMO
www.rbc.com Symbol:RY

Key points for examination are operating ratios such as the gross profit and operating profit margins. The firm would like to examine how these margins compare to competitors and how they improve or deteriorate over time.

Before concluding this brief interpretation of ratios it is important to recap some of the limitations of ratio analysis. Of major concern is whether or not financial statements correctly portray a company's financial situation, particularly in comparison to other companies that may use different methods to report financial performance. The question of market values versus book values has been raised. The impact of inflation and other sources of distortion on the financial reporting of the firm are discussed more fully in the next sections.

Ratios do not by themselves suggest whether or not the firm is operating optimally. There are no accepted standards, although comparison with industry averages may be of some help. However, even in comparison with industry averages, we must raise questions. Are we comparing to the appropriate industry? What if the firm is a conglomerate? Furthermore, we may want to compare to the industry leader and not the average. Firms tend to follow the financing patterns of their competition, and one should wonder whether or not the industry norms are indeed appropriate. Is the industry operating optimally? Financial ratios are based on the past performance of a firm. Are they indicative of future performance? And finally, how are conflicting signals between ratios resolved?

Distortion in Financial Reporting

Coincident with the computation of financial ratios, we should also identify possible distortions that can occur in the reported results of companies. Historical-based accounting in an environment of changing prices due to inflation, **disinflation,** and possible deflation will distort financial results. Price changes will show immediately in revenues but the impact of changing prices will be delayed in asset values, such as inventory and capital assets. Accrual-based accounting is subject to interpretation and the discretion of those who prepare the results. This can result in significant differences in the reporting of revenue, the treatment of cost of goods sold, and the write-off policies

TABLE 3–4
Common-size income statement and balance sheet

SAXTON COMPANY
Income Statement
For year ended Dec. 31, 2002

Sales	100%
Cost of goods sold	75%
Gross profit	25%
Selling and administration	11%
Operating profit	14%
Interest expense	1%
Extraordinary loss	3%
Net income before taxes	10%
Taxes	5%
Net income	5%

Balance Sheet
As of December 31, 2002

Assets

Cash	2%
Marketable securities	3%
Accounts receivable	22%
Inventory	23%
Total current assets	50%
Net plant and equipment	50%
Total assets	100%

Liabilities and Shareholders' Equity

Accounts payable	3%
Notes payable	16%
Total current liabilities	19%
Long-term liabilities	19%
Total liabilities	38%
Common stock	25%
Retained earnings	37%
Total liabilities and shareholders' equity	100%

of the firm. These distortions cause a number of problems for the financial manager or analyst who is evaluating a company.

Inflationary Impact

Bank of Canada
www.bankofcanada.ca/en/inflation_calc.htm

The major problem during inflationary times is that revenue is almost always stated in current dollars, whereas plant and equipment or inventory may have been purchased at lower price levels. Thus, profit may be more a function of increasing prices than of satisfactory performance.

Consider the Stein Corporation's income statement for 2001, in Table 3–5. At year-end the firm also has 100 units still in inventory at $1.00 per unit and $200 worth of plant and equipment with a 20-year life.

Assume that in 2002, the number of units sold remains constant at 100. However, inflation causes a 10 percent increase in price, from $2.00 to $2.20. Total sales go up

Combat in 3D

ATI Technologies Inc. of Thornhill, Ontario, listed on the TSX (www.tsx.ca) and NVidia Corporation of Santa Clara, California, listed on NASDAQ (www.nasdaq.com) are serious competitors in 3D graphics, video, and multimedia technology, including 3D graphics accelerators. NVidia and ATI are about equal in total sales, but in late 2001 NVidia was growing at a faster pace. To win back market share, ATI was investing heavily in research and development. However it remained less cost effective than NVidia. This can be seen by an examination of their common-size income statements.

	NVidia	ATI
Gross margin	38.3%	23.2%
R & D	12.6	14.4
General, selling, and administration	7.3	10.9
Operating margin	18.1	−2.1
Profit margin	13.5	3.0

Each operating ratio reveals that NVidia is more cost effective than ATI. The question is whether ATI can improve its margins and if the extra resources devoted to R & D by ATI will pay off in the long run.

The latest financial statements of ATI and NVidia will reveal if ATI is improving its cost competitiveness. The longer run share price performances of these companies will be the result of cost efficiencies if R & D expenditures pay off.

FINANCE IN ACTION

Q1 Has ATI improved its margins?

Q2 Which share price has performed better over the last year?

www.ati.com

Symbol: ATY

www.nvidia.com

Symbol: NVDA (NASDAQ)

TABLE 3–5
Stein Income Statement, 2001

STEIN CORPORATION
Net Income for 2001

Sales	$200	(100 units at $2)
Cost of goods sold	100	(100 units at $1)
Gross profit	100	
Selling and administrative expense	20	
Amortization	10	
Operating profit	70	
Taxes (40%)	28	
Aftertax income	$ 42	

to $220, but with no actual increase in physical volume. Assume that the firm uses FIFO inventory pricing, so inventory first purchased will be written off against current sales. In this case, 2001 inventory will be written off against 2002 sales revenue.

The 2002 income statement of the Stein Corporation is shown in Table 3–6 on the next page. The company appears to have increased profit by $11.00 simply as a result of inflation. These are **inventory profits**. But not reflected is the increased cost of replacing inventory. Presumably, its **replacement cost** has increased in an inflationary environment.

A replacement cost accounting method would reduce income, but at the same time increase assets. This increase in assets would lower the debt-to-assets ratio since debt is a monetary asset that is not revalued because it is paid back in nominal dollars. A decreased debt-to-assets ratio would indicate the financial leverage of the firm has decreased. However the interest coverage ratio which measures the operating income available to cover interest expense will have decreased.

TABLE 3–6
Stein Income Statement, 2002

STEIN CORPORATION Net Income for 2002		
Sales	$220	(100 units at 1999 price of $2.20)
Cost of goods sold	100	(100 units at $1.00)
Gross profit	120	
Selling and administrative expense	22	(10% of sales)
Amortization	10	
Operating profit	88	
Taxes (40%)	35	
Aftertax income	$ 53	

Disinflation Effect

As long as prices continue to rise in an inflationary environment, profits appear to feed on themselves. However when price increases moderately (**disinflation**), there will be a rude awakening for management and unsuspecting shareholders as expensive inventory is charged against softening retail prices. A 15 or 20 percent growth rate in earnings may be little more than an inflationary illusion. Industries most sensitive to inflation-induced profits are those with cyclical products, such as commodities, and also those in which inventory is a significant percentage of sales and profits. The value of assets must also be challenged if deflation comes into play. Additionally the real value of debt will rise if deflation occurs.

Valuation Basics with Changing Prices

Inflation-induced corporate profits may go down during disinflation periods, but investors may be more willing to place their funds in financial assets such as stocks and bonds. The reason for the shift may be a belief that declining inflationary pressures will no longer seriously impair the purchasing power of the dollar. Lessening inflation means that the required return investors demand on financial assets will be lower and future expected earnings or interest should receive a higher current valuation.

None of the above happens with a high degree of certainty. Lower rates of inflation will not necessarily produce high stock and bond prices unless the price pattern appears sustainable over a reasonable period and disinflation or deflation is not coincident with a recessionary economy. Recessions will significantly lower the future returns from stocks and bonds.

While financial assets such as stocks and bonds have the potential (whether realized or not) to do well during disinflation, such is not the case for tangible (real) assets. Precious metals, such as gold and silver, gems, and collectibles that boomed in the highly inflationary environment of the late 1970s fell off sharply in the 1980s as softening prices caused less perceived need to hold real assets as a hedge against inflation. Some commodities, such as copper and nickel, achieved strong price gains in the late 1980s due to supply shortages. Generally in the 1990s, financial assets outperformed real assets during a period of low inflation.

Accounting Discretion

Accrual-based accounting allows certain leeway in matching the revenues and expenses of the firm. This can result in a wide variance in reported results across different firms. Furthermore, many companies have taken to producing pro forma or adjusted earnings statements that are significantly different from accounting standards. These adjusted statements often receive more public attention.

To illustrate some of these discretions in financial reporting, the income statements for two hypothetical companies in the same industry are presented in Table 3–7. Both firms had identical operating performances for 2002, but Company A is very conservative in reporting its results, while Company B has attempted to maximize its reported income. If both companies had reported income of $200,000 in 2001, Company B would be thought to be showing substantial growth in 2002, with net income of $780,000, while Company A is reporting a "flat" or no-growth year of $240,000. Let us examine how the inconsistencies in Table 3–7 could occur. Emphasis is given to a number of key elements on the income statement.

TABLE 3–7

Income Statement
For the Year 2002

	Conservative (A)	High Reported Income (B)
Sales	$4,000,000	$4,200,000
Cost of goods sold	3,000,000	2,400,000
Gross profit	1,000,000	1,800,000
Selling and administrative expense	450,000	450,000
Operating profit	550,000	1,350,000
Interest expense	50,000	50,000
Net income before taxes	500,000	1,300,000
Taxes (40%)	200,000	520,000
Net income	300,000	780,000
Extraordinary loss (net of tax)	60,000	—
Net income transferred to retained earnings	$ 240,000	$ 780,000

Sales Company B reported $200,000 more in sales although actual volume was the same. This may be the result of different concepts of revenue recognition.

For example, certain assets may be sold on an installment basis over a long period. A conservative firm may defer recognition of the revenue until each payment is received, while other firms may attempt to recognize a fully effected sale at the earliest possible date. A matter for debate is the question of when the risks and rewards of ownership are effectively transferred. Although the accounting profession attempts to establish appropriate methods of financial reporting through generally accepted accounting principles, reporting varies among firms.

Cost of Goods Sold Conservative Company A may well be using **LIFO** accounting in an inflationary environment, thus charging the last-purchased, more expensive items against

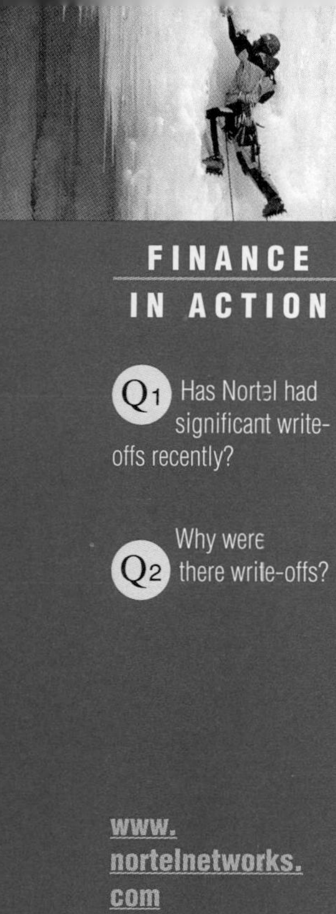

Symbol: NT

Taking a Big Bath

The Big Bath is the tendency of corporations to write-off large portions of corporate assets during times of financial stress in order to restart with a leaner balance sheet. The large write-offs usually result in substantial losses recorded on the income statement for one year. However, the substantial loss will likely increase future reported earnings because the amortization expense is lowered due to the decrease in capitalized assets. Often the Big Bath is taken during reorganization or a change in CEO. If a firm has to report a loss, why not report a big one? A large loss can be blamed on the past leadership. With lower amortization costs and thus higher earnings in the future, the new CEO will look better. Interestingly, executive compensation, which is often tied into profits, will also be better.

In 2001, a lot of companies reported substantial losses in the midst of a recession. These losses were often the result of write-offs. The most substantial was at Nortel which reported a loss of $19.4 billion in the second quarter as seen in Chapter 2. Write-offs included;

Goodwill	$12.4 billion
Restructuring	1.2 billion
Inventory	0.8 billion
Receivables	0.3 billion

The goodwill related to companies that had been acquired within the last few years, but were no longer worth what Nortel had paid for them. Fortunately Nortel had paid for these companies with its own stock and had not incurred any debt in the purchases. The restructuring costs related to thousands of employees terminated by Nortel in 2001 and the breaking of leases in over 200 office buildings. Inventory write-offs were part of "Cost of Goods Sold" and reflected lower values for telecom equipment. The receivables write-offs were part of 'Selling, General and Administrative Expense' and were related to the financing extended by Nortel to its customers, to buy Nortel products. Some of these customers had gone bankrupt.

Without these "one time write-offs" Nortel's results didn't look too bad considering the downturn in the economy at the time.

All figures in U.S. dollars

sales, while Company B uses **FIFO** accounting, charging off less expensive inventory against sales. The $600,000 difference in cost of goods sold may also be explained by varying treatment of research and development costs.

Extraordinary Gains/Losses Nonrecurring gains or losses may occur from the sale of corporate capital assets, lawsuits, the write-down in value of certain assets, or similar nonrecurring events. Unfortunately, there is not always agreement on when those extraordinary gains or losses should be recognized in the income statement. Conservative Company A has taken a write-off of $100,000 ($60,000 aftertax). This is shown as an extraordinary loss. Company B, which holds similar assets, has chosen not to take a write-down in asset value and has thus avoided the extraordinary loss. Extraordinary gains and losses occur among large companies fairly often. In this age of mergers, tender offers, divestments, and corporate restructurings, understanding the finer points of financial statements becomes more important than ever.

Net Income Company A has reported net income of $240,000, while Company B claims $780,000 before subtraction of extraordinary losses. The $540,000 difference is attributed to different methods of financial reporting, and it should be recognized as such by the analyst. No superior performance has actually occurred. The analyst must remain ever alert in examining each item in the financial statements rather than accepting bottom-line figures.

Distortions occur in reported financial statements despite the best efforts and intentions of accountants. Basic financial statements can hide much of what they purport to represent, but by careful examination and inquiry, including ratio calculations and analysis, we can gain a truer picture of the performance of a firm. This will allow us to better estimate the value of the assets held by the firm and in turn the value of the firm itself.

Summary

1. Under ratio analysis, we develop four categories of ratios: profitability, asset utilization, liquidity, and debt utilization. We used the balance sheet and income statement to construct the 13 ratios.
2. The DuPont system of analysis breaks return on equity, the shareholders' investment, into three components. The profit margin, asset turnover, and debt usage each contribute to return on equity.
3. Each ratio should be compared to industry averages to identify possibilities for inquiry. Ratio analysis is rather like solving a mystery in which each clue leads to a new area of inquiry.
4. Each ratio should also be developed over a number of time periods to identify any positive or negative trends.
5. Financial analysis calls for an awareness of the distortions that can occur in the financial reports of the firm. Historical-based accounting can report values significantly different from the current values of assets and can misrepresent income, especially in periods of inflation or deflation. Alternate methods of financial reporting may allow firms with equal performance to report different results.

Review of Formulas

A. Profitability Ratios

3–1. $\text{Profit margin} = \dfrac{\text{Net income}}{\text{Sales}}$

3–2. Return on assets (investment) = (ROA) =

a. $\dfrac{\text{Net income}}{\text{Total assets}}$

b. $\dfrac{\text{Net income}}{\text{Sales}} \times \dfrac{\text{Sales}}{\text{Total assets}}$

3–3. Return on equity (ROE) =

a. $\dfrac{\text{Net income}}{\text{Shareholders' equity}}$

b. $\text{Equity multiplier} = \dfrac{\text{Total assets}}{\text{Equity}}$

c. ROA × Equity multiplier

B. Asset utilization ratios

3–4a. $\text{Receivables turnover} = \dfrac{\text{Sales (credit)}}{\text{Receivables}}$

3–4b. $\text{Average collection period} = \dfrac{\text{Accounts receivable}}{\text{Average daily credit sales}}$

3–5a. $\text{Inventory turnover} = \dfrac{\text{Cost of goods sold}}{\text{Inventory}} \text{ or } \dfrac{\text{Sales}}{\text{Inventory}}$

3–5b. $\text{Inventory holding period} = \dfrac{\text{Inventory}}{\text{Average daily COGS}}$

3–6a. Accounts payable turnover $= \frac{\text{Cost of goods sold}}{\text{Account payable}}$

3–6b. Accounts payables period $= \frac{\text{Accounts payable}}{\text{Average daily purchases (COGS)}}$

3–7. Capital asset turnover $= \frac{\text{Sales}}{\text{Capital assets}}$

3–8. Total asset turnover $= \frac{\text{Sales}}{\text{Total assets}}$

C. Liquidity ratios

3–9. Current ratio $= \frac{\text{Current assets}}{\text{Current liabilities}}$

3–10. Quick ratio $= \frac{\text{Current assets} - \text{Inventory}}{\text{Current liabilities}}$

D. Debt Utilization Ratios

3–11. Debt to total assets $= \frac{\text{Total debt}}{\text{Total assets}}$

3–12. Times interest earned $= \frac{\text{Income before interest and taxes}}{\text{Interest}}$

3–13. Fixed charge coverage $= \frac{\text{Income before fixed charges and taxes}}{\text{Fixed charges}}$

List of Terms

Discussion Questions

1. If we divide users of ratios into short-term lenders, long-term lenders, and shareholders, which ratios would each group be most interested in, and for what reasons?
2. Inflation can have significant effects on income statements and balance sheets and, therefore, on the calculation of ratios. Discuss the possible impact of inflation on the following ratios and explain the direction of the impact based on your assumptions.
   a. Return on investment.
   b. Inventory turnover.
   c. Capital asset turnover.
   d. Debt-to-assets ratio.
3. Explain how the DuPont system of analysis breaks down return on assets. Also explain how it breaks down return on shareholders' equity.
4. What advantage does the fixed charge coverage ratio offer over simply using times interest earned?

5. How would our analysis of profitability ratios be distorted if we used income before taxes? Income before interest and taxes?
6. Is there any validity in rule-of-thumb ratios for all corporations; for example, a current ratio of 2 to 1 or debt to assets of 50 percent?
7. Why is trend analysis helpful in analyzing ratios?
8. What effect will disinflation following a highly inflationary period have on the reported income of the firm?
9. Why might disinflation prove to be favorable to financial assets?
10. Comparing the incomes of two companies can be very difficult even though they sell the same products in equal volume. Why?

INTERNET RESOURCES AND QUESTIONS

Electronic documents including financial statements filed with the Canadian Securities Commissions are available through the System for Electronic Document Analysis and Retrieval (SEDAR): www.sedar.com

MPL Communications Inc. (MPZ on TSX-V) publishes *The Investment Reporter* and *Investor's Digest of Canada*. Financial ratios on Canadian companies are available at: www.adviceforinvestors.com

Ratios are also available on individual companies at: www.globeinvestor.com and www.nasdaq-canada.com

Industry Canada has available industry statistics, and its section entitled company fact sheets calculates financial ratios for individual corporations: www.strategis.ic.gc.ca

Dun & Bradstreet outlines its services and describes its directories: www.dnb.ca

The Business Development Bank has a ratio calculator for many of the common financial ratios. www.bdc.ca

1. Using a site, such as www.adviceforinvestors.com, select industry groupings for analysis.
   a. Compare two companies within an industry group over four years on the basis of return on equity, profit margin, market to book value, and P/E ratio.
   b. Compare two companies within different industry groups over four years on the basis of return on equity, profit margin, market to book value, and P/E ratio.
2. Using a site, such as SEDAR, locate the financial statements of any corporation and calculate the thirteen ratios used in this chapter over a three-year period.
3. Update the trends exhibited in Table 3–3. Has there been a change?

Problems

1. Neon Light Company has $1,000,000 in assets and $600,000 of debt. It reports net income of $100,000.
   a. What is its return on assets?
   b. What is the return on shareholders' equity?
   c. If the firm has an asset turnover ratio of 3 times, what is the profit margin?

www.mcgrawhill.ca/college/block

2. Bass Chemical, Inc., is considering expanding into a new product line. New assets to support expansion will cost $800,000. It is estimated that Bass can generate $2 million in annual sales, with a 5 percent profit margin. What would net income and return on assets (investment) be for the year?
3. Fonda Pistol and Gun Shop can open a new store that have annual sales of $750,000. It will turn over its assets 2.5 times per year. The profit margin on sales will be 6 percent. What would net income and return on assets (investment) for the year be?
4. Billy's Crystal Stores has assets of $5 million and turns over its assets 1.2 times per year. Return on assets is 8 percent. What is the firm's profit margin?
5. Gate Appliances has a return on assets (investment) ratio of 8 percent.
   a. If the debt-to-total-assets ratio is 40 percent, what is the return on equity?
   b. If the firm had no debt, what would the return on equity be?
6. Using the Du Pont method, please evaluate the effects of the following relationships for the Butters Corporation.
   a. Butters Corporation has a profit margin of 7 percent and its return on assets (investment) is 25.2 percent. What is its asset turnover?
   b. If Butters Corporation has a debt-to-total-assets ratio of 50 percent, what would the firm's return on equity be?
   c. What would happen to the return on equity if the debt-to-total-assets ratio decreased to 35 percent?
7. Baker Oats has an asset turnover of 1.6 times per year.
   a. If the return on total assets (investment) was 11.2 percent, what was Baker's profit margin?
   b. The following year, on the same level of assets, Baker's asset turnover declined to 1.4 times and its profit margin was 8 percent. How did the return on total assets change from that of the previous year?
8. Joe Jackson's Shoe Stores, Inc., has $2 million in sales and turns over its assets 2.5 times per year. The firm earns 3.8 percent on each sales dollar. It has $60,000 in current liabilities and $140,000 in long-term liabilities.
   a. What is its return on shareholders' equity?
   b. If the asset base remains the same as computed in part *a,* but total asset turnover goes up to 3, what will be the new return on shareholders' equity? Assume the profit margin stays the same as does current and long-term liabilities.
9. Assume the following data for Cable Corporation and Multi-Media Corp.

	Cable Corporation	Multi-Media Corp.
Net income	$ 30,000	$ 100,000
Sales	300,000	2,000,000
Total assets	400,000	900,000
Total debt	150,000	450,000
Shareholders' equity	250,000	450,000

   a. Compute return on shareholders' equity. Which firm has the higher return?
   b. Compute the following ratios for both firms:
      Net income/sales
      Net income/total assets

Sales/total assets

Debt/total assets

c. Discuss the factors that added or detracted from each firm's return on shareholders' equity.

10. A firm has sales of $3 million, and 10 percent of the sales are for cash. The year-end accounts receivable balance is $285,000. What is the average collection period?

11. Martin Electronics has accounts receivable turnover equal to 15 times. If accounts receivable are $80,000, what is the value for average daily credit sales?

12. Kamin Corporation the following financial data for the years 2001 and 2002:

	2001	2002
Sales	$4,000,000	$5,000,000
Cost of goods sold	3,000,000	4,500,000
Inventory.	400,000	500,000

a. Compute inventory turnover based on sales for each year.

b. Compute inventory turnover based on cost of goods sold for each year.

c. What observations can you reach based on the calculations in parts *a* and *b?*

13. The balance sheet for Stud Clothiers is given below. Sales for the year were $3,040,000, with 75 percent of sales sold on credit.

STUD CLOTHIERS
Balance Sheet Dec. 31, 2002

Assets		Liabilities and Equity	
Cash	$ 50,000	Accounts payable	$220,000
Accounts receivable	280,000	Accrued taxes	80,000
Inventory	240,000	Bonds payable (long term)	118,000
Plant and equipment	380,000	Common stock	250,000
		Retained earnings	282,000
Total assets	$950,000	Total liabilities and equity	$950,000

Compute the following ratios:

a. Current ratio.

b. Quick ratio.

c. Debt-to-total-assets ratio.

d. Asset turnover.

e. Average collection period.

14. The Neeley Office Supplies income statement is given below.

a. What is the times interest earned ratio?

b. What would be the fixed charge coverage ratio?

NEELEY OFFICE SUPPLIES	
Sales	$200,000
Cost of goods sold	115,000
Gross profit	85,000
Fixed charges (other than interest)	25,000
Income before interest and taxes	60,000
Interest	15,000
Income before taxes	45,000
Taxes	15,300
Income aftertaxes	$ 29,700

15. Using the income statement for Paste Management Company, compute the following ratios:
    a. The interest coverage
    b. The fixed charge coverage

    The total assets for this company equal $80,000. Set up the formula for the DuPont system of ratio analysis, and compute *c, d,* and *e.*
    c. Profit margin
    d. Total asset turnover
    e. Return on assets (investment).

PASTE MANAGEMENT COMPANY	
Sales	$126,000
Less: Cost of goods sold	93,000
Gross profit	33,000
Less: Selling and administrative expense	11,000
Less: Lease expense	4,000
Operating profit*	18,000
Less: Interest expense	3,000
Earnings before taxes	15,000
Less: Taxes (30%)	4,500
Earnings after taxes	$ 10,500

*Equals income before interest and taxes

16. A firm has net income before interest and taxes of $120,000 and interest expense of $24,000.
    a. What is the times interest earned ratio?
    b. If the firm's lease payments are $40,000, what is the fixed charge coverage?
17. In January 1993 the Status Quo Company was formed. Total assets were $500,000, of which $300,000 consisted of capital assets. Status Quo uses straight-line amortization, and in 1993 it estimated its capital assets to have useful lives of 10 years. Aftertax income has been $26,000 per year each of the last 10 years. Other assets have not changed since 1993.
    a. Compute return on assets at year-end for 1993, 1995, 1998, 2000, and 2002. (Use $26,000 in the numerator for each year.)
    b. To what do you attribute the phenomenon shown in part *a?*

c. Now assume income increased by 10 percent each year. What effect would this have on your above answers? Comment.

18. Jodie Foster Care Homes Corp., shows the following data:

Year	Net income	Total assets	Shareholders Equity	Total debt
1999	$118,000	$1,900,000	$ 700,000	$1,200,000
2000	131,000	1,950,000	950,000	1,000,000
2001	148,000	2,010,000	1,100,000	910,000
2002	175,700	2,050,000	1,420,000	630,000

a. Compute the ratio of net income to total assets for each year and comment on the trend.

b. Compute the ratio of net income to shareholders' equity and comment on the trend. Explain why there may be a difference in the trends between parts *a* and *b*.

19. Calloway Products has the following data. Industry information is also shown.

	Company Data		Industry Data on Net Income/ Total Assets
Year	Net Income	Total Assets	
2000	$360,000	$3,000,000	11%
2001	380,000	3,400,000	8
2002	380,000	3,800,000	5

Year	Debt	Total Assets	Industry Data on Debt/Total Assets
2000	$1,600,000	$3,000,000	52%
2001	1,750,000	3,400,000	40
2002	1,900,000	3,800,000	31

As an industry analyst comparing the firm to the industry, are you likely to praise or criticize the firm in terms of.

a. Net income/total assets

b. Debt/total assets.

20. The United World Corporation has three subsidiaries.

	Computers	Magazines	Cable TV
Sales	$16,000,000	$4,000,000	$8,000,000
Net income (aftertaxes)	1,000,000	160,000	600,000
Assets	5,000,000	2,000,000	5,000,000

a. Which division has the lowest return on sales?

b. Which division has the highest return on assets?

c. Compute the return on assets for the entire corporation.

d. If the $5 million investment in the Cable TV division is sold and redeployed in the computer subsidiary at the same rate of return on assets currently achieved in the computer division, what will be the new return on assets for the entire corporation?

21. Bard Corporation shows the following income statement. The firm uses FIFO inventory accounting.

BARD CORPORATION
Income Statement for 2002

Sales	$200,000	(10,000 units at $20)
Cost of goods sold	100,000	(10,000 units at $10)
Gross profit	100,000	
Selling and administrative expense	10,000	
Amortization	20,000	
Operating profit	70,000	
Taxes (30%)	21,000	
Aftertax income	$ 49,000	

a. Assume that the same 10,000 unit volume is maintained in 2003, but the sales price increases by 10 percent. Because of FIFO inventory policy, old inventory will still be charged off at $10.00 per unit. Also assume that selling and administrative expense will be 5 percent of sales and amortization will be unchanged. The tax rate is 30 percent. Compute aftertax income for 2003.

b. In part *a,* by what percent did aftertax income increase as a result of a 10 percent increase in the sales price? Explain why this impact occurred.

c. Now assume in 2004 the volume remains constant at 10,000 units, but that the sales price decreases by 15 percent from its 2003 level. Also, because of FIFO inventory policy, cost of goods sold reflects the inflationary conditions of the prior year and is $11.00 per unit. Further assume that selling and administrative expense will be 5 percent of sales and amortization will be unchanged. The tax rate is 30 percent. Compute aftertax income.

22. Construct the current assets section of the balance sheet from the following data.

Yearly sales (credit)	$730,000
Inventory turnover	6 times
Current liabilities	$105,000
Current ratio	2
Quick ratio	1
Average collection period	35 days
Current assets:	
Cash	$ ______
Accounts receivable	______
Inventory	______
Total current assets	______

23. The Griggs Corporation has sales of $1,200,000, all on credit. Given the following ratios, fill in the balance sheet below.

Total assets turnover	2.4 times
Cash to total assets	2.0%
Accounts receivable turnover	8.0 times
Inventory turnover	10.0 times
Current ratio	2.0 times
Debt to total assets	61.0%

GRIGGS CORPORATION
Balance Sheet Dec. 31, 2002

Assets		Liabilities and Shareholders' Equity	
Cash	______	Current debt	______
Accounts receivable	______	Long-term debt	______
Inventory	______	Total debt	______
Total current assets	______	Equity	______
Capital assets	______	Total debt and	
Total assets	______	shareholders' equity	______

24. We are given the following information for Coleman Machine Tools Corporation.

Sales (credit)	$7,200,000
Cash	300,000
Inventory	2,150,000
Current liabilities	1,400,000
Asset turnover	1.20 times
Current ratio	2.50 times
Debt-to-assets ratio	40%
Receivables turnover	8 times

Current assets are composed of cash, marketable securities, accounts receivable, and inventory.
Calculate the following balance sheet items:

a. Accounts receivable

b. Marketable securities

c. Capital assets

d. Long-term debt

25. The following data are from Stone Cold Corporation's financial statements. The firm manufactures home decorative material. Sales (all credit) were $60 million for 2002.

Sales to total assets	3.0 times
Total debt to total assets	40%
Current ratio	2.0 times
Inventory turnover	10.0 times
Average collection period	18.0 days
Capital asset turnover	7.5 times

Fill in the brief balance sheet:

Cash	______	Current debt	______
Accounts receivable	______	Long-term debt	______
Inventory	______	Total debt	______
Total current assets	______	Equity	______
Capital assets	______	Total debt and	
Total assets	______	shareholders' equity	______

26. Using the financial statements for the Hot Air Corporation, calculate the 13 basic ratios found in the chapter.

THE HOT AIR COMPANY
Balance Sheet
December 31, 2002

Assets

Current assets:	
Cash	$ 40,000
Marketable securities	30,000
Accounts receivable (net)	120,000
Inventory	180,000
Total current assets	370,000
Investments	40,000
Plant and equipment	450,000
Less: Accumulated amortization	100,000
Net plant and equipment	350,000
Total assets	$760,000

Liabilities and Shareholders' Equity

Current liabilities:	
Accounts payable	$ 90,000
Notes payable	10,000
Accrued taxes	10,000
Total current liabilities	110,000
Long-term liabilities:	
Bonds payable	170,000
Total liabilities	280,000
Shareholders' equity	
Preferred stock	90,000
Common stock	290,000
Retained earnings	100,000
Total shareholders' equity	480,000
Total liabilities and shareholders' equity	$760,000

THE HOT AIR COMPANY
Income Statement
Year ending December 31, 2002

Sales (on credit)	$2,000,000
Less: Cost of goods sold	1,300,000
Gross profit	700,000
Less: Selling and administrative expenses*	400,000
Operating profit (EBIT)	300,000
Less: Interest expense	20,000
Earnings before taxes (EBT)	280,000
Less: Taxes	112,000
Earnings aftertaxes (EAT)	$ 168,000

*Includes $10,000 in lease payments.

27. Using the financial statements of Jet Boat Ltd., calculate the 13 basic ratios found in this chapter. Comment briefly on the ratios that might be worth further investigation. Explain why.

JET BOAT LTD.
Balance Sheet
December 31, 2002

Assets

Current assets:	
Cash	$ 40,000
Marketable securities	85,000
Accounts receivable (net)	100,000
Inventory	375,000
Total current assets	600,000
Net plant and equipment	600,000
Total assets	$1,200,000

Liabilities and Shareholders' Equity

Current liabilities:	
Accounts payable	$ 100,000
Bank loans	125,000
Accrued expenses	25,000
Total current liabilities	250,000
Long-term liabilities:	
Bonds payable*	500,000
Total liabilities	750,000
Shareholders' equity:	
Common stock	350,000
Retained earnings	100,000
Total shareholders' equity	450,000
Total liabilities and shareholders' equity	$1,200,000

*Sinking fund provision of $50,000 a year.

JET BOAT LTD.
Income Statement
Year ending December 31, 2002

Sales (on credit)	$2,900,000
Less: cost of goods sold	2,465,000
Gross profit	435,000
Less: selling and administrative expenses	250,000
Operating profit (EBIT)	185,000
Less: interest expense	94,000
Earnings before taxes (EBT)	91,000
Less: taxes (20%)	18,200
Earnings aftertaxes (EAT)	$ 72,800

28. The financial statements for Turner Corporation and Brady Corporation are shown below.
    a. To which company would you, as credit manager for a supplier, approve the extension of (short-term) trade credit? Why? Compute all ratios before answering.
    b. In which corporation would you buy shares? Why?

TURNER CORPORATION

Current Assets		Liabilities	
Cash	$ 5,000	Accounts payable	$110,000
Accounts receivable	90,000	Bonds payable (long-term)	80,000
Inventory	55,000		
Long-Term Assets		**Shareholders' Equity**	
Capital assets	600,000	Common stock	210,000
Less: Accumulated amortization	(150,000)	Retained earnings	200,000
Net capital assets	450,000		
	$600,000		$600,000

Sales (on credit)	$1,500,000
Cost of goods sold	1,000,000
Gross profit	500,000
Selling and administrative expense*	244,500
Less: Amortization expense	50,000
Operating profit	205,500
Interest expense	8,000
Earnings before taxes	197,500
Tax expense (40%)	79,000
Net income	$ 118,500

*Includes $9,000 in lease payments.

Note: Turner Corporation has 75,000 shares outstanding.

BRADY CORPORATION

Current Assets		Liabilities	
Cash	$ 30,000	Accounts payable	$ 75,000
Marketable securities	7,500	Bonds payable—10%	
Accounts receivable	70,000	(long-term)	210,000
Inventory	72,500		
Long-Term Assets		**Shareholders' Equity**	
Capital assets	$500,000	Common stock	$105,000
Less: Accumulated amortization	(250,000)	Retained earnings	40,000
Net capital assets	250,000		
	$430,000		$430,000

Sales (on credit)	$1,000,000
Cost of goods sold	650,000
Gross profit	350,000
Selling and administrative expense*	175,000
Amortization expense	69,000
Operating profit	106,000
Interest expense	21,000
Earnings before taxes	85,000
Tax expense (40%)	34,000
Net income	$ 51,000

*Includes $6,000 in lease payments.

Note: Brady Corporation has 75,000 shares outstanding.

29. The following ratio calculations are based on three years of financial statements and are compared to the industry standards. The retail company has had some growth during this period but has found that its profitability is less than satisfactory. Examine the ratios to identify possible reasons for the profitability concerns.

	2002	2001	2000	Industry
Profit margin	3.5%	4.0%	4.3%	4.2%
Return on assets	3.9%	4.8%	5.6%	6.4%
Return on equity	7.7%	9.6%	11.2%	13.7%
Gross margin	43.0%	43.0%	43.0%	40.0%
Receivables turnover	8.1×	7.9×	7.8×	7.3×
Average collection period	45/days	46/days	47/days	50/days
Inventory turnover	8.3×	8.2×	8.1×	8.3×
Capital asset turnover	2.7×	3.0×	3.3×	3.5×
Total asset turnover	1.1×	1.2×	1.3×	1.5×
Current ratio	2.3	2.3	2.2	2.1
Quick ratio	2.0	2.0	1.9	1.7
Debt to total assets	50.0%	50.0%	50.0%	54.0%
Times interest earned	8.1×	8.2×	8.1×	7.2×
Fixed charge coverage	4.0×	4.5×	5.5×	5.1×

COMPREHENSIVE PROBLEM

30. You are the manager of a credit department. The sales team has presented a large order from a new purchaser, Wizard Industries. For approximately 12 years, Wizard has been installing security and water sprinkler systems in office buildings.

The salespeople have been well trained, as they have also presented you with the following financial statements and industry ratios (from your files). In their report they note that sales have increased in the last two years due to Wizard's more aggressive selling approach.

The sales team is eager for you to grant credit to Wizard Industries. Of course, you must do a complete analysis noting any ratios that are cause for concern or require a further explanation.

What is your recommendation? Do you grant credit?

WIZARD INDUSTRIES
Income Statements Year ended

	2002	2001	2000
Sales (all on credit)	$1,605,100	$1,841,300	$1,542,700
Cost of goods sold	1,258,900	1,397,400	1,174,800
Gross profit	346,200	443,900	367,900
Selling and administrative expense	265,650	256,850	294,200
Amortization	14,000	14,400	16,000
Operating profit	66,550	172,650	57,700
Interest expense	65,100	50,550	50,100
Earnings before taxes	1,450	122,100	7,600
Taxes	350	27,100	2,200
Earnings available to common shareholders	$ 1,100	$ 95,000	$ 5,400
Dividends declared	$ 70,000	$ 65,000	$ 60,000

WIZARD INDUSTRIES
Balance Sheets
December 31

	2002	2001	2000
Assets			
Cash	$ 14,900	$ 24,700	$ 11,500
Marketable securities	7,000	7,000	7,000
Accounts receivable	410,800	361,800	297,300
Inventory	256,600	330,000	289,900
Prepaid expenses	5,200	800	5,500
Total current assets	694,500	724,300	611,200
Net plant and equipment	162,000	172,900	184,300
Goodwill	25,400	28,200	30,600
Total assets	$881,900	$925,400	$826,100
Liabilities and Shareholders' Equity			
Accounts payable	$145,900	$196,700	$209,700
Bank loan	254,000	202,000	169,000
Accrued expenses	3,700	23,700	14,400
Total current liabilities	403,600	422,400	393,100
Long-term debt	225,800	181,600	141,000
Total liabilities	629,400	604,000	534,100
Common stock	14,000	14,000	14,000
Retained earnings	238,500	307,400	278,000
Total shareholders' equity	252,500	321,400	292,000
Total liabilities and shareholders' equity	$881,900	$925,400	$826,100

Selected industry ratios

Profit margin	5.8%
Return on assets (investment)	8.1%
Return on equity	20.3%
Receivables turnover	6.3×
Average collection period	58.3 days
Inventory turnover	4.3×
Capital asset turnover	8.0×
Current ratio	1.6
Total asset turnover	1.7×
Quick ratio	1.1
Debt to total assets	60.0%
Times interest earned	4.3×

31. Bob Adkins has recently been approached by his first cousin, Ed Lamar, with a proposal to buy a 15 percent interest in Lamar Swimwear. The firm manufactures stylish bathing suits and sunscreen products.

Mr. Lamar is quick to point out the increase in sales that has occurred over the past three years as indicated in the following income statement. The annual growth rate is 25 percent. A balance sheet for a similar time period and selected industry ratios are also presented. Note the industry growth rate in sales is only 10 to 12 percent per year.

There was a steady real growth of 3 to 4 percent in gross domestic product during the period under study. The rate of inflation was in the 5 to 6 percent range.

The stock in the corporation has become available due to the ill health of a current shareholder, who needs cash. The issue here is not to determine the exact price for the stock but rather to determine whether Lamar Swimwear represents an attractive investment situation. Although Mr. Adkins has a primary interest in the profitability ratios, he will take a close look at all the ratios. He has no fast and firm rules about required return on investment; rather, he wishes to analyze the overall condition of the firm. The firm does not currently pay a cash dividend, and return to the investor must come from selling the stock in the future. After doing a thorough analysis (including ratios for each year and comparisons to the industry), what comments and recommendations can you offer to Mr. Adkins?

LAMAR SWIMWEAR
Income Statements Year ended

	2002	2001	2000
Sales (all on credit)	$1,875,000	$1,500,000	$1,200,000
Cost of goods sold	1,310,000	1,040,000	800,000
Gross profit	565,000	460,000	400,000
Selling and administrative expense*	304,700	274,000	239,900
Operating profit (EBIT)	260,300	186,000	160,100
Interest expense	85,000	45,000	35,000
Net income before taxes	175,300	141,000	125,100
Taxes	55,600	49,200	36,900
Net income	$ 119,700	$ 91,800	$ 88,200
Shares	38,000	30,000	30,000
Earnings per share	$3.15	$3.06	$2.94

*Includes $15,000 in lease payments for each year.

LAMAR SWIMWEAR
Balance Sheets Dec. 31

Assets

	2002	2001	2000
Cash	$ 30,000	$ 40,000	$ 30,000
Marketable securities	30,000	25,000	20,000
Accounts receivable	360,000	259,000	170,000
Inventory	290,000	261,000	230,000
Total current assets	710,000	585,000	450,000
Net plant and equipment	1,390,000	765,000	650,000
Total assets	$2,100,000	$1,350,000	$1,100,000

Liabilities and Shareholders' Equity

	2002	2001	2000
Accounts payable	$ 505,000	$ 310,000	$ 200,000
Accrued expenses	35,000	30,000	20,400
Total current liabilities	540,000	340,000	220,400
Long-term liabilities	703,900	363,600	325,000
Total liabilities	1,243,900	703,600	545,400
Common stock	340,000	250,000	250,000
Retained earnings	516,100	396,400	304,600
Total shareholders' equity	856,100	646,400	554,600
Total liabilities and shareholders' equity	$2,100,000	$1,350,000	$1,100,000

Selected Industry Ratios

	2002	2001	2000
Growth in sales	12.00%	10.00%	—
Profit margin	7.96%	7.82%	7.71%
Return on assets (investment)	8.95%	8.68%	8.09%
Return on equity	16.01%	15.26%	14.31%
Receivables turnover	9.31×	8.86×	9.02×
Average collection period	38.7 days	40.6 days	39.9 days
Inventory turnover	5.11×	5.10×	4.24×
Capital asset turnover	1.75×	1.64×	1.60×
Total asset turnover	1.12×	1.10×	1.05×
Current ratio	2.40×	2.25×	1.96×
Quick ratio	1.38×	1.41×	1.37×
Debt to total assets	44.10%	43.11%	43.47%
Times interest earned	6.61×	5.99×	6.50×
Fixed charge coverage	4.73×	4.69×	4.70×
Growth in earnings per share	13.30%	10.10%	—

Selected References

Artz, William A., and Raymond N. Neihengen, Jr. "Analysis of Finance Company Ratios." *Journal of Lending and Credit Risk Management* 80 (September 1997), pp. 32–36.

Brooks, Raymond M., Marilyn F. Johnson, and Tie Su. "CEO Presentations to Financial Analysts: Much Ado About Nothing?" *Financial Practice and Education* 7 (Fall–Winter 1997), pp. 19–28.

Chen, Carl R., and Nancy J. Mohan. "Timing the Disclosure of Information: Management's View of Earnings Announcements." *Financial Management* 23 (August 1994), pp. 63–69.

Fama, Eugene F., and Kenneth R. French. "Size and Book-to-Market Factors in Earnings and Returns." *Journal of Finance* 50 (March 1995), pp. 131–55.

Ferguson, Robert, and Ean Leistikow, "Search for the Best Financial Performance Measure, Basic are Better." *Financial Analysts Journal* 54 (January–February 1998), pp. 81–85.

Firer, Colin. "Driving Financial Performance through the DuPont Identity: A Strategic Use of Financial Analysis and Planning." *Financial Practice and Education* 9 (Spring–Summer 1999), pp. 34–45.

Froot, Kenneth A., David S. Scharfstein, and Jeremy C. Stein. "Heard on the Street: Informational Inefficiencies in a Market with Short-Term Speculation." *Journal of Finance* 47 (September 1992), pp. 1461–84.

Hollingsworth, Danny P., and Walter T. Harrison, Jr. "Deducting the Cost of Intangibles." *Journal of Accounting* 174 (July 1992), pp. 85–90.

Park, Kwangwoo, and Ronald A. Ratti. "Real Activity Inflation, Stock Returns, and Monetary Policy." *Financial Review* 36 (May 2000), pp. 59–78.

Ramakrisnan, Ram T. S., and Jacob K. Thomas. "What Matters from the Past: Market Value, Book Value or Earnings?" *Journal of Accounting, Auditing & Finance* 7 (Fall 1992), pp. 423–64.

Schukat, Ann. "Inside the Retrenchment: Profits Matter." *Fortune* 142 (August 14, 2000), p. 280.

CHAPTER | FOUR

Financial Forecasting

LEARNING | OBJECTIVES

1 Explain why financial forecasting is essential for the healthy growth of the firm.

2 Prepare the three financial statements for forecasting—the pro forma income statement, the cash budget, and the pro forma balance sheet.

3 Perform the percent-of-sales method for forecasting on a less precise basis.

4 Determine the need for new funding resulting from sales growth.

Forecasting the future has never been easy, but today our vision of that future changes constantly. The Internet provides us with instant access to these changes, however, we have to be prepared to use this constant stream of information effectively. The old notion of the corporate treasurer burning the midnight oil to find new avenues of financing before dawn is no longer realistic. One talent that is essential to the financial manager is the ability to plan ahead and to make necessary adjustments before actual events occur. We likely could construct the same set of external events for two corporations (inflation, recession, severe new competition, and so on), and one would survive, while the other would not. The outcome might be a function not only of their risk-taking desires, but also of their ability to hedge against risk with careful planning.

Although we may assume that no growth or a decline in volume is the primary cause for a shortage of funds, this is not necessarily the case. A rapidly growing firm may witness a significant increase in accounts receivable, inventory, and plant and equipment to facilitate that growth and these increasing investments in assets cannot be financed solely through profits. Suppliers, the bank, and perhaps the shareholders will be required to contribute more capital to the firm. A comprehensive financing plan with pro forma statements must be developed to anticipate these capital needs. Too often the small businessperson (and sometimes the big one as well) is mystified by an increase in sales and profits but a decrease of cash in the till. Recognizing the differences between income statements and actual cash is often crucial to ensure the continuing success of a business.

Real Time Forecasts at Dell

Dell Computers was founded in 1984 and today it has annual sales of U.S.$32 billion. Its business model is to sell customized computers directly to the customer, saving money and making the latest technology available quickly. This is identified through its web site as the "Dell Direct Method." Another key advantage of direct sales is that Dell is aware immediately of customer concerns and expectations. By 1994 Dell began to sell PCs over the Internet and this has been highly successful, but it was Dell's ability to deliver that made it successful.

Sales information from across the globe is collected, summarized, and reported daily to Michael Dell in Texas. Immediate areas of soft or changing sales become known. This is a real time forecasting model. Being on top of the revenue side of the business is complemented on the variable cost side by holding less than a week's worth of inventory. Cost reductions can be passed on to customers immediately and inventory needs can respond to changing customer dynamics.

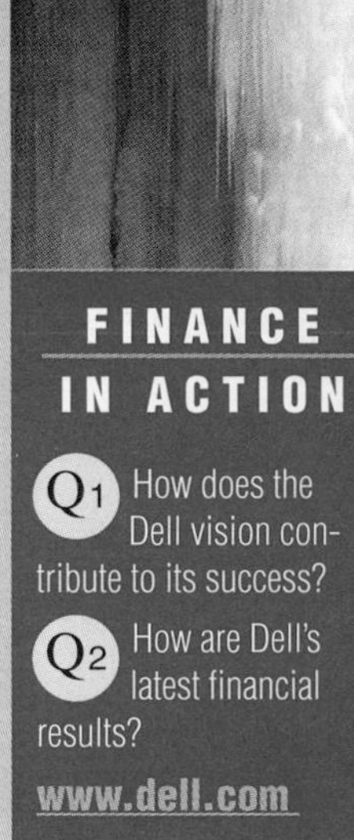

FINANCE IN ACTION

Q1 How does the Dell vision contribute to its success?

Q2 How are Dell's latest financial results?

www.dell.com

The Financial Planning Process

Financial forecasting is just part of the larger financial planning process, in which long-run investment and financing decisions of the firm are molded into an overall corporate strategy. The financial plan of the firm is built after carefully identifying financial goals and then examining the available investment alternatives. These alternatives should be analyzed with the capital budgeting techniques, which will be examined in Chapter 12. Scenarios that cover the best case, worst case, and most likely case outcomes often are produced to enable management to better appreciate the possible results of the different investment alternatives. Long-run strategies will have significant impact on the short-run operations of the firm.

In the process of building a financial plan, it is important that consensus is built amongst all stakeholders of the company, such as the marketing, production, treasury, and accounting personnel. If certain stakeholders are alienated from the process of building the plan, it will not have their support, and the financial plan will likely fail. If stakeholders don't feel part of the process they will be reluctant or unwilling to contribute reliable information that will be needed to construct an effective plan.

Financial forecasting tends to focus more on the short run and is usually based on the overall strategies developed as part of the financial plan. Forecasting financial results, particularly over the next 12 months, is essential to ensure the firm has sufficient cash to remain in business. This helps the firm avoid surprises and the forecasts can be used by the firm to measure performance. Difficulties arise in preparing the financial forecasts because there seldom are direct relationships between projected sales and cash requirements. Furthermore, sales projections, cost estimates, and the timing of cash flows often rely on the estimates of persons within the company based on past experience and these must be tempered with the changing business environment. This is why it is essential that those people see the value of the process and feel their participation gives tangible results.

Results are usually different than forecasted, sometimes to a great extent. The importance of a forecasted plan is that it allows the firm to identify what went wrong and hopefully to correct it in the future. A plan allows the firm to adjust to changing conditions; it shows the firm where it should be going and helps them identify when things are amiss. A good plan will be altered continually but it still allows the firm to better see where it is going and where it has been.

Constructing Pro Forma Statements

The most comprehensive means of financial forecasting is to develop a series of pro forma, or projected, financial statements. We give particular attention to the *pro forma income statement*, the *cash budget*, and the *pro forma balance sheet*. Based on the projected statements, the firm can judge its future level of receivables, inventory, payables, and other corporate accounts as well as its anticipated profits and borrowing requirements. Then the financial officer can carefully track actual events against the plan and make necessary adjustments.

For the small business these statements are essential. A lack of realistic financial forecasts often results in liquidity problems and the eventual failure of the business. Furthermore, bankers and other lenders will ask for financial forecasts when deciding on whether or not to lend money. If the pro forma statements are poorly prepared, bankers will be unwilling to lend to the business because the lack of effective planning reflects on management's ability to run and control the resources of a successful business. The banker should be able to see from the financial forecasts how repayment will occur.

A systems approach is necessary to develop pro forma statements. Projections should be based on knowledge of the local and broad economic environment, on awareness of social and political change, on anticipation of competitors' strategies, and on our prediction of innovation in product markets. With these considerations we first construct a pro forma income statement based on sales projections and the production plan; then, we translate this material into a cash budget; and finally, we assimilate all previously developed material into a pro forma balance sheet; as depicted in Figure 4–1.

FIGURE 4–1
Development of pro forma statements

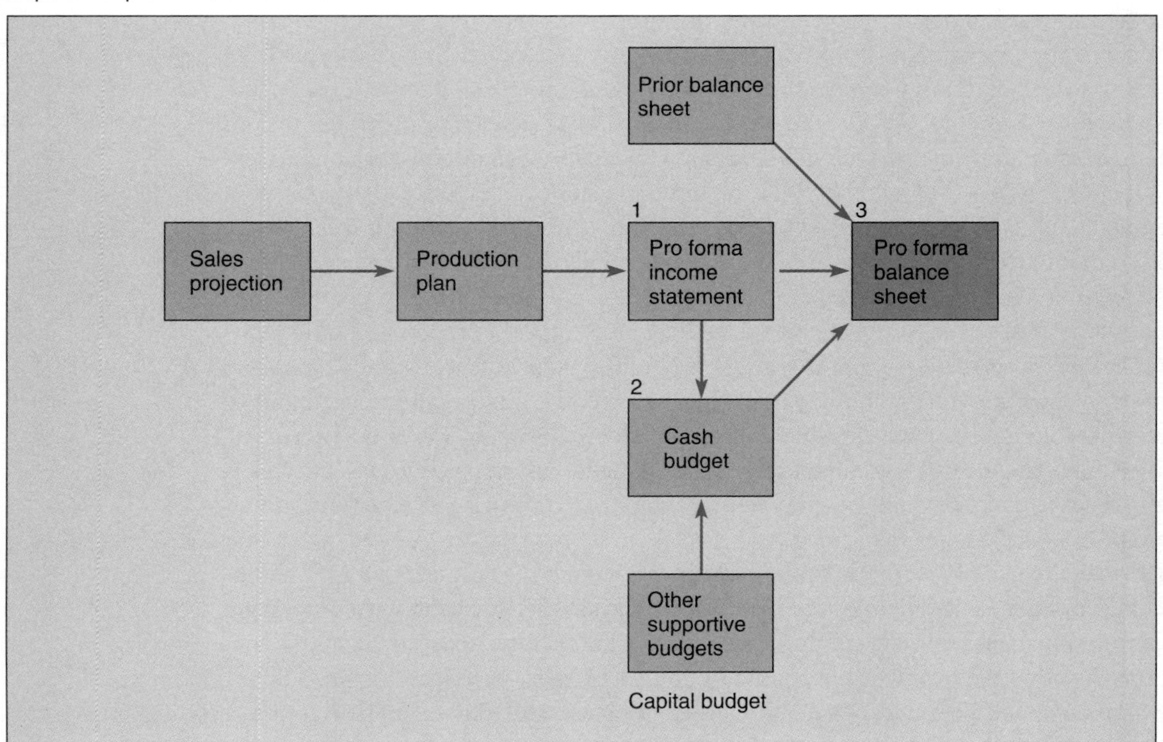

The construction of pro forma statements is greatly enhanced by computerized spreadsheets. Furthermore, sensitivity analysis is fairly simple once the spreadsheets are set up on the computer.

Pro Forma Income Statement

Assume the Goldman Corporation has been requested by its bank to provide pro forma financial statements for midyear 2003. The **pro forma income statement** provides a projection of how much profit the firm anticipates making over the ensuing time period. In developing the pro forma income statement, we will follow four important steps:

1. Establish a sales projection.
2. Determine a production schedule and the associated use of new material, direct labour, and overhead to arrive at gross profit.
3. Compute other expenses.
4. Determine profit by completing the actual pro forma statement.

Ultimately, a firm's continued success is written with income statement results showing an acceptable return to investors. However, it is the appropriate management of the firm's short-term cash position that allows the long-term success to be realized.

Establish a Sales Projection

For purposes of analysis we assume the Goldman Corporation has two primary products: wheels and casters. Our sales projection calls for the sale of 1,000 wheels and 2,000 casters at prices of $30.00 and $35.00, respectively. As indicated in Table 4–1 we anticipate total sales of $100,000.

TABLE 4–1
Projected wheel and caster sales (first six months, 2003)

	Wheels	Casters	
Quantity	1,000	2,000	
Sales price	$30	$35	
Sales revenue	$30,000	$70,000	
Total			$100,000

Sales estimates are the cornerstone of the entire process of constructing pro forma statements. Sales revenue, we are reminded, is the product of demand for a company's products or services and their prices. A firm's financial results will likely prove to be sensitive to differences between projected demand and realized demand. Our concern for the precision of forecasted demand depends on the seriousness attached to a potential cash shortfall. This in turn determines if daily, weekly, or monthly estimates are required.

The projected price is based on the firm's cost structure, the marketing effort, and the anticipated response of competitors to the firm's price. A forecast of the quantity sold needs to consider price, knowledge of the continuing and growing needs of a firm's clientele, and estimates of new clients. The forecast uses past relationships and ratios, builds on the estimates suggested by the sales force, and is tempered by considerations of economic, social, and political events. In addition, the limitations and opportunities of the production facilities must be considered.

Sales projections are best derived from both an external and internal viewpoint. Using the former, we analyze our prospective sales in light of economic conditions affecting our industry and our company. Statistical techniques such as regression and time series analysis may be employed in the process. Internal analysis calls for the sales department to survey our own salespeople within their territories. Ideally, we would proceed along each of those paths in isolation of the other and then assimilate the results into one meaningful projection.

Determine a Production Schedule and the Gross Profit

We determine the necessary production plan for the six-month period based on anticipated sales. The number of units produced depends on the beginning inventory of wheels and casters, our sales projection, and the desired level of ending inventory. Assume that on January 1, 2003, the Goldman Corporation has in stock the items shown in Table 4–2.

TABLE 4–2
Stock of beginning inventory

	Wheels	Casters	
Quantity	85	180	
Cost	$16	$20	
Total value	$1,360	$3,600	
Total			$4,960

We add the projected quantity of unit sales for the next six months to our desired ending inventory and subtract our stock of beginning inventory (in units) to determine our production requirements.

Units
+ Projected sales
+ Desired ending inventory
− Beginning inventory
= Production requirements

In Table 4–3 we see a required production level of 1,015 wheels and 2,020 casters.

TABLE 4–3
Production requirements for six months

	Wheels	Casters
Projected unit sales (Table 4–1)	+1,000	+2,000
Desired ending inventory (assumed to represent 10% of unit sales for the time period)	+100	+200
Beginning inventory (Table 4–2)	−85	−180
Units to be produced	1,015	2,020

We must now determine the cost to produce these units. In Table 4–2 we saw that the cost of units in stock was $16.00 for wheels and $20.00 for casters. However, we

Oil Prices! How about a Forecast?

FINANCE IN ACTION

For oil producers and marketers, the future price of oil is very important for their projections of the firm's revenues and costs. The future price of oil will also determine their spending plans and the returns to shareholders. In early 1999 the price of oil was just above U.S.$12.00 per barrel, but in November of 2000 it topped U.S.$36.00. By November of 2001 it had dipped below U.S.$18.00. What could be expected for the future? OPEC was squabbling with non-OPEC producers over the reduction of production to support prices, but Russia the world's second largest oil exporter, was reluctant to cooperate.

We might look to the past for guidance as to where oil prices might go in the future (www.bp.com and www.wtrg.com). In 1974 when the OPEC oil embargo was in its infancy (or infamy) stage the price of oil had jumped to U.S. $10.41, about the same price it was in early 1999. By 1980 the price of oil had reached U.S.$36.00, and some were predicting that oil would reach U.S.$100.00 a barrel before the end of the decade. In real dollars (with adjustment for inflation, with 2001 as reference) the 1974 price was over U.S.$37.00 and the 1980 price well over U.S.$54.00.

If we look at the price of a barrel of oil over the last century, in 2001 dollars, we find that the average price has been about U.S.$19.00 and the median price about U.S.$15.00. The average price is about where the price of oil was in late 2001. It would seem that the oil prices of the 1970s, the 1980s and even 2000 were abnormal and that late 2001's price was about right.

Estimates from various sources in late 2001 for average oil prices in 2002 were in the range of U.S.$20.00 to U.S.$26.00, and for about U.S.$21.00 out to 2005. It is on these prices that oil firms would forecast their revenues and cash flows for the immediate future. Current oil prices can be found at: www.bloomberg.com/energy/index.html .

Q1 What is the current price of West Texas Intermediate (WTI) oil?

Price Forecasts:
www.madisonenergy.com
www.glja.com

assume the price of materials, labour, and overhead going into the products is now $18.00 for wheels and $22.00 for casters, as indicated in Table 4–4.

TABLE 4–4
Unit costs

	Wheels	Casters
Materials	$10	$12
Labour	5	6
Overhead	3	4
Total	$18	$22

The *total* cost to produce the required items for the next six months is shown in Table 4–5.

TABLE 4–5
Total production costs

	Wheels	Casters	
Units to be produced (Table 4–3)	1,015	2,020	
Cost per unit (Table 4–4)	$18	$22	
Total cost	$18,270	$44,440	$62,710

We must also determine whether the firm has the production facilities to meet the projected demand. Sales and production should be equated only over the long term, as seasonal and cyclical patterns will cause demand to fluctuate. Inventory positions and price adjustments can be used to handle the short-term differences between demand and production. However, without the required long-run production capabilities, the firm must reconsider its sales projections or make capital investments. Either of these possibilities affects financial forecasts. Capital investments in particular require large fund-raising efforts with concurrent costs.

Cost of Goods Sold The main consideration in constructing a pro forma income statement is the costs specifically associated with units sold during the time period. Note that in the case of wheels, we anticipate sales of 1,000 units, as indicated in Table 4–1, but are producing 1,015, as indicated in Table 4–3, to increase our inventory level by 15 units. For profit measurement purposes we do *not* charge these extra 15 units against current sales.[1] Furthermore, in determining the cost of the 1,000 units sold during the current time period, we do *not* assume all of the items sold represent inventory manufactured in this period. We assume Goldman Corporation uses FIFO (first-in, first-out) accounting, and it first allocates the cost of current sales to beginning inventory and then to goods manufactured during the period.

In Table 4–6 we look at the revenue, associated cost of goods sold, and gross profit for both products. For example, 1,000 units of wheels are to be sold at a total revenue of $30,000. Of the 1,000 units, 85 units are from beginning inventory at a $16.00 cost (see Table 4–2), and the balance of 915 units are from current production at an $18.00 cost. The total cost of goods sold for wheels is $17,830, yielding a gross profit of $12,170. The pattern is the same for casters, with sales of $70,000, cost of goods sold of $43,640, and gross profit of $26,360. The combined sales for the two products are $100,000, with cost of goods sold of $61,470 and gross profit of $38,530.

TABLE 4–6

Allocation of manufacturing cost and determination of gross profits

		Wheels		Casters	Combined
Quantity sold (Table 4–1)		1,000		2,000	3,000
Sales price		$ 30		$ 35	
Sales revenue		$30,000		$70,000	$100,000
Cost of goods sold:					
Old inventory (Table 4–2)					
Quantity (units)	85		180		
Cost per unit	$ 16		$ 20		
Total		$ 1,360		$ 3,600	
New inventory (the remainder):					
Quantity (units)	915		1,820		
Cost per unit (Table 4–4)	$ 18		$ 22		
Total		16,470		40,040	
Total cost of goods sold		17,830		43,640	$ 61,470
Gross profit		$12,170		$26,360	$ 38,530

At this point we also compute the value of ending inventory for later use in constructing financial statements. As indicated in Table 4–7, the value of ending inventory is $6,200.

[1]Later on in the analysis we show the effect these extra units have on the cash budget and the balance sheet.

+ Beginning inventory (Table 4–2)	$ 4,960
+ Total production costs (Table 4–5)	62,710
Total inventory available for sales	67,670
− Cost of goods sold (Table 4–6)	61,470
Ending inventory	$ 6,200

Other Expense Items

Having computed total revenue, cost of goods sold, and gross profits, we must now subtract other expense items to arrive at a net profit figure. We deduct selling, marketing, general, and administrative expenses; research and development; as well as interest expenses from gross profit to arrive at earnings before taxes. We then subtract taxes to determine aftertax income, and finally we deduct dividends to ascertain the contribution to retained earnings. Goldman Corporation's selling, general, and administrative expenses are $12,000, interest expense is $1,500, and dividends are $1,500.

Actual Pro Forma Income Statement

Combining the gross profit in Table 4–6 with our assumptions on other expense items, we arrive at the pro forma income statement presented in Table 4–8. We anticipate earnings aftertaxes of $20,024, dividends of $1,500, and an increase in retained earnings of $18,524.

TABLE 4–8

Pro Forma Income Statement
June 30, 2003

Sales revenue	$100,000
Cost of goods sold	61,470
Gross profit	38,530
Selling, general, and administrative expense	12,000
Operating profit (EBIT)	26,530
Interest expense	1,500
Earnings before taxes (EBT)	25,030
Taxes (20%)	5,006
Earnings aftertaxes (EAT)	20,024
Common stock dividends	1,500
Increase in retained earnings	$ 18,524

Cash Budget

The cash budget is perhaps the most important forecast. It is the ability to meet cash flow demands on a timely basis that allows a firm to survive in the long term. The cash flow demands identified by a good cash budget will be met by efficient management of working capital, including having short-term financing available at the required time. As previously indicated, the generation of sales and profits does not necessarily ensure adequate cash on hand to meet financial obligations as they come due. A profitable sale may generate accounts receivable in the short run but no immediate cash to

[illegible]anCanadian Energy Expects Strong Cash Flow

[illegible]INANCE IN ACTION

Q1 What are current oil and gas prices?

Q2 Have PanCanadian's financial results been affected?

PanCanadian Energy Corporation is one of Canada's largest producers and marketers of crude oil and natural gas. Although the bulk of its activity is in Canada, PanCanadian has operations in the Gulf of Mexico, the North Sea, Australia, South Africa, Libya, and Venezuela. PanCanadian's drilling success rate is over 80 percent, which suggests capital expenditures on exploration should bring good returns.

Back in 1998 the average price of crude oil dropped to U.S.$15.11. In January 1999 the crude oil price tenuously hovered above U.S.$12.00, with few projections for upward movement. The drop in oil prices significantly impacted PanCanadian's operations. PanCanadian reduced its labour force by over 10 percent, lowered operating costs by 18 percent and reduced projected capital expenditures for 1999 to $650 million, almost half the expenditure of 1997. Most of these expenditures were slated for natural gas exploration and development.

However prices for crude oil and natural gas began to pick up, cash flow improved and capital expenditures once again increased significantly. The impact of oil and gas prices can be seen in PanCanadian's results between 1997 and 2000. The weak prices of 1998 resulted in the drop in capital expenditures of 1999 followed by increasing expenditures as prices improved.

	2000	1999	1998	1997
Revenue	$7,476	$4,020	$2,986	$3,400
Cash flow	2,473	1,110	802	961
Net income	1,039	350	150	330
Capital expenditures	1,415	825	884	1,136
ROE	29.4%	12.2%	5.6%	13.2%
Average oil price (/bbl)	$32.49	$21.51	$15.11	$20.26
Average gas price (/mcf)	$4.74	$2.55	$2.06	$2.07

PanCanadian prepares a sensitivity analysis in its annual report based on how major variables will impact on net income. Notice the significant change in sensitivity to natural gas price changes as compared to crude oil. PanCanadian's stated strategy from 1997 was to refocus its activities towards natural gas.

		Net Income	
		2000	1998
Crude oil	US$1/barrel (WTI)	$16	$30
Natural gas	Cdn.$0.10/1,000 cu. ft.	32	18
Exchange rate	US$0.01 per Cdn.$	13	6

These sensitivity impacts show the potential for weakened results at PanCanadian as energy prices dropped in late 2001. PanCanadian was able to offset the declining prices by increased production and from its hedging activities, by presetting the prices on the future oil and gas production. In 2002 PanCanadian merged with Alberta Energy to form EnCana.

www.pancanadianenergy.com

Symbol: PCE

www.bloomberg.com/energy/index.html

meet maturing obligations. For this reason we must translate the pro forma income statement into cash flows, producing a **cash budget**. In this process, we divide the longer-term pro forma income statement into smaller and more precise time frames to appreciate the seasonal and monthly patterns of cash inflows and outflows. Some months may represent particularly high or low sales volume or may require the payment of dividends or taxes, or capital expenditures.

The timing of cash flows is particularly crucial. One must consider the nature of the firm's business, terms of trade, and general economic conditions to appropriately reflect the timing of cash flows in the cash budget. The cash flow cycle, discussed further in Chapter 6, outlines the process from inventory to sale to accounts receivable to cash.

Cash Receipts

In the case of the Goldman Corporation, we break down the pro forma income statement for the first half of 2003 into a series of monthly cash budgets. In Table 4–1 we showed anticipated sales of $100,000 over this time period; we shall now assume these sales can be divided into monthly projections, as indicated in Table 4–9.

TABLE 4–9
Monthly sales pattern

January	February	March	April	May	June
$15,000	$10,000	$15,000	$25,000	$15,000	$20,000

A careful analysis of past sales and collection records indicates that 20 percent of sales are collected in the month of sales and 80 percent are collected in the following month. The cash receipt pattern related to monthly sales is shown in Table 4–10. It is assumed that sales for December 2002 were $12,000. The cash receipts could be adjusted to reflect any uncollectible accounts based on previous experience and future expectations.

TABLE 4–10
Monthly cash receipts

	December	January	February	March	April	May	June
Sales	$12,000	$15,000	$10,000	$15,000	$25,000	$15,000	$20,000
Collections:							
(20% of current sales)		3,000	2,000	3,000	5,000	3,000	4,000
Collections:							
(80% of previous month's sales)		9,600	12,000	8,000	12,000	20,000	12,000
Total cash receipts		$12,600	$14,000	$11,000	$17,000	$23,000	$16,000

The cash inflows vary between $11,000 and $23,000, with the high point in receipts coming in May. We now examine the monthly outflows.

Cash Payments

The primary considerations for cash payments are monthly costs associated with inventory manufactured during the period (material, labour, and overhead) and disbursements for general and administrative expenses, interest payments, taxes, and dividends. We must also consider cash payments for any new plant and equipment, an item that does not show up on our pro forma income statement.

Costs associated with units manufactured during the period may be taken from the data provided in Table 4–5, Total Production Costs. In Table 4–11 we simply recast these data in terms of material, labour, and overhead.

TABLE 4–11
Component costs of manufactured goods

	Wheels			Casters			
	Units Produced	Cost per Unit	Total Cost	Units Produced	Cost per Unit	Total Cost	Combined Cost
Materials	1,015	$10	$10,150	2,020	$12	$24,240	$34,390
Labour	1,015	5	5,075	2,020	6	12,120	17,195
Overhead	1,015	3	3,045	2,020	4	8,080	11,125
							$62,710

We see that the total costs for components in the two products are material, $34,390; labour, $17,195; and overhead, $11,125. We assume that all these costs are incurred on an equal monthly basis over the six-month period. Even though the sales volume varies from month to month, we assume we are employing level monthly production to ensure maximum efficiency in the use of various productive resources. Average monthly costs for materials, labour, and overhead are as shown in Table 4–12.

TABLE 4–12
Average monthly manufacturing costs

	Total Costs	Time Frame	Average Monthly Cost
Materials	$34,390	6 months	$5,732
Labour	17,195	6 months	2,866
Overhead	11,125	6 months	1,854

We pay for materials one month after the purchase has been made. Labour and overhead represent direct monthly cash outlays. Other major expenses occur at less frequent but fairly predictable intervals. These include interest (coupon payments), taxes, dividends, and new equipment purchases. We summarize all of our cash payments in Table 4–13. Past records indicate that $4,500 in materials was purchased in December.

Actual Budget

We are now in a position to bring together our monthly cash receipts and payments into a cash flow statement, illustrated in Table 4–14. The difference between monthly receipts and payments is net cash flow for the month.

The primary purpose of the cash budget is to allow the firm to anticipate the need for outside funding at the end of each month. In the present case we assume the Goldman Corporation wishes to have a minimum cash balance of $5,000 at all times. If it goes below this amount, the firm borrows funds from the bank. If it goes above $5,000 and the firm has a loan outstanding, it uses the excess funds to reduce the loan. This

TABLE 4–13

Summary of all monthly cash payments

	Dec.	Jan.	Feb.	March	April	May	June
From Table 4–12:							
Monthly material purchase	$4,500	$5,732	$5,732	$5,732	$5,732	$5,732	$5,732
Payment for material (prior month's purchase)		$4,500	$5,732	$5,732	$5,732	$5,732	$5,730*
Monthly labour cost		2,866	2,866	2,866	2,866	2,866	2,866
Monthly overhead		1,854	1,854	1,854	1,854	1,854	1,854
From Table 4–8:							
Selling, general, and administrative expense ($12,000 over 6 months)		2,000	2,000	2,000	2,000	2,000	2,000
Interest expense							1,500
Taxes (two equal payments) ...				2,503			2,503
Cash dividend							1,500
Also:							
New equipment purchases			8,000				10,000
Total payments		$11,220	$20,452	$14,955	$12,452	$12,452	$27,953

*Adjusted for rounding.

TABLE 4–14

Monthly cash flow

	Jan.	Feb.	March	April	May	June
Total receipts (Table 4–10)	$12,600	$14,000	$11,000	$17,000	$23,000	$16,000
Total payments (Table 4–13)	11,220	20,452	14,955	12,452	12,452	27,953
Net cash flow	$ 1,380	($ 6,452)	($ 3,955)	$ 4,548	$10,548	($11,953)

pattern of financing is demonstrated in Table 4–15—a fully developed cash budget with borrowing and repayment provisions.

The first line in Table 4–15, on the next page, shows net cash flow, which is added to the beginning cash balance to arrive at the cumulative cash balance. The fourth entry is the additional monthly loan or loan repayment, if any, required to maintain a minimum cash balance of $5,000. To keep track of our loan balance, the fifth entry represents cumulative loans outstanding for all months. Finally, we show the cash balance at the end of the month, which becomes the beginning cash balance for the next month.

At the end of January the firm has $6,380 in cash, but by the end of February, the cumulative cash position of the firm is negative, necessitating a loan of $5,072 to maintain a $5,000 cash balance. The firm has a loan on the books until May, at which time there is an ending cash balance of $11,069. During the months of April and May the cumulative cash balance is greater than the required minimum cash balance of $5,000, so loan repayments of $4,548 and $4,479 are made to retire the loans completely in May. In June the firm is once again required to borrow $5,884 to maintain a $5,000 cash balance.

TABLE 4–15
Cash budget with borrowing and repayment provisions

	Jan.	Feb.	March	April	May	June
1. Net cash flow	$1,380	($6,452)	($3,955)	$4,548	$10,548	($11,953)
2. Beginning cash balance	5,000*	6,380	5,000	5,000	5,000	11,069
3. Cumulative cash balance	6,380	(72)	1,045	9,548	15,548	(884)
4. Monthly loan or (repayment)	—	5,072	3,955	(4,548)	(4,479)	5,884
5. Cumulative loan balance	—	5,072	9,027	4,479	—	5,884
6. Ending cash balance	6,380	5,000	5,000	5,000	11,069	5,000

*We assume the Goldman Corporation has a beginning cash balance of $5,000 on January 1, 2003, and it desires a minimum monthly ending cash balance of $5,000.

Adjustments could be made at this time. The cash budget indicates that operating loans will be required at certain times, which will necessitate the payment of monthly interest. Operating loans or self-liquidating loans are required as temporary current assets are built up in a firm due to seasonal fluctuations in demand. This buildup requires the use of short-term financing and is examined later in Chapters 6 and 8. We have included only interest on long-term debt on the summary of cash payments. Offsetting the payment of interest on short-term loans to a certain extent will be the receipt of interest from marketable securities received during periods with excess cash balances. These adjustments have not been included in our example.

Before proceeding to the pro forma balance sheet, we may want to return to the income statement and make some adjustments based on the results from the cash budget. For example, severe cash shortages may require additional borrowing, which in turn would increase the interest expense.

Pro Forma Balance Sheet

Now that we have developed a pro forma income statement and a cash budget, it is relatively simple to integrate all of these items into a **pro forma balance sheet**. Because the balance sheet represents cumulative changes in the corporation over time, we first examine the *prior* period's balance sheet and then translate these items through time to represent June 30, 2003. The last balance sheet, dated December 31, 2002, is shown in Table 4–16.

In constructing our pro forma balance sheet for June 30, 2003, some of the accounts from the old balance sheet remain unchanged, while others will take on new values, as indicated by the pro forma income statement and cash budget. The process is depicted in Figure 4–2 on page 114.

We present the new pro forma balance sheet as of June 30, 2003, in Table 4–17.

Explanation of Pro Forma Balance Sheet

Each item in Table 4–17 (on page 114) can be explained on the basis of a prior calculation or assumption.

1. Cash ($5,000)—minimum cash balance as shown in Table 4–15.
2. Marketable securities ($3,200)—remains unchanged from prior period's value in Table 4–16. Note that firms will likely liquidate marketable securities

TABLE 4–16
Balance Sheet

Balance Sheet December 31, 2002	
Assets	
Current assets:	
Cash	$ 5,000
Marketable securities	3,200
Accounts receivable	9,600
Inventory	4,960
Total current assets	22,760
Plant and equipment	27,740
Total assets	$50,500
Liabilities and Shareholders' Equity	
Accounts payable	$ 4,500
Long-term debt	15,000
Common stock	10,500
Retained earnings	20,500
Total liabilities and shareholders' equity	$50,500

positions before increasing short-term borrowings. In that case, Table 4–15 would require revision. To simplify matters, that has not been done in this example. Furthermore, due to cash flow timing considerations, firms often have positions in marketable securities and short-term loans on reporting dates.

3. Accounts receivable ($16,000)—based on June sales of $20,000 in Table 4–10 (see page 109). Twenty percent is collected that month, while 80 percent becomes accounts receivable at the end of the month.

$20,000	sales
× 80%	receivables
$16,000	

4. Inventory ($6,200)—ending inventory as shown in Table 4–7 (see page 107).
5. Plant and equipment ($45,740).

Initial value (Table 4–16)	$27,740
Purchases* (Table 4–13)	18,000
Plant and equipment	$45,740

*For simplicity, amortization is not explicitly considered.

6. Accounts payable ($5,732)—based on June purchases in Table 4–13. They are not to be paid until July and thus are accounts payable.
7. Notes payable ($5,884)—the amount we must borrow to maintain our cash balance of $5,000, as shown in Table 4–15.
8. Long-term debt ($15,000)—remains unchanged from the prior period's value in Table 4–15. The firm may increase long-term debt to hedge the additional purchase of plant and equipment. The hedging concept is explored in Chapter 6.

FIGURE 4–2
Development of a pro forma balance sheet

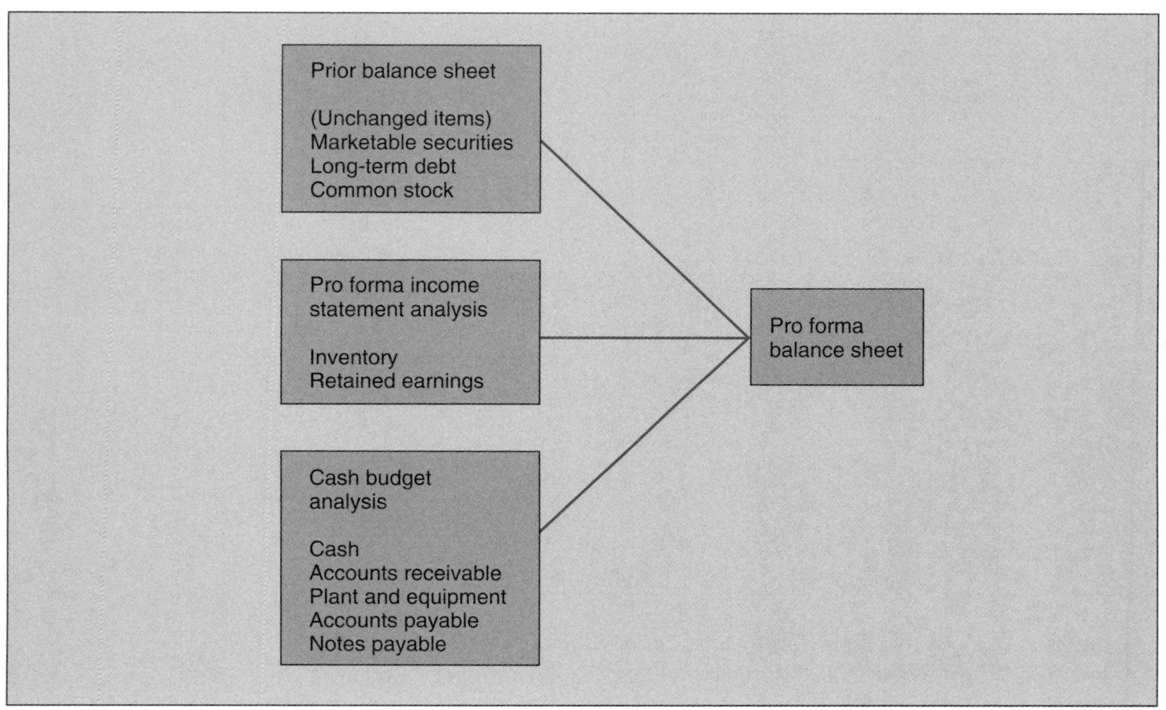

TABLE 4–17
Pro forma balance sheet

Pro Forma Balance Sheet
June 30, 2003

Assets

Current assets:	
1. Cash	$ 5,000
2. Marketable securities	3,200
3. Accounts receivable	16,000
4. Inventory	6,200
Total current assets	30,400
5. Plant and equipment	45,740
Total assets	$76,140

Liabilities and Shareholders' Equity

6. Accounts payable	$ 5,732
7. Notes payable	5,884
8. Long-term debt	15,000
9. Common stock	10,500
10. Retained earnings	39,024
Total liabilities and shareholders' equity	$76,140

9. Common stock ($10,500)—remains unchanged from prior period's value in Table 4–16.
10. Retained earnings ($39,024).

Initial value (Table 4–16)	$20,500
Transfer of pro forma income to retained earnings (Table 4–8)	18,524
Retained earnings	$39,024

Analysis of Pro Forma Statement

In comparing the pro forma balance sheet (Table 4–17) to the prior balance sheet (see Table 4–16), we note that assets are up by $25,640.

Total assets (June 30, 2003)	$76,140
Total assets (Dec. 31, 2002)	50,500
Increase	$25,640

The growth must be financed by accounts payable, notes payable, and profit (as reflected by the increase in retained earnings). Though the company enjoys a high degree of profitability, it must still look to bank financing. At the end of June this amounts to $5,884 to support the increase in assets. This represents the difference between the $25,640 buildup in assets and the $1,232 increase in accounts payable, as well as the $18,524 buildup in retained earnings.

However the cash budget, Table 4–15, reveals that the borrowing need peaks at $9,027 in March. If Goldman has not anticipated this peak in borrowing need and had not made arrangements with the bank to advance funds to meet this peak requirement, there may be liquidity problems.

The small business by failing to properly anticipate the fluctuations in borrowing requirements is often forced to return to the bank to renegotiate further loan advances. Bankers are obviously not too pleased by surprises resulting from poor forecasts and may view this as evidence of ineffective planning. This is not to say that forecasts turn out exactly as planned. However, by knowing the forecasts and the underlying assumptions the firm is able to adapt its plan as conditions change.

Percent-of-Sales Method

An alternative to tracing cash and accounting flows to determine financial needs is to assume accounts on the balance sheet maintain a given percentage relationship to sales. This method makes some strong assumptions and is probably more applicable to longer-term and generalized forecasting. For immediate cash needs, a budget is more exacting. However, by indicating a change in the sales level, we can ascertain our related financing needs. This is known as the **percent-of-sales method.** For example, for the Howard Corporation, introduced in Table 4–18 (on the next page), we show the following balance sheet accounts in dollars and their percent of sales, based on a sales volume of $200,000. The percent-of-sales method relies on the assumption that certain assets and liabilities spontaneously increase with sales. This spontaneity without any conscious action by management is discussed in Chapter 7.

TABLE 4–18
Howard Corporation

HOWARD CORPORATION
Balance Sheet and Percent-of-Sales Table

Assets		**Liabilities and Shareholders' Equity**	
Cash	$ 5,000	Accounts payable	$ 40,000
Accounts receivable	40,000	Accrued expenses	10,000
Inventory	25,000	Notes payable	15,000
Total current assets	$ 70,000	Common stock	10,000
Equipment	50,000	Retained earnings	45,000
Total assets	$120,000	Total liabilities and shareholders' equity	$120,000

$200,000 Sales
Percent of Sales

Cash	2.5%	Accounts payable	20.0%
Accounts receivable	20.0	Accrued expenses	5.0
Inventory	12.5		25.0%
Total current assets	35.0		
Equipment	25.0		
	60.0%		

We observe that cash of $5,000 represents 2.5 percent of sales of $200,000; receivables of $40,000 are 20 percent of sales; and so on. No percentages are computed for notes payable, common stock, and retained earnings because they are not assumed to maintain a direct relationship with sales volume. Note that any dollar increase in sales necessitates a 60 percent increase in assets, of which 25 percent is spontaneously or automatically financed through accounts payable and accrued expenses, leaving 35 percent to be financed by profit or additional outside sources of financing.[2] We assume the Howard Corporation has an after-tax return of 6 percent on the sales dollar and 50 percent of profits are paid out as dividends.[3]

If sales increase from $200,000 to $300,000, the $100,000 increase in sales necessitates $35,000 (35 percent) in additional financing. Since we earn 6 percent on total sales of $300,000, we show a profit of $18,000. With a 50 percent dividend payout, $9,000 remains for internal financing. This means that $26,000 out of the $35,000 must be financed from outside sources. Our formula to determine the need for new funds (required new funds, or RNF) is:

Increase in assets − spontaneous increase in liabilities −
increase in retained earnings = Required New Funds

$$RNF = \frac{A}{S_1}(\Delta S) - \frac{L}{S_1}(\Delta S) - PS_2(1 - D) \qquad (4\text{–}1)$$

[2]We are assuming equipment increases in proportion to sales. In certain cases there may be excess capacity, and equipment (or plant and equipment) will not increase, which will decrease the total financing needs.

[3]Some may wish to add back amortization under the percent-of-sales method. Most, however, choose the assumption that funds generated through amortization (in the sources and uses of funds sense) must be used to replace the capital assets to which amortization is applied.

where

$\frac{A}{S_1}$ = Percentage relationship of assets varying with sales to sales [60%]

ΔS = Change in sales [$100,000]

$\frac{L}{S_1}$ = Percentage relationship of liabilities varying with sales to sales [25%]

P = Profit margin [6%]

S_1 = Existing sales level

S_2 = New sales level [$300,000]

D = Dividend payout ratio

Plugging in the values, we show:

RNF = 60% ($100,000) − 25% ($100,000) − 6% ($300,000) (1 − 0.5)
= $60,000 − $25,000 − $18,000 (0.5)
= $35,000 − $9,000
= $26,000 required sources of new funds

Presumably, the $26,000 can be financed at the bank or through some other appropriate source.

We can see how this formula works by comparing pro forma balance sheets before and after the sales expansion, as in Table 4–19. The spontaneous increase in current assets and capital assets (equipment) from the increased sales is $60,000 and is the first term in the formula. This requirement for new funding is partially offset by the increase in current liabilities of $25,000 and by the increase in retained earnings of $9,000. The increase in retained earnings is based on the profit generated from total sales less the dividend payout. These increases are tied to the sales increase by a fixed percentage, but could be changed if we have superior knowledge.

We notice in Table 4–19, on the next page, that in order to achieve balance the amount of required new funds, $26,000, is entered on the new balance sheet as notes payable. These required new funds are needed to support the sales expansion and are the same value given by the formula. If the firm was not operating at capacity and did not require the $25,000 in additional equipment to support the new sales the required new funds would only be $1,000. Therefore, our assumptions about what assets will increase proportionately with a sales increase are quite important.

If the required new funds are financed through operating loans (notes payable), as is suggested in this example, there will be a significant change in certain relevant ratios. The debt to total assets increases from 0.54 to 0.64 and the current ratio decreases from 1.08 to 0.91. This would likely be interpreted as deterioration in these ratios. It is important to determine if the firm can obtain this funding from its financial institution(s).

If the firm cannot obtain additional short-term financing or perhaps long-term financing, sales and growth will have to be scaled back or alternatively additional equity contributions will have to be made by shareholders with a cash injection or by decreasing the dividend payout. Alternatively the firm might improve its asset utilization ratios which would generate additional cash flow. These utilization ratios were identified in Chapter 3.

TABLE 4–19

HOWARD CORPORATION				
Sales		$200,000		
Sales increase	50.00%	$100,000		
Assets	**Before**	**Increase**	**RNF**	**After**
Cash	$ 5,000	$ 2,500	$ 7,500	$ 7,500
Accounts receivable	40,000	20,000	60,000	60,000
Inventory	25,000	12,500	37,500	37,500
Total current assets	$ 70,000	35,000	$105,000	$105,000
Equipment	50,000	25,000	75,000	75,000
Total assets	$120,000	$ **60,000**	$180,000	$180,000
Liabilities and Shareholders' Equity				
Accounts payable	$ 40,000	$ 20,000	$ 60,000	$ 60,000
Accrued expenses	10,000	5,000	15,000	15,000
Notes payable	15,000	0	15,000	**41,000**
Total current liabilities	$ 65,000	**25,000**	$ 90,000	$116,000
Common stock	10,000		10,000	10,000
Retained earnings	45,000	**9,000**	54,000	54,000
Total liabilities and shareholders' equity	$120,000	$ 34,000	$154,000	$180,000
Required new funds			**26,000**	
Selected Ratios				
Debt/Total assets	65/120	= 0.54	116/180	= 0.64
Debt/Equity	65/(10+45)	= 1.18	116/(10+54)	= 1.81
Current ratio	70/65	= 1.08	105/116	= 0.91

It may be appropriate in this example to obtain long term financing to match the increase in capital assets. This matching of the maturity of assets with liabilities is called a hedging approach and is discussed in Chapter 6. For Howard Corporation long-term funding has already been supplied by equity of $9,000. Further long-term financing of $16,000 would match the long-term investment in capital assets totalling $25,000. With this mix of long-term debt and a smaller portion of short-term debt, the current ratio would exhibit an improvement.

Observe that using the percent-of-sales method is much easier than tracing through the various cash flows to arrive at the pro forma statements. Nevertheless, the output is much less meaningful, and we do not get a month-to-month breakdown of the data. The percent-of-sales method is a broadbrush approach, while the development of pro forma statements is more exacting. Of course, whatever method we use, the results are only as meaningful or reliable as the assumptions about sales and production that went into the numbers.

Sustainable Growth Rate

From the preceding discussion, the question arises: What level of growth can the corporation encounter and still be able to raise the required new funds through additional bank borrowings? The general answer is that highly profitable companies can sustain a high rate of growth, but marginally profitable companies can sustain only low growth.

We use the following formula to determine the maximum rate of growth obtainable without increasing the debt ratio. The formula, known as the **sustainable growth rate** (SGR), assumes that the performance ratios and balance sheet-to-sales ratios remain the same and that no new shares are issued.

$$SGR = \frac{\Delta S}{S_1} = \frac{P(1-D)\left(1+\frac{D_T}{E}\right)}{\frac{A}{S_1} - P(1-D)\left(1+\frac{D_T}{E}\right)}^{4} \qquad (4\text{–}2)$$

where

$$\frac{D_T}{E} = \text{Debt to equity ratio}$$

For the Howard Corporation, the calculation is

$$SGR = \frac{.06\,(1-.5)\,(1+1.1818)}{.60 - .06\,(1-.5)\,(1+1.1818)}$$

$$= .1224 \text{ or } 12.24\%$$

This suggests that sales can increase by 12.24 percent or $24,480 while maintaining the debt to equity ratio at 1.18. Using the RNF formula, assets will increase by $14,688, current liabilities by $6,120, and retained earnings by $6,734. This will require new funds of $1,834, as shown in Table 4–20 on the next page. With the required new funds financed by an operating loan (notes payable), the key ratios remain the same.

---

[4] $\frac{A}{S_1}(\Delta S) = P(S_1+\Delta S)(1-D) + P(S_1+\Delta S)(1-D)\left(\frac{D_T}{E}\right)$

$\frac{A}{S_1}(\Delta S) = P(S_1+\Delta S)(1-D)\left(1+\frac{D_T}{E}\right)$

$\frac{A}{S_1}(\Delta S) = S_1\left[P(1-D)\left(1+\frac{D_T}{E}\right)\right] + \Delta S\left[P(1-D)\left(1+\frac{D_T}{E}\right)\right]$

$\frac{A}{S_1}(\Delta S) - \Delta S\left[P(1-D)\left(1+\frac{D_T}{E}\right)\right] = S_1\left[P(1-D)\left(1+\frac{D_T}{E}\right)\right]$

$\Delta S\left[\frac{A}{S_1} - P(1-D)\left(1+\frac{D_T}{E}\right)\right] = S_1\left[P(1-D)\left(1+\frac{D_T}{E}\right)\right]$

$SGR = \frac{\Delta S}{S_1} = \frac{P(1-D)\left(1+\frac{D_T}{E}\right)}{\frac{A}{S_1} - P(1-D)\left(1+\frac{D_T}{E}\right)}$

[4] An approximate formula is $SGR = ROE\,(1-D)$.

TABLE 4–20

HOWARD CORPORATION				
Sales		$200,000		
Sales increase	12.24%	$ 24,480		
Assets	**Before**	**Increase**	**RNF**	**After**
Cash	$ 5,000	$ 612	$ 5,612	$ 5,612
Accounts receivable	40,000	4,896	44,896	44,896
Inventory	25,000	3,060	28,060	28,060
Total current assets	$ 70,000	8,568	$ 78,568	$ 78,568
Equipment	50,000	6,120	56,120	56,120
Total assets	$120,000	**$14,688**	$134,688	$134,688
Liabilities and Shareholders' Equity				
Accounts payable	$ 40,000	$ 4,896	$ 44,896	$ 44,896
Accrued expenses	10,000	1,224	11,224	11,224
Notes payable	15,000	0	15,000	**16,834**
Total current liabilities	$ 65,000	**6,120**	$ 71,120	$ 72,954
Common stock	10,000		10,000	10,000
Retained earnings	45,000	**6,734**	51,734	51,734
Total liabilities and shareholders' equity	$120,000	$12,854	$132,854	$134,688
Required new funds			**1,834**	
Selected Ratios				
Debt/Total assets	65/120	= 0.54	73/135	= 0.54
Debt/Equity	65/(10+45)	= 1.18	73/(10+52)	= 1.18
Current ratio	70/65	= 1.08	79/73	= 1.08

Summary

1. Financial forecasting allows the financial manager to anticipate events before they occur, particularly the need for raising funds externally. Growth itself may call for additional sources of financing because profit is often inadequate to cover the net buildup in receivables, inventory, and other asset accounts.
2. We develop pro forma financial statements from an overall corporate systems viewpoint. Today computerized spreadsheets greatly facilitate this process. The time perspective is usually six months to a year in the future. In developing a pro forma income statement, we begin by making sales projections; then, we construct a production plan. Finally, we consider all other expenses. From the pro forma income statement we proceed to a cash budget in which the monthly or quarterly cash inflows and outflows related to sales, expenditures, and capital outlays are portrayed. All of this information can be assimilated into a pro forma balance sheet in which asset, liability, and shareholders' equity accounts are shown. Any shortage of funds is assumed to be financed through notes payable (bank loans).
3. We may take a shortcut to financial forecasting through the use of the percent-of-sales method. Under this approach, selected balance sheet accounts are assumed to maintain a constant percentage relationship to sales, and thus we can ascertain balance sheet values for any given sales amount. Once again, a shortage of funds is assumed to be financed through notes payable.
4. Required new funding can be estimated by using the RNF formula (4–1).

Review of Formulas

$$RNF = \frac{A}{S_1}(\Delta S) - \frac{L}{S_1}(\Delta S) - PS_2(1 - D) \quad (4\text{–}1)$$

$$SGR = \frac{P(1 - D)\left(1 + \frac{D_T}{E}\right)}{\frac{A}{S_1} - P(1 - D)\left(1 + \frac{D_T}{E}\right)} \quad (4\text{–}2)$$

List of Terms

pro forma income statement 103
cash budget 108
pro forma balance sheet 112
percent-of-sales method 115
sustainable growth rate 119

Discussion Questions

1. What are the basic benefits and purposes of developing pro forma statements and a cash budget?
2. Explain how the collections and purchases schedules are related to the borrowing needs of the corporation.
3. With inflation, what are the implications of using LIFO and FIFO inventory methods? How do they affect the cost of goods sold?
4. Explain the relationship between inventory turnover and purchasing needs.
5. Rapid corporate growth in sales and profits can cause financing and other problems. Elaborate on this statement.
6. Discuss the advantage and disadvantage of level production schedules in firms whose sales are cyclical.
7. What conditions would help make a percent-of-sales forecast as accurate as pro forma financial statements and cash budgets?

INTERNET RESOURCES AND QUESTIONS

The major financial institutions have economic departments that regularly report on economic trends and their possible impact on the economy, regions of the country, and industries.
www.bmo.com/economic/index.html
www.rbcds.com/english/literature/gm/edr.html

The New York based U.S. Conference Board regularly reports on consumer confidence in the United States. Consumer spending is the major component of U.S. economic activity.
www.conference-board.org/index.cfm

Decisioneering has a demo of their time series forecasting tool for sales projections called CB Predictor.
www.decisioneering.com

1. Research the current forecasts for GDP growth, inflation and unemployment in Canada, Europe, and your particular region of the country.

Problems

1. Bill Gates and Fence Company had sales of 3,000 units at $200 per unit last year. The marketing manager projects a 20 percent increase in unit volume this year, with a 10 percent price increase. Returned merchandise will represent 5 percent of total sales. What is your net dollar sales projection for this year?
2. Blinky Morris Ltd. is excited because sales for his clothing company are expected to double from $500,000 to $1,000,000 next year. Blinky's net assets (assets − liabilities) will remain at 50 percent of sales. His clothing firm will enjoy a 9 percent return on total sales. He will begin the year with $100,000 in the bank and is already bragging about the two Mercedes he will buy and the European vacation he will take. Compute the likely cash balance for the end of the year. Does his optimistic outlook for his cash position appear to be justified?
3. In the previous problem, with Blinky Morris, if there is no increase in sales and all other facts remain the same, what would be Blinky's ending cash balance? What observation can be reached from these two problems?
4. The Alliance Corporation expects to sell the following number of units of copper cables at the prices indicated, under three different scenarios in the economy. The probability of each outcome is indicated. What is the expected value of the total sales projection?

Outcome	Probability	Units	Price
A	0.30	200	$15
B	0.50	320	30
C	0.20	410	40

5. Sales for Western Boot Stores are expected to be 40,000 units for October. The company likes to maintain 15 percent of unit sales for each month in ending inventory (that is, end of October). Beginning inventory for October is 8,500 units. How many units should Western Boot produce for the coming month?
6. Vitale Hair Spray had sales of 8,000 units in March. A 50 percent increase is expected in April. The company will maintain 5 percent of expected unit sales for April in ending inventory. Beginning inventory for April was equal to 400 units. How many units should the company produce in April?
7. Sam's Leather Goods has beginning inventory of 16,000 units, will sell 60,000 units for the month, and desires to reduce ending inventory to 30 percent of beginning inventory. How many units should Sam's produce?
8. Laser Systems Inc. anticipates sales of 125,000 units for the first six months of the year. Beginning inventory is maintained at 15 percent of anticipated sales. Ending inventory will be equal to 25 percent of the projected sales of 140,000 units for the last six months of the year. How many units should the firm produce during the first six months of the year?
9. On December 31 of last year, Barton Air Filters had in inventory 600 units of its product, which cost $28.00 per unit to produce. During January, the company produced 1,200 units at a cost of $32.00 per unit. Assuming Barton Air Filters sold 1,500 units in January, what was the cost of goods sold (assume FIFO inventory method)?
10. At the end of January, Lemon Auto Parts had an inventory of 825 units, which cost $12.00 per unit to produce. During February the company produced 750 units at a cost of $16.00 per unit. If the firm sold 1,050 units in February, what was its cost of goods sold?
    a. Assume LIFO inventory accounting.
    b. Assume FIFO inventory accounting.

11. Convex Mechanical Supplies produces a product with the following costs as of July 1, 2002:

Material	$6 per unit
Labour	4 per unit
Overhead..............	2 per unit

Beginning inventory at these costs on July 1, was 5,000 units. From July 1 to December 1, Convex produced 15,000 units. These units had a material cost of $10 per unit. The costs for labour and overhead were the same. Convex uses FIFO inventory accounting.

Assuming Convex sold 17,000 units during the last six months of the year at $20 each, what would gross profit be? What is the value of ending inventory?

12. Assume in the previous problem that Convex used LIFO inventory accounting instead of FIFO. What would gross profit be? What is the value of ending inventory?

13. Sprint Shoes, Inc., had a beginning inventory of 9,000 shoes on January 1, 2002. The costs associated with the inventory were:

Material	$13.00 per shoe
Labour	8.00 per shoe
Overhead..........	6.10 per shoe

During 2002, the firm produced 42,500 shoes with the following costs:

Material	$15.50 per shoe
Labour	7.80 per shoe
Overhead..........	8.30 per shoe

Sales for the year were 47,250 units at $39.60 each. Sprint uses LIFO accounting. What was the gross profit? What was the value of ending inventory?

14. Harris Flower Shops has forecast credit sales for the fourth quarter of the year as follows:

September (actual)	$70,000
Fourth quarter	
October	60,000
November	55,000
December	80,000

Experience has shown 30 percent of sales are collected in the month of sale, 60 percent are collected in the following month, and 10 percent are never collected. Prepare a schedule of cash receipts schedule for Harris Flower Shops covering the fourth quarter (October through December).

15. Pirate Video Company has made the following sales projections for the next six months. All sales are credit sales.

July	$24,000	October	$28,000
August	30,000	November	35,000
September	18,000	December	38,000

Sales in May and June were $27,000 and $26,000, respectively.

Experience has shown that of total sales, 10 percent are uncollectible, 30 percent are collected in the month of sale, 40 percent are collected in the following month, and 20 percent are collected two months after sale.

Prepare a monthly cash receipts schedule for the firm for July through December.

Of the sales expected to be made during the six months from July through December, how much will still be uncollected at the end of December? How much of this is expected to be collected?

16. Ultravision Limited anticipates sales of $240,000 from January through April. Materials will represent 50 percent of sales and because of level production, material purchases will be equal for each month during these four months.

    Materials are paid for one month after the month purchased. Materials purchased in December of last year were $20,000 (half of $40,000 in sales). Labour costs for each of the four months are slightly different due to a provision in the labour contract in which bonuses are paid in February and April. The labour figures are:

January	$10,000
February	13,000
March	10,000
April	15,000

    Prepare a schedule of cash payments for January through April.

17. The Elway Corporation has forecast the following sales for the first seven months of the year.

Month	Sales	Month	Sales
January	$12,000	May	$12,000
February	16,000	June	20,000
March	18,000	July	22,000
April	24,000		

    Monthly material purchases are set equal to 20 percent of forecasted sales for the next month. Of the total material costs, 40 percent are paid in the month of purchase and 60 percent are paid in the following month. Labour costs will run $6,000 per month, and fixed overhead is $3,000 per month. Interest payments on the debt will be $4,500 for both March and June. Finally, Elway salespeople will receive a 3 percent commission on total sales for the first six months of the year, to be paid on June 30. Prepare a monthly summary of cash payments for the six months from January through June. (Note: Compute prior December purchases to help get total material payments for January.)

18. Wright Lighting Fixtures forecasts its sales in units for the next four months as follows:

March	4,000
April	10,000
May	8,000
June	6,000

    Wright maintains an ending inventory for each month in the amount of one and one-half times the expected sales in the following month. The ending inventory for February (March's beginning inventory) reflects this policy. Materials cost $7.00 per unit and are paid for in the month after production. Labour cost is $3.00 per unit and is paid for in the month incurred. Fixed overhead is $10,000 per month. Dividends of $14,000 are to be paid in May. Eight thousand units were produced in February. Complete a production schedule and a summary of cash payments for March, April, and May. Remember that production in any one month is equal to sales plus desired ending inventory minus beginning inventory.

19. Dina's Dress Company has forecast its sales in units as follows:

January	1,000	May	1,550
February	800	June	1,800
March	900	July	1,400
April	1,400		

Dina always keeps an ending inventory equal to 120 percent of the next month's expected sales. The ending inventory for December (January's beginning inventory) is 1,200 units, which is consistent with this policy.

Materials cost $14.00 per unit and are paid for in the month after production. Labour cost is $7.00 per unit and is paid in the month the cost is incurred. Overhead costs are $8,000 per month. Interest of $10,000 is scheduled to be paid in March, and employee bonuses of $15,500 will be paid in June.

Prepare a monthly production schedule and a monthly summary of cash payments for January through June. Dina produced 800 units in December.

20. Ed's Bowling Alley has made the following sales projections for the next six months. All sales are credit sales.

March	$18,000	June	$12,000
April	19,000	July	10,000
May	15,000	August	9,000

Sales in January and February were $15,000 and $12,000 respectively.

Experience has shown that of total sales 5 percent are uncollectible, 60 percent are collected in the month of sale, 25 percent are collected in the following month, and 10 percent are collected 2 months after sale.

Prepare a monthly cash receipts schedule for the firm for March through August.

Of the sales expected to be made during the six months from March to August, how much will still be uncollected at the end of August? How much of this is expected to be collected later?

21. Graham Potato Company has expected sales of $6,000 in September, $10,000 in October, $16,000 in November, and $12,000 in December. Of the company's sales, 20 percent are paid for by cash and 80 percent are on credit. Experience shows that 40 percent of accounts receivable are paid in the month after the sale, while the remaining 60 percent are paid two months after. Determine collections for November and December.

Assume that Graham's cash payments for November and December are $13,000 and $6,000, respectively. The beginning cash balance in November is $5,000, which is the desired minimum balance.

Prepare a cash budget with borrowing needed or repayments made for November and December.

22. Paco's Pizza Company has restaurants in five college towns. Paco wants to expand into Normal and French Lick and needs a bank loan to do this. Mr. Sousse, the banker, will finance construction if Paco can present an acceptable three-month financial plan for January through March. Following are actual and forecasted sales figures:

Actual		Forecast		Additional information	
November	$120,000	January	$190,000	April forecast	$230,000
December	140,000	February	210,000		
		March	230,000		

a. Using a percent-of-sales method, determine whether Jordan Aluminum has external financing needs.

b. Prepare a pro forma balance sheet with any financing adjustment made to notes payable.

c. Calculate the current ratio and total debt to assets ratio for each year.

26. Clyde's Well Servicing has the following financial statements. The balance sheet items, profit margin, and dividend payout have maintained the same relationships the past couple of years; these relationships are anticipated to hold in the future. Clyde's has excess capacity, so there is no expected increase in capital assets.

Income Statement

Sales	$2,000,000
Cost of goods sold	1,260,000
Gross profit	740,000
Selling and administrative expense	400,000
Amortization	55,000
Earnings before interest and taxes	285,000
Interest	50,000
Earnings before taxes	235,000
Taxes	61,000
Earnings available to common shareholders	$ 174,000
Dividends	$ 104,400

Balance Sheet

Assets		Liabilities and Shareholders' Equity	
Cash	$30,000	Accounts payable	$105,000
Accounts receivable	260,000	Accruals	20,000
Inventory	210,000	Bank loan	150,000
Current assets	500,000	Current liabilities	275,000
Capital assets	550,000	Long-term debt	200,000
		Common stock	175,000
		Retained earnings	400,000
Total assets	$1,050,000	Total liabilities and equity	$1,050,000

a. Using a percent-of-sales method, determine whether Clyde's can handle a 30 percent sales increase without using external financing. If so, what is the need?

b. If the average collection period of receivables could be held to 43 days, what would the need be for external financing? All other relationships hold.

c. Suppose the following results with the increased sales of $600,000.

Cash increases by	$5,000
Average collection period	43 days
Inventory turnover (COGS)	6 ×
Capital assets increase by	$125,000
Accounts payable increase	in proportion to sales
Accruals	no change
Long-term debt decreases by	$25,000
Gross profit margin	40%
Selling, general, and administrative expense increase by	$50,000

Amortization increases by	$12,500
Interest decreases by	$10,000
Tax rate	35%
Dividends increase to	$120,000

What new funds would be required? The first $75,000 of any new funds would be short-term debt and then long-term debt. Prepare the pro forma balance sheet.

27. Cambridge Prep Shops, a national clothing chain, had sales of $200 million last year. The business has a steady net profit margin of 12 percent and a dividend payout ratio of 40 percent. The balance sheet for the end of last year is shown below:

Balance Sheet
Dec. 31, 2002
($ millions)

Assets		**Liabilities and Shareholders' Equity**	
Cash	$ 10	Accounts payable	$ 15
Accounts receivable	15	Accrued expenses	5
Inventory	50	Other payables	40
Plant and equipment	75	Common stock	30
		Retained earnings	60
Total assets	$150	Total liabilities and equity	$150

Cambridge's marketing staff tells the president that in this coming year, there will be a large increase in the demand for tweed sport coats and various shoes. A sales increase of 15 percent is forecast for the Prep Shop.

All balance sheet items are expected to maintain the same percent-of-sales relationships as last year, except for common stock and retained earnings. No change in the number of common stock shares outstanding is scheduled, and retained earnings will change as dictated by the profits and dividend policy of the firm.

a. Will external financing be required for the Prep Shop during the coming year?

b. What would the need for external financing be if the net profit margin went up to 14 percent and the dividend payout ratio was increased to 70 percent? Explain.

COMPREHENSIVE PROBLEMS

28. The Landis Corporation had 2002 sales of $100 million. The balance sheet items that vary directly with sales and the profit margin are as follows:

	Percent
Cash	5%
Accounts receivable	15
Inventory	25
Net capital assets	40
Accounts payable	15
Other payables	10
Profit margin aftertaxes	6

The dividend payout rate is 50 percent of earnings, and the balance in retained earnings at the beginning of 2003 was $33 million. Common stock and the company's long-term bonds are constant at $10 million and $5 million, respectively. Notes payable are currently $12 million.

a. How much additional external capital will be required for next year if sales increase 15 percent? (Assume that the company is already operating at full capacity.)

b. What will happen to external fund requirements if Landis Corporation reduces the payout ratio, grows at a slower rate, or suffers a decline in its profit margin? Discuss each of these separately.

c. Prepare a pro forma balance sheet for 2003, assuming that any external funds being acquired will be in the form of notes payable. Disregard the information in part *b* in answering this question (that is, use the original information and part *a* in constructing your pro forma balance sheet).

d. Calculate debt to total assets, debt to equity, current ratio, return on assets, and return on equity before and after the sales increase.

e. Calculate Landis's sustainable growth rate.

29. The Adams Corporation makes standard-size 2.5 cm fasteners, which it sells for $155 per thousand. Mr. Adams is the majority owner and manages the inventory and finances of the company. He estimates sales for the following months to be:

January	$263,500 (1,700,000 fasteners)
February	$186,000 (1,200,000 fasteners)
March	$217,000 (1,400,000 fasteners)
April	$310,000 (2,000,000 fasteners)
May	$387,500 (2,500,000 fasteners)

Last year Adams Corporation's sales were $175,000 in November and $232,500 in December (1.5 million fasteners).

Mr. Adams is preparing for a meeting with his banker to arrange the financing for the first quarter. Based on his sales forecast and the following information provided by him, your job as his new financial analyst is to prepare a monthly cash budget, a monthly and quarterly pro forma income statement, a pro forma quarterly balance sheet, and all necessary supporting schedules for the first quarter.

Past history shows that Adams Corporation collects 50 percent of its accounts receivable in the normal 30-day credit period (the month after the sale) and the other 50 percent in 60 days (two months after the sale). It pays for its materials 30 days after receipt. In general, Mr. Adams likes to keep a two-month supply of inventory on hand in anticipation of sales. Inventory at the beginning of December was 2.6 million units. (This was not equal to his desired two-month supply.)

The major cost of production is the purchase of raw materials in the form of steel rods that are cut, threaded, and finished. Last year raw material costs were $52.00 per 1,000 fasteners, but Mr. Adams has just been notified that material costs have risen, effective January 1, to $60.00 per 1,000 fasteners. The Adams Corporation uses FIFO inventory accounting. Labour costs are relatively constant at $20.00 per thousand fasteners, since workers are paid on a piecework basis. Overhead is allocated at $10.00 per thousand units, and selling and administrative expense is 20 percent of sales. Labour expense and overhead are direct cash outflows paid in the month incurred, while interest and taxes are paid quarterly.

The corporation usually maintains a minimum cash balance of $25,000, and it puts its excess cash into marketable securities. The average tax rate is 40 percent, and Mr. Adams usually pays out 50 percent of net income in dividends to shareholders. Marketable securities are sold before funds are borrowed when a cash shortage is faced. Ignore the interest on any short-term borrowings. Interest on the long-term debt is paid in March, as are taxes and dividends.

ADAMS CORPORATION
Balance Sheet
December 31, 2002

Assets

Current assets:		
Cash	$ 30,000	
Accounts receivable	320,000	
Inventory	237,800	
Total current assets		587,800
Capital assets:		
Plant and equipment	1,000,000	
Less: Accumulated amortization	200,000	800,000
Total assets		$1,387,800

Liabilities and Shareholders' Equity

Accounts payable	$ 93,600	
Notes payable	0	
Long-term debt, 8 percent	400,000	
Common stock	504,200	
Retained earnings	390,000	
Total liabilities and shareholders' equity		$1,387,800

30. Toys for You, a manufacturing company, has been growing quickly but has found that its financial situation is continually under pressure. Production has fluctuated to meet demand in an attempt to provide first-class service, resulting in larger inventory positions. Also, the collection of accounts has worsened to approximately 60 days, which is well above the terms of 30 days. To address the financial concerns, Toys for You has proposed level production and an effort by the credit department to bring the average collection period down to 35 days.

Estimated sales for the upcoming months are:

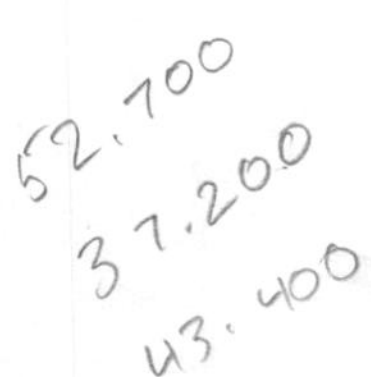

July	$1,957,500
August	2,070,000
September	2,205,000
October	2,362,500
November	2,475,000
December	2,565,000

Sales for May were $1,732,500 and will be approximately $1,845,000 for the current month of June.

It is projected that the current collection period of 60 days will be reduced to 50 days for July and August, 42 days for September and October, and will meet the target of 35 days in November and December.

Purchases are forecast to be $585,000 a month beginning in July. In May they were $675,000, and in June they are expected to be $607,500. The purchases are paid in 40 days. Materials used per month beginning in July will be $744,000. Labour expense will be paid as incurred and will be $195,000 a month. Other expenses of manufacturing will also be paid as incurred and are expected to be $375,000 a month. Cost of goods sold has regularly been 70 percent of sales.

Amortization is $38,000 per month. Selling and administrative expenses are expected to be 13 percent of sales. The tax rate is 42 percent.

There will be payments on notes of $675,000 in each of August and November. Interest of $270,000 and income taxes of $338,000 are both due in October. Dividends of $22,500 are payable in July and October.

TOYS FOR YOU
Balance Sheet (estimated)
June 30, 2003
($ thousands)

Assets		
Current assets:		
Cash		$ 666
Accounts receivable		3,578
Inventory		8,231
Total current assets		12,475
Capital assets:		
Plant and equipment	11,273	
Less: Accumulated amortization	4,784	6,489
Total assets		$18,964
Liabilities and Shareholders' Equity		
Current liabilities		
Accounts payable		$ 945
Notes payable		3,700
Accrued liabilities		2,596
Total current liabilities		7,241
Long-term debt		4,725
Common stock		4,500
Retained earnings		2,498
Total liabilities and shareholders' equity		$18,964

Using the information above, prepare pro forma statements for Toys for You for the three months ending September and December 2003. Also construct a cash budget for the six-month period and identify any need for short-term financing. There are no changes in accounts not mentioned above. Comment on the policy changes and examine the consequences if the collection period remains at 60 days. Assume capital assets are sufficient for increased sales.

Selected References

Carter, J. R. "A Systematic Integration of Strategic Analysis and Cash Flow Forecasting." *Journal of Commercial Lending* 74 (April 1992), pp. 12–23.

Chase, Charles W., Jr. "The Realities of Business Forecasting." *The Journal of Business Forecasting Methods and Systems* 14 (Spring 1995), p. 2.

Coller, Maribeth, and Teri Lombardi Yohn. "Management Forecasts: What Do We Know?" *Financial Analysts Journal* 54 (January–February 1998), pp. 58–62.

Gage, Theodore Justin. "Forecasts Get Clearer When Current Data, Not History, Is Used." *Corporate Cashflow* 9 (November 1990), pp. 7–8.

Hamm, Richard A. "The Art of Making Financial Statement Projections: A Six-Step Visual Model." *Journal of Commercial Lending* 77 (April 1995), pp. 30–38.

Kumst, R. M., and P. H. Franses. "The Impact of Seasonal Constants on Forecasting Seasonally Cointegrated Time Series." *Journal of Forecasting* 17 (March 1998), pp. 109–24.

Lam, Kin, and King Chung Lam. "Forecasting for the Generation of Trading Signals in Financial Markets." *Journal of Forecasting* 19 (July 2000), pp. 39–52.

Strischek, Dev. "Cash Flow Projections for Contractors Revisited." *Journal of Commercial Lending* 77 (June 1995), pp. 17–37.

Tay, Anthony S., and Kenneth F. Wallis. "Density Forecasting: A Survey." *Journal of Forecasting* 19 (January 2000), pp. 235–54.

Tergesen, Anne. "Fearless Forecast." *Business Week* (January 3, 2000), pp. 122–24.

CHAPTER | FIVE

5 Operating and Financial Leverage

LEARNING | OBJECTIVES

1 Define leverage as a method to magnify earnings available to the firm's common shareholders.

2 Define and calculate operating leverage and assess its opportunities and limitations.

3 Define and calculate financial leverage and assess its opportunities and limitations.

4 Calculate the indifference point between financing plans using EBIT/EPS analysis.

5 Define and calculate combined leverage.

In the physical sciences, as well as in politics, the term **leverage** has been popularized to mean the use of special force and effects to produce more than normal results from a given action. In business the same concept is applied. The use of fixed cost items, in particular capital assets and debt, can magnify returns to shareholders at high levels of operation. Although leverage may produce highly favourable results when things go well, it is a two-edged sword. The opposite will occur under negative economic conditions. This potential for higher gains or greater losses is an exposure to a greater variability of returns, which we define as risk. We explore this concept in Chapter 13. This greater risk will impact on share value as will the higher expected gains/losses. In this chapter the Finance in Action boxes discuss how leverage goes wrong at Air Canada and how it continues to go right at the Royal Bank.

Leverage in a Business

Assume you are approached with an opportunity to start your own business. You are to manufacture and market industrial parts, such as ball bearings, wheels, and casters. You are faced with two primary decisions.

First you must determine the amount of fixed cost plant and equipment you wish to use in the production process. By installing modern, sophisticated equipment, you can virtually eliminate labour in the production of inventory. At high volume, you can do quite well, as most of your costs are fixed. At low volume, however, you could face difficulty in making your fixed payments for plant and equipment. If you decide to use expensive labour rather than machinery, you will lessen your opportunity for profit, but at the same time you lower your exposure to risk (you can lay off part of the work force).

Second, you must determine how to finance the business. If you rely on debt financing and the business is successful, you generate substantial profits as an owner, paying only the fixed costs of debt. Of course, if the business starts off poorly, the contractual obligations related to debt could mean bankruptcy. As an alternative, you might decide to sell equity rather than borrow, a step that lowers your own profit potential (you must share with others) but minimizes your risk exposure.

In both decisions you are making very explicit decisions about the use of leverage. To the extent that you go with a heavy commitment to fixed costs in the operation of the firm, you are employing operating leverage. To the extent that you use debt in the financing of the firm, you are engaging in financial leverage. We carefully examine each type of leverage and then show the combined effect of both. The amount of leverage a firm employs is often conditioned by its type of business and its pattern of cash flows. The cash flows are required to service the fixed costs incurred with leverage. In the discussion to follow, be careful to realize that the goal of the firm is the maximization of shareholders' wealth by increasing the share price. Although the expected value of earnings per share can be affected by leverage, so can risk. Share price is a complicated mixture of many things, including a trade-off between expected cash flows and risk.

Operating Leverage

Operating leverage reflects the extent to which capital assets and associated fixed costs are utilized in the business firm. It results from the capital budgeting decisions (Chapter 12) used by the firm in its investment strategy. Larger capital projects demand substantial revenues to repay the investment, but if healthy revenues can be generated by the project, then economies of scale can be exploited. Efficiency is obtained through better profit margins, although the firm's risk increases and will be evident if the capital projects do not generate the expected returns. As indicated in Table 5–1, a firm's operational costs may be classified as fixed, variable, or semivariable.

TABLE 5–1
Classification of costs

Fixed	Variable	Semivariable
Rental	Raw material	Utilities
Amortization	Factory labour	Repairs and maintenance
Executive salaries	Sales commissions	
Property taxes		

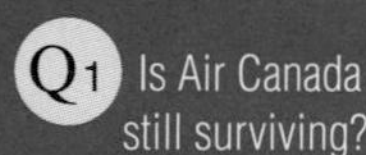

FINANCE IN ACTION

Q1 Is Air Canada still surviving?

Q2 Does it still have high operating and financial leverage?

www.aircanada.ca
Symbol: AC

www.boeing.com
Symbol: BA (NYSE)

Big Leverage! Big Losses! Big Gains at Air Canada!

Air Canada is an international air carrier that again experienced financial difficulties in late 2001 due to a slowing global economy and a high cost structure resulting in part from the takeover of Canadian Airlines. The airline incurred losses of $470 million and $340 million respectively in 1992 and 1993. The global recovery throughout the 1990s did have a positive impact on air travel. By 1997 Air Canada's earnings had reached $352 million, but losses returned in 1998 due in some part to a pilot's strike and in 2000 due to labour and restructuring costs related to the Canadian takeover. By the 3rd quarter of 2001 the situation grew worse.

Despite these troubles Air Canada still was committed to over $2 billion in capital expenditures between 2001 and 2003. The huge capital requirements for aircraft (U.S.$183 to U.S.$211 million for a 747) ensure that the airline business is one of high operating leverage. By the end of 2001 Air Canada owned 66 aircraft and had operating leases on another 160. The book value after amortization of its capital assets (primarily aircraft) was $2.8 billion. If operating leases were included the use of capital would be even more significant. Its gross margin in 2000 was 14.8 percent and its operating margin was 2.8 percent indicating the heavy fixed charges.

Increasing the risk of the airline was the heavy reliance on debt to finance the large capital expenditures. Air Canada's debt represented 98 percent of its booked capital structure in 1993. Losses from 1991 to 1993 had depleted the equity in the company. By 1998, debt still represented 80 percent of the capital structure and by 2000 it was back to almost 97 percent. On operating income of $264 million, interest payments were $210 million. A high degree of financial leverage is in evidence.

The combined effect of operating and financial leverage in the airline business requires the generation of large revenues and good control of operating costs to remain profitable. Air Canada's revenue of $9.3 billion in 2000 generated operating profit of $264 million down from $293 million in 1997 on revenue of $5.5 billion. After interest and other corporate expenses Air Canada experienced a loss in 2000 versus a profit of $352 million in 1997.

Return on equity that had been −103 percent in 1992 and −199 percent in 1993 was over 50 percent in 1994 and again over 36 percent in 1997, but was −24 percent in 2000. This demonstrates the high risk combined with the potential for reward and the downside from the combined leverage at Air Canada. Air Canada shares that were worth $12.00 in 1989 dropped to almost $3.00 by 1993 and were back up to $14.75 in 1997, before dropping below $2.00 in 2001. The high leverage at Air Canada is demonstrated through the dramatic swings experienced by return on equity. When earnings are positive, leverage magnifies return on equity, but when the earnings are negative, deterioration in return on equity can be huge.

For purposes of analysis, variable and semivariable costs are combined. To evaluate the implications of heavy capital asset use, we employ the technique of break-even analysis. We are unable to change the **fixed costs** that come with capital assets in the short run.

Break-Even Analysis

Simulated break-even tool www.bized.ac.uk/virtual/vla/break_even_analysis/

How much do changes in volume affect cost and profit? At what point does the firm break even? What is the most efficient level of capital assets to employ in the firm? A break-even chart is presented in Figure 5–1 to answer some of these questions. The number of units produced and sold is shown along the horizontal axis, and revenue and costs are shown along the vertical axis.

Note that our fixed costs are $60,000 regardless of volume and that our **variable costs** (at $0.80 per unit) are added to fixed costs to determine total costs at any point.[1] The total revenue line is determined by multiplying price ($2.00) times volume.

[1]Fixed costs, as used in the operating leverage analysis, include only fixed operating costs and do not include fixed financing charges.

FIGURE 5–1
Break-even chart: leveraged firm

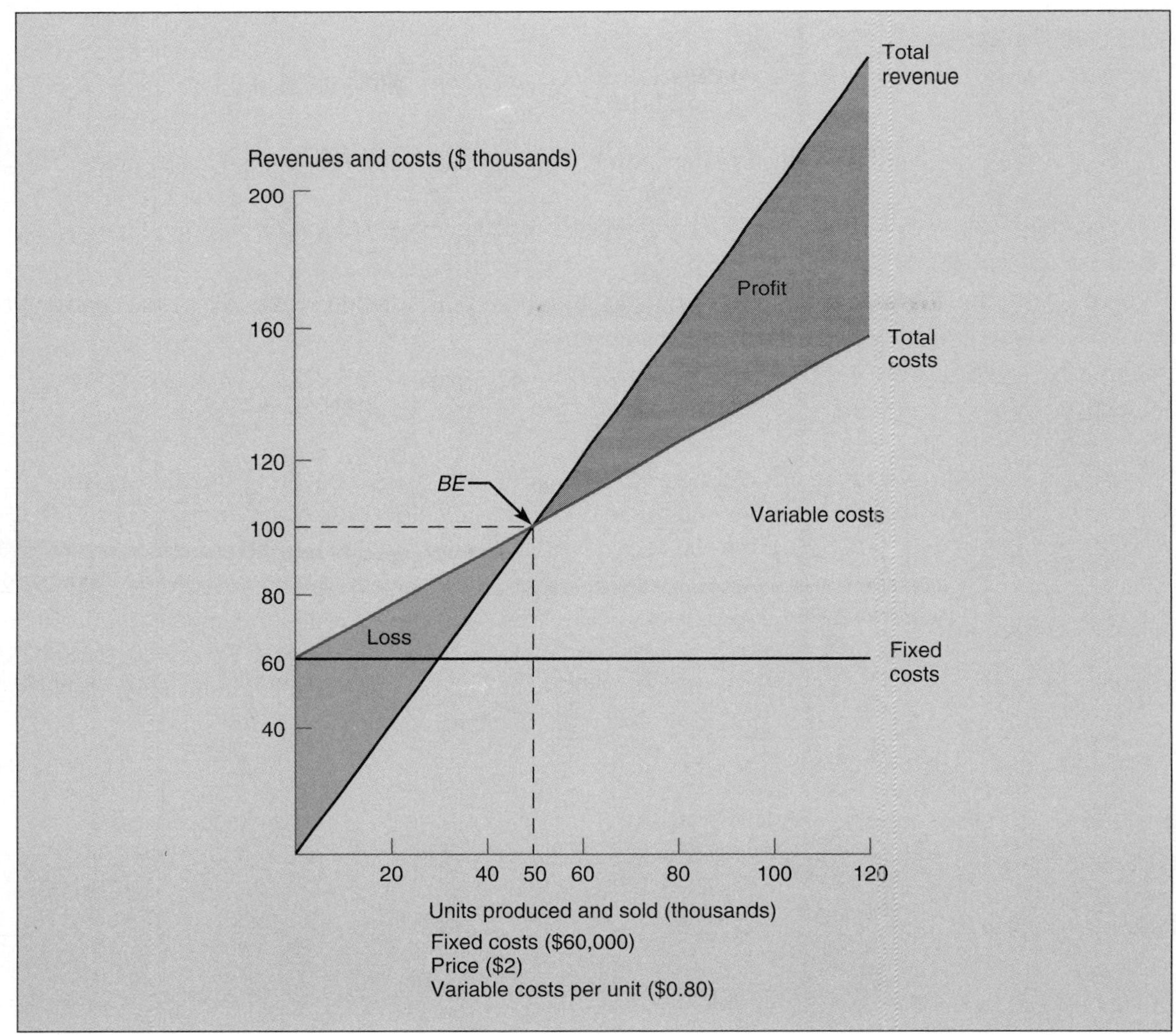

Of particular interest is the break-even (BE) point at 50,000 units, where the total costs and total revenue lines intersect. The numbers are as follows:

		Units = 50,000		
Total Variable Costs (TVC)	**Fixed Costs (FC)**	**Total Costs (TC)**	**Total Revenue (TR)**	**Operating Income (loss)**
(50,000 × $0.80)			(50,000 × $2)	
$40,000	$60,000	$100,000	$100,000	0

The break-even point for the company may also be determined by use of a simple formula in which we divide fixed costs by the contribution margin on each unit sold, with the **contribution margin** defined as price minus variable cost per unit.

$$BE = \frac{\text{Fixed costs}}{\text{Contribution margin}} = \frac{\text{Fixed costs}}{\text{Price} - \text{Variable costs per unit}} = \frac{FC}{P - VC} \quad (5\text{–}1)$$

$$\frac{\$60{,}000}{\$2.00 - \$0.80} = \frac{\$60{,}000}{\$1.20} = 50{,}000 \text{ units}$$

Contribution margin may also be expressed as a percentage. In this example:

$$\frac{P - VC}{P} = \frac{\$2.00 - \$0.80}{\$2.00} = 0.60 = 60\%$$

To calculate breakeven on sales basis fixed costs should be divided by the contribution margin expressed as a percentage.

$$\frac{FC}{CM\%} = \frac{\$60{,}000}{0.60} = \$100{,}000$$

Since we are getting a $1.20 contribution toward covering fixed costs from each unit sold, minimum sales of 50,000 units will allow us to cover our fixed costs (50,000 units × $1.20 = $60,000 fixed costs). Beyond this point we move into a highly profitable range in which each unit of sales brings an increase in operating profit of $1.20 to the company. As sales increase from 50,000 to 60,000 units, operating profits increase by $12,000 as indicated in Table 5–2; as sales increase from 60,000 to 80,000 units, profits increase by another $24,000; and so on. As further indicated in Table 5–2, at low volumes such as 40,000 or 20,000 units, our losses are substantial ($12,000 and $36,000 in the red).

TABLE 5–2
Volume-cost-profit analysis: leveraged firm

Units Sold	Total Variable Costs	Fixed Costs	Total Costs	Total Revenue	Operating Income (loss)
0	0	$60,000	$ 60,000	0	$(60,000)
20,000	$16,000	60,000	76,000	$ 40,000	(36,000)
40,000	32,000	60,000	92,000	80,000	(12,000)
50,000	40,000	60,000	100,000	100,000	0
60,000	48,000	60,000	108,000	120,000	12,000
80,000	64,000	60,000	124,000	160,000	36,000
100,000	80,000	60,000	140,000	200,000	60,000

Assume that the firm depicted in Figure 5–1 is operating with a high degree of leverage. The situation is analogous to that of an airline, which must carry a certain number of people on board to break even; a very profitable range, however, is beyond that point.

The student should note that this break-even analysis does not consider the timing of cash flows. This is of major importance, as the fixed costs are usually incurred at the beginning of a project and the sales of the product come later. Those cash flows received later are less valuable than those received earlier. The timing of cash flows is considered with present value analysis in Chapter 9. At this time we can note that the break-even point does not consider the opportunity cost of having monies invested in the capital assets. This break-even analysis is based on accounting income. We will look at cash break-even in a moment.

A More Conservative Approach

Not all firms would choose to operate at the high degree of operating leverage exhibited in Figure 5–1. Fear of falling short of the 50,000-unit break-even level may discourage some companies from heavy utilization of fixed assets. More expensive variable costs may be substituted for automated plant and equipment. Assume that fixed costs for a more conservative firm can be reduced to $12,000—but that variable costs go from $0.80 to $1.60. If the same price assumption of $2.00 per unit is employed, the break-even level is 30,000 units.

$$BE = \frac{\text{Fixed costs}}{\text{Price} - \text{Variable costs per unit}} = \frac{FC}{P - VC} = \frac{\$12{,}000}{\$2 - \$1.60} = \frac{\$12{,}000}{\$0.40} = 30{,}000 \text{ units}$$

With fixed costs reduced from $60,000 to $12,000, the loss potential is small. Furthermore, the break-even level of operations is a comparatively low 30,000 units. Nevertheless, the use of a virtually unleveraged approach has cut into the potential profitability of the more conservative firm, as indicated in Figure 5–2 on the next page.

Even at high levels of operation, the potential profit is rather small. As indicated in Table 5–3, at a 100,000-unit volume, operating income is only $28,000—some $32,000 less than that for the leveraged firm previously analyzed in Table 5–2.

TABLE 5–3
Volume-cost-profit analysis: conservative firm

Units Sold	Total Variable Costs	Fixed Costs	Total Costs	Total Revenue	Operating Income (loss)
0	0	$12,000	$ 12,000	0	$(12,000)
20,000	$ 32,000	12,000	44,000	$ 40,000	(4,000)
30,000	48,000	12,000	60,000	60,000	0
40,000	64,000	12,000	76,000	80,000	4,000
60,000	96,000	12,000	108,000	120,000	12,000
80,000	128,000	12,000	140,000	160,000	20,000
100,000	160,000	12,000	172,000	200,000	28,000

The Risk Factor

In general, firms in relatively new markets and industries tend to select less leveraged positions, while firms in more mature industries choose to employ more operating leverage. For example, for a small business competing in an emerging industry where the market potential is not yet fully understood and the technology is not standardized, locking the firm into fixed costs that require high sales volume based on an as yet unproven technology is highly risky. On the other hand, a firm competing in the pulp and paper industry, where the markets are large but growing slowly and the production

FIGURE 5–2

Break-even chart: conservative firm

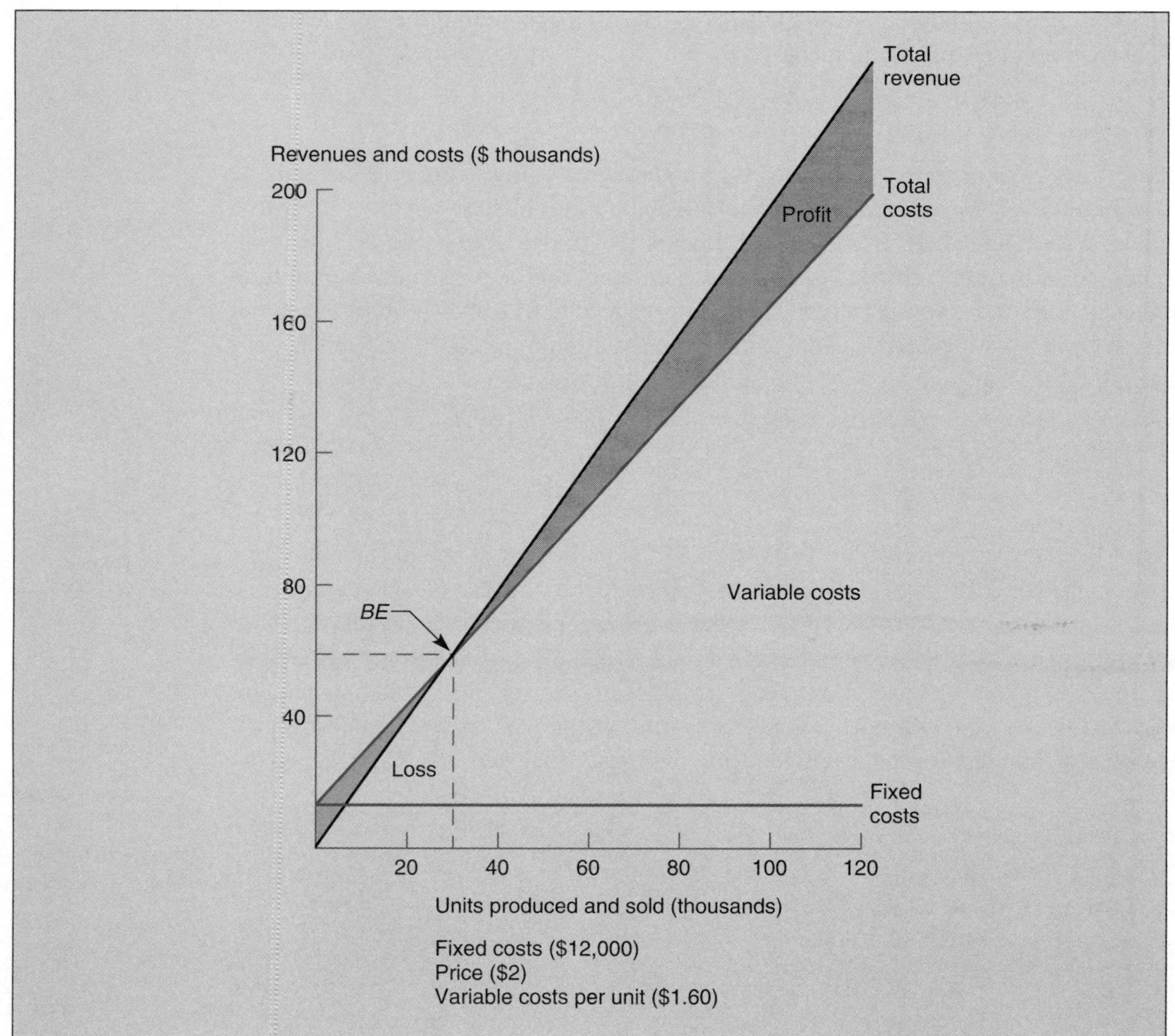

processes are highly developed, cannot afford to do anything but invest in high-cost (but very efficient at high volumes) plant and equipment. Furthermore, most likely, the expected cash flows are known with greater certainty and therefore are less risky. One can feel more comfortable with leverage when the source of repayment appears to have greater certainty.

Whether management follows the path of high leverage or conservatism also depends on its perceptions about the future. If top management is apprehensive about economic conditions, a more conservative plan may be undertaken. For a growing business in times of relative prosperity, management might maintain a more aggressive, leveraged position. The firm's competitive position within its industry is also a factor. Does the firm desire to merely maintain stability or to become a market leader? To a certain extent, management should tailor the use of leverage to meet its own risk-taking desires. Those who are risk averse (prefer less risk to more risk) should anticipate a particularly high return before contracting for heavy fixed costs. Others, less averse to risk, may be willing to leverage under more normal conditions. Simply taking risks is not a virtue—bankruptcy courts are filled with risk takers. The important idea, which is stressed throughout the text, is to achieve the best possible return within an acceptable level of risk. The pace of technological change today may dictate the need to reinvest continually to remain competitive.

Cash Break-Even Analysis

Our discussion to this point has dealt with **break-even analysis** in accounting flows rather than cash flows. For example, amortization has been implicitly included in fixed expenses, but it represents an accounting entry rather than an explicit expenditure of funds. To the extent that we were doing break-even analysis on a strictly cash basis, amortization would be excluded from fixed expenses. Accounting break-even analysis by including amortization gives a longer-term perspective to our analysis. In the example of the leveraged firm in Formula 5–1, if we eliminate \$20,000 of assumed amortization from fixed costs, the break-even level is reduced to 33,333 units.

$$\frac{FC - \text{Amortization}}{P - VC} = \frac{(\$60{,}000 - \$20{,}000)}{\$2.00 - \$0.80} = \frac{\$40{,}000}{\$1.20} = 33{,}333 \text{ units}$$

Other adjustments could also be made for noncash items. For example, sales may initially take the form of accounts receivable rather than cash, and the same can be said for the purchase of materials and accounts payable. An actual weekly or monthly cash budget would be necessary to isolate these items.

While cash break-even analysis is helpful in analyzing the short-term outlook of the firm, particularly when it may be in trouble, most break-even analysis is conducted on the basis of accounting flows rather than strictly cash flows. Most of the assumptions throughout the chapter are based on concepts broader than pure cash flows. This is a longer-term focus. In the short term nothing is more important than cash flow.

Degree of Operating Leverage

Degree of operating leverage (DOL) may be defined as the percentage change in operating income that occurs as a result of a percentage change in units sold.

$$DOL = \frac{\text{Percent change in operating income}}{\text{Percent change in unit volume}} \quad (5\text{–}2)$$

Highly leveraged firms, such as those in the auto or construction industry, are likely to enjoy a rather substantial increase in income as volume expands, while more conservative firms will participate to a lesser extent. Degree of operating leverage should be computed only over a profitable range of operations. However, the closer DOL is computed to the company break-even point, the higher the number is, due to a large percentage increase in operating income.[2]

[2]While the value of DOL varies at each level of output, the beginning level of volume determines the DOL regardless of the location at the end point.

Let us apply the formula to the leveraged and conservative firms previously discussed. Their income or losses at various levels of operation are summarized in Table 5–4.

TABLE 5–4
Operating income or loss

Units	Leveraged Firm (Table 5–2)	Conservative Firm (Table 5–3)
0	\$(60,000)	\$(12,000)
20,000	(36,000)	(4,000)
40,000	(12,000)	4,000
60,000	12,000	12,000
80,000	36,000	20,000
100,000	60,000	28,000

We now consider what happens to operating income as volume moves from 80,000 to 100,000 units.

Leveraged Firm

$$DOL = \frac{\text{Percent change in operating income}}{\text{Percent change in unit volume}} = \frac{\dfrac{\$24{,}000}{\$36{,}000} \times 100}{\dfrac{20{,}000}{80{,}000} \times 100} = \frac{67\%}{25\%} = 2.7$$

Conservative Firm

$$DOL = \frac{\text{Percent change in operating income}}{\text{Percent change in unit volume}} = \frac{\dfrac{\$8{,}000}{\$20{,}000} \times 100}{\dfrac{20{,}000}{80{,}000} \times 100} = \frac{40\%}{25\%} = 1.6$$

We see that the DOL is much greater for the leveraged firm, indicating at 80,000 units a 1 percent increase in volume will produce a 2.7 percent change in operating income versus a 1.6 percent increase for the conservative firm. The DOL measures the sensitivity of a firm's operating income to a change in sales. The higher the DOL, the more concerned the firm should be to any potential decrease in sales because of the potential impact on operating results. For instance, our leveraged firm is more susceptible to the loss of a major client.

The formula for degree of operating leverage may be algebraically manipulated to read:

$$DOL = \frac{Q(P - VC)}{Q(P - VC) - FC} \qquad (5\text{–}3a)$$

where

Q = Quantity at which DOL is computed.
P = Price per unit.
VC = Variable costs per unit.
FC = Fixed costs.

Using the newly stated formula for the first firm at $Q = 80{,}000$, with $P = \$2$, $VC = \$0.80$, and $FC = \$60{,}000$:

$$DOL = \frac{80{,}000(\$2.00 - \$0.80)}{80{,}000(\$2.00 - \$0.80) - \$60{,}000}$$

$$= \frac{80{,}000(\$1.20)}{80{,}000(\$1.20) - 60{,}000} = \frac{96{,}000}{96{,}000 - 60{,}000} = 2.67$$

We once again derive an answer of 2.67. The same type of calculation could also be performed for the conservative firm.

The formula for DOL may also be rewritten as:

$$DOL = \frac{Q(P - VC)}{Q(P - VC) - FC}$$

$$= \frac{QP - QVC}{QP - QVC - FC}$$

We can rewrite the second terms as:

QP = S, or Sales (Quantity × Price)
QVC = TVC, or Total variable costs (Quantity × Variable costs per unit)
FC = Total fixed costs (remains the same term)

We then have:

$$DOL = \frac{S - TVC}{S - TVC - FC} \tag{5–3b}$$

$$= \frac{\$160{,}000 - \$64{,}000}{\$160{,}000 - \$64{,}000 - \$60{,}000}$$

$$= \frac{\$96{,}000}{\$36{,}000} = 2.67$$

Examine formula 5–3b closely and relate it to the income statement. Sales less variable costs is contribution margin. Sales less variable costs less fixed costs is operating profit or earnings before interest and taxes (EBIT). Therefore contribution margin divided by operating profit will give us the degree of operating leverage (DOL).

$$DOL = \frac{\text{Contribution margin}}{\text{Operating profit } (EBIT)}$$

Limitations of Analysis

Throughout our analysis of operating leverage we have assumed that a constant or linear function exists for revenues and costs as volume changes. For example, we have used $2.00 as the hypothetical sales price at all levels of operation. In the real world, however, we may face price weakness as we attempt to capture an increasing market, or we may face cost overruns as we move beyond an optimum-size operation. Relationships are not so fixed as we have assumed.

Nevertheless, the basic patterns we have studied are reasonably valid for most firms over an extended operating range (in our example that might be between 20,000 and

100,000 units). It is only at the extreme levels that linear assumptions break down and **nonlinear break-even analysis** is required, as indicated in Figure 5–3.

FIGURE 5–3
Nonlinear break-even analysis

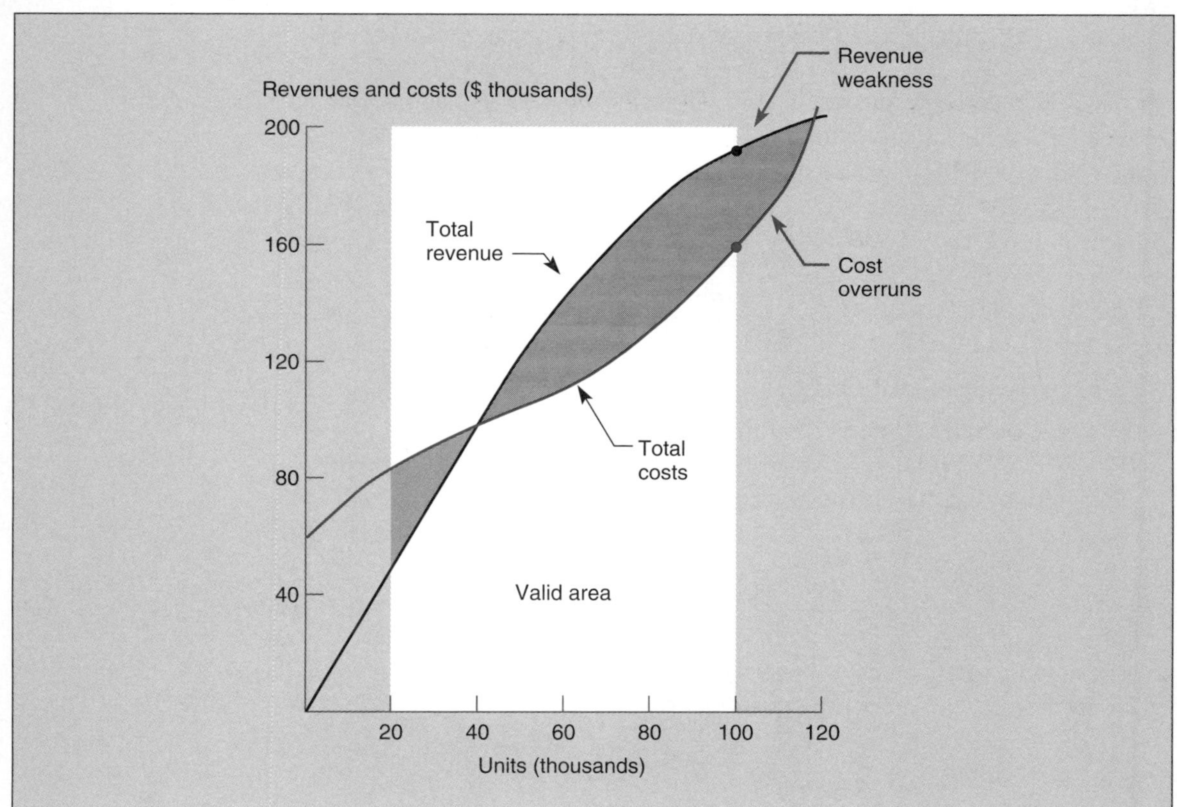

A further word of caution relating to break-even analysis is in order. Although the analysis period is generally one year, a product or venture new to the company probably will not break even within the first few years of operation. It takes time to nurture and realize the market potential. Thus, for such cases, one should analyze the break-even possibilities for the situation a few years hence when the market has developed rather than consider just the immediately upcoming year. Although companies commonly require that a new product introduction be profitable by its third year, an important study found that it took eight years, on average, for new products to actually turn a profit.[3] Furthermore, as we pointed out earlier, our break-even analysis does not account for the timing of cash flows. Therefore, opportunity costs of an investment are not considered.

[3]Ralph Biggadike, "The Risk Business of Diversification," *Harvard Business Review,* May–June 1979, pp. 103–111.

Financial Leverage

Having discussed the effect of fixed costs on the operations of the firm (operating leverage), we now turn to the second form of leverage. **Financial leverage** reflects the amount of debt used in the capital structure of the firm. Because debt carries a fixed obligation of interest payments, we can greatly magnify our results at various levels of operations. You may have heard of the real estate developer who borrows 100 percent of the costs of his project and enjoys an infinite return on his zero investment if all goes well.

It is the firm's capital structure choice (debt to equity) that determines its financial leverage. The overall financial choices available between short- and long-term financing options are identified in later chapters through Figures 6–11 and 8–1. Corporate use of the money and capital markets in Canada is highlighted in Figures 14–1 and 14–4, with the tradeoffs for short-term financing alternatives examined in Chapter 8 and the longer-term choices covered in Chapters 16 and 17.

It is helpful to think of *operating leverage* as primarily affecting the left-hand side of the balance sheet and *financial leverage* as affecting the right side.

Balance Sheet

Assets	Liabilities and Net Worth
Operating leverage	Financial leverage

Whereas operating leverage influences the mix of plant and equipment, financial leverage determines how the operation is to be financed. Two firms can have equal operating capabilities and yet show widely different results because of differing uses of financial leverage.

Impact on Earnings

In studying the impact of financial leverage, we examine two financial plans for a firm, each employing a significantly different amount of debt in the capital structure. Financing totalling $200,000 is required to carry the assets of the firm.[4]

Total Assets—$200,000

	Plan A (Leveraged)	Plan B (Conservative)
Debt (8% interest)	$150,000 ($12,000 interest)	$ 50,000 ($4,000 interest)
Common stock	50,000 (8,000 shares at $6.25)	150,000 (24,000 shares at $6.25)
Total financing	$200,000	$200,000

Under *leveraged* Plan A, we borrow $150,000 and sell 8,000 shares of stock at $6.25 to raise an additional $50,000; *conservative* Plan B calls for borrowing only $50,000 and acquiring an additional $150,000 in stock with 24,000 shares.

[4]We have assumed that the share price does not change under the different plans for purposes of illustration. In reality, the different risk exposure of leverage and the potential for greater returns to shareholders would affect the share price.

In Table 5–5 we compute earnings per share for the two plans at various levels of earnings before interest and taxes (EBIT). These earnings represent the operating income of the firm—before deductions have been made for financial charges or taxes. We assume EBIT levels of 0, $12,000, $16,000, $36,000, and $60,000.

TABLE 5–5
Impact of financing plan on earnings per share

	Plan A (Leveraged)	Plan B (Conservative)
1. EBIT (0)		
Earnings before interest and taxes (EBIT)	0	0
– Interest (I)	$(12,000)	$ (4,000)
Earnings before taxes (EBT)	(12,000)	(4,000)
– Taxes (T)*	(6,000)	(2,000)
Earnings aftertaxes (EAT)	$ (6,000)	$ (2,000)
Shares	8,000	24,000
Earnings per share (EPS)	$(0.75)	$(0.08)
2. EBIT ($12,000)		
Earnings before interest and taxes (EBIT)	$ 12,000	$12,000
– Interest (I)	12,000	4,000
Earnings before taxes (EBT)	0	8,000
– Taxes (T)	0	4,000
Earnings aftertaxes (EAT)	$ 0	$ 4,000
Shares	8,000	24,000
Earnings per share (EPS)	0	$0.17
3. EBIT ($16,000)		
Earnings before interest and taxes (EBIT)	$ 16,000	$16,000
– Interest (I)	12,000	4,000
Earnings before taxes (EBT)	4,000	12,000
– Taxes (T)	2,000	6,000
Earnings aftertaxes (EAT)	$ 2,000	$ 6,000
Shares	8,000	24,000
Earnings per share (EPS)	$0.25	$0.25
4. EBIT ($36,000)		
Earnings before interest and taxes (EBIT)	$ 36,000	$36,000
– Interest (I)	12,000	4,000
Earnings before taxes (EBT)	24,000	32,000
– Taxes (T)	12,000	16,000
Earnings aftertaxes (EAT)	$ 12,000	$16,000
Shares	8,000	24,000
Earnings per share (EPS)	$1.50	$0.67
5. EBIT ($60,000)		
Earnings before interest and taxes (EBIT)	$ 60,000	$60,000
– Interest (I)	12,000	4,000
Earnings before taxes (EBT)	48,000	56,000
– Taxes (T)	24,000	28,000
Earnings aftertaxes (EAT)	$ 24,000	$28,000
Shares	8,000	24,000
Earnings per share (EPS)	$3.00	$1.17

*The assumption is that large losses can be written off against other income, perhaps in other years, thus providing the firm with a tax savings benefit. The tax rate is 50 percent.

Leverage of 21 Times Equity

The Royal Bank is the largest bank in Canada with assets of $359 billion as of late 2001. With these assets the Royal Bank only received a 0.74% return on its assets. This still represented a rather large net income of $2.4 billion. Personally we might expect to receive a higher return on our savings accounts at the banks. However, the shareholders at the Royal Bank did receive a 16.4% return on their equity (book value) of $16.1 billion

This large difference in the return to equity as compared to return on assets is the result of the tremendous financial leverage employed the Royal Bank. The majority of the bank's liabilities are loans from the general public by way of deposit accounts. Our chequing and savings accounts are loans to the bank! The Royal Bank's debt at over 95 percent of total liabilities and equities was over 21 times its equity. This allowed it to magnify its low return on assets to achieve a quite satisfactory return to shareholders. In effect the ROA is multiplied by the degree of financial leverage to obtain the ROE. The leverage employed by our banks helps to explain their conservative lending practices. They must ensure that revenues are maintained or the leverage will work against them.

FINANCE IN ACTION

Q1 What is the latest ROA and ROE at the Royal Bank?

www.rbc.com

Symbol: RY

The impact of the two financing plans is dramatic. Although both plans assume the same operating income, or EBIT, for comparative purposes at each level (say $36,000 in calculation 4), the reported income per share is vastly different ($1.50 versus $0.67). It is also evident that the conservative plan produces better results at low income levels, but the leveraged plan generates much better earnings per share as operating income, or EBIT, goes up. The firm would be indifferent between the two plans at an EBIT level of $16,000, as indicated in Table 5–5.

In Figure 5–4, on the next page, we graphically demonstrate the effect of the two financing plans on earnings per share.

With an EBIT of $16,000 we are earning *8 percent* on total assets of $200,000—precisely the percentage cost of borrowed funds to the firm. The use or nonuse of debt does not influence the answer. Beyond $16,000, Plan A, employing heavy financial leverage, really goes to work, allowing the firm to greatly expand earnings per share as a result of a change in EBIT.

Degree of Financial Leverage

As was true of operating leverage, degree of financial leverage measures the effect of a change in one variable on another variable. **Degree of financial leverage (DFL)** may be defined as the percentage change in earnings (EPS) that occurs as a result of a percentage change in earnings before interest and taxes (EBIT).

$$DFL = \frac{\text{Percent change in } EPS}{\text{Percent change in } EBIT} \tag{5–4}$$

For purposes of computation, the formula for DFL may be conveniently restated as:

$$DFL = \frac{EBIT}{EBIT - \text{I}} \tag{5–5}$$

If we relate this formula to the income statement we notice that operating profit is divided by earnings before taxes (EBT).

$$DFL = \frac{\text{Operating profit}}{\text{Earnings before taxes } (EBT)}$$

FIGURE 5–4

Financing plans and earnings per share

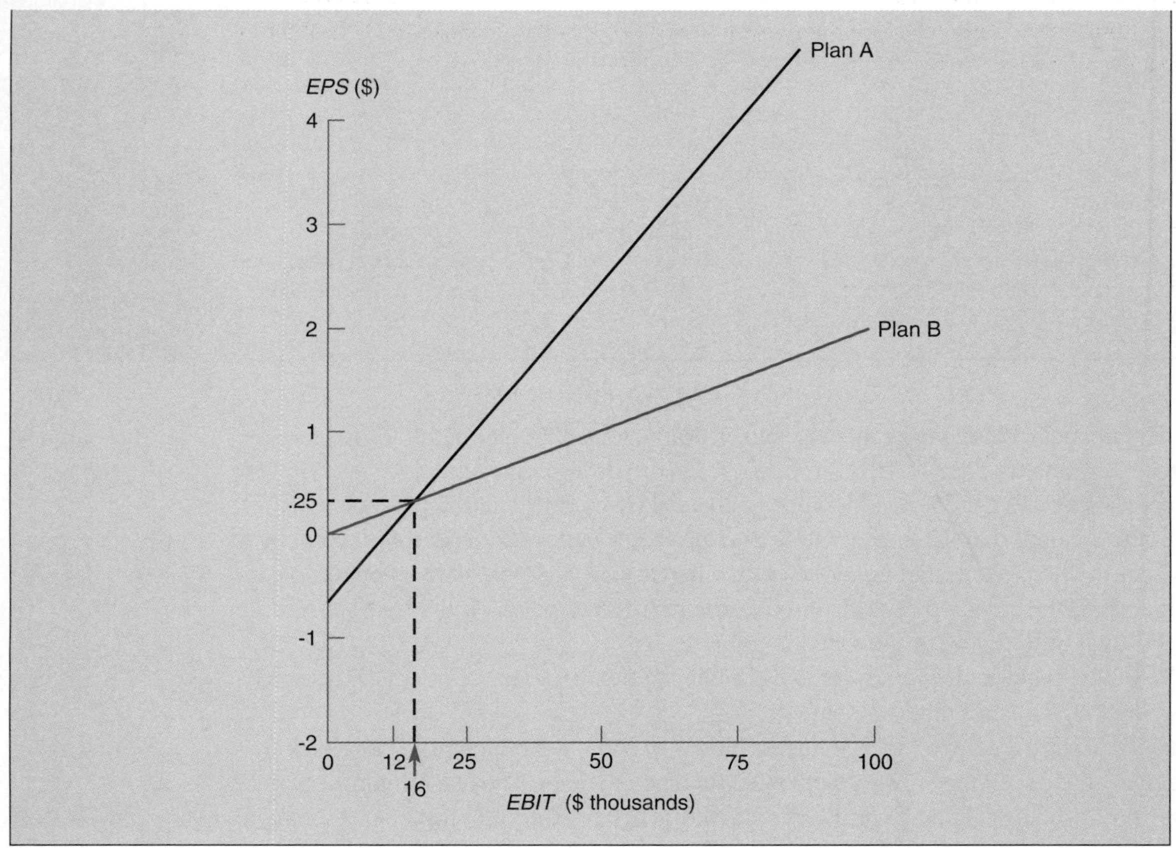

Let's compute the degree of financial leverage for Plan A and Plan B, presented in Table 5–5, at an EBIT level of $36,000. Plan A calls for $12,000 of interest at all levels of financing, and Plan B requires $4,000.

Plan A (Leveraged)

$$DFL = \frac{EBIT}{EBIT - I} = \frac{\$36,000}{\$36,000 - \$12,000} = \frac{\$36,000}{\$24,000} = 1.5$$

Plan B (Conservative)

$$DFL = \frac{EBIT}{EBIT - I} = \frac{\$36,000}{\$36,000 - \$4,000} = \frac{\$36,000}{\$32,000} = 1.1$$

As expected, Plan A has a much higher degree of financial leverage. At an EBIT level of $36,000, a 1 percent increase in earnings produces a 1.5 percent increase in earnings per share under Plan A. The same increase in earnings produces only a 1.1 percent increase under Plan B. DFL may be computed for any level of operation, and it changes from point to point, but Plan A always exceeds Plan B.

The DFL measures the sensitivity of a firm's earnings available to shareholders (EPS) to a change in operating profits. The higher the DFL, the more concerned the firm should be to any potential decrease in operating results because of the potential impact on earnings. As with operating leverage, sales changes can have a magnified impact the greater the leverage.

The Indifference Point

A firm may be interested in determining the point (EBIT) where the impact between one financing plan and another has an equal impact on earnings per share (EPS). This is the **EBIT/EPS indifference point** and will occur where net income per share is equal for both plans. It is worth noting that this point may not have an equal impact on share price because investors may assign a lower P/E ratio to earnings with the higher risk associated with greater leverage. For the firm, it is important to assess the likelihood of exceeding or not exceeding the indifference point in operating results when deciding on a financing plan.

The indifference point between two financing plans is determined mathematically by:

$$\frac{(EBIT^* - I_A)(1 - t)}{S_A} = \frac{(EBIT^* - I_B)(1 - t)}{S_B}$$

where

$EBIT^*$ = operating income at the indifference point
I = interest costs under plan A and B
S = shares outstanding under plan A and B
t = corporate tax rate.

This formula can be simplified to:

$$EBIT^* = \frac{(S_B \times I_A - S_A \times I_B)}{S_B - S_A} \tag{5–6}$$

For our example the indifference point is:

$$EBIT^* = \frac{(24{,}000 \times \$12{,}000) - (8{,}000 \times \$4{,}000)}{24{,}000 - 8{,}000}$$

$$= \$16{,}000$$

This is the same result we obtained in Table 5–5.

Valuation Basics with Financial Leverage

The alert student may quickly observe that if debt is such a good thing, why sell any stock? (Perhaps one share for yourself!) With exclusive debt financing at an EBIT level of $36,000, we would have a degree of financial leverage factor of 1.8.

$$DFL = \frac{EBIT}{EBIT - I} = \frac{\$36{,}000}{\$36{,}000 - \$16{,}000} = 1.8$$

(With no stock, we would borrow the full $200,000.)

$$(8\% \times \$200{,}000 = \$16{,}000 \text{ interest})$$

As stressed throughout the text, debt financing and financial leverage offer unique advantages, but only up to a point. Beyond that point, debt financing may be detrimental to the firm. As the firm expands the use of debt in its capital structure, lenders may perceive a greater risk for the firm. They may then raise the interest rate to be paid, and may demand that certain restrictions be placed on the firm. Furthermore, concerned common shareholders may drive down the price of the stock because of their increased risk. This moves the firm away from the objective of maximizing the firm's overall value in the market. The overall impact of financial leverage must be carefully weighed.

This is not to say that financial leverage does not work to the benefit of the firm. It does if properly used. Further discussion of appropriate debt-equity mixes is covered in Chapter 11. For now, we accept the virtues of financial leverage, knowing that we face a trade-off between the higher potential returns to shareholders and the greater risk of failing to meet our financial obligations.

The use of some debt is recommended for firms in industries that offer some stability, are in positive stages of growth, and are operating in favourable economic conditions. In the cases of large utilities operating cash flows can be forecasted within narrow ranges, thus favouring the use of higher leverage to maximize share values. This is because of the relative certainty of the cash flows. On the other hand, for companies in industries open to cyclicality or other causes of revenue volatility, the use of high levels of leverage may become the cause of significant financial distress and depressed share prices. The small business may be limited in its ability to borrow from the banks or the capital markets, but it should consider the use of trade credit from suppliers as a means of leveraging its investment. Trade credit is a debt obligation that if prudently used can enhance the performance of the small firm.

Leveraged Buyout

During the late 1980s the term **leveraged buyout** became familiar. This is the act of purchasing a corporation's common shares with borrowed money. Buyers hope to eventually repay that borrowed money by selling assets of the acquired corporation or by borrowing monies against the remaining assets of the corporation. These borrowings are often referred to as junk bonds, as the security is tenuous with leverage ratios, or debt-to-equity ratios, often in double digits. In effect, a corporation is bought with its own assets and borrowing power. It is, however, a much riskier corporation after the changes. During this period, the Canadian firm Campeau Corporation acquired Federated Department Stores and Allied Stores of the U.S. for a total of $11.6 billion, mostly with borrowed money. Both companies subsequently went into bankruptcy protection (Chapter 11 in U.S. bankruptcy law), as their cash flows were insufficient to meet the huge debt burden. Campeau Corporation had its common share price plunge below $1.00 from above $22.00 in less than half a year. It was a spectacular failure. The leveraged buyout is still in use today.

Federated Department Stores, Inc.
www.federated-fds.com

However because firms in a given industry tend to face similar levels of business risk, investors and financial analysts often compare a firm's level of financial leverage to industry averages to estimate whether it is excessive. It is, therefore, incumbent on management to justify any decision to employ a higher amount of leverage than most other firms in its industry. Information on financial leverage for selected Canadian industries is presented in Figure 5–5.

Canada's Leveraged Buyout Specialist

In 1998 Long-Term Capital Management, a so-called hedge fund, was rescued by several large U.S. banks when its failure threatened the stability of the world financial system. On a capital base of $4 billion it had borrowed over $100 billion from the banks and had then had further leveraged its investment in the derivative markets to over $1 trillion. Its investments had lost money and its meager equity of $4 billion had quickly disappeared. This is the downside to the double-edged sword of leverage!

Onex is a Canadian leveraged buyout specialist that takes equity stakes in companies. Its objective is to use debt to effectively create value in these companies as it turns them into global leaders. Onex emphasizes value creation throughout its web site and identifies eight principles for building value. For example Sky Chefs Inc., the world's largest airline caterer, was sold by Onex in 2001 for $1.8 billion which represented a 30% annual return from its original investment of $99 million. Another key company in which Onex has an equity stake is Celestica, a major electronics manufacturer.

Onex Corporation is fairly conservative in its leveraged investments, in the Canadian tradition. It finances perhaps 30 percent of an investment from equity and uses debt financing to enhance its capital base. The 2000 capital structure of Onex reveals a long-term debt to book value of equity of 3.4 to 1. Onex in 2000 had a ROA of less than 1%, but through leverage its ROE was over 13%, which was down from 23.5% in 1999.

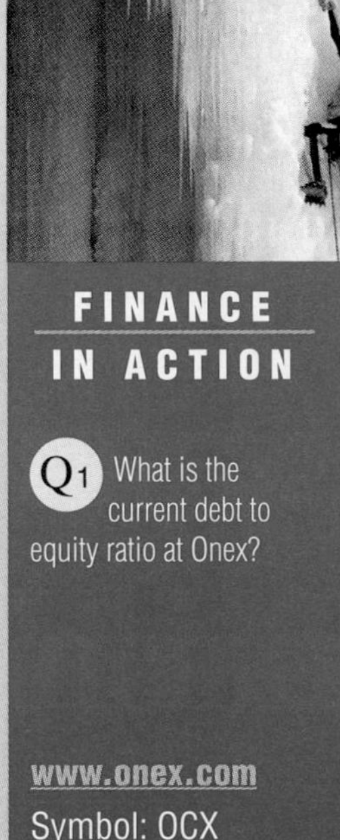

FINANCE IN ACTION

Q1 What is the current debt to equity ratio at Onex?

www.onex.com

Symbol: OCX

FIGURE 5–5

Financial leverage in selected industries

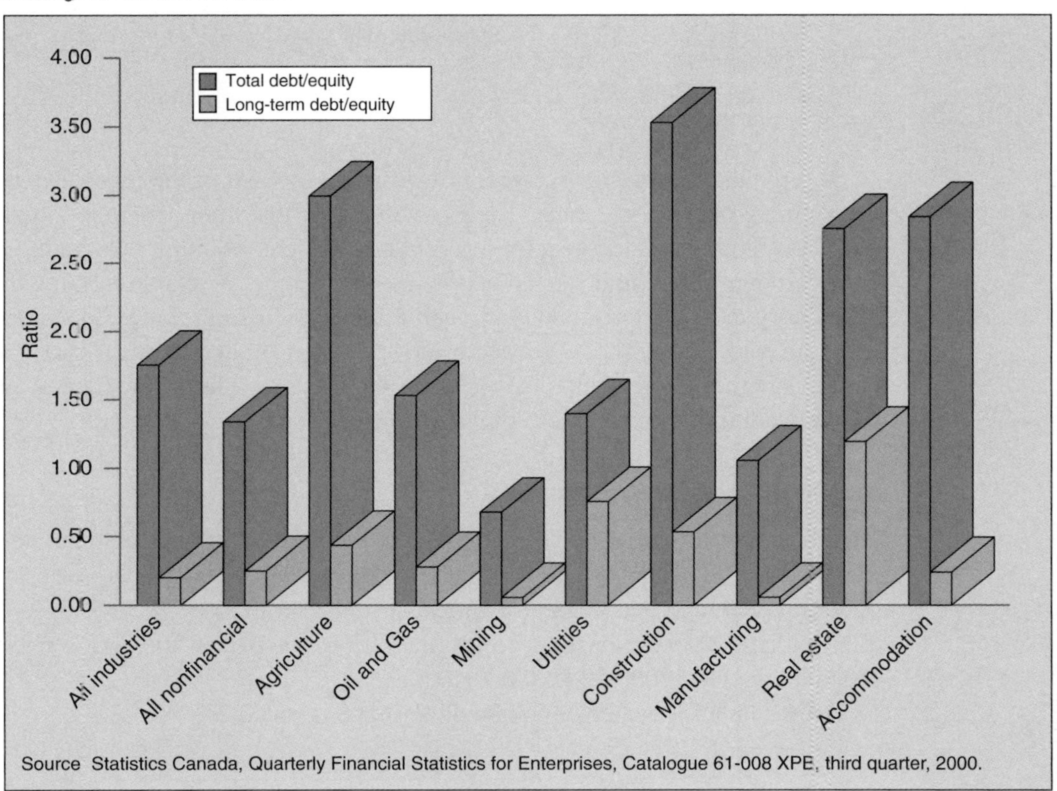

Source Statistics Canada, Quarterly Financial Statistics for Enterprises, Catalogue 61-008 XPE, third quarter, 2000.

Combining Operating and Financial Leverage

If both operating and financial leverage allow us to magnify our returns, we get maximum leverage through **combined leverage**. We have said that operating leverage affects primarily the asset structure of the firm, while financial leverage affects the debt-equity mix. From an income statement viewpoint, operating leverage determines return from operations, while financial leverage determines how the fruits of our labour are allocated to debt holders and, more importantly, to shareholders in the form of earnings per share. Table 5–6 shows the combined influence of operating and financial leverage on the income statement. The values in Table 5–6 are drawn from earlier material in the chapter (see Tables 5–2 and 5–5). We assumed in both cases a high degree of operating and financial leverage. The sales volume is 80,000 units.

TABLE 5–6
Income statement

Sales (total revenue) (80,000 units @ $2)	$160,000	Operating leverage
– Variable costs ($0.80 per unit)	64,000	
Contribution margin	96,000	
– Fixed costs	60,000	
Operating income	$ 36,000	
Earnings before interest and taxes	$ 36,000	Financial leverage
– Interest	12,000	
Earnings before taxes	24,000	
– Taxes	12,000	
Earnings aftertaxes	$ 12,000	
Shares	8,000	
Earnings per share	$1.50	

Observe that operating leverage influences the top half of the income statement—determining operating income. The last item under operating leverage, operating income, becomes the initial item for determining financial leverage. "Operating income" and "earnings before interest and taxes" are one and the same, representing the return to the corporation after production, marketing, and so forth, but before interest and taxes are paid. In the second half of the income statement, we show the extent to which earnings before interest and taxes are translated into earnings per share. A graphical representation of these points is provided in Figure 5–6.

Degree of Combined Leverage

Degree of combined leverage (DCL) uses the entire income statement and shows the impact of a change in sales or volume on bottom-line earnings per share. Degree of operating leverage and degree of financial leverage are, in effect, being combined. Table 5–7 shows what happens to profitability as the firm's sales go from $160,000 (80,000 units) to $200,000 (100,000 units).

The formula for degree of combined leverage is stated as:

$$DCL = \frac{\text{Percent change in } EPS}{\text{Percent change in sales (or volume)}} \tag{5–7}$$

$$\frac{\text{Percent change in } EPS}{\text{Percent change in sales}} = \frac{\frac{\$1.50}{\$1.50} \times 100}{\frac{\$40,000}{\$160,000} \times 100} = \frac{100\%}{25\%} = 4$$

FIGURE 5–6

Combining operating and financial leverage

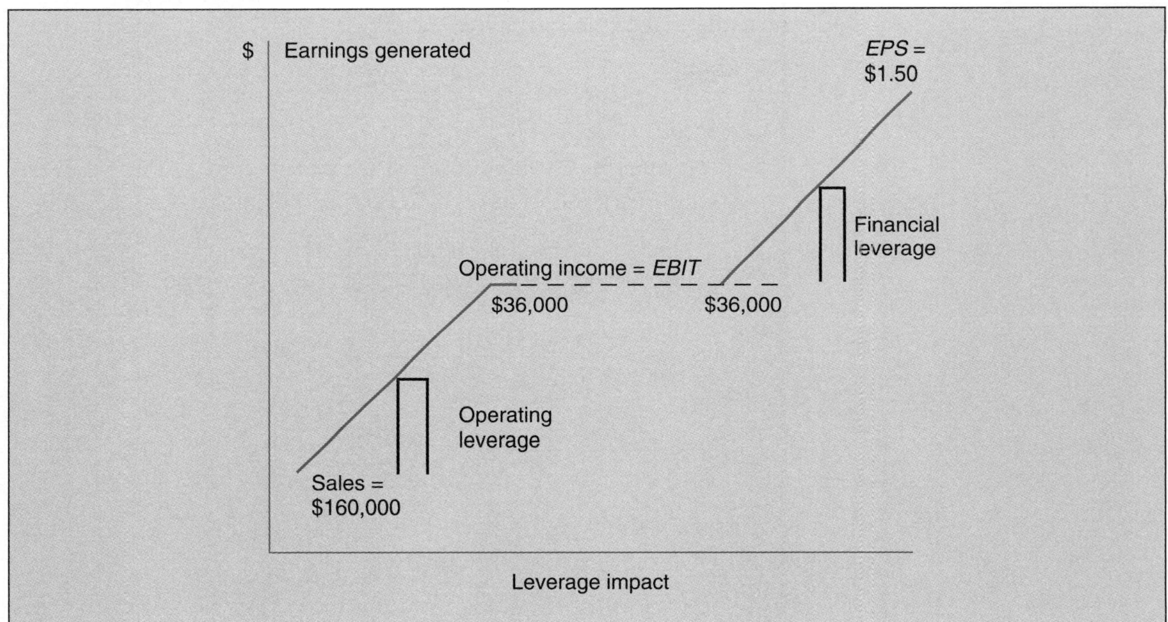

TABLE 5–7

Operating and financial leverage

	(Taken from Table 5–6)		
Sales (total revenue) (80,000 units @ $2)	$160,000	(100,000 →	$200,000
− Variable costs ($0.80 per unit)	64,000	units)	80,000
Contribution margin	96,000		120,000
− Fixed costs	60,000		60,000
Operating income = EBIT	36,000		60,000
− Interest	12,000		12,000
Earnings before taxes	24,000		48,000
− Taxes	12,000		24,000
Earnings aftertaxes	$ 12,000		$ 24,000
Shares	8,000		8,000
Earnings per share	$1.50		$3.00

Using our previous calculations we find:

$$\begin{array}{c}\text{Degree of operating} \\ \text{leverage } (DOL)\end{array} \times \begin{array}{c}\text{Degree of financial} \\ \text{leverage } (DFL)\end{array} = \begin{array}{c}\text{Degree of combined} \\ \text{leverage } (DCL)\end{array}$$

$$\frac{\%\text{ change in } EBIT}{\%\text{ change in unit volume}} \times \frac{\%\text{ change in } EPS}{\%\text{ change in } EBIT} = \frac{\%\text{ change in } EPS}{\%\text{ change in unit volume}}$$

Plan A (leveraged)

$$2.67 \times 1.5 = 4$$

Every percentage point change in sales will be reflected in a 4 percent change in earnings per share at this level of operation (quite an impact).

An algebraic statement of the formula is

$$DCL = \frac{Q(P - VC)}{Q(P - VC) - FC - I} \tag{5–8a}$$

From Table 5–7: Q (quantity) = 80,000; P (price per unit) = \$2.00; VC (variable costs per unit) = \$0.80; FC (fixed costs) = \$60,000; and I (interest) = \$12,000.

$$DCL = \frac{80{,}000(\$2.00 - \$0.80)}{80{,}000(\$2.00 - \$0.80) - \$60{,}000 - \$12{,}000}$$

$$= \frac{80{,}000(\$1.20)}{80{,}000(\$1.20) - \$72{,}000}$$

$$= \frac{\$96{,}000}{\$96{,}000 - \$72{,}000} = \frac{\$96{,}000}{\$24{,}000} = 4$$

The answer is once again shown to be 4.

The formula for DCL may be rewritten as:

$$DCL = \frac{Q(P - VC)}{Q(P - VC) - FC - I}$$

$$= \frac{QP - QVC)}{QP - QVC - FC - I}$$

We can rewrite the second terms as:

QP = S, or Sales (Quantity × Price)
QVC = TVC, or Total variable costs (Quantity × Variable cost per unit)
FC = Total fixed costs (remains the same term)
I = Interest (remains the same term)

We then have:

$$DCL = \frac{S - TVC}{S - TVC - FC - I} \tag{5–8b}$$

$$= \frac{\$160{,}000 - \$64{,}000}{\$160{,}000 - \$64{,}000 - \$60{,}000 - \$12{,}000}$$

$$= \frac{\$96{,}000}{\$24{,}000} = 4$$

A Word of Caution

In a sense, we are piling risk on risk as the two different forms of leverage are combined. Perhaps a firm carrying heavy operating leverage may wish to moderate its position financially, and vice versa. One thing is certain—the decision will have a major impact on the operations of the firm.

Summary

1. Leverage may be defined as the use of fixed cost items to magnify returns at high levels of operation.
2. Operating leverage primarily affects fixed versus variable cost utilization in the operation of the firm. An important concept, degree of operating leverage (DOL), measures the percentage change in operating income as a result of a percentage change in volume. With heavier utilization of fixed cost assets, DOL is likely to be higher. Once the break-even point is reached, returns are magnified by the more efficient use of the fixed resource. Break-even is often calculated on accounting income for a longer-term perspective, while cash flow break-even focuses on more immediate needs.
3. Financial leverage reflects the extent to which debt is used in the capital structure of the firm. Substantial use of debt places a great burden on the firm at low levels of profitability, but helps to magnify earnings per share as volume or operating income increases. The degree of financial leverage (DFL) measures the percentage change in earnings per share (EPS) for a percentage change in earnings before interest and taxes (EBIT).
4. A level of operating income where the firm's results based on earnings per share are equal between two financing plans is calculated as the indifference point.
5. We combine operating and financial leverage to assess the impact of all types of assets on the firm. There is a multiplier effect when we use the two different types of leverage. Because leverage is a two-edged sword, management must be sure the level of risk assumed is in accord with its desires for risk and its perceptions of the future. High operating leverage may be balanced against lower financial leverage if this is deemed desirable, and vice versa.

Review of Formulas

1. $$BE = \frac{FC}{P - VC} \qquad (5\text{–}1)$$

BE is break-even point
FC is fixed costs
P is price per unit
VC is variable cost per unit

$$BE \text{ (cash basis)} = \frac{FC - \text{Amortization}}{P - VC}$$

2. $$DOL = \frac{Q(P - VC)}{Q(P - VC) - FC} \qquad (5\text{–}3a)$$

DOL is degree of operating leverage
Q is quantity at which DOL is computed
P is price per unit
VC is variable cost per unit
FC is fixed costs

3. $$DOL = \frac{S - TVC}{S - TVC - FC} \qquad (5\text{–}3b)$$

DOL is degree of operating leverage
S is sales (*QP*) at which DOL is computed
TVC is total variable costs
FC is fixed costs

4. $DFL = \dfrac{EBIT}{EBIT - I}$ (5–5)

DFL is degree of financial leverage
$EBIT$ is earnings before interest and taxes
I is interest

5. $EBIT^* = \dfrac{(S_B \times I_A - S_A \times I_B)}{S_B - S_A}$ (5–6)

$EBIT^*$ is operating income at the indifference point
I is interest costs under plan A and B
S is shares outstanding under plan A and B

6. $DCL = \dfrac{Q(P - VC)}{Q(P - VC) - FC - I}$ (5–8a)

DCL is degree of combined leverage
Q is quantity at which DCL is computed
P is price per unit
VC is variable cost per unit
FC is fixed costs
I is interest

7. $DCL = \dfrac{S - TVC}{S - TVC - FC - I}$ (5–8b)

DCL is degree of combined leverage
S is sales (QP) at which DCL is computed
TVC is total variable costs
FC is fixed costs
I is interest

List of Terms

leverage (concept in general) 134
operating leverage 135
fixed costs 136
variable costs 136
contribution margin 137
break-even analysis 141
degree of operating leverage (DOL) 141
nonlinear break-even analysis 144
financial leverage 145
degree of financial leverage (DFL) 147
EBIT/EPS indifference point 149
leveraged buyout 150
combined leverage 151
degree of combined leverage (DCL) 152

Discussion Questions

1. Discuss the various uses for break-even analysis.
2. Which factors would cause a difference between the use of financial leverage for a utility company and an automobile company?
3. Explain how the break-even point and operating leverage are affected by the choice of manufacturing facilities (labour-intensive versus capital-intensive).
4. What role does amortization play in break-even analysis based on accounting flows? Based on cash flows? Which perspective is longer-term in nature?
5. What does risk taking have to do with the use of operating and financial leverage?
6. Discuss the limitations of financial leverage.
7. How does the interest rate on new debt influence the use of financial leverage?

8. Explain how combined leverage brings together operating income and earnings per share.
9. Explain why operating leverage decreases as a company increases sales and shifts away from the break-even point.
10. Why does the starting level of sales determine the degree of operating leverage rather than the ending level of sales?
11. One could say that financial leverage has its most important impact on earnings per share rather than net income after taxes. How would you support this statement?
12. Does being at the EPS indifference point mean that you are always indifferent between two financing plans? Explain.
13. Discuss the concept of operating leverage as you think it would apply to a major, independent television broadcaster.
14. Explore the failure of the leveraged buyouts by Campeau Corporation. (Research of financial newspapers from the 1989 to early 1990 period is suggested, or *Foundations of Financial Management,* 4th ed., Chapter 20.)

INTERNET RESOURCES AND QUESTIONS

The latest financial statements of publicly traded Canadian companies are available at www.sedar.com

1. Based on the latest available financial results (note the date) calculate and comment on the DOL, DFL, and DCL of the following companies:
   a. Air Canada
   b. Royal Bank
   c. Onex
   d. EnCana

   Explain the relationship between operating and financial leverage for each company and the resultant combined leverage. What accounts for the differences in leverage among these companies?

www.mcgrawhill.ca/college/block

Problems

1. Shock Electronics sells portable heaters for $25.00 per unit, and the variable cost to produce them is $17.00. Mr. Amps estimates that the fixed costs are $96,000.
   a. Compute the break-even point in units.
   b. Fill in the table below (in dollars) to illustrate that the break-even point has been achieved.

Sales	______
− variable costs	______
Contribution margin	______
− fixed costs	______
Total operating profit (loss)	______

2. The Hazardous Toys Company produces boomerangs that sell for $8.00 each and have a variable cost of $7.50. There are $15,000 in fixed costs involved in the production process.
   a. Compute the break-even point in units.
   b. Find the sales (in units) needed to earn a profit of $25,000.

3. Therapeutic Systems sells its products for $8.00 per unit. It has the following costs.

Rent	$120,000	Factory labour	$1.50 per unit
Executive salaries	112,000	Raw materials	0.70 per unit

Separate the expenses between fixed and variable costs per unit. Using this information and the sales price per unit of $8.00, compute the break-even point.

4. Jay Linoleum Company has fixed costs of $70,000. Its product currently sells for $4.00 per unit and has variable costs per unit of $2.60. Mr. Thomas, the head of manufacturing, proposes to buy new equipment that will cost $300,000 and drive up fixed costs to $105,000. Although the price will remain at $4.00 per unit, the increased automation will reduce variable costs per unit to $2.25.
   a. Calculate the break-even point before and after acquiring the new equipment.
   b. Find the required sales (in units) to generate a profit that represents a 20 percent return on the fixed costs before and after acquiring the new equipment.
5. Gibson & Sons, an appliance manufacturer, computes its break-even point strictly on the basis of cash expenditures related to fixed costs. Its total fixed costs are $1.2 million, but 25 percent of this value is represented by amortization. Its contribution margin (price minus variable cost) for each unit sold is $2.40. How many units does the firm need to sell to reach the cash break-even point?
6. Draw two break-even graphs—one for a conservative firm using labour-intensive production and another for a capital-intensive firm. Assuming these companies compete within the same industry and have identical sales, explain the impact of changes in sales volume on both firms' profits.

7. The Ripken Company produces baseball gloves. The company's income statement for 2002 is as follows:

RIPKEN COMPANY
Income Statement
Year ended December 31, 2002

Sales (30,000 gloves at $70 each)	$2,100,000
Less: Variable costs (30,000 gloves at $30)	900,000
Contribution margin	1,200,000
Less: Fixed costs	700,000
Earnings before interest and taxes (EBIT)	500,000
Interest expense	120,000
Earnings before taxes (EBT)	380,000
Income tax expense (30%)	114,000
Earnings aftertaxes (EAT)	$ 266,000

Given this income statement, compute the following:
   a. Degree of operating leverage.
   b. Degree of financial leverage.
   c. Degree of combined leverage.
   d. Break-even point in units.
   e. Break-even point considering the interest expense as a fixed cost.

8. Freudian Slips and Gowns, Inc., income statement for 2002 is as follows:

FREUDIAN SLIPS AND GOWNS
Income Statement
Year ended December 31, 2002

Sales (30,000 units at $25)	$750,000
Less: Variable costs (30,000 units at $7)	210,000
Contribution margin	540,000
Less: Fixed costs	270,000
Operating profit or (EBIT)	270,000
Interest expense	170,000
Earnings before taxes (EBT)	100,000
Income tax expense (35%)	35,000
Earnings aftertaxes (EAT)	$ 65,000

Given this income statement, compute the following:

a. Degree of operating leverage.

b. Degree of financial leverage.

c. Degree of combined leverage.

d. Break-even point in units.

e. Break-even point considering the interest expense as a fixed cost.

9. University Catering sells 50-kilo bags of popcorn to university dormitories for $10.00 a bag. The fixed costs of this operation are $80,000, while the variable costs of the popcorn are $0.10 per pound.

a. What is the break-even point in bags?

b. Calculate the profit or loss on 12,000 bags and 25,000 bags.

c. What is the degree of operating leverage at 20,000 bags and 25,000 bags? Why does the degree of operating leverage change as quantity sold increases?

d. If University Catering has an annual interest payment of $10,000, calculate the degree of financial leverage at both 20,000 and 25,000 bags.

e. What is the degree of combined leverage at both sales levels?

10. Leno's Drug Stores and Hall Pharmaceuticals are competitors in the discount chain drugstore business. The separate capital structures for Leno's and Hall are presented below.

Leno's		**Hall**	
Debt @ 10%	$100,000	Debt @ 10%	$200,000
Common stock	200,000	Common stock	100,000
Total	$300,000	Total	$300,000
Common shares	20,000	Common shares	10,000

a. Compute earnings per share if earnings before interest and taxes are $20,000, $30,000, and $120,000 (assume a 30 percent tax rate).

b. Explain the relationship between earnings per share and level of EBIT.

c. If the cost of debt went up to 12 percent and all other factors remained equal, what would be the point of indifference point for EBIT?

11. In the previous problem, compute the stock price for Hall Pharmaceuticals if it sells at 13 times earnings per share and EBIT is $80,000.
12. Firms in Japan often employ both high operating and financial leverage because of the use of modern technology and close borrower-lender relationships. Assume the Susaki Company has a sales volume of 100,000 units at a price of $25.00 per unit; variable costs are $5.00 per unit and fixed costs are $1,500,000. Interest expense is $250,000. What is the degree of combined leverage for this Japanese firm?
13. Glynn Enterprises and Monroe, Inc., both produce fluid control products. Their financial information is as follows:

Capital Structure		
	Glynn	**Monroe**
Debt @ 10%	$1,500,000	0
Common stock, $10 per share	500,000	2,000,000
	$2,000,000	$2,000,000
Common shares	50,000	200,000
Operating Plan		
Sales (200,000 units at $5 each)	$1,000,000	$1,000,000
Less: Variable costs	600,000	200,000
	($3 per unit)	($1 per unit)
Fixed costs	0	400,000
Earnings before interest and taxes (EBIT)	$ 400,000	$ 400,000

a. If you combine Glynn's capital structure with Monroe's operating plan, what is the degree of combined leverage?

b. If you combine Monroe's capital structure with Glynn's operating plan, what is the degree of combined leverage?

c. Explain why you got the results you did in parts *a* and *b.*

d. In part *b,* if sales double, by what percentage will EPS increase?

14. DeSoto Tools, Inc. is planning to expand production. The expansion will cost $300,000, which can either be financed by bonds at an interest rate of 14 percent or by selling 10,000 shares of common stock at $30.00 per share. The current income statement before expansion is as follows:

DESOTO TOOLS, INC.
Income Statement
Year ended Dec. 31, 2002

Sales	$1,500,000
Variable costs	450,000
Contribution margin	1,050,000
Fixed costs	550,000
Earnings before interest and taxes	500,000
Interest expense	100,000
Earnings before taxes	400,000
Taxes @ 34%	136,000
Earnings aftertaxes	$ 264,000
Shares	100,000
Earnings per share	$2.64

After the expansion, sales are expected to increase by $1 million. Variable costs will remain at 30 percent of sales, and fixed costs will increase to $800,000. The tax rate is 34 percent.

a. Calculate the degree of operating leverage, the degree of financial leverage, and the degree of combined leverage before expansion.

b. Construct the income statement for the two financial plans after expansion.

c. Calculate the degree of operating leverage, the degree of financial leverage, and the degree of combined leverage, after expansion, for the two financing plans.

d. Calculate the EBIT/EPS indifference point.

e. Explain which financing plan you favor and the risks involved.

15. Dickinson Company has $12 million in assets. Currently half of these assets are financed with long-term debt at 10 percent and half are financed with common stock. Ms. Smith, vice-president of finance, wishes to analyze two refinancing plans, one with more debt (D) and one with more equity (E). The company earns a return on assets before interest and taxes of 10 percent. The tax rate is 45 percent.

Under Plan D, a $3 million long-term bond would be sold at an interest rate of 12 percent and 375,000 shares of stock would be purchased in the market at $8.00 per share and retired.

Under Plan E, 375,000 shares of stock would be sold at $8.00 per share and the $3 million in proceeds would be used to reduce long-term debt.

a. How would each of these plans affect earnings per share? Consider the current plan and the two new plans.

b. Which plan would be most favourable if return on assets fell to 5 percent? Increased to 15 percent? Consider the current plan and the two new plans.

c. Calculate the EBIT/EPS indifference point.

d. If the market price for common stock rose to $12.00 before the restructuring, which plan would then be most attractive? Continue to assume that $3 million in debt will be used to retire stock in Plan D and $3 million of new equity will be sold to retire debt in Plan E. Also assume that return on assets is 10 percent.

e. Calculate the EBIT/EPS indifference point at the new share price.

16. Johnson Grass and Garden Centres has $20 million in assets, 75 percent financed by debt and 25 percent financed by common stock. The interest rate on the debt is 12 percent, and the stock book value is $10.00 per share. President Johnson is considering two financing plans for an expansion to $30 million in assets.

Under Plan A, the debt-to-total-assets-ratio will be maintained, but new debt will cost 15 percent! New stock will be sold at $10.00 per share. Under Plan B, only new common stock at $10 per share will be issued. The tax rate is 40 percent.

a. If EBIT is 12 percent on total assets, compute earnings per share (EPS) before the expansion and under the two alternatives.

b. What is the degree of financial leverage under each of the three plans?

c. Calculate the EBIT/EPS indifference point.

d. If shares could be sold at $20.00 each due to increased expectations for the firm's sales and earnings, what impact would this have on earnings per share for the two expansion alternatives? Compute earnings per share for each.

e. Calculate the EBIT/EPS indifference point at the new share price.

f. Explain why corporate financial officers are concerned about their share values!

17. Mr. Katz is in the widget business. He currently sells 2 million widgets a year at $4 each. His variable cost to produce the widgets is $3.00 per unit, and he has $1.5 million in fixed costs. His

sales-to-assets ratio is 4 times, and 40 percent of his assets are financed with 9 percent debt, with the balance financed by common stock at $10.00 per share. The tax rate is 30 percent.

His brother-in-law, Mr. Doberman, says he is doing it all wrong.

By reducing his price to $3.75 a widget, he could increase his volume of units sold by 40 percent. Fixed costs would remain constant, and variable costs would remain $3.00 per unit. His sales-to-assets ratio would be 5 times. Furthermore, he could increase his debt-to-assets ratio to 50 percent, with the balance in common stock. It is assumed that the interest rate would go up by 1 percent and the price of stock would remain constant.

a. Compute earnings per share under the Katz plan.

b. Compute earnings per share under the Doberman plan.

c. Mr. Katz's wife does not think that fixed costs would remain constant under the Doberman plan; she believes they would go up by 20 percent. If this is the case, should Mr. Katz shift to the Doberman plan, based on earnings per share?

18. Highland Cable Company is considering an expansion of its facilities. Its current income statement is as follows:

Sales	$4,000,000
Less: Variable expense (50% of sales)	2,000,000
Fixed expense	1,500,000
Earnings before interest and taxes (EBIT)	500,000
Interest (10% cost)	140,000
Earnings before taxes (EBT)	360,000
Tax (30%)	108,000
Earnings aftertaxes (EAT)	$ 252,000
Shares of common stock	200,000
Earnings per share	$1.26

Highland Cable Company is currently financed with 50 percent debt and 50 percent equity (common stock, par value of $10.00). To expand facilities, Mr. Highland estimates a need for $2 million in additional financing. His investment dealer has laid out three plans for him to consider:

1. Sell $2 million of debt at 13 percent.
2. Sell $2 million of common stock at $20 per share.
3. Sell $1 million of debt at 12 percent and $1 million of common stock at $25.00 per share.

Variable costs are expected to stay at 50 percent of sales, while fixed expenses will increase to $1.9 million per year. Mr. Highland is not sure how much this expansion will add to sales, but he estimates that sales will rise by $1 million per year for the next five years.

Mr. Highland is interested in a thorough analysis of his expansion plans and methods of financing. He would like you to analyze the following:

a. The break-even point for operating expenses before and after expansion (in sales dollars).

b. The degree of operating leverage before and after expansion. Assume sales of $4 million before expansion and $5 million after expansion.

c. The degree of financial leverage before expansion at sales of $4 million and for all three methods of financing after expansion. Assume sales of $5 million for the second part of this question.

d. Compute EPS under all three methods of financing the expansion at $5 million in sales (first year) and $9 million in sales (last year).

e. What can we learn from the answer to part *d* about the advisability of the three methods of financing the expansion? Make your selection of the financing method that best suits Mr. Highland's objective of maximizing shareholders' wealth.

COMPREHENSIVE PROBLEMS

19.

ASPEN SKI COMPANY
Balance Sheet
December 31, 2002

Assets		**Liabilities and Shareholders' Equity**	
Cash	$ 40,000	Accounts payable	$1,800,000
Marketable securities	60,000	Accrued expenses	100,000
Accounts receivable	1,000,000	Notes payable (current)	600,000
Inventory	3,000,000	Bonds (10%)	2,000,000
Gross plant and equipment	5,000,000	Common stock	
less: accumulated		(1.5 million shares)	1,500,000
amortization	2,000,000	Retained earnings	1,100,000
Total assets	$7,100,000	Total liabilities and shareholders' equity	$7,100,000

Income Statement
Year ended Dec. 31, 2002

Sales (credit)	$6,000,000
Variable costs (0.60)	3,600,000
Contribution margin	2,400,000
Fixed costs*	1,800,000
Operating profit	600,000
Less: Interest	200,000
Earnings before taxes	400,000
Less: Taxes @ 40%	160,000
Earnings after taxes	$ 240,000
Dividends	43,200
Increased retained earnings	$ 196,800

*Fixed costs include (*a*) lease expense of $190,000 and (*b*) amortization of $400,000.

Note: Aspen Ski also has $100,000 per year in sinking fund obligations associated with its bond issue. The sinking fund represents an annual repayment of the principal amount of the bond. It is not tax deductible.

Ratios

	Aspen Ski (to be Filled in)	Industry
Profit margin		6.1%
Return on assets		6.5%
Return on equity		8.9%
Receivables turnover		4.9×
Inventory turnover		4.4×
Accounts payable turnover		5.8×
Capital-asset turnover		2.1×
Total-asset turnover		1.06×
Current ratio		1.4×
Quick ratio		1.1×
Debt to total assets		27%
Interest coverage		4.2×
Fixed charge coverage		3.0×

a. Analyze Aspen Ski Company using ratio analysis. Compute the ratios above for Aspen and compare them to the industry data that is given. Discuss the weak points, strong points, and what you think should be done to improve the company's performance.

b. In your analysis, calculate the overall break-even point in sales dollars and the cash break-even point. Also compute the degree of operating leverage, degree of financial leverage, and degree of combined leverage.

c. Use the information in parts *a* and *b* to discuss the risk associated with this company. Given the risk, decide whether a bank should loan funds to Aspen Ski. Aspen Ski Company is trying to plan the funds needed for 2003. The management anticipates an increase in sales of 20 percent, which can be absorbed without increasing capital assets.

d. What would be Aspen's needs for external funds based on the current balance sheet? Compute RNF (required new funds). Notes payable (current) and bonds are not part of the liability calculation.

e. What would be the required new funds if the company brings its ratios into line with the industry average during 2003? Specifically examine receivables turnover, inventory turnover, and the profit margin. Use the new values to recompute the factors in RNF (assume liabilities stay the same).

f. Do not calculate, only comment on the following questions. How would required new funds change if the company:

1. Were at full capacity?
2. Raised the dividend payout ratio?
3. Suffered a decreased growth in sales?
4. Faced an accelerated inflation rate?

20. Rockway Framers Ltd. has requested a bank loan for a one-year period to refinance most of its notes payable. It would be supported by Rockway's current assets. The following statements and industry averages accompanied the loan request.

Prepare a statement of changes in financial position for Rockway and complete a ratio analysis. Also prepare pro forma statements for 2003 on the basis of the same financial relationships as in 2002, no new capital asset purchases, and a sales increase of 25 percent. Recommend support or rejection of the loan request.

ROCKWAY FRAMERS LTD.
Balance Sheets
December 31

	2002	2001
Current assets:		
Cash	$ 1,300	$ 20,000
Accounts receivable	36,000	28,000
Inventories	101,000	64,500
Total current assets	138,300	112,500
Land	57,700	44,500
Buildings and equipment	222,000	155,000
Less: Accumulated amortization	85,000	62,000
Total assets	$333,000	$250,000
Current liabilities:		
Accounts payable	$ 48,770	$ 23,250
Notes payable	104,500	37,750
Total current liabilities	153,270	61,000
Long-term debt	51,000	64,000
Common stock	70,000	70,000
Retained earnings	58,730	55,000
Total liabilities and equity	$333,000	$250,000

ROCKWAY FRAMERS LTD.
Income Statements
Year ended Dec. 31

	2002	2001
Sales	$355,200	$277,500
Cost of goods sold	213,120	166,500
Gross profit	142,080	111,000
Sales and administration expenses	82,140	74,370
Amortization	23,000	10,000
Operating income	36,940	26,630
Interest	14,200	6,800
Earnings before taxes	22,740	19,830
Taxes	5,685	4,958
Net income	$ 17,055	$ 14,872

Industry Averages

Profit margin	3.50%
Return on assets	4.00%
Return on equity	8.20%
Gross margin	38.00%
Receivables turnover	9.73 times
Average collection period	37.51 days
Inventory turnover	2.50 times
Capital asset turnover	2.08 times
Total asset turnover	1.14 times
Current ratio	1.80
Quick ratio	0.70
Debt to total assets	58.00%
Times interest earned	3.80 times

21. Furniture magnate Carl Thompson couldn't believe the amount of pressure security analysts could put on a firm. The Glen Mount Furniture Company was a leading manufacturer of fine home furnishings and distributed its products directly to department stores, independent home furnishing retailers, and a few regional furniture chains. The firm specialized in bedroom, dining room, and living room furniture and had three plants in Quebec and two in Ontario. Its home office was in Granby, Quebec.

In a recent presentation to the Montreal chapter of the Financial Analysts Federation, Carl Thompson barely had taken a bite out of his salad when two analysts from a stock brokerage firm began asking questions. They were particularly concerned about Glen Mount's growth rate in earnings per share.

Carl was aware that security analysts considered earnings performance to be important, but he was somewhat distressed by the fact that this seemed to be their overriding concern. It bothered him that the firm had just spent over $10 million to develop exciting new product lines, modernize production facilities, and expand distribution capabilities, and yet all the questions seemed to deal with near-term earnings performance. He believed he would eventually have an opportunity to discuss the above-mentioned management initiatives and their impact on the company for the next decade, but current earnings per share seemed to gather the attention of the analysts.

Carl knew only too well from past experience that the earnings performance of the firm would affect the company's price-earnings ratio and its market value. Furthermore, before Carl became president of Glen Mount Furniture Company, he had attended a six-week executive development program at the Western Business School in which he heard a number of professors stress the importance of the goal of shareholder wealth maximization. He often wondered if other items were not equally important to the company, such as community service. (The firm donated $60,000 a year to a local university to help supplement faculty salaries for outstanding professors.) He also had a sense of pride that his firm provided employment to over 500 people in the area. He was not sure that the security analysts would consider these items important.

With all of these thoughts in mind, his upcoming meeting with Chief Financial Officer Barbara Bainesworth became particularly important.

When Barbara arrived, she had a number of financial documents to review before making key decisions. In Figure 1, she showed the earnings performance of the company over the past five years. Figure 2 provided a current balance sheet, and Figure 3 represented an abbreviated income statement for 2002.

The firm was considering buying back 625,000 shares of stock outstanding at $16.00 per share. This would represent $10 million in total. The funds to purchase the shares would be acquired from a new bond issue that would carry an interest rate of 11.25 percent. The bond would have a 15-year life. The firm was in a 34 percent tax bracket.

a. Project earnings per share for 2003 assuming that sales increase by $500,000. Use Figure 3 as the model for the calculation. Further assume that the capital structure is not changed.

b. By what percent did earnings per share increase from 2002 to 2003?

c. Now assume $10 million of debt replaces 625,000 shares of common stock as described in the case. The interest on the new debt will be 11.250 percent. What will projected earnings per share be for 2003 based on the anticipated sales increase of $500,000?

d. Based on your answer to part *c*, by what percent would earnings per share increase from 2002 to 2003?

e. Compute the degree of financial leverage (DFL) for the answer to part *a* and for the answer to part *c*.

f. Compute degree of combined leverage (DCL) for the answer to part *a* and the answer to part *c*.

g. What is the total-debt-to-total-assets ratio as shown in the 2002 balance sheet (Figure 2)? What will it be if $10 million worth of shareholders' equity is replaced with debt?

h. What do you think might happen to the share price as a result of replacing $10 million worth of shareholders' equity with debt? Consider any relevant factors.

FIGURE 1

Earnings per share for the past five years

Year	1st Quarter	2nd Quarter	3rd Quarter	4th Quarter	Yearly Total
1998	$0.23	$0.25	$0.19	$0.34	$1.01
1999	$0.26	$0.28	$0.27	$0.41	$1.22
2000	$0.34	$0.36	$0.33	$0.48	$1.51
2001	$0.35	$0.37	$0.34	$0.49	$1.55
2002	$0.35	$0.36	$0.36	$0.49	$1.56

FIGURE 2

GLEN MOUNT FURNITURE COMPANY
Comparative Balance Sheets
December 31, 2002
Assets

Current Assets:		
Cash		$ 350,000
Marketable securities		90,000
Accounts receivable		5,000,000
Inventory		7,000,000
Total current assets		12,440,000
Other assets:		
Investments		5,000,000
Capital assets:		
Plant and equipment	$27,060,000	
Less: accumulated amortization	4,000,000	
Net plant and equipment		23,060,000
Total assets		$40,500,000

Liabilities and Shareholders' Equity

Current liabilities:	
Accounts payable	$ 4,400,000
Wages payable	150,000
Accrued expenses	950,000
Total current liabilities	5,500,000
Long-term liabilities:	
Bonds payable, 10.625%	12,000,000
Shareholders' equity:	
Common stock	10,000,000
Retained earnings	13,000,000
Total shareholders' equity	23,000,000
Total liabilities and shareholders' equity	$40,500,000

FIGURE 3

GLEN MOUNT FURNITURE COMPANY
Abbreviated Income Statement
For the Year ending Dec. 31, 2002

Sales	$45,000,000
Less: Variable costs	26,100,000
Fixed costs	12,900,000
Operating profit (EBIT)	6,000,000
Interest	1,275,000
Earnings before taxes (EBT)	4,725,000
Taxes @ 34%	1,606,500
Earnings aftertaxes	$ 3,118,500
Shares	2,000,000
Earnings per share	$1.56

Selected References

Akers, Michael D., and Grover L. Porter. "Strategic Planning at Five World-Class Companies." *Management Accounting* 77 (July 1995), pp. 24–31.

Biais, Bruno, and Catherine Casamatta. "Optimal Leverage and Aggregate Investment." *Journal of Finance* 54 (August 1999), pp. 1291–1323.

Dennis, David J. "The Benefits of High Leverage from Kroger's Leveraged Recap and Safeway's LBO." *Journal of Applied Corporate Finance* 7 (Winter 1995), pp. 38–52.

D'Souze, Juliet, and William L. Megginson. "The Financial and Operating Performance of Privatized Finns during the 1990s." *Journal of Finance* 54 (August 1999), pp. 1397–1438.

Eales, Robert, and Edward Bosworth. "Severity of Loss in the Event of Default in Small Business and Larger Consumer Loans." *Journal of Lending and Credit Risk Management* 80 (May 1998), pp. 58–65.

Holthausen, Robert W., and David F. Larcker. "Performance, Leverage, and Ownership Structure in Reverse LBOs." *Journal of Applied Corporate Finance* 10 (Spring 1997), pp. 8–20.

Hull, Robert M. "Leverage Ratios, Industry Norms, and Stock Price Reaction: An Empirical Investigation of Stock-for-Debt Transactions." *Financial Management* 28 (Summer 1999), pp. 32–45.

Miller, Merton. "Leverage." *Journal of Applied Corporate Finance* 4 (Summer 1991), pp. 6–12.

O'Brien, Thomas J., and Paul A. Vanderheiden. "Empirical Measurement of Operating Leverage for Growing Firms." *Financial Management* 16 (Summer 1987), pp. 43–53.

Prezas, Alexandros P. "Effects of Debt on the Degree of Operating and Financial Leverage." *Financial Management* 16 (Summer 1987), pp. 329–44.

Sarig, Oded, and James Scott. "The Puzzle of Financial Leverage Clienteles." *Journal of Finance* 40 (December 1985), pp. 1459–67.

PART | THREE

WORKING CAPITAL MANAGEMENT

The financial manager's major focus is the efficient management of the firm's short-term assets and liabilities. Inventories and accounts receivable are significant investments and there are several competing financing sources available to the financial manager. The proper use of the techniques for managing these resources allows the firm to plan and implement its long-run strategies.

CHAPTER I SIX

6 Working Capital and the Financing Decision

LEARNING I OBJECTIVES

1 Define working capital management.

2 Describe the impact, asset growth has on working capital positions.

3 Identify working capital management considerations for; permanent components, the impact of sales/production schedules, and liquidity versus risk.

4 Identify the cash flow cycle of the firm.

5 Explain financing of assets in terms of hedging.

6 Describe the term structure of interest rates, explain the theories that suggest its shape, and identify how it may be of use to a financial manager.

7 Identify risk and profitability in determining the financing plan for current assets.

Working capital management entails arranging short-term financing to facilitate investment in the current assets of the firm. Financial managers probably devote more time to working capital management than to any other activity, in order to ensure adequate liquidity for the firm. For the small business, the maintenance of liquidity is critical to its survival, as the small firm is unlikely to have as much flexibility in short-term financing as the larger corporation. While long-term decisions involving capital assets or market strategy may determine the eventual success of the firm, short-term decisions on working capital determine whether the firm gets to the long term.

Changing sales levels impact inventory, receivables, and payables immediately, putting pressure on the cash resources of the firm. More and more cash (capital) will likely be tied up in current assets, as was demonstrated in Chapter 4. Some of the increased investment in current assets can be financed from profits reinvested in the firm. But in most cases, internal funds do not provide enough financing, and some external sources of funds must be found, particularly when sales growth accelerates. These funds may come from the sale of stock, long-term bonds, short-term securities, **trade credit,** and bank loans or from a combination of funding sources. As all these sources of capital have a cost to the firm, the financial manager must maintain liquidity while ensuring appropriate returns on the current asset investments.

In this chapter we examine the theories and general considerations in the interaction between current assets and liabilities that contribute to the firm's success. Asset growth, sales and production schedules, the cash flow cycle and their impact on liquidity are examined. The financial risk and return aspects of working capital management are identified in light of

Working Capital Is a Large Investment at Loblaw

Loblaw Companies Ltd. is Canada's largest food distributor, with sales reaching $20.0 billion in 2000. It is represented in all provinces at both the wholesale and retail levels. Many people may recognize President's Choice brand-name products or the Real Canadian Superstore. These are both part of Loblaw, that has George Weston Limited, as a majority shareholder.

The food business operates on very narrow margins. In 2000, Loblaw's gross profit, or trading margin, was $976 million or approximately 5 percent of sales. Net earnings were $473 million, for a profit margin of about 2.4 percent (Formula 3-1).

What is striking about Loblaw in comparison to companies in other industries is the large investment in current assets at over 32 percent of total assets. In 2000, $2.9 billion was invested in current assets, primarily in inventory. Total assets were $9.0 billion. To finance this position in current assets, Loblaw relied heavily on its suppliers. Accounts payable totalled $2.24 billion, with short-term loans and commercial paper adding $629 million. Net working capital was a negative $291 million. With equity of $3.1 billion, the suppliers of short-term capital had almost as much stake in Loblaw as the shareholders.

On a continuing basis, inventories, accounts receivable, and accounts payable are perhaps the most significant components of Loblaw's balance sheet. In a business with a low profit margin it is important that Loblaw maintain a high degree of liquidity.

FINANCE IN ACTION

Q1 What is Loblaw's latest working capital position?

Q2 Have the margins at Loblaw improved or deteriorated?

www.loblaw.com

Symbol: L

different financing patterns and interest rate changes, which leads to the development of an optimum policy. Chapter 7 will examine effective management of current assets and Chapter 8 will examine the effective management of current liabilities.

The Nature of Asset Growth

Any company that produces and sells a product, whether the product is consumer- or industry-oriented, has current assets and capital assets. If a firm grows, those assets are likely to increase over time. The key to current asset planning is the ability of management to forecast sales accurately and then to match the production schedules with the sales forecast. Whenever actual sales are different from forecasted sales, unexpected buildups or reductions in inventory occur that eventually affect receivables and cash flow.

In the simplest case (stage one), all of the firm's current assets are **self-liquidating assets** (sold at the end of a specified time period). For example, assume that at the start of the summer you buy 100 tires to be disposed of by September. It is your intention that all tires be sold, receivables collected, and bills paid over this time period. In this case, your working capital (current asset) needs are truly short term.

Now let us begin to expand the business. In stage two you add radios, seat covers, and batteries to your operation. Some of your inventory is again completely liquidated, while other items form the basic stock for your operation. To stay in business you must maintain floor displays and multiple items for selection. Furthermore, not all items will sell. As you eventually grow to more than one store, this permanent aggregate stock of current assets continues to increase. Problems of inadequate financing arrangements are often the result of the businessperson's failure to realize that the firm is carrying not only self-liquidating inventory, but is also likely to require **permanent current assets.**

If we look at the balance sheet at any time during the year, we are likely to see minimum levels of cash, accounts receivable, and inventory necessary to maintain sales. Although the individual receivable or inventory item is not always with the business, one can say these minimum levels are a permanent component of current assets.

FIGURE 6-1
The nature of asset growth

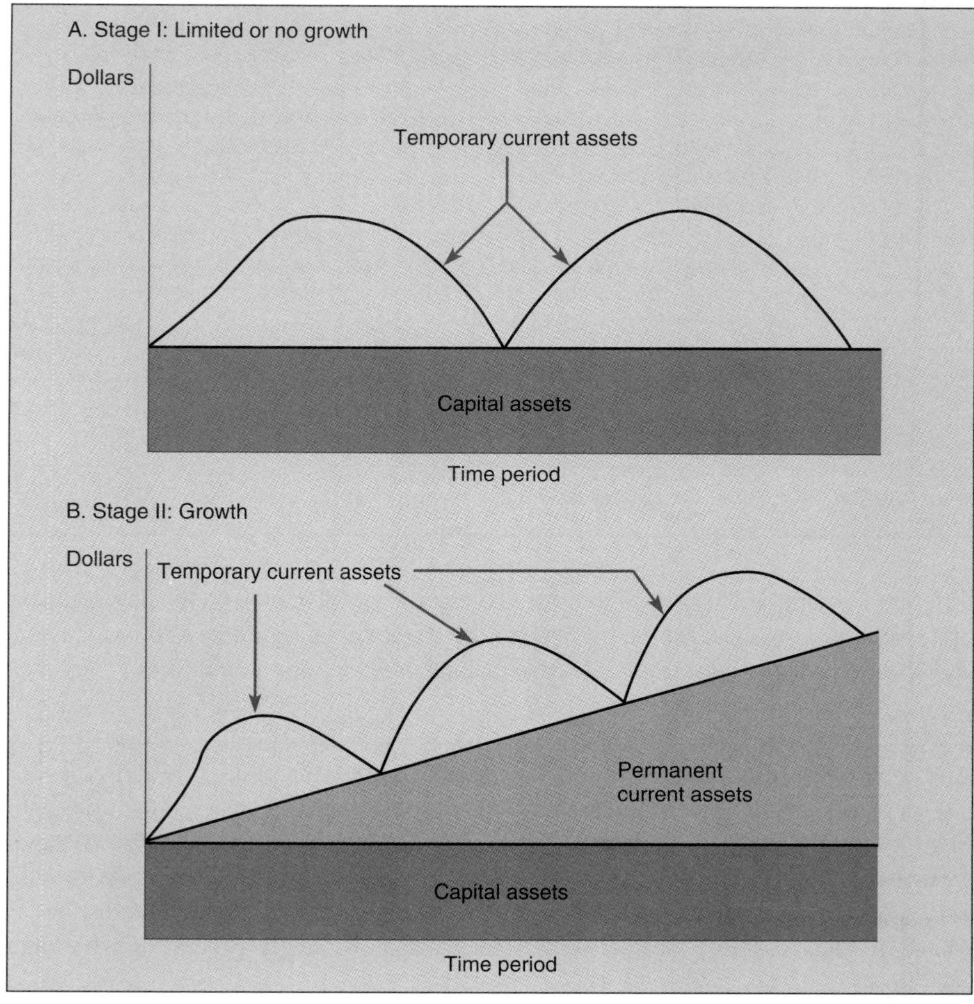

Figure 6-1 depicts the movement from stage one to stage two growth for a typical business. Panel A shows a buildup in **temporary current assets,** while in Panel B part of the growth in current assets is temporary and part is permanent. (Capital assets are included in the illustrations, but they are not directly related to the present discussion.)

Controlling Assets—Matching Sales and Production

In most firms capital assets grow slowly as productive capacity is increased and old equipment is replaced, but current assets fluctuate in the short run, depending on the level of production versus the level of sales. When the firm produces more than it sells, inventory rises. When sales rise faster than production, inventory declines and receivables rise.

As discussed in the treatment of the cash budgeting process in Chapter 4, some firms employ **level production** methods to smooth production schedules and to use labour and equipment efficiently at a lower cost. One consequence of level production is that current assets go up and down when sales and production are not equal. Other firms may try to match sales and production as closely as possible in the short run. This allows current assets to increase or decrease with the level of sales and eliminates the large seasonal bulges or sharp reductions in current assets that occur under level production.

Publishing companies are good examples of companies with seasonal sales and an inventory problem. By the nature of the textbook market, heavy sales are made in the third quarter of the year for fall semester sales. The bulk of the sales occurs in July and August and again in December for the second semester. The actual printing and binding of a book has fixed costs that make printing a large number of copies more efficient. Since publishing companies cannot reproduce books on demand, they contract with the printing company to print a fixed number of copies, depending on expected sales over at least a one-year period and sometimes based on sales over several years. If the books sell better than expected, the publishing company orders a second or a third printing. Orders may have to be placed as much as nine months before the books are actually needed, and reorders are placed as much as three or four months ahead of actual sales. If the book declines in popularity, the publisher could get stuck with a large inventory of obsolete books.

Figure 6-2 on the next page depicts quarterly sales and earnings of a Canadian book publisher, McGraw-Hill Ryerson. This is a good example of a company with seasonal sales. Note that the largest sales and earnings occur in the third quarter of each year. If company management has not planned its inventory correctly, the lost sales or excess inventory could be a serious problem. In 1994 large write-offs were incurred related to McGraw-Hill Ryerson's discontinued legal division. The assets were written off and were disposed of with no proceeds.

McGraw-Hill Ryerson Limited
www.mcgrawhill.ca/about+mhr

Retail firms such as Hudson's Bay and Sears Canada also have seasonal sales patterns. Figure 6-3 on page 177 shows the quarterly sales and earnings of these two companies. These retail companies do not stock a year or more of inventory at one time as do the publishers. They generally sell products made by other firms. Therefore, retail stores are not involved in deciding level versus seasonal production, but rather, they must match sales and inventory. Their suppliers must make the decision to produce on either a level or a seasonal basis. Since the selling seasons are very much affected by the weather and holiday periods, the suppliers and retailers cannot avoid inventory risk. The fourth quarter beginning in October and ending in December is the biggest quarter for retailers and usually accounts for 50 percent or more of their annual earnings. Of course, inventory not sold during the Christmas season probably ends up being discounted in January. Hudson's Bay took large write-offs in 1996 and again in 1997, revaluing its inventory.

Hudson's Bay Company
www.shareholder.com/hbc
Sears Canada
www.sears.ca/press.nsf/efinpr

These seasonal peaks and troughs are also reflected in cash, receivables, and inventory. We see that sales in the fourth quarter are usually 60 to 70 percent higher than those in the first quarter. Note how both companies demonstrate the impact of operating leverage on earnings, as discussed in Chapter 5. In fact, Sears often incurred losses in all but the fourth quarters over the period charted.

As we go through the chapter, we see that such highly seasonal sales can cause asset management problems. A financial manager must be aware of these to avoid getting caught short of cash or unprepared to borrow if necessary.

Many retail firms have been more successful in matching sales and orders in recent years because of new, computerized inventory control systems linked to online

FIGURE 6-2

Sales and Earnings for McGraw-Hill Ryerson, 1991–2001

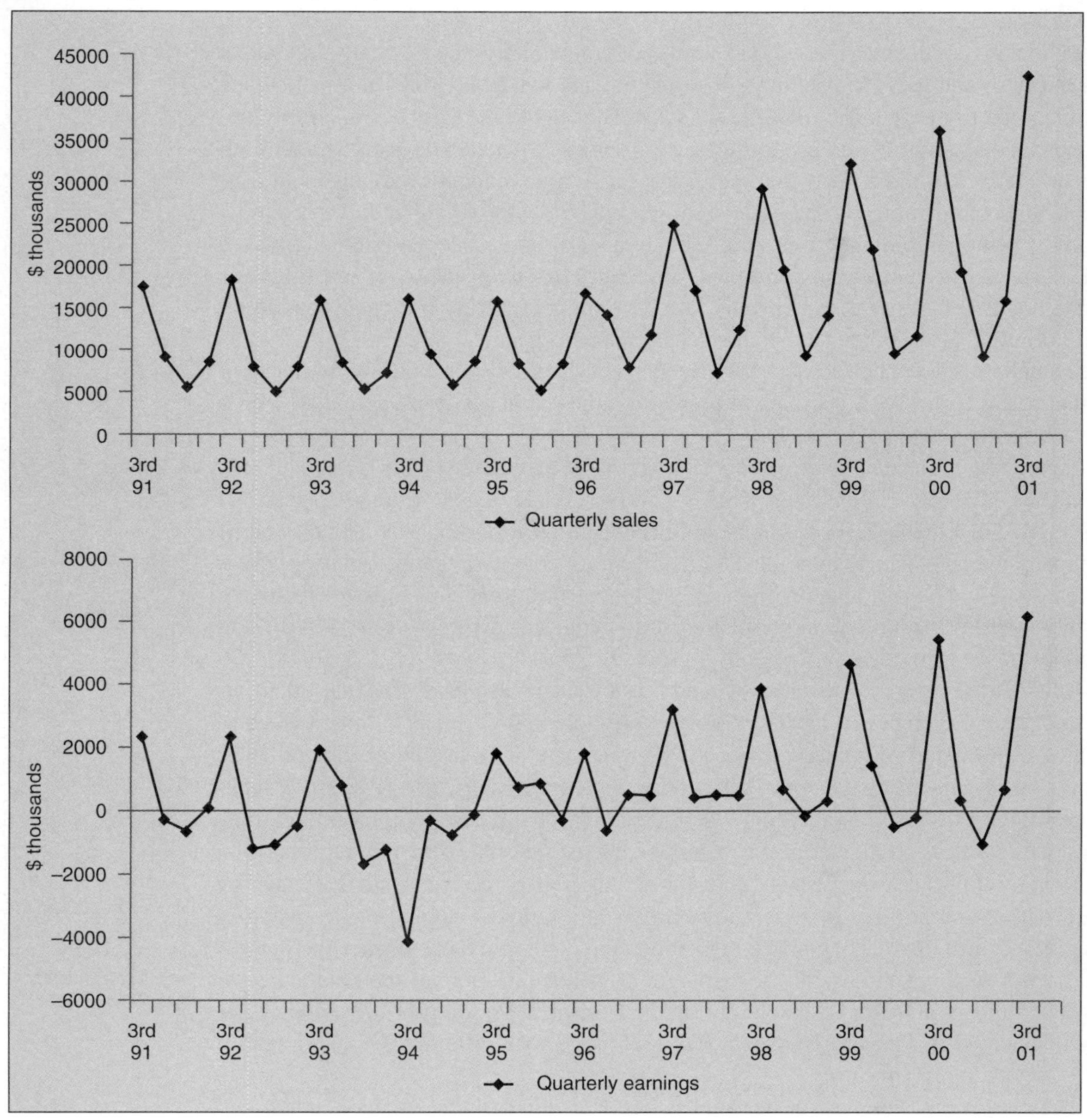

point-of-sale terminals. These point-of-sale terminals allow either digital input or use of optical scanners to record the inventory numbers and the amount of each item sold. At the end of the day managers can examine sales and inventory levels item by item and, if need be, adjust orders or production schedules. The predictability of the market influences the speed with which the manager reacts to this information, while the length and complexity of the ordering or production process dictate how fast inventory levels can be changed.

Managers are very concerned with the company's ability to quickly convert assets into cash. This is referred to as **liquidity.** The nature of many businesses requires that

FIGURE 6-3
Sales and earnings for Hudson's Bay Company and Sears Canada

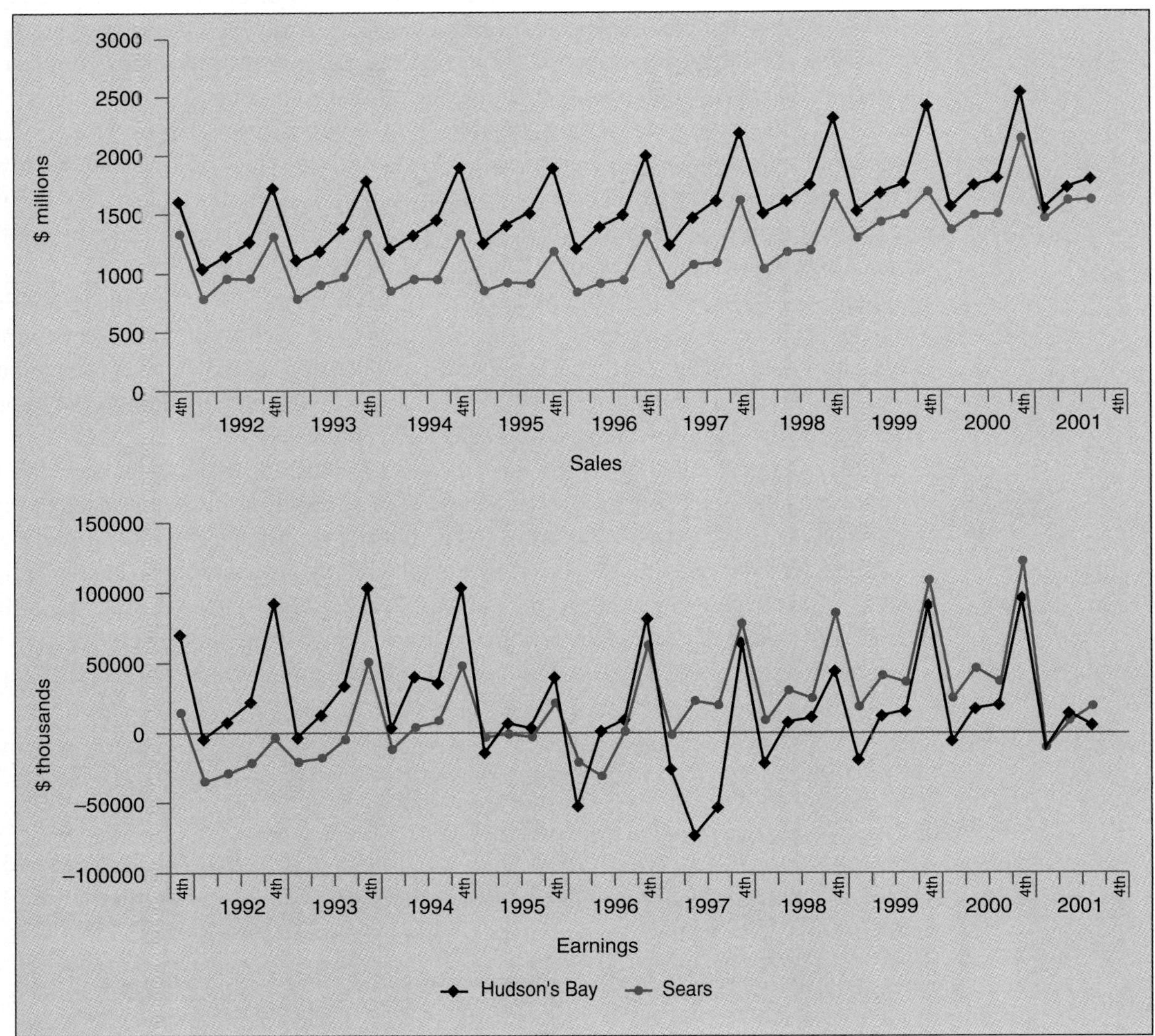

current assets be held to better serve clients. The onus is on managers to continually monitor the state of these current assets to ensure that they remain liquid, that is, readily converted to cash as the need arises. In Chapter 3, we identified the ratios that can be used to monitor the firm's liquidity.

On the other side of the ledger, it is important that management have well-developed credit facilities with support of suppliers and financial institutions to enhance the firm's liquidity. When a firm's liquidity is called into question it often is difficult to continue in business.

Cash Flow Cycle

Liquidity is largely determined by cash flowing through the company on a daily, weekly, and monthly basis as determined by the **cash flow cycle.** As discussed in

Chapter 4, the cash budget is a common tool used to track cash flows and resulting cash balances. Cash flow relies on the payment pattern of customers, the speed at which suppliers and creditors process cheques, and the efficiency of the banking system. These are the treasury functions of a corporation. Cash flow also relies on the efficiency of the production process to complete a finished product from raw materials, the ability to sell the product, and the collection of funds from clients. The primary consideration in managing the cash flow cycle is to ensure that inflows and outflows of cash are properly synchronized for transaction purposes. In this chapter we discuss the cyclical nature of asset growth and its impact on cash, receivables, and inventory, and we expand on that by examining the cash flow process more fully.

Figure 6-4 illustrates the simple cash flow cycle where the sale of finished goods or services produces either a cash sale or an account receivable for future collection. Eventually, the account receivable is collected and becomes cash, which is used to buy or produce inventory that is then sold. Thus, the cash-generating process is continuous even though the cash flow may be unpredictable and uneven.

McDonald's
www.mcdonalds.com

IBM
www.ibm.com

Sales, receivables, and inventory form the basis for cash flow, but other activities in the firm can also affect cash inflows and outflows. The cash flow cycle presented in Figure 6-6 on page 180 expands the detail and activities that influence cash. Cash inflows are driven by sales and are influenced by the type of customers, their geographical location, the product being sold, and the industry. A sale can be made for cash (e.g., McDonald's) or on credit (e.g., IBM). Some industries, such as textbook publishing, will grant credit terms of 60 days to bookstores; others, such as department stores, will grant

FIGURE 6-4
The cash flow cycle

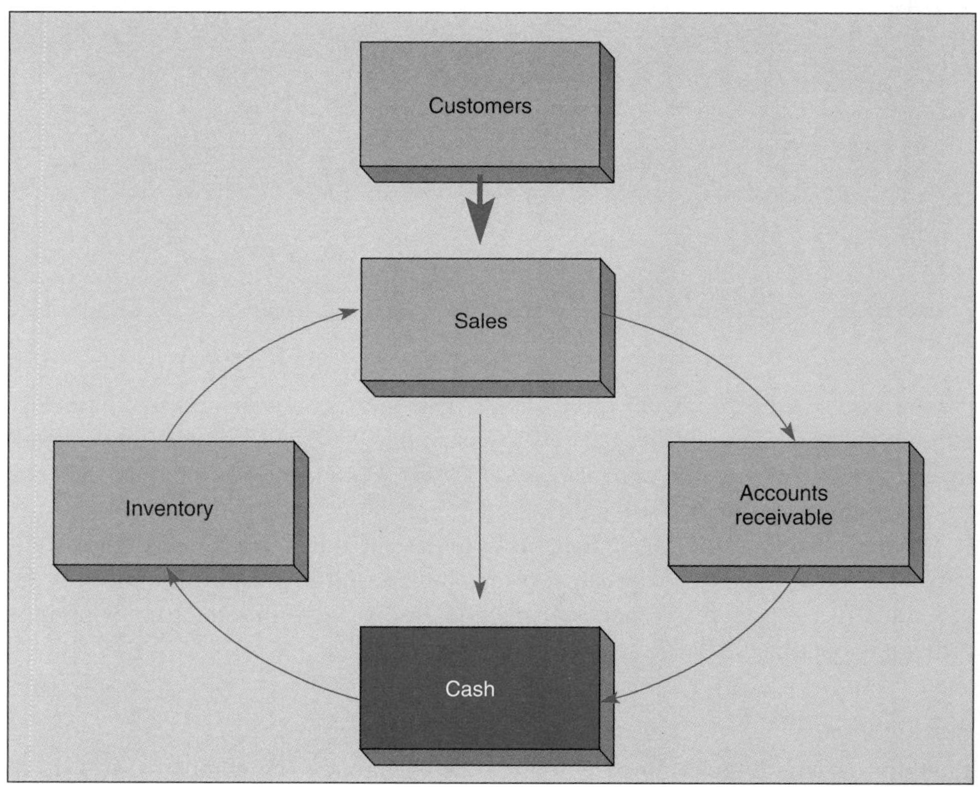

customers credit for 30 days. When receivables are paid, cash balances increase and the firm uses cash to pay interest to lenders, dividends to shareholders, taxes, suppliers, and wages, and to repurchase inventory. When the firm has excess cash, it invests in marketable securities, and when it needs cash for current assets, it usually either sells marketable securities or borrows funds from short-term lenders.

Beyond the cash flow cycle, the firm might calculate the time it takes from the initial outlay of funds for raw materials until the firm collects funds from its clients for the finished product. The time required to complete the cycle illustrated in Figure 6-4 will be offset to some degree by the firm's purchases bought on credit. This is shown in Figure 6-5. The combination of these time periods is referred to as the **cash conversion cycle** and utilizes the asset utilization formulas developed in Chapter 3. Realizing that cash flow is so vital to the firm we can understand why the utilization of assets is a major focus of management. Basically, the cash conversion cycle will consist of:

1. The time materials are in inventory (calculated as the inventory holding period, Formula 3-5b).
2. Plus the time it takes to collect sales from clients (calculated as the average collection period, Formula 3-4b).
3. Less the time the firm is allowed to delay payment to its suppliers (calculated as the accounts payable period, Formula 3-6b).

Examining Figure 6-5 we observe that there is a cash gap between the funds required for the inventory holding period through the collection period, and the funds provided from the accounts payable period. This time period gap will require that the firm obtain

FIGURE 6-5
Cash conversion cycle

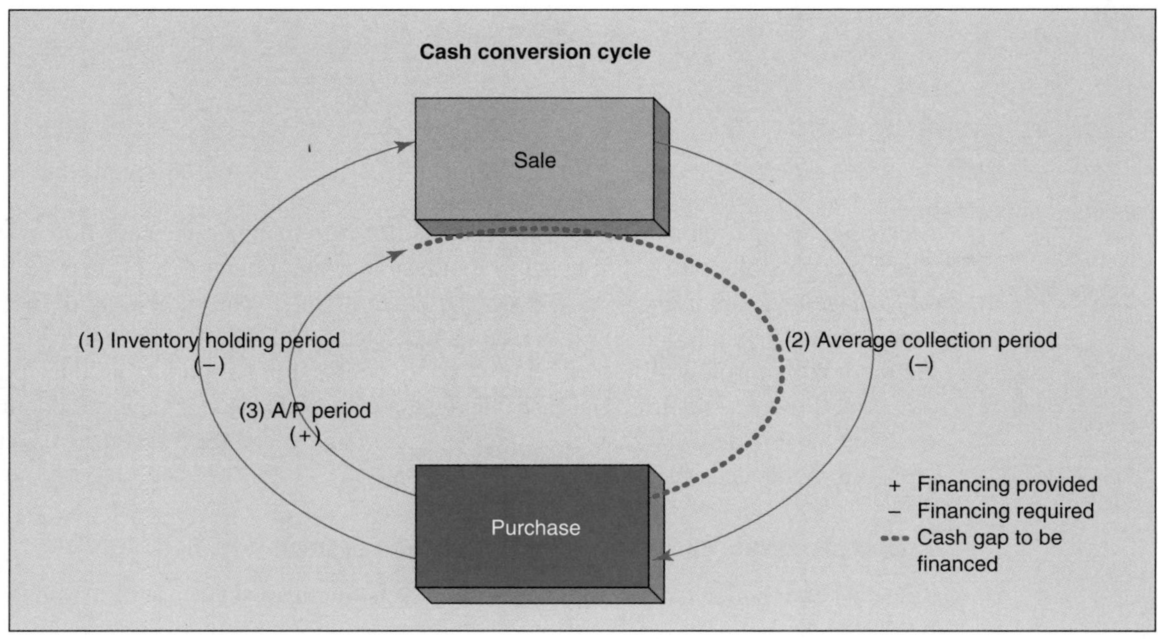

FIGURE 6-6
Expanded cash flow cycle

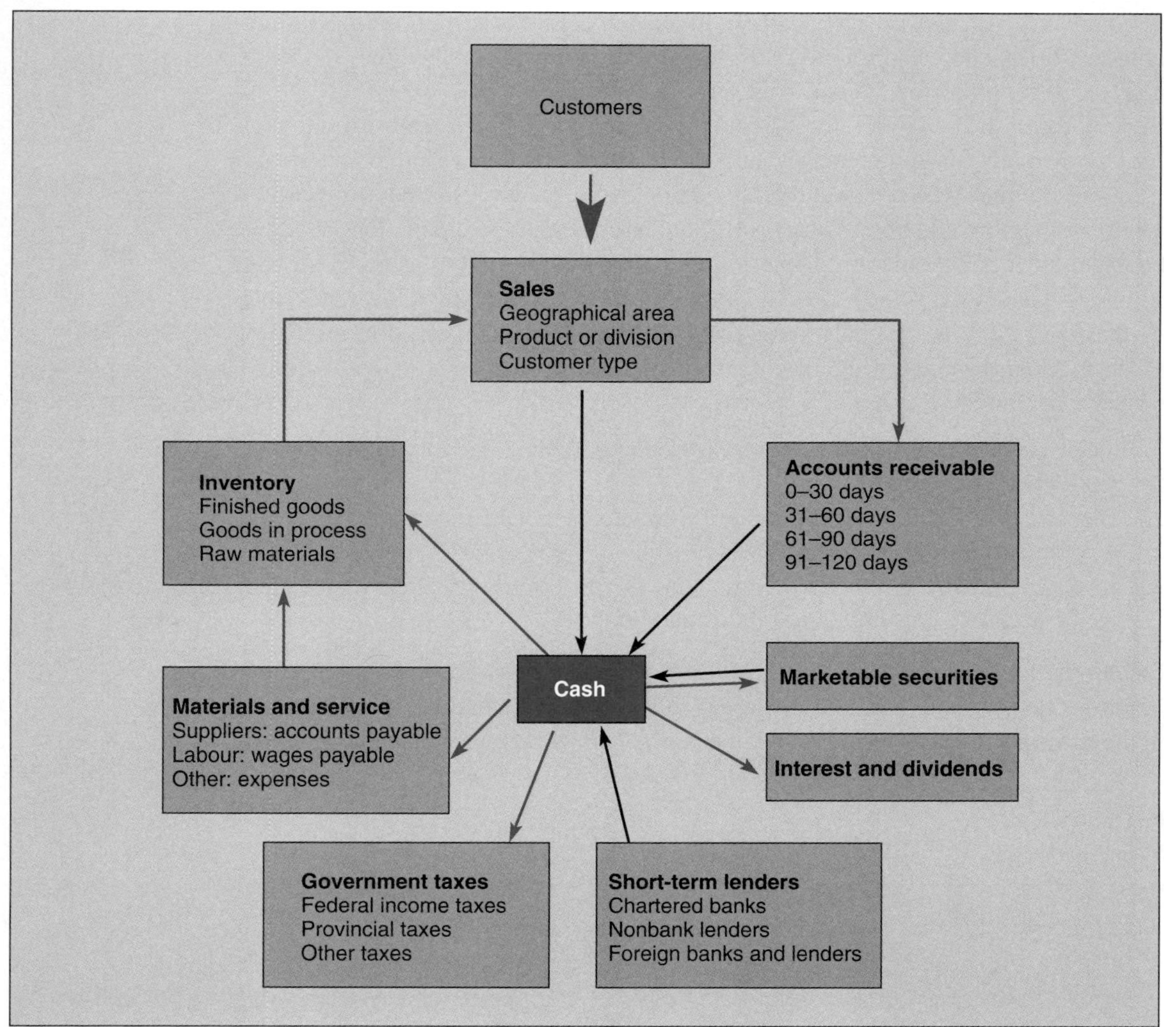

financing, likely from nonspontaneous sources if it is to maintain the cash flow cycle. The many possible sources of financing are illustrated later in Figure 6-11 on page 190.

Management can improve cash flow by shortening its inventory holding or collection periods or by lengthening its accounts payable period. The Loblaw's Finance in Action box that follows illustrates how the cash conversion period can produce positive cash flows for the firm. The cash conversion cycle because it is repeated continuously by most firms will create an ongoing or permanent need for financing to fill the cash gap, if it is negative as shown in Figure 6-5.

Temporary Assets under Level Production—An Example

To get a better understanding of how current assets fluctuate, let us use the example of the Yawakuzi Motorcycle Company, which manufactures in southern Ontario and sells throughout Canada. Not many Canadians buy motorcycles during October through

Loblaw's Cash Conversion Cycle Generates Cash

The assets at Loblaw must be turned over quickly to obtain reasonable returns for shareholders because of its low profit margin. The profit margin of 2.4 percent becomes a return on equity of over 15 percent by way of the high turnover of assets. In 2000 Loblaw's inventory position was $1.3 billion, with cost of goods sold at $18.9 billion, representing an inventory turnover rate of 14.4 times a year (Formula 3-5a), or put another way, inventory was held for about 25 days (Formula 3-5b). Accounts receivable at $381 million on sales of $20.1 billion had an average collection period of 7 days (Formula 3-4b), or a turnover rate of 53 times a year (Formula 3-4a). The accounts payable of $2.2 billion turned over 8.4 times a year (Formula 3-6a), which represented an accounts payable period of 43 days (Formula 3-6b).

Based on these numbers from its annual report, Loblaw actually had a positive cash conversion cycle of 11 days. The cash conversion cycle was determined from the inventory period of 25 days plus the collection period of 7 days less the accounts payable period of 43 days. This suggests that Loblaw received payment for its product before it had to pay its suppliers. By closely monitoring the components of its cash cycle, Loblaw generates a positive cash flow from its working capital investment.

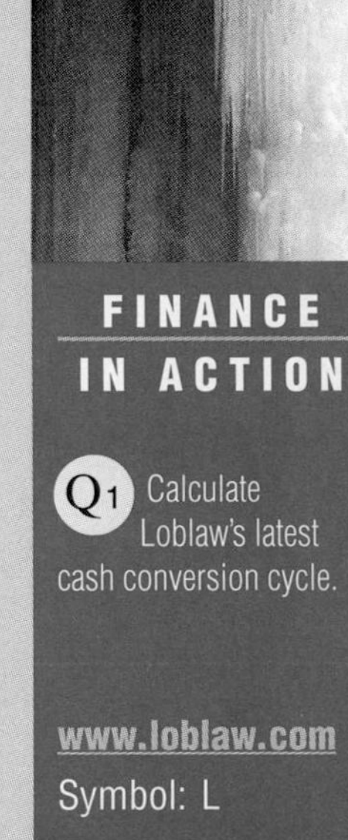

FINANCE IN ACTION

Q1 Calculate Loblaw's latest cash conversion cycle.

www.loblaw.com

Symbol: L

TABLE 6-1

Yawakuzi sales forecast (in units)

1st Quarter		2nd Quarter		3rd Quarter		4th Quarter	
October	300	January	0	April	1,000	July	2,000
November	150	February	0	May	2,000	August	1,000
December	50	March	600	June	2,000	September	500

Total sales of 9,600 units at $3,000 each = $28,800,000 in sales.

March, but sales pick up in early spring and summer and trail off during the fall. Because of the fixed assets and the skilled labour involved in the production process, Yawakuzi decides that level production is the least expensive and the most efficient production method. The marketing department provides a sales forecast for October through September (see Table 6-1).

After reviewing the sales forecast, Yawakuzi decides to produce 800 motorcycles per month, or one year's production of 9,600 divided by 12. A look at Table 6-2 on the next page shows how level production and seasonal sales combine to create fluctuating inventory. Assume October's beginning inventory is one month's production of 800 units. The production cost per unit is $2,000.

The inventory level at cost fluctuates from a high of $9 million in March, the last consecutive month in which production is greater than sales, to a low of $1 million in August, the last month in which sales are greater than production. Table 6-3 on page 183 combines a sales forecast, a cash receipts schedule, a cash payments schedule, and a brief cash budget to examine the buildup in accounts receivable and cash.

In Table 6-3 the *sales forecast* is based on assumptions in Table 6-1. The unit volume of sales is multiplied by a sales price of $3,000 to get sales dollars in millions. Next, *cash receipts* represent 50 percent collected in cash during the month of sale and 50 percent from the prior month's sales. For example, in October this would represent $0.45 million from the current month plus $0.75 million from the prior month's sales.

TABLE 6-2

Yawakuzi's production schedule and inventory

	Beginning Inventory	+	Production	−	Sales	=	Ending Inventory	Inventory (at cost of $2,000 per unit)
October	800		800		300		1,300	$2,600,000
November	1,300		800		150		1,950	3,900,000
December	1,950		800		50		2,700	5,400,000
January	2,700		800		0		3,500	7,000,000
February	3,500		800		0		4,300	8,600,000
March	4,300		800		600		4,500	9,000,000
April	4,500		800		1,000		4,300	8,600,000
May	4,300		800		2,000		3,100	6,200,000
June	3,100		800		2,000		1,900	3,800,000
July	1,900		800		2,000		700	1,400,000
August	700		800		1,000		500	1,000,000
September	500		800		500		800	1,600,000

Cash payments in Table 6-3 are based on an assumption of level production of 800 units per month at a cost of $2,000 per unit, or $1.6 million, plus payments for overhead, dividends, interest, and taxes.

Finally, the *cash budget* in Table 6-3 represents a comparison of the cash receipts and cash payments schedules to determine cash flow. We further assume that the firm desires a minimum cash balance of $0.25 million. Thus, in October a negative cash flow of $1.1 million brings the cumulative cash balance to a negative $0.85 million, and $1.1 million must be borrowed to provide an ending cash balance of $0.25 million. Similar negative cash flows in subsequent months necessitate expanding the bank loan. For example, in November there is a negative cash flow of $1.325 million. This brings the cumulative cash balance to $−1.075 million, requiring additional borrowings of $1.325 million to ensure a minimum cash balance of $0.25 million. The cumulative loan through November (October and November borrowings) now adds up to $2.425 million. Our cumulative bank loan is highest in the month of March.

We now wish to ascertain our total current asset buildup as a result of level production and fluctuating sales for October through September. The analysis is presented in Table 6-4 on page 184. The cash figures come directly from the last line of Table 6-3. The accounts receivable balance is based on the assumption that accounts receivable represent 50 percent of sales in a given month, as the other 50 percent is paid for in cash. Thus, the accounts receivable figure in Table 6-4 represents 50 percent of the sales figure from the second numerical line in Table 6-3. The inventory figure is taken directly from the last column of Table 6-2, which presented the production schedule and inventory data.

Total current assets start at $3.3 million in October and rise to $10.35 million in the peak month of April. From April through August, sales are larger than production and inventory falls to its low of $1.0 million in August, but accounts receivable peak at

TABLE 6-3

Sales forecast, cash receipts and payments, and cash budget ($millions)

	Oct.	Nov.	Dec.	Jan.	Feb.	March	April	May	June	July	Aug.	Sept.
Sales Forecast												
Sales (units)	300	150	50	0	0	600	1,000	2,000	2,000	2,000	1,000	500
Sales (unit price, $3,000)	$ 0.9	$ 0.45	$ 0.15	$ 0	$ 0	$ 1.8	$ 3.0	$ 6.0	$6.0	$ 6.0	$ 3.0	$ 1.5
Cash Receipts Schedule												
50% cash	$ 0.45	$ 0.225	$0.075	$ 0.000	$ 0	$ 0.9	$ 1.5	$ 3.0	$ 3.0	$ 3.0	$ 1.5	$0.75
50% from prior month's sales	0.75*	0.450	0.225	0.075	0	0.0	0.9	1.5	3.0	3.0	3.0	1.50
Total cash receipts	$ 1.20	$ 0.675	$0.300	$ 0.075	$ 0	$ 0.9	$ 2.4	$ 4.5	$ 6.0	$ 6.0	$ 4.5	$2.25
Cash Payments Schedule												
Constant production of 800 units/month (cost, $2,000 per unit)	$ 1.6	$ 1.6	$ 1.6	$ 1.6	$ 1.6	$ 1.6	$ 1.6	$ 1.6	$ 1.6	$ 1.6	$ 1.6	$ 1.6
Overhead	0.4	0.4	0.4	0.4	0.4	0.4	0.4	0.4	0.4	0.4	0.4	0.4
Dividends and interest	—	—	—	—	—	—	—	—	—	—	1.0	—
Taxes	0.3	—	—	0.3	—	—	0.3	—	—	0.3	—	—
Total cash payments	$ 2.3	$ 2.0	$ 2.0	$ 2.3	$ 2.0	$ 2.0	$ 2.3	$ 2.0	$ 2.0	$ 2.3	$ 3.0	$ 2.0
Cash Budget (required minimum balance is $0.25 million)												
Cash flow	$(1.10)	$(1.325)	$ (1.70)	$(2.225)	$(2.00)	$(1.10)	$0.10	$2.50	$4.00	$3.70	$ 1.5	$0.25
Beginning cash	0.25†	0.250	0.25	0.250	0.25	0.25	0.25	0.25	0.25	0.25	1.1	2.60
Cumulative cash balance	$(0.85)	$(1.075)	$ (1.45)	$(1.975)	$(1.75)	$(0.85)	$0.35	$2.75	$4.25	$3.95	$ 2.6	$2.85
Monthly loan or (repayment)	1.10	1.325	1.700	2.225	2.000	1.10	(0.10)	(2.50)	(4.00)	(2.85)	0	0
Cumulative loan	1.10	2.425	4.125	6.350	8.350	9.45	9.35	6.85	2.85	0.0	0	0
Ending cash balance	$ 0.25	$ 0.250	$ 0.250	$ 0.250	$ 0.250	$ 0.25	$0.25	$0.25	$0.25	$1.1	$ 2.6	$2.85

*Assumes September sales of $1.5 million.

†Assumes cash balance of $0.25 million at the beginning of October and that this is the desired minimum cash balance.

TABLE 6-4

Total current assets, first year ($millions)

	Cash	Accounts Receivable	Inventory	Total Current Assets
October	$0.25	$0.45	$2.6	$3.30
November	0.25	0.225	3.9	4.375
December	0.25	0.075	5.4	5.725
January	0.25	0.000	7.0	7.25
February	0.25	0.000	8.6	8.85
March	0.25	0.90	9.0	10.15
April	0.25	1.50	8.6	10.35
May	0.25	3.00	6.2	9.45
June	0.25	3.00	3.8	7.05
July	1.10	3:00	1.4	5.50
August	2.60	1.50	1.0	5.10
September	2.85	0.75	1.6	5.20

$3.0 million in the highest sales months of May, June, and July. The cash budget in Table 6-3 explains the cash flows and external funds borrowed to finance asset accumulation. From October to March, Yawakuzi borrows more and more money to finance the inventory buildup, but from April to July it eliminates all borrowing as inventory is liquidated and cash balances rise to complete the cycle. In October the cycle starts again; but now the firm has accumulated cash it can use to finance next year's asset accumulation, pay a larger dividend, replace old equipment or—if growth in sales is anticipated—invest in new equipment to increase productive capacity. Table 6-5 presents the cash budget and total current assets for the second year. Under a simplified, no-growth assumption, the monthly cash flow is the same as that of the first year, but beginning cash in October is much higher from the first year's ending cash balance. This lowers the borrowing requirement and increases the ending cash balance and total current assets at year-end. Higher current assets are present despite the fact accounts receivable and inventory do not change.

Figure 6-7 on page 186 is a graphic presentation of the current asset cycle. It corresponds to Figure 6-1 B, which demonstrates the nature of asset growth. Figure 6-7 includes the two years covered in Tables 6-4 and 6-5, assuming level production and no sales growth. We observe that there are minimum levels of current assets. These we consider permanent current assets.

Patterns of Financing

The financial manager's selection of external sources of funds to finance current assets may be one of the firm's most important decisions. The axiom that all current assets should be financed by current liabilities (accounts payable, bank loans, commercial paper, etc.) is subject to challenge when one sees the permanent buildup that can occur in current assets. In the Yawakuzi example, the buildup in inventory was substantial at $9 million. The example had a logical conclusion in that the motorcycles were sold, cash was generated, and current assets became very liquid. What if a much smaller sales level had occurred? Yawakuzi would be sitting on a large inventory that needed to be financed and would be generating no cash. Theoretically, the firm could be declared technically insolvent (bankrupt) if short-term sources of funds were used but were

TABLE 6-5

Cash budget and assets for second year with no growth in sales ($millions)

	End of First Year—	Second Year											
	Sept.	Oct.	Nov.	Dec.	Jan.	Feb.	March	April	May	June	July	Aug.	Sept.
Cash flow	$0.25	$(1.10)	$(1.325)	$(1.700)	$(2.225)	$(2.00)	$ (1.10)	$0.10	$2.50	$4.00	$3.70	$1.5	$0.25
Beginning cash	2.60	2.85	1.750	0.425	0.250	0.25	0.25	0.25	0.25	0.25	0.25	3.7	5.20
Cumulative cash balance		1.75	0.425	(1.275)	(1.975)	(1.75)	(0.85)	0.35	2.75	4.25	3.95	5.2	5.45
Monthly loan or (repayment)		—	—	1.525	2.225	2.00	1.10	(0.10)	(2.50)	(4.00)	(0.25)	—	—
Cumulative loan		—	—	1.525	3.750	5.75	6.85	6.75	4.25	0.25	0.00	—	—
Ending cash balance	$2.85	$1.75	$0.425	$0.25	$0.25	$0.25	$0.25	$0.25	$0.25	$0.25	$3.70	$5.2	$5.45
		Total Current Assets											
Ending cash balance	$2.85	$1.75	$0.425	$0.250	$0.25	$0.25	$0.25	$0.25	$0.25	$0.25	$3.70	$5.2	$5.45
Accounts receivable	0.75	0.45	0.225	0.075	0.00	0.00	0.90	1.50	3.00	3.00	3.00	1.5	0.75
Inventory	1.60	2.60	3.900	5.400	7.00	8.60	9.00	8.60	6.20	3.80	1.40	1.0	1.60
Total current assets	$5.20	$4.80	$4.550	$5.725	$7.25	$8.85	$10.15	$10.35	$9.45	$7.05	$8.10	$7.7	$7.80

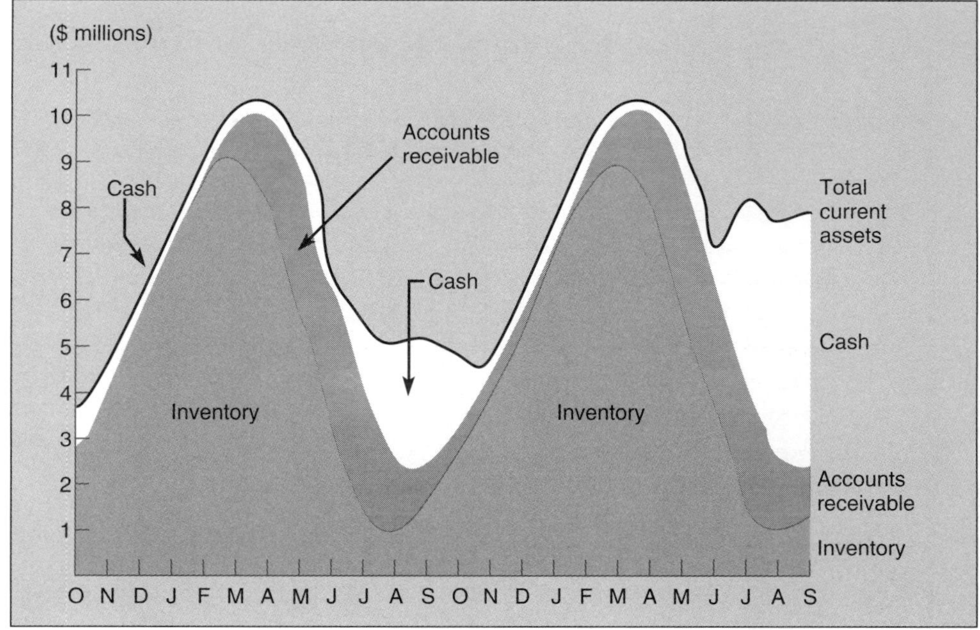

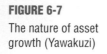

FIGURE 6-7
The nature of asset growth (Yawakuzi)

unable to be renewed when they came due. How would the interest and principal be paid without cash flow from inventory liquidation? The most appropriate financing pattern would be one in which asset buildup and length of financing terms are perfectly matched, as indicated in Figure 6-8.

In the upper part of Figure 6-8 we see that the temporary buildup in current assets is financed by short-term funds. More important, however, permanent current assets, as well as capital assets, are financed with long-term funds from the sale of stock, the issuance of bonds, or retention of earnings. This is known as a hedged approach. **Hedging** is the matching of the maturities of assets and liabilities to reduce risk. A financial manager is interested in techniques that help deal with risk. In this instance of a hedged approach, financial liabilities are matched so that they are covered by assets

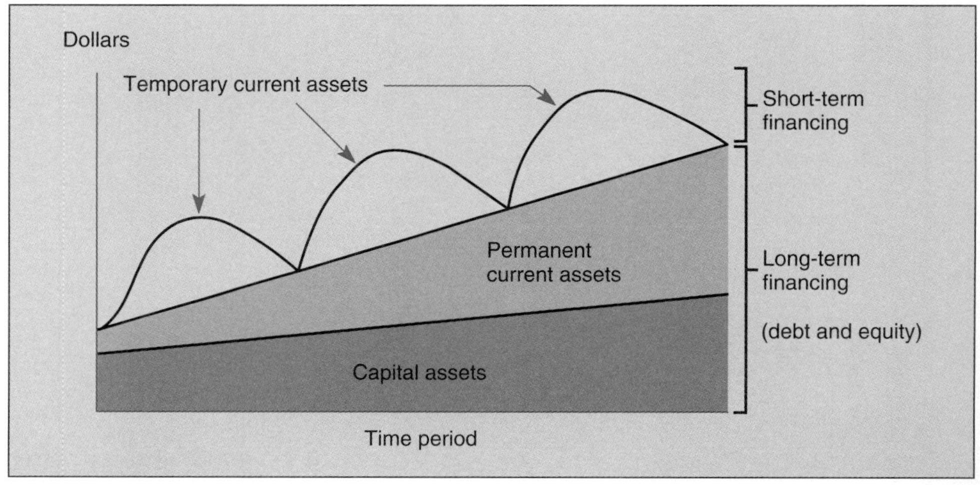

FIGURE 6-8
Matching long-term and short-term needs

that are being converted to cash when they come due. Of course, a perfectly hedged approach is almost impossible to achieve in practice.

The balance sheet for the perfectly hedged firm as illustrated in Figure 6-8 might look as follows.

HEDGED CORPORATION
Balance Sheet
As at December 31, 2002
(000's)

Temporary current assets	6	Accounts payable	2
		Bank loans	4
Permanent current assets	10	Debt	15
Capital assets	20	Equity	15

Alternate Plans

Only a financial manager with unusual insight and timing could construct a financial plan for working capital that adhered perfectly to the design in Figure 6-8. The difficulty rests in precisely determining which part of current assets is temporary and which part is permanent. Even if dollar amounts could be ascertained, the exact timing of asset liquidation is a difficult matter. To compound the problem, we are never quite sure how much short-term or long-term financing is available at a given time. While the precise synchronization of temporary current assets and short-term financing depicted in Figure 6-8 may be the most desirable and logical plan, other alternatives must be considered.

Long-Term Financing

To protect against the danger of not being able to provide adequate short-term financing in tight money periods, the financial manager may rely on long-term funds to cover some short-term needs. As indicated in Figure 6-9, long-term capital is now being used to finance capital assets, permanent current assets, and part of *temporary current assets.*

By using long-term capital to cover short-term needs, the firm virtually assures itself of having adequate capital at all times. The firm may prefer to borrow a million

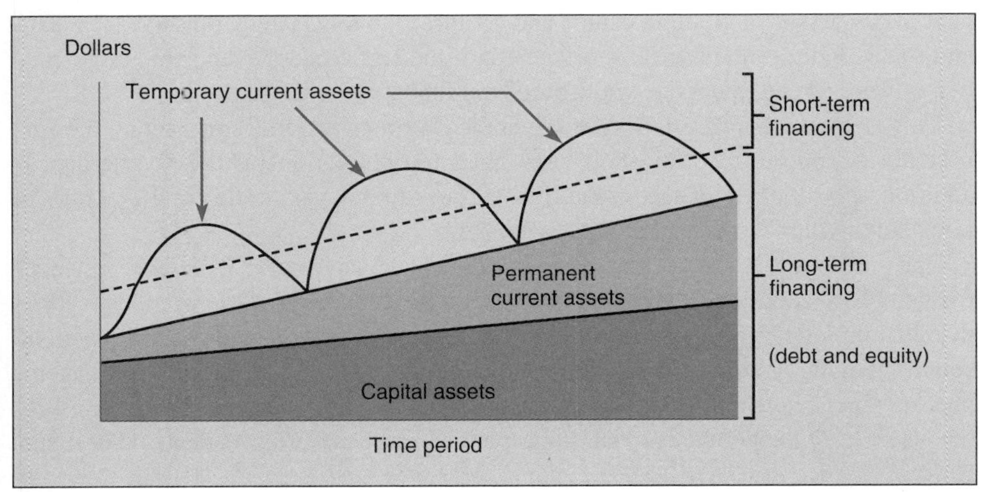

FIGURE 6-9
Using long-term financing for part of short-term needs

FINANCE IN ACTION

Q1 Determine Canada Choice's current ratio now?

Q2 Determine the working capital and hedging approach of another S&P/CDNX firm?

www.canadian.com

Source: CHW

www.tse-cdnx.com

Hedging: Balancing Working Capital

Canada Choice Spring Water Inc. of High River, Alberta is a small business with the objective of becoming the premier North American supplier of bottled water. It is a publicly traded company traded on the TSX Venture Exchange (TSX-V). Although it had gained access to the capital markets through bond and share issues, it is interesting to look at its financing of their current assets, which represented about 20 percent of total assets as at June 2001.

Small businesses may have access to bank loans, but they tend to be expensive and therefore it is important to make good use of the trade credit available through suppliers. If a firm is offering its customers credit it should seek to balance this accounts receivable position with trade credit (accounts payable) available to it. Trade credit is generally available without interest charges, whereas bank loans definitely have an explicit cost.

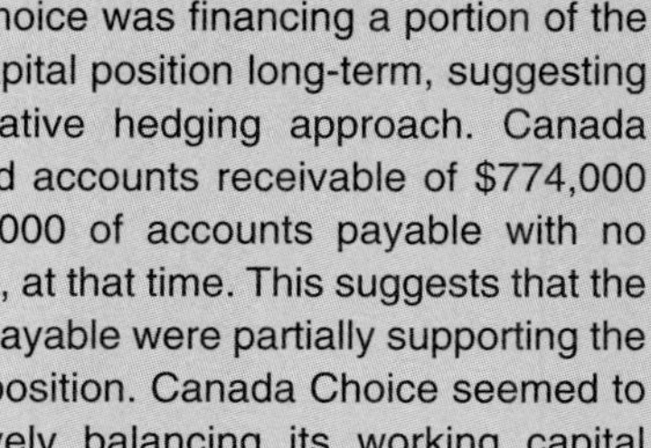

With a current ratio was 1.42 in June 2001, Canada Choice was financing a portion of the working capital position long-term, suggesting a conservative hedging approach. Canada Choice had accounts receivable of $774,000 and $916,000 of accounts payable with no bank loans, at that time. This suggests that the accounts payable were partially supporting the inventory position. Canada Choice seemed to be effectively balancing its working capital position.

Company web sites generally have financial statements available under investor relations. The TSX-V site lists the securities that make up its S&P/TSX Composite Index through its site map. The TSX Venture Exchange (TSX-V) focuses on small Canadian businesses.

dollars for 10 years—rather than attempt to borrow a million dollars at the beginning of each year for 10 years and paying it back at the end of each year.

This is a conservative approach. Although it provides adequate funds, it is less profitable. Generally, longer-term interest rates are more expensive. Additionally, as can be seen from Figure 6-9, the firm pays interest on funds during periods when the funds are not needed.

Short-Term Financing (Opposite Approach)

This is not to say that all financial managers utilize long-term financing on a large scale. To acquire long-term funds, the firm must generally go to the capital markets with a bond or stock offering or must privately place longer-term obligations with insurance companies, wealthy individuals, and so forth. Many small businesses do not have access to such long-term capital and are forced to rely heavily on short-term bank and trade credit. In the capital shortage era of the last decade, even some large businesses were forced to operate with short-term funds.

This is a risky approach. If sales lag and cash flows are not as projected, the firm may not be able to meet its short-term financing obligations as they come due. In addition, the suppliers of credit, the financial institutions and trade creditors, may be reluctant or unable to extend credit any longer.

The upside is that short-term financing offers some advantages over more extended financial arrangements. As a general rule, the interest rate on short-term funds is lower than that on long-term funds. In addition, short-term obligations are generally paid off sooner. We might surmise then that a firm could develop a working capital financing plan in which short-term funds are used to finance not only temporary current assets, but also part of the permanent working capital needs of the firm. As depicted in Figure

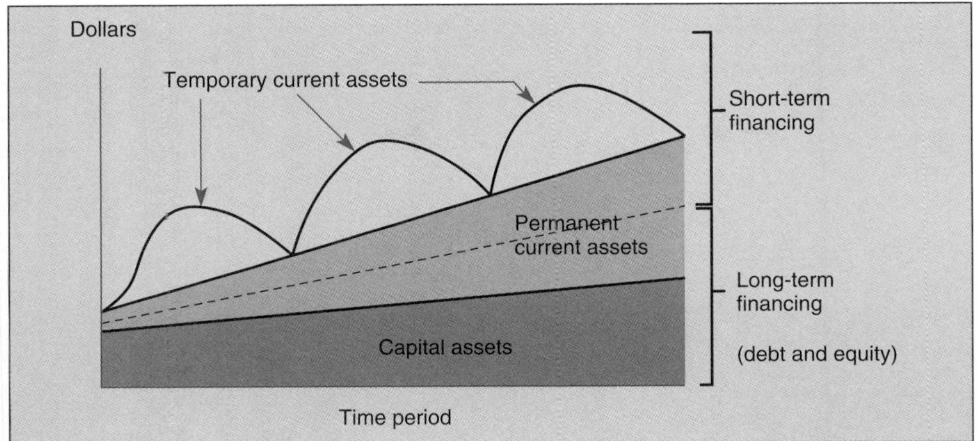

FIGURE 6-10
Using short-term financing for part of long-term needs

6-10, bank and trade credit as well as other sources of short-term financing are now supporting part of the permanent current asset needs of the firm.

The Financing Decision

Some corporations are more flexible than others because they are not locked into a few available sources of funds. Corporations would like many financing alternatives to minimize their cost of funds at any point in time. Unfortunately, not many firms are in this enviable position through the duration of a business cycle. During an economic boom period, a shortage of low-cost alternatives exists, and firms often minimize their financing costs by raising funds in advance of forecasted asset needs.

Not only does the financial manager encounter a timing problem, but the manager also needs to select the right type of financing. Even for companies having many alternative sources of funds, there may be only one or two decisions that look good in retrospect. At the time the financing decision is made, the financial manager is never sure it is the right one. Should the financing be long term or short term, debt or equity, and so on? Figure 6-11 (on the next page) is a decision-tree diagram that shows many of the financing decisions that can be made. At each point a decision is made until a final financing method is reached. In most cases corporations use a combination of these financing methods. At all times the financial manager balances short-term versus long-term considerations against the composition of the firm's assets and the firm's willingness to accept risk. The ratio of long-term financing to short-term financing at any time is greatly influenced by the financial manager's consideration of the risks and potential payoffs from each financing alternative, and also by the term structure of interest rates.

Term Structure of Interest Rates

The term structure of interest rates is often referred to as a yield curve. It shows the interest rate at a specific time for all securities having equal risk but differing maturity dates (term). Therefore, we graph yield (return) against time to maturity. Generally, Government of Canada securities are used to construct yield curves because they have many maturities, and each of the securities has an equally low risk of default. Corporate securities of similar grade (or rating) move in the same direction as government

FIGURE 6-11

Decision tree and the financing decision

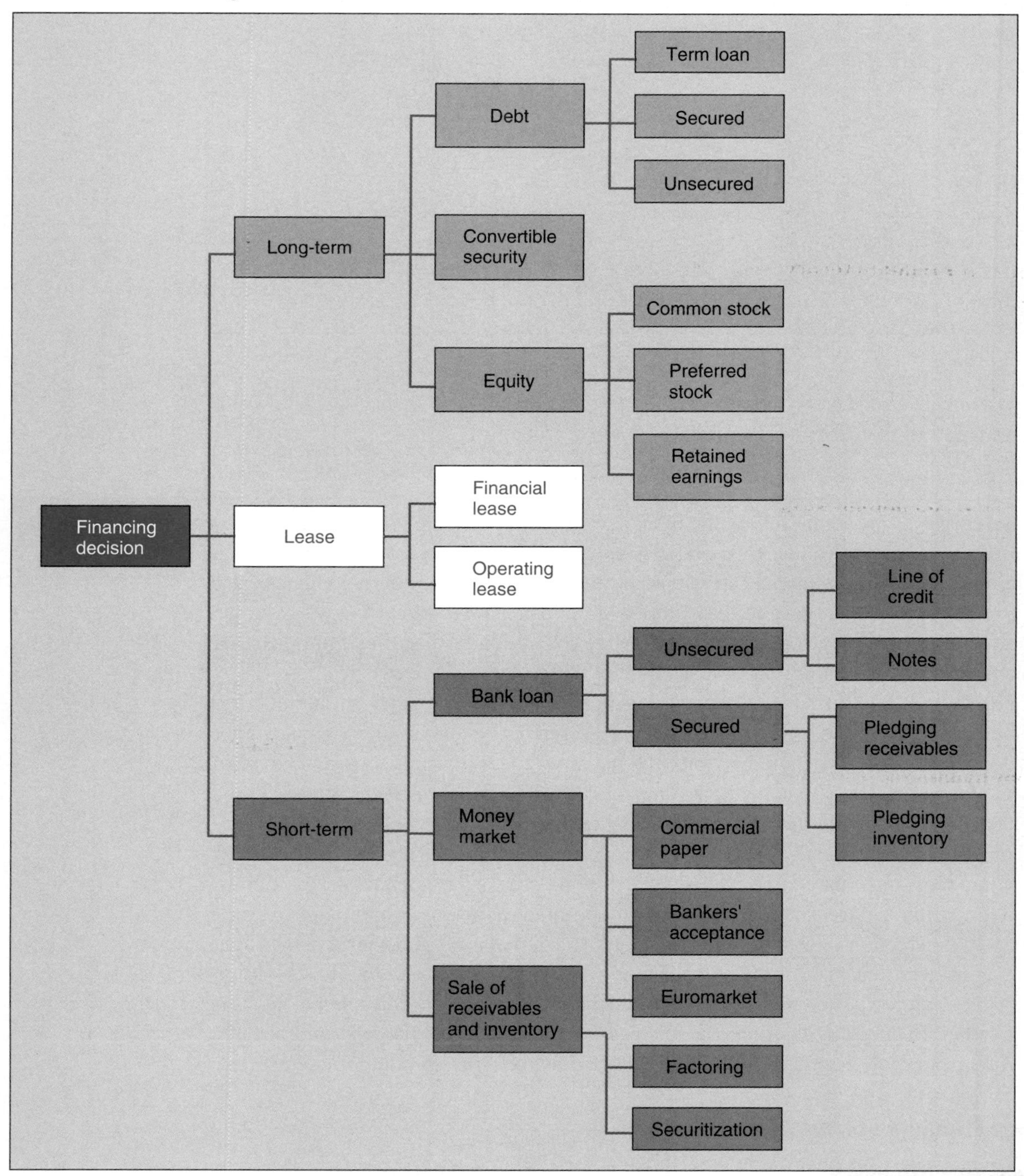

securities, but have higher interest rates because of their greater default risk. The yield curves for both corporate and government securities change daily to reflect current competitive conditions in the money and capital markets, expected inflation, changes in economic conditions, and the strength of the Canadian dollar in international currency markets.

The term structure of interest rates presents valuable information to the financial manager. At any time it shows the yields for various lengths of time (maturities), but the shape of the yield curve is also of interest. Its shape is the result of the daily buying and selling actions of bond market participants, investing monies in a volume that far exceeds that of the equity (stock) markets. It is this quick action of incorporating new information in the pricing and yields of securities that makes these markets efficient. The markets are efficient because they fairly represent risks and promised returns. The shape of the yield curve thus shows the beliefs, based on new information, that market participants have about interest rates now and in the future.

Three basic theories describe the shape of the yield curve. The first theory, the **liquidity premium theory,** states that long-term rates should be higher than short-term rates. This premium of long-term rates over short-term rates exists because short-term securities have greater liquidity, and therefore higher rates have to be offered to potential long-term bond buyers to entice them to hold these less liquid and more price-sensitive securities. The greater liquidity of short-term securities is partly because there is less uncertainty about their future, in particular their payments. Short-term securities are less price sensitive because underlying yield changes in the economy do not affect their prices to the same extent as longer-term securities.

The **segmentation theory** (the second theory) states that Treasury securities are divided into market segments by the various financial institutions investing in the market. Chartered banks prefer short-term securities of one year or less to match their short-term lending strategies. Mortgage-oriented financial institutions prefer the intermediate-length securities of between five and seven years, while life insurance companies prefer long-term, 20- to 30-year securities to offset the long-term nature of their commitments to policyholders. The changing needs, desires, and strategies of these investors tend to strongly influence the nature and relationship of short-term and long-term interest rates.

The third theory describing the term structure of interest rates is called the **expectations hypothesis.** This theory explains the yields on long-term securities as a function of the short-term rates. The expectations theory says long-term rates reflect the average of short-term expected rates over the time period that the long-term security is outstanding. Using a four-year example and a simple arithmetic mean, we demonstrate this theory in Table 6-6. In the left panel of the table, we show the anticipated one-year rate on T-bill (Treasury bill) securities at the beginning of each of four years in the future. Treasury bills are short-term securities issued by the government. In the right panel, we show averages of the one-year anticipated rates.

For example, the two-year security rate is the average of the expected yields of two one-year T-bills, while the rate on the four-year security is the average of all four one-year rates. In this example, the progressively higher rates for two-, three-, and

TABLE 6-6
The expectations theory

1 yr. T-bill at beginning of yr. 1 = 7%	
1 yr. T-bill at beginning of yr. 2 = 8%	2 yr. security (7% + 8%)/2 = 7.5%
1 yr. T-bill at beginning of yr. 3 = 9%	3 yr. security (7% + 8% + 9%)/3 = 8%
1 yr. T-bill at beginning of yr. 4 = 10%	4 yr. security (7% + 8% + 9% + 10%)/4 = 8.5%*

*Exact calculation is [(1.07)(1.08)]1/2 − 1 × 100% = 7.4988%
[(1.07)(1.08)(1.09)]1/3 − 1 × 100% = 7.997%
[(1.07)(1.08)(1.09)(1.10)]1/4 − 1 × 100% = 8.494%

four-year securities represent a reflection of higher anticipated one-year rates in the future. The expectations hypothesis is especially useful in explaining the shape and movement of the yield curve.

The result of the expectations hypothesis is that when long-term rates are much higher than short-term rates, the market is saying that it expects short-term rates to rise. When long-term rates are lower than short-term rates, the market is expecting short-term rates to fall. This theory is useful to financial managers in helping them set expectations for the cost of financing over time and, especially, in making choices about when to use short-term debt or long-term debt.

All three theories presented have some impact on interest rates. At times, the liquidity premium or segmentation theory dominates the shape of the curve, and at other times, the expectations theory is most important. The financial manager cannot escape making judgments about future developments, and sometimes, knowledge of yield curve theories provides a managerial edge for more accurate judgments.

Term Structure Shapes

Figure 6-12 depicts the three common shapes taken by the term structure of interest rates (yield curves). The lower curve of January 2002 is upward sloping, generally referred to as a **normal yield curve,** and the November 2000 term structure is a flat yield curve. The downward sloping yield curve of January 1990 is referred to as an **inverted yield curve.**

Under economic conditions that are expected to be positive, we usually see a normal yield curve. However as signs appear that the economy is slowing down, yield curves usually invert on the expectations that the weaker economy will bring lower inflationary pressures and thus lower interest rates. The Bank of Canada generally cooperates in lowering interest rates to help stimulate the economy as it weakens. When the economy is overheating the Bank of Canada often raises interest rates to slow economic activity and borrowing by adopting a restrictive (or **tight money**) monetary policy, sometimes bringing on a recession.

Bank of Canada
www.bankofcanada.ca/en

In late 2000 and throughout 2001 the North American economy slowed dramatically and the central banks in Canada and the United States dropped interest rates dramatically, trying to stimulate the economy. By early 2002 the economic slowdown appeared to be ending and the term structure reflected this belief with a return to the normal yield curve. The expected slowdown was reflected in the flat yield curve of November 2000 and slightly inverted yield curves found in early 2001. In 1990 we see an inverted yield curve foreshadowing a recession and falling interest rates. By 1991, with the moderate recession under way, the yield curve was quite flat, but by 1992 the normal-shaped yield curve had returned.

Interest rates are influenced by many variables, but inflationary levels have a major influence on the height of the yield curve and inflationary expectations have influence on its shape. In 1990 inflation was in excess of 5 percent, but by 2000 it had dropped to about 2 percent. This is demonstrated by the higher level of the 1990 yield curve in Figure 6-12. When inflation increases, lenders charge a premium for the purchasing power they will lose when the loan is repaid in cheaper, inflated dollars. Although short-term rates are influenced more by current demands for money than by inflation, long-term rates are greatly affected by the expected rate of inflation over the life of an investment.

FIGURE 6-12
Yield curves showing term structure of interest rates

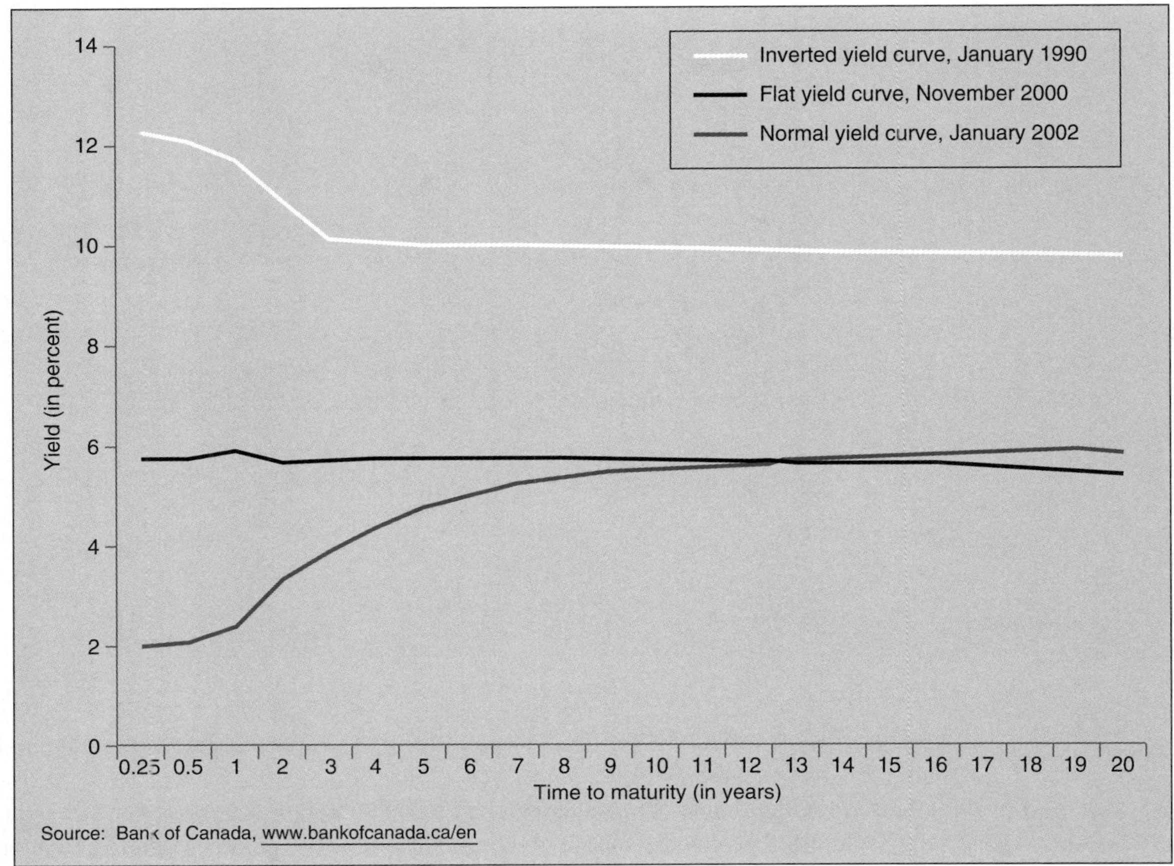

Within Canada, inflation and the value of the Canadian dollar are major determinants of interest rates. The relationship between interest rates and the foreign exchange value of the Canadian dollar is covered in Chapter 21, which deals with international finance.

Interest Rate Volatility

In designing working capital policy, the astute financial manager is interested not only in the term structure of interest rates, but also in the relative volatility and the historical level of short-term and long-term rates. Figure 6-13 (on the next page) uses long-term corporate bonds and short-term commercial paper to provide insight into interest rate volatility over a long time period.

Short-term rates are much more volatile than long-term rates. As a general rule, short-term rates have been lower than long-term rates, but there have been a number of exceptions. Short-term rates exceeded long-term rates in the early 1980s, for a brief time in 1986 and in the early 1990s. These were all periods of tight monetary policy and were followed by economic slowdowns, Note that while short-term rates have fluctuated wildly about long-term rates, long-term rates have fallen from the historic

FIGURE 6-13

Long- and short-term interest rates

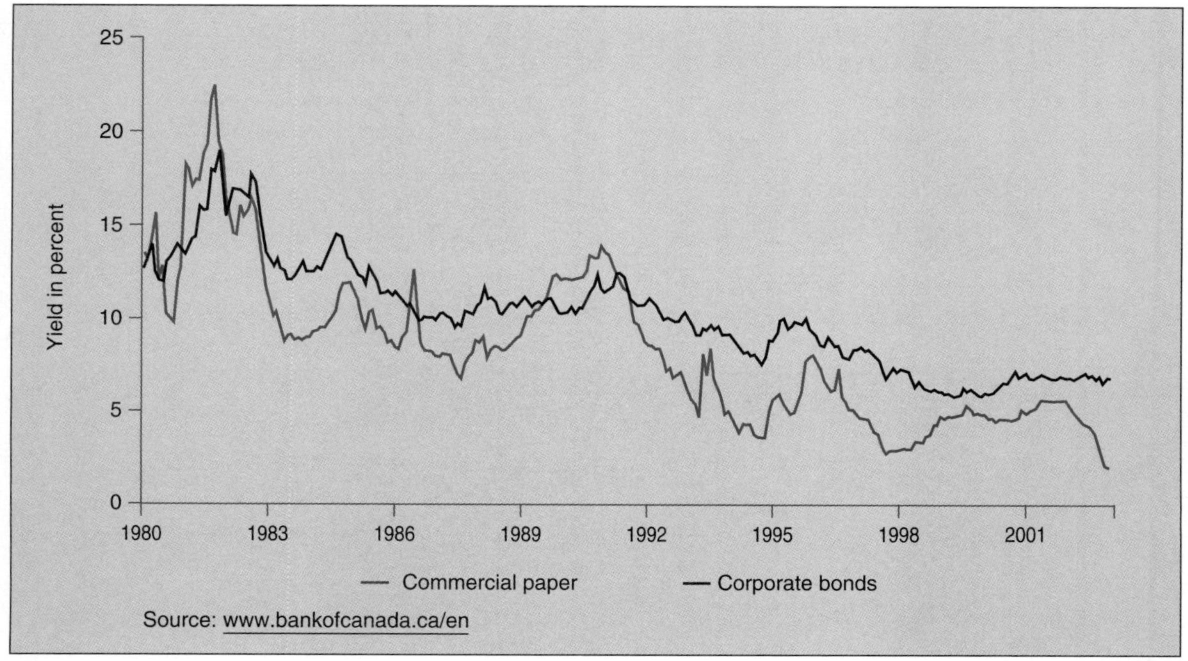

peak of 1982 as inflation rates have declined from in excess of 12 percent annually to about 2 percent by the 1990s.

How should a financial manager respond to fluctuating interest rates and changing term structures? Managers should always be aware of the greater volatility of short-term rates relative to longer-term rates, so as to not get caught offside. They do not want to be holding a lot of short-term financial obligations that might prove difficult to service if interest rates move up quickly. As financial managers plan investment and financing decisions, they should keep in mind the shape of the yield curve because it embeds the expectations of market participants about future interest rates.

When interest rates are high, especially with an inverted yield curve, financial managers generally prefer to temporarily borrow short term if funds are available. This is because the inverted yield curve suggests that interest rates, both short and long term, will decline in the future. As rates decline, the financial officers try to lock in lower rates with long-term borrowing. Some of these long-term funds are used to reduce short-term debt, and the rest are available for future expansion. Expansion generally requires additional investment in both capital assets (plant and equipment) and in working capital.

A Decision Process

Assume we are comparing alternative financing plans for working capital. As indicated in Table 6-7, $500,000 of working capital (current assets) must be financed for the Edwards Corporation. Under Plan A we finance all our current asset needs with short-term funds, while under Plan B we finance only a relatively small portion of working capital with short-term money—relying heavily on long-term funds. In either case, we carry $100,000 of capital assets with long-term financing commitments. As indicated in part 3 of Table 6-7, under Plan A we finance total needs of $600,000 with $500,000 of short-term financing and $100,000 of long-term financing, whereas with Plan B we finance $150,000 short term and $450,000 long term.

TABLE 6-7
Alternative financing plans

EDWARDS CORPORATION	Plan A	Plan B
Part 1. Current assets		
Temporary	$250,000	$250,000
Permanent	250,000	250,000
Total current assets	500,000	500,000
Short-term financing (6%)	500,000	150,000
Long-term financing (10%)	0	350,000
	$500,000	$500,000
Part 2. Capital assets		
Plant and equipment	$100,000	$100,000
Long-term financing (10%)	$100,000	$100,000
Part 3. Total financing (summary of parts 1 and 2)		
Short-term (6%)	$500,000	$150,000
Long-term (10%	100,000	450,000
	$600,000	$600,000

Plan A carries the lower cost of financing, with interest of 6 percent on $500,000 of the $600,000 required. We show the impact of both plans on bottom line earnings in Table 6-8 on page 196.[1] Assuming the firm generates $200,000 in earnings before interest and taxes, Plan A provides aftertax earnings of $80,000, while Plan B generates only $73,000.

Introducing Varying Conditions

Although Plan A, employing cheaper short-term sources of financing, appears to provide $7,000 more in return, this is not always the case. During tight money periods, short-term financing may be difficult to find or may carry exorbitant rates.

Furthermore, inadequate financing may mean lost sales or financial embarrassment. For these reasons, the firm may wish to evaluate Plans A and B based on differing assumptions about the economy and the money markets.

An Expected Value Approach

The maximization of shareholder wealth has been identified as an important goal of the firm and management will make many decisions attempting to meet this objective.

[1]Common stock is eliminated from the example to simplify the analysis. If it were included, all of the basic patterns would still hold.

TABLE 6-8
Impact of financing plans on earnings

EDWARDS CORPORATION	
Plan A	
Earnings before interest and taxes	$200,000
Interest (short-term): 6% × $500,000	−30,000
Interest (long-term): 10% × $100,000	−10,000
Earnings before taxes	160,000
Taxes (50%)	80,000
Earnings aftertaxes	$ 80,000
Plan B	
Earnings before interest and taxes	$200,000
Interest (short-term): 6% × $150,000	−9,000
Interest (long-term): 10% × $450,000	−45,000
Earnings before taxes	146,000
Taxes (50%)	73,000
Earnings aftertaxes	$ 73,000

However, in spite of the best possible planning process , irregular economic conditions may have an adverse impact on the results achieved by the firm. To increase wealth over time the firm must have more correct decisions than incorrect decisions. Put another way the firm's average decision should increase firm value.

An **expected value** approach will identify the possible results for the firm under differing economic conditions, as well as assign a probability to the occurrence of each economic condition. The expected value is then calculated as the average result based on the probable economic conditions. If the firm makes decisions based on the expected value approach it will sometimes exceed expectations and sometimes not meet expectations, but on average it will have results that add value to the firm.

As an example let us suggest that past history combined with economic forecasting may indicate an 80 percent probability of normal events and a 20 percent chance of extremely tight money. To determine these probabilities a firm could use the economic and financial information supplied by financial institutions. The financial institutions, through their economic departments, regularly suggest the future direction of interest rates. The firm could combine these predictions with its knowledge based on experience of how interest rates impact on the particular firm. Financial institutions provide market assessments and comments on a daily basis through their web sites. We should also be able to use the term structure of interest rates to determine the market's expectations of the direction of future interest rates.

Using Plan A, under normal conditions the Edwards Corporation enjoys a $7,000 superior return over Plan B (as indicated in Table 6-8). Let us now assume that under disruptive tight money conditions, Plan A would provide a $15,000 lower return than Plan B because of high short-term interest rates. These conditions are summarized in Table 6-9, and an expected value of return is computed. The expected value represents the sum of the expected outcomes under the two conditions.

TABLE 6-9
Expected returns under different economic conditions

EDWARDS CORPORATION						
1. Normal conditions	Expected higher return under Plan A		Probability of normal conditions		Expected outcome
	$7,000	×	.80	=	+ $5,600
2. Tight money	Expected lower return under Plan A		Probability of tight money		
	($15,000)	×	.20	=	(3,000)
Expected value of return for Plan A versus Plan B				=	+ $2,600

We see that even when downside risk is considered, Plan A carries a higher expected return of $2,600. For another firm in the same industry that might suffer $50,000 lower returns during tight money conditions, Plan A becomes too dangerous to undertake, as indicated in Table 6-10. Plan A's expected return is now $4,400 less than that of Plan B.

TABLE 6-10
Expected returns for high-risk firm

THE OTHER CORPORATION					
1. Normal conditions	Expected higher return under Plan A		Probability of normal conditions		Expected outcome
	$7,000	×	.80	=	+ $5,600
2. Tight money	Expected lower return under Plan A		Probability of tight money		
	($50,000)	×	.20	=	(10,000)
Expected value of return for Plan A versus Plan B				=	−$4,400

Shifts in Asset Structure

Thus far our attention has been directed to the risk associated with various financing plans. We have said that short-term financing is generally cheaper, and thus more profitable, but carries a higher risk. The manager faces a risk-return trade-off. Risk-return analysis must also be carried to the asset side and to the interaction between both sides of the balance sheet. On the asset side, we note that as we proceed down the balance sheet, assets generally become less liquid. Longer-term assets carry greater risks but higher potential returns. Again, the trade-off. Keep in mind the relationship between both sides of the balance sheet. A firm with heavy risk exposure due to short-term borrowing may compensate in part by carrying highly liquid assets. Conversely, a firm with established long-term debt commitments may choose to carry a heavier component of less liquid, highly profitable assets.

Either through desire or compelling circumstances, business firms have decreased the liquidity of their current asset holdings since the early 1960s. The increased cost of financing current assets resulting from the general rise in interest rates may be one reason for this decline. The diminishing liquidity can also be traced in part to more sophisticated, profit-oriented financial management, as well as to a better utilization of cash balances via computer. Less liquidity can also be traced to the long-term effect inflation has had on the corporate balance sheet—forcing greater borrowing to carry more expensive assets—and to decreasing profitability during recessions.

FIGURE 6-14
Industrial corporations' current ratio

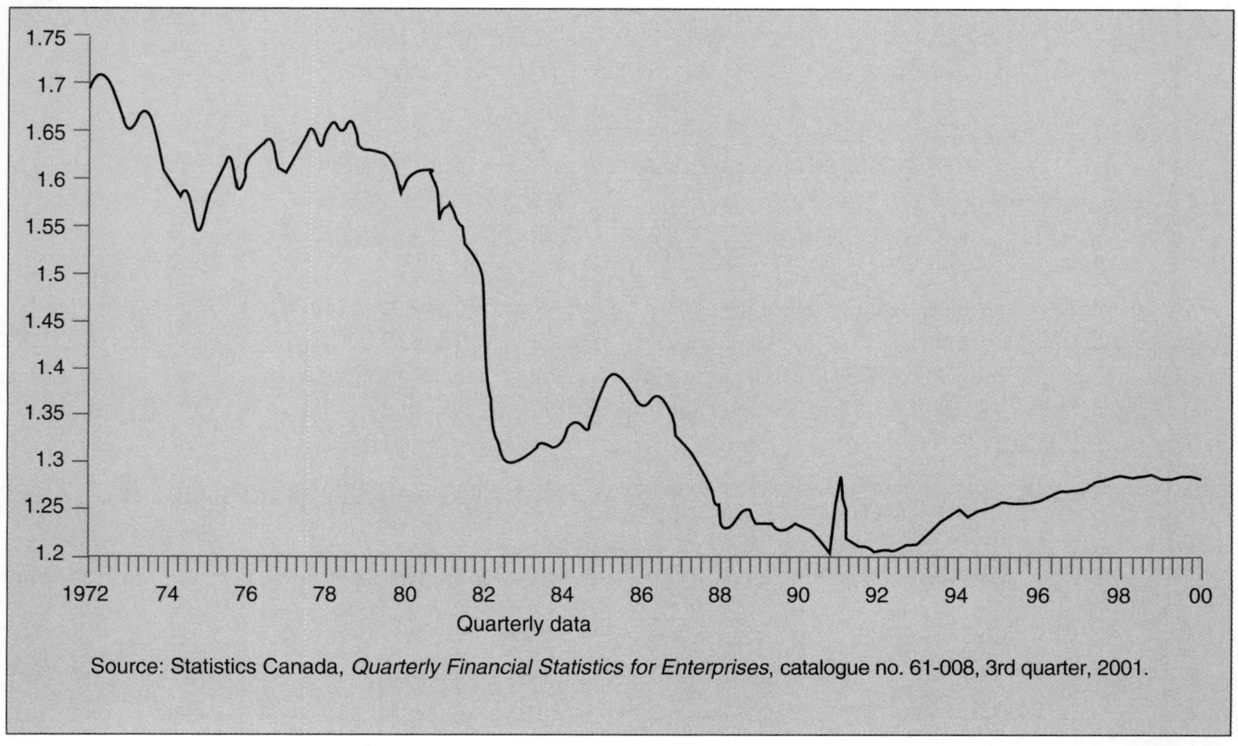

Source: Statistics Canada, *Quarterly Financial Statistics for Enterprises*, catalogue no. 61-008, 3rd quarter, 2001.

To demonstrate these effects in current ratio changes, Figure 6-14 graphs the average current ratio over time for Canadian nonfinancial corporations. In the early 1960s the average current ratio was slightly above 2.0:1. That ratio steadily declined from that time until it reached 1.5:1 at the end of 1974. After the recession of 1974–75, corporate liquidity increased slightly, with the average current ratio remaining between 1.6 and 1.7:1 until the long and severe recession of 1981–82. By the end of that recession, the average current ratio had fallen to about 1.3:1. Even after that recession was over, the ratio recovered only modestly to stay at historically low levels of between 1.3 and 1.4:1. The ratio declined even further in the late 1980s and reached 1.2:1 in the recession of the early 1990s. It has recovered through the 1990s.

Toward an Optimal Policy

As previously indicated, the firm should attempt to relate financing patterns to asset liquidity, and vice versa. The firm should also consider its financing in relation to the risks it is prepared to face and the potential returns. Table 6-11 presents a number of different working capital alternatives. Along the top of the table is asset liquidity and along the side, the type of financing arrangement. The combined impact of the two variables is shown in each of the four panels of the table. Each represents a trade-off between risk and return.

Each firm must decide how it wishes to combine asset liquidity and financing needs. The aggressive, risk-oriented firm in Panel 1 of Table 6-11 borrows short term and maintains relatively low levels of liquidity, hoping to increase profit. It benefits from low-cost short-term financing and has a greater investment in high-return assets. It does not tie up funds in low-return current assets. The aggressive firm, however, is vulnerable to a credit crunch. Short-term interest rates are more volatile, and funding may temporarily become more expensive or unavailable. At these times the aggressive firm may have difficulties continuing in business because it does not have the liquidity cushion to sustain itself through the difficult times.

TABLE 6-11
Current asset liquidity and asset financing plan

	Asset Liquidity	
Financing Plan	**Low Liquidity**	**High Liquidity**
Short-term	1 High profit High risk	2 Moderate profit Moderate risk
Long-term	3 Moderate profit Moderate risk	4 Low profit Low risk

The more conservative firm, following the plan in Panel 4, utilizes established long-term financing and maintains a high degree of liquidity. The conservative firm pays more in the long run on its financing and has more money tied up in low-return current assets. Both these factors reduce its return on assets and equity. However, the conservative firm builds a cushion in the buildup of current assets and by putting long-term financing in place that may allow it to survive market downturns and periods of high interest rates.

In Panels 2 and 3, we see more moderate positions in which the firm compensates for short-term financing with highly liquid assets (2) or balances off low liquidity with precommitted, long-term financing (3).

Each financial manager must structure his or her working capital position and the associated risk-return trade-off to meet the company's needs. For firms whose cash flow patterns are predictable—typified by the public utilities sector—a low degree of liquidity can be maintained without significant risk increases. Immediate access to capital markets, such as that enjoyed by large, prestigious firms, also allows a greater risk-taking capability. Firms with volatile cash flow patterns, on the other hand, probably should be more conservative by maintaining higher liquidity to meet cash flow slowdowns and by establishing solid longer-term financing. In each case the ultimate concern must be for maximizing the overall valuation of the firm through a judicious consideration of risk-return options.

In the next two chapters we examine the various methods for managing the individual components of working capital. In Chapter 7 we consider the techniques for managing cash, marketable securities, receivables, and inventory. In Chapter 8 we look at trade and bank credit and also at other sources of short-term funds.

Summary

1. Working capital management involves the financing and management of the current assets of the firm. A firm's ability to properly manage current assets and the associated liabilities may determine how well it can survive in the short run. The financial manager probably spends the most time on working capital management.
2. As sales increase, a firm requires an increasing investment in current assets to support the increased sales.
3. Production processes are usually more operationally efficient on a level basis. However, sales volumes are likely to fluctuate over time. Although production and sales should be roughly matched over the long run, the short-term differences will result in the buildup of current assets. If part of this buildup in current assets is permanent, and sales levels continue, financial arrangements should carry longer maturities. This demands more careful financial planning and attention to the firm's liquidity. As assets become less liquid their risk increases.
4. The cash flow cycle of the firm is determined by the inventory holding period plus the collection period less the accounts payable period.
5. A hedged approach is an attempt by a financial manager to reduce risk. Hedging attempts to match the maturities of debt obligations to the maturities of assets. Assets should convert to cash as liabilities become payable.
6. The astute financial manager must keep an eye on the general cost of borrowing, the term structure of interest rates, and the relative volatility of short- and long-term rates. The term structure relates yields on similar risk obligations to the time until maturity. The shape of the term structure tells us the expectations and demands of market participants in regards to interest rates.
7. The firm has a number of risk-return decisions to consider. Though long-term financing provides a safety margin in availability of funds, its higher cost may reduce the profit potential of the firm. On the asset side, carrying highly liquid current assets assures the bill-paying capability of the firm but detracts from profit potential. Each firm must tailor the various risk-return trade-offs to meet its own needs. The peculiarities of a firm's industry have a major impact on the options open to management.

List of Terms

working capital management 172
trade credit 172
self-liquidating assets 173
permanent current assets 173
temporary current assets 174
level production 174
point-of-sale terminals 176
liquidity 176
cash flow cycle 177
cash conversion cycle 179
hedging 186
term structure of interest rates 189
liquidity premium theory 191
segmentation theory 191
expectations hypothesis 191
normal yield curve 192
inverted yield curve 192
tight money 192
expected value 196

Discussion Questions

1. Explain how rapidly expanding sales can drain the cash resources of the firm.
2. What is the significance to working capital management of matching sales and production?
3. How is a cash budget used to help manage current assets?
4. Discuss the impact of inflation on working capital management.

5. "The most appropriate financing pattern would be one in which asset buildup and length of financing terms are perfectly matched." Discuss the difficulty involved in achieving this financing pattern.
6. By using long-term financing to finance part of temporary current assets, a firm may have less risk but lower returns than a firm with a normal financing plan. Explain the significance of this statement.
7. A firm that uses short-term financing methods for a portion of permanent current assets is assuming more risk but expects higher returns than a firm with a normal financing plan. Explain.
8. What does the term structure of interest rates indicate?
9. What are the three theories for describing the shape of the term structure of interest rates (the yield curve)? Briefly describe each theory.
10. What might an inverted yield curve suggest to the financial manager?
11. Discuss macroeconomic factors that would influence the yield curve.
12. Suppose a bond trader believes that interest rates will begin to fall in the near future. Which strategy should the trader adopt? If the trader controls lots of money, what impact will the trader's action have on the yield curve?
13. Discuss the relative volatility of short- and long-term interest rates.
14. Since the early 1960s corporate liquidity has been declining. What reasons can you give for this trend?

INTERNET RESOURCES AND QUESTIONS

The Bank of Canada provides weekly financial statistics, including yields on T-bills and benchmark bonds that can be used to construct current and historical yield curves:
www.bankofcanada.ca/en

Royal Bank Dominion Securities offers market reports through its economics department that provides a weekly comment on economic events and financial indicators. Beside comments, *Basic Points,* include yields on short- and long-term government obligations for Canada, the United States, Japan, Germany, and the United Kingdom:
www.rbcds.com

Scotia Capital Markets provides current short-term yields as well as yields on Canadian, provincial, and corporate bonds in its daily market update:
www.scotiacapital.com

Bloomberg provides a wealth of information including the U.S. yield curve and under "Rates and Bonds" provides yields from the major industrialized countries:
www.bloomberg.com/markets/index.html

1. Construct the Canadian yield curve using information from the Bank of Canada. Construct the most current yield curve and a yield curve of one year ago.
   a. How would you describe the yield curves?
   b. What are your expectations for future interest rates?
2. Using a site, such as Bloomberg, construct current yield curves for Canada, the United States, Britain, another European country, and Japan on the same chart, using excel. Label appropriately including date and source. Identify the similarities and differences in the curves. What do the yield curves suggest about the different economies?

3. Discuss the predictions for the future trends in interest rates in Canada and identify the factors that are driving interest rate changes. Use a market commentary from a major financial institution.

Problems

1. Tobin Supplies Company expects sales next year to be $500,000. Inventory and accounts receivable will have to be increased by $90,000 to accommodate this sales level. The company has a steady profit margin of 12 percent, with a 40 percent dividend payout. How much external funding will Tobin Supplies Company have to seek? Assume there is no increase in liabilities other than that which will occur with the external financing.
2. Sherwin Paperboard Company expects to sell 600 units in January, 700 units in February, and 1,200 units in March. January's beginning inventory is 800 units. Expected sales for the whole year are 12,000 units. Sherwin has decided on a level monthly production schedule of 1,000 units (12,000 units/12 months = 1,000 units per month). What is the expected end-of-month inventory for January, February, and March? Show the beginning inventory, production, and sales for each month to arrive at ending inventory.
3. Antonio Banderos & Scarves sells headwear that is very popular in the fall-winter season. Units sold are anticipated as:

October	1,000
November	2,000
December	4,000
January	3,000
	10,000

If seasonal production is used, it is assumed that inventory will directly match sales for each month and there will be no inventory buildup.

Antonio thinks the above assumption is too optimistic and decides to go with level production to avoid being out of merchandise. He will produce the 10,000 items at a level of 2,500 per month.

a. What is the ending inventory at the end of each month? Compare the units sold to the units produced and keep a running total.

b. If the inventory costs $5.00 per unit and will be financed through the bank at 10 percent per annum, what is the monthly financing cost and the total for the four months?

4. Sharpe Computer Graphics Corporation has forecasted the following monthly sales:

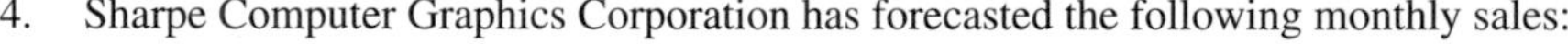

Month	Sales	Month	Sales
January	$80,000	July	$ 30,000
February	70,000	August	31,000
March	10,000	September	40,000
April	10,000	October	70,000
May	15,000	November	90,000
June	20,000	December	110,000
	Total sales = $576,000		

The firm sells its graphic forms for $5.00 per unit, and the cost to produce the forms is $2.00 per unit. A level production policy is followed. Each month's production is equal to annual sales (in units) divided by 12.

Of each month's sales, 30 percent are for cash and 70 percent are on account. All accounts receivable are collected in the month after the sale is made.

a. Construct a monthly production and inventory schedule in units. Beginning inventory in January is 15,000 units. (Note: To do part *a*, you should work in terms of units of production and units of sales.)

b. Prepare a monthly schedule of cash receipts. Sales in the December before the b planning year were $90,000. Work part *b* using dollars.

c. Determine a cash payments schedule for January through December. The production costs of $2.00 per unit are paid for in the month in which they occur. Other cash payments, besides those for production costs, are $30,000 per month.

d. Prepare a monthly cash budget for January through December. The beginning cash balance is $5,000, and that is also the minimum desired.

5. Seasonal Products Corporation expects the following monthly sales:

January	$20,000	July	$10,000
February	15,000	August	14,000
March	5,000	September	20,000
April	3,000	October	25,000
May	1,000	November	30,000
June	3,000	December	22,000
	Total sales = $168,000		

Sales are 20 percent for cash in a given month, with the remainder going into accounts receivable. All 80 percent of the credit sales are collected in the month following the sale. Seasonal Products sells all of its goods for $2.00 each and produces them for $1.00 each. Seasonal Products uses level production, and average monthly production is equal to annual production divided by 12.

a. Generate a monthly production and inventory schedule in units. Beginning inventory in January is 5,000 units. (Note: To do part *a*, you should work in terms of units of production and units of sales.)

b. Determine a cash receipts schedule for January through December. Assume dollar sales in the prior December were $15,000. Work using dollars.

c. Determine a cash payments schedule for January through December. The production costs ($1 per unit produced) are paid for in the month in which they occur. Other cash payments, besides those for production costs, are $6,000 per month.

d. Construct a cash budget for January through December. The beginning cash balance is $1,000, and that is also the required minimum.

e. Determine total current assets for each month. (Note: Accounts receivable equal sales minus 20 percent of sales for a given month.)

6. Modern Tombstones has estimated monthly financing requirements for the next six months as follows:

January	$20,000	April	$10,000
February	6,000	May	22,000
March	8,000	June	12,000

Short-term financing will be utilized for the next six months. Projected annual interest rates are:

January	9.0%	April	15.0%
February	8.0%	May	12.0%
March	12.0%	June	9.0%

a. Compute total dollar interest payments for the six months. To convert an annual rate to a monthly rate, divide by 12.

b. If long-term financing at 12 percent had been utilized throughout the six months, would the total-dollar interest payments be larger or smaller?

7. In the previous problem, what long-term interest rate would represent a break-even point between using short-term financing as described in part *a* and long-term financing? Hint: Divide the interest payments in 6*a* by the amount of total funds provided for the six months and multiply by 12.

8. Gabriel Health Services Ltd. requires $1.5 million in financing over the new two years. The firm can borrow at 5 percent per year, over the two years. However with some economic forecasting it has been suggested that financing in the first year will be 3.5 percent and 6.25 in the second year. Determine the total interest charges under both possibilities. Which action is less costly?

9. Sauer Food Company has decided to buy a new computer system with an expected life of three years. The cost is $150,000. The company can borrow $150,000 for three years at 10 percent annual interest or for one year at 8 percent annual interest.

How much would Sauer Food Company save in interest over the three-year life of the computer system if the one-year loan is utilized and the loan is rolled over (reborrowed) each year at the same 8 percent rate? Compare this to the 10 percent, three-year loan. What if interest rates on the 8 percent loan go up to 13 percent in year two and 18 percent in year three? What is the total interest cost now compared to the 10 percent, three-year loan?

10. Goniff Steel has $4.2 million in assets.

Temporary current assets	$1,000,000
Permanent current assets	2,000,000
Capital assets	1,200,000
Total assets	$4,200,000

Short-term rates are 8 percent. Long-term rates are 13 percent. Earnings before interest and taxes are $996,000. The tax rate is 40 percent.

If long-term financing is perfectly matched (hedged) with long-term asset needs, and the same is true of short-term financing, what will earnings aftertaxes be? For an example of perfectly hedged plans, see Figure 6-8.

11. In the previous problem, assume the term structure of interest rates becomes inverted, with short-term rates going to 12 percent and long-term rates 4 percentage points lower than short-term rates.

If all other factors in the problem do not change, what will earnings be aftertaxes? Why has the company benefited?

12. Currently Atlas Tours has $5.4 million in assets. This is a peak six month period. During the other six months temporary current assets drop to $400,000.

Temporary current assets	$1,200,000
Permanent current assets	1,800,000
Capital assets	2,400,000
Total assets	$5,400,000

Short-term rates are 4 percent. Long-term rates are 5 percent. Annual earnings before interest and taxes are $1,080,000. The tax rate is 38 percent.

a. If the assets are perfectly hedged throughout the year what will earnings be aftertaxes?

b. If short term interest rates increase to 5 percent when assets are at their lowest level what will earnings be aftertaxes?

13. Guardian, Inc., is trying to develop an asset-financing plan. The firm has $400,000 in temporary current assets and $300,000 in permanent current assets. Guardian also has $500,000 in capital assets. Assume a tax rate of 40 percent.

a. Construct two alternative financing plans for Guardian. One of the plans should be conservative, with 75 percent of assets financed by long-term sources, and the other should be aggressive, with only 56.25 percent of assets financed by long-term sources. The current interest rate is 15 percent on long-term funds and 10 percent on short-term financing.

b. Given that Guardian's earnings before interest and taxes are $200,000, calculate earnings aftertaxes for each of your alternatives.

c. What would happen if the short- and long-term rates were reversed?

14. Lear, Inc., has $800,000 in current assets, $350,000 of which are considered permanent current assets. In addition, the firm has $600,000 invested in capital assets.

a. Lear wishes to finance all capital assets and half of its permanent current assets with long-term financing costing 10 percent. Short-term financing currently costs 5 percent. Lear's earnings before interest and taxes are $200,000. Determine Lear's earnings aftertaxes under this financing plan. The tax rate is 30 percent.

b. As an alternative, Lear might wish to finance all capital assets and permanent current assets plus half of its temporary current assets with long-term financing. The same interest rates apply as in part *a*. Earnings before interest and taxes will be $200,000. What will be Lear's earnings aftertaxes? The tax rate is 30 percent.

c. What are some of the risks associated with each of these alternative financing strategies?

15. Date Wireless has the following assets:

Current assets:	Temporary	$1,000,000
	Permanent	1,000,000
Capital Assets		7,000,000
Total		$9,000,000

Its operating profit (EBIT) is expected to be $1.0 million. Its tax rate is 40 percent. Shares are valued $25. Capital structure is either short term financing at 6 percent or equity. There is no long term debt.

a. Calculate expected earnings per share (e.p.s.) if the firm is perfectly hedged.

b. Calculate expected earnings per share (e.p.s.) it has a capital structure of 40% debt.

c. Recalculate *a* and *b* if short term rates go to 11 percent.

16. Pick a day within the past week and construct a yield curve for that day. Pick a day approximately a year ago and construct a yield curve for that day. How are interest rates different? *The Globe and Mail* or the *Financial Post* should be of help in solving this problem. What does the term structure suggest to you as a financial manager?

17. Using the expectations hypothesis theory for the term structure of interest rates, determine the expected return for securities with maturities of two, three, and four years based on the following data. Do a similar analysis to that in Table 6-6.

1-year T-bill at beginning of year 1	6%
1-year T-bill at beginning of year 2	7%
1-year T-bill at beginning of year 3	9%
1-year T-bill at beginning of year 4	11%

18. The government currently promises a return of 5 percent annually on a one-year bond and 6 percent annually on a two-year bond. What is your expectation for the interest rate you would receive on a one-year government bond one year from now?

19. The following information was available as of the close of business March 1, 2002, on government of Canada bonds.

Coupon	Maturity	Price	Yield
8.25%	Mar. 1, 2003	102.75	5.78
3.75%	Mar. 1, 2004	95.70	5.85
5.75%	Mar. 1, 2005	98.65	6.22

Calculate the anticipated one-year interest rate for 2004 (up to March 2005).

20. The following information was available as of the close of business March 1, 1999, on government of Canada bonds.

Coupon	Maturity	Price	Yield
5.00%	Mar. 1, 2000	99.89	5.11
10.50%	Mar. 1, 2001	109.99	5.18
8.50%	Mar. 1, 2002	109.00	5.22

Calculate the anticipated one-year interest rate for 2001 (up to March 2002).

21. Gary's Pipe and Steel Company expects next year's sales to be $800,000 if the economy is strong, $500,000 if the economy is steady, and $350,000 if the economy is weak. Gary believes there is a 20 percent probability the economy will be strong, a 50 percent probability of a steady economy, and a 30 percent probability of a weak economy. What is the expected level of sales for next year?

22. Assume Stratton Health Clubs, Inc., has $3 million in assets. If it goes with a low liquidity plan for the assets, it can earn a return of 20 percent, but with a high liquidity plan, the return will be 13 percent. If the firm goes with a short-term financing plan, the financing costs on the $3 million will be 10 percent; with a long term financing plan, the financing costs on the $3 million will be 12 percent. (Review Table 6-11 for parts *a, b,* and *c* of this problem.)

    a. Compute the anticipated return after financing costs on the most aggressive asset financing mix.

    b. Compute the anticipated return after financing costs on the most conservative asset-financing mix.

    c. Compute the anticipated return after financing costs on the two moderate approaches to the asset-financing mix.

    d. Would you necessarily accept the plan with the highest return after financing costs? Briefly explain.

COMPREHENSIVE PROBLEM

23. During mid-October 2002 the top managers of the Gale Force Corporation, a leading manufacturer of windsurfing equipment and surfboards, were gathered in the president's conference room reviewing the results of the company's operations during the past fiscal year (which runs from October 1 to September 30).

"Not a bad year, on the whole," remarked the president, 32-year-old Charles (Chuck) Jamison. "Sales were up, profits were up, and our return on equity was a respectable 15 percent. In fact," he continued, "the only dark spot I can find in our whole annual report is the profit-on-sales ratio, which is only 2.25 percent. Seems like we ought to be making more than that, don't you think, Tim?" He looked across the table at the vice-president for finance, Timothy Baggitt, age 28.

"I agree," replied Tim, "and I'm glad you brought it up, because I have a suggestion on how to improve that situation." He leaned forward in his chair as he realized he had captured the interest of the others. "The problem is, we have too many expenses on our income statement that are eating up the profits. Now I've done some checking, and the expenses all seem to be legitimate except for interest expense. We paid over $250,000 last year to the bank just to finance our short-term borrowing. If we could have kept that money instead, our profit-on-sales ratio would have been 4.01 percent, which is higher than that of any other firm in the industry."

"But, Tim, we have to borrow like that," responded Roy ("Pop") Thomas, age 35, the vice-president for production. "After all, our sales are seasonal, with almost all occurring between March and September. Since we don't have much money coming in from October to February, we have to borrow to keep the production line going." "Right," Tim replied, "and it's the production line that's the problem. We produce the same number of products every month, no matter what we expect sales to be. This causes inventory to build up when sales are slow and to deplete when sales pick up.

That fluctuating inventory causes all sorts of problems, not the least of which is the excessive amount of borrowing we have to do to finance the inventory accumulation." (See Tables 1 through 5 for details of Gale Force's current operations based on equal monthly production.)

"Now, here's my idea," said Tim. "Instead of producing 400 items a month, every month, we match the production schedule with the sales forecast. For example, if we expect to sell 150 windsurfers in October, then we only make 150. That way we avoid borrowing to make the 250 more that we don't expect to sell, anyway. Over the course of an entire year, the savings in interest expense could really add up."

"Hold on, now," Pop responded, feeling that his territory was being threatened. "That kind of scheduling really fouls up things in the shop where it counts. It causes a feast or famine environment—nothing to do for one month, then a deluge the next. It's terrible for the employees, not to mention the supervisors who are trying to run an efficient operation. Your idea may make the income statements look good for now, but the whole company will suffer in the long run."

Chuck intervened. "OK, you guys, calm down. Tim may have a good idea or he may not, but at least it's worth looking into. I propose that you all work up two sets of figures, one assuming level production and one matching production with sales. We'll look at them both and see if Tim's idea really does produce better results. If it does, we'll check it further against the other issues Pop is concerned about and then make a decision on which alternative is better for the firm."

a. Tables 1 through 5 contain the financial information describing the effects of level production on inventory, cash flow, loan balances, and interest expense. Reproduce these tables as if Tim's suggestion were implemented; that is, change the *Production This Month* column in Table 3 from 400 each month to 150, 75, 25, and so on, to match Sales in the next column. Then, recompute the remainder of Table 3, and Tables 1, 4, and 5 based on the new production numbers. Beginning inventory is still 400 units. Beginning cash is still $125,000 and that remains the minimum required balance.

b. Given that Gale Force is charged 12 percent annual interest (1 percent a month) on its cumulative loan balance each month (Table 5), how much would Tim's suggestion save in interest expense in a year?

c. Until now we have not considered any inefficiencies that have been introduced as a result of going from level to seasonal production. Assume there is an added expense for each sales dollar of .5 percent (.005). Based on this fact and the information computed in part *b*, is seasonal production justified?

TABLE 1

Sales forecast, cash receipts and payments, and cash budget

	October	November	December	January	February	March
Sales Forecast						
Sales (units)	150	75	25	0	0	300
Sales (unit price: $3,000)	$ 450,000	$ 225,000	$ 75,000	0	0	$ 900,000
Cash Receipts Schedule						
50% cash	$ 225,000	$ 112,500	$ 37,500	0	0	$ 450,000
50% from prior month's sales*	375,000	225,000	112,500	37,500	0	0
Total cash receipts	$ 600,000	$ 337,500	$ 150,000	$ 37,500	0	$ 450,000
Cash Payments Schedule						
Production in units	400	400	400	400	400	400
Production costs (each: $2,000)	$ 800,000	$ 800,000	$ 800,000	$ 800,000	$ 800,000	$ 800,000
Overhead	200,000	200,000	200,000	200,000	200,000	200,000
Dividends and interest	0	0	0	0	0	0
Taxes	150,000	0	0	$ 150,000	0	0
Total cash payments	$1,150,000	$1,000,000	$1,000,000	$1,150,000	$1,000,000	$1,000,000
Cash Budget; Required Minimum Balance Is $125,000						
Cash flow	$−550,000	−662,000	−850,000	−1,112,500	−1,000,000	−550,000
Beginning cash	125,000	125,000	125,000	125,000	125,000	125,000
Cumulative cash balance	−425,000	−537,500	−725,000	−987,500	−875,000	−425,000
Monthly loan or (repayment)	550,000	662,500	850,000	1,112,500	1,000,000	550,000
Cumulative loan	550,000	1,212,500	2,062,500	3,175,000	4,175,000	4,725,000
Ending cash balance	$ 125,000	$ 125,000	$ 125,000	$ 125,000	$ 125,000	$ 125,000

*Note: September sales assumed to be $750,000.

TABLE 1 ***(concluded)***

Sales forecast, cash receipts and payments, and cash budget

	April	May	June	July	August	September
Sales Forecast						
Sales (units)	500	1,000	1,000	1,000	500	250
Sales (unit price: $3,000)	$1,500,000	$3,000,000	$3,000,000	$3,000,000	$1,500,000	$750,000
Cash Receipts Schedule						
50% cash	$ 750,000	$1,500,000	$1,500,000	$1,500,000	$ 750,000	$ 375,000
50% from prior month's sales*	450,000	750,000	1,500,000	1,500,000	1,500,000	750,000
Total cash receipts	$1,200,000	$2,250,000	$3,000,000	$3,000,000	$2,250,000	$1,125,000
Cash Payments Schedule						
Production in units	400	400	400	400	400	400
Production costs (each: $2,000)	$ 800,000	$ 800,000	$ 800,000	$ 800,000	$ 800,000	$ 800,000
Overhead	200,000	200,000	200,000	200,000	$ 200,000	200,000
Dividends and interest	0	0	0	0	$1,000,000	0
Taxes	$ 150,000	0	0	$ 300,000	0	0
Total cash payments	$1,150,000	$1,000,000	$1,000,000	$1,300,000	$2,000,000	$1,000,000
Cash Budget; Required Minimum Balance Is $125,000						
Cash flow	50,000	1,250,000	2,000,000	1,700,000	250,000	125,000
Beginning cash	125,000	125,000	125,000	125,000	400,000	650,000
Cumulative cash balance	175,000	1,375,000	2,125,000	1,825,000	650,000	775,000
Monthly loan or (repayment)	(50,000)	(1,250,000)	(2,000,000)	(1,425,000)	0	0
Cumulative loan	4,675,000	3,425,000	1,425,000	0	0	0
Ending cash balance	$ 125,000	$ 125,000	$ 125,000	$ 400,000	$ 650,000	$ 775,000

*Note: September sales assumed to be $750,000.

TABLE 2

Sales forecast (in units)

First Quarter		Second Quarter		Third Quarter		Fourth Quarter	
October	150	January	0	April	500	July	1,000
November	75	February	0	May	1,000	August	500
December	25	March	300	June	1,000	September	250

TABLE 3

Production schedule and inventory (equal monthly production)

	Beginning Inventory	Production This Month	Sales	Ending Inventory	Inventory ($2,000/ per unit)
October	400	400	150	650	$1,300,000
November	650	400	75	975	1,950,000
December	975	400	25	1,300	2,600,000
January	1,350	400	0	1,750	3,500,000
February	1,750	400	0	2,150	4,300,000
March	2,100	400	300	2,250	4,500,000
April	2,200	400	500	2,150	4,300,000
May	2,100	400	1,000	1,550	3,100,000
June	1,500	400	1,000	950	1,900,000
July	900	400	1,000	350	700,000
August	300	400	500	250	500,000
September	200	400	250	400	800,000

TABLE 4

Total current assets, first year

	Cash	Accounts Receivable*	Inventory	Total Current Assets
October	$125,000	$225,000	$1,300,000	$1,650,000
November	125,000	112,500	1,950,000	2,187,500
December	125,000	37,500	2,600,000	2,762,500
January	125,000	0	3,500,000	3,625,000
February	125,000	0	4,300,000	4,425,000
March	125,000	450,000	4,500,000	5,075,000
April	125,000	750,000	4,300,000	5,175,000
May	125,000	1,500,000	3,100,000	4,725,000
June	125,000	1,500,000	1,900,000	3,525,000
July	400,000	1,500,000	700,000	2,600,000
August	650,000	750,000	500,000	1,900,000
September	775,000	375,000	800,000	1,950,000

*Equals 50 percent of monthly sales.

TABLE 5

Cumulative loan balance and interest expense (1% per month)

	October	November	December	January	February	March
Cumulative loan balance	$550,000	$1,212,500	$2,062,500	$3,175,000	$4,175,000	$4,725,000
Interest expense at (prime, 8.0% + 4 = 12.00%)	$5,500	$12,125	$20,625	$31,750	$41,750	$47,250
	April	**May**	**June**	**July**	**August**	**September**
Cumulative loan balance	$4,675,000	$3,425,000	$1,425,000	0	0	0
Interest expense at (prime, 8.0% +4 = 12.00%)	$46,750	$34,250	$14,250	0	0	0
Total interest expense for the year: $254,250.						

Selected References

Acheson, Marcus W. "From Cash Management to Bank Reform." *Journal of Applied Corporate Finance* 4 (Summer 1991), pp. 105–16.

Billett, Mathew T., Mark J. Flannery, and Jon A. Garfinkel. "The Effect of Lender Indemnity on a Borrowing Firm's Equity Return." *Journal of Finance* 50 (June 1995), pp. 699–718.

Boudoukh, Jacob, Mark J. Flannery, and Jon A. Garfinkel. "The Effect of Lender Indemnity on a Borrowing Firm's Equity Return." *Journal of Finance* 50 (June 1995), pp. 699–718.

Brown, Cathy. "Getting a Grip: Year 2000 Credit Risk." *Journal of Lending and Credit Risk Management* 80 (January 1998), pp. 62–68.

Coulter, David A. "Risk Management in a Time of Technological Change." *Journal of Lending and Credit Risk Management* 80 (January 1998), pp. 44–49.

Fass, Greg. "Capital Allocation and Pricing Credit Risk." *Journal of Commercial Lending* 75 (September 1992), pp. 35–53.

Jarrow, Robert A., and Stuart M. Turnbull. "The Intersection of Market and Credit Risk." *Journal of Banking and Finance* 24 (January 2000), pp. 271–99.

Scholtens, Bert, and Dick van Wensveen. "A Critique of the Theory of Financial Intermediation." *Journal of Banking and Finance* 24 (August 2000), pp. 1243–51.

CHAPTER | SEVEN

7 Current Asset Management

LEARNING | OBJECTIVES

1 Extend Chapter 6 concepts of liquidity and risk to current asset management recognizing that a firm's investment in current assets should achieve an adequate return for its liquidity and risk.

2 Discuss cash management as the control of receipts and disbursements to minimize nonearning cash balances while providing liquidity and describe techniques to make cash management more efficient.

3 Define the various marketable securities available for investment by the firm and calculate the yield on these instruments.

4 Describe accounts receivable as an investment resulting from the firm's credit policies, outline the considerations in granting credit, and evaluate a credit decision that changes credit terms to stimulate sales.

5 Describe inventory as an investment and apply techniques to reduce the costs of this investment.

The financial manager must carefully allocate resources among the current assets of the firm—cash, marketable securities, accounts receivable, and inventory. In managing cash and marketable securities, the primary concern should be for safety and liquidity, with secondary attention placed on maximizing returns. As we consider accounts receivable and inventory, a stiffer profitability test must be met as liquidity risk increases. The investment level should not be a matter of happenstance or historical determination; it must meet the same return-on-investment criteria applied to any decision. We may need to choose between an increase in inventory, a new plant location, or a major research program. We shall examine the decision techniques that are applied to the various forms of current assets in order to provide an appropriate return while providing timely liquidity for the firm's operations.

Cost-Benefit Analysis

We have identified the goal of the firm as the maximization of shareholder wealth, but in practice, this is a demanding objective for the financial manager. Many decisions are made within the firm, that collectively add up to its successes or failures. It is important that each decision consider all the factors that will result from new procedures or projects. **Cost-benefit analysis** provides a framework to identify all the resultant changes arising from a decision. Some results will be incremental, increasing the firm's value and some will be decremental, decreasing value. Good value-adding decisions will ensue when the benefits exceed the costs.

Cost-benefit analysis must consider explicit and implicit costs and benefits. Opportunity costs (benefits) are forgone alternatives. Employee time and effort resulting from a new procedure must be considered if it could have been directed elsewhere, if not for the new procedure. Capital that is tied up as a result of a new project could have been earning a return elsewhere in the firm. As we examine and analyze techniques for working capital management let us consider the following:

- Employee costs for training, implementation, and monitoring
- New technology required
- Capital tied up (or freed up)
- Rates of return on capital
- Timeliness of information provided (whether better or worse)
- Exposure to risk
- Fees or charges

Careful thought and information gathering must be the inputs into cost-benefit analysis. We will use this technique as a foundation for many of the techniques that follow.

Cost-benefit analysis is first examined in this chapter under cash management analysis.

Cash Management

Managing cash has become more sophisticated in the new global and electronic age as financial managers try to squeeze the last dollar of profit out of their cash management strategies. Despite whatever lifelong teachings you might have learned about the virtues of cash, the corporate manager actively seeks to keep this nonearning asset to a minimum. Generally, the less cash you have the better off you are, however, you still do not want to get caught without cash when you need it. The penalties imposed by short-term creditors and bankers when a company runs out of cash may have a lasting impact on relationships. Highly liquid securities or standby lines of credit available through banking arrangements can meet cash needs quickly. **Liquidity**, a desirable characteristic of financial assets, may be defined as the degree to which a financial asset can be converted into cash quickly and at fair market value.

Minimizing cash balances as well as having accurate knowledge of when cash moves into and out of the company can improve overall corporate profitability. Knowledge of the cash flow cycle discussed in Chapter 6 can assist in understanding cash management, while the financial forecasting pro formas of Chapter 4 are invaluable tools for identifying the cash requirements of the firm. The small business often runs into difficulties when these cash requirements are not properly identified and appropriate arrangements are not made to provide financing as it is needed.

FINANCE IN ACTION

Q1 Identify some of the products currently available for bidding at these online sites.

www.freemarkets.com

www.commerceone.com

The Impact of the Internet on Working Capital Management

The Internet is significantly effecting the way companies manage the purchase of their inventory, sell their goods, collect their money, and manage their cash. Electronic funds transfer (EFT) systems have been around for over 20 years and their use continues to accelerate.

Business-to-business (B2B) industry supply exchanges are having a major impact on industry. Perhaps the exchange with the biggest potential is the alliance of Ford, General Motors, and DaimlerChrysler. They have created, with the aid of Oracle and Commerce One, an online auction house, a B2B Internet exchange for purchasing that will open up the bidding process amongst their suppliers, pushing prices down and profits up. Between these three car companies there is U.S.$230 billion of annual purchasing volume and savings that are expected to be shared between the manufacturers and their suppliers. Other companies are copying this model. Sears U.S. and Carrefour of France have created a web supply exchange and Compaq, Hewlett-Packard, Gateway, and NEC of Japan are creating an online electronic marketplace.

Another trend in current asset management is the use of B2B online auction companies such as FreeMarkets and Commerce One. FreeMarkets has created specialties and qualified buyers and suppliers in product categories such as coal, injection molded plastic parts, metal fabrications, chemicals, printed circuit boards, and more. In 1999 they auctioned more than U.S.$2.7 billion worth of purchase orders with estimated savings to buyers of about 20 to 25 percent.

The advantage of these B2B auction sites is that they eliminate geographical barriers and allow suppliers from all over the world to bid on business that was unavailable to them before the Internet. The bidding process has time limits and the participants get feedback on bids and can compete on price. The suppliers are prequalified so that they meet manufacturer's standards.

These online efforts are significantly reducing costs in working capital management, the explicit cost of products, and will encourage growth throughout the industrialized world.

Reasons for Holding Cash Balances

There are several reasons for holding cash: for transactions balances, for compensating balances for banks, and for precautionary needs. The transactions motive involves the use of cash to pay for planned corporate expenses such as supplies, payrolls, and taxes, but it also can include infrequent planned acquisitions of long-term capital assets. The second major reason for holding cash results from the practice of holding balances to compensate a bank for services provided rather than to pay directly for those services.

Holding cash for precautionary motives assumes that management wants cash for emergency purposes when cash inflows are less than projected. Precautionary cash balances are more likely to be important in seasonal or cyclical industries where cash inflows are more uncertain. Interest-paying marketable securities held for precautionary purposes should be transferred into cash only when there is a scheduled need for disbursement. Firms with precautionary needs may also rely on untapped lines of bank credit. For most firms, the primary motive for holding cash is the transactions motive.

Collections and Disbursements

Managing a firm's cash inflows and payments is a function with many variables such as float, the mail system, electronic funds transfer mechanisms, lockboxes, international sales, and more. These are presented in the following section.

Float

Some people are shocked to realize that even the most trusted asset on a corporation's books, cash, may not portray the actual dollars available for use at any given moment.

There are, in fact, two cash balances of importance: (1) the corporation's recorded amount and (2) the amount available for use by the corporation at the bank. The difference between the two is labelled **float.** Float exists as a result of the time lag between when a payment or receipt is recorded in the corporation's ledgers and the eventual acknowledgement that it has altered the corporate bank account.

Float arises from the payments or receipts, being in the mail, clearing the banking system, processing time, or from a slow information acknowledgement system. Any of these components of float can result in funds that belong to the firm not being deployed effectively or conversely the firm can take advantage of float opportunities. The Canadian banking system is extremely efficient with same-day clearing, which virtually eliminates the banking system's clearing float. Nevertheless float still remains, but with large volumes of payments and receipts, float time can become fairly predictable and therefore can be effectively managed.

Canadian Payments Association
www.cdnpay.ca

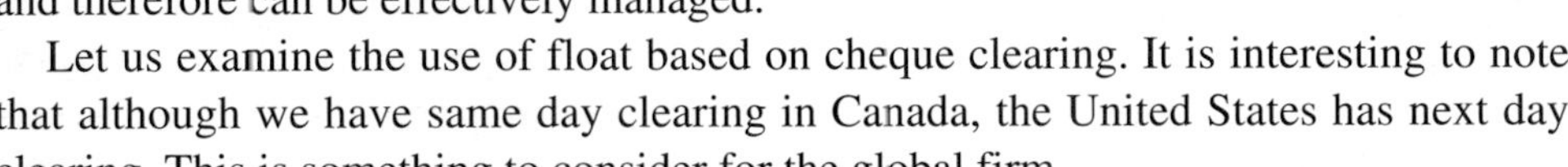

Let us examine the use of float based on cheque clearing. It is interesting to note that although we have same day clearing in Canada, the United States has next day clearing. This is something to consider for the global firm.

A firm has received $1 million in cheques from customers during the week and has written $900,000 in cheques to suppliers. If the initial balance were $100,000, the corporate books would show $200,000. But what will the bank records show in the way of usable funds? Perhaps only $800,000 of the cheques from customers have been processed and deposited to the firm's account, while only $400,000 of our cheques may have completed a similar cycle. As indicated in Table 7–1, the firm has used float to provide $300,000 extra in available short-term funds.

TABLE 7–1
The use of float to provide funds

	Corporate Books		Bank Books (usable funds) (amounts actually cleared)
Initial amount	$ 100,000		$100,000
Deposits	+ 1,000,000		800,000
Cheques	− 900,000		− 400,000
Balance	+$ 200,000		+$500,000
		+ $300,000 float	

Some companies actually operate with a negative cash balance on the corporate books, knowing that float will carry them through at the bank. In the preceding example, the firm may write $1.2 million in cheques on the assumption that only $800,000 will clear by the end of the week, thus leaving it with surplus funds in its bank account. The results, shown in Table 7–2 on next page, represent the phenomenon known as "playing the float." A float of $200,000 turns a negative balance on the corporation's books into a positive temporary balance on the bank's books. Obviously, float can also work against you if cheques going out are being processed more quickly than cheques coming in.

Improving Collections and Extending Disbursements

A firm must be diligent in collecting monies owed to it, in depositing those monies into a bank account, and in holding on to monies as long as possible, so that the funds can be utilized efficiently by the corporate treasurer. Having monies in a bank account

TABLE 7–2
Playing the float

	Corporate Books		Bank Books (usable funds) (amounts actually cleared)
Initial amount	$ 100,000		$100,000
Deposits	+ 1,000,000*		+ 800,000*
Cheques	− 1,200,000		− 800,000
Balance	−$ 100,000		+$100,000
		+ $200,000 float	

*Assumed to remain the same as in Table 7–1.

even one day longer can make a significant difference to the firm. The objective of faster collections is met by encouraging customers to effect payment on a timely basis, by cutting down on the time monies take to arrive in the firm's possession through the mail or electronic transfer, by accounting for and processing monies quickly upon receipt, and by depositing monies quickly into the firm's bank accounts. These steps serve to cut down on negative float.

Once in the firm's bank accounts, the funds can be more efficiently deployed, and this usually involves moving the funds to one location or at least administering the funds from one location. The advantages of concentration are many. The treasury has better control of the funds, and with only the head office making investment decisions, transaction and administration costs are lower. Furthermore, with one large, concentrated sum, the firm can invest the monies overnight in marketable securities and earn better rates of return (i.e., $100,000 receives a higher rate than 20 × $5,000).

The chartered banks have numerous services available to assist in any or all facets of improving a firm's collections. Many improve the collection and cheque-posting process, although, as we will discuss later, the electronic transfer of monies between firms and banks is increasingly replacing the use of cheques. A popular method for dealing with cheques is to have customers make payment to the firm's local offices throughout the country rather than to the corporate headquarters. The local office would then deposit the cheques into a bank account at its local bank branch. At the local branch, the deposits will be credited directly to the corporate account in a centralized location. Details of the various deposits will be available to the corporate treasurer by way of bank-produced reports or by viewing the bank accounts directly from a personal computer tied into the bank's system. Such a system reduces the time the customer's cheque is in the mail because of the proximity of the branch offices.

Bank of Montreal Cash Management www.bmo.com: under business banking, click cash management

For those who wish to enjoy the benefits of expeditious cheque processing at lower costs, a **lockbox system** may replace the role of the local collection offices. This system is particularly effective when there are no local branch offices or when customers are scattered across and outside the country. Under this plan, customers are requested to forward their cheques to a post office box in one of the cities that serve as regional data processing centres for the chartered banks. This allows the bank to process the cheques immediately through its computer network and credit the firm's account on a more timely basis. The firm is notified of the deposit and can do its accounting after the funds have already been put to work. The company thus retains many of the benefits of regional branch office collections, but with reduced corporate overhead.

On the other side of the ledger, it is important that disbursements be made only when due and not before. This allows a firm to retain the use of these funds for a longer period and to utilize them to increase returns. In Canada, because of the efficiency of the banking system in cheque clearing, any attempt to extend float has little effect. The one opportunity to extend disbursements in Canada may involve mailing cheques from dispersed locations so that the time in the mail might be extended. However, this method may impose extra administration costs and antagonize customers.

Electronic Funds Transfer

We are moving into an era where the collection and disbursement of monies is increasingly initiated through the techniques of **electronic funds transfer,** a system in which funds are moved between computer terminals without the use of a cheque. For instance, through the use of terminal communication between a store and your bank, your payment to a supermarket will be automatically charged against your account at the bank before you walk out the door. This is done with the debit card. For the customer, it is a quick and safe way to pay. For the supermarket, it cuts down on cheque handling and nonsufficient funds (NSF) cheques and provides immediate funds settlement. People also spend more. For the banks, it is another chargeable service, and it cuts down on their float.

Many large corporations have computerized cash management systems. For example, a firm may have 55 branch offices and 56 bank branches, one branch for each branch office and a lead bank branch in which the major corporate account is kept. At the end of each day the financial manager can check all the company's bank accounts through an on-line computer terminal. He or she can then transfer through the computer all excess cash balances from each bank branch to the corporate lead bank for overnight investment in money market securities.

Canadian banks have developed sophisticated cash management systems for their clients. On the disbursement side, payment can be initiated the same day to almost anywhere in Canada for payroll, pension, or dividend payments. Although float time is reduced, accuracy and security are improved and cheques are eliminated. As for collections, automated same day bill payments occur for mortgages, insurance premiums, and cable charges through preauthorized cheques, speeding up the collection process.

The banking establishment is currently promoting electronic data interchange (EDI) in conjunction with electronic funds transfer. EDI involves the exchange of payments and remittance information between the computers of business trading partners. Besides the electronic transfer of funds directly from the bank account of one business to its supplier, information that can update the inventory, accounts receivable, and payables accounts of the trading partners is initiated at the same time without direct involvement of staff. EDI is eliminating cheques, float, mail, and processing costs generated by the preparation and posting of such documents as purchase orders, invoices, and receiving reports. These transactions are facilitated through the regional data centres operated by the Canadian Payments System. Some companies, such as Sears Canada, will not purchase from suppliers that are not set up to handle EDI transactions. Today the vast majority of large companies use computers to initiate money transfers and to receive reports from their banks on lockbox receipts and bank balances, thus allowing them to judge the amount of float available.

FINANCE IN ACTION

Cash Management Systems at TD Canada Trust

International electronic funds transfer is mainly carried out through SWIFT, which is an acronym for the Society for Worldwide Interbank Financial Telecommunications (www.swift.com). SWIFT provides around-the-clock international payments between banks-foreign exchange, derivatives and trade transactions, and cash flows due to international securities transactions. Currently there are over 6,500 users, including 3,000 member banks in over 178 countries. The size of SWIFT's messaging (electronic funds transfers) is staggering and is estimated to be over $3.5 trillion per day and growing.

Rigid security standards are enforced. Each message is encrypted (secretly coded), and every money transaction is authenticated by another code. These security measures are important to the bank members as well as SWIFT, which assumes the financial liability for the accuracy, completeness, and confidentiality of transaction instructions from and to the point of connection to member bank circuits. One area of increasing concern has been electronic fraud, and SWIFT is using advanced smart card technology to improve its security system. Additionally, it will automate the process by which banks exchange secret authentication keys with each other.

Q1 Examine TD Canada Trust's cash management system by taking its web business banking tour at www.tdcommercialbanking.com

Cash Management Analysis

An efficiently maintained cash management program can be an expensive operation. Using a **cost-benefit analysis,** the expenses of setting up a program must be compared to the benefits that may accrue. Suppose a firm has average daily collections of $2 million and 1.5 days can be saved in the collection process by establishing a sophisticated collection network. Also, through stretching the disbursement schedule by one day, perhaps another $2 million becomes available for alternative uses. The money that could be earned on this freed-up capital represents a significant opportunity benefit to the firm. An example of this process is shown in Figure 7–1.

To complete the example, suppose the bank that will set up the cash management system will charge monthly fees of $15,000, but will also provide you with more timely information worth $40,000 a year to your firm. If the firm is able to earn 4 percent on the funds freed up, is the bank's system worth it?

Benefits			
Freed up funds	$2,000,000 × 1.5 days =	$3,000,000	
	2,000,000 × 1.0 days =	2,000,000	
		$5,000,000	
Opportunity benefit at 4% (interest earned on funds freed up)		$5,000,000 × 4% =	$200,000
Value of more timely information			40,000
			$240,000
Costs			
Bank fees		$15,000 × 12 =	$180,000
Net benefit			$60,000
The new system is worth it!			

FIGURE 7–1
Cash management network

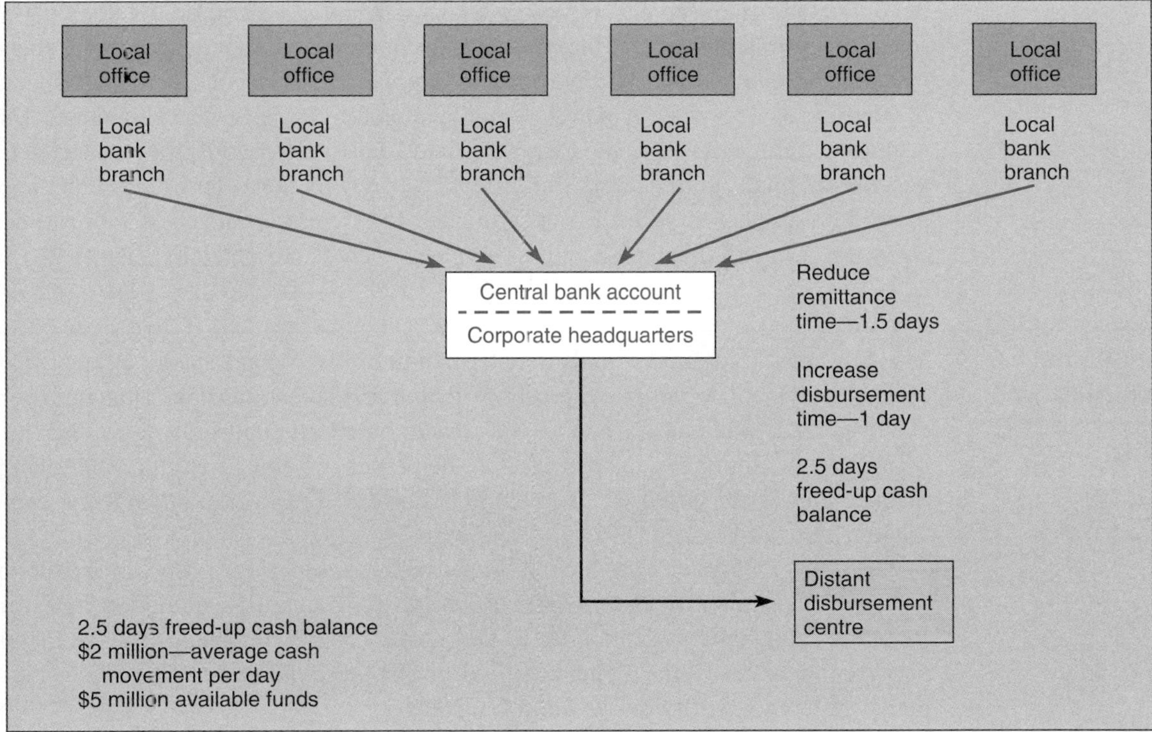

International Cash Management

Multinational corporations can shift funds around from country to country much as a firm may transfer funds from a local branch bank account in Halifax to the corporation's headquarters account in Montreal. An international electronic funds transfer system called SWIFT has been developed to facilitate this international payments system.

International cash management has many differences compared to domestic-based cash management systems. Payment methods differ from country to country. For example, in Poland, Russia, and other eastern European countries, cheques are seldom used in preference to cash, while electronic payments are more common than in the United States. International cash management is more complex because liquidity management involving short-term cash balances and deficits has to be managed across international boundaries and time zones and is subject to the risks of currency fluctuations and interest rate changes in all countries. There are also differences in banking systems, cheque-clearing processes, account balance management, information reporting systems, cultural beliefs, and tax and accounting procedures.

SWIFT
www.swift.com

A company may prefer to hold cash balances in one currency rather than another. This may occur either because of future expectations regarding foreign currency rate changes or because of interest rate differentials on short-term investments. In periods when one country's currency has been rising relative to others, financial managers often try to keep as much cash as possible in the country with the strong currency. For example, in the last decade the U.S. dollar was rising relative to most currencies. At that time the tendency was to try to keep balances in U.S. bank accounts or in U.S.-dollar-denominated bank accounts in foreign banks. The latter are commonly known as Eurodollar deposits. Because of the growth of the international money markets in size and in scope, Eurodollar deposits have become an important aspect of cash management. At the international level, cash managers employ domestic management techniques. Using such forecasting devices as the cash budget and daily cash reports, they collect and invest excess funds, until needed, in Eurodollar money market securities or other appropriate investments in securities denominated in strong currencies. A more in-depth coverage of international cash and asset management is presented in Chapter 21.

Marketable Securities

The firm may hold excess funds in anticipation of some major cash outlay such as a dividend payment or partial retirement of debt or as a precaution against an unexpected event. Indeed, when cash flow projections are based on expected values, the firm is bound to have shortages and surpluses. When funds are being held for other than immediate transaction purposes, they should be converted from cash into interest-earning marketable securities.[1]

The financial manager has a virtual supermarket of securities from which to choose. Among the factors influencing that choice are yield, maturity, minimum investment required, safety, and marketability. Under normal conditions the longer the maturity period of the security, the higher the yield, as displayed in Figure 7–2.[2] This is the liquidity preference theory discussed in Chapter 6.

The problem in stretching out the maturity of your investment is not that you are legally locked in (you can generally sell your security when you need funds) but that you may have to take a loss to convert the security to cash. A $5,000 government bond issued initially at 9.5 percent, with three years to maturity, may bring only $4,500 if the going interest rate climbs to 11 percent. This risk of price change increases as the maturity date is extended. A complete discussion of interest rate risk is included in Chapter 16. This is why the financial manager would want to closely match expected cash flows with the maturity schedule of marketable securities. A hedged approach is based to a certain extent on the reliability of the forecasted cash flows.

Various forms of marketable securities and investments, emphasizing the short term, are presented in Table 7–3, on page 222. These short-term securities are bought and sold in what is known as the **money market.** The key characteristics of each investment are delineated along with examples of yields for January 3, 2002. Rates are compared with those at March 22, 1990, when rates were considerably higher.

Money market securities are bought and sold based on their promised yield. Yield calculations for most money market securities are done on a discount basis, meaning the return received is the difference between the price paid and the maturity value. (For tax purposes the return is considered interest, not capital gain.) As an example, suppose

[1] The one possible exception to this principle is found in the practice of holding compensating balances at chartered banks—a topic for discussion in Chapter 8.

[2] Chapter 6 identified some of the different yield-maturity relationships encountered in recent history.

FIGURE 7–2
An examination of yield and maturity characteristics

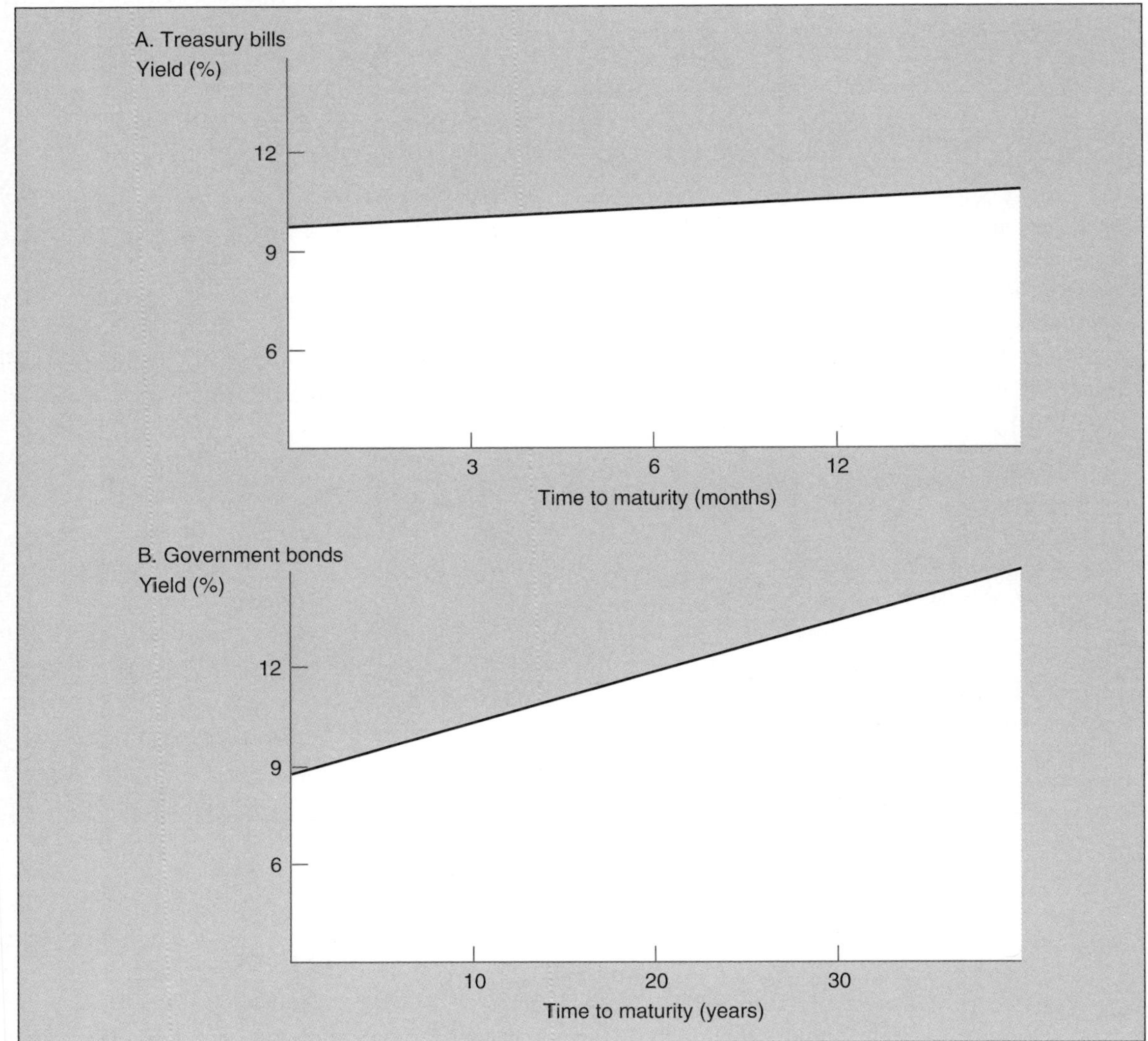

a financial security sells at 99.531 of its maturity value, with maturity occurring in 90 days. The annualized yield that would be quoted in the marketplace is given by the formula

$$\frac{100 - P}{P} \times \frac{365}{d} = r \qquad (7\text{–}1a)^3$$

P = Discounted price as percentage of maturity value
d = Number of days to maturity
r = Annualized yield

[3]Formula 7–1 is derived from the basic formula for determining the interest earned on an investment, which is $I = Prt$ ($I = 100 - 99.531$, $P = 99.531$, $t = 90/365$, r = to be determined). In the United States, 360 days is used in this calculation.

TABLE 7–3
Short-term investments

Investment	Maturity*	Minimum Amount	Safety	Marketability	Yield March 22, 1990‡	Yield January 3, 2002
Federal government securities						
Treasury bills§	91	$ 1,000	Excellent	Excellent	13.13%	1.91
Treasury bills	182	1,000	Excellent	Excellent	13.25	1.97
Provincial government securities						
Treasury bills	91	25,000	Excellent	Excellent	13.18	1.95
Nongovernment securities						
Term deposits (large)	90	100,000	Good	None†	12.75	1.45
Term deposits (small)	90	5,000	Good	None	10.00	1.35
Commercial paper	90	100,000	Good	Fair	13.33	2.04
Bankers' acceptances	90	25,000	Good	Good	13.27	2.05
Eurodollar deposits (bid)	90	25,000	Good	Excellent	12.81	2.11
LIBOR (London Interbank Offered Rate)	90	100,000	Good	Excellent	12.94	2.14
Savings accounts	Open	None	Excellent	None†	8.75	.10–1.00
Bank swap deposits	90	100,000	Excellent	None	13.23	1.98
Money market deposits (financial institutions)	Open	500	Excellent	None	10.15	1.00–1.75
Overnight (call) money	1 day	100,000	Excellent	Excellent	—	2.24

*Many of these securities can be purchased with different maturities than those indicated.
†Though not marketable, these investments are highly liquid and can often be withdrawn without penalty.
‡Quoted yields are often for wholesale amounts above $(million).
§In the summer of 1981, 91-day Treasury bills offered yields in excess of 20 percent.

In our example

$$\frac{100 - 99.531}{99.531} \times \frac{365}{90} = .0191 \text{ or } 1.91\%$$

The above calculation does not consider the potential compounding effects on the interest earned (return) after the 90-day period. The yield is expressed as an annual rate that ignores interest earned on interest—in other words, the compounding effects. An annualized effective yield calculation considers the compounding and is expressed by the formula

$$\left(1 + \frac{100 - P}{P}\right)^{\frac{365}{d}} - 1 = r \qquad (7\text{–}1b)$$

In our example this is .0192, or 1.92 percent. With a hand calculator, this is easy to determine if we identify 100 = *FV*, −99.531 = *PV*, 90/365 = *n*, and 0 = *pmt*. We then compute *i*.

At the foundation of interest rates in the economy is the rate at which financial institutions lend money to each other for one day to meet temporary cash shortfalls. The banks exchange billions of dollars a day through their clearing systems, and often are left with deficit or surplus positions with the Bank of Canada. This requires them to borrow from each other or from the Bank of Canada at the overnight rate. The **overnight, or call, money rate** is the rate at which the major financial institutions lend money to each other for this short period. In other countries the rate may have other names, such as the federal funds rate in the United States, but regardless of its name there is a strong relationship between the overnight rate and the other short-term interest rates of the marketplace.

Bank of Canada
www.bankofcanada.ca/en/backgrounders/bg-p9.htm

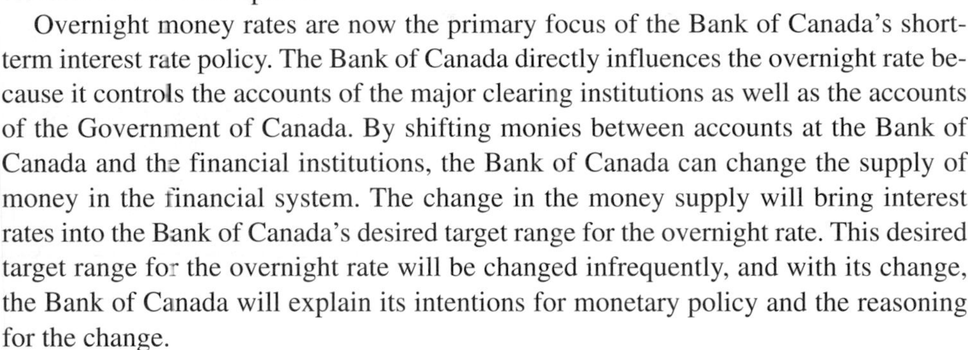

Overnight money rates are now the primary focus of the Bank of Canada's short-term interest rate policy. The Bank of Canada directly influences the overnight rate because it controls the accounts of the major clearing institutions as well as the accounts of the Government of Canada. By shifting monies between accounts at the Bank of Canada and the financial institutions, the Bank of Canada can change the supply of money in the financial system. The change in the money supply will bring interest rates into the Bank of Canada's desired target range for the overnight rate. This desired target range for the overnight rate will be changed infrequently, and with its change, the Bank of Canada will explain its intentions for monetary policy and the reasoning for the change.

Financial institutions may occasionally borrow from the Bank of Canada, although it is more convenient to borrow in the overnight market. The **bank rate** is the interest rate charged to Canadian chartered banks when they borrow from our lender of last resort—the Bank of Canada. The bank rate is set at the upper limit of the overnight rate target band determined by the Bank of Canada.

From 1980 until early 1996 the average yield of 91-day T-bills sold at the Tuesday auction by the Bank of Canada set the bank rate for one week at one-quarter of 1 percent (25 basis points) above the average yield. For example, if the average yield on the 91-day T-bills at the auction was .0512, or 5.12 percent, the bank rate would have been set at .0537, or 5.37 percent. The supply and demand forces in the market primarily determine Treasury bill yields, and this caused frequent changes in the bank rate. Therefore, the Bank of Canada's desire for interest rates in the economy was not always clear. The shift from 91-days to one day also reflected the current realities of the faster-paced market of today. Daily fluctuations of the Treasury bill rate or the overnight rate do not reset the bank rate.

Let us examine the characteristics of each security offered in the money market. **Treasury bills** are short-term obligations of the Government of Canada and are a popular place to park funds because of a large and active market. The market is large and active because the Government of Canada stands behind these IOUs and is prepared to repurchase them at any time, making T-bills virtually risk free. In addition, because they are in bearer form—meaning ownership resides with the individual in possession—they can be resold over and over again until maturity. It is the level of activity generated by the security of the Treasury bill that makes it an extremely liquid financial asset. In 1997 to aid market liquidity it was decided that T-bills would only be auctioned biweekly, with maturities of 98 days, 182 days, and one year. However, the investor may buy an outstanding T-bill with as little as two days remaining to maturity (perhaps two prior investors have held it for 48 days each). Treasury bills trade on a discount basis. Although federal government T-bills can be bought at retail in amounts as small as $1,000, the rates quoted are generally for transactions of $1 million or

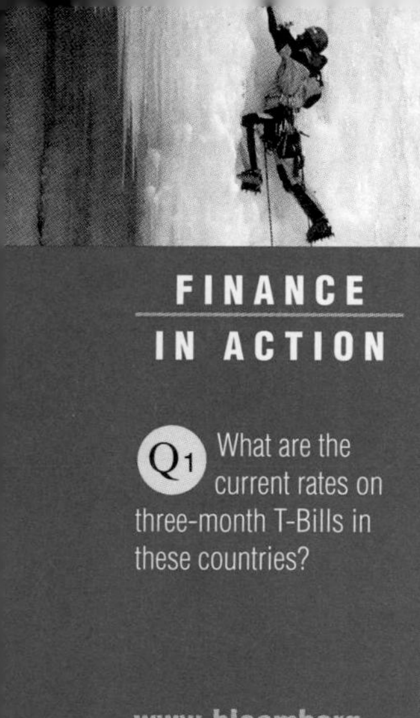

FINANCE IN ACTION

Treasury Bills around the Globe

The three-month treasury bill issued by federal governments is perhaps the safest and most liquid investment available. Most major countries offer treasury bills or something similar. How do the yields compare in different countries? Comparisons are available at the Bloomberg market site under government bonds.

In January 2002 the following rates were available on three-month government securities:

Canada	1.95%
United States	1.72
Britain	3.77
France	3.20
Germany	3.29
Italy	3.11
Japan	0.014

The rates in Canada and the United States had been lowered dramatically through 2001 to stimulate the economy. Japan had yields that were virtually zero. The Japanese economy was experiencing deflationary pressures, and its economy had been stagnant for several years. The interest rates in the three European countries were virtually the same. These countries were all part of the European Economic Union that has introduced the Euro, a common currency. A common currency requires similar monetary policies and interest rates in all the countries that join the monetary union. Britain maintained a separate monetary policy.

Q1 What are the current rates on three-month T-Bills in these countries?

www.bloomberg.com

more. The yields on the smaller denominations are substantially less. The fact that the market for Government of Canada T-bills services about $100 billion in monthly securities trading attests to their popularity as short-term investment vehicles.

Canadian provinces and municipalities, along with their agencies and crown corporations, also issue short-term securities such as Treasury bills. There is a good secondary market for these securities, and they generally provide a slightly higher return than do Government of Canada T-bills.

Commercial paper represents unsecured promissory notes issued to the public by large business corporations. Over 200 major corporations in Canada issue commercial paper, and over $125 billion was outstanding in early 2002. Finance companies such as the mortgage subsidiaries of the major banks and sales finance companies are very active in the commercial paper market, issuing what is commonly referred to as *finance company paper.* Commercial paper is usually sold only in amounts of $100,000 or more. Maturities range from 30 days to one year, with the shorter terms being most popular. Commercial paper is sold in bearer form and is discounted. Although the market for industrial commercial paper is relatively small, it has grown rapidly in Canada. Canadian banks are encouraging industrial commercial paper as new regulations concerning bankers' acceptances make the banks' returns from guaranteeing these securities less attractive.

Bankers' acceptances are short-term securities that generally arise from foreign trade. This is explored more fully in Chapter 8. The acceptance is a draft drawn on a bank for payment when presented to the bank. The difference between a draft and a cheque is that a company does not have to deposit funds at the bank to cover the draft until the bank has accepted the draft for *future* payment of the required amount. This means the exporter who now holds the bankers' acceptance may have to wait 30, 60, or 90 days to collect the money. There is an active market involving approximately $50 billion in bankers' acceptances. This market has developed as the exporter, wanting cash now, sells the draft at a discount into the market. Purchasers are reassured by the banks' guarantee of payment. Banks themselves hold bankers' acceptances to meet their liquidity needs.

Another popular short-term investment arising from foreign trade is the **Eurocurrency deposit.** The most common Eurocurrency is the U.S. Eurodollar, which is a U.S. dollar held on deposit by foreign banks that is, in turn, loaned out by those banks to anyone seeking dollars. There is a large market for Eurodollar deposits and loans mostly centred in the London international banking market. Because this is a market for large deposits of $1 million or more, only large companies such as Bell Canada and HydroOne are active in it.

HydroOne
www.HydroOne.com

LIBOR (London Interbank Offered Rate) is the rate offered for dollar deposits in the London market. Thus, companies can lend money (that is, deposit) to banks at that rate. Although this is essentially a Eurodollar deposit, the difference is that it is centred only in London rather than in Paris or Frankfurt or some other part of Europe. LIBOR is often used as a base lending rate for companies that may borrow at a floating interest rate of LIBOR plus a small premium. The use of LIBOR is discussed further in Chapter 21.

Another outlet for investment is the **term deposit.** Depending on the issuing bank or trust company, these deposits may be called certificates of deposit (CDs), term notes, term deposit receipts, or some other similar name. The investor places his or her funds on deposit at a specified rate over a given time period as evidenced by the certificate received. This is a market for smaller amounts ($1,000 to $100,000), with no secondary market. In these cases the money is invested for specified periods of from one month to seven years.

If the company wants to invest $100,000 or more in a bank deposit, however, it can do so via **bearer deposits,** which are transferable from one investor to another. Although this feature makes bearer deposits somewhat liquid, they are still not a very attractive place for temporary excess funds. Part of the reason bearer deposit notes are not attractive is that they pay no interest, unlike other money market instruments that sell at a discount. In the United States bearer deposit notes are known as **certificates of deposit.** Canadian CDs are not transferable.

The lowest yielding investment may well be a passbook *savings account.* Its relative advantages are that it can accommodate small investments and that it can usually be liquidated with no notice. Thus, although not attractive to the large corporations that have other more lucrative options available, the savings account is still a good short-term investment alternative for small businesses and individuals.

Bank **swapped deposits** have arisen as Canadian companies take advantage of differences in international short-term interest rates. For example, in a typical case, the Canadian company would convert Canadian dollars to U.S. dollars and deposit them in a U.S. bank. Concurrently, the company would execute a futures contract to sell the U.S. dollars for Canadian dollars when the deposit matures. Thus, the company ends up with a **hedged** U.S. dollar investment.[4] This is attractive if the combination of direct yield and foreign exchange cost or yield generates a higher return than would a straight deposit in Canada.

For the small investor there is the **money market fund,** a product that pools the monies of many small investors and invests in a collection of short-term, highly liquid securities. For as little as $500, the investor can have part of the higher-yielding

[4]Hedged means the investor has no foreign exchange risk.

securities with returns only slightly lower to cover management and administrative fees. Some financial institutions also offer accounts that invest in T-bills or other money market securities to allow their customers more attractive deposit returns.

Management of Accounts Receivable

Despite the expansion of credit via bank credit cards and the creation of finance subsidiaries, a substantial portion of the investment in assets by industrial companies continues to be in accounts receivable. This granting of credit by companies as an alternative to the banks or the capital markets occurs because trade credit facilitates sales. Credit is a part of the complete marketing package presented to a potential customer. It does however require careful monitoring and analysis by the financial manager.

Of course the accounts receivable of one firm is an account payable at another firm. The smaller firm, in fact, may lack access to the capital markets or to bank financing. Banks may be unwilling to lend to the small firm because the security it can offer is insufficient or the risks are too high and the profit margins too low. Larger firms with higher profit margins on their product, by extending **trade credit**, in effect provide access for the smaller firm to these financing sources. Remember, the large firm likely supports its accounts receivable position with short-term financing through the banks or the capital markets. Examine Figure 8–1, on page 253, to see the extent of trade credit financing in Canada.

Trade credit is readily available and convenient. According to Statistics Canada, accounts receivable as a percentage of total assets for industrial corporations in Canada have remained between 12 and 15 percent since 1962. In absolute terms, accounts receivable have risen from $7 billion to over $212 billion by late 2001.

Accounts Receivable as an Investment

As is true of other current assets, accounts receivable should be thought of as an investment. The level of accounts receivable should not be adjudged too high or too low based on historical standards of industry norms, but rather, the test should be whether the level of return we are able to earn from this asset equals or exceeds the potential gain from other commitments. For example, if we allow our customers 10 extra days to clear their accounts, our accounts receivable balance increases—draining funds from marketable securities and perhaps drawing down the inventory level. We must ask whether we are optimizing our return in light of appropriate risk and liquidity considerations.

Suppose a company's annual sales are $10.95 million and the company sells on terms of net 30, meaning customers are expected to pay their bills 30 days after purchase. Therefore, the

$$\text{Average daily sales} = \$10.95 \text{ million} \times \tfrac{1}{365} = \$30{,}000$$

$$\text{Average accounts receivable} = \$30{,}000 \times 30 \text{ days} = \$900{,}000$$

$$\text{or Average accounts receivable} = \$10.95 \text{ million} \times \tfrac{30}{365} = \$900{,}000.$$

If annual credit sales remain at $10.95 million and customers pay in 30 days, on average, the daily accounts receivable balance is $900,000. This is the company's investment as a result of its credit policy.

Vendor Funding at Nortel

In 2001 Nortel's optical network business fell 80 percent. For the overall company, sales that had been projected to reach $40 billion fell to $16 billion. Over 50,000 Nortel employees were laid off, 248 offices vacated, product lines slashed, and R & D expenditures reduced. The slowdown in sales was dramatic, as was the plunge in the price of Nortel shares. Nortel was Canada's largest company with a market value for equity of over $300 billion. Less than a year later the market value was less than $30 billion.

As a result of its sales slowdown, Nortel was left with a lot of inventory that it could not sell and accounts receivable it could not collect. However throughout 2001 it aggressively reduced its inventory from $4.3 billion to less than $2 billion and accounts receivable from over $8 billion to less than $4 billion. This was done to provide liquidity. However a lot of the uncollectible accounts receivable were written off, including over $750 million in the third quarter of 2001.

Nortel despite its accounts receivable problems was again providing vendor financing in 2002. This is the practice of lending money to customers to purchase Nortel products. Nortel like any business is dependent on the success of its customers and when they struggle so does Nortel. This is what happened so dramatically in 2001. Apparently Nortel was expecting (or hoping) that its clients would be more successful in 2002 and be able to eventually pay for the products purchased from Nortel. Otherwise the value of Nortel's accounts receivable would again come under stress.

FINANCE IN ACTION

Q1 Has Nortel had additional loss provisions for accounts receivable?

Q2 Is Nortel's accounts receivable position growing?

www.nortel.com

Symbol: NT

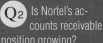

Notice that if the customers pay 10 days later,

$$\text{Average accounts receivable} = \$10.95 \text{ million} \times \frac{40}{365} = \$1{,}200{,}000.$$

This is an increased investment of $300,000 on average every day of the year. That investment could have been in marketable securities as an alternative. If those securities offered a return of 6 percent, the annual opportunity cost of allowing customers to pay 10 days later would be $18,000 ($300,000 × 6%).

An example of a buildup in accounts receivable is presented in Figure 7–3, on the next page, with supportive financing provided through reducing lower-yielding assets and increasing lower-cost liabilities. For example, if accounts receivable are increasing, they are supported by bank loans or perhaps a less significant position in marketable securities. Both have a cost to the firm.

Credit Policy Administration

In the extension of credit, three primary policy variables to consider in conjunction with our profit objective are:

1. Credit standards.
2. Terms of credit.
3. Collection policy.

Credit Standards A firm must decide on the degree of credit risk it is prepared to accept. We have seen that large sums of "potential" cash can be invested in accounts receivable. Any receivable that becomes uncollectible affects the firm's success. Accounts receivable are self-liquidating assets. This depends on the ability of a firm's customers to sell their product so the firm granting credit can be paid. The degree of acceptable credit risk is influenced by several factors. These factors include whether or not the firm is attempting to establish a market, if the firm is responding to competitive

FIGURE 7–3
Financing growth in accounts receivable

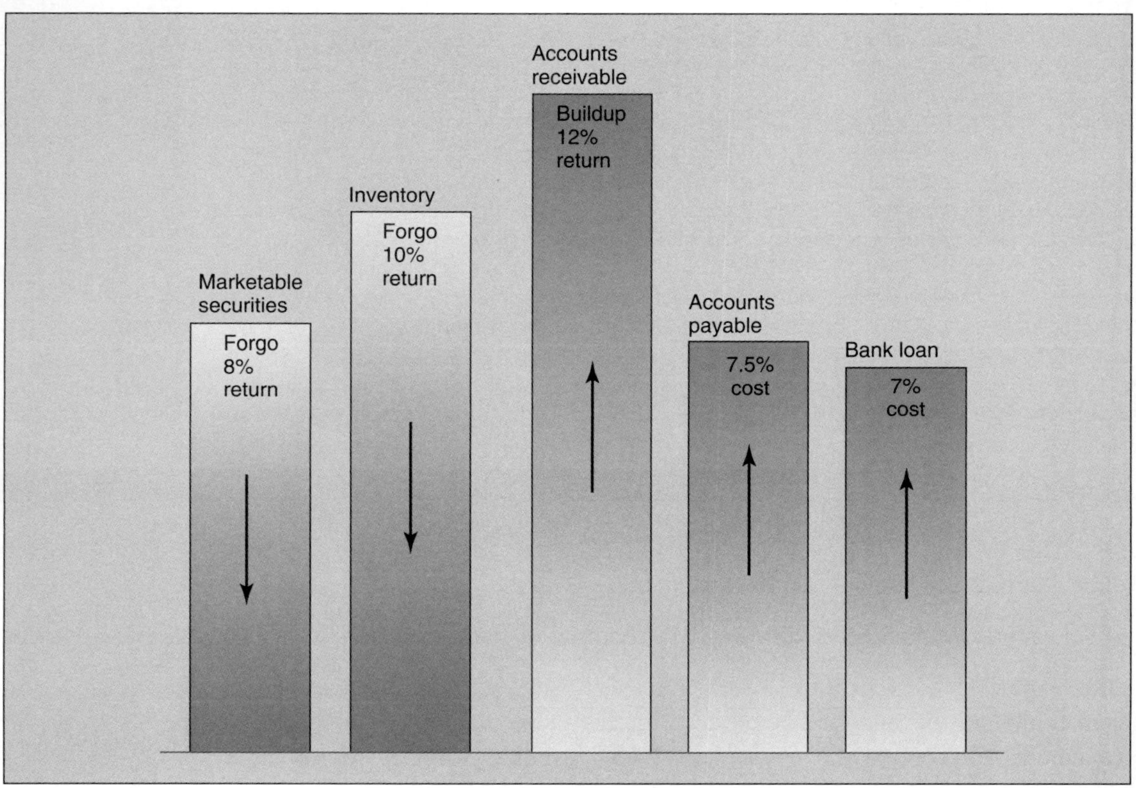

pressures, and the degree of utilization of plant capacity. In early 1990, and again in late 2001, the automobile companies offered credit direct to the ultimate customer. At the same time, North America had an oversupply of cars, automakers laid off workers, and plant capacity was underutilized.

To establish the degree of credit risk of a potential customer, a firm should develop a credit profile. This profile establishes the customer's strengths and weaknesses. Most important, it questions if customers are able to pay and if they can buy enough. Companies that analyze credit risk tend to develop a system in some way related to the 4 Cs of credit.

Character is the first C. An analyst attempts to determine the customer's willingness to pay. If things get rough, does the customer go into hiding or attempt to work things out? Clues as to the strength of corporate character come from information on fraudulent activities, legal disputes, union problems, dealings with other suppliers, and even the willingness to supply credit information.

Perhaps most important is the second C—the customer's capacity, which is the ability to pay. Capacity is built on marketing abilities, experience in the business, the management team, and overall, the ability to generate profits. To judge a customer's ability to generate profits is a difficult process. Financial ratio analysis can be of considerable assistance, however, as is an investigation of the customer's abilities based on past experience.

The third C is a customer's capital. This is a look at assets and net worth. Strong net worth is evidence of past success and a commitment by shareholders to the firm. Growing assets demonstrate an ongoing successful business. In difficult economic times when its ability to generate profits is diminished, a strong net worth helps a company survive.

The final C is conditions. This is the state of the economy and the industry in general. One's experience and knowledge best help an analyst in getting a fix on conditions. One tries to foresee how existing conditions impact the potential credit customer. How the customer adapts to changing conditions in the marketplace is also a consideration.

The preceding is a very sketchy outline of the four Cs of credit. An analyst examines information and attempts to determine the potential customer's degree of credit risk. Regardless of the amount of information and analysis, judgments must be made because credit analysis is not an exact science. Once the degree of credit risk is established, it must be measured against company policy to determine whether or not granting credit is acceptable.

Determining a credit profile of a potential customer requires gathering information. An extensive network of credit information has been developed by credit agencies throughout the country. The most prominent source is **Dun & Bradstreet**, which publishes the *Reference Book,* listing many thousands of business establishments. Information is given on the firm's line of business, net worth, and creditworthiness. An example of the rating system used by Dun & Bradstreet is presented in Table 7–4.

Dun & Bradstreet
www.dnb.com

TABLE 7–4
Dun & Bradstreet credit rating system

Key to Ratings

Estimated Financial Strength			Composite Credit Appraisal			
			High	Good	Fair	Limited
5A	Over	$50,000,000	1	2	3	4
4A	$10,000,000 to	50,000,000	1	2	3	4
3A	1,000,000 to	10,000,000	1	2	3	4
2A	750,000 to	1,000,000	1	2	3	4
1A	500,000 to	750,000	1	2	3	4
BA	300,000 to	500,000	1	2	3	4
BB	200,000 to	300,000	1	2	3	4
CB	125,000 to	200,000	1	2	3	4
CC	75,000 to	125,000	1	2	3	4
DC	50,000 to	75,000	1	2	3	4
DD	35,000 to	50,000	1	2	3	4
EE	20,000 to	35,000	1	2	3	4
FF	10,000 to	20,000	1	2	3	4
GG . . .	5,000 to	10,000	1	2	3	4
HH	Up to	5,000	1	2	3	4

A firm with a BB2 rating has estimated financial strength, based on net worth, of $200,000 to $300,000, with an overall composite credit rating of "Good." Besides the *Reference Book,* Dun & Bradstreet can also provide extensive individualized credit reports on potential customers.

Dun & Bradstreet has created a statistical model to analyze the risk of a bad debt. Some of the more important variables they put into their model are the age of the company in years, negative public records, total number of employees, facility owned, financial statement data, payment index, percent of satisfactory payment experiences, and the percent of slow or negative payment experiences. The model is able to predict payment problems and bankruptcy with a high probability 12 months before they occur.

Given that the world is doing more and more business on a global scale, the fact that you can track companies around the world on a database that lists 39 million companies is helpful. The companies on the database can be accessed through a D-U-N-S number, which is accepted by the United Nations as a global business identification standard. The **Data Universal Number System (D-U-N-S)** is a unique nine-digit code assigned by Dun & Bradstreet to each business in its information base. The D-U-N-S number can be used to track a whole family of companies that are related through ownership. Subsidiaries, divisions, and branches can be tracked to their ultimate parent company at the top of the family pyramid. For example, this tracking ability helps to determine who would ultimately be responsible for a bad debt that occurred in a subsidiary.

Certain industries have also developed their own special credit reporting agencies. Even more important are the local credit bureaus that keep close tabs on day-to-day transactions in a given community.

In addition, information can be gathered from

- Sales reports and visits to the potential customer's place of business.
- Customer's financial statements.
- Financial institutions.
- Other suppliers and industry contacts.
- Other credit reporting agencies such as Equifax.

Equifax
www.equifax.com

Terms of Trade *Terms of trade* refers to the length of time credit is granted and whether or not a discount is allowed for early payment. The credit period is often set in response to what the competition is doing. However, a company may set a different credit period to increase sales or perhaps to make up for product deficiencies. Discounts are usually offered to encourage early payment to address cash flow concerns, rather than to stimulate sales. We have already seen how the length of the credit period allowed (not necessarily the stated term) can have a dramatic impact on the level of investment in accounts receivable. Offering the **credit terms** 2/10, net 30 enables the customer to deduct 2 percent from the face amount of the bill when paying within the first 10 days, but if the discount is not taken, the customer must remit the full amount within 30 days. As later demonstrated in Chapter 8, the annualized cost of not taking a cash discount may be substantial.

Collection Policy A third area for consideration under credit policy administration is the collection function. A company must establish collection procedures that get after delinquent accounts in a timely and regular manner. The procedures should be applied consistently with the goal not only of collecting the debt, but also of maintaining the customer. A number of quantitative measures may be applied to the credit department of the firm.

1. **Average collection period** $= \dfrac{\text{Accounts receivable}}{\text{Average daily credit sales}}$

   (See Formula 3–4b in Chapter 3.) As discussed in Chapter 6, the average collection period is part of the cash conversion period. An increasing collection period will have implications for financial planning, as it will take longer to turn the accounts receivable investment into cash. When applying this formula, a company must be careful if sales vary throughout the year, as it can give distorted signals. A trend toward a longer collection period could be the result of a predetermined plan to extend credit terms or the consequence of poor credit administration. Management should monitor this measure closely as compared to the collection department's credit terms and industry averages. If the collection period extends beyond these standards, management should seek corrective action, as it is likely that increasing amounts of capital are being tied up unproductively in accounts receivable.
2. **Ratio of bad debts to credit sales.** An increasing ratio may indicate too many weak accounts or an aggressive market expansion policy. On the other hand, too low a ratio may indicate an overly restrictive credit policy that is limiting sales. The standard for this ratio should be past experience and industry averages.
3. **Aging of accounts receivables.** We may wish to determine the amounts of time the various accounts have been on our books. The likelihood of accounts becoming uncollectible increases dramatically the further the account extends beyond its credit terms. Furthermore, older receivables represent less profitable investments. If there is a buildup in receivables beyond our normal credit terms, we may wish to take remedial action. Such a buildup is shown in the following table.

Age of Receivables, June 30, 2002

Month of Sales	Age of Account (days)	Amounts
May	0–30	$ 60,000
April	31–60	25,000
March	61–90	5,000
February	91–120	10,000
Total receivables		$100,000

If our normal credit terms are 30 days, we may be doing a poor job of collecting our accounts, with particular attention required on the over-90-day accounts. It is important to examine the nature of the accounts receivable because their characteristics can change quickly due to their rapid turnover.

An Actual Credit Decision

We now examine a credit decision that brings together the various elements of accounts receivable management. In arriving at a credit decision, it is best to focus on the incremental changes that result from a potential change in credit policy. These are identified by comparing the firm's financial situation under the present credit policy with what it would be under the proposed credit policy. Only those financial variables that change are relevant for analysis. Our analysis and decision are good if we improve the wealth of the shareholders. Generally, credit policy changes affect the level of sales by changing credit standards or by changing the length of the credit period. Often, changes are a response to competitive pressures.

For example, let us assume a firm is considering a credit decision to sell to a group of customers that will result in sales increasing from $100,000 to $110,000, an increase of $10,000 in new annual sales. The cost of producing the product is 67 percent of sales, and selling expenses are expected to be 10 percent of sales. Additionally, collection costs are projected at 5 percent of sales, and because the new customers are risky, we forecast 10 percent of the new sales to be uncollectible. While this is a very high rate of nonpayment, the critical question is, What is the potential contribution of these incremental sales to profitability? These incremental revenues and expenses are fairly easy to identify with the traditional income statement approach.

Sales	$100,000	$110,000
Cost of goods sold	67,000	73,700
Gross profit margin	33,000	36,300
Selling expenses	10,000	11,000
Bad debt expense	10,000	11,000
Collection expense	5,000	5,500
Income before interest and taxes	$ 8,000	$ 8,800

However, other costs may be more elusive, in particular the opportunity costs that will arise if the firm commits to the new credit policy. A major consideration is the increased investment in accounts receivable and the opportunity cost on the firm's funds tied up in this asset. This cost is often taken from the rate on short-term demand loans, which are sometimes used to finance accounts receivable. If bank financing is used for the incremental investment, this cost would be described fully by an income statement approach. However, the cost of an increased investment in accounts receivable is not always easily identified by such a direct cost. Sometimes the increased investment is provided by an increased equity contribution and expected return to the shareholders does not show up on the income statement. The use of an opportunity cost in the analysis captures the broader possibilities for financing the accounts receivable position.

Additionally, our analysis might consider possible investments in inventories or plant or equipment that may result from increased sales. We do not, however, consider them in this example.

In our example, our firm expects its receivables to turn over six times a year, and we assume that the opportunity cost is 15 percent. The analysis, set out below, proceeds on the basis of the incremental revenues and costs that we have identified from selling to the new group of customers and includes the opportunity cost on the increased investment in accounts receivable. Incremental analysis isolates and identifies only the relevant changes that result from a shift in credit policy.

			Summary of Costs/Benefits
Incremental sales		$10,000	
Incremental contribution margin	(100%-67%)		$ 3,300
Incremental selling expense	10%		<1,000>
Incremental bad debts (uncollectibles)	10%		<1,000>
Incremental collection costs	5%		<500>
Incremental accounts receivable[5]		10,000/6 = 1,667	
Incremental opportunity cost on investment in accounts receivable	15%		<250>
Total incremental change			$ 550

Our decision would be to proceed with the new credit policy. Not only have the increased profits and costs been considered in the analysis, but most important from an investor or shareholder perspective, consideration also has been given to the opportunity cost of having funds tied up or invested in accounts receivable. This opportunity cost of funds in our example is a before-tax cost. This analysis is basically for one time period and assumes that the incremental changes are perpetual. It may neglect considerations such as the time value of money, changes to product life, earlier capital expenditure requirements as increasing sales wear out machinery sooner, and tax changes due to the previously noted considerations.

Another Example of a Credit Decision

Assume that the firm currently has annual sales of $121,667 and collection occurs in 30 days. It is expected that sales will increase to $146,000 if 45 days of credit are extended to customers. Additionally, administration costs are projected to increase by $1,000. Another cost is the expected increase in bad debt expense from 1 to 1.5 percent of sales. The firm has an opportunity cost of capital of 12 percent and its variable costs are 80 percent of sales.

[5]We could actually argue that our out-of-pocket commitment to sales is 82 percent times $10,000, or $8,200. This would indicate an even smaller commitment to receivables. However, does this best capture the opportunity cost of an investment that has changed in substance from inventory to credit with the concurrent change in the profit and equity accounts and their subsequent expectation of return?

	Current	Projected	Summary
Sales	$121,667	$146,000	
Incremental sales		24,333	
Incremental contribution margin (100%-80%)		4,867	$4,867
Incremental administration costs		1,000	<1,000>
Bad debts:			
1%	1,216		
1.5%		2,190	
Incremental bad debts		974	<974>
Accounts receivable	121,667	146,000	
	× 30/365 =	× 45/365 =	
	10,000	18,000	
Incremental accounts receivable investment		8,000	
Incremental opportunity cost on investment in accounts receivable	12%	960	<960>
Total incremental change			$1,933

Decision: Implement new credit terms! On an incremental basis, with consideration given to the investment in accounts receivable, there is positive value added to the firm from changing the credit policy.

Inventory Management

Inventory needs to be financed, and its efficient management can increase a firm's profitability. Just like accounts receivable, inventory can represent a sizable investment by a company. An adequate return is expected on this investment. The amount of inventory is not totally controlled by company management; it also is affected by sales, production, and economic conditions.

GM Canada
www.gmcanada.com

A good case study is the automobile industry. Its inventory management is influenced by cyclical sales that are highly sensitive to the economy. Automakers often suffer from inventory buildups when sales decline because adjusting production levels takes time. In late 2001 as the economy slowed the car manufacturers implemented buyer incentive programs such as zero percent financing and cash rebates. These programs cut profit margins per car, but generated cash flow and reduced investment expenses associated with holding high inventories. By 2002 layoffs and plant closings were being announced and efforts were being made to make the production lines more flexible by running several makes of cars to allow quicker response to changing consumer tastes.

Inventory management has been changing. Seeking to reduce the large costs that can be tied up in inventory, companies have been developing ways to control overinvestment. The just-in-time (JIT) process that brings parts to the assembly line just as they are needed has helped to reduce inventories. We have also seen the benefits of on-line inventory reporting systems that allow management to quickly respond to changing market conditions. Excess inventory buildups do not appear to be as prevalent as in the past.

Inventory is the least liquid of current assets, and it should provide the highest yield to justify investment. While the financial manager may have direct control over cash management, marketable securities, and accounts receivable, control over inventory policy is generally shared with production management and marketing.

In Chapter 3 we noted the relationship between cost of goods sold (COGS) and inventory, which was expressed either as the inventory holding period or inventory turnover ratio. This relationship is expressed in the following example:

$$\text{COGS/day} \times \text{holding period} = \text{Average inventory}$$
$$\$1{,}216{,}667/365 \times 30 = \$100{,}000$$

or it can also be expressed as a turnover ratio of 12 (365/30). The average inventory position may fluctuate dramatically above the average if sales of the firm's product vary throughout the year. Also note how the average inventory and the cost of financing the inventory position will change as the holding period (turnover) or level of sales (and thus COGS) changes.

Level versus Seasonal Production

A manufacturing firm must determine whether a plan of level or seasonal production should be followed. Production scheduling is complicated by uncertain demand and the desire to provide immediate service. Furthermore, inventory buildups may be used to take advantage of quantity discount offers. In addition, an inventory buildup is a hedging technique to deal with anticipated resource shortages or price increases. Level production was discussed in Chapter 6. While level (even) production throughout the year allows for maximum efficiency in the use of labour and machinery, it may result in unnecessarily high inventory buildups before shipment, particularly in a seasonal business. We may have 10,000 bathing suits in stock in November.

If we produce on a seasonal basis, the inventory problem is eliminated, but we then have unused capacity during slack periods. Furthermore, as we shift to maximum operations to meet seasonal needs, we may be forced to pay overtime wages to labour and to sustain other inefficiencies as equipment is overused.

We have a classic problem in financial analysis. Are the cost savings from level production sufficient to justify the extra expenditure in carrying inventory? Let us look at a typical case.

	Production	
	Level	Seasonal
Average inventory	$100,000	$70,000
Operating costs—aftertaxes	50,000	60,000

Though we have to invest $30,000 more in average inventory under level production, we save $10,000 in operating costs. This represents a 33 percent return on investment. If our required rate of return is 10 percent, this would clearly be an acceptable alternative.[6]

[6]The problem may be further evaluated by using the capital budgeting techniques presented in Chapter 12.

Inventory Policy in Inflation (and Deflation)

While the consumer price index has risen consistently from 93 in 1990 to 117 by late 2001, the commodity price index on industrial materials has been quite volatile over the same period. From 100 in 1990, it was up over 132 by late 1995, and was down to 93 in late 2001.

Price increases on nickel and copper were so great in the late 1980s that Inco almost didn't know what to do with the cash flow it was generating. A dividend of over $1 billion was paid to shareholders. Only the most astute inventory manager can hope to prosper in this environment. The problem can be partially controlled by taking moderate inventory positions (that is, do not fully commit at one price).

New York Mercantile Exchange
www.nymex.com

Another way of protecting an inventory position is by use of a **futures contract,** a hedging technique. A futures contract is an agreement to sell (buy) a commodity at a specific price and on a specific date in the future, regardless of the actual price of the commodity at that future date. Although a company gives up the ability to make a potentially large gain if prices move up, it also avoids a potential loss if prices go down. The advantage to the financial manager is that uncertainty, or risk, is removed, as the manager knows the price that will be received at the future date. Planning can occur with a known cash flow. Futures are traded on organized exchanges that ensure that the contracts are fulfilled.

Rapid price movements in inventory may also have a major impact on the reported income of the firm, a process described in Chapter 3. A firm using FIFO (first-in, first-out) accounting may experience large inventory profits when old, less expensive inventory is written off against new high prices in the marketplace. The benefits may be transitory, as the process reverses itself when prices decline. Nevertheless, profits that result from holding inventories are subject to tax, if they are carried to the bottom line. This reduces cash flow when increasing costs are being incurred to purchase new inventories. Additionally, escalating financing expenses are required to finance the inflating inventory position although the actual number of inventory items may remain constant.

The Inventory Decision Model

Substantial research has been devoted to the problem of determining optimum inventory size, order quantity, usage rate, and similar considerations. An entire branch in the field of operations research is dedicated to the subject. We examine a somewhat simple model that is dependent on the certainty of the variables used—in particular, the certainty of steady demand for the product.

In developing an inventory model, we must evaluate the two basic costs associated with inventory: the carrying costs and the ordering costs. Through a careful analysis of both of these variables, we can determine the optimum order size to place to minimize costs.

Carrying Costs **Carrying costs** include interest on funds tied up in inventory and the cost of warehouse space, insurance premiums, and material handling expenses. There is also an implicit cost associated with the dangers of obsolescence and rapid price change. The larger the order we place, the greater the average inventory we will have on hand, and the higher the carrying cost.

Ordering Costs As a second factor, we must consider the **ordering costs** and the processing of inventory into stock. If we maintain a relatively low average inventory in stock, we must order many times, and total ordering cost will be high. The opposite patterns associated with the two costs are portrayed in Figure 7–4.

FIGURE 7–4
Determining the optimum inventory level

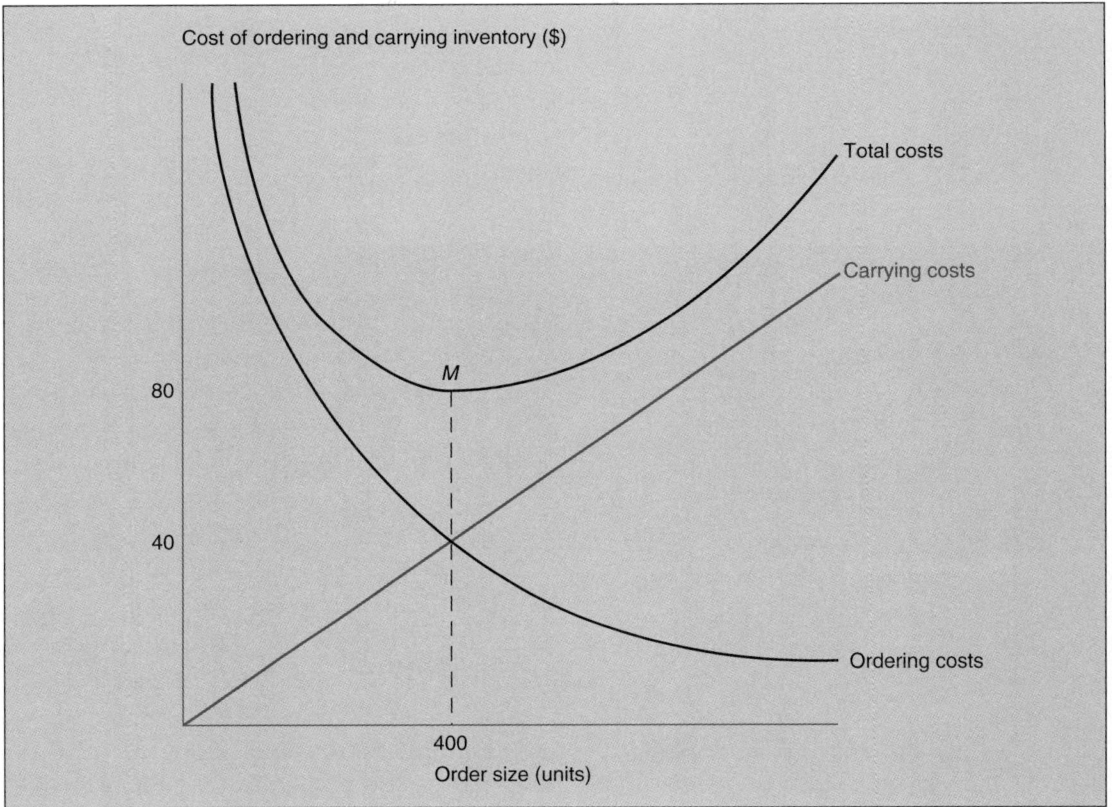

As the order size increases, carrying costs go up because we have more inventory on hand. With larger orders, we will order less frequently and overall ordering costs will go down. The approximate trade-off between the two can best be judged by examining the total cost curve. At point *M,* we have appropriately played the advantages and disadvantages of the respective costs against each other. With larger orders, carrying costs will be excessive, while at a reduced order size, constant ordering will put us at an undesirably higher point on the ordering cost curve.

The question becomes, How do we mathematically determine the minimum point (*M*) on the total cost curve? Under certain fairly reasonable assumptions, we may use the following formula as the first step.[7]

[7]The assumptions are that inventory usage is at a constant rate, that the amount of time to deliver each order is consistent, and that the delivery date coincides with the point at which we reach a zero level of inventory. It does not consider the problem of stock-outs. A stock-out occurs when a firm is out of a specific inventory item and is unable to sell or deliver the product. Relaxation of these assumptions does not greatly change the calculations.

$$EOQ = \sqrt{\frac{2SO}{C}} \tag{7–2}$$

Economic Ordering Quantity EOQ is the **economic ordering quantity,** the amount most advantageous for the firm to order each time. We determine this value, translate it into average inventory size, and determine the minimum total cost amount (M). The terms in the EOQ formula are defined as follows:

S = Total sales in units
O = Ordering cost for each order
C = Carrying cost per unit in dollars
Q = Quantity per order

Our total inventory costs are given by the following formula:

$$TC = \frac{SO}{Q} + \frac{CQ}{2} \tag{7–3}$$ [8]

This formula represents total costs as ordering costs times the number of times we order each year (S/Q) plus carrying costs times the average inventory ($Q/2$).

Let us assume we anticipate selling 2,000 units, it will cost us \$8.00 to place each order, and the price per unit is \$1.00, with a 20 percent carrying cost to maintain the average inventory (the carrying charge per unit is \$0.20). Plugging these values into our formula, we show:

$$EOQ = \sqrt{\frac{2SO}{C}} = \sqrt{\frac{2 \times 2{,}000 \times \$8}{\$0.20}} = \sqrt{\frac{\$32{,}000}{\$0.20}} = \sqrt{160{,}000}$$

$$= 400 \text{ units}$$

[8]To achieve minimum total costs (M), we must take the first derivative and set it equal to zero.

$$\frac{dTC}{dQ} = \frac{-SO}{Q^2} + \frac{C}{2}$$

$$\frac{-SO}{Q^2} + \frac{C}{2} = 0$$

$$\frac{C}{2} = \frac{SO}{Q^2}$$

$$Q^2 = \frac{2SO}{C}$$

$$Q = \sqrt{\frac{2SO}{C}}$$

We note that minimum costs are achieved in Figure 7–4, where

$$\frac{SO}{Q} = \frac{CQ}{2}$$

$$SO = \frac{CQ^2}{2}$$

$$2SO = CQ^2$$

$$\frac{2SO}{C} = Q^2$$

$$Q = \sqrt{\frac{2SO}{C}}$$

The optimum order size is 400 units. On the assumption we use up inventory at a constant rate throughout the year, our average inventory on hand will be 200 units, as indicated in Figure 7–5. Average inventory equals *EOQ*/2.

FIGURE 7–5
Inventory usage pattern

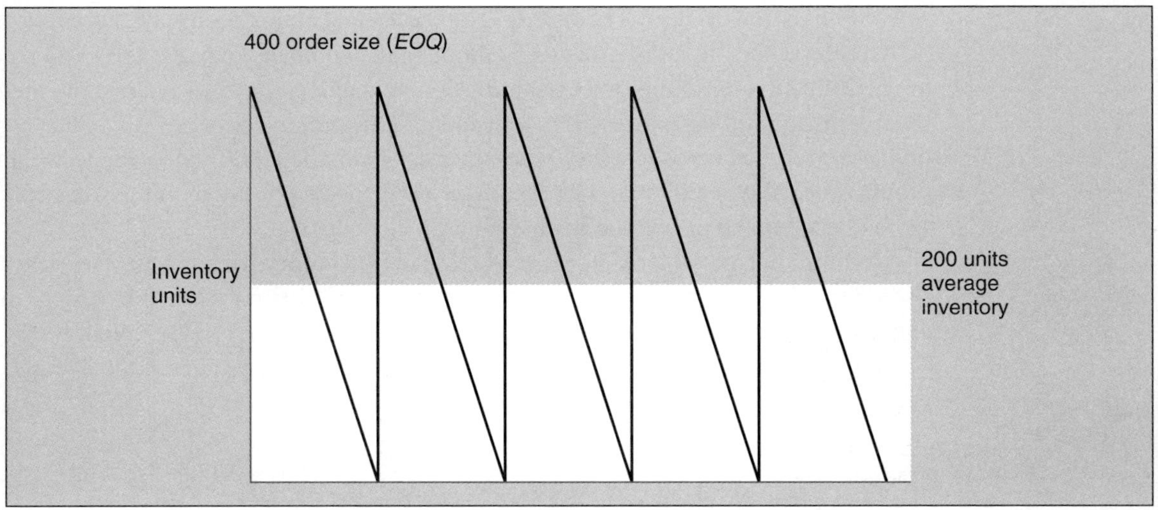

Our total costs with an order size of 400 and an average inventory size of 200 units are computed in Table 7–5.

TABLE 7–5
Total costs for inventory

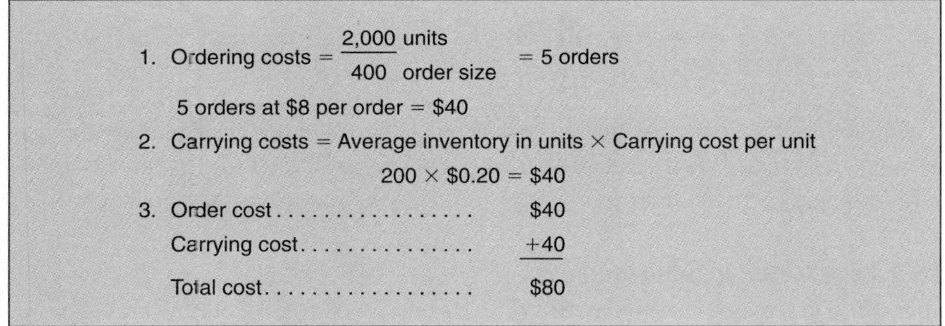

1. Ordering costs $= \dfrac{2{,}000 \text{ units}}{400 \text{ order size}} = 5$ orders

   5 orders at \$8 per order = \$40
2. Carrying costs = Average inventory in units × Carrying cost per unit

   200 × \$0.20 = \$40
3. Order cost \$40

   Carrying cost .... +40

   Total cost \$80

Point *M* on Figure 7–4 can be equated to a total cost of \$80.00 at an order size of 400 units. At no other order point can we hope to achieve lower costs. The same basic principles of total cost minimization that we have applied to inventory can be applied to other assets as well. For example, we may assume cash has a carrying cost (opportunity cost of lost interest on marketable securities as a result of being in cash) and an ordering cost (transaction costs of shifting in and out of marketable securities) and then work toward determining the optimum level of cash. In each case we are trying to minimize the overall costs and increase profit.

Safety Stock and Stock-outs

In our analysis thus far we have assumed that we would use up inventory at a constant rate and that we would receive new inventory when the old level of inventory reached zero. To verify this point, you may wish to reexamine Figure 7–5. We have not specifically considered the problem of being out of stock.

A stock-out occurs when a firm is out of a specific inventory item and is unable to sell or deliver the product. The risk of losing sales to a competitor may cause a firm to hold a safety stock to reduce this risk. Although the company may use the EOQ model to determine the optimum order quantity, management cannot always assume the delivery schedules of suppliers will be constant or assure delivery of new inventory when inventory reaches zero. A **safety stock** guards against late deliveries due to weather, production delays, equipment breakdowns, and the many other things that can go wrong between the placement of an order and its delivery.

A minimum safety stock increases the cost of inventory because the carrying cost rises. This cost should be offset by eliminating lost profits on sales due to stock-outs and also by increased profits from unexpected orders that can now be filled.

In the prior example, if a safety stock of 50 units were maintained, the average inventory figure would be 250 units.

$$\text{Average inventory} = \frac{EOQ}{2} + \text{Safety stock}$$

$$\text{Average inventory} = \frac{400}{2} + 50$$

$$= 200 + 50 = 250$$

The inventory carrying cost now increases to $50.

$$\text{Carrying costs} = \text{Average inventory in units} \times \text{Carrying cost per unit}$$
$$= 250 \times \$0.20 = \$50$$

The amount of safety stock that a firm carries is likely to be influenced by the predictability of inventory usage and the time period necessary to fill inventory orders. The following discussion indicates safety stock may be reduced in the future.

Just-in-Time Inventory Management

Just-in-time inventory management (JIT) was designed for Toyota by the Japanese firm Shigeo Shingo and found its way to other countries. Just-in-time inventory management is part of a total production concept that often interfaces with a total quality control program. A JIT program has several basic requirements: (1) quality production that continually satisfies customer requirements; (2) close ties between suppliers, manufacturers, and customers; and (3) minimization of the level of inventory.

Usually suppliers are located near manufacturers that can make orders in small lot sizes because of short delivery times. One side effect has been for manufacturers to reduce their number of suppliers to assure quality as well as to ease the complexity of ordering and delivery. Computerized ordering/inventory tracking systems both on the assembly line and in the supplier's production facility are necessary for JIT to work.

A Strike Exposes Just-in-Time Management

The auto industry in Canada, as in other countries, has implemented just-in-time management practices in its assembly plants. The discipline of the process has imposed a rigor on the assembly of automobiles that is extraordinary. The General Motors plant in Oshawa requires deliveries by 600 to 700 transports a day, often with only 20 minute delivery windows for arrival at the plant. The impact of this heavy delivery schedule can be seen on the truck-congested highways of Ontario.

In 1992, the Ford Motor Company of Canada, using its computers and telecommunications networks, set up its just-in-time management system to assemble the Crown Victoria and Grand Marquis cars at its St. Thomas, Ontario, plant. The operations at this plant require the coordinating of shipments by air, sea, and land from all parts of the globe. As a result, the plant has become more efficient, has reduced its inventory investment, and has improved quality.

In May 1995 a rail strike demonstrated how dependent the auto industry in Canada has become on the just-in-time process and the smooth coordination of deliveries with suppliers. Ford was forced to shut down three plants in Canada for more than a week because a body panel for the Windstar could not be delivered by rail from the United States. The part was needed just-in-time to keep the assembly lines operating. Unfortunately, Ford had not developed an alternative plan to transport the required part in the event of disrupted delivery.

Cost Savings from Lower Inventory Cost savings from lower levels of inventory and the reduced financing cost are expected. Harley-Davidson reduced its in-process and in-transit inventory by $20 million at a single plant, and General Electric trimmed inventory by 70 percent in 40 plants. In one sense, the manufacturer pushes some of the cost of financing onto the supplier. If the supplier also imposes JIT on *its* suppliers, these efficiencies work their way down the supplier chain to create a leaner production system for the whole economy. Lower inventory levels are facilitated by computer control systems that incorporate point-of-sale terminals and electronic ordering systems to keep track of extensive selections of inventory. Ordering of additional inventory occurs automatically when current stocks hit trigger order points.

Other Benefits There are other, not-so-obvious cost savings to just-in-time systems. A JIT automotive plant may use 70 percent less space than the standard automobile plant and therefore saves construction costs and reduces its overhead expenses for utilities and manpower. General Electric increased productivity by 35 percent in its 40 plants operating under JIT. The computerized ordering systems and EDI systems between suppliers, production, and manufacturing reduce rekeying errors and duplication of forms for the accounting and finance functions. Xerox implemented a quality process along with JIT and reduced its supplier list to 450, which created a $15 million savings in quality control programs. JIT can reduce quality control costs as much as 60 percent, but these costs can often be overlooked by financial analysts because JIT prevents defects rather than detecting poor quality; therefore no cost savings are recognized. One last item is the elimination of waste, which is one of the side benefits of a total quality control system coupled with JIT.

Xerox
www.xerox.com

It is important to realize that the just-in-time inventory system is very compatible with the concept of economic ordering quantity. The focus is to balance reduced carrying costs from maintaining less inventory with increased ordering costs. Fortunately, electronic data interchange minimizes the impact of having to place orders more often.

Summary

1. Current assets of the firm entail a sizable investment that must be financed. The concepts of asset growth in relation to sales, hedging, risk, liquidity and profitability are important as we study current assets. The more liquid an asset, the easier it is to convert that asset to cash, allowing the firm greater flexibility. This flexibility is sacrificed when monies are committed to less liquid assets, therefore we must have higher expectations for the return on those assets; otherwise, the firm will become less efficient.
2. In cash management, the primary goal should be to keep the balances as low as possible, consistent with the notion of maintaining adequate funds for transactions purposes and compensating balances. Cash moves through the firm in a cycle as customers make payments and the firm pays its bills. We try to speed the inflow of funds and defer their outflow in managing the company's float. The increased use of electronic funds transfer systems both domestically and internationally is reducing float and is making for timelier collections and disbursements. .
3. Excess short-term funds may be placed in marketable securities. There is a wide selection of issues, maturities, and yields from which to choose. Safety and liquidity are primary considerations for marketable securities.
4. Accounts receivable are an investment of the firm based on its credit policies, and a test of profitability should be applied. Management of accounts receivable calls for determining credit standards and the forms of credit to be offered as well as the development of an effective collection policy. There is no such thing as bad credit—only unprofitable credit extension. Incremental analysis of credit policies highlights the critical variables in determining profitability.
5. Inventory is the least liquid of the current assets, so it should provide the highest yield. We recognize three different inventory types: raw materials, work-in-progress, and finished goods inventory. We manage inventory levels through models such as the economic ordering quantity (EOQ) model, which helps us determine the optimum average inventory size that minimizes the total cost of ordering and carrying inventory. The just-in-time inventory management model (JIT) focuses on the minimization of inventory through quality production techniques and close ties between manufacturers and suppliers. Both EOQ and JIT models are compatible and can work together in the management of inventory.

Review of Formulas

Annualized yield marketplace

1. $$\frac{100 - P}{P} \times \frac{365}{d} = r \qquad (7\text{–}1a)$$

Annualized effective yield

2. $$\left(1 + \frac{100 - P}{P}\right)^{\frac{365}{d}} - 1 = r \qquad (7\text{–}1b)$$

P = Discounted price as percent of maturity value
d = Number of days to maturity

3. $$EOQ = \sqrt{\frac{2SO}{C}} \qquad (7\text{–}2)$$

4. $$TC = \frac{SO}{Q} + \frac{CQ}{2} \qquad (7\text{–}3)$$

List of Terms

Discussion Questions

1. In the management of cash and marketable securities, why should the primary concern be for safety and liquidity rather than profit maximization?
2. Define liquidity.
3. Why are cash flows of more interest than income to the treasury manager?
4. Explain briefly how a corporation may use float to its advantage.
5. Why does float exist, and what effect does our national banking system have on it?
6. How can a firm operate with a negative cash balance on its corporate books?
7. Explain the similarities and differences between lockbox systems and regional collection offices.
8. Why would a financial manager want to slow down disbursements?
9. Use a financial publication to find the going interest rates for the list of marketable securities in Table 7–3. Which security would you choose for a short-term investment? Why?
10. Why are Treasury bills a favourite place for financial managers to invest excess cash?
11. Why are U.S. money market rates generally lower than Canadian money market rates on instruments of similar risk?
12. Differentiate between the money market and the Eurobond market.
13. Explain why the bad debt percentage or any other similar credit-control percentage is not the ultimate measure of success in the management of accounts receivable. What is the key consideration?
14. Precisely what does the EOQ formula tell us? What assumption is made about the usage rate for inventory?
15. Why might a firm keep a safety stock? What effect is it likely to have on carrying cost of inventory?
16. If a firm uses a just-in-time inventory system, what effect is that likely to have on the number and location of suppliers?

INTERNET RESOURCES AND QUESTIONS

The Bank of Canada provides some current and historical money market yields under financial statistics:
www.bankofcanada.ca/en

The Globe and Mail, under money and markets-money rates, provides extensive current money market yields for Canada and the United States:
www.globeandmail.com

Bloomberg provides government yields for several maturities and for several countries under rates and bonds-international:
www.bloomberg.com

The central banks of several countries maintain sites that are linked through the Federal Reserve of the United States. These sites outline the purpose and function of central banks and maintain historical interest rates:
www.federalreserve.gov

The Department of Finance provides definitions of debt instruments, describes the auction process, and demonstrates how yields and prices are calculated on money market instruments:
www.fin.gc.ca/invest/tech-e.html

The chartered banks provide descriptions of their cash management services. The Bank of Montreal is a good example:
www.bmo.com

1. Provide current yields on four different money market securities in Canada, and from similar securities from the United States, using a site such as the *Globe and Mail* site. How do the rates compare?
2. Compare yields on three-month government securities using a site such as Bloomberg. Why are the rates similar or different?
3. List the cash management services provided by a chartered bank.
4. Compare the overnight call rate in Canada and Japan, using the Bank of Japan site. Why the difference in rates?
   www.boj.or.jp/en/index.htm

Problems

1. Porky's Sausage Co. shows the following values on its corporate books.

Corporate Books	
Initial amount	$10,000
Deposits	+ 80,000
Cheques	− 50,000
Balance	$40,000

The initial amount on the bank's books is also $10,000. However, only $70,000 in deposits has been recorded and only $25,000 in cheques have cleared. Fill in the table below and indicate the amount of float.

Bank Books	
Initial amount	$10,000
Deposits	
Cheques	
Balance	
Float	______

2. City Farm Insurance has collection centres around the country to speed up cash collections. The company also makes its disbursements from remote disbursement centres, so cheques written by City Farm take longer to clear the bank. Collection time has been reduced by two days and disbursement time has been increased by one day because of these policies. Excess funds are being invested in short-term instruments yielding 12 percent per annum.
   a. If City Farm has $5 million per day in collections and $3 million per day in disbursements, how many dollars has the cash management system freed up?
   b. How much can City Farm earn per year on short-term investments made possible by the freed-up cash?
3. Neon Lights Company of Kanata ships lights and appliances throughout the country. Ms. Neon has determined that through the establishment of local collection centres around the country, she can speed up the collection of payments by one and one-half days. Furthermore, the cash management department of her bank has indicated to her that she can defer her payments on her accounts by one-half day without offending suppliers. The bank has a remote disbursement centre in the Yukon.
   a. If Neon Lights Company has $2 million per day in collections and $1 million per day in disbursements, how many dollars will the cash management system free up?
   b. If Neon Light Company can earn 5 percent per annum on freed-up funds, how much income can be generated?
   c. If the total cost of the system is $210,000 should it be implemented?
4. The current cash management system of Low Ash Cat Foods requires five days to collect its daily receipts of $225,000. Now Bank offers to reduce the collection time by four days for an annual fee of $49,000. If the opportunity cost of funds is 6 percent, should Low Ash accept the bank's offer?
5. Leeft Bank offers to reduce the collection time for your company's daily cash receipts by two days with its cash management system. This service will cost you $15,000 per year. Currently, short-term money market rates average 5 percent. If you anticipate annual sales of $46.355 million, would you accept the bank's offer?
6. Your banker has analyzed your company account and has suggested that her bank has a cash management package for you. She suggests that with a concentration banking system, your float can be reduced by three days on average. You, of course, are delighted (you're not sure why), but you do know your average daily collections amount to $305,000. Your opportunity cost of funds is 9 percent. The bank provides this service for $52,500 plus a compensating balance in your current account of $75,000. (A compensating balance is the amount you are required to maintain interest free at that bank.) Is this package worth it? By how much?
7. Ron's chequebook shows a balance of $400. A recent statement from the bank (received last week) shows that all cheques written as of the date of the statement have been paid, except numbers 325 and 326, which were for $35.00 and $58.00, respectively. Since the statement date, cheques 327, 328, and 329 have been written for $22.00, $45.00, and $17.00, respectively.

There is an 80 percent probability that cheques 325 and 326 have been paid by this time. There is a 50 percent probability that cheques 327, 328, and 329 have been paid.

a. What is the total value of the five cheques outstanding?

b. What is the expected value of payments for the five cheques outstanding?

c. What is the difference between parts *a* and *b?* This represents a type of float.

8. Camembert's commercial paper is presently selling at a discount. It sells for 97.92 of par and matures in 120 days.

   a. Calculate its yield as quoted in the market.

   b. Calculate its effective annual yield.

9. A bankers' acceptance is discounted by Canmex Inc. at 98.71 of par. It matures in 60 days.

   a. What is the cost to the company on a nominal basis?

   b. What is the effective annual cost to the company?

10. A 91-day Treasury bill with a face value of $1 million is sold to yield 5.27 percent.

    a. At what price did the T-bill sell if the yield was quoted by the market?

    b. At what price did the T-bill sell if the yield was an effective annual yield?

11. Thompson Wood Products has credit sales of $2,007,500 and accounts receivable of $220,000. Compute the value for the average collection period.

12. Darla's Cosmetics had annual credit sales of $1,003,750 and an average collection period of 36 days in 2002. What was the company's average accounts receivable balance?

13. In the previous problem, if accounts receivable change in 2003 to $138,600, and credit sales increase to $1,204,500, should we assume that the firm has a more or less lenient credit policy?

14. Hubbell Electronic Wiring Company has an average collection period of 35 days. The accounts receivable balance is $144,375. What is the value of credit sales?

15. Guitar Girl Company has an opportunity cost of funds of 11 percent and a credit policy based on net 30 days. If all of its customers adhere to the stated terms and annual sales increase from $4.21 million to $5.37 million, what will be the increased cost of funds tied up in accounts receivable?

16. Wontaby Ltd. is extending its credit terms from 30 to 45 days. Sales are expected to increase from $4.7 million to $5.8 million as a result. Wontaby finances short-term assets at the bank at a cost of 10 percent annually. Calculate the additional annual financing cost of this change in credit terms.

17. Standard Business Forms is considering extending trade credit to some customers previously considered poor risks. Sales would increase by $100,000 if credit is extended to these new customers. Of the new accounts receivable generated, 12 percent will prove to be uncollectible. Additional collection costs will be 4 percent of sales, and production and selling costs will be 77 percent of sales.

    a. Compute the incremental income before taxes.

    b. What will the firm's incremental return on sales be if these new credit customers are accepted?

    c. If the receivable turnover ratio is 5 to 1, and no other asset buildup is needed to serve the new customers, what will Standard Business Forms' incremental return on new average investment be?

18. Collins Office Supplies is considering a more liberal credit policy to increase sales, but it expects that 9 percent of the new accounts will be uncollectible. Collection costs are 5 percent

of new sales, production and selling costs are 78 percent, and accounts receivable turnover is five times. Assume an increase in sales of $80,000. No other asset buildup will be required to service the new accounts.

a. What is the level of accounts receivable to support this sales expansion?

b. What would be Collins's incremental before-tax return on investment?

c. Should Collins liberalize credit if a 21.43 percent before-tax return is required (opportunity cost of capital)?

Assume Collins also needs to increase its level of inventory to support new sales and that inventory turnover is four times.

d. What would be the total incremental investment in accounts receivable and inventory to support an $80,000 increase in sales?

e. Given the income determined in part *b* and the investment determined in part *d,* should Collins extend more liberal credit terms? (Use text format.)

19. Curtis Toy Manufacturing Company is evaluating extending credit to a new group of customers. Although these customers will provide $240,000 in additional credit sales, 12 percent are likely to be uncollectible. The company will incur $21,000 in additional collection expenses. Production and marketing expenses represent 72 percent of sales. The company has a receivables turnover of six times. No other asset buildup will be required to service the new customers. The firm has a 14.5 percent desired return on investment.

a. Should Curtis extend credit to these customers?

b. Should credit be extended if 14 percent of the new sales prove uncollectible?

c. Should credit be extended if the receivables turnover drops to 1.5 and 12 percent of the accounts are uncollectible (as was the case in part *a*)?

20. Reconsider Curtis Toy. Assume the average collection period is 120 days. All other factors are the same (including 12 percent uncollectibles). Should credit be extended?

21. Maddox Resources has credit sales of $180,000 yearly with credit terms of net 30 days, which is also the average collection period. Maddox does not offer a discount for early payment, so its customers take the full 30 days to pay.

a. What is the average receivables balance? What is the receivables turnover?

b. If Maddox offered a 2 percent discount for payment in 10 days and every customer took advantage of the new terms, what would the new average receivables balance be? Use the full sales of $180,000 for your calculation of receivables.

c. If Maddox reduces its bank loans, which cost 12 percent, by the cash generated from reduced receivables, what will be the net gain or loss to the firm? Should it offer the discount?

d. Assume the new trade terms of 2/10, net 30 will increase sales by 20 percent because the discount makes Maddox price competitive. If Maddox earns 16 percent on sales before discounts, should it offer the discount?

22. Lipto Biomedic has credit sales of $740,000 yearly with credit terms of net 60 days, with an average collection period of 75 days. Lipto does not offer a discount for early payment.

a. What is the average receivables balance? What is the receivables turnover?

b. If Lipto offered a 3 percent discount for payment in 10 days and every customer took advantage of the new terns and pay on the tenth day, what would the new average receivables balance be? Use the full sales of $740,000 for your calculation of receivables.

c. If Lipto reduces its bank loans, which cost 8 percent, by the cash generated from reduced receivables, what will be the net gain or loss to the firm? Should it offer the discount?

d. Assume the new trade terms of 2/10, net 30 will increase sales by 12 percent because the discount makes Lipto price competitive. If Lipto earns 19 percent on sales before discounts, should it offer the discount?

23. Tobin Fisheries presently sells to its customers on terms of 2/10, net 30. Its average collection period is 15 days, with 80 percent currently taking the discount. All sales are credit sales. Upper management has expressed concern about sluggish sales, and the marketing department would like a more attractive credit package. Next year's sales are projected to be $3.1 million. It has been estimated that with terns of 3/10, net 60, sales next year would jump to S4.2 million and 60 percent of sales would take the discount, but the average collection period would increase to 34 days. Tobin's contribution margin of 5.5 percent would hold with the expansion of sales, as would its short-term financing cost of 10 percent. Should Tobin initiate the change in credit policy?

24. Happy Trail Adventure Products is reevaluating its credit policy. Current terms are 2/10, net 30, resulting in annual sales of 400,000 units. Cash sales that qualify for the discount account for 10 percent of sales, 65 percent qualify for the discount by paying on the 10th day, and the other 25 percent pay, on average, in 40 days. Unit sales price is $24.00 and variable production costs are $21.00 per unit. Bad debts are 1.5 percent of credit sales.

    The new policy of 2/10, net 60 is expected to increase sales by 12 percent annually. Cash sales are expected to remain at 10 percent of sales, but those qualifying for the discount by paying in 10 days would drop to 25 percent; the other 65 percent would, on average, pay in 70 days. It is expected that variable production costs would remain at $21.00 per unit but that bad debt expense would increase to 2 percent of credit sales. Happy Trail's banker would continue to finance working capital requirements at 13 percent. Should the new policy be implemented?

25. Power Play, Inc., has seen profits drop acutely because of the economic downturn. To enhance profitability and to preserve cash, Power Play is considering shortening its credit period and eliminating its cash discount. Terms are currently 3/10, net 60 and would be changed to net 30. Currently, 60 percent of customers, on average, pay at the end of the credit period (60 days); the other 40 percent pay, on average, in 10 days and receive the discount. It is anticipated that under the new policy customers will pay, on average, in 30 days. At present, average monthly sales are $450,000, but they are expected to fall to $400,000 with the tightening of credit. Variable production costs are 78 percent, and bank financing is currently floating at 11 percent. Bad debt losses at 2 percent of sales are expected to drop to 1.75 percent of sales.

    a. Should Power Play's credit policy be tightened?

    b. What is the average accounts receivable balance under both policies?

    c. Discuss the choice of discount rate for this analysis.

26. OB1 Sabres Ltd. has determined that product sales are not what they could be because they have unused capacity; as a result, the company is considering adjusting its marketing strategy. At present, all sales to distributors are on a cash basis, but the competition offers credit terms. Similar credit terms for OB1 Sabres have been suggested. Research suggests that sales in the upcoming year would jump from $4.3 million annually to $5.5 million with credit terms of 2/10, net 30. Furthermore, research estimates that 75 percent of the customers would take the discount and the remainder would pay on average on the 30th day. Inventory turnover would remain at 15 times a year. Cost of goods sold (variable costs) are 75 percent of gross sales. Bad debts are estimated to be .75 percent of credit sales. Credit department expenses would be $50,000 per year plus the salary of two individuals at S35,000 per year each. One of the staff would be reassigned from another division without affecting costs or produc-

tivity as that individual is currently redundant in that division. Marketing expenses are 4 percent of gross sales. Bank financing of working capital requirements is at 11 percent. Should OB1 Sabres Ltd. adopt the proposed policy? Show your calculations.

27. First Picked Fruits, Inc., is considering two alternatives to stimulate sales. Currently, the policy is net 30 and the average collection period is 40 days, with bad debt losses of 1.25 percent of sales. All sales are credit sales and are expected to be $6.1 million annually under this policy.

Under policy 1, credit terms would be lengthened to 45 days to a select group of new customers, with an expected increase in sales to $6.9 million annually. However, it is expected that the incremental sales would experience bad debt losses of 1.75 percent and that their average collection period would be 50 days. No change would occur in the average collection period or bad debt loss experience on the existing credit sales. Under policy 2, credit terms would be lengthened to 60 days to a select group of new customers (not completely overlapping with the first group). Sales would be expected to rise to $7.2 million annually. Incremental sales expectations would be payment, on average, after 65 days, and bad debt losses of 2 percent. No change would occur in the average collection period or bad debt losses on the original credit sales. First Picked Fruits has an opportunity cost of funds of 16 percent, and its variable costs are 94 percent of sales.

a. Is either alternative advantageous?

b. Any concerns with this analysis as stated?

c. Any theoretical concerns with an apparent one-year time horizon for analysis?

28. Route Canal Shipping Company has the following schedule for aging of accounts receivable:

AGE OF RECEIVABLES
April 20, 2003

(1) Month of Sales	(2) Age of Account	(3) Amounts	(4) Percent of Amount Due
April	0–30	$105,000	________
March	31–60	60,000	________
February	61–90	90,000	________
January	91–120	45,000	________
Total receivables		$300,000	100%

a. Fill in column (4) for each month.

b. If the firm had $1,440,000 in credit sales over the four month period, compute the average collection period. Average daily sales should be based on a 120-day period.

c. If the firm likes to see its bills collected in 30 days, should it be satisfied with the average collection period?

d. Disregarding your answer to part c and considering the aging schedule for accounts receivable, should the company be satisfied?

e. What additional information does the aging schedule bring to the company that the average collection period may not show?

29. Nowlin Pipe & Steel has expected sales of 72,000 pipes this year, an ordering cost of $6.00 per order, and carrying costs of $2.40 per pipe.

a. What is the economic ordering quantity?

b. How many orders will be placed during the year?

c. What will the average inventory be?

d. What is the total cost of ordering and carrying inventory?

30. Friendly Home Services has expected sales of 5,000 baskets this year, an ordering cost of $75.00 per order, and carrying costs of $3.00 per basket.

    a. What is the economic ordering quantity?

    b. How many orders will be placed during the year?

    c. What will the average inventory be?

    d. What is the total cost of ordering and carrying inventory?

31. Howe Corporation is trying to improve its inventory control system and has installed an online computer at its retail stores. Howe anticipates sales of 126,000 units per year, an ordering cost of $4.00 per order, and carrying costs of $1.008 per unit.

    a. What is the economic ordering quantity?

    b. How many orders will be placed during the year?

    c. What will the average inventory be?

    d. What is the total cost of inventory expected to be?

32. (See previous problem for basic data.) In the second year, Howe Corporation finds that it can reduce ordering costs to $1.00 per order, but carrying costs will stay the same at $1.008 per unit.

    a. Recompute *a, b, c,* and *d* in the previous problem for the second year.

    b. Now compare years one and two and explain what has happened.

33. Higgins Athletic Wear has expected sales of 22,500 units a year, carrying costs of $1.50 per unit, and an ordering cost of $3.00 per order.

    a. What is the economic order quantity?

    b. What is average inventory? What is the total carrying cost?

    c. Assume an additional 30 units will be required as safety stock. What will the new average inventory be? What will the new total carrying cost be?

34. Joseph Sports Equipment, Inc., is considering a switch to level production. Under level production, cost efficiencies would occur and aftertax costs would decline by $35,000, but inventory would increase by $400,000. Joseph would have to finance the extra inventory at a cost of 10.5 percent.

    a. Should the company go ahead and switch to level production?

    b. How low would interest rates need to fall before level production would be feasible?

35. Minty Airfresheners Ltd. maintains an inventory of bottles with chemical disinfectants to meet its annual demand for 81,600 bottles to service restrooms. Each package costs $4.75, and the order cost is $106.25 per order. Carrying costs have been identified as $1.50 per package. Minty Airfresheners bases its orders on the economic ordering quantity. Recently, the wholesaler of the bottles, in an attempt to shift the inventory burden to Minty Airfresheners, has offered a 10 percent discount if orders are placed quarterly. Should the present ordering policy of Minty Airfresheners be changed?

36. Baktoo Basics Ltd. is considering introducing an inventory control system that will increase inventory turnover from 10 to 15 times per year. Its annual cost of goods sold is expected to be $6 million, and its financing costs are at 11 percent. Should Baktoo Basics consider an expenditure of $17,500 on the new control system?

COMPREHENSIVE PROBLEM

37. Logan Distributing Company of Lethbridge sells fans and heaters throughout the west. Joe Logan, the president of the company, is thinking about changing the credit policies offered by the firm to attract customers away from competitors. The current policy calls for a 1/10, net 30, and the new policy would call for a 3/10, net 50. Currently, 30 percent of Logan customers are taking the discount, and it is anticipated that this number would go up to 50 percent with the new discount policy. It is further anticipated that annual sales would increase from a level of $400,000 to $600,000 as a result of the change in the cash discount policy.

    The increased sales would also affect the inventory level carried by Logan. The average inventory carried by Logan is based on a determination of an EOQ. Assume unit sales of fans and heaters will increase from 15,000 to 22,500 units. The ordering cost for each order is $200 and the carrying cost per unit is $1.50 (these values will not change with the discount). Each unit in inventory has an average cost of $12.00. Cost of goods sold is equal to 65 percent of net sales, general and administrative expenses are equal to 15 percent of net sales, and interest payments of 14 percent will be necessary only for the increase in the accounts receivable and inventory balances. Taxes will equal 40 percent of before-tax income.

    a. Compute the accounts receivable balance before and after the change in the cash discount policy. Use the net sales (Total sales – Cash discounts) to determine the average daily sales and the accounts receivable balances.

    b. Determine EOQ before and after the change in the cash discount policy. Translate this into average inventory (in units and dollars) before and after the change in the cash discount policy.

    c. Complete an income statement before and after the policy change.

    d. Should the new cash discount policy be utilized? Briefly comment.

Selected References

Altman, Edward I., and Robert Haldeman. "Credit Scoring Models: Approaches and Tests for Successful Implementation." *Journal of Commercial Lending* 77 (May 1995), pp. 10–22.

Daniels, Carol. "Timing Cash Flow: Will Finality Changes Delay Funds Availability?" *Corporate Cashflow* 11 (January 1990), pp. 40–41.

Frazer, Douglas H. "Issues in Lending: A Primer for Avoiding Contests Over Collateral." *Journal of Commercial Lending* 77 (June 1995), pp. 58–62.

Goerner, Peter. "How to Use a Customer-Focused Quality Program to Improve the Loan Approval Process." *Journal of Commercial Lending* 77 (April 1995), pp. 20–29.

Hill, Claire A. "Securitization: A Low Cost Sweetener for Lemons." *Journal of Applied Corporate Finance* 10 (Spring 1997), pp. 64–71.

Mian, Schzad L., and Clifford W. Smith, Jr. "Accounts Receivable Management Policy: Theory and Evidence." *Journal of Finance* 47 (March 1992), pp. 169–99.

Scholl, William C. "Commercial Lenders' Guide to Cash Management." *Journal of Commercial Lending* 75 (December 1992), pp. 44–48.

Store, Charles A. "Asset Backed Commercial Paper: Get with the Program." *Journal of Applied Corporate Finance* 10 (Spring 1997), pp. 72–78.

Strischek, Dev. "The Quotable Five C's." *Journal of Lending and Credit Risk Management* 82 (April 2000), pp. 47–49.

CHAPTER | EIGHT

8 Sources of Short-Term Financing

LEARNING | OBJECTIVES

1 Describe trade credit as an important form of short-term financing and calculate its cost to the firm if a discount is forgone.

2 Describe bank loans as self-liquidating, as short-term, and as having their interest cost tied to the prime rate. Also, calculate interest rates under differing conditions.

3 Describe commercial paper as a short-term, unsecured promissory note of the firm.

4 Review borrowing in foreign markets as a cost-effective alternative for the firm.

5 Explain that offering accounts receivable and inventory as collateral may lower the interest costs on a loan.

6 Demonstrate the hedging of interest rates to reduce borrowing risk.

In this chapter we examine the cost and availability of various short-term funds, which we record as current liabilities. Attention is focused on trade credit from suppliers, bank loans, corporate promissory notes, foreign borrowing, and loans against receivables and inventory. Although it is often suggested that loans are only available to those who already have money, it is the objective of this chapter is to demonstrate how required funds could be made available on a short-term basis from the various suppliers of credit.

Figure 8–1 on the next page shows the overall profile of various sources and forms of debt in financing nonfinancial Canadian corporations as of the third quarter of 2000. Among these Canadian companies, short-term financing comprised 66 percent of the overall total debt. In this chapter we deal with the sources that provide that short-term financing. Chapter 16 explores in depth the longer-term sources of that debt, while Chapter 21 examines the international sources.

Trade Credit

The largest provider of short-term credit is usually at the firm's doorstep—the manufacturer or seller of goods and services. This is a true alternative form of borrowing as compared to bank loans. Over 50 percent of short-term financing is in the form of accounts payable or trade credit. Trade payables are a **spontaneous source of funds,** growing as the business expands on a seasonal or long-term basis and contracting in a like fashion.

For example, if annual purchases of a company are $7.3 million and are paid on terms of net 30 days, the average accounts payable balance will be $600,000. An expansion in business, and thus purchases, by 20 percent to $8.76 million increases the accounts payable balance to $720,000. This represents an expansion in available credit by $120,000 as long as purchases remain at the higher level. Unlike bank credit, this expansion occurs somewhat painlessly. We see this relationship develop from the accounts payable period ratio examined in Chapter 3 and again used to examine the cash conversion cycle in Chapter 6.

Annual purchases		Credit period/365		Average accounts payable balance	
$7,300,000	×	30/365	=	$600,000	
					$120,000 increase
$8,760,000	×	30/365	=	$720,000	

FIGURE 8–1
Structure of corporate debt, 2000

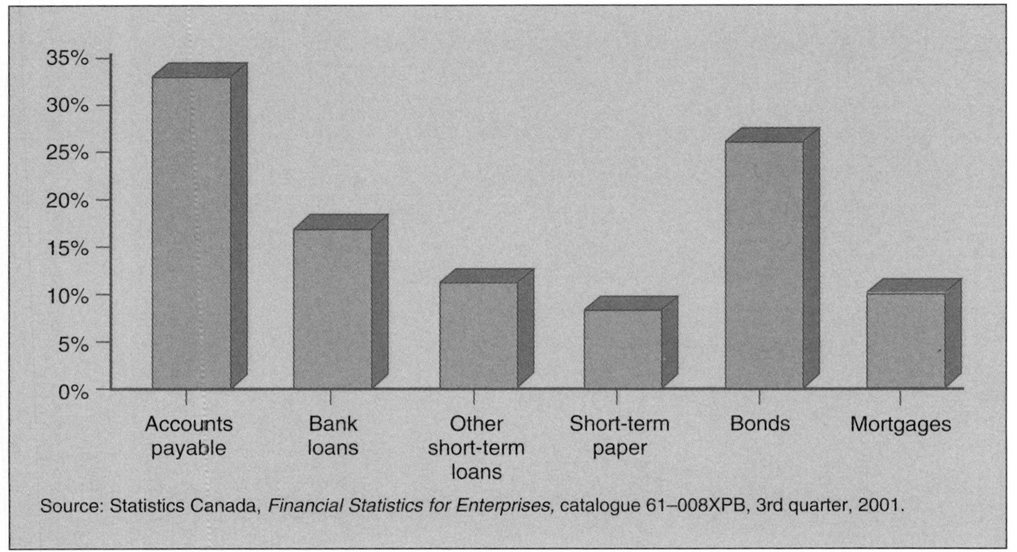

Source: Statistics Canada, *Financial Statistics for Enterprises,* catalogue 61–008XPB, 3rd quarter, 2001.

Payment Period

Trade credit is extended for 30 to 60 days, although that varies by industry. For example, many suppliers of foodstuffs such as ice cream to small retailers give only 10 days to pay. Many firms attempt to stretch the payment period to provide additional short-term financing. This is an acceptable form of financing as long as it is not carried to an

Dun & Bradstreet Corporation www.dnb.ca

abusive extent. Going from a 30- to a 35-day average payment period may be tolerated within the trade, while stretching payments to 65 days might alienate suppliers and cause a diminishing credit rating with Dun & Bradstreet and local credit bureaus. A major variable in determining the payment period is the possible existence of a cash discount.

Going back to our previous example, see how stretching payables to 35 days on annual purchases of \$8.76 million increases accounts payable to \$840,000, which represents an increase in available credit of \$120,000.

Annual purchases		Credit period/365		Average accounts payable balance	
\$8,760,000	×	30/365	=	\$720,000	
					\$120,000 increase
\$8,760,000	×	35/365	=	\$840,000	

Cash Discount Policy

A cash discount allows for a reduction in price if payment is made within a specified time period. A 2/10, net 30 cash discount means we can deduct 2 percent if we remit our funds within 10 days after billing, but failing this, we must pay the full amount by the 30th day.

On a \$100 billing we could pay \$98.00 up to the 10th day or \$100.00 at the end of 30 days. If we fail to take the cash discount, we get to use \$98.00 for 20 more days for a \$2.00 fee. The interest rate on the use of that money is then a whopping 37.24 percent. Note that we first consider the interest cost and then convert this to an annual basis. The standard formula for approximating this interest cost is:

The cost of forgoing the discount (8–1)

$$K_{DIS} = \frac{d\%}{100\% - d\%} \times \frac{365}{f\,(\text{date}) - d\,(\text{date})}$$

$$\begin{aligned} d\% &= \text{discount percentage} \\ f\,(\text{date}) &= \text{final payment period} \\ d\,(\text{date}) &= \text{discount period} \end{aligned}$$

$$= \frac{2\%}{100\% - 2\%} \times \frac{365}{30 - 10} = 37.24\%^{1}$$

This formula fails to account for the cumulative effect of being able to earn interest on the interest in each succeeding 20-day period after the first period. The methods and rationale for such compounding are covered in Chapter 9. This can be formulated as

$$i = \left(1 + \frac{2}{98}\right)^{\frac{365}{20}} - 1 = .4459$$

[1]Note the similarity of this formula with Formula 7–1b.

Calculator

$PV = (98)$	$FV = 100$
$PMT = 0$	$n = \frac{20}{365}$

Compute $i = 44.59\%$.
Therefore, the real rate of interest is more like 44.59 percent.

Again, going back to our example with annual purchases of $8.76 million, note that if the discount is taken, the accounts payable balance is $235,200. If not taken, this balance is $705,600. Not taking the discount provides additional credit of $470,400 on an average daily basis. The cost is the discount forgone, which amounts to 2 percent of $8.76 million, or $175,200. This represents an annualized cost of $175,200/$470,400, or .3724 (37.24%). This is the result obtained by the formula.

Annual purchases		Credit period/365		Average accounts payable balance
$8,760,000 × 98%	×	10/365	=	$235,200
				$470,400 increase
$8,760,000 × 98%	×	30/365	=	$705,600

Cash discount terms may vary. For example, on a 2/10, net 90 basis, it would cost us only 9.3 percent not to take the discount and to pay the full amount after 90 days.

$$= \frac{2\%}{100\% - 2\%} \times \frac{365}{90 - 10} = 9.30\%$$

The compounded rate of interest is 9.65%.

Calculator

$PV = (98)$	$FV = 100$
$PMT = 0$	$n = \frac{80}{365}$

Compute $i = 9.65\%$.

In each case we must ask ourselves whether bypassing the discount and using the money for a longer period is the cheapest means of financing. In the first example, with an approximated cost of 37.24 percent, it probably is not. We would be better off borrowing $98.00 for 20 days at some lesser rate. For example, at 10 percent interest we would pay $0.54 in interest as opposed to $2.00 under the cash discount policy.[2] With the 2/10, net 90 arrangement, the cost of missing the discount is only 9.3 percent, and we may choose to let our suppliers carry us for an extra 80 days.

Net Credit Position

In Chapter 2 we defined accounts receivable as a use of funds and accounts payable as a source. The manager should closely watch the relationship between the two to determine the firm's net credit position. If a firm has average daily sales of $5,000 and

[2] $\frac{20}{365} \times 10\% \times \$98 = \$0.54$

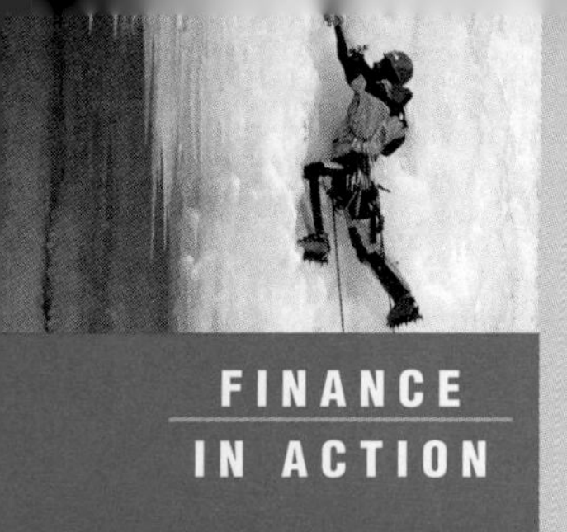

FINANCE IN ACTION

Small Business Financing Sources

SB For the busy small-business owner it is often difficult to find sources of financing as sales expand. The Government of Canada through Industry Canada provides lots of information and links to many useful sites. The many varied sources of financing available to the small business, including government assistance programs are outlined at the Government's web site: http://strategis.ic.gc.ca/sc_mangb/sources/engdoc/homepage.html

1. What are the different sources of financing available?
2. What is an angel?

collects in 30 days, the accounts receivable balance is $150,000. If this is associated with average daily purchases of $4,000 and a 25-day average payment period, the average accounts payable balance is $100,000—indicating $50,000 more in credit extended than received. This is a positive **net trade credit** position. Changing this situation to an average payment period of 40 days increases the accounts payable to $160,000 ($4,000 × 40). Accounts payable would then exceed accounts receivable by $10,000, thus leaving funds for other needs. Larger firms tend to be net providers of trade credit (relatively high receivables), with smaller firms in the user position (relatively high payables). Anyone who has dealt with the large retail chains knows how carefully they manage their payables, using them as important sources of funds.

Bank Credit

Banks may provide funds to finance seasonal needs, product line expansions, long-term growth, and so on. The preferred type of loan from the point of view of most bankers is a **self-liquidating loan,** the use of which generates cash flows that form a built-in or automatic repayment scheme. Although Canadian banks have traditionally lent monies for short-term needs, through renewing old loans, many of the 90- or 180-day agreements take on the characteristics of longer-term financing.

The major changes occurring in banking today are centred on the concept of full-service banking. The modern banker's function is much broader than merely accepting deposits, making loans, and processing cheques. A banking institution may be providing investment services, a credit card operation, real estate lending, data processing services, trust services, and helpful advice in cash management or international trade. This wide array of services has become possible because of periodic changes in the Bank Act that continually expand the types of operations with which a bank may become involved.

Canadian Bankers Association
www.cba.ca

Unlike the U.S. situation, where banking has traditionally been a state-by-state industry, banking in Canada has been national. Ongoing deregulation of the financial industries in Canada seems destined to create one-stop financial institutions. Approximately 32 foreign banks from countries such as Japan, Germany, Britain, and the United States do business in Canada as Schedule II banks. Banking today is international in scope, with Canadian banks operating in foreign countries with reciprocal banking arrangements. Canada has perhaps the most competitive banking environment in the world.

We now look at a number of terms generally associated with banking (and other types of lending activity) and consider the significance of each. Attention focuses on the prime interest rate, compensating balances, the term loan arrangement, and methods of computing interest.

Prime Rate

This is the rate the bank charges its most creditworthy customers, and it is scaled up proportionally to reflect the various credit classes. At certain slack loan periods in the economy, banks may actually charge top customers less than the published prime rate; however, such activities are difficult to track. The average customer can expect to pay 1 or 2 percent above prime, while in tight money periods a builder in a speculative construction project may pay 5 or more percentage points over prime.

The **prime rate** is competitively set by the chartered banks, but tends to be at least 1.5 percent (150 basis points) above the Bank of Canada rate. It has at times actually been below the **bank rate**, which is the rate at which the chartered banks can borrow from the Bank of Canada. The bank rate is set at the upper limit of the Bank of Canada's target overnight money rate. The overnight rate is the interest rate at which financial institutions lend to each other for one day.

Bank of Canada
www.bankofcanada.ca/en

Interest rates are determined by the supply of and demand for money in the marketplace, and these forces naturally cause interest rates to move up and down over time. The prime rate is no exception and this results in the interest rate charged on bank loans changing on a regular basis. Therefore, if the money supply tightens and interest rates go up, the interest charges on bank loans will become more expensive. Prudent managers factor this cost consideration into their decision to hold current assets that are likely financed to some extent with bank loans.

Figure 8–2 presents the average prime rate from 1971 until early 2002 for Canada compared with the United States. While the period before 1971 does not show up, it should be pointed out that interest rates in the 1950s and early 1960s were relatively stable. Beginning in 1965 and continuing into the 1990s, the prime rate became highly

FIGURE 8–2

Prime interest rate movements

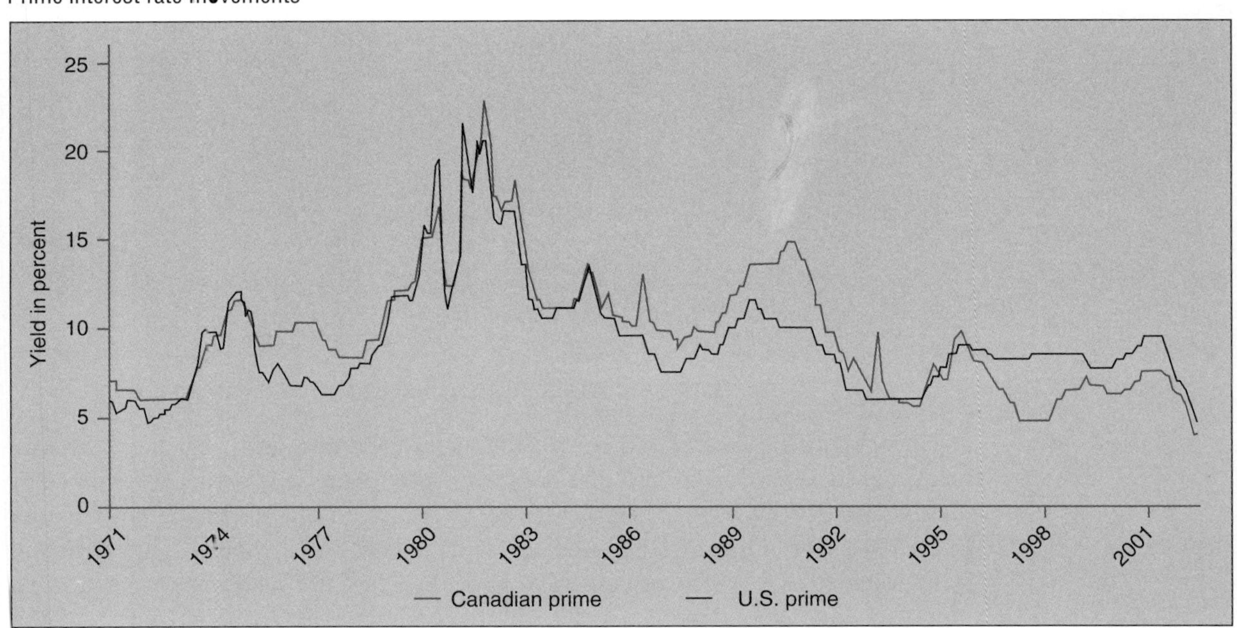

volatile, moving as much as 10 percent in the 12-month period leading up to August 1981 when it hit a high point of 22.75 percent. Figure 8–2 shows the prime rate in the early 1980s above 20 percent for several months before sharply declining. With lower inflation in the 1990s the prime rates in both countries came down significantly. By 2002 the prime in Canada was 3.75 percent, a rate not seen since the 1930s.

Compensating Balances

In providing loans and other services, rather than charging fees, banks sometimes require that business customers maintain a minimum average account balance, herein referred to as a **compensating balance**. The required amount is usually computed as a percentage of customer loans outstanding or as a percentage of bank commitments toward future loans to a given account. A common ratio used to be 20 percent against outstanding loans, though market conditions tended to influence the percentages. Increasingly, fees for services are being charged by the banking industry. In the past loan rates were "padded" to subsidize other bank services, but with direct costing of each service loan rates can become very competitive.

Some view the compensating balance requirement as an unusual arrangement. Where else would you walk into a business establishment, buy a shipment of goods, and then be told you could not take 20 percent of the purchase home with you? If you borrowed $100,000, paying 8 percent interest on the full amount with a 20 percent compensating balance requirement, you would be paying $8,000 for the use of $80,000 in funds, or an effective rate of 10 percent.

The amount that must be borrowed to end up with the desired sum of money is simply figured by taking the needed funds and dividing by $(1 - c)$, where c is the compensating balance expressed as a decimal. For example, if you need $100,000 in funds, you must borrow $125,000 to ensure that the intended amount is available. This would be calculated as follows:

$$\text{Amount to be borrowed} = \frac{\text{Amount needed}}{(1 - c)}$$

$$= \frac{\$100{,}000}{(1 - .20)} = \$125{,}000$$

A check on this calculation could be done to see if we actually end up with the use of $100,000:

$125,000	Loan
−25,000	20% compensating balance requirement
$100,000	Available funds

Bank Act
http://laws.justice.gc.ca/en/B-2/index.html

Under the Bank Act, borrowers must agree to the compensating balance requirement, and Canadian banks must disclose the full cost of the loan, which is increased by the need for a compensating balance. However, banks seem to be making most of their loans these days without the requirement for the compensating balance, preferring instead to charge interest rates consistent with their cost of funds. The emphasis has turned to doing more intensive analysis of the profitability of each loan.

Maturity Provisions

Bank loans have been traditionally short term in nature (though perhaps renewable). In the last decade there has been a movement to the use of the **term loan** in which credit is extended for one to seven years. The loan is usually repaid in monthly or quarterly installments over its life rather than in one single payment. Only superior credit applicants, as measured by working capital strength, potential profitability, and competitive position, can qualify for term loan financing.

Bankers are hesitant to fix a single interest rate to a term loan. The more common practice is to allow the interest rate to change with market conditions. Thus, the interest rate on a term loan may be tied to the prime rate and changes (floats) with it. A good customer may have its rate set at prime plus 1 percent, for example. More is said on term loans in Chapter 16 when we discuss longer-term financing.

Cost of Commercial Bank Financing

The annual interest rate on a loan is based on the loan amount, the dollar interest paid, the length of the loan, and the method of repayment. It is easy enough to observe that \$60.00 interest on a \$1,000 loan for one year would carry a 6 percent interest rate; but what if the same loan were for 120 days? To come to an approximate answer to that question we use the formula:

$$R_{ANNUAL} = \frac{I}{P} \times \frac{365}{d} \qquad (8\text{–}2)$$

R_{ANNUAL} = annual rate
I = interest
P = principal
d = days loan is outstanding

$$= \frac{\$60}{\$1{,}000} \times \frac{365}{120} = 18.25\%$$

Since we have use of the funds for only 120 days, the annual rate is approximately 18.25 percent. If we considered the accumulation of interest on the interest in the second and third 120-day periods, we would come to an annual interest rate of 19.39 percent.

Calculator

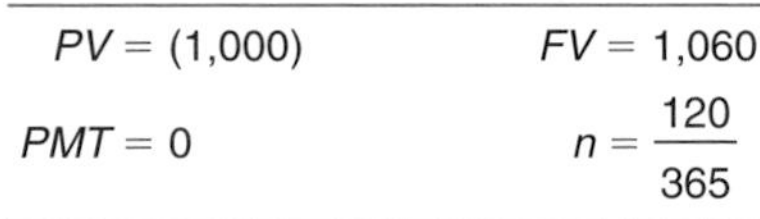

$PV = (1{,}000)$	$FV = 1{,}060$
$PMT = 0$	$n = \frac{120}{365}$

Compute $i = 19.39\%$.

To highlight the effect of time, if you borrowed \$20 for only 10 days and paid back \$21.00, the effective interest rate would be almost 500 percent, a gross violation of our sense of what is ethical.

Calculator

$PV = (20)$	$FV = 21$
$PMT = 0$	$n = \frac{10}{365}$

Compute $i = 493.38\%$.

Not only is the time dimension of a loan important, but also the way in which interest is charged. We have assumed interest would be paid when the loan comes due. If the bank deducts the interest in advance **(discounted loan),** the effective rate of interest will increase. For example, a $1,000, 120-day loan with $60.00 of interest deducted in advance represents the payment of interest on only $940.00, or an annual rate of 19.41 percent.

Annual rate on discounted loan (8–3)

$$R_{DIS} = \frac{I}{P - I} \times \frac{365}{d}$$

$$= \frac{\$60}{\$1{,}000 - \$60} \times \frac{365}{120} = .1941 = 19.41\%$$

The effective annual rate is 20.71 percent.

Calculator

$PV = (940)$	$FV = 1{,}000$
$PMT = 0$	$n = \frac{120}{365}$

Compute $i = 20.71\%$.

Interest Costs with Compensating Balances

If a loan is made with compensating balances, the annual interest rate is the stated interest rate divided by (1 − c), where c is the compensating balance expressed as a decimal. Assume 6 percent is the stated annual rate and a 20 percent compensating balance is required.

Annual rate with compensating balances (8–4)

$$R_{COMP} = \frac{I}{(1 - c)}$$

$$= \frac{6\%}{(1 - 0.2)} = 7.5\%$$

If dollar amounts are used and the stated rate is unknown, Formula 8–5 can be used. The assumption is that we are paying $60.00 interest on a $1,000.00 loan, but are able to use only $800.00 of the funds. The loan is for a year.

$$R_{COMP} = \frac{I}{P - B} \times \frac{365}{d} \qquad (8\text{–}5)$$

B = Compensating balance in $$

$$= \frac{\$60}{\$1{,}000 - \$200} \times \frac{365}{365} = 7.5\%$$

Calculator

$PV = (800)$	$FV = 860$
$PMT = 0$	$n = 1$

Compute $i = 7.50\%$.

Of course, the firm may have ongoing cash needs greater than the compensating balance required. In theory the compensating balance is supposed to be above and beyond those needs. However, in some cases the compensating balance requirement does not require the firm to have more cash on hand than it otherwise would. In such cases the firm would not use Formula 8–4 or 8–5 to adjust the annual rate of the loan.

Rate on Installment Loans

The most confusing borrowing arrangement to the average bank customer or consumer is the installment loan. **An installment loan** calls for a series of equal payments over the life of the loan. Financial institutions provide these fixed-rate loans for up to several years by matching the required funds with a fixed-rate obligation on funds they have borrowed by way of term deposits. This reduces the financial institution's risk. Though federal legislation prohibits a misrepresentation of interest rates on loans to customers, it would be possible for a loan officer or an overeager salesperson to quote a rate on an installment loan that is approximately half the true rate.

Assume you borrow $1,000 on a 12-month installment basis, with regular monthly payments to apply to interest and principal, and the interest requirement is $60.00. Though it might be suggested that the rate on the loan is 6 percent ($60/$1,000), this is not the case. It is true that you pay a total of $60.00 in interest, but you do not have the use of $1,000 for one year. Rather, you are paying back the $1,000 on a monthly basis, with an average outstanding loan balance for the year of a little more than $500. The effective annual rate of interest is 11.46 percent.

Calculator

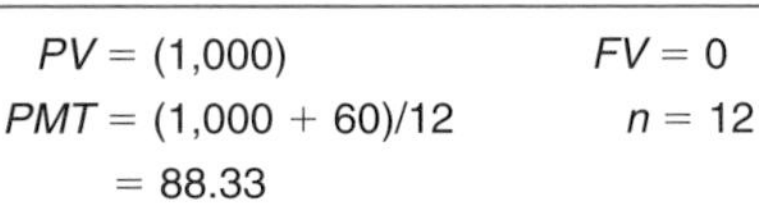

$PV = (1{,}000)$	$FV = 0$
$PMT = (1{,}000 + 60)/12$	$n = 12$
$= 88.33$	

Compute $i = .9080312\%$.

This is a monthly effective interest rate and must be converted to an annual effective rate. Multiply by 12 to get an annual rate:

$$.9080312 \times 12 = 10.896375$$

For an annual effective rate APR▶ or EFF▶ is used (dependent on calculator).

12 [2nd] [APR ▶] 10.896375 = 11.457

or

12 [2nd] [EFF ▶] 10.896375 = 11.457

The formula for compounding the monthly effective rate is:

$$(1 + .009080312)^{12} - 1$$

Formula 8–6 can be used for approximating the effective rate of interest on an installment loan.

$$R_{INSTALL} = \frac{2 \times \text{Annual number of payments} \times I}{(\text{Total number of payments} + 1) \times P} \qquad (8\text{–}6)$$

$$= \frac{2 \times 12 \times \$60}{13 \times \$1{,}000} = \frac{1{,}440}{\$13{,}000} = 11.08\%$$

The Credit Crunch Phenomenon

In 1969–70, 1973–74, 1979–81, 1990–92, and to some extent in 2001, the economy went through a period of credit shortage in the banking sector and other financial markets. The anatomy of such a credit crunch is as follows. The Bank of Canada tightens the growth in the money supply in its battle against inflation, causing a decrease in funds available for lending and an increase in interest rates. The battle against inflation is waged to help create a more stable business and economic environment. To compound difficulties, business requirements for funds may be increasing to carry inflation-laden or slow moving inventory and receivables. The increase in general interest rates causes a third problem—the withdrawal of savings deposits from our financial institutions, all in search of higher returns. The net result is that there simply are not enough lendable funds to go around. Recent policy changes instituted by the Bank of Canada, in an effort to revert away from trying to control the growth of the money supply directly, mean that future credit shortages, if they develop, will arise in an at least slightly different fashion.

Recent history has taught us that the way not to deal with credit shortages is to impose artificial limits on interest rates in the form of restrictive usury laws or extreme governmental pressure. In 1969–70 the prime rate went to 8.5 percent in a tight money period, a level not high enough to bring the forces of demand and supply together, and little credit was available. In 1974 the prime rose to 11.5 percent, a rate truly reflecting market conditions, and funds were available. The same was true in 1980 and 1981 as the prime went to 20 percent and higher, but funds were available for borrowers.

The Bank of Canada has put increasing emphasis on attempting to control the rate of growth in the money supply at a steady pace and allowing interest rates to move freely. This helps to explain part of the volatility in interest rates in recent years. Bank of Canada policy in the late 1980s and 1990s was seemingly aimed at lowering the rate of inflation in Canada and, to a certain extent, at influencing the level of the Canadian dollar on international markets. As such, monetary policy could not ignore economic circumstances in the major industrial countries. This is explored in Chapter 21. Borrowed funds when measured against the rate of inflation can represent expensive money to financial managers. Furthermore, in 2001 bankers became more risk averse, again due this time to large losses experienced on loans to the high-tech industry. This risk aversion resulted in added difficulties for borrowers in securing bank financing.

Financing through Commercial Paper

As an alternative to bank financing, large, prestigious firms may issue commercial paper in the wholesale money markets. **Commercial paper** is a short-term, unsecured promissory note issued to the public in minimum units of $50,000. To the borrower, commercial paper usually carries an effective interest rate below that available through borrowing from the banks. Bypassing the bank's function as intermediary, commercial paper allows more direct contact between the borrower and lender of funds without the overhead. Rather than paying interest, commercial paper is sold at a discount from the maturity value, with the depth of the discount determining the rate of return.

It has been suggested that the spread between borrowing and lending rates on large sums is about 2 percent (200 basis points) when funds are passed through an intermediary like a bank. However, the spread drops to about 1/2 percent (50 basis points) when funds are transferred through the wholesale money markets.

As Figure 8–3 indicates, the amount of commercial paper outstanding has increased dramatically, rising from $2 billion in 1970 to over $130 billion by 2002. This large increase in the commercial paper market reflects the eagerness of qualified companies to borrow at the lowest possible rate available. It also reflects the growth of securitized paper to $60 billion by 2002 from zero in 1993. The larger market that has emerged in the last five years has improved the ability of corporations to raise short-term funds.

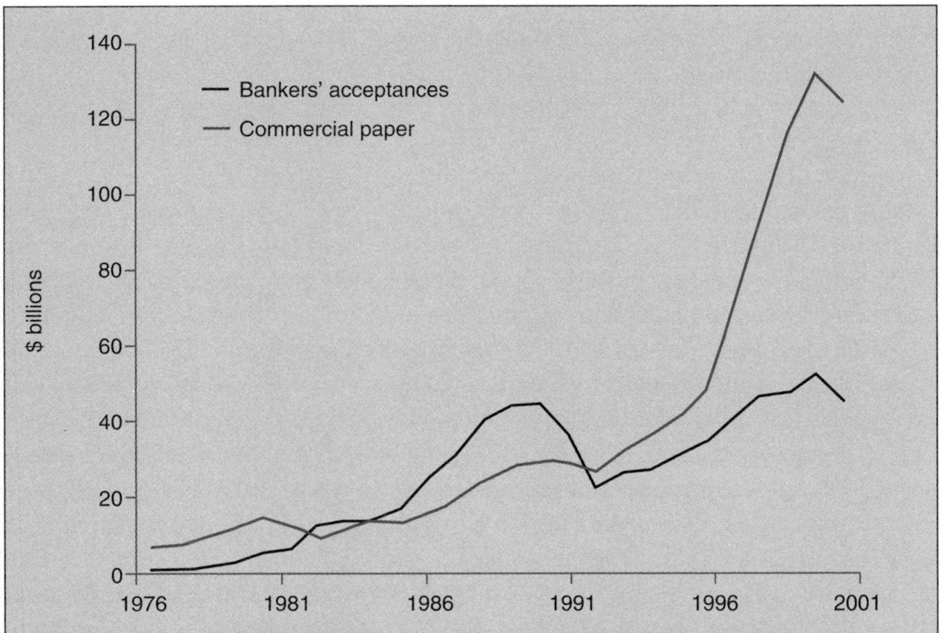

Source: *Bank of Canada Banking and Financial Statistics*, March 2002. www.bankofcanada.ca/en

FIGURE 8–3
Corporate short-term paper outstanding

FINANCE IN ACTION

Q1 What is the present composition of Canadian Tire's short-term financing?

Bank Loan, Commercial Paper or Accounts Payable at Canadian Tire

Canadian Tire is one of Canada's largest retailers, selling automotive, sport, leisure and household products through over 400 stores nationwide. It maintains large working capital positions in accounts receivables and inventories that must be financed on a short-term basis. In the second quarter of 2001 Canadian Tire's balance sheet showed loans of $18 million, commercial paper of $150 million, and accounts payable of $676 million. The commercial paper was rated R-1(high) which suggested a yield of slightly over 2 percent at the time and its unsecured loans were at a prime of 4 percent. These positions change from time to time and can be seen if you examine the latest financials under investor info at the Canadian Tire web site at www.canadiantire.com.

Today over 200 major corporations are active in the Canadian commercial paper market. The banks are encouraging large corporations to borrow by way of commercial paper rather than by bankers' acceptances, which have become less attractive as a revenue source to the banks. This is because under international agreements, banks are required to set aside reserves for their contingent liabilities under the guarantees of bankers' acceptances. Reserves earn low or no return for the banks and thus lower their profits.

Commercial paper falls into two categories. First, there are finance companies, such as Household Finance Corporation, that issue *"finance paper"* primarily to institutional investors such as pension funds, insurance companies, and money market mutual funds. It is also referred to as direct paper. Sales finance, consumer loan, and other financial institutions use the commercial paper market to fund their ordinary course of business. The second type of commercial paper is sold by industrial or utility firms, such as Stelco or Bell Canada Enterprises, which use an intermediate dealer network to distribute their paper. This is referred to as dealer paper. Nonfinancial corporations account for almost $25 billion in commercial paper debt, often issuing it to fund seasonal fluctuations in inventory or accounts receivable. Securitized paper, new since 1993, has now reached almost $60 billion in outstanding paper. This is discussed later in the chapter.

Traditionally, commercial paper is just that. A paper certificate is issued to the lender to signify the lender's claim to be repaid. This certificate could be lost, stolen, misplaced, or damaged, and in rare cases, someone could fail to cash it in at maturity. Although the investments are fairly sound, there is increasing clearing and settlement risk from the increased volume of transactions in the money markets. The **Canadian Depository for Securities Ltd. (CDS)** has established an online, real-time national clearinghouse for money market securities. CDS is owned by the banks, investment dealers, and trust companies and provides a similar service for equity market transactions. Paper certificates are held by CDS as the underlying security, but subsequent transactions will involve electronic transfers and a book-entry ledger. The use of computer-based electronic issuing methods lowers costs, simplifies administration, increases security, and links the lender or lender's bank and the issuing company. Bank lines of credit, call loans, and security loans will be tied into the system to produce net fund positions for companies. Better service and increased liquidity will result from this new clearing mechanism.

Canadian Depository for Securities
www.cds.ca

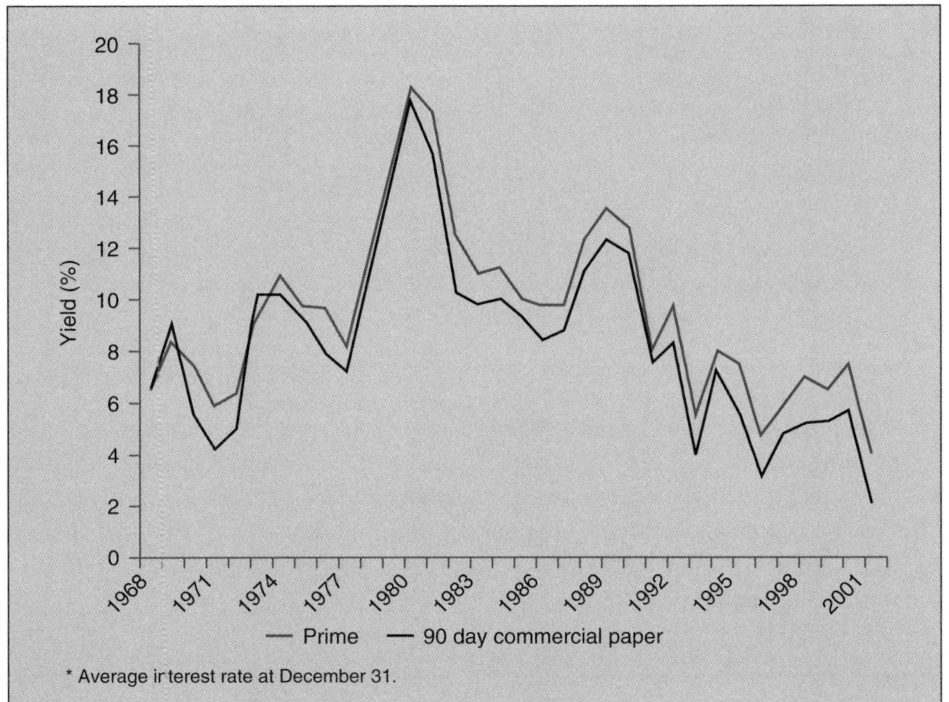

FIGURE 8–4
Comparison of commercial paper rate to prime rate*

Advantages of Commercial Paper

The growing popularity of commercial paper can be attributed largely to its relative cheapness compared to short-term bank debt. For example, commercial paper may be issued below the prime interest rate. As indicated in Figure 8–4, this rate differential is generally between .5 and 2 percent except during times of extremely tight money. Differentials of over 2 percent during the tight money periods account for the surge in commercial paper activity at that time. In 1982, the differential in the U.S. market had reached 5 percent, causing an even greater expansion of commercial paper in that market.

A second advantage of commercial paper is that no compensating balance requirements are associated with its issuance, though the firm is generally required to maintain commercial bank lines of approved credit equal to the amount of the paper outstanding (a procedure somewhat less costly than compensating balances). Finally, a number of firms enjoy the prestige associated with being able to float their commercial paper in what is considered an exclusive market for funds.

Limitations on the Issuance of Commercial Paper

Historically, commercial paper activity has sometimes led to problems. In 1965 the default of the Atlantic Acceptance Corporation was a reminder to the lenders of the risks involved. In recent memory, the failures of corporations such as Olympia and York, and Confederation Life Insurance Company, have left many holding their unsecured IOU's. Confederation Life had about $400 million outstanding at the time it was seized by regulators. At the time its commercial paper was rated R1 (low) by the Dominion Bond Rating Service and was still considered to be of investment grade.

FINANCE IN ACTION

www.banamex.com/eng

Mexican Bankers' Acceptances

Bankers' Acceptances because of the ever-increasing volumes of international trade are a common investment option throughout the world. One of the most popular futures contracts on the Montreal Exchange is the 90-day Bankers' Acceptance. Mexico is increasing its presence in the international arena and its banks are there to assist its traders and investors. Banamex is a leading financial services institution from Mexico with worldwide operations. Its web site is quite instructive on money market instruments and has a good description of bankers' acceptances under corporate investing/money markets.

1. What is the face value and withholding tax on the Mexican bankers' acceptance?
2. What is CETES?

The lesson to be learned is that although the funds provided through the issuance of commercial paper are cheaper than bank loans, they are also less predictable. Along with the higher rate on a bank loan, a firm may be buying a degree of loyalty and commitment that is unavailable in the commercial paper market. Therefore, lines of credit at a commercial bank are important in protecting the firm against adverse turns of events in the money markets.

Bankers' Acceptances

Figure 8–3 displays the prominent role played by **bankers' acceptances** in short-term debt financing in recent years. These instruments accounted for almost $50 billion of borrowings in 2002. There was a drop in bankers' acceptances outstanding by 1992 due to the recession and bank reporting changes. In recent years the use of bankers acceptances has remained steady. The main use of bankers' acceptances has been to finance inventories of finished goods in transit to the buyers. As you can imagine, companies engaged in foreign trade find this form of financing especially helpful given the long lead times involved.

Banks began in the 1990s to encourage companies to enter the commercial paper market rather than using bankers' acceptances to borrow short-term funds. To comply with international banking regulations, Canadian banks set aside reserves to cover contingent liabilities, such as bankers' acceptances. This made it more expensive for banks to guarantee bankers' acceptances, and they were less willing to do so. The banks new growth market for financing has been asset-based securities.

As an example of a bankers' acceptance, a Canadian company is importing machinery from a German manufacturer, and agreeing to pay in 180 days. The Canadian company would arrange a letter of credit with a Canadian bank. Under the letter of credit, the bank agrees to accept a draft drawn by the German company on the Canadian importer. Hence, the term bankers' acceptance is used to signify the accepted draft once it has been sent by the exporter to the importer's bank. By accepting the draft, the bank has substituted its creditworthiness for that of the customer. If the bank is one of our major banks, the draft becomes a highly marketable money market instrument. This means that the German manufacturer does not have to hold the draft until the due date, but rather, it can sell it in the money market at a discount from its face value. The discount allows the buyer of the bankers' acceptance to realize a return for holding the acceptance until the 180-day payment period is up.

Foreign Borrowing

An increasing source of funds for Canadian firms has been the large Eurocurrency market. Loans from foreign banks denominated in U.S. dollars (the most common currency) are called **Eurodollar loans** and are usually short term to intermediate term in maturity. Many multinational corporations are finding cheaper ways of borrowing in foreign markets. In the 1980s financial managers began to borrow foreign currencies either directly or through foreign subsidiaries at very favourable interest rates. The companies then converted the borrowed francs or pounds to dollars, which where then sent to Canada to be used by the parent company. There is, however, foreign exchange exposure risk associated with these loans. Eurodollar loans are also available in Canadian dollars; thus, foreign exchange risk is avoided while allowing Canadian firms to access capital from markets beyond our borders. This topic is given greater coverage in Chapter 21.

Use of Collateral in Short-Term Financing

Almost any firm would prefer to borrow on an unsecured (no-collateral) basis, but if the borrower's credit rating is too low or its need for funds is too great, the lending institution requires that certain assets be pledged. A secured credit arrangement might help the borrower to obtain funds that would otherwise be unavailable.

In any loan, the lender's primary concern, however, is whether the borrower's capacity to generate cash flow is sufficient to liquidate the loan as it comes due. Few lenders would make a loan strictly on the basis of collateral. Collateral is merely a stopgap device to protect the lender when all else fails. The bank or finance company is in business to collect interest, not to repossess and resell assets.

Though a number of different assets may be pledged, we direct our attention to accounts receivable and inventory. The authority to assign accounts receivable as security on a loan comes under provincial legislation. Section 178 of the Bank Act covers inventories of manufactured goods as loan collateral. It gives banks the ability to take possession of, to look after, and to sell the inventories, if required.

Lines of Credit Credit lines are usually established on a year-to-year basis between a bank and its customer. This allows the firm to finance temporary cash needs. The **line of credit** is an agreement whereby the bank sets out the maximum amount it allows the firm to owe it at any one time. The amount of the line depends on an assessment of the firm's creditworthiness. Major considerations are the management capabilities of the firm, its profitability, and its net worth position. The line of credit is usually evidenced by a letter from the bank. However, the letter does not legally bind the bank to extend credit to the customer on demand. If the creditworthiness of the customer were to change or if the market were to become tight for funds, the bank might refuse to lend money under the line of credit agreement. In practice, however, a bank would be very reluctant not to honour its commitments under lines of credit.

Arranging lines of credit is an important role of the financial manager. Credit lines are available at floating interest rates tied into the prime rate. The best customers are able to get prime, which may be in Canadian funds, U.S. funds, or at a LIBOR rate.

Revolving Credit Agreements The basic differences between the revolving credit agreement and the lines of credit are that the **revolving credits** are usually for periods longer than one year, and they usually involve a fee calculated as a fraction of the unused portion of the credit. Technically, because they are for periods longer than one year, revolving credits are generally classed as intermediate rather than short-term financing.

Transaction Loans Sometimes a borrower needs a loan to fund one particular project. In such cases a line of credit or a revolving credit agreement would not make sense. The bank might finance a company to finish work on a piece of machinery that is to be delivered on contract to a large customer. When the machine is delivered and paid for, the firm would repay its debt to the bank.

Accounts Receivable Financing

Accounts receivable financing may include **pledging receivables** as collateral for a loan or an outright sale **(factoring)** of receivables. Receivables financing is popular because it permits borrowing to be tied directly to the level of asset expansion at any time. As the level of accounts receivable goes up, we are able to borrow more.

A drawback is that this is a relatively expensive method of acquiring funds, so it must be carefully compared to other forms of credit. Accounts receivable represent valuable short-term assets, and they should be committed only where the appropriate circumstances exist. An ill-advised accounts receivable financing plan may exclude the firm from a less expensive bank term loan. Let us investigate more closely the characteristics and the costs associated with the pledging and selling of receivables.

Pledging Accounts Receivable

The lending institution generally stipulates which of the accounts receivable are of sufficient quality to serve as collateral for a loan. For example, banks generally do not accept accounts receivable more than 90 days old. The firm may borrow up to 75 percent of the value of the acceptable collateral from a bank. The loan percentage depends on the financial strength of the borrowing firm and on the credit risk of its accounts. The lender has full recourse against the borrower in the event any of the accounts go bad. The interest rate in a receivables borrowing arrangement is generally 1 to 3 percent in excess of the prime rate.

The interest is computed against the loan balance outstanding, a figure that may change quite frequently, as indicated in Table 8–1. In the illustration, interest is assumed to be 12 percent annually, or approximately 1 percent per month. In month 1, the firm can borrow $6,000 against $10,000 in acceptable receivables and must pay $60.00 in interest. Similar values are developed for succeeding months.

TABLE 8–1
Receivable loan balance

	Month 1	Month 2	Month 3	Month 4
Total accounts receivable	$11,000	$15,100	$19,400	$16,300
Acceptable receivables (to bank)	10,000	14,000	18,000	15,000
Loan balance (60%)	6,000	8,400	10,800	9,000
Interest—1% per month	60	84	108	90

Additionally, the bank will require the firm to report regularly on its accounts receivable position and will likely establish other requirements covering insurance, withdrawal of funds, and obtaining of additional debt.

Factoring Receivables

As an alternative to borrowing funds from the bank, a firm may be able to sell its receivables to a factoring company. Factoring companies deal only with companies that produce physical products rather than service companies. Smaller manufacturers in the apparel, consumer electronics, furniture, and automotive aftermarket industries are the prime users of factoring services. Factoring companies may provide accounts receivable management alone or combined with receivables-based financing.

The factoring company may be used as a direct substitute for the firm's accounts receivable department. The client firm sells its product and sends a copy of the invoice to the factor, which then takes over collection responsibility. The invoiced customers still pay the client firm, but the factor keeps track of payments, sends follow-up notices to late payers, and so forth. As part of the service, the factor usually provides a credit guarantee. This guarantee provides that if a factor cannot collect a legitimate account receivable within a specified period, often 180 days, the factor will pay the client firm for the receivable and take possession of it. Rates for this management service, including the credit guarantee, are 1 to 2 percent per month. Thus, although the factor's service is not cheap, the client firm may save on bad debt expenses as well as administrative costs related to managing collections.

Factoring companies also provide financing based on receivables as collateral. For a rate of prime plus 1 to 3 percent, the factor might actually advance a higher proportion of the value of receivables, sometimes as much as 80 to 90 percent. Accounts receivable may be purchased by a factoring company at a discount of between 4 to 10 percent to the face value of invoices depending on their size and the estimated time to collection. If the factoring company cannot collect a receivable purchased on a recourse basis, it retains the right to return the receivable to the company that sold it for payment.

Consider, as an illustration, a case where a factor administers all of a client's receivables and advances 80 percent of their value as an operating loan. If $100,000 a month is processed at a 1 percent commission and a 12 percent annual borrowing rate is charged on the loan, the total cost of the borrowing is calculated as approximately 24 percent on an *annual* basis.

1.0%	Commission
1.0%	Interest for one month (12% annual/12)
2.0%	Total fee monthly
2.0%	Monthly × 12 = 24% annual rate

The important part of the factoring analysis, however, is to determine what portion of the cost relates to the administration and credit guarantee service and to determine if that is reasonable. If the equivalent cost of a secured loan from the bank was also 12 percent, the company would have to determine if the commission costs of 1 percent per month or $12,000 per year are justified by administrative and credit loss savings. For example, if the firm estimated that factoring would save $10,000 in credit checking and clerical costs as well as avoid a 1/2 percent bad debt experience, the estimated savings would be $16,000 per year versus a cost of $12,000.

FINANCE IN ACTION

www.accordfinancial.com

Factoring for the Small Growing Business

There are many factoring companies in Canada that are more than willing to compete to provide financing on the strength of a firm's accounts receivable. Accord Financial Corp. is listed on the TSE and provides a variety of factoring services to small- and medium-sized businesses through its subsidiaries Montcap Financial and Accord Business Credit. Other factoring companies operating in Canada are listed at Industry Canada's web site: www.strategis.ic.gc.ca/SSG/so01924e.html

1. What are the factoring services available at the Accord Group of companies?

$10,000	Administrative cost savings
$ 6,000	Bad debt savings ($100,000 × .005 × 12)
$16,000	

Choosing to factor its receivables would therefore be a sound financial decision.

Asset-Backed Public Offerings

A new wrinkle in accounts receivable financing is the sale of receivables by large firms in public offerings arranged by securities dealers. While factoring has long been one way of selling receivables, public offerings of securities backed by receivables as collateral gained respectability when General Motors Acceptance Corporation (GMAC) made a public offering of $500 million of asset-backed securities in December 1985.

These **asset-backed securities** are nothing more than the sale of receivables through public offerings. By 2002 asset-backed securities totalled almost $60 billion outstanding. In former years, companies that sold receivables were viewed as short of cash, financially shaky, or in some sort of financial trouble. However, there is growing acceptance of this form of financing in Canada. There have been asset-backed security offerings by Chrysler based on car loans and by Sears based on credit card receivables.

Investment dealers continue to develop new types of asset-backed securities, and they are optimistic that the use of all asset-backed securities will continue to grow because of the predictable cash flows they offer investors. The public offerings of asset-backed securities have ranged from commercial paper with a short term to maturity to five-year term notes. Asset-backed commercial paper trades at 5 to 50 basis points above bankers' acceptances.

Dominion Bond Rating Service
www.dbrs.com

One of the benefits to the issuer is that they trade future cash flows for immediate cash. The asset-backed security is likely to carry a high credit rating of AA or better, even when the issuing firm may have a low credit rating. This allows the issuing firm to acquire lower-cost funds than it could with a bank loan or a bond offering. While this short-term market is still relatively small by money market standards, it does provide an important avenue for corporate liquidity and short-term financing.

There are also several problems facing the public sale of receivables. Computer systems need to be upgraded to service securities and to handle the paperwork that is needed to keep track of the loans for the investors in the securities. A second consideration for the buyer of these securities is the probability that the receivable will actually be paid. Even though the loss rates on loans were about one half of 1 percent in the

Liquid Assets as Collateral—It Goes Down Well

In 1999 and 2000 Pubmaster Ltd., a U.K. pub company, issued £414 million of securitized credit notes using the cash flow from its pubs as collateral. Many thought the cash flow stream to be quite reliable and Pubmaster received an A credit rating. The yield was 100 basis points above LIBOR for its floating notes. Pubmaster was purchasing pubs throughout Great Britain and in 1999 sold 368,000 barrels of beer.

In November 1991 Sears Canada Receivables Trust (SCRT) was formed to buy accounts receivable from Sears Canada. These accounts receivable were credit card balances. Commercial paper and debentures were issued to provide financing for the trust. The buyers of these financial instruments would have credit card receivables as their security. Credit card receivables have a low default rate and offer very good security. In fact, SCRT received a better credit rating than Sears Canada itself.

In 1998 CIBC Visa raised over $2 billion in asset-backed securities based on credit card receivables. The average size of asset-backed offerings was $100 to $150 million, although deals for as low as $10 million have been done in Canada.

In August 1982 Mexico told the international investment community it could no longer repay its loans. Lenders were reluctant to lend to crown and private corporations of Mexico, except at high interest rates.

Telephonos de Mexico in 1992, raised funds by securitizing its future receivables of American Telephone and Telegraph Co. (AT&T). Investors were willing to purchase these securities at about 2 percent below the telephone company's normal borrowing costs. This was because the investor would have a claim on AT&T assets if Telephonos de Mexico defaulted on its loan repayments.

And of particular "note" was the an offering by David Bowie, the rock singer, who raised U.S.$55 million at a 7.9 percent interest rate over 15 years based on future royalties from over 300 songs that he had written.

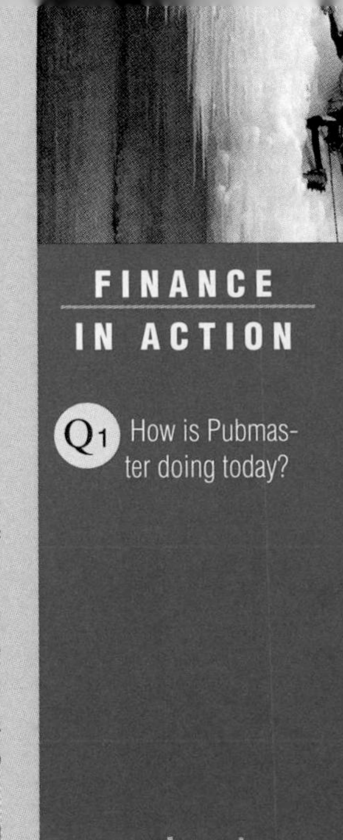

FINANCE IN ACTION

Q1 How is Pubmaster doing today?

www.pubmaster.co.uk

www.asset-backed.com

1980s, bad debts can be as much as 5 to 10 percent in tight money markets.[3] During a serious recession the owners of the asset-backed securities might find themselves without the promised cash flows as people can't make payments on their receivables. To counteract these fears, many issuers set up a loan-loss reserve fund to partially insure against the possibility of a loss.

Inventory Financing

We may also borrow against inventory to acquire funds. The extent to which inventory financing may be employed is based on the liquidity or marketability of the pledged goods, their associated price stability, and the perishability of the product. Another significant factor is the degree of physical control that can be exercised over the product by the lender. We can relate some of these factors to the stages of inventory production and the nature of lender control.

Stages of Production

Raw materials and finished goods are likely to provide the best collateral, while goods in process may qualify for only a small percentage loan. For a firm holding such widely traded raw materials as lumber, metals, grain, cotton, and wool, a loan of 70 to 80 percent is possible. The lender may only have to place a few quick phone calls to dispose of the goods at market value if the borrower fails to repay the loan. For standardized

[3]Ann Monroe, "Sales of Receivables By Big Firms Gain Respect in Public Offerings," the *Wall Street Journal*, December 2, 1985, p. 41.

finished goods, such as tires, canned goods, and building products, the same principle would apply. On the other hand, goods in process, representing altered but unfinished raw materials, may qualify for a loan of only one-fourth their value or less.

Nature of Lender Control

The methods for controlling pledged inventory go from the simple to the complex, providing ever-greater assurances to the lender, but progressively higher administrative costs.

Blanket Inventory Liens The simplest method is a **blanket inventory lien** in which the lender has a general claim against the inventory of the borrower. Specific items are not identified or tagged, and there is no physical control.

Trust Receipts A **trust receipt** is an instrument acknowledging that the borrower holds the inventory and proceeds from sales in trust for the lender. Each item is carefully marked and specified by serial number. When sold, the proceeds are transferred to the lender, and the trust receipt is cancelled. Also known as *floor planning*, this financing device is very popular among auto and industrial equipment dealers and in the television and home appliance industries. Although it provides tighter control than does the blanket inventory lien, it still does not give the lender direct control over inventory—only a better and more legally enforceable system of tracing the goods.

Warehousing Under this arrangement goods are physically identified, segregated, and stored under the direction of an independent warehousing company. The firm issues a warehouse receipt to the lender, and goods can be moved only with the lender's approval.

The goods may be stored on the premises of the warehousing firm, an arrangement known as **public warehousing,** or on the borrower's premises under a **field warehousing** agreement. When field warehousing is utilized, an independent warehousing company still exercises control over inventory.

Appraisal of Inventory Control Devices

Although the more structured methods of inventory financing appear somewhat restrictive, they are well accepted in certain industries. For example, field warehousing is popular in grain storage and food canning. Well-maintained control measures do involve substantial administrative expenses, and they raise the overall costs of borrowing. The costs of inventory financing may run 15 percent or higher. As is true of accounts receivable financing, the extension of funds is well synchronized with the need.

Hedging to Reduce Borrowing Risk

Those firms that need to borrow funds or to lend funds for the continuing operations of their firm are exposed to the risk of interest rate changes. One way to partially reduce that risk is through **interest rate hedging** activities in the **financial futures market**. Hedging means to engage in a transaction that partially or fully reduces a prior risk exposure. The financial futures market is set up to allow for the trading of a financial instrument at a future time. This instrument is separate from the firm's requirement,

Montreal Exchange Opts for Futures

The Montreal Exchange is Canada's oldest stock exchange, but in 1999 it agreed, subject to government approval, to abandon its stock trading to the Toronto Stock Exchange and concentrate on derivatives trading. During the 1990s it had lost significant trading volume to Toronto.

However, the Montreal Futures Exchange www.me.org had carved out a strong niche in derivatives that offer a means for firms to hedge their interest rate risk. The bankers' acceptance future (BAX) and bond futures on 5- and 10-year Government of Canada bonds have proved quite popular. In fact, they have nicely withstood a challenge from the Chicago Mercantile Exchange, www.cme.com, the world's largest futures exchange which recently began offering EuroCanada futures and options. The MER's contracts are based on EuroCanadian LIBOR, which is a short-term interest rate that closely tracks the interest rate on bankers' acceptances.

Hedgers have so far preferred the BAX offered by the Montreal Exchange (Bourse de Montreal). Under quotes for the BAX contracts at the Montreal Exchange the open interest position is given. This gives an idea of the contract's liquidity.

Many Canadian companies with global business engage in hedging activities. The company's latest financial statements will identify hedging activities in the notes, perhaps listed under derivative instruments.

FINANCE IN ACTION

Q1 What are the hedging activities at Bombardier?

Q2 What is the trading unit of the BAX ?

Q3 What is the open interest of the first BAX to expire?

www.bombardier.com

Symbol: BBD.B

through a business transaction, to borrow or lend funds at a fixed rate at some time in the future. Chapter 19 further discusses the futures market.

Let us suppose it is January 2003 and a firm will be required to borrow funds for equipment sometime between then and June 2003 at a fixed rate of interest and for an extended period of time. This exposes the firm to the risk that interest rates might go up in the future, forcing it to pay higher interest rates than the current market rates. To hedge this risk, the firm might sell a Canadian government bond future contract that is to be closed out in June 2003, through the financial futures market. The sale price of this contract is established by the initial January transaction. A subsequent purchase of a June 2003 contract at a currently unknown price will be necessary to close out the transaction.

In the futures market you do not physically deliver the goods (in this case the government bond). What you do is execute a later transaction that reverses your initial position. Thus, if you initially sell a futures contract, you later buy a contract that covers your initial sale. If you initially buy a futures contract, the opposite is true, and you later sell a contract that covers your initial purchase position.

In the case of selling a Canadian government bond futures contract, the subsequent pattern of interest rates determines whether the futures contract is profitable or not. If interest rates go up, Canadian government bond prices go down and you can buy a subsequent contract at a lower price than the sales value that you originally established. The result is a profitable transaction that can be used to offset the higher costs the firm will incur when borrowing to pay for its equipment. Note the following example:

Sale price, June government bond contract[4] (sale occurs in January 2003)	$95,000
Purchase price, June 2003 government bond contract (the purchase occurs in June 2003)	90,000
Profit on futures contract	$ 5,000

[4]Only a small percentage of the actual dollars involved must be invested to initiate the contract. This is known as a margin.

The reason government bond prices went down is because, as previously mentioned, interest rates and bond prices move in opposite directions, and interest rates went up. If the reverse were true and bond prices had increased with lower interest rates, the futures contract would show a loss. The firm, however, would be able to borrow at more desirable lower rates of interest, so once again the firm is covered or hedged. The lesson to be learned from this example is that rising interest rates can mean profits in the financial futures market if you initially sell a contract and later buy it back. This can offset higher interest rates on borrowed funds that might be required in the future course of business.

The financial futures market can be used to partially or fully hedge against almost any financial event. In addition to the Government of Canada bond future, there is the bankers' acceptance future, which is used to hedge short-term interest rates. Both of these contracts are available through the Montreal Exchange. The level of activity in these futures is minimal when compared to the financial futures available in the United States, where besides Treasury bonds, trades may be initiated in Treasury bills, certificates of deposit, GNMA certificates,[5] and many other instruments.[6] The trades may be executed on such exchanges as the Chicago Board of Trade, the Chicago Mercantile Exchange, or the New York Mercantile Exchange.

New York Mercantile Exchange
www.nymex.com

[5]GNMA stands for the Government National Mortgage Association, also known as Ginnie Mae.

[6]For a more complete discussion of corporate hedging in the futures market, see "Commodities and Financial Futures" in Chapter 16 of Geoffrey Hirt and Stanley Block, *Fundamentals of Investment Management*, 6th ed. (New York: McGraw Hill, 1999).

Summary

1. The easiest access to short-term financing is through trade credit provided by suppliers as a natural outgrowth of the buying and reselling of goods. Larger firms tend to be net providers of trade credit, while smaller firms are net users. Firms that do not take advantage of discounts in order to provide themselves with additional financing may find it quite expensive.
2. Bank financing is usually in the form of short-term, self-liquidating loans. A financially strong customer is offered the prime, or lowest rate, with the rates to other accounts scaled up appropriately. Economic factors cause the prime to change frequently, and thus the interest rate on loans changes as well. Short-term loans are usually on a demand basis, which allows the amount outstanding to move up and down based on business conditions. Compensating balances and discount loans change the actual interest rate stated.
3. An alternative to bank credit for the large, prestigious firm is the use of commercial paper. Though generally issued at a rate below prime, it is an impersonal means of financing that may dry up during difficult financing periods.
4. Firms are also turning to foreign sources of funds, either through the Eurodollar market or through borrowing foreign currency directly. These markets represent alternative sources of capital often at cheaper rates, but they may introduce foreign exchange risk.
5. By using a secured form of financing, the firm ties its borrowing requirements directly to its asset buildup. We may pledge our accounts receivable as collateral or sell them outright, as well as borrow against inventory. Though secured-asset financing devices may be expensive, they may fit the credit needs of the firm, particularly those of a small firm that cannot qualify for premium bank financing or the commercial paper market.

6. The financial manager may wish to consider the use of hedging through the financial futures market. The consequences of rapid interest rate changes can be reduced through participation in the financial futures market.

Review of Formulas

1. The cost of forgoing the discount (8–1)

$$K_{DIS} = \frac{d\%}{100\% - d\%} \times \frac{365}{f(\text{date}) - d(\text{date})}$$

$d\%$ = discount percentage
$f(\text{date})$ = final payment period
$d(\text{date})$ = discount period

2. $$\text{Amount to be borrowed} = \frac{\text{Amount needed}}{(1 - c)}$$

c is compensating balance requirement expressed as a decimal.

3. $$R_{ANNUAL} = \frac{I}{P} \times \frac{365}{d}$$ (8–2)

R_{ANNUAL} = annual rate
I = interest
P = principal
d = days loan is outstanding

4. Annual rate on discounted loan (8–3)

$$R_{DIS} = \frac{I}{P - I} \times \frac{365}{d}$$

5. Annual rate with compensating balances (8–4)

$$R_{COMP} = \frac{I}{(1 - c)}$$

c is compensating balance requirement expressed as a decimal.

6. $$R_{COMP} = \frac{I}{P - B} \times \frac{365}{d}$$ (8–5)

B = Compensating balance in $$

7. Annual rate on an installment loan (8–6)

$$R_{INSTALL} = \frac{2 \times \text{Annual number of payments} \times I}{(\text{Total number of payments} + 1) \times P}$$

List of Terms

spontaneous source of funds 253
net trade credit 256
self-liquidating loan 256
prime rate 257
bank rate 257
compensating balance 258
term loan 259
discounted loan 260
installment loan 261
commercial paper 263
Canadian Depository for Securities Ltd. (CDS) 264
bankers' acceptances 266
Eurodollar loans 267
line of credit 267
revolving credits 267
pledging receivables 268
factoring receivables 268
asset-backed securities 270
blanket inventory lien 272

trust receipt 272
public warehousing 272
field warehousing 272
interest rate hedging 272
financial futures market 272

Discussion Questions

1. Under which circumstances would it be advisable to borrow money to take a cash discount?
2. Discuss the relative use of credit between large and small firms. Which group is generally in the net creditor position? Why?
3. What is the prime interest rate? How does the average bank customer fare in regard to the prime interest rate? Are companies ever allowed by banks to borrow at less than prime?
4. What advantages do compensating balances have for banks? Are the advantages to banks necessarily disadvantages to corporations?
5. A borrower is often confronted with a stated interest rate and an effective interest rate. What is the difference, and which one should the financial manager recognize as the true cost of borrowing?
6. Commercial paper may show up on corporate balance sheets as either a current asset or a current liability. Explain this statement.
7. What are the advantages of commercial paper in comparison with bank borrowing at the prime rate? What are the disadvantages?
8. What is the major advantage of a bankers' acceptance?
9. Discuss the major types of collateralized short-term loans.
10. What is an asset-backed public offering?
11. What is meant by hedging in the financial futures market to offset interest rate risks?

INTERNET RESOURCES AND QUESTIONS

The Canadian exchange for interest rate futures is the Montreal Exchange. It includes a history of the exchange and specifications for the bankers' acceptances and government bond contracts:
www.me.org

The Chicago Mercantile Exchange is the world's largest futures exchange. It lists several Canadian interest rate products:
www.cme.com

Quicken, under its banking and credit section, compares interest rates on loans and investments at various Canadian financial institutions:
www.quicken.ca

The *National Post* also provides a comparison of interest rates under money rates in its money section.
www.nationalpost.com

1. Identify the Canadian dollar interest rate futures contracts, including the contract size and how settlement prices are determined, available on:
   a. The Montreal Exchange.
   b. The Chicago Mercantile Exchange.
2. Compare interest rates on secured and unsecured lines of credit, as well as unsecured loans, at Canadian financial institutions.

Problems

1. Compute the cost of not taking the following trade discounts:
   a. 2/10, net 50.
   b. 2/15, net 40.
   c. 3/10, net 45.
   d. 3/10, net 180.
2. To finance additional inventory, Arbutus Ltd. is considering forgoing the cash discount on all of its purchases presently offered on terms of 2/10, net 45. No payments will be stretched. Annual purchases are $9.21 million.
   a. Calculate the additional financing available to Arbutus Ltd. by forgoing the cash discount.
   b. Calculate the annual cost of forgoing the cash discount.
3. S. Pumpkins has an average inventory of $630,000, with an annual turnover rate of eight times. The average accounts receivable balance is $520,250, and customers pay on average in 30 days. S. Pumpkins pays accounts in 45 days.
   a. Calculate S. Pumpkins' average accounts payable balance.
   b. Calculate its annual sales.
4. Mr. Paul Promptly is a very cautious businessman. His suppliers offer trade credit terms of 3/10, net 70. Mr. Promptly never takes the discount offered, but he pays his suppliers in 60 days rather than the 70 days allowed so that he is sure the payments are never late. What is Mr. Promptly's cost of not taking the cash discount?
5. Regis Clothiers can borrow from its bank at 11 percent to take a cash discount. The terms of the cash discount are 2/15 net 60. Should the firm borrow the funds?
6. The average price on 91-day Treasury bills at a recent Tuesday auction was 98.671 with maturity value 100. Calculate the T-bill's annualized yield.
7. The average price on 182-day Treasury bills was 98.097 with maturity value at 100. Calculate the T-bill's annualized yield.
8. McGriff Dog Food Company normally takes 20 days to pay for average daily credit purchases of $9,000. Its average daily sales are $10,000 and it collects accounts in 25 days.
   a. What is its net credit position?
   b. If the firm extends its average payment period from 20 days to 32 days (and all else remains the same), what is the firm's new net credit position?
9. Your bank will lend you $3,000 for 50 days at a cost of $45.00 interest. What is your annual rate of interest? What is your effective annual rate?
10. I. M. Boring is going to borrow $5,000 for one year at 13 percent interest. What is the annual rate of interest if the loan is discounted?
11. Simpson Orange Juice Company normally takes 20 days to pay for its average daily credit purchases of $6,000. Its average daily sales are $7,000, and it collects its accounts in 28 days.
    a. What is its net credit position?
    b. If the firm extends its average payment period from 20 days to 35 days (and all else remains the same), what is the firm's new net credit position? Has it improved its cash flow?
12. Carey Company is borrowing $200,000 for one year at 12 percent from Second National Bank. The bank requires a 20 percent compensating balance. What is the annual rate of interest? What would the annual rate be if Carey were required to make 12 equal monthly

payments to retire the loan? The principal, as used in Formula 8–6, refers to funds the firm can effectively utilize.

13. Capone Child Care Centres, Inc., plans to borrow $250,000 for one year at 10 percent from the Chicago Bank and Trust Company. There is a 20 percent compensating balance requirement. Capone keeps minimum transaction balances of $18,000 in the normal course of business. This idle cash counts toward meeting the compensating balance requirement. What is the annual rate of interest?

14. The treasurer of Hi-Cost Supermarkets is seeking a $30,000 loan for 180 days from Midland Bank. The stated interest rate is 10 percent and there is a 15 percent compensating requirement. The treasurer always keeps a minimum of $2,500 in the firm's checking account. These funds could count toward meeting any compensating balance requirements. What is the annual rate of interest on this loan?

15. Tucker Drilling Corp. plans to borrow $200,000. Northern Dominion Bank will lend the money at one-half percentage point over the prime rate of 8 percent and requires a compensating balance of 20 percent. What is the annual rate of interest?

16. Your company plans to borrow $5 million for 12 months, and your banker gives you a stated rate of 14 percent interest. You would like to know the annual rate of interest for the following types of loans. (Each of the following parts stands alone.)
    a. Simple 14 percent interest with a 10 percent compensating balance.
    b. Discounted interest.
    c. An installment loan (12 payments).
    d. Discounted interest with a 5 percent compensating balance.

17. If you borrow $12,000 at $900 interest for one year, what is your annual interest cost for the following payment plan?
    a. Annual payment.
    b. Semiannual payments.
    c. Quarterly payments.
    d. Monthly payments.

18. Vroom Motorcycle Company is borrowing $30,000 from First Prairie Bank. The total interest charge is $9,000. The loan will be paid by making equal monthly payments for the next three years. What is the annual rate of interest on this installment loan?

19. Morrisette Records' commercial paper is currently selling at 98.512 percent of maturity value; it matures in 75 days. What annualized yield is it offering to investors?

20. Calculate the cost of discounting a $100,000 bankers' acceptance if it is due in 90 days and is sold at $97,285. Ignore bank fees.

21. Blue Grass Filters requires additional financing. Presently, it pays for all purchases on the discount date under terms of 2/15, net 75. Its banker will lend funds at 11 percent.
    a. Should Blue Grass Filters obtain funding from the bank or by forgoing the cash discount?
    b. Assuming the bank is the cheaper alternative, why might Blue Grass Filters still choose to forgo the cash discount to obtain financing?

22. The Ogden Timber Company buys from its suppliers on terms of 2/10, net 35. Ogden has not been utilizing the discount offered and has been taking 50 days to pay its bills. The suppliers seem to accept this payment pattern, and Ogden's credit rating has not been hurt.

Mr. Wood, Ogden Timber Company's vice-president, has suggested that the company begin to take the discount offered. Mr. Wood proposes the company borrow from its bank at a stated rate of 15 percent. The bank requires a 25 percent compensating balance on these loans. Current account balances would not be available to meet any of this compensating balance requirement. Do you agree with Mr. Wood's proposal?

23. In the previous problem, if the compensating balance requirement were 10 percent instead of 25 percent, would you change your answer? Do the appropriate calculation.

24. Bosworth Petroleum needs $500,000 to take a cash discount of 2/10, net 70. A banker will loan the money for 60 days at an interest cost of $8,100.

   a. What is the annual rate on the bank loan?

   b. How much would it cost (in percentage terms) if Bosworth did not take the cash discount and paid the bill in 70 days instead of 10 days?

   c. Should Bosworth borrow the money to take the discount?

   d. If the banker requires a 20 percent compensating balance, how much must Bosworth borrow to end up with the $500,000?

   e. What would be the interest rate in part *d* if the interest charge for 60 days were $13,000? Should Bosworth borrow with the 20 percent compensating balance? (There are no funds to count against the compensating balance requirement.)

25. Rockford Filing Ltd. requires $1 million in financing for a 45-day period. Three alternatives are being considered:

   a. Establish a line of credit with the bank at an interest rate of 10 percent. The bank will charge an annual commitment fee of 1 percent to establish the line of credit.

   b. Forgo trade discounts from suppliers on terms of 2/15, net 60.

   c. Issue commercial paper for 45 days at a discount of 1.25 percent. Which alternative should be selected?

26. Bernie's Macs requires $600,000 in financing for a 60-day period. Three alternatives are being considered.

   a. Establish a line of credit with the bank at an interest rate of 7 percent. The bank will charge an annual commitment fee of $4,750 to establish the line of credit.

   b. Forgo trade discounts from suppliers on terms of 2/30, net 90.

   c. Issue commercial paper for 60 days at a discount of 1.91 percent. Which alternative should be selected?

27. Nanaimo Shipping Company is negotiating with two banks for a $100,000 loan. Bankcorp of B.C. requires a 20 percent compensating balance, discounts the loan, and wants to be paid back in four quarterly payments. Victoria Bank requires a 10 percent compensating balance and does not discount the loan, but it wants to be paid back in 12 monthly installments. The stated rate at both banks is 10 percent. Compensating balances and any discounts will be subtracted from the $100,000 in determining the available funds in part *a*.

   a. Which loan should Nanaimo accept?

   b. Recompute the annual cost of interest, assuming Nanaimo ordinarily maintains $20,000 at each bank in deposits that will serve as compensating balances.

   c. How much did the compensating balances inflate the percentage interest costs? Does your choice of banks change if the assumption in part *b* is correct?

28. Alberta Oil Supplies sells to the 12 accounts listed on the next page.

Account	Receivable Balance Outstanding	Average Age of the Account over Last Year
A	$ 50,000	35
B	80,000	25
C	120,000	47
D	10,000	15
E	250,000	35
F	60,000	51
G	40,000	18
H	180,000	60
I	15,000	43
J	25,000	33
K	200,000	41
L	60,000	28

J&J Financial Corporation will lend 90 percent against account balances that have averaged 30 days or less; 80 percent for account balances between 30 and 40 days; and 70 percent for account balances between 40 and 45 days. Customers that take over 45 days to pay their bills are not considered as adequate accounts for a loan. The current prime rate is 12 percent, and J&J Financial Corporation charges 3 percent over prime to Alberta Oil Supplies as its annual loan rate.

a. Determine the maximum loan for which Alberta Oil Supplies could qualify.

b. Determine how much one month's interest expense would be on the loan balance determined in part *a*.

29. Towers Arcades currently borrows $560,000 per month from its bank on the strength of receivables, which average $800,000 per month. Credit terms are net 30. The bank's interest rate is 10 percent annually, with an additional charge of .5 percent to process the accounts receivable used as security. The processing charge is based not on the loan amount but on the dollar value of the underlying receivables pledged as collateral.

Towers has an offer from a factoring company to buy all of its receivables without recourse for a fee of 2 percent of the value of the receivables purchased. The factoring firm is prepared to lend Towers Arcades $560,000 per month at an interest rate of 11 percent. The factoring company would eliminate Tower's credit department expense, including bad debts costs, of $15,000 a month. Should Towers Arcades switch to the factoring company?

30. The treasurer for Thornton Pipe and Steel Company wishes to use financial futures to hedge her interest rate exposure. She will sell five Canadian bond futures contracts at $105,000 per contract. It is July and the contracts must be closed out in December of this year. Long-term interest rates are currently 7.4 percent. If they increase to 8.5 percent, assume the value of the contracts will go down by 10 percent. Also, if interest rates do increase by 1.1 percentage points, assume the firm will have additional interest expense on its business loans and other commitments of $60,800. This expense, of course, is separate from the futures contract.

a. What will be the profit or loss on the futures contract if interest rates go to 8.5 percent?

b. Explain why a profit or loss occurred on the futures contracts.

c. After considering the hedging in part *a,* what is the net cost to the firm of the increased interest expense of $60,800? What percent of this increased cost did the treasurer effectively hedge away?

d. Indicate whether there would be a profit or loss on the futures contracts if interest rates went down.

COMPREHENSIVE PROBLEM

31. Fresh & Fruity Foods is a mail-order company operating out of a winery near Summerland, British Columbia. The company specializes in sending British Columbian specialties to catalogue customers nationwide. Sales are seasonal, with most occurring in November and December—when people select Fresh & Fruity's Famous Fruit Fantasy boxes as Christmas gifts. Although seasonal, the company's sales are fairly predictable, because the bulk of Fresh & Fruity's customers are regulars who purchase year after year. The company has also managed to smooth out its sales somewhat by offering incentives, such as the Fruit of the Month Club, which encourages customers to buy throughout the year.

The nature of the mail-order business is such that most of Fresh & Fruity's sales are on credit; therefore, the company has historically had a high accounts receivable balance relative to sales. It has also historically been short of cash; forcing it to delay payments to suppliers as long as possible (its average time to pay accounts in 2002 was 67 days).

In January 2003, Tom Appleby and Alice Plummer, the president and treasurer of Fresh & Fruity, respectively, were discussing the cash flow problem over lunch. "You know, Tom," Alice said as she sliced a piece of avocado, "I was reading the other day about a company called Kringle's Candles & Ornaments, and it occurred to me that we're a lot like them. Most of our assets are current ones like their accounts receivable and inventory; and over half of ours are financed just like theirs, by current liabilities—that is, accounts payable." She paused for a sip of chardonnay, and continued, "They got around their cash flow problems by issuing long-term debt, which took the pressure off their current obligations. I've been looking at that for our company, too; but then I got to thinking, there's another way that's a good deal easier and would produce results just as quickly."

"Oh? And what's that?" Tom replied, his interest captured.

"All we have to do," she said, "is to reduce our accounts receivable balance. That will help reduce our accounts payable balance, since, as our customers begin paying us earlier, we can, in turn, pay our suppliers earlier. If we could get enough customers to pay us right away, we could even pay some of the suppliers in time to take advantage of the 2 percent discount they offer for payments within 10 days." (Fresh & Fruity's suppliers operated on a 2/10, net 60 basis.) "That would increase our net income and free up even more cash to take advantage of even more discounts!" She looked excited at the prospect.

"Sounds great, but how do we get people to pay us earlier?" Tom inquired, doubtfully.

"Easy," Alice continued. "Up to now we've been giving them incentives to pay later. Remember our 'Buy Now, No Payments for Two Months' program? Well, a lot of our customers use it, and it's caused our accounts receivable balance to run way up. So what we have to do now is give them incentives to pay earlier. What I propose is to cancel the buy now/pay later plan and instead, offer a 10 percent discount to everyone who pays with their order."

"But won't that cause our revenues to drop?" Tom asked, again still doubtful.

"Yes, but the drop will be offset by even more new customers who will come in to take advantage of the discount. I figure the net effect on sales will be just about zero, but our accounts receivable balance could be cut in half! Now here's a kicker that I just thought of: After we've reduced our accounts receivable balance as far as practical, I'd like to look into the possibility of reducing our accounts payable still further by replacing them with a bank loan. The effective rate of interest that we pay by not taking our suppliers' discounts is, after all, pretty high. So what I'd like to do is take out a loan once a year of a sufficient size that would enable us to take all the discounts our suppliers offer. The interest that we'll pay on the loan is bound to be less than what we pay in discounts lost—so we'll see another gain in earnings on our income statement. In fact, these two initiatives together might have a really significant impact!"

"You've convinced me," Tom said. "Let's go back to the office and run some figures to see what happens!"

Assume that Alice Plummer's first initiative to offer a 10 percent discount was to be implemented, and the company's average collection period would drop to 32 days. As a result of Alice's first initiative Fresh & Fruity would be able to take advantage of the 2 percent discount on one-third of its purchases. Fresh & Fruity can obtain an 8 percent loan for one year.

Prepare a report outlining the costs and benefits of the various alternatives. (Guided questions are available in the instructor's manual.) Include recommendations.

FRESH & FRUITY FOODS, INC.
Income Statement
For year ending Dec. 31, 2002

Revenue from sales:			
Gross sales (credit)			$1,179,000
Cost of goods sold:			
Beginning inventory		$ 141,000	
Purchases	$969,000		
Less: cash discounts	0		
Net purchases		969,000	
Goods available for sale		1,110,000	
Less: ending inventory		79,557	
Cost of goods sold			1,030,443
Gross profit			148,557
Selling and administrative expenses			73,000
Earnings before interest and tax			75,557
Interest expense			0
Earnings before tax			75,557
Income taxes @ 33%			24,934
Net income			$ 50,623

FRESH & FRUITY FOODS, INC.
Balance Sheet
As of December 31, 2002

Assets:		
Cash	$ 3,560	
Accounts receivable	209,686	
Inventory	79,557	
Total current assets		$292,803
Property, plant, and equipment, net		11,430
Total asset		$304,233
Liabilities and equity:		
Accounts payable	$180,633	
Notes payable (bank loans)	0	
Total current liabilities		$180,633
Long-term debt		0
Total liabilities		180,633
Common stock	96,600	
Retained earnings	27,000	
Total equity		123,600
Total liabilities and equity		$304,233
Selected ratios:		
Return on sales	4.29%	
Return on equity	40.96%	
Inventory turnover	14.82	
Receivables turnover	5.62	
Average payment period	67	

Selected References

Agin, William E. "Websites—Obtaining and Perfecting a Security Interest." *Journal of Lending and Credit Risk Management* 82 (July-August 2000), pp. 78–83.

Altman, Edward L, and Robert Haldeman. "Credit Scoring Models: Approaches and Tests for Successful Implementation." *Journal of Commercial Lending* 77 (May 1995), pp. 10–22.

Carey, Mark, Mitch Post, and Steven Sharp. "Does Corporate Lending by Banks and Finance Companies Differ? Evidence of Specialization in Private Debt Contracting." *Journal of Finance* 53 (June 1998), pp. 845–78.

Crabbe, Leland, and Mitchell A. Post. "The Effect of a Rating Downgrade on Outstanding Commercial Paper." *Journal of Finance* 49 (March 1994), pp. 39–56.

Daniels, Carol. "Timing Cash Flow: Will Finality Changes Delay Funds Availability?" *Corporate Cashflow* 11 (January 1990), pp. 40–41.

Frazer, Douglas H. "Issues in Lending: A Primer for Avoiding Contests Over Collateral." *Journal of Commercial Lending* 77 (June 1995), pp. 58–62.

Goerner, Peter. "How to Use a Customer-Focused Quality Program to Improve the Loan Approval Process." *Journal of Commercial Lending* 77 (April 1995), pp. 20–29.

Hill, Claire A. "Securitization: A Low Cost Sweetener for Lemons." *Journal of Applied Corporate Finance* 10 (Spring 1997), pp. 64–71.

Mian, Schzad L., and Clifford W. Smith, Jr. "Accounts Receivable Management Policy: Theory and Evidence." *Journal of Finance* 47 (March 1992), pp. 169–99.

Scholl, William C. "Commercial Lenders' Guide to Cash Management." *Journal of Commercial Lending* 75 (December 1992), pp. 44–48.

Store, Charles A. "Asset Backed Commercial Paper: Get with the Program." *Journal of Applied Corporate Finance* 10 (Spring 1997), pp. 72–78.

Strischek, Dev. "The Quotable Five C's." *Journal of Lending and Credit Risk Management* 82 (April 2000), pp. 47–49.

PART | FOUR

4 THE CAPITAL BUDGETING PROCESS

Establishing the value of assets (capital budgeting) that produce cash flows for future periods is a major consideration of finance. Estimating the cash flows, determining returns required by investors, considering the risks involved, and placing a current price (present worth) on these cash flows are significant endeavours. Both the cost of capital and the capital asset pricing model will assist us in this endeavour, as will the financial markets.

CHAPTER | NINE

9 The Time Value of Money

LEARNING | OBJECTIVES

1 Explain the concept of the time value of money.

2 Calculate present values, future values, and annuities based on the number of time periods involved and the going interest rate.

3 Calculate yield based on the time relationships between cash flows.

In 1624 Native Americans sold Manhattan Island at the ridiculously low figure of $24.00. But was it really ridiculous? If the Native Americans had merely taken the $24.00 and reinvested it at 6 percent annual interest up to 2003, they would have had $94 billion, an amount sufficient to repurchase most of New York City. If the Natives had been slightly more astute and had invested the $24.00 at 7.5 percent compounded annually, they would now have over $18,000,000,000,000 ($18 trillion)—and tribal chiefs would now rival oil sheiks and Bill Gates as the richest people in the world. Another popular example is that $1.00 received 2,000 years ago, invested at 6 percent, could now be used to purchase all of the wealth in the world.

While not all examples are this dramatic, the time value of money applies to many day-to-day decisions. Understanding the effective rate on a business loan, the mortgage payment in a real estate transaction, or the true return on an investment is dependent on understanding the time value of money. As long as an investor can garner a positive return on idle dollars, distinctions must be made between money received today and money to be received in the future. The investor/lender essentially demands that a financial "rent" be paid on his or her funds as current dollars are set aside today in anticipation of higher returns in the future.

This chapter outlines how to use a financial calculator to solve time value problems (calculators carry answers to several decimals and are quite accurate). Appendix E provides additional guidance on the calculator functions. This chapter also outlines the use of tables, which are found in Appendixes A through D. A calculator, a set of tables, or a computer are tools for time value calculations. What is important is for the student to visualize the timing patterns of the cash flows in order to solve problems.

Calculator To evaluate time value problems with the calculator, it is important to become familiar with five keys of the calculator. After the problem is visualized, often with a time line, we can use the calculator to express any cash flow or cash flows at a particular time. The keys of importance are present value (PV), future value (FV), payment (PMT) or annuity (ANN), the number of times interest is compounded (n), and the interest rate ($\%i$) per compounding period. The begin (BGN) or (DUE) key will also be valuable when cash flows occur at the beginning of a time period, such as with leases, for example. The tables and calculator normally assume that any cash flows occur at the end of time periods.

Relationship to the Capital Budgeting Decision

The decision to purchase new plant and equipment or to introduce a new product in the market requires the use of funds with benefits over several time periods and is referred to as capital budgeting. Essentially, we must determine whether the future benefits from these projects are sufficiently large to justify the current outlays. It is important that we develop the mathematical tools of the time value of money as the first step toward making capital allocating decisions. This technique will allow us to evaluate the present worth of these future benefits, which can then be compared properly with the current outlays. Let us now examine the basic terminology of "time value of money."

Interest Rate

The interest rate used in time value of money calculations is also referred to as a discount rate, rate of return, or yield. It specifies a relationship between a value today and a value or series of values tomorrow. It allows us to equate values that occur at different points in time. In effect, from our previous example, the $24.00 in 1624 was equivalent to $94 billion in 2003 if the going interest rate was 6 percent over that period. Only when values are specified at the same point in time can we add or subtract them if we are working with the time value of money.

Future Value—Single Amount

In determining the **future value**, we measure the value of an amount that is allowed to grow at a given interest rate over a time period. The future value is also referred to as the compound value. Assume an investor has $1,000 and wishes to know its worth after four years if it grows at 10 percent per year. Each year the investor is credited with the interest earned so that, in subsequent years, interest is earned on interest. This is known as compounding, and the more frequently it occurs, the higher the future value. At the end of the first year, the investor will have $1,000 × 1.10, or $1,100. By the end of year two, the $1,100 will have grown to $1,210 ($1,100 × 1.10). The four-year pattern is indicated below.

1st year	$1,000 × 1.10 = $1,100
2nd year	$1,100 × 1.10 = $1,210
3rd year	$1,210 × 1.10 = $1,331
4th year	$1,331 × 1.10 = $1,464

After the fourth year, the investor has accumulated $1,464. Because compounding problems often cover a long time period, a more generalized formula is necessary to describe the compounding procedure. We shall let:

FV = Future value
PV = Present value
i = Interest rate
n = Number of periods

The formula is:

$$FV = PV(1 + i)^n \quad (9\text{–}1)^1$$

In this case, $PV = \$1{,}000$, $i = 10$ percent, and $n = 4$, so we have:

$$FV = \$1{,}000(1.10)^4 = \$1{,}464$$

Calculator

	$FV = ?$
$PV = \$1{,}000$	
	$i = 10$
	$n = 4$
	$PMT = 0$

Compute $FV = -\$1{,}464.10$.

With the known variables input into the calculator, we compute $FV = -\$1{,}464.10$. The result is negative (dependent on calculator) to indicate that \$1,464.10 must be given up in the future to receive \$1,000 today, or vice versa. We will often ignore the negative sign in our illustrations, as the meaning should be clear.

Tables (optional) The term $(1.10)^4$ is found to equal 1.464 by multiplying 1.10 four times itself (the fourth power) or by using logarithms. Using an interest rate table, such as presented at the back of the text in Appendix A, can also reveal the future value of a dollar. With $n = 4$ and $i = 10$ percent, the value is also found to be 1.464.

The table also tells us the amount that \$1 would grow to if it were invested for any number of periods at a given interest rate. We multiply this factor times any other amount to determine the future value.

In determining the future value, we will change our formula from $FV = PV(1 + i)^n$ to:

$$FV = PV \times FV_{IF}$$

where FV_{IF} equals the **interest factor** found in the table.

As another example, suppose \$10,000 was invested for 10 years at 8 percent. The future value would be:

[1]All formulas are developed at the end of this chapter, in Appendix 9A.

Calculator

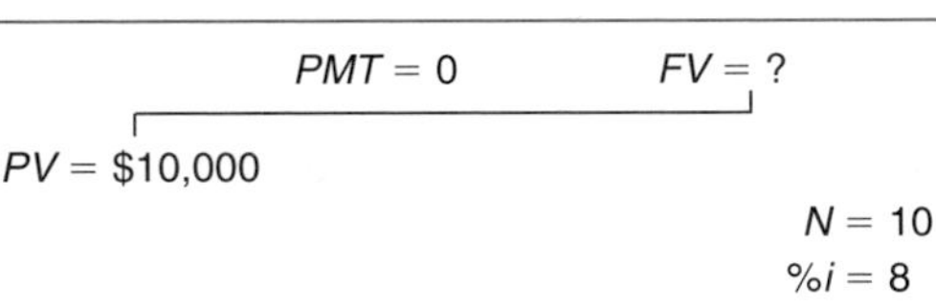

Compute $FV = \$21{,}589.25$.

Effective and Nominal Interest Rates

In the previous future value example, the investor earned an annual rate of interest of 10 percent. If we had simply multiplied the 10 percent annual rate of interest by the four years the monies were invested, we would get a 40 percent rate of return. This would only be a return of $400.00. However we would have missed the compounding effects of interest on interest. The 40 percent rate of return is referred to as a **nominal rate of interest,** an interest rate that does not capture the effects of compounding. Generally at the end of a period of time, often a year, the investor receives interest and can reinvest it, along with the original investment, for another year. The investor will earn interest on interest as well as the original investment.

In our example, after four years of reinvestment, $464.00 in interest was earned. Over the four-year period this represents a 46.4 percent rate of return. This is the **effective rate of interest,** an interest rate that includes any compounding effects. An effective rate of interest is more informative because we can calculate the actual interest earned or, if we are borrowing, the actual cost of the loan.

When compounding is called for, a formula to calculate the effective rate of interest can be developed. At the end of the first compounding period the return on the original investment plus the interest earned is given by the principal (1.00), representing 100 percent of the investment, and the interest rate (0.10) added together (1.00 + 0.10 = 1.10). This suggests 110% of the original investment value. This value is then raised to an exponent (4) representing the number of compounding periods. The original principal (1.00), which does not represent any return of interest, is then subtracted to isolate the effective interest rate or return of 46.4%. To demonstrate the increasing value of the investment (principal plus interest);

$$
\begin{array}{llll}
1.00 & \times & (1 \times i) = & (1 \times i)^1 \\
(1+i)^1 & \times & (1 \times i) = & (1 \times i)^2 \\
(1+i)^2 & \times & (1 \times i) = & (1 \times i)^3 \\
(1+i)^3 & \times & (1 \times i) = & (1 \times i)^4
\end{array}
$$

Note the similarity to the future value development in the previous section.

By formula the effective interest rate,

$$(1+i)^n - 1 = \text{Effective interest rate} \qquad (9\text{–}2)$$
$$i = \text{interest rate per compounding period}$$

Calculator

	PMT = 0			FV = ?	
	1	2	3	4	
PV = <1>					N = 4
					%i = 10

PV	= 1	PMT	= 0
N	= 4	%i	= 10

CPT FV = 1.4641 (includes principal).

If we multiply our future value of 1.4641 by the original investment of $1,000 we get the value of $1,464.10, the same amount as derived in the previous section on future values. The $464.10 is 46.4% of the $1,000.

Interest rates are usually expressed as annual rates, but not all annual rates are equal. Quite often annual rates of interest are expressed as nominal rates and do not include the compounding effects that may be in effect. For example, an institution may quote a rate of 10 percent, compounded quarterly. Each quarter an investor will receive 2.5 percent on the investment. By formula,

$$(1 + i/m)^m - 1 = \text{effective annual interest rate}$$

where

$$m = \text{number of compounding periods per year}$$

For this example,

$$(1 + .10/4)^4 - 1 = .1038, \text{ or } 10.38\%$$

Calculator

PV	= 1	PMT	= 0
N	= 4	%i	= 10/4

CPT FV = 1.1038 (includes principal)

also The calculator has an APR→ or EFF→ function key that will convert nominal annual interest rates to effective annual interest rates. Depending on the calculator, the directional arrow is relevant to which key is used, as effective annual rates will be larger than nominal annual rates.

4 2nd *EFF*→ 10 = 10.38

It is important that we distinguish between nominal and effective interest rates because, over time, they can represent a significant difference in the time value of money. Effective interest rates that include compounding effects give accurate results and allow us to better compare interest rates from different investments.

Present Value—Single Amount

In recent years the sports pages have been filled with stories of athletes who receive multimillion-dollar contracts for signing with sports organizations. Perhaps you have wondered how the Canucks or Blue Jays can afford to pay such fantastic sums. The

Starting Salaries 50 Years from Now—Will $248,734 Be Enough?

The answer is probably yes if inflation averages 4 percent over the next 50 years. Over the last 50 years the inflation rate was in the 4 to 5 percent range, so $248,734 might allow a college graduate to pay his or her bills in 50 years if inflation rates stay about the same. The $248,734 is based on a starting salary of $35,000 today and the future value of a dollar for 50 periods at 4 percent. Of course, $35,000 may be too low for some majors and too high for others.

Inflation in Canada actually was as high as 12.7 percent in 1981 and in 2002 it was about 2 percent. Conversely, there were declining prices during the Depression of the 1930s. Suppose inflation averaged 6 percent over the next 50 years; then, it would require $644,705 to replace a $35,000 salary today. At 10 percent inflation, the college graduate would need to ask an employer for a starting salary of $4,108,680 in 50 years to be as well off as his or her predecessor of today. Those in more popular majors would certainly not take a penny under $5 million. While 10 percent inflation seems high for Canada, in countries such as Bolivia, Israel, and Mexico, 10 percent inflation might be a happy occurrence. Bolivia's estimated inflation rate in 1985 was 3,400 percent.

The intent of this discussion is to demonstrate the effect of the time value of money. So far, all of the discussion has been forward looking. Now, let's look back. How much would one of your grandparents have had to make 50 years ago to equal a $35,000 salary today, assuming a 4 percent rate of inflation? The answer is $4,925. The Bank of Canada's inflation target and the core inflation rate is provided at its web site.

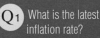

FINANCE IN ACTION

Q1 What is the latest inflation rate?

Q2 In 50 years, with this inflation rate, what will be equivalent to $35,000 today?

www.bankofcanada.ca/en

answer may lie in the concept of present value—a sum payable in the future is worth less today than the stated amount.

The **present value** is the exact opposite of the future value. For example, earlier we determined that the future value of $1,000 for four periods at 10 percent was $1,464. We could reverse the process to state that $1,464 received four years into the future, with a 10 percent interest or **discount rate,** is worth only $1,000 today–its present value. Present value is also referred to as the discounted value. The relationship is depicted in Figure 9–1 on the next page.

The formula for present value is derived from the original formula for future value.

$$FV = PV(1 + i)^n \quad \text{Future value}$$

$$PV = FV\left[\frac{1}{(1 + i)^n}\right] \quad \text{Present value} \qquad (9\text{–}3)$$

Calculator

$FV = \$1,464.10$

$PV = ?$

$\%i = 10$
$n = 4$
$PMT = 0$

Compute $PV = \$1,000$.

FIGURE 9–1
Relationship of present value and future value

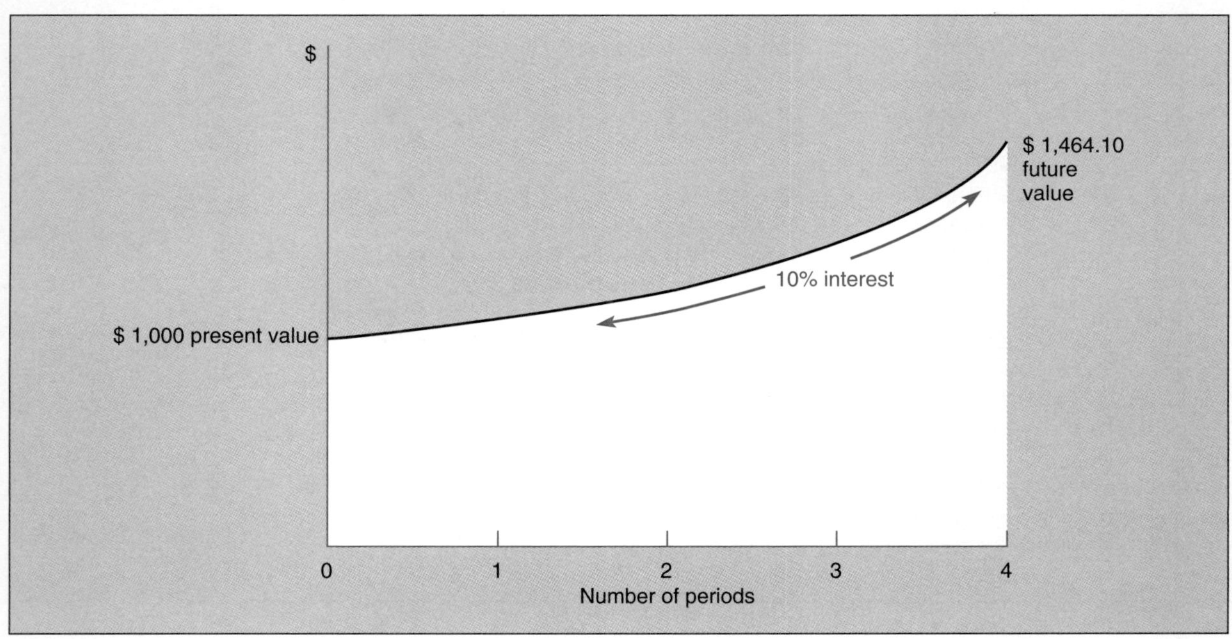

Tables (optional) The present value can be determined by using Appendix B, the present value of a dollar. In the latter instance, we restate the formula for present value as:

$$PV = FV \times PV_{IF}$$

Once again, PV_{IF} represents the interest factor found in Appendix B.

Let's demonstrate that the present value of $1,464, based on our assumptions, is $1,000 today.

$$PV = FV \times PV_{IF} \qquad (n = 4, i = 10\%) \text{ [Appendix B]}$$
$$PV = \$1{,}464 \times 0.683 = \$1{,}000$$

Future Value—Annuity

Up to now our calculations have dealt with single amounts rather than an **annuity**, which may be defined as a series of consecutive payments or receipts of equal amount. The annuity values are generally assumed to occur at the end of each period. If we invest $1,000 at the end of each year for four years and our funds grow at 10 percent, what is the future value of this annuity? We may find the future value for each payment and then total to find the **future value of an annuity** (Figure 9–2). The future value of an annuity is also referred to as a cumulative future value.

The future value for the annuity in Figure 9–2 is $4,641. Although this is a four-period annuity, the first $1,000 comes at the *end* of the first period and has but three periods to run, the second $1,000 at the *end* of the second period, with two periods

FIGURE 9–2
Compounding process for annuity

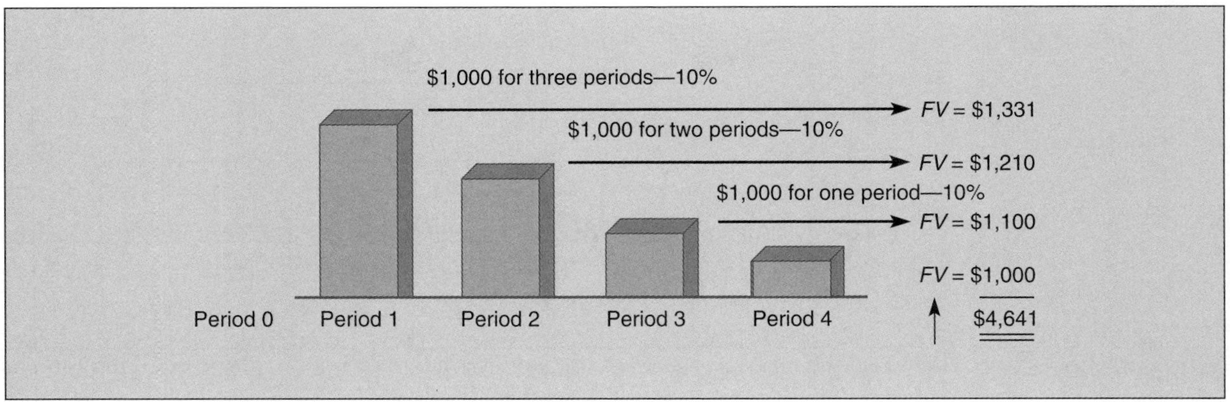

remaining—and so on down to the last $1,000 at the end of the fourth period. The final payment (period 4) is not compounded at all.

We shall let A = Series of equal payments.

The formula for the future value of an annuity is as follows:

$$FV_A = A\left[\frac{(1+i)^n - 1}{i}\right] \qquad (9\text{–}4a)$$

Calculator

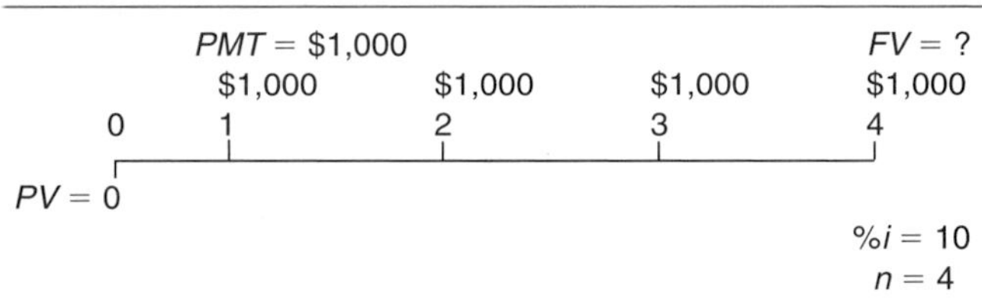

Compute FV = $4,641.00.

Tables (optional) Special tables are also available for annuity computations. We shall refer to Appendix C, the future value of an annuity of $1.00. Let us define A as the annuity value and use Formula 9–3 for the future value of an annuity. Note that the A part of the subscript on both the left and right sides of the formula indicates that we are dealing with tables for an annuity rather than a single amount. Using Appendix C:

$$FV_A = A \times FV_{IFA} \qquad (n = 4, i = 10\%)$$
$$FV_A = \$1{,}000 \times 4.641 = \$4.641$$

Suppose a wealthy relative offered to set aside $2,500 a year for you for the next 20 years, how much would you have to your credit after 20 years if the funds grew at 8 percent?

Calculator

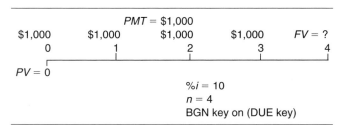

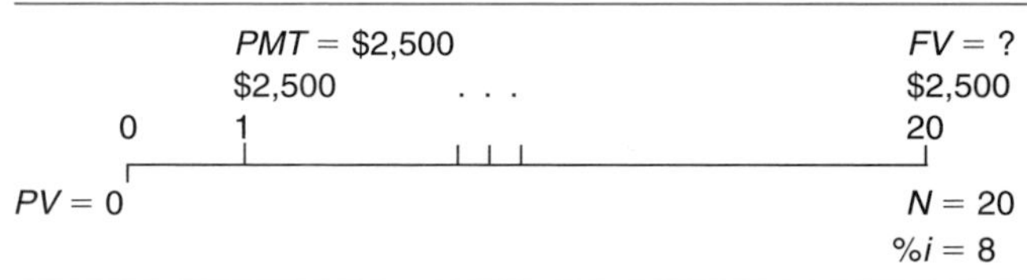

Compute $FV = \$114{,}404.91$.

A rather tidy sum considering that only a total of $50,000 has been invested over the 20 years.

Future Value—Annuity in Advance

There may be an occasion when the annuity payments occur at the beginning of the time period instead of the end, as we have assumed to this point. These earlier payments increase the future value because the payments have a longer time to earn interest. An **annuity in advance** places payments at the beginning of each period. This is also referred to as an **annuity due**. Some older calculators use this term rather than a begin key. Annuity in advance tables are available, but a financial calculator handles the problem easily.

We shall let A_{BGN} = Series of equal payments at the beginning of each period.

The formula for the future value of an annuity (in advance) is as follows:

$$\text{(in advance) } FV_A = A_{BGN}\left[\frac{(1+i)^{n+1} - (1+i)}{i}\right] \qquad (9\text{–}4b)$$

Calculator

PMT = $1,000

$1,000	$1,000	$1,000	$1,000	FV = ?
0	1	2	3	4

PV = 0

%i = 10
n = 4
BGN key on (DUE key)

$FV = \$5{,}105.10$.

Also note that (in advance) $FV_A = FV_A \times (1 + i)$
[e.g. $\$5{,}105.10 = \$4{,}641 \times (1 + .10)$]

> **Tables (optional)** We note that this result could be obtained with the tables (Appendix C) with $n = 5$. This gives the factor 6.105, which is reduced by 1 to indicate the payment that does not occur at $t = 4$.

Present Value—Annuity

To find the **present value of an annuity**, the process is reversed. In theory, each individual payment is discounted back to the present and then all of the discounted payments are added up, yielding the present value of an annuity. The present value of an annuity is also referred to as a cumulative present value.

The formula for the present value of an annuity is as follows:

$$PV_A = A\left[\frac{1 - \dfrac{1}{(1+i)^n}}{i}\right] \qquad (9\text{–}5a)$$

Calculator

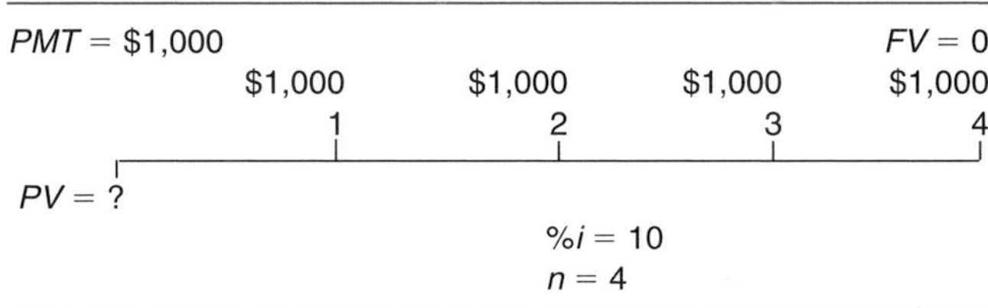

$PV = \$3{,}169.87.$

Tables (optional) Appendix D allows us to eliminate extensive calculations and to find our answer directly. In Formula 9–5*a* the term PV_A refers to the present value of the annuity. Once again, assume $A = \$1{,}000$, $n = 4$, and $i = 10$ percent—only now we want to know the present value of the annuity. Using Appendix D:

$$PV_A = A \times PV_{IFA} \qquad (n = 4, i = 10\%)$$
$$PV_A = \$1{,}000 \times 3.170 = \$3{,}170$$

Present Value—Annuity in Advance

We may want to determine the value of an annuity when the first contribution is made immediately. Calculations follow as compared to the previous annuity, with the contributions at the end of each time period.

The formula for the present value of an annuity (in advance) or annuity due is as follows:

$$\text{(in advance) } PV_A = A_{BGN}\left[\frac{(1+i) - \dfrac{1}{(1+i)^{n-1}}}{i}\right] \qquad (9\text{–}5b)$$

Calculator

$1,000	$1,000	$1,000	$1,000	FV = 0 0
0	1	2	3	4

PV = ?

%i = 10
n = 4
BGN key on (DUE key)

$PV = \$3{,}486.85.$

Also note that (in advance) $PV_A = PV_A \times (1 + i)$

Tables (optional) We note that this result could be obtained with the tables (Appendix D) with $n = 3$. This gives the factor 2.487, to which we add 1 to indicate the payment that occurs at $t = 0$ and is already stated at present value.

Determining the Annuity Value

In our prior discussion of annuities, we assumed the unknown variable was the future value or the present value—with specific information available on the annuity value (A), the interest rate, and the number of periods or years. In certain cases our emphasis may shift to solving for one of these other values (on the assumption that future value or present value is given). For now we will concentrate on determining an unknown annuity rate.

Annuity Equalling a Future Value

Assuming we wish to accumulate $4,641 after four years at a 10 percent interest rate, how much must be set aside at the end of each of the four periods? The annuity equalling a future value is also referred to as a sinking fund value.

The formula for an annuity equal to a future value is as follows:

$$A = FV_A\left[\frac{i}{(1 + i)^n - 1}\right] \tag{9–6a}$$

Calculator

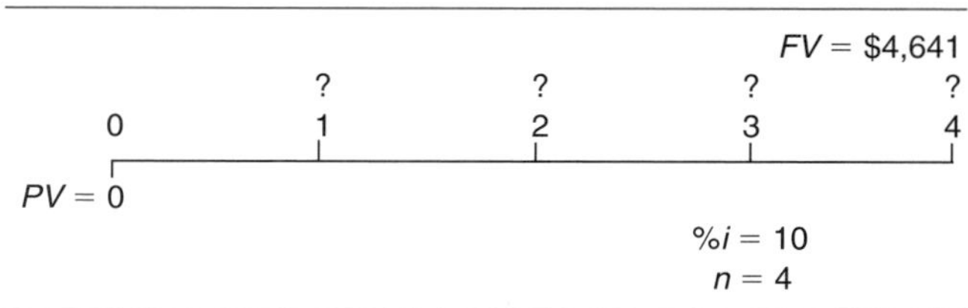

$PMT = \$1,000.00$.

The solution is the exact reverse of that previously presented under the discussion of the future value of an annuity.

Tables (optional) Or we could take the previously developed statement for the future value of an annuity and solve for A.

$$FV_A = A \times FV_{IFA}$$

$$A = \frac{FV_A}{FV_{IFA}}$$

(continued)

(continued)

The future value of an annuity (FV_A) is given as \$4,641, and FV_{IFA} may be determined from Appendix C (future value for an annuity). Whenever you are working with an annuity problem relating to future value, you employ Appendix C, regardless of the variable that is unknown. For n = 4, and i = 10 percent, FV_{IFA} is 4.641. Thus, A equals \$1,000.

$$A = \frac{FV_A}{FV_{IFA}} = \frac{\$4,641}{4.641} = \$1,000$$

As a second example, assume the director of the Women's Tennis Association must set aside an equal amount for each of the next 10 years to accumulate \$100,000 in retirement funds and that the return on deposited funds is 6 percent.

Calculator

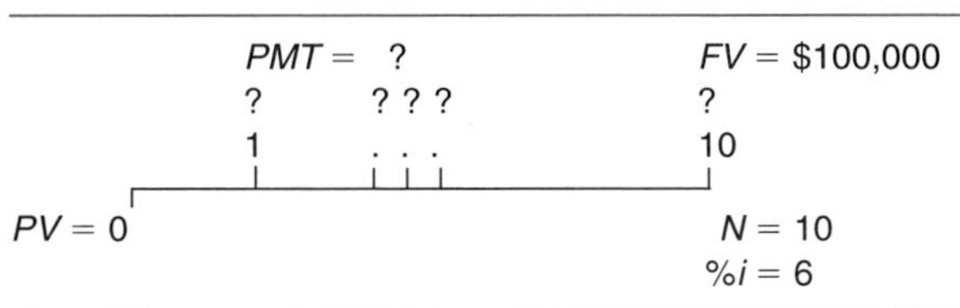

Compute PMT = \$7,586.80.

The formula for an annuity in advance equalling a future value is as follows:

$$A_{BGN} = FV_A\left[\frac{i}{(1 + i)^{n+1} - (1 + i)}\right] \qquad (9\text{–}6b)$$

For the same example as above the required payment or annuity would be \$7,157.35.

Annuity Equalling a Present Value

In this instance we assume that you know the present value and you wish to determine what size annuity can be equated to that amount. Suppose your wealthy uncle presents you with \$10,000 now to help you get through the next four years of college. If you are able to earn 6 percent on deposited funds, how much can you withdraw at the end of each year for four years? We need to know the value of an annuity equal to a given present value. The annuity equalling a present value is also referred to as a capital recovery value.

The formula for an annuity equal to a present value is as follows:

$$A = PV_A\left[\frac{i}{1 - \frac{1}{(1 + i)^n}}\right] \qquad (9\text{–}7a)$$

Calculator

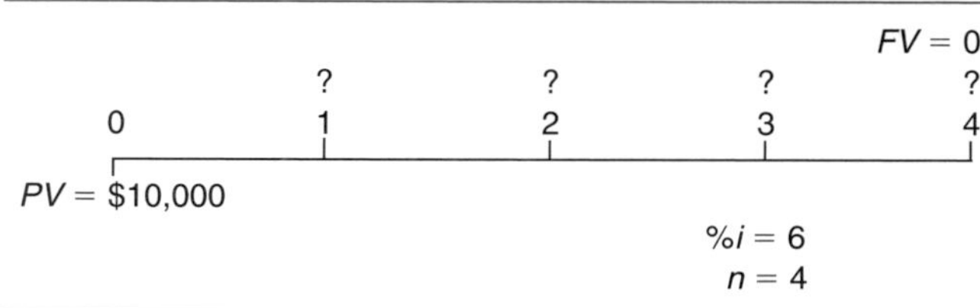

$PMT = \$2{,}885.91.$

Tables (optional) We can take the previously developed statement for the present value of an annuity and reverse it to solve for A.

$$PV_A = A \times PV_{IFA}$$

$$A = \frac{PV_A}{PV_{IFA}}$$

The appropriate table is Appendix D (present value of an annuity). We determine an answer of \$2,886.

$$A = \frac{PV_A}{PV_{IFA}} \qquad (n = 4,\ i = 6\%)$$

$$A = \frac{\$10{,}000}{3.465} = \$2{,}886$$

The flow of funds would follow the pattern in Table 9–1. Annual interest is based on the beginning balance for each year.

TABLE 9–1
Relationship of present value to annuity

Year	Beginning Balance	Annual Interest (6 percent)	Annual Withdrawal	Ending Balance
1	\$10,000.00	\$600.00	\$2,886.00	\$7,714.00
2	7,714.00	462.84	2,886.00	5,290.84
3	5,290.84	317.45	2,886.00	2,722.29
4	2,722.29	163.71	2,886.00	0

The formula for an annuity in advance equalling a present value is as follows:

$$A_{BGN} = PV_A\left[\frac{i}{(1+i) - \dfrac{1}{(1+i)^{n-1}}}\right] \qquad (9\text{–}7b)$$

For the same example as above the available payment or annuity would be \$2,722.56.

The same process can be used to indicate necessary repayments on a loan. Suppose a homeowner signs a \$40,000 mortgage to be repaid over 20 years at 8 percent interest.

How much must he or she pay annually to eventually liquidate the loan? In other words, what annuity paid over 20 years is the equivalent of a $40,000 present value with an 8 percent interest rate?

Calculator

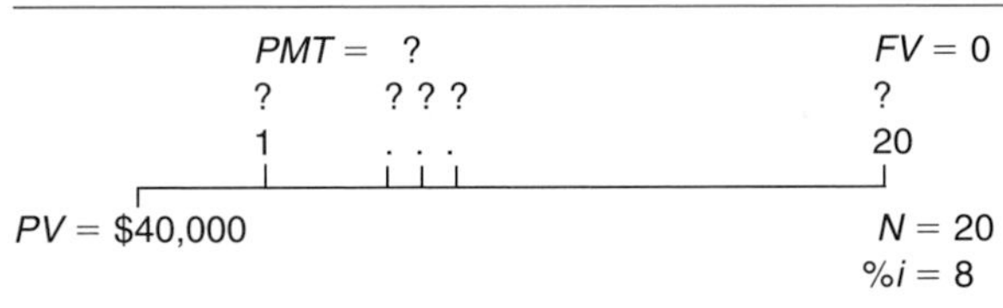

Compute PMT = $4,074.09.

Part of the payment to the mortgage company will go toward the payment of interest, with the remainder applied to debt reduction, as indicated in Table 9–2.

If this same process is followed over 20 years, the balance will be reduced to zero. The student might note that the homeowner will pay over $41,000 of *interest* during the term of the loan, as indicated below.

Total payments ($4,074 for 20 years)	$ 81,480
Repayment of principal	−40,000
Payments applied to interest	$ 41,480

TABLE 9–2
Payoff table for loan (amortization table)

Period	Beginning Balance	Annual Payment	Annual Interest (8 percent)	Repayment on Principal	Ending Balance
1	$40,000	$4,074	$3,200	$ 874	$39,126
2	39,126	4,074	3,130	944	38,182
3	38,182	4,074	3,055	1,019	37,163

Determining the Yield on an Investment

In our discussion thus far, we have considered the following time-value-of-money problems with our calculator, by formula, or with tables.

		Formula	Appendix
Future value—single amount	(9–1)	$FV = PV(1 + i)^n$	A
Present value—single amount	(9–3)	$PV = FV\left[\frac{1}{(1 + i)^n}\right]$	B
Future value—annuity	(9–4*a*)	$FV_A = A\left[\frac{(1 + i)^n - 1}{i}\right]$	C
Future value—annuity in advance	(9–4*b*)	$FV_A = A_{BGN}\left[\frac{(1 + i)^{n+1} - (1 + i)}{i}\right]$	–
Present value—annuity	(9–5*a*)	$PV_A = A\left[\frac{1 - \frac{1}{(1 + i)^n}}{i}\right]$	D

Present value—annuity in advance	(9–5b)	$PV_A = A_{BGN}\left[\frac{(1+i) - \frac{1}{(1+i)^{n-1}}}{i}\right]$	–
Annuity equalling a future value	(9–6a)	$A = FV_A\left[\frac{i}{(1+i)^n - 1}\right]$	C
Annuity in advance equalling a future value	(9–6b)	$A_{BGN} = FV_A\left[\frac{i}{(1+i)^{n+1} - (1+i)}\right]$	–
Annuity equalling a present value	(9–7a)	$A = PV_A\left[\frac{i}{1 - \frac{1}{(1+i)^n}}\right]$	D
Annuity in advance equalling a present value	(9–7b)	$A_{BGN} = PV_A\left[\frac{i}{(1+i) - \frac{1}{(1+i)^{n-1}}}\right]$	–

In each case we knew three out of the four variables and solved for the fourth. We will follow the same procedure once again, but now the unknown variable will be i, the interest rate, or yield, on the investment.

Yield—Present Value of a Single Amount

An investment producing $1,464 after four years has a present value of $1,000. What is the interest rate, or **yield**, on the investment?

The formula is as follows:

$$i = \left(\frac{FV}{PV}\right)^{\frac{1}{n}} - 1 \qquad (9\text{–}8)$$

Calculator

	$PMT = 0$			$FV = \$1,464.10$
0	1	2	3	4
$PV = -\$1,000$				$n = 4$

$i = 10\%$.

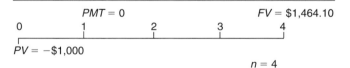

Tables (optional) We can also use the basic formula for the present value of a single amount and rearrange the terms.

$$PV = FV \times PV_{IF}$$

$$PV_{IF} = \frac{PV}{FV} = \frac{\$1,000}{\$1,464} = 0.683$$

(continued)

(continued)

The determination of PV_{IF} does not give us the final answer, but it scales down the problem so that we may ascertain the answer from Appendix B, the present value of $1. A portion of Appendix B is reproduced below.

Periods	1%	2%	3%	4%	5%	6%	8%	10%
2	0.980	0.961	0.943	0.925	0.907	0.890	0.857	0.826
3	0.971	0.942	0.815	0.889	0.864	0.840	0.794	0.751
4	0.961	0.924	0.888	0.855	0.823	0.792	0.735	0.683

Read down the left-hand column of the table until you have located the number of periods in question (in this case $n = 4$), and read across the table for $n = 4$ until you have located the computed value of PV_{IF} from above. We see that for $n = 4$ and PV_{IF} equal to 0.683, the interest rate, or yield, is 10 percent. This is the rate that will equate $1,464 received in four years to $1,000 today.

If a PV_{IF} value does not fall under a given interest rate, an approximation is possible. For example, with $n = 3$ and $PV_{IF} = 0.861$, 5 percent may be suggested as an approximate answer.

Interpolation may also be used to find a more precise answer. In the above example, we write out the two PV_{IF} values between which the designated PV_{IF} (0.861) falls and take the difference between the two.

PV_{IF} at 5%	0.864
PV_{IF} at 6%	0.840
	0.024

We then find the difference between the PV_{IF} value at the lowest interest rate and the designated PV_{IF} value.

PV_{IF} at 5%	0.864
PV_{IF} designated	0.861
	0.003

We next express this value (0.003) as a fraction of the preceding value (0.024) and multiply by the difference between the two interest rates (6 percent minus 5 percent). The value is added to the lower interest rate (5 percent) to get a more exact answer of 5.125 percent rather than the estimated 5 percent.

$$5\% + \frac{0.003}{0.024}(1\%) =$$

$$5\% + 0.125\,(1\%) =$$

$$5\% + 0.125\% = 5.125\%$$

Yield—Present Value of an Annuity

Assuming a \$10,000 investment will produce \$1,490 a year for the next 10 years, what is the yield on the investment?

Calculator

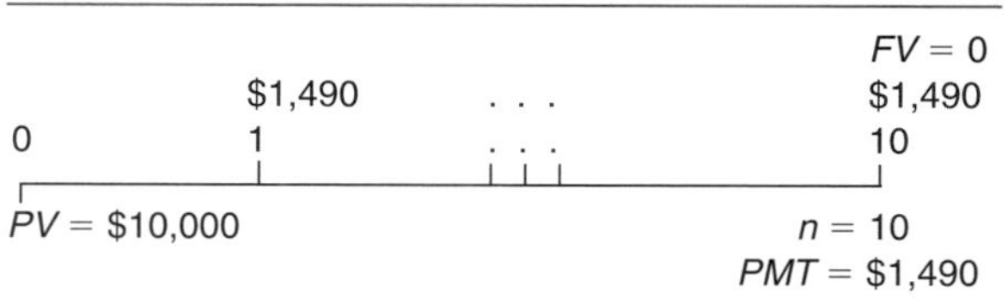

Compute i = 7.996%.

Tables (optional) Let's look at the present value of an annuity. Take the basic formula for the present value of an annuity, and rearrange the terms.

$$PV_A = A \times PV_{IFA}$$

$$PV_{IFA} = \frac{PV_A}{A}$$

The appropriate table is Appendix D (the present value of an annuity of \$1).

$$PV_{IFA} = \frac{PV_A}{A} = \frac{\$10{,}000}{\$1{,}490} = 6.710$$

If the student will flip to Appendix D and read across the columns for n = 10 periods, he or she will see that the yield is 8 percent.

The same type of approximated or interpolated yield that applied to a single amount can also be applied to an annuity when necessary.

Special Considerations in Time Value Analysis

We have assumed that interest was compounded or discounted on an annual basis. This assumption will now be relaxed. Contractual arrangements, such as an installment purchase agreement or a corporate bond contract, may call for semiannual, quarterly, or monthly compounding periods. The adjustment to the normal formula is simple. To determine n, multiply the number of years by the number of compounding periods during the year. The factor for i is then determined by dividing the quoted annual interest rate by the number of compounding periods.

Case 1—Find the future value of a \$1,000 investment after five years at 8 percent annual interest, **compounded semiannually**.

What Is the $10 Million Publishers Clearing House Sweepstakes Really Worth?

In January 1997 Beata Sankiewicz of Sudbury won the Publishers Clearing House grand prize. One year later K.J. Macalister of Edmonton also won it. Publishers Clearing House officials knocked on the door of their homes in the middle of the afternoon and not only filmed the excitement, but also brought along flowers, champagne, and balloons for the occasion.

These persons might have felt they could now qualify for "Lifestyles of the Rich and Famous." Actually, they were probably considerably more modest than this, but they would find many new friends. Previous winners had reported that their appeal to the opposite sex had gone up considerably once their names were published as sweepstakes winners. They received amorous correspondence from throughout the world.

But what is the $10 million Publishers Clearing House Sweepstakes really worth? The $10 million is paid out as $500,000 the first year, $250,000 a year for the next 29 years, and an additional final payment of $2,500,000. Assuming a discount rate of 10 percent, the present value of the rewards is only $2,985,673.* The final payment of $2,500,000 after 30 years only has a present value of $143,271. Publishers Clearing House in the fine print discusses the impact of present value assumptions.

However, $2.9 million isn't too bad. You can enter yourself to win at the Publishers Clearing House web site. Good luck!

*The value will change slightly depending on whether the inflows occur at the beginning, middle, or end of the year.

$$n = 5 \times 2 = 10 \qquad i = 8 \text{ percent} \div 2 = 4 \text{ percent}$$

Calculator

PMT = 0 FV = ?

0 5

PV = $1,000

Years = 5 n = 10
%i = 8/2 = 4% per compounding period

$FV = \$1{,}480.24$.

Tables (optional) Since the problem calls for the future value of a single amount, the formula is $FV = PV \times FV_{IF}$. Using Appendix A for $n = 10$ and $i =$ 4 percent, the answer is $1,480.

$$FV = PV \times FV_{IF}$$
$$FV = \$1{,}000 \times 1.480 = \$1{,}480$$

Case 2—Find the present value of 20 quarterly payments of $2,000 each to be received over the next five years. The stated interest rate is 8 percent per annum. The problem calls for the present value of an annuity.

Calculator

	$2,000	. . .	$FV = 0$ $2,000
0		. . .	5
$PV = ?$			
			Years = 5 $n = 20$ $\%i = \frac{8}{4} = 2\%$ per compounding period $PMT = \$2,000$

$PV = \$32,702.87.$

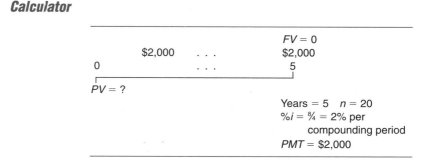

Tables (optional) We again follow the same procedure as in Case 1 in regard to *n* and *i*.

$$PV_A = A \times PV_{IFA}\ (n = 20, i = 2\%)\ [\text{Appendix D}]$$
$$PV_A = \$2,000 \times 16.351 = \$32,702$$

Patterns of Payment

Time-value-of-money problems may evolve around a number of different payment or receipt patterns. Not every situation will involve a single amount or an annuity. For example, a contract may call for the payment of a different amount each year over a three-year period. To determine present value, each payment is discounted to the present and then summed. (Assume 8% discount rate.)

1. 1,000	$FV =$ $ 926
2. 2,000	$FV =$ 1,714
3. 3,000	$FV =$ 2,382
	$5,022

A more involved problem might include a combination of single amounts and an annuity. If the annuity will be paid at some time in the future, it is referred to as a deferred annuity, and it requires special treatment. Assume the same problem as above, but with an annuity of $1,000 that will be paid at the end of each year from the fourth through the eighth year. With a discount rate of 8 percent, what is the present value of the cash flows?

1.	$1,000	Present value = $5,022
2.	2,000	
3.	3,000	
4.	1,000	Five-year annuity
5.	1,000	
6.	1,000	
7.	1,000	
8.	1,000	

We know that the present value of the first three payments is $5,022, but what about the annuity? Let's diagram the five annuity payments.

Present value				A_1 $1,000	A_2 $1,000	A_3 $1,000	A_4 $1,000	A_5 $1,000
0	1	2	3	4	5	6	7	8

Calculator

$FV = 0$	$PMT = \$1,000$
$N = 5$	$\%i = 8$

Compute $PV = \$3,992.71$.

However, this result is only discounted to the beginning of the first stated period of an annuity—in this case the beginning of the fourth year, as diagrammed below.

Beginning of fourth period

Present value			$3,993	A_1 $1,000	A_2 $1,000	A_3 $1,000	A_4 $1,000	A_5 $1,000
0	1*	2	3	4	5	6	7	8

*Each number represents the end of the period; that is, 4 represents the end of the fourth period.

The $3,993 must finally be discounted back to the present. Since this single amount falls at the beginning of the fourth period—in effect, the equivalent of the end of the third period—we discount back for three periods at the stated 8 percent interest rate.

Calculator

$FV = \$3,992.71$	$PMT = 0$
$N = 3$	$\%i = 8$

Compute $PV = \$3,169.54$.

The last step in the discounting process is shown below.

End of the third period—beginning of the fourth period

$3,170 Present value			$3,993 (single amount)	A_1 $1,000	A_2 $1,000	A_3 $1,000	A_4 $1,000	A_5 $1,000
0	1	2	3	4	5	6	7	8

Calculator To calculate the present value of uneven cash flows, calculators have special function keys requiring the net present value concept. This is discussed in Appendix E.

Canadian Mortgages

In Canada it is common to have mortgages that have interest compounded semiannually, with payments made monthly. The potential problem with blended payments of principal and interest made on a monthly basis is that the interest is being paid before it is actually due. Calculations must acknowledge the early payment of interest. We cannot just divide the semiannual interest rate by six. To adjust, we must calculate a monthly effective interest rate that, when compounded over a six-month period, is equivalent to the semiannual effective interest rate. It is with this monthly effective interest rate that we calculate the monthly payment.

Say the interest rate offered at the bank is 8 percent annually. Therefore, the rate for six months is 4 percent (8/2). We now need a rate that, when compounded six times, will equal 4 percent; by formula $(1 + r)^6 = 1.04$. Solving for r gives us .6558 percent.

Calculator

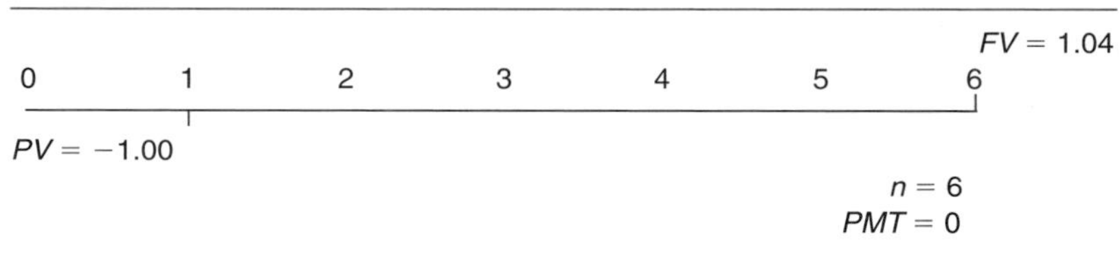

$i = .655819692\%$.

Also with APR→ or EFF→ (dependent on calculator)

6	2nd	EFF→	4	=
(number of payment periods in compounding period)			(six-month interest rate)	
3.9349174		(6-month equivalent)		

Then divide by 6

3.9349174/6 = .6558196% (monthly effective interest rate)

We begin with 1 and six months later it is 1.04. We have determined the interest rate for one of the six periods, a monthly effective interest rate.

Now we can calculate the monthly payment on the mortgage. Suppose the mortgage is for $80,000, to be paid off over 20 years at our interest rate of 8 percent annually.

Calculator

FV = 0

??????????????????????????????

0 240

PV = $80,000

n = 240 (20 yrs. × 12)

%i = .655819692

PMT = $662.69.

FINANCE IN ACTION

Is a Weekly Mortgage a Good Idea?

The banks often promote the weekly mortgage as a great way to pay off your mortgage early. It is suggested that you can reduce the time to pay off a mortgage by perhaps four to five years, depending on circumstances. However, do these claims identify the complete picture?

We have noted that a mortgage for $80,000 paid monthly over 20 years at an 8 percent interest rate would require a monthly payment of $662.69. If you were to pay weekly, the bank would likely take that monthly payment and divide by 4 to represent the weeks in a month. The weekly payment will therefore be $165.67. Some banks do identify this as an accelerated payment schedule.

Principal amount	$80,000	Weekly payment	$165.67
Annual interest rate	8%	Number of payments	865.48
Weekly interest rate	.15096273%*	Number of years	16.64

*$\left(1 + \frac{.08}{2}\right)^{26} - 1 \times 100\%$ For 26 weeks in a six-month period.

Sounds great until the situation is examined more closely. With weekly payments a mortgagee is actually making an extra monthly payment each year.

Weekly	52	×	$165.67	=	$8,614.84
Monthly	12	×	$662.69	=	7,952.28
Extra payment					$ 662.56

Presumably if a homeowner can afford $8,614.84 as weekly payments over one year, the homeowner could pay the same amount as monthly payments. In that case the monthly payment would be $717.90

Principal amount	$80,000	Monthly payment	$717.90
Annual interest rate	8%	Number of payments	200.77
Monthly interest rate	.655819691%	Number of years	16.73

This is very similar to the weekly plan. So what is a homeowner to do? The key is to match your cash inflows with your cash outflows. A mortgage is the major obligation (outflow) for most people, and salary the major inflow. If the homeowner is paid monthly, take out a monthly mortgage! If the homeowner is paid weekly, take out a weekly mortgage! Otherwise cash flows to the household will be inefficiently allocated. The homeowner with a weekly mortgage, but monthly pay, would be forced to save money from each pay to meet the weekly obligation or, even worse, to borrow until the next monthly pay period. The best strategy for the homeowner is to determine the largest payment out of each pay that can be afforded and to match the amortization period and payment period to that payment.

A Final Note

The key foundation tool of financial management is the ability to understand and to calculate the time value of money. Value is determined by the ability to generate cash flows. The time value of money allows us to properly value cash flows that occur at different points in time. As such, it is essential that the student of finance be able to comfortably handle the problems of this chapter.

Summary

1. The time value of money suggests that a dollar today is worth more than a dollar tomorrow. Alternatively, a dollar invested today will grow to a larger value tomorrow. Through the discounting technique, that dollar tomorrow is equated (discounted) to a value today. Discounting values to a common time period allows for comparison.

2., 3. In working a time-value-of-money problem, the student should determine, first, whether the problem deals with future value or present value and, second, whether a single sum or an annuity is involved. The major calculations in Chapter 9 are summarized below if a calculator is not used.

A. *Future value of a single amount.*

Formula: $FV = PV(1 + i)^n$ (9–1)

Appendix A.

When to use: In determining the future value for a single amount.

Sample problem: You invest $1,000 for four years at 10 percent interest. What is the value at the end of the fourth year?

B. *Effective interest rate.*

Formula: $(1 + i)^n - 1 =$ effective interest rate (9–2)

When to use: In determining an interest rate that captures interest compounding.

C. *Present value of a single amount.*

Formula: $PV = FV\left[\frac{1}{(1 + i)^n}\right]$ (9–3)

Appendix B.

When to use: In determining the present value of an amount to be received in the future.

Sample problem: You will receive $1,000 after four years at a discount rate of 10 percent. How much is this worth today?

D. *Future value of an annuity.*

Formula: $FV_A = A\left[\frac{(1 + i)^n - 1}{i}\right]$ (9–4*a*)

Appendix C.

When to use: In determining the future value of a series of consecutive, equal payments (an annuity).

Sample problem: You will receive $1,000 at the end of each period for four periods. What is the accumulated value (future worth) at the end of the fourth period if money grows at 10 percent?

When the payments are at the beginning of each period:

Formula: $FV_A = A_{BGN}\left[\frac{(1 + i)^{n+1} - (1 + i)}{i}\right]$ (9–4*b*)

E. *Present value of an annuity.*

Formula: $PV_A = A\left[\frac{1 - \frac{1}{(1 + i)^n}}{i}\right]$ (9–5*a*)

Appendix D.

When to use: In determining the present worth of an annuity.

Sample problem: You will receive $1,000 at the end of each period for four years. At a discount rate of 10 percent, what is the current worth?

When the payments are at the beginning of each period:

Formula: $PV_A = A_{BGN}\left[\frac{(1 + \mathrm{i}) - \frac{1}{(1 + i)^{n-1}}}{i}\right]$ (9–5*b*)

F. Annuity equalling a future value.

Formula: $A = FV_A \left[\frac{i}{(1+i)^n - 1}\right]$ (9–6a)

Appendix C.

When to use: In determining the size of an annuity that will equal a future value.

Sample problem: You need $1,000 after four periods. With an interest rate of 10 percent, how much must be set aside at the end of each period to accumulate this amount?

When the payments are at the beginning of each period:

Formula: $A_{BGN} = FV_A \left[\frac{i}{(1+i)^{n+1} - (1+i)}\right]$ (9–6b)

G. Annuity equalling a present value.

Formula: $A = PV_A \left[\frac{i}{1 - \frac{1}{(1+i)^n}}\right]$ (9–7a)

Appendix D.

When to use: In determining the size of an annuity equal to a given present value.

Sample problems:

a. What four-year annuity is the equivalent of $1,000 today with an interest rate of 10 percent?

b. You deposit $1,000 today and wish to withdraw funds equally over four years. How much can you withdraw at the end of each year if funds earn 10 percent?

c. You borrow $1,000 for four years at 10 percent interest. How much must be repaid at the end of each year?

When the payments are at the beginning of each period:

Formula: $A_{BGN} = PV_A \left[\frac{i}{(1+i) - \frac{1}{(1+i)^{n-1}}}\right]$ (9–7b)

H. Determining the yield on an investment.

Formulas	Tables	
a. $i = \left(\frac{FV}{PV}\right)^{1/n}$	Appendix B	Yield—present value of a single amount
b. Interpolation required	Appendix D	Yield—present value of an annuity

When to use: In determining the interest rate (i) that will equate an investment with future benefits.

Sample problem: You invest $1,000 now, and the funds are expected to increase to $1,360 after four periods.

What is the yield on the investment?

I. Less than annual compounding periods.

Semiannual	Multiply $n \times 2$	Divide i by 2	then use
Quarterly	Multiply $n \times 4$	Divide i by 4	normal
Monthly	Multiply $n \times 12$	Divide i by 12	formula

When to use: If the compounding period is more (or perhaps less) frequent than once a year.

Sample problem: You invest $1,000 compounded semiannually at 8 percent per annum over four years.

Determine the future value.

J. Patterns of payment—deferred annuity.

Formulas	Tables
$PV_A = \left[\frac{1 - \frac{1}{(1+i)^n}}{i}\right]$	Appendix D
$PV = FV\left[\frac{1}{(1+i)^n}\right]$	Appendix B

When to use: If an annuity begins in the future.

Sample problem: You will receive $1,000 per period, starting at the end of the fourth period and running through the end of the eighth period. With a discount rate of 8 percent, determine the present value.

4. ***Calculator***

Use a time line to set up the problem.

Use $\%i =$, $n =$, $PV =$, $FV =$, $PMT =$.

Input the known values for the above including a zero if necessary (this ensures memory is cleared).

Calculate the unknown value.

The student is encouraged to work the many problems found at the end of the chapter.

List of Terms

future value 287
interest factor 288
nominal rate of interest 289
effective rate of interest 289
present value 291
discount rate 291
annuity 292
future value of an annuity 292
annuity in advance 294
annuity due 294
present value of an annuity 294
yield 300
compounded semiannually 302

Discussion Questions

1. How is the future value (Appendix A) related to the present value of a single sum (Appendix B)?
2. How is the present value of a single sum (Appendix B) related to the present value of an annuity (Appendix D)?
3. Why does money have a time value?
4. Does inflation have anything to do with making a dollar today worth more than a dollar tomorrow?
5. Adjust the annual formula for a future value of a single amount at 12 percent for 10 years to a semiannual compounding formula. What are the interest factors (FV_{IF}) for the two assumptions? Why are they different?
6. If, as an investor, you had a choice of daily, monthly, or quarterly compounding, which would you choose? Why?
7. What is a deferred annuity?

8. List five different financial applications of the time value of money.
9. Discuss why the compounding of interest within a tax sheltered plan is so effective, as opposed to paying taxes each year.

INTERNET RESOURCES AND QUESTIONS

Sun Media has a news and information site that includes a mortgage calculator, as well as interest rates on various mortgages, loans, and investments. It is the Canoe site (Canadian online explorer): www.webfin.com/en/

Quicken has a site that includes a mortgage calculator and a retirement calculator: www.quicken.ca

Bloomberg, under money and tools, has a mortgage calculator for U.S. mortgages: www.bloomberg.com

The Canadian banks have sites that have mortgage calculators. The Royal Bank calculator has a breakdown for weekly and bi-weekly accelerated mortgage payments: www.rbc.com

The Bank of Montreal site, under tools and number cruncher, has a mortgage calculator, as well as a retirement planning calculator: www.bmo.com

1. The last few problems (40 to 43) in this chapter include mortgage calculations. After you have completed these problems use a mortgage calculator such as the one available at a site listed above to redo the calculations. Are the results the same, and if not, why is there a difference?
2. Redo the above calculations using a mortgage calculator from a U.S. financial institution or from Bloomberg. Why is there a difference in the numbers calculated?

Problems

1. What is the present value of
   a. $9,000 in 7 years at 8 percent?
   b. $20,000 in 5 years at 10 percent?
   c. $10,000 in 25 years at 6 percent?
   d. $1,000 in 50 years at 16 percent?
2. If you invest $9,000 today, how much will you have:
   a. in 2 years at 9 percent?
   b. in 7 years at 12 percent?
   c. in 25 years at 14 percent?
   d. in 25 years at 14 percent (compounded semiannually)?
3. How much would you have to invest today to receive:
   a. $15,000 in 8 years at 10 percent?
   b. $20,000 in 12 years at 13 percent?
   c. $6,000 each year for 10 years at 9 percent?
   d. $6,000 each year, at the beginning, for 10 years at 9 percent?
   e. $75,000 for 50 years at 7 percent?
   f. $75,000 for 50 years, at the beginning, at 7 percent?

4. If you invest $10,000 per period for the following number of periods, how much would you have?
   a. 6 years at 8 percent
   b. 12 years at 4 percent
   c. 40 periods at 12 percent
5. Rework the previous problem, assuming that the $10,000 per period is received at the beginning of each year. (Annuity in advance)
6. Jean Splicing will receive $8,500 a year for the next 15 years from her trust. A 7 percent interest rate is appropriate.
   a. What is the current value of the future payments?
   b. What is the current value, if they are received at the beginning of each year?
7. Rapt Carter will receive $250,000 in 60 years. Sounds great! However if current interest rates suggested for discounting are 10 percent what is the present worth of this payment?
8. "Red" Herring will receive $11,000 a year for the next 18 years as a result of his patent. At present 9 percent is an appropriate discount rate.
   a. Should he be willing to sellout his future rights now for $100,000?
   b. Would he be willing to sell his future rights now for $100,000, if the payments will be made at the beginning of each year?
9. General Mills will receive $27,500 for the next 10 years as a payment for a weapon he invented. Currently a 12 percent discount rate is appropriate.
   a. Should he be willing to sell his future rights now for $160,000?
   b. Should he be willing to sell his future rights now for $160,000, if payments will be made at the beginning of the year?
10. Larry Doby invests $50,000 in a mint condition 1952 "Rocket" Richard Topps hockey card. He expects the card to increase in value 8 percent per year for the next five years. How much will his card be worth after five years?
11. Dr. Ruth has been secretly depositing $2,500 in her savings account every December starting in 1991. Her account earns 5 percent compounded annually. How much did she have in December 2002? (Assume a deposit is made in 2002.) Make sure to carefully count the years.
12. At a growth (interest) rate of 9 percent annually, how long will it take for a sum to double? To triple? Select the year that is closest to the correct answer.

13. If you owe $40,000 at the end of seven years, how much should your creditor accept in payment immediately if she could earn 12 percent on her money?
14. Les Moore retired as president of Goodman Snack Foods Company, but he is currently on a consulting contract for $35,000 per year for the next 10 years.
   a. If Mr. Moore's opportunity cost (potential return) is 10 percent, what is the present value of his consulting contract?
   b. Assuming Mr. Moore will not retire for two more years and will not start to receive his 10 payments until the end of the third year, what would be the value of his deferred annuity?
   c. Recalculate part *a* assuming the contract stipulates that payments are to be made at the beginning of each year.
15. Juan Garza invested $20,000 10 years ago at 12 percent, compounded quarterly.
   a. How much has he accumulated?

b. What is his effective annual interest rate (rate of return)?

16. Determine the amount of money in a savings account at the end of five years, given an initial deposit of $5,000 and a 12 percent annual interest rate when interest is compounded (*a*) annually, (*b*) semiannually, and (*c*) quarterly. Calculate the effective annual interest rate of each compounding possibility.

17. Joe Macro wishes to accumulate $60,000 10 years from today by making an equal annual deposit into an account that pays 10 percent, compounded quarterly.

    a. What is the effective annual interest rate?

    b. How large an annual deposit is required to meet Joe's objective?

    c. How large an annual deposit is required if the deposits are made at the beginning of each year?

18. Sally Gravita has received a settlement from an insurance company that will pay her $23,500 annually for 12 years. Current interest rates are 8 percent, compounded semiannually.

    a. What is the effective annual interest rate?

    b. How much is the present worth of Sally's settlement?

    c. How much is the present worth of Sally's settlement if payments are made at the beginning of each year?

19. Your rich uncle has offered you a choice of one of the three following alternatives: $10,000 now; $2,000 a year for eight years; or $24,000 at the end of eight years. Assuming you could earn 11 percent annually, which alternative would you choose? If you could earn 12 percent annually, would you still choose the same alternative?

20. You need $28,974 at the end of 10 years, and your only investment outlet is an 8 percent long-term certificate of deposit (compounded annually). With the certificate of deposit, you make an initial investment at the beginning of the first year.

    a. What single payment could be made at the beginning of the first year to achieve this objective?

    b. What amount could you pay at the end of each year annually for 10 years to achieve this same objective?

21. Carol Travis started a paper route on January 1, 1997. Every three months, she deposits $500 in her bank account, which earns 4 percent annually but is compounded quarterly. On December 31, 2000, she used the entire balance in her bank account to invest in a contract that pays 9 percent annually. How much will she have on December 31, 2003?

22. On January 1, 2000, Mike Irwin, Jr., bought 100 shares of stock at $14.00 per share. On December 31, 2002, he sold the stock for $21.00 per share. What was his annual rate of return?

23. Al Counsel purchased 357 shares of Eco-Survival Tours on July 1, 1996 for $5.00 per share. Find his annual rate of return if he sold the stock:

    a. On June 30, 1997, for $6.00 per share.

    b. On December 31, 1999, for $10.92 per share.

    c. On June 30, 2002, for $8.39 per share.

24. Dr. I.N. Stein has just invested $6,250 for his son (age one). The money will be used for his son's education 17 years from now. He calculates that he will need $50,000 for his son's education by the time the boy goes to school. What rate of return will Dr. I.N. Stein need to achieve this goal?

25. Ester Seals has just given an insurance company $41,625. In return, she will receive an annuity of $5,000 for 15 years.

    a. At what rate of return must the insurance company invest this $41,625 to make the annual payments?

b. What rate of return is required if the annuity is payable at the beginning of each year?

26. Mr. G. Day has approached his bank about a loan. He expects to receive $30,000 in three years and $85,000 nine years from now. These funds will be applied against the loan as they are received. The bank suggests that interest rates will be 9 percent for the next five years and 7 percent in subsequent years. Calculate the maximum amount Mr. G. Day can borrow.

27. Ms. R. Emm has purchased land for $90,000 in cash today and another $45,000 four years from today. Interest rates over a four-year period are currently 8 percent, compounded semi-annually. Calculate the cash value of the property.

28. Count Crow wishes to have a large celebration eight years from today costing $150,000. Currently, he has an investment of $625,000 in a financial institution earning 7.5 percent interest annually. Count Crow also wishes to receive an annual payment from his investment over this period at the beginning of each year starting today. Calculate how much of an annual payment the Count can expect.

29. Robert Watts has just retired after 25 years with the electric company. His total pension funds have an accumulated value of $180,000, and his life expectancy is 15 more years. His pension fund manager assumes he can earn a 9 percent return on his assets. What will be his yearly annuity for the next 15 years?

30. Dr. Jordan Rivers, a geography professor, invests $50,000 in a parcel of land that is expected to increase in value by 12 percent per year for the next five years. He will take the proceeds and provide himself with a 10-year annuity. Assuming a 12 percent interest rate, how much will this annuity be?

31. Blackie Knight is planning to retire in 25 years, at which time she hopes to have accumulated enough money to receive an annuity of $21,000 a year for 26 years of retirement. During her pre-retirement period she expects to earn 7 percent annually, while during retirement she expects to earn 6 percent annually on her money. What annual contributions to this retirement fund are required for Blackie to achieve her objective and sleep well at night?

32. You wish to retire after 30 years, at which time you want to have accumulated enough money to receive an annuity of $55,000 a year for 18 years of retirement. During the period before retirement, you can earn 9 percent annually, while after retirement you can earn 7 percent on your money.

    a. What annual contributions to the retirement fund will allow you to receive the $55,000 annually?

    b. What annual contributions are required if the contributions are made at the beginning of each year?

33. Your retirement planning suggests a goal of $57,000 a year in today's dollars for 30 years of retirement. Retirement will begin 35 years from today, at which time you will expect your first annuity payment. Inflation between now and retirement is expected to be 4 percent annually (do not consider inflation during retirement). The anticipated yield over the pre-retirement period is 7 percent annually, and 8 percent per annum is anticipated during retirement. Calculate how much you should set aside each year between now and retirement to achieve your goal. (Ignore taxes.)

34. For your retirement you would like to receive $75,000 a year in today's dollars for a period of 25 years. A problem, of course, is that you expect inflation to average 2.5 percent a year for the next 33 years until your retirement. (Inflation will not be a concern during retirement.) Interest rates (borrowing rates equal lending rates in this perfect market without taxes) are expected to be 7 percent until retirement and 5 percent during retirement. Your first retirement annuity is to be received 33 years from today, and your first contribution to your retirement will be at the end of this year and will be made 33 times. You will also require $125,000 (do

not inflate) from your retirement funds in 17 years for a sabbatical that you are planning. Calculate the equal annual (33) contributions to your retirement fund required for this all to happen.

35. Sybil White has just purchased an annuity to begin payment at the end of 2006 (that is the date of the first payment). Assume it is now the beginning of 2003. The annuity is for $8,000 per year and is designed to last 10 years. If the interest rate for this problem is 13 percent, what is the most she should have paid for the annuity?

36. If you borrow $15,618 and are required to pay back the loan in seven equal annual installments of $3,000, what is the interest rate associated with the loan?

37. Jim Busby owes $10,000 now. A lender will carry the debt for five more years at 10 percent interest. That is, in this particular case, the amount owed will go up by 10 percent per year for five years. The lender then will require that Jim pay off the loan over the next 12 years at 11 percent interest. What will his annual payment be?

38. If your uncle borrows $60,000 from the bank at 10 percent interest over the seven-year life of the loan, what equal annual payments must be made to discharge the loan, plus pay the bank its required rate of interest (round to the nearest dollar)? How much of his first payment will be applied to interest? To principal? How much of his second payment will be applied to each?

39. Dan Rogers borrows $80,000 at 14 percent interest toward the purchase of a home. His mortgage is for 25 years.

    a. How much will his annual payments be? (Although home payments are usually on a monthly basis, we shall do our analysis on an annual basis for ease of computation. We get a reasonably accurate answer.)

    b. How much interest will he pay over the life of the loan?

    c. How much should he be willing to pay to get out of a 14 percent mortgage and into a 10 percent mortgage with 25 years remaining on the mortgage? Assume current interest rates are 10 percent. Carefully consider the time value of money. Disregard taxes.

40. Peter Piper has applied for a mortgage of $120,000. Interest is computed at 8.5 percent compounded semiannually. The mortgage will be paid off over 20 years.

    a. Calculate Peter's monthly payment.

    b. Calculate Peter's weekly payment.

    c. Calculate Peter's bi-weekly payment.

41. Ocean Spray has applied for a mortgage of $200,000. Interest is computed at 4.5 percent compounded semiannually. The mortgage will be paid off over 25 years.

    a. Calculate Ocean's monthly payment.

    b. Calculate Ocean's weekly payment.

    c. Calculate Ocean's bi-weekly payment.

42. Bing and Monica Cherrie require a mortgage of $145,000 and can afford monthly payments of $1,150 on the mortgage. Current interest rates are 4 percent compounded semiannually. How long should the Cherries select to pay off the mortgage (the amortization period)?

43. Deidre Hall can afford monthly payments of $690 on a mortgage. Current mortgage rates are 3.5 percent, compounded semiannually. The longest period over which a mortgage can be amortized is 25 years. What size mortgage can Deidre afford?

44. Your younger sister, Linda, will start college in five years. She has just informed your parents that she wants to go to Gatineau University, which will cost $17,000 per year for four years (assumed to come at the end of each year). Anticipating Linda's ambitions, your parents started investing $2,000 per year five years ago and will continue to do so for five more

years. How much more will your parents have to invest each year for the next five years to have the necessary funds for Linda's education? Use 10 percent as the appropriate interest rate throughout this problem (for discounting or compounding).

45. Linda (from previous problem) is now 18 years old (five years have passed), and she wants to get married instead of going to school. Your parents have accumulated the necessary funds for her education.

    Instead of her schooling, your parents are paying $8,000 for her upcoming wedding and plan to take a year-end vacation costing $5,000 per year for the next three years. How much will your parents have at the end of three years to help you with graduate school, which you will start then? You plan to work on a master's and perhaps a Ph.D. If graduate school costs $14,045 per year, approximately how long will you be able to stay in school based on these funds? Use 10 percent as the appropriate interest rate throughout this problem.

46. You are chairperson of the investment fund for Eastern Football League. You are asked to set up a fund of semiannual payments to be compounded semiannually to accumulate a sum of $100,000 after 10 years at an 8 percent annual rate (20 payments). The first payment into the fund is to occur six months from today, and the last payment is to take place at the end of the 10th year.

    a. Determine how much the semiannual payment should be. (Round to whole numbers.) On the day after the fourth payment is made (the beginning of the third year) the interest rate goes up to a 10 percent annual rate, and you can earn a 10 percent annual rate on funds that have been accumulated as well as all future payments into the fund. Interest is to be compounded semiannually on all funds.

    b. Determine how much the revised semiannual payments should be after this rate change (there are 16 payments and compounding dates). The next payment will be in the middle of the third year. (Round all values to whole numbers.)

COMPREHENSIVE PROBLEM

47. Allison Boone had been practising medicine for seven years. Her specialty was neurology. She had received her bachelor's degree in chemistry from the University of Toronto and her M.D. from McMaster University. She did her residency at Toronto General Hospital. Allison practised neurology in a clinic with three other doctors in Toronto.

    Her husband, Samuel L. Boone, held an administrative position at the Toronto Dominion Bank. Allison and Samuel had been married for five years and were the parents of young twin sons, Todd and Trey. They lived in the Beaches area in a beautiful four-room house overlooking Lake Ontario.

    Allison normally left for work at 7:30 a.m. and closed her office at 5:30 p.m. to return home. On Tuesday, July 6, 2002, at 5:15 p.m., she received an emergency call from Toronto General Hospital and immediately went to the hospital to help a patient who had suffered serious brain damage. By the time she had administered aid and helped prepare the patient for surgery it was 11:00 p.m.

    On her way home as she passed Woodbine Racetrack, she was confronted head on by a drunken driver going over 110 kilometres an hour. A crash was inevitable, and Allison and the other driver were killed instantly. The drunken driver was making a late delivery for Wayland Frozen Foods, Inc.

    ### *Legal Considerations*

    The families of both drivers were devastated by the news of the accident. After the funeral and explaining the situation to the children, Samuel Boone knew he must seek legal redress for his family's enormous loss. Following interviews with a number of lawyers, he decided to hire Sloan Whitaker.

Sloan was with a Toronto law firm (Hanson, Sloan, and Thomason) that specialized in plaintiff's lawsuits. He had been in practice for over 20 years since graduating from Osgoode Law School in 1980.

When Sloan Whitaker began his investigation on behalf of Samuel Boone and his family, he was surprised to find out the driver of the delivery vehicle had a prior record of alcohol abuse and that Wayland Frozen Foods, Inc. had knowledge of the problem when they hired him. It appears the driver was a relative of the owner, and at the time of employment he revealed what he termed "a past alcoholic problem that was now under control." In any event, he was acting as an employee for Wayland Frozen Foods in using their truck to make a business-related delivery at the time of the accident. The fact that he was speeding and intoxicated at the time of the impact only increased the legal exposure for Wayland Frozen Foods.

After much negotiating with the law firm that represented Wayland Frozen Foods (and its insurance company), Sloan Whitaker received three proposals for an out-of-court settlement to be paid to Allison Boone's family. The intent of the proposals was to replace the future earning's power of Allison Boone, less any of the earnings she would have personally needed for her normal living requirements. Also, the value that she provided for her family as a wife and mother, quite aside from her earning power, had to be considered. Finally, there was the issue of punitive damages that Wayland Frozen Foods was exposed to as a result of letting an unqualified driver operate its truck. If the case went to court, there was no telling how much a jury might assign to this last factor.

The three proposals are listed below. An actuarial table indicated that Allison, age 37 at the time of the accident, had an anticipated life expectancy of 40 more years.

Proposal 1 Pay the family of Allison Boone $300,000 a year for the next 20 years, and $500,000 a year for the remaining 20 years.

Proposal 2 Pay the family a lump sum payment of $5 million today.

Proposal 3 Pay the family of Allison Boone a relatively small amount of $50,000 a year for the next 40 years, but also guarantee them a final payment of $75 million at the end of 40 years.

In order to analyze the present value of these three proposals, attorney Sloan Whitaker called on a financial expert to do the analysis. You will aid in the process.

a. Using a current long-term interest rate, recommend a proposal to the Boone family. Justify your choice of discount rate.

b. Now assume that a discount rate of 11 percent is used. Which of the three alternatives provides the highest present value?

c. Explain why the change in outcome takes place between part *a* and part *b*.

d. If Sloan Whitaker thinks punitive damages are likely to be $4 million in a jury trial, should he be more likely to settle out-of-court or go before a jury?

Selected References

Black, Fischer. "A Simple Discounting Rule." *Financial Management* 17 (Summer 1988), pp. 7–11.

Crosby, Mark, and Glenn Oho. "Inflation and the Capital Stock." *Journal of Money, Credit, and Banking* 32 (May 2000), pp. 237–53.

Schlolnick, Barry. "Interest Rate Asymmetrics in Long-Term Loan and Deposit Markets." *Journal of Financial Services Research* 16 (September 1999), pp. 5–26.

APPENDIX 9A

Derivation of Time-Value-of-Money Formulas

Equation 9–1 (Future value)

$$FV_1 = PV_1 + iPV = PV(1+i)$$

$$FV_2 = PV(1+i) + iPV(1+i) = PV(1+i) \times (1+i) = PV(1+i)^2$$

$$FV_3 = PV(1+i)^2 + iPV(1+i)^2 = PV(1+i)^2 \times (1+i) = PV(1+i)^3$$

$$FV_n = PV(1+i)^{n-1} + iPV(1+i)^{n-1} = PV(1+i)^{n-1} \times (1+i) = PV(1+i)^n$$

$$FV = PV(1+i)^n$$

Equation 9–3 (Present value)

$$FV = PV(1+i)^n \qquad PV = FV\left[\frac{1}{(1+i)^n}\right]$$

Equation 9–4*a* (Future value—annuity)

$$FV_1 = A + Ø = A$$

$$FV_2 = A + A + Ai = A + A(1+i)$$

$$FV_3 = A + A(1+i) + i[A + A(1+i)] = [A + A(1+i)](1+i) = A + A(1+i) + A(1+i)^2$$

$$FV_4 = A + A(1+i) + A(1+i)^2 + i[A + A(1+i) + A(1+i)^2] = A + A(1+i) + A(1+i)^2 + A(1+i)^3$$

$$FV_A = A + A(1+i) + A(1+i)^2 + A(1+i)^3 + \ldots A(1+i)^{n-1}$$

To get the sum of this geometric series, multiply by $(1 + i)$ and deduct the original equation.

$$FV_A(1+i) = A(1+i) + A(1+i)^2 + A(1+i)^3 + \ldots A(1+i)^{n-1} + A(1+i)^n$$

$$-FV_A \qquad - A + A(1+i) + A(1+i)^2 + A(1+i)^3 + \ldots A(1+i)^{n-1}$$

$$FV_A(1+i) - FV_A = A(1+i)^n - A$$

$$FV_A + iFV_A - FV_A = A(1+i)^n - A$$

$$iFV_A = A[(1+i)^n - 1]$$

$$FV_A = A\left[\frac{(1+i)^n - 1}{i}\right]$$

Equation 9–4*b* (Future value—annuity in advance)

$$FV_1 = A + iA = A(1+i)$$

$$FV_2 = A + iA + A(1+i) + i[A(1+i)] = A(1+i) + (1+i)[A(1+i)] = A(1+i) + A(1+i)^2$$

$$FV_3 = A + iA + A(1+i) + A(1+i)^2 + i[A(1+i)] + A(1+i)^2] = A(1+i) + A(1+i)^2 + A(1+i)^3$$

$$FV_A = A(1+i) + A(1+i)^2 + A(1+i)^3 + \ldots A(1+i)^n$$

To get the sum of this geometric series, multiply by $(1 + i)$ and deduct the original equation.

$$FV_A(1 + i) = A(1 + i)^2 + A(1 + i)^3 + A(1 + i)^4 + \ldots A(1 + i)^n + A(1 + i)^{n+1}$$

$$-FV_A \quad - A(1 + i) + A(1 + i)^2 + A(1 + i)^3 + A(1 + i)^4 \ldots A(1 + i)^n$$

$$FV_A(1 + i) - FV_A \quad - A(1 + i)^{n+1} - A(1 + i)$$

$$FV_A + iFV_A - FV_A \quad - A(1 + i)^{n+1} - A(1 + i)$$

$$iFV_A = A[(1 + i)^{n+1} - (1 + i)]$$

$$FV_A = A_{BGN}\left[\frac{(1 + i)^{n+1} - (1 + i)}{i}\right]$$

Equation 9–5*a* (Present value of an annuity)

$$PV_1 = A(1 + i)^{-1}$$

$$PV_2 = A(1 + i)^{-1} + A(1 + i)^{-2}$$

$$PV_3 = A(1 + i)^{-1} + A(1 + i)^{-2} + A(1 + i)^{-3}$$

$$PV_n = A(1 + i)^{-1} + A(1 + i)^{-2} + A(1 + i)^{-3} + \ldots + A(1 + i)^{-n}$$

To get the sum of this geometric series, multiply by $(1 + i)$ and deduct the original equation.

$$PV_n(1 + i) = A(1 + i)^0 + A(1 + i)^{-1} + A(1 + i)^{-2} + A(1 + i)^{-3} + \ldots + A(1 + i)^{-(n-1)}$$

$$-PV_n = A(1 + i)^{-1} + A(1 + i)^{-2} + A(1 + i)^{-3} + \ldots + A(1 + i)^{-n}$$

$$PV_n(1 + i) - PV_n = A - A(1 + i)^{-n}$$

$$PV_n + iPV_n - PV_n = A[1 - (1 + i)^{-n}]$$

$$iPV_n = A[1 - (1 + i)^{-n}]$$

$$PV_A = A\left[\frac{1 - \dfrac{1}{(1 + i)^n}}{i}\right]$$

Equation 9–5*b* (Present value of an annuity in advance)

$$PV_1 = A$$

$$PV_2 = A + A(1 + i)^{-1}$$

$$PV_3 = A + A(1 + i)^{-1} + A(1 + i)^{-2}$$

$$PV_n = A + A(1 + i)^{-1} + A(1 + i)^{-2} + \ldots + A(1 + i)^{-(n-1)}$$

To get the sum of this geometric series, multiply by $(1 + i)$ and deduct the original equation.

$$PV_n(1 + i) = A(1 + i) + A(1 + i)^0 + A(1 + i)^{-1} + A(1 + i)^{-2} + \ldots + A(1 + i)^{-n}$$

$$-PV_n = A + A(1 + i)^{-1} + A(1 + i)^{-2} + \ldots + A(1 + i)^{-(n-1)}$$

$$PV_n(1 + i) - PV_n = A(1 + i) - A(1 + i)^{-(n-1)}$$

$$PV_n + iPV_n - PV_n = A[(1 + i) - (1 + i)^{-(n-1)}]$$

$$iPV_n = A[(1 + i) - (1 + i)^{-(n-1)}]$$

$$PV_A = A_{BGN}\left[\frac{(1 + i) - \dfrac{1}{(1 + i)^{n-1}}}{i}\right]$$

Equation 9–6*a* (Annuity equalling a future value)

$$FV_A = A\left[\frac{(1+i)^n - 1}{i}\right] \qquad A = FV_A\left[\frac{i}{(1+i)^n - 1}\right]$$

(9–4*a*)

Equation 9–6*b* (Annuity in advance equalling a future value)

$$FV_A = A_{BGN}\left[\frac{(1+i)^{n+1} - (1+i)}{i}\right] \qquad A_{BGN} = FV_A\left[\frac{i}{(1+i)^{n+1} - (1+i)}\right]$$

(9–4*b*)

Equation 9–7*a* (Annuity equalling a present value)

$$PV_A = A\left[\frac{1 - \frac{1}{(1+i)^n}}{i}\right] \qquad A = PV_A\left[\frac{i}{1 - \frac{1}{(1+i)^n}}\right]$$

(9–5*a*)

Equation 9–7*b* (Annuity in advance equalling a present value)

$$PV_A = A_{BGN}\left[\frac{(1+i) - \frac{1}{(1+i)^{n-1}}}{i}\right] \qquad A_{BGN} = PV_A\left[\frac{i}{(1+i) - \frac{1}{(1+i)^{n-1}}}\right]$$

(9–5*b*)

CHAPTER | TEN

10

Valuation and Rates of Return

LEARNING | OBJECTIVES

1 Describe the valuation of a financial asset as based on the present value of future cash flows.

2 Explain that the required rate of return in valuing an asset is based on the risk involved.

3 Calculate the current value (price) of bonds, preferred shares (perpetuals), and common shares based on the future benefits (cash flows).

4 Calculate the yields on financial claims based on the relationship between current price and future expected cash flows.

5 Describe the use of a price-earnings ratio to determine value.

In Chapter 9 we considered the basic principles of the time value of money. In this chapter we use many of those concepts to determine how financial assets (bonds, preferred stock, and common stock) are valued and how investors establish the rates of return they demand for investing in these assets. In the next chapter we use material from this chapter to determine the overall cost of financing to the firm. Once we know how much bondholders and shareholders demand in the way of rates of return, we then observe what the corporation is required to pay them to attract their funds. The cost of corporate financing (capital) is subsequently used in analyzing whether a project is acceptable for investment or not. These relationships are depicted in Figure 10–1 on the next page.

Financial calculators are used to work the problems in this chapter. Your answer will be slightly different if it is determined using the tables. Whether you use tables, calculators, or computers to do these calculations, you must firmly comprehend the concept behind present value analysis to be successful.

FIGURE 10-1

The relationship between time value of money, required return, cost of financing, and investment decisions

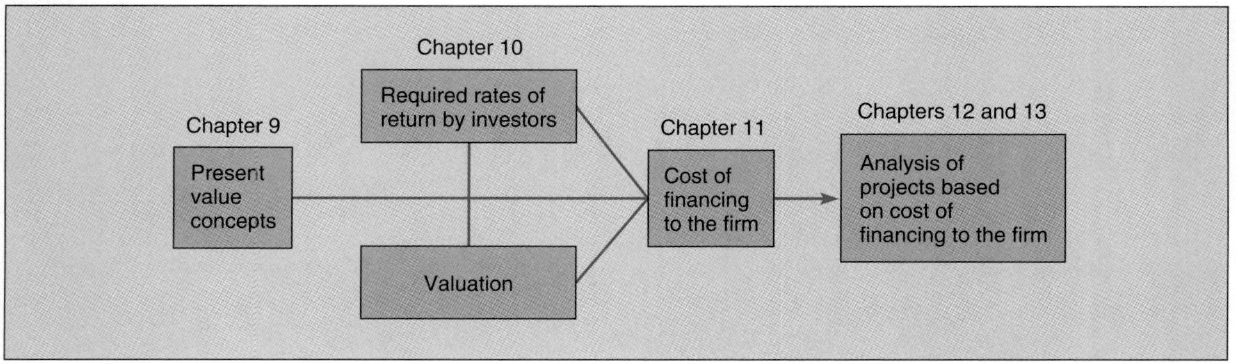

Valuation Concepts

The valuation of a financial asset is based on determining the present value of future expected cash flows. Thus, we need to know the value of future anticipated cash flows and the **discount rate** to be applied to the future cash flows to determine the current value. The financial assets that we study in this chapter usually trade in secondary markets, where their prices change minute by minute as investors change their expectations about future cash payouts and their required rates of return. These changes cause prices or present values to move up or down in these markets as financial assets are exchanged between investors.

Bell Canada Enterprises Inc.
www.bell.ca

The market-determined **required rate of return,** which is the discount rate, depends on the market's perceived level of risk associated with the individual security. Also important is the idea that required rates of return are competitively determined among the many companies seeking financial capital. For example, Bell Canada, due to its low financial risk, reasonable return, and strong market position in telecommunications, is likely to raise debt capital at a significantly lower cost than can Air Canada which has had significant financial difficulties. This implies that investors are willing to accept a lower return for a lower risk, and vice versa. As just described, the market allocates capital to companies based on estimates of risk, efficiency, and expected returns–which are based to a large degree on past performance. The reward to the manager for efficient use of capital in the past is a lower required return for investors than that of competing companies that did not manage their financial resources as well.

Throughout the balance of this chapter, concepts of valuation to corporate bonds, preferred stock, and common stock are applied. Although we describe the basic characteristics of each form of security as part of the valuation discussion, extended discussion of each security is deferred until later chapters.

Valuation of Bonds

As previously stated, the value of a financial asset is based on the concept of determining the present value of future cash flows. Let's start our exploration of this process by applying it to bond valuation. A bond promises an annuity stream of interest

Nortel—A Valuation Journey

In mid 1998 Nortel shares traded at about \$20.00 per share, however, by July 2000 they were worth over \$120.00 per share. Based on its equity value or the market capitalization of its common shares (number of shares outstanding × market share price) Nortel became Canada's first \$100 billion, \$200 billion, \$300 billion and then \$350 billion company. However, within a year of this peak, the price of a share fell below \$10 and the market capitalization below \$30 billion. Still Nortel was Canada's largest market capitalized company. What had happened?

At its peak Nortel was projecting revenues of \$40 billion for the year 2001, up from the \$30 billion it reported in 2000. Investors, of course, determine the market share price based on future earnings, but it is hoped that revenues filter down to a firm's earnings. Microsoft in its first five years of existence had achieved revenue growth of 53 percent a year and was a great story in value creation. In 2000 Nortel shares were being priced by the market based on similar growth projections, and yet Nortel at the time was a much larger company than Microsoft had been at the beginning.

As the year 2001 approached investors began to realize that Nortel and the other high-tech companies were not going to realize their stellar growth projections. The market for Nortel products such as fibre optic and wireless networks had become saturated. Sales were about to fall! In 2001 Nortel sales were only \$17.5 billion and Nortel suffered an earnings loss of \$26.7 billion as it wrote down overvalued assets. The reduction in share prices correctly anticipated this drastic drop in Nortel fortunes.

At the TSX web site you can find the listing for Nortel. Clicking on the Nortel stock symbol (NT) will display its current price and market capitalization. Clicking on the chart for the last five years will show Nortel's share price journey up and then down.

FINANCE IN ACTION

Q1 How does Nortel's current price compare to the \$10 of 2001?

Q2 Why do think that Nortel's shares changed so drastically in value?

www.nortelnetworks.com

www.tsx.ca
Symbol: NT

payments (coupon payments) and a \$1,000 principal payment at maturity. Both the par or maturity value and the coupon payments are fixed over the term of the bond. Most corporate bonds have a \$1,000 par value. If the par value is higher or lower, that value would be used. The par value is also referred to as the face value.

Investors discount these future cash flows to determine the current price of the bond. The discount factor used is called the **yield to maturity** (*Y*). Yield, therefore, is the relationship between the price investors are prepared to pay and future expected cash flows—in this case, coupon payments and the maturity value. The value of *Y* is determined in the bond markets and represents the required rate of return demanded by investors on a bond of a given risk and maturity.

Because the coupon payments and maturity values are fixed, the price of the bond will move up or down as those payments become more or less desirable. The price changes as the market requires a different yield or rate of return, based on changing economic conditions. More is said about the concept of yield to maturity in the next section.

The price of a bond is equal to the present value of regular interest payments discounted by the yield to maturity added to the present value of the principal (also discounted by the yield to maturity).

This relationship can be expressed mathematically as follows:

$$P_b = \sum_{t=1}^{n} \frac{I_t}{(1 + Y)^t} + \frac{P_n}{(1 + Y)^n} \qquad (10\text{–}1)$$

or graphically as

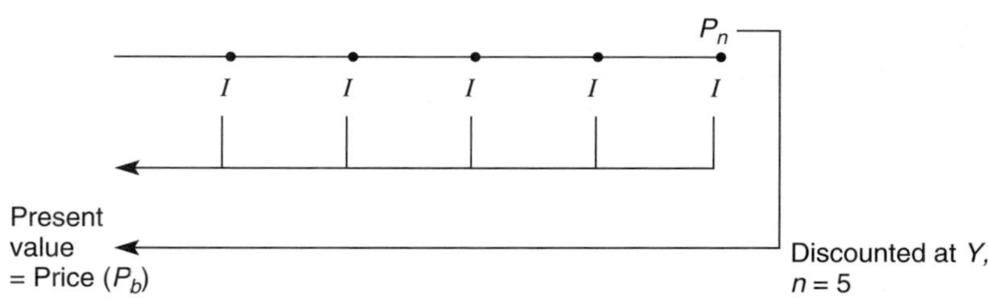

where

P_b = Price of the bond
I_t = Interest payments
P_n = Principal payment at maturity
t = Number corresponding to a period; running from 1 to n
n = Total number of periods
Y = Yield to maturity (or required rate of return)

The first term in the formula says to take the sum of the present values of the interest payments (I_t); the second term directs you to take the present value of the principal payment at maturity (P_n). The discount rate used throughout the analysis is the yield to maturity (Y). The answer derived is referred to as P_b (the price of the bond). The analysis is carried out for n periods.

Let's consider an example where I_t (interest payments) equals \$100; for now we are using annual interest payments for simplicity. Later in the discussion we will shift to semiannual payments, allowing us to more appropriately determine the value of a bond. P_n (principal payment at maturity) equals \$1,000; Y (yield to maturity) is 10 percent; and n (total number of periods) equals 20. This means P_b (the price of the bond) would equal:

$$P_b = \sum_{t=1}^{20} \frac{\$100}{(1 + .10)^t} + \frac{\$1,000}{(1 + .10)^{20}}$$

Calculator

From our graphical representation:
$P_n = FV = \$1,000$
$I = PMT = \$100$
$n = 20$
$Y = i = 10\%$

Compute $PV = P_b = \$1,000$.

Tables (optional) We could use present value tables. We take the present value of the interest payments (Appendix D) and then add this value to the present value of the principal payment at maturity (Appendix B).

(continued)

(continued)

(PV_A) Present value of interest payments	$ 851.40
(PV) Present value of principal payment at maturity	149.00
Total present value, or price, of the bond	$1,000.40

The price of the bond in this case is essentially the same as its par, or stated, value to be received at maturity of $1,000. This is because the annual interest rate is 10 percent (the annual interest payment of $100 divided by $1,000), and the yield to maturity, or discount rate, is also 10 percent. When the interest rate on the bond and the yield to maturity are equal, the bond trades at par value. Later we examine the mathematical effects of varying the yield to maturity above or below the interest rate on the bond. But first let's more fully examine the concept of yield to maturity.

Concept of Yield to Maturity

In the previous example, the yield to maturity that was used as the discount rate was 10 percent. The yield to maturity, or discount rate, is the rate of return required by investors. The investor allows *three* factors to influence his or her required rate of return.

1. *The Required Real Rate of Return.* This is the rate of return that the investor demands for giving up current use of the funds on a non-inflation-adjusted basis. It is the financial rent the investor charges for using his or her funds for one year, five years, or any given time period. Historically, the **real rate of return** demanded by investors has been about 2 to 3 percent. Throughout the 1980s and early 1990s, the real rate of return was much higher; that is, 5 to 7 percent.
2. *Inflation Premium.* In addition to the real rate of return, the investor requires a premium to compensate for the eroding effect of inflation on the value of the dollar. It would hardly satisfy an investor to have a 3 percent total rate of return in a 5 percent inflationary economy. Under such circumstances the lender (investor) would be paying the borrower 2 percent (in purchasing power) for use of the funds. This would be irrational. No one wishes to *pay* another party to use his or her funds. The **inflation premium** added to the real rate of return ensures that this does not happen. The size of the inflation premium is based on the investor's expectations about future inflation. Through the 1980s the inflation premium was 4 to 5 percent. In the late 1970s it was in excess of 10 percent. After 1992 to the end of the decade inflation was about 2 percent.

Bank of Canada
www.bankofcanada.ca/en

If one combines the real rate of return and the inflation premium, the **risk-free rate of return** is determined. This is the rate that compensates the investor for the current use of his or her funds and for the loss in purchasing power due to inflation, but not for taking risks. The risk-free rate of return is often considered to be the yield on Government of Canada treasury bills. As an example, if the real rate of return were 3 percent and the inflation premium were 4 percent, we would say the risk-free rate of return was 7 percent.[1]

In Chapter 6 we examined the term structure of interest rates by looking at the yields for various maturities of Government of Canada securities. We discovered first that because of a liquidity preference to deal with uncertainty, longer-term rates are higher than short-term rates. Second, a yield curve is a reflection of the expectations of investors as to what they believe interest rates or yields will be in the future. Those expectations are formulated by many factors, including inflationary expectations, government monetary policy, government fiscal policies (in particular, the upward pressure on interest rates created by the demands of debt financing), and the influences on Canadian interest rates from the global financial community.

3. *Risk Premium.* We must now add the **risk premium** to the risk-free rate of return. This is a premium associated with the special risks of a given investment. Of primary interest to us are two types of risks: business risk and financial risk. **Business risk** relates to the possible inability of the firm to hold its competitive position and maintain stability and growth in its earnings. We can relate this to the firm's capital assets and operating leverage. **Financial risk** relates to the possible inability of the firm to meet its debt obligations as they come due. This relates to the firm's capital structure and the maturity of its financial obligations. This is the financial leverage we examined in Chapter 5. From an investor's viewpoint, we often speak of different risks such as default risk, liquidity risk, and maturity risk. Whatever the label, risk concerns add to the required rate of return.

In addition to these two forms of risk, the risk premium is greater or less for different investments. For example, because bonds possess a contractual obligation for the firm to pay interest and repay principal to bondholders, they are considered less risky than common stock, where no such obligation exists. On the other hand, common stock carries the potential for unlimited return when the corporation is very profitable.

The risk premium of an investment may range from as low as zero on a very short-term Canadian government-backed security to 10 to 15 percent on a gold mining expedition. Typical risk premiums range from 2 to 6 percent. We assume that in the investment we are examining, the risk premium is 3 percent. If we add this risk premium to the two components of the risk-free rate of return, we arrive at an overall required rate of return of 10 percent.

+ Real rate of return	3%
+ Inflation premium	4
= Risk-free rate	7%
+ Risk premium	3
= Required rate of return	10%

[1]Actually a slightly more accurate representation would be:

$$\text{Risk-free rate} = \left(1 + \text{Real rate of return}\right)\left(1 + \text{Inflation premium}\right) - 1$$

We would show:

$$(1.03)(1.04) - 1 = .0712 = 7.12 \text{ percent}$$

The Ups and Downs of Bond Prices

Unlike Canada savings bonds, Canadian government and corporate bonds trade in the markets among investors. Investors are promised a fixed semiannual coupon payment and the face value, or maturity value, at the maturity of the bond. Since these cash flows are fixed, it is the price of bonds in the markets that must change to reflect investor expectations about the future and required rates of return. The daily dollar trading in bonds exceeds stock market trading by at least 10 times.

Let's examine the price changes on an issue of Air Canada bonds. After the terrorist attacks on America in September of 2001, the airline business around the world experienced great difficulties as air travel dropped significantly. However, even before the attacks, Air Canada was experiencing financial difficulties. As revenues dropped through the fall of 2001, Air Canada was concerned that its cash flow might dry up. The bond holders of Air Canada were also concerned as they feared the possible bankruptcy of Air Canada or at least a restructuring of the interest payments due on their bonds.

On November 26, 2001, Air Canada bonds due in February 2004 and promising an annual coupon of 6.75 percent, traded at 50 percent of maturity value, or at $500 on a $1,000 par value bond. This suggested a yield to maturity of 45.07 percent, if Air Canada was able to meet its obligations. In 2002 the financial situation at Air Canada was somewhat more stable and the same bonds traded at $720 on January 18th for a suggested yield to maturity of 25.08 percent.

An investor that had purchased the Air Canada bonds in November and sold them in January would have earned $220 for every $500 invested. This represents a 44 percent return over 52 days. This is a nominal annual return of over 300 percent. The trick would be to repeat this success throughout the year, while assuming tremendous risk.

Bond quotes can be obtained from *The Globe and Mail* site noted by clicking print edition, then money and markets, and then the article on bonds.

FINANCE IN ACTION

Q1 Are revenues, earnings, and cash flow up or down at Air Canada?

Q2 What is the current price and yield to maturity of the Air Canada bonds maturing in 2004?

www.aircanada.com

www.globeandmail.com/business

Symbol: AC

In this instance we assume that we are evaluating the required return on a bond issued by a firm. If the security had been the common stock of the same firm, the risk premium might have been 5 to 6 percent, thus making the required rate of return 12 to 13 percent.

As we conclude this section, please recall that the required rate of return on a bond is effectively identical to the required yield to maturity. The required rates of return and their components are common to the valuation of all financial securities.

Changing the Yield to Maturity and the Impact on Bond Valuation

In the earlier bond value calculation, the interest rate (coupon rate) was 10 percent ($100 annual interest on a $1,000 par value bond), while the yield to maturity was also 10 percent. Under those circumstances, the price of the bond was basically equal to its par value. Let us now assume that conditions in the market cause the yield to maturity to change.

Increase in Inflation Premium Although other factors will cause the required rate of return to change almost continually, inflation tends to be a major factor. For example, assume that the inflation premium goes up from 4 to 6 percent while all else remains constant. The required rate of return would now become 12 percent.

+ Real rate of return	3%
+ Inflation premium	6
= Risk-free rate	9%
+ Risk premium	3
= Required rate of return	12%

This increase in the required rate of return, or yield to maturity, on the bond causes its price to change. Of course, the required rate of return on all other financial assets also goes up proportionately. A bond that pays only 10 percent interest when the required rate of return (yield to maturity) is 12 percent has its price fall below its former value of approximately $1,000. The new price of the bond, $850.61, is computed as follows:

Calculator

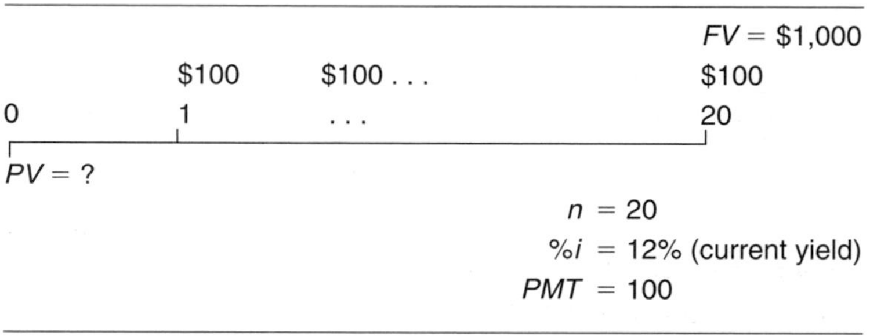

Price = *PV* = $850.61.

Tables (optional) *Total present value*

(PV_A) Present value of interest payments	$746.90
(PV) Present value of principal payment at maturity	104.00
Total present value, or price, of the bond	$850.90

In this example we assumed that increasing inflation caused the required rate of return (yield to maturity) to go up and the bond price to fall by approximately $150. The same effect would occur if the business risk increased or if the demanded level for the *real* rate of return became higher.

Decrease in Inflation Premium Of course, the opposite effect would happen if the required rate of return went down because of lower inflation, less risk, or other factors. Let's assume that the inflation premium declines and the required rate of return (yield to maturity) goes down to 8 percent. The 20-year bond with the 10 percent interest rate would now sell for $1,196.36.

Calculator

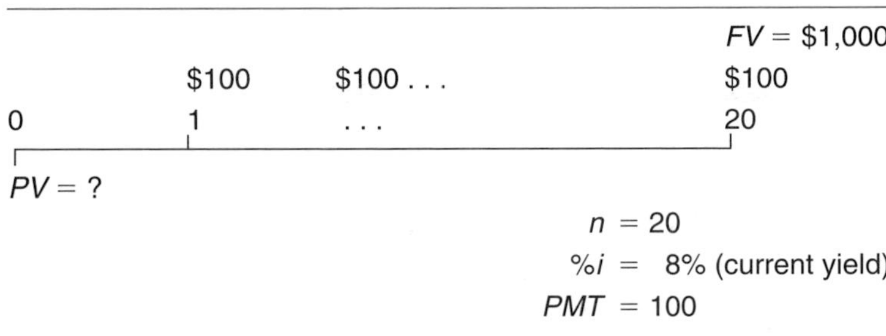

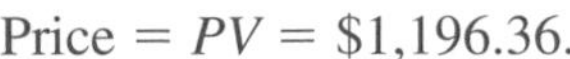

Price = PV = $1,196.36.

Tables (optional) *Total present value*

(PV_A) Present value of interest payments	$ 981.80
(PV) Present value of principal payment at maturity	215.00
Total present value, or price, of the bond	$1,196.80

The price of the bond has now risen $196.36 above par value. This is certainly in line with the expected result because the bond is paying 10 percent interest when the required yield in the market is only 8 percent. The 2 percent differential on a $1,000 par value bond represents $20.00 per year. The investor receives this differential for the next 20 years. The present value of $20.00 for the next 20 years at the current market rate of interest of 8 percent is $196.36. This explains why the bond is trading at $196.36 over its stated, or par, value.

The further the yield to maturity on a bond falls away from the stated interest rate on the bond, the greater the price change effect is. This is illustrated in Table 10–1 (on the next page) for the 10 percent interest rate, 20-year bonds discussed in this chapter. Also note the inverse relationship between price and yield. As required yield increases, price decreases, and as yield decreases, price increases.

Clearly, different yields to maturity have a significant impact on the price of a bond.[2]

Time to Maturity

The impact of a change in yield to maturity on valuation is also affected by the remaining time to maturity. The effect of a bond paying 2 percent more or less than the going

[2]Observe that the impact of a decrease or increase in interest rates is not equal. For example, a 2 percent decrease in interest rates produces a $196.36 gain in the bond price, and an increase of 2 percent causes a $149.39 loss. While price movements are not symmetrical around the price of the bond when the time dimension is the maturity date of the bond, they are symmetrical around the duration of the bond. The duration represents the weighted average time period to recapture the interest and principal on the bond. While these concepts go beyond that appropriate for an introductory finance text, the interested reader may wish to consult Geoffrey A. Hirt and Stanley B. Block, *Fundamentals of Investment Management,* 4th ed. (Homewood, Ill.: Richard D. Irwin, 1993), or Frank K. Reilly, *Investments,* 2nd ed. (Hinsdale, Ill.: Dryden Press, 1985).

TABLE 10–1
Bond price table

(10 Percent Interest Payment, 20 Years to Maturity)	
Yield to Maturity	**Bond Price**
2%	$2,308.11
4	1,815.42
6	1,458.80
7	1,317.82
8	1,196.36
9	1,091.29
10	1,000.00
11	920.37
12	850.61
13	789.26
14	735.07
16	644.27
20	513.04
25	406.92

TABLE 10–2
Impact of time to maturity on bond prices

Time Period in Years (of 10 percent bond)	Bond Price with 8 Percent Yield to Maturity	Bond Price with 12 Percent Yield to Maturity
0	$1,000.00	$1,000.00
1	1,018.52	982.14
5	1,079.85	927.90
10	1,134.20	887.00
15	1,171.19	863.78
20	1,196.36	850.61
25	1,213.50	843.14
30	1,225.16	838.90

rate of interest is much greater for a 20-year bond than it is for a 1-year bond. In the latter case, the investor only gains or gives up $20.00 for one year. That is not the same as having this differential for an extended time. Let's once again return to the 10 percent interest rate bond and show the impact of a 2 percent decrease or increase in yield to maturity for varying *times* to maturity. The values are shown in Table 10–2 and graphed in Figure 10–2. The upper part of Figure 10–2 shows how the amount (premium) above par value is reduced as the number of years to maturity becomes smaller and smaller. Figure 10–2 should be read from left to right. The lower part of the figure shows how the amount (discount) below par value is reduced with progressively fewer years to maturity. Clearly, the longer the maturity, the greater the impact of changes in yield.

Determining Yield to Maturity from the Bond Price

Recall from Chapter 6 that our discussion of the term structure of interest rates revealed an investor preference for liquidity. This resulted in higher required yields for

FIGURE 10–2

Relationship between time to maturity and bond price*

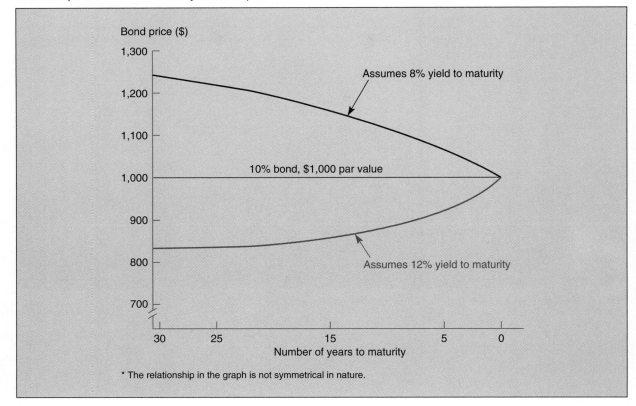

* The relationship in the graph is not symmetrical in nature.

longer-term maturities, all other things being equal. The preference for liquidity can be explained by the impact of yield changes on longer-term maturities, in that they experience greater price fluctuations for a given yield change. This subjects the holder of a longer-term security to greater risk, and therefore a higher expected yield is required.

Table 10–3 (on the next page) taken from *The Globe and Mail* identifies several government and corporate bond issues that trade regularly in the financial markets. Prices are expressed as a percentage of the face value of the bond. For example the Air Canada bond price at 72.00 is 72 percent of a $1,000 face value bond or $720. The coupon rate of 6.750 percent, calculated on the $1,000 face value, obligates Air Canada to pay $67.50 a year on a semiannual basis. Therefore $33.75 every six months is to be paid.

Air Canada
www.aircanada.ca/about-us

Notice the variations in yields based on maturity dates and the different risks of the bonds. The Air Canada bond is set to mature on February 2, 2004 when the face value is payable, Based on the price and future expected coupon and face value payment the bond promises a yield to maturity of 25.22 percent. The high yield suggests high risk and the market's expectation that all those future commitments may not be paid.

Until now we have used yield to maturity as well as other factors, such as the interest rate on the bond and number of years to maturity, to determine the price of the bond. We now assume we know the price of the bond, the interest rate on the bond, and the years to maturity, and we wish to determine the yield to maturity. Once we have

TABLE 10–3

An example of bond quotes, January 19, 2002

CANADIAN BONDS

Provided by RBC Capital Markets. Selected quotations, with changes since the previous day, on actively traded bond issues yesterday. Yields are calculated to full maturity. Price is the final bid-side price as of 5 pm yesterday.

issuer	coupon	maturity	price	yield	price $ chg
GOVERNMENT OF CANADA					
Canada	11.750	Feb 01/03	109.48	2.36	-0.01
Canada	7.250	Jun 01/03	106.22	2.55	0.04
Canada	5.750	Jun 01/03	104.24	2.55	0.04
Canada	5.250	Sep 01/03	103.82	2.80	0.05
Canada	7.500	Dec 01/03	108.06	3.00	0.05
Canada	5.000	Dec 01/03	103.57	3.01	0.05
Canada	10.250	Feb 01/04	113.80	3.17	0.05
Canada	6.500	Jun 01/04	106.99	3.39	0.06
Canada	5.000	Sep 01/04	103.48	3.59	0.07
Canada	9.000	Dec 01/04	114.05	3.76	0.07
Canada	12.000	Mar 01/05	123.02	4.03	0.12
Canada	12.250	Sep 01/05	127.07	4.09	0.15
Canada	6.000	Sep 01/05	106.24	4.12	0.14
Canada	8.750	Dec 01/05	115.98	4.21	0.15
Canada	5.750	Sep 01/06	105.17	4.49	0.20
Canada	14.000	Oct 01/06	139.63	4.52	0.23
Canada	7.000	Dec 01/06	110.45	4.57	0.21
Canada	7.250	Jun 01/07	111.87	4.71	0.27
Canada	4.500	Sep 01/07	98.67	4.77	0.28
Canada	6.000	Jun 01/08	105.72	4.94	0.34
Canada	10.000	Jun 01/08	127.58	4.89	0.43
Canada	5.500	Jun 01/09	102.38	5.11	0.36
Canada	9.750	Mar 01/10	129.05	5.29	0.45
Canada	9.500	Jun 01/10	128.96	5.18	0.46
Canada	5.500	Jun 01/10	101.78	5.23	0.40
Canada	9.000	Mar 01/11	126.35	5.31	0.55
Canada	6.000	Jun 01/11	105.25	5.28	0.47
Canada	5.250	Jun 01/12	99.40	5.33	0.51
Canada	10.250	Mar 15/14	142.76	5.40	0.64
Canada	11.250	Jun 01/15	155.13	5.40	0.72
Canada	9.750	Jun 01/21	147.70	5.66	0.66
Canada	9.250	Jun 01/22	142.29	5.71	0.64
Canada	8.000	Jun 01/23	127.59	5.74	0.69
Canada	9.000	Jun 01/25	141.45	5.75	0.75
Canada	8.000	Jun 01/27	130.29	5.72	0.77
Canada	5.750	Jun 01/29	101.95	5.61	0.70
Canada	5.750	Jun 01/33	103.45	5.52	0.68
CMBT	5.527	Jun 15/06	103.98	4.52	0.19
CMBT	4.750	Mar 15/07	99.91	4.77	0.22
CMHC	5.000	Jun 01/04	103.44	3.46	0.07
PROVINCIAL					
Alberta	6.375	Jun 01/04	106.53	3.46	0.06
B C	7.750	Jun 16/03	106.89	2.68	0.04
B C	5.250	Dec 01/06	102.04	4.77	0.21
B C	6.000	Jun 09/08	104.34	5.19	0.32
B C	6.375	Aug 23/10	105.25	5.60	0.41
B C	5.750	Jan 09/12	100.39	5.70	0.47
B C	8.500	Aug 23/13	122.66	5.79	0.59
Ontario	7.600	Jun 02/27	118.88	6.12	0.78
Ontario	6.500	Mar 08/29	105.48	6.08	0.68
Ontario Hyd	9.000	Jun 24/02	102.87	2.06	-0.01
Ontario Hyd	5.375	Jun 02/03	103.60	2.65	0.04
Ontario Hyd	7.750	Nov 03/05	111.89	4.30	0.15
Ontario Hyd	5.600	Jun 02/08	102.35	5.16	0.31
Ontario Hyd	8.250	Jun 22/26	126.44	6.14	0.60
Quebec	7.500	Dec 01/03	107.90	3.08	0.05
Quebec	6.500	Dec 01/05	107.45	4.38	0.17
Quebec	6.500	Oct 01/07	107.06	5.05	0.26
Quebec	11.000	Apr 01/09	132.46	5.47	0.35
Quebec	5.500	Jun 01/09	99.91	5.51	0.31
Quebec	6.250	Dec 01/10	103.56	5.73	0.37
Quebec	8.500	Apr 01/26	126.63	6.33	0.68
Quebec	6.000	Oct 01/29	96.17	6.29	0.58
Quebec	6.250	Jun 01/32	99.82	6.26	0.62
Saskatchewan	5.500	Jun 02/08	101.51	5.22	0.31
Saskatchewan	8.750	May 30/25	131.17	6.20	0.75
Toronto -Met	6.100	Aug 15/07	104.81	5.09	0.27
Toronto -Met	6.100	Dec 12/17	100.19	6.08	0.58
CORPORATE					
AGT Limited	8.800	Sep 22/25	101.77	8.62	0.49
Air Canada	6.750	Feb 02/04	72.00	25.22	0.00
Avco Fin	5.750	Jun 02/03	103.85	2.83	0.04
Bank Of Mont	7.000	Jan 28/10	108.63	5.65	0.39
Bank Of Mont	6.903	Jun 30/10	103.80	6.31	0.39
Bank Of Mont	6.647	Dec 31/10	101.84	6.37	0.40
Bank Of Mont	6.685	Dec 31/11	101.48	6.48	0.46
Bank Of N S	5.400	Apr 01/03	102.98	2.82	0.03
Bank Of N S	6.250	Jul 16/07	105.22	5.14	0.27
Bank Of N S	7.310	Dec 31/10	106.58	6.33	0.42
Bell Canada	6.250	Dec 01/03	104.98	3.45	0.05
Bell Canada	6.500	May 09/05	106.54	4.34	0.09
Can Cred Tst	5.625	Mar 24/05	103.92	4.29	0.11
Cards Trust	5.510	Jun 21/03	103.60	2.88	0.05
Coca-Cola	5.650	Mar 17/04	103.66	3.85	0.06
DlmrCCFin	6.600	Jun 03/03	103.53	3.90	0.04
DlmrCCFin	6.600	Jun 21/04	103.95	4.84	0.06
Domtar Inc	10.000	Apr 15/11	108.88	8.58	0.39
Ford Credit	5.730	Dec 01/03	101.63	4.80	0.05
Ford Credit	6.000	Mar 08/04	102.18	4.90	0.06
Ford Credit	6.650	Jun 20/05	102.22	5.92	0.13
Genesis Trus	6.869	Feb 15/05	107.82	4.12	0.11
GoldCred	5.700	Aug 15/06	103.84	4.75	0.20
Grtr TTO Air	5.400	Dec 03/02	102.45	2.50	0.01
Grtr TTO Air	5.950	Dec 03/07	102.90	5.36	0.28
Grtr TTO Air	6.700	Jul 19/10	104.38	6.03	0.40
Grtr TTO Air	6.450	Dec 03/27	94.12	6.94	0.54
Grtr TTO Air	6.450	Jul 30/29	93.37	7.00	-0.10
Grtr TTO Air	7.050	Jun 12/30	101.33	6.94	0.59
Grtr TTO Air	7.100	Jun 04/31	101.97	6.94	0.60
Gtc Trans	6.200	Jun 01/07	97.71	6.71	0.24
Gulf Can Res	6.450	Oct 01/07	102.06	6.01	0.27
HolRecTst	5.672	Apr 26/06	103.96	4.63	0.18
HSBC	7.780	Dec 31/10	106.87	6.74	0.41
HydroOne	6.940	Jun 03/05	108.52	4.19	0.09
HydroOne	7.150	Jun 03/10	108.60	5.83	0.41
HydroOne	7.350	Jun 03/30	109.95	6.57	0.66
IADB	5.625	Jun 29/09	102.25	5.26	0.79
Interprv Pip	8.200	Feb 15/24	114.35	6.92	0.59
Legacy	5.930	Nov 15/02	100.96	4.70	0.01
Loblaws Co	6.650	Nov 08/27	97.92	6.82	0.56
Milit - Air	5.750	Jun 30/19	99.34	5.81	0.67
MLI	5.700	Feb 16/06	104.02	4.60	0.16
MLI	6.240	Feb 16/11	102.14	5.93	0.44
MLI	6.700	Jun 30/12	102.02	6.43	0.48

Source: Data provided by ILX Systems, a division of Thomson Information Services Inc.

computed this value, we have determined the rate of return investors are demanding in the marketplace to provide for inflation, risk, and other factors.

Let's once again present Formula 10–1.

$$P_b = \sum_{t=1}^{n} \frac{I_t}{(1 + Y)^t} + \frac{P_n}{(1 + Y)^n}$$

We now try to determine the value of Y, the yield to maturity, that equates the interest payments (I_t) and the principal payment (P_n) to the price of the bond (P_b). This is similar to the calculations to determine yield in the previous chapter.

Assume a 15-year bond pays $110.00 per year (11 percent) in interest and $1,000 after 15 years in principal repayment. The current price of the bond is $932.89.

We wish to determine the yield to maturity, or discount rate, that equates future flows with the current price.[3]

---

[3]An approximate yield formula is given by:

$$\text{Approximate yield to maturity } (Y') = \frac{\text{Annual interest payment} + \dfrac{\text{Principal payment} - \text{Price of the bond}}{\text{Number of years to maturity}}}{0.6\,(\text{Price of the bond}) + 0.4\,(\text{Principal payment})}$$

This formula is recommended by Gabriel A. Hawawini and Ashok Vora, "Yield Approximations: A Historical Perspective," *Journal of Finance* 37 (March 1982), pp. 145–56. It tends to provide the best approximation.

Calculator

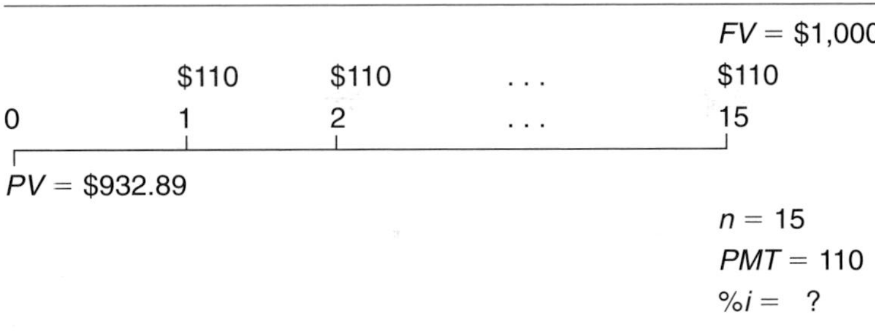

$i = 12\%$.

Tables (optional) Tables require a trial-and-error process (as does the calculator when its screen temporarily goes blank). The first step is to choose an initial percentage in the tables to try as the discount rate. Since the bond is trading below the par value of $1,000, we know the yield to maturity (discount rate) must be above the quoted interest rate of 11 percent. By the trial-and-error process, a 12 percent discount rate brings us:

Total Present Value

Present value of interest payments	$749.21
Present value of principal payment at maturity	183.00
Total present value, or price, of the bond	$932.21

The answer closely approximates the price of $932.89 for the bond being evaluated. That indicates that the correct yield to maturity for the bond is 12 percent. If the computed value were slightly different from the price of the bond, we could use interpolation to arrive at the correct answer. An example of interpolating to derive yield to maturity is presented in Appendix 10A.

Semiannual Interest and Bond Prices

Until now in our bond analysis, we have been considering examples where interest was paid annually. However, most bonds in Canada and the United States pay interest semiannually. Thus, a 10 percent interest rate bond may actually pay $50.00 twice a year instead of $100.00 annually. To make the conversion from an annual to semiannual analysis, we follow three steps.

1. Divide the annual interest rate by two.
2. Multiply the number of years by two.
3. Divide the annual yield to maturity by two.

Deutsche Bundesbank
www.bundesbank.de/index_html_en.htm
(check out Federal Securities under financial markets)

Assume a 10 percent, $1,000 par value bond has a maturity of 20 years. The annual yield to maturity is 12 percent. In following the preceding three steps, we would show:

1. 10%/2 = 5% semiannual interest rate; therefore, 5% × \$1,000 = \$50 semiannual interest.
2. 20 × 2 = 40 periods to maturity.
3. 12%/2 = 6% yield to maturity, expressed on a semiannual basis.

In computing the price of the bond issued, on a semiannual analysis, we show:

Calculator

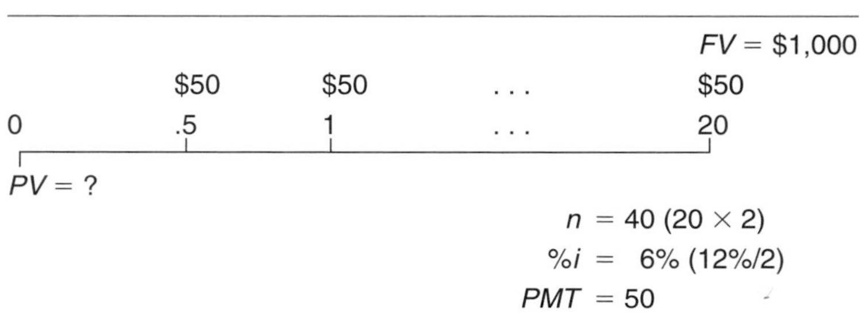

PV = \$849.54.

The answer of PV = \$849.54 is slightly below that which we found previously for the same bond, assuming an annual interest rate (\$850.61). In terms of accuracy, the semiannual analysis is a more acceptable method and is the method used in bond tables. As is true in many finance texts, the annual interest rate approach is given first for ease of presentation, and then the semiannual basis is given. In the problems at the back of the chapter, you will be asked to do problems on both an annual and semiannual interest payment basis.

Tables (optional) *Total present value*

(PV_A) Present value of interest payments	\$752.30
(PV) Present value of principal payment at maturity	97.00
Total present value, or price, of the bond	\$849.30

Valuation and Preferred Stock

Preferred stock usually represents a **perpetuity**. In other words, it has no maturity date. It is valued in the market without any principal payment since it has no ending life. If preferred stock had a maturity date, the analysis would be similar to that of the preceding bond example. Preferred stock has a fixed, expected dividend payment carrying a higher order of precedence than common stock dividends, but not the binding contractual obligation of interest on debt. Preferred stock, being a hybrid security, has neither the ownership privilege of common stock nor the legally enforceable provisions of debt. To value a perpetuity such as preferred stock, we first consider the formula:

$$P_p = \frac{D_p}{(1 + K_p)^1} + \frac{D_p}{(1 + K_p)^2} + \frac{D_p}{(1 + K_p)^3} + \ldots + \frac{D_p}{(1 + K_p)^x} \qquad (10\text{–}2)$$

represented graphically as

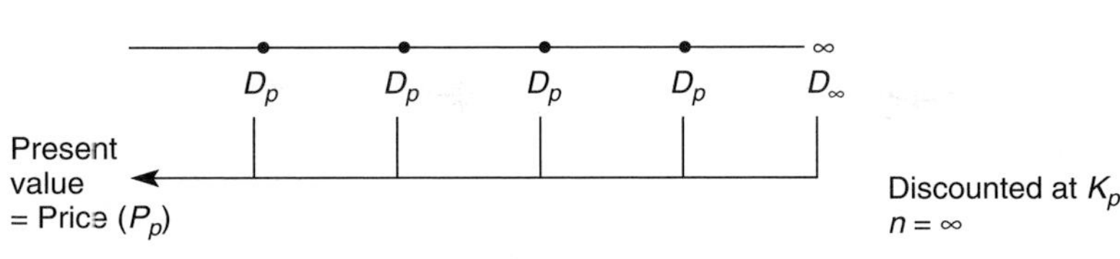

where

P_p = Price of preferred stock
D_p = Annual dividend for preferred stock (a constant value)
K_p = Required rate of return, or discount rate, applied to preferred stock dividends

Note that the formula calls for taking the present value of an infinite stream of constant dividend payments at a discount rate equal to K_p. This discount rate of K_p also consists of the three factors influencing yield that were discussed under bond valuation. Because we are dealing with an infinite stream of payments, Formula 10–2 can be reduced to a much more usable form, as indicated in Formula 10–3.

$$P_p = \frac{D_p}{K_p} \qquad (10\text{–}3)$$

According to Formula 10–3, all we have to do to find the price of preferred stock (P_p) is to divide the constant annual dividend payment (D_p) by the required rate of return that preferred shareholders are demanding (K_p). For example, if the annual dividend were $10.00 and the shareholder required a 10 percent rate of return, the price of preferred stock would be $100.00.

$$P_p = \frac{D_p}{K_p} = \frac{\$10}{.10} = \$100$$

As was true in our bond valuation analysis, if the rate of return required by security holders changes, the value of the financial asset (in this case, preferred stock) changes. You may also recall that the longer the life of an investment, the greater the impact of a change in required rate of return. It is one thing to be locked into a low-paying security for one year when the rate goes up; it is quite another to be locked in for 10 or 20 years. With preferred stock, you have a *perpetual* security, so the impact is at a maximum. Assume in the prior example that because of higher inflation or increased business risk, K_p (the required rate of return) increases to 12 percent. The new value for the preferred stock shares then becomes:

$$P_p = \frac{D_p}{K_p} = \frac{\$10}{.12} = \$83.33$$

If the required rate of return were reduced to 8 percent, the opposite effect would occur. The preferred stock price would be recomputed as:

$$P_p = \frac{D_p}{K_p} = \frac{\$10}{.08} = \$125$$

It is not surprising that preferred stock is now trading well above its original price of \$100.00. It is still offering a \$10.00 dividend (10 percent of original offering price of \$100.00), while the market is demanding only an 8 percent yield. To match the \$10.00 dividend with the 8 percent rate of return, the market price will advance to \$125.00.

Determining the Required Rate of Return (Yield) from the Market Price

In our analysis of preferred stock, we have used the value of the annual dividend (D_p) and the required rate of return (K_p) to solve for the price of preferred stock (P_p). We could change our analysis to solve for the required rate of return (K_p) as the unknown, given that we knew the annual dividend (D_p) and the preferred stock price (P_p). We take Formula 10–3 and rewrite it as Formula 10–4, where the unknown is the required rate of return (K_p).

$$P_p = \frac{D_p}{K_p} \text{ (reverse the position of } K_p \text{ and } P_p\text{)} \qquad (10\text{–}3)$$

$$K_p = \frac{D_p}{P_p} \qquad (10\text{–}4)$$

Using Formula 10–4, if the annual preferred dividend (D_p) is \$10.00 and the price of preferred stock (P_p) is \$100.00, the required rate of return (yield) would be 10 percent.

$$K_p = \frac{D_p}{P_p} = \frac{\$10}{\$100} = 10\%$$

If the price goes up to \$130, the yield will be only 7.69 percent.

$$K_p = \frac{\$10}{\$130} = 7.69\%$$

We see that the rise in market price causes quite a decline in the yield.

Valuation of Common Stock

Investors place value on common shares based on the firm's ability to generate cash flow or earnings and the risks attached to those expected earnings. The value of a common share to the shareholder is the claim on the residual earnings of the firm. These earnings will flow to the shareholder as dividends in current periods or at some time in the future, possibly as a liquidating dividend at the end of the corporation's life. Therefore, the value of a share of common stock can be seen as the *present value* of an expected stream of *future dividends.*

Shareholders will be influenced by a change in earnings, a change in the risks faced by the firm, or by other variables, but the ultimate value of any holding rests with the distribution of earnings in the form of dividend payments. Though the shareholder may benefit from the retention and reinvestment of earnings by the corporation, at some point the earnings must be translated into cash flow for the shareholder. A stock valuation model based on future expected dividends can be stated as:

$$P_0 = \frac{D_1}{(1 + K_e)^1} + \frac{D_2}{(1 + K_e)^2} + \frac{D_3}{(1 + K_e)^3} + \ldots + \frac{D_x}{(1 + K_e)^x} \qquad (10\text{–}5)$$

where

P_0 = Price of the stock today
D = Dividend for each year
K_e = Required rate of return for common stock (discount rate)

With modification, this **dividend valuation model** formula is generally applied to three different circumstances:

1. No growth in dividends.
2. Constant growth in dividends.
3. Variable growth in dividends.

No Growth in Dividends

Under the no-growth circumstance, common stock is similar to preferred stock. The common stock pays a constant dividend each year. For that reason we merely translate the terms in Formula 10–4, which applies to preferred stock, to apply to common stock. This is shown as new Formula 10–6.

$$P_0 = \frac{D_0}{K_e} \tag{10–6}$$

where

P_0 = Price of common stock today
D_0 = Current annual common stock dividend (a constant value)
K_e = Required rate of return for common stock

Assume D_0 = \$1.86 and K_e = 12 percent; the price of stock would be \$15.50.

$$P_0 = \frac{\$1.86}{.12} = \$15.50$$

A no-growth policy for common stock dividends does not hold much appeal for investors and so is seen infrequently in the real world.

Constant Growth in Dividends

A firm that increases dividends at a constant rate is a more likely circumstance. Perhaps a firm decides to increase its dividends by 5 or 7 percent per year. Under such a circumstance, Formula 10–5 converts to Formula 10–7.

$$P_0 = \frac{D_0(1+g)^1}{(1+K_e)^1} + \frac{D_0(1+g)^2}{(1+K_e)^2} + \frac{D_0(1+g)^3}{(1+K_e)^3} + \ldots + \frac{D_0(1+g)^x}{(1+K_e)^x} \tag{10–7}$$

represented graphically as

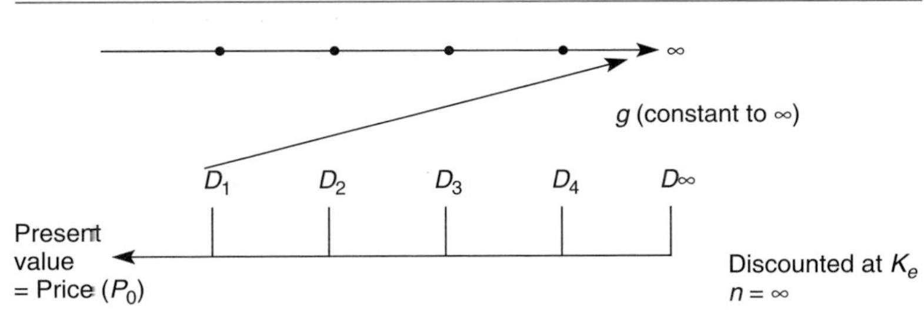

where

$$\begin{aligned} P_0 &= \text{Price of common stock today} \\ D_0(1+g)^1 &= \text{Dividend in year 1, } D_1 \\ D_0(1+g)^2 &= \text{Dividend in year 2, } D_2\text{, and so on} \\ g &= \text{Constant growth rate in dividends} \\ K_e &= \text{Required rate of return for common stock (discount rate)} \end{aligned}$$

In other words, the current price of the stock is the present value of the future stream of dividends growing at a constant rate. If we can anticipate the growth pattern of future dividends and determine the discount rate, we can ascertain the price of the stock.

For example, assume the following information:

$$\begin{aligned} D_0 &= \text{Latest 12-month dividend (assume \$1.87)} \\ D_1 &= \text{First year, \$2.00 (growth rate, 7\%)} \\ D_2 &= \text{Second year, \$2.14 (growth rate, 7\%)} \\ D_3 &= \text{Third year, \$2.29 (growth rate, 7\%) etc.} \\ K_e &= \text{Required rate of return (discount rate), 12\%} \end{aligned}$$

then

$$P_0 = \frac{\$2.00}{(1.12)^1} + \frac{\$2.14}{(1.12)^2} + \frac{\$2.29}{(1.12)^3} + \ldots + \frac{\text{Infinite dividend}}{(1.12)^x}$$

To find the price of the stock, we take the present value of each year's dividend. This is no small task when the formula calls for us to take the present value of an *infinite* stream of growing dividends. Fortunately, Formula 10–7 can be compressed into a much more usable form if two circumstances are satisfied.

1. The dividend growth rate (g) must be constant to infinity.
2. The discount rate (K_e) must exceed the growth rate (g).

These assumptions are usually made to reduce the complications in the analytical process. They then allow us to reduce or rewrite Formula 10–7 as Formula 10–8. Formula 10-8 is the basic formula for finding the value of common stock and is referred to as the dividend valuation model.

$$P_0 = \frac{D_1}{K_e - g} \qquad (10\text{–}8)$$

This is an extremely easy formula to use in which:[4]

[4]To derive this relationship we multiply both sides of Formula 10–7 by $(1 + K_e)/(1 + g)$ and subtract Formula 10–7 from the product. The result is

$$\frac{P_0(1 + K_e)}{(1 + g)} - P_0 = D_0 - \frac{D_0(1 + g)^\infty}{(1 + K_e)^\infty}$$

Because K_e is larger than g, the last term on the right side goes to zero because of the infinite exponent. That leaves us with

$$P_0\left[\frac{1 + K_e}{1 + g} - 1\right] = D_0$$

$$P_0\left[\frac{(1 + K_e) - (1 + g)}{1 + g}\right] = D_0$$

$$P_0(K_e - g) = D_0(1 + g)$$

$$P_0 = \frac{D_1}{K_e - g}$$

P_0 = Price of the stock today
D_1 = Dividend at the end of the first year (or period)
K_e = Required rate of return (discount rate)
g = Constant growth rate in dividends

Based on the current example:

$$D_1 = \$2.00$$
$$K_e = .12$$
$$g = .07$$

and P_0 is computed as:

$$P_0 = \frac{D_1}{K_e - g} = \frac{\$2.00}{.12 - .07} = \frac{\$2.00}{.05} = \$40$$

Thus, given that the stock has a \$2.00 dividend at the end of the first period, a discount rate of 12 percent, and a constant growth rate of 7 percent, the current price of the stock is \$40.00.

Let's take a closer look at Formula 10–8 and the factors that influence valuation. For example, what is the anticipated effect on valuation if K_e (the required rate of return, or discount rate) increases as a result of inflation or increased risk? Intuitively, we would expect the stock price to decline if investors demand a higher return and the dividend and growth rate remain the same. This is precisely what happens.

If D_1 remains at \$2.00 and the growth rate (g) is 7 percent but K_e increases from 12 percent to 14 percent, using Formula 10–8, the price of the common stock would now be \$28.57. This is considerably lower than its earlier value of \$40.00.

$$P_0 = \frac{D_1}{K_e - g} = \frac{\$2.00}{.14 - .07} = \frac{\$2.00}{.07} = \$28.57$$

Similarly, if the growth rate (g) increases while D_1 and K_e remain constant, the stock price can be expected to increase. Assume D_1 = \$2.00, K_e is set at its earlier level of 12 percent, and g increases from 7 percent to 9 percent. Using Formula 10–8 once again, the new price of the stock would be \$66.67.

$$P_0 = \frac{D_1}{K_e - g} = \frac{\$2.00}{.12 - .09} = \frac{\$2.00}{.03} = \$66.67$$

We should not be surprised to see that an increasing growth rate has enhanced the value of the stock.

Determining the Inputs for the Dividend Valuation Model

Our model for valuation based on future dividends seems reasonable, but where do we find the numbers for the model that allow us to determine the share price. Dividends are fairly accessible, if they are paid, and are found in annual reports or at various investment sites. An appropriate required return for the common shares (K_e) can be estimated using CAPM, examined further in Appendix 11-A, or by using the current yield for long-term Government of Canada bonds to which a risk premium is added, based on the riskiness of the common shares. This yield to maturity concept is discussed briefly under bond valuation earlier in this chapter.

FINANCE IN ACTION

Estimating Value with the Dividend Capitalization Model

Q1 Can you suggest any reasons for a difference between the market share price and the model's share value?

www.thomsoninvest.net

www.globeinvestor.com

Symbol: RY

Historical earnings are available in annual reports, accessible at company web sites or at the SEDAR site (www.sedar.com) for publicly traded companies. Several investment sites provide earnings estimates for Canadian companies, although the information is often in U.S.$ (watch carefully). An example is www.nasdaq-canada.com.

We will estimate the share value of the Royal Bank of Canada (RY) using the dividend capitalization model as of the first week of February 2002.

$D_0 = \$1.38$
from TSX site: financial snapshot

$K_e = 11.67\%$
6% (for risk) plus 5.67% (Government of Canada bond rate (10+)) from Bank of Canada site (www.bankofcanada.ca/en)

$g = 8.51\%$
Average of 7.74% (www.thomson-invest.net) and 9.28% (Globeinvestor through www.tse.com)

$$D_1 = D_0 \times (1 + g) = \$1.38 \times (1.0851) = \$1.50$$

$$P_0 = \frac{D_1}{K_e - g} = \frac{\$1.50}{} = \$47.47$$

The actual price of Royal Bank shares at this time was $47.90. With the same methodology you should be able to calculate a value for a Royal Bank's share today with the dividend capitalization model.

It is the value for growth (g) that will require some effort on our part. This is the long-run growth rate for the firm. What we can do is examine the historical growth rate of the firm and project it into the future, adjusting for any micro (firm related) or macro (overall economy) factors that we believe will cause the growth rate to change. New technologies, changing government regulations, economic slowdowns, and external shocks such as wars may be some of the events that might alter our growth estimates.

The historical growth rates are best estimated from dividends, but we could also use the growth in earnings per share, revenues per share or cash flow per share if one or the other of these items is not readily available. We might also use an alternative entry if there is possible distortion of one or more of the historical growth rates. In fact, determining the growth rates for all of these entries would give us a broader picture of the probable growth rate for the firm.

If for example, the earnings per share figure five years ago was $1.50 and the last reported earnings per share was $2.10, the historical growth rate would be 7 percent.

Calculator

$PV = (1.50)$	$FV = 2.10$
$PMT = 0$	$n = 5$

Compute $i = 7\%$.

Stock Valuation Based on Future Stock Value The discussion of stock valuation to this point has related to the concept of the present value of future dividends. This is a valid concept, but suppose we wish to approach the issue from a slightly different viewpoint. Assume we are going to buy a stock and hold it for three years and then sell it. We wish to know the present value of our investment. This is somewhat like the bond valuation analysis. We receive a dividend for three years (D_1, D_2, D_3) and then a price (payment) for the stock at the end of three years (P_3). What is the present value of the benefits? What we do is add the present value of three years of dividends and the present value of the stock price after three years. Assuming a constant-growth dividend analysis, the stock price after three years is simply the present value of all future dividends after the third year (from the fourth year on). Thus, the current price of the stock in this case is nothing other than the present value of the first three dividends, plus the present value of all future dividends (which is equivalent to the stock price after the third year). Saying the price of the stock is the present value of all future dividends is also the equivalent of saying it is the present value of a dividend stream for a number of years plus the present value of the price of the stock after that time period. The appropriate formula is still $P_0 = D_1/(K_e - g)$, which we have been using throughout this part of the chapter.

Determining the Required Rate of Return from the Market Price

In our analysis of common stock, we have used the first year's dividend (D_1), the required rate of return (K_e), and the growth rate (g) to solve for the stock price (P_0) based on Formula 10–8.

$$P_0 = \frac{D_1}{K_e - g} \quad \text{(previously presented Formula 10–8)}$$

We could change the analysis to solve for the required rate of return (K_e) as the unknown, given that we know the first year's dividend (D_1), the stock price (P_0), and the growth rate (g). We take Formula 10–8 and algebraically change it to provide Formula 10–9.

$$P_0 = \frac{D_1}{K_e - g} \qquad (10\text{–}8)$$

$$K_e = \frac{D_1}{P_0} + g \qquad (10\text{–}9)$$

This formula allows us to compute the required return (K_e) from the investment. Returning to the basic data from the common stock example:

K_e = Required rate of return (to be solved)
D_1 = Dividend at the end of the first year \$2.00
P_0 = Price of the stock today \$40.00
g = Constant growth rate .07

$$K_e = \frac{\$2.00}{\$40.00} + 7\% = 5\% + 7\% = 12\%$$

In this instance we would say that the shareholder demands a 12 percent return on the common stock investment. Of particular interest are the individual parts of the formula for K_e that we have been discussing. Let's write out Formula 10–9 again.

$$K_e = \frac{\text{First year's dividend}}{\text{Common stock price}} \left(\frac{D_1}{P_0}\right) + \text{Growth } (g)$$

The first term represents the **dividend yield** the shareholder receives, and the second term represents the anticipated growth in dividends, earnings, and stock price. While we have been describing the growth rate primarily in terms of dividends, it is assumed that the earnings and stock price also grow at that same rate over the long term if all else holds constant. Observe that the preceding formula represents a total return concept. The shareholder is receiving a current dividend plus anticipated growth in the future. If the dividend yield is low, the growth rate must be high to provide the necessary return. Conversely, if the growth rate is low, a high dividend yield is expected. The concepts of dividend yield and growth are clearly interrelated.

The Price-Earnings Ratio Concept and Valuation

In Chapter 2 we introduced the concept of the **price-earnings ratio (P/E).** The price-earnings ratio represents a multiplier applied to current earnings to determine the value of a share of stock in the market. It is considered a pragmatic, everyday approach to valuation. If a stock has earnings per share of $3.00 and a price-earnings (P/E) ratio of 12 times, it carries a market value of $36.00. Another company with the same earnings but a P/E ratio of 15 times enjoys a market price of $45.00.

The price-earnings ratio is influenced by the earnings and sales growth of the firm, the risk (or volatility in performance), the debt-equity structure of the firm, the dividend policy, the quality of management, and a number of other factors. Firms that have bright expectations for the future tend to trade at high P/E ratios, while the opposite is true of low P/E firms. It is because of those future expectations of earnings that one should be careful in applying historical P/E ratios to current earnings.

Toronto Stock Exchange
www.tsx.ca

In early 2002 the average P/E for the top 300 companies of the Toronto Stock Exchange (the S&P/TSX Composite Index) was negative 46 to 1. Normally this is a positive number, but Nortel and JDS Uniphase had suffered losses of about $70 billion in 2001. This overwhelmed the P/E ratio for the S&P/TSX Composite Index companies' average. The S&P/TSX Composite Index Unweighted Index had a positive P/E ratio of 33.31.

There was a large variation among firms based on their future earnings expectations and earnings at that moment. The fabricating firms of the industrial products section, which included Nortel and JDS had a P/E of negative 469, whereas the transportation sector had a positive P/E ratio of 58 to 1.

Globe and Mail
www.globeandmail.com

Price-earnings ratios can be looked up in many financial newspapers and at several web sites. Quotations from the Saturday *Globe and Mail* are presented in Table 10–4. Note the columns that show the annual dividend and the dividend yield. The P/E ratio is also given. For Bank of Montreal (BMO) it was 12.8, indicating that the current price closing price of $34.71 represented 12.8 times current annual earnings of $2.72 per share.[5] The remaining columns show the high and low prices for the year; high, low, and closing prices for the week; dividend yield; P/E ratio; and earnings per share. Also included is the stock symbol, which is used by the exchange and many web sites to identify the stock.

The P/E ratio represents an easily understood, pragmatic approach to valuation that is widely used by stockbrokers and individual investors. The dividend valuation approach (based on the present value of dividends) we have been using throughout the chapter is more theoretically sound and is likely to be used by sophisticated financial

[5]The price-earnings ratio is not shown for some companies because they do not have positive earnings on which to base the calculation, or because the preferred stock of the company is shown, in which case the P/E ratio is not relevant because preferred stock does not have earnings per share as such.

TABLE 10–4

An example of stock quotations, January 19, 2002

Source: Data Provided by ILX Systems, a division of Thomson Information Services Inc.

ILX Systems
www.ILX.com

stock trends	RSI	365-day high	365-day low	stock	sym	div	friday hi/bid	friday lo/ask	friday chg	friday vol(h)	this week hi/bid	this week lo/ask	this week close	this week chg	this week vol(h)	yld	shr prof	p/e ratio
⬇	74–	10.50	0.86	Bakbone	BKB		1.27	1.20	–0.03	778	1.44	1.20	1.20	–0.15	4253		–0.43	
⇩	130–	118.00	22.00	Ballard	BLD		54.66	53.27	–1.59	1440	55.00	51.20	53.39	–0.60	8272		–1.59	
⇩	84+	1.27	0.34	Band Ore	BAN		0.55	0.52	–0.04	284	0.58	0.51	0.52	–0.05	1027		–0.02	
⬇	87–	44.40	32.75	♣ Bank Mtl	BMO	1.12	35.28	34.58	–0.44	17243	36.35	34.58	34.71	–1.44	81108	3.23	2.72	12.8
☆	90+	27.20	25.01	♣ BkMtl	BMO.PR.F	1.39	26.64	26.64	–0.06	z 1	26.75	26.49	26.64	+0.14	287	5.21		
	92+	26.20	24.25	♣ BkMt	BMO.PR.G	1.20	26.18	26.10	+0.15	467	26.18	26.00	26.15	+0.06	1385	4.59		
⬆	89+	25.30	22.60	♣ BkMt	BMO.PR.H	1.32	25.00	24.80	–0.10	68	25.00	24.50	24.80	+0.22	630	5.34		
☆	92+	26.05	24.00	♣ Bk Mtl	BMO.PR.I	1.19	26.02	25.90	+0.07	373	26.05	25.85	26.02	–0.03	870	4.56		
⬆	96–	50.74	37.30	♣ Bank NS	BNS	1.36	48.10	47.50	+0.42	10788	48.39	47.13	48.10	–0.01	57856	2.83	4.12	11.7
☆	89+	26.99	25.50	♣ Bk NS	BNS.PR.E	1.79	26.00	26.00	+0.15	3	26.00	25.85	26.00	–0.20	114	6.87		
☆	91+	27.60	26.21	♣ Bk NS	BNS.PR.F	1.77	26.50	26.50	–0.20	5	26.70	26.21	26.50	–0.15	50	6.70		
☆	90+	28.20	26.54	♣ Bk NS	BNS.PR.G	1.75	27.26	27.26	–0.18	9	27.45	27.22	27.26	+0.06	208	6.42		
☆	90+	28.00	26.75	♣ Bk NS	BNS.PR.H	1.69	27.70	27.65	+0.35	10	27.70	27.35	27.70	+0.20	58	6.09		
☆	90+	28.00	26.00	♣ Bk NS	BNS.PR.I	1.50	27.45	27.45	+0.25	24	27.60	26.95	27.45	+0.51	116	5.46		
⬆☆	91+	25.10	22.50	♣ Bk NS	BNS.PR.J	1.31	24.80	24.60	–0.20	86	24.80	23.90	24.60	+0.60	729	5.33		
		.514	.514	♣ Barnwell	BNW	0.50				nt			.514		nt	97.28	4.48	0.1
⇩	98+	29.65	21.10	♣ Barrick	ABX	0.35	27.48	26.89	–0.67	21305	28.08	26.89	27.03	–0.47	131742	1.31	–3.03	
⬆	**104+**	**4.40**	**0.99**	**Basis 100**	**BAS**		**4.34**	**4.01**	**–0.39**	**7462**	**4.40**	**3.79**	**4.01**	**–0.09**	**18071**		**–1.05**	
⇩☆	147–	0.63	0.12	Battery Tech	BTI		.315	.305	+.005	337	0.33	0.30	.315	–.005	4241		–0.03	
⬇☆	80–	14.84	3.00	Baytex Enr	BTE		4.20	4.07	–0.05	891	4.28	3.95	4.10	–0.18	6417		0.32	12.8
	87–	0.76	0.09	Beamscop	BSP					nt			0.13		nt		–9.03	
⬆☆	101–	7.00	4.50	Becker	BEK.B	0.60	6.80	7.25		nt	6.75	6.75	6.75	–0.25	1	8.89	0.76	8.9
⬇	65+	4.96	1.65	♣ BelAir En	BEC		1.88	1.80		85	1.88	1.75	1.80		731		0.54	3.3
⬆	88+	26.85	24.10	Bell	BC.PR.A	1.38	25.70	25.50	+0.20	12	25.70	25.20	25.70	+0.20	122	5.35		
	90+	26.25	24.00	Bell	BC.PR.B	1.31	25.39	25.30	+0.19	16	25.39	25.05	25.39	+0.39	297	5.17		
	88+	27.00	24.51	BellCd	BC.PR.C	1.39	25.25	25.25	–0.05	5	25.50	25.10	25.25	+0.01	298	5.49		
⇩★	115–	14.00	3.00	Belzberg	BLZ		5.50	5.10		74	5.50	4.40	5.40	+0.85	4186		–0.14	
⬆★	82–	0.87	0.30	♣ Bema Gl j	BGO		0.60	0.56		1440	0.61	0.55	0.58	–0.02	28421		0.45	1.3
⬆☆	179–	11.25	3.40	♣ Bennett	BEV		10.90	10.55	+0.20	175	10.98	10.55	10.90	–0.05	643		0.07	155.7
⇧☆	90–	3.10	2.40	Benvest Ca	BCI		2.45	2.70		nt	2.45	2.45	2.45	–0.01	1			
⬇	72–	1.60	0.80	Best Pacifi	BPG		0.99	0.98	–0.01	64	1.04	0.98	0.99	–0.03	568		0.19	5.2
⇩	137+	1.85	0.90	Bestar	BES		1.36	1.50		nt	1.50	1.31	1.40	+0.09	55		0.06	23.3
□☆	66–	1.13	0.50	Big Horn	BGH					nt			0.50		nt		0.09	5.6
⇩☆	95+	5.75	4.00	Big Rock	BR		4.51	4.75		nt	4.75	4.50	4.75	+0.15	13		0.27	17.6
⬇	79–	14.80	5.33	Biomira	BRA		6.51	6.33	–0.03	253	6.51	6.27	6.44	–0.09	1814		–0.82	
⇩	111+	3.70	2.05	Bioniche Li	BNC		3.38	3.30	+0.15	608	3.40	3.15	3.35	+0.10	2004		–0.09	
⇩	72–	3.90	1.00	Bioscrypt	BYT		1.98	1.85	+0.01	420	2.00	1.85	1.86	–0.14	3804		–0.60	
⬆	106+	91.00	45.80	Biovail Crp	BVF		88.10	85.50	+0.54	3221	88.10	82.10	86.00	+0.71	15871		3.69	23.3
⇩	103+	0.31	0.13	♣ Birim Gold	BGI		0.20	0.20	–0.04	165	0.24	0.19	0.20	+0.02	749		–0.03	
⬇	86+	.195	.065	Black Ha j	BHK		0.10	.095		2535	.105	0.09	0.10		7979		0.02	5.0
⬇	79–	0.38	0.14	Black Swn	BSW		0.18	0.18	–.005	36	0.20	0.18	0.18		1456		–0.01	
⬆★	**83+**	**1.30**	**0.81**	**BlackRock**	**BVI**		**1.25**	**1.12**	**+0.10**	**962**	**1.25**	**1.00**	**1.20**	**+0.10**	**14365**		**0.01**	**120.0**
⬇	89–	13.00	10.00	♣ Boardwalk	BEI	0.05	11.88	11.80		7	12.25	11.65	11.80	–0.10	4228	0.42	0.06	196.7
⬆☆	114–	0.89	0.31	Bocenor	GBO		0.65	0.70		nt	0.65	0.62	0.62	–0.06	24		–1.00	
☆		19.904	2.58	Boliden	BLS		6.75	6.75	–0.01	30	7.25	6.75	6.75	–0.50	60		–2.55	
⇩	119+	24.95	9.25	BombrA	BBD.A	0.18	15.44	15.06	–0.10	447	15.44	14.20	15.15	–0.06	18235	1.19	0.36	42.1
⇩	121+	24.74	9.19	BmbrB	BBD.B	0.18	15.44	15.00		20193	15.44	14.25	15.25		173664	1.19	0.36	42.4
⬇☆	95+	26.50	22.00	BmbrB	BBD.PR.B	1.38	23.60	23.60	–0.10	50	24.05	23.51	23.60	–0.25	442	5.83		
⬇	84–	34.75	21.75	Bonavista	BNP		26.91	25.60	+0.80	134	26.91	25.60	26.80	+0.35	1942		3.35	8.0
⬇	79–	5.20	1.85	♣ Boomrng	BMG		2.80	2.71	–0.05	282	2.90	2.71	2.75	–0.15	908		0.10	27.5
⬆	143+	11.95	5.48	Boralex	BLX.A		10.00	9.75	–0.15	1749	10.00	9.50	9.75	–0.06	2736		0.31	31.4
⇩	103–	0.30	0.04	Bovar	BVR.A	0.20	.065	0.06		2515	.075	0.06	0.06	–0.01	5252		0.12	0.5
⬆☆	92+	1.85	0.86	Bow Valley	BVX		1.45	1.40	–0.05	822	1.45	1.35	1.40		2178		0.25	5.6
⬆☆	95–	82.00	65.00	Bowater	BWX	1.22	74.00	73.75	–0.25	5	74.07	72.40	73.75	–2.25	52	1.65	3.34	22.1
⇩★	163–	2.40	1.01	♣ Boyd	BYD.A		2.20	2.15		172	2.30	2.10	2.15	+0.14	1067		0.19	11.3
⬇★	1–	10.00	0.04	♣ Bracknell	BRK					nt			0.06		nt		0.83	0.1
⇩	140+	2.10	0.21	Bradst	BEP.A		0.75	0.75	+0.10	10	0.75	0.60	0.75	+0.15	557		–0.14	
⇩☆	215+	2.00	0.21	Bradston	BEP.B		0.75	0.75	+0.15	10	0.75	0.60	0.75	+0.15	25			
⬇☆	95+	0.50	0.05	Brainium	BNU		0.10	0.08	+0.01	860	0.10	0.08	0.09	+.015	1580		–0.16	
⬆★	147–	11.95	5.40	Bram	BBL.A		11.25	11.25	–0.05	13	11.75	11.25	11.25	–0.10	181		0.99	11.4
⇩☆	90+	0.15	.005	Brandselite	BNT					nt			.015		nt		–0.11	
	89–	44.00	40.75	Brasc	BCA.PR.B	3.23	43.50	43.90		nt	43.35	43.25	43.25	–0.75	5	7.46	0.97	44.6
⬆	100+	29.60	21.20	Brascan	BNN.A	1.00	29.04	28.50	–0.50	1202	29.60	28.45	28.59	–0.21	13056	3.50	1.75	16.3
⬆	**90+↑**	**26.25**	**18.50**	**Bras**	**BNN.PR.A**	**0.82**	**26.25**	**26.25**	**+2.25**	**2**	**26.25**	**26.25**	**26.25**	**+2.25**	**2**	**3.13**		
⬇☆	85+	18.75	16.00	Bras	BNN.PR.B	0.89	17.00	17.00	+0.16	3	17.00	16.84	17.00		37	5.21		
⬇☆	84–	19.25	16.00	Bras	BNN.PR.C	0.89	17.00	17.00	+0.50	z 81	17.55	16.55	17.00	+0.50	z 94	5.21		
⬇☆	92–	25.00	22.50	Brasc	BNN.PR.E	0.92	24.30	24.20	+0.20	5	24.30	24.00	24.20	–0.19	47	3.79		
★		26.00	23.75	Bras	BNN.PR.G		25.50	25.50		3	25.60	25.39	25.50		205			
	91+	26.39	24.75	Bras	BNN.PR.H	1.44	26.00	25.75		74	26.39	25.75	26.00		1272	5.53		
		24.85	24.40	Brasc	BNN.PR.S		24.60	24.53		500	24.60	24.53	24.58	–0.02	2640			
⇩	129+	1.65	0.14	Breakwatr	BWR		0.32	0.30	+0.02	3470	0.32	0.24	0.32	+0.07	15741		–1.45	
⬇☆	76+	0.75	0.30	Brick j	BRB		.415	.415	–.005	10	0.44	0.40	.415	–.075	224		0.12	3.5
⬇	41–↓	0.67	0.04	BridgePoint	BDG		.045	0.04	–.005	1237	0.05	0.04	0.04	–0.01	13960		–0.29	
⬆	151–	4.20	1.25	♣ Bridges.co	BIT		3.90	3.75	+0.15	45	3.95	3.75	3.90	–0.05	152		–0.13	
⬇☆	153+	87.00	65.00	British Air	BAB	3.91	48.50	53.50		nt	48.50	53.50	65.00		nt	6.02	6.80	9.6
⇩	136+	3.60	0.20	Brocker Tec	BKI		0.45	0.40	+0.05	57	0.45	0.35	0.45	+0.10	197		–1.35	
⬇	91+	31.90	23.10	Brookfield	BPO	0.64	27.41	27.19	+0.21	413	27.41	26.70	27.40	+0.40	5377	2.35	2.07	13.2
⇩	121+	11.75	7.00	Budd Cda	BUD	1.00	10.25	10.95		nt	10.75	10.00	10.75	+1.00	50	9.30	–25.00	
⬆	95+	3.86	3.20	Buhler	BUI	0.11	3.85	3.75	+0.17	39	3.85	3.68	3.85	+0.07	420	2.86	0.30	12.8
⇩	125+	5.70	1.25	Burntsand	BRT		2.52	2.40	+0.07	773	2.52	2.15	2.42	+0.22	3381		–0.18	
★	82–	2.59	1.09	Bushmils	BSH		1.17	1.17		12	1.20	1.17	1.17	–0.03	239		–0.01	
☆	91+	10.05	9.20	BusinDvl	BDB.O		9.58	9.64		nt	9.52	9.52	9.52	+0.01	10			
⬇	90+	10.10	8.50	BusinDvl	BDB.Q		10.00	10.00	+0.15	5	10.00	9.80	10.00	+0.20	550			
		11.00	9.90	Busine	BDB.RT		10.10	10.00	+0.10	350	10.10	9.95	10.10	–0.20	455			
☆	93+	10.05	9.71	BusnsDv	BDB.X		9.93	10.00		nt	9.98	9.98	9.98	+0.06	31			
		10.00	9.50	Busine	BDB.WD		9.80	9.79	+0.30	12	9.80	9.50	9.80		17			
	92+	10.03	9.52	Business	BDB.C		9.85	10.25		nt	10.00	9.85	9.85	+0.09	37			
⬆☆	91–	9.20	7.25	BusinDvl	BDB.G		8.25	8.40		nt	8.25	8.25	8.25	–0.10	8			
☆	92+	9.35	7.68	Busines	BDB.M		7.99	7.99	–0.03	11	8.05	7.99	7.99	–0.01	43			
	93–	**11.25**	**8.25**	**BusnsDv**	**BDB.Y**		**10.50**	**10.00**	**+0.75**	**5**	**10.50**	**9.75**	**10.50**	**+0.50**	**35**			

FINANCE IN ACTION

Valuation of Small Businesses

SB The value of a small business takes on importance when the business is sold as part of a divorce settlement, for estate purposes, or when the owner wishes to retire. Unlike a firm trading in the public securities market, there is no ready market for a local bookstore, a bowling alley, or an accountant's practice. Lower liquidity decreases the value assigned the business.

Another factor affecting value is the importance of a key person in the operation of the business. If the founder of the business is critical to its functioning, the goodwill established by the owner will often diminish after he or she departs, resulting in declining cash flows and a loss of value.

Earnings of a small business are often lower than a publicly traded company. The owners of small businesses often intermingle personal and business expenses. Family use of cars, health insurance, travel, and so on, may be charged as business expenses even when Revenue Canada tries to restrict the practice. Furthermore small, private businesses try to report earnings as low as possible to minimize taxes. Publicly traded companies report quarterly often attempting to show ever increasing profits to boost share prices. Analysts will carefully examine the earnings reports of the small business making necessary adjustments that may increase the stated earnings.

The average small business usually sells at 5 to 10 times average adjusted earnings for the previous three years. Sale prices on comparable businesses are also considered in the valuation. Accountants and financial analysts with experience in similar business valuations can be of immense help.

analysts. To some extent, the two concepts can be brought together. A stock that has a high required rate of return (K_e) because of its risky nature generally has a low P/E ratio. Similarly, a stock with a high expected growth rate (g) normally has a high P/E ratio. In the first example, both methods provide a low valuation, while in the latter case, both methods provide a high valuation.

Variable Growth in Dividends

In the discussion of common stock valuation, we have considered procedures for firms that had no growth in dividends and for firms that had a constant growth. Most of the discussion and literature in finance assumes a constant growth dividend model. However, there is also a third case, and that is one of variable growth in dividends. The most common variable growth model is one in which the firm experiences very rapid or **supernormal growth** for a number of years and then levels off to more normal, constant growth. The supernormal growth pattern is often experienced by firms in emerging industries, such as in the early days of electronics or microcomputers.

In evaluating a firm with an initial pattern of supernormal growth, we first take the present value of dividends during the exceptional growth period. We then determine the price of the stock at the end of the supernormal growth period by taking the present value of the normal, constant dividends that follow the supernormal growth period. We discount this price to the present and add it to the present value of the supernormal dividends. This gives us the current price of the stock. A numerical example of a supernormal growth rate evaluation model is presented in Appendix 10B at the end of this chapter.

Finally, in the discussion of common stock valuation models, readers may ask about the valuation of companies that currently pay no dividends. Since virtually all of our

Diamonds, Nickel, Gold, or the Internet; for Value?

Share prices for several Canadian companies over the last decade represent a fascinating look at valuation based on future expected cash flows that were highly speculative.

In 1991 Dia Met Minerals Ltd., shares traded between $0.26 and $6.50. In 1992 the shares traded as high as $60.00 and the equity in Dia Met was worth $600 million. One year earlier, with a share price of $0.26, the equity value had been less than $2 million. Dia Met Minerals, which had little in the way of hard assets, had never paid a dividend and was worth $600 million. Investors had bid up the price of the shares based on the promise of future cash flows. Quality diamonds had been discovered in the Northwest Territories. By 1999, mining production began to generate cash flows from those diamonds. Diamet was acquired by BHP Ltd. trading on the Australian Stock Exchange.

As a result of the rush to find diamonds in Canada, another company, Diamond Fields Resources, Inc., was formed to locate diamonds and for $450,000 they sponsored two prospectors. In 1993 a rust-coloured outcrop of rock on a hill near Voisey's Bay, Labrador contained one of the world's richest deposits of nickel, copper, and cobalt. In the fall of 1994 Diamond Fields stock traded for $3.55, and by 1996 it was trading at over $160 per share (adjusted for stock splits). Inco purchased Diamond Fields for $4.3 billion, even though no full-scale mining had begun. The value, established by Inco bidding in the securities market, was based on the promised returns from this rich mineral deposit in the future. In 1996 nickel sold at about $3.80 a pound and the future looked bright, but by 1998 nickel sold for less than $2.00 per pound and Voisey's Bay was mothballed. By 2002 Inco was again looking at production at Voisey's Bay.

On the Alberta Stock Exchange, a share in the company Bre-X soared in value from a few dollars in early 1995 to over $240.00 by mid-1996 on the strength of possibly one of the largest gold finds in the world. Bre-X was touted as having perhaps 200 million ounces of gold in the wilds of Borneo, and value was established on the belief of future earnings that would come from this discovery. However, by 1997 it was apparent that Bre-X was a hoax, and the shares plunged in value to almost nothing. Some people were prepared to pay a few pennies for Bre-X shares, as souvenirs.

Investors become excited about future potential revenues that may hopefully result in profits. Internet companies created a 'bubble' in share prices for high-tech companies through 1999 and 2000. Some suggested that the Internet, with its effect on the economy, had changed valuation standards. Our earlier study of Nortel showed that valuation standards may vary but seem to eventually show their true worth.

FINANCE IN ACTION

Q1 Is Inco planning at present to develop Voisey's Bay?

Q2 How have the share prices of Nortel, Inco, and BHP performed over the last year?

www.inco.com
Symbol: N

www.nortelnetworks.com
Symbol: NT

www.diamet.com

www.asx.com.au

discussion has been based on values associated with dividends, how can this no-dividend circumstance be handled? One approach is to assume that even for the firm that pays no current dividends, at some point in the future shareholders will be rewarded with cash dividends. We then take the present value of their deferred dividends.

A second approach to valuing a firm that pays no cash dividend is to take the present value of earnings per share for a number of periods and add that to the present value of the last earnings per share, valued as a perpetuity. The discount rate applied to future earnings is generally higher than the discount rate applied to future dividends.

Chapter Summary and Review of Formulas

1. The primary emphasis in this chapter is on valuation of financial assets: bonds, preferred stock, and common stock. Regardless of the security being analyzed, valuation is normally based on the concept of determining the present value of future cash flows. Thus, we draw on many of the time-value-of-money techniques developed in Chapter 9.
2. Inherent in the valuation process is a determination of the rate of return demanded by investors. The rate of return is also referred to as the discount rate, or yield to maturity. We note

that the required rate of return is composed of a real rate of return, an inflation premium, and a risk premium based on the uncertainty of the future expected cash flows. When we have identified the rate of return required by investors, we have also identified what it will cost the corporation to raise new capital.

3., 4. In the section below, we specifically review the valuation techniques associated with bonds, preferred stock, and common stock.

Bonds

The price, or current value, of a bond is equal to the present value of interest payments (I_t) over the life of the bond plus the present value of the principal payment (P_n) at maturity. The discount rate used in the analytical process is the yield to maturity (Y). The yield to maturity (required rate of return) is determined in the marketplace by such factors as the *real* rate of return, an inflation premium, and a risk premium.

The formula for bond valuation was presented as Formula 10–1.

$$P_b = \sum_{t=1}^{n} \frac{I_t}{(1 + Y)^t} + \frac{P_n}{(1 + Y)^n} \qquad (10\text{–}1)$$

Calculator

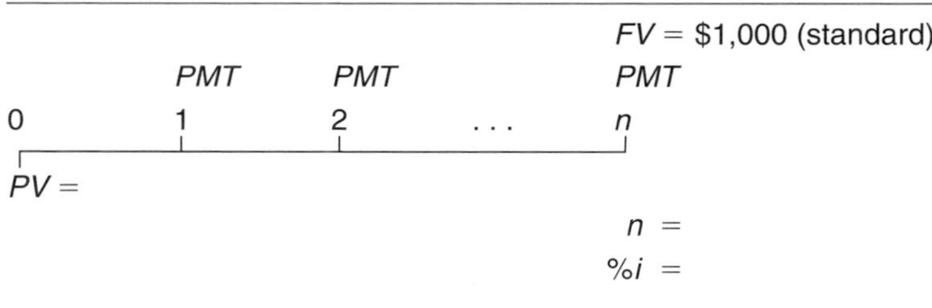

Bonds fit the pattern described by the above graphical representation. Usually, we are concerned with determining the current price of the bond or its yield. The other variables are likely known.

Tables (optional)

We say the present value of interest payments is:

$PV_A = A \times PV_{IFA}$ (n =________, i =________) (Appendix D)

while the present value of the principal payment at maturity is:

$PV = FV \times PV_{IF}$ (n =________, i =________ ,) (Appendix B)

Adding these two values together gives us the price of the bond. We may use annual or semiannual analysis.

The value of the bond is strongly influenced by the relationship of the yield to maturity in the market to the interest rate on the bond and also the length of time to maturity.

If we know the price of the bond, the size of the interest payments, and the maturity of the bond, we can solve for the yield to maturity, as discussed in Appendix 10A.

Preferred Stock

In determining the value of preferred stock, we are taking the present value of an infinite stream of level dividend payments. This would be a tedious process if it were not for the fact that the mathematical calculations can be compressed into a simple formula. The appropriate formula is Formula 10–3.

$$P_p = \frac{D_p}{K_p} \tag{10–3}$$

According to Formula 10–3, to find the preferred stock price (P_p) we take the constant annual dividend payment (D_p) and divide this value by the rate of return that preferred shareholders are demanding (K_p).

If, on the other hand, we know the price of the preferred stock and the constant annual dividend payment, we can solve for the required rate of return on preferred stock as:

$$K_p = \frac{D_p}{P_p} \tag{10–4}$$

Common Stock

The value of common stock is also based on the concept of the present value of an expected stream of future dividends. Unlike preferred stock, the dividends are not necessarily level. The firm and shareholders may experience:

1. No growth in dividends.
2. Constant growth in dividends.
3. Variable or supernormal growth in dividends.

It is the second circumstance that receives most of the attention in the financial literature. If a firm has constant growth (g) in dividends (D) and the required rate of return (K_e) exceeds the growth rate, Formula 10–8 can be utilized.

$$P_0 = \frac{D_1}{K_e - g} \tag{10–8}$$

In using Formula 10–8, all we need to know is the value of the dividend at the end of the first year, the required rate of return, and the discount rate. Most of our valuation calculations with common stock utilize Formula 10–8.

If we need to know the required rate of return (K_e) for common stock, Formula 10–9 can be employed.

$$K_e = \frac{D_1}{P_0} + g \tag{10–9}$$

The first term represents the dividend yield on the stock, and the second term represents the growth rate. Together they provide the total return demanded by the investor.

5. The price-earnings ratio represents a multiplier applied to earnings to determine share price. It is an easy rule of thumb used to determine value, but it does not incorporate the dynamics of the other models, including future expected cash flows and today's required rate of return.

List of Terms

discount rate 322
required rate of return 322
yield to maturity 323
real rate of return 325
inflation premium 325
risk-free rate of return 325
risk premium 326
business risk 326
financial risk 326
perpetuity 334

dividend valuation model 337
dividend yield 341
price-earnings ratio (P/E) 342
supernormal growth 344

Discussion Questions

1. How is valuation of financial assets by investors related to the cost of financing (cost of capital) for the firm?
2. How is valuation of any financial asset related to future cash flows?
3. Why might investors demand a lower rate of return for an investment in BCE as compared to Air Canada?
4. What are the three factors that influence the required rate of return by investors?
5. What is meant by real rate of return?
6. If inflationary expectations increase, what is likely to happen to the yield to maturity on bonds in the marketplace? What is also likely to happen to the price of bonds?
7. Why is the remaining time to maturity an important factor in evaluating the impact of a change in yield to maturity on bond prices?
8. These valuation models are based on investors' required rates of return and their reflection in the prices of the assets. Does the change in price always occur according to the model?
9. What three adjustments have to be made in going from annual to semiannual bond analysis?
10. Why is a change in required yield for preferred stock likely to have a greater impact on price than a change in required yield for bonds?
11. What type of dividend pattern for common stock is similar to the dividend payment for preferred stock?
12. What two conditions must be met to go from Formula 10–7 to Formula 10–8 in using the dividend valuation model?

$$P_0 = \frac{D_1}{K_e - g} \quad (10\text{–}8)$$

13. What two components make up the required rate of return on common stock?
14. What factors might influence a firm's price-earnings ratio?
15. How does a firm's price-earnings ratio relate to K_e? to g?
16. How is the supernormal growth pattern likely to vary from the more normal, constant growth pattern?
17. What approaches can be taken in valuing a firm's stock when there is no cash dividend payment?

INTERNET RESOURCES AND QUESTIONS

CIBC WoodGundy has a daily fixed income/daily fact sheet that includes prices and yields on several bond issues:
www.cibcwg.com/research

The Globe and Mail's print edition under money and markets has daily bond prices and yields:
www.globeandmail.com

Ebond is a centre with selected live quotes for Canadian fixed income securities.
www.ebond.ca

Canpx, a bond pricing service of the Investment Dealers Association and Interdealer Brokers Association, has a web site with moneyline telerate and featuring some demos and discussion of the quote services used in the bond trading industry:
www.moneyline.com

ScotiaCapital provides a daily market update for fixed income securities, including a selection of daily benchmark bonds:
www.scotiacapital.com

The Toronto Stock Exchange (TSX) site includes information on listed stocks that include daily and yearly high and low prices, opening prices, volume, e.p.s., P/E ratios, and dividend yields:
www.tsx.ca

Sun Media through its canoe site has stock quotes that include highs, lows, open, e.p.s., P/E ratios, dividend yields, and volumes. It also breaks stocks into industrial groupings:
www.webfin.com/en

The Government of Canada Finance Department provides a technical guide on determining bond prices and yields, as well as definitions of various government bonds:
www.fin.gc.ca/invest/tech-e.html

The Bank of Canada provides current money market and long-term bond yields.
www.bankofcanada.ca/en/rates.htm.

1. What is the price and yield of Government of Canada bonds of 1, 2, 5, 10, and 30 years.
2. Find the price-earnings ratio and dividend yield for today for the following corporations: Abitibi (A), Bell Canada Enterprises (BCE), Imperial Oil (IMO), Molson (MOL.A), Nortel (NT), Open Text (OTC), and Royal Bank Preferred (RY.PR.J). Discuss the reasons for differences in the ratios among these securities.

Problems

1. Burns Fire and Casualty Company has $1,000 par value (maturity value) bonds outstanding at 11 percent interest. The bonds will mature in 20 years with annual payments. Compute the current price of the bonds if the present yield to maturity is:
   a. 6 percent.
   b. 8 percent.
   c. 12 percent.
2. Albert's Imports has $1,000 par value (maturity value) bonds outstanding at 5 percent interest. The bonds will mature in 15 years with annual payments. Compute the current price of the bonds if the present yield to maturity is:
   a. 3 percent.
   b. 4 percent.
   c. 7 percent.
3. Kilgore Natural Gas has a $1,000 par value bond outstanding that pays 9 percent interest with annual payments. The current yield to maturity on such bonds in the market is 12 percent. Compute the price of the bonds for these maturity dates:
   a. 30 years.
   b. 15 years.
   c. 1 year.

4. ClearBell Telecom has a $1,000 par value bond outstanding that pays 8 percent interest with annual payments. The current yield to maturity on such bonds in the market is 5 percent. Compute the price of the bonds for these maturity dates:
   a. 30 years.
   b. 15 years.
   c. 1 year.

5. For the previous problem, graph the relationship in a manner similar to the top half of Figure 10–2. Also explain why the pattern of price change occurs.
6. Al Simmons calls his broker to inquire about purchasing a bond of Disk Storage Systems. His broker quotes a price of $1,180. Al is concerned that the bond might be overpriced based on the facts involved. The $1,000 par value bond pays 14 percent annual interest payable semiannually, and it has 25 years remaining until maturity. The current yield to maturity on similar bonds is 12 percent. Compute the new price of the bond and comment on whether you think it is overpriced in the marketplace.
7. Westlake Drilling Company issued bonds in 1998 at $1,000 per bond. The bonds had a 30-year life when issued, with semiannual payments at the then annual rate of 11 percent. This return was in line with required returns by bondholders at that point as described below:

Real rate of return	3%
Inflation premium	3
Risk premium	5
Total return	11%

   Assume that in 2003 the inflation premium is 2 percent, the risk premium has declined to 3 percent and both are appropriately reflected in the required return (or yield to maturity) of the bonds. The bonds have 25 years remaining until maturity. Compute the new price of the bond.
8. Tom Cruise Lines, Inc., issued bonds ten years ago at $1,000 per bond. The bonds had a 20-year life when issued, with semiannual payments at the then annual rate of 9 percent. This return was in line with required returns by bondholders at that point as described below:

Real rate of return	2%
Inflation premium	5
Risk premium	2
Total return	9%

   Assume that today the inflation premium is only 2 percent and is appropriately reflected in the required return (or yield to maturity) of the bonds. Compute the new price of the bond.

9. Bo Boatler specializes in buying deep discount bonds. These represent bonds that are trading at well below par value. He has his eye on a bond issued by the Quantum Corporation. The $1,000 par value bond with semiannual payments has 5 percent annual interest and has 10 years remaining to maturity. The current yield to maturity on similar bonds is 11 percent.
   a. What is the current price of the bonds?
   b. By what percent will the price of the bonds increase between now and maturity?
   c. What is the annual compound rate of growth in the value of the bonds? (An approximate answer is acceptable.)

10. Bonds issued by the Crane Optical Company have a par value of $1,000, which is also the amount of principal to be paid at maturity. The bonds are currently selling for $942. They have 8 years to maturity. Annual interest is 7 percent ($70) paid semiannually. Compute the yield to maturity.

11. Bonds issued by the West Motel Chain have a par value of $1,000, are selling for $1,100, and have 20 years remaining to maturity. Annual interest payment is 13.5 percent ($135), paid semiannually. Compute the yield to maturity.

12. Ann Nichols is considering a bond investment in the Southwest Technology Company. The $1,000 bonds have a quoted annual interest rate of 8 percent, and the interest is paid semiannually. The yield to maturity on the bonds is 10 percent annually. There are 25 years to maturity. Compute the price of the bonds.

13. You are called in as a financial analyst to appraise the bonds of the Holtz Corporation. The $1,000 par value bonds have a quoted annual interest rate of 14 percent, which is paid semiannually. The yield to maturity on the bonds is 12 percent annually. There are 15 years to maturity.
    a. Compute the price of the bonds.
    b. With 10 years remaining to maturity, if yield to maturity goes down substantially to 8 percent, what will be the new price of the bonds?

14. Douglas bonds mature in 10 years and have an annual coupon rate of 10.5 percent with semiannual payments. The $1,000 par value bond currently trades at $1,105 in the market. Compute the annual yield to maturity on the Douglas bond.

15. A $1,000 par value bond has a 5 percent coupon, which is paid on a semiannual basis. It matures in either 1 year or 15 years. Current yields on similar bonds are either 3 percent or 7 percent.
    a. Calculate the price of the bond for the 4 possibilities.
    b. What is the relationship between price and yield?
    c. What is the relationship between bond price changes and time to maturity?

16. A preferred share of Ultra Corp. pays an annual dividend of $6.30. It has a required rate of return of 9 percent. Compute the price of a preferred share.

17. Airdrie Lanes preferred shares pay an annual dividend of $1.20, payable on a quarterly basis. Current yields of similar risk preferred shares are 3 percent. What is the price of each preferred share?

18. North Pole Cruise Lines issued preferred shares many years ago. They carry a fixed dividend of $6.00 per share. With the passage of time, yields have soared from the original 6 percent to 14 percent (yield is the same as required rate of return).
    a. What was the original issue price?
    b. What is the current value of a North Pole preferred share?
    c. If the yield on the Preferred Stock Index declines, how will the price of these preferred shares be affected?

19. Venus Sportswear Corporation has preferred shares outstanding that pay an annual dividend of $12.00. Each has a price of $110.00. What is the required rate of return (yield) on the preferred stock?

20. B2Y Solutions has preferred shares outstanding that pay an annual dividend of $3, payable quarterly. Each has a price of $75.00. What is the required rate of return (yield) on the preferred stock?

www.mcgrawhill.ca/college/block

21. Static Electric Co. currently pays a \$2.10 annual cash dividend (D_0). It plans to maintain the dividend at this level for the foreseeable future, as no future growth is anticipated. If the required rate of return by common shareholders (K_e) is 12 percent, what is the price of each common share?

22. BioScience, Inc., will pay a common share dividend of \$3.20 at the end of the year (D_1). The required return on common shares (K_e) is 14 percent. The firm has a constant growth rate (g) of 9 percent. Compute the current price of the shares (P_0).

23. Husky Kennels will pay a quarterly common share dividend of \$0.20 at the end of the next quarter. The required return on common shares is 8 percent and the firm has a constant growth rate of 3 percent. Compute the price of a common share of Husky.

24. Ecology Labs, Inc., will pay a dividend of \$3.00 per share in the next 12 months (D_1). The required rate of return (K_e) is 9 percent and the constant growth rate is 4 percent.

    a. Compute P_0.

    (For the remaining questions in this problem, all variables remain the same except the one specifically changed. Each question is independent of the others.)

    b. Assume K_e, the required rate of return, goes up to 11 percent, what will be the new value of P_0?

    c. Assume the growth rate (g) goes up to 6 percent, what will be the new value of P_0?

    d. Assume D_1 is \$2, what will be the new value of P_0?

25. Maxwell Communications paid a dividend of \$3.00 last year. Over the next 12 months, the dividend is expected to grow at 8 percent, which is the constant growth rate for the firm. The new dividend after 12 months will represent D_1. The required rate of return is 14 percent. Compute the price of a common share.

26. Haltom Enterprises has had the following pattern of earnings per share over the last five years:

Year	Earnings per Share
1998	\$3.00
1999	3.18
2000	3.37
2001	3.57
2002	3.78

    The earnings per share have grown at a constant rate (on a rounded basis) and will continue to do so in the future. Dividends represent 30 percent of earnings.

    a. Project earnings and dividends for the next year (2003). Round all values in this problem to two places to the right of the decimal point.

    b. If the required rate of return is 10 percent, what is the anticipated share price at the beginning of 2003?

27. Inferno Firewalls Ltd. will pay a \$4.90 dividend at the end of year one, has a share price of \$70.00, and a constant growth rate of 6 percent. Compute the required rate of return.

28. Triple Peaks Playhouse will pay a quarterly dividend of \$0.40 at the end of the next quarter, has common share price of \$32.00, and a constant growth rate of 4 percent. Compute the required rate of return.

29. A firm pays a \$1.90 dividend at the end at year one, has a share price of \$40.00 (P_0), and a constant growth rate (g) of 8 percent.

a. Compute the required rate of return (K_e). Also indicate whether each of the following changes would make the required rate of return (K_e) go up or down.

(In each question below, assume only one variable changes at a time. No actual numbers are necessary.)

b. The dividend payment increases.

c. The expected growth rate increases.

d. The stock price increases.

30. Cellular Systems paid a \$3.00 dividend last year. The dividend is expected to grow at a constant rate of 5 percent forever. The required rate of return is 12 percent (this will also serve as the discount rate in this problem). Round all values to three places to the right of the decimal point where appropriate.

a. Compute the anticipated value of the dividends for the next three years. That is, compute D_1, D_2, and D_3; for example, D_1 is \$3.15 (\$3.00 × 1.05). Round all values throughout this problem to three places to the right of the decimal point.

b. Discount each of these dividends back to the present at a discount rate of 12 percent and then sum them.

c. Compute the price of the stock at the end of the third year (P_3).

$$P_3 = \frac{D_4}{K_e - g}$$

(D_4 is equal to D_3 times 1.05)

d. After you have computed P_3, discount it back to the present at a discount rate of 12 percent for three years.

e. Add together the answers in part *b* and part *d* to get P_0, the current value of the stock. This answer represents the present value of the first three periods of dividends, plus the present value of the price of the stock after three periods (which, in turn, represents the value of all future dividends).

f. Use Formula 10–8 to show that it will provide approximately the same answer as part *e*.

$$P_0 = \frac{D_1}{K_e - g} \qquad (10\text{–}8)$$

For Formula 10–8 use $D_1 = \$3.15$, $K_e = 12$ percent, and $g = 5$ percent. (The slight difference between the answers to part *e* and part *f* is due to rounding.)

(And for more fun and review, do these valuation problems.)

31. What is the value of a common share that has just paid a dividend of \$2.25, is expecting an indefinite annual growth rate of 5 percent, and requires a return of 17 percent based on perceived market risks?

32. Calculate the price of a bond originally issued seven years ago that pays semiannual interest at the rate of 11 percent and matures in eight years at \$1,000. The market currently requires a 7 percent return for a bond of this risk.

33. The Tahitian Lottery has promised an annual stipend of \$75,000 forever and permanent residency on Tahiti. Assuming interest rates of 6 percent, how much must the Tahitian authorities set aside today to guarantee this stipend?

34. A bond just purchased pays annual interest of 10 percent. In seven years it matures at its face value of \$25,000. What price was paid if current yields on a bond of this risk are 8.5 percent?

35. Burrito Bell issued a series of $1,000 bonds eight years ago with an annual coupon rate of $100. The bonds mature 12 years from now. If an investor requires a 6 percent return on this investment, what would be the price of a Burrito Bell bond?

36. Current yields are 9 percent on a preferred share that pays a perpetual annual dividend of $6.00. What is the appropriate price of one preferred?

37. With an anticipated dividend of $1.20, continual annual growth of 8 percent, and a market expectation of a 19 percent yield, at what price would a common share sell?

38. You wish to invest $175,000 in a 12-year annuity. Current yields over the same time to maturity are 8 percent. What could you expect as an annual payment?

39. You have purchased a preferred share that promises a $3.00 dividend. If you expect a 14 percent yield, what price did you pay for the preferred?

40. Waterman Company has had a fantastic growth of 22 percent per year, but this growth rate is expected to fall to 6 percent in the near future and then continue at that rate for a long time. Shareholders expect a 17 percent annual rate of return and a dividend of $0.75 next year. What is the share price of Waterman's common stock?

41. Lou Spence bought a stock seven years ago for $15.00 a share. If it is now selling for $42.39 a share, what is the stock's compound annual growth rate? (No dividends were paid.)

42. You are interested in receiving a true yield on a government bond investment of 8 percent. Your broker suggests a 20-year issue with 12 years to maturity, an original coupon rate of 10 percent, payable semiannually, and a face value of $10,000. The bond has had its coupons stripped, so you won't receive the coupon payments. What price will you pay?

43. A national financial institution is currently offering $50,000 a year for life as a special promotion. Current inflation is 2 percent a year, and the real rate of return is assumed to be 3 percent. One could suggest that this financial institution would receive a 2 percent premium for the risk inherent in its long-term investments. Assuming you will live forever, how much will this promise cost the financial institution today when you win?

44. Thunderbay Ltd. has a 20-year bond outstanding that matures in 14 years. The annual coupon rate is 11 percent, paid semiannually. Current annual nominal yields for bonds of similar risk are 9 percent. What is the price of this bond?

45. Royal Blue Bonds were purchased nine years ago at $1,000, with a 13 percent annual coupon. Today they are sold for $1,215. Assuming the coupons were reinvested at 9 percent, what was the annual yield actually received?

46. Baffin College has an endowment that pays one lucky student $7,500 a year forever; of course, it is a different student each year. Long-term yields are 10 percent.
    a. How much is currently required to fund the endowment?
    b. If the endowment will not commence until five years from today, how much is required?

COMPREHENSIVE PROBLEM

47. Tom Gilbert, founder and chairman of the board of Gilbert Enterprises, could not believe his eyes as he read the quote about his firm in *The Globe and Mail.* The stock had closed at $35.25, down $3.75 for the week. He called his vice president of finance, Jane Arnold, and they agreed to meet on Saturday morning at 9:00 a.m. for breakfast.

    When Jane arrived, they reviewed the stock's performance for the last few months. Although the stock opened the year (2002) at $28.50 per share, it had reached a high of $50.00 in

March, but had steadily slid in value to its current level of $35.25 in mid-May. Tom and Jane both thought the stock was undervalued in the marketplace and were seriously considering an announcement that the firm was going to repurchase up to one million of its own shares in the open market beginning on June 1 of 2002. They thought that would send a message to investors that the market had placed the stock at an unrealistically low level.

Before taking any action, they decided to consult with their investment banking representative, Albert Roth, senior vice president at the investment firm of Baker, Green and Roth. Roth had aided the firm in initially selling its stock to the public (going public) five years ago and was quite familiar with its operations. Although he was surprised to receive their call during an early Saturday morning round of golf at the country club, he promised to get back to them in the next few days with his recommendation on a stock repurchase.

Gilbert Enterprises was the third largest firm in the auto parts replacement industry, specializing in brake parts, power transmissions, batteries, cables, and other products related to used automobiles. Although most of the auto industry advertising relates to flashy new cars, Albert Roth knew that the auto parts replacement industry was becoming increasingly important.

His research indicated that the average age of an automobile life had reached eight years in 2002, up from a mere 6.8 years in the mid-1990s. Why? New vehicle price increases have far surpassed the rise in consumer income. People are forced to keep their old cars longer whether they want to or not. Furthermore, environmental legislation mandated more emission inspections and maintenance programs. Consumers were being forced to spend more money to update older automobiles to meet these standards.

Gilbert Enterprises had the most advanced just-in-time (JIT) inventory management system in the industry. For that reason, Albert Roth believed the firm would enjoy supernormal growth beyond industry standards for the next three years. His best estimate was that a 15 percent growth rate during that time period was entirely reasonable. After that time span, a more normal growth rate of 6 percent was expected. Current dividends were $1.20 per share, and he decided to use a discount or required rate of return of 10 percent.

He discussed this approach with his partners, and while they generally agreed, they suggested that he also consider a more traditional approach of comparing the firm's price-earnings ratio to other firms in the industry. Price-earnings data along with other information are shown in Figure 1 for Gilbert Enterprises and three other firms in the industry.

a. What recommendation would you suggest that Albert Roth make? Do you suggest the firm is under- or overvalued?

	Gilbert Enterprises	Reliance Parts	Standard Auto	Allied Motors
Annual growth in EPS (Last five years)	12.0%	8.0%	7.0%	9.0%
Return on shareholders' equity	18.0%	25.3%	14.0%	15.3%
Return on total assets	12.1%	8.1%	10.5%	9.8%
Debt to total assets	33.0%	68.0%	25.0%	36.0%
Market value	$35.25	$70.50	$24.25	$46.75
Book value	$16.40	$50.25	$19.50	$50.75
Replacement value	$43.50	$68.75	$26.00	$37.50
Dividend yield	3.40%	2.18%	5.26%	3.12%
P/E ratio	16.8	24.1	14.2	18.1

FIGURE 1
Comparative Data for Auto Parts Replacement Firms

Selected References

Arnold, Tom, and Jerry James. "Finding Firm Value without a Pro Forma Analysis." *Financial Analysts Journal* 56 (March–April 2000), pp. 77–84.

Beaves, Robert G. "A Comment on Interpreting Rates of Return: A Modified Rate-of-Return Approach." *Financial Practice and Education* 4 (Fall–Winter 1994), pp. 136–37.

Evans, Martin D. "Real Rates, Expected Inflation, and Inflation Risk Premia," *Journal of Finance* 53 (February 1998), pp. 187–218.

Good, Walter R. "When Are Price/Earnings Ratios Too High-or Too Low?" *Financial Analysts Journal* 47 (July–August 1991), pp. 9–12, 15.

Klein, Linda S., and Dogan Tirtirogiu. "Valuation Process and Market Efficiency for U.S. Treasury Bonds." *Financial Management* 26 (Winter 1997), pp. 74–80.

Linsmeier, Thomas J., and Neil D. Pearson. "Value at Risk." *Financial Analysts Journal* 56 (March–April 2000), pp. 57–67.

Patrick, Steven C. "Three Pieces to the Capital Structure Puzzle: The Cases of Alco Standard, Comdisco and Revco." *Journal of Applied Corporate Finance* 7 (Winter 1995), pp. 53–61.

Raad, Elias, and Robert Ryan. "Capital Structures and Ownership Distribution of Tender Offer Targets: An Empirical Study." *Financial Management* 25 (Spring 1995), pp. 46–57.

Sinquefield, Rex A. "Are Small-Stock Returns Achievable?" *Financial Analysts Journal* 47 (January-February 1991), pp. 45–50.

APPENDIX 10A

The Bond Yield to Maturity Using Interpolation

As demonstrated in the body of the chapter, this calculation is much easier and more accurate if a financial calculator is used. However, here we use a numerical example to demonstrate this process. Assume a 20-year bond pays $118 per year (11.8 percent) in interest and $1,000 after 20 years in principal repayment. The current price of the bond is $1,085. We wish to determine the yield to maturity, or discount rate, that equates the future flows with the current price.

Because the bond is trading above par value at $1,085, we can assume the yield to maturity must be below the quoted interest rate of 12 percent (the yield to maturity would be the full 12 percent at a bond price of $1,000). As a first approximation, we try 10 percent. Annual analysis is used.

Present value of interest payments—

$$PV_A = A \times PV_{IFA} \quad (n = 20, i = 10\%) \qquad \text{(Appendix D)}$$
$$PV_A = \$118 \times 8.514 = \$1{,}004.65$$

Present value of principal payment at maturity—

$$PV = FV \times PV_{IF} \quad (n = 20, i = 10\%) \qquad \text{(Appendix B)}$$
$$PV = \$1{,}000 \times .149 = \$149$$

Total present value—

Present value of interest payments	$1,004.65
Present value of principal payment at maturity	149.00
Total present value, or price, of the bond	$1,153.65

The discount rate of 10 percent gives us too high a present value in comparison to the current bond price of $1,085. Let's try a higher discount rate to get a lower price. We will use 11 percent.

Present value of interest payments—

$$PV_A = A \times PV_{IFA} \quad (n = 20, i = 11\%) \qquad \text{(Appendix D)}$$
$$PV_A = \$118 \times 7.963 = \$939.63$$

Present value of principal payment at maturity—

$$PV = FV \times PV_{IF} \quad (n = 20, i = 11\%) \qquad \text{(Appendix B)}$$
$$PV = \$1{,}000 \times .124 = \$124$$

Total present value—

Present value of interest payments	$ 939.63
Present value of principal payment at maturity	124.00
Total present value, or price, of the bond	$1,063.63

The discount rate of 11 percent gives us a value slightly lower than the bond price of $1,085. The rate for the bond must fall between 10 and 11 percent. Using linear interpolation, the answer is 10.76 percent.

$1,153.65	*PV*@ 10%	$1,153.65	*PV* @ 10%
1,063.63	*PV* @ 11%	1,085.00	bond price
$ 90.02		$ 68.65	

$$10\% + \frac{\$68.65}{\$90.02}(1\%) = 10\% + .76(1\%) = 10.76\%$$

Problems

1. Bonds issued by the Peabody Corporation have a par value of $1,000, are selling for $890, and have 18 years to maturity. The annual interest payment is 8 percent. Find yield to maturity by combining the trial-and-error approach with interpolation, as shown in this appendix. (Use an assumption of annual interest payments.)
2. Bonds issued by the Bullwinkle Corporation have a par value of $1,000, are selling for $1,100, and have 7 years to maturity. The annual interest payment is 9 percent, payable semiannually. Find yield to maturity by combining the trial-and-error approach with interpolation, as shown in this appendix.

APPENDIX 10B

Valuation of a Supernormal Growth Firm

The formula for the valuation of a supernormal growth firm is:

$$P_0 = \sum_{t=1}^{n} \frac{D_t}{(1 + K_e)^t} + P_n\left(\frac{1}{(1 + K_e)}\right)^n \qquad \text{(10B–1)}$$

(Supernormal growth period) (After supernormal growth period)

represented graphically as

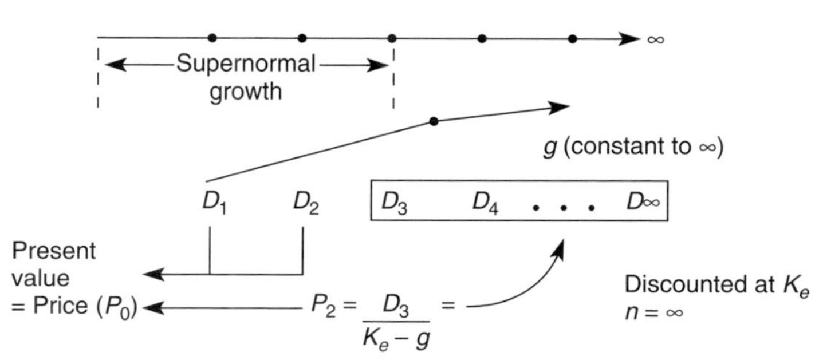

The formula is not difficult to use. The first term calls for determining the present value of the dividends using the supernormal growth period. The second term calls for computing the present value of the future stock price as determined at the end of the supernormal growth period. If we add the two together, we arrive at the current stock price. We are adding together the two benefits the shareholder will receive: (1) a future stream of dividends during the supernormal growth period, and (2) the future stock price.

Let's assume that the firm paid a dividend over the last 12 months of $1.67; this represents the current dividend rate. Dividends are expected to grow by 20 percent per year over the supernormal growth period (n) of three years. They will then grow at a normal constant rate (g) of 5 percent. The required rate of return (discount rate) as represented by K_e is 9 percent. We first find the present value of the dividends during the supernormal growth period.

1. Present Value of Supernormal Dividends

D_0 = $1.67. We allow the value to grow at 20 percent per year over the three years of supernormal growth.

$$D_1 = D_0\,(1 + .20) = \$1.67\,(1.20) = \$2.00$$

$$D_2 = D_1\,(1 + .20) = \$2.00\,(1.20) = \$2.40$$

$$D_3 = D_2\,(1 + .20) = \$2.40\,(1.20) = \$2.88$$

We then discount these values back at 9 percent to find the present value of dividends during the supernormal growth period.

	Supernormal Dividends	Present Value of Dividends during the Supernormal Period (K_e = 9%)
D_1	$2.00	$1.83
D_2	2.40	2.02
D_3	2.88	2.22
		$6.07

The present value of the supernormal dividends is $6.07. We now turn to the future stock price.

2. Present Value of Future Stock Price

We first find the future stock price at the end of the supernormal growth period. This is found by taking the present value of the dividends that will be growing at a normal, constant rate after the supernormal period. This will begin *after* the third (and last) period of supernormal growth.

Since after the supernormal growth period the firm is growing at a normal, constant rate ($g = 5$ percent) and K_e (the discount rate) of 9 percent exceeds the new, constant growth rate of 5 percent, we have fulfilled the two conditions for using the constant dividend growth model after three years. That is, we can apply Formula 10–8 (without subscripts for now).

$$P = \frac{D}{K_e - g}$$

In this case, however, D is really the dividend at the end of the fourth period because this phase of the analysis starts at the beginning of the fourth period, and D is as of the *end* of the first period of analysis in the formula. Also, the price we are solving for now is the price at the beginning of the fourth period, which is the same concept as the price at the end of the third period (P_3).

We thus say:

$$P_3 = \frac{D_4}{K_e - g} \qquad \text{(10B–2)}$$

D_4 is equal to the previously determined value for D_3 of \$2.88 moved forward one period at the constant growth rate of 5 percent.

$$D_4 = \$2.88\,(1.05) = \$3.02$$

Also:

$$K_e = .09 \text{ discount rate (required rate of return)}$$

$$g = .05 \text{ constant growth rate}$$

$$P_3 = \frac{D_4}{K_e - g} = \frac{\$3.02}{.09 - .05} = \frac{\$3.02}{.04} = \$75.50$$

This is the value of the stock at the end of the third period. We discount this value back to the present.

Stock Price after Three Years	Present Value of Future Price (K_e = 9%)
\$75.50	\$58.30

The present value of the future stock price (P3) of \$75.50 is \$58.30.

By adding together the answers in part 1 and part 2 of this appendix, we arrive at the total present value, or price, of the supernormal growth stock.

1. Present value of dividends during the normal growth period	\$ 6.07
2. Present value of the future stock price	58.30
Total present value, or price	\$64.37

The process we have just completed is presented in Figure 10B–1. Students who wish to develop skills in growth analysis should work the problems on the next page.

FIGURE 10B–1
Stock valuation under supernormal growth analysis

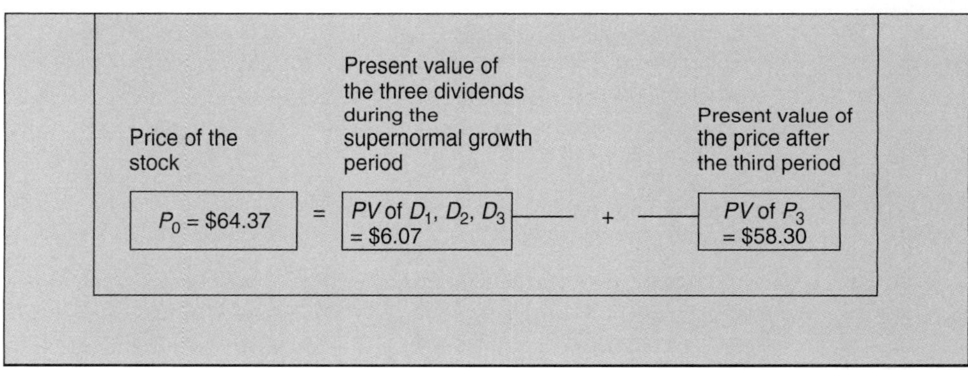

Review of Formulas

1. $$P_0 = \sum_{t=1}^{n} \frac{D_t}{(1 + K_e)^t} + P_n \left(\frac{1}{(1 + K_e} \right)^n \quad (10B\text{–}1)$$

2. $$P_3 = \frac{D_4}{K_e - g} \quad (10B\text{–}2)$$

Problems

1. Surgical Supplies Corporation paid a dividend of $1.12 over the last 12 months. The dividend is expected to grow at a rate of 25 percent over the next three years (supernormal growth). It will then grow at a normal, constant rate of 7 percent for the foreseeable future. The required rate of return is 12 percent (this will also serve as the discount rate).
   a. Compute the anticipated value of the dividends for the next three years (D_1, D_2, and D_3).
   b. Discount each of these dividends back to the present at a discount rate of 12 percent and then sum them.
   c. Compute the price of the stock at the end of the third year (P_3). $P_3 = \frac{D_4}{K_e - g}$ [Review appendix 10B for the definition of D_4]
   d. After you have computed P_3, discount it back to the present at a discount rate of 12 percent for three years.
   e. Add together the answers in part *b* and part *d* to get the current value of the stock. (This answer represents the present value of the first three periods of dividends plus the present value of the price of the stock after three periods.)
2. You are considering investing in Black Tie Co., a holding enterprise that will pay a dividend of $2.00, which will increase by 12 percent each year over the following three years and then grow at an annual rate of 5 percent indefinitely. You expect a 22 percent return on your invested capital. What price would you pay for a share in this company?

3. Sleepy Ltd. expects its present $1.25 dividend (just paid) to grow by 20 percent over the next three years, after which it will remain the same with no growth forever. If an investor requires a return of 16 percent for investing in Sleepy, what would be its current price?

4. Clarinet Inc.. has an expected yield of 18 percent. It anticipates paying the same dividend of $1.10 for four more years, after which the dividend will grow at 7 percent a year indefinitely. Based on the dividend valuation (capitalization) model, at what price should Clarinet currently sell?

5. March Hair Ltd. just paid a dividend of $1.80, which it expects to be $2.90 next year and $4.00 the next year After that time, the dividend will likely decline to 5 percent per year forever. With required rates of return at 14 percent, what should investors pay for March Hair?

CHAPTER | ELEVEN

11 Cost of Capital

LEARNING | OBJECTIVES

1 Explain that the cost of capital represents the overall cost of financing to the firm.

2 Define the cost of capital as the discount rate normally used to analyze an investment. It is an evaluation tool.

3 Calculate the cost of capital based on the various valuation techniques from Chapter 10 as applied to bonds, preferred stocks, and common shares.

4 Describe how a firm attempts to find a minimum cost of capital by varying the mix of its sources of financing.

5 Explain the marginal cost of capital concept.

Throughout the previous two chapters, a number of references were made to discounting future cash flows in solving for the present value. The vexing problem at this point is: How do you determine the appropriate discount rate in a given situation? To demonstrate the importance of the answer to this question, it might be helpful to explore a rather simple, but not uncommon, type of problem. Suppose a young doctor is rendered incapable of practicing medicine due to an auto accident in the last year of her residency. In a subsequent legal action, the court determines that the best approximation of her future earning potential before the accident was $100,000 a year for the next 30 years. How much, then, should the court award the young woman as a single payment to compensate her for the lost earning power? To assign a settlement value, the court must still determine the appropriate rate to use to discount those future earnings estimates. Suppose further that her lawyer argues for a 5 percent discount rate while the insurance company lawyers argue for a 12 percent rate. What present value would the court assign to these inflows? If it accepts the arguments of the doctor's lawyer, the settlement value becomes $1,537,300. If, on the other hand, it accepts the arguments made by the insurance company's lawyers, the assigned value becomes $805,500. The choice between these two discount rates represents a $730,000 difference in the amount awarded to the injured doctor. As you see, the difference is not trivial.

In the corporate finance setting, the more likely circumstance is one in which an investment, if made today, promises a set of inflows in the future. To decide whether the expected future inflows justify the current investment, we need to know the appropriate discount rate. The discount rate we choose becomes the evaluation yardstick by which an investment proposal is deemed acceptable or not acceptable, in the attempt to maximize shareholders' wealth. This chapter sets down the methods and procedures for making that determination.

If we invest money today to receive benefits in the future, how much must we earn on it? If you said we must be certain that we are earning at least as much as it costs us to acquire the funds for investment, you were right. That amount, in essence, is the minimum acceptable return. Thus, if the firm's cost of funds is 12 percent, then all normal projects must be tested to make sure they earn at least 12 percent. The term *normal* is used because the method under discussion would not be appropriate for considering a new venture in a high-risk area, for example. By using this as the discount rate, we can decide whether we can reasonably expect to earn the financial cost of doing business. The student is again encouraged to reproduce the present value calculations of this chapter using a financial calculator.

The Overall Concept

Decisions made by the financial manager are aimed at increasing shareholder value and should be judged against the standard of the **cost of capital.** The cost of capital is derived from the cost of funds that will be borrowed or assembled by the firm. The cost of those funds must be based on the costs (or yields) currently found in the financial markets, as investors will demand these yields for the use of their funds. Those funds (capital) will be invested in the firm's assets to produce future cash flows and the firm must value these cash flows in the present, comparing their value (benefit) against the cost of acquiring the assets. This requires a discount rate or a cost of capital. The cost of capital is the tool used to evaluate (discount) future cash flows and assign a value to them. It is the standard that will satisfy shareholders.

To illustrate this concept, let's suppose that a plant superintendent wishes to borrow funds at 6 percent (aftertax cost) to purchase a conveyor system, while the division manager suggests that common shares be sold at an effective cost of 15 percent to finance the development of a new digital component for one of the company's products. Judging each investment against the specific means of financing used to fund it, runs the risk of making investment selection decisions arbitrary and inconsistent. Evaluating the conveyor system having an 8 percent return with 6 percent debt while evaluating the digital component project having a 14 percent return against the 15 percent cost of common stock is inappropriate. If projects and financing are matched in this way, the project with the lower return would be accepted and the project with the higher return would be rejected.

In reality, if stock and debt are sold in equal proportions, the average cost of financing would be 10.5 percent (one-half debt at 6 percent and one-half stock at 15 percent). With a 10.5 percent average cost of financing, we would now reject the 8 percent conveyor system and accept the 14 percent component project. This would be a rational and consistent decision. Though an investment financed by low-cost debt might appear acceptable at first glance, the use of debt might increase the overall risk of the firm (as discussed in Chapter 5), eventually making all forms of financing more expensive. Therefore, the general conclusion has been that each project must be measured against the overall cost of funds to the firm.

The use of the cost of capital to analyze investment projects, as subsequently determined with the Baker Corporation example below, rests on two important assumptions. The first assumption, which is alluded to above, is that the capital structure of the firm must remain in the same proportions as that currently in place, or the cost of capital calculation must be revised. If the financial leverage of the firm is altered, the risks to the investors from holding debt or equity will change. Investors will then require different rates of return, and these required rates of return are the firm's costs of financing.

The second assumption is that the investment proposals being analyzed are of the same risk as those investments currently undertaken by the firm. If, for instance, the new proposals are riskier than the current investments of the firm, investors, through their debt or equity holdings, will expect and demand higher returns from their investments, and the cost of capital calculation must be revised upwards accordingly. Otherwise, projects might be accepted that do not satisfy the risk and return preferences of investors, thus causing the firm value to drop.

The determination of cost of capital can best be understood by examining the **capital structure** of a hypothetical firm, the Baker Corporation, in Table 11–1. Note that the aftertax costs of the individual sources of financing are determined, weights are then assigned to each, and finally, a weighted average cost is determined. The relevant costs are those related to new funds that might be raised in future financings rather than the costs of funds raised to fund investments in the past. The remainder of the chapter examines each of these procedural steps.

TABLE 11–1
Cost of capital–Baker Corporation

		Cost (aftertax)	Weights	Weighted Cost
Debt	K_d	6.55%	30%	1.97%
Preferred stock	K_p	10.94	10	1.09
Common equity (retained earnings)	K_e	12.00	60	7.20
Weighted average cost of capital	K_a			10.26%

Each element in the capital structure (on the right side of the balance sheet) has an explicit or opportunity cost associated with it, herein referred to by the symbol *K*. Although all liabilities have some cost associated with them, we usually only determine the cost of longer-term liabilities for simplicity in a cost of capital calculation. Nevertheless, current liabilities can sometimes be significant in the capital structure of a firm.

This cost is directly related to the valuation concepts developed in the previous chapter. The cost of a security is a function of how the security is valued in the marketplace by investors. Once we decide on the proper method for valuing a particular security, the mathematics involved are relatively simple. In Chapter 10 we examined the valuation techniques for financial assets. Let us now examine how the various components of the capital structure might be calculated by a firm's financial analyst.

Cost of Debt

The cost of debt is measured by the interest rate, or yield, that would have to be paid to bondholders to persuade them to buy our bonds. The present market-determined yield that we have seen in the term structure of interest rates is a reflection of future interest rate expectations. This is an appropriate yield to use because the investment proposals to be evaluated will be successful, or not successful, in the future as well. A simple case might involve our being able to sell $1,000 bonds, paying $100 in annual interest for $1,000. Our cost of debt would thus be 10 percent. Of course, the compu-

EVA, the Music of Shareholder Value

EVA stands for economic value added and is a concept for financial decision-making that was developed by Stern Stewart & Co., a New York City consulting firm, over two decades ago. Worldwide Stern Stewart & Co. has over 300 EVA clients, who claim great success. The concept reduces to the following formula:

EVA = Net Operating Profit after Taxes (NOPAT) − [Capital × The Cost of Capital]

EVA stresses that decisions should be made or projects accepted only if this formula's results are positive. Simply put, it maintains that you should only make an investment decision if the return exceeds the cost. So what's the big deal? The "big deal" is that it is one thing for managers of corporations to understand the concept, but it is quite another for them to implement it. Often companies do not properly measure the cost of capital or are incorrectly focused on growth rather than shareholder wealth. Joel M. Stern and G. Bennett Stewart III, as developers of the EVA concept, maintain that they can teach corporate managers a program that ensures the return on capital exceeds the cost. In the process, shareholder wealth is maximized.

EVA practioneers in Canada include Alcan and Domtar. Alcan actually includes the calculation of EVA as part of the consolidated review of its financial statements and in its presentations to analysts. In the 3rd quarter of 2001 Alcan had \$8 million of EVA, which was down from previous quarters. The value of the EVA technique is that it focuses the organization on creating value for the shareholders and it is an extension of the cost of capital concept examined in the chapter.

FINANCE IN ACTION

Q1 What are the 4Ms of EVA?

Q2 Was EVA increasing or decreasing during the latest financial quarter at Alcan?

www.alcan.com

Symbol: AL

www.sternstewart.com

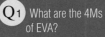

tation becomes a little more difficult if our \$1,000 bonds sell for an amount more or less than \$1,000. If this is the case, we could use the yield-to-maturity techniques discussed in Chapter 10.

For example, assume the firm is preparing to issue new debt. To determine the likely cost of the new debt in the marketplace, the firm computes the yield on its currently outstanding debt. This is not the rate at which the old debt was issued; it is the rate that investors are demanding today. Assume the debt issue pays \$100 per year in interest, has a 20-year life, and is currently selling for \$940.

Calculator

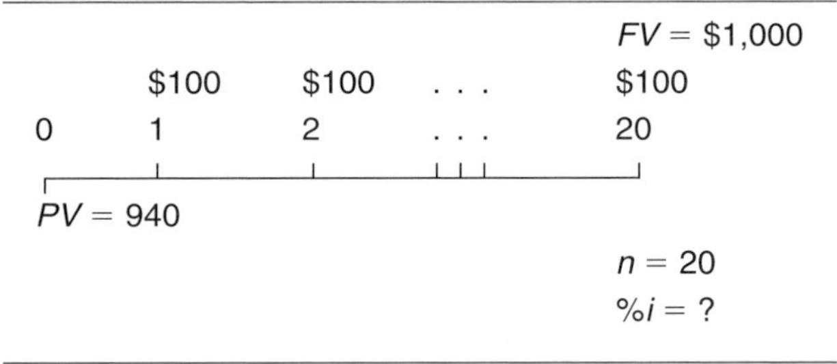

$i = 10.74\%$.

In many cases, we do not have to compute the yield to maturity. It is available from other sources, such as the financial pages of various daily and weekly newspapers, from one of the larger investment dealers who deal in bond trading, or from several web sites. The type of information available on a sample of outstanding bonds is presented in Table 11–2 (on the next page). If the firm involved is the Bank of Nova Scotia, for example, the financial manager could observe that debt maturing in 2025 would have a yield to maturity of 6.92 percent. This is true even though the debt was

Scotia Capital
www.scotiacapital.com

originally issued at close to 8.90 percent, the established coupon rate. The financial manager should also observe that lower-rated bonds typically offer the investing public a higher rate of return. Rogers Cable with a BB+ rating yields 8.94 percent, while Nav Canada with a similar maturity yields 5.02 percent.

TABLE 11–2
Sample bond information

Issuer	Interest Payable	Maturity	Price	Yield	Rating
Nav Canada	6.60%	Dec 2006	106.71	5.02	AA+
	6.50	June 2009	105.01	5.66	AA+
	7.56	Mar 2027	113.07	6.50	AA+
Bank of Nova Scotia	5.75	May 2009	100.25	5.71	A+
	8.90	June 2025	122.76	6.92	A+
Loblaw	7.10	May 2010	107.89	5.88	A
	6.65	Nov 2027	97.92	6.82	A
Thomson	6.90	June 2008	105.02	5.94	A–
	6.85	June 2011	102.06	6.55	A–
Domtar	10.00	Apr 2011	108.88	8.58	BBB–
Rogers Cable	8.75	Jul 2007	99.25	8.94	BB+
Sask. Wheat Pool	6.60	July 2007	70.00	14.77	B+

Note: Pricing for Friday, January 18, 2002.

Source: *The Globe and Mail: Monday's Report on Business*
ScotiaCapital: www.scotiacapital.com
National Post: Saturday's FP Investing
Standard & Poors: www.standardandpoors.com/canada/ratingsactions/ratingslists/index.html

Once the bond yield is determined through the formula or the tables (or is given) we must adjust the yield for tax considerations. In other words, yield to maturity indicates how much the corporation has to pay on a before-tax basis. The interest payment on debt, however, is a tax-deductible expense. Since interest is tax deductible, the true cost of the bond is less than the interest paid because the government is picking up part of the cost by allowing the firm to pay less taxes. The aftertax cost of debt is actually the yield to maturity times one minus the tax rate. This is presented as Formula 11–1*a*.

$$K_d = Y(1 - T) \qquad (11\text{–}1a)$$

where

$$K_d = \text{Cost of debt}$$
$$Y = \text{Yield}$$

The yield may also be thought of as representing the interest cost to the firm after consideration of all selling and distribution costs, known as **flotation costs**, though no explicit representation is given to these costs in relationship to debt. These costs are usually quite small, and they are often bypassed in some types of loans. For those who wish to explicitly include this factor we would have:[1]

[1]Better still, we could use a time line development to compute the aftertax yield with a present value calculation. We would adjust the initial proceeds by the flotation costs and by the present value of the tax savings resulting from the flotation costs over the first five years of the bond's life. The annual interest payments would be included at one minus the tax rate. The final payment on the debt would be included in the calculation as a future value. This would only have a minor impact on the final cost of debt.

$$K_d = \frac{Y(1 - T)}{1 - F} \quad (11\text{–}1b)$$

where

$$F = \text{Flotation, or selling, cost}$$

Flotation cost (F) in this formula is expressed as a percentage of the funds raised. Therefore $1 - F$ will also be a percentage, equal to net proceeds (P_n) as a percentage of gross proceeds. A dollar value for costs can be converted to net proceeds.

The term *yield* in the formula is interchangeable with yield to maturity. Earlier we determined that *current* yield on existing debt was 10.74 percent. We assume that new debt can be issued at the same going market rate and that the firm is in a 39 percent tax bracket.[2] Applying the tax adjustment factor, the aftertax cost of debt would be 6.55 percent.

$$\begin{aligned} K_d &= Y(1 - T) \\ &= 10.74\% \, (1 - .39) \\ &= 10.74\% \, (.61) \\ &= 6.55\% \end{aligned}$$

Please refer back to Table 11–1 and observe in column 1 that the aftertax cost of debt for Baker Corporation is the 6.55 percent that we have just computed.

Cost of Preferred Stock

The cost of preferred stock is similar to the cost of debt in that a constant annual payment is made, but it is dissimilar in that there is no maturity date on which a principal payment must be made. Thus, the determination of the yield on preferred stock is simpler than determining the yield on debt. One must examine the actual preferreds quite closely for the attached bells and whistles, as their maturity dates often make their valuation similar to bonds. All you have to do is divide the annual dividend by the current price (this process was discussed in Chapter 10). This represents the rate of return to preferred shareholders as well as the annual cost to the corporation for the preferred stock issue.

To determine the cost of a new issue of preferred shares we have to make one slight alteration by dividing the dividend payment by the *net* price (P_n) or proceeds received by the firm. Since a new share of preferred stock has a selling cost (**flotation cost**), the proceeds to the firm are equal to the selling price in the market minus the flotation cost. The cost of preferred stock is presented as Formula 11–2.[3]

$$K_p = \frac{D_p}{P_p - F} \quad (11\text{–}2)$$

[2]Actually, the rate might be slightly higher to reflect that bonds trading at a discount from par ($940 in this case) generally pay a lower yield to maturity than par value bonds because of potential tax advantages and higher leverage potential. This is not really a major issue in this case.

[3]Note that in Chapter 10, K_p was presented with no adjustment for flotation charges. Some may wish to formally add an additional subscript to K_p to indicate we are now talking about the cost of *new* preferred stock. The adjusted symbol would be K_{pn}. If the yield is determined it can be divided by the net proceeds of an issue expressed as a percentage out of 100. In our example $10.50/ $100 = 10.50%. Then 10.50%/96% = 10.94%

FINANCE IN ACTION

Q1 What are the current yields on 10 year bonds in the above countries?

Q2 What is the current situation regarding Argentina's economy?

www.bloomberg.com

Debt Costs around the Globe

A corporation needing long-term debt financing usually looks first in its own backyard, that is, the country where it is going to invest the capital. However, multinational corporations will carefully investigate global interest rates to find the most cost-effective. The risk of borrowing in a foreign country is the likelihood that exchange rates will change before the debt is paid back. This may make the debt cost far greater than anticipated.

In January 2002 the following long-term interest rates were demanded in capital markets for government securities with 10 years to maturity. Top-rated corporations would expect to pay 1 to 2 percent above these rates.

Canada	5.313%
Germany	4.805
Japan	1.445
New Zealand	6.520
Argentina (3 yrs)	153.750

Notice the low rate in Japan compared to Canada and Germany. The Japanese economy had stagnated for a decade with deflationary pressures; low rates are an attempt to stimulate economic activity. Also examine the rate of borrowing in Argentina, a country with significant economic troubles in 2002 as the government began to miss bond payments. Of course, the key from a Canadian perspective would be how exchange rates moved as debt borrowed abroad was paid back.

where

$$K_p = \text{Cost of preferred stock}$$
$$D_p = \text{Annual dividend on preferred stock}$$
$$P_p = \text{Price of preferred stock}$$
$$F = \text{Flotation, or selling, cost}$$

In the case of the Baker Corporation, the annual dividend is \$10.50, the preferred stock price is \$100, and the flotation, or selling, cost is estimated at \$4.00. The effective cost of preferred shares becomes:

$$K_p = \frac{D_p}{P_p - F} = \frac{\$10.50}{\$100 - 4} = \frac{\$10.50}{\$96} = 10.94\%$$

Because a preferred stock dividend is not a tax-deductible expense, there is no downward tax adjustment. Now refer back to Table 11–1 and observe in column 1 that 10.94 percent is the cost of preferred stock in the Baker Corporation example.

Cost of Common Equity

Determining the cost of **common equity** in the capital structure is a much more involved task than was the case for debt or preferred shares. Those instruments were much simpler because a stated coupon or dividend rate was in evidence. Now we are trying to determine the required yields of investors when the expected payouts are not as clear. The out-of-pocket cost is the cash dividend, but one cannot merely assume the percentage cost of common stock is simply the current year's dividend divided by the market price.

$$\frac{\text{Current dividend}}{\text{Market price}}$$

CN Rail
www.cn.ca

If such an approach were followed, the common stock costs for selected Canadian corporations based on their dividend yields of January 2002 would have been 3.4 percent for Abitibi Consolidated, 3.4 percent for BCE, Inc., 1.1 percent for CN Rail, and 2.7 percent for the Toronto Dominion Bank. If new common stock were thought to be so cheap, those firms would have no need to issue other securities and could profitably finance projects that earned only 2 to 6 percent. On the other hand, who would invest in a corporation with such inadequate yields? The question still remaining, then, is: How do we determine the correct effective cost of common stock to the firm?

Valuation Approach (Dividend Model)

The cost of common stock is a function of the pricing and performance demands of current and future shareholders. An appropriate approach is to develop a model for valuing common stock that is dependent on the required return demanded from it. Investors receive their return from dividends and the increase in share price. Our **dividend valuation model** or **dividend capitalization model** uses both components to derive a cost of equity capital.

In Chapter 10 the constant dividend growth model yielded the following relationship between stock price and demanded return:

$$P_0 = \frac{D_1}{K_e - g}$$

where

P_0 = Price of the stock today
D_1 = Dividend at the end of the first year (or period)
K_e = Required rate of return/cost of equity
g = Constant growth rate in dividends

We then found we could rearrange the terms in the formula to solve for K_e instead of P_0. This was presented in Formula 10-9 and once again here as Formula 11–3.

$$K_e = \frac{D_1}{P_0} + g \qquad (11\text{–}3)$$

The required rate of return (K_e) is equal to the dividend at the end of the first year (D_1), divided by the price of the stock today (P_0), plus a constant growth rate (g). Although the growth rate applies directly to dividends, it must also apply to earnings over the long term. The formula's assumption that there is a constant relationship between earnings per share and dividends per share (that is, a constant payout ratio) assures the ability to sustain the growth in dividend payments.

In the Baker Corporation example, the expected dividend for this year is \$2.00, the current stock price is \$40.00, and the dividends have been and are expected to continue to grow at a rate of 7 percent. Given that information, we would calculate K_e to be equal to 12 percent.

$$K_e = \frac{D_1}{P_0} + g = \frac{\$2}{\$40} + 7\% = 5\% + 7\% = 12\%$$

This result assumes shareholders expect to receive a 5 percent return on their investment by way of dividends and a 7 percent return by way of an increase in the price of their shares. Thus, they are investing in this stock on the basis that they demand and expect to receive a 12 percent return on their investment.

FINANCE IN ACTION

Capital Availability for Small Business

The options for raising capital in a small business are limited because the full scope of the capital market is not available to the smaller firm. Investors and the investment dealers that put together financing packages in the capital markets shy away from the small business because of the risks perceived in the small business and because the amount of capital required is limited. Capital markets operate as wholesale markets, and require financing deals of a sufficient size to achieve economies of scale. Small business risks may relate only to a lack of understanding of the business by the capital markets, but nevertheless the small business owner will likely have to raise capital elsewhere.

Debt financing is generally limited to bank operating loans that are used to support liquid current assets and term loans secured by capital assets. The cost of these loans is often several percentage points above the prime rate unless special government or bank programs are available.

As for equity; personal savings, love money (from family and good friends), government assistance, and venture capital funding are the options. The sale of shares (equity) in the capital markets is pretty well impossible in the start up phase of the business. Money from "Angels" or venture capital firms is also difficult to access in the early stages and if available, is advanced to the firm on the expectations of rates of return of between 25 to 40 percent annually. Family and friends may have similar expectations.

MacDonald and Associates Ltd. (www.canadavc.com) is a significant source of information on the venture capital business in Canada.

Considering the higher debt costs and the high expectations for equity returns by investors, the cost of capital in the small business will be substantial. This places a significant demand on the returns that need to be achieved by the business. Cost of capital is used to evaluate the desirability of capital investment projects by the firm.

Q1 From "Strategis" what are the financing options available to the small firm?

Q2 Can you describe two recent venture capital deals?

www.strategis.ic.gc.ca/engdoc/main.html

www.canadavc.com

SB

Alternative Calculation of the Required Return on Common Stock

An alternative model for calculating the required return on common stock is represented by the **capital asset pricing model (CAPM).** The attributes of this model are covered in Appendix 11A, so we consider it only briefly at this point. Some proclaim the capital asset pricing model as an important advance in our attempts at common stock valuation, while others suggest that it is not a valid description of how the real world operates.

Under the capital asset pricing model, the required return for common stock (or other investments) can be described by the following formula:

$$K_j = R_f + \beta_j(R_m - R_f) \qquad (11\text{–}4a)$$

where

K_j = Required return on common stock/cost of equity

R_f = Risk-free rate of return; often taken as equivalent to the current rate on short-term Government of Canada treasury bills.

β_j = Beta coefficient. The beta measures the historical volatility of an individual stock's (j) return relative to a stock market index. A beta greater than 1 indicates greater volatility (as measured by price movements) than the market, while the reverse would be true for a beta less than 1.

R_m = Return in the market as measured by an appropriate index.

A flotation cost adjustment can be achieved, for new equity, by adjusting the formula by:

$$K_{jn} = K_j\left(\frac{P_0}{P_n}\right) \qquad (11\text{–}4b)$$

where

K_{jn} = cost of new equity (CAPM)
P_0 = current price
P_n = net proceeds received on a new share issue after flotation costs (and any underpricing of the share price).

In the Baker Corporation example, the following values might apply:

$$R_f = 9\%$$
$$R_m = 11\%$$
$$\beta_j = 1.5$$

K_j, based on Formula 11–4, would then equal:

$$K_j = 9\% + 1.5(11\% - 9\%) = 9\% + 1.5(2\%)$$
$$= 9\% + 3\% = 12\%$$

In this case we have structured the data so that K_j (the required return under the capital asset pricing model) would equal K_e (the required return under the dividend valuation model). In both cases the computations lead to a 12 percent estimate as the cost of common equity. In real life the two models rarely give exactly the same estimate. Nevertheless, both models are attempting to determine the same thing—the expected or required return of investors.

For now, we use the dividend valuation model, that is, $K_e = D_1/P_0 + g$. Those who wish to study the capital asset pricing model further are referred to Appendix 11A.

Cost of Retained Earnings

Up to this point we have discussed the cost (required return) of common stock in a general sense. We have not really specified who is supplying these funds. One obvious supplier of common stock equity capital is the purchaser of new shares of common stock. This is not the only source, however. Retained earnings constitute what is referred to as an internal, as opposed to external, funding source. Statistics Canada reported that as of late 2000, Canadian nonfinancial corporations' balance sheets showed \$271 billion of their historical equity financing came from retained earnings and \$469 billion from common share issues.[4] Thus, for the universe of firms as a whole, retained earnings form an important source of ownership or equity capital investment funds.

Statistics Canada
www.statcan.ca

Accumulated retained earnings represent the past and present earnings of the firm minus previously distributed dividends. Retained earnings, by law, belong to the current shareholders. They can either be paid out to the current shareholders in the form of dividends or reinvested in the firm. Thus, as current earnings are retained in the firm for reinvestment, they represent a source of equity capital supplied by the current shareholders. Just because the firm did not have to go to the market to raise new funds

[4]This represents the most recent published data. Statistics Canada, *Quarterly Statistics for Enterprises*, catalogue 61-008, third quarter 2001.

does not mean, however, that these internally generated funds are free. In other words, an opportunity cost is involved—the funds could be paid out as dividends to the current shareholders who could then redeploy them by buying other stocks, bonds, real estate, and so forth. The expected rate of return on these alternative investments becomes the opportunity cost of not having paid out the earnings in dividends. It seems reasonable to assume shareholders could earn a return equivalent to that provided by their present investment in the firm (on an equal risk basis).[5] This is represented by $D_1/P_0 + g$. Given that in the securities markets there are thousands of investments from which to choose, it is not implausible to assume the shareholder can take dividend payments and reinvest them to provide a comparable yield.

Computing the cost of retained earnings takes us back to where we began our discussion of the cost of common stock. The cost of retained earnings is equivalent to the rate of return on the firm's common stock. This is the opportunity cost. Thus, we say the cost of common equity in the form of retained earnings is equal to the required rate of return on the firm's stock.[6]

$$K_e = \frac{D_1}{P_0} + g \tag{11–5}$$

Thus, K_e not only represents the required return on common stock as previously defined, but it also represents the cost of equity in the form of retained earnings. It is a symbol that has double significance.

For ease of reference, the terms in Formula 11–5 are reproduced below. They are based on prior values presented in this section on the cost of common equity.

K_e = Cost of common equity in the form of retained earnings
D_1 = Dividend at the end of the first year, \$2
P_0 = Price of the stock today, \$40
g = Constant growth rate in dividends, 7%

We arrive at the value of 12%.

$$K_e = \frac{D_1}{P_0} + g = \frac{\$2}{\$40} + 7\% = 5\% + 7\% = 12\%$$

The cost of common equity in the form of retained earnings is equal to 12 percent. Please refer back to Table 11–1 and observe in column (1) that 12 percent is the value we have used for common equity.

[5]Chapter 14, in dealing with the concept of efficient markets, provides more insight as to why this assumption is reasonable.

[6]One could make the seemingly logical suggestion that this is not a perfectly equivalent relationship. For example, if shareholders receive a distribution of retained earnings in the form of dividends, they may have to pay taxes on the dividends before they can reinvest them in equivalent yield investments. Additionally, the shareholder may incur brokerage costs in the process. For these reasons, one might suggest that the opportunity cost of retained earnings is less than the rate of return on the firm's common stock. The current majority view, however, is that the appropriate cost for retained earnings is equal to the rate of return on the firm's common stock. The strongest argument for this equality position is that for a publicly traded company, a firm always has the option of buying back some of its shares in the market. Given that this is so, it is assured a return of K_e. Thus, the firm should never make an alternative investment that has an expected equity return of less than K_e. Nevertheless, some students may wish to look into the minority view as well. In the event a tax adjustment is made, the cost of retained earnings can be represented as $K_r = K_e(1 - t_r)$, where K_r is the cost of retained earnings, K_e is the required return on common stock, and t_r is the average shareholder marginal tax rate on dividend income.

Cost of New Common Stock

Let's now consider the other source of equity capital, new common stock. If we are issuing *new* common stock, we must pay a slightly higher return than K_e, which represents the required rate of return of *present* shareholders. The higher return is needed to cover the distribution costs of the new securities. If the required return for present shareholders were 12 percent and shares were quoted to the public at $40.00, a new distribution of securities would need to earn slightly more than 12 percent to compensate for sales commissions and other expenses. The corporation does not receive the full $40.00 because of these costs. The formula for K_e is restated as K_n (the cost of new common stock) to reflect this requirement.

$$\text{Common stock} \quad K_e = \frac{D_1}{P_0} + g$$

$$\text{New common stock} \quad K_n = \left(\frac{D_1}{P_0} + g\right)\left(\frac{P_0}{P_n}\right) \qquad (11\text{–}6)$$

The only new term is P_n (net proceeds received on a new share issue after flotation costs and any underpricing of the share price).

If net proceeds are expressed as a percentage we can divide K_e by the net proceeds to get $K_{e.}$

Assume

$$D_1 = \$2 \qquad P_n = P_0 - F$$
$$P_0 = \$40 \qquad = \$40 - \$4$$
$$F = \$4 \qquad = \$36$$
$$g = 7\%$$

then

$$K_n = \left(\frac{\$2}{\$40} + 7\%\right)\left(\frac{\$40}{\$36}\right)$$
$$= (5\% + 7\%)(1.111) = 13.33\%$$

The cost of new common stock to the Baker Corporation is 13.3 percent. This value is used more extensively later in the chapter. New common stock was not included in the original assumed capital structure for the Baker Corporation presented in Table 11–1.

Overview of Common Stock Costs

For those of you who are suffering from an overexposure to *K*s in the computation of cost of common stock, let us reiterate the two common stock formulas you will use in the rest of the chapter and to solve the problems at the end of the chapter.

$$K_e \begin{pmatrix}\text{Cost of common equity in the} \\ \text{form of retained earnings}\end{pmatrix} = \frac{D_1}{P_0} + g$$

$$K_n \text{ (Cost of new common stock)} = \left(\frac{D_1}{P_0} + g\right)\left(\frac{P_0}{P_n}\right)$$

The primary emphasis is on K_e for now, but later in the chapter we also use K_n when we discuss the marginal cost of capital.

Optimal Capital Structure—Weighting Costs

Having established the techniques for computing the cost of the various elements in the capital structure, we must now discuss methods of assigning weights to these costs to determine our **weighted average cost of capital**. We attempt to weight capital components in accordance with our desire to achieve a minimum overall cost of capital. That will be the **optimum capital structure** because at that point the value of shareholders' wealth is maximized. For purposes of this discussion, Table 11–1 (Cost of Capital for the Baker Corporation) is reproduced here.

		Cost (aftertax)	Weights	Weighted Cost
Debt	K_d	6.55%	30%	1.97%
Preferred stock	K_p	10.94	10	1.09
Common equity (retained earnings)	K_e	12.00	60	7.20
Weighted average cost of capital	K_a			10.26%

How does the firm decide on the appropriate weights for debt, preferred stock, and common stock financing? In other words, why not use all debt for future financing since the preceding chart indicates that it is substantially cheaper than the alternatives? The use of debt beyond a reasonable point will probably greatly increase the firm's financial risk and thereby drive up the costs of all sources of financing. For a more complete discussion of the theory related to this point, please see Appendix 11B, "Capital Structure Theory and Modigliani and Miller."

One way for us to explore this critical point is to assume that you are going to start your own company and are considering the following three different capital structures. For ease of presentation, only debt and equity (common stock) are being considered. As it happens, the costs of the components in the capital structure change each time you vary the proposed debt-equity mix (weights).

	Cost (aftertax)	Weights	Weighted Cost
Financial Plan A:			
Debt	6.5%	20%	1.3%
Equity	12.0	80	9.6
			10.9%
Financial Plan B:			
Debt	7.0%	40%	2.8%
Equity	12.5	60	7.5
			10.3%
Financial Plan C:			
Debt	9.0%	60%	5.4%
Equity	15.0	40	6.0
			11.4%

Canadian Utilities and Its Cost of Capital

Canadian Utilities is primarily a holding company for electrical and natural gas utilities and in 2001 it had assets exceeding $5 billion. Canadian Utilities' electric and natural gas utilities produce the overwhelming majority of its revenues and profits. Although nonregulated subsidiaries are playing a significant role, and although utilities are having their business deregulated, Canadian Utilities continues to face the demands of government regulation. Its gas subsidiaries, ATCO Pipelines and ATCO Gas, must appear before the Alberta Energy Utilities Board (AEUB) to determine cost of service rates. These rates become the charges customers pay for their gas.

To determine the cost of service rates, each utility prepares for an intensive hearing to establish the cost of financing the utility's operation. Often there are divergent views on the costs of the different components of the firm's capital structure. These costs are debated, attempting to reach a "consensus" on the firm's cost of capital. Eventually customer gas rates are set based on these cost calculations, from revenue projections and a "fair rate of return" is established. For 2001 Canadian Utilities had the following:

Capital Structure	(Book Value)
Current liabilities	17%
Commercial paper	4
Long-term debt	43
Preferreds	6
Common equity	30

In 1998 ATCO Gas, and ATCO Pipelines established cost of service rates with the AEUB for the period 1998 to 2002. These called for returns based on a spread over or under the National Energy Board's determined return. Other regulatory decisions established fixed rates of return. Regulatory matters are discussed in the management discussion and analysis of the financial statements.

FINANCE IN ACTION

Q1 What is the fair return that the AEUB established for the utilities?

Q2 What is the rating on Canadian Utilities commercial paper, debentures, and preferred shares?

www.canadian-utilities.com

Symbol: CU

www.dbrs.com

www.standardandpoors.com/canada/

We see that the firm can reduce the cost of capital by including more debt financing as we consider Plan B versus Plan A. Beyond a point, however, the continued use of debt becomes unattractive, causing increases in the costs of the various sources of financing that more than offset the benefit of substituting cheaper debt for more expensive equity. In our example, that point seems to occur somewhere around the debt-equity mix represented by Plan B. Traditional financial theory maintains that there is a U-shaped cost of capital curve relative to debt-equity mixes for the firm, as illustrated in Figure 11–1, on the next page. In this illustration the optimum capital structure occurs at a 40 percent debt-to-equity ratio.

Most firms are able to use 40 to 70 percent total debt in their capital structure without exceeding norms acceptable to creditors and investors. Distinctions should be made, however, between firms that carry high or low business risks. As discussed in Chapter 5, a growth firm in a reasonably stable industry can afford to absorb more debt than its counterparts in cyclical industries. Examples of debt used by companies in various industries are presented in Table 11–3, on the next page.

In determining the appropriate capital mix, the firm generally begins with its present capital structure and ascertains whether that structure is optimal. If it is not, subsequent financing should carry the firm toward a financing mix deemed more desirable. Note that only the costs of new or incremental financing should be considered. The historical costs of financing to the firm are not relevant except to the extent that they provide clues as to what future financing costs are likely to be.

FIGURE 11–1
Cost of capital curve

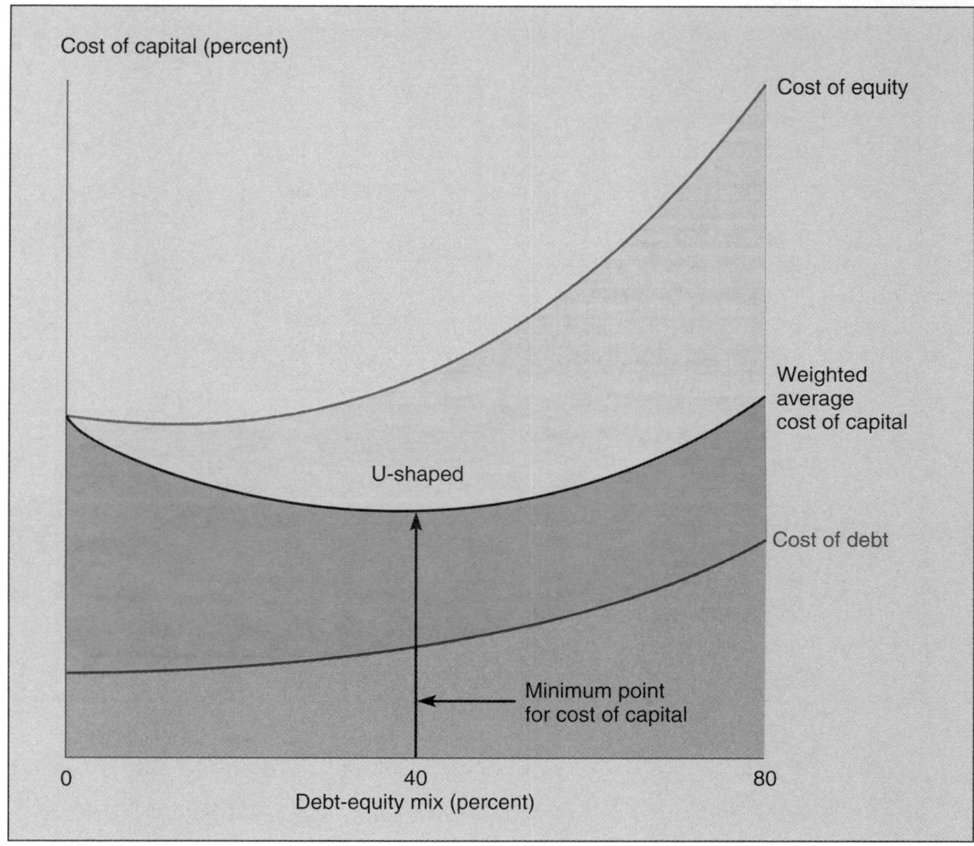

TABLE 11–3
Debt (total) to total assets, 2002

Selected Companies with Industry Designation	Percent
Abitibi Consolidated (forest products)	72
Air Canada (airlines)	106
Bank of Montreal (banking)	96
Canadian Tire (consumer products)	60
Dofasco (steel)	46
Molson (breweries and beverage)	77
Noranda (mining)	58
Nortel (networks)	72
Nova Corp. (petrochemicals)	59
TrizecHahn (real estate)	76

These ratios were calculated as follows: 1 − (equity/total assets) from the latest balance sheet available at each companies web site. Company web sites can be accessed through the TSX web site under listed companies. Please note that these are based on book values not market values. Nortel for instance had a market capitalization of equity in early 2002 that exceeded the book value of its total assets. Search symbol (NT) at the TSX web site.

1. What are the latest debt ratios for the above companies?
2. Compare the book value of equity of these companies with their market capitalization.

www.tsx.ca

Market Value Weightings

To calculate the cost of capital, we use weights for each component of the capital structure based on how the corporation will raise funds in the future (presumably its optimal capital structure) and it is with that capital structure mix that new investments must find their success. If the firm is to be successful, the new investments must achieve a rate of return equal to the overall cost of the financing used. Past costs are not relevant. Unless the corporation has calculated its optimal capital structure, we presume that the present structure will be maintained and is appropriate for cost of capital calculations.

However that present capital structure should be based on the market value of debt and equity. It should not be based on book values from the financial statements. Why? Remember that the cost of funding for each component in the capital structure is based on the expectations of investors for the returns they require from the corporation. In Chapter 6 we discovered that expectations about the future are part of today's interest rates (the expectations hypothesis) and that the returns expected by investors from their investment are based on what they have at stake—the market value of their investment.

For example, suppose an investor purchased shares in a corporation several years ago for $1,000 and those shares are now worth $10,000. If that investor expected the investment to generate a 12 percent return over the next year, by way of dividends or capital gain from an increasing share price, the expectation would be for $1,200 based on the market value, and not $120 based on the book value. What is relevant to investors and their required rate of return is the market value of their investment.

Toronto Stock Exchange
www.tsx.ca

Let's examine how we would calculate the market value weightings for a corporation. If there is an active market for the securities of the corporation, it is easy to identify their market value, as we do below for equity. The market value will be available in the newspaper or by calling an investment dealer. Without an active market for a firm's securities we must use the present value models from Chapter 10 to determine market value, as we do below for debt and preferreds.

To use the present value models, we must identify from the firm's financial statements the book values of debt, preferreds, common stock, and retained earnings. The footnotes should disclose the historical costs for each of these components of the capital structure. The historical costs and book values from the financial statements will identify the cash flows (future values, payments, time periods) for the present value models.

For our example, let us suppose that the debt has 20 years to maturity with an annual coupon rate of 16 percent. The preferreds are paying dividends at the rate of 7 percent and there are 1 million common shares outstanding.

Finally, to calculate the current market values of each component of the capital structure we will need discount rates. We will use the current yields (interest rates) from the market. Current yields on securities of similar risk are found in newspapers, on many web sites, and from investment dealers. Table 11–2 illustrates how these yields are found.

Again, for our example, we will suppose that the common shares currently trade at $8.00 per share in the market, while present yields are 12 percent on debt and 10 percent on preferreds.

prices cause a downward shift in K_a. This graph illuminates two basic points: (1) The firm wants to keep its debt-to-equity ratio between x and y at all times; and (2) the firm would rather finance its long-term needs at K_{at+2} than at K_{at}. Corporations do have some leeway in the money and capital markets such that it is not uncommon for the debt-to-equity ratio to fluctuate between x and y over a business cycle. Note, however, that the firm at point y has lost the flexibility of increasing its debt-to-equity ratio without incurring the penalty of higher capital costs.

Cost of Capital in the Capital Budgeting Decision

The current cost of capital for each source of funds is always important when making a capital budgeting decision. Historical costs for past funding may have little to do with current costs against which future potential returns must be measured. When raising new financial capital, a company taps the various sources of financing over a reasonable time period. Regardless of the particular source of funds the company is using for the purchase of an asset, the required rate of return or discount rate is the weighted average cost of capital. As long as the company earns its cost of capital, the common share value of the firm is maintained since shareholders' expectations are being met. For example, assume the Baker Corporation was considering making an investment in eight projects with the returns and costs shown in Table 11–4. These projects could be viewed graphically and merged with the weighted average cost of capital to make a capital budgeting decision, as indicated in Figure 11–3.

TABLE 11–4
Investment projects available to the Baker Corporation

Projects	Expected Returns	Cost ($millions)
A	16.00%	$10
B	14.00	5
C	13.50	4
D	11.80	20
E	10.40	11
F	9.50	20
G	8.60	15
H	7.00	10
		$95

Notice that the Baker Corporation is contemplating $95 million in projects. Given that the weighted average cost of capital is 10.26 percent, however, it should choose only projects A through E, or $50 million in new assets. Selecting assets F, G, and H would probably reduce the market value of the common stock because these projects do not provide a return equal to the overall costs of raising funds. We cannot forget that using the weighted average cost of capital assumes that the Baker Corporation is in its optimum capital structure range and will employ that structure in the future. Furthermore, when using the cost of capital to evaluate capital projects, we are assuming those projects will not adjust the risk complexion of the corporation. If they do, investors will change their required rates of return, and the cost of capital as calculated will be inappropriate.

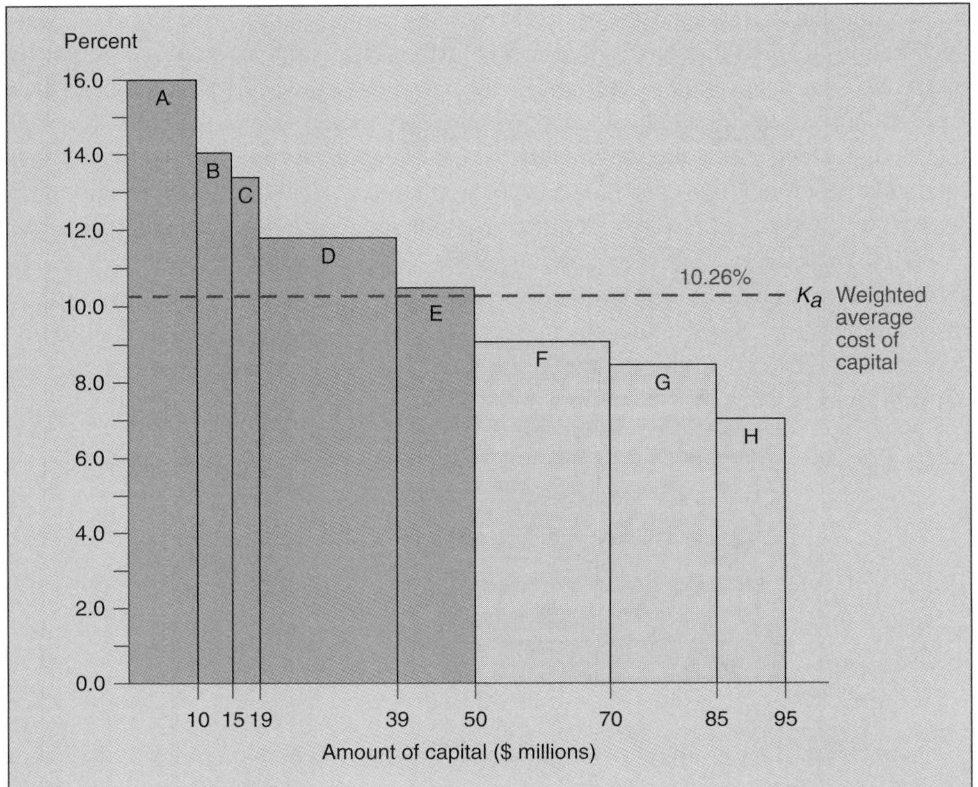

FIGURE 11–3
Cost of capital and investment projects for the Baker Corporation

The Marginal Cost of Capital

Nothing guarantees the Baker Corporation that its component cost of capital will stay constant for as much money as it wants to raise even if a given capital structure is maintained. If a large amount of financing is desired, the market may demand a higher cost of capital for each extra increment of funds desired. The point is analogous to the fact that you may be able to go to your relatives and best friends and raise funds for an investment at 10 percent. After exhausting the lending or investing power of those closest to you, and you have to look to other sources, your **marginal cost of capital will probably go up**.

As a background for this discussion, the cost of capital table for the Baker Corporation is reproduced again.

		Cost (aftertax)	Weights	Weighted Cost
Debt	K_d	6.55%	30%	1.97%
Preferred stock	K_p	10.94	10	1.09
Common equity (retained earnings)	K_e	12.00	60	7.20
Weighted average cost of capital	K_a			10.26%

We need to review the nature of the firm's capital structure to explain the concept of marginal cost of capital as it applies to the firm. Note that 60 percent of the firm's capital is in the form of common equity. This equity (ownership) capital is represented initially by share capital and subsequently by share capital and retained earnings. Management has learned through experience that 60 percent is the amount of equity capital the firm must maintain to keep a balance, acceptable to security holders, between fixed income securities and ownership interest. The astute reader has already realized, however, that depending on how quickly the firm's capital needs expand, the growth in internally generated funds that are recorded as retained earnings may not be enough to support the investment needs of the firm and to maintain a balanced capital structure.

For example, if the Baker Corporation generates \$23.4 million in earnings, it will be recorded as retained earnings and will be deployed with other capital in the investments of the firm.[8] Since management has determined that equity should represent 60 percent of the capital structure, these internally generated funds recorded as retained earnings will be adequate to support investments of \$39 million. More formally, we say that:

$$X = \frac{\text{Retained earnings}}{\text{Percent of equity in the capital structure}} \qquad (11\text{–}7)$$

(Where X represents the size of the investments that retained earnings will support.)

$$X = \frac{\$23.4 \text{ million}}{.60}$$
$$= \$39 \text{ million}$$

Once \$39 million of investments are made, internally generated funds, recorded as retained earnings, are no longer adequate to keep the equity portion of the capital structure above 60 percent. Lenders and investors become concerned if common equity (ownership) capital falls below 60 percent. Because of this, *new* common stock is needed to supplement retained earnings to provide the 60 percent common equity component for the firm. That is, after \$39 million of investments are made, additional common equity capital will be in the form of new common stock rather than retained earnings.

In the upper portion of Table 11–5, we see the original cost of capital that we have been discussing throughout the chapter. This applies up to a total capital amount of \$39 million. After \$39 million, the concept of marginal cost of capital becomes important, and as shown on the lower portion of the table, the cost of capital goes up.

K_{mc}, in the lower portion of the table, represents the *marginal* cost of capital, which becomes 11.06 percent after \$39 million. The cost of capital increases for capital above \$39 million because the invested common equity is now in the form of new common stock rather than retained earnings. The cost of the latter is slightly more than the former because of flotation costs (F). The formula for the cost of new common stock was shown earlier in the chapter as Formula 11–6. In this circumstance it is calculated:

[8]This basic concept, known as sustainable growth rate, is an important one for the student or practitioner of finance to grasp. Too often managers have assumed that as long as their firms were profitable, they could continue to grow as quickly as possible. Rude awakenings sometimes followed when banks refused to advance any more loans to the cash-strapped firms. The basic formula for determining the internally sustainable growth rate of the firm is discussed in Chapter 4. Assuming the firm's debt ratio is optimal, the rest of the balance sheet can grow no faster than the equity portion.

TABLE 11–5
Cost of capital for different amounts of financing

		Aftertax Cost	Weights	Weighted Cost
First $39 million:				
Debt	K_d	6.55%	.30	1.97%
Preferred	K_p	10.94	.10	1.09
Common equity*	K_e	12.00	.60	7.20
				K_a = 10.26%
Next $11 million:				
Debt	K_d	6.55%	.30	1.97%
Preferred	K_p	10.94	.10	1.09
Common equity†	K_n	13.33	.60	8.00
				K_{mc} = 11.06%

*Retained earnings.
†New common equity.

$$K_n = \left(\frac{D_1}{P_0} + g\right)\left(\frac{P_0}{P_n}\right) = \left(\frac{\$2}{\$40} + 7\%\right)\left(\frac{\$40}{\$36}\right)$$

$$= \frac{\$2}{\$46} = 13.33\%$$

The flotation cost (F) of $4.00 reduces the net share proceeds (P_n) to $36.00 and makes the cost of new common stock 13.33 percent. This is higher than the 12 percent cost of retained earnings we have been using and therefore causes the increase in the marginal cost of capital.

To carry the example a bit further, let us assume the cost of debt of 6.55 percent applies to the first $15 million of debt the firm raises. After that, the aftertax cost of debt rises to 7.9 percent because of the need to tap more expensive sources. Since debt represents 30 percent of the capital structure for the Baker Corporation, the cheaper form of debt is available to support the capital structure up to $50 million. We derive the $50 million by using Formula 11–8.

$$Z = \frac{\text{Amount of lower-cost debt}}{\text{Percent of debt in the capital structure}} \quad (11\text{–}8)$$

(Where Z represents the size of the investments in which lower-cost debt can be utilized.)

$$Z = \frac{\$15 \text{ million}}{.30}$$

$$= \$50 \text{ million}$$

After the first $50 million of capital is raised, lower-cost debt is no longer available to make up 30 percent of the capital structure. After $50 million in total financing, the aftertax cost of debt goes up to the previously specified 7.9 percent. The marginal cost of capital for over $50 million in financing is shown in Table 11–6, on the next page.

TABLE 11–6
Cost of capital for increasing amounts of financing

		Cost (aftertax)	Weights	Weighted Cost
Over \$50 million:				
Debt (higher cost)	K_d	7.90%	.30	2.37%
Preferred stock	K_p	10.94	.10	1.09
Common equity (new common stock)	K_n	13.33	.60	8.00
				K_{mc} = 11.46%

This increase in the cost of debt causes another rise in the marginal cost of capital (K_{mc}) to 11.46 percent after \$50 million of financing. Observe that the capital structure with over \$50 million of financing reflects both the increase in the cost of debt and the continued exclusive use of new common stock to represent additional common equity capital.

We could carry on this process by next considering at what point an increase in the cost of preferred stock would be demanded by investors, or at what points the costs of debt or new common stock increase as more and more capital is required. For now, however, it is important that you merely understand the basic process and can think it through when the details of an actual situation are at hand.

To summarize, then, we have calculated that the Baker Corporation has a basic weighted average cost of capital of 10.26 percent. This chapter was devoted to demonstrating the development of that value. Table 11–1 presented it originally. We found, however, that as the firm's investment plans required it to substantially expand its capital structure, the weighted average cost of capital increased. This process demonstrated the concept of marginal cost of capital. The first increase, or break point, occurred at \$39 million. At that point the marginal cost of capital went up to 11.06 percent as a result of having to raise new common stock (in other words we passed the firm's sustainable growth rate). The second increase in the cost of capital occurred when the total required capital structure passed \$50 million. Past there, the marginal cost of capital increased to 11.46 percent as a result of the need to utilize more expensive sources of debt. These marginal changes are summarized as:

Amount of Financing	Marginal Cost of Capital
0–\$39 million	10.26
\$39–50 million	11.06
Over \$50 million	11.46

Remember that this discussion of marginal cost of capital is highly dependent on the investment opportunities available to the firm and, in turn, has a great effect on them. Figure 11–3 showed the estimated returns from investment for Projects A through H. Figure 11–4 reproduces the returns originally shown in Figure 11–3 and includes the concept of marginal cost of capital. Observe that the marginal cost of capital (dotted lines) increases even as the marginal returns (straight lines) decrease.

In the earlier Figure 11–3 presentation, the Baker Corporation seemed justified in choosing projects A through E, representing capital expenditures of $50 million. Figure 11–4 represents a more sophisticated consideration of the investment alternatives and, as such, tells a slightly different story. Because of the increasing marginal cost of capital, the returns exceed the cost of capital for only the first $39 million of projects. This means that only projects A through D are deemed acceptable.

For most of our discussion of capital budgeting decisions in the next chapter, we assume we are operating on the initial flat part of the marginal cost of capital curve shown in Figure 11–4. This means that most of our decisions are made based on the initial weighted average cost of capital. Such an approach is generally acceptable, but it is up to the astute financial analyst to realize when this will not be the case. If there seem to be very real financing consequences involved with taking on marginal projects, he or she must consider them.

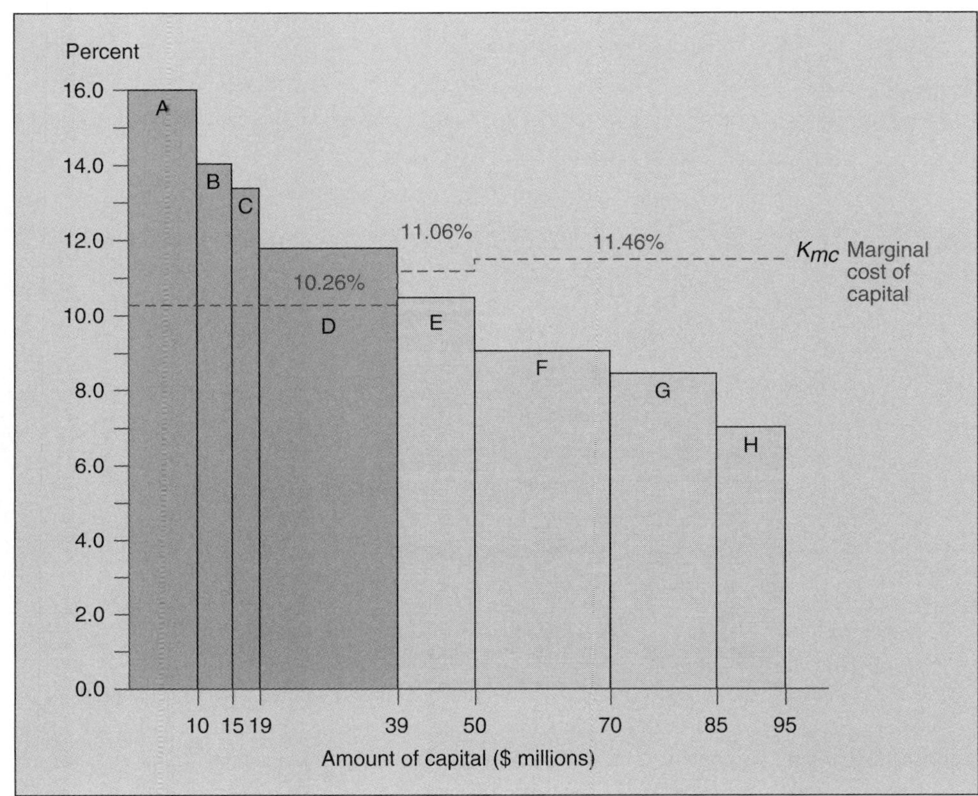

FIGURE 11–4
Marginal cost of capital and Baker Corporation investment alternatives

Summary

1. The cost of capital is determined by computing the costs from the various sources of financings and weighting them in proportion to their expected representation in future financings. As such, it is the overall cost of financing of the firm at the present time based on expectations of the future.
2. The cost of capital is a critical component in the valuation of a firm and its future prospects. An investment is expected to generate cash flows in the future. To evaluate the worth of these cash flows, we want to discount them to the present and compare their value with the investment cost.

By using the cost of capital as the discount rate, we suggest that the cash flows are valued on the basis of the financing required to make the investment that will produce those cash flows. The cost of capital is used under the assumption that the investment evaluated is of the same risk as the average investment of the firm. It is important to realize that the cost of capital is a concept used as an evaluation tool to analyze investment proposals.

3. A cost of capital calculation requires the determination of the appropriate weightings of the components of the firm's capital structure and the current costs of those components. We saw how to determine the weightings based on the market value of the existing capital structure. The cost of each component in the capital structure is closely associated with the valuation of that source. For debt and preferred stock, the cost is directly related to the current yield determined by investors, with the cost of debt reduced downward to reflect the tax deductibility of interest costs.

   For common stock the cost of retained earnings (K_e) is the current dividend yield on the security plus the anticipated future rate of growth in dividends. Minor adjustments must be made to the formula to determine the cost of new common stock issues. A summary of the Baker Corporation's capital costs, as developed throughout the chapter, is presented in Table 11–7.

TABLE 11–7

Cost of components in the capital structure

1. Cost of debt	K_d = Yield $(1 - T)$ = 6.55%	Yield = 10.74% T = Corporate tax rate, 39.0%
2. Cost of preferred stock	$K_p = \frac{D_p}{P_p - F} = 10.94\%$	D_p = Preferred dividend, \$10.50 P_p = Price of preferred stock, \$100 F = Flotation costs, \$4.00
3. Cost of common equity (retained earnings)	$K_e = \frac{D_1}{P_0} + g = 12.0\%$	D_1 = First year common dividend, \$2.00 P_0 = Price of common stock, \$40.00 g = Growth rate, 7.0%
4. Cost of new common stock	$K_n = \left(\frac{D_1}{P_0} + g\right)\left(\frac{P_0}{P_n}\right) = 13.33\%$	Same as above, with F = Flotation costs of \$4.00, P_n = \$36.00

4. The weights for each of the elements in the capital structure should be chosen with a view to minimizing the overall cost of capital. While debt is usually the cheapest form of financing, excessive use of debt may increase the financial risk of the firm and drive up the costs of all sources of financing. The wise financial manager attempts to ascertain which level of debt will result in the lowest overall cost of capital. That level of debt defines the optimum capital structure. Once the optimum capital structure has been established, the weighted average cost of capital is used as the discount rate in converting future cash flows to their present value. The major decision rule, then, is to determine if an investment proposal will earn at least the cost of the firm's financing. Investments that earn more than that cost increase the value of the firm or create value.

5. The marginal cost of capital is important in considering what happens to a firm's cost of capital as it tries to finance large requirements for funds. At first the company uses up its access to retained earnings, with the cost of financing rising as higher-cost new common stock is substituted for retained earnings. Common stock is needed to maintain the optimum capital structure (that is, the appropriate debt-to-equity ratio). Needs for larger amounts of financial capital can also cause the

costs of the individual means of financing to rise by raising the interest rates the firm must pay or by depressing the price of the stock because more is offered for sale than the market wants to absorb at the old price. The marginal cost of capital is the cost of the next dollar of financing required based on the presumption that the next dollar comes from a weighted mix of the optimal financing sources.

Review of Formulas

1. $K_d = Y(1 - T)$ (11–1*a*)
   K_d is cost of debt
   Y is yield
   T is corporate tax rate
2. $K_d = \frac{Y(1 - T)}{1 - F}$ (11–1*b*)
   F is flotation, or selling, cost
3. $K_p = \frac{D_p}{P_p - F}$ (11–2)
   K_p is cost of preferred stock
   D_p is the annual dividend on preferred stock
   P_p is the price of preferred stock
4. $K_e = \frac{D_1}{P_0} + g$ (11–3)
   K_e is cost of common equity
5. $K_j = R_f + \beta_j(R_m - R_f)$ (11–4*a*)
   K_j is required return on common equity
   R_f is risk-free rate of return
   β_j is beta coefficient
   R_m is return in the market as measured by an appropriate index
6. $K_{jn} = K_j \frac{P_0}{P_r}$ (11–4*b*)
   K_j is cost of new equity (CAPM)
7. $K_e = \frac{D_1}{P_0} + g$ (11–5)
   K_e is cost of common equity in the form of retained earnings
8. $K_n = \left(\frac{D_1}{P_0} + g\right)\frac{P_0}{P_n}$ (11–6)
   K_n is cost of new common stock
9. X (size of the investments that retained earnings will support $= \frac{\text{Retained earnings}}{\text{\% of equity in the capital structure}}$ (11–7)
10. Z (size of the investments that lower-cost debt will support) $= \frac{\text{Amount of lower-cost debt}}{\text{\% of lower-cost debt in the capital structure}}$ (11–8)

F is flotation, or selling cost (as a percentage)
P_0 is current selling price
P_n is net proceeds received on a new share issue after flotation costs
D_1 is dividend at end of the first year (or period)
g is the growth rate in dividends

List of Terms

cost of capital 363
capital structure 364
flotation costs 366
common equity 368
dividend valuation model 369
dividend capitalization model 369
capital asset pricing model (CAPM) 370
weighted average cost of capital 374
optimum capital structure 374
marginal cost of capital 381

Discussion Questions

1. Why do we use the overall cost of capital for investment decisions even when an investment will be funded by only one source of capital (for example, debt)?
2. How does the cost of a source of capital relate to the valuation concepts presented in Chapter 10?
3. In computing the cost of capital, do we use the historical costs of existing debt and equity or the current costs as determined in the market? Why?
4. Why is the cost of debt less than the cost of preferred stock if both securities are priced to yield 10 percent in the market?
5. What are the two sources of equity (ownership) capital for the firm?
6. Explain why retained earnings has an opportunity cost associated with it.
7. Why is the cost of retained earnings the equivalent of the firm's own required rate of return on common stock (K_e)?
8. Why is the cost of new common stock (K_n) higher than the cost of retained earnings (K_e)?
9. How are the weights determined to arrive at the optimal weighted average cost of capital?
10. Explain the traditional, U-shaped approach to the cost of capital.
11. Identify other variables (ratios) besides the debt-to-equity ratio that influence a company's cost of capital. You may wish to refer to Chapter 3 for possibilities.
12. It has often been said that if the company can't earn a rate of return greater than the cost of capital, it should not make investments. Explain.
13. What effect would inflation have on a company's cost of capital? (Hint: Think about how inflation influences interest rates, stock prices, corporate profits, and growth.)
14. What is the concept of marginal cost of capital?
15. What limitations are there in using the dividend valuation model to determine the cost of equity capital?
16. What is the justification for using market value weightings rather than book value weightings?

INTERNET RESOURCES AND QUESTIONS

Two Canadian sites rate and grade debt. The ratings determine the spread corporations pay above Government of Canada securities:
www.standardandpoors.com/canada
www.dbrs.com

Two sites identify current yields on bond issues:
www.globeandmail.com
www.scotiacapital.com

The Canoe site identifies current pricing on preferreds and common stock, including P/E ratios, and dividend yields:
www.webfin.com/en

Betas and other useful share information is available on many Canadian companies at Nasdaq Canada and Thomson Financial
www.thomsoninvest.net
www.nasdaq-canada.com

1. Calculate the cost of capital for a corporation listed on one of the major exchanges in Canada. Use current pricing on debt and equity from the sites identified above, and use the latest filed financial statement of the selected company. The financial statements will be available at www.sedar.com.
2. Update the information included in Table 11–2. Have any of the ratings changed? Can you suggest why the ratings have changed?
3. Find the betas, P/E ratios and dividend yields for the companies listed in Table 11–2. What do they tell you about the relative riskiness of the companies?

Problems

1. Sullivan Cement Company can issue debt yielding 13 percent. The company is paying a 39 percent tax rate. What is the aftertax cost of debt?
2. Calculate the aftertax cost of debt under each of the following conditions.

	Yield	Corporate Tax Rate
a.	8.0%	30.0%
b.	12.0%	42.0%
c.	10.6%	22.0%

3. Calculate the aftertax cost of debt on a bond issue yielding 10 percent. The issuing company pays tax at a rate of 34 percent and will incur distribution costs of 1 percent on this bond issue.
4. Airborne Airlines has a $1,000 par value bond outstanding with 15 years to maturity. The bond carries an annual interest payment of $98.00, payable semiannually, and is currently selling for $1,150. Airborne is in a 25 percent tax bracket. The firm wishes to know what the aftertax cost of a new bond issue is likely to be. The yield to maturity on the new issue will be the same as the yield to maturity on the old issue because the risk and maturity date will be similar.
   a. Compute the yield to maturity on the old issue and use this as the yield for the new issue.
   b. Make the appropriate tax adjustment to determine the aftertax cost of debt.
5. Addison Glass Company has a $1,000 par value bond outstanding with 25 years to maturity. The bond carries an annual interest payment of $88.00, payable semiannually, and is currently selling for $925. Addison is in a 25 percent tax bracket. The firm wishes to know what the aftertax cost of a new bond issue is likely to be. The yield to maturity on the new issue will be the same as the yield to maturity on the old issue because the risk and maturity date will be similar.

   a. Compute the yield to maturity on the old issue and use this as the yield for the new issue.
   b. Make the appropriate tax adjustment to determine the aftertax cost of debt.

6. For Addison Glass Company, described in the previous problem, assume the yield on the bonds goes up by one percentage point and that the tax rate is now 40 percent.
   a. What is the new aftertax cost of debt?
   b. Has the aftertax cost of debt gone up or down from the previous problem? Explain why.
7. Loblaw is planning to issue debt that will mature in the year 2027. In many respects the issue is similar to currently outstanding debt of the corporation. Using Table 11–2 in the chapter, identify:
   a. The yield to maturity on similarly outstanding debt for the firm, in terms of maturity.
   b. Assume that because the new debt will be issued at par, the required yield to maturity will be 0.15 percent higher than the value determined in part *a*. Add this factor to the answer in *a*. (New issues at par sometimes require a slightly higher yield than old issues that are trading below par. There is less leverage and fewer tax advantages.)
   c. If the firm is in a 40 percent tax bracket, what is the aftertax cost of debt?
8. Burger Queen can sell preferred shares for $70.00 with an estimated flotation cost of $2.50. The preferred stock is anticipated to pay $6.00 per share in dividends.
   a. Compute the cost of preferred stock for Burger Queen.
   b. Do we need to make a tax adjustment for the issuing firm?

9. Wallace Container Company issued $100.00 par value preferred shares 12 years ago. The shares provided a 9 percent yield at the time of issue. Each preferred share is now selling for $72.00. What is the current yield or cost of preferred stock? (Disregard flotation costs.)
10. The treasurer of BioScience, Inc., is asked to compute the cost of fixed income securities for her corporation. Even before making the calculations, she assumes the aftertax cost of debt is at least 2 percent less than that for preferred stock. Based on the following facts, is she correct?

    Debt can be issued at a yield of 11 percent, and the corporate tax rate is 30 percent. Preferred shares will be priced at $50.00 and pay a dividend of $4.80. The flotation cost on the preferred stock is $2.10.
11. Murray Motor Company wants you to calculate its cost of common stock. During the next 12 months, the company expects to pay dividends (D_1) of $2.50 per share, and the current price of its common stock is $50.00 per share. The expected growth rate is 8 percent.
    a. Compute the cost of retained earnings (K_e).
    b. If a $3.00 flotation cost is involved, compute the cost of new common stock (K_n).
12. Compute K_e and K_n under the following circumstances:
    a. $D_1 = \$4.20$; $P_0 = \$55.00$; $g = 5\%$; $F = \$3.80$.
    b. $D_1 = \$0.40$; $P_0 = \$15.00$; $g = 8\%$; $F = \$1.00$.
    c. E_1 (earnings at the end of period one) = $8.00; payout ratio equals 25 percent; $P_0 = \$32.00$; $g = 5\%$; $F = \$2.00$.
    d. D_0 (dividend at the beginning of the first period) = $3.00; growth rate for dividends and earnings (g) = 9%; $P_0 = \$60.00$; $F = \$3.50$.
13. Business has been good for Keystone Control Systems, as indicated by the four-year growth in earnings per share. The earnings have grown from $1.00 to $1.63.
    a. Determine the compound annual rate of growth in earnings ($n = 4$).
    b. Based on the growth rate determined in part *a*, project earnings for next year (E_1). Round to two places to the right of the decimal point.

c. Assume the dividend payout ratio is 40 percent. Compute D1. Round to two places to the right of the decimal point.

d. The current price of the stock is $50. Using the growth rate (g) from part *a* and D_1 from part *c*, compute K_e.

e. If the flotation cost is $3.75, compute the cost of new common stock (K_n).

14. Global Technology's capital structure is as follows:

Debt	35%
Preferred stock	15
Common equity	50

The aftertax cost of debt is 6.5 percent; the cost of preferred stock is 10 percent; and the cost of common equity (in the form of retained earnings) is 13.5 percent.

Calculate Global Technology's weighted average cost of capital in a manner similar to Table 11–1.

15. As an alternative to the capital structure shown in the previous problem for Global Technology, an outside consultant has suggested the following modifications.

Debt	60%
Preferred stock	5
Common equity	35

Under this new and more debt-oriented arrangement, the aftertax cost of debt is 8.8 percent, the cost of preferred stock is 11 percent, and the cost of common equity (in the form of retained earnings) is 15.6 percent.

Recalculate Global's weighted average cost of capital. Which plan is optimal in terms of minimizing the weighted average cost of capital?

16. Given the following information, calculate the weighted average cost of capital for Glamour Girl Cosmetics. Line up the calculations in the order shown in Table 11–1.

Percent of capital structure:	
Debt	40%
Preferred stock	10
Common equity	50
Additional information:	
Bond coupon rate	12%
Bond yield	10%
Dividend, expected common . . .	$ 3.00
Dividend, preferred	$ 9.20
Price, common	$60.00
Price, preferred	$99.00
Flotation cost, preferred	$ 4.00
Corporate growth rate	9%
Corporate tax rate	30%

17. Given the following information, calculate the weighted average cost of capital for Digital Processing, Inc. Line up the calculations in the order shown in Table 11–1.

Percent of capital structure:	
Preferred stock	15%
Common equity	40
Debt	45
Additional information:	
Corporate tax rate	34%
Dividend, preferred	$ 8.50
Dividend, expected common . . .	$ 2.50
Price, preferred	$105.00
Corporate growth rate	7%
Bond yield	9.5%
Flotation cost, preferred	$3.60
Price, common	$75.00

18. Carr Auto Parts is trying to calculate its cost of capital for use in a capital budgeting decision. Mr. Horn, the vice president of finance, has given you the following information and has asked you to compute the weighted average cost of capital.

The company currently has outstanding a bond with a 12 percent coupon rate and a convertible bond with an 8.1 percent rate. The firm has been informed by its investment dealer, Axle, Wiell, and Axle, that bonds of equal risk and credit rating are now selling to yield 14 percent. The common stock has a price of $30.00 and an expected dividend (D_1) of $1.30 per share. The firm's historical growth rate of earnings and dividends per share has been 15.5 percent, but security analysts on Bay Street expect this growth to slow to 12 percent in the future. The preferred stock is selling at $60.00 per share and carries a dividend of $6.80 per share. The corporate tax rate is 30 percent. The flotation costs are 3 percent of the selling price for preferred stock.

The optimum capital structure for the firm seems to be 40 percent debt, 5 percent preferred stock, and 55 percent common equity in the form of retained earnings.

Compute the cost of capital for the individual components in the capital structure, and then calculate the weighted average cost of capital.

19. First Yukon Utility Company faces increasing needs for capital. Fortunately it has an A+ credit rating. The corporate tax rate is 36 percent. First Yukon's treasurer is trying to determine the corporation's current weighted average cost of capital to assess the profitability of capital budgeting projects. Historically, the corporation's earnings and dividends per share have increased at about a 6 percent annual rate.

First Yukon's common stock is selling at $60.00 per share, and the company will pay a $4.80 per share dividend (D_1). The company's $100.00 preferred stock has been yielding 9 percent in the current market. Flotation costs for the company have been estimated by its investment dealer to be $1.50 for preferred stock. The company's optimum capital structure is 40 percent debt, 10 percent preferred stock, and 50 percent common equity in the form of retained earnings. Refer to the table below on bond issues for comparative yields on bonds of equal risks to First Yukon, maturing in 2011. Compute the answer to questions *a, b, c,* and *d* from the information given.

Data on Bond Issues

Issue	Rating	Price	Yield to Maturity
Utilities:			
NAV 6.5%, 2009	AA+	105.01	5.66%
HydroOne 6.4% 2011	AA−	103.83	5.88
Bell Canada 6.9%, 2011	A+	105.11	6.20
Epcor 6.6%, 2011	A−	100.48	6.53
Alberta Energy 7.1%, 2011	BBB+	99.77	7.13
Industrials:			
Clarica 6.65%, 2010	AA	105.02	5.90
BMO 6.647%, 2010	A+	101.48	6.37
Suncor 6.7%, 2011	A−	101.19	6.53
Nova 7.85%, 2010	BBB−	91.90	9.23

a. Cost of debt, K_d.

b. Cost of preferred stock, K_p.

c. Cost of common equity in the form of retained earnings, K_e.

d. Weighted average cost of capital.

20. The McGee Corporation finds that it is necessary to determine its marginal cost of capital. McGee's current capital structure calls for 40 percent debt, 5 percent preferred stock, and 55 percent common equity. Initially common equity will be in the form of retained earnings (K_e) and then new common stock (K_n). The costs of the various sources of financing are as follows: debt, 7.4 percent; preferred stock, 10.0 percent; retained earnings, 13.0 percent; and new common stock, 14.4 percent.

a. What is the initial weighted average cost of capital? (Include debt, preferred stock, and common equity in the form of retained earnings, K_e.)

b. If the firm has $27.5 million in retained earnings, at what size of investment will the firm run out of retained earnings?

c. What will the marginal cost of capital be immediately after that point? (Equity will remain at 55 percent of the capital structure, but it will all be in the form of new common stock, K_n.)

d. The 7.4 percent cost of debt referred to above applies only to the first $32 million of debt. After that the cost of debt will be 8.6 percent. At what size of investment will there be a change in the cost of debt?

e. What will the marginal cost of capital be immediately after that point? (Consider the facts in both parts *c* and *d*.)

21. The Flying Burrito Corporation finds that it is necessary to determine its marginal cost of capital. Burrito's current capital structure calls for 60 percent debt, 10 percent preferred stock, and 30 percent common equity. Initially common equity will be in the form of retained earnings (K_e) and then new common stock (K_n). The costs of the various sources of financing are as follows: debt, 4.2 percent; preferred stock, 6 percent; retained earnings, 11 percent; and new common stock, 12.5 percent.

a. What is the initial weighted average cost of capital? (Include debt, preferred stock, and common equity in the form of retained earnings, K_e.)

b. If the firm has $10 million in retained earnings, at what size of investment will the firm run out of retained earnings?

c. What will the marginal cost of capital be immediately after that point? (Equity will remain at 30 percent of the capital structure, but it will all be in the form of new common stock, K_n.)

d. The 4.2 percent cost of debt referred to above applies only to the first $15 million of debt. After that the cost of debt will be 5.8 percent. At what size of investment will there be a change in the cost of debt?

e. What will the marginal cost of capital be immediately after that point? (Consider the facts in both parts *c* and *d*.)

COMPREHENSIVE PROBLEMS

22. Medical Research Corporation is expanding its research and production capacity to introduce a new line of products. Current plans call for the expenditure of $100 million on four projects of equal size ($25 million) but different returns. Project A is in blood clotting proteins and has an expected return of 18 percent. Project B relates to a hepatitis vaccine and carries a potential return of 14 percent. Project C, dealing with a cardiovascular compound, is expected to earn 11.8 percent, and Project D, an investment in orthopedic implants, is expected to show a 10.9 percent return.

    The firm has $15 million in retained earnings. After a capital structure with $15 million in retained earnings is reached (in which retained earnings represent 60 percent of the financing), all additional equity financing must come in the form of new common stock.

    Common stock is selling for $25.00 per share, and underwriting costs are estimated at $3.00 if new shares are issued. Dividends for the next year will be $0.90 per share ($D_1$), and earnings and dividends have grown consistently at 11 percent per year.

    The yield on comparative bonds has been hovering at 11 percent. The investment dealer believes the first $20 million of bonds could be sold to yield 11 percent, while additional debt might require a 2 percent premium and be marketed to yield 13 percent. The corporate tax rate is 30 percent. Debt represents 40 percent of the capital structure.

    a. Based on the two sources of financing, what is the initial weighted average cost of capital? (Use K_d and K_e.)

    b. At what size capital structure will the firm run out of retained earnings?

    c. What will the marginal cost of capital be immediately after that point?

    d. At what size capital structure will there be a change in the cost of debt?

    e. What will the marginal cost of capital be immediately after that point?

    f. Based on the information about potential returns on investments in the first paragraph and information on marginal cost of capital (in parts *a*, *c*, and *e*), how large a capital investment budget should the firm use?

    g. Graph the answer determined in part *f*.

23. Masco Oil and Gas Company is a very large company with common stock listed on the Toronto Stock Exchange and bonds traded over the counter. As of the current balance sheet, it has three bond issues outstanding:

$150 million of 10% series	2016
$ 50 million of 7% series	2010
$ 75 million of 5% series	2005

The vice president of finance is planning to sell $75 million of bonds next year to replace the debt due to expire in 2005. Present market yields on similar BB rated bonds are 12.1 percent. Masco also has $90 million of 7.5 percent noncallable preferred stock outstanding, and it has no intentions of selling any more preferred stock in the future. The preferred stock is currently priced at $80.00 per share, and its dividend per share is $7.80.

The company has had very volatile earnings, but its dividends per share have had a very stable growth rate of 8 percent and this will continue. The expected dividend (D_1) is $1.90 per share and the common stock is selling for $40.00 per share. The company's investment dealer has quoted the following flotation costs to Masco: $2.50 per share for preferred stock and $2.20 per share for common stock.

On the advice of its investment dealer, Masco has kept its debt at 50 percent of assets and its equity at 50 percent. Masco sees no need to sell either common or preferred stock in the foreseeable future as it generates enough internal funds for its investment needs when these funds are combined with debt financing. Masco's corporate tax rate is 40 percent.

Compute the cost of capital for the following:

a. Bond (debt) (K_d).

b. Preferred stock (K_p).

c. Common equity in the form of retained earnings (K_e).

d. New common stock (K_n).

e. Weighted average cost of capital.

24. A Dozen Monkeys Ltd. has the following right-hand side of its balance sheet:

Debt: 8% coupon, 12 years to maturity	$ 8,000,000
Preferred shares: 5% dividend	1,000,000
Common shares: 750,000 outstanding	1,500,000
Retained earnings	4,500,000
	$15,000,000

New debt could be issued to yield 10 percent, with flotation costs netting the firm $970 on each $1,000 bond. Preferred shares would require a current yield of 8 percent, with aftertax flotation costs of 4 percent. Common shares currently trade at $15.00, but new shares would be discounted to $14.25 to encourage sales. Aftertax flotation costs on new common shares would be 5 percent. The anticipated dividend growth rate is 6 percent. The expected dividend is $1.50.

A Dozen Monkeys Ltd. has a 40 percent tax rate and would require new share capital to fund new investments. Based on market value weightings, calculate Monkey's weighted average cost of capital.

25. Island Capital has the following capital structure:

Bonds	$20,000,000
Perpetuals (preferred shares)	4,000,000
Common shares	20,000,000
Retained earnings	19,500,000
	$63,500,000

The existing bonds have a coupon rate of 8 percent with 18 years left to maturity, but current yields on these bonds are 11 percent. Flotation costs of $25.00 per $1,000 bond would be expected on a new issue.

The existing perpetuals have a $25.00 par value and an annual dividend rate of 9 percent. New perpetuals could be issued at a $50.00 par value with an 8 percent yield. Flotation costs would be 3 percent.

There are 4 million common shares outstanding that currently trade at $18.00 per share and expect to pay a dividend next year of $1.75 that will continue to grow at 7 percent per annum for the foreseeable future. New shares could be issued at $17.50 and would require flotation expenses of 5 percent of proceeds.

Island's tax rate is 39 percent, and it is expected that internally generated funds will be sufficient to fund capital projects in the near future.

a. Compute Island Capital's current cost of capital with market value weightings.

b. How would the cost of capital calculation change if new shares are required to fund the equity component of the capital structure?

26. Trois-Rivières Manufacturing has the following capital structure:

Debt: 10% coupon, due in 8 years	$10,000,000
Preferreds: 7.5% dividend (100,000 shares)	2,500,000
Common shares: 600,000 outstanding	6,000,000
Retained earnings	4,500,000
	$23,000,000

During the last five years Trois-Rivières Manufacturing has enjoyed steady growth, with common stock dividends growing from $0.80 to $1.23 (just recently paid). The common share price currently trades at $15.00. If new shares were issued at $15.00, they would require flotation expenses of 7 percent of proceeds.

The preferred shares currently trade at $26.50, and any new issue would require flotation expenses of 5 percent of price to investors.

The bonds currently pay interest semiannually and are trading at a price that yields a nominal 12 percent annual rate (12.36 effective annual rate). Flotation costs of new debt would be 4 percent of proceeds.

Trois-Rivières' tax rate is 38 percent, and equity financing would require a new share issue. Calculate the weighted average cost of capital of Trois-Rivières Manufacturing.

27. Murchie's is considering diversification by way of acquisition to reduce its reliance on its volatile core business. Mad Max, the CEO, has asked for your calculation of a discount rate to be used to analyze the potential acquisition targets. The following information has been assembled.

Long-term bonds	$10,000,000
Subordinated perpetual bonds	2,000,000
Common shares capital	2,062,500
Retained earnings	937,500
	$15,000,000

The yield on 98-day treasury bills is 7.38 percent. Long-term debt has 15 years to maturity and has a coupon rate of 12 percent paid semiannually. Currently the bonds are trading at a premium of 15 percent to face value. A new debt issue would incur flotation costs of 3 percent of the issue price.

The perpetual bonds were issued at a yield of 9 percent but currently are trading to yield 12 percent. The flotation costs of a new issue would be 4 percent.

There are 750,000 common shares outstanding, presently priced at $4.50. Murchie's, with a beta of 1.7, is planning a dividend of $0.10. Future growth is suggested at a compound annualized rate of 15 percent. A new issue of common shares would net the firm $4.10 per share. Murchie's tax rate is 43 percent. Internally generated funds will not be sufficient to fund future expansion plans.

a. Calculate Murchie's weighted average cost of capital.

b. Calculate Murchie's weighted average cost of capital if it has negative income for tax purposes.

c. Comment on the appropriateness of Murchie's present capital structure.

d. Comment on the use of the weighted average cost of capital as calculated to analyze the suggested acquisitions.

Selected References

Amihud, Yakov, and Hiam Mendelson. "The Liquidity Route to a Lower Cost of Capital." *Journal of Applied Corporate Finance* 12 (Winter 2000), pp. 8–25.

Beranek, William, and Christopher Cornwell. "External Financing, Liquidity and Capital Expenditure." *Journal of Financial Research* 18 (Summer 1995), pp. 207–22.

Botosan, Christine A. "Evidence That Greater Disclosure Lowers the Cost of Equity Capital." *Journal of Applied Corporate Finance* 12 (Winter 2000), pp. 60–69.

Durand, David. "Costs of Debt and Equity Funds for Business: Trends and Problems of Measurement." *Conference on Research in Business Finance.* National Bureau of Economic Research, New York, 1952.

———. "Afterthoughts on a Controversy with MM, Plus New Thoughts on Growth and the Cost of Capital." *Financial Management* 18 (Summer 1989), pp. 12–18.

Johnson, Shane A. "The Effect of Bank Debt on Optimal Capital Structure." *Financial Management* 27 (Spring 1998), pp. 47–56.

Krueger, Mark K., and Charles M. Linke. "A Spanning Approach for Estimating Divisional Cost of Capital." *Financial Management* 23 (Spring 1994), pp. 64–70.

McDaniel, William R. "Techniques for Including Flotation Costs in Capital Budgeting: Materiality, Generality, and Circularity." *Financial Practice and Education* 4 (Spring–Summer 1994), pp. 139–48.

Miller, Merton H. "Debt and Taxes." *Journal of Finance* 32 (May 1977), pp. 262–73.

Modigliani, Franco, and Merton H. Miller. "The Cost of Capital, Corporation Finance and the Theory of Investment." *American Economic Review* 48 (June 1958), pp. 261–96.

———. "Taxes and the Cost of Capital: A Correction." *American Economic Review* 53 (June 1963), pp. 433–43.

Pastor, Lubos, and Robert F. Stamborough. "Cost of Equity Capital and Model Mispricing." *Journal of Finance* 54 (February 1999), pp. 67–121.

Roden, Dianne M., and Wilbur G. Lewellen. "Corporate Capital Structure Decisions: Evidence from Leveraged Buyouts." *Financial Management* 24 (Summer 1995), pp. 76–87.

www.mcgrawhill.ca/college/block

APPENDIX | 11A

Cost of Capital and the Capital Asset Pricing Model (optional)

The work of Harry Markowitz, examined in Chapter 13, highlighted the importance of thinking of investments, their returns, and their risks in a portfolio context. The risk of an investment is not so much its individual risk but the risk it adds to a portfolio or collection of assets. Individual or unique risks tend to disappear (they cancel each other out) within a portfolio. However some risk still remains and it is this risk that is of interest as it will shape the value that investors or shareholders place on assets. William Sharpe and others developed a model that focused on the risk that cannot be diversified away, which suggests that the nondiversifiable risk will determine the pricing of assets in an efficient market. Efficient markets are examined in Chapter 14.

The Capital Asset Pricing Model

The **capital asset pricing model (CAPM)** relates the risk-return trade-offs of individual assets to market returns. It suggests the expected return of an asset based on the asset's risk that cannot be diversified away. Common stock returns over time have generally been used to test this model since stock prices are widely available and efficiently priced, as are market indexes of stock performance. In theory the CAPM encompasses all assets, but in practice it is difficult to measure returns on all types of assets or to find an all-encompassing market index. For our purposes we use common stock returns to explain the model, and occasionally we generalize to other assets.

The basic form of the CAPM is a linear relationship between returns on individual stocks and stock market returns over time. By using least squares regression analysis, the return on an individual stock, K_j, is expressed in Formula 11A–1.

$$K_j = \alpha + \beta_j R_m + e \qquad (11A–1)$$

where

K_j = Return on individual common stock of a company
α = Alpha, the intercept on the y axis
β_j = Beta, the coefficient of stock (j)
R_m = Return on the stock market (an index of stock returns is used, usually the S&P/TSX Composite Index)
e = Error term of the regression formula

As indicated in Table 11A–1 and Figure 11A–1, this formula uses historical data to generate the alpha coefficient (α) and the **beta** coefficient (β_j), a measurement of the return performance of a given stock versus the return performance of the market. Assume we want to calculate a beta for Parts Associates, Inc. (PAI), and we have the performance data for that company and the market shown in Table 11A–1. The relationship between PAI and the market appears graphically in Figure 11A–1.

TABLE 11A–1
Performance of PAI and the market

	Rate of Return on Stock	
Year	**PAI**	**Market**
1	12.0%	10.0%
2	16.0	18.0
3	20.0	16.0
4	16.0	10.0
5	6.0	8.0
Mean return	14.0%	12.4%
Standard deviation	4.73%	3.87%

The alpha term in Figure 11A–1 of 2.8 percent is the y intercept of the linear regression. It is the expected return on PAI stock if returns on the market are zero. However, if the returns on the market are expected to approximate the historical rate of 12.4 percent, the expected return on PAI would be $K_j = 2.8 + 0.9(12.4) = 14.0$ percent. This maintains the historical relationship. If the returns on the market are expected to rise to 18 percent next year, expected return on PAI would be $K_j = 2.8 + 0.9(18.0) = 19$ percent.

FIGURE 11A–1

Linear regression of returns between PAI and the market

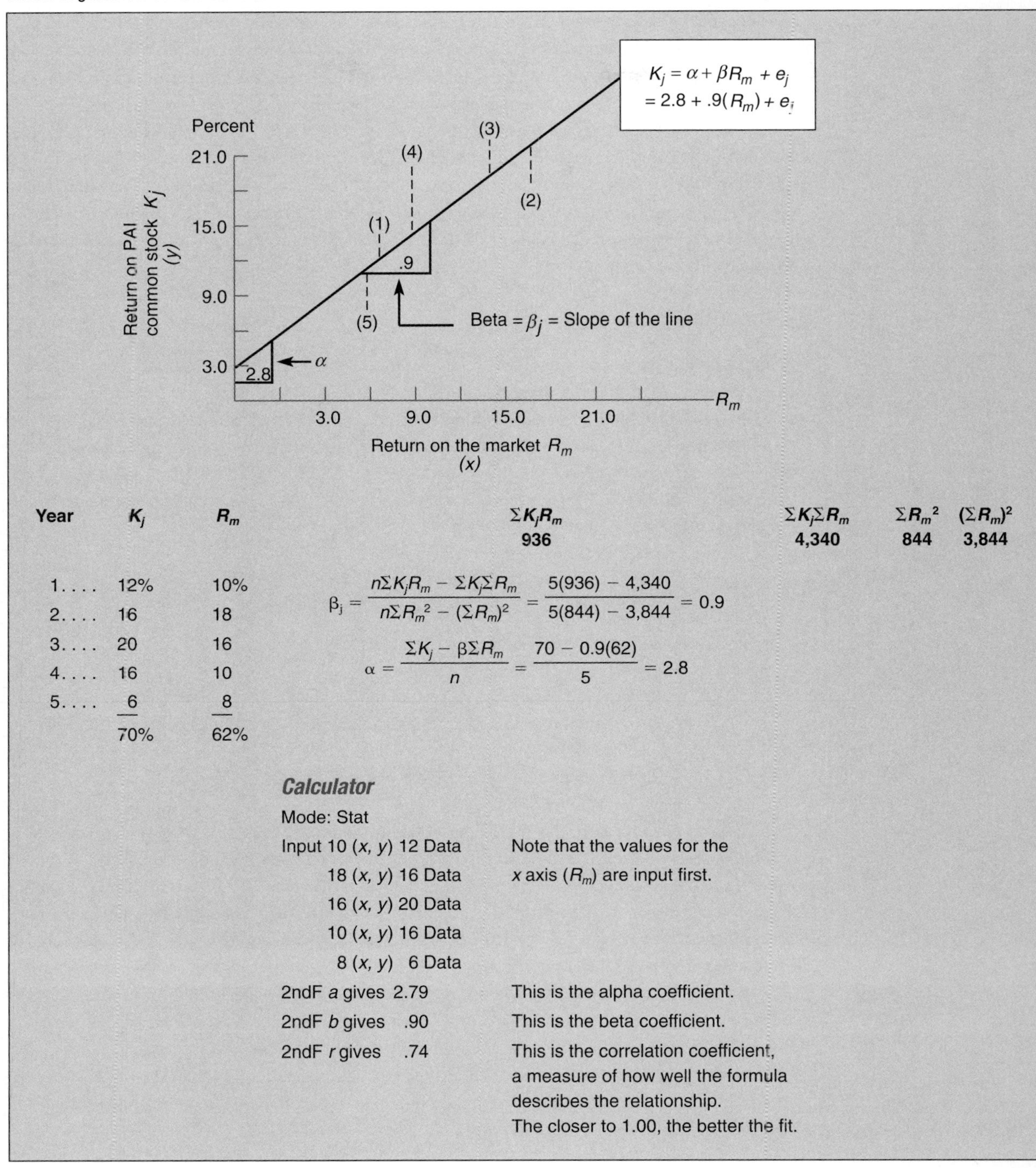

Year	K_j	R_m
1. . . .	12%	10%
2. . . .	16	18
3. . . .	20	16
4. . . .	16	10
5. . . .	6	8
	70%	62%

$\Sigma K_j R_m$	$\Sigma K_j \Sigma R_m$	ΣR_m^2	$(\Sigma R_m)^2$
936	4,340	844	3,844

$$\beta_j = \frac{n\Sigma K_j R_m - \Sigma K_j \Sigma R_m}{n\Sigma R_m^2 - (\Sigma R_m)^2} = \frac{5(936) - 4{,}340}{5(844) - 3{,}844} = 0.9$$

$$\alpha = \frac{\Sigma K_j - \beta \Sigma R_m}{n} = \frac{70 - 0.9(62)}{5} = 2.8$$

Calculator

Mode: Stat

Input 10 (*x*, *y*) 12 Data	Note that the values for the
18 (*x*, *y*) 16 Data	*x* axis (R_m) are input first.
16 (*x*, *y*) 20 Data	
10 (*x*, *y*) 16 Data	
8 (*x*, *y*) 6 Data	
2ndF *a* gives 2.79	This is the alpha coefficient.
2ndF *b* gives .90	This is the beta coefficient.
2ndF *r* gives .74	This is the correlation coefficient, a measure of how well the formula describes the relationship. The closer to 1.00, the better the fit.

The error term (*e*) is useful in determining the degree of confidence we would have in estimates of returns based on the regression line. From the historical data it is evident that all observations do not lie on the regression line, and yet we propose to use the relationship that it suggests to predict return expectations in the future. Based on the historical observations that do not fit on the line, the error terms, we can express the likelihood that our predicted returns are within an acceptable range of the prediction. Statistically this involves calculating the standard error of the estimate.

As the capital asset pricing model is developed, our focus will be on the beta term. If we plot only excess returns—that is, asset and market returns above the risk-free rate of return—it is found that alpha is not significantly different from zero. In addition, our expectation for the error term is also zero. In a diversified portfolio, the error terms tend to offset each other.

Notice that we are talking in terms of expectations. The CAPM is an expectational (ex ante) model, and there is no guarantee that historical data will reoccur. One area of empirical testing involves the stability and predictability of the beta coefficient based on historical data. Research has indicated that betas are more useful in a portfolio context (for groupings of stocks) because the betas of individual stocks are less stable from period to period than portfolio betas. In addition, research indicates betas of individual common stocks have a tendency to approach 1.0 over time.

The Security Market Line

The capital asset pricing model evolved from Formula 11A–1 into a risk premium model where the basic assumption is that investors expected to take more risk must be compensated by larger expected returns. Investors should also not accept returns that are less than they can get from a riskless asset. For CAPM purposes, it is assumed that short-term government Treasury bills may be considered a riskless asset.[1] When viewed in this context, an investor must achieve an extra return above that obtainable from a Treasury bill to induce the assumption of more risk. This brings us to the more common and theoretically useful model:

$$K_j = R_f + \beta_j(R_m - R_f) \qquad (11A\text{–}2)$$

where

R_f = Risk-free rate of return

β_j = Beta coefficient from Formula 11A–1

R_m = Return on the market index

$R_m - R_f$ = Premium or excess return of the market versus the risk-free rate (since the market is riskier than R_f, the assumption is that the expected R_m will be greater than R_f)

$\beta_j(R_m - R_f)$ = Expected return above the risk-free rate for the stock of Company *j,* given the level of risk

The model centres on *beta,* the coefficient of the premium demanded by an investor to invest in an individual stock. For each individual security, beta measures the sensitivity (volatility) of the security's return to the market. By definition, the market has a beta of 1.0, so if an individual company's beta is 1.0, it can expect to have returns as volatile as the market and total returns equal to the market. A company with a beta of 2.0 would be twice as volatile as the market and would be expected to generate more returns, whereas a company with a beta of 0.5 would be half as volatile as the market.

Ibbotson Associates
www.ibbotson.com/Research

The term $(R_m - R_f)$ indicates common stock is expected to generate a rate of return higher than the return on a Treasury bill. This makes sense since common stock has more risk. In fact, research by Roger Ibbotson shows that this risk premium over the last 60 years is close to 6.5 percent on average, but exhibits a wide standard deviation.[2] In the actual application of the CAPM to cost of capital, companies often use this historical risk premium in their calculations. In our example we use 6.5 percent to represent the expected $(R_m - R_f)$.

[1]A number of studies have also indicated that longer-term government securities may appropriately represent R_f (the risk-free rate).

[2]Ibbotson Associates, *Stocks, Bonds, Bills and Inflation: 1986 Yearbook* (Chicago, Ill.: Ibbotson Associates and Capital Market Research Center, 1987).

Risks and Returns

In January 2002 the following betas were reported for three companies listed on the Toronto Stock Exchange.

Big Rock Brewery	0.34
G.T. Group Telecom	1.04
Ballard Power	2.20

These betas give us a sense of the performance we should expect from each of the companies. We measure performance based on changes in the company's market share price. Big Rock Brewery would be least sensitive to market movements, while Ballard, a world leader in fuel cell technology, would be most sensitive to market movements. In an up market, Ballard's share price would be expected to outperform the two other companies. This would, however, be appropriate, given that with a higher beta, Ballard would be riskier. In a down market, Ballard would be expected to underperform the other companies. G.T. Telecom would tend to mirror the performance of the market as a whole.

A portfolio with equal value weightings of the three stocks would have a beta of 1.19 (0.34 × 0.33 + 1.04 × 0.33 + 2.20 × 0.33). This portfolio, with its higher beta, would be expected to moderately outperform the market, which has a beta of 1. A portfolio beta would be a more reliable estimate of performance because, through the benefits of diversification, the individual risks of each company would be reduced. Although beta measures risk in relation to the market fairly well, it does not capture the individual risk of a company's performance (the error term in formula 11A–1).

In constructing an individual's portfolio of investments, betas can be used (and are by investment managers) to assemble a collection of stocks. Betas would be used to construct a portfolio based on an investor's attitude toward risk and expected returns. Higher beta portfolios would expect greater returns, but with greater risks.

FINANCE IN ACTION

Q1 What are the current betas of these companies?

Q2 Can you find any Canadian companies with higher betas?

www.thomsoninvest.net

www.nasdaq-canada.com

For example, assuming the risk-free rate is 5.5 percent and the market risk premium ($R_m - R_f$) is 6.5 percent, the following returns would occur with betas of 2.0, 1.0, and 0.5:

$$K_2 = 5.5\% + 2.0\,(6.5\%) = 5.5\% + 13.0\% = 18.5\%$$
$$K_1 = 5.5\% + 1.0\,(6.5\%) = 5.5\% + 6.5\% = 12.0\%$$
$$K_{.5} = 5.5\% + 0.5\,(6.5\%) = 5.5\% + 3.25\% = 8.75\%$$

The beta term measures the riskiness of an investment relative to the market. To outperform the market, one would have to assume more risk by selecting assets with betas greater than 1.0. Another way of looking at the risk-return trade-off would be that if less risk than the market is desired, an investor would choose assets with a beta of less than 1.0. Beta is a good measure of a stock's risk when the stock is combined into a portfolio, and therefore it has some bearing on the assets a company acquires for its portfolio of real capital.

In Figure 11A–1 individual stock returns were compared to market returns and the beta from Formula 11A–1 was shown. From Formula 11A–2, the risk-premium model, a generalized risk-return graph called the **security market line** (SML) can be constructed that identifies the risk-return trade-off of any common stock (asset) relative to the company's beta. This is shown in Figure 11A–2.

The required return for all securities can be expressed as the risk-free rate plus a premium for risk. Thus, we see that a stock with a beta of 1.0 would have a risk premium of 6.5 percent added to the **risk-free rate of interest**, 5.5 percent, to provide a required return of 12 percent. Since a beta of 1.0 implies risk equal to the stock market, the return is also at the overall market rate. If the beta is 2.0, twice the **market risk premium** of 6.5 percent must be earned, and we add 13 percent to the risk-free rate of 5.5 percent to determine the required return of 18.5 percent. For a beta of 0.5, the required return is 8.75 percent.

FIGURE 11A–2
The security market line (SML)

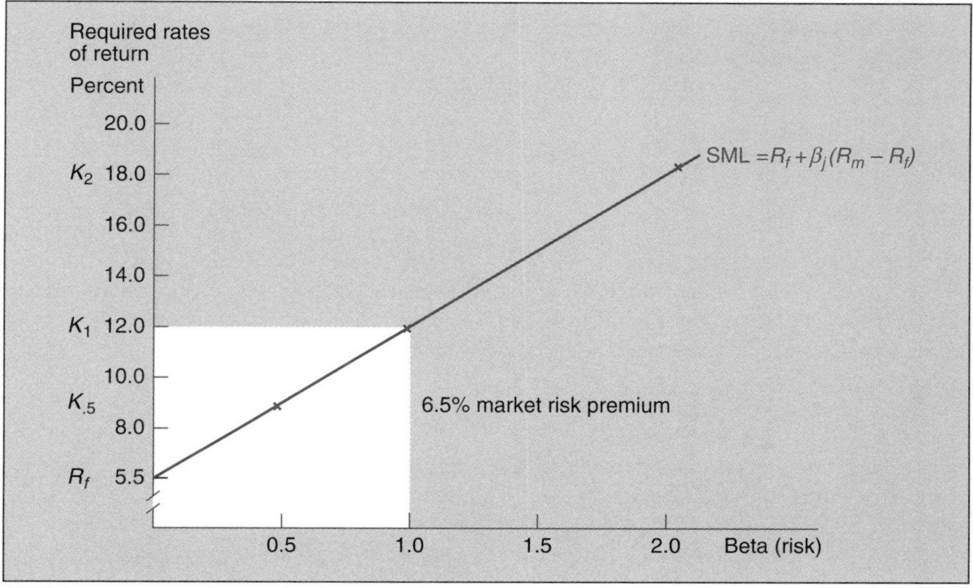

Cost of Capital Considerations

When calculating the cost of capital for common stock, remember that K_e is equal to the expected total return from the dividend yield and capital gains.

$$K_e = \frac{D_1}{P_0} + g$$

K_e is the return required by investors based on expectations of future dividends and growth. The SML provides the same information, but in a market-related risk-return model. As required returns rise, prices must fall to adjust to the new equilibrium return level, and as required returns fall, prices rise. Stock markets are generally efficient, and when stock prices are in equilibrium, the K_e derived from the dividend model is equal to K_j derived from the SML. However, just as with the dividend valuation model we had to allow for flotation costs on a new share issue, we must do the same for the CAPM. We adjust K_j by multiplying by P_0 / P_n.

The SML helps us to identify several circumstances that can cause the cost of capital to change. Figure 11–2 examined required rates of returns over time with changing interest rates and stock prices. Figure 11A–3 does basically the same thing, only through the SML format.

When interest rates increase from the initial period (R_{f1} versus R_{f0}), the security market line in the next period is parallel to SML_0, but higher. This means that required rates of return have risen for every level of risk, as investors desire to maintain their risk premium over the risk-free rate.

One very important variable influencing interest rates is the rate of inflation. As inflation increases, lenders try to maintain their real dollar purchasing power, so they increase the required interest rates to offset inflation. The risk-free rate can be thought of as:

$$R_f = RR + IP$$

where

RR = the real rate of return on a riskless government security when inflation is zero
IP = an inflation premium that compensates lenders (investors) for loss of purchasing power

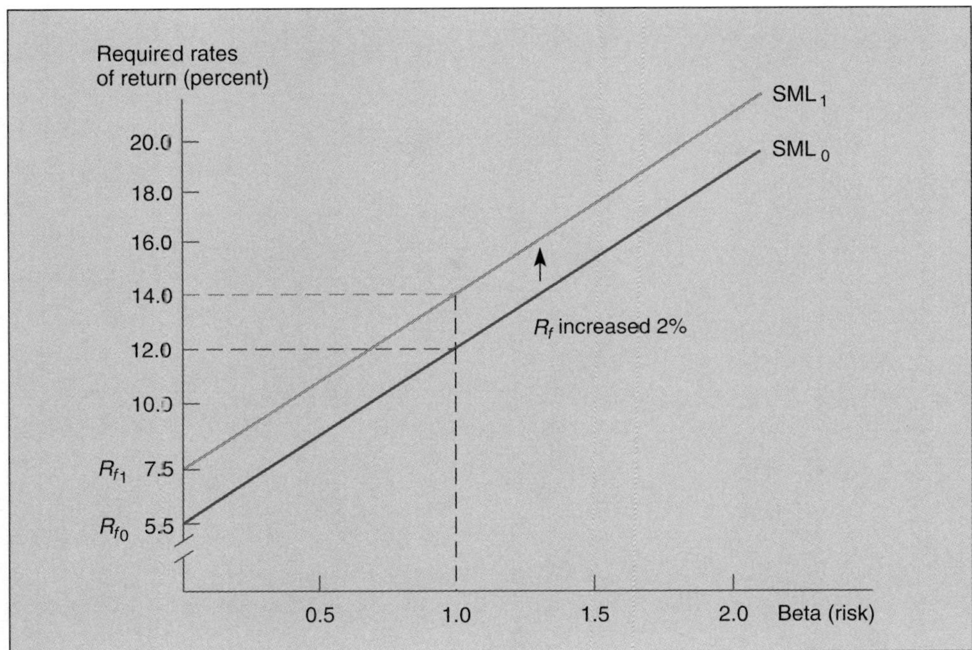

FIGURE 11A–3
The security market line and changing interest rates

An upward shift in the SML indicates that the prices of all assets shift downward as interest rates move up. In Chapter 10 this was demonstrated in the discussion showing that when market interest rates went up, bond prices adjusted downward to make up for the lower coupon rate (interest payment) on the old bonds.

Another factor affecting the cost of capital is a change in risk preferences by investors. As investors become more pessimistic about the economy, they require larger premiums for assuming risks. Even though the historical average market risk premium may be close to 6.5 percent, this is not stable and investors' changing attitudes can have a big impact on the market risk premium. A more risk-averse attitude shows up in higher required stock returns and lower stock prices. For example, if investors raise their market risk premium to 8 percent, the rates of return from the original formulas increase as follows:

$$K_2 = 5.5\% + 2.0\,(8.0\%) = 5.5\% + 16.0\% = 21.5\%$$
$$K_1 = 5.5\% + 1.0\,(8.0\%) = 5.5\% + 8.0\% = 13.5\%$$
$$K_{.5} = 5.5\% + 0.5\,(8.0\%) = 5.5\% + 4.0\% = 9.5\%$$

The change in the market risk premium causes the required market return (beta = 1.00) to be 13.5 percent instead of the 12 percent from Figure 11A–2. Any asset riskier than the market would have a larger increase in the required return. For example, a stock with a beta of 2.0 would need to generate a 21.5 percent return, instead of the 18.5 percent in Figure 11A–2. The overall shape of the new security market line (SML_1) is shown in Figure 11A–4. Note the higher slope for SML_1, in comparison to SML_0.

In many instances rising interest rates and pessimistic investors go hand in hand, so the SML may change its slope and intercept at the same time. This combined effect would cause severe drops in the prices of risky assets and much larger required rates of return for such assets.

The capital asset pricing model and the security market line have been presented to further your understanding of market-related events that affect the firm's cost of capital, such as market returns and risk, changing interest rates, and changing risk preferences.

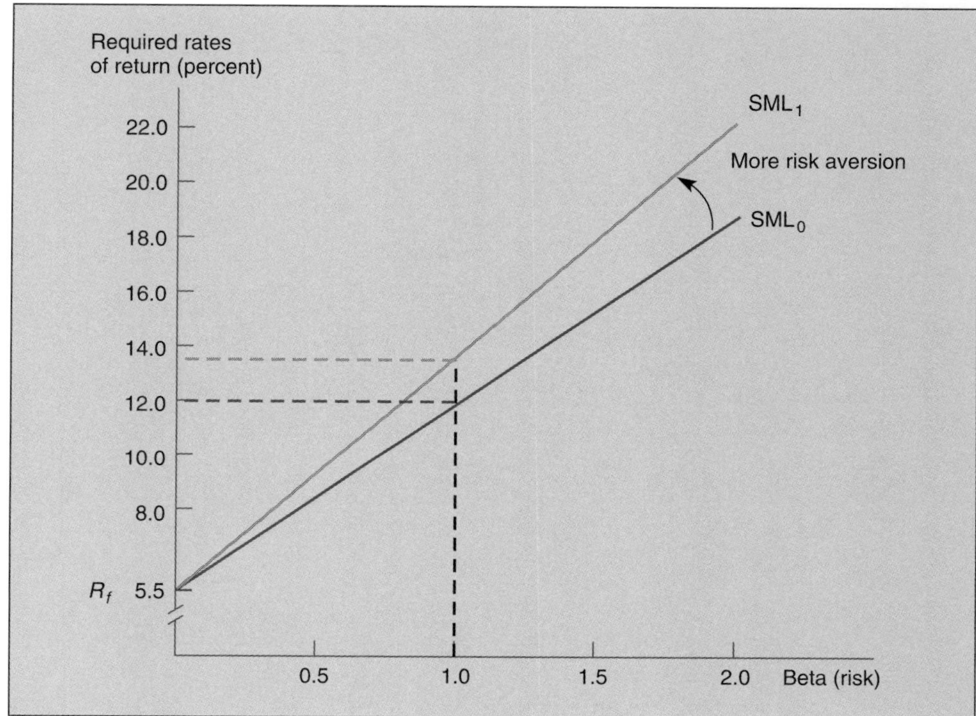

FIGURE 11A–4
The security market line and changing investor expectations

While the capital asset pricing model has received criticism because of the difficulties of dealing with the betas of individual securities and because of the problems involved in consistently constructing the appropriate slope of the SML to represent reality, it provides some interesting insights into risk-return measurement.

Review of Formulas

1. $K_j = \alpha + \beta_j R_m + e$ (11A–1)
2. $K_j = R_f + \beta_j (R_m - R_f)$ (11A–2)

List of Terms

capital asset pricing model (CAPM) 398
beta 398
security market line 401
risk-free rate of interest 401
market risk premium 401

Discussion Questions

11A–1. How does the capital asset pricing model help explain changing costs of capital?

11A–2. Why does K_e approximate K_j, or why does $D_1/(P_0 - g)$ approximate $R_f + \beta_j (R_m - R_f)$?

11A–3. How does the SML react to changes in the rate of interest, changes in the rate of inflation, and changing investor expectations?

11A–4. If an individual stock lay above the SML, what would be an appropriate investment strategy? Why?

11A–5. Why would an efficient market be an important assumption for the development of the CAPM?

11A–6. Why do you think the CAPM is or is not useful to the financial manager?

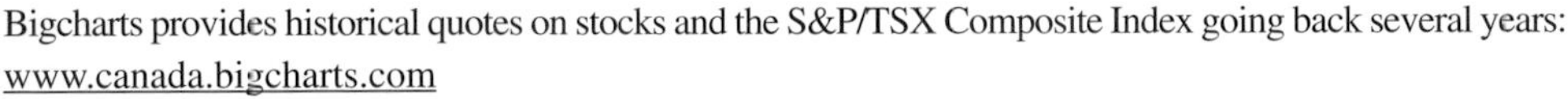

Betas and other useful share information is available on many Canadian companies at Nasdaq Canada and Thomson Financial
www.thomsoninvest.net
www.nasdaq-canada.com

Bigcharts provides historical quotes on stocks and the S&P/TSX Composite Index going back several years:
www.canada.bigcharts.com

The Globe and Mail and ScotiaCapital sites identify yields on Government of Canada bonds that can represent the risk-free rate:
www.globeandmail.com
www.scotiacapital.com

The Bank of Canada provides some current and historical yields on securities:
www.bankofcanada.ca/en

11A–1. Calculate the expected yield for the following securities using current information and the framework of the CAPM: BCE, Nortel, Abitibi Talisman, Hudson Bay, and the S&P/TSX Composite Index. For the market portfolio, determine the average annual return on the S&P/TSX Composite Index over the last five years. Do your results seem reasonable in today's market?

Problems

1. Assume $R_f = 4$ percent and $R_m = 8$ percent. Compute K_j for the following betas, using Formula 11A–2.
   a. 0.7
   b. 1.4
   c. 1.7
2. In the preceding problem, assume an increase in interest rates changes R_f to 7.0 percent; also assume that the market premium $(R_m - R_f)$ changes to 6.5 percent. Compute K_j for the three betas of 0.7, 1.4, and 1.7.
3. The risk-free interest rate on one-year debt is 7 percent and the return on the market is expected to be 13 percent. A stock with a beta of 1.2 pays no dividends over the next year. If it is currently priced at $15.00, what will its price be at the end of the year?
4. Currently, Treasury bills yield 4.75 percent and the market prices risk at 6.90 percent. You have invested in a stock efficiently priced by the CAPM with a beta of 1.15 that will pay an expected dividend of $1.80 in one year. If the stock expects no capital appreciation in value over the next year, compute its current price.
5. You have invested in a stock with some systematic risk. It has a beta of 1.05. The current anticipated market portfolio return for the upcoming year is 16 percent, and the anticipated market risk premium is 7 percent. Calculate the expected yield on this stock based on the CAPM.
6. The risk-free rate is projected to be 5 percent for the upcoming year. Investor expectations concerning the market portfolio reveal expected excess returns of 8 percent during the same period. You have been closely following Y Ltd.'s stock with a beta of 1.2.

a. What would be Y's anticipated return based on the SML?

b. If your analysis reveals an expected return of 16 percent, what investment strategy would you suggest? Justify and fully explain your position.

[And now for some WACC (weighted average cost of capital) calculations using the CAPM for the cost of equity.]

7. Austen Sensibles Ltd. has the following capital structure, which it expects to maintain into the foreseeable future:

Debt	35%
Preferreds	10%
Common Stock	35%
Retained Earnings	20%

Current yields on similar risk bonds are 11 percent. Flotation costs would be negligible and can be ignored for calculation purposes.

New preferred shares are presently being considered and are expected to be offered at $100.00 with a dividend of 8 percent. Flotation costs would be 5 percent.

Austen has a beta of 0.9. Currently, treasury bills are yielding 8.5 percent for one year, and the market portfolio (the S&P/TSX Composite Index) is expected to yield 16 percent over the next year.

Austen has a tax rate of 44 percent and expects internally generated funds to be sufficient to fund new investments.

Calculate the cost of capital of Austen Sensibles Ltd.

8. Huron Ltd. has the following capital structure:

16% Debentures, due in 14 years	$30,000,000
Preferreds (8% dividend, 40,000 shares)	3,000,000
Common shares: 3,600,000 outstanding	7,200,000
Retained earnings	5,600,000
Foreign currency translation	2,200,000
	$58,000,000

In today's capital markets, a company with risk characteristics similar to Huron's would be subject to the following yields:

- Bank prime rate is 7 percent.
- The average yield on 91 day T-bills is 5 percent.
- Debentures would require a yield of 9.5 percent. Flotation costs aftertax would be 4 percent.
- Preferreds would require a yield of 6.5 percent. Flotation costs aftertax would be 5 percent.
- The market portfolio is anticipated to yield 13 percent over the next year.
- Huron's historical beta is 1.25.

Huron's shares currently trade at $15.50. A new issue would net $15.00 including aftertax flotation costs. Internally generated funds will be sufficient to fund Huron's upcoming enterprises. Huron's tax rate is 40 percent.

a. Calculate Huron Ltd.'s cost of capital.

b. A major new investor in Huron is concerned with the possible rejection of viable business proposals based on the calculations just performed. The shareholder suggests that Huron can borrow at prime plus 1 percent and that should be good enough as a discount rate. Prepare a reply to the shareholder. (A "Yes, sir" or "No, ma'am" is not a correct answer.)

9. Orbit Corp. has the following balance sheet:

Cash	$ 500,000	Demand loans at prime + 1%	$ 3,000,000
A/R	2,500,000	Subordinated debentures	
Inventory	4,000,000	8% coupon, 12 years to maturity	12,000,000
Land	15,000,000	Preferred issue 6%	7,000,000
Equipment	20,000,000	Common stock: 5,000,000 shares	
		outstanding	5,000,000
		Retained earnings	15,000,000
	$42,000,000		$42,000,000

Today's market is subject to different supply/demand factors and underlying economic events than when Orbit's capital structure was put in place. This has been translated into the following current yields, which are demanded by the marketplace for a company exhibiting the same risk characteristics as Orbit Corp.:

- The bank's prime rate is now 9.5 percent. The average yield on 91-day T-bills is now 8.5 percent.
- Subordinated debentures would now demand 12 percent; the underwriter would float them for 5 percent of par.
- Preferreds would now call for a stated yield of 11 percent. The underwriters would take 6 percent of issue price for their fee.
- Orbit's stock currently trades on the market at $25.00. Flotation costs would be 8 percent of the current market price.

This high-growth stock, 12 percent per year, pays no dividends but it has been determined to have a beta of 1.7. A well-diversified market portfolio of stocks would yield excess returns of 9 percent above the risk-free rate of interest in the foreseeable future.

Retained earnings will be insufficient to contribute the equity portion of funding of new investments. Orbit's tax rate is 23 percent.

a. Calculate Orbit's cost of capital.

b. Would you suggest that Orbit consider paying a small dividend?

c. Explain how Orbit might improve its capital structure. Justify your position.

APPENDIX I 11B

Capital Structure Theory and Modigliani and Miller

The foundation supporting cost of capital theories was primarily developed by Professors Modigliani and Miller in the late 1950s and mid-1960s.[1] They actually went through an evolutionary process in which they proposed many different theories and conclusions about cost of capital.

Nobel
www.nobel.se

However, before we discuss Modigliani and Miller, we briefly touch on the work of David Durand in the early 1950s, which was the first written attempt to describe the effect of financial lever-

[1]Franco Modigliani and Merton H. Miller, "The Cost of Capital, Corporation Finance and the Theory of Investment," *American Economic Review,* June 1958, and "Taxes and the Cost of Capital: A Correction," *American Economic Review,* June 1963, pp. 433–43.

age on cost of capital and valuation. Professor Durand described three different theories of cost of capital: the net income (NI) approach, the net operating income (NOI) approach, and the traditional approach.[2]

Net Income (NI) Approach

Under the **net income (NI) approach,** it is assumed that the firm can raise all the funds it desires at a constant cost of equity and debt. Since debt tends to have a lower cost than equity, the more debt utilized, the lower the overall cost of capital and the higher the evaluation of the firm, as indicated in Figure 11B–1.

Under the net income (NI) approach, the firm would be foolish not to use 100 percent debt to minimize cost of capital and maximize valuation. However, the assumption of constant cost of all forms of financing regardless of the level of utilization was severely challenged by practitioners.

FIGURE 11B–1
Net income (NI) approach

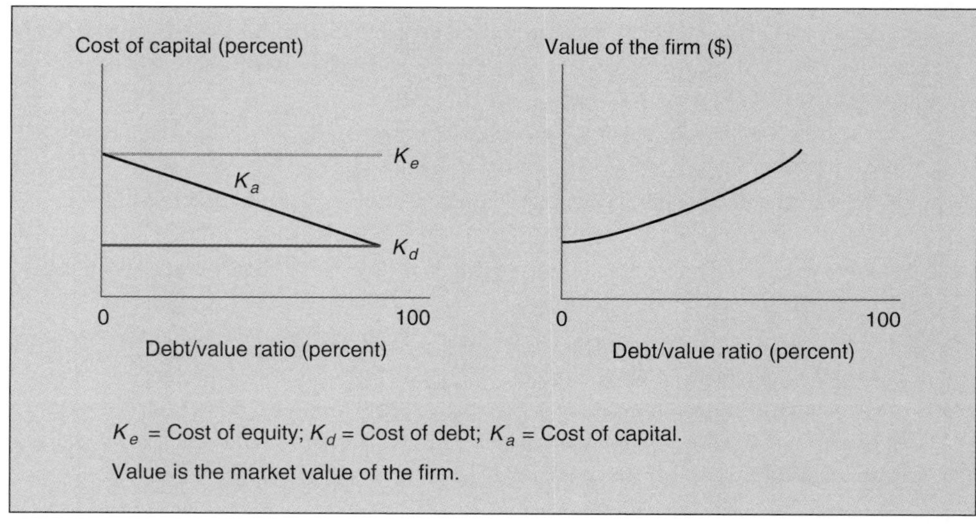

K_e = Cost of equity; K_d = Cost of debt; K_a = Cost of capital.
Value is the market value of the firm.

Net Operating Income (NOI) Approach

A second approach covered by Professor Durand was the **net operating income (NOI) approach.** Under this proposition the low cost of debt is assumed to remain constant with greater debt utilization, but the cost of equity increases to such an extent that the cost of capital remains unchanged. Essentially, only operating income matters, and how you finance it makes no difference in terms of cost of capital or valuation. In Figure 11B–2 we see the effects of the net operating income (NOI) approach.

Finally, Professor Durand described the **traditional approach,** which falls somewhere between the net income approach and the net operating income approach. In the traditional approach there are benefits from increased debt utilization, but only up to a point. After that point, the cost of capital begins to turn up and the valuation of the firm begins to turn down. A graphic representation of the traditional approach is seen in Figure 11B–3.

[2]See David Durand, "Costs of Debt and Equity Funds for Business: Trends and Problems of Measurement," *Conference on Research in Business Finance,* National Bureau of Economic Research, New York, 1952.

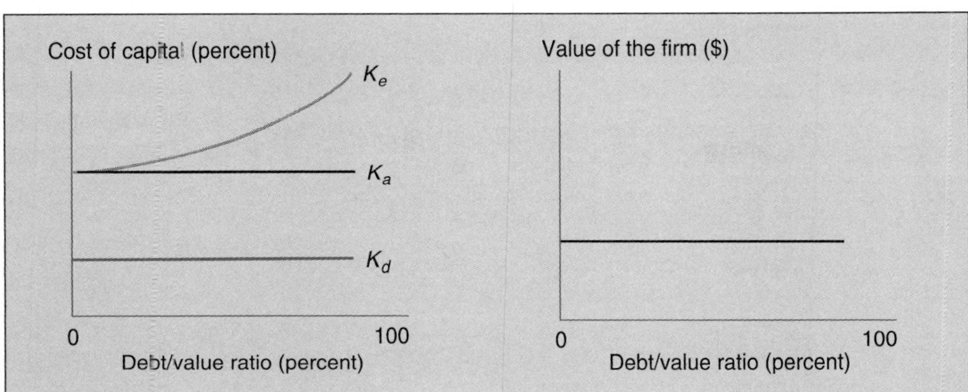

FIGURE 11B–2
Net operating income (NOI) approach

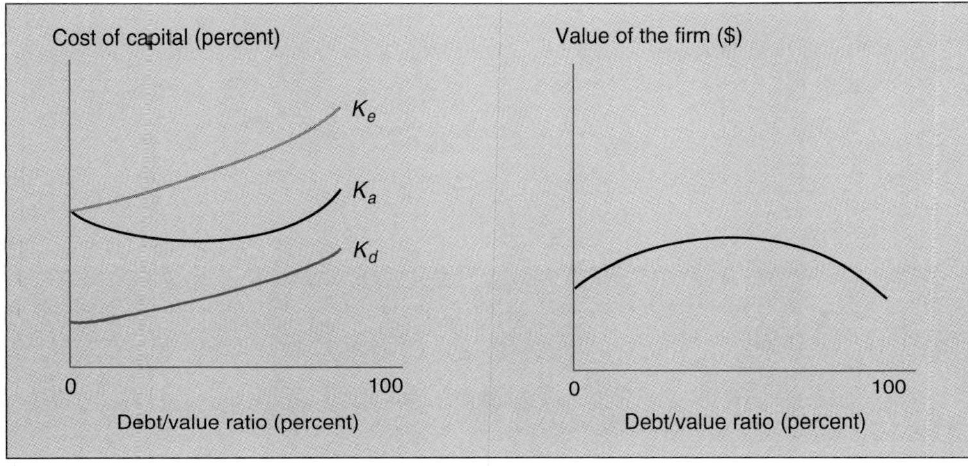

FIGURE 11B–3
Traditional approach as described by Durand

The student will perhaps realize that the traditional approach described by Durand in 1952 is similar to what is accepted today (as described in the main body of the chapter), but the many theories of Modigliani and Miller had a major impact as we went from 1952 to the currently existing theory.

Modigliani and Miller's Initial Approach

The approaches described by Durand were largely unsupported by theories and mathematical proofs. The major contribution by Modigliani and Miller (M&M) was to add economic and financial theories to naive assumptions. Although it is beyond the scope of this text to go through all the various mathematical proofs of M&M, their basic positions are presented.

Under the initial Modigliani and Miller approach, it is assumed that the value of the firm and its cost of capital are independent of the means of financing that occurs. This is similar to the NOI approach described by Durand, but the rationale or mechanism for arriving at this conclusion is different.

M&M stipulate that the value of the firm equals the following:

$$V = \frac{EBIT}{K_a} \tag{11B–1}$$

where

V = Value
$EBIT$ = Earnings before interest and taxes
K_a = Cost of capital

They further stipulate that:

$$K_a = K_{eu} \tag{11B–2}$$

K_{eu} represents the cost of equity for an unlevered firm (one with no debt).

But what if a firm decides to include debt in its capital structure? Then the cost of equity for this leveraged firm increases by a risk premium to compensate for the additional risk associated with the debt.

$$K_{eL} = K_{eu} + \text{Risk premium} \tag{11B–3}$$
$$K_{eL} = K_{eu} + (K_{eu} - I)(D/S)$$

K_{eL} represents the cost of equity to the leveraged firm, I is the interest rate on the debt, D is the amount of debt financing, S is the amount of stock (equity) financing. The actual symbols aren't important for our purposes. The important point to observe in Formula 11B–3 is that a risk premium is associated with the cost of equity financing (K_e) when leverage is involved.

M&M thus say a firm cannot reduce the cost of capital or increase the valuation of the firm because any benefits from cheaper debt are offset by the increased cost of equity financing. That is:

$$K_{eL} = K_{eu} + \text{Risk premium}$$

M&M then go on to demonstrate that, if a leveraged firm could increase its value over another firm not using leverage (when all else is equal in terms of operating performance), then investors would simply sell the overpriced leverage firm and use **homemade leverage** (borrow on their own) to buy the underpriced, unleveraged firm's stock. Since both firms are equal in operating performance, investors would simply arbitrage between the values of the two to bring them into equilibrium (sell the overpriced firm and buy the underpriced one using their own personally borrowed funds as part of the process).

In summary, under the initial M&M hypothesis, the value of a firm and its cost of capital are unaffected by the firm's capital structure.

Modigliani and Miller with the Introduction of Corporate Taxes

As is true of many economic models, M&M made a number of assumptions in their initial theory of cost of capital that tended to simplify the analysis. The most critical simplifying assumption was to ignore the impact of corporate taxes on the cost of capital to the firm (Durand made similar simplifying assumptions). Once M&M began to consider the effect of taxes, their whole outlook changed. Because interest on debt is a tax-deductible expense, the tax effect greatly reduces the cost of debt and the associated cost of capital. Furthermore, with a reduced cost of capital, there is an increased valuation for the firm.

A key adjustment to a basic valuation formula is that:

$$V_L = V_U + TD \tag{11B–4}$$

Formula 11B–4 says the value of a leveraged firm (V_L) is equal to the value of an unleveraged firm (V_U), plus an amount equal to the corporate tax rate (T) times the amount of debt (D) the firm has. If an unleveraged firm has a value of \$1,000,000 (V_U), then a leveraged firm with \$400,000 in debt and a tax rate of 34 percent will have a value of \$1,136,000.

$$\begin{aligned} V_L &= V_U + TD \\ &= \$1{,}000{,}000 + 0.34\ (\$400{,}000) \\ &= \$1{,}000{,}000 + \$136{,}000 \\ &= \$1{,}136{,}000 \end{aligned}$$

A firm with \$600,000 in debt has a value of \$1,204,000, and so on.

$$V_L = V_U + TD$$
$$= \$1{,}000{,}000 + 0.34\ (\$600{,}000)$$
$$= \$1{,}000{,}000 + \$204{,}000$$
$$= \$1{,}204{,}000$$

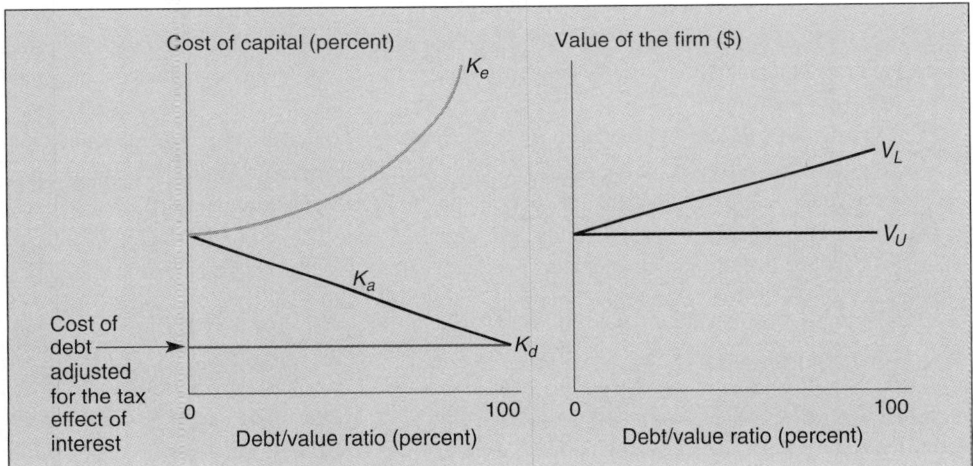

FIGURE 11B–4
Modigliani and Miller with corporate taxes

Graphically, we are led to the positions presented in Figure 11B–4.

As can be viewed in Figure 11B–4, once corporate taxes are introduced, it is assumed that every increment of debt reduces the cost of capital, eventually down to the cost of debt itself. Furthermore, the more debt a firm has, the higher its valuation.[3]

Under the second version of M&M, every firm should be 100 percent (perhaps 99.9 percent) financed by debt to lower its cost of capital and increase its valuation. With corporate taxes our cost of equity capital becomes:

$$K_{eL} = K_{eu} + (K_{eu} - 1)\ (D/S)\ (1 - T) \qquad (11B\text{–}5)$$

Modigliani and Miller with Bankruptcy Considerations

Since no firm or investor in the real world operates on the basis of the just described M&M hypothesis, there must be some missing variables. One of the disadvantages of heavy borrowing is that the firm may eventually go bankrupt (a topic discussed in Appendix 16A). A firm that does not borrow has *no* such threat. All things being equal, the threat of bankruptcy increases as the amount of borrowing increases.

When bankruptcy occurs, the firm may be forced to sell assets at a fraction of their value. Furthermore, there are likely to be substantial legal fees, court costs, and administrative expenses. Even if a firm does not go bankrupt, but is on the verge of bankruptcy, customers may hesitate to do business with the firm. Suppliers may demand advanced payments, and so on.

Also, as a firm increases the amount of debt it has, there are likely to be restrictive covenants or provisions in debt agreements that hinder the normal operations of the firm (the current ratio must be at a given level or no new projects can be undertaken without lender approval).

All of these bankruptcy-related considerations have an implicit cost. If the potential cost of bankruptcy were $10 million, then the probability of that bankruptcy must also be considered. Of course, if the firm has no debt, then the probability of bankruptcy is zero and the obvious cost is zero. If the

[3]The only constraint to this proposition is that the amount of debt cannot exceed the amount of assets.

firm has 50 percent debt, there may be a 10 percent probability of bankruptcy and the expected cost is \$1 million (\$10,000,000 × 10 percent). Finally, with 90 percent debt, there may be a 25 percent probability of bankruptcy and the expected cost is \$2.5 million (\$10,000,000 × 25 percent). Once these expected costs of bankruptcy are present valued, they must be deducted from the current, unadjusted value of the firm to determine true value. Similarly, the expected value of the threat of future bankruptcy also tends to increase the cost of capital to the firm as progressively more debt is utilized.

In Figure 11B–5 we combine the effect of the corporate tax advantage (M&M II) with the effect of the bankruptcy threat (M&M III) to show the impact of financial leverage on the cost of capital and valuation of the firm.

As you can see in Panel (A) of Figure 11B–5, the black line, which combines the tax effect with the bankruptcy effect, takes us all the way back to the initial proposition first discussed in the main body of the chapter, which is that cost of capital tends to be U-shaped in nature. We have simply added some additional theory to support this proposition. In Panel (B) of Figure 11B–5, we also see from the black line that the combined effect of taxation and bankruptcy allows the firm to maximize valuation at a given debt level and then the valuation begins to diminish.

The Miller Model

As if to temporarily confuse an already settled issue, Professor Miller announced at the annual meeting of the American Finance Association in 1976 that he was rejecting his own latest version of the M&M hypothesis (M&M III, as indicated by the black lines in Figure 11B–5).[4] His new premise was that he had considered corporate taxes but not personal taxes in the earlier M&M models. He suggested that, when one began considering personal taxes in the process, share ownership had substantial advantages over debt ownership. Why? Because, at the time, gains from share ownership were potentially taxed at a much lower rate than interest income, due to the capital gains component that was part of the anticipated return to shareholders. Long-term capital gains have traditionally been taxed at a rate lower than other income. Miller said that once you factored all tax considerations (corporate and personal) into the analysis, there was not an overall advantage to debt utilization to the firm, and therefore, the cost of capital was unaffected by the capital structure of the firm.

Subsequent research has partially taken issue with Professor Miller. We can somewhat safely return to the U-shaped approach generally described in the chapter and in this appendix.

Review of Formulas

1. $V = \dfrac{EBIT}{K_a}$ (11B–1)
2. $K_a = K_{eu}$ (11B–2)
3. $K_{eL} = K_{eu} + (K_{eu} - I)(D/S)$ (11B–3)
4. $V_L = V_U + TD$ (11B–4)
5. $K_{eL} = K_{eu} + (K_{eu} - 1)(D/S)(1 - T)$ (11B–5)

List of Terms

net income (NI) approach 408
net operating income (NOI) approach 408
traditional approach 408
homemade leverage 410

[4] Merton H. Miller, "Debt and Taxes," *Journal of Finance,* May 1977, pp. 261–75.

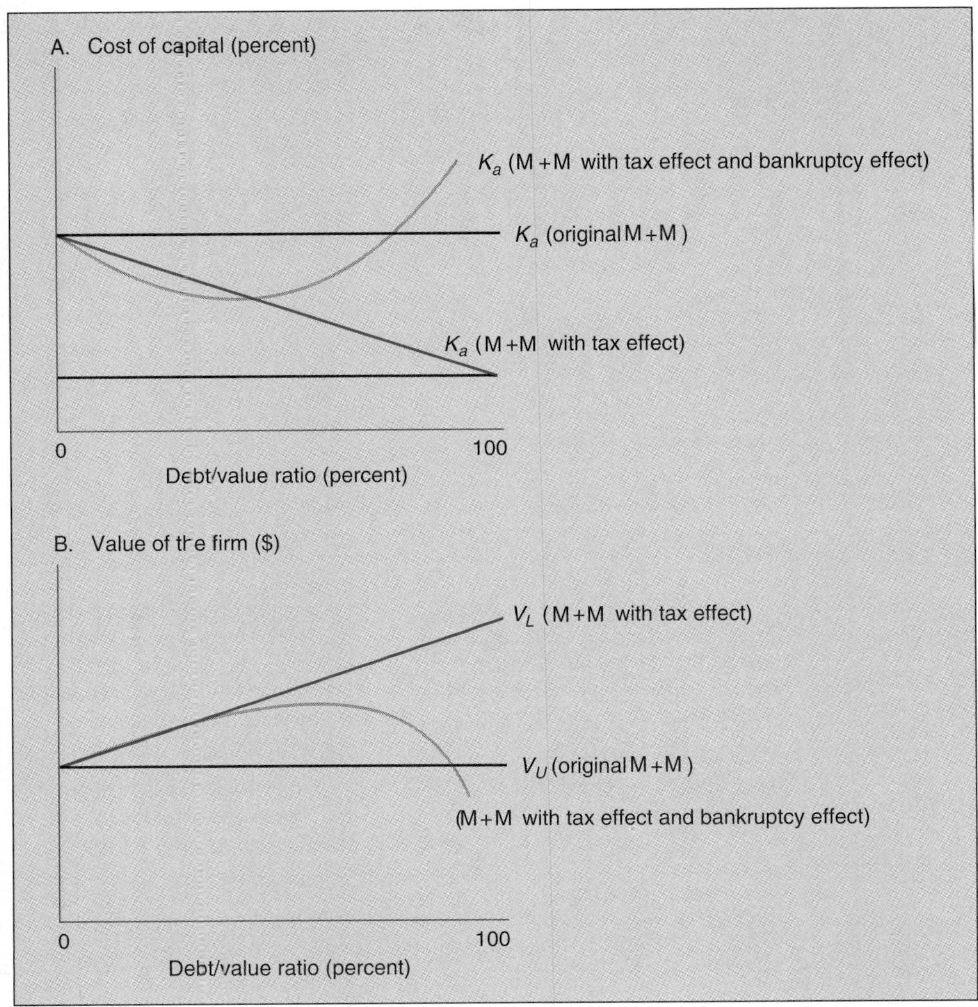

FIGURE 11B–5
Combined impact of the corporate tax effect and bankruptcy effect on valuation and cost of capital

Discussion Questions

11B–1. What is the difference between the net income (NI) approach, the net operating income (NOI) approach, and the traditional approach?

11B–2. Under the initial Modigliani and Miller approach, does the use of debt affect the cost of capital? Explain.

11B–3. How do corporate taxes and bankruptcy considerations change the initial Modigliani and Miller approach? What is the net effect?

CHAPTER | TWELVE

12 The Capital Budgeting Decision

LEARNING | OBJECTIVES

1 Define capital budgeting decisions as long-run investment decisions.

2 Explain that cash flows rather than accounting earnings are evaluated in the capital budgeting decision.

3 Evaluate investments by the average accounting return, the payback period, the internal rate of return, the net present value, and the profitability index.

4 Discuss the use of the cost of capital as the discount rate in capital budgeting analysis.

5 Identify the resultant cash flows that result from an investment decision, including the aftertax operating benefits and the tax shield benefits of capital cost allowance (amortization).

6 Perform NPV analysis to assist in the decision-making process concerning long-run investments.

One of the most significant decisions that the management of a firm will ever have to make concerns capital investment. Capital budgeting decisions are important as they usually involve the long-term commitment of a firm's resources and because a large amount of capital is usually involved; management is setting the firm into a strategic direction that is difficult to change. A decision to build a new plant, develop a new technology, purchase another company, or expand into a foreign market may influence the performance of the firm over the next decade or more. A wrong decision can lead to great financial stress and even bankruptcy for a firm.

The capital budgeting decision involves the planning of expenditures for a project with a life of at least one year and usually considerably longer. In general, the capital expenditure decision requires extensive planning to ensure that engineering and marketing information is available, product design is completed, necessary patents are acquired, production costs are fully understood, and the capital markets are tapped for the necessary funds. Throughout this chapter we use the techniques developed in our discussion of the time value of money to equate future cash flows to present ones. The firm's cost of capital is used as the basic discount rate.

One problem that a manager faces is that as the time horizon moves further into the future, uncertainty becomes a greater hazard. The manager is uncertain about annual costs and inflows, product life, interest rates, economic conditions, and technological change. The personal computer industry beginning in the 1980s is a prime example of rapid change. IBM and Apple took the early lead in product development and had no difficulty selling products in the $2,000 to $5,000 range, with little more than ten-page text memory. As Tandy, Compaq, and overseas competitors moved into the market, prices dropped by 50

Strategy: Right or Wrong?

During 2000 Nortel Networks (www.nortelnetworks.com)purchased three companies in the network infrastructure business; Alteon for U.S.$7.8 billion, Xros for U.S.$3.25 billion, and Qtera for $3.25 billion. Then in early 2001 Nortel purchased a JDS Uniphase subsidiary in the photonics business for $2.5 billion. Nortel paid for most of these purchases with Nortel stock. This, fortunately, involved limited cash although the shareholders might disagree based on the dilution of their ownership! In the second quarter of 2001, with Internet and network business suffering a dramatic decline in demand, Nortel took a write-off of U.S.$12.4 billion related primarily to these acquisitions.

Canada's important but cyclical resource industries are also faced with decisions regarding large capital investments to modernize or expand their operations. Often massive projects are envisioned, constructed, and become operative just as the demand for their product has declined, exposing the firms to declining revenues despite the increased costs created by the new investments. In 1996 Inco (www.inco.com) purchased a rich nickel deposit at Voisey's Bay, Labrador, for $4.3 billion with further capital expenditures of $1.4 billion planned for a mine, mill, smelter, and refinery. At the time of the Voisey's Bay purchase, nickel sold for U.S.$3.61 per pound. By early 1999, with nickel prices at about U.S.$2.00 per pound, the project was mothballed. In 2001 the project was again being considered as nickel prices rose to U.S.$2.76 a pound.

The business of Inco with tangible assets like nickel is quite different from the knowledge assets of the information age represented by Nortel's ideas and its fibre optic networks.

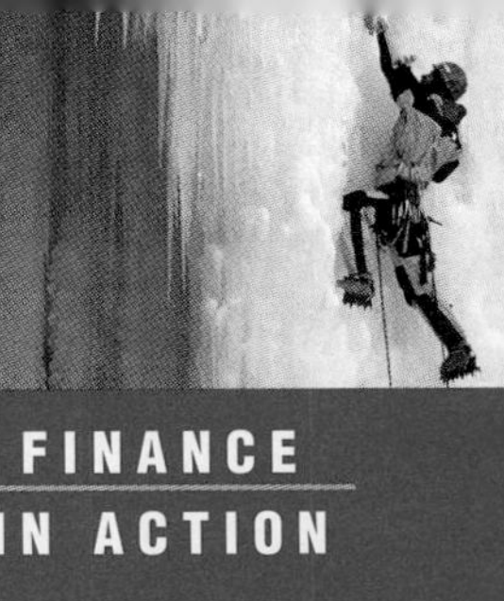

FINANCE IN ACTION

Q1 Explain which company you consider a better investment based on its type of assets.

Q2 How have the share prices of Nortel (NT) and Inco (N) performed over the last year?

www.tsx.ca

percent and consumer demand for quality went up. The computer business morphed into the explosive Internet business in the 1990s. Many high-tech companies rose on great dreams and then failed when their promised cash flows did not materialize. Not all new developments are so perilous, and a number of techniques, which will be treated in the next chapter, have been devised to cope with the impact of uncertainty on decision making.

IBM
www.ibm.com
Apple
www.apple.com
Tandy Corporation
www.tandy.com
Compaq
www.compaq.com

In this chapter capital budgeting is studied under the following major topical headings: administrative considerations, accounting flows versus cash flows, methods of ranking investment proposals, selection strategy, combining cash flow analysis and selection strategy, and analysis of a long-run investment decision. These decisions might be to replace machinery, start new projects, or diversify into new areas. In addition, part of this chapter is devoted to exploring the impact of Canadian tax law and development incentives on amortization and capital budgeting decisions.

Administrative Considerations

A good capital budgeting program requires that a number of steps be taken in the decision-making process.

1. Search and discovery of investment opportunities.
2. Collection of data.
3. Evaluation of alternatives and decision making.
4. Plan implementation.
5. Ongoing reevaluation and adjustment.

The search for new opportunities is the least emphasized, though perhaps the most important, of the five steps. Although it is outside the scope of this book to suggest procedures for developing an organization that is conducive to innovation and creative

FINANCE IN ACTION

Q1 What are the latest R&D and capital expenditures, to revenues for these three companies?

Q2 Which share prices have performed the best over the last 1 and 5 years?

www.nortelnetworks.com
Symbol: NT

www.ballard.com
Symbol: BLD

www.alcan.com
Symbol: AL

Research and Development: The Start of Capital Investment

Where do the ideas come from that are then transformed into capital expenditures and then into products that eventually produce the revenues to grow a business? To varying degrees, firms commit resources to research and development (R&D) activities, hoping that new products and processes will be the result of these expenditures.

Northern Telecom (Nortel) is a world leader in the development and production of wireless networks and it is one of Canada's largest companies, employing thousands of engineers, designers, and scientists worldwide. In 2001 it spent approximately $3.2 billion on R&D, which represented over 18 percent of its revenues, despite an extremely difficult year for Nortel financially. In the same year Nortel incurred capital expenditures of about 8 percent of revenues.

However, the most significant R&D spender, relative to its size, was Ballard Power Systems. Ballard spent $94 million on R&D in 2001 for expenditures related primarily to its proton exchange fuel cell, which was 138 percent of its revenues. This cell converts gas, methanol, or hydrogen directly into electricity without producing any pollutants. Ballard has begun to move towards commercial uses for its technology and capital expenditures that were once almost nil have reached 30 percent of revenues. Obviously Ballard continues to borrow from the capital markets to finance these aggressive expenditures.

A minimal R&D spender was Alcan Aluminum, involved in the mining, refining, and manufacturing of aluminum. An established company with established technology, Alcan spent about 1 percent of its revenues on R&D. However, capital expenditures were almost 9 percent of revenues as Alcan renewed existing technology.

Share price performance in 2001 was poor, but from a five-year perspective Ballard would rank first, followed by Alcan, and then Nortel. Nortel has had particular difficulties in the last year but we should expect better results in the future from its R&D efforts. Charting, using the TSX web site (www.tsx.ca) can show share price performance over various time periods.

thinking, the marginal return of such an organization is likely to be high (and a high marginal return is the essence of capital budgeting).[1]

The collection of data should go beyond engineering data and market surveys. It must attempt to identify possible important events and capture the relative likelihood of their occurrence. The probabilities of increases or slumps in product demand may be evaluated from statistical analysis, while other outcomes may have to be estimated subjectively. The likely competitive reaction of other industry participants to any new investment by our firm is an important element to be considered in this analysis. The collection of data, however, is not a perfect process. Eventually a decision must be made based on the best available data. Although more information collection is possible, the cost becomes too high when compared to the marginal benefit.

After all data have been collected and evaluated, the final decision must be made. Generally, determinations involving relatively small amounts are made at the department or division level, while major expenditures can be approved only by top management. Once a plan is developed and implemented, constant monitoring of the results of a given decision may indicate that a whole new set of probabilities must be developed based on actual experience. This may cause an initial decision to then be reevaluated and perhaps reversed. This process is outlined in Figure 12–1.

[1]See, for example, H. Allan Conway and N. A. McGuinness, "Idea Generation in Technology-Based Firms," *Journal of Product Innovation Management* 4 (1986), pp. 276–91, for an investigation of the factors that influence the new product search process.

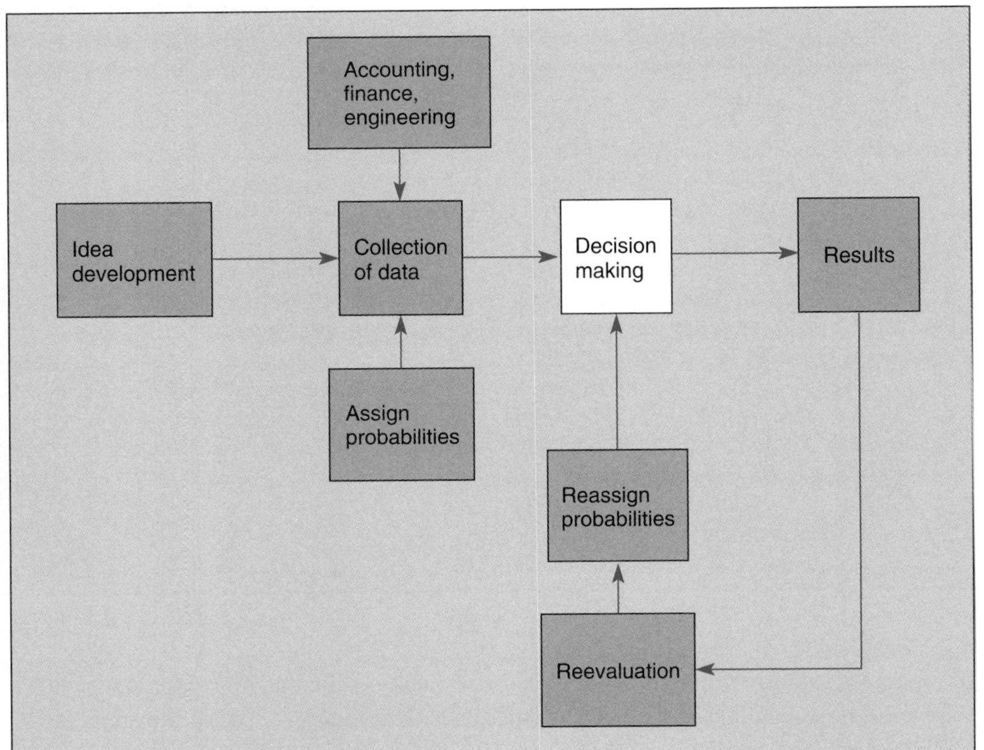

FIGURE 12–1
Capital budgeting procedures

The Notion of Resultant Cash Flows

Capital budgeting is about investment decisions and the value that those investment decisions can create for the firm. In most cases the investment decisions will produce benefits and costs to the firm over several time periods. Those benefits and costs for the most part can be identified as cash flows. Furthermore, the investments will likely entail the commitment of a substantial amount of capital.

From an analytical standpoint, the task in capital budgeting is to identify the amount and timing of all the **resultant cash flows** stemming from a possible investment decision. By the term *resultant cash flows* we mean those **incremental cash flows (inflows)** and **decremental cash flows (outflows)** that occur only if we decide to make a given capital investment. Those cash flows that would continue to be generated by the firm regardless of the investment decision are irrelevant for the investment analysis. Once the resultant cash flows have been identified, it is necessary to value them. The use of the discounting techniques explored in Chapter 9 is the best method to equate the resultant cash flows to present values for comparison with the cost of the investment. The choice of an appropriate discount rate based on the risk of the project will be an important consideration.

Let us suppose that we consider the replacement of an older machine with a new one. The cost of the new machine would be a decremental cash flow, while any money we received on the sale of the old machine would be an incremental cash flow. Alternatively we could consider the net cash flow of the investment, which would be the cost of the new machine minus the resale value of the old one. If the same operator, at

FINANCE IN ACTION

Q1 What was reason for the depletion (increase) in AirIQ's cash resources over the last quarter?

Q2 What other equity investments have been made by Bell Mobility Investments?

www.airiq.com

www.bell.ca

Symbol: AirIQ

Cash Flow Mobility

Bell Mobility Investments (BMI), a subsidiary of Bell Canada, was established in early 2001 with $30 million in capital to invest in innovative firms in "wireless Internet space." Check out "about Bell" at the web site. BMI was prepared to make R&D and equity investments in the $3 to $5 million range. The CEO of BMI was on record as stating that return on investment (ROI) was certainly an objective of the firm.

However an overriding objective was to invest in firms with commercial potential that would provide an increased customer and revenue base for Bell Mobility. Bell Mobility wanted to develop products and services that could use its network. Although the investments themselves might not provide an adequate return the increased cash flows through the expanded use of Bell Mobility's network could justify the investments.

Furthermore in the fast paced high-technology business, investments are important to keep firms "in the game." If firms like Bell Mobility are not involved in many of these projects then they effectively exclude themselves from some markets that have yet to be envisioned and that may develop in the future. By making these investments now Bell Mobility keeps its options open.

One of its investments was in AirIQ (IQ). AirIQ, which is listed on the TSX, has technology used by vehicle and trucking fleets. The technology can locate their vehicles across North America, determine their speeds, unlock their doors, and perform many other functions from a central location.

the same wage, were required to operate either machine, the machine operator's wages would not be a resultant cash flow and, therefore, would be ignored in the analysis. If, on the other hand, the new machine required a more skilled operator at a higher wage, the difference in operators' wages would be the resultant cash flow.

The relevant or resultant cash flows should be included in the analysis at market value and should include any opportunity costs or benefits that may not be explicitly stated. This may take the form of an alternative decision imbedded in the major decision under analysis. For example, we might consider the value of building on a property we own. There will be no cash flow resulting from using the property, but there is the opportunity cost of not selling the property at today's value. That cost should form part of an analysis.

Identification of the resultant cash flows attached to a particular capital budgeting decision is a critical task and requires careful thought and judgment on the part of the capital budgeting analyst. It may be helpful to conceptualize the appropriate resultant cash flows by developing a time line. Much of the rest of this chapter is devoted to considering methods of identifying the timing and amounts of all resultant cash flows.

Accounting Flow versus Cash Flows

In capital budgeting decisions the emphasis is on cash flow rather than reported income. In accounting the consideration is on assigning the costs of an asset to those periods during which the asset provides economic benefit to the firm. To analyze a capital investment proposal, we often have to be able to translate accounting profit figures into actual cash flows. Furthermore, it is essential to identify the timing of those cash flows. The presence of many working capital accounts attests to the difference between accounting flows and cash flows.

One of the most important differences between accounting profits and the timing of cash flows relates to amortization.[2] Because amortization does not represent an actual expenditure of current funds, it is added back to profit to determine the amount of cash flow generated in the current period.

Table 12–1 tries to capture the effect of adding back amortization to the accounting profit to arrive at the actual cash flow. In that table the Alston Corporation has $50,000 of new equipment to be amortized on a straight-line basis over 10 years ($5,000 per year). The firm has $20,000 in earnings before amortization and taxes and is in a 50 percent tax bracket. The firm shows $7,500 in earnings aftertaxes. To arrive at the cash flow figure of $12,500, we add the noncash deduction of $5,000 in amortization to the accounting profit number. An even more dramatic illustration of the difference between accounting and cash flow is provided by the situation shown in Table 12–2. That table demonstrates what would happen if the amortization expense for Alston had been $20,000 rather than $5,000. Net earnings before and aftertaxes would have been zero, but the company ends the year with $20,000 more in the bank than it had at the beginning.

TABLE 12–1
Cash flow for Alston Corporation

Earnings before amortization and taxes (cash flow)	$20,000
Amortization (noncash expense)	5,000
Earnings before taxes	15,000
Taxes (cash outflow)	7,500
Earnings aftertaxes	7,500
Amortization	+5,000
Cash flow	$12,500
Alternative method of cash flow calculation	
Cash inflow (EBAT)	$20,000
Cash outflow (taxes)	−7,500
Cash flow	$12,500

TABLE 12–2
Revised cash flow for Alston Corporation

Earnings before amortization and taxes	$20,000
Amortization	20,000
Earnings before taxes	0
Taxes	0
Earnings aftertaxes	0
Amortization	+20,000
Cash flow	$20,000

[2]Chapter 2 explores amortization in further detail. It notes that amortization is not a new source of funds (except as tax savings), but represents a noncash expense. Furthermore, it is noted that the term amortization is a generic term to represent the loss of utility in capital assets. Past practice suggested the use of the term depreciation for tangible assets, amortization for intangible assets, and depletion for natural resource assets. The use of these terms by corporations is still common.

FINANCE IN ACTION

Government Capital Budgeting Techniques

In 1997 the Clinton administration of the United States commissioned a study of capital budgeting and suggested that the Federal Government might benefit from employing capital budgeting techniques in its decision processes. Some of the observations and conclusions identified in the committee's report were the following:

1. Capital spending produces benefits over the long run and these benefits are neglected without appropriate capital budgeting considerations.
2. Without capital budgeting considerations, borrowing activities are inefficient.
3. Cost/benefit determinations are central to capital budgeting.
4. Capital rationing and NPV analysis are standard considerations in the private sector.
5. The financing of capital projects and the decision to undertake them are not necessarily linked.

The commission also found that governments around the world have been reluctant to apply capital budgeting techniques in their decision-making processes. Because their focus has often been short term, the long-term costs and benefits of capital allocations have often been overlooked. Furthermore the upkeep of existing assets has also been neglected.

Q1 Do you think Governments would benefit from using capital budgeting techniques?

www.clinton4.nara.gov/pcscb/

To the capital budgeting specialist, the concentration on cash flow rather than accounting figures seems obvious. It is sometimes harder for practicing managers to consider cash flows, therefore ignoring the effects reported in the historical cost accounting statements. Assume, for example, you are the president of a widely held firm listed on the Toronto Stock Exchange and must select between two investment alternatives. Over the next year it is estimated that Proposal A will provide zero in aftertax earnings and $100,000 in cash flow, while Proposal B, calling for no amortization, will provide $50,000 in both aftertax earnings and cash flow. As president of a publicly traded firm, you realize that security analysts are constantly pencilling in their projections of your earnings for the next quarter, and you fear your stock may drop dramatically if earnings are lower than they project, even if by a small amount. Although a capital budgeting analysis indicates that Proposal A is a superior investment, you may be more sensitive to reported aftertax earnings than to cash flow and so select Proposal B. This type of understandable sensitivity among managers leads to periodic criticism of them for being overly concerned with the short-term impact of a decision rather than its longer-term economic benefits. Nevertheless, we should all realize that after the tax person cometh, it is the coin in our pockets, not the accountant's income, that matters.

Toronto Stock Exchange
www.tsx.ca

Be sensitive therefore to the concessions to short-term pressures that are sometimes made by top executives. Some observers have held that modern financial decision-making tools reinforce this tendency.[3] Nevertheless, in the material that follows, the emphasis is on the use of proper evaluation techniques aimed at identifying the best economic choice and, therefore, at providing long-term wealth maximization.

[3]See, for example, Robert Hayes and William Abernathy, "Managing Our Way to Economic Decline," *Harvard Business Review,* July–August 1980, pp. 67–77, for a widely read and quoted criticism of the tendency of users of modern financial decision-making techniques to become very short-term oriented.

Methods of Evaluating Investment Proposals

Five methods for evaluating capital expenditures are considered, along with the shortcomings and advantages of each.

1. Average accounting return (AAR).
2. Payback period.
3. Net present value.
4. Internal rate of return.
5. Profitability index.

The average accounting return and payback period methods are widely used even though each method has some serious theoretical shortcomings. The net present value and internal rate of return methods are more comprehensive, and one or the other should be applied to most situations. The profitability index can be used in ranking from the most to least desirable project and is really a variation of the NPV method.

Average Accounting Return

The **average accounting return (AAR)** is a simple evaluation technique for investment projects given by the following formula:

$$\frac{\text{Average earnings aftertax}}{\text{Average book value}}$$

Let us suppose that an investment project has the following projected earnings and amortized cost for the capital asset over the next four years. The asset can be purchased for $30,000 and is expected to last four years, at which time it would have no value. Therefore, it is amortized on a straight-line basis over that period.

	Earnings Aftertax	Amortized capital asset
Capital cost		$30,000
Year 1	$2,000	22,500
Year 2	4,000	15,000
Year 3	8,000	7,500
Year 4	2,000	0
Average	16,000/4 = $4,000	75,000/5 = 15,000
Average accounting return	$4,000/15,000 =	26.7%

The average accounting return is fairly easy to calculate and makes use of information readily prepared by the accounting conventions. In this example the average earnings aftertax for the four years is $4,000, and this is divided by the average investment of $15,000. This gives an AAR of 26.7 percent.

Firms frequently calculate the AAR, but it has serious flaws. We have noted earlier that asset values come from the amount and timing of cash flows. The AAR method for evaluating investments uses accounting earnings, not cash flows, and it gives equal treatment to all the earnings. The $2,000 earned in the first and fourth years is assigned the same value. We have learned from the study of the time value of money that this is not correct. A further flaw is that the AAR does not use market values, but rather book values to establish the value of the investment. The final problem with this method is that it does not suggest an evaluation yardstick, such as the acceptable rate of return used by the NPV and IRR methods.

Establishing Cash Flows

To examine the next four approaches to capital budgeting analysis, consider a situation in which the cash flow patterns of two investments are estimated. We are called on to select between Investment A and Investment B, both requiring an initial capital investment of $10,000 (an outflow). The resultant, and in this case incremental, aftertax cash flows for these investments are shown in Table 12–3.

To arrive at the aftertax cash flows of Table 12–3 we must begin with revenues and include consideration of tax-allowable amortization (capital cost allowance) and taxes. In our example, both investments qualify for a 20 percent capital cost allowance (CCA) rate. Capital cost allowance is discussed in detail later in the chapter, where the calculation of the tax-allowable amortization for this machine is calculated in Table 12–9 on page 440. The relevant tax rate is 40 percent. Note that the net cash flow increment is calculated by subtracting any additional taxes incurred from the increased revenue. Column 5 is the resultant cash flow that is produced for each investment in Table 12–3.

Net Operating Cash Flows (on a $10,000 net capital outlay)
Investment A

Year	(1) Increased Revenue	(2) Increased CCA	(3) Increased Taxable Income	(4) Increased Taxes (@40%)	(5) Increased Cash Flow (1) − (4)
1	$7,667	$1,000	$6,667	$2,667	$5,000
2	7,133	1,800	5,333	2,133	5,000
3	2,373	1,440	933	373	2,000

Net Operating Cash Flows (on a $10,000 net capital outlay)
Investment B

Year	(1) Increased Revenue	(2) Increased CCA	(3) Increased Taxable Income	(4) Increased Taxes (@40%)	(5) Increased Cash Flow (1) − (4)
1	$1,833	$1,000	$833	$333	$1,500
2	2,133	1,800	333	133	2,000
3	3,207	1,440	1,767	707	2,500
4	7,565	1,152	6,413	2,565	5,000
5	7,719	922	6,797	2,719	5,000

Payback Period

The **payback period** method simply computes the time required to recoup the initial investment. We can examine Table 12–3.

It would take two years to receive net cash inflows of $10,000, the amount of the initial investment, under Investment A. Thus, we say the payback period for Investment A is 2 years, while for Investment B it is 3.8 years. In the latter case we would recover

TABLE 12–3
Investment alternatives

Year	Net Cash Inflows (of a $10,000 investment)	
	Investment A	Investment B
1	$5,000	$1,500
2	5,000	2,000
3	2,000	2,500
4		5,000
5		5,000

$6,000 in the first three years, $4,000 short of the full $10,000 investment. Since the fourth year has a total inflow of $5,000, we assume we would be 80 percent of the way through the fourth year ($4,000/$5,000) before we had recovered the additional $4,000 needed to make up the original $10,000. Thus, the payback period for Investment B is computed as 3.8 years.

In using the payback period to select Investment A, two important considerations are ignored. First, there is no consideration of the amount of cash flow generated after the initial investment is recaptured. The $2,000 in Year 3 for Investment A is ignored, as is the $5,000 in Year 5 for Investment B. Even if the $5,000 inflow in Year 5 were $50,000, it would have no impact on the decision. Therefore, the payback period places a premium on liquidity and tends to emphasize the shorter time horizon. Second the method fails to consider the time value of money. If we had two possible $10,000 investments with the following inflow patterns, the payback period would rank them equally.

Year	Early Returns	Late Returns
1	$9,000	$1,000
2	1,000	9,000
3	1,000	1,000

Although both investments have a payback period of two years, the first alternative is clearly superior because the $9,000 comes in the first year rather than the second. We could overcome this drawback by developing a discounted payback method.

The payback period has some features that help to explain its use by corporate management. It is easy to understand, and it places a heavy emphasis on liquidity. A proposed project must recoup the initial investment quickly, or it will not qualify (most corporations use a maximum time horizon of three to five years). A rapid payback may be particularly important to firms in industries characterized by rapid technological developments or other sources of uncertainty. Payback may give the financial analyst or manager the initial view of an investment's risk. Given that some decisions may be justifiable only on the basis of cash flow estimates far in the future (and therefore relatively more uncertain), managers often opt for the decisions with the more predictable cash flow estimates.

Nevertheless, the payback period method, concentrating as it does on only the initial years of investment, fails to definitively discern the optimum or most economic solution to a capital budgeting problem. By ignoring cash flows beyond the payback period this method may fail to accept projects that can add substantial value to the firm. The analyst is therefore required to consider the more comprehensive and more

Capital Budgeting Practices Utilized by Smaller, Privately Held Businesses

SB While the techniques described in this chapter are intended to be used by the modern, sophisticated financial manager, not everyone uses them. Surveys of large firms show usage of discounted cash flow techniques (NPV and IRR) and usage of the weighted average cost of capital. These are essential tools for today's financial manager.

However studies of smaller privately held firms reveal that only a small percentage of these firms use discounted cash flow methods. For example Runyon* found only 14 percent of his questionnaire respondents in small firms used the internal rate of return (IRR) or net present value (NPV) approaches. Most used the payback period or another simple approach.

There are perhaps two reasons why large firms use the more sophisticated and theoretically correct techniques, while smaller firms do not employ them to any great extent. The first is that the small business owner is likely to be less familiar with the discounted cash flow techniques. Although the small business owner likely understands the time value of money concept and applies it in a general fashion, he or she is unlikely equipped with the time or knowledge to apply the detailed techniques and inputs required by discounted cash flow analysis. The small business owner's skills are more likely to be in designing products, meeting customer's demands, and in hiring and satisfying employees.

The second reason may be because they spend more time with bankers rather than shareholders or bondholders. When approaching a banker for a loan for capital investments, the owner must be prepared to demonstrate the capacity to repay the loan within a set period of time rather than show the investment's NPV or IRR. The payback period is often the maturity period the bank will allow for the loan.

*__L.R. Runyon.__ "Capital Budgeting Decision Making in Small Firms." *Journal of Business Research* 11 (September 1983), pp. 389–97.

theoretically correct capital budgeting methods. These methods will value all possible cash flows.

Net Present Value

The **net present value (NPV)** of an investment discounts all the cash inflows over the life of the investment to determine whether they equal or exceed the required investment. If the present value of the inflows less the initial capital outflow is positive, value is added to the firm. The basic discount rate is usually the cost of capital to the firm.

If we once again evaluate Investments A and B from Table 12–3—using an assumed cost of capital or a discount rate of 10 percent—we arrive at the following figures for net present value:

Calculator—Investment A

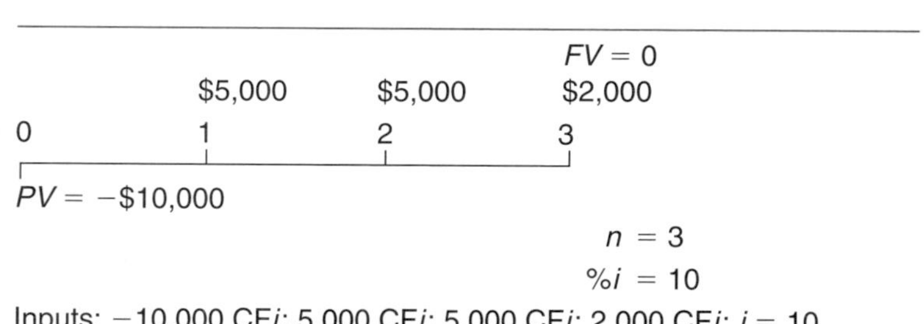

$NPV = 180.32.$

Calculator-Investment B

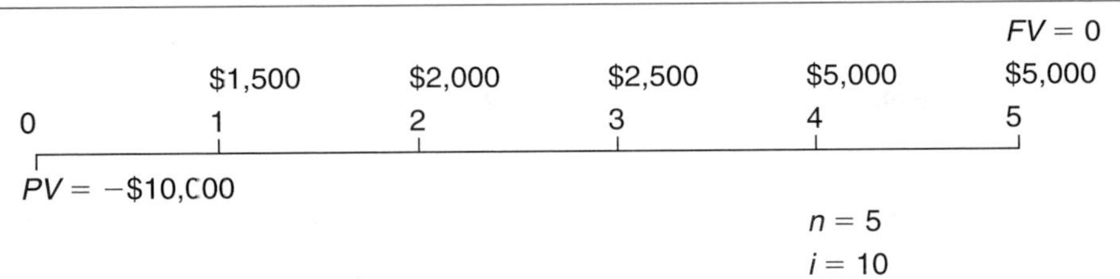

Inputs: −10,000 CF*i*; 1,500 CF*i*; 2,000 CF*i*; 2,500 CF*i*; 5,000 CF*i*; 5,000 CF*i*; *i* = 10.

NPV = $1,414.49.

$10,000 Investment, 10 percent discount rate

Year	Investment A		Year	Investment B	
1	$5,000 *PV* =	$ 4,545	1	$1,500 *PV* =	$ 1,364
2	5,000 *PV* =	4,132	2	2,000 *PV* =	1,653
3	2,000 *PV* =	1,503	3	2,500 *PV* =	1,878
		$10,180	4	5,000 *PV* =	3,415
			5	5,000 *PV* =	3,105
					$11,415
Present value of inflows		$10,180	Present value of inflows		$11,415
Present value of outflows		10,000	Present value of outflows		10,000
Net present value		$ 180	Net present value		$ 1,415

While both proposals have a positive NPV and thus are acceptable, Investment B has a considerably higher net present value than Investment A. Investment B will add the most value to the firm today. This is a different conclusion than suggested by the payback period. The NPV method is superior to the payback period because it includes all cash flows and the time value of money as part of the analysis. The internal rate of return method to be examined next, and which also incorporates the time value of money in its analysis, is a special case of the NPV method. However, for theoretical reasons, the NPV method is also preferred to the internal rate of return method and is easier to handle in more complex problems that may require more than one discount rate.

Internal Rate of Return

The **internal rate of return (IRR)** calls for determining the yield on an investment; that is, calculating the discount rate that equates the cash outflows (cost) of an investment with the subsequent cash inflows. It is that discount rate that produces an NPV of zero. We believe the net present value method is the superior evaluation technique, but some still prefer IRR. This may be because yield sometimes appears more comprehensible than the absolute value derived from the NPV analysis. We are more used to seeing rates of return, interest rates, and yields in our daily lives, and these seem to equate with the IRR. The IRR calculation requires a trial-and-error or interpolation procedure to determine a discount rate. This is true for a calculator or a computer, although they can perform the procedure fairly quickly.

The simplest case would be an investment of $100.00 that provides $120.00 after one year, or a 20 percent internal rate of return. For more complicated situations we must use the techniques developed in Chapter 9. For example, a $1,000 investment returning an annuity of $244.00 per year for five years provides an internal rate of return of 7.02 percent.

Calculator

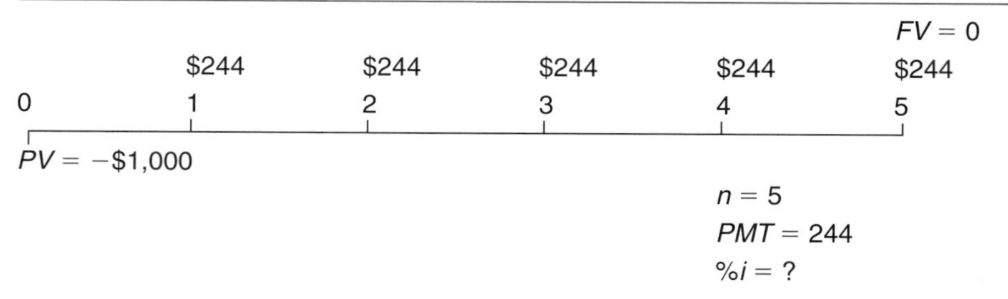

$i = 7.02\%$.

Tables (optional)

1. First divide the investment (present value) by the annuity.

$$\frac{\text{(Investment)}}{\text{(Annuity)}} = \frac{\$1{,}000}{\$244} = 4.1(PV_{IFA})$$

2. Then proceed to Appendix D (present value of an annuity). The factor of 4.1 for five years indicates a yield of 7 percent.

If an uneven cash inflow is involved, the process becomes somewhat more complicated, particularly when using tables.

Let us again evaluate the two investment alternatives in Table 12–3, only this time using the internal rate of return to rank the two projects. Neither proposal represents a precise annuity stream. We begin with Investment A, which qualifies for a 20 percent capital cost allowance (CCA) rate for income tax allowable amortization. Tax-allowable amortization for this machine is discussed later in the chapter and is calculated in Table 12–9. The relevant tax rate is 40 percent. Net cash flow increment is calculated by subtracting any additional taxes incurred from the increased revenue. Column 5 is the cash flow produced earlier for Investment A in Table 12–3. We set out to determine the discount rate equating the future increased cash flows with the initial investment.

Year	(1) Increased Revenue	(2) Increased CCA	(3) Increased Taxable Income	(4) Increased Taxes (@40%)	(5) Increased Cash Flow (1) − (4)
1	$7,667	$1,000	$6,667	$2,667	$5,000
2	7,133	1,800	5,333	2,133	5,000
3	2,373	1,440	933	373	2,000

Calculator

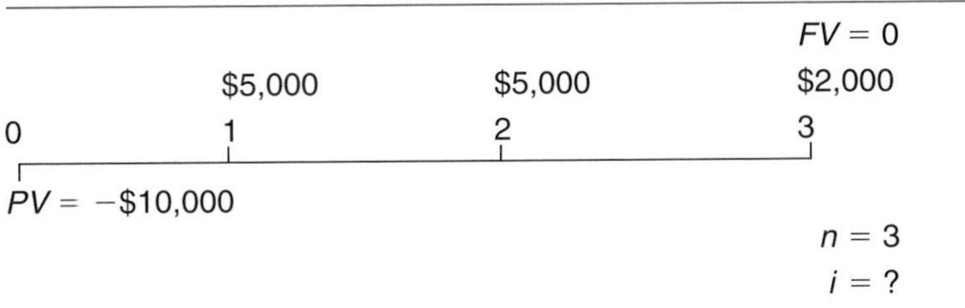

Inputs: −10,000 CF*i*; 5,000 CF*i*; 5,000 CF*i*; 2,000 CF*i*.

IRR = 11.16%.

Tables (optional)

1. To find a beginning value to start our first trial, average the inflows as if we were really getting an annuity.

$$\begin{array}{r} \$\ 5{,}000 \\ 5{,}000 \\ \underline{2{,}000} \\ \$12{,}000 \div 3 = \$4{,}000 \end{array}$$

2. Then divide the investment by the "assumed" annuity value in step 1.

$$\frac{\text{(Investment)}}{\text{(Annuity)}} = \frac{\$10{,}000}{\$4{,}000} = 2.5(PV_{IFA})$$

3. Proceed to Appendix D to arrive at a *first approximation* of the internal rate of return, using:

$$(PV_{IFA}) \text{ factor} = 2.5$$
$$n \text{ (period)} = 3$$

The factor falls between 9 and 10 percent. This is only a first approximation—our actual answer will be closer to 10 percent or higher because our method of average cash flows theoretically moved receipts from the first two years into the last year. This averaging understates the actual internal rate of return. The same method would overstate the IRR for Investment B because it would move cash from the last two years into

(continued)

(concluded)

the first three years. Since we know that cash flows in the early years are worth more and increase our return, we can usually gauge whether our first approximation is overstated or understated.

4. Next enter into a trial-an-error process to arrive at an answer. Because these cash flows are uneven rather than an annuity, we need to use Appendix B. We begin with 10 percent and then try 12 percent.

Year	10 Percent		Year	12 Percent	
1	$5,000 × 0.909 =	$ 4,545	1	$5,000 × 0.893 =	$ 4,465
2	5,000 × 0.826 =	4,130	2	5,000 × 0.797 =	3,985
3	2,000 × 0.751 =	1,502	3	2,000 × 0.712 =	1,424
		$10,177			$9,874

At 10 percent, the present value of the inflows exceeds $10,000—we therefore use a higher discount rate.

At 12 percent, the present value of the inflows is less than $10,000—thus, the discount rate is too high.

The answer must fall between 10 percent and 12 percent, indicating an approximate answer of 11 percent.

If we want to be more accurate, the results can be *interpolated.* Because the internal rate of return is determined when the present value of the inflows (PV_I) equals the present value of the outflows (PV_O), we need to find a discount rate that equates the PV_I to the cost of $10,000 ($PV_O$), where $NPV = 0$. The total difference in present values between 10 percent and 12 percent is $303.

$10,177	.... PV_I@10%	$10,177	.... PV_I@10%
9,874	.... PV_I@12%	10,000	..........(cost)
$ 303		$ 177	

The solution at 10 percent is $177 away from $10,000. Actually, the solution is ($177/$303) percent of the way between 10 and 12 percent. Because there is a 2 percent difference between the two rates used to evaluate the cash inflows, we need to multiply the fraction by 2 percent and then add our answer to 10 percent for the final answer of:

$$10\% + (\$177/\$303)(2\%) = 11.17\% \text{ IRR}$$

Note that this answer is not as accurate as the calculator.

The calculator is more accurate.

For Investment B the same process yields an answer of 14.33 percent (you may wish to confirm this).

Year	(1) Increased Revenue	(2) Increased CCA	(3) Increased Taxable Income	(4) Increased Taxes (@40%)	(5) Increased Cash Flow (1) − (4)
1	$1,833	$1,000	$833	$333	$1,500
2	2,133	1,800	333	133	2,000
3	3,207	1,440	1,767	707	2,500
4	7,565	1,152	6,413	2,565	5,000
5	7,719	922	6,797	2,719	5,000

The use of the internal rate of return method calls for the prudent selection of Investment B, with an IRR of 14.33 percent, in preference to Investment A with an IRR of 11.16 percent. The final selection of any investment, under the internal rate of return method, depends on the yield exceeding some minimum cost standard, usually based on the cost of capital to the firm. Again, in this example, with a cost of capital of 10 percent, both investments would be acceptable.

This conclusion is the same one reached with the NPV method. Under most circumstances the net present value and internal rate of return methods suggest the same conclusion, and the subsequent discussion is restricted to these two approaches.

A small correction to the above investment calculations is in order. Under the Canadian tax system, amortization for tax purposes is called capital cost allowance. On many capital items, capital cost allowance is calculated on a declining-balance method. If this applies to the investments in question, the calculations of internal rate of return and net present value become more complicated because the value of the capital cost allowance tax shield may continue at ever diminishing amounts well past the economic life of the asset. For simplicity we have ignored the value of tax savings past Year 3 for Investment A and Year 5 for Investment B. Since there are leftover tax savings in these examples, however, the true internal rates of return and net present values are slightly higher than those calculated. The handling of declining-balance, capital cost allowance tax shields in capital budgeting decision making is discussed later in this chapter.

Profitability Index

The **profitability index** is the ratio of cash inflows to cash outflows in present value terms. It is an alternative presentation of the net present value method and is used to place returns from different size investments onto a common measuring standard.

$$(PI) \text{ Profitability index} = \frac{\text{Present value of the inflows}}{\text{Present value of the outflows}}$$

Using the information from the NPV analysis we find for Investment A, the profitability index is 1.0180 ($10,180/$10,000), and for Investment B it is 1.1414 ($11,414/$10,000). As both investments have a profitability index greater than 1, they will add value to the firm because the present value of cash inflows exceeds the initial capital investment (cash outflow). Furthermore, Investment B has a higher relative value than Investment A based on the size of the investment, which in this example is the same for both investments.

Summary of Evaluation Methods

A summary of the results and various conclusions reached under the four capital budgeting methods based on cash flows is presented in Table 12–4.

TABLE 12–4
Capital budgeting results

	Investment A	Investment B	Selection
Payback period	2 years	3.8 years	Quickest payback: Investment A
Net present value	$180	$1,414	Highest net present value: Investment B
Internal rate of return	11.16%	14.33%	Highest yield: Investment B
Profitability index	1.0180	1.1414	Highest relative profitability: Investment B

Selection Strategy

The net present value, internal rate of return, and profitability index methods must have the profitability based on the time value of money equal or exceed the cost of capital for the project to be potentially acceptable. If profitability in these methods exceeds the cost of the investment, value will be added to the firm. These methods are similar and generally lead to the same decision. The profitability index, it should be noted, is really only a variation of the NPV method.

The IRR and NPV methods are clearly superior to the payback period and the average accounting return (AAR) methods, because they evaluate all the resultant cash flows from an investment decision and employ the time value of money. Furthermore, the acceptance of an investment when using the IRR and NPV methods is determined by the cost of capital. This is an objective criterion determined in the financial markets. The payback period and AAR methods fail to produce such an objective yardstick upon which to accept or reject an individual project.

However, the IRR method does have some flaws when compared to the NPV method that may produce unclear results. These flaws are discussed below under mutually exclusive projects, discounting considerations, and multiple internal rates. These reasons are why the NPV is a better methodology. The NPV method can also handle more complex problems that require more than one discount rate. The nature of the IRR method is that there can be only one discount rate.

Mutually Exclusive Projects

Under certain circumstances the IRR method will suggest a different decision than the NPV, in particular whether the projects are **mutually exclusive** *or not.* If investments are mutually exclusive, the selection of one alternative precludes the selection of any other alternative.

To illustrate mutually exclusive projects, let us assume we are going to build a specialized assembly plant in central Canada. Four cities are under consideration, only one of which will be picked. In this situation we select the alternative with the highest acceptable yield or the highest net present value and disregard all others. Even if certain

Continual Capital Budgeting

In the 1970s the development of the vast tar sands of Northern Alberta commenced on a large scale. This region has reserves of oil to rival any deposit in the world. The problem, and hence the cost, of recovering the oil was that it was mixed with sticky tar sand, unlike the oil from conventional oil sites. By the turn of the millennium George Bush, the U.S. president, was showing interest in the "tar pits."

Syncrude Canada Ltd. was a joint venture formed by governments and private sector oil companies to extract oil from these sands. By 1994 the governments had sold their stakes in Syncrude to the private sector. With the increasing oil prices of the 1970s, the capital budgeting numbers on full-scale development of the tar sands looked good. Even with the high costs of extracting the oil and the huge initial capital costs, the expectation of future oil prices suggested that this would be a profitable venture.

Syncrude was built in the 1970s for $2.3 billion. Its first barrel of oil cost $30.00, and in 1981 its unit cost of a barrel of oil had declined to $24.50 Canadian. However, with oil prices dropping as low as $10.00 a barrel in the 1980s, the joint venture had its difficulties. Syncrude persisted by "de-bottlenecking" the production process and reducing its cost structure by way of continual capital budgeting projects of approximately $500 million a year.

Today Syncrude is the largest source of oil in Canada and supplies 25 percent of our oil needs by producing over 200,000 barrels of synthetic sweet crude oil per day. By 1999 Syncrude's unit cost of synthetic light crude oil was as low as $11.29 Canadian per barrel, although by 2000 it increased to $17.45 per barrel. Extensive maintenance and higher purchased energy costs were responsible for the increase. Even with low oil prices of below U.S.$20.00 per barrel, a profit was being made.

Capital expenditures for 2002 were projected at $2 billion, with $1.75 billion for expansion and the rest to sustaining and maintenance. The expenditures were for the third stage of expansion of an upgrader (which turns heavy oil to light crude), and for the second bitumen production train for the Aurora mine. The process of transport to the upgrader includes the world's largest trucks (320 tonnes) and largest shovels (42 cubic metres) and a hydrotransport technology.

Continual capital budgeting has allowed Syncrude to reduce it's per unit costs of oil production to a profitable level, even at depressed sale prices.

FINANCE IN ACTION

Q1 Can Syncrude produce at profit based on the latest cost per barrel of oil?

Q2 What were the capital expenditures for the latest quarter at Syncrude?

www.syncrude.ca

locations provide a marginal return in excess of the cost of capital, they may be rejected. In the following table, the possible alternatives are presented.

Mutually Exclusive Alternatives	IRR	Net Present Value (thousands)
Oakville	15%	$300
Sarnia	12	200
Ottawa	11	100
Cost of capital	**10**	—
Windsor	9	(100)

Among the mutually exclusive alternatives, only Oakville would be selected. Of course, if the alternatives were not a mutually exclusive need for multiple specialized plants, we would accept all of the alternatives that provided a return in excess of our cost of capital. Only Windsor would then be rejected.

Applying this logic to Investments A and B in the prior discussion and assuming a cost of capital of 10 percent, only Investment B would be accepted if the alternatives were mutually exclusive, while both would clearly qualify if they were not mutually exclusive.

	Investment A	Investment B	Accepted if Mutually Exclusive	Accepted if Not Mutually Exclusive
Internal rate of return	11.16%	14.33%	B	A, B
Net present value	$180	$1,414	B	A, B

The discussion to this point has assumed the internal rate of return and net present value methods call for the same decision. Although this is generally true, there are exceptions. Two rules may be stated:

1. Both methods accept or reject the same investments based on minimum return or cost of capital criteria. If an investment has a positive net present value, it also has a yield in excess of the cost of capital.
2. In certain limited cases, however, the two methods may give different answers in selecting the best investment from a range of acceptable alternatives. This will be demonstrated later after the net present value profile is presented.

Discounting Consideration

The methodology for the internal rate of return discounts all cash flows from the future to the present at the same discount rate. The internal rate of return is that discount rate that makes the present value of those cash flows equal to the initial investment or, in other words, produces an NPV of zero. However, with our knowledge of the term structure of interest rates and our later study of risk, we should wonder whether the same discount rate is appropriate over time and whether the same discount should be applied to cash flows of a differing nature. Table 12–5 demonstrates the use of different discount rates for different time periods with the NPV method. Fortunately, the NPV methodology allows us to handle these considerations if they are appropriate to the analysis. This makes the NPV method of discounted cash flow analysis more flexible than the IRR method.

TABLE 12–5
Internal rate of return and net present value ($10,000 investment)

Investment A (11.16% IRR)			Investment A		
Year	Cash Flow		Year	Cash Flow	
1	$5,000 →		1	$5,000 →	10%
2	5,000 →		2	5,000 →	11%
3	2,000 →	Discounted at 11.16%	3	2,000 →	12% Discounted at various rates if desired
	NPV = 0			NPV = $27	

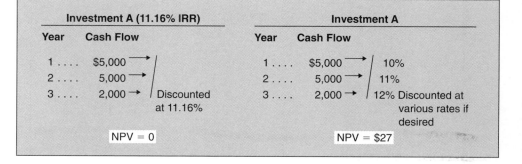

Multiple Internal Rates

It is possible with the IRR method to have more than one discount rate that equates the future cash flows and the initial investment, depending on the pattern of cash flows. For example, suppose an investment has the following pattern of cash flows.

Calculator

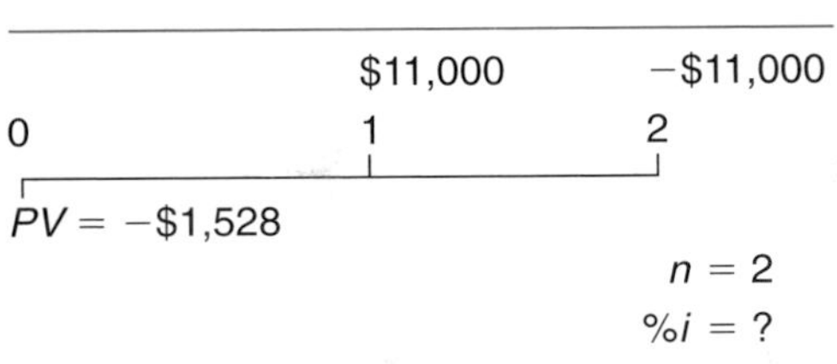

i = 20% and 500%.

The present value of the cash flows in years 1 and 2 is shown in Table 12–6. The pattern of cash flows is what one might find on an environmentally sensitive project where rehabilitation costs have to be incurred at the end of the project. The project would have an initial capital investment (cash outflow) to start the project, followed by positive cash flows and finally a negative cash flow. This occurs when the project can no longer yield positive profits and the firm is then obligated to incur costs (cash outflow) to restore the property to its original condition.

TABLE 12–6
Multiple IRRs

	Cash Flow	@20%	@500%
0	−1,528	−1,528	−1,528
1	11,000	9,167	1,833
2	−11,000	−7,639	−305
NPV		0	0

We are left with a dilemma when we calculate the IRR in this example. Both 20 percent and 500 percent are correct because they produce an NPV equal to zero, but which IRR should be used to decide whether or not to proceed with the project? With the NPV method and an acceptable discount rate employed in the calculations, we can easily decide if the project is worthwhile. It turns out in our example that any discount rate between 20 percent and 500 percent produces a positive NPV. However, if our cost of capital is 15 percent the NPV would be negative and the project would not add value to the firm. The IRRs of 20 percent or 500 percent would suggest that this would be a worthwhile project. Thus, the NPV method gives a better decision rule under these circumstances.

It turns out that there can be as many IRRs as there are changes of sign from positive to negative in the cash flows. This flaw in the IRR method could lead to incorrect decisions, or at best vague results. The NPV method handles this situation well and produces a clear decision result.

Capital Rationing

At times management may place a dollar constraint on the amount of funds that can be invested in a given period. This is **capital rationing.** The executive planning committee may emerge from a lengthy capital budgeting session to announce that only $5 million may be spent on new capital projects this year. Although $5 million may represent a large sum, it is still an artificially determined constraint and not the product of marginal analysis in which all projects with positive net present values are accepted.

Perhaps a management team may adopt a posture of capital rationing because it fears the risks attached to rapid growth strategies or because it is hesitant to use external sources of financing. However, in a purely theoretical sense, capital rationing hinders a firm from maximizing value.

If capital budgeting analysis is performed correctly, risk will be captured in the discount rate (cost of capital) used to evaluate an investment. Then, if the NPV is positive the investment, with appropriate consideration for risk, will add value to the firm. With capital rationing as indicated in Table 12–7, acceptable projects must be ranked, and only those with the highest positive net present value are accepted. Under capital rationing only Projects A through C, calling for $5 million in investment, will be accepted. Although Projects D and E have returns exceeding the cost of funds, as evidenced by a positive net present value, they will not be accepted under capital rationing.

Why would experienced managers impose a capital constraint? Besides the periodic reluctance to go to external sources for funding, many times the reason probably derives from one or two other sources. External sources of funding expose management to greater scrutiny by the impersonal capital markets and may dilute control of the firm.

TABLE 12–7
Capital rationing

	Project	Investment	Total Investment	Net Present Value
Capital rationing solution	A	$2,000,000		$400,000
	B	2,000,000		380,000
→	C	1,000,000	$5,000,000	150,000
	D	1,000,000		100,000
Best solution →	E	800,000	6,800,000	40,000
	F	800,000		(30,000)

In some cases the concern is with how many new projects the current management team can oversee at one time. In other words, the constraint being imposed is actually one related to available management talent, even though it is presented as a restriction on the amount of capital available. Thus, although the projects might look good under the assumption that their implementation will be supervised by experienced company managers, they are less attractive if additional new managers must be employed.

Canadian Institute of Forestry
www.cif-ifc.org

Another case relates to industries where the experience with forecasting future demand has been so unsuccessful that management deliberately funds new projects in relation to cash near at hand. This has often been the situation with Canada's forest products industry, which accounts for about 10% of the jobs in the country. This latter form of capital rationing is really a qualitative way of dealing with high levels of uncertainty. A variation on the forecasting problem is upper management's experience with capital budgeting analysis in which estimated cash flows are biased in an upward direction to promote certain projects. To limit the "rigging" of acceptable projects, management rations capital.

Net Present Value Profile

An interesting way to summarize the characteristics of an investment is through the use of the **net present value profile.** The profile allows us to graphically portray the net present value of a project at different discount rates. Let's apply the profile to the investments we have been discussing. The projects are summarized again:

	Aftertax Cash Inflows (of a $10,000 investment)	
Year	Investment A	Investment B
1	$5,000	$1,500
2	5,000	2,000
3	2,000	2,500
4		5,000
5		5,000

To apply the net present value profile, you need to know *three* characteristics about an investment:

1. *The net present value at a zero discount rate.* That is easy to determine. With no discount rate, the present values and future values are the same. For Investment A, the net present value would be $2,000 ($5,000 + $5,000 + $2,000 − $10,000). For Investment B, the answer is $6,000 ($1,500 + $2,000 + $2,500 + $5,000 + $5,000 − $10,000).
2. *The net present value as determined by a normal discount rate* (such as the cost of capital). For these two investments we used a discount rate of 10 percent. As summarized in Table 12–4 on page 430, the net present values for the two investments at that discount rate were $180 for Investment A and $1,414 for Investment B.
3. *The internal rate of return for the investments.* Once again referring to Table 12–4, we see the internal rate of return is 11.16 percent for Investment A and 14.33 percent for Investment B. Also realize that the internal rate of return is the discount rate that allows the project to have a net present value of zero. This characteristic becomes more important when we present our graphic display.

We summarize the information about discount rates and net present values for each investment below and graphically in Figure 12–2 on the next page.

Investment A	
Discount Rate	Net Present Value
0	$2,000
10%	180
11.16% (IRR)	0

Investment B	
Discount Rate	Net Present Value
0	$6,000
10%	1,414
14.33% (IRR)	0

Note that in Figure 12–2 we have graphed the three points for each investment. Investment A shows a $2,000 net present value at a zero discount rate, a $180 net present value at a 10 percent discount rate, and a zero net present value at an 11.16 percent

FIGURE 12–2

Net present value profile

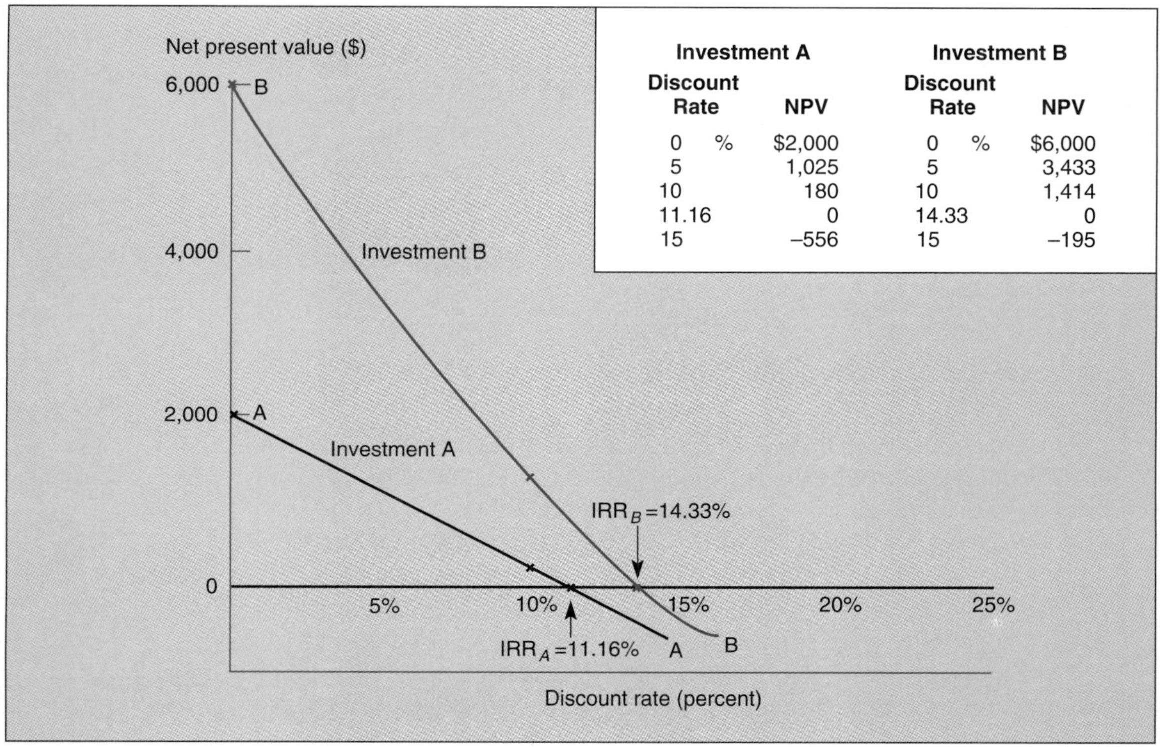

Investment A		Investment B	
Discount Rate	NPV	Discount Rate	NPV
0 %	$2,000	0 %	$6,000
5	1,025	5	3,433
10	180	10	1,414
11.16	0	14.33	0
15	–556	15	–195

discount rate. We then connected the points. The same procedure was applied to Investment B. The reader can also visually approximate what the net present value for the investment projects would be at other discount rates (such as 5 percent).

In the preceding example the net present value of Investment B was superior to Investment A at every point. This is not always the case in comparing projects. To illustrate, let's introduce a new project, Investment C, and then compare it with Investment B.

Characteristics of Investment C

Investment C ($10,000 investment)	
Year	Aftertax Cash Inflows
1	$9,000
2	3,000
3	1,200

1. The net present value at a zero discount rate for this project is $3,200 ($9,000 + 3,000 + 1,200 − 10,000).
2. The net present value at a 10 percent discount rate is $1,563.
3. The internal rate of return is 22.49 percent.

You could compute these values for yourself, but that is not necessary at this point.

Comparing Investment B to Investment C in Figure 12–3, we observe that at low discount rates, Investment B has a higher net present value than Investment C. However, at high discount rates, Investment C has a higher net present value than Investment B. The actual crossover point is at approximately 8.7 percent. That is to say, if you had to choose between Investment B and Investment C, your answer would depend on the discount rate. At low rates (below 8.7 percent) you would opt for Investment B. At higher rates (above 8.7 percent) you would select Investment C. Since the cost of capital is presumed to be 10 percent, you would probably prefer Investment C (remember though that the cost of capital can change).

FIGURE 12–3

Net present value profile with crossover

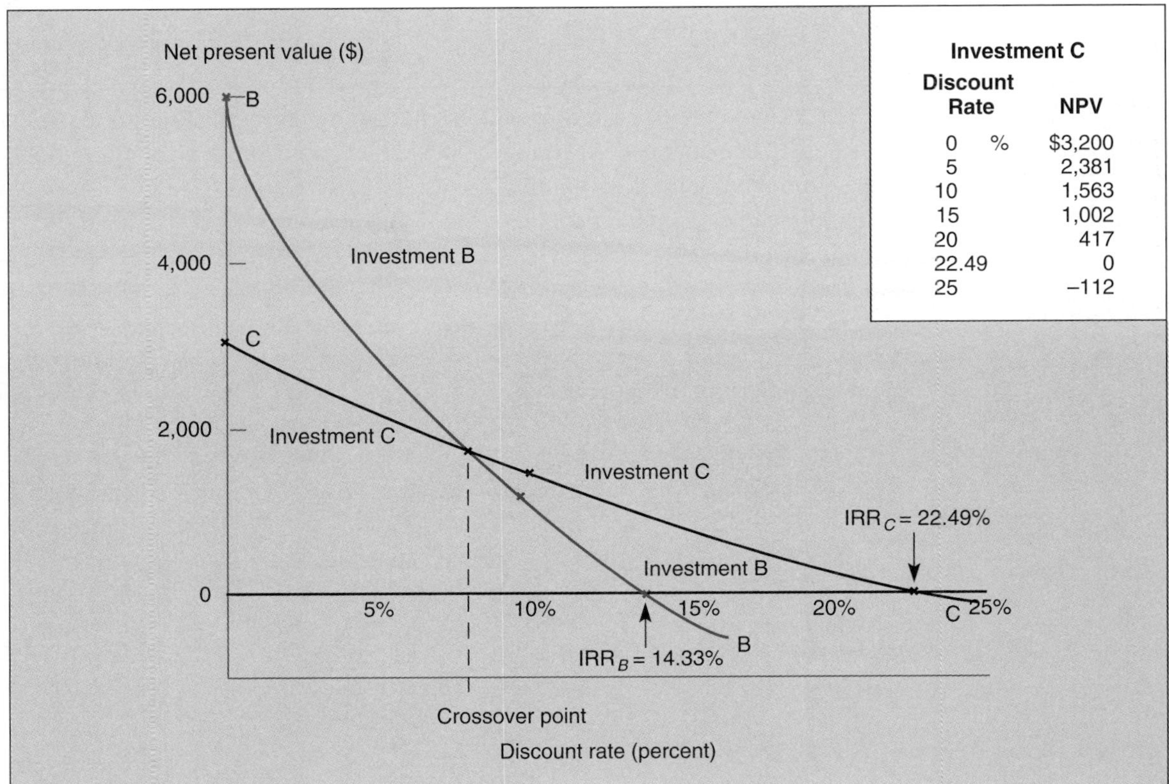

Investment C

Discount Rate	NPV
0 %	$3,200
5	2,381
10	1,563
15	1,002
20	417
22.49	0
25	–112

Why does Investment B do well compared to Investment C at low discount rates and relatively poorly compared to Investment C at high discount rates? This difference is related to the timing of inflows. Let's examine the inflows.

	Cash Inflows (of a $10,000 investment)	
Year	Investment B	Investment C
1	$1,500	$9,000
2	2,000	3,000
3	2,500	1,200
4	5,000	
5	5,000	

Investment B has heavy late inflows ($5,000 in both the fourth and fifth years), and these are more strongly penalized by high discount rates. Investment C has extremely high early inflows that are less affected by high discount rates than are later flows.

As previously mentioned in the chapter, if the investments are not mutually exclusive and capital is not being rationed, we would probably accept both Investment B and Investment C at discount rates below 14.33 percent. Below that discount rate they both have positive net present values. On the other hand, if we can select only one, the decision may well turn on the choice of a discount rate. Observe in Figure 12–3 that at a discount rate of 5 percent, we would select Investment B, at 10 percent we would select Investment C, and so on, because the NPV is greater. The net present value profile helps us make such decisions. This also suggests that the NPV method is superior to the IRR method when projects are mutually exclusive.

Capital Cost Allowance

To analyze the anticipated cash flow patterns under any investment proposal, we have to know how to consider the effects of tax-allowable amortization on our cash flow estimates. Although financial accounting entries for amortization have no cash flow effects, tax-allowable amortization expenses do. The Income Tax Act of Canada lays out a system of allocating amortization, called **capital cost allowance (CCA),** that reduces the tax payable for profitable firms and therefore is important in estimating the cash flow effects of proposed project investments. Capital cost allowance creates tax shields or tax savings.

As an example:

Before CCA Expense		After CCA Expense		
Income (cash flow)	$12,000	Income (cash flow)		$12,000
		CCA		5,000
		Taxable income		7,000
Tax @ 40%	4,800	Tax @ 40%		2,800
Income (cash flow) aftertaxes	$ 7,200	Income aftertaxes		$ 4,200
		Add back CCA		5,000
		Income/cash flow aftertax		$ 9,200
		Aftertax expense	$5,000 (1 − T) =	$ 3,000
		Tax savings	$5,000 (T) =	$ 2,000
		Before-tax expense		$ 5,000

Amortization was originally authorized under the Income War Tax Act of 1917, which made it tax deductible on any straight-line basis acceptable to the minister. During World War II, accelerated amortization was introduced to encourage expansion of wartime production capacity. Virtually every federal budget in recent years has included measures implementing new government policy directions through amendments to the system of capital cost allowances.

The amount of amortization allowable under the tax act is called *capital cost allowance (CCA).* For tax-deductible CCA purposes, assets are divided into a number of

Tax Savings Disappear into the Air!

In the third quarter of 2001, Air Canada wrote-off $410 million related to an intangible tax asset. Although there was no immediate cash flow consequence to Air Canada, the write-off represented the loss of future expected tax flows. At the time and for the foreseeable future, Air Canada expected to experience substantial losses.

Tax savings can only be realized by a profitable firm. If no taxes have to be paid because earnings are nonexistent there can be no tax savings and the value of accumulated write-offs decreases significantly. Air Canada was acknowledging this fact in its financial statements.

FINANCE IN ACTION

www.aircanada.ca

classes, each of which is assigned a CCA rate. All of the assets of a given class form what is called an asset pool. Unfortunately for those of us trying to calculate the tax shield resulting from capital cost allowance, most of the asset classes call for declining-balance CCA as a result of the income tax act implemented in 1949. A sampling of CCA classes (subject to the declining-balance rule), their accompanying CCA rates, and some of the items that might be assigned to a particular class are included in Table 12–8.

TABLE 12–8
Some declining-balance CCA classes

Class	Rate	Assets
Class 1	4%	Bridges, buildings, dams
Class 3	5	Windmills, telegraph poles
Class 6	10	Greenhouses, hangars, wood jetties
Class 7	15	Boats, ships
Class 8	20	Most machinery, radio communications equipment
Class 9	25	Aircraft
Class 10	30	Automobile equipment, computer hardware, feature films
Class 12	100	Cutlery, television commercials, computer software
Class 16	40	Taxicabs, autos for short-term rental, video games (coin)
Class 17	8	Roads, storage area
Class 30	40	Telecommunications spacecraft
Class 33	15	Timber resource property
Class 42	12	Fibre optic cable

Of the CCA classes, some of the larger amounts involving capital investment projects often fall under Class 1 (buildings) and Class 8 (machinery). Table 12–9, on the next page, calculates the CCA for the assets (Class 8) involved in Investments A and B considered earlier in this chapter.

Note that any increases in a pool are eligible for only half the normal CCA in the year of addition. Under the *half-rate rule,* introduced in November 1981, only half the normal CCA for most assets is allowed as a tax-deductible expense in the year of acquisition. This rule does not apply to some Class 12 assets, normally written off 100 percent in the first year. Property in Classes 14 and 15 (see Table 12–11) is also exempt from the half-rate rule because of the depletion nature of those allowances.

Once an asset has been assigned to a given CCA pool, capital cost allowance is calculated on the **undepreciated capital cost (UCC)** of the pool of assets rather than on a single individual asset. What we have just calculated is the maximum CCA a firm can deduct for a given year. There may be circumstances where a firm would want to claim less than the maximum allowable CCA. For example, if the firm were in a loss situation and expected to be for many years hence, it might decide that taking the maximum CCA allowable might only reduce the tax shield available in the future while there is no income to shield from tax presently.[4]

TABLE 12–9
Capital cost allowance for Investment A or B

Year 1:	
Net original cost	$10,000
Less: capital cost allowance 1/2($10,000 × .20)	1,000
Undepreciated capital cost*	$ 9,000
Year 2:	
Less: capital cost allowance ($9,000 × .20)	1,800
Undepreciated capital cost	$ 7,200
Year 3:	
Less: capital cost allowance ($7,200 × .20)	1,440
Undepreciated capital cost	$ 5,760
Year 4:	
Less: capital cost allowance ($5,760 × .20)	1,152
Undepreciated capital cost	$ 4,608
Year *n*:	
Undepreciated capital cost (for year $n - 1$)	
Less: capital cost allowance (UCC in year $n - 1 \times .20$)	
Equals: undepreciated capital cost (for year *n*)	

*UCC for short.

$$UCC_n = (1 - \frac{d}{2})(1 - d)^{n-1}$$

Capital Cost Allowance
www.ccra-adrc.gc.ca/E/pbg/tf/t2sch8eq/t2sch8-e.pdf

Addition and Disposal of Assets

When an asset is purchased, its purchase price is added to the pool. When an asset is sold, on the other hand, the lower of the sale price or its original cost is deducted. A pool can have CCA applied to it forever as long as there is at least one asset in it. If an asset is sold for more than its original cost, the difference is treated as a capital gain for tax purposes.

A capital gain for tax purposes is the difference between the purchase price of an asset and its sale price, assuming the price has gone up and the asset was not held primarily for resale as part of doing business. In that case, it would be considered as income. For tax purposes, only 50 percent of a capital gain, known as the taxable capital gain, is added to taxable income for the year. Tax is then paid on the increased amount of taxable income.

Assume Firm XYZ chose to buy Investment A in Year 1 and then also bought Investment B in Year 2. This is our example from Table 12–3, with both investments costing $10,000. Assume also that these are the only assets in Class 8. The undepreciated capital cost balance for Class 8 assets at the end of Year 3 would then be $12,960 (from Table 12–9 we see it would include $5,760 from A and $7,200 from B).

[4]For losses incurred in 1983 or later, the carryover rule is forward seven or back three years to be applied against taxable income. Thus, the consideration to delay or not to delay CCA expenses is not a straightforward one, although the later rule makes delay a less likely choice.

Suppose that in Year 4, XYZ sells both of the assets in Class 8, after which no assets remain in that pool. The liquidation of the pool could give rise to a number of different tax effects depending on the amounts for which the assets were sold. (See Table 12–10.)

TABLE 12–10
Liquidation of asset pool

	Outcome 1	Outcome 2	Outcome 3	Outcome 4
Year 3:				
UCC	$12,960	$12,960	$12,960	$12,960
Year 4:				
Sale price—A	5,000	7,000	7,500	12,000
Sale price—B	5,000	5,960	7,500	7,200
Balance in pool	$ 2,960	$ 0	$ (2,040)	$ (4,240)
Capital gain	$ 0	$ 0	$0	$ 2,000
Tax consequences (@40%)				
Positive values are tax savings:				
From CCA pool	$ 1,184	$ 0	$ (816)	$ (1,696)
From capital gain	$0	$ 0	$0	$(600)
	$ 1,184	$ 0	$ (816)	$ (2,296)

Under Outcome 1, the pool has a leftover balance of $2,960, as the resale value of the assets declined more quickly than allowed for under the CCA schedule. That left-over balance is called a **terminal loss** and is tax deductible in Year 4, creating a tax savings. Under Outcome 2, the amount realized on the sale of the assets is exactly equal to the previous UCC, and the pool balance is zero, leaving no need for further adjustment. In Outcome 3, the sale price exceeds the UCC. More CCA was taken than the difference between the purchase and resale prices. The $2,040 is added to revenue in Year 4, creating taxes payable, and is termed **recapture.** Outcome 4 generates both a capital gain of $2,000 on the resale of A and recapture of $4,240 to eliminate the negative balance that would still be left in the pool after accounting for the capital gain.

Straight-Line CCA Classes

Some classes of capital items are not subject to rules of declining balance, but rather may be amortized for tax purposes on a straight-line basis. Table 12–11 lists some examples of classes subject to straight-line CCA.

TABLE 12–11
Straight-line CCA classes

Class 13	Certain leasehold improvements (to be amortized over the life of the lease)
Class 14	Certain patents, franchises, or licenses for a limited period (to be amortized over the life of the asset)
Class 15	Woods assets (amortized depending on the amount cut in the year)

Investment Tax Credit

The current **investment tax credit (ITC)** was originally a temporary measure that provided a 5 percent tax credit with respect to qualified buildings or equipment acquired between June 23, 1975, and June 30, 1976. Since that time, various governments have added qualified scientific research expenditures, qualified transportation equipment, and certified property to the list of assets that qualify for the investment tax credit. Besides being used to encourage expansion of the types of businesses favored by government policymakers, the investment tax credit has been used to encourage investment in certain geographical regions. Investment tax credits available in 2002 include:

Qualified scientific research expenditures:	
CCPC	35%
Other corporations and for expenditures above $2,000,000	20
Qualified property for use in manufacturing, processing in selected incentive areas	10

Canada Customs and Revenue Agency
www.ccra-adrc.gc.ca/taxcredit/business/menu-e.html

Unlike the CCA tax shield that reduces taxable income and then taxes indirectly, investment tax credits, by reducing taxes otherwise payable, represent direct dollar cash flow. Under certain conditions, where a corporation is not in a position to pay taxes, there is a provision for a cash refund.[5] For simplicity, the method of present value analysis that we use assumes that all cash flows related to tax consequences occur at the end of each appropriate year.

In the case of a new $100,000 machine (Class 8) bought by a profitable firm with a 38 percent tax rate, the first-year cash flow effect generated by tax savings or tax shield would be

$$\tfrac{1}{2}(20\% \times \$100{,}000 \times 38\%) = \$3{,}800$$

This cash flow effect occurs at the end of the year.

If this machine qualified as a scientific research expenditure in Alberta, it would be eligible for a 20 percent investment tax credit. Taxes would first be reduced by $20,000 (20% × $100,000). An investment tax credit, however, reduces the amount available for capital cost allowance in the year following acquisition by the amount of the credit, which in this case is $20,000. Therefore, the undepreciated capital cost (UCC) in the second year before capital cost allowance is taken would be

$$\$100{,}000 - [\tfrac{1}{2}(20\% \times \$100{,}000)] - \$20{,}000 = \$70{,}000$$

In addition, the scientific research expenditure is fully deductible as an expense. The corporation is therefore entitled to the full write-off of the expense and the investment tax credit.

To summarize, the ITC produces a direct cash flow and a reduction in the CCA pool in the year following acquisition.

Combining Cash Flow Analysis and Selection Strategy

To explore how the system affects the project cash flow, consider a situation in which a firm with a tax rate of 39 percent is deciding whether to add two new vehicles to its fleet of delivery vans. By referring to Table 12–8 we see that these vehicles would be placed in the CCA Class 10 asset pool, which carries a 30 percent CCA rate. Consider

[5]Section 127.1 of the Income Tax Act.

also that since the Class 10 pool had a balance of $52,000 coming into the current year, these vans would be purchased for $30,000, and no other assets will be added to the pool in the current year. The sale of an old van for $500 is the only other transaction expected to cause an adjustment to the balance in the asset pool. The sale of the old van is included in the analysis because its sale was a result of the decision to purchase the new vans. The undepreciated capital cost of the pool would thus become $81,500 ($52,000 + $30,000 − $500) if the vans were purchased.

Beginning UCC	$52,000
Additions to the pool	30,000
Dispositions from the pool	500
Undepreciated capital cost	$81,500

In the current year the maximum allowable CCA in respect to automobile equipment would be

$$[\text{Beginning UCC} + ½(\text{Additions} - \text{Dispositions})] \times \text{CCA rate}$$

If the vans are purchased, the balance in the Class 10 asset pool increases by $29,500. Table 12–12 demonstrates the change in the CCA tax shield available in the first few years that results if the vans are purchased. It is, of course, this incremental change in the pool that is relevant. What was in the pool before continues regardless of the decision.

TABLE 12–12
Capital cost allowance for vans

Year	Beginning UCC Effect	CCA Calculation	Change in CCA Available
2002	$29,500	½(29,500 × .30)	$4,425
2003	25,075	25,075 × .30	7,523
2004	17,552	17,552 × .30	5,266
2005	12,286	12,286 × .30	3,686
2006	8,600	8,600 × .30	2,580

After Year 1 we have created a steadily declining balance in perpetuity as long as the asset pool continues in existence. For the investment decision analysis, we need to calculate the present value of the tax savings resulting from the yearly allowable capital allowance expense, or in other words, the **CCA tax shield.** Given how the CCA system operates, we must provide the present value of a perpetual CCA tax shield. The general formula to account for the tax shield effect can be developed then as:[6]

$$\frac{CdT_c}{r + d}$$

[6]The development is exactly the same as for the dividend growth model derived in Chapter 10. The major conceptual difference is only that g (growth rate) is negative. Thus we have

$$PV = \frac{C_1}{1 + r} + \frac{C_1(1 - d)}{(1 + r)^2} + \frac{C_2(1 - d)^2}{(1 + r)^3} + \cdots$$
$$= \frac{C_1}{r - (-d)}$$

where

C = Change in capital cost pool resulting from acquiring the asset
d = CCA rate for the asset class
T_c = Corporate tax rate
r = Discount rate

In adjusting this formula for the half-rate rule, we obtain

$$\frac{CdT_c}{r+d} \times \frac{1+.5r}{1+r}$$

One further complication to the present value calculation must be included to make it complete. In the normal course of events we would expect at some time in the future to sell or salvage those two vans. An asset sold must be subtracted from the UCC of the asset pool. We would expect to have other values still in the Class 10 CCA pool. Therefore, we would realize a cash inflow on the sale of the vans, but lose the CCA tax shield associated with that value in future years. This causes a need to adjust the CCA tax shield formula as follows to take into account the estimated timing and amount of the salvage value:[7]

$$\text{PV of CCA tax shield} = [C - S_{\text{pv}}]\left(\frac{dT_c}{r+d}\right)\left(\frac{1+.5r}{1+r}\right) \quad (12\text{–}1)$$

where

S_{pv} = Change in capital cost pool resulting from the salvage value, as a present value
n = Number of years in the future we intend to sell the asset

If we examine Formula 12–1 we note three components. Within the square brackets is the present value of all changes in the CCA pool as a result of an investment decision, including any additions and deletions. These changes, assuming an asset pool remains open, will effect tax savings on a declining-balance basis forever, and this is handled by the term in the first round brackets following the square brackets. The final round bracket adjusts for the half-year rule. What the formula achieves is the present value of tax savings from all resultant changes in a CCA pool from an investment decision.

In the case of the proposed van purchases (net $29,500), if we expected to sell them after four years' usage at an estimated value of $2,000 each, and if the company's estimated cost of capital was 12 percent, the present value of the CCA tax shield from the vans would be:

$$PV = [\$29{,}500 - \$4{,}000_{\text{pv}}\ (\text{n} = 4, \text{r} = 12\%)]\left(\frac{(.30)(.39)}{.12 + .30}\right)\left(\frac{1 + .5(.12)}{1 + .12}\right)$$

$$= [\$29{,}500 - \$2{,}542](.27857)(.94643)$$
$$= \$7{,}107$$

[7]Some prefer not to apply the half-year rule to the salvage value. The half-year rule does not apply to salvage if the asset is sold by itself. However this formula is developed on the assumption that the asset pool continues (this makes the formula work). If the pool continues it is likely that a new asset will be purchased and its price is netted against the salvage value to be added to the pool. The half-year rule then applies to the salvage value. In any case, whether we do or do not apply the half-year rule to the salvage value should not have a material effect on the NPV and should not be the critical basis for any investment decision.

The estimated value of $2,000 for each of the vans in four years is referred to as the salvage value. This is the estimated market value at that time. The vans would probably be able to generate cash flows beyond the four years, but our analysis would require the value of those cash flows. We perhaps make a rather simplifying assumption by suggesting the salvage value captures the present value of the cash flows beyond the fourth year.

What remains to be done in order to decide whether or not to buy the vans? That decision rests on whether the estimated increase in future cash flows resulting from the purchase and use of the vans in the business more than offsets their initial cost. This means that we must next estimate the resultant cash flow effects (in addition to the CCA tax shield effect). Say, for example, we estimate that the new vans will allow the business to generate $33,000 per year in extra sales and that those extra sales will also require $16,000 per year in extra operating costs. The net present value of the resultant operating cash flows, the salvage value, and the tax shield less the capital outlay would be as shown in Table 12–13.

Thus, on the basis of this financial analysis, the investment in the vans clearly creates value. However, there may be other effects of this decision that have not been quantified or are difficult to quantify. For example, the addition of the two vans may implicitly reduce the amount of time a supervisor spends on his or her present duties. Management should then factor in any additional overall company effects against the favorable result of the information already included.

TABLE 12–13
Net present value of resultant cash flows @ 12%

Year	Cash Flow	Amount	(1 − *t*)	Aftertax Cash Flow	Present Value
0	Investment	−$29,500	—		−$29,500
1–4	Operating	17,000	.61	$10,370	31,497
4	Salvage	4,000	—		2,542
Present value of CCA tax shields ($29,500 − $2,542)(.263647)*					7,107
Net present value of resultant cash flows and initial investment					$11,646

*This number is from our calculation using Formula 12–1.

IRR Solution

For IRR analysis we can use the framework we have employed for the NPV analysis. Our purpose, however, is to find the discount rate that reduces the NPV to zero. This will involve trial and error complicated by the CCA formula in particular, because the IRR is part of the formula as *r*.

Since our NPV is fairly large, let us try 25 percent as our discount rate (see Table 12–14 on the next page). We are closer to an NPV of zero, but we are going to have to try again. Normal calculator functions will not work because the cash flow related to CCA, unlike the other cash flows, changes with each new discount rate. Therefore, we continue with trial and error. At a discount rate of 28 percent the NPV is $261; at 29 percent the NPV is −$272. We are close enough.

TABLE 12–14
IRR solution framework using 25%

Year	Cash Flow	Amount	(1 − *t*)	Aftertax Cash Flow	Present Value
0	Investment	−$29,500	—		−$29,500
1–4	Operating	17,000	.61	$10,370	24,490
4	Salvage	4,000	—		1,638
Present value of CCA tax shields					
$(\$29{,}500 - \$1{,}638)\left(\frac{(.30)(.39)}{.25 + .30}\right)\left(\frac{1 + .5(.25)}{1 + .25}\right)$					5,334
Present value of resultant cash flows and initial investment					$ 1,962

The Replacement Decision

Our discussion of capital budgeting thus far has centred on projects being considered as net additions to the present plant and equipment. Many capital budgeting decisions are made, however, because of the availability of new machinery to replace older models. Such decisions are referred to as replacement decisions. For example, plant engineers are constantly faced with the need to determine if a new machine incorporating the latest in technology can do a job more efficiently than the one currently used.

These replacement decisions bring additional considerations to the capital budgeting problem. For example, the sale of the old machine must be included in the analysis. This sale produces a cash inflow that partially offsets the purchase price of the new machine. In Canada, unlike in the United States, the sale of the old machinery generally does not have any tax consequences that require special handling because of the manner in which CCA works. In the unlikely case that it is sold for more than its original purchase price, however, an allowance must be made for capital gains tax payable.

The replacement decision can be analyzed by using a total analysis of both the old and the new machines or by using a differential analysis. We use the differential approach, which emphasizes the changes in cash flow between using the old and the new machines.

The Dalton Corporation purchased a computer two years ago for $100,000. The asset is included under CCA Class 10 (30 percent rate). It can currently be sold in the market for $40,000. A new replacement computer would cost $150,000 and would also become a Class 10 asset. A 15 percent investment tax credit would be available on the new computer.

The estimated cost savings and other benefits attributable to installing the new computer are between $20,000 and $45,000 per year for each of the next five years. This would show up as a net increase in earnings before amortization and taxes. The estimate is that at the end of that period, either of the old or the new computers would be replaced. At that time it is estimated the new computer under consideration could be sold for only $30,000 while the old computer would have no salvage value. The firm is in a 39 percent tax bracket and has a 14 percent cost of capital.

As the first step, we have to determine the net additional cost of the new computer. The purchase price of $150,000 is partially offset by the investment tax credit and by the cash inflow from the sale of the old computer (see Table 12–15).

The effect of the lost tax shield attached to the old computer need not be considered here as there will be tax calculations related to the sale. That is despite the fact that the

TABLE 12–15
Net price of the new computer

Price of the new computer	$150,000
– Investment tax credit (15%) or $22,500	19,737*
Net price of new computer	130,263
– Cash inflow from sale of old computer	40,000
Net cost of new computer	$90,263

*Our assumption about cash flows (revenues, expenses) and tax-initiated cash flows is that they occur at the end of the year. Therefore, the tax credit of $22,500 is discounted one year. The CCA pool is affected in the year after acquisition. The CCA tax shield formula is constructed assuming tax savings effects occur at the end of the year.

CCA taken thus far on the computer would have been less than the difference between its purchase price and the realization on its sale. Instead it is handled by the fact that we consider the net change in the Class 10 UCC balance rather than the salvage value and new purchase effects separately.

The basic capital budgeting question in this circumstance becomes, then: *Are the anticipated incremental gains from the replacement of the old computer by the new large enough to justify the net cost of $90,263?*

The answer to that question depends on a cash flow analysis of (1) the incremental increase in capital cost allowance and the related tax shield benefits, (2) the operating benefits, and (3) other resultant costs such as working capital adjustments.

Incremental Amortization (CCA)

If the replacement decision is taken, we note three changes in the undepreciated capital cost. In the first year the net increase would be $110,000 ($150,000 – $40,000). In the second year a decrease of $22,500 would result from the investment tax credit. The half-rate rule does not apply to the change due to the investment tax credit. In the fifth year the undepreciated capital cost would decrease by $30,000 as a result of the salvage value. The present value of the CCA tax shield using Formula 12–1 takes care of the net first year investment and the salvage value.

$$PV = [\$110{,}000 - \$30{,}000_{pv}\ (n = 5, r = 14\%)]\left(\frac{(.30)(.39)}{.14 + .30}\right)\left(\frac{1 + .5(.14)}{1 + .14}\right)$$

$$= [\$110{,}000 - \$15{,}581](.26591)(.93860)$$
$$= \$23{,}565$$

However, some CCA tax shield is lost from the second year forward due to the investment tax credit. This effect is handled by using Formula 12–1 (without the half-rate rule) and discounting the result back one year.

$$PV = -[\$22{,}500_{pv}\ (n = 1, r = 14\%)]\left(\frac{(.30)(.39)}{.14 + .30}\right)]$$

$$= -[\$19{,}737(.26591)]$$
$$= -\$5{,}248$$

In total, the present value of the CCA tax shield is $18,317 ($23,565 – $5,248), and is included in Table 12–16, on the next page, the summary of this investment decision.

Cost Savings

The second type of benefit that requires consideration relates to the cost savings that can be realized by installing the new computer. As previously stated, these are estimated at between $20,000 and $45,000 per year over the next five years. The aftertax benefits are summarized in Table 12–16, where the cost savings are multiplied by one minus the tax rate to calculate the value of the savings on an aftertax basis. The cost savings are combined with the other resultant costs and benefits of the computer installation in Table 12–16.

Other Resultant Costs

In any analysis all changes that are a result of an investment decision must be considered to correctly determine the value of an investment. One change that should not be overlooked is a change in working capital. In Chapters 6 and 7 it was pointed out that often with increasing sales a firm finds it has more capital tied up in accounts receivable, inventory, and other current assets. These current assets support the new sales level.

A benefit of many new investments is the increased level of sales that can be obtained, and it is likely that incremental increases in working capital will result from new investments. This working capital investment resulting from the decision to invest in a new project must be considered in the analysis as a resultant cost. Of course, when the project ends, through salvage of equipment or for other reasons, the working capital position would be unwound, resulting in a positive cash flow to the project.

TABLE 12–16
Differential analysis of new computer

Year	Cash Flow	Amount	(1 − tax rate)	Aftertax Cash Flow	Present Value (@14%)
0	New computer	−$90,263	—	—	−$90,263
0	Working capital investment	−5,000	—	—	−5,000
1	Cost savings	20,000	.61	12,200	10,702
2	Cost savings	38,000	.61	23,180	17,836
3	Cost savings	40,000	.61	24,400	16,469
4	Cost savings	45,000	.61	27,450	16,253
5	Cost savings	45,000	.61	27,450	14,257*
5	Salvage	30,000	—	—	15,581
0	Working capital recovery	5,000	—	—	2,597
Present value of CCA tax shield benefits . . . (from calculation)					18,317
Net present value					$16,749

*The present value of all the cost savings may be handled in one output from the calculator, particularly if it is an annuity.

In our computer example, we will suppose that as a result of this investment decision the firm will increase its investment in working capital by $5,000. Notice in Table 12–16 that a negative cash flow occurs at time 0, and a positive cash flow occurs when the project ends in Year 5. The working capital recovered in Year 5 in present value terms is only worth \$2,597. The working capital investment during the length of the project will cost the firm \$2,403 (\$5,000 − \$2,597).

In practice, projects are ongoing, and working capital positions will continue in support of the next project. However, for analysis purposes we should isolate and assign resultant cash flows properly to each project in order to make correct decisions. The ongoing working capital position now is related to the next project. The best analysis comes when we think of a project with a clear beginning and a definitive end.

According to the estimates used in this investment analysis and presented in Table 12–16, the net present value is positive. Thus, the purchase of the new computer can be recommended on the basis of the financial analysis. The company will be better off by \$16,749 today if the new computer is put into use. There may be other costs attached to this decision that have not yet been quantified. If so, the fact that the financial analysis thus far revealed a positive net present value should not dissuade management from analyzing whether there will be other costs (or benefits) that have not been included in this analysis. The analysis would be aided by the development of a time line.

One can extend this analysis to evaluate investment decisions that don't involve replacement of equipment. If the analysis is used to evaluate mutually exclusive projects of different lives, caution should be exercised. It is important that projects be analyzed over the same period to ensure equal treatment.

Discounted Cash Flow Models—The Difficulties

Although conceptually the discounted cash flow models, the NPV and IRR, are straightforward and theoretically strong, in practice they encounter some problems. Both models require the estimation of future expected cash flows and the selection of an appropriate opportunity cost of capital or discount rate, as per the following model:

$$PV = \sum_{n=1}^{n} \frac{CF_n}{(1 + r)^n}$$

where

PV = present or market value
CF = resultant aftertax cash flows
r = discount rate appropriate to project's risk

There can be difficulties and mistakes in estimating the future expected cash flows. Projects may entail the use of new products or technologies where there is no past data on which to base future projections. For those projects that have past results, practitioners often just extrapolate, assuming trends will continue as they have in the past. New economic and societal developments are not considered. Furthermore, there is often bias built into estimates by those who want to see a project accepted, and therefore the cash flow projections become overly optimistic. As well, cash flow projections may not properly reflect the influence of inflation in boosting the nominal value of the cash flows over time. In preparing the resultant cash flows from a proposed project, analysts may fail to identify all the relevant cash flows. Impact on other product lines, opportunity costs, and the possible benefits to future projects are often missed in the preparation of the discounted cash flow analysis.

Cash Flow
www.fool.com/School/CashFlowBasedValuations.htm

The determination of the discount rate is also problematic. Theoretically it should be the rate that is equated with the risk of the project under consideration. How is that rate determined in practice? Several models have been developed to assist us in this task, and this question of risk is explored further in Chapter 13. However, in the end, there must be a judgement call based on knowledge and experience. The use of the cost of capital has been developed in Chapter 11, but we have learned that there are many inputs into the cost of capital calculation that call for estimation. The cost of capital relies on well-developed, efficient capital markets to establish the cost components of the capital structure. These markets may not always be efficient or available. The market costs based on current yields capture anticipated inflation, and therefore the cash flows must capture the same assumptions about inflation as mentioned above. In addition, the risk of the cash flows may vary over time, and this would suggest the use of different discount rates. The NPV method can handle this adjustment, unlike the IRR method, but it adds to the complexity of the analysis.

Finally, management must be convinced that the decisions suggested by cash flow analysis produce value. Management should be concerned with increasing the value of share prices that is suggested by the discounted cash flow analysis, but we noted in Chapter 1 that management's focus may be more on goals such as increasing earnings per share or the book rate of return. These goals do not always increase shareholder value, but they may increase the benefits paid to management or look good in the financial press. Furthermore, management may feel that discounted cash flow analysis does not capture all of the benefits produced by a project. A better image for the company, fairer treatment of employees, and the development of new technologies and competencies for the corporation often cannot be captured by the analysis. These qualitative factors are important, however.

When NPV analysis suggests that a project can add value to the firm, we should examine the results carefully. In an efficient market, which is discussed further in Chapter 14, it is stated that all transactions should have an NPV equal to zero. If this is the case, how could our analysis produce a positive NPV? Either we have a competitive advantage over other corporations or we have made a mistake in the analysis.

Suggested Considerations for NPV Analysis

1. Identify events along a time line. Also note relevant variables such as the discount rate, CCA rate, tax rate, and time period.
2. Identify cash flows, not income, and on an aftertax basis.
3. Present individual sources of cash flows one at a time. Each cash flow identified along your time line is to be brought to the same point, time 0, and then summed to determine the NPV. Cash flows that appear as annuities can be handled in one calculation. Capital items are best handled by the CCA formula, which deals with the cash flow and the tax consequences separately.
4. Interest costs should not be identified as cash flows because they are already considered in the discount rate used, the cost of capital. To include the interest costs and their tax consequences in the cash flows would amount to double counting.
5. Include all resultant costs and benefits. This is perhaps the most important and difficult step. Take time to think! As a result of the decision being considered, what will change for the firm? Consider additional staffing, the impact on other divisions of the organization, and the required buildup in working

capital to support the decision under consideration. Include all opportunity costs and ignore costs already incurred because nothing can be done about those costs now. For example, land already owned has had its original cost already spent, but if we use the land in a project under consideration we forgo the opportunity of selling it and receiving the proceeds.

6. Use market values for the cash flows. The land mentioned in point 5 should be entered into the analysis at the market value forgone if the land is used in the project rather than sold.
7. Consider risk. This is discussed in Chapter 13.

Summary

1. The capital budgeting decision involves the planning of expenditures for a project with a life of at least one year and usually considerably longer. Although top management is often anxious about the impact of decisions on short-term reported income, the planning of capital expenditures dictates adopting a longer time horizon. Although effective short-term decisions allow the firm to continue in operation for the long term, effective long-term decisions impact the most on shareholder wealth.
2. Cash flows and their timing are important for capital budgeting analysis because we are using the time value of money. When we receive the cash is important. Accounting income that includes accruals and does not consider opportunity costs fails in the important decision-making framework of identifying the timing of cash flows and opportunity costs.
3. Five methods are used to analyze capital investment proposals: average accounting return, payback period, net present value, internal rate of return, and the profitability index. The first two methods, although widely used, have serious theoretical flaws. The latter methods, because they consider the timing and overall amount of cash flows, are more complete methods for assessing capital budgeting decisions. Under certain circumstances, the net present value method is superior to the internal rate of return.

   Investment alternatives may be classified as either mutually exclusive or not mutually exclusive. If they are mutually exclusive, the selection of one alternative precludes the selection of all other alternatives, and projects with a positive net present value may be eliminated. The same may also be true under capital rationing, a method under which management determines the maximum amount that can be invested in any one time period.
4. The cost of capital is used as the discount rate for analyzing an investment under the assumption that the investment is of the same risk as the average collection of current investments owned by the firm. This seems somewhat unlikely, but the cost of capital is a good starting point in determining the discount rate to be used in the analysis.

   Although capital budgeting techniques are economically rational by design, the combination of future uncertainty and information complexity means that decision inputs are highly dependent on managerial judgment. Projects with large initial investments, with long time horizons, and facing a high degree of future uncertainty are particularly difficult to justify using capital budgeting or any other analytical technique. In Chapter 13 we examine how differing levels of risk can be factored into the capital budgeting decision-making process.
5. A capital budgeting decision will likely have a major impact on the firm. Therefore, careful consideration should be given to all the costs and benefits that will result from a decision to proceed with an investment. The NPV analysis suggests that the moment a decision is made to proceed with an investment having a positive NPV, the wealth of the shareholders is increased by the amount of that NPV. All incremental cash flows should be identified.

Tax considerations are also a major factor in capital budgeting decisions. In this chapter we have considered the effects of tax-allowable amortization (capital cost allowance) and investment tax credits (ITC) in relation to the analysis. At this time in Canada, the tax system is being used to attempt to encourage investment in some of the less-affluent regions of the country and also to attempt to channel investments toward research and development.

6. NPV analysis is best performed by carefully developing the cash flows that will likely result from an investment decision before proceeding to the calculations.

Review of Formulas

$$\begin{matrix} PV\text{ of CCA} \\ \text{tax shield} \end{matrix} = [C - S_{pv}]\left(\frac{dT_c}{r + d}\right)\left(\frac{1 + .5r}{1 + r}\right) \quad (12\text{–}1)$$

where

C = Change in capital cost pool resulting from acquiring the asset
S_{pv} = Change in capital cost pool resulting from the salvage value, as a present value
r = Discount rate
d = CCA rate for the asset class
T_c = Corporate tax rate
n = Number of years in the future we intend to sell the asset

List of Terms

resultant cash flows 417
incremental cash flows (inflows) 417
decremental cash flows (outflows) 417
average accounting return (ARR) 421
payback period 422
net present value (NPV) 424
internal rate of return (IRR) 425
profitability index 429
mutually exclusive 430
capital rationing 433
net present value profile 434
capital cost allowance (CCA) 438
undepreciated capital cost (UCC) 439
terminal loss 441
recapture 441
investment tax credit (ITC) 441
CCA tax shield 443

Discussion Questions

1. What are the important administrative considerations in the capital budgeting process?
2. Why does capital budgeting rely for analysis on cash flows rather than net income effects?
3. What are the weaknesses of the payback period? Why do many managers use it?
4. What is normally used as the discount rate under the net present value method? Why?
5. What does the term *mutually exclusive investments* mean?
6. If a corporation has projects that will earn more than the cost of capital, should it ration capital?
7. What is the net present value profile? What three points (characteristics) should be determined to create the profile?
8. What else, besides the forecast IRR and NPV, might top management consider in making capital budgeting decisions?
9. Generally, what effect does the capital cost allowance system have on the timing of CCA tax shield benefits?

10. What is the investment tax credit? How does it affect the capital budgeting decision?
11. How would you modify your capital budgeting analysis (NPV methodology) to account for expected inflation?
12. What implications does an efficient market (Chapter 14) have for NPV calculations?

INTERNET RESOURCES AND QUESTIONS

Information on ITCs and CCA is available at Canada Customs and Revenue Agency.
www.ccra-adrc.gc.ca

Problems

www.mcgrawhill.ca/college/block

1. Assume a corporation has earnings before amortization and taxes of $90,000 and amortization of $40,000, and it has a 30 percent tax rate. Compute its cash flow.
2. *a.* In the previous problem, how much would cash flow be if there was only $10,000 in amortization? All other factors are the same.

   b. How much cash flow is lost due to the reduced amortization between problems 1 and 2*a*?
3. Blink 281 Corporation is considering an investment that will cost $80,000 and last for five years. The investment will be amortized on a straight-line basis over that period. Earnings generated by the investment before amortization and taxes over this period are as follows:

Year 1	$35,000
Year 2	37,000
Year 3	41,000
Year 4	45,000
Year 5	50,000

   Elias Corporation has a tax rate of 40 percent.

   a. What is the average accounting return of this project?

   b. Should this project be accepted? What criteria would you use to accept or decline the project?

   c. What are the problems with this type of analysis?
4. Pluto Corporation is considering an investment that will cost $210,000 and last for three years. The investment will be amortized on a straight-line basis over that period. Earnings generated by the investment before amortization and taxes over this period are as follows:

Year 1	$110,000
Year 2	120,000
Year 3	150,000

   Pluto Corporation has a tax rate of 40 percent. What is the average accounting return of this project?
5. Assume a $40,000 investment and the following cash flows for two alternatives:

Year	Investment X	Investment Y
1	$ 6,000	$15,000
2	8,000	20,000
3	9,000	10,000
4	17,000	—
5	20,000	—

Which of the alternatives would you select under the payback period?

6. Referring to the previous problem, if the inflow in the fifth year for Investment X were $20,000,000 instead of $20,000, would your answer change under the payback period?
7. Again referring to problem 5, analyze the two investment alternatives under the net present value method using a 15 percent discount rate. Would your answer change?
8. Boardwalk Company is considering a $90,000 investment in either of two companies. The cash flows are as follows:

Year	Reading Railway	St. Charles Place
1	$60,000	$10,000
2	10,000	10,000
3	10,000	10,000
4	10,000	60,000
4–10	15,000	15,000

a. Using the payback period, what decision should be made?

b. Explain why the answer in part a can be misleading.

9. Diaz Camera Company is considering two investments, both of which cost $10,000. The cash flows are as follows:

Year	Project A	Project B
1	$6,000	$5,000
2	4,000	3,000
3	3,000	8,000

a. Which of the two projects should be chosen based on the payback period?

b. Which of the two projects should be chosen based on the net present value method? Assume a cost of capital of 10 percent.

c. Should a firm normally have more confidence in answer *a* or answer *b*.

10. Hand Salsa buys a new piece of equipment for $11,778 and will receive a cash flow of $2,000 per year for 10 years. What is the internal rate of return?
11. Generation Thumbs buys a new piece of equipment for $16,980, and you receive a cash inflow of $3,000 per year for 12 years. What is the internal rate of return?

12. Warner Business Products is considering the purchase of a new machine at a cost of $11,070. The machine will provide $2,000 per year in cash flow for eight years. Warner's cost of capital is 13 percent. Using the internal rate of return method, evaluate this project and indicate whether it should be undertaken.
13. Home Security Systems is analyzing the purchase of manufacturing equipment that will cost $40,000. The annual cash inflows are as follows

Year	Cash Flow
1.	$20,000
2.	18,000
3.	13,000

a. Determine the internal rate of return.

b. With a cost of capital of 12 percent, should the machine be purchased?

c. With information from part *b*, compute the profitability index.

14. Aerospace Dynamics will invest $110,000 in a project that will produce the following cash flows. The cost of capital is 11 percent. Should the project be undertaken?

Year	Cash Flow
1.	$36,000
2.	44,000
3.	38,000
4.	(44,000)
5.	81,000

15. The Horizon Corporation will invest $60,000 in a temporary project that will generate the following cash inflows:

Year	Cash Flow
1.	$15,000
2.	25,000
3.	40,000

The firm will also be required to spend $10,000 to close the project at the end of the three years. If the cost of capital is 10 percent, should the investment be undertaken? Use the NPV method.

16. Skyline Corp. will invest $130,000 in a project that will not begin to produce returns until after the third year. From the end of the 3rd year until the end of the 12th year (10 periods), the annual cash flow will be $34,000. If the cost of capital is 12 percent, should this project be undertaken?

17. The Ogden Corporation makes an investment of $25,000 which yields the following cash flows:

Year	Cash Flow
1.	$ 5,000
2.	5,000
3.	8,000
4.	9,000
5.	10,000

a. What is the present value with a 9 percent discount rate (cost of capital)?

b. What is the internal rate of return?

c. In this problem would you make the same decision in parts *a* and *b*?

www.mcgrawhill.ca/college/block

18. The Danforth Tire Company is considering the purchase of a new machine that would increase the speed of manufacturing tires and save money. The net cost of the new machine is $66,000. The annual cash flows have the following projections.

Year	Cash Flow
1.	$21,000
2.	29,000
3.	36,000
4.	16,000
5.	8,000

a. If the cost of capital is 10 percent, what is the net present value?

b. What is the internal rate of return?

c. Should the project be accepted? Why?

19. You are asked to evaluate the following two projects for Adventures Club, Inc. Using the net present value method, combined with the profitability index approach, which project would you select? Use a discount rate of 12 percent.

Project X (trips to Disneyland) ($10,000 Investment)		Project Y (International Film Festivals) ($22,000 Investment)	
Year	**Cash Flow**	**Year**	**Cash Flow**
1	$4,000	1	$10,800
2	5,000	2	9,600
3	4,200	3	6,000
4	3,600	4	7,000

20. Cablevision, Inc., will invest $48,000 in a project. The firm's discount rate (cost of capital) is 9 percent. The investment will provide the following inflows:

Year	Inflow
1.	$10,000
2.	10,000
3.	16,000
4.	19,000
5.	20,000

The internal rate of return is 15 percent.

a. If reinvestment is assumed at the cost of capital rate used by the net present value method, what will be the total value of the inflows after five years? (Assume the inflows come at the end of each year.)

b. If the reinvestment is assumed at the internal rate of return, what will be the total value of the inflows after five years?

c. Generally, is one investment reinvestment assumption likely to be better than another?

21. Oliver Stone and Rock Company uses a process of capital rationing in its decision making. The firm's cost of capital is 12 percent. It will invest only $80,000 this year. It has determined the internal rate of return for each of the following projects:

Project	Project Size	Internal Rate of Return
A	$15,000	14%
B	25,000	19
C	30,000	10
D	25,000	16.5
E	20,000	21
F	15,000	11
G	25,000	18
H	10,000	17.5

a. Pick out the projects that the firm should accept.

b. If projects B and G are mutually exclusive, how would that affect your overall answer? That is, which projects would you accept in spending the $80,000?

22. Miller Electronics is considering two new investments. Project C calls for the purchase of a coolant recovery system. Project H represents the investment in a heat recovery system. The firm wishes to use a net present value profile in comparing the projects. The investment and cash flow patterns are as follows:

Project C ($25,000 Investment)		Project H ($25,000 Investment)	
Year	Cash Flow	Year	Cash Flow
1	$ 6,000	1	$20,000
2	7,000	2	6,000
3	9,000	3	5,000
4	13,000		

a. Determine the net present value of the projects based on a zero discount rate.

b. Determine the net present value of the projects based on a 9 percent discount rate.

c. The internal rate of return on Project C is 13.0 percent, and the internal rate of return on Project H is 15.69 percent. Graph a net present value profile for the two investments similar to Figure 12–3. (Use a scale up to $10,000 on the vertical axis, with $2,000 increments. Use a scale up to 20 percent on the horizontal axis, with 5 percent increments.)

d. If the two projects are not mutually exclusive, what would your acceptance or rejection decision be if the cost of capital (discount rate) is 8 percent? (Use the net present value profile for your decision; no actual numbers are necessary.)

e. If the two projects are mutually exclusive (the selection of one precludes the selection of the other), what would be your decision if the cost of capital is (1) 5 percent, (2) 13 percent, (3) 19 percent? Use the net present value profile for your answer.

23. Software Systems is considering an investment of $20,000, which produces the following inflows:

Year	Cash Flow
1	$11,000
2	9,000
3	5,800

You are going to use the net present value profile to approximate the value for the internal rate of return. Please follow these steps:

a. Determine the net present value of the project based on a zero discount rate.

b. Determine the net present value of the project based on a 10 percent discount rate.

c. Determine the net present value of the project based on a 20 percent discount rate (it will be negative).

d. Draw a net present value profile for the investment (use a scale up to $6,000 on the vertical axis, with $2,000 increments. Use a scale up to 20 percent on the horizontal axis, with 5 percent increments.). Observe the discount rate at which the net present value is zero. This is an approximation of the internal rate of return on the project.

e. Actually compute the internal rate of return. Compare your answers in parts *d* and *e*.

24. Zebra Corporation has decided to sell one of its jetties for $5 million. This non-wood structure is part of the Class 3 (5 percent) CCA pool, and Zebra had it built five years ago at a cost of $4.5 million. Zebra's tax rate is 40 percent. Zebra uses 12 percent as its cost of capital.

    a. If the Class 3 UCC at the start of the year in question was $12 million (and this was the only disposal), what would be the tax consequences of the sale of the building?

    b. If the Class 3 UCC at the start of the year of the sale was $4 million, what would be the tax effect of the sale?

    c. If the UCC at the start of the year was $6 million and this was the last building in the pool, what would be the tax effects?

25. A $95,000 investment is to be amortized for tax purposes using the maximum capital cost allowance available.

    a. If the investment represents a fleet of automobiles for a telephone utility, what will be the allowable CCA rate?

    b. How much will the addition of the automobiles increase the allowable dollar CCA in Year 1? in Year 2?

    c. If the investment had been for machinery, what difference would that have made in the CCA rate allowed?

    d. What difference will it make when the cars are scrapped for next to nothing after five years? (The company's autos tend to accumulate very high mileage, and the company has adopted the practice of giving them away to interested employees when their usefulness to the company ceases.)

26. Coastal Shipping Corporation has decided to sell one of its vessels for $1 million. This vessel is part of the Class 7 (15 percent) CCA pool, and Coastal Shipping had it built three years ago at a cost of $1.2 million. Coastal Shipping's tax rate is 40 percent. Coastal Shipping uses 10 percent as its cost of capital.

    a. If the Class 7 UCC at the start of the year in question was $2 million (and this was the only disposal), what would be the tax consequences of the sale of the vessel?

    b. If the Class 7 UCC at the start of the year of the sale was $0.8 million, what would be the tax effect of the sale?

    c. If the UCC at the start of the year was $0.6 million and this was the last vessel in the pool, what would be the tax effects?

27. Nexus Corp. has made a $1.5 million investment that is to be amortized for tax purposes using the maximum capital cost allowance available.

    a. If the investment represents an aircraft, what will be the allowable CCA rate?

    b. How much will the addition of the aircraft increase the allowable dollar CCA in Year 1? in Year 2?

c. If the investment had been for a hangar for the aircraft, what difference would that have made in the CCA rate allowed?

d. What will be the tax consequences when the aircraft is scrapped for $200,000 after ten years?

28. The Thorpe Corporation will purchase a $50,000 piece of production machinery with an estimated useful life of five years. The new machine is expected to allow an increase in sales of $80,000 per year, while increased incremental costs amount to $45,000 per year. The firm is in a 38 percent income tax bracket. Complete the following table to determine the first-year cash flow effect of the investment.

Increased sales	______
Increased costs	______
Earnings before amortization and taxes	______
Amortization	______
Earnings before taxes	______
Taxes	______
Earnings aftertaxes	______
Amortization	______
Net cash flow	______

29. Cellular Spacephones Ltd. has gained approval for an eligible scientific research and experimental development on Cape Breton Island and is intending to invest $1.7 million.

a. Assuming the tax rules governing investment tax credits and CCA remain the same as represented in this chapter, compute the investment tax credit available to Cellular.

b. What will be the original capital cost base for CCA purposes?

c. Compute the present value of the investment tax credit and capital cost allowance combined (Cellular uses 10 percent as its discount rate). Cellular's tax rate is 22 percent.

30. Medicine Hat Enterprises has purchased three greenhouses over the past five years, but today it sold them all for $400,000. Five years ago Medicine Hat purchased the first greenhouse for $250,000, two years later it purchased the second for $300,000, and last year it purchased one for $400,000. Medicine Hat Enterprises has a marginal tax rate of 43 percent. Capital cost allowance on greenhouses is 10 percent.

a. Calculate the tax shields and any taxes payable to Medicine Hat on an annual basis over the five-year period resulting from these investments.

b. Assuming the asset pool continues, calculate the tax shields on an annual basis over the five-year period.

c. Calculate the present value of the tax shields and any taxes payable under the assumptions of part *a* and *b*. Calculate the present value of the CCA tax shields with Formula 12–1 and compare your results. Medicine Hat's cost of capital is 13 percent.

31. The Elite Car Rental Corporation is contemplating expanding its short-term rental fleet by 30 automobiles at a cost of $900,000. It expects to keep the autos for only two years and to sell them at the end of that period for 60 percent, on average, of what they cost. The plan is to generate $10,500 of incremental revenue per additional auto in each year of operation. The controller estimates that other costs will amount to 14 cents per kilometre on an average of 40,000 kilometres per car per year. She also estimates that the new business will require an investment of $10,000 in additional working capital. The firm is in a 40 percent tax bracket and uses 12 percent as a cost of capital.

Should Elite purchase the automobiles? Do all of the necessary calculations to substantiate your recommendation.

32. Albert I. Stein Ltd. is considering the investment of $75,000 in a new machine that will allow it to do research on developing a new microchip for use in video games. The machine will be assigned to CCA Class 8. The firm is considered a Canadian-controlled private corporation eligible for the small-business tax deduction. (The tax rate is therefore 23 percent.) A 20 percent investment tax credit is available.

    If the machine is purchased, Albert I. Stein expects to be able to develop a new product for the video game market that would be ready for sale about two years after the machine is purchased. This new product is anticipated to provide new revenues of $121,000 per year for the seven years after introduction and to have associated expenses of $90,000 per year for the first five of those years and $105,000 for the last two. Other development costs associated with the new product in the initial two years are estimated at $17,500 per year. The firm's controller estimates its cost of capital at 13 percent and that $0.10 in additional working capital is required for every $1.00 in extra sales.

    Should Albert I. Stein Ltd. purchase the new machine? Do all relevant calculations to support your recommendation.

33. Pierce Labs, located in Gaspe Bay, purchased a radio communication system three years ago for $310,000. It has a potential buyer for the system who is willing to pay $85,000. A new system will cost $390,000 and is eligible for a 15 percent investment tax credit.

    It is estimated the new system would provide the following stream of cost savings over the next five years:

Year	Cost Savings
1	$99,000
2	88,000
3	77,000
4	66,000
5	55,000

    The tax rate is 44 percent, and the estimated cost of capital is 12 percent. Should the new system be purchased?

COMPREHENSIVE PROBLEMS

34. On graduating from college, Steven MacLean joined the financial analysis section of a large Canadian industrial concern, Ontario Corporation. Soon after, MacLean was assigned to help in the financial analysis of a proposed acquisition by Ontario of a firm in a business unlike any of Ontario's traditional businesses. After a month of searching, MacLean had assembled the following additional information:

    a.

TARGET FIRM
Balance Sheet at 12/31/02
(000s)

Cash	$ 150	Current liabilities	$ 150
Accounts receivable	400		
Inventory	600	Long-term debt	750
Net capital assets	2,100	Equity	2,350
Total	$3,250		$3,250

b. Target Firm's sales for 2002 had been $3.5 million, and because it was operating at full capacity, it looked as if all classes of assets would increase at a pace directly proportional to any increase in sales.

c. The interest rate on Target's long-term debt was 12.5 percent with annual interest payments being made at the end of each year.

d. MacLean recommended the long-term debt be maintained after the acquisition.

e. Target had 2 million shares outstanding at the end of 2002, which had traded recently at prices around $1.50 per share.

f. The following estimates of sales and earnings before interest and taxes were the most reliable MacLean had come across:

Year	Annual Sales (millions)	Annual EBIT
1	$3.7	$650,000
2	4.0	700,000
3	4.1	720,000
4	4.2	720,000
5	4.0	690,000
6–10	4.3	700,000

In arriving at EBIT, amortization expenses of $140,000 per year had been deducted.

g. Expenditures on capital assets would be necessary to allow for growth and to replace worn-out equipment. MacLean estimated that $200,000 per year would be required in Years 1–5, with $80,000 per year thereafter.

h. The income tax rate for both firms was expected to remain at 46 percent.

i. Ontario Corporation used 13 percent as its cost of equity and had a weighted average cost of capital of 11 percent.

Compute the price MacLean should recommend that Ontario Corporation offer to pay for each of Target Firm's shares.

35. Signs For Fields Machinery Ltd. is considering the replacement of some technologically obsolete machinery with the purchase of a new machine for $65,000. Although the older machine has no market value, it could be expected to perform the required operation for another 10 years. The older machine has an unamortized capital cost of $27,000.

The new machine with the latest in technological advances will perform essentially the same operations as the older machine but will effect cost savings of $17,500 per year in labour and materials. The new machine is also estimated to last 10 years, at which time it could be salvaged for $11,500. To install the new machine will cost $7,000.

Signs For Fields has a tax rate of 39 percent, and its cost of capital is 15 percent. For accounting purposes, it uses straight-line amortization, and for tax purposes its capital cost allowance is 20 percent.

a. Should Signs For Fields Machinery purchase the new machine?

b. If the old machine has a current salvage value of $9,000, should Signs For Fields purchase the new machine?

c. Calculate the IRR and PI for part *a*.

36. H. Improvements Ltd. is evaluating the replacement of an older machine. There are two possible replacements under consideration—the OuOu and the Major OuOu. The existing machine was purchased a few years ago for $32,000 and currently has a book value of $8,500. If sold today, it would probably be worth $4,500.

today. In 10 years the older machine could be scrapped for $8,000, whereas the new machine would still be worth $32,000.

Also, the older machine requires a spare parts inventory (not eligible for tax-related amortization) of $5,000 that is not required by the newer machine. Blue Sky's tax rate is 40 percent, and its cost of capital is 15 percent. Would you advise Blue Sky to replace the older machine?

43. Midnight Oil and Gas is considering building a pipeline from a remote source of gas with only a 10-year supply of reserves. This qualifies the pipeline for a CCA rate of 20 percent rather than the normal 4 percent. The pipeline will cost $1 million; accompanying buildings will cost another $200,000. The buildings are Class 1 with a CCA rate of 4 percent.

Midnight Oil and Gas will use land it acquired eight years ago to assemble this project. The land was purchased for $500,000, and it is now worth $2 million. Annual cash flows before amortization from the pipeline and taxes for the 10-year period are estimated at $625,000.

In 10 years the buildings and pipeline will be worthless, but the land will be worth $4.5 million. Environmental clean-up costs at the end of the project are expected to be $1.2 million.

Midnight Oil and Gas has a tax rate of 42 percent, and its cost of capital is 14 percent. Capital gains are taxed at 50 percent of the gain. Should Midnight Oil and Gas build the pipeline?

44. Investigation and a reasonable amount of footwork brought the following information to the attention of April Kehg, executive assistant to the board of Swiss Ventures, Inc. She, with your able assistance, will prepare a proposal to submit to the board under the heading "the St. Bernard Venture."

Capital outlays on the project are expected to occur over the next two years, and the project, which will produce widgets for the wireless communication business, will be a unique entity to the Swiss Ventures family of projects. An immediate outlay of $600,000 will be required for the land to house the specialized building that will be constructed over the next year. Final payment on the building will amount to $1.1 million inclusive and will be due in exactly one year. Payment for the machinery to produce the widgets will amount to $175,000 and will be due after the initial test period, which will take to the end of the second year.

After the testing period, cash flows will begin in the third year. It is assumed that the revenues and expenses will be acknowledged at the end of each year. Beginning in the 3rd year, revenues are expected to amount to $875,000 until the 12th year. Expenses are projected at $325,000 to the 12th year from the 3rd year. These estimates are the averages of estimates obtained from the marketing staff and the production department. The expected values have been determined through preliminary work by Kehg.

In 12 years everything will end, as the market for the widget will be gone. The building will be scrapped for $225,000, and the machinery will be sold for $50,000. It is anticipated that the land will appreciate in value by 9 percent a year.

The following additional information is available:

CCA rates	building	4%
	machinery	30%
Corporate tax rate		40%
Cost of capital		15%
Capital gain		50% of gain taxable

Would you recommend proceeding with the St. Bernard Venture?

45. Marceline Enterprises is considering an expansion to its amusement park. The cost of this expansion is pegged at $1 million, but will require additional capital expenditures of $200,000 every three years. In nine years it is expected that the expansion, which will be separated from the existing amusement park, can be sold for $150,000. Amusement parks belong to CCA Class 37, with a CCA rate of 15 percent.

Along with the capital investment, Marceline expects to increase its working capital requirements by 5 percent of any capital investment during the period of this investment.

Operating cash flows for the entire operation are expected to increase by $250,000 in each of the first two years, by $325,000 in each of the following three years, and by $375,000 for the final four years.

Marceline Enterprises has a corporate tax rate of 40 percent and at the current time its cost of capital is 11 percent.

Should it proceed with the investment? Show your analysis.

46. As she headed toward her boss's office, Emily Hamilton, chief operating officer for the Aerocomp Corporation—a computer services firm that specialized in airborne support—wished she could remember more of her training in financial theory that she had been exposed to in college. Emily had just completed summarizing the financial aspects of four capital investment projects that were open to Aerocomp during the coming year, and she was faced with the task of recommending which should be selected. What concerned her was the knowledge that her boss, Kay Marsh, a "street smart" chief executive, with no background in financial theory, would immediately favour the project that promised the highest gain in reported net income. Emily knew that selecting projects purely on that basis would be incorrect; but she wasn't sure of her ability to convince Kay, who tended to assume financiers thought up fancy methods just to show how smart they were.

As she prepared to enter Kay's office, Emily pulled her summary sheets from her briefcase and quickly reviewed the details of the four projects, all of which she considered to be equally risky.

A. A proposal to add a jet to the company's fleet. The plane was only six years old and was considered a good buy at $300,000. In return, the plane would bring over $600,000 in additional revenue during the next five years with only about $56,000 in operating costs. (See Table 1 for details.)

TABLE 1

Financial analysis of Project A: Add a twin-jet to the company's fleet

	Initial Expenditures	Year 1	Year 2	Year 3	Year 4	Year 5
Net cost of new plane	$300,000					
Additional revenue		$43,000	$76,800	$112,300	$225,000	$168,750
Additional operating costs		11,250	11,250	11,250	11,250	11,250
Amortization		45,000	66,000	63,000	63,000	63,000
Net increase in income		(13,250)	(450)	38,050	150,750	94,500
Less: Tax at 33%		0	0	12,557	49,748	31,185
Increase in after-tax income		($13,250)	($ 450)	$25,494	$101,003	$ 63,315
Add back amortization		$45,000	$66,000	$63,000	$ 63,000	$ 63,000
Net change in cash flow	($300,000)	31,750	65,550	88,494	164,003	126,315

B. A proposal to diversify into copy machines. The franchise was to cost $700,000, which would be amortized over a 40-year period. The new business was expected to generate over $1.4 million in sales over the next five years, and over $800,000 in aftertax earnings. (See Table 2 for details.)

TABLE 2

Financial analysis of Project B: Diversify into copy machines

	Initial Expenditures	Year 1	Year 2	Year 3	Year 4	Year 5
Net cost of new franchise	$700,000					
Additional revenue		$87,500	$175,000	$262,500	$393,750	$525,000
Additional operating costs		26,250	26,250	26,250	26,250	26,250
Amortization		17,500	17,500	17,500	17,500	17,500
Net increase in income		43,750	131,250	218,750	350,000	481,250
Less: Tax at 33%		14,438	43,313	72,188	115,500	158,813
Increase in aftertax income		$29,313	$ 87,938	$146,563	$234,500	$322,438
Add back amortization		$17,500	$ 17,500	$ 17,500	$ 17,500	$ 17,500
Net change in cash flow	(700,000)	46,813	105,438	164,063	252,000	339,938

C. A proposal to buy a helicopter. The machine was expensive and, counting additional training and licensing requirements, would cost $40,000 a year to operate. However, the versatility that the helicopter was expected to provide would generate over $1.5 million in additional revenue, and it would give the company access to a wider market as well. (See Table 3 for details.)

TABLE 3

Financial analysis of Project C: Add a helicopter to the company's fleet

	Initial Expenditures	Year 1	Year 2	Year 3	Year 4	Year 5
Net cost of helicopter	$800,000					
Additional revenue		$100,000	$200,000	$300,000	$450,000	$600,000
Additional operating costs		40,000	40,000	40,000	40,000	40,000
Amortization		120,000	176,000	168,000	168,000	168,000
Net increase in income		(60,000)	(16,000)	92,000	242,000	392,000
Less: Tax at 33%		0	0	30,360	79,860	129,360
Increase in aftertax income		($ 60,000)	($ 16,000)	$ 61,640	$162,140	$262,640
Add back amortization		$120,000	$176,000	$168,000	$168,000	$168,000
Net change in cash flow	(800,000)	60,000	160,000	229,640	330,140	430,640

D. A proposal to begin operating a fleet of trucks. Ten could be bought for only $51,000 each, and the additional business would bring in almost $700,000 in new sales in the first two years alone. (See Table 4 for details.)

In her mind, Emily quickly went over the evaluation methods she had used in the past: payback, internal rate of return, and net present value. Emily knew that Kay would add a fourth, size of reported earnings, but she hoped she could talk Kay out of using it this time.

TABLE 4

Financial analysis of Project D: Add fleet of trucks

	Initial Expenditures	Year 1	Year 2	Year 3	Year 4	Year 5
Net cost of new trucks	$510,000					
Additional revenue		$382,500	$325,125	$ 89,250	$ 76,500	$ 51,000
Additional operating costs		19,125	19,125	25,500	31,875	38,250
Amortization		76,500	112,200	107,100	107,100	107,100
Net increase in income		286,875	193,800	(43,350)	(62,475)	(94,350)
Less: Tax at 33%		94,669	63,954	0	0	0
Increase in aftertax income		$192,206	$129,846	($ 43,350)	($ 62,475)	($ 94,350)
Add back amortization		$ 76,500	$112,200	$107,100	$107,100	$107,100
Net change in cash flow	(510,000)	268,706	242,046	63,750	44,625	12,750

Note: For figures, assume amortization is CCA and no tax savings extend beyond Year 5.

Emily herself favoured the net present value method, but she had always had a tough time getting Kay to understand it.

One additional constraint that Emily had to deal with was Kay's insistence that no outside financing be used this year. Kay was worried that the company was growing too fast and had piled up enough debt for the time being. She was also against a stock issue for fear of diluting earnings and her control over the firm. As a result of Kay's prohibition of outside financing, the size of the capital budget this year was limited to $800,000, which meant that only one of the four projects under consideration could be chosen. Emily wasn't too happy about that, either, but she had decided to accept it for now and concentrate on selecting the best of the four.

As she closed her briefcase and walked toward Kay's door, Emily reminded herself to have patience; Kay might not trust financial analysis, but she would listen to sensible arguments. Emily only hoped her financial analysis sounded sensible!

a. Refer to Tables 1 through 4. Add up the total increase in aftertax income for each project. Given what you know about Kay Marsh, to which project do you think she will be attracted?

b. Compute the payback period, internal rate of return (IRR), and net present value (NPV) of all four alternatives based on cash flow. Use 10 percent for the cost of capital in your calculations. For the payback period, merely indicate the year in which the cash flow equals or exceeds the initial investment. You do not have to compute midyear points.

c. (1) According to the payback method, which project should be selected?

(2) What is the chief disadvantage of this method?

(3) Why would anyone want to use this method?

d. (1) According to the IRR method, which project should be chosen?

(2) What is the major disadvantage of the IRR method that occurs when high IRR projects are selected?

(3) Can you think of another disadvantage of the IRR method?

(4) If Kay had not put a limit on the size of the capital budget, would the IRR method allow acceptance of all four alternatives? If not, which one(s) would be rejected and why?

e. (1) According to the NPV method, which project should be chosen? How does this differ from the answer under the IRR?

(2) If Kay had not put a limit on the size of the capital budget, under the NPV method which projects would be accepted? Do the NPV and IRR both reject the same project(s)? Why?

(3) Given all the facts of the case, are you more likely to select Project A or C?

f. (1) According to the PI method, which project should be chosen?

(2) Does your answer conflict with the NPV method? Why? Which method suggests the best project?

Selected References

Canadian Institute of Chartered Accountants. *CICA Handbook.* Toronto: CICA, 2001.

Chan, Su Han, George W. Gau, and Ko Wang. "Stock Market Reaction to Capital Investment Decisions: Evidence from Business Relocation Decisions." *Journal of Financial and Quantitative Analysis* 30 (March 1995), pp. 81–100.

Dixit, Avinash K., and Robert S. Pindyck. "The Options Approach to Capital Investment." *Harvard Business Review* 63 (May–June 1995), pp. 105–15.

Eccles, Robert G., and Philip J. Pyburn. "Creating a Comprehensive System to Measure Performance." *Management Accounting* 74 (October 1992), pp. 41–51.

Kite, Devaun. "Capital Budgeting: Integrating Environmental Impact." *Journal of Cost Management* 9 (Summer 1995), pp. 11–14.

Lipscomb, Joseph. "Real Estate Capital Budgeting." *The Real Estate Appraiser and Analyst* 48 (Summer 1982), pp. 23–31.

Mukherje, Tarun K., and Vineeta L. Hingorani. "Capital-Rationing Decision of Fortune 500 Firms: A Survey." *Financial Practice and Education* 9 (Spring–Summer 1999), pp. 7–15.

Payne, Janet D., Will Carrington Heath, and Lewis R. Gale. "Comparative Financial Practice in the U.S. and Canada: Capital Budgeting and Risk Assessment Techniques." *Financial Practice and Education* 9 (Spring–Summer 1999), pp. 25–33.

Smith, Kimberly J. "Postauditing Capital Investments." *Financial Practice and Education* 4 (Spring–Summer 1994), pp. 129–37.

Visscher, Sue L., and Timothy S. Stansfield. "Illustrating Capital Budgeting Complexities with JIT Justification Data." *Financial Practice and Education* 7 (Fall–Winter 1997), pp. 29–34.

Vogt, Stephen C. "Cash Flow and Capital Spending: Evidence from Capital Expenditure Announcements." *Financial Management* 26 (Summer 1997), pp. 44–57.

CHAPTER | THIRTEEN

13 Risk and Capital Budgeting

LEARNING | OBJECTIVES

1 Describe the concept of risk based on the uncertainty of future cash flows.

2 Define risk as standard deviation, coefficient of variation, or beta.

3 Describe most investors as risk averse.

4 Utilize the basic methodology of risk-adjusted discount rates for dealing with risk in capital budgeting analysis.

5 Describe and apply the techniques of certainty equivalents, simulation models, sensitivity analysis, and decision trees to help assess risk.

6 Discuss how a project's risk may be considered in a portfolio context.

No one area is more essential to financial decision making than the evaluation and management of risk. The price of a firm's stock is strongly influenced by the amount of risk investors perceive as inherent in the firm's operations. We are constantly trying to achieve the appropriate mix between profitability and risk to satisfy those with a stake in the affairs of the firm and to realize the goal of wealth maximization for shareholders.

Our valuation models are built on future expected cash flows and the rate at which we discount those expectations to the present. The discount rate is based on the market's perception of the risks inherent in those cash flows. In Chapter 12 we often used the cost of capital as the discount rate in our analysis, but it was based on the assumption that the project under consideration had the same risk as the firm. This was a strong assumption!

The difficulty is not in finding viable investment alternatives, but in determining where we want to be on the risk-return scale. Would we prefer a 30 percent potential return on a new product in Russia or a safe 8 percent return on an extension of our current product line in our home territory? The question can be answered only in terms of profitability, the risk position of the firm, and the disposition toward risk of both management and shareholders. In this chapter we examine additional definitions of risk, its measurement, its incorporation into the *capital budgeting* process, and the basic tenets of portfolio theory.

Definition of Risk in Capital Budgeting

When we consider the term risk, we often think of the exposure we will have to the chance of peril or of loss. There may also be the possibility of great gain. The greater the peril and the greater the gain, the greater the risk. **Risk** may be defined in terms of the variability of possible outcomes from a given investment. If funds are invested in a Government of Canada treasury bill, the outcome is certain and there is no variability—hence, there is no risk. On the other hand, if we invest the same funds in a gold-mining expedition in the deepest wilds of Borneo, the variability of possible outcomes is great, and we say the project is replete with risk.

The student should observe that risk is measured not only in terms of losses, but also uncertainty.[1] We say gold mining carries a high degree of risk not just because you may lose your money, but also because there is a wide range of possible outcomes. Observe in Figure 13–1 examples of three investments that have different possible

FIGURE 13–1

Variability and risk

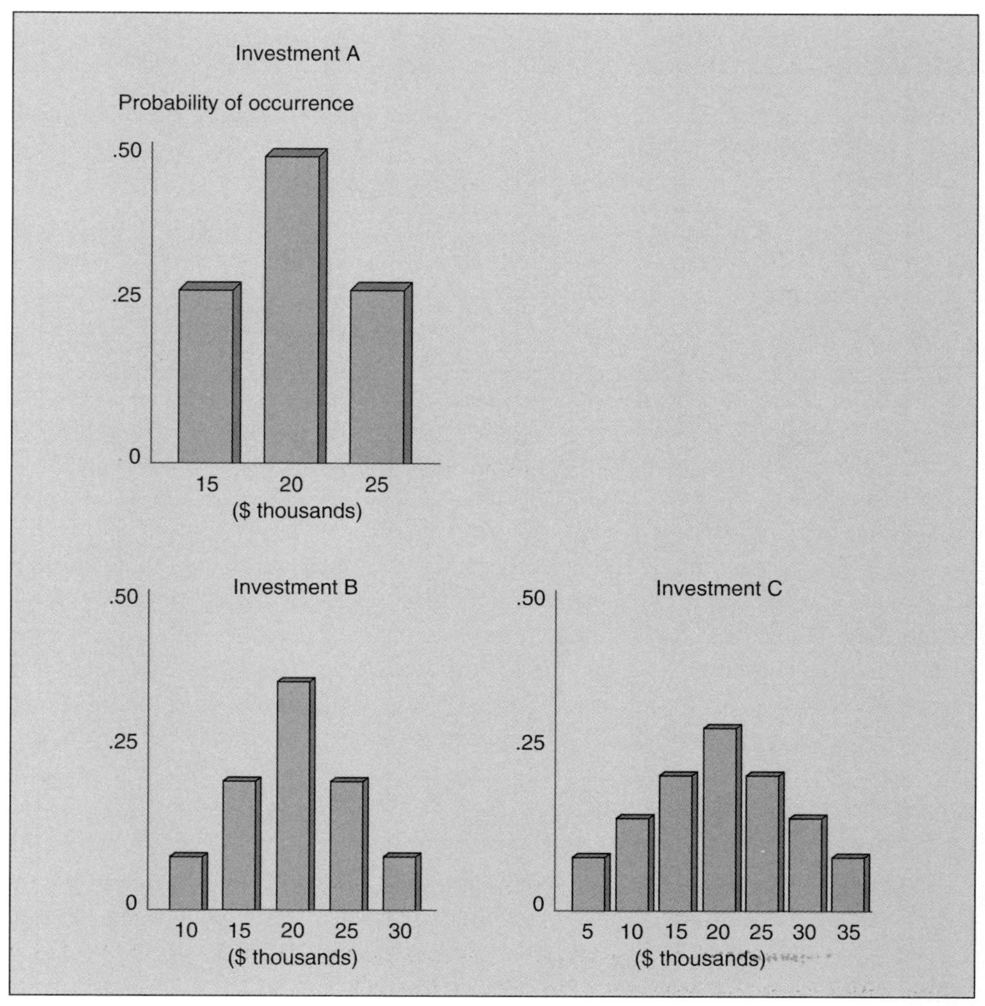

[1]We use the term *uncertainty* in its normal sense, rather than in the more formalized sense in which it is sometimes used in decision theory to indicate that insufficient evidence is available to estimate a probability distribution.

Risk After September 11th

After September 11th the world seemed a much more dangerous and riskier place in which to live and do business. People were unsure about the future and this uncertainty affected their willingness to spend money. Increased risk and lower cash flow expectations combined to decrease asset values, a fact reflected in the world's stock markets.

Bombardier (www.bombardier.com) is one of Canada's most dynamic firms with business divisions manufacturing recreational craft, transportation vehicles, and aircraft. It was expected that air travel would drop on the commercial airlines but there was also an expectation that interest in private aircraft would increase as businesses sought other means to get their staff around the world. This would be positive for Bombardier and its share price. (www.tsx.ca)

However dealer and manufacturer inventories went up as business dropped off. Prices for aircraft dropped about 25 percent and a significant portion of the worldwide fleet was for sale. This increased the difficulties for Bombardier in selling its aircraft. Apparently businesses embarked on general cost cutting schemes and began to better utilize the telecommunications infrastructure to keep in touch with their customers. Furthermore, Bombardier experienced setbacks in its operations in Germany in early 2002.

FINANCE IN ACTION

Q1 Has Bombardier's share price outperformed the S&P/TSX Composite Index since September 11th?

Q2 What were Bombardier's (Symbol: BBD.A) 2002 setbacks?

outcomes, all of which are centred on the same value ($20,000). It is important to recall that in finance, we are evaluating cash flows that we expect to occur in the future. These expected cash flows represent an average of several possibilities. When our evaluation techniques, such as those used in Chapter 12, consider only the expected value, we may miss important information.

In our example, each investment is expected to return $20,000, as this is the average of the possible outcomes. Note, however, that as we move from Investment A to Investment C, the dispersion of possible outcomes widens or the variability (risk) increases. Because you may gain or lose the most in Investment C, it is considered the riskiest of the three. Therefore, the greater the dispersion, the greater the risk.

The Concept of Risk Averse

A basic assumption in financial theory is that most investors and managers are **risk averse**—that is, for a given situation they would prefer relative certainty to uncertainty. In Figure 13–1, therefore, they would prefer Investment A over Investments B and C, despite the fact that all three investments have the same expected value of $20,000. You are probably risk averse too. Assume you have saved $3,000 for your last year in college and are challenged to flip a coin, double or nothing. Heads, you end up with $6,000; tails, you are broke. Given that you are not enrolled at the University of Nevada at Las Vegas or that you are not an inveterate gambler, you would probably stay with your certain $3,000.

This is not to say that investors or businesspeople are unwilling to take risks—but rather that they require a higher expected value or return for risky investments. In Figure 13–2, on the next page, we compare a low-risk proposal with an expected value of $20,000 to a high-risk proposal with an expected value of $30,000. The higher expected return may well compensate investors for absorbing greater risk.

Throughout the chapter we develop methods for incorporating a higher demanded return for risky investments. For Evel Knievel, back in the 1970s, it was $7 million to

FIGURE 13–2
Risk-return trade-off

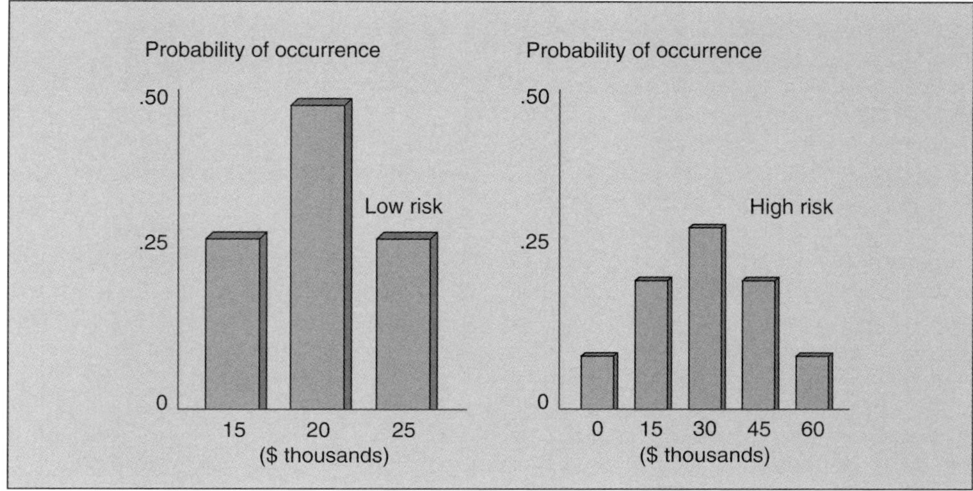

jump over the Snake River Canyon; for a corporation, it may be a bonus return of 5 percent over its normal cost of capital.

Actual Measurement of Risk

A number of basic statistical devices may be employed to measure the extent of risk inherent in any given situation. Assume we are examining an investment with the probability of possible outcomes shown in Table 13–1.

TABLE 13–1
Probability distribution of outcomes

Outcome	Probability of Outcome	Assumptions
$300	.2	Pessimistic
600	.6	Moderately successful
900	.2	Optimistic

Probabilities such as those in Table 13–1 are generally based on some combination of past experience, industry ratios and trends, interviews with company executives, and sophisticated simulation techniques. The probability values may be easy to estimate for the introduction of a mechanical stamping process for which the manufacturer has 10 years of past data, but they are difficult to assess for a new product in a foreign market. In one study that compared the present value of actual results with that of forecasted results for capital projects, new products were found, on average, to realize only 10 percent of the forecasted returns. Sales expansion projects realized an average of 60 percent, while cost reduction projects realized, on average, 110 percent of their forecasted returns.[2] Because of the difficulty of estimating future results, it is important to analyze carefully the range and probability of possible outcomes.

[2]Reported in Joseph L. Bower, *Managing the Resource Allocation Process* (Homewood, Ill.: Richard D. Irwin, 1972), pp. 9–10.

Bankers: Getting Risk Adverse

Risk and its management are a major preoccupation for today's bankers. More and more frequently, we see banks experience huge losses, despite their careful lending practices. During the early 1990s as the economy suffered through a slowdown, Canadian banks reported loan losses in the billions. Things improved for the later part of the decade but as the economy slowed though 2001, loan losses were again on the rise. In Japan the banking system is in terrible shape, the result of a stagnant economy throughout the 1990s. Loan losses in the hundreds of billions of dollars have been experienced on loans secured by declining real estate and stock assets. As economies do poorly, so do the banks.

How do bankers deal with risk in a world of increasing volatility and competition brought on by the deregulation of the financial markets? In the past bankers learned to deal with liquidity risk (not having enough cash on hand) and credit risk (the chance that a borrower might experience cash flow problems) within rules set in the 1930s. To deal with liquidity risk, lines of credit were established with central banks and with other commercial banks. By diversifying their loans, not lending too much to one borrower, and matching the maturities of their loans and deposits (hedging), the banks dealt with credit risk.

However, by the 1970s new risks appeared. The banks had begun to do a significant amount of their business outside of Canada, and the world had entered an era of floating exchange rates. With inflation and market shocks such as the oil crisis, exchange rates fluctuated dramatically, exposing the banks and their clients to large risks. To deal with the exchange rate volatility, the banks developed forward markets in which exchange rates could be set in advance.

In the 1980s the markets had become increasingly sophisticated and interrelated. The banks were experiencing competition from money market funds, and they were losing large corporate clients to the wholesale markets, where cheaper funds could be raised and better rates received on excess funds. This was the process of disintermediation. As money moved faster and faster, banks were subjected to increasing risks as their collection of loans and deposits became mismatched and as large sums were exchanged between financial institutions. To better manage these new risks, banks began the "securitization" of their loans. This allowed the banks to sell loans that no longer fit appropriately with their other assets as conditions continually changed in the dynamic market.

To reduce other risks, the banks also entered the derivative markets that had developed to prefix the prices on such items as interest and exchange rates. As reported by the Bank of International Settlements (BIS), the worldwide market for derivatives in the OTC market had over $3 trillion in outstanding derivatives by the end of 2001.

Banking has become a continual process of managing risk in an increasingly complex financial marketplace.

FINANCE IN ACTION

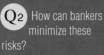

Q1 What risks do you see that bankers face today?

Q2 How can bankers minimize these risks?

www.bis.org

With the data before us, we compute two important statistical measures—the expected value and the standard deviation. **The expected value** is a weighted average of the outcomes times their probabilities.

$$\bar{D}\text{ (expected value)} = \Sigma DP \qquad (13\text{–}1)$$

$$\begin{array}{rcl} D & P & DP \\ 300 \times & .2 = & \$\ 60 \\ 600 \times & .6 = & 360 \\ 900 \times & .2 = & \underline{\$180} \\ & & \$600 = \Sigma DP \end{array}$$

The expected value is $600. We then compute the **standard deviation**—the measure of dispersion or variability around the expected value. The formula for the standard deviation is quite simple:

$$\sigma\text{ (standard deviation)} = \sqrt{\Sigma(D - \bar{D})^2 P} \qquad (13\text{–}2)$$

These steps should be followed:

Step 1: Subtract the Expected Value ($\bar{D}$) from Each Outcome (D)	Step 2: Square $(D - \bar{D})$	Step 3: Multiply by P and Sum	Step 4: Determine the Square Root
D $\bar{D}$ $(D - \bar{D})$	$(D - \bar{D})^2$	P $(D - \bar{D})^2 P$	
300 − 600 = −300	90,000	× .20 = 18,000	
600 − 600 = 0	0	× .60 = 0	
900 − 600 = 300	90,000	× .20 = 18,000	
		36,000	$\sqrt{36{,}000}$ = \$190

The standard deviation of \$190 gives us a rough average measure of how far each of the three estimated possible outcomes falls away from the expected value. Generally, the larger the standard deviation (or spread of possible outcomes), the greater is the risk, as indicated in Figure 13–3.

Note that in Figure 13–3 we compare the standard deviation of three investments with the same expected value of \$600. However, the dispersion of possible outcomes is different for each investment. The investment with the greater standard deviation would be considered the riskiest. If the expected values of the investments were quite

FIGURE 13–3
Probability distribution with differing degrees of risk

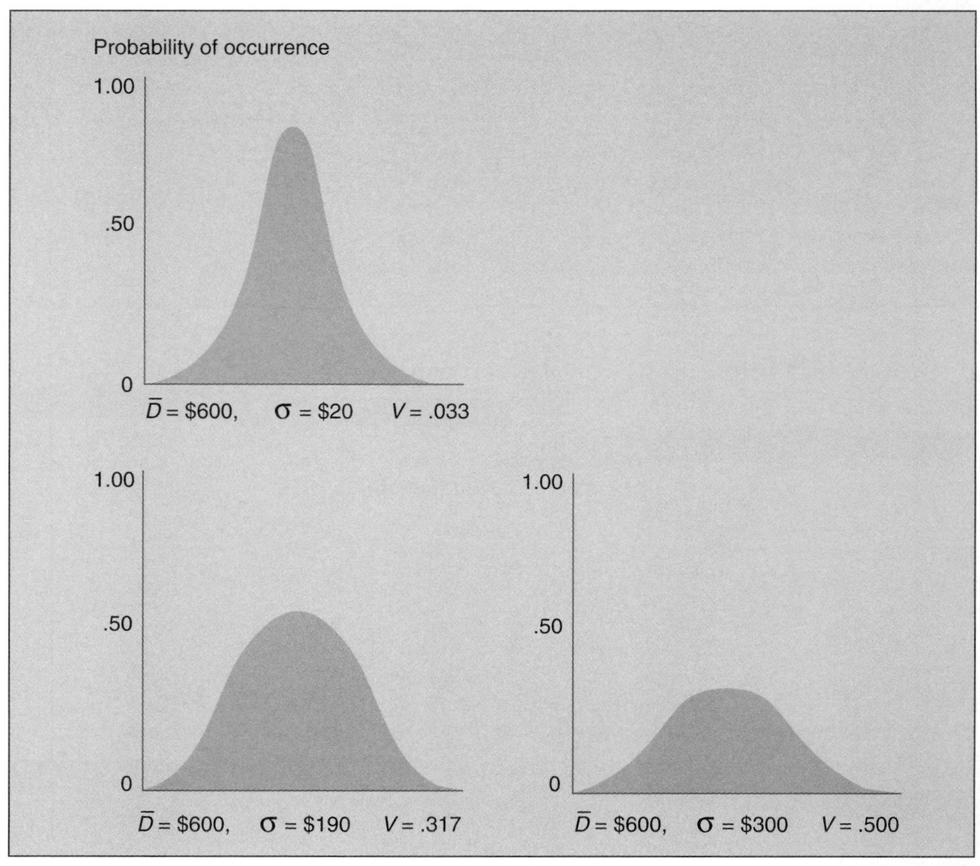

different (such as \$600 versus \$6,000), a direct comparison of the standard deviations for each distribution would not be very helpful in measuring risk. This is because standard deviation is measured in the same scale as the expected value for each investment. The same standard deviation is much more significant on \$600 as compared to \$6,000. Figure 13–4 shows this comparison.

Note that the investment in Panel A of Figure 13–4 appears to have a high standard deviation—but not when related to the expected value of the distribution. A standard deviation of \$600 on an investment with an expected value of \$6,000 may indicate less risk than a standard deviation of \$190 on an investment with an expected value of only \$600.

We can eliminate the size difficulty by developing a third measure, the **coefficient of variation** (*V*), which allows for a comparable scale across different investments. This rather imposing term calls for nothing more difficult than dividing the standard deviation of an investment by the expected value. Generally, the larger the coefficient of variation, the greater is the risk.

$$\text{Coefficient of variation } (V) = \frac{\sigma}{\bar{D}} \tag{13–3}$$

For the investments in Panels A and B of Figure 13–4, we show:

$$A: \quad V = \frac{600}{6{,}000} = .10 \qquad\qquad B: \quad V = \frac{190}{600} = .317$$

We have correctly identified the second investment as carrying the greater risk.

The standard deviation and coefficient of variation of an investment measure its unique risk—that is, the risk of the investment based only on its possible outcomes. However, an investment is not usually undertaken in isolation, and it may be worth considering its interrelationships with the possible outcomes of other investments.

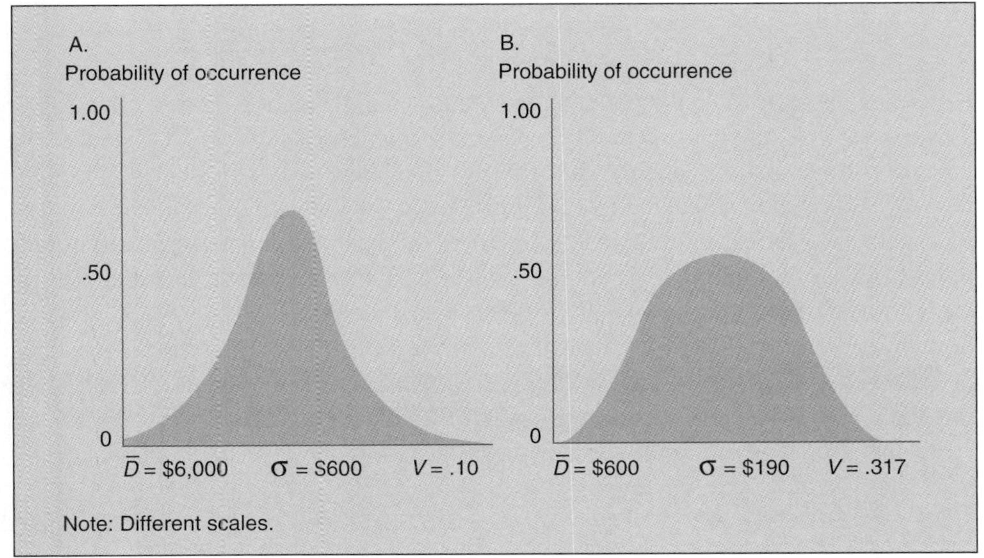

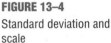

FIGURE 13–4
Standard deviation and scale

TABLE 13–2
Betas, 2002

Company Name	Beta
Air Canada	1.81
Alcan Aluminum	1.28
BCE Inc.	1.30
Inco	1.32
Nortel	2.21
Royal Bank	0.82

1. Betas for several Canadian companies are available at a couple of web sites. Update the above betas. Why have the betas changed and why are they not the same at each site?
2. Check out the Stern site for industry betas.

Source: www.nasdaq-canada.com
www.thomsoninvest.net
www.stern.nyu.edu/~adamodar/New_Home_Page/datafile/Betas.html

Toronto Stock Exchange
www.tsx.ca

Another risk measure, **beta** (b), is discussed in Appendix 11A in the context of portfolios of common stock. Beta may be useful in considering investments and how they relate to other investments of the firm, particularly in the context of a diversified collection of assets. Beta measures the volatility of returns on an individual stock relative to a stock market index of returns such as the Toronto Stock Exchange (S&P) stock index.[3] A common stock with a beta of 1.0 is said to be of equal risk with the market. Stocks with betas greater than 1.0 are riskier than the market, while stocks with betas of less than 1.0 are less risky than the market. Table 13–2 presents a sample of betas calculated for several well-known companies.

If we are to gauge risk, the coefficient of variation best captures total risk, while beta best captures market related risk (systematic) when diversification has significantly reduced the risk that is unique to a project or firm. For the financial manager it is important to identify whether investments require a consideration of total or market related risk.

Risk and the Capital Budgeting Process

How can risk analysis be used effectively in the capital budgeting process? In Chapter 12 we made no explicit distinction between risky and nonrisky events.[4] We showed the amount of the investment and the annual returns—making no comment about the riskiness or likelihood of achieving these returns. We know that enlightened investors and managers need further information. A $1,400 investment that produces certain returns of $600 a year for three years is not the same as a $1,400 investment that produces returns with an expected value of $600 for three years but has a high coefficient of variation. Investors, being risk averse by nature, apply a stiffer test to the second investment.

Remember that the capital budgeting process involves estimating future cash flows and that each estimate of those cash flows is the average of many possibilities. The more dispersed those possibilities, the greater the risk of the investment proposal. Our

[3]Other market measures may also be utilized.

[4]Our assumption was that the risk factor could be considered as constant for various investments.

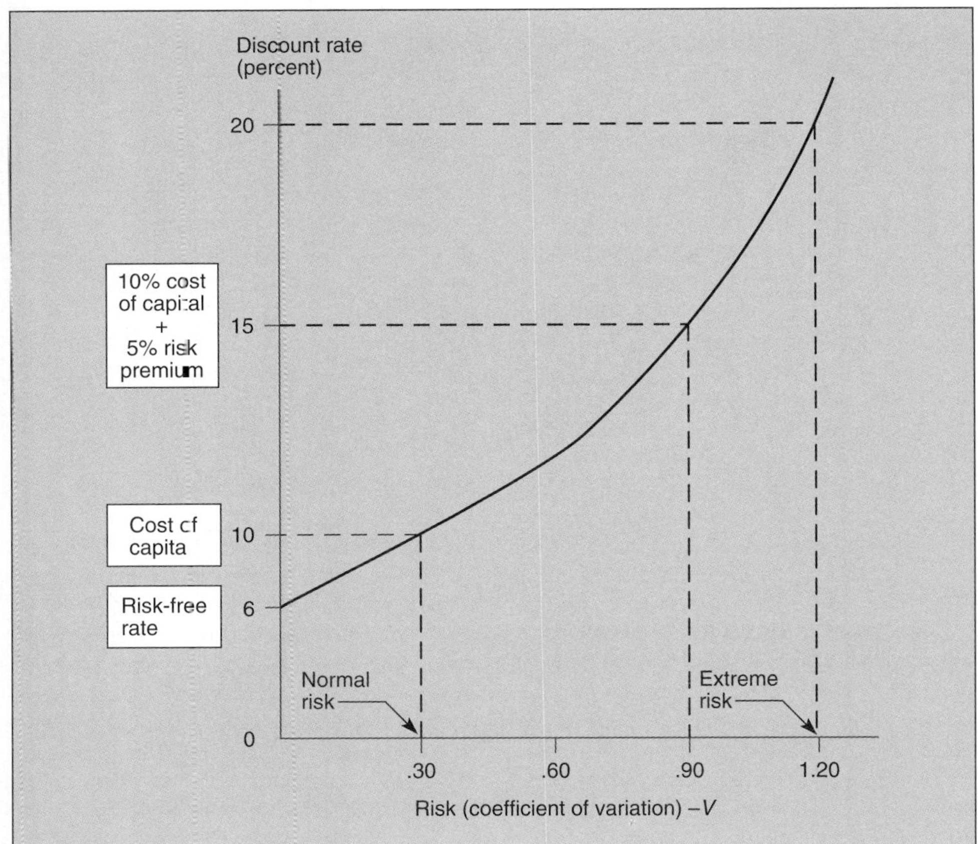

FIGURE 13–5
Relationship of risk to discount rate

task is to consider the risk in our capital budgeting analysis. Many techniques have been developed to assist in gaining a better appreciation and understanding of the risks inherent in investment projects available to the firm. We now describe briefly some of these techniques.

Risk-Adjusted Discount Rate

A favoured approach to adjusting for risk is to use different **risk-adjusted discount rates** for proposals with different risk levels. A project that carries a normal amount of risk and does not change the overall risk composure of the firm should be discounted at the firm's cost of capital. Investments carrying greater than normal risk should be discounted at a higher rate, and so on. Figure 13–5 shows a possible risk/discount rate trade-off scheme. In that figure, risk is measured by the coefficient of variation (V). Higher discount rates will make future expected cash flows worth less today, but of course, that is generally how we value riskier cash flows.

In Figure 13–5 the normal risk for the firm is represented by a coefficient of variation of 0.30. An investment with this risk would be discounted at the firm's normal cost of capital of 10 percent. As the firm selects riskier projects with, for example, a V of 0.90, a risk premium of 5 percent is added for an increase in V of 0.60. If the company selects a project with a coefficient of variation of 1.20, it adds another 5 percent risk premium for this additional V of 0.30. Notice that the same risk premium of 5 percent

FINANCE IN ACTION

What Risk Adjusted Discount Rate To Use for Russian Investments?

Q1 How does Russia's credit rating compare to Argentina's? To India's? To Mexico's?

Let's talk about real risk! We're not talking about risk such as the Toronto Maple Leafs by one goal over the Edmonton Oilers, or working up the nerve to ask someone out this weekend—we're talking about investing in Russia.

Among Russia's positive features is its abundant natural resources, particularly in the form of oil and gold. It also has a well-educated population with a 98 percent literacy rate. The economy has been privatized to a large degree over the last several years, with companies and individuals now controlling 70 percent of what were formerly government assets. The annual rate of inflation, which had been an astronomical 1,526 percent in 1992, fell to below 10 percent by 1998. Furthermore, Russia broke a string of six straight years of negative GDP growth between 1990 and 1996 to post its first positive growth rate of the decade in 1997.

But before you change your dollars to rubles, let's consider risks. First of all, the banking system stands in constant peril because of the declining value of the ruble. In early 1997, one dollar purchased 4.2 rubles. By February 2002, one dollar would net 19.3 rubles. An investment valued in rubles would have plunged in value by 80 percent over the period. The newly formed stock market in Russia is extremely volatile, with overall market movements of 70 percent or more in even briefer periods of time. Many previously government-owned companies continue to produce their old products even though there is no demand in the marketplace. This, of course, means workers are often not paid, and there is little taxable revenue for the government.

Shareholders' rights are close to nonexistent, with many privatized companies being managed by former communists. Not only are shareholder rights frequently ignored, but the free market system is, at times, overlooked as well. In 2002 Canadian oil firm, Norex Exploration, alleged racketeering and money laundering by the U.S. businesses controlling Russia's Tyumen Oil, in a takeover of Norex's equity position in Yugraneft Oil.

With all these factors in mind, what should the risk-adjusted rate of return (discount rate) be for Canadian investors going into Russia? Standard and Poors ratings (ratings lists) for sovereign debt might help us to establish a discount rate. Russia's credit rating has improved over the last few years. What impact do you suggest this would have on the risk adjusted discount rate? In spite of all the problems, there are still potentially profitable startup opportunities in technology, manufacturing, and the service areas. As we examine Table 13–3 (see page 480), a seventh category could probably be added with a risk-adjusted discount rate of well over 20 percent.

www.standardandpoors.com

Symbol: CDNX

was added for a smaller increase in risk. This is an example of being increasingly risk averse at higher levels of risk and potential return.

Another method for adjusting the discount rate to account for differing risk is to use the capital asset pricing model. By identifying the beta of a particular proposal and with knowledge of the capital markets, we can determine the required return on the proposal given its risk. There are difficulties with the model, but it does provide a framework for adjusting discount rates based on risk.

Imperial Oil
www.imperialoil.ca/index.html

Shell
www.shell.ca/investor.htm

Syncrude
www.syncrude.ca

Increasing Risk over Time

Our ability to forecast accurately diminishes as we forecast further in time. As the time horizon becomes longer, more uncertainty enters the forecast. In 1985 Esso Resources was planning a $13 billion investment in a steam-injection oil sands plant at Cold Lake, Alberta, while Shell Canada had plans for a similar plant at Peace River. The rapid decline in world oil prices in early 1986 (from about U.S.$26.00 per barrel to less than $10.00), due to Saudi Arabia's policy of flooding the market with cheap oil, led Esso and Shell to postpone these huge capital investments. Today they have revived these projects. This contrasts with Syncrude, which had already committed large sums of money to tar sands extraction, as discussed in the Finance in Action box in Chapter

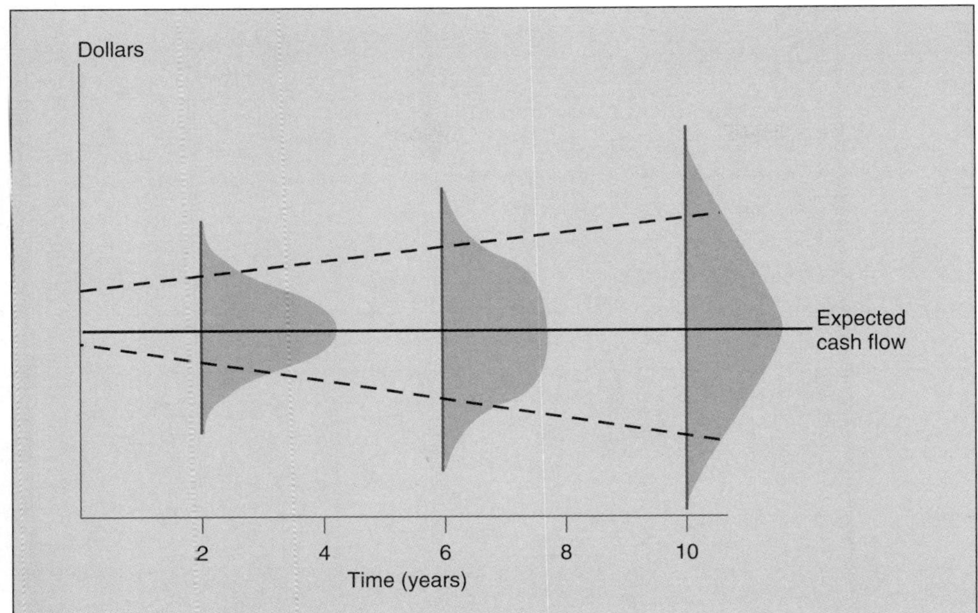

FIGURE 13–6
Risk over time

12. These unexpected events create a higher standard deviation in cash flow estimates and increase the risk associated with long-lived projects. Figure 13–6 depicts the relationship between risk and time.

Even though a forecast of cash flows shows a constant expected value, Figure 13–6 shows that the range of outcomes and probabilities increases as we move from Year 2 to Year 10. The standard deviations increase for each forecast of cash flow. If cash flows were forecast as easily for each period, all distributions would look like the first one for Year 2. However, as later expected cash flows are more uncertain and exhibit increasing standard deviations, there is greater risk in the longer-term cash flows forecasts than in the near-term forecasts.

Both the time value of money and risk are included in a risk-adjusted discount rate. The nature of discounting as a compounding process is such that cash flows further out in time do bear greater risk. This is consistent with the notion that later cash flows should bear more risk. However, it could be suggested that risk lessens as a project continues because the firm has become more knowledgeable about its operation and the cash flows are more predictable. Certainty equivalents and decision trees help us to address this consideration.

Qualitative Measures

Rather than relate the discount rate—or required return—to the coefficient of variation or the beta, management may wish to set up risk classes based on qualitative considerations. Examples are presented in Table 13–3. Once again we are assigning the discount rate based on the perceived risk.[5]

[5]Throughout all of this, note the difficulty implied for managers trying to gain approval for "new" ideas with long development time horizons. Considering Canada's relatively inferior position with respect to most new technologies, its relatively high manufacturing costs, its need to depend on selling into foreign markets, and the purported risk averseness of the Canadian people, you have the definition of a very serious impediment to investment for the long-term development of the Canadian industrial economy.

TABLE 13–3
Risk categories and associated discount rates

	Discount Rate
Low or no risk (repair to old machinery)	6%
Moderate risk (new equipment)	8
Normal risk (addition to normal product line)	10
Risky (new product in related market)	12
High risk (completely new market)	16
Highest risk (new product in foreign market)	20

TABLE 13–4
Capital budgeting analysis

Year	Investment A (10% discount rate)		Year	Investment B (10% discount rate)	
1	$5,000	$ 4,545	1	$1,500	$ 1,364
2	5,000	4,132	2	2,000	1,653
3	2,000	1,503	3	2,500	1,878
		$10,180	4	5,000	3,415
			5	5,000	3,105
					$11,415
Present value of inflows		$10,180	Present value of inflows		$11,415
Investment		10,000	Investment		10,000
Net present value		$ 180	Net present value		$ 1,415

TABLE 13–5
Capital budgeting decision adjusted for risk

Year	Investment A (10% discount rate)		Year	Investment B (20% discount rate)	
1	$5,000	$ 4,545	1	$1,500	$ 1,250
2	5,000	4,132	2	2,000	1,389
3	2,000	1,503	3	2,500	1,447
		$10,180	4	5,000	2,411
			5	5,000	2,009
					$ 8,506
Present value of inflows		$10,180	Present value of inflows		$ 8,506
Investment		10,000	Investment		10,000
Net present value		$ 180	Net present value		$(1,494)

Example—Risk-Adjusted Discount Rate In Chapter 12 we compared two $10,000 investment alternatives and indicated that each had a positive net present value (at a 10 percent cost of capital). That analysis is reproduced in Table 13–4.

Though both proposals are acceptable, if they were mutually exclusive, only Investment B would be undertaken. But what if we add a risk dimension to the problem? Assume Investment A calls for an addition to the normal product line and is assigned a discount rate of 10 percent. Further, assume Investment B represents a new product in a foreign market and must carry a 20 percent discount rate to adjust for the large risk component. As indicated in Table 13–5, our answers are reversed; Investment A is now the only acceptable alternative.

Other methods besides the risk-adjusted discount rate are also used to evaluate risk in the capital budgeting process. The spectrum runs from a seat-of-the-pants executive preference approach to sophisticated computer-based statistical analysis. All methods, however, include a common approach—they must recognize the riskiness of a given investment proposal and make an appropriate adjustment for risk.

Certainty Equivalents

The **certainty equivalent** approach adjusts each cash flow based on its probability distribution to a value that is equal on the basis of having no inherent risk and is therefore certain. In effect, a decision maker would be indifferent between choosing the risky cash flow and the certain cash flow. The certain cash flows would be smaller because of the risk aversion of individuals. These adjusted cash flows would then be discounted at the risk-free discount rate or, effectively, on the basis of the time value of money alone.

In practice, the expected value for a given year is multiplied by a percentage figure indicating the degree of certainty and then translated back to the present at a risk-free discount rate (less than the cost of capital). Items with a high degree of certainty might be multiplied by 100 percent, less certain items by 75 percent, and so on down the scale. This approach is difficult to apply because it calls for certainty equivalents for each distribution of possible outcomes and depends on the individual decision maker's attitude toward risk.

For example, we might establish that the final decision maker for the firm values uncertain cash flows in the following manner:

Year of Uncertain Cash Flow	Value as Certain Cash Flow
1	85%
2	80%
3	65%

The company's cost of capital is 13 percent, and the risk-free rate of return is 5 percent.

A proposal costing $1,100 has the following pattern of cash flows and certainty equivalents:

Year	Cash Flow	Certainty Equivalent
1	$500	$425 (500 × 85%)
2	600	480 (600 × 80%)
3	800	520 (800 × 65%)

The net present value (NPV) of this proposal using certainty equivalents and the risk-free rate for discount purposes is $189.

Year	Certainty Equivalent	Present Value
0	−$1,100	−$1,100
1	425	405
2	480	435
3	520	449
		NPV = $ 189

Risk has been considered and a positive NPV has been achieved, so this would be an acceptable proposal.

Computer Simulation Models

Computers make it possible to simulate various economic and financial outcomes, using a large number of variables. Thus, **simulation** is one way of dealing with the uncertainty involved in forecasting the outcomes of capital budgeting projects or other types of decisions. A Monte Carlo simulation model uses random variables for inputs. By programming the computer to randomly select inputs from probability distributions, the outcomes generated by a simulation are distributed about a mean; thus, instead of generating one return or net present value, a range of outcomes with standard deviations is provided. A simulation model relies on repetition of the same random process as many as several hundred times. Because the inputs are representative of what one might encounter in the real world, many possible combinations of returns are generated.

Decisioneering
www.crystalball.com/crystal_ball

One of the benefits of simulation is its ability to test various possible combinations of events. This sensitivity testing allows the planner to ask "what if" questions, such as: What will happen to the returns on this project if oil prices go up? Go down? What effect will a 5 percent increase in interest rates have on the net present value of this project? The analyst can use the simulation process to test possible changes in economic policy, sales levels, inflation, or any other variable included in the modelling process. Some simulation models are driven by sales forecasts with assumptions to derive income statements and balance sheets. Others generate probability acceptance curves for capital budgeting decisions by informing the analyst about the probabilities of having a positive net present value.

For example, each distribution in Figure 13–7 would have a value picked randomly and used for one simulation. The simulation would be run many times, each time selecting a new random variable to generate the final probability distribution for the net present value (at the bottom). For that probability distribution, the expected values are on the horizontal axis and the probability of occurrence is plotted on the vertical axis. The outcomes also indicate something about the riskiness of the project, which is indicated by the overall dispersion.

Sensitivity Analysis

Another method for employing the power of the computer is known as sensitivity analysis. However, it is not as complex, nor as expensive, as the Monte Carlo simulation. **Sensitivity analysis** sets up the project analysis with the methodology developed in Chapter 12, but with the intent of changing one variable at a time. The resulting impact on the NPV of the project and, ultimately, our decision is observed. We thus determine the variables to which the project's success is sensitive. Identifying these

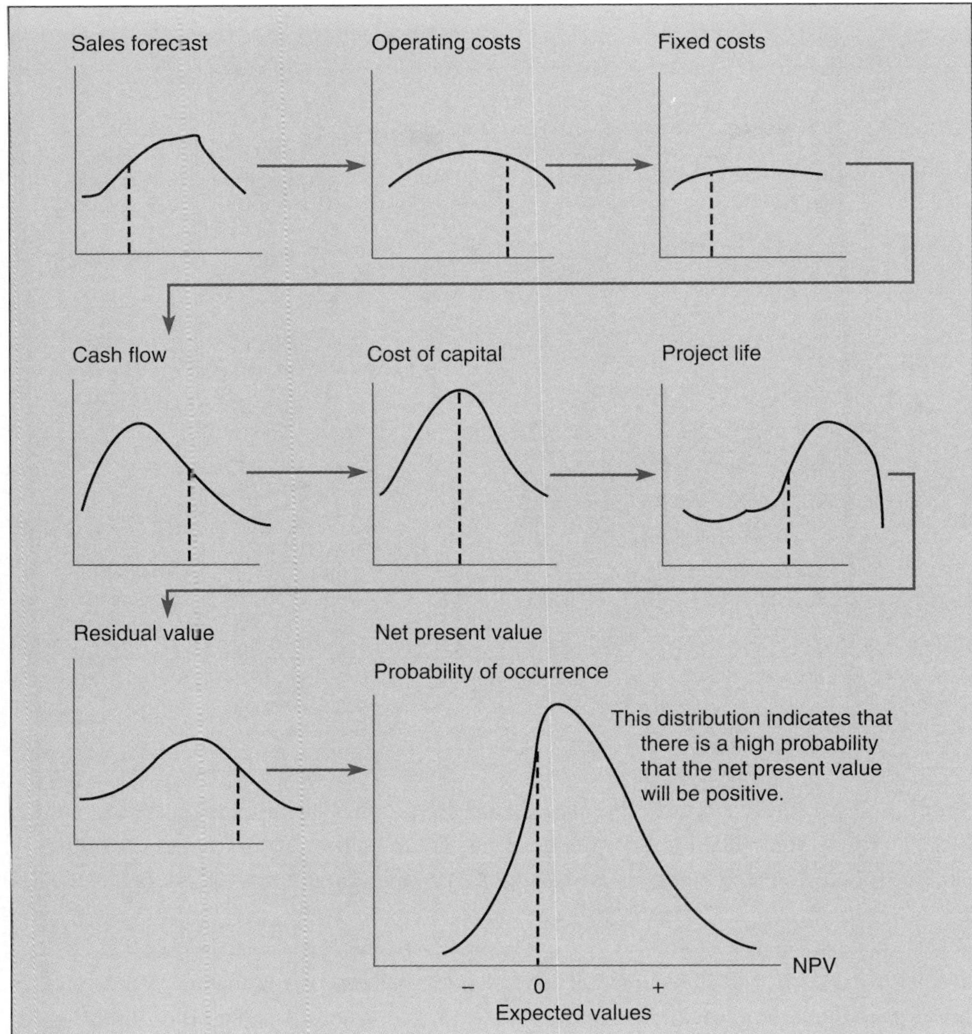

FIGURE 13–7
Simulation flow chart

variables may suggest further research to more closely define their expected values. Through sensitivity analysis we can observe the different results possible if the project is implemented.

Sensitivity analysis is not without its problems. Variables generally do not change in isolation. The variables tend to be related. For example, if the discount rate decreases, it likely reflects lower inflation rates, and lower inflation rates would likely affect our cash flow projections. We have to be careful with the results when one variable at a time is changed without considering the impact on the other variables in the analysis.

Also, sensitivity analysis only determines the impact a variation in a particular variable will have on the project. It does not identify the probability of that variation. We do not truly identify risk in sensitivity analysis. We might conclude that an adverse result rules out accepting a project, even though the probability of that result is quite

FIGURE 13–8
Decision trees

	(1) Expected Sales	(2) Probability	(3) Present Value of Cash Flow from Sales ($ millions)	(4) Initial Cost ($ millions)	(5) NPV (3) – (4) ($ millions)	(6) Expected NPV (2) x (5) ($ millions)
A: Expand semiconductor capacity	High	.50	$100	$60	$40	$20.00
	Moderate	.25	75	60	15	3.75
	Low	.25	40	60	(20)	(5.00)
					Expected NPV =	$18.75 ($ millions)
B: Enter home computer market	High	.20	$200	$60	$140	$28.00
	Moderate	.50	75	60	15	7.50
	Low	.30	25	60	(35)	(10.50)
					Expected NPV =	$25.00 ($ millions)

small. It is therefore important that we consider the probabilities of variations in the key variables. With the aid of computers, one also must be careful to plan the output of sensitivity analysis because it is easy to generate lots of meaningless paper.

Decision Trees

Decision trees lay out the sequence of decisions that can be made and present a tabular or graphical comparison that resembles the branches of a tree and highlight the differences between investment choices. Figure 13–8, examines a semiconductor firm's consideration of two choices: (A) expanding the production of semiconductors for sale to computer manufacturers, or (B) forward integrating into the highly competitive home computer market. The cost of both projects would be the same, $60 million, but the net present value (NPV) and risk are different.

If the firm expanded its semiconductor capacity (Project A), it would be assured of some demand, so a high likelihood of a positive rate of return exists. The market demand for these products is volatile over time, but long-run growth seems to be a reasonable expectation as the emphasis on technology increases. If the firm expanded into the home computer market (Project B), it would face stiff competition from many existing firms. It stands to lose more money under low expected sales conditions than under option A, but it will make more under high expected sales conditions. Even though Project B has a higher expected NPV than Project A, its extra risk makes for a difficult choice. Clearly, more analysis would have to be done before management made the final choice between these two projects. Nevertheless, the decision tree has identified critical areas where managerial judgment must be exercised.

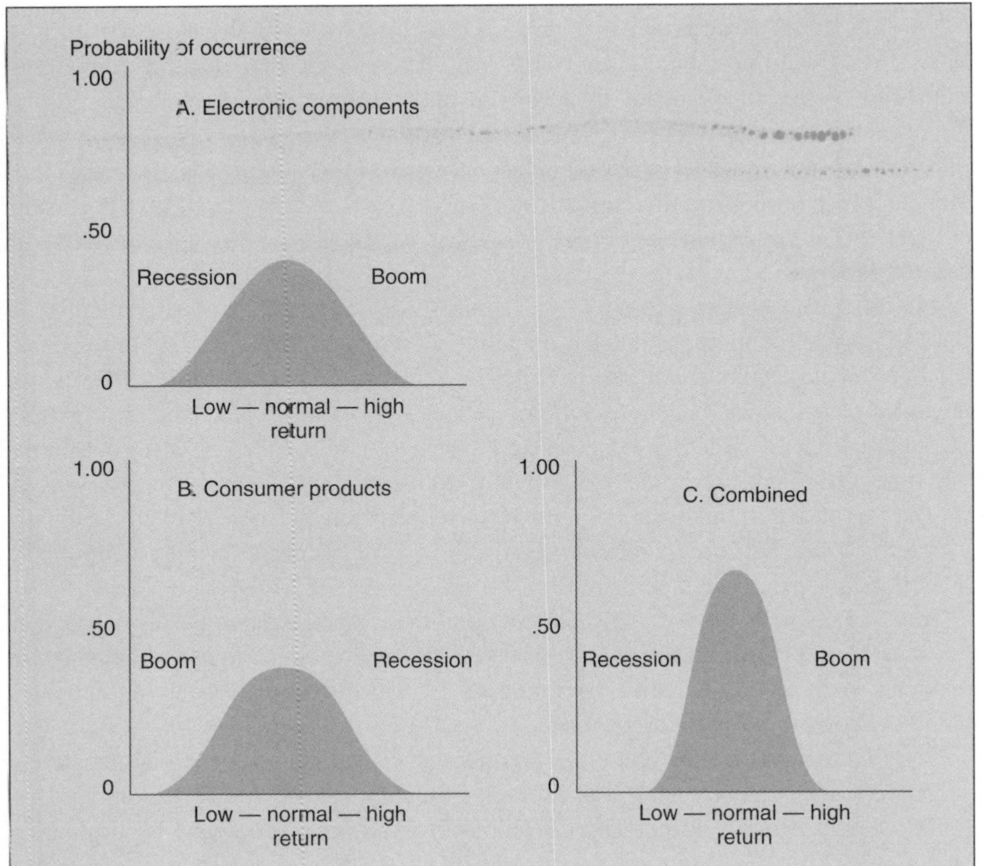

FIGURE 13–9
Portfolio considerations in evaluating risk

The Portfolio Effect

Up to this point we have been primarily concerned with the risk inherent in an *individual* investment proposal. While this approach is very useful, we also need to consider the impact of a given investment on the overall risk of the firm—the **portfolio effect**.[6] For example, we might undertake a particular investment in the consumer products industry that appears to carry a high degree of risk, but if our primary business is the manufacture of electronic components for industrial use, that investment may actually diminish the overall risk exposure of the firm. Why? Because electronic component sales generally expand when the economy does well and falter in a recession. The consumer products industry often reacts in the opposite fashion—performing poorly in boom periods and reacting well relative to other industries in recessionary periods. By investing in the consumer products industry, an electronic components manufacturer could actually smooth out the cyclical fluctuations inherent in its business and reduce overall risk exposure, as indicated in Figure 13–9.

Harry Markowitz
www.nobel.se/economics/laureates/1990/markowitz-autobio.html

The risk reduction phenomenon is demonstrated by a less dispersed probability distribution. We say that the standard deviation for the entire company (the portfolio of investments) has been reduced.

[6]Here the portfolio of investments refers to plant, equipment, new products, and so forth, rather than stocks and bonds.

Portfolio Risk

Whether a given investment changes the overall risk of the firm depends on its relationships to other investments. If one airline purchases another, there is little risk reduction. Highly correlated investments—that is, projects that move in the same direction in good times as well as bad—do little or nothing to diversify away risk. Projects moving in opposite directions (for example, consumer products and electronic components) are referred to as being negatively correlated and provide a high degree of risk reduction.

Finally, projects that are totally uncorrelated provide some overall reduction in portfolio risk, though not as much as negatively correlated investments. For example, if a beer manufacturer purchases a textile firm, the projects are neither positively nor negatively correlated, but the purchase reduces the overall risk of the firm simply through the law of large numbers. If you have enough unrelated projects going on at one time, good and bad events will probably even out.

The extent of correlation among projects is represented by a new term called the **coefficient of correlation**—a measure that may take on values anywhere from −1 to +1.[7] Examples are presented in Table 13–6.

In the real world, very few investment combinations take on values as extreme as −1 or +1 or, for that matter, exactly 0. The more likely case is a point somewhere in between, such as −.2 negative correlation or +.3 positive correlation, as indicated along the continuum in Figure 13–10.

The fact that risk can be reduced by combining risky assets with low or negatively correlated assets can be seen by the example of Conglomerate, Inc. Conglomerate has fairly average returns and standard deviations of returns. The company is considering

TABLE 13–6
Measures of correlation

Coefficient of Correlation	Condition	Example	Impact on Risk
−1	Negative correlation	Electronic components, consumer products	Large risk reduction
0	No correlation	Beer, textiles	Some risk reduction
+1	Positive correlation	Two airlines	No risk reduction

[7]Coefficient of correlation is not to be confused with coefficient of variation—a term used earlier in the chapter.

$$\text{The coefficient of correlation } \rho_{AB} = \frac{\text{Covariance}_{AB}}{\sigma_A \sigma_B}$$

The covariance

$$Cov_{AB} = \Sigma P(D - \bar{D})(F - \bar{F}),$$

with D and F representing the outcomes of the events.

Standard deviation of a portfolio

$$\sigma_{AB} = \sqrt{x_A^2\sigma_A^2 + x_B^2\sigma_B^2 + 2cov_{AB}x_Ax_B}$$

or

$$\sigma_{AB} = \sqrt{x_A^2\sigma_A^2 + x_B^2\sigma_B^2 + 2\rho_{AB}\sigma_A\sigma_Bx_Ax_B}$$

where

$$x = \text{\% weighting in the portfolio of each investment.}$$

Diversification: Go By Country or By Corporation

In the last number of years Canadian investors have increasingly sought to diversify their stock holdings by investing abroad. Decreased restrictions on our ability to invest overseas and a growing awareness that we can improve our returns by investing outside of Canada have lead to this trend. Canada only represents about 2 percent of the world's capital markets.

International diversification has meant including investments in various countries around the globe whose economies are not highly correlated. However as the world becomes increasingly integrated we are observing that the global economy is increasingly correlated. In other words, countries tend to move through expansions and recessions together. Therefore less diversification occurs. One only has to look at Europe. At one time it was important to diversify across several currencies; currencies that no longer exist.

Instead we may be able to achieve effective diversification by investing in globally based companies such as Microsoft or Nokia that have already achieved international diversification. We can then supplement our portfolios with companies that are subject to unique local events. We could think of entertainment and travel companies or utilities subject to local deregulation activities.

Regardless of our choice, as the world becomes increasingly integrated through trading patterns and cultural "sameness" it will become harder to find investments that can effectively diversify risk.

the purchase of two separate but large companies with sales and assets equal to its own. Management is struggling with the decision since both companies have a 14 percent rate of return, which is 2 percent higher than that of Conglomerate, and they have the same standard deviation of returns as that of Conglomerate, at 2.83 percent. This information is presented in the first three columns of Table 13–7 on the next page.

Because management desires to reduce risk (σ) and to increase returns at the same time, it decides to analyze the results of each combination.[8]

These combinations are shown in the last two columns in Table 13–7. A combination with Positive Correlation, Inc., increases the mean return to 13 percent, but maintains the same standard deviation of returns (no risk reduction). Why? This occurs because the coefficient of correlation is +1.0 and no diversification benefits are achieved. A combination with Negative Correlation, Inc., also increases the mean return to 13 percent, but it reduces the standard deviation of returns to 0.63 percent, a significant reduction in risk. This occurs because of the offsetting relationship of returns between the two companies, as evidenced by the coefficient of correlation of −.9. When one company has high returns, the other has low returns, and vice versa.

Extreme risk reduction	Significant Risk Reduction		Some Risk Reduction		Minor Risk Reduction		No reduction
	−1	−.5	−.2	0	+.3	+.5	+1	

FIGURE 13–10
Levels of risk reduction as measured by the coefficient of correlation

[8]In Chapter 20 you evaluate a merger situation in which there is no increase in earnings, only a reduction in the standard deviation. Because the lower risk may mean a higher price-earnings ratio, this could be beneficial.

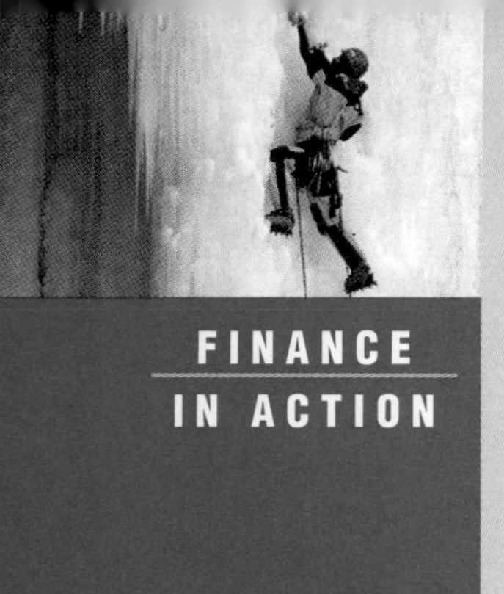

FINANCE IN ACTION

Diversifying Product Lines

SB Nadir, owns and operates a retail business that sells silver jewellery in a large Canadian city. Silversmith, his firm, has several outlets in malls across the city. He must however be careful in buying his inventories because decreased sales can have a dramatic impact on the business. Despite the slowdown in the economy in late 2001 his business has done reasonably well.

Jewellery however happens to be a fashion statement subject to quick change. In order to reduce his risk due to changing customer tastes Nadir has diversified some of his risk by buying product from around the globe. The Middle East, Europe, and Southeast Asia represent the sources of his varied product. The silver jewellery produced in the different countries tends to be unique to the cultures and allows the firm to meet the changing needs and desires of the customer. Not only does this diversification allow Nadir to diversify some of his product risk, it also allows him to visit several exotic locations.

Evaluation of Combinations

The firm should evaluate all possible combinations of projects, determining which provides the best trade-off between risk and return. In Figure 13–11 we see a number of alternatives that might be available to a given firm. Each point represents a combination of different possible investments. For example, point *F* might represent a semiconductor manufacturer combining three different semiconductors, two calculators, and two unrelated products. In choosing between the various points or combinations, management should have two primary objectives:

1. Achieve the highest possible return at a given risk level.
2. Allow the lowest possible risk at a given return level.

All the best opportunities fall along line *CFG*. Each point on the line satisfies the two objectives of the firm. Any point to the right is less desirable than any point below.

TABLE 13–7

Rates of return for Conglomerate, Inc., and two merger candidates

Year	(1) Conglomerate, Inc.	(2) Positive Correlation Inc. +1.0	(3) Negative Correlation Inc. −.9	(1) + (2) Conglomerate, Inc. + Positive Correlation, Inc.	(1) + (3) Conglomerate, Inc. + Negative Correlation, Inc.
1	14%	16%	10%	15%	12%
2	10	12	16	11	13
3	8	10	18	9	13
4	12	14	14	13	13
5	16	18	12	17	14
Mean return	12%	14%	14%	13%	13%
Standard deviation of returns (σ)*	2.83%	2.83%	2.83%	2.83%	.63%
Correlation coefficients with Conglomerate, Inc				+1.0	−.9

*Technically the calculation of the standard deviation is based on whether we are dealing with a population or a sample. For a sample an adjustment is made to get an unbiased estimate.

Flying the Friendly but Risky Skies

In early 1996 Westjet Airlines Ltd. decided to form a western Canadian discount airline, despite the fact that in the United States and Canada 9 out of 10 cut-rate airlines fail, including over 100 since 1971.

One successful discount airline is Southwest Airlines of the United States. Southwest has been able to achieve a profit for over 25 years by keeping operating costs about 60 percent below the major carriers and by increasing passenger traffic on carefully selected short-haul routes. The new discount airline in Canada would operate cheap flights with no meals, no tickets, self-serve baggage handling, and flexible air routes.

Westjet bought three, 22-year-old Boeing 737s for $15 million, spent $2 million for spare parts, and $0.75 million on computers in 1996. By 2002 Westjet operated 28 aircraft and had a contract with Boeing to purchase 48 more. Westjet's original financing came primarily from equity invested by successful Albertan oil and gas entrepreneurs and the Ontario Teachers Pension Plan Board. In 1999 it had a successful share issue at $100 per share. Shares were split 3 for 1 the next year.

The experience of Southwest Airlines was that, on certain routes, decreased fares could increase passenger volumes by two or three times. Westjet would make money if its planes were 60 percent full and if air travel between the major cities in western Canada would expand. Westjet's expectations were that 300,000 passengers would generate about $50 million in revenues in its first year of operation. By 2001 revenues approached $500 million and Westjet had expanded in a limited way across the country

Westjet in 2001 had a load factor of 80 percent versus Air Canada's 70 percent. Its revenue per seat mile was 16.7 cents versus costs of 14.2 cents per seat mile. For Air Canada revenue was 14.7 cents versus expenses of 16.9 per seat mile. No wonder Westjet earned its 19th consecutive profit while Air Canada lost over $700 million in 2001.

Westjet remains successful as it watches its costs, expands the travel market, and weathers the competition from Air Canada. Risky! You bet. But with careful planning, the risks can be controlled, and large returns are the prize.

FINANCE IN ACTION

Q1 Has Westjet or Air Canada's share price performed better over the last three years?

Q2 Which airline has better revenue to expenses per seat mile (ASM) in the latest financial quarter?

www.westjet.com
Symbol: WJA

www.aircanada.ca
Symbol: AC

After we have developed our best risk-return line, known in the financial literature as the **efficient frontier**, we must determine where on the line our firm should be. There is no universally correct answer. To the extent that we are willing to take large risks for superior returns, we would opt for some point on the upper portion of the line—such as *G*. A more conservative selection might be *C* or *F*.

Combining assets with less than perfect positive correlation reduces risk. This is the benefit of diversification. However, we might want to question whether or not

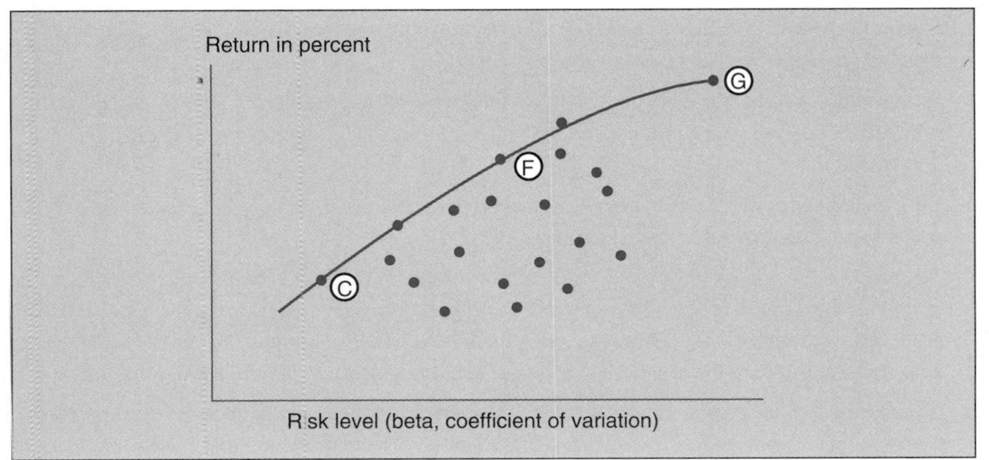

FIGURE 13–11
Risk-return trade-offs

diversification is useful at the firm level. If investors already hold diversified portfolios, might the firm's attempts at diversification only duplicate the investors' actions? Perhaps the firm should stick to what it knows best and let investors achieve diversification through the marketplace.

John Labatt Inc.
www.labatt.com
Interbrew
www.bestbelgianbeers.com

In the past few years several corporations have announced divestitures and a return to concentrating on the business they know best. This follows a period in which corporate diversification seemed to be the thing to do. BCE Inc., after a period of diversification, has concentrated more on the telecommunications business, with expansion into Great Britain and with an alliance with MCI of the United States. John Labatt Ltd. diversified into the dairy business, but encountered difficulties and recently refocused the corporate strategy primarily on the beer and entertainment business. With Interbrew's purchase of Labatt, even its entertainment division, which includes the Toronto Blue Jays, has been divested.

The Share Price Effect

The firm must be sensitive to the wishes and demands of shareholders. To the extent that unnecessary or undesirable risks are taken, a higher discount rate and lower valuation will probably be assigned to the shares in the market. Higher profits, resulting from risky ventures, could have a result opposite from that intended. In raising the coefficient of variation, or beta, we could be lowering the overall valuation of the firm.

The aversion of investors to unpredictability (and the associated risk) is confirmed by observing the relative valuation given to cyclical stocks versus highly predictable growth stocks in the market. Metals, autos, and housing stocks generally trade at earnings multipliers well below those for industries with level, predictable performance, such as drugs, soft drinks, and even alcohol or cigarettes. Each company must carefully analyze its own situation to determine the appropriate trade-off between risk and return. The changing desires and objectives of investors tend to make the task somewhat more difficult.

Summary

1. Risk may be defined as the variability of the potential outcomes from an investment. The less predictable the outcomes, the greater is the risk.
2. Standard deviation is the statistical measure that defines risk. The coefficient of variation is the standard deviation divided by the expected value; it brings the same scale to our statistical measures of risk.
3. Both management and investors tend to be risk averse; that is, all things being equal, they would prefer to take less risk rather than greater risk.
4. The most commonly employed method to adjust for risk in the capital budgeting process is to alter the discount rate based on the perceived risk level. High-risk projects carry a risk premium, producing a discount rate well in excess of the average cost of capital. The CAPM may prove helpful in establishing the appropriate discount rate based on the risk inherent in a project.
5. In assessing the risk components of a given project, management may employ several techniques. Certainty equivalents adjust cash flows rather than the discount rate and use a risk-free discount rate. Simulation models can be quite elaborate. They generate probabilities of possible outcomes.

Sensitivity analysis examines the impact on a project of changing one variable at a time. Decision trees model the possible outcomes from an investment and highlight dependencies between sequential events.

5. Management must consider not only the risk inherent in a given project, but also the impact of a new project on the overall risk of the firm (the portfolio effect). Negatively correlated projects have the most favorable effect on smoothing out business cycle fluctuations. The firm may wish to consider all combinations and variations of possible projects and to select only those that provide a total risk-return trade-off consistent with its goals.

Review of Formulas

1. $\bar{D}$ (expected value) $= \Sigma DP$ (13–1)
   D is outcome
   P is probability of outcome
2. σ (standard deviation) $= \sqrt{\Sigma(D - \bar{D})^2 P}$ (13–2)
   D is outcome
   $\bar{D}$ is expected value
   P is probability of outcome
3. V (coefficient of variation) $= \dfrac{\sigma}{\bar{D}}$ (13–3)
   σ is standard deviation
   $\bar{D}$ is expected value

List of Terms

risk 470
risk averse 471
expected value 473
standard deviation 473
coefficient of variation 475
beta 476
risk-adjusted discount rates 477
certainty equivalent 481
simulation 482
sensitivity analysis 482
decision trees 484
portfolio effect 485
coefficient of correlation 486
efficient frontier 489

Discussion Questions

1. If corporate managers are risk averse, does this mean they will not take risks? Explain.
2. Discuss the concept of risk and how it might be measured.
3. When is the coefficient of variation a better measure of risk than the standard deviation?
4. Explain how the concept of risk can be incorporated into the capital budgeting process.
5. If risk is to be analyzed in a qualitative way, place the following investment decisions in order from the lowest risk to the highest risk:
   a. New equipment.
   b. Completely new market.
   c. Repair of old machinery.
   d. New product in a foreign market.
   e. New product in a related market.
   f. Addition to a product line.
6. Assume a company whose performance is highly correlated with the general economy is evaluating six projects, of which two are positively correlated with the economy, two are negatively correlated, and two are not correlated with it at all. Which two projects would you select to minimize the company's overall risk?

7. Why use certainty equivalents in a capital budgeting analysis?

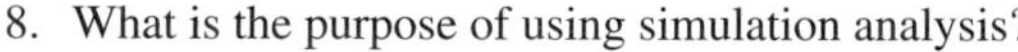

8. What is the purpose of using simulation analysis?

9. Why must one be careful when using sensitivity analysis?
10. Why might an analyst set up a decision tree in attempting to make a decision?
11. Assume a firm has several hundred possible investments and wants to analyze the risk-return trade-off for portfolios of 20 projects. How should it proceed with the evaluation?
12. Explain the effect of the risk-return trade-off on the market value of common stock.

INTERNET RESOURCES AND QUESTIONS

Decisioneering and Vanguard, are software companies that develop and market decision-analysis tools. Several demos are available on their web sites. Included is a Monte Carlo simulation-type model, and a time-series forecasting model. The demos give a sense of the models required in risk analysis:
www.crystalball.com/crystal_ball
www.vanguardsw.com/decisionpro/

1. Using the Standard and Poors web site and your knowledge of the components of yield to maturity from Chapter 10, construct an appropriate discount rate for an investment (for a known technology) from a Canadian viewpoint in the following countries: Finland, Estonia, Chile, Ecuador.

   www.standardandpoors.com

   www.bankofcanada.ca/en

Problems

1. Myers Business Systems is evaluating the introduction of a new product. The possible levels of unit sales and the probabilities of occurrence are given.

Possible Market Reaction	Sales in Units	Probabilities
Low response	20	.10
Moderate response	40	.30
High response	55	.40
Very high response	70	.20

   a. What is the expected value of unit sales for the new product?

   b. What is the standard deviation of unit sales?

2. Shack Homebuilders Limited is evaluating a new promotional campaign that could increase home sales. Possible outcomes and probabilities of the outcomes are shown below. Compute the coefficient of variation.

Possible Outcomes	Additional Sales in Units	Probabilities
Ineffective campaign	40	.20
Normal response	60	.50
Extremely effective	140	.30

3. Five investment alternatives have the following returns and standard deviations of returns.

Alternative	Returns: Expected Value	Standard Deviation
A	$ 5,000	$1,200
B	4,000	600
C	4,000	800
D	8,000	3,200
E	10,000	900

Rank the five alternatives from lowest risk to highest risk using the coefficient of variation.

4. In the previous problem, if you were to choose between Alternative B and C only, would you need to use the coefficient of variation? Why?

5. Tim Trepid is highly risk-averse while Mike Macho actually enjoys taking a risk.
   a. Which of the four investments should Tim choose?
   b. Which of the four investments should Mike choose?

Investments	Returns: Expected Value	Standard Deviation
Buy stocks	$ 7,000	$ 4,000
Buy bonds	5,000	1,560
Buy commodities	12,000	15,100
Buy options	8,000	8,850

6. Wildcat Oil Company was set up to take large risks and is willing to take the largest risk possible. Richmond Construction Company is more typical of the average corporation and is risk-averse.
   a. Which of the following four projects should Wildcat Oil Company choose?
   b. Which of the following four projects should Richmond Construction Company choose?

Projects	Returns: Expected Value	Standard Deviation
A	$262,000	$138,000
B	674,000	403,000
C	88,000	108,000
C	125,000	207,000

7. Possible outcomes for three investment alternatives and their probabilities of occurrence are given below.

	Alternative 1		Alternative 2		Alternative 3	
	Outcomes	Probability	Outcomes	Probability	Outcomes	Probability
Failure	50	.2	90	.3	80	.4
Acceptable	80	.4	160	.5	200	.5
Successful	120	.4	200	.2	400	.1

Rank the three alternatives in terms of risk.

8. Bridge's Modelling Studios is considering opening in a new location in White Rock. An after-tax cash flow of $120 per day (expected value) is projected for each of the two locations being evaluated.

Which of these sites would you select based on the distribution of these cash flows (use the coefficient of variation as your measure of risk):

Site A		Site B	
Probability	**Cash Flows**	**Probability**	**Cash Flows**
.15	$ 80	.10	$ 50
.50	110	.20	80
.30	140	.40	120
.05	220	.20	160
		.10	190
Expected value	$120	Expected value	$120

9. Micro Systems is evaluating a $50,000 project with the following cash flows.

Years	Cash Flows
1	$ 9,000
2	12,000
3	18,000
4	16,000
5	24,000

The coefficient of variation is .726.

Based on the following table of risk-adjusted discount rates, should the project be undertaken? An NPV calculation is appropriate.

Coefficient of Variation	Discount Rate
0.00–0.25	6%
0.26–0.50	8
0.51–0.75	12
0.76–1.00	16
1.01–1.25	20

10. Payne Medical Labs is evaluating two new products to introduce into the marketplace. Product 1 (a new form of plaster cast) is relatively low in risk for this business and will carry a 10 percent discount rate. Product 2 (a knee joint support brace) has a less predictable outcome and will require a higher discount rate of 15 percent. Either investment will require an initial capital outlay of $90,000. The inflows from projected business over the next five years are given below. Which method should be selected using net present value analysis?

Years	Product 1	Product 2
1	$25,000	$16,000
2	30,000	22,000
3	38,000	34,000
4	31,000	29,000
5	19,000	70,000

11. Debby's Dance Studios is considering the purchase of new sound equipment that will enhance the popularity of its aerobics dancing. The equipment will cost $25,000 and has an estimated life of five years. Debby is not sure how many members the new equipment will attract, but she estimates that her increased annual cash flows for each of the next five years will have the following probability distribution. Debby's cost of capital is 11 percent.

Probability	Cash Flow
.2	$3,600
.3	5,000
.4	7,400
.1	9,800

   a. What is the expected cash flow?

   b. What is the expected net present value and internal rate of return?

   c. Should Debby buy the new equipment?

12. Silverado Mining Company is analyzing the purchase of two silver mines. Only one investment will be made. The Yukon mine will cost $2 million and will produce $400,000 per year in years 5 through 15 and $800,000 per year in years 16 through 25. The Labrador mine will cost $2.4 million and will produce $300,000 per year for the next 25 years. The cost of capital is 10 percent.

   a. Which investment should be made?

   b. If the Yukon mine justifies an extra 5 percent premium over the normal cost of capital because of its riskiness and relative uncertainty of flows, does the investment decision change?

13. Mr. Monty Terry, a real estate investor, is trying to decide about two potential small shopping centre purchases. His choices are the Wrigley Village and Crosley Square. The anticipated annual cash inflows from each are as follows:

Wrigley Village		Crosley Square	
Yearly Aftertax Cash Inflow	Probability	Yearly Aftertax Cash Inflow	Probability
10,000	.1	20,000	.1
30,000	.2	30,000	.3
40,000	.3	35,000	.4
50,000	.3	50,000	.2
60,000	.1		

   a. Find the expected value of the cash flow for each shopping centre.

   b. What is the coefficient of variation for each shopping centre?

   c. Which shopping centre has more risk?

14. Referring to the previous problem, Mr. Terry is likely to hold the shopping centre of his choice for 25 years and will use this period for decision-making purposes. Either shopping centre can be purchased for $300,000. Mr. Terry uses a risk-adjusted discount rate approach when evaluating investments. His scale is related to the coefficient of variation (for other types of investments, he also considers other measures).

Coefficient of Variation	Discount Rate
0–0.30	8%
0.31–0.60	11 (cost of capital)
0.61–0.90	14
Over 0.90	18

a. Compute the risk-adjusted net present value for Wrigley Village and Crosley Square using cash flow figures from the previous problem.

b. Which investment should Mr. Terry accept if the two investments are mutually exclusive? If the investments are not mutually exclusive and no capital rationing is involved, how would your decision be affected?

15. Allison's Dresswear Manufacturers is planning strategy for the fall season. One option is to expand its traditional ensemble of wool sweaters. A second option would be to enter the cashmere sweater market with a new line of high-quality designer label products. The marketing research department has determined that the wool and cashmere sweater lines offer the following probabilities of outcomes and related cash flows:

	Expanded Wool Sweaters Line		Enter Cashmere Sweaters Line	
Expected Sales	**Probability**	**Present Value of Cash Flows from Sales**	**Probability**	**Present Value of Cash Flows from Sales**
Fantastic	.2	$180,000	.4	$300,000
Moderate	.6	130,000	.2	230,000
Dismal	.2	85,000	.4	0

The initial cost to expand the wool line is $110,000. To enter the cashmere sweater line the initial cost in designs, inventory, and equipment is $125,000.

a. Diagram a complete decision tree of the possible outcomes similar to Figure 13–8. Take the analysis all the way through the process of computing expected NPV for each investment.

b. Given the analysis in part *a*, would you automatically make the investment indicated?

16. When returns from a project can be assumed to be normally distributed, such as those shown in Figure 13–6 (represented by a symmetrical, bell-shaped curve), the areas under the curve can be determined from statistical tables based on standard deviations. For example, 68.26 percent of the distribution will fall within one standard deviation of the expected value ($D \pm 1\sigma$). Similarly, 95.44 percent will fall within two standard deviations ($D \pm 2\sigma$), and so on. An abbreviated table of areas under the normal curve is shown here.

Number of σs from Expected Value	+ or −	+ and −
0.5	0.1915	0.3830
1.0	0.3413	0.6826
1.5	0.4332	0.8664
1.96	0.4750	0.9500
2.0	0.4772	0.9544

Assume Project A has an expected value of $40,000 and a standard deviation (σ) of $8,000.

a. What is the probability the outcome will be between $32,000 and $48,000?

b. What is the probability the outcome will be between $28,000 and $52,000?

c. What is the probability the outcome will be greater than $32,000?

d. What is the probability the outcome will be less than $55,680?

e. What is the probability the outcome will be less than $32,000 or greater than $52,000?

17. The Palo Alto Microchip Corporation projects a pattern of inflows from the investment shown in the following table. The inflows are spread over time to reflect delayed benefits. Each year is independent of the others.

Year 1		Year 5		Year 10	
Cash Inflow	**Probability**	**Cash Inflow**	**Probability**	**Cash Inflow**	**Probability**
50	.20	40	.25	30	.30
60	.60	60	.50	60	.40
70	.20	80	.25	90	.30

The expected value for all three years is $60.00.

a. Compute the standard deviation for each of the three years.

b. Diagram the expected values and standard deviations for each of the three years in a manner similar to Figure 13–6.

c. Assuming a 5 percent and 10 percent discount rate, complete the table for present value factors.

Year	PV_{IF} 5 Percent	PV_{IF} 10 Percent	Difference
1	0.952	0.909	0.043
5	______	______	______
10	______	______	______

d. Is the increasing risk over time, as diagrammed in part *b*, consistent with the larger differences in PV_{IFs} over time as computed in part *c*?

e. Assume the initial investment is $110. What is the net present value of the expected values of $60.00 for the investment at a 10 percent discount rate? Should the investment be accepted?

18. Gifford Western Wear makes blue jeans and cowboy shirts. It has seven manufacturing outlets in British Columbia and Alberta. It is seeking to diversify its business and lower its risk. It is examining three companies—a toy company, a boot company, and a highly exclusive jewellery store chain. Each of these companies can be bought at the same multiple of earnings. The following represents information about all the companies.

Company	Correlation with Gifford Western Wear	Sales ($ millions)	Average Earnings ($ millions)	Standard Deviation in Earnings ($ millions)
Gifford Western Wear	+1.0	$150	$10	$3
Toy Company	+.2	150	10	6
Boot Company	+.9	150	10	5
Jewellery Company	−.6	150	10	7

a. What would happen to Gifford Western Wear's portfolio risk-return if it bought Toy Company? Boot Company? Jewellery Company? Pay particular attention to the first column of correlation data.

b. If you were going to buy one company, which would you choose? Why?

c. If you wanted to buy two companies, which would you choose? Why?

19. Hooper Chemical Company, a major chemical firm that uses such raw materials as carbon and petroleum as part of its production process, is examining a plastics firm to add to its operations. Before the acquisition the normal expected outcomes for the firm were as follows:

	Outcomes ($ millions)	Probability
Recession	$20	.30
Normal economy	40	.40
Strong economy	60	.30

After the acquisition the expected outcomes for the firm would be:

	Outcomes ($ millions)	Probability
Recession	$10	.30
Normal economy	40	.40
Strong economy	80	.30

a. Compute the expected value, standard deviation, and coefficient of variation before the acquisition.

After the acquisition these values are as follows:

Expected value	43.0 ($ millions)
Standard deviation	27.2 ($ millions)
Coefficient of variation	.633

b. Comment on whether this acquisition appears desirable to you.

c. Do you think the firm's share price is likely to go up as a result of this acquisition?

d. If the firm were interested in reducing its risk exposure, which of the following three industries would you advise it to consider for an acquisition? Briefly comment on your answer.

(1) Chemical company

(2) Oil company

(3) Computer company

20. Mr. Boone is looking at a number of different types of investments for his portfolio. He identifies eight possible investments.

	Return	Risk		Return	Risk
A	10%	1.5%	E	14%	4.0%
B	11	3.0	F	14	5.0
C	13	3.5	G	15	5.5
D	13	4.0	H	17	7.0

a. Graph the data in a manner similar to Figure 13–11.

b. Draw a curved line representing the efficient frontier.

c. What two objectives do points on the efficient frontier satisfy?

d. Is there one point on the efficient frontier that is best for all investors?

COMPREHENSIVE PROBLEMS

21. Tobacco Company of Southern Ontario is a very stable billion-dollar company with sales growth of about 5 percent per year in good or bad economic conditions. Because of this stability (a correlation coefficient with the economy of +.3 and a standard deviation of sales of about 5 percent from the mean), Mr. Weed, the vice president of finance, thinks the company can absorb some small risky company that could add quite a bit of return without increasing the company's risk very much. He is trying to decide which of two companies he will buy. Tobacco Company's cost of capital is 10 percent.

Computer Whiz Company (cost $75 million)		Atlantic Micro-Technology (AMT) (cost $75 million)	
Probability	Aftertax Cash Flows for 10 Years ($ millions)	Probability	Aftertax Cash Flows for 10 Years ($ millions)
.3	$ 6	.2	$ (1)
.3	10	.2	3
.2	16	.2	10
.2	25	.3	25
		.1	31

a. What is the expected cash flow from both companies?
b. Which company has the lower coefficient of variation?
c. Compute the net present value of each company.
d. Which company would you pick based on net present values?
e. Would you change your mind if you added the risk dimensions to the problem? Explain.
f. What if Computer Whiz had a correlation coefficient with the economy of +.5 and AMT had one of −.1? Which of the companies would give you the best portfolio effects for risk reduction?
g. What might be the effect of the acquisitions on the market value of Tobacco Company's shares?

22. Ace Trucking Company is considering buying 50 new diesel trucks that are 15 percent more fuel-efficient than the ones the firm is now using. Mr. King, the president, has found that the company uses an average of 30 million litres of diesel fuel per year at a price of $0.40 per litre. If he can cut fuel consumption by 15 percent, he will save $1.8 million per year.

Mr. King assumes the price of diesel fuel is an external market force he cannot control, and any increased costs of fuel will be passed on to the shipper through higher rates. If this is true, then fuel efficiency would save more money as the price of diesel fuel rises (at $0.45 per litre, he would save $2,025,000 in total if he buys the new trucks).

Mr. King has come up with two possible forecasts as shown below—each of which he believes has about a 50 percent chance of coming true. Under assumption one, diesel prices will stay relatively low; under assumption two, diesel prices will rise considerably.

Fifty new trucks will cost Ace Trucking $5 million. They will qualify for a 30 percent CCA. The firm has a tax rate of 40 percent and a cost of capital of 11 percent.

a. First, compute the yearly expected costs of diesel fuel for both assumption one (relatively low diesel prices) and assumption two (high diesel prices) from the forecasts below.

Forecast for assumption one:

Probability (same for each year)	Price of Diesel Fuel per Litre		
	Year 1	Year 2	Year 3
.1	$.25	$.30	$.35
.2	.30	.35	.40
.3	.35	.40	.45
.2	.40	.45	.50
.2	.45	.50	.55

Forecast for assumption two:

Probability (same for each year)	Price of Diesel Fuel per Litre		
	Year 1	Year 2	Year 3
.1	$.45	$.50	$.65
.3	.50	.55	.75
.4	.65	.75	.90
.2	.75	.85	1.00

b. What will be the dollar savings in diesel expenses for each year for assumption one and for assumption two?

c. Find the increased cash flow aftertaxes for both forecasts.

d. Compute the net present value of the truck purchases for each fuel forecast assumption and the combined net present value (that is, weigh the NPVs by .5).

e. If you were Mr. King, would you go ahead with this capital investment?

f. How sensitive to fuel prices is this capital investment?

23. John Churchill, instead of taking a job with a large company on graduation, had started his own chain of muffin shops. The menu featured different varieties of freshly baked muffins, along with coffee and cookies. It also included a soup and sandwich luncheon special and some fancy pies and pastries.

The first Churchill's opened in Toronto in 1996. Because Churchill's family had owned a bakery, he had grown up in the old-style bakery business and was aware that it was a dying industry. On the other hand, his summer work for the bakery division of a large supermarket had alerted him to the potential for a muffin-based food concept. Financing for the start-up was provided from the proceeds of a mortgage his parents took out on their previously debt-free home plus $400,000 from James Henson, a local businessman who had great faith in Churchill's abilities. The outside investor's $400,000 had come in the form of $100,000 in common equity and $300,000 in 12 percent preferred shares. John Churchill, Henson, and John's father, Henry, each had a third of the voting power in the corporation. John was concerned about his parent's house being at risk.

After six years, 79 restaurants were in operation across the country, 30 owned by the company and 49 owned by franchisees. In addition, two company and four franchisee stores were under construction. The balance sheet as of December 31, 2002 is shown in Exhibit 1.

Each of the shops was built to the same specifications for exterior style and interior decor; each had seating for 30. Many customers ate their purchases in their cars or elsewhere.

The buildings were located on approximately three quarters of an acre of land and were designed with parking for 20 to 25 cars. All of the restaurants featured the same menu.

Franchisee agreements generally provided the option of operating a specified number of Churchill's outlets in a defined geographical area. Each new location required an initial payment of $20,000, while an additional royalty of 6 percent of sales was paid to corporate. Franchisees were required to spend at least 1 percent of sales on local advertising. All store

EXHIBIT 1
Balance sheet

CHURCHILL'S MUFFINS LTD.
Balance Sheet
as of December 31, 2002

Assets		
Current assets:		
Cash	$ 345	
Accounts receivable	425	
Inventory	320	
Other current assets	900	$ 1,990
Plant and equipment:		
Buildings	5,100	
Leasehold improvements	2,942	
Restaurant equipment	3,992	
Motor vehicles	498	
Office equipment	430	
Lease rights	210	
	13,172	
Less: accumulated amortization	3,450	9,722
Land	3,655	
Construction in progress	433	
Other assets	522	4,610
		$16,322
Liabilities and Shareholders' Equity		
Current liabilities:		
Notes payable to banks	$ 550	
Accounts payable	2,755	
Taxes payable	534	
Accrued liabilities	987	
Current portion, term debt	799	$ 5,625
Long-term debt, over one year		7,585
Deferred		
Income taxes	332	
Franchise fees	1,238	1,570
Shareholders' equity:		
Preferred stock	300	
Common stock	300	
Retained earnings	942	1,542
		$16,322

www.mcgrawhill.ca/college/block

managers and company trainees were required to attend a three-week training program in Toronto that covered all aspects of restaurant operations.

Churchill's was planning to start construction on another four new company-owned restaurants during 2003. Although the exact size of these had not been determined, John Churchill believed a bigger size with capacity for 50 persons versus the current 30 would be more profitable.

The company faced at least the following two choices—going with their standard units or going to the larger size. The initial cost for the four smaller shops would be $1.6 million in total, while it would be $3 million for the larger shops. Probabilities were estimated at 30 percent for high demand, 40 percent for medium demand, and 30 percent for low demand. Historically, Churchill had used a higher estimated probability of low demand for company stores than for franchisees', based on experience. The present values of the two proposals are given in Table 1.

TABLE 1
Present value of cash flows

		Outcomes (NPV)	
Restaurant Size	**Level of Demand**	**Company**	**Franchise**
	High	$1,450,000	$520,000
Standard	Medium	630,000	300,000
	Low	(200,000)	150,000
	High	3,812,000	1,040,000
Expanded	Medium	740,000	540,000
	Low	(900,000)	(150,000)

Churchill knew this decision facing the company was critical. Although the returns attached to the larger shops seemed more attractive than with the smaller shops, he wondered if the risks were justified.

24. Indigo Ltd. is faced with three investment proposals with the following information:

Project	Cost	Cash flow (10 years)	Beta
A	$200,000	$37,000	1.6
B	160,000	27,500	1.1
C	180,000	27,000	.5

The cash flow is aftertax and includes the tax savings on CCA. Indigo has a cost of capital of 10 percent, the market portfolio is expected to earn 11 percent, and the risk-free rate is 3 percent.

a. Which projects would you recommend based on analysis using the firm's cost of capital? Show your analysis.

b. Which projects would you recommend based on the individual risk of each project? Show your analysis.

25. Sam McGee, the financial analyst in the service of Labarge Ltd., is investigating the Midnight Sun project that is quite unlike any of its existing projects. It would require an initial investment of $320,000 and the probable increase in current assets by 15 percent of this initial investment. The anticipated revenues have been estimated at $90,000 a year for three years, followed by revenues of $115,000 for the remaining four years of the project's life. At end of seven years any remaining equipment would be salvaged for $25,000. Labarge Ltd. has a tax

rate of 38 percent, and the appropriate CCA rate for this capital project is 30 percent. Currently the firm has 44 percent debt and 56 percent equity in its capital structure based on market values. It plans to maintain this capital structure in the foreseeable future. The existing shareholders expect a return of 15 percent on their investment, and new debt would require a 9.53 percent yield. The market risk premium is 8 percent, and the risk-free rate is 3 percent. Sam McGee has examined the betas of firms in the Midnight Sun business, with capital structures similar to Labarge Ltd., and this has revealed an average firm beta of 1.5 for these firms.

a. Calculate the two possible discount rates to analyze the Midnight Sun project.

b. Justify the choice of one of the discount rates.

c. Should Labarge Ltd. proceed with the Midnight Sun project? Show your analysis.

d. How would analysis and decision change if the average beta determined from similar businesses was 2.0 and was based on their equity rather than the overall firm.

Selected References

Chow, George. "Portfolio Selection Based on Return, Risk, and Relative Performance." *Financial Analysts Journal* 51 (March–April 1995), pp. 54–69.

Culp, Christopher L., and Andrea M. P. Neves. "Risk Management by Securities Settlement Agents." *Journal of Applied Corporate Finance* 10 (Fall 1997), pp. 96–103.

Moore, James, Jay Culver, and Bonnie Masterman. "Risk Management for Middle Market Companies." *Journal of Applied Corporate Finance* 12 (Winter 2000), pp. 112–19.

Neyens, Andrew W., and Ruth Lane Neyens. "Decision Tree Analysis: Formalizing the Workout Decision." *Journal of Commercial Lending* 75 (September 1992), pp. 6–22.

Rusate, David A., Erroll Harris, Paul Collier, and A. John Kearney. "The Reins on Risk." *Financial Executive* 11 (July–August 1995), pp. 18–23.

Sealy, Tom. "Risk and Assessment in a New World Environment." *Journal of Lending and Credit Risk Management* 82 (June 2000), pp. 18–22.

Sick, Gordon A. "A Certainty-Equivalent Approach to Capital Budgeting Forecasts." *Financial Management* 15 (Winter 1986), pp. 22–32.

Trencher, Jeffrey W. "Risk-Adjusted Performance Measurement." *Journal of Lending and Credit Risk Management* 80 (May 1998), pp. 17–21.

Williams, Edward J. "Risk Management Comes of Age." *Journal of Commercial Lending* 77 (January 1995), pp. 17–26.

PART | FIVE

LONG-TERM FINANCING

Raising capital in an appropriate mix (capital structure) is another major consideration of finance. Understanding Canadian and international financial markets, the process of raising capital, and the features of debt and equity are important knowledge bases for the financial manager. Will the investor prefer dividends or reinvestment in the firm? Derivatives can be an exotic means to raise capital or may be used to reduce the firm's risk in volatile financial markets.

CHAPTER | FOURTEEN

14 Capital Markets

LEARNING | OBJECTIVES

1. Define money markets and capital markets.
2. Outline the primary participants raising funds in the capital markets.
3. Describe the Canadian economy as three major sectors allocating funds between themselves.
4. Outline the organization of the securities markets.
5. Discuss the concept of market efficiency and its benefits to the economic system.
6. Describe the changing financial environment.

Security markets are generally separated into short-term and long-term markets. The short-term markets are composed of government treasury bills and bonds with maturities up to three years and of other fixed income securities with maturities of one year or less. These short-term markets are referred to as **money markets**. The securities most commonly traded in these markets, treasury bills, commercial paper, bankers' acceptances, and negotiable certificates of deposit, were previously discussed under working capital in Chapter 7.

The long-term markets are called **capital markets** and consist of securities having maturities greater than one year. The most common corporate securities in this category are bonds, common stock, preferred stock, and convertible securities. These **securities** are found on the firm's balance sheet under the designation of long-term liabilities and equities. Taken together with the retained earnings, these long-term securities comprise the firm's capital structure.

In the following chapters of Part 5, we will look at how the capital markets are organized and integrated into the corporate and economic system of Canada. Increasingly, capital markets are international in scope, as suppliers of financial capital seek the best risk-return opportunities in the global economy. We will also see how corporate securities are sold by investment dealers and examine the rights, contractual obligations, and unique features of each type of security.

Competition for Funds in the Capital Markets

To put corporate securities into perspective, it is necessary to look at the other securities available in the capital markets. The federal government, provincial governments, and local municipalities all compete with one another for a limited supply of financial capital, with the capital markets serving as a way of allocating the available capital to the most efficient users. The ultimate investor chooses among many kinds of securities of differing maturities, both corporate and noncorporate. The investor generally does this so as to maximize the return for any given level of risk. Thus, the expected return from the universe of securities acts as an allocating mechanism in the markets.

The size and composition of these markets reflect the growth of our society's wealth, the changing roles of the participants within our society and the increasing role of the international capital markets. Furthermore the changes in these financial markets reveal new challenges for the management of the financial resources of the firm. Figures 14–1 and 14–2 show the size and composition of the money and bond markets in 1991 and in 2001.

If we examine the outstanding securities in the money market, in Figure 14–1, we observe the decreasing significance of Government of Canada treasury bills and the increase in other money market securities, particularly asset-backed securities. The total dollar value of outstanding securities is only slightly larger in 2001 as compared to 1991. These observations reflect the shrinking needs of the federal government as it begins to run budgetary surpluses and its shift to longer-term securities as interest rates have dropped to lows not seen in decades. For the financial manager it means that investments in short-term marketable securities will have to assume more risk with the decreasing availability of risk free treasury bills and it also suggests increased use of asset-backed securities for short term financing needs.

FIGURE 14–1

Canadian money market: securities outstanding

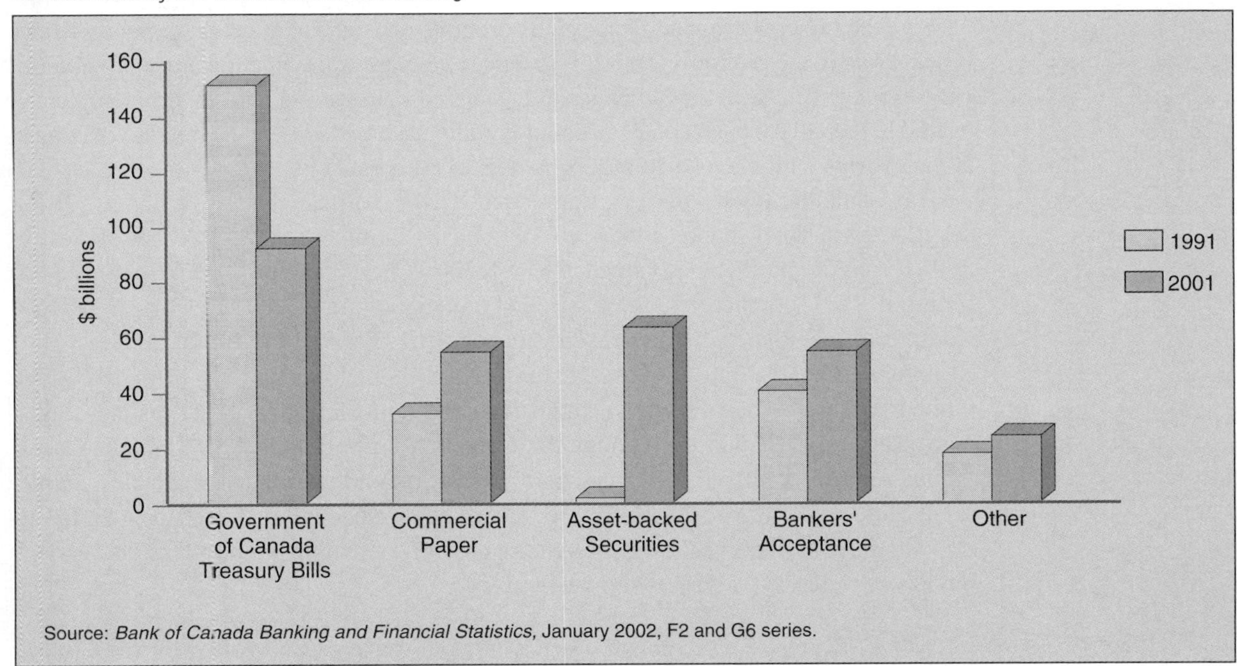

Source: *Bank of Canada Banking and Financial Statistics,* January 2002, F2 and G6 series.

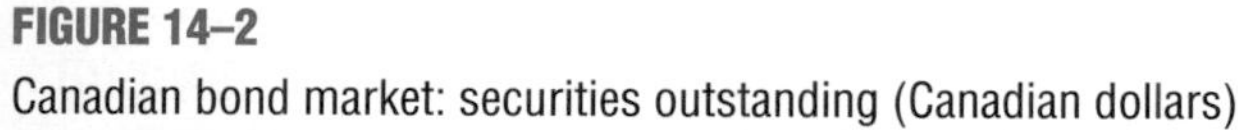

FIGURE 14–2
Canadian bond market: securities outstanding (Canadian dollars)

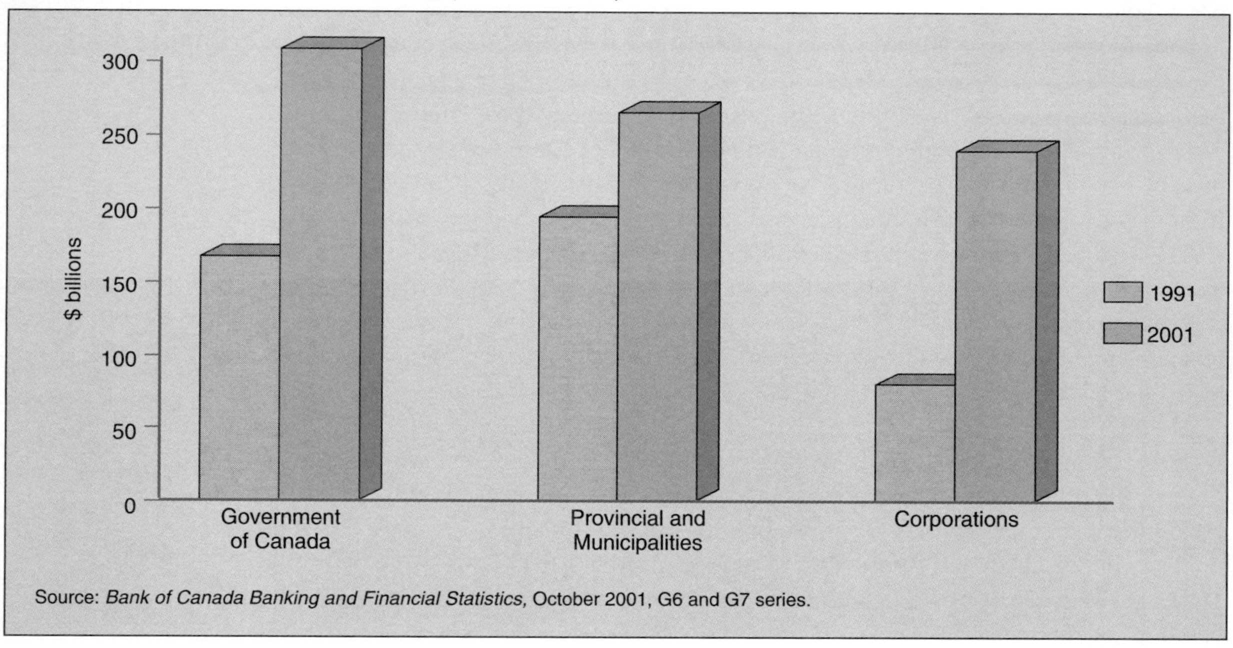

Source: *Bank of Canada Banking and Financial Statistics,* October 2001, G6 and G7 series.

The bond market, illustrated in Figure 14–2, shows a healthy increase over the last decade almost doubling in size. Although the Government of Canada bonds and provincial bonds outstanding have increased over this period it is primarily a shift from the shorter term maturities of the money markets. There had been a heavy reliance on the short-term money markets in the 1980s during a period of high inflation and high interest rates. Overall, however, the government's outstanding debt is shrinking. We should observe the rather significant increase in corporate debt as business takes on a more significant role in the economy. The shift to longer-term securities and towards corporate securities is causing structural changes in the capital markets. As less government debt is available there have been concerns about liquidity in the markets, and bondholders must come to grips with the risks of buying increased corporate obligations.

The Canadian equity market, dominated by the Toronto Stock Exchange (TSX), surpassed the bond market in size in 1999 based on the book value of securities. In 2001 the equity market was valued at $1.1 trillion,[1] growing from approximately $400 billion in 1991, compared to the domestic bond market of $779 billion. The S&P/TSX Composite Index had a market based value of $2.2 trillion at the end of 2001.

Figure 14–3 illustrates the use of capital markets beyond Canada, primarily in the United States, for raising funds. Bonds outstanding in foreign currencies are almost equivalent to Canadian obligations for Canadian corporations. The Canadian bond market represents only about 2 percent of the world bond market while the U.S. market represents about 50 percent. Therefore the Canadian financial manager must be familiar with these markets as they represent larger pools of capital, greater liquidity and often lower yields to the firm when raising funds.

[1] *Quarterly Financial Statistics of Enterprises*, Statistics Canada, Catalogue No. 61-008-X1B

Looking for Capital Abroad

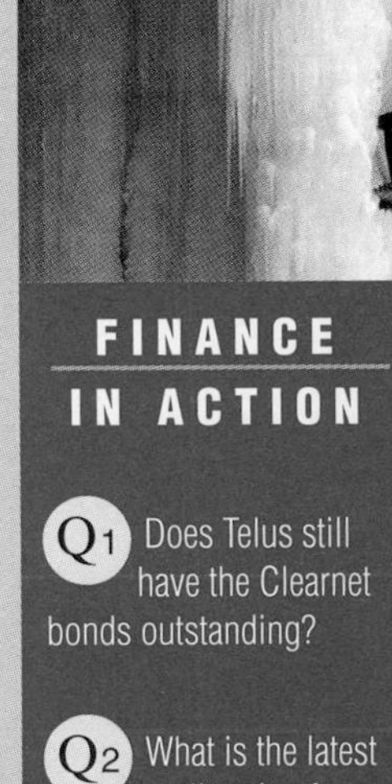

Of some concern to the Canadian capital markets is the trend for Canadian corporations to seek new capital in international markets, in particular in the United States or the Euromarket. Several Canadian firms have their common shares listed on foreign exchanges or sell debt outside of Canada in order to access larger pools of capital than are available in Canada. On a daily basis, the trades in these shares are increasingly being executed outside of Canada, particularly on the New York Stock Exchange and on Nasdaq, the U.S. market that trades shares in companies over the phone and by computer.

In October of 2000, Telus Corporation acquired Clearnet and its financial obligations. Clearnet had required capital to fund the expansion of its Canadian wireless network and for the operating cash flows to service its subscriber base. Although it had relied on its Canadian bankers for its operating lines of credit of $350 million, it sought out the U.S. capital markets to sell its high yield bonds. The bonds were sold in the United States by T.D. Securities as discount bonds for U.S.$265 million in 1999. In May 2009 the bonds would mature at U.S.$420 million. The effective yield on the bonds would be 10.125 percent, which at the time was 4.88 percent above comparable U.S. government bonds. High yield securities tend to have a less enthusiastic reception in Canada due to Canadians' greater risk aversion and the smaller pool of available high yield debt instruments.

When Telus acquired Clearnet the credit rating (available at DBRS) on these bonds improved to investment grade. With the better rating investors required a lower yield and the price of these bonds jumped dramatically.

FINANCE IN ACTION

Q1 Does Telus still have the Clearnet bonds outstanding?

Q2 What is the latest credit rating for Telus bonds?

www.telus.com

Symbol: T

www.dbrs.com

FIGURE 14–3

Canadian bonds outstanding: foreign currencies

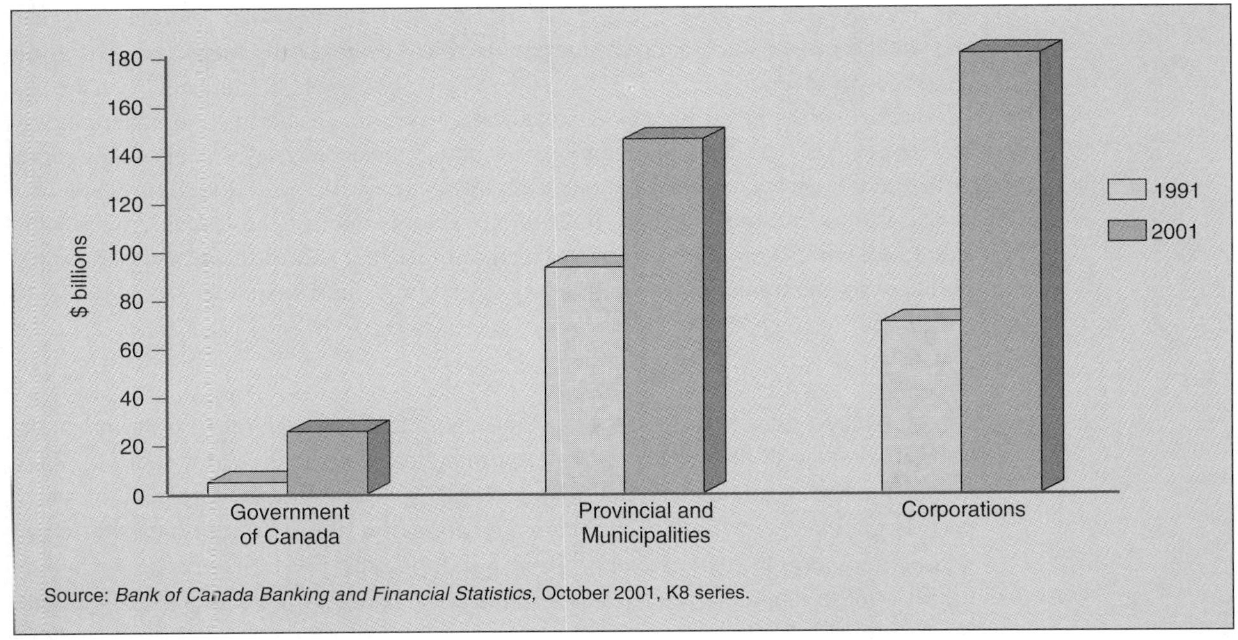

Source: *Bank of Canada Banking and Financial Statistics,* October 2001, K8 series.

Government Securities

Government of Canada Securities

In accordance with government fiscal policy, the Bank of Canada manages the federal government's debt to balance budgetary inflows and outflows. When deficits are incurred, the government can sell short-term or long-term securities to finance the shortfall.

Bank of Canada
www.bankofcanada.ca/en

After a budgetary surplus in 1973, until recently (1998), the federal government has been a significant borrower in the capital and money markets. Annual deficits continued to add to the federal debt, and by early 1997 it stood at about $588 billion. The government had to go to the bond markets at least once a month either to roll over maturing debt or to finance revenue shortfalls. Canada savings bonds, which are longer-term sources of government funding, have become less important over the years. After 1998, the move again to budget surpluses shifted government funding to the net reduction of debt outstanding.

The biweekly auction of treasury bills also plays an important role in government finances. However with the lower interest rates of the 1990s, the government has returned to a greater reliance on longer-term financing. Treasury bills outstanding have dropped by about 50 percent since 1993 and with lower availability there have been instances of liquidity problems in the money markets.

In 2001 about 19 percent of the federal debt position was held by nonresidents. The payment of interest on this nonresident-held debt is a drain of funds out of Canada. As the Government of Canada reduces the annual deficit and thus the accumulated debt its dependence on borrowing from nonresidents will also decline.

The government's demand for long-term capital also depends on the relationship between long-term and short-term interest rates. The discussion of the term structure of interest rates in Chapter 6 demonstrated the volatile nature of short-term rates. In 1979, the average term to maturity on the federal government debt exceeded 10 years, but had dropped below 4 years by 1989. However, in 2001, the average term had lengthened to over 6.5 years, as interest rates had established themselves at significantly lower levels.

The size of the government's debt causes concern for instability and uncertainty in both the money and the capital markets. As noted, the accumulated debt of the federal government reached a peak of about $588 billion in early 1997. Not all of this debt is traded in the financial markets. In 2001 marketable debt of the federal government stood at $418 billion, down from $441 billion in 1997, and of this about $38 billion was held by the Bank of Canada.

Provincial and Municipal Government Bonds

The provinces, municipalities, and crown corporations are important borrowers in the bond markets with the provinces representing about 90 percent of the total. In 2002, they had a total accumulated debt of approximately $380 billion, 38 percent, of which was denominated in foreign currencies. Historically, the provinces have borrowed mainly long term to fund capital projects, but during the 1990s they became active in the short-term market as well. Treasury bills outstanding by the end of 2001 were approximately $17 billion. Annual financing requirements exceeded $30 billion in 1993, but by 2001, a net $1 billion per year was being repaid.

As seen in Figure 14–3, the provinces, municipalities, and certain crown corporations borrow actively in the foreign markets, and in many years, foreign borrowings are larger than domestic financings. In 1993, a heavy year of borrowing, approximately 75 percent of provincial funding occurred in capital markets outside of Canada.

Bond Auctions

The Government of Canada, through its agent the Bank of Canada (www.bankofcanada.ca/en), holds auctions on a scheduled basis to sell its bonds through investment dealers into the market. These auctions allocate bonds to the dealers that offer to pay the best price. Bids are submitted electronically and in secret by 12:30 EST on the date of the auction. This is one of the ways in which the Government funds its capital requirements. The Bank of Canada (under bonds—results) gives details of the latest bond auction.

What is the average price and yield of the latest GoC bond auction?

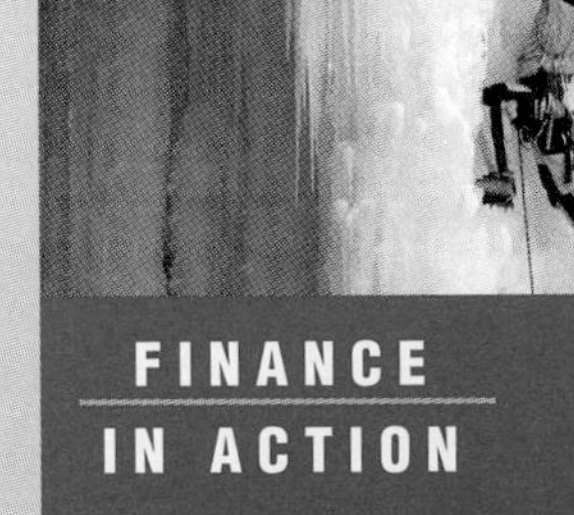

FINANCE IN ACTION

Municipal bonds comprise a small portion of the bond market. Some of these new financings occur abroad. Because most municipal debentures are relatively illiquid, they tend to be purchased mainly by institutions.

Historically, provincial and municipal bonds have been a significant component of the long-term securities market in Canada, although in recent years the federal government has become a dominant player. The provinces continue to go abroad for much of their financing needs.

Corporate Securities

Corporate Bonds

The corporate bond has been an important element of Canadian markets in the past, although the overall balance between raising new capital via stock or bond issues has been volatile, as seen in Figure 14–4. In some years bond financings dominate, while in other years equity issues are more significant. In stronger equity markets with higher share prices, management is more enthusiastic about issuing stock. The weak economy in the early 1990s is demonstrated in the lack of demand for corporate funding in general, while the weak stock market of 2001 forced corporate financings into the bond markets.

FIGURE 14–4

Net new corporate financings by type of security

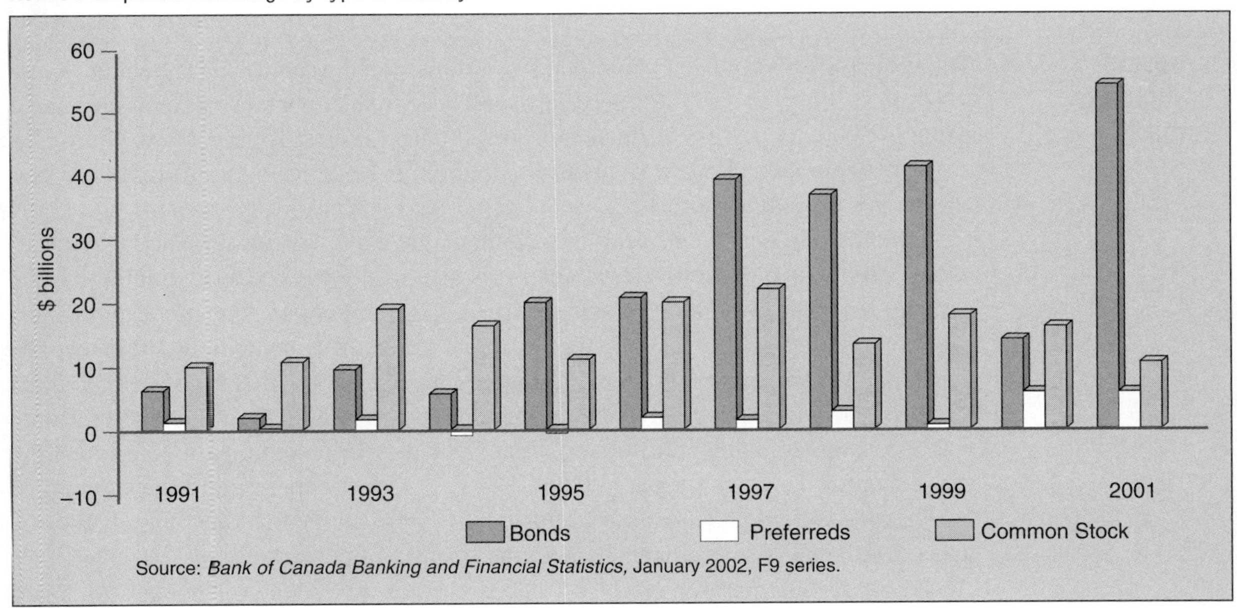

Source: *Bank of Canada Banking and Financial Statistics,* January 2002, F9 series.

Preferred Stock

Figure 14–4 shows that preferred stock is a source of corporate financing in Canada, although far less significant than bonds or common shares. Preferred stock financings have a role in balancing the capital structure of the corporation.

Preferred share funding in Canada is more significant than in the United States due to the differences in the tax treatment of corporate dividends, coupled with the use of holding companies controlling ownership of Canadian companies. In both countries, interest payments are tax deductible to a corporation, while dividends are not. In the United States dividends received are taxed at the full personal rate. Regulated public utilities, which can pass the tax disadvantage of preferred shares versus debt on to the customer, are the major issuers of preferred shares in the United States. In Canada, dividend income is generally not taxable when paid from one Canadian corporation to another. A dividend tax credit is accorded to individual investors and is examined further in Chapter 18. The tax advantage of debt over preferred share financing is thus erased in certain circumstances and is reduced in most others.

Common Stock

The sale of common stock has been significant during the 1990s, although bond financings have been somewhat higher in total value. The healthy equity financing through the 1990s was to a large extent the result of the booming stock markets. As a result equity has now surpassed debt in total value (book value) of market traded securities for Canadian corporations. However when the total long-term funding activity, including that by governments, in the Canadian capital markets is considered, common stock financing is a smaller proportion. Stock financing outside Canada has become increasingly significant and in some years represents 25 percent of new funds raised. This is a concern as it represents a threat to the Canadian capital markets by decreasing their level of activity and lowering the liquidity of financial securities.

Corporate Financing in General

The year-to-year variance in common stock versus debt issuance, as shown in Figure 14–4, is striking. In 1994, 78 percent of net new financings were done with equity, while in 2000, 77 percent of financings were by debt issues. Total net new issues also vary greatly, reaching a low of about $13 billion in 1992 during a difficult year, and almost $70 billion in 2001.

Although one must be careful in assigning simple explanations to such variations, some partial explanations are available. It is safe to say the general bumpiness of financing issues can lead a given firm to issue a large amount of debt at one point. This is often followed by a large amount of equity at the next financing in order to keep the debt-to-equity ratio in the appropriate range. This does not explain, however, general trends by the whole population of firms toward debt or equity. In the early 1990s there was a considerable downturn in new financings due to the anticipation and then the realization of a sluggish economy, but by 1993, with the increase in the economy's health, corporations again returned dramatically to the capital markets. Initially they financed with equity to take advantage of the strong equity markets.

The interesting question is why so much debt was used in the financings. We touch on this issue again in Chapter 20, but part of the reason lies in the very rationale for

FIGURE 14–5

Debt-to-equity ratios for nonfinancial private corporations

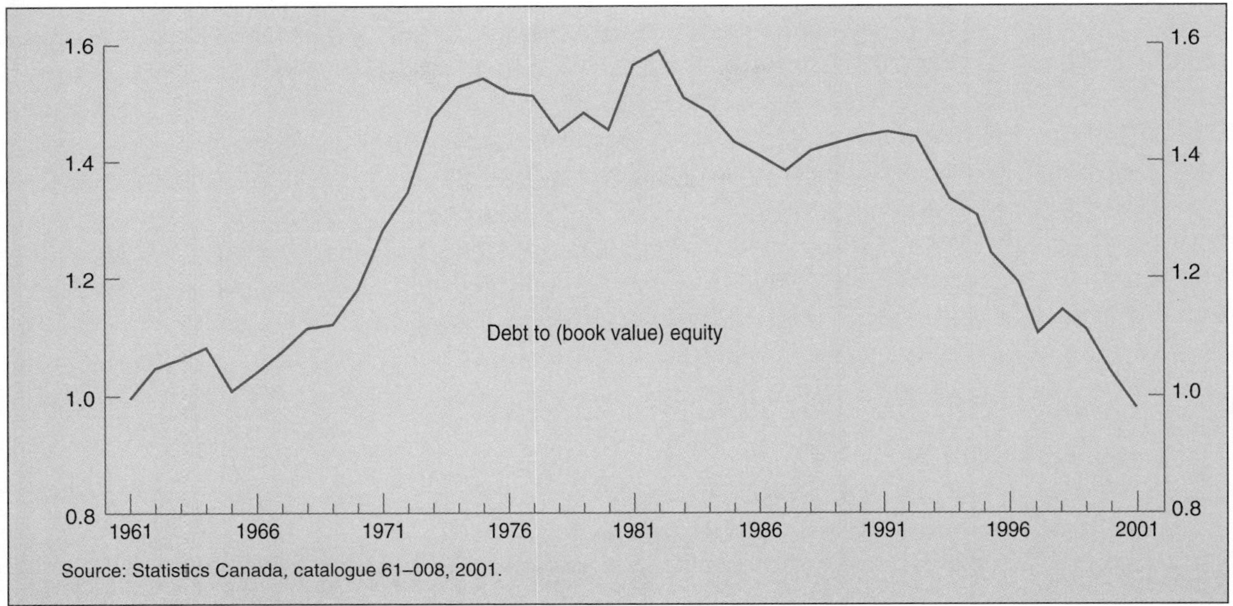

making the acquisitions in the first place. Low stock market values made managers reluctant to sell shares in their own firms even though they made them eager to buy those of other firms. Conversely, beginning in 1993 and continuing through most of the 1990s, when the stock market was assigning much higher valuations than earlier, corporate managements undertook to rebuild the corporate balance sheets by issuing equity to achieve more normal debt-to-equity ratios.

Such an explanation of debt versus equity issuance means managers attempt to time their issues of common stock. Empirical studies in the United States and in Great Britain have shown that stock issues tend to be more popular after prices have risen than after they have fallen.[2] At least two observations on this behaviour should be of interest to all serious students and/or practitioners of financial management. First, an increased market value for a firm's shares increases its capacity to incur debt, yet firms substitute equity for debt on their balance sheets at that time. Second, managers seem to believe equity is expensive when stock markets are low by historic standards (and vice versa). This implies that they have some notion of the stock market generally underpricing and overpricing equity rather than placing a rational value on it at all points in time.

Figure 14–5 is a graphic representation of debt-to-equity ratios among Canadian nonfinancial private corporations. It shows that the debt-to-book-equity ratio rose through the 1970s and 1980s, so that by 1981 it was about 1.6:1, versus 1:1 in the early 1960s. However, with the lower inflation of the 1990s and stronger equity markets, we have moved towards lower debt equity ratios, dropping below 1:1 by 2000. When

[2]R.A. Taggart, "A Model of Corporate Financing Decisions," *Journal of Finance* 32 (December 1977), pp. 1467–84; and P. Marsh, "The Choice between Equity and Debt: An Empirical Study," *Journal of Finance* 37 (March 1982), pp. 121–44.

FIGURE 14–6

Internal versus external generation of corporate funding requirements

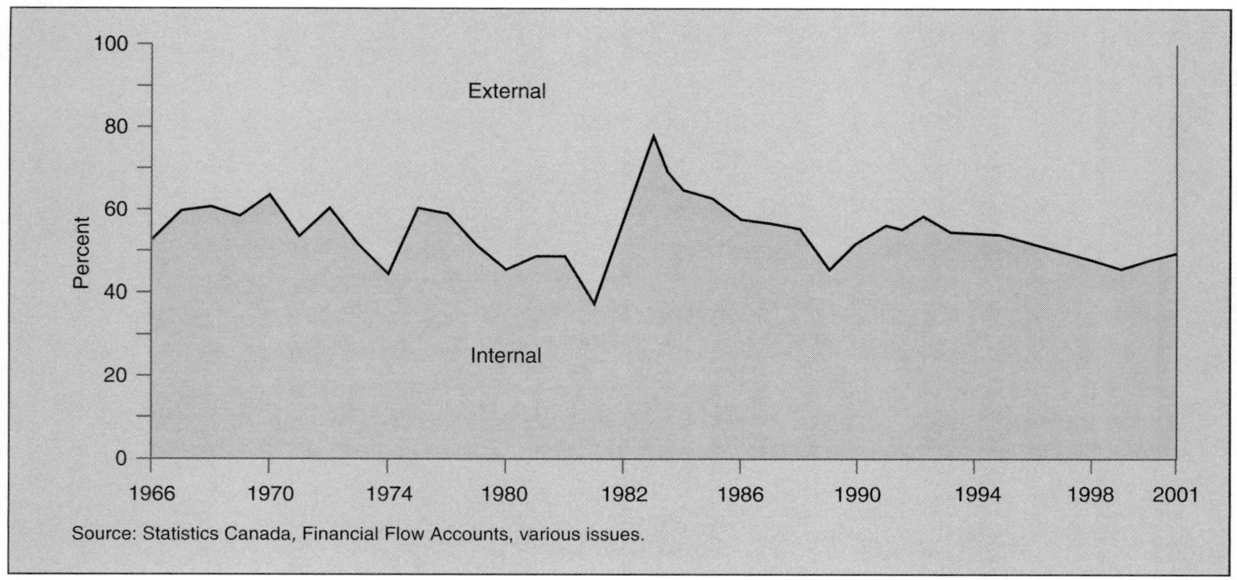

Source: Statistics Canada, Financial Flow Accounts, various issues.

some value for equity based on current value accounting is used the debt-to-equity ratio seems to be trending down from a peak reached in 1973.[3]

Internal versus External Sources of Funds

Thus far the discussion has centred on corporations raising long-term financing externally using bonds, preferred stock, and common stock. However, funds generated and retained from ongoing operations have historically been an equally important source of funds to the corporation. These internally generated funds are generally designated as retained earnings and accounting expense amounts for amortization and other noncash items. In the previous discussion of cost of capital in Chapter 11, the cost of retained earnings was considered, while Chapter 12 demonstrated how the capital budgeting decision is significantly affected by the noncash nature of amortization charges. Figure 14–6 shows the ratio of **internally generated funds** versus **externally generated corporate funds** from 1966 until 2001. Although corporations had relied primarily on internally generated funds before the mid-1960s, Figure 14–6 shows an approximate equal weighting of internal and external funding over the whole period since 1966. This demonstrates the increasing development of the capital markets. Because the inflationary spiral that began in the mid-1960s made equipment amortization amounts inadequate for the replacement investment required, one would have suspected a more dramatic shift toward external financing sources. Amortization has contributed the major share of internally generated funds, ranging as high as 97 percent in 1991 when profits were down.

[3]See Chapter 11 for a discussion of debt capacity.

FIGURE 14–7
Flow of Funds through the economy

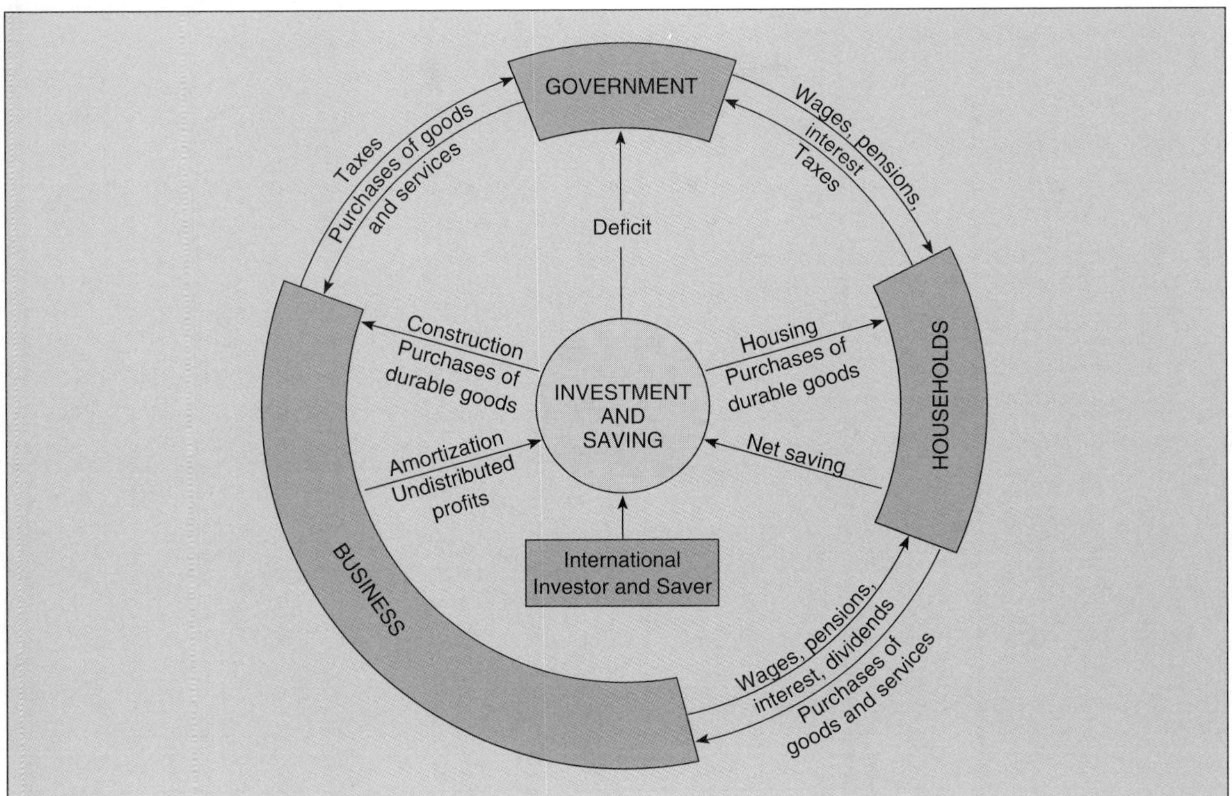

The ability to reinvest internally generated funds insulates managerial decision making to some extent from the scrutiny of objective outside analysts.[4] It is not uncommon for firms that have limited investment opportunities in traditional businesses to look elsewhere to invest internally generated funds rather than pay them out to shareholders. Although it is probably true that managers would make fewer investment decisions if they had to approach external sources for each investment, it is not clear that this would result in better investment decisions by managers. First, such a system would be awkward and costly. Second, it might require managers to make public every detail of their planned competitive strategy, which might deprive their companies of the benefits of a unique industrial initiative. The current system, whereby managers are held accountable for the outcomes of their decisions after the fact and only on an aggregated basis, is probably necessary for good management practice, although it may also allow mediocre practices to go undetected for some time. Investors cannot monitor each management decision. Since investors must trust in management's ability to choose the best options, it is extremely important to ensure that the best possible individuals occupy managerial positions.

[4]Remember, earnings could be paid out to shareholders as dividends requiring firms to raise and justify to external investors the funds for new investments.

FIGURE 14–8

Total assets of financial intermediaries

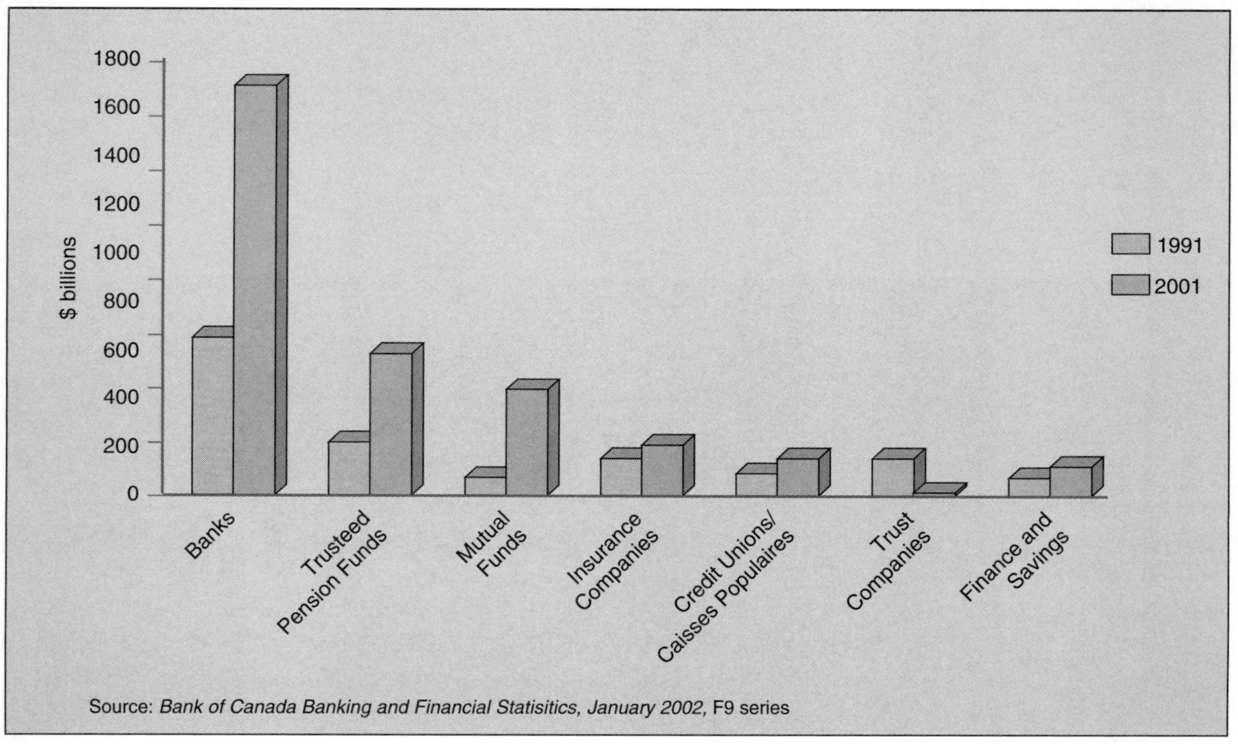

Source: *Bank of Canada Banking and Financial Statisitics, January 2002,* F9 series

The Supply of Capital Funds

In a **three-sector economy** consisting of business, government, and households, the major supplier of funds for investment is the household sector. As we have seen in a previous discussion of competition for funds, corporations and governments have traditionally been net demanders of funds. Figure 14–7, on page 515, diagrams the flow of funds through our basic three-sector economy.

As households receive wages and transfer payments from the government and wages and dividends from corporations, they generally save some portion of their income. A well-developed financial system will facilitate the funnelling of these savings to the most efficient users or borrowers of funds. This transfer of funds from savers to borrowers can be accomplished directly by investing in the capital markets. Alternatively, a saver of funds can invest with a financial intermediary, or middleperson, that in turn invests the collected pool of funds from many investors in the capital markets. This is known as indirect investment.

The types of **financial intermediaries** that channel funds into the capital markets are specialized and diverse. The major intermediaries and their total assets are seen in Figure 14–8. Although the banks dominate the other intermediaries, increasingly pension and mutual funds play a vital and growing role in the capital markets. These financial intermediaries help make the flow of funds from one sector of the economy to another very efficient and competitive. They are able to assemble vast pools of funds and, through risk management techniques such as diversification and hedging, reduce risk. Also, because they can generate economies of scale, the cost of funds is lowered,

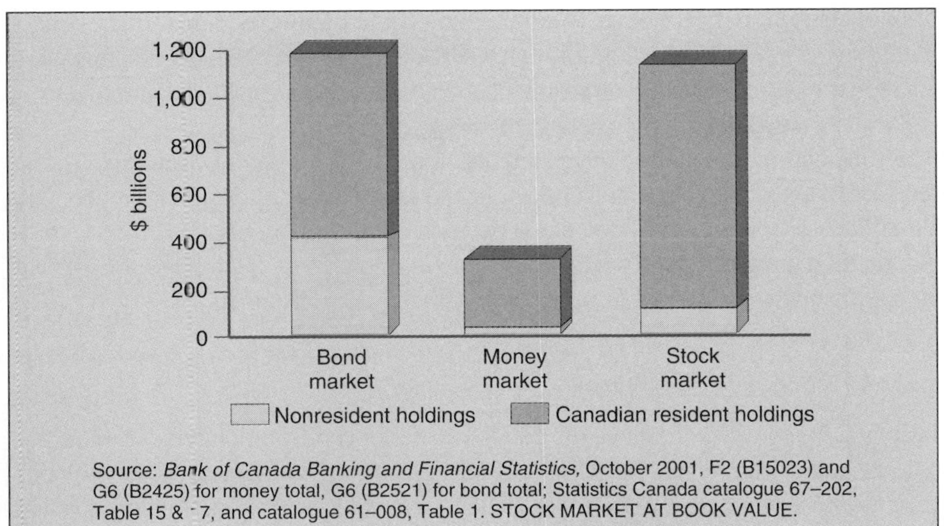

FIGURE 14–9
Nonresident holdings of Canadian securities, 2001

FIGURE 14–10
Secondary market: daily trading averages

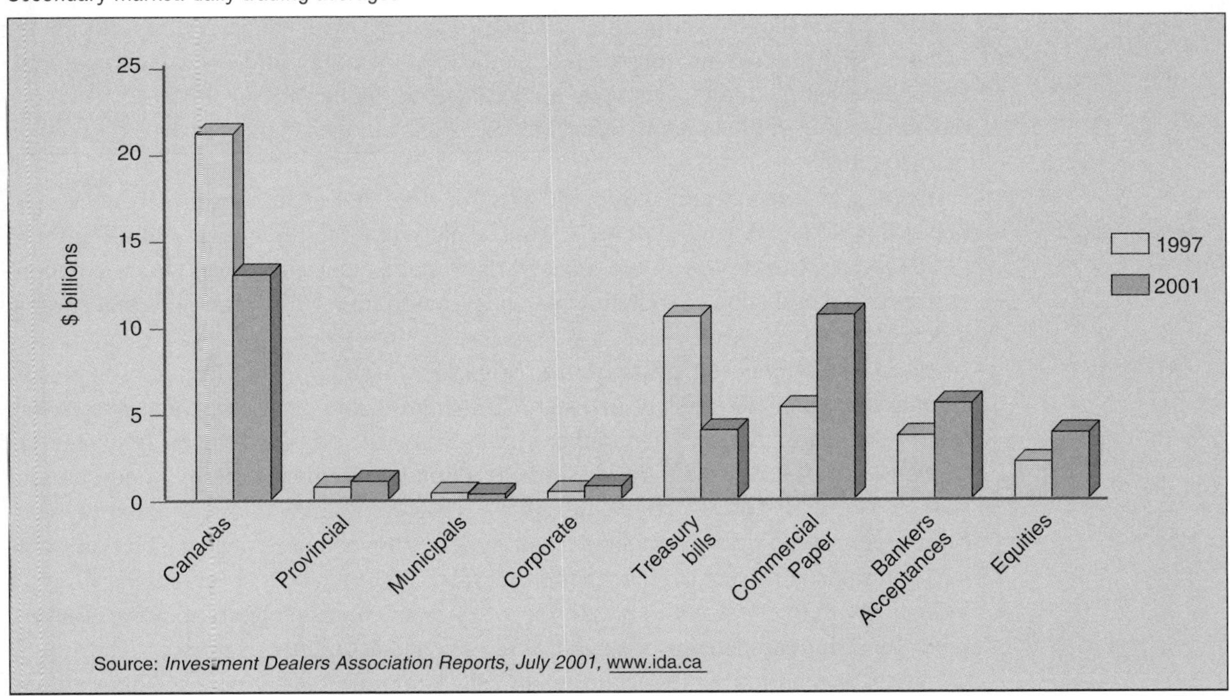

and the efficient allocation of funds to the best users is accomplished at the lowest cost. The international saver and investor has become a critical supplier of funds to the Canadian capital markets. At the end of 2000, nonresidents had supplied over $1,023 billion of investment to Canada. Although Canadians supplied funds to the international markets, Canada's net international investment position was a negative $244 billion by the end of 2000. This position is improving. Figure 14–9 shows the portion of outstanding capital market obligations held by nonresidents. Interestingly, Canadians held over $177 billion in foreign stocks, over twice what nonresidents hold of Canadian stocks. However, nonresidents held $381 billion in Canadian bonds versus $35 billion of foreign bonds held by Canadians.

The financial intermediary is very important in this three-sector economy. The intermediary is a key element in the allocation and reallocation of capital. Our economy could not possibly have developed to the extent that it has without this ability to move vast sums of capital efficiently. The ability to get a loan or to have numerous investment options is the product of a sophisticated financial environment.

The Role of the Security Markets

Security markets exist to facilitate the direct transfer of capital among households, corporations, and governments. Initially, securities or financial claims are issued by borrowers to raise funds, and these securities are sold in the capital markets. If well-developed securities or secondary markets are not available, the initial sale of securities will be made more difficult. The capital markets are generally divided into the money, bond, and stock markets, with each market offering a certain type of security. The daily volume of trading in each of these markets is shown in Figure 14–10, on page 517. We should contrast the volume of trading with the actual amount dollar value of securities outstanding in each market as shown in Figure 14–9. Although trading volumes in the money and bond markets are far greater than in the equity markets, the outstanding value of equity securities exceeds both these other markets if based on market value.

Trading volumes declined through 2001 for a number of reasons. Weak stock markets reduced the willingness of investors to participate in the markets, the supply of fixed income securities declined particularly from the government perspective, and investors in general adopted more passive index-based investment strategies that suggest less trading.

After a security is sold initially as an original offering, it then trades in its appropriate market among all kinds of investors. This trading activity is known as **secondary trading** since funds flow only among investors and the original borrower gets no further funds when these securities are traded. Secondary trading is vitally important as it provides liquidity for investors and keeps prices competitive among alternative security investments. Furthermore, it is because a well-developed secondary market exists that securities are easier to issue in the first place.

Security markets provide liquidity in two ways. They enable corporations to raise funds by selling new issues of securities rapidly and at competitive prices. They allow the investor who purchases securities to sell them with relative ease and speed and thereby to turn a paper asset into cash at will. Ask yourself the question, "Would I buy securities if there were no place to sell them?" You would probably think twice before committing funds to an illiquid investment. It follows that without markets, corporations and governmental units would not be able to raise the large amounts of capital necessary for economic growth. Therefore, the presence and efficient management of security markets in Canada is vitally important to individuals, corporations, and governments alike.

The Organization of the Security Markets

The competitive structure and organization of the security markets have and will continue to change considerably. In this section we present the current organization of the markets and provide an update of significant events of the last few years. The most common division of security markets is between organized exchanges and over-the-counter markets. Each is examined separately.

The Organized Exchanges

An organized stock exchange is a marketplace where buyers and sellers of securities come together to trade securities. This trading is undertaken through an investment dealer that has a "seat" on the exchange. Prices on an exchange are established competitively according to conditions of supply and demand. It is important that an organized or "auction" exchange allow for a bidding process to establish fair prices and that this process be transparent to investors. Transparency requires that investors are aware of pricing and trading volumes on a timely basis. Canadian exchanges facilitate the trading of common and preferred shares, rights and warrants, listed options, financial instrument futures, and some commodities.

Organized exchanges are either regional or national. Each exchange has a central location where all buyers and sellers meet in an auction market to transact purchases and sales. Buyers and sellers are not actually present on the floor of the exchange, but are represented by brokers who act as their agents. These brokers are registered members of the exchange by virtue of having purchased one or more seats on the particular exchange.

Each exchange has its own governing body whose job it is to do the administration and policy-setting for the stock exchange. Each governing body is made up of permanent officers of the exchange, members of the brokerage community, and individuals representing the community outside of the brokerage industry.

Toronto Stock Exchange
www.tsx.ca

Until the 1990s there were five stock exchanges in Canada, located in Montreal, Toronto, Winnipeg, Calgary, and Vancouver. Today stock trading takes place through the **Toronto Stock Exchange (TSX)** for senior securities and through the TSX Venture Exchange, owned by the TSX, for junior securities. The Montreal Exchange (ME) now specializes in derivative securities, which will be examined in Chapter 19. At the end of 2001, over 120 firms were represented on the Toronto Stock Exchange, the largest exchange in Canada and second to the New York Stock Exchange in North America. To trade securities a firm must purchase a seat on the exchange. The price of a seat on the Toronto Stock Exchange peaked at $370,000 in 1987, but had fallen to about $50,000 in the late 1990s.

The Toronto Stock Exchange (TSX) accounts for over 95 percent of the dollar volume of trading in listed stocks in Canada. There are over 1,400 companies listed on the TSX, with a total quoted market value of over $2 trillion. The TSX Venture Exchange has over 2,600 firms listed but their market values are considerably lower and trading volumes dropped off dramatically in 2001. This has caused some liquidity concerns.

Foreign Exchanges

As the industrialized world has grown, capital markets around the globe have increased in size and importance. As a result, many Canadian international companies have listed their shares on more than one exchange outside the country, just as many

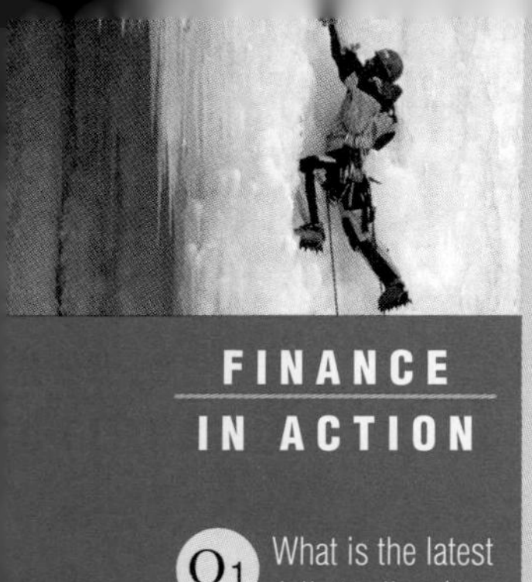

FINANCE IN ACTION

Moving to the "Show"

Q1 What is the latest daily trading $ value for the TSX Venture Exchange?

The TSX Venture Exchange is Canada's junior equity market. It assists smaller firms in accessing capital through public offerings of securities and in 2001 helped to place over $1 billion in new equity placements. By providing a secondary market where continual trading in these junior securities can take place, the Venture Exchange assists in capital formation within Canada.

In 2001 twenty-six companies moved from the TSX Venture Exchange to the senior TSX. As they gained more experience with being a public company and their financial positions improved these firms wanted to move to an exchange that offered greater liquidity and more prestige. The TSX Venture Exchange provides information on the requirements to go public as Tier 1 and Tier 2 companies.

www.tse-cdnx.com and www.tsx.ca

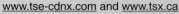

foreign companies have listed their shares on Canada's exchanges. BCE, for instance, is listed on the New York, London, and Swiss exchanges. Many global companies such as Sony and DaimlerChrysler are listed on the TSX.

New York Stock Exchange www.nyse.com
NASDAQ www.nasdaq.com

Canadian-based companies are primarily interlisted on U.S. exchanges with over 200 companies interlisted in both Canada and the United States. Canadian companies listed on the TSX and one of the New York, American, or Nasdaq exchanges are seeing almost 50 percent of their daily volume in trades come from those exchanges. The New York Stock Exchange (NYSE) is the largest in the world by dollar volume, followed by NASDAQ, the London Stock Exchange, and the Japanese (Nikkei) Stock Exchange. The Toronto Stock Exchange ranks twelfth in the world in daily trading volumes.

Table 14–1 lists the major global stock markets by country, alphabetically. Not all are large, but most are flourishing, with growing volume, new listings, and increased interest by investors worldwide. By capitalized market value, the United States represented over 45 percent of the world's capital markets, followed by Japan and the United Kingdom with over 10 percent each. Canada's capital markets represented less than 2 percent of the world's capital markets.

TABLE 14–1
Global stock markets

Australia	Germany	Norway
Austria	Hong Kong	Singapore/Malaysia
Belgium	Italy	Spain
Brazil	Japan	Sweden
Canada	Korea	Switzerland
Denmark	Mexico	United Kingdom
France	Netherlands	United States

Chicago Mercantile Exchange www.cme.com

As more companies have their common stock listed on exchanges around the world, the easier it will be for trading to be continuous for 24 hours per day. Several exchanges have already linked their trading floors so that trading can be maintained at all hours of the day. For example, the Chicago Mercantile Exchange, which specializes in metals, foreign exchange currencies, and interest rate futures contracts, has instituted 24-hour computer trading by linking with Reuters Holding PLC. This system, called Globex, enables customers around the world to trade financial futures products when

Listing requirements

For the shares of a corporation to be traded on an exchange, the corporation must meet certain requirements and be accepted by the board of governors of the exchange. The listing requirements differ from exchange to exchange. Generally, the more senior an exchange, tougher listing requirements are imposed and the exchange becomes more stringent on the disclosure of "material" information. These disclosure requirements impose greater reporting costs on the firm in addition to higher listing and maintenance fees required by the exchange.

Corporations desiring to be listed on exchanges have decided that public availability of the stock on an exchange benefits their shareholders. The benefits occur either by providing liquidity to owners or by allowing the company a more viable means for raising external capital for growth and expansion. In return, the company must disclose information about the company and any proposed transactions in a timely manner.

The exchanges have the authority to withdraw a listed security's trading or listing privileges either temporarily or permanently. Such actions would be taken to protect the interests of the investors or at the request of the company in respect to its own securities.

FINANCE IN ACTION

Q1 Compare the listing requirements on three exchanges.

Q2 Compare the listing fees on three exchanges.

www.tse-cdnx.com

www.tsx.ca

www.nyse.com

www.nasdaq.com

their own exchange is closed. The TSX is joining with the NYSE, Euronext (Paris, Brussels, Amsterdam), Tokyo, Hong Kong, Australia, Mexico, and Brazil to create 24-hour equity trading through a Global Equity Market (GEM).

The Over-the-Counter Markets

Investment dealers maintain large inventories of securities and facilitate trading activity in the **over-the-counter (OTC) market**, a market where securities are not listed on the exchange. There is no central location for the OTC market; instead, a network of brokers and dealers is linked by computer display terminals, telephones, and teletypes. While the organized exchanges trade by auction, the OTC market carries out trading by negotiation.

Many **dealers** who act on their own account, and **brokers**, who act as agents, make markets in the same security and thus create prices on the active stocks. With the advent of a centralized computer to keep track of all trades and prices, potential traders have up-to-the-minute price information on all competing traders. The Canadian Dealing Network (CDN) is Canada's over-the-counter market and is owned by the TSX.

According to the Investment Dealers Association, the overall OTC market in North America involves over 50,000 stocks and 14,000 bonds. Although the shares of a few conservative industrial companies trade over the counter, the average price of securities traded is lower, making the dollar volume traded much less than that of the organized exchanges. Since 1969 Quebec brokers have been required to report statistics on unlisted trading in Quebec to the Quebec Securities Commission. Since 1970 the Investment Dealers Association and the Ontario Securities Commission have operated a reporting system for designated unlisted industrial stocks.

In contrast to the Canadian situation where very few stocks trading over the counter could obtain listing on the TSX, many large companies are trading over the counter in

National Association of Securities Dealers
www.nasd.com

the United States. Such well-known companies as Apple Computer, MCI Communications, and Intel are included in that group. The National Association of Securities Dealers in the United States estimates that at least 600 of the over-the-counter stocks would meet the very stringent listing requirements of the New York Stock Exchange (NYSE).

Historically, trading in bonds and debentures in Canada has occurred in the OTC market. This market has traditionally been somewhat reluctant to reveal all of the trades that take place between dealers. The Bank of Canada and the Investment Dealers Association have been working on a plan that will require all trades and prices to be reported to a service called CanPx. This will allow these markets to become more transparent to investors. The best prices for bonds and Treasury bills would be displayed for any investor.

Recent Developments in Trading

The Canadian capital markets face several challenges in the immediate future. In raising capital, corporations seek the most competitive market to ensure the least expensive sources of capital. That often meant looking beyond Canada's borders, often to the capital markets of the United States. Well-functioning capital markets require secondary markets with good trading volumes to ensure that prices are fair and reliable. To address this threat from U.S. markets the Canadian markets have coordinated their efforts and have specialized. The TSX as the senior equities exchange is seeking links with other global markets to allow 24-hour trading and is considering trading interlisted stocks in both Canadian and U.S. dollars. The TSX will also become a public traded company itself in 2002.

Another threat to the Canadian exchanges is common share trading that takes place in the "upstairs rooms" of the investment dealers or through alternative trading systems that make use of the Internet. The "upstairs rooms" of investment dealers refers to the practice of dealers matching large trades in shares between institutional investors through their own trading floors, without first putting the trade to open cry and competition through the stock exchange. The Internet enabled trading to occur with insignificant brokerage fees compared to the traditional fees. The concern with these challenges is that the Canadian stock exchanges may become irrelevant in the execution of trading and the pricing of securities. This will weaken their regulatory role and their function of providing efficient markets with fair prices.

The TSX has announced plans to establish an electronic call market for the Canadian markets to counteract "upstairs trading." With this system, institutional investors would be able to trade blocks of shares, and possibly fixed income products through a computer that would match buy and sell orders. All orders through this system would go on the TSX's books to receive the best available prices. Fortunately the TSX has replaced its outdated **Computer Assisted Trading System (CATS)** that in recent years had several breakdowns, which prevented the efficient execution of trades. The TSX is now fully automated for equity trading, with floor trading closed in April 1997. Bidding by open cry of quotes has disappeared.

In 1986, a system called Canadian Over-the-Counter Automated Trading System (COATS) was introduced by the Ontario Securities Commission for trading unlisted stocks. By 1991 the Canadian Dealing Network (CDN) was established to ensure quality reporting and quotation in the OTC market.

In comparison to the New York markets, the secondary markets in Canada are thin, with few buyers and sellers. This condition makes it difficult to carry out large transactions without a significant price effect. While the Canadian equities market has consisted almost entirely of exchange-listed stocks, New York has a large over-the-counter market as well as a third market that occurs among the dealers outside of the exchanges. Even in exchange trading on the NYSE, dealers play a much larger role, acting as specialists who make markets in given stocks. All of this has historically meant that a seller would have to give up the stock at a lower price, on the TSE versus the NYSE, to make it marketable. The extremely liquid markets in the United States have tended to attract business away from Canadian markets. To reduce this relatively higher price of liquidity, the Toronto Stock Exchange has been urging a larger role for dealers acting as principals rather than brokers in stock trading.

It is probably safe to say that over the next decade securities markets will become more competitive as computer systems are employed to do more and more of the trading and as innovations are found to make the secondary markets more liquid.

Market Efficiency

This chapter has discussed the capital markets that allocate monies from those who save to those who borrow. Capital is employed to increase the productive capacity and thus the wealth of our society. It has been suggested that competitive and efficient markets accomplish this beneficial allocation of capital. However, we have not yet given criteria to judge whether the Canadian securities markets are competitive and efficient markets. **Efficient markets** allocate capital to its best use without undue costs. The best use of capital as defined by finance refers to its commitment to investments from which we expect to achieve the highest returns based on a given amount of risk. Returns from an investment are generated from its cash flows, and the market's expectations for those cash flows are derived from the market's knowledge about the investment.

In a well-functioning capital market, monies will move quickly into investments that promise superior returns, and those investments will rise in price. As the price of an investment rises its expected return will diminish. We explored this concept in Part 4, the Capital Budgeting Process. Capital will continue to move into an investment and its price will continue to rise until a balance is achieved between the price paid for an investment and the returns that the investment is expected to generate. That balance is achieved when investors perceive a fair return is offered based on the known facts about an investment's expected risks and returns. Therefore, the wide availability of relevant information about an investment's risks and expected returns, upon which investors can base their buying and selling decisions, is essential to an efficient market. Those decisions determine price! Within a risk-return framework such as the CAPM, market efficiency gives rationality to the pricing mechanism of our markets. We could say that all we need to know about an investment in an efficient market is already included in the current price.

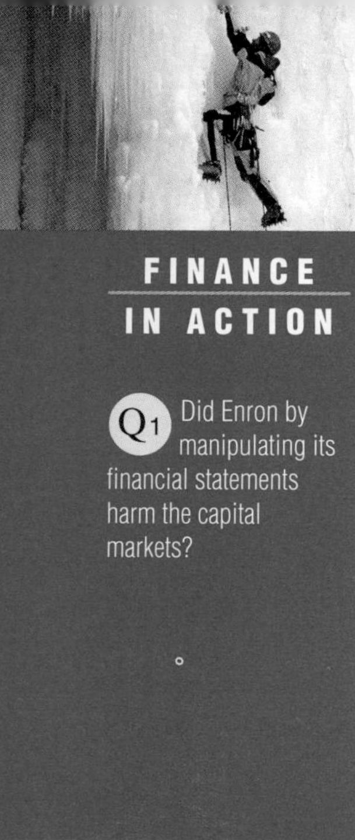

FINANCE IN ACTION

Enronitis

Q1 Did Enron by manipulating its financial statements harm the capital markets?

www.enron.com

In little over a decade, Enron became the seventh largest company in the United States. In the end, it dealt to a large degree in derivatives (discussed in Chapter 19) based on the deregulated energy market. Then within a few months, towards the end of 2001, it became the largest bankruptcy in American history.

One of the results of Enron's crash and burn was investor concern for the "truth" in published financial statements. Apparently Enron did not disclose the full extent of its liabilities when entering into highly leveraged partnership deals. These statements had been signed off by accounting firms, but were now being called into question. The concern was that many firms and their accountants were aggressively interpreting the rules of disclosure in reporting their financial results.

IBM for example reported the sale of a division as selling, general, and administration expense. This produced no difference in earnings, but by not reporting this sale as a separate line it made IBM's operating profit look significantly better. The market reacted by dropping the price of IBM shares. General Electric, the world's largest company, suffered the same result when the public learned that through 26 business units that were not reported separately, General Electric had been for years "massaging" its earnings.

Investors began to question the integrity of financial statements. This would suggest that all information that could be known was not available to the investing public, despite a system of regulatory safeguards. This would allow market inefficiencies to develop and then investing would no longer be a fair game. The concern is that investors have lost some faith in the proper functioning of the capital markets and will be less willing to invest. This will slow capital formation and the pace of economic activity.

Criteria of Efficiency

There are several concepts of market efficiency, and there are many degrees of efficiency, depending on which market we are discussing. Markets in general are efficient when: (1) prices adjust rapidly to new information; (2) there is a continuous market in which each successive trade is made at a price close to the previous price (the faster the price responds to new information and the smaller the differences in price changes, the more efficient the market); and (3) the market can absorb large dollar amounts of securities without destabilizing the price. The New York Stock Exchange is the world's most efficient capital market on these criteria, while the Toronto Stock Exchange also appears quite efficient. Let us examine the TSX on these criteria.

During the late 1990s and into the 2000, the technology market as exemplified by the NASDAQ soared to staggering heights. Firm values rose and many individuals became wealthy based on their stock market investments. However during 2001, the technology markets plunged with many top-rated stocks, such as Nortel, dropping 90 percent in value. Although many would argue that a "bubble" and speculative mentality had been at play in the markets, to a large extent the markets were reacting to the weakening economy. The technology industry in some instances was growing at 60 percent a year, but in 2001 there was no more growth to be had for the foreseeable future. Our earlier discussions on the valuation of securities suggested that the market set the current price of a security by the discounting of future expected cash flows. With dramatically decreased profit expectations for companies, investors reduced the present value of expected future cash flows from their equity investments and responded accordingly by selling shares. This new information was quickly reflected in the value of the securities on the exchanges.

Do Mutual Funds Achieve Superior Returns?

FINANCE IN ACTION

If the markets are not efficient in so much as they do not fully incorporate all available information into share prices in a timely manner, it is possible that those who are "in the know" can exploit the market's inefficiency. This would mean that by developing a trading strategy based on patterns of stock return predictability, an investor should be able to "beat the market." Who would be more in the know than the managers of mutual funds? It is their task to uncover private information by which they can readjust the portfolio of stocks in a mutual fund to take advantage of this new knowledge before the rest of the market.

In a study in 1968, Michael Jensen concluded that mutual funds, after expenses, did worse than randomly selected portfolios of stocks. However, there was some evidence in the 1980s from various studies that some mutual funds did achieve superior returns. However, in a recent study that spanned the period 1971 to 1991, Burton G. Malkiel reports in the *Journal of Finance* that mutual funds underperformed the market. His conclusion, based on U.S. markets, was that an investor could do best by purchasing a mutual fund with low management fees and that only invested in a basket of stocks such as S&P/TSX Composite Index. This index fund would do better than a fund that is actively managed. The active manager who trades back and forth between different sectors of the market would probably achieve returns less than the index, would generate excess transaction fees, and would trigger more tax burden for the investor.

Source: *Journal of Finance* (June 1995), pp. 549–72.

If we examine the Toronto Stock Exchange during the 1990s, we find that almost 99 percent of all the volume traded is within five cents of its previous trade. This until recently was the smallest allowed change in the price of securities listed on the exchange. These small price changes suggest a deep, continuous market and one that is reasonably efficient. Prices are now based on one cent increments.

On the other hand, we have seen instances where a large buyer of securities has significantly moved the values on the Toronto market, which has had a destabilizing effect. This has occurred because of the size of the transaction in relation to the total volume of the entire market. The impact of a large buy order is much more prevalent in the Toronto market as compared to one in the much larger New York market. This indicates market inefficiency.

Markets are more efficient as certain characteristics become more in evidence. These characteristics serve to improve the quality of information available to investors. In efficient markets there are many buyers and sellers of securities making numerous trades that reflect their perceptions of new information, as it becomes available. This level of activity creates liquidity in the market. Efficient markets also have a great deal of analysis performed and published on the securities that are traded. Thus, more information becomes available to be reflected in the price of securities. Furthermore, an efficient market is well regulated with high standards for the disclosure of information to ensure that all market participants have the same information available to them at the same time.

A key variable affecting efficiency is the certainty of the income stream. As price movements are less volatile with more certain income streams, investors are more willing to purchase the securities. Fixed-income securities, with known maturities, have reasonably efficient markets. The most efficient market is that for Government of Canada securities. The vast majority of trades in the bond market are with Government of Canada bonds, and in the money markets it is Government of Canada treasury bills. This is changing as the government retires more of these securities. Corporate bond markets are somewhat efficient, but less so than government bond markets. A question still widely debated and researched by academics is whether markets for common stock are truly efficient.

The Efficient Market Hypothesis

Eugene Fama
http://gsb.uchicago.edu/tac/eugene.fama/

If stock markets are efficient, it is very difficult for investors to select portfolios of common stocks that can outperform the stock market in general. That is because all relevant and available information would already be reflected in the stock prices. Share prices move up and down quickly as new information is learned. In the terminology of capital budgeting, purchases and sales of stocks in an efficient market are zero-NPV transactions. An investor receives only the going return for an investment based on its risk. The investor does not receive an abnormal return. An **abnormal return** would be a return above (or below) what the capital market suggests is fair for the risk of an investment. Furthermore, in an efficient market, since all relevant information is reflected in security prices, the same investor has no need to pay for expensive information.

This concept of market efficiency is called the efficient market hypothesis, and it has been stated in three forms, which have been designated the weak, semistrong, and strong forms. The efficient market hypothesis was developed after research suggested that the markets followed a random walk. Researchers had been seeking to discover cycles in stock market movements, but were unable to find any patterns. A random walk is the noncorrelation of future price movements with past price movements. It is what we should expect from efficient markets where new information is rapidly reflected in prices and new information arrives randomly. New information must arrive randomly, as it cannot be known ahead of time. The three forms of market efficiency are grades as to the degree of market efficiency. All three forms refer to the nature of information that is included in the price of a security.

The first level of efficiency, the **weak form** simply states that prices reflect all of the information contained in the past price history. This implies that past price information is unrelated to future prices, so attempting to extrapolate trends generates no additional gains to investors. This noncorrelation of future price movements with past price movements has been referred to as a random walk and has received much empirical validation. Despite such empirical validation of the random walk theory of stock price movements, some analysts chart past price movements in the belief that the patterns suggest future price movements. These people are known as technical analysts.

The second level of efficiency is the **semistrong form.** It states that prices reflect all public information, such as announcements of company earnings forecasts. Most of the research in this area focuses on changes in public information and on the measurement of how rapidly prices converge to a new equilibrium after the release of new information.[5] This research has concluded that this information is rapidly reflected in the stock price.

A third level of efficiency, the **strong form**, states that all information, both private and public, is immediately reflected in stock prices. Under this form of market effi-

---

[5]See, for example, G. Mandelker, "Risk and Return: The Case of Merging Firms," *Journal of Financial Economics* 1 (December 1974), pp. 303–35; and G. Charest, "Returns to Dividend Splitting Stocks on the Toronto Stock Exchange," *Journal of Business Administration* 12 (Fall 1980), pp. 1–18.

Be Careful What You Say and How You Say It!

In late 2001, product markets in the technology sector had "virtually" disappeared. The stock markets were nervous and any apparent information that was discouraging was enough to send stock prices lower. The market was beginning to look for signs of recovery but was jittery.

One of the obligations of a publicly traded company is that it must disclose any material changes in its prospects. This usually involves a press release or a public conference, more often being done over the Internet.

In November 2001, the president of Wire One Technologies Inc. held a conference call to discuss the company's videoconferencing abilities. He stated that interest in Wire One's products had been "piqued." Those listening, without their dictionaries, thought they heard peaked and thinking the business was headed downward sold off the stock. It dropped 21 percent that day. The share price of Wire One was approximately U.S.$6.50 at the time of the conference call.

FINANCE IN ACTION

Q1 What is Wire One's current share price?

www.wireone.com

Symbol: WONE

ciency, efficient markets should prevent insiders and large institutions from being able to make profits in excess of the market in general. A number of analyses of the portfolio performance of mutual fund managers have shown that this group of investors does no better than the market as a whole. Other research on the buying patterns of insiders has tended to show that strong form market efficiency does not exist.

Much research in recent years had focused on the measurement of market efficiency. Researchers have generally accepted that markets such as the New York Stock Exchange and, to a lesser extent, the Toronto Stock Exchange are efficient. They search for abnormalities where some sort of trading rule or market strategy can consistently earn an investor above-normal profits. When these inefficiencies are discovered the researchers generally seek reasons why abnormal profits can be achieved and do not suggest that the market is inefficient. Some abnormalities have been found related to small-firm portfolios, certain days of the week, or the so-called January effect. Research has, in some cases, tended to show that abnormally high profits can be earned during January. The abnormal profits are usually attributed to incomplete or poorly distributed information. However, once this information is given on the 6 o'clock news, as has been done in recent years, the abnormal profit opportunities usually disappear. Disseminating this information makes the market more efficient.

As communications systems advance, information is being disseminated more quickly and accurately. The Internet brings information directly to investors, quickly bypassing investment brokers and advisors. Furthermore, securities laws are forcing fuller disclosure of inside corporate data. The research has shown that our capital markets generally function well. Disclosure of more and better information, therefore, should be digested and reflected in stock prices, allowing for even better valuations.

The belief—or nonbelief—in market efficiency is important to those who participate in the financial markets. The efficient market hypothesis suggests that the purchase and sale of financial assets is a fair game in which participants receive an appropriate return based on risk. This means there are no big winners or big losers. For the financial manager, it suggests that prices in the market should be accepted as true reflections of value. If the manager believes otherwise, there should be a strong reason as to why the markets do not reflect the manager's beliefs.

It is likely that in certain markets, prices may not fully reflect all available information. This is what drives analysts, investors, and fund managers to change their portfolios to take advantage of new information before other market participants do. Their buying and selling provides the market with liquidity and to a large extent ensures that prices reflect the new information. The market may be efficient for the general population. Those who study and track it on a regular basis may find it inefficient at times, allowing them to profit from their effort and research.

Securities Regulation—A Changing Environment

Much of our previous discussion of the role of the organized exchanges centred on the self-regulatory role of the exchanges with regard to their members and clients. Stock exchanges impose listing requirements, demand regular financial statements, demand notice of material changes in corporate affairs, establish trading rules to protect the public, and enact special rules to govern takeover bids exercised through the exchanges.

Besides the stock exchanges, the **Investment Dealers Association**, a trade organization of approximately 150 firms, is an important player in the self-regulation of securities markets. The Investment Dealers Association establishes minimal capital limits for member firms, maintains a fund to reimburse clients in case of a member firm's failure, monitors the ethics of clients' conduct, and sets up courses of instruction for securities industry employees.

Investment Dealers Association
www.ida.ca
Ontario Securities Commission
www.osc.gov.on.ca

Despite the conscientious attempts at self-regulation by the industry, governments still have little confidence in the adequacy of self-regulation. As mentioned in Chapter 1, the policing of fraudulent or unfair practices has been a major concern of these regulatory bodies since the 1930s.

Because regulation of the securities industry is a provincial responsibility, each of the provinces has its own securities commission. However, most provinces adopt the regulations of the **Ontario Securities Commission (OSC),** as the majority of companies are listed and trade on the Toronto Stock Exchange. The general exception to that uniformity of provincial approach is Quebec. Recognizing that the need to generally improve the policing of market-related activities is an ongoing priority, there is a move to have the federal government regulate the securities business to cut down on bureaucratic overlap.

The Four Pillars of Finance

To understand the current changing regulatory situation in the securities industry, we must review the philosophies that underlay the historical regulation of the whole financial sector in Canada. Because of concerns over conflicts of interest, the basic structural foundation has been one called the **four pillars of finance**. There were to be banks, trust companies, insurance companies, and securities dealers. Thus, the reasoning went, a bank would not be caught in the bind of having to decide whether to lend money from a trust account to a corporate client.

Over the past 20 years, however, the separation of function among these four sectors has significantly eroded. Trust companies have to a large extent been taken over by the banks. Securities firms are also under the umbrella of the banks. The Insurance companies have merged and have demutualized to compete with the banks. Since changes to the 1967 and 1980 Bank Acts, banks have moved into mortgage lending, personal lending, leasing, factoring, discount brokerage, and full service securities dealing. The banks have also been pressing for mergers within Canada and have been rapidly expanding their business into the United States.

Canadian Bankers Association
www.cba.ca

Another hallmark of the financial sector has been restrictions on nonresident ownership. This was ostensibly to safeguard investors and depositors, as regulators would have more control over Canadian residents. These restrictions have been questioned as financial institutions seek access to larger capital pools from around the globe.

In addition, various rules have been aimed at preventing self-dealing. Thus, regulations prevent nonfinancial firms from owning financial firms. Banking restrictions have been aimed at preventing one individual or group from buying control for the same reason. The traditional separation of the real and financial sectors in Canada has been long gone with financial conglomerates in place. Peter and Edward Bronfman's Trilon Corporation, one of the largest financial institution in Canada, controlled Hees International Bankcorp, London Life, Triathlon Leasing, Eurobrokers Investment Corp., and Trilon Bancorp. Paul Desmarais's Power Financial Corp. controlled Investors Syndicate and Great West Life Assurance. The Caisse dépôt et placement du Québec, the eighth largest financial institution, was controlled by the Quebec government.

Current Directions in Regulation

There is still a need for a coordinated approach between the federal and provincial governments to deal with the rapidly changing financial environment. The exchanges have recently taken the first steps. Generally, governments, through legislative change, have sought more competition and less concentration of power and decision making. At the same time, recognition has been given to the need to compete effectively in the global financial market.

The country's investment industry needs financial muscle to compete with the investment goliaths of the United States and other countries. In addition, Ottawa has looked at banks and financial service, already a major component of Canada's export activity, to become major factors in future export growth. Canada's banks are well positioned to become major players in the U.S. banking industry as it deregulates.

We will see more one-stop financial service institutions at the retail level especially, but they will be regulated carefully to prevent conflicts of interest and to control their power. While the banks continue to channel funds to corporations, it will be in different forms from the past. They will take equity positions in corporations as investment bankers and accept more fee income by arranging financing for corporations directly with savers rather than acting as an intermediary. Increasingly, market activity has been generated by dealers acting on their own account, as opposed to acting as brokers in buying securities directly for an interested party. Yet while we see the global influence on our financial institutions, there has also been a move by those institutions to find a regional niche.

Summary

1. Money markets refer to the wholesale trading of financial assets with less than one year to maturity. The capital markets, comprising the equity, bond, and mortgage markets, are of longer terms to maturity.

2. In the capital and money markets, corporations compete for funds not only among themselves, but also with government units of all kinds. Corporations account for only about one-third of all funds raised in the Canadian capital market. Nonresidents have become significant holders of Canadian financial assets. Canadian corporations and governments increasingly seek funds from outside of Canada. Both bonds and stock are important sources of funding for the corporation, although their use shows wide variation from year to year.
3. The three-sector economy consists of households, corporations, and governmental units, and funds flow through the capital markets from suppliers of funds to the ultimate users. This process is highly dependent on the efficiency of the financial institutions that act as intermediaries in channelling the funds to the most productive users.
4. Security markets are divided into organized exchanges and over-the-counter markets. Brokers act as agents for stock exchange transactions, and dealers make markets over the counter at their own risk as owners of the securities they trade. The Toronto Stock Exchange is Canada's senior organized stock exchange. Although the OTC market for stock is not significant in Canada, corporate bond trades and trades in municipal, provincial, and federal government securities are transacted over the counter.
5. Throughout this chapter we have tried to present the concept of efficient markets doing an important job in allocating financial capital. We find the existing markets struggling to provide liquidity for both the corporation and the investor while they adjust efficiently to new information. Because of the laws governing the markets, much information is available for investors, and this in itself creates more competitive prices. Moreover, there are few cases of fraud and manipulation. In the future we expect even more efficient markets, with expanded roles for the investment dealers aimed at increasing liquidity for secondary trading.
6. The financial environment in Canada is changing rapidly. Traditionally we have had the four pillars of banks, trusts, insurance, and securities, but those pillars have faded. Although governments continue to be concerned about potential conflicts of interest, they have allowed the move toward one-stop financial services. Financial institutions will grow larger to compete effectively in the global financial market. There will be closer links between commercial banking that has tended to take only loan positions and investment banking that takes equity positions in corporations requiring funding.

List of Terms

money markets 506
capital markets 506
securities 506
internally generated funds 514
externally generated corporate funds 514
three-sector economy 516
financial intermediary 516
secondary trading 518
Toronto Stock Exchange (TSX) 519
over-the-counter (OTC) market 521
dealers 521
brokers 521
Computer Assisted Trading System (CATS) 522
efficient markets 523
abnormal return 526
weak form 526
semistrong form 526
strong form 526
Investment Dealers Association 528
Ontario Securities Commission (OSC) 528
four pillars of finance 528

Discussion Questions

1. Name the major competitors for funds in the capital markets.
2. How does the economy influence the amount of funds raised by the federal government in the long-term markets?
3. Discuss the average maturity of the federal government's marketable interest-bearing public debt and the implications for the money and capital markets if the present trend continues.
4. What implications are there for the capital markets as the Federal Government reduces its accumulated debt?
5. What has been the composition of long-term financing by corporations from 1991 through 2001?
6. Comment on the use of external versus internal sources of funds by corporations in the 1970s, 1980s, and 1990s. What has caused this shifting pattern?
7. Explain the role of financial intermediaries in the flow of funds through the economy.
8. Discuss the importance of security markets for both the corporation and the shareholder or bondholder.
9. What is the difference between organized exchanges and over-the-counter markets?
10. Why does the Toronto Stock Exchange have listing requirements? What are the major requirements? How do they compare with the listing requirements of the other exchanges?
11. How would you define efficient securities markets?
12. The efficient market hypothesis is interpreted in a weak form, a semistrong form, and a strong form. How can we differentiate its various forms?
13. What is meant by abnormal profits?
14. Discuss the characteristics that would make a market efficient.
15. Discuss tests you would develop to prove market inefficiencies.
16. Why do we have the four pillars of finance concept in Canada?
17. What are the implications of the changing regulations governing the Canadian securities industry?
18. Why is the 24-hour trading day becoming more important?
19. Discuss the changes currently occurring in Canada's financial environment.

INTERNET RESOURCES AND QUESTIONS

Market information about the history of exchanges, listing requirements, and quotes on securities is available at the exchange web sites:
www.tsx.ca
www.me.org
www.tse-cdnx.com
www.nyse.com
www.nasdaq.com

Market information on the bond market will soon be available at CanPx:
www.canpx.ca

For securities and exchange commissions:

www.osc.gov.on.ca	Ontario
www.sec.gov	United States
www.iosco.org	International Organization of Securities Commissions

For worldwide stock exchanges there is the International Federation of Stock Exchanges: www.fibv.com

1. Identify the listing costs and the various exchanges in Canada and the United States.
   a. Does it make sense to have so many exchanges in Canada?
   b. Why might a firm prefer to list on Nasdaq compared to the New York Stock Exchange?
   c. Why might a Canadian firm prefer to list on the New York Stock Exchange compared to Toronto?
2. Find the amount of protection afforded investors through the Canadian Investor Protection Fund www.cipf.ca

Selected References

Aggarwal, Reena, and Sandeep Dahiya. "Capital Formation and the Internet." *Journal of Applied Corporate Finance* 13 (Spring 2000), pp. 108–13.

Baker, H. Kent, and Richard B. Edelman. "The Effect of Spread and Volume of Switching to the NASDAQ Market System." *Financial Analysts Journal* 83 (January-February 1992), pp. 83–86.

Bank of Canada Review, selected issues.

Canadian Securities Institute. Canadian Securities Course. Toronto, 2000.

Chan, K. C., William C. Christie, and Paul H. Schultz. "Market Structure and the Intraday Pattern of Bid-Ask Spreads for NASDAQ Securities." *Journal of Business* (January 1995), pp. 35–60.

Clyde, Paul, Paul Schultz, and Mir Zaman. "Trading Costs and Exchange Delisting: The Case of Firms that Voluntarily Move from the American Stock Exchange to the Nasdaq." *Journal of Finance* 52 (December 1997), pp. 2103–12.

Cowan, Arnold R., Richard B. Carter, Frederick H. Dark, and Ajai K. Singh. "Explaining the NYSE Listing of NASDAQ Firms." *Financial Management* 21 (Winter 1992), pp. 73–86.

Eleswarapu, Venkat. "Cost of Transactions and Expected Returns in the Nasdaq Market." *Journal of Finance* 52 (December 1997), pp. 2113–27.

Malkiel, Burton. *A Random Walk down Wall Street*, 4th ed. New York: W. W. Norton, 1985.

Modhavan, Ananth. "Trading Mechanisms in Securities Markets." *Journal of Finance* 47 (June 1992), pp. 607–41.

Shearer, R. A., J. F. Chant, and D. E. Bond. *The Economics of the Canadian Financial System*, 3rd ed. Toronto: Prentice-Hall Canada, 1995.

CHAPTER | FIFTEEN

15 Investment Underwriting: Public and Private Placement

LEARNING | OBJECTIVES

1 Describe investment dealers as intermediaries between corporations and governments in need of funds and the investing public.

2 Outline the various roles investment dealers play in distributing and pricing corporate securities. Evaluate the impact of issued securities on earnings per share and share market price.

3 Indicate how the distribution spread is allocated and calculate the potential returns to syndicate participants.

4 Outline the other functions the investment dealer performs for clients, including advice on potential mergers and acquisitions.

5 Outline the changes in the investment industry in Canada.

6 Discuss the pros and cons of going public versus going private when raising funds.

7 Describe a leveraged buyout.

In Chapter 15 we examine the role of the investment dealer in finding capital, the advantages and disadvantages of selling securities to the public, and the private placement of securities with insurance companies, pension funds, and other lenders.

The Investment Industry

The term *investment dealer* tends to be a Canadian term, whereas Americans use *investment banker* for a securities corporation that generally performs the same functions. Although we will concentrate on the investment dealer's underwriting function we should identify the scope of the dealer's activities. One may hear the terms *investment house, securities house, brokerage*, or *dealer* used interchangeably; they are generally one and the same. But there is an important distinction between the dealer and the broker functions, although the same firms often perform both functions.

An **investment dealer** acts as a true intermediary; buying securities on its own behalf and taking the risk that it can resell the securities at a profit. This means that a dealer through its trading desks will take significant positions in financial assets of the money markets, bond markets and equity markets. The dealer will split the trading function of the secondary markets from the corporate financing function of the primary market.

Investment Dealers Association
www.ida.ca

A **broker** acts as an agent, receiving a commission by acting for a buyer or seller of securities. This is a commission-based function at the discount brokerage level for retail customers and at the wholesale institutional level. Additionally a dealer will have a department to give advice and plan merger and acquisition activities (M&A), sometimes taking capital positions. There will be a management services department to manage client capital and a department that carries on research related to the capital markets, analyzing the economy and specific financial securities.

The so-called corporate finance fraternity within the investment dealer community has long been thought of as an elite group; with appropriate memberships in country clubs, yacht clubs, and other such venerable institutions. The roller coaster performances of the securities markets in the last number of years has altered the picture somewhat. Competition has become the new way of doing business. Even the fittest must merge to survive, while others are forced to drop out of the game. Today the Canadian chartered banks and large foreign investment banking firms dominate the securities business. Individuals in the securities business, and there are about 38,000 in Canada, can be compensated well, but they are well trained and work long and hard hours because of the increasingly competitive environment.

The Role of Investment Underwriting

The investment dealer or underwriter is the great link between the corporation in need of funds and the investor. As it grows, the firm has a great need for funds to invest in receivables, inventories, and capital assets. It is unlikely that these funds can all be generated internally from profits and cash flow. The firm must seek outside funding. The capital markets where these funds may be available are impersonal and highly specialized. They impose requirements on the firm as to the disclosure of information and the costs associated with that disclosure. This is where the investment dealer can assist the firm. As a middleperson, the investment dealer is responsible for designing and packaging a security offering and selling the securities to the public.

Enumeration of Functions

The investment dealer plays a number of key roles in the distribution of securities.

Underwriter The underwriting function involves the purchase of a new issue of securities from an issuer at an agreed price. As **underwriter**, the investment dealer assumes the risk of reselling the securities to those sectors of the economy with excess funds. Usually, the underwriter is a group of investment dealers that share the task of selling the issue. Often, their risk is reduced by an "out clause" that allows them to back away from selling the securities if the market drops suddenly.

The underwriting function has increasingly included the **bought deal**. With this process, one dealer assumes all the risk and operates over a shorter time period. The dealer purchases the whole issue from well-established firms that qualify for the short-time filing procedures with the securities commission by way of a short-form prospectus. The dealer sells it either publicly or privately, but usually to customers who have expressed a solid interest in the issue. Of some concern has been the potential exclusion of the retail client in these quick prepackaged bought deals. Today, the bought deal is often being done on an overnight basis and thus the underwriting fees can be reduced significantly because the risk to the underwriter has been reduced.

By giving a firm commitment to purchase the securities from the corporation, the dealer is said to underwrite any risks that might be associated with a new issue. The trend to the bought deal is also partially responsible for the increased need for capital in the investment business. Therefore, we have seen mergers and the entry of the large banks into the investment business. While the risk may be fairly low in handling a bond offering for Bell Canada Enterprises or for the Royal Bank in a stable market, such may not be the case in selling the shares of a lesser-known firm in a very volatile market environment.

Though the public offerings of most large, well-established firms usually require the investment dealers to assume the risk of distribution, issues for relatively unknown corporations are still handled on a "best-efforts" or commission basis. These investment offerings are also referred to as a marketed deal and often involve a "roadshow" where management of the firm must make presentations about the company across the country with the assistance of the underwriters. This practice is more common in the United States, even for the largest firms.

An issue of securities by a corporation that adds to its securities already outstanding in the public hands is referred to as a **seasoned offering**. The first time securities are offered for sale to the public is referred to as an **initial public offering (IPO)**.

Market Maker During distribution and later, the investment dealer may become a **market maker** in a given security—that is, engage in the buying and selling of the security to ensure a liquid market. By maintaining an inventory in various securities, the dealer stands ready to buy and sell securities even if a buyer and seller are not available at the same time. A well-functioning secondary market enhances the attractiveness of securities by providing liquidity. The dealer may also provide research on the firm to encourage active investor interest.

Advisor The investment dealer may advise clients on a continuing basis about the securities to be sold, whether a foreign issue would be appropriate, the number of shares or units for distribution, the pricing including special features, and the timing of the sale. A company considering a stock issuance to the public may be persuaded, in

IPSCO Goes to Market

In February 2002, a syndicate of investment dealers, with TD Securities as the lead underwriter purchased 5.4 million IPSCO (www.ipsco.com) shares at $23.25 each. The next day they sold most of the shares into the market with a closing price for the day of $23.85. This was an overnight bought deal with a spread of 2.5 percent.

IPSCO is a producer of steel and steel products and periodically requires additional capital for its operations. In this case IPSCO went to the capital markets. Details of this "seasoned" issue are available at the SEDAR (System for the Electronic Document Analysis and Retrieval) web site (www.sedar.com). This site maintains press releases of publicly traded companies.

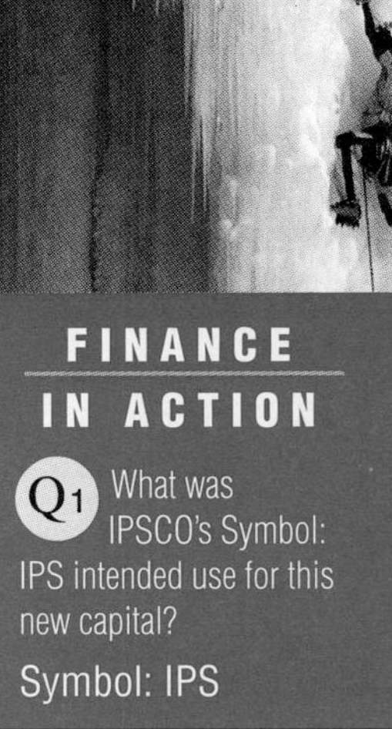

FINANCE IN ACTION

Q1 What was IPSCO's intended use for this new capital?

Symbol: IPS

counsel with an investment dealer, to borrow the funds from an insurance company or, if stock is to be sold, to wait for two more quarters of earnings before going to the market. The investment dealer also provides important advisory services in the area of mergers and acquisitions, leveraged buyouts, and corporate restructuring.

Agency Functions The investment dealer may act as an agent for a corporation that wishes to place its securities privately with an insurance company, a pension fund, or a wealthy individual. In this instance the investment dealer shops around among potential investors and negotiates the best possible deal for the corporation. It may also serve as an agent in merger and acquisition transactions. Because of the many critical roles the investment dealer plays, it may be requested to have a representative sit on the board of directors of the client company.

The Distribution Process

The actual distribution process requires the active participation of a number of parties. The principal, or **managing investment dealer**, usually calls on other investment houses to share the burden of risk and to aid in the distribution. To this end, they form an **underwriting syndicate**, composed of as few as two or as many as one hundred investment houses. This is also referred to as the banking group because they are on the hook for the financing of the issue. In Figure 15–1, on the next page, we see a typical case in which a hypothetical firm, the Maxwell Corporation, wishes to issue 250,000 additional shares of stock, with CIBC Wood Gundy as the managing underwriter and an underwriting syndicate of 15 firms.

CIBC Wood Gundy
www.canada.cibcwg.com

The managing investment dealer also helps prepare a prospectus for the corporation issuing the securities. The governing bodies of securities exchanges require full disclosure of all relevant information on publicly traded securities. A prospectus must be prepared for any issue of securities. It includes audited financial statements, information on the firm's operations and history, the major shareholders, and other relevant information. The securities body that examines the prospectus does not pass judgement on the advisability of an investment in the securities offered to the public. It does, however, ensure that adequate information is contained in the prospectus to allow an investor to make an informed decision.

If a corporation already has publicly traded shares outstanding with a market value in excess of $75 million, it may be able to shorten the time and effort required for preparation by filing a short-form prospectus. A corporation that has filed annual and

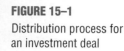

FIGURE 15–1
Distribution process for an investment deal

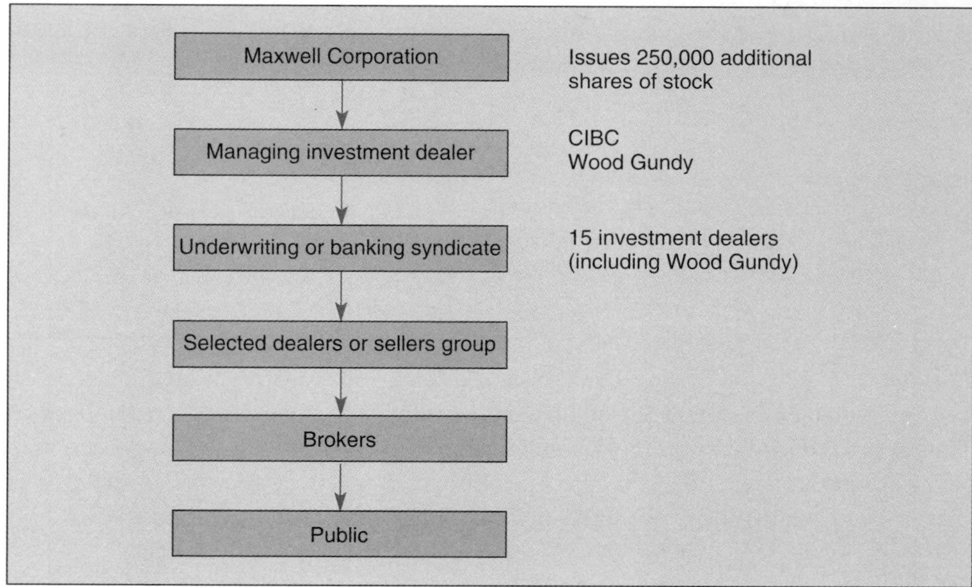

interim financial statements for at least three years can focus its attention on the specific security offering. Matters of price, the features of the security, and the use of the proceeds of the issue are the important considerations. This process is known as the prompt offering qualification system (POP) and has greatly assisted the bought deal. Putting the full prospectus or POP together is an important role of the managing investment dealer.

The banking or underwriting syndicate purchases shares from the Maxwell Corporation and distributes them through channels to the selected dealers or selling group. Although the selling group can purchase the securities at a discount, the group is not financially responsible for underwriting of the issue beyond its own purchases. Syndicate members act as wholesalers in distributing the shares to brokers and dealers who eventually sell the shares to the public. Large investment houses are usually vertically integrated, acting as underwriter-dealer-broker and capturing more fees and commissions.

The Spread

The **underwriting spread** represents the total compensation available to those who participate in the distribution process. As an example, we look at an initial issue of 2 million shares of West Fraser Timber Company stock when it went public. The shares were offered at a public, or retail, price of \$20.50 each. The underwriters paid a price of \$19.3725 per share to West Fraser. The \$1.1275 differential between the public price and the proceeds to the issuing company is known as the total spread. In a typical case, such a spread of \$1.1275 might be divided up among the participants in a manner like that depicted in Figure 15–2.

The spread is often calculated as a percentage based on the price to the public. In this example it would be:

$$\frac{\$1.1275}{\$20.50} = 0.055 = 5.5\%$$

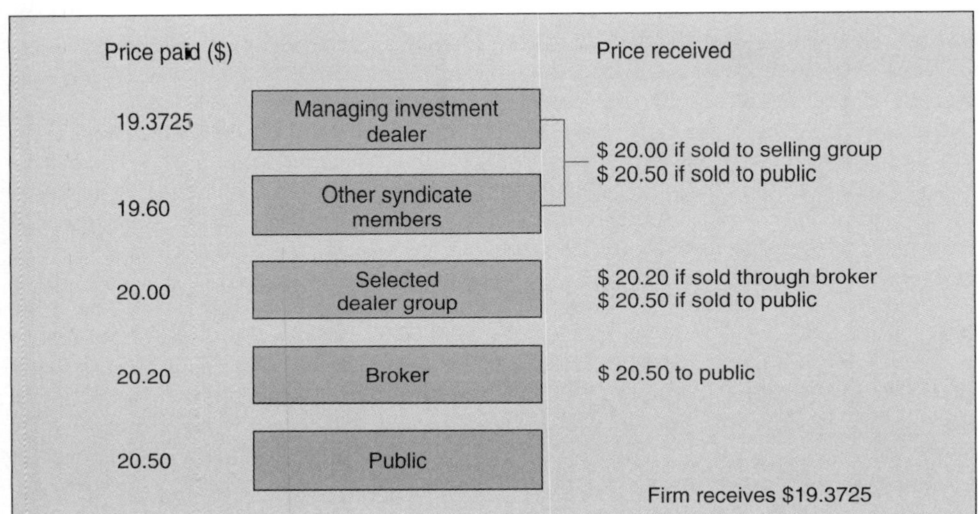

FIGURE 15–2
Allocation of underwriting spread

However the return to the underwriter or cost to the firm is based on the price they pay (or receive) for the securities after underwriting costs are deducted. In this example the return (cost) would be:

$$\frac{\$1.1275}{\$19.3725} = 0.0582 = 5.82\%$$

The farther down the dealer is in the distribution process, the higher the price the investment firm must pay for shares. The managing underwriter pays $19.3725, while dealers in the selling group syndicate pay $20.00. This also means that a dealer, by reselling as far down the distribution chain as it can, stands to make a higher profit. If, for example, the managing underwriter resells a volume of shares to a member of the selling group syndicate, it earns $0.6225 per share; for each share the managing underwriter resells directly to the public, it makes $1.1275. This will also alter the return the investment firm receives.

The total spread of $1.1275 in the sample case represents 5.5 percent of the offering price. In general, the larger the dollar value of an issue, the smaller the spread as a percentage of the offering price. Certain company expenses like printing and legal costs are largely fixed, again increasing the **flotation cost** percentages for smaller versus larger issues. For the West Fraser Timber Company issue, the company's direct issue expenses were estimated at $275,000, or about two-thirds of 1 percent of the total issue proceeds. Thus, the total flotation costs for the issue were just over 6 percent of the total proceeds. For a larger stock issue this percentage might be closer to 4 percent, while for a $5 million issue, a percentage cost of 8 percent or more might be reasonably expected. When the spread plus out-of-pocket costs are considered, the total cost of a new issue is substantial.

Before leaving the subject of flotation costs, it is important to realize that for the purposes of Figure 15–2, we assumed the shares were sold at their offering price of $20.50. However, an issue may not be salable at the offering price; in that case it will have to be sold for a lesser amount. Such a situation may result from adverse market conditions arising before the distribution is completed or simply because the issue was

FINANCE IN ACTION

Get Ready for the Next Big One

Governments around the world have embarked on the divestiture of their assets based on a need to raise capital and a shift in the philosophy as to their roles in the economy. In November 1995 the Canadian government continued its own privatization movement by selling CN Rail (CNR) to the public for $2.2 billion. The government had previously privatized portions of enterprises such as Air Canada (AC) and PetroCan (PCA) for $1.7 billion.

CN Rail went to market at a price $27.00 each for 83 million shares, which was to be paid in two installments of $16.25 initially and another of $10.75 in late November 1996. The issue, which was listed on the Toronto, Montreal, and New York Stock exchanges, has been well received by the market. CN Rail was considered a good investment because it eliminated a large portion of debt and it traded at a lower price earnings ratio than comparable U.S. rail companies. Canadian investment dealers were given 60 percent of the issue; foreign dealers were given 40 percent. Retail clients in Canada were allocated 20 percent of the domestic sales. The investment dealers earned an underwriting fee of somewhat less than 4 percent of the issue price, while the Air Canada issue had earned 5 percent.

In 2002, HydroOne (Ontario's power assets) will go public (an IPO), by selling shares in the market totalling $5 billion, the largest underwriting in Canada history. The underwriting fee will only be 2.25 percent, but $112.5 million isn't too bad. The equity issue will likely be sold in Canada (40 percent), the United States (40 percent) and Europe (20 percent). The lead underwriters will be RBC Dominion Securities, BMO Nesbitt Burns and Goldman Sachs and Company, of the United States. A recent court decision has suggested that the Government of Ontario does not have the right to sell shares in HydroOne. This has put the underwriting on hold. Meanwhile, other financing options are being explored, such as a trust offering. This will be one to watch in 2002.

You might want to examine how the share price of these firms has performed over the last three years.

Q1 What was the price to the public and the underwriter and the number of shares sold of the HydroOne offering?

www.tsx.ca

www.sedar.com

www.HydroOne.com

mispriced relative to the prices of other competing securities. In situations where the issue is sold to the public for less than the offering price, the actual realized commissions of the underwriting group are less than the amounts originally planned.

Pricing the Security

Because the syndicate members purchase the stock for redistribution in the marketing channels, they must be careful about the pricing of the stock. When a stock is sold to the public for the first time (that is, when the firm is going public), the managing investment dealer does an in-depth analysis of the company to determine its value. The study includes an analysis of the firm's industry, financial characteristics, and anticipated earnings and dividend-paying capability.

Based on appropriate valuation techniques that include the formulas from Chapter 10, a tentative price is assigned and compared to that commanded by the common shares of similar firms in a given industry. If the industry's average price-earnings ratio is 10, for example, the issue price should probably not be set far above this norm. Besides the fundamental valuation and the industry comparison, the anticipated public demand for the new issue is a major factor in pricing.

Rather than new issues, however, the majority of common stock flotations handled by investment dealers are additional issues of stocks or bonds for companies already trading publicly, in the secondary markets. In such cases, the price is generally set at a level slightly below the current market price for the company's common stock. This process, known as underpricing, helps create a receptive market for the securities, thereby reducing somewhat the pricing risk borne by the underwriting syndicate.

At times an investment dealer handles large blocks of securities for existing shareholders. Because the number of shares may be too large to trade in normal channels, the investment dealer manages the issue and prices the stock below current prices to the public. Such a process of selling the shares of an existing shareholder, is known as a secondary offering, in contrast to a primary offering in which corporate securities are sold directly by the corporation.

Dilution

The actual or perceived **dilutive effect on shares** currently outstanding is a problem facing companies when they issue additional securities. In the case of the Maxwell Corporation, the issuance of 250,000 new shares may represent a 10 percent increment to the 2.5 million shares currently in existence. Let us suppose that earnings are currently \$5 million and the capital raised from the public issue will eventually generate additional earnings of \$775,000. We will calculate 3 e.p.s. figures:

1. Before the issue

$$e.p.s. = \frac{earnings}{number\ of\ shares} = \frac{\$5{,}000{,}000}{2{,}500{,}000} = \$2.00$$

2. After initial issue

$$e.p.s. = \frac{earnings}{number\ of\ shares} = \frac{\$5{,}000{,}000}{2{,}750{,}000} = \$1.82$$

3. After the issue, when capital raised impacts to increase earnings

$$e.p.s. = \frac{earnings}{number\ of\ shares} = \frac{\$5{,}775{,}000}{2{,}750{,}000} = \$2.10$$

The proceeds from the sale of new shares may well be expected to provide the increased earnings necessary to bring earnings back to or to surpass \$2.00 per share as in our example. While financial theory dictates that a new equity issue should not be undertaken if it diminishes the overall wealth of current shareholders, there may be a time lag in the recovery of earnings per share as a result of the increased shares outstanding, especially if the proceeds are invested in a relatively new business development. For this reason, there may be a temporary weakness in a stock when an issue of additional shares is proposed. In most cases this is overcome with the passage of time as the wisdom of management's financial decision making is demonstrated.

Market Stabilization

Another problem may set in when the actual public distribution begins—namely, unanticipated weakness in the stock or bond market. Since the sales group has made a firm commitment to purchase stock at a given price for redistribution, it is essential that the price of the stock remain relatively strong. If, in the West Fraser Timber Company situation, syndicate members were committed to purchasing the stock at \$19.60 or better, they could be in trouble if the sales price fell to \$19.00 or \$18.00. The managing investment dealer or underwriter is generally responsible for stabilizing the offering during the distribution period and may accomplish this by repurchasing securities as the market price moves below the initial public offering price. This is **market stabilization**.

The period of stabilization usually lasts two or three days after the initial offering, but it may extend up to 30 days for difficult-to-distribute securities. In a very poor market environment, stabilization may be virtually impossible to achieve. Investment dealers may be forced to take substantial losses due to deteriorating stock prices.

Aftermarket

As its ultimate reputation rests on bringing strong securities to the market, the investment dealer is also interested in how well the underwritten security behaves after the distribution period. This is particularly true for initial public offerings.

Research has indicated that initial public offerings often do well in the immediate aftermarket. For example, one of these studies examined approximately 500 firms and determined that there were excess returns of 10.9 percent, on average, one week after issue (the term *excess return* refers to movement in the price of the stock above and beyond the market). There were also positive excess returns of 11.6 percent for a full month after issue but a negative market-adjusted performance of −3.0 percent one full year after issue.[1] Because the managing underwriter may underprice the issue initially to ensure a successful offering, the value often jumps after the issue first goes public. The efficiency of the market eventually takes hold, so sustained long-term performance is very much dependent on the quality of the issue and the market conditions at play.

Changes in the Investment Industry

Until recently, investment dealers were somewhat protected from a wide-open and competitive marketplace. This resulted in market inefficiencies and the potential in many years for large profits. Dramatic changes in the investment business in Canada have occurred due to the deregulation of the industry in the 1980s, the internationalization of the capital markets, and the technological advances that have become available. Besides the underwriting function, the investment firms have expanded their corporate finance, merger/acquisition advisory service, derivatives, and bond trading activities. However, as the markets gain in efficiency, the investment firms are in some cases consolidating and focusing their activities on those functions in which they have a competitive advantage.

Traditionally in Canada, banks looked after the short-term funding needs of businesses, investment dealers took care of long-term funding, and the insurance business was there to reduce risk exposure. In 1987 the federal government began to dismantle the framework that separated these functions, and this allowed the banks fuller participation in investment dealer and insurance activities. The Canadian banks moved quickly, buying up existing investment dealers or setting up their own investment houses. Although they had to go through several years of adjustment, the banks began to produce solid returns on these investments by the mid-1990s.

The major investment dealers in Canada today are listed in Table 15–1. This exhibit shows clearly the dominant presence of the Canadian banks. Although there are over 150 investment firms in the industry, there are only a handful of dominant players. The difficulty that the investment firms of Canada face is a limited capital base. A solid capital base is required in an era when investment firms must risk large amounts of

---

[1]Frank K. Reilly, "New Issues Revisited," *Financial Management* 6 (Winter 1977), pp. 28-42.

capital to compete by way of the bought deal. However, one should consider securities firms today in association with their parent company. This would rank the Canadian firms with the investment firms of the world.

TABLE 15–1
Largest investment dealers in Canada

	Major shareholder
CIBC World Markets	CIBC
National Bank Financial	National Bank
BMO Nesbitt Burns	Bank of Montreal
RBC Dominion Securities	Royal Bank
Scotia Capital	Bank of Nova Scotia
TD Securities	T.D. Bank
Griffiths McBurney	Independent
UBS Warburg	Foreign owned
Merrill Lynch	Foreign owned
HSBC	Foreign owned
Goldman Sachs	Foreign owned

One key trend has been a movement toward the integration of services. Large investment firms owned by the large banks have moved to combine their banking and investment trading operations. Immense trading floors combine the trading operations of the equity, debt, money, and forward markets. Specialized sections for derivatives and corporate banking have been set up in New York, which is better placed to service the demands of clients. Derivatives present an alternative to the risk-reduction capabilities of the insurance business.

With the equity markets moving toward computerized trading and the bond and money markets already operating an over-the-counter market, the trading of securities is increasingly occurring in the trading rooms of the large investment dealers. Our concern with this should be for the transparency of these trades. To ensure market efficiency, it is important that information on the prices of executed trades be widely available to all participants in the markets.

Another trend in the investment industry in Canada has been the movement to global trading units. With growing international trade investment, dealers have expanded to other countries, following their clients. Canadian investment dealers operate in the large capital markets of the world, raising capital for Canadian governments and corporations. It has already been noted that 40 percent of the 1995 issue of CN Rail was sold in the U S. markets, and often the debt issues of the provinces and other borrowers are sold in the Euromarkets, centred primarily in London. In Chapter 14, Figure 14-1, we saw the large amounts of funding raised abroad. These international markets, besides offering access to large capital pools, have highly skilled professionals, more services than the Canadian markets, and provide greater liquidity for the securities. This all translates into cost savings.

As noted in the chart on the next page, Canadian banks have also moved to create North American discount brokerage services with the purchases of U.S. firms. This is a result of the dramatic increase in participation in the capital markets by the retail investor.

TD Bank	Waterhouse Investors Services
CIBC	Oppenheimer & Company
Royal Bank	Bull & Bear Securities, Dain Rauscher
BMO	CSFBDirect

The globalization of the capital markets is also leading to 24-hour trading in many financial assets. Trading desks of the large firms already pass their "book" of securities from Toronto to Tokyo to London and back to Toronto so that clients can adjust their portfolios of financial assets at any time. The demands of the worldwide competitive capital markets are leading the Canadian investment firms to integrate and specialize in the services in which they enjoy the best advantage. Sometimes this can best be done in Canadian capital markets, and sometimes it can best be done in other capital markets around the globe.

Underwriting Activity in Canada

Corporate issues are presented in Figure 15–3. From Figure 15–3 we note that equity issues of seasoned companies (with shares already outstanding) and IPOs (initial public offerings) were less significant than debt as a source of new external funding for corporations in 2000. The year 2001 saw a dramatic drop in equity underwriting activity due to the weak stock markets. Debt issues that saw a drop in 2000, particularly in the foreign markets were the dominant choice for underwriting activity in 2001. In Chapter 14 we observed that equity and debt issues switch from year to year as the dominant source of funding.

The average size of an equity issue was $3.3 million in late 2001 down from $5.4 million in 2000. There were several large equity issues, but the majority of public issues are considerably smaller, although no less important to the companies or under-

FIGURE 15–3

New corporate issues underwritten in 2000, in Canada

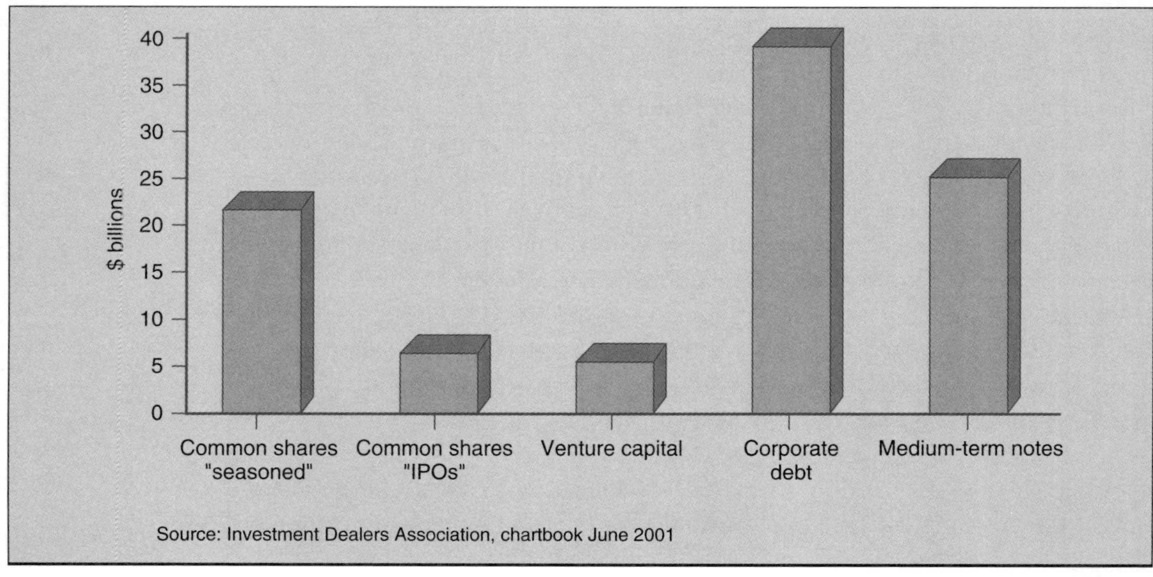

writers involved with the issue. As for debt issues, the underwriting activity in Canada has moved significantly to asset-backed securities.

Underwriting activity often involves a bought deal where the investment dealer is at risk financially to ensure the placement of funds by the borrower. A bought deal often does not involve a syndicate, which increases the investment dealer's risk exposure. Concern has also been expressed that the bought deal may exclude the retail customer from participating in the initial offering of securities.

In 2001 securities firms received their revenue as follows; from commissions 41 percent, investment banking 19 percent, fixed income trading 13 percent, interest 12 percent, equity trading 1 percent, other 14 percent.

As activity in Canadian markets becomes more open to international competition, and as more activity becomes centred on the large markets of New York, London, and Tokyo, the needs for size and efficiency strike many Canadian securities firms as being paramount.

Size Criteria for Going Public

Although there are no prescribed, or official, size criteria for approaching the public markets, the well-informed corporate financial officer of a private company should have some feel for what his or her options are. Can a company with $10 million in sales even consider a public offering?

In the United States, the most prestigious investment houses tend to concentrate on underwriting large companies. Because of the absolute difference in size of American versus Canadian investment firms, it is not surprising that even the largest of Canadian firms are often involved in relatively small securities issues.

Public versus Private Financing

Our discussion to this point has assumed that the firm was distributing stocks or bonds in the public markets (through the organized exchanges or over the counter, as explained in Chapter 14). However, many companies, by choice or circumstance, prefer to remain private, restricting their financial activities to direct negotiations with bankers, insurance companies, and so forth. Let us evaluate the advantages and the disadvantages of public versus private financing and then explore the avenues open to a privately financed firm.

Advantages of Being Public

First, the corporation may tap the security markets for a greater amount of funds by selling securities directly to the public through a **public placement**. With millions of individual shareholders in the country, combined with hundreds of institutional investors, the greatest pool of funds is channeled toward publicly traded securities. Furthermore, the attendant prestige of a public security may be helpful in bank negotiations, executive recruitment, and the marketing of products.

Second, shareholders of a heretofore private corporation may also sell part of their holdings if the corporation decides to go public. The shareholder is able to achieve a higher degree of liquidity and to diversify his or her portfolio. A publicly traded stock with an established price may also be helpful for estate-planning purposes.

Finally, going public allows the firm to play the merger game, using marketable securities for the purchase of other firms. The high visibility of a public offering may even make the firm a potential recipient of attractive offers for its own securities. This may not be viewed as an advantage by firms that do not wish to be acquired.

Disadvantages of Being Public

New York Stock Exchange
www.nyse.com

The company must make all information available to the public through a securities' commission filing. Not only is this tedious, time consuming, and expensive, but also important corporate information on profit margins and product lines must be divulged. For Canadian firms that are also listed on the New York Stock Exchange, the filings required by the U.S. Securities and Exchange Commission are even more extensive than those required by Canadian regulators. Because of the need to provide information, a company president must become a public relations representative to all interested members of the securities industry.

Another disadvantage of being public is the tremendous pressure for short-term performance placed on the firm by security analysts and large institutional investors. Quarter-to-quarter earnings reports can become more important to top management than providing a long-run stewardship plan for the company. A capital budgeting decision calling for the selection of Alternative A—carrying a million dollars higher net present value than Alternative B—may be discarded in favour of the latter because Alternative B adds two cents more to next quarter's earnings per share.

In a number of cases, the blessings of having a publicly quoted security may become quite the opposite. Although a security may have had an enthusiastic reception in a strong new issues market, a dramatic erosion in value may later occur, causing embarrassment and anxiety for shareholders and employers.

A final disadvantage is the high cost of going public. For example, for issues of under a million dollars, the underwriting spread plus the out-of-pocket cost may run well over 10 percent.

Initial Public Offerings

When a corporation first sells shares to the public and is thus no longer a private company, it has initiated an initial public offering (IPO). Firms seem more likely to bring an IPO to market when it is "hot", that is, when share prices are moving upwards in value and there is a lot of investor interest in the stock market. The IPO market dried up considerably in the weak equity market of 2001. Figure 15–3 shows that "seasoned" issues, that is, issues that add to company shares already outstanding, are more significant in dollar value than IPOs.

Table 15–2 shows the price performance and net proceeds of a selected group of IPOs. Their subsequent price performance demonstrates the considerable volatility of returns that one can expect from these issues. This is what should be expected from these newly listed companies that are offering shares to the public for the first time. These companies have not yet been subject to intense public scrutiny. As a publicly traded company, there are certain disclosure requirements demanded of companies by the securities commission, resulting in more information being available to investors.

A Defiant IPO

In late 2001, Defiant Energy Corporation (www.definatenergy.com) listed its shares on the TSX (www.tsx.ca) at the same time as it raised $1.5 million through an IPO. This was a difficult time to go to the equity markets.

Defiant issued two types of shares; common and flow through to raise capital for its operations. Defiant explores for, develops, and produces oil and gas properties in Western Canada.

IPOs tend to enjoy initial success in share price appreciation but over the longer term the results are less impressive. The TSE supplies information on new listings and IPOs.

The SEDAR web site (www.sedar.com) maintains an electronic version of any prospectus filings. The prospectus identifies the price to the public and the net proceeds to the firm after underwriting fees.

How have the common shares performed since the IPO?

FINANCE IN ACTION

Q1 What were the net proceeds of each issue?

Symbol: DEF

As this previously unknown information is revealed about these companies, their share prices exhibit volatility.

TABLE 15–2 IPOs on the TSX, 1998–1999

Date of IPO	Public Company	Offering Price	February 23, 2002 Price	Net Proceeds (millions)
7 July 98	Celestica Inc. (CLS)	$23.75	$52.20	$338
9 Nov. 98	Husky Injection (HKY)	10.50	5.10	162
8 Feb. 99	Tundra Semiconductor	9.25	14.85	31

Private Placement

Private placement refers to the selling of securities directly to insurance companies, pension funds, and wealthy individuals rather than through the security markets. The financing device may be employed by a growing firm that wishes to avoid or defer an initial public stock offering or by a publicly traded company that wishes to incorporate private funds into its financing package. The relative importance of private versus public placement is indicated in Figure 15–4, on the next page, over the last decade. New equity raised privately through the facilities of the TSX represented slightly under 20 percent of all equity raised.

The advantages of private placement are worthy of note. There is no lengthy, expensive registration process with the securities commissions. The firm also has considerably greater flexibility in negotiating with one or a handful of insurance companies, pension funds, or bankers than is possible in a public offering. Because there is no securities registration or underwriting, the initial costs of a private placement may be considerably lower than those of a public issue. However, on an interest-bearing security, the interest rate is usually higher to compensate the investor for holding a less liquid obligation.

Going Private and Leveraged Buyouts

In the 1970s a number of firms gave up their public listings to go private, but these were usually small firms. Management figured they could save several hundred thousand dollars a year in annual report expenses, legal and auditing fees, and security analysts' meetings—a significant amount for a small company.

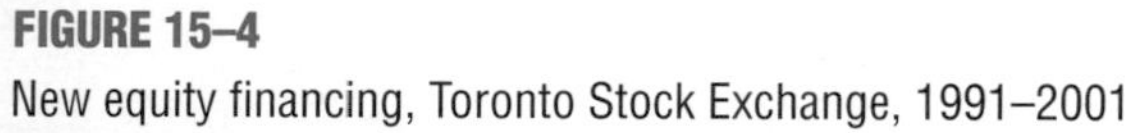

FIGURE 15–4

New equity financing, Toronto Stock Exchange, 1991–2001

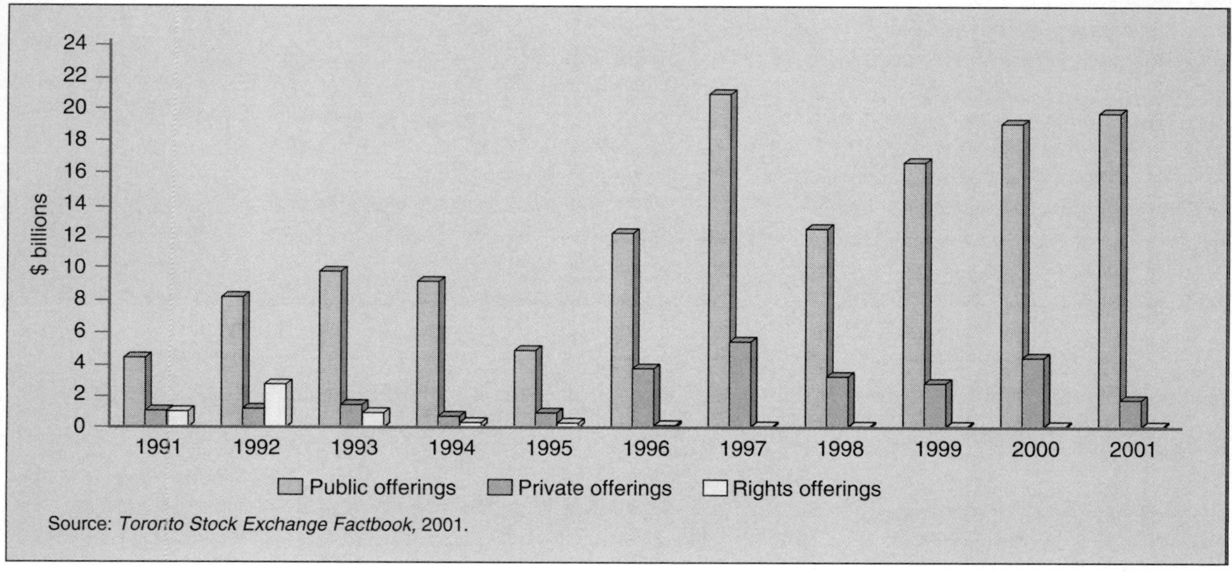

Source: *Toronto Stock Exchange Factbook*, 2001.

In the 1980s, however, a number of very large U.S. corporations went private, and not just to save several hundred thousand dollars. The answer seems to be in management's desire to manage for the long term without the short-term performance demands that the stock market places on corporations. Private firms do not have to please analysts with short-term performance. Nevertheless, many corporations that went private in 1985 were resold to the public in the up markets of 1987 for handsome profits. Although large Canadian firms have not yet followed suit in going private, many chief executives wish from time to time to be subject to less intense demands relating to current reported profits.

There are basically two ways to accomplish **going private**. A publicly owned company can be purchased by a private company, or the company can repurchase all publicly traded shares from the shareholders. Both methods have been popular and can be accomplished through the use of a leveraged buyout. In a **leveraged buyout**, the management or some other investor group borrows the needed cash to repurchase all the shares of the company. After the repurchase, the company exists with a lot of debt and heavy interest expense. However, many analysts worry that the borrowing is done at banks rather than through the securities markets. They claim that this may cause a misdirection of capital into nonproductive activities (leveraged buyouts) instead of capital formation for new ventures and products. Also when a large firm goes private common stock outstanding tends to disappear, leaving fewer investment choices for investors.

Usually, management of the private company must sell assets to reduce the debt load, and a corporate restructuring occurs, wherein divisions and products are sold and assets are redeployed into new, higher-return areas. As specialists in the valuation of assets, investment dealers try to determine the "break-up value" of a large company. This is its value if all of its divisions were divided and sold separately. Over the long run, these strategies can be rewarding, and these companies may again become publicly owned. For example, Beatrice Foods went private in 1986 for $6.2 billion. One year later, it sold various pieces of the company—Avis, Coke Bottling, International Playtex—and other assets worth $6 billion and still had assets left valued at $4 billion for a public offering.

In Canada, leveraged buyouts have been used for repatriating ownership of what were formerly Canadian divisions of foreign multinationals. For example, a group of Canadian managers successfully negotiated the purchase of B. F. Goodrich's Canadian industrial products division; it is now run as a private corporation under the name Epton Industries. In another case, a group of Canadian investors bought American Can Inc.'s Canadian subsidiary. That group followed up its acquisition with a $55 million issue of subordinate voting shares, presumably to ease the debt load caused by the buyout. The availability of these Canadian subsidiaries to be bought stems from a number of global corporate strategic conditions. As the multinational corporations switch to global product production strategies, smaller Canadian operations established to serve only the Canadian market may no longer make sense in the overall corporate plan. In other cases, the traditional businesses around which the Canadian subsidiaries were founded may have become deemphasized by corporate decision makers as newer, more exciting market developments are pursued.

The leveraged buyout has not taken hold in Canada, although Onex Corporation exists largely as a specialist in this field. In 1995 Onex lost out to Interbrew of Belgium in the $2.7 million takeover of John Labatt. There are perhaps two reasons for the limited amount of activity in Canada. First, Canadian corporations are not as widely held as U.S. corporations, and only a few entities dominate our market. Second, being more resource based, Canadian corporations are much more susceptible to cyclical swings in the economy. In a leveraged buyout with heavy debt loads, stability in the generation of cash flow to meet interest payments is very important.

Onex Corporation
www.onexcorp.com

The lack of leveraged buyout activity in Canada did not prevent the now infamous takeovers of Federated Stores for $6.6 billion (in Canadian equivalent $) and Allied Stores for $5.0 billion (in Canadian equivalent $), in 1988 and 1986 respectively, by Campeau Corporation of Toronto. Both purchases were almost completely financed with borrowed money. With increasing interest rates and a slowdown in activity in retail department stores in the late 1980s, Campeau could not service the debt it had accumulated on these leveraged buyouts. This was despite a large selloff of assets. By mid-1990, Campeau Corporation was on the verge of bankruptcy, with its share price having declined from over $22.00 per share to less than $1.00 per share in about six months. Federated Stores and Allied Stores were forced to declare a form of bankruptcy protection known as Chapter 11, and Campeau Corporation went bankrupt. Campeau serves to emphasize the risks in the leveraged buyout game.

Large Investment Deals

Investment dealers are key players in the mergers and acquisitions (M&As) that take place each year. In 1998 Seagram took over Polygram for $15.6 billion. Only three years before, in 1995, Seagram had sold its stake in DuPont for $12.2 billion and immediately bought MCA from Matsushita Electric. In May 2001 Seagram was sold to Vivendi. In early 2002 PanCanadian Energy and Alberta Energy announced a $20 billion merger.

Canada and the provinces have followed a worldwide trend toward privatization, which is the selling of property previously held by governments by way of public share offerings. These large and small public offerings are shown in Table 15–3.

TABLE 15–3
Big international deals ($ millions)

Country	Company	Business	Year	Sale Price	Percent Private	Major Buyers
The Americas						
Argentina	YPF	Oil and gas	1993	$ 2,500	80%	Public offering
Bolivia	Corani (part of Ende)	Power plant	1995	$ 58	51%	Dominion Energy (U.S.)
Brazil	Cia. Siderurgica Nacional	Steelmaker	1993	$ 1,056	100%	Banco Bamerindus, Grupo Vicunha, Banco Gradesco, Banco Itau, Docenave (Brazil)
Canada	Petro-Canada	Oil and gas	1991	$ 1,980	80%	Public offering
Chile	CTC	Telecommunications	1988	$ 115	100%	Bond Corp. (Aus.)
Colombia	Banco de Colombia	Banking	1994	$ 490	99%	Group led by Jaime Gilinski (Col.)
Cuba	Etecsa	Telecommunications	1994	$ 706	49%	Grupo Domos (Mex.)
Jamaica	Telecommunications of Jamaica	Telecommunications	1987	$ 61	72%	Cable & Wireless (U.K.)
Mexico	Telmex	Telecommunications	1990	$ 7,000	100%	Grupo Carso (Mex.), SBC Communications (U.S.), France Cable et Radio (France)
Panama	Cementos Bayano	Cement	1994	$ 60	100%	Cemex (Mexico)
Peru	ENTEL-CPT	Telecommunications	1994	$ 2,000	35%	Telefonica de Espana (Spain)
Venezuela	Cia. Anonima Nacional Telefonos de Venezuela	Telecommunications	1991	$ 1,900	40%	Group led by GTE (U.S.)
Western Europe						
Austria	OMV	Energy	1987	$ 736	50%	Public offering
Belgium	ASLK-CGER	Banking	1993	$ 1,200	50%	Fortis (Neth./Belgium)
France	Elf-Aquitaine	Oil	1994	$ 6,220	90%	Public offering
Germany	VEBA	Energy, telecommunications, chemicals	1984	$ 1,670	100%	Public offering
Greece	AGET Heracles General Cement	Cement	1992	$ 560	70%	Calcestruzzi (Italy) and National Bank of Greece (Greece)
Italy	Istituto Nazionale delle Assicurazioni	Insurance	1994	$ 4,150	66%	Public offering

TABLE 15–3
(continued)

Country	Company	Business	Year	Sale Price	Percent Private	Major Buyers
Western Europe *(continued)*						
The Netherlands	Koninklijke PTT Nederland	Telecommunications	1994	$ 3,750	30%	Public offering
Spain	Repsol	Oil, gas, and chemicals	1989	$ 4,160	80%	Public offering
Sweden	Pharmacia	Pharmaceuticals	1994	$ 1,200	87%	Public offering, Volvo
United Kingdom	British Telecom	Telecommunications	1984	$21,990	100%	Public offering
Eastern Europe						
Estonia	Viru Hotell	Hotel	1994	$ 12	100%	Estonia/Finnish Investment Group
Hungary	MATAV	Telecommunications	1993	$ 875	5%	Consortium of Deutsche Telekom (Ger.) and Ameritech (U.S.)
Latvia	Latvijas Universala Banka	Banking	1995	$ 23	50%	Clients, employees, public (Latvia)
Lithuania	Klaipeda Tobacco Factory	Tobacco products	1993	$ 13	100%	Philip Morris (U.S.)
Poland	FSM	Automaker	1994	$ 1,230	90%	Fiat (Italy)
Russia	Lukoil	Oil company	1994	$ 3,900	62%	N.A.
Asia						
Australia	Commonwealth Bank of Australia	Banking	1991	$ 2,280	50%	Public offering
China	Huaneng International	Power	1994	$ 555		Public offering
Indonesia	Indosat	Telecommunications	1994	$ 1,120	35%	Public offering
Japan	NTT	Telecommunications	1987	$73,490	35%	Public offering
New Zealand	Telecom New Zealand	Telecommunications	1990	$ 2,460	100%	BellAtlantic/Ameritech (U.S.)
The Philippines	Petron	Oil refining and distribution	1993	$ 931	60%	Saudi Aramco (Saud.)
Singapore	Singapore Telecommunications	Telecommunications	1993	N.A.	11%	Public offering
South Korea	Korea Electric Power	Electric utility	1989	$ 1,930	22%	Individual investors
Taiwan	China Steel	Steelmaker	1989	$ 3,020	52%	Public offering
Thailand	PTT Exploration & Production	Petroleum	1994	$ 258	29%	Public offering

Source: Reprinted with permission of *The Wall Street Journal*,

Summary

1. The role of the investment dealer is critical to the distribution of securities in the Canadian economy. The investment dealer serves as an underwriter or risk taker by purchasing the securities from the issuing corporation or government and redistributing them to the public.
2. The dealer may act as managing underwriter, which will include assistance in the pricing and features of the security. The dealer may also be part of the banking group that underwrites the issue or the selling group that sells only a portion of the issue, or the dealer may act as a broker only and assume no risk. Estimation of market prices uses the formulas and concepts developed in Chapter 10.
3. The spread is the difference between the price the managing underwriter pays the corporation or government and the price expected from the public. The greater the risk taken by the dealer, the greater will be the spread. Spread is calculated on the price to the public. The dealer may continue to maintain a market in the distributed securities long after they have been sold to the public. The dealer can help sell a new issue on a best-efforts basis. Alternatively, the dealer may assume all of the risk with a bought deal.
4. Investment dealers also serve as advisors to corporations and have become more important to corporations in providing advice on mergers, acquisitions, leveraged buyouts, and hostile takeover attempts. Dealers also maintain large inventories of securities, helping to maintain liquid markets.
5. Investment dealers have become larger and consolidated into fewer firms in just the past few years. The industry may become dominated by the large dealers that can take down large blocks of securities and compete in a more international market. Despite their exceptional historical profitability, Canadian investment dealers face the future with serious concerns about competition from the mammoth foreign investment bankers, and the effects of 24-hour worldwide trading centred in the New York, London, and Tokyo markets.
6. The advantages of selling securities in the public markets must be weighed against the disadvantages. While going public may give the corporation and major shareholders greater access to funds as well as additional prestige, these advantages may quickly disappear in a down market. Furthermore, the corporation must open its books to the public and orient itself to the supposed short-term emphasis of investors. Private placement—or the direct distribution of securities to large insurance companies, pension funds, and wealthy individuals—may bypass the rigours of securities commission registration and allow more flexibility in terms. A number of U.S. corporations actually changed their structure from public to private during the bear market of 1973–74. This trend was evident again in the 1980s, with many large companies going private through leveraged buyouts. Some became public again, realizing substantial gains.
7. A leveraged buyout occurs when an acquiring firm purchases all the equity in a target firm, generally using the assets of the target firm as collateral for the funds required for the takeover. After acquisition, the targeted firm has many of its assets sold to pay off debt, the operations of the firm are rationalized including layoffs, and a great deal of debt is added to the capital structure of the acquired firm. While much of the debt used in leveraged buyouts comes from the banking industry, only the public markets can meet the vast capital needs of Canadian corporations. Leveraged buyouts provide a mechanism for former subsidiaries of foreign multinationals to become controlled by Canadian investors, who were often the subsidiary managers.

Review of Formulas

Please refer to Chapter 10.

List of Terms

Discussion Questions

1. In what way is an investment dealer a risk taker?
2. What is the purpose of market stabilization activities during the distribution process?
3. Discuss how an underwriting syndicate decreases risk for each underwriter and at the same time facilitates the distribution process.
4. Discuss the reason for the differences between underwriting spreads for stocks and bonds.
5. Explain how the price-earnings ratio is related to the pricing of a new security issue and the dilution effect.
6. Explain why the new issues market periodically becomes extremely popular. What are the dangers of a hot new issues market?
7. Comment on the market performance of companies going public, both immediately after the offering has been made and some time later. Relate this to research that has been done in this area.
8. Discuss key changes going on in the investment dealer-brokerage community in terms of vertical integration. Also who are some of the new participants in the industry?
9. Discuss the benefits accruing to a company traded in the public securities market.
10. What are some reasons a corporation may prefer to remain privately held?
11. If a company wished to raise capital by way of a private placement, where would it look for funds?
12. How does a leveraged buyout work? What does the debt structure of the firm normally look like after a leveraged buyout? What might be done to reduce the debt?
13. What effect does a leveraged buyout have on the future strategic choices open to the company's management?
14. Comment on whether or not you believe leveraged buyouts are good for an economy.

www.mcgrawhill.ca/college/block

INTERNET RESOURCES AND QUESTIONS

To identify recent listings, including IPOs on stock exchanges, try the listed companies section of the exchanges:
www.tsx.ca

The SEDAR site provides recent press releases and prospectus information:
www.sedar.com

1. Select three IPOs that have come to market in the last three months and indicate the following:
   a. Issue price.
   b. Gross proceeds.

c. Net proceeds.

d. The reasons for the difference between gross and net proceeds.

e. The reasons for raising the capital.

Problems

1. Blaine and Company is the managing investment dealer for a major new underwriting. The price of the stock to the managing investment dealer is $24.00 per share. Other syndicate members may buy at $24.30. The price to the selected dealer group is $24.90, with a price to the brokers of $25.32. The price to the public is $25.60.
   a. If Blaine and Company sells its shares to the dealer group, what will its percentage return be?
   b. If Blaine and Company performs the dealers' function also and sells to brokers, what will its percentage return be?
   c. If Blaine and Company fully integrates its operation and sells directly to the public, what will its percentage return be?
2. R. David and Company is the managing investment dealer for a major new underwriting. The price of the stock to the investment dealer is $26.00 per share. Other syndicate members may buy at $26.25. The price to the selected dealer group is $26.80, with a price to the brokers of $27.00. The price to the public is $27.50.
   a. If R. David and Company sells its shares to the dealer group, what will the percentage return be?
   b. If R. David and Company performs the dealers' function also and sells to brokers, what will its percentage return be?
   c. If R. David and Company fully integrates its operation and sells directly to the public, what will its percentage return be?
3. The Canadian Loonie Company needs to raise $40 million. The investment dealer Wayne and Shuster will handle the transaction.
   a. If stock is utilized, 2 million shares will be sold to the public at $20.95 per share. The corporation will receive a net price of $20.00 per share. What is the percentage of underwriting spread per share?
   b. If bonds are utilized, slightly over 40,000 bonds will be sold to the public at $1,001 per bond. The corporation will receive a net price of $997 per bond. What is the percentage of underwriting spread per bond?
   c. Which alternative has the larger percentage of spread? Is this the normal relationship between the two types of issues?
4. Gagnon Skates, Inc. has earnings of $6.4 million with 3.2 million shares outstanding before a public distribution. Six hundred thousand shares will be included in the sale, of which 400,000 are new corporate shares and 200,000 are shares currently owned by Marcus Gagnon, the founder and CEO. The 200,000 shares that Marcus is selling are referred to as a secondary offering and all proceeds will go to him.
   a. What was the corporation's earnings per share before the offering?
   b. What are the corporation's earnings per share expected to be after the offering?
5. The Western Slope Timber Company currently has 5 million shares of stock outstanding and will report earnings of $9 million in the current year. The company is considering the issuance of 1 million additional shares of stock that will net $40.00 per share to the corporation.
   a. What is the immediate dilution potential for this new share issue?

b. Assume the Western Slope Timber Company can earn 10.5 percent on the proceeds of the share issue in time to include it in the current year's results. Should the new issue be undertaken based on earnings per share?

6. In the previous problem, if the 1 million additional shares can be issued only at $32.00 per share and the company can earn 5 percent on the proceeds, should the new issue be undertaken based on earnings per share?

7. The In The Net Fishing Corp. has 6 million shares of stock outstanding at a current market price of $12.00. It is considering a new share offering that will net it $11.00 per share on 400,000 shares. Earnings this year are expected to be $8 million.

   a. What is the immediate dilution potential for this new share issue?

   b. Assume In The Net Fishing Corp. can earn 14 percent on the proceeds of the share issue and these can be realized with this year's results. Should the new issue be undertaken based on earnings per share? Can you suggest why or why not?

   c. If the 400,000 additional shares can only be issued at $5.00 per share and the company can earn 12 percent on the proceeds, should the new issue be undertaken based on earnings per share?

8. Catriona Sporting Goods is considering a public offering of common shares. Its investment dealer has informed the company that the retail price will be $24.00 per share for 800,000 shares. The company will receive $22.50 per share and will incur $175,000 in registration, accounting, and printing fees.

   a. What is the spread on this issue in percentage terms?

   b. What are the total expenses of the issue as a percentage of total value (at retail)?

   c. If the firm wants to net $22 million from this issue, how many shares must be sold?

9. Skyway Airlines will issue stock at a retail (public) price of $15.00. The company will receive $13.80 per share.

   a. What is the spread on the issue in percentage terms?

   b. If Skyway Airlines demands receiving a net price only $0.75 below the public price suggested in part *a*, what will the spread be in percentage terms?

   c. To hold the spread down to 3 percent based on the public price in part *a*, what net amount should Skyway Airlines receive?

10. Lynch Brothers is the managing underwriter for a 1 million share issue by Overcharge Healthcare Inc. Lynch Brothers is "handling" 10 percent of the issue. Its price is $30.00, and the price to the public is $31.50. Lynch also provides the market stabilization function. During the issuance, the market for the stock turned soft, and Lynch was forced to repurchase 45,000 shares in the open market at an average price of $29.90. It later sold the shares at an average value of $26.00. Compute Lynch Brothers' overall gain or loss from managing the issue.

11. Richmond Rent-A-Car is about to go public. The investment firm of Tinkers, Evers, and Chance is attempting to price the issue. The car rental industry generally trades at a 10 percent discount below the P/E ratio on the S&P/TSX Composite Index. Assume that index currently has a P/E ratio of 20. The firm can be compared to the car rental industry as follows:

	Richmond	**Car Rental Industry**
Growth rate in earnings per share	15 percent	10 percent
Consistency of performance	Increased earnings 4 out of 5 years	Increased earnings 3 out of 5 years
Debt to total assets	52 percent	39 percent
Turnover of product	Slightly below average	Average
Quality of management	High	Average

www.mcgrawhill.ca/college/block

Assume, in assessing the initial P/E ratio, the investment dealer will first determine the appropriate industry P/E based on the S&P/TSX Composite Index. Then a half point will be added to the P/E ratio for each case in which Richmond Rent-A-Car is superior to the industry norm, and a half point will be deducted for an inferior comparison. On this basis, what should the initial P/E be for the firm?

12. The investment firm of Luther King Inc., will use a dividend valuation model to appraise the shares of the Pyramid Corporation. Dividends (D_1) at the end of the current year will be \$1.20. The growth rate (g) is 9 percent and the discount rate (K_e) is 13 percent.
    a. What should be the price of the stock to the public? (Refer to Chapter 10.)
    b. If there is a 6 percent total underwriting spread on the stock, how much will the issuing corporation receive?
    c. If the issuing corporation requires a net price of \$29.00 (proceeds to the corporation) and there is a 6 percent underwriting spread, what should be the price of the stock to the public? (Round to two places to the right of the decimal point.)

13. The investment dealer of IB12 Inc. uses a dividend valuation model to appraise the shares of Lambert Aerospace Company. Dividends (D_1) at the end of the current year will be \$1.50. The growth rate (g) is 6 percent and the discount rate (K_e) is 14 percent.
    a. What should be the price of the stock to the public?
    b. If there is a 5 percent total underwriting spread on the stock, how much will the issuing corporation receive?
    c. If the issuing corporation requires a net price of \$18.00 (proceeds to the corporation) and there is a 5 percent underwriting spread, what should be the price of the stock to the public?

14. The Alston Corporation needs to raise \$1 million of debt on a 20-year issue. If it places the bonds privately, the interest rate will be 11 percent, and \$25,000 in out-of-pocket costs will be incurred. For a public issue, the interest rate will be 10 percent, and the underwriting spread will be 5 percent. There will be \$75,000 in out-of-pocket costs.

    Assume interest on the debt is paid semiannually, and the debt will be outstanding for the full 20 years, at which time it will be repaid.

    Which plan offers the higher net present value? For each plan, compare the net amount of funds initially available—inflow—to the present value of future payments of interest and principal to determine net present value. Assume the stated discount rate is 12 percent annually, but use 6 percent semiannually throughout the analysis. (Disregard taxes.)

15. Warner Drug Co. has a net income of \$18 million and 9 million shares outstanding. Its common stock is currently selling for \$30.00 per share. Warner plans to sell common stock to set up a major new production facility with a net cost of \$21,280,000. The production facility will not produce a profit for one year, and then it is expected to earn a 16 percent return on the investment. Roth and Stern, an investment dealer, plans to sell the issue to the public for \$28.00 per share with a spread of 5 percent.
    a. How many shares of stock must be sold to net \$21,280,000? (Note: No out-of-pocket costs must be considered in this problem.)
    b. Why is the investment dealer selling the stock at less than its current market price?
    c. What are the earnings per share (EPS) and the price-earnings ratio before the issue (based on a stock price of \$30.00)? What will be the price per share immediately after the sale of stock if the P/E stays constant? (based on including the additional shares computed in part *a*).
    d. Compute the EPS and the price (P/E stays constant) after the new production facility begins to produce a profit.

e. Are the shareholders better off because of the sale of stock and the resultant investment? What other financing strategy could the company have tried to increase earnings per share?

16. The Presley Corporation is about to go public. It currently has aftertax earnings of $7.5 million, and 2.5 million shares are owned by the present stockholders (the Presley family). The new public issue will represent 600,000 new shares. The new shares will be priced to the public at $20.00 per share, with a 5 percent spread on the offering price. There will also be $200,000 in out-of-pocket costs to the corporation.

a. Compute the net proceeds to the Presley Corporation.

b. Compute the earnings per share immediately before the stock issue.

c. Compute the earnings per share immediately after the stock issue.

d. Determine what rate of return must be earned on the net proceeds to the corporation so that there will not be a dilution in earnings per share during the year of going public.

e. Determine what rate of return must be earned on the proceeds to the corporation so that there will be a 5 percent increase in earnings per share during the year of going public.

17. B. P. Hart has a chance to participate in a new public offering by Cardiovascular Systems, Inc. His broker informs him demand for the 800,000 shares to be issued is very strong. His broker's firm is assigned 20,000 shares in the distribution and will allow Hart, a relatively good customer, 1.5 percent of its 20,000 share allocation.

The initial offering price is $40.00 per share. There is a strong aftermarket, and the stock goes to $44.00 one week after issue. After the first full month after issue, Mr. Hart is pleased to observe his shares are selling for $46.25. He is content to place his shares in a lockbox and eventually use their anticipated increased value to help send his son to college many years in the future. However, one year after the distribution, he looks up the shares in *The Globe and Mail* and finds that they are trading at $38.50.

a. Compute the total dollar profit or loss on Mr. Hart's shares one week, one month, and one year after the purchase. In each case, compute the profit or loss against the initial purchase price.

b. Also compute this percentage gain or loss from the initial $40.00 price and compare this to the results that might be expected in an investment of this nature based on prior research. Assume the overall stock market was basically unchanged during the period of observation.

c. Why might a new public issue be expected to have a strong aftermarket?

18. The management of Rowe Boat Co. decided to go private in 2000 by buying all 2 million outstanding shares at $16.50 per share. By 2002 management had restructured the company by selling the scuba diving division for $7.5 million, the pleasure cruise division for $9 million, and the military contract aqua division for $11 million.

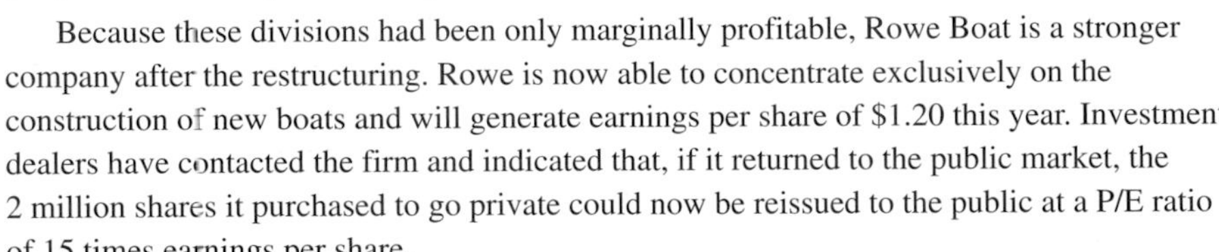

Because these divisions had been only marginally profitable, Rowe Boat is a stronger company after the restructuring. Rowe is now able to concentrate exclusively on the construction of new boats and will generate earnings per share of $1.20 this year. Investment dealers have contacted the firm and indicated that, if it returned to the public market, the 2 million shares it purchased to go private could now be reissued to the public at a P/E ratio of 15 times earnings per share.

a. What was the initial total cost to Rowe Boat Co. to go private?

b. What is the total value to the company from (1) the proceeds of the divisions that were sold, and (2) the current value of the 2 million shares (based on current earnings and an anticipated P/E of 15)?

c. What is the percentage return to the management of Rowe Boat Co. from the restructuring? Use answers from parts *a* and *b* to determine this value.

COMPREHENSIVE PROBLEM

19. The Anton Corporation, a manufacturer of radar control equipment, is planning to sell its shares to the general public for the first time. The firm's investment dealer is working with the Anton Corporation in determining a number of items. Information on the Anton Corporation follows:

ANTON CORPORATION
Income Statement
For the year ending Dec. 31, 2002

Sales (all on credit)	$22,428,000
Cost of goods sold	16,228,000
Gross profit	6,200,000
Selling and administrative expenses	2,659,400
Operating profit	3,540,600
Interest expense	370,600
Net income before tax	3,170,000
Taxes	1,442,000
Net income	$ 1,728,000

Balance Sheet
As of December 31, 2002

Assets

Cash	$ 150,000
Marketable securities	100,000
Accounts receivable	2,000,000
Inventory	3,800,000
Total current assets	6,050,000
Net plant and equipment	6,750,000
Total assets	$12,800,000

Liabilities and Shareholders' Equity

Accounts payable	$ 1,000,000
Notes payable	1,200,000
Total current liabilities	2,200,000
Long-term liabilities	2,380,000
Total liabilities	4,580,000
Shareholders' equity	
Common stock (1,200,000 shares)	4,000,000
Retained earnings	4,220,000
Total shareholders' equity	8,220,000
Total liabilities and shareholders' equity	$12,800,000

a. Assume that 500,000 new corporate shares will be issued to the general public. What will earnings per share immediately after public offering be? (Round to two places to the right of the decimal point.) Based on the price-earnings ratio of 10, what will the initial price of the stock be? Use earnings per share after the distribution in the calculation.

b. Assuming an underwriting spread of 7 percent and out-of-pocket costs of $150,000, what will be the net proceeds to the corporation?

c. What return must the corporation earn on the net proceeds to equal the earnings per share before the offering? How does this compare with current return on the total assets on the balance sheet?

d. Now assume that, of the initial 500,000 share distribution, 250,000 shares belong to current shareholders and 250,000 are new corporate shares, and these will be added to the 1.2 million corporate shares currently outstanding. What will earnings per share immediately after the public offering be? What will the initial market price of the stock be? Assume a price-earnings ratio of 10 and use earnings per share after the distribution in the calculation.

e. Assuming an underwriting spread of 7 percent and out-of-pocket costs of $150,000, what will be the net proceeds to the corporation?

f. What return must the corporation now earn on the net proceeds to equal earnings per share before the offering? How does this compare with current return on the total assets on the balance sheet?

Selected References

Barry, Christopher. "Initial Public Offering Underpricing: The Issuer's View—A Comment." *Journal of Finance* 44 (September 1989), pp. 1099–1103.

Barry, Christopher, Chris Muscarella, and Michael Vetsuypens. "Underwriter Warrants, Underwriter Compensation and Cost of Going Public." *Journal of Financial Economics* 18 (March 1991), pp. 113–35.

Carow, Kenneth A. "Underwriting Spreads and Reputational Capital: An Analysis of New Corporate Securities." *Journal of Financial Research* 22 (Spring 1999), pp. 15–28.

Ferreira, Eurico, Michael F. Spivey, and Charles E. Edwards. "Pricing New Issues and Seasoned Preferred Stock: A Comparison of Valuation Models." *Financial Management* 21 (Summer 1992), pp. 52–62.

Hanley, Kathless Weiss, and William J. Wilhelm, Jr. "Evidence on the Strategic Allocation of Initial Public Offerings." *Journal of Financial Economics* 37 (February 1995), pp. 239–57.

Pagano, Marco, Fabio Panetta, and Luigi Zingales. "Why Do Companies Go Public? An Empirical Analysis." *Journal of Finance* 53 (February 1998), pp. 27–64.

Reilly, Frank K. "New Issues Revisited." *Financial Management* 6 (Winter 1977), pp. 28–42.

Ritler, Jay R. "The Long-Term Performance of Initial Public Offerings." *Journal of Finance* 46 (March 1991), pp. 3–27.

Sherman, Ann E. "Underwriter Certification and the Effect of Shelf Registration on Due Diligence." *Financial Management* 28 (Spring 1999), pp. 5–19.

www.mcgrawhill.ca/college/block

CHAPTER | SIXTEEN

16 Long-Term Debt and Lease Financing

LEARNING | OBJECTIVES

1 Identify and describe the key features of long-term debt.

2 Discuss bond yields and prices as influenced by how corporations and governments are rated by bond rating services.

3 Analyze the decision of whether or not to call in and reissue debt (refund the obligation) when interest rates have declined.

4 Outline some of the features of innovative forms of raising long-term financing, including zero-coupon rate bonds, floating rate bonds, and real return bonds.

5 Outline the characteristics of long-term lease financing that make it an alternative form of long-term financing.

6 Analyze a lease-versus-borrow-to-purchase decision.

Shakespeare's advice, "Neither a borrower nor a lender be," hardly applies to corporate financial management. The virtues and drawbacks of debt usage were considered in Chapter 5 and in Chapter 11. One can only surmise that today's financial managers, although sometimes cautious in assuming debt, nevertheless find debt financing an essential component of the firm's capital structure. Over the last decade the corporate sector has shown the greatest increase in debt financing through bonds, as identified in Figure 14–2 of an earlier chapter.

In Chapter 16 we consider the diverse features of long-term debt instruments. These features and the creditworthiness of the issuing corporation have a direct influence on the important measure of return for bonds, which is the yield to maturity. Creditworthiness is examined through the credit rating firms. Furthermore, the analytical framework for the cost/benefit decision to call back or refund an existing bond issue is examined.

Lease financing is considered as a special case of long-term or intermediate debt financing. Particular attention is given to the accounting rules changes that affect leasing and the decision analysis for examining a lease versus borrow-to-purchase decision. A well-run business will make prudent use of both long-term debt and leases in its capital structure. Both are necessary to help build the capital needed for a firm's growth.

The Expanding Role of Debt

Rapid expansion of the economy has pressured corporations to raise even larger amounts of borrowed capital to facilitate their own growth. This continuously expanded level of borrowing has forced those evaluating the quality of corporate bond issues to reevaluate the benchmarks used to judge capital adequacy. The borrowing quality of the average corporation has deteriorated significantly since the 1960s, but this has been offset to a large degree by the increased efficiencies of the modern corporation that we have examined in earlier chapters.

Figure 16–1 attempts to capture the effects of this extra borrowing on the safety margin of pretax, pre-interest earnings (operating and non-operating) over interest charges, referred to as interest coverage or times interest earned. This is formula 3-12 from Chapter 3. From about six times interest earned in the early 1970s, the average interest coverage ratio has steadily declined for Canadian non-financial corporations. Interest coverage slipped to 0.9 times in the final quarter of 1991, rebounded to over 3 times by early 2000, but has fallen back to about 2 times by the end of 2001.

FIGURE 16–1
Interest coverage—Canadian nonfinancial corporations, 1978–2001

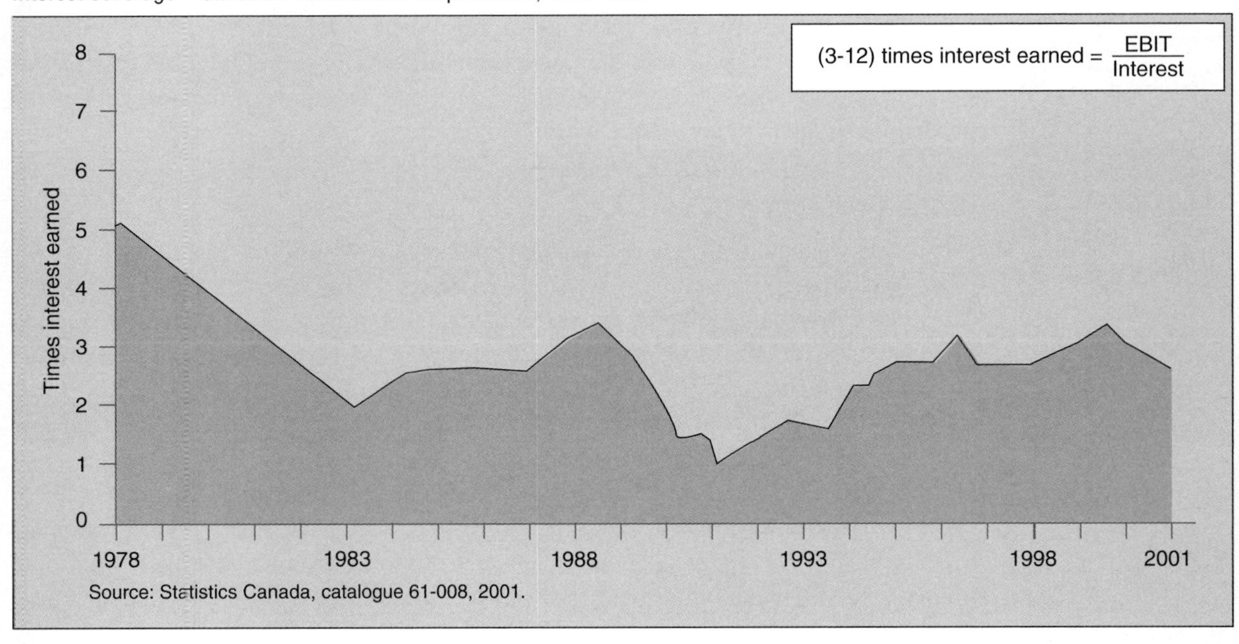

With the decline in the interest-paying capability of corporate borrowers, it is not uncommon for large and small corporations to default on their obligations resulting in the reorganization or liquidation of the firm's assets. In these situations the debt contract dictates the relative bargaining position of the lenders and the borrowing corporation in the reorganization or liquidation efforts.

The Debt Contract

The corporate bond represents the basic long-term debt instrument for most large corporations. The bond agreement specifies such basic items as the par value, the coupon rate, and the maturity date. These features are important in establishing value for the bond.

Par Value (Face Value) The initial value of the bond is its **par value (face value)** and the bond is initially sold at close to this value. This value is fixed and does not change. Most corporate bonds are traded in $1,000 units.

Coupon Rate The actual interest rate on the bond is its **coupon rate,** usually payable in semiannual installments. This is a contractual payment and does not change. To the extent that interest rates or yields in the market go above or below the coupon rate, after the bond has been issued, the market price on the bond will change from the par value. A bond paying a 10 percent coupon rate on par value will be considered a good investment when current yields are 6 percent. Therefore this bond will trade at a premium from par value in a market when the market yields have declined.

Maturity Date The final date on which repayment of the bond principal is due is the **maturity date.** The par or face value is due on this date.

The bond agreement is supplemented by a much longer document termed a **bond indenture.** The indenture, often containing over 100 pages of complicated legal wording, covers every detail surrounding the bond issue, including restrictions on the corporation, collateral pledged, methods of repayment, and procedures for initiating claims against the corporation. An independent trustee (for example, AGF Trust) is appointed by the corporation to administer the bond indenture provisions under the guidelines of the trust acts of the individual provinces.

AGF Trust
www.agf.com
Trusts
www.cdnpay.ca/eng/member/trusts.Eng.htm

Restrictive Covenants

To prevent weakening the claims that debt holders have against the assets or cash flows of a borrowing firm, certain promises or **covenants** are made by the firm in the indenture. These covenants to some degree limit the flexibility of management in running the firm but are meant to protect the investment of the debt holder. A common covenant limits the securing of subsequent debt ahead of debt already outstanding and may also limit additional borrowing. This can also be referred to as a negative pledge.

Restrictions may also require maintaining minimum ratios, such as debt/equity and working capital, and a covenant may limit the payment of dividends to a percentage of earnings. When ratio restrictions are in force, management must carefully monitor them to ensure the company is not technically in violation of its agreement with debt holders. The formulation of these ratios as identified in Chapter 3 may become quite important.

Security Provisions

A **secured claim** is one in which specific assets are pledged to bondholders in the event of default. Only infrequently are pledged assets actually sold and the proceeds distributed to bondholders. Typically, the defaulting corporation is reorganized, and existing claims are partially satisfied by issuing new securities to the participating parties. Of course, the stronger and better secured the initial claim, the higher the quality of the new security to be received in exchange. When a defaulting corporation is reorganized for failure to meet obligations, existing management may be terminated and, in extreme cases, be held legally responsible for any imprudent actions.

Continental Airline Bonds: Don't Forget to Read the Fine Print

In 1983, Continental Airlines went into Chapter 11 of the Bankruptcy Act, allowing it to reorganize, and in 1996, it came out of bankruptcy protection.

In March 1987, Continental Airlines issued $350 million of bonds that were secured by 53 planes and 55 spare engines having a total appraised value of $467 million. Bonds of this type are common in the airline industry and are sometimes referred to as equipment bonds or equipment trust certificates. Investors assume that the equipment listed as collateral for the bond will protect them from default, and therefore they agree to lend money at a rate lower than those of unsecured bonds of equal risk. What bondholders found out after Continental again declared bankruptcy in 1990 was that Continental had put its oldest and least salable planes into the asset pool used as collateral.

The $467 million in planes appeared to more than secure the bond issue and provided 4.7 times the indebtedness of the $100 million in first-class bonds. This particular bond issue had three classes of bondholders: first class, second class, and third class. It was assumed that the first-class bondholders were most protected because they could claim the whole asset pool as collateral, while the third-class bondholders were at more risk because they would be satisfied only after the first two classes of bondholders had been paid off.

With bankruptcy, many investors realized that they failed to read the fine print in the bond indenture (or didn't understand the implications), which stated that Continental could remove planes from the collateral pool and sell them to raise cash. If Continental did exercise this option and sold planes, it was required to either replace the planes or buy back bonds. After selling planes for about $167 million, Continental repurchased bonds at a discount in the open market. Because it could retire $167 million in par value at a discount, Continental paid much less than $167 million in cash to reduce this liability on the balance sheet. It then used the leftover dollars for other corporate purposes rather than protecting the bondholders. The riskiest third-class bonds were selling at the biggest discount from par value and so Continental maximized its bond repurchase program by buying third-class bonds rather than first-class. Continental took more money out of the asset pool than it put back into it.

The first-class bondholders, who were supposed to be the most secure, found themselves unprotected by the asset pool. What was left were mostly old models that were not fuel efficient and had very little value in the resale market. Covenants are there to protect the investor when times are bad and investors should not overlook permissive covenants with the hope of squeezing out a slightly higher interest rate. The investor may be trading off significant protection for very little "extra" return.

In 1993 Air Canada, as one of several airlines, paid $85 million for a stake in Continental which helped to bring Continental out of bankruptcy. By 1996 Air Canada had sold warrants on Continental for over $58 million, almost recouping its original investment, and had begun selling some of its common shares in Continental. Continental since 1993 has posted 24 consecutive quarters of positive earnings. This is little consolation to those original bondholders.

Source: Linda Sandler, "Continental Air Bonds' Terms Spur Turbulence," the *Wall Street Journal*, December 17, 1990, pp. C1-C2.

FINANCE IN ACTION

Q1 Did Continental achieve positive earnings during the difficult period of 2001-2002?

Q2 How has Continental's share price performed over the last year? Last five years?

www.continental.com/corporate/

Symbol: CAL (NYSE)

www.nyse.com

A number of terms denote collateralized or secured debt. Under a **mortgage agreement,** real property (plant and equipment) is pledged as security for the loan. A mortgage may be senior or junior in nature, with the former requiring satisfaction of claims before payment is given to the latter. Bondholders may also attach an **after-acquired property clause,** requiring that any new property be placed under the original mortgage.

Note that not all secured debt carries every protective factor; rather, its provisions result from careful negotiations through which some safeguards are included and others are rejected. Generally, the greater the protection offered a given class of bondholders, the lower the interest rate on the bond. Bondholders willing to assume some degree of risk receive a higher yield.

Unsecured Debt

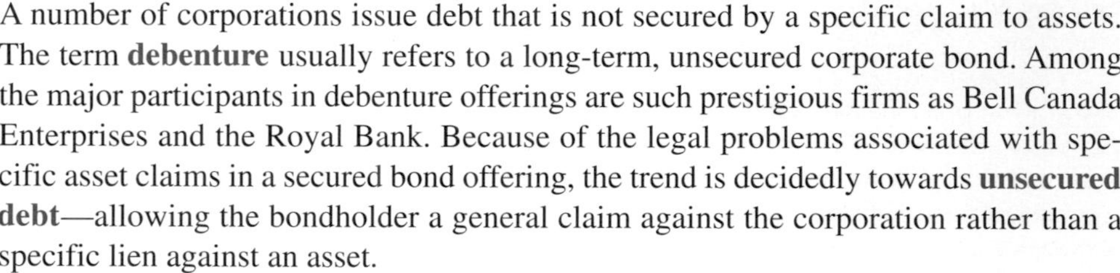

A number of corporations issue debt that is not secured by a specific claim to assets. The term **debenture** usually refers to a long-term, unsecured corporate bond. Among the major participants in debenture offerings are such prestigious firms as Bell Canada Enterprises and the Royal Bank. Because of the legal problems associated with specific asset claims in a secured bond offering, the trend is decidedly towards **unsecured debt**—allowing the bondholder a general claim against the corporation rather than a specific lien against an asset.

The Royal Bank of Canada
www.rbc.ca

Even unsecured debt may be divided between high-ranking and subordinated debt. A **subordinated debenture** is an unsecured bond in which payment to the holder occurs only after designated senior debenture holders are satisfied. The hierarchy of creditor obligations for secured as well as unsecured debt is presented in Figure 16–2 along with consideration of the position of shareholders. For a further discussion of payment of claims and the hierarchy of obligations, see Appendix 16A, "Financial Alternatives for Distressed Firms," which also covers bankruptcy considerations.

FIGURE 16–2
Priority of Claims

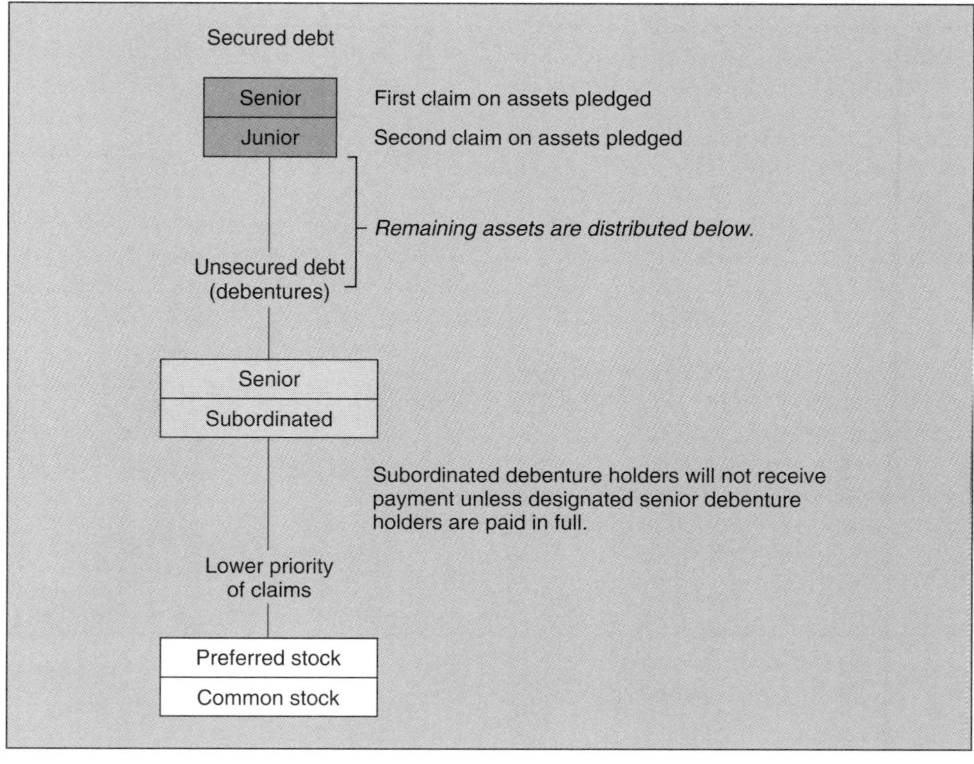

A **junk bond** is a bond that is not in default, but is of questionable quality and is speculative in nature. On the bond rating scale referred to later in this chapter, bonds that are rated BBB or above are generally considered to be investment grade debt. Those rated BB or below are considered junk or, more politely, high-yield debt. By this definition of a junk bond, a number of Canadian companies qualify. However these companies have been able to successfully raise long-term debt, but often at substantial premiums over top-quality corporate debt. Furthermore, high-yield securities are easier to sell in the more developed and greater risk-taking U.S. capital market.

Junk or High-Yield Bonds?

In Canada, bonds that are rated below triple B by the bond rating services are not considered to be of investment grade by many pension funds and other institutional buyers. Although the press prefers to call bonds that are rated below investment grade "junk bonds," the investment dealers that trade in these securities like to use the term "high-yield bonds or debt." The Dominion Bond Rating Service (DBRS) and Standard and Poors rate bonds in Canada (www.standardandpoors.com/canada).

The lack of interest in high-yield debt by Canadian buyers has forced many Canadian companies that do not have the ratings or stable cash flow of a bank or utility company to raise funds in the U.S. market. Often, the reason given for using the U.S. market was the breadth of the market and the greater liquidity it gave the issue.

However, Canadian underwriters have established a high-yield debt market in Canadian issues and a demand for these issues both within Canada and the United States. Portfolio managers such as Deans Knight Capital Management invest significant amounts in high-yielding debt for institutional investors. There are many high-yield mutual funds offered in the Canadian marketplace, which can be identified through the Globe fund web site.

With a clear majority of TSX listings ranking below investment grade, there is a large market for junk bonds. The debt of companies such as Air Canada, Hudson's Bay, Nortel, and Rogers Communication rate below investment grade, but these well-established companies offer an above average return to investors.

www.globefund.com
www.dbrs.com

FINANCE IN ACTION

Q1 Identify the holdings of a high yield bond (mutual) fund. Search the globefund site?

Q2 Identify five "junk" bonds as per the rating sites of Dominion Bond Rating Service (DBRS) or Standard & Poors?

Q3 Are the four companies listed above still rated "junk"?

A junk bond does have a high expected yield. Some studies have shown that a diversified portfolio of high-yielding junk bonds can be a satisfactory investment. However, one would want to look out for economic downturns. Junk bonds, which are not very prevalent in Canada, have been used to finance leveraged buyouts.

Methods of Repayment

The method of repayment for bond issues may not always call for one lump-sum disbursement at the maturity date. Historically, some Canadian and British government bond issues were perpetual in nature. In the case of one unusual U.S. issue, West Shore Railroad, 4 percent bonds are not scheduled to mature until 2361 (almost 400 years in the future). Nevertheless, most bonds have some orderly or preplanned system of repayment. In addition to the simplest arrangement—a single-sum payment at maturity—bonds may be retired by serial payments, through sinking-fund provisions, through conversion, or through a call feature.

Serial Payments Bonds may be paid off in installments, or **serial payments**, over the life of the issue. Each bond has its own predetermined date of maturity and receives interest only to that point. Although the total issue may span 20 years, 15 or 20 maturity dates may be assigned specific dollar amounts.

Sinking-Fund Provision A less structured but considerably more popular method of debt retirement is directed by a **sinking-fund provision**. Under this arrangement, semiannual or annual contributions are made by the corporation into a fund administered by the trustee for purposes of debt retirement. The calculation of the sinking fund provision is the annuity calculation based on a future value (amount to be repaid at

TABLE 16–1

Bonds: Corporate

BOMBARDIER INC.
(formerly Bombardier-MLW Ltd.)

8.3% Debentures, due July 28, 2003

DBRS Rating:	A	Aug 4, 2000
Issued:	$150,000,000	July 28, 1993
O/S	$150,000,000	Jan 31, 2001
Interest:	8.30% (S)	Jan 28/Jul 28

Redemption: Redeem, at any time at the greater of Canada Yield Price (Canada Yield + 0.30%) and par.
Lead Underwriter(s): ScotiaMcLeod Inc.
Trustee: Computershare Investor Services Inc.
CUSIP: 097751AB7

6.08% Notes, due Sept. 1, 2003

DBRS Rating:	A	Aug 4, 2000
Issued:	U.S.$69,000,000	Sep 1, 1993
O/S	U.S.$12,627,000	Jan 31, 2001
Interest:	6.08% (S)	Mar 1/Sep 1

Private Placement
Sinking Fund: Sufficient to retire the following principal amount of debt on:

Sep 1, 1994	U.S.$4,295,250	Sept 1, 1998	U.S.$18,630,000
Sep 1, 1995	U.S.$4,295,250	Sept 1, 1999	U.S.$11,040,000
Sep 1, 1996	U.S.$4,295,250	Sept 1, 2000	U.S.$9,522,000
Sep 1, 1997	U.S.$4,295,250	Sept 1, 2002	U.S.$4,209,000

Lead Underwriter(s): Bank of Montreal
Trustee: Computershare Investor Services Inc.

6.32% Notes, due Sept. 1, 2003

DBRS Rating:	A	Aug 4, 2000
Issued:	U.S.$31,000,000	Sep 1, 1993
O/S	U.S.$13,284,716	Jan 31, 2001
Interest:	6.32% (S)	Mar 1/Sep 1

Private Placement
Sinking Fund: Sufficient to retire U.S.$4,428,571 principal amount of debt on Sep 1, in each of the years 1997 to 2003 inclusive.
Lead Underwriter(s): Bank of Montreal
Trustee: Computershare Investor Services Inc.

6.58% Notes, due Jan. 25, 2006

DBRS Rating:	A	Aug 4, 2000
Issued:	U.S.$150,000,000	Jan 25, 1996
O/S	U.S.$150,000,000	Jan 31, 2001
Interest:	6.58% (S)	Jan 25/Jul 25

Private Placement
Redemption: Redeem, at any time at the greater of U.S. Treasury Yield + 0.50% and par.
Lead Underwriter(s): CS First Boston Corporation
Trustee: Computershare Investor Services Inc.

6.25% Bonds, due Feb. 23, 2006

Issued:	£175,000,000	Feb 22, 2001	Euro
O/S	£175,000,000	Feb 22,2001	
Interest:	6.25% (A)	Feb 23	

Lead Underwriter(s): ABN AMRO Bank N.V., Credit Suisse First Boston (Europe) Ltd., Deutsche Bank AG London, J.P. Morgan Securities Inc.

6.4% Debentures, due Dec. 22, 2006

DBRS Rating:	A	Aug 4, 2000
Issued:	$150,000,000	Dec 20, 1996
O/S	$150,000,000	Jan 31, 2001
Interest:	6.40% (S)	Jun 22/Dec 22

TABLE 16–1
Bonds: Corporate (concluded)

Redemption: Redeem, at any time on min. 30 and max. 60 days' notice at the greater of Canada Yield Price (Canada Yield + 0.10%) and par.
Lead Underwriter(s): RBC Dominion Securities Inc.
Trustee: Computershare Investor Services Inc.
CUSIP: 097751AD3

<u>5.75% Bonds, due Feb. 22, 2008</u>

Issued:	Euro500,000,000	Feb 22, 2001	Euro
O/S	Euro500,000,000	Feb 22,2001	
Interest:	5.75% (A)	Feb 22	

Lead Underwriter(s): ABN AMRO Bank N.V., Credit Suisse First Boston (Europe) Ltd., Deutsche Bank AG London, J.P. Morgan Securities Inc.

<u>7.35% Debentures, due Dec. 22, 2026</u>

DBRS Rating:	A	Aug 4, 2000
Issued:	$150,000,000	Dec 20, 1996
O/S	$150,000,000	Jan 31, 2001
Interest:	7.35% (S)	Jun 22/Dec 22

Redemption: Redeem, at any time on min. 30 and max. 60 days' notice at the greater of Canada Yield Price (Canada Yield + 0.15%) and par.
Lead Underwriter(s): RBC Dominion Securities Inc.
Trustee: Computershare Investor Services Inc.
CUSIP: 09775[illegible]AE1

maturity) that we saw in Chapter 9. The trustee takes the proceeds and goes into the market to purchase bonds from willing sellers. If no willing sellers are available, a lottery system is used among outstanding bondholders.

Conversion A more subtle method of reducing debt outstanding is to provide for debt **conversion** into common stock. Although this feature is exercised at the option of the bondholder, a number of incentives or penalties may be utilized to encourage conversion. The mechanics of convertible bond trading are discussed at length in Chapter 19.

Call Feature A call provision allows the corporation to call in or force in the debt issue before maturity. In the event that it exercises the **call feature**, the corporation pays a premium over par value of 5 to 10 percent. Bonds with call features are redeemable issues. Modern call provisions usually do not take effect until the bond has been outstanding at least 5 to 10 years in order to allow an original investor to reap some reward if he or she timed the purchase to buy the bonds before a general decrease in interest rates. Generally, the call premium declines over time, usually by ½ to 1 percent per year after the call period begins. A corporation may decide to call in outstanding debt issues when interest rates on new securities are considerably lower than those on previously issued debt. (The purpose would be to get the high-cost, old debt off the books.)

Table 16–1 presents information from *Financial Post Bonds: Corporate* on Bombardier, as of December 31, 2001. The bonds carried an A rating and were issued in Canadian dollars, U.S. dollars, and euros. Outstanding were bonds, debentures, and medium-term notes. Some were redeemable before maturity, the euro bonds had interest payments on an annual basis, and one issue with sinking funds payments was a private placement. Underwriters were from both Canada and abroad.

FINANCE IN ACTION

www.sedar.com

www.comdev.ca
Symbol: CDV

www.nortelnetworks.com
Symbol: NT

Exchangeable, Redeemable, Floating Rate Debentures

In April 1999, Teck Corporation raised $125 million with the private placement of exchangeable debentures with maturity in 2024. TD Securities and Griffiths McBurney were the underwriters for the issue. The interest payment on the issue "floated" at 2 percent above Teck's dividend rate (at the time 3.28 percent). Teck debentures were then rated A (low) at the time (now BBB high), which would have suggested a yield of over 6 percent for regular debentures. However, Teck received a lower interest rate because each debenture was "exchangeable" into 42.5532 shares of Cominco Ltd., a company partially owned by Teck. This feature gave each debenture added value and afforded Teck a lower interest payment rate. For a premium above the par value of $1,000 Teck could "redeem" (buy back) the debentures before their maturity. The premium began at $112.00, decreasing to $19.00 over time.

In 2001, Teck and Cominco merged to become Teck Cominco. These bonds had to be reset based on the exchange rate of 1.8 Teck for 1 Cominco. The face value of the bond was reduced to $745 and was now exchangeable into 76.5958 Teck class B shares.

In late 2001, Com Dev International, a wireless communications firm and Nortel ($1.8 billion), issued convertible debentures that were well received by the market. Information on these issues is available at the SEDAR Web site.

1. For each debenture issue identify the following: private or public, rate of conversion, interest rate, underwriting spread, net proceeds to the firm, currency.

Bond Prices, Yields, and Ratings

The financial manager must be sensitive to interest rate changes and price movements in the bond market. The treasurer's interpretation of market conditions influences the timing of new issues, the coupon rate offered, the maturity date, and the necessity for a call provision.

Let's examine the erratic bond pricing during the period 1977 to 1982. When the market interest rate on outstanding 30-year, AAA corporate bonds went from 9.5 percent to 18.3 percent, the average price of such existing bonds dropped about 48 percent. Imagine the disillusionment of a conservative investor during that period as $1,000, 9.5 percent, top-quality bonds declined to be quoted at $525.[1] Though most bonds are virtually certain to be redeemed at their face value at maturity ($1,000 in this case), this is small consolation to the bondholder who has many decades to wait while his or her capital is tied up making below-market returns. On the other hand, there have been tremendous returns on bonds, particularly when yields declined in late 1982.

As just indicated, the price of a bond is intimately tied to current interest rates. A bond paying 9.5 percent ($95.00 per year) fares quite poorly when the going market rate is 18.3 percent ($183.00 per year). To maintain a market in the older issue, the price is adjusted downward to reflect current market demands. The longer the life of the issue, the greater the influence of interest rate changes on the price of the bond.[2] The same process works in reverse if interest rates go down. The value of a 30-year, $1,000 bond initially issued to yield 18.3 percent would rise to $1,800 if interest rates declined to 9.5 percent (assuming the bond is not callable). An illustration of interest rate effects on bond prices is presented in Table 16–2 for a bond paying 12 percent interest. Observe that year to maturity as well as market interest rates have a strong influence on bond prices.

[1]Bond prices are generally quoted as a percentage of original par value. In this case, the quote would be read 52.5.

[2]This is known as Malkiel's second theory of bonds. It is completely true only when the coupon rate of the bond is equal to or greater than the original discount rate.

TABLE 16–2
Interest rates and bond prices (the bond pays 12 percent interest)

Years to Maturity	Rate in the Market (percent)				
	8%	10%	12%	14%	16%
1	$1,037.72	$1,018.59	$1,000	$981.92	$964.33
15	1,345.84	1,153.72	1,000	875.91	774.84
25	1,429.64	1,182.56	1,000	861.99	755.33

Note: This table is based on semiannual interest payments, with annualized interest rates.

Over the past couple of decades, long-term interest rates have shown a definite downward trend from the high inflation era of the late 1970s and early 1980s, as Figure 16–3 illustrates. As we observed in Chapter 14 there has been a definite trend towards longer-term maturities in the last number of years as firms try to lock in the lower interest rates. At the same time, firms have broadened their debt structure with money market instruments and medium-term notes.

FIGURE 16–3
Long-term yields on corporate debt

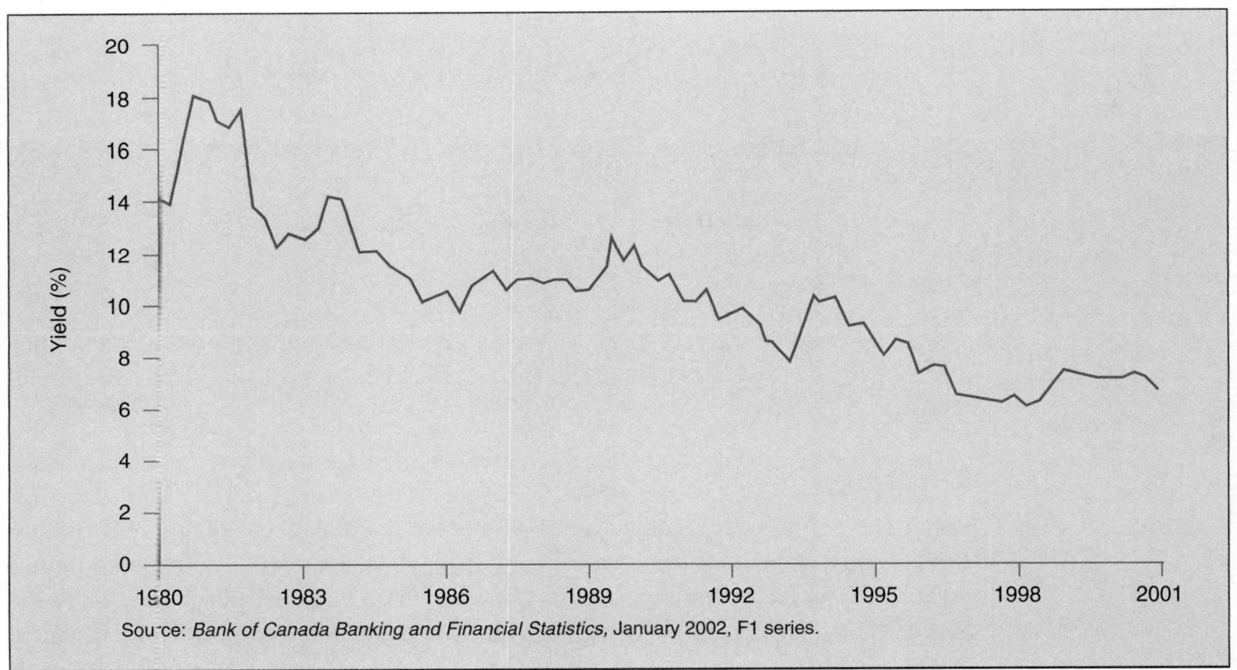

Source: *Bank of Canada Banking and Financial Statistics,* January 2002, F1 series.

Bond Yields

Bond yields are quoted on three different bases: coupon rate, current yield, and yield to maturity. To illustrate we apply each to a $1,000 par value bond paying $100 per year interest for 10 years and currently selling in the market for $900.

Coupon Rate (Nominal Yield) Stated interest payment divided by the par value is the coupon rate. Generally the coupon rate is fixed under the terms of the indenture.

$$\frac{\$100}{\$1,000} = 10\%$$

Current Yield The stated interest payment divided by the current price of the bond gives the **current yield.** The current yield is focused short-term and does not consider the time to maturity.

$$\frac{\$100}{\$900} = 11.11\%$$

Yield to Maturity The interest rate that equates future interest payments and the payment at maturity to the current market price is the **yield to maturity.** This represents the concept of the internal rate of return. Although the yield to maturity (YTM) has its flaws it is the most instructive yield calculation.

In our illustration we determine an internal rate of 11.75 percent. Recall that this is the discount rate, we call yield (YTM) that equates the annual interest payments of $100 for 10 years and the final payment of $1,000 to the current price of $900.

Calculator

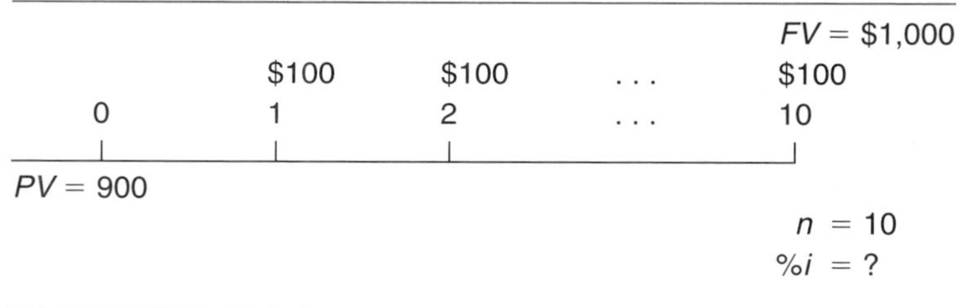

Yield = 11.75%.

When financial analysts speak of bond yields, the general assumption is that they are speaking of yield to maturity. This is deemed to be the most significant measure of return.

Bond Ratings

Dominion Bond Rating Service
www.dbrs.com

Rating services provide an objective assessment of the investment quality of securities. Both issuing corporations and investors alike pay close attention to the bond ratings assigned by **bond rating** services. In Canada, Dominion Bond Rating Services and Standard & Poor's Rating Service provide independent bond ratings. In the United States, Moody's Investor Service, and Standard & Poor's Corporation perform a similar service.

The higher the rating assigned a given issue, the lower the interest payments required to satisfy potential investors. A higher rating indicates a lower amount of risk. A major industrial corporation may be able to issue a bond with a 5 percent yield to maturity because it is rated AA by the Dominion Bond Rating Service, while a smaller, riskier firm may qualify for only a B rating and be forced to pay in excess of 10 percent as noted in Table 16–3.

The rating systems of Dominion Bond Rating Service and Standard and Poor's Rating Service are outlined on the next page:

	Description
AAA	Highest quality
AA	
A	
BBB	
BB	Speculative or medium quality
B	
CCC	
D	Default

High(+) and low(−) modifiers are also added to each of the ranges to make the rating even more precise. Both services have web sites that outline the criteria for each category more completely.

TABLE 16–3

Outstanding debt issues, March 1, 2002

Rating/Issuer	Coupon	Maturity Date	Price	Yield to Maturity
AAA				
CARDS Trust Receivables	5.630	Dec. 21/05	102.94	4.77
Government of Canada	5.750	Sept. 01/06	104.10	4.72
Government of Canada	8.000	Jun 01/27	127.72	5.88
AA				
BMO	8.150	May 9/06	111.29	5.11
BMO	6.685	Dec. 31/11	101.69	6.45
Nav Canada	6.600	Dec 01/06	106.13	5.12
Nav Canada	7.400	Jun 01/27	109.78	6.60
A				
Bell Canada	6.700	June 28/07	105.74	5.44
Bell Canada	7.850	Apr. 02/31	106.11	7.34
Loblaw	6.000	June 02/08	101.92	5.63
Loblaw	6.650	Nov. 08/27	96.67	6.93
BBB				
Domtar	10.000	Apr. 15/11	108.21	8.68
Talisman	5.800	Jan. 30/07	97.69	6.35
BB				
Rogers Cable	10.500	June 01/06	103.00	9.61
B				
Air Canada	6.750	Feb 02/04	72.00	26.29
Saskatchewan Wheat Pool	6.600	July 18/07	71.00	14.56

1. Do these securities still have the same ratings and yields?

Check out bond ratings at:
www.dbrs.com
www.standardandpoors.com/canada

Check out yields at:
www.globeandmail.com/businessPE

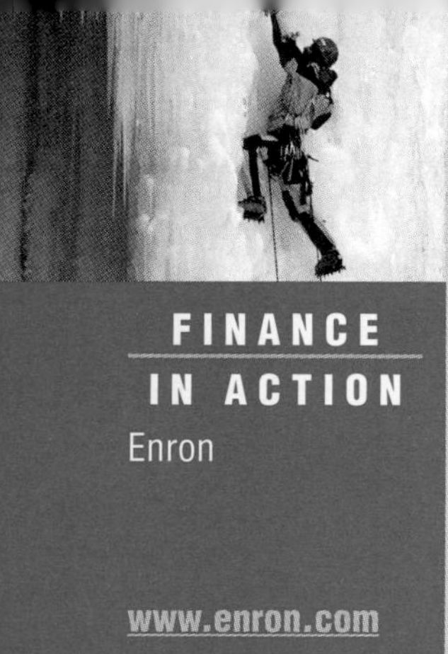

FINANCE IN ACTION

Enron

Before the Fall

Before Enron filed for the biggest corporate bankruptcy in U.S. history it was negotiating to be bought out and merged with Dynegy Inc. Until October of 2001 it had a solid bond rating from both Standard and Poor's and Moody's bond rating services. However in November 2001, both bond rating organizations lowered Enron's bond rating to junk bond status. This violation of bond indenture covenants immediately resulted in $3.9 billion of debt becoming due and payable.

The Dynegy deal was abandoned partly as a result of the lower rating and Enron shortly thereafter filed for bankruptcy protection under Chapter 11. Although the rating services claimed they were looking at bondholder protection with the downgrade, their announcements only came after the markets had already dramatically decreased the value of Enron stock. Were the rating services providing valuable insight into the market or reflecting what the market already knew?

www.enron.com

Bonds receive ratings based on the corporation's ability to make interest payments, its consistency of performance, its size, its debt-equity ratio, its working capital position, and a number of other factors. Rating services are extremely interested in the quality of the corporation's management, although it seems this judgement is often a function of the consistency and adequacy of the firm's financial ratios. The yield spread between higher- and lower-rated bonds varies with economic conditions. If investors are pessimistic about the economic outlook, they may accept as much as 3 percent less to hold high-quality securities, while in normal times the spread may be only 1 percent.

In a manner similar to Chapter 3, on financial analysis, the rating service calculates ratios such as profit margins, coverage ratios, debt to equity, and total liabilities to equity. There is also a close examination of the debt indenture to identify the protection afforded the debt holder.

Examining Actual Bond Offerings

Information on actual outstanding debt issues as of March 2002 is shown in Table 16–3 to illustrate the various terms we have used. Recall that the true return on a bond issue is measured by yield to maturity (the last column of Table 16–3). Air Canada, with the lowest rating of B, which is below investment grade in Canada, offers the highest expected yield to maturity for a short-term maturity, over 20 percent above a comparable AA-rated bond. This suggests extreme risk and the strong possibility that an investor may not get fully paid. The CARDS Trust Receivable, which is an asset-backed security based on credit card receipts, was trading at a comparable yield to the Government of Canada bonds with the same approximate maturity date.

Talisman Energy
www.talisman-energy.com

Bond issues are often quoted by how many basis points they trade above Government of Canada issues. For example the BMO bond rated AA and maturing in 2006 was trading 39 basis points above the Canada issue. Notice that the Talisman bond trades at a reasonable yield compared to the Domtar bond. Bonds that trade at a discount are often more desirable and therefore have somewhat lower yields.

The Refunding Decision

From time to time a firm may decide to refund a bond issue. For example, assume you are the financial vice president for a corporation that has issued bonds at 12.5 percent only to witness a drop in interest rates to 10 percent. If you believe interest rates will not go down further and will go back up, you may wish to redeem the expensive 12.5 percent bonds and issue new debt at the prevailing 10 percent rate. This process is called a refunding operation. It is made feasible by the call provision that enables a corporation to buy back bonds at close to par rather than at high market values when interest rates are declining. The decline in long-term interest rates over the last couple of decades has provided a good environment for refunding.

Because bond indenture agreements in Canada normally contain the financial advantage clause, refunding of high-cost debt has been more infrequent than one would expect.[3] Dofasco's call in July 1986 of its 17 percent debentures, issued in 1982 and due in 1997, thus had particular significance in the investment community. Before the call, each $1,000 worth of these bonds traded for $1,250. The day after the call announcement they were worth $1,113, precisely the redemption value. The investment community was not pleased and took issue with Dofasco's call. Bond indentures were rewritten thereafter.

Dofasco
www.dofasco.ca

Besides refunding an issue to achieve a lower interest rate, the corporation may want to remove restrictive covenants in the bond indenture, reissue new debt with a longer term than the issue currently outstanding or reorder the firm's capital structure.

A Capital Budgeting Problem

The **refunding decision** involves outflows in the form of financing costs related to redeeming and reissuing securities and inflows represented by savings in annual interest costs and some tax savings. The task of an analyst is to determine whether or not the refunding of bonds will add to the value of the firm.

In the present case, assume the corporation issued $10 million worth of 12.5 percent debt with a 25-year maturity and the debt has been on the books for 5 years. The corporation now has the opportunity to buy back the old debt and effectively replace it with new debt at 10 percent interest with a 20-year life. The underwriting cost for the old issue was $125,000, and the underwriting cost for the new issue is $200,000. Other issue costs (legal, accounting, advertising, and printing) were $25,000 for the old issue and $30,000 for the new issue. We also assume that the corporation is in the 40 percent tax bracket and uses a 6 percent discount rate for refunding decisions.

Since the savings from a refunding decision are certain—unlike the savings from most other capital budgeting decisions—the **aftertax cost of new debt** is used as the discount rate rather than the more generalized cost of capital.[4] In this case then, the aftertax cost of new debt is 10 percent × (1 − tax rate), or 6 percent.

[3] This clause states that borrowers cannot use money raised more cheaply to finance the redemption of high-cost debt.

[4] A minority opinion would be that there is sufficient similarity between the bond refunding decision and other capital budgeting decisions to disallow any specialized treatment. Also note that although the bondholders must still bear some risk of default, for which they are compensated, the corporation assumes no risk.

Restatement of facts

	Old Issue	New Issue
Size	$10,000,000	$10,000,000
Interest rate	12.5%	10.0%
Total life	25 years	20 years
Remaining life	20 years	20 years
Call premium	10%	—
Underwriting costs	$125,000	$200,000
Other issue costs	25,000	30,000
Tax bracket 40%		
Discount rate 6%		

Let's go through the capital budgeting process of defining the costs (outflows) and benefits (inflows) and determining the net present value attached to the refunding decision.

Step A—Costs (Outflow Considerations)

1. *Payment of Call Premium.* The first cost is the 10 percent call premium on $10 million, or $1 million. This prepayment penalty is necessary to call in the original issue. Because it is considered a capital item, the $1 million cash expenditure will cost $1 million on an aftertax basis.[5]

Net cost of call premium	$1,000,000

2. *Borrowing Expenses on the New Issue.* The second cost is the $200,000 underwriting cost of the new issue and the $30,000 in other expenses. The actual aftertax costs of these expenses is somewhat less because their payment is tax deductible. Expenses related to the borrowing of money or issuing of shares, such as printing and advertising costs, legal and accounting expenses, filing fees, and underwriting commissions (the investment dealer's fee), are deductible for tax purposes.

   These financing expenses are considered capital in nature and, for tax purposes, must be amortized over five years on a straight-line basis. This amounts to 20 percent per year. If the debt is repaid, any undeducted balance of these borrowing costs is deductible in the year the debt is fully repaid, unless the repayment is part of a refinancing. Therefore, in a refunding decision, unamortized borrowing costs on the old issue must be expensed on the original amortization schedule.

   In our example, equal deductions of $46,000 ($230,000/5) a year will occur over the next five years. The tax savings from a noncash write-off are equal to the amount times the tax rate. For a company in a 40 percent tax bracket, $46,000 of annual tax deductions will provide $18,400 ($46,000 × .4) of tax savings each year for the next five years. The present value of the annual tax savings is:

   Calculator computation: $77,507
   ($n = 5$; $i = 6\%$)

[5]This is unlike the situation in the United States, where the call premium is tax deductible.

The net borrowing costs (underwriting and other flotation expenses) of the reissue equal the actual expenditure less the present value of the future tax savings.

Actual expenditure	$230,000
Less: PV of future tax savings	77,507
Net cost of borrowing costs	$152,493

3. *Duplicate Interest during Overlap Period.* An overlap period generally occurs because the new bonds must be sold before the old ones are redeemed. We allow one month as an estimate of the overlap period, although it could be longer. Offsetting this payment of interest on two bond issues during the overlap period is the fact that the company earns interest on the proceeds from the new issue until it employs them. Since interest is a tax-deductible expense, the net cash flow effect of having to continue paying interest on the old issue during the overlap period is the difference between what is paid on the old issue and what is earned on the new (say 8½ percent in this case):

125 × 1⁄12 × $10,000,000 × (1 − .40)	$62,500
.085 × 1⁄12 × $10,000,000 × (1 − .40)	42,500
	$20,000

The firm will not likely earn interest on the full $10 million because the underwriter pays the firm a reduced amount after the underwriting fees. We use $10 million for ease of calculation.

Step B—Benefits (Inflow Considerations) The major inflows in the refunding decision are related to the reduction of annual interest expense.

4. *Cost Savings in Lower Interest Rates.* The corporation enjoys a 2.5 percentage point drop in interest rates, from 12.5 percent to 10 percent, on $10 million of bonds if it refunds the bond issue:

12.5% × $10,000,000	$1,250,000
10.0% × $10,000,000	1,000,000
Savings	$ 250,000

Since the firm is in the 40 percent tax bracket, this is equivalent to $150,000 of aftertax benefits per year for 20 years. Just take the savings and multiply by one minus the tax rate to get the aftertax benefits. Applying a 6 percent discount rate for a 20-year annuity:

$$PMT = \$150{,}000;\ n = 20;\ i = 6\%;\ FV = 0$$
$$CPT\ PV = \$1{,}720{,}488$$

Cost savings in lower interest rates: $1,720,488

The borrowing expenses of the old issue, the underwriting, and other costs are irrelevant for the decision analysis on a refunding decision. Unamortized borrowing expenses cannot be brought forward and written off as part of a refinancing. The unamortized borrowing expenses are written off as scheduled.

FINANCE IN ACTION

www.canpx.ca

www.moneyline.com

Transparency in the Bond Markets

The Canadian bond market executes billions of dollars in trades on a daily basis, and yet these trades are not readily "visible" to all market participants. Trades occur over phones, by telex, and through computer terminals without necessarily passing on pricing information for full public view. Without full information being available to all investors, one should question the complete efficiency of this market. Could some players obtain abnormal returns?

To bring these transactions and the prices paid into full view and to make the transactions "transparent," the Investment Dealers Association (IDA) and the Interdealer Brokers Association, with the approval of the Ontario Securities Commission, instituted a bond pricing service called CanPx. CanPx has partnered with Moneyline Telerate to provide this service.

This service will provide information about the lowest prices offered and the highest prices bid on bonds and Treasury bills. Investment dealers will be required to supply the information. It is expected that this increased transparency in the bond market will increase trading volumes, decrease the spreads between the buy and sale prices of bonds, lower interest rates generally, and improve the market's efficiency.

Step C—Net Present Value We now compare our outflows and our inflows.

Costs (Outflows)	
1. Net cost of call premium	$1,000,000
2. Net cost of borrowing expenses on new issue	152,493
3. Duplicate interest during overlap period	20,000
Present value of costs	$1,172,493
Benefits (Inflows)	
4. Cost savings in lower interest rates	$1,720,488
Present value of benefits	$1,720,488
Net present value	$ 547,995

The refunding decision has a positive net present value, suggesting that interest rates have dropped sufficiently to favour refunding. The only question is: Will interest rates go lower—indicating an even better time for refunding? This is a consideration all firms must face, and there is no easy answer.

A number of other factors may complicate the problem. For example, the overlapping time period in the refunding procedure when both issues are outstanding and the firm is paying double interest could be longer than one month. If the bonds were issued at a discount, the difference between the redemption value and the amount the company received for the bond would be tax deductible in the year of redemption.

In working problems, students should have minimum difficulty if they follow these four suggested calculations. Note, by way of review, that in the calculations we had the following tax implications:

1. Payment of call premium—non-tax-deductible.
2. New issue expenses—underwriting commissions and legal, accounting, and printing costs are all flotation costs. We pay an amount now and then amortize it over a five-year period for tax purposes. This subsequent amortization represents a *noncash write-off* of a tax-deductible expense. The annual tax savings from the amortization are equal to the write-off times the tax rate. The five-year annuity is then taken to a present value.

3. Duplicate interest during the overlap period, both interest earned and the interest expense on the old issue must be considered aftertax.
4. Cost savings in lower interest rates—cost savings are like any form of income, and we retain the cost savings times (1 − tax rate).

The underwriting cost on the old issue is irrelevant for a refunding decision. The approximate discount rate for a refunding decision is the aftertax cost of the new debt.

Other Forms of Bond Financing

As interest rates continued to show increasing volatility in the 1980s, innovative forms of bond financing were presented to the market.

The **zero-coupon rate bond**, as the name implies, does not pay interest. It is, however, sold at a deep discount from face value. The return to the investor is the difference between the investor's cost and the face value received at the end of the life of the bond.

The zero-coupon bond has had limited appeal in Canada, particularly after an unfavourable tax ruling late in 1991. However, several of these bonds went to market, including an Ontario Hydro $765 million zero-coupon Canadian dollar issue that paid no interest. Ontario Hydro was responsible for a total of $3.99 billion in principal maturing yearly for various amounts until the year 2031. The investor would receive principal repayments that produced a yield of about 10 percent annually, depending on when the principal payments were due. Zero-coupon bonds have been issued in Canadian dollars in the eurobond market. Furthermore, Canadian companies have issued zero-coupon bonds in the U.S. and Canadian markets based on cash flow considerations in recent years.

The advantage to the corporation of a zero-coupon bond is the immediate cash inflow, without any outflow until the bonds mature. Furthermore, the difference between the initial bond price and the maturity value may be amortized for tax purposes by the corporation over the life of the bond. This means that the corporation takes annual deductions without current cash outflow.

A similar investment is the **strip bond,** which is arranged by an investment dealer and is based on government securities and, more recently, on corporate bonds. The actual coupons and the face value of the security are sold separately with differing maturities to suit the investor. The securities, which are held in custody for the benefit of investors, are sold at a fraction of face value and are ultimately redeemed at full value. The investor receives a multiple of the original investment and no interest.

Strips
www.donations.utoronto.ca/bonds.htm

Strip Bond Illustrated

An investor desires an 8 percent yield or return for a 10-year investment. The investment dealer locates a Government of Canada bond that matures in 10 years, strips the coupons or semiannual payments from the bond (to sell to other clients), and agrees to sell the face or maturity value of the bond to the investor for $463.19. In 10 years the investor collects $1,000. (Larger multiples of the $1,000 bond are possible.) The investor has realized a holding period or true yield to maturity (YTM) of 8 percent, without the risk of having to reinvest the coupons at lower interest rates.

Calculator

no coupons	FV = $1,000
PV = ?	n = 10
	%i = 8%
	PMT = 0

Compute PV = $463.19.

From the investor's viewpoint, the strip bonds allow him or her to lock in a fixed return on the initial investment. For example, an investor may know he will more than double the investment in 10 years. The investor does not have to be concerned about reinvesting coupon payments every six months, possibly at lower rates of return. The major drawback is that the difference in value between the purchase price and the maturity must be amortized on a straight-line basis as interest income over the number of years to maturity. Tax must be paid annually on this interest income, even though the bondholder does not have a cash return until maturity.

Many investors in strip bonds have tax-exempt or deferred status. These include pension funds, foundations, charitable organizations, registered retirement savings plans (RRSPs), and the like. Strip bonds are also favoured by institutional investors that like to more precisely match their assets (the bonds) with their future liabilities.

The prices of strip bonds tend to be highly volatile when there are changes in interest rates. This is due to the fact that the initial yield to maturity comes solely from the face value payment at maturity with no annual interest payment to modify the effects of interest rate changes in the marketplace.

Another type of innovative bond issue is the **floating-rate bond** (quite popular in European capital markets). In this case, instead of a change in the price of the bond, the interest rate paid on the bond changes with market conditions (usually monthly or quarterly). Thus, a bond that was initially issued to pay 6 percent may lower the interest payments to 4 percent during some years and raise them to 9 percent in others. The interest rate is usually tied to some overall market rate, such as the yield on treasury bills or the prime rate.

The advantage is that the investor has a constant (or almost constant) market value for the security, even though interest rates vary. The one exception that can cause a change to this principle is that floating-rate bonds often have broad limits that interest payments cannot exceed. For example, the interest rate on a 6 percent initial offering may not be allowed to go over 13 percent or below 4 percent. If long-term interest rates dictated an interest payment of 15 percent, the payment would still remain at 13 percent. This could cause some short-term loss in market value. To date, floating-rate bonds have been relatively free of this problem.

Real return bonds
www.fin.gc.ca/invest/instru-e.html

To keep matters in perspective, floating-rate bonds still represent a relatively small percentage of the total market of new debt offerings.

As an alternative to adjusting the interest payments due to changing yields in the market, the **real return bond** adjusts the principal amount based on inflationary changes. In November 1991 the government of Canada issued Canada's first real return bond. The bond would provide a real yield of 4.25 percent above the inflation rate as measured by the Canadian consumer price index (CPI). This security had its

Innovation with CRESTS and Linked Notes

Two interesting debt issues were offered in the Canadian market in early 1999. Both were innovative financings to raise capital for the corporation and to attract the buying interest of increasingly sophisticated investors. Details of public issues are found in a prospectus which is filed electronically at SEDAR.

PanCanadian Petroleum sold $125 million of Coupon Reset Subordinated Term Securities (CRESTS) set to mature in 2034. Every five years the interest payment would be reset at 200 basis points (2 percent) above a comparable 5-year Government of Canada bond. The PanCanadian bonds in 1999 would pay interest at 7 percent semiannually and were sold at $993.54 to offer a yield slightly above 7 percent. DBRS rated them pfd-2 (high), which was a preferred share rating. Did DBRS not consider these bonds?

Barrington Petroleum, in a bought deal with CIBC WoodGundy, raised $50 million with 5-year natural gas linked subordinated notes. The notes were to pay an interest rate of 6.5 percent and up to an additional 5.5 percent interest based on the price of natural gas.

FINANCE IN ACTION

Q1 Identify a recently issued "exotic" bond?

www.sedar.com

principal adjusted to reflect changes in value due to inflation. A coupon payment of 4.25 percent was paid semiannually on the adjusted principal. By historical standards, a 4.25 percent return was quite good on long-term government securities.

The **revenue bond** has always been a factor in the U.S. market, but it was brought to the Canadian market in 1996. The revenue bond is based on an enterprise that generates a dependable stream of cash flow, and this, rather than the firm's assets, is the security for investors. NAV Canada, with RBC Dominion Securities as lead underwriter, issued $3 billion in revenue bonds to assist in the purchase of the air traffic control network from Transport Canada. With no competition allowed, the ability to set rates, a surcharge on all airline tickets, and a levy on foreign aircraft over Canadian skies, cash flow to NAV Canada would seem assured. NAV Canada has since issued several well-received revenue bonds

Eurobond Market

Another component in the bond market is the **eurobond.** A eurobond is a bond payable in currency and sold where that currency is not legal tender. Eurobonds take us out of the purely domestic framework and into foreign markets. Eurocurrencies are units of currency deposited in banks outside of the country issuing the currencies. Of such deposits, the U.S. eurodollar is the most prevalent. International investment dealer syndicates place eurobonds all over the world. An example might be a bond of a Canadian corporation that is payable in U.S. dollars and sold in London, Paris, Tokyo, or Singapore. Table 16–4 presents several outstanding eurobond issues.

TABLE 16–4
Examples of eurobonds

	Rating	Coupon	Maturity	Amount Outstanding ($ millions)	Currency Domination*
Petro-Canada	Baa1	9.25%	2021	300.0	U.S.$
Procter & Gamble Co.	Aa2	10.88	2003	200.0	C$
Sony Corporation	Aa3	1.40	2005	300.0	Yen
Telecom Corporation	Aa1	7.50	2003	100.0	NZ$

*C$ is Canadian dollar and NZ$ is New Zealand dollar.
Source: Mergent Bond Report, July 2000

Moody's
www.moodys.com

Looking back at Table 16–1, we note that the Bombardier had eurobonds outstanding. These issues allowed Bombardier to tap the resources of this large market of funds. While these issues in EUROs carry exchange risk, an issue in Canadian dollars in the euromarket would not be subject to exchange rate fluctuations.

Disclosure requirements in the eurobond market are less demanding than those of Canadian domestic regulatory agencies. Investors in eurobonds are generally not able to rely on bond rating agencies, though Moody's and Standard & Poor's have been rating selected eurobond issues for a fee.

Advantages and Disadvantages of Debt

The financial manager must consider whether debt contributes to or detracts from the firm's operations. In certain industries, such as the airlines, very heavy debt utilization is a way of life, whereas in other industries (drugs, photographic equipment) reliance is placed on other forms of capital.

Benefits of Debt

The advantages of debt are as follows:

1. Interest payments are tax deductible. Because the corporate tax rate approximates 40 percent, the effective aftertax cost of interest is about 60 percent of the dollar amount expended.
2. The financial obligation is clearly specified and is of a fixed nature (with the exception of floating-rate bonds). Contrast this with selling an ownership interest in which shareholders have open-ended participation in the sharing of profits.
3. In an inflationary economy, debt may be paid back with cheaper dollars. A $1,000 bond obligation may be repaid in 10 or 20 years with dollars that have shrunk in value by 50 or 60 percent. In terms of real dollars, or purchasing power equivalents, one might argue that the corporation should be asked to repay something in excess of $2,000. Presumably, high interest rates in inflationary periods compensate the lender for loss in purchasing power, but this is not always the case.
4. The use of debt, up to a prudent point, may lower the cost of capital to the firm. To the extent that debt does not strain the risk position of the firm, its low aftertax cost may aid in reducing the weighted overall cost of financing to the firm.

Drawbacks of Debt

The disadvantages of debt are as follows:

1. Interest and principal payment obligations are set by contract and must be met regardless of the economic position of the firm.
2. Bond indenture agreements may place burdensome restrictions on the firm such as maintenance of working capital at a given level, limits on future debt offerings, and guidelines for dividend policy. Although bondholders generally do not have the right to vote, they may take virtual control of the firm if important indenture provisions are not met.
3. Utilized beyond a given point, debt may depress outstanding common stock values.

Intermediate Term Loans and Medium-Term Notes

Instead of issuing debentures, a corporation might borrow the sum needed from a financial intermediary. Banks and other commercial lenders may extend to a corporation an operating loan or a **term loan.** Although the differences between these types of loans are many, two stand out. First, the money on the operating loan is generally advanced based on current asset security, while the term loan is advanced against capital asset security. Second, the operating loan is payable on demand, while the term loan is not. The choice of lenders for term loans in Canada is wide and includes banks, trust companies, life insurance companies, credit unions and caisses populaires, specialized equipment lenders, Business Development Bank of Canada, pension funds, and term lending specialists such as Commercial Capital Corporation.

Business Development Bank of Canada www.bdc.ca/bdc/home

Funding that often includes equity participation is available from venture capitalists and from "angels,"—wealthy individuals looking for good growth prospects in a company. Besides funding, these sources can also provide valuable advice and assistance.

The length of time on a term loan is generally from 3 to 10 years, although it is occasionally longer, depending on the nature of the security and the financial strength of the borrower. The interest rate charged is often floating (for example, prime +1½ percent), although lenders sometimes, depending on economic and market circumstances, fix the rate for the full term of the loan. Principal and interest repayments are usually made monthly or quarterly, with a balloon payment of principal required at the end of the term. Figure 16–4 provides a sample of a credit offer from a term lender to a potential borrower. Take special note of the legal covenants governing the credit as extended.

FIGURE 16–4
Sample credit offer

Term Loan Offer
Acme Company Limited

We are pleased to make the following offer to finance:

BORROWER:	Acme Company Limited
LENDER:	XYZ Insurance Company of Canada
AMOUNT:	$3,000,000
REPAYMENT:	$25,000 per month, including principal and interest, to liquidate in 10 years. Subject to adjustment to reflect changes in Prime Lending Rate.
INTEREST:	Prime (average of 5 largest banks) + 1½%, payable monthly or fixed rate option at rates for 1-, 2-, 3- or 5-year term as set from time to time.
SECURITY:	A first fixed charge on all land, buildings, and equipment. A first floating charge on all other assets subject only to the bank charge on accounts receivable and inventory.
LEGAL COVENANTS:	1. Annual audited financial statements provided to XYZ Insurance within 90 days after fiscal year end. 2. Quarterly financial statements to be provided within 30 days of quarter end. 3. Net worth of the borrower including capital, retained earnings, and shareholders' loans is not to fall below $2,000,000 during the term of the loan. 4. Debt/equity ratio not to exceed 2:1. 5. Working capital ratio is not to be less than 1.5:1. 6. Capital expenditures not to exceed $500,000 in any fiscal year without XYZ's approval. 7. Management salaries and bonuses not to exceed $750,000 per annum without XYZ's approval. 8. An annual list of capital assets is to be provided.

In 2002 **medium-term notes (MTNs)** issued by companies in Canada exceeded $24 billion and were a very significant source of financing, as seen in Figure 15–3. Additionally, MTNs were issued in the U.S. and the Euro-MTN market. Medium-term notes can be issued by companies that have already filed a "shelf prospectus" with the appropriate securities commissions. This process allowed companies that have already issued public securities to bring further securities to market on the basis of information already filed with the commission.

The advantage of an MTN to a company is that it can issue the notes and receive settlement in about five days, as compared to the two weeks normally required by a public issue with full prospectus. The MTN can be issued for as little as several million dollars, which makes it more flexible as a funding vehicle compared to the larger public bond issues. Investment dealers only act as agents to the company, and sets the spread on the issue above government bonds. The dealers do not act as underwriters on MTNs and therefore receive about 40 percent less in commissions because they do not assume the risk that the issue will sell.

This market began in the 1980s when the big car companies issued 3- to 5-year commercial paper by way of the shelf prospectus. The market is still developing and is somewhat "illiquid," as the term notes are generally sold to specific buyers and the MTNs do not trade frequently.

Leasing as a Form of Debt

When a corporation contracts to lease an oil tanker or a computer and signs a noncancellable, long-term agreement, the transaction has all the characteristics of a debt obligation. Long-term leasing was not recognized as a debt obligation in the early post-World War II period, but since the mid-1960s there has been a strong movement by the accounting profession to force companies to fully divulge all information about leasing obligations and to indicate the equivalent debt characteristics.

This position was made official for financial reporting purposes as a result of a Canadian Institute of Chartered Accountants (CICA) ruling in December 1978. In essence, this ruling said that certain types of leases must be shown as long-term obligations on the financial statements of the firm. Before that, lease obligations could merely be divulged in footnotes to financial statements, and large lease obligations did not have to be included in the debt structure (except for the upcoming payment). Consider the case of firm ABC, whose balance sheet is shown in Table 16–5. Before the CICA recommendation on leases, a footnote to the financial statements might have indicated a lease obligation of $12 million a year for the next 15 years, with a present value of $100 million. Under current practice, however, this information has been moved directly to the balance sheet, as indicated in Table 16–6.

We see that both a new asset and a new liability have been created, as indicated by the asterisks. The essence of this treatment is that a long-term, noncancellable lease is tantamount to purchasing the asset with borrowed funds, and this should be reflected on the balance sheet. Note that between the original balance sheet (Table 16–5) and the revised balance sheet (Table 16–6), the total-debt-to-total-assets ratio has gone from 50 percent to 66.7 percent.

TABLE 16–5

Balance Sheet (in $ millions)

Current assets	$ 50	Current liabilities	$ 50
Capital assets	150	Long-term liabilities	50
		Total liabilities	$100
		Shareholders' equity	100
Total assets	$200	Total liabilities and shareholders' equity	$200

TABLE 16–6

Revised Balance Sheet (in $ millions)

Current assets	$ 50	Current liabilities	$ 50
Capital assets	150	Long-term liabilities	50
*Leased property under capital lease	100	*Obligation under capital lease	100
		Total liabilities	$200
		Shareholders' equity	100
Total assets	$300	Total liabilities and shareholders' equity	$300

*New categories.

$$\text{Original} \qquad \frac{\textit{Total debt}}{\textit{Total assets}} = \frac{\$100 \textit{ million}}{\$200 \textit{ million}} = 50\%$$

$$\text{Revised} \qquad \frac{\textit{Total debt}}{\textit{Total assets}} = \frac{\$200 \textit{ million}}{\$300 \textit{ million}} = 66.7\%$$

Though this represents a substantial increase in the ratio, the impact on the firm's credit rating or stock price may be minimal. To the extent that the financial markets are efficient, the information was already known by analysts who took the data from footnotes or other sources and made their own adjustments. Nevertheless, corporate financial officers fought long, hard, and unsuccessfully to keep the lease obligation off the balance sheet. They seem to be much less convinced about the efficiency of the marketplace than are financial theorists.

Capital Lease versus Operating Lease

Not all leases must be capitalized (present value) and placed on the balance sheet. Only under circumstances in which substantially all the benefits and risks of ownership are transferred in a lease is this treatment necessary. Under these circumstances we have a **capital (or financing) lease.** Identification as a capital lease and the attendant financial treatment are required whenever any one of the four following conditions is present:

1. The arrangement transfers ownership of the property to the lessee (the leasing party) by the end of the lease term.
2. The lease contains a bargain purchase price at the end of the lease. The option price has to be sufficiently low so exercise of the option appears reasonably certain.

3. The lease term is equal to 75 percent or more of the estimated life of the leased property.
4. The present value of the minimum lease payments equals 90 percent or more of the fair value of the lease property at the inception of the lease.[6]

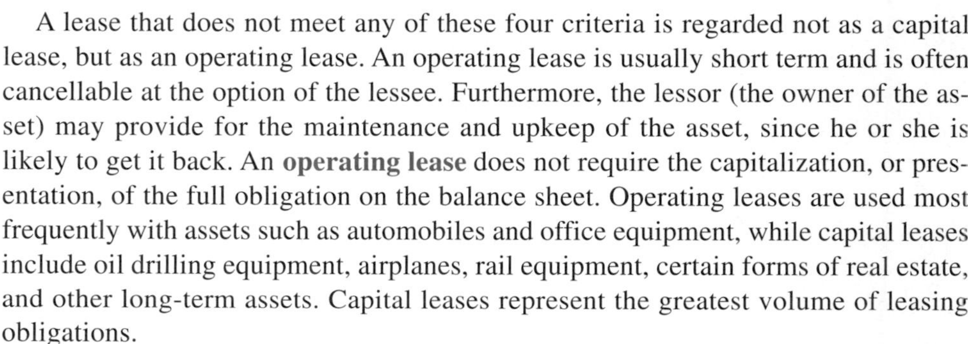

A lease that does not meet any of these four criteria is regarded not as a capital lease, but as an operating lease. An operating lease is usually short term and is often cancellable at the option of the lessee. Furthermore, the lessor (the owner of the asset) may provide for the maintenance and upkeep of the asset, since he or she is likely to get it back. An **operating lease** does not require the capitalization, or presentation, of the full obligation on the balance sheet. Operating leases are used most frequently with assets such as automobiles and office equipment, while capital leases include oil drilling equipment, airplanes, rail equipment, certain forms of real estate, and other long-term assets. Capital leases represent the greatest volume of leasing obligations.

Canadian Finance and Leasing Association www.canadianleasing.ca/welcome.cfm

Besides a straightforward direct lease, where a firm acquires the use of an asset offered in general to the market by a lessor, there are also **sale-and-leaseback** arrangements and **leveraged leases.** Under a sale-and-leaseback arrangement, a firm would sell an asset it already owns to another party. It would then lease the asset back from that party. In leveraged leases, three parties are involved: a lessee, a lessor, and a lender. In these instances the asset is generally financed by an equity investment by the lessor (often about 20 percent) and a loan to the lessor from a financial institution for the remainder. Leveraged leasing is common where the asset in question requires a large capital outlay.

In the 1989 federal budget, the lessor's ability to claim capital cost allowance (CCA) was further restricted. Tax-exempt institutions had been entering into sale-and-leaseback arrangements, which traded off CCA for lower rental payments. For cash-strapped institutions such as universities and colleges, this was a viable means of freeing much-needed capital. The University of Ottawa actually sold its entire library collection and then leased it back. However, the budget has now limited the ability to undertake such transactions. Furthermore, it will affect large capital acquisitions. Leasing companies have been leasing items such as airplanes and construction equipment, and these transactions will likely diminish. This has forced some Canadian corporations to enter into lease arrangements with offshore firms that can take advantage of tax laws in other jurisdictions.

Income Statement Effect

The capital lease calls not only for present valuing the lease obligation on the balance sheet, but also for treating the arrangement for income statement purposes as if it were somewhat similar to a purchase-borrowing arrangement. Thus, under a capital lease, the asset account shown in Table 16–6 as "Leased property under capital lease" is amortized or written off over the life of the lease with an annual expense deduction. Also the liability account shown in Table 16–6 as "Obligation under capital

---

[6]The discount rate used for this test is the leasing firm's new cost of borrowing or the lessor's (the firm that owns the asset) implied rate of return under the lease. The lower of the two must be used when both are known.

Sale and Leaseback in the Airline Business

In late 2001 Air Canada entered into a sale and leaseback arrangement with GE Capital Aviation Services. Air Canada received $565 million for sixteen Airbus 320s and one 319 Airbus. Besides leasing back these aircraft, Air Canada would also lease another six newer aircraft under the terms of the lease. Air Canada was under severe financial duress in late 2001 and suggested that these leasing arrangements would provide them with greater liquidity and allow cost efficiencies from maintenance cost reductions. Cash flow from sale and leasebacks in 2001 was over $1.4 billion.

As of late 2001 the majority of Air Canada's fleet was leased.

FINANCE IN ACTION

www.aircanada.ca

Symbol: AC

lease" is written off through regular amortization, with an implied interest expense on the remaining balance. Thus, for financial reporting purposes, the annual deductions are amortization of the asset plus implied interest expense on the remaining present value of the liability. Though the actual development of these values and accounting rules is best deferred to an accounting course, the finance student should understand the close similarity between a capital lease and borrowing to purchase an asset for financial reporting purposes.

An operating lease, on the other hand, usually calls for an annual expense deduction equal to the lease payment, with no specific amortization.

Advantages of Leasing

Why is leasing so popular? In the United States it has emerged as a $500 billion-plus industry, with such firms as Clark Equipment, GE Capital, and U.S. Leasing International providing an enormous amount of financing. Although industry figures for the Canadian leasing market are not publicly tabulated, the Canadian market is significant but less spectacular. There are approximately 100 lessors in the Canadian equipment leasing business. The banks are poised to become major players in the car leasing business in which as many cars are now leased as purchased.

Major reasons for the popularity of leasing include the following:

1. The lessee may lack sufficient funds or the credit capability to purchase the asset from a manufacturer that is willing, however, to accept a lease agreement or to arrange a lease obligation with a third party.
2. The provisions of a lease obligation may be substantially less restrictive than those of a bond indenture.
3. There may be no downpayment requirement, as would generally be the case in the purchase of an asset (leasing allows for a larger indirect loan).
4. The lessor may possess particular expertise in a given industry—allowing for expert product selection, maintenance, and eventual resale. Through this process the negative effects of obsolescence may be lessened.
5. Creditor claims on certain types of leases, such as real estate, are restricted in bankruptcy and reorganization proceedings. Leases on chattels (non-real estate items) have no such limitation.

There are also some tax factors to be considered. Where one party to a lease is in a higher tax bracket than the other party, certain tax advantages, such as an investment tax credit, may be better utilized. For example, a wealthy party may purchase an asset and take an investment tax credit then lease the asset to another party in a lower tax bracket for actual use. Also, lease payments on the use of land are tax deductible, whereas land ownership does not allow a similar deduction for amortization. Note that to be treated as a legitimate lease contract for tax purposes, the Canada Customs and Revenue Agency requires that lease payments not include an excess amount, implying the lessee is purchasing the underlying asset on an installment basis.

Canada Customs and Revenue Agency
www.ccra-adrc.gc.ca

Finally, a firm may wish to engage in a sale-and-leaseback arrangement to provide it with an infusion of capital while allowing it to continue to use the asset. Even though the dollar costs of a leasing arrangement are often higher than the dollar costs of owning an asset, the advantages just cited may outweigh the direct cost factors.

Lease-versus-Purchase Decision

A corporation is often faced with the decision as to whether to purchase an asset or to enter into a lease arrangement to allow the use of the asset without the large capital commitment. Assuming the capital asset will add value to the firm based on a capital budgeting analysis, as outlined in Chapter 12, there must be a further decision as to the best financing alternative.

The classic lease-versus-purchase decision does not fit most capital leasing decisions anymore because of the similar financial accounting and tax treatment accorded to a capital lease and borrowing to purchase. An exception may occur when land is part of the lease arrangement. Furthermore, the classic lease-versus-purchase decision is still appropriate for the operating lease, and this is where we concentrate our analysis.

Take, for instance, a firm considering the purchase of a $5,000 asset with a five-year life as opposed to entering into two sequential operating leases for two years and three years each. Under the operating leases, the annual payments would be $1,250 on the first lease and $1,800 on the second lease. If the firm purchased the asset, it would pay $1,319 annually to amortize a $5,000 loan over five years at 10 percent interest.

Year	0	1	2	3	4	5
Lease obligations	$1,250	$1,250	$1,800	$1,800	$1,800	
Loan obligations		$1,319	$1,319	$1,319	$1,319	$1,319

The purchaser of the asset would be entitled to deduct interest charges on the loan, effecting a tax shield, and be able to claim capital cost allowance (CCA). The asset may also have salvage value. On the lease the payments are deductible for tax purposes, effecting a tax savings.

In the analysis of the lease-versus-borrow decision we are looking at a type of capital budgeting problem. Besides determining the appropriate cash flows, it is important to discount the future expected cash flows to the present at a proper discount rate. Because the costs associated with both leasing and borrowing are contractual and certain, we use the **aftertax cost of debt** as the discount rate rather than the cost of capital used in most capital budgeting decisions. The aftertax cost of debt is a lower discount rate representing greater certainty in the cash flow stream.

However, if a salvage value is relevant in a lease-versus-borrow decision, we usually discount it at the higher cost of capital to acknowledge the greater uncertainty in its estimation. All other cash flows in the analysis are relatively more certain than the salvage value. Therefore, these cash flows are discounted at the lower discount rate, the aftertax borrowing rate.

Let us first analyze the costs and benefits of borrowing to purchase. This is laid out in Table 16–7. The loan payments (column 2) are costs, and the tax shields on the interest portion of the loan payments are benefits. To determine the interest payments, we could set up an amortization schedule to separate the annual payment into the interest and principal components. The interest portion has been identified and then multiplied by the tax rate to determine the tax shields (column 3). The tax shields have been deducted from the annual loan payment (column 4) to determine the aftertax cost of the loan. Finally, we have calculated the present value of the aftertax costs at a discount rate of 6 percent (column 5). The 6 percent is the aftertax cost of borrowing. It was computed by multiplying the interest rate of 10 percent by (1 − tax rate): [10% (1 − .4) = 6%].

TABLE 16–7
Net present value of borrow-purchase

Year	(1) PV of CCA Shield	(2) Payment	(3) Interest Tax Shield	(4) Aftertax Cost of (2) − (3)	(5) Present Value at 6%
1		($1,319)	$500 × .4	($1,119)	($1,056)
2		(1,319)	$418 × .4	(1,152)	(1,025)
3		(1,319)	$328 × .4	(1,188)	(997)
4		(1,319)	$229 × .4	(1,227)	(972)
5		(1,319)	$120 × .4	(1,271)	(950)
					(5,000)
or	Cost of asset				(5,000)
	PV of CCA shield				1,495
	PV of borrowing alternative				($3,505)

Notice that the present value of the aftertax cost of the annual loan payments is $5,000, which equals the cost of the asset and the original amount of the loan. This is always the case when the aftertax borrowing rate is used as the discount rate. From a calculation standpoint, this means we may avoid setting up an amortization schedule. The amount borrowed will equal the present value of the loan payments plus the tax savings on the interest portion of the loan payment.

The next task is to calculate the CCA tax shield. In this example the asset falls into CCA Class 8, which allows a 20 percent CCA deduction. Thus, using Formula 12-1, the present value of the CCA tax shield (assuming a zero salvage value) would be:

$$\text{PV of CCA tax shield} = \frac{Cdt}{r + d}\left[\frac{1 + .5r}{1 + r}\right]$$

$$= \frac{\$5{,}000 \times .20 \times .40}{.06 + .20}\left[\frac{1 + .03}{1 + .06}\right]$$

$$= \$1{,}495$$

The CCA tax shield has been included in Table 16–7. The total cost of the loan alternative is $3,505. If we had a salvage value on the asset, this could be included as an additional line of the table.

Next, we analyze the cash outflows from leasing. To consider the time value of money, we have discounted the annual values in the borrowing alternative at an interest rate of 6 percent, the aftertax cost of debt to the firm. To treat the analysis of each financing alternative equally we must use the same discount rate for the cash flows of the leasing alternative. The net present value calculation for the operating lease option is shown in Table 16–8.

TABLE 16–8
Net present value of operating lease outflows

Year	Payment	Tax Shield	Aftertax Cost of Leasing	Present Value at 6%
0	($1,250)	$ 0	($1,250)	($1,250)
1	(1,250)	500	(750)	(708)
2	(1,800)	500	(1,300)	(1,157)
3	(1,800)	720	(1,080)	(907)
4	(1,800)	720	(1,080)	(855)
5	0	720	720	538
				($4,339)

Note the adjustments in Table 16–8 for the timing of the cash flows related to the lease payments and tax shields on the lease payments. While the lease payments are generally made at the start of the year, the tax deductions related to them can be claimed only over the year for which the payment applies.

The borrow-purchase alternative has a lower present value of aftertax costs ($3,505 versus $4,339) that would appear to make it the more desirable alternative. The NPV of borrow to purchase is $834. However, many of the previously discussed qualitative factors that support leasing must also be considered in the decision-making process.

Summary

1. The use of debt financing by corporations has grown rapidly since the 1960s, and the degree to which earnings are sufficient to cover interest payments has deteriorated. Corporate bonds may be secured by a lien on a specific asset or may carry an unsecured designation, indicating that the bondholder possesses a general claim against the corporation. A special discussion of the hierarchy of claims for firms in financial distress is presented in Appendix 16A. Long-term debt may have sinking-fund provisions, a call feature, or conversion provisions that cause the debt to be repaid or converted to equity before maturity.
2. Bond prices and yields are inversely related. The yields on which corporate and government bonds are evaluated are generally based on the level of interest rates in the economy and particularly by the inflation rate. More specifically, the yield required on an issue is based on its rating as determined by one of the bond rating services. The rating is determined by the rating agency's analysis of the corporation or government's ability to pay its financial commitments.
3. During periodic cyclical downturns in interest rates, corporations have an opportunity for refunding debt if the issue has a call provision. This allows the replacement of high interest rate bonds with lower interest rate bonds. This is a capital budgeting decision in which the financial manager

must consider whether the savings in lower aftertax interest payments will compensate for the additional costs of calling the old issue and selling a new one. The discount rate for this analysis is the aftertax borrowing rate on the new issue.

4. Innovative forms of raising long-term debt are attempts to serve a market that is not completely satisfied by the current offerings. New types of debt can meet the needs of both the investor and the issuer and earn healthy returns to the innovators.
5. The long-term, noncancellable lease should be considered as a special debt form available to the corporation. It is capitalized on the balance sheet to represent both a debt and an asset account and is amortized on a regular basis. Leasing offers a means of financing in which lessor expertise and other financial benefits can be imparted to the lessee (leasing party).
6. A lease-versus-borrow-to-purchase decision for an operating lease requires careful consideration of all cash flows, including loan and lease payments, tax shields from interest payments and CCA, and any salvage value. The appropriate discount rate is the aftertax cost of debt.

List of Terms

par value (face value) 562
coupon rate 562
maturity date 562
bond indenture 562
covenants 562
secured claim 562
mortgage agreement 563
after-acquired property clause 563
debenture 564
unsecured debt 564
subordinated debenture 564
junk bond 564
serial payments 565
sinking-fund provision 565
conversion 567
call feature 567
current yield 570
yield to maturity 570
bond ratings 570
refunding decision 573
aftertax cost of new debt 573
zero-coupon rate bond 577
strip bond 577
floating-rate bond 578
real return bond 578
revenue bond 579
eurobond 579
term loan 581
medium-term notes (MTNs) 582
capital (or financing) lease 583
operating lease 584
sale-and-leaseback 584
leveraged leases 584

Discussion Questions

1. Corporate debt has been expanding very dramatically since World War II. What has been the impact on interest coverage, particularly since 1973?
2. What are some basic features of bond agreements?
3. What is the difference between a bond agreement and a bond indenture?
4. Discuss the relationship between the coupon rate (original interest rate at time of issue) on a bond and its security provisions.
5. Take the following list of securities and arrange them in order of their priority of claims:

Preferred stock	Senior debentures
Subordinated debenture	Senior secured debt
Common stock	Junior secured debt

6. Which method of bond repayment reduces debt and increases the amount of common stock outstanding?

7. What is the purpose of serial repayments and sinking funds?
8. Under which circumstances would a call on a bond be exercised by a corporation? What is the purpose of a deferred call?
9. Discuss the relationship between bond prices and interest rates. What impact do changing interest rates have on the price of long-term bonds versus short-term bonds?
10. What is the difference between the following yields: coupon rate, current yield, yield to maturity?
11. How does the bond rating affect the interest rate paid by a corporation on its bonds?
12. Bonds of different risk classes have a spread between their interest rates. Is this spread always the same? Why?
13. Use Table 16–3 to answer the following questions.
    a. Why would the Talisman bond have a lower yield to maturity than the Rogers Cable bond?
    b. What do you suggest is the spread above Government of Canada bonds for a long-term bond of Nav Canada, or for Loblaw? Why the difference?
14. Explain how the bond refunding problem is similar to a capital budgeting decision.
15. What cost of capital is generally used in evaluating a bond refunding decision? Why?
16. Discuss the advantages and disadvantages of debt.
17. Explain how the zero-coupon rate bond, or stripped bond, provides return to the investor. What are the advantages to the corporation?
18. Explain how floating-rate bonds can save the investor from potential embarrassments in portfolio valuation.
19. What is a eurobond?
20. What do we mean by capitalizing lease payments?
21. Explain the close parallel between a capital lease and the borrow-purchase decision from the viewpoint of both the balance sheet and the income statement.
22. In the lease-versus-purchase decision, why is the discount rate the aftertax cost of debt?

www.mcgrawhill.ca/college/block

INTERNET RESOURCES AND QUESTIONS

Bond ratings and the criteria for bond ratings on Canadian, U.S., and international sovereign debt securities are available at several sites:
www.dbrs.com
www.moodys.com
www.standardandpoors.com/canada

Historical yields for a broad selection of Canadian and U.S. bonds are available at the Bank of Canada site:
www.bankofcanada.ca/en

The current pricing and yield to maturity on bonds is available at several sites:

www.scotiacapital.com	(market update)
www.cibcwg.com	(daily fixed income/daily fact sheet)
www.globeandmail.com	(money and markets)
www.bloomberg.com	(international bonds)

Eurobond information and pricing is available at the Swiss Exchange site:
www.bourse.ch

Prospectus information on new debt securities is available at SEDAR (System for Electronic Document Analysis and Retrieval), a subsidiary of the Canadian Depository for Securities:
www.sedar.com

Problems

(Assume the par value of the bonds in the following problems is $1,000 unless otherwise specified.)

1. The Pioneer Petroleum Corporation has a bond outstanding with an $85.00 annual interest payment, a market price of $800.00, and a maturity date in five years. Find the following:
   a. The coupon rate.
   b. The current rate.
   c. The yield to maturity.
   d. The yield an investor would realize if coupon payments were reinvested at 6 percent (holding period return).
2. Preston Corporation has a bond outstanding with a $110.00 annual coupon payment, a market price of $1,200, and a maturity date in 10 years. Find the following:
   a. The coupon yield.
   b. The current yield.
   c. The yield to maturity.
   d. The yield an investor would realize if coupon payments were reinvested at 12 percent.
3. Harold Reese must choose between two bonds:

   Bond X pays $95.00 annual interest and has a market value of $900.00. It has 10 years to maturity.

   Bond Z pays $95.00 annual interest and has a market value of $920.00. It has two years to maturity.

   a. Compute the current yield on both bonds.
   b. Which bond should he select based on your answer to part *a*?
   c. A drawback of current yield is that it does not consider the total life of the bond. What is the yield to maturity on these bonds?
   d. Has your answer changed between part *b* and *c* of this question?
4. The Prairie Investment Fund buys 70 bonds of the Hillary Bakery Corporation through its broker. The bonds pay 9 percent annual interest. The yield to maturity (market rate of interest) is 12 percent. The bonds have a 25-year maturity. Using an assumption of semiannual interest payments:

   a. Compute the price of a bond (refer to "semiannual interest and bond prices" in Chapter 10 for review if necessary).

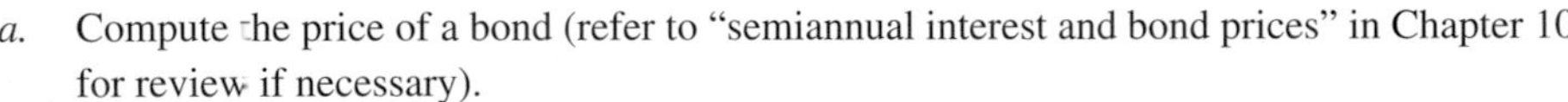

   b. Compute the total value of the 70 bonds.
5. Barry, Sanders & Co. pays a 12 percent coupon rate on debentures due in 20 years. The current yield to maturity on bonds of similar risk is 10 percent. The bonds are currently callable at $1,060. The theoretical value of the bonds will be equal to the present value of the expected cash flow from the bonds. This is the normal definition we use.
   a. Find the theoretical market value of the bonds using semiannual analysis.
   b. Do you think the bonds will sell for the price you arrived at in part *a*? Why?

6. The yield to maturity for 25-year bonds is as follows for four different bond rating categories.

AAA	9.4%	A	10.0%
AA	9.6	BBB	10.2

The bonds of Evans Corporation were rated as AA and issued at par a few weeks ago. The bonds have just been downgraded to A. Determine the new price of the bonds, assuming a 25-year maturity and semiannual interest payments.

7. The 25-year B-rated bonds of Parker Optical Company were initially issued at a 12 percent yield (paid semiannually). After 10 years, the bonds have been upgraded to AA. Such bonds are currently yielding 10 percent. Determine the price of the bonds with 15 years remaining to maturity.

8. A previously issued AA, 20-year industrial bond provides a return one-third higher than the prime interest rate of 6 percent. Previously issued public utility bonds provide a yield of three-fourths of a percentage point higher than previously issued industrial bonds of equal quality. Finally, new issues of AA public utility bonds pay one-fourth of a percentage points more than previously issued public utility bonds. What should the interest rate be on a newly issued AA public utility bond?

9. A 15-year, $1,000 par value strip bond is to be issued to yield 12 percent.
   a. What should be the initial price of the bond?
   b. If immediately upon issue, interest rates dropped to 10 percent, what would be the value of the strip bond?
   c. If immediately upon issue, interest rates increased to 14 percent, what would be the value of the strip bond?

10. What is the effective yield to maturity on a strip bond that sells for $338.83 and will mature in 15 years?

11. You purchased a 7 percent, 30 year, $1,000 par value, floating rate bond in 1999. If rates on similar risk bonds are up to 9 percent in 2004, what is your estimate as to the bond's value?

12. It was 14 years ago, that ALS Aluminum Corporation borrowed $9.9 million. Since then, cumulative inflation has been 98 percent (a compound rate of approximately 5 percent per year).
   a. When the firm repays the original $9.9 million loan this year, what will be the effective purchasing power of the $9.9 million?
   b. To maintain the original $9.9 million purchasing power, how much should the lender be repaid?
   c. If the lender knows he will receive only $9.9 million in payment after 14 years, how might he be compensated for the loss in purchasing power? A descriptive answer is acceptable.

13. A $1,000 par value bond was issued 25 years ago at a 12 percent coupon rate. It currently has 15 years remaining to maturity. Interest rates on similar debt obligations are now 8 percent.
   a. What is the current price of the bond?
   b. Assume Ms. Bright bought the bond three years ago, when it had a price of $1,050. What is her dollar profit based on the bond's current price?
   c. Further assume Ms. Bright paid 30 percent of the purchase price in cash and borrowed the rest (known as buying on margin). She used the interest payments from the bond to cover the interest costs on the loan. How much of the purchase price of $1,050 did Ms. Bright pay in cash?

d. What is Ms. Bright's percentage return on her cash investment? Divide the answer to part *b* by the answer to part *c*.

e. Explain why her return is so high.

14. The Delta Corporation has a $30 million bond obligation outstanding, which it is considering refunding. Though the bonds were initially issued at 9 percent, the interest rates on similar issues have declined to 7.5 percent. The bonds were originally issued for 20 years and have 14 years remaining. The new issue would be for 14 years. There is a 7 percent call premium on the old issue. The underwriting cost on the new $30 million issue is $600,000, and the underwriting cost on the old issue was $750,000. The company is in a 40 percent tax bracket, and it will allow a 30 day overlap period. Treasury bills currently yield 3 percent. Should the old issue be refunded with new debt?

15. The Sunshine Corporation has $40 million of bonds outstanding that were issued at a coupon rate of $12\frac{7}{8}$ percent seven years ago. Interest rates have fallen to 12 percent. Mr. Heath, the vice president of finance, does not expect rates to fall any further. The bonds have 18 years left to maturity, and Mr. Heath would like to refund the bonds with a new issue of equal amount also having 18 years to maturity. The Sunshine Corporation has a tax rate of 36 percent. The underwriting cost on the old issue was 2.5 percent of the total bond value. The underwriting cost on the new issue will be 1.8 percent of the total bond value. The original bond indenture contained a five-year protection against a call, with an 8 percent call premium starting in the sixth year and scheduled to decline by one-half percent each year thereafter (consider the bond to be seven years old for purposes of computing the premium). Should the Sunshine Corporation refund the old issue?

16. In the previous problem, what would be the aftertax cost of the call premium at the end of Year 11 (in dollar value)?

17. Providence Industries has an outstanding debenture of $25 million that was issued when flotation costs could be expensed immediately. It carries a coupon rate of 12 percent and has 15 years to maturity. Currently, similar risk bonds are yielding 9.5 percent over a 15-year period, and Providence is wondering if a refunding would be economically sound. The existing debenture has a call premium of 11 percent at present. It is estimated that a new issue would require underwriting costs of $470,000 and other costs of $80,000. No overlap period would be required. Providence Industries has a tax rate of 43 percent. Its cost of capital is 16 percent.

    a. Should Providence Industries refund the old issue? Show your calculations.

    b. Discuss your choice of discount rate.

    c. Suppose the refunding was not justified economically. What other reasons might Providence have for refunding the old issue?

18. United Oui Stand Ltd. has a bond outstanding that carries a 12 percent coupon rate paid annually. Current bond yields are 9.5 percent. It has $40 million outstanding and 10 years left to maturity. A new issue would require $1 million for flotation costs, and the existing issue has written off all its flotation expenses. An overlap period of 30 days would be anticipated, during which money market rates would be 7 percent. United Oui Stand Ltd. has a tax rate of 40 percent. The call premium on the outstanding issue is currently at 7 percent. Calculate if refunding would be justified.

19. Daedulus Wings has had several successful years in the airline business and had received recognition from many quarters for flying higher, further and cheaper than the competition. Its financial state of affairs has not been as successful. The new vice-president of finance is reviewing some debentures that carry fairly high semiannual payments.

The vice president notes in particular a bond issue that was issued 8 years ago with 15 years to maturity at an annual rate of 12 percent, payable semiannually. It has a call provision at a premium of 8 percent above par value. The bond issue has $50 million outstanding.

Current long-term interest rates are 7.5 percent, payable on a semiannual basis and short-term rates are 3 percent. If the old bonds are called the vice-president will require a 15-day overlap period. Wings has a tax rate of 35 percent. Underwriting and other financing expenses will be $1 million.

Should the old issue be refunded and replaced with a debt issue with a comparable maturity? Show your calculations.

20. Webber Musicals Corporation is considering replacing its $2 million preferred share issue because market yields have declined. The existing preferreds carry a dividend of $5.00 per share, which is a rate of 10 percent on the par value. Current market yields on Webber preferreds are estimated to be 7 percent. Webber preferreds are currently trading at $71.43. Flotation expenses on a new preferred issue would be $160,000. Webber's tax rate is 38 percent. There is no call provision. Should Webber Musicals consider replacing its existing preferred shares? Show your calculations.

21. The Richmond Corporation has just signed a 144-month lease on an asset with an 18-year life. The minimum lease payments are $3,000 per month ($36,000 per year) and are to be discounted back to the present at an 8 percent annual discount rate. The estimated fair value of the property is $290,000. Should the lease be recorded as a capital lease or an operating lease?

22. The Bradley Corporation has heavy lease commitments. Before the 1978 CICA recommendation on leases, it merely footnoted lease obligations in the balance sheet, which appeared as follows:

BRADLEY CORPORATION
($ millions)

Current assets	$150	Current liabilities	$ 50
Capital assets	250	Long-term liabilities	100
		Total liabilities	150
		Shareholders' equity	250
Total assets	$400	Total liabilities and equity	$400

The footnotes stated that the company had $22 million in annual capital lease obligations over the next 20 years.

a. Discount these annual lease obligations back to the present at a 7 percent discount rate (round to the nearest million dollars).

b. Construct a revised balance sheet that includes lease obligations, as in Table 16–6.

c. Compute total debt to total assets on the original and revised balance sheets.

d. Compute total debt to equity on the original and revised balance sheets.

e. In an efficient capital market environment, should the consequences of the CICA recommendation, as viewed in the answers to parts *c* and *d,* change stock prices and credit ratings?

f. Comment on management's perception of market efficiency (the viewpoint of the financial officer).

23. The Lollar Corporation plans to lease an $800,000 asset to the Pierce Corporation. The lease will be for 12 years.

a. If the Lollar Corporation desires a 10 percent return on its investment, how much should the lease payments be?

b. If the Lollar Corporation is able to generate $120,000 in immediate tax shield benefits from the asset to be purchased for the lease arrangement and will pass the benefits along to the Pierce Corporation in the form of lower lease payments, how much should the revised lease payments be? Continue to assume the Lollar Corporation desires a 10 percent return on the 12-year lease.

24. Edison Electronics is considering whether to borrow funds and purchase an asset or to lease the asset under an operating lease arrangement. If it purchases the asset, the cost will be $8,000. It can borrow funds for four years at 12 percent interest. The asset will qualify for a 25 percent capital cost allowance. Assume a tax rate of 35 percent.

The other alternative is to sign two operating leases, one with payments of $2,100 for the first two years and the other with payments of $3,700 for the last *two* years. In your analysis, round all values to the nearest dollar. The leases would be treated as operating leases.

a. Compute the aftertax cost of the lease for the four years.

b. Compute the annual payment for the loan (round to the nearest dollar).

c. Compute the amortization schedule for the loan. (Disregard a small difference from a zero balance at the end of the loan. It is due to rounding.)

d. Determine the cash flow effect of the capital cost allowance.

e. Compute the aftertax cost of the borrow-purchase alternative.

f. Compute the present value of the aftertax cost of the two alternatives.

g. If the objective is to minimize the present value of aftertax costs, which alternative should be selected?

25. Kumquat Farms Ltd. has decided to acquire a kumquat picking machine. The cost of the picking machine is $45,000, and it has an economic life of 10 years. At the end of seven years, the market (salvage) value is estimated to be $11,000. Seven years is the time horizon for analysis.

The owner of Kumquat Farms Ltd. has discussed this acquisition with his financial services conglomerate. It has agreed to lend him the purchase price at 10 percent per year, payable in equal blended payments at the end of each year, for seven years.

An alternative method of financing the equipment would be to lease it from the local leasing store. Annual lease payments, payable at the beginning of each of the next seven years, would be $7,750. This would be considered an operating lease.

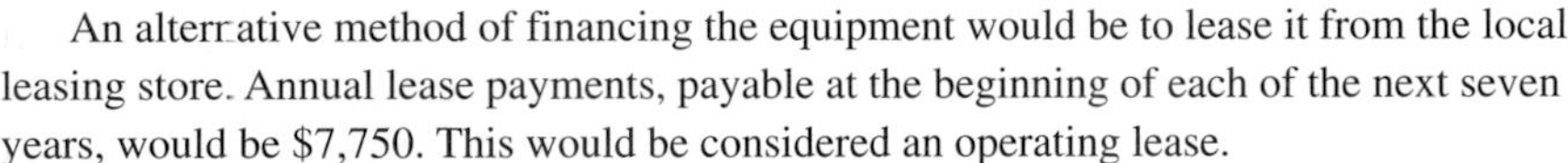

The equipment has a capital cost allowance of 20 percent. The benefits of any tax shields are realized at the end of each year. The company's tax rate is 25 percent. Kumquat Farms's cost of capital is 16 percent. Should Kumquat Farms Ltd. lease or buy the picking machine? Show all calculations.

26. I2C Beams Ltd., a manufacturer of lighted hockey pucks, is negotiating with the Hat Trick Company to purchase or to lease a machine that produces red-lighted pucks. The machine would cost $139,890. In five years the machine would have an estimated salvage value of $33,000. Its useful economic life is nine years.

I2C Beams can borrow funds at 12.5 percent from its Playoff Bank and has a tax rate of 36 percent. The capital cost rate on this machine is 30 percent, and I2C Beam's cost of capital is 16 percent. Lease payments would be at the beginning of each year, and tax savings would occur at the end of each year. Lease payments would be $32,500 over a five-year term.

Should I2C Beams Ltd. lease or borrow to purchase the machine? Show your calculations. We note that of all the cash flows, the salvage value has the greatest uncertainty. We recognize this by discounting the salvage value at a higher discount rate—the cost of capital.

27. Dan Teasin's Furs And Coats Ltd. has decided to acquire a cooling machine. Its cost is $50,000. In five years it can be salvaged for $15,000. The Cloister Bank has agreed to advance funds for the entire purchase price at 8 percent per annum payable in equal installments at the end of each year over the five years.

    As an alternative, the machine could be leased over the five years from the manufacturer, Snowbird Ltd., with annual lease payments of $10,000 payable at the beginning of each year.

    Dan Teasin's tax rate is 40 percent. Its cost of capital is 15 percent, and its tax shields are realized at the end of the year. Cooling machines have a CCA rate of 20 percent. If the machine is owned, annual maintenance costs will be $500. Should Dan Teasin's lease or buy its machine? Show all calculations.

28. Koss Leasing requires a 14 percent return on its investments. It is prepared to lease you a truck for two years, provided that it can achieve this return. The lease payments are to be made at the beginning of the year.

    The truck, which has a useful economic life of six years, cost Koss $60,000. Its estimated value in two years is $17,000.

    The capital cost allowance rate is 30 percent, and Koss's tax rate is 42 percent. Calculate the annual lease payment required by Koss Leasing.

COMPREHENSIVE PROBLEM

29. Leland Industries is the country's fifth largest producer of bakery and snack goods, with operations primarily located in central Canada. Over the last 10 years, Leland had been one of the most efficient bakeries in the country, with a 10-year average sales growth of 9.8 percent and an average return on equity of 16.8 percent. Management goals for the company include 10 percent earnings growth per year, and an average return of 16.8 percent on equity over time.

    Late in 2002, Leland reached an agreement with a major food chain to provide private label bakery service in addition to its own products that are sold to Loblaw, Safeway, and many other grocery stores. The new private label program had significant start-up costs, including new packaging techniques and the addition of 250 sales routes.

    Al Oliver, the vice president of finance, believed in maintaining a balanced capital structure, and since a 1 million common share issue totaling $25 million in value had been offered earlier in the year, he thought this was a good time to go to the debt market. Previously, the firm's debt issues had been privately placed with insurance companies and pension funds, but Al believed this was an appropriate time to approach the public markets based on the company's recent strong performance.

    He called his investment dealer and was told that the rating that the firm received from Standard and Poors and DBRS would be a key variable in determining the interest rate that would be paid on the debt issue. Leland Industries intended to issue $20 million of new debt.

    A comparison of Leland Industries to other bakeries is shown in Table 1. The other five firms all had issued debt publicly according to Ben Gilbert, who was Leland Industries' major contact at the investment dealing firm of Gilbert, Rollins, and Ross.

    As an alternative to a straight bond issue, Ben Gilbert suggested that the firm consider issuing floating-rate or even zero-coupon rate bonds. He said the principal advantage to the floating-rate bonds was that they could be issued at 1¼ percent below the going market rate for straight debt issues. Al Oliver was pleasantly surprised to hear this, and asked his investment dealer what the catch was. Al had heard too many times that "there is no such thing as a free lunch." His investment dealer explained that with a floating-rate bond the problem of interest rate changes was shifted from the borrower to the lender. To quote Ben Gilbert:

TABLE 1
Bond ratings of comparative firms

	International Bakeries		
Debt to total assets	30%	Bond price	$1,100
Times interest earned	7.1X	Annual interest	10.35%
Fixed charge coverage	5.0X	Maturity	25 years
Current ratio	3.1X	Par value (principal payment)	$1,000
Return on shareholders' equity	22%		
Rating	AA (high)		
	Gates Bakeries		
Debt to total assets	42%	Bond price	$920
Times interest earned	5.5X	Annual interest	9.45%
Fixed charge coverage	4.2X	Maturity	20 years
Current ratio	2.3X	Par value (principal payment)	$1,000
Return on shareholders' equity	17.1%		
Rating	A (high)		
	Prairie Products		
Debt to total assets	65%	Bond price	$1,150
Times interest earned	2.0X	Annual interest	15.75%
Fixed charge coverage	1.7X	Maturity	15 years
Current ratio	1.2X	Par value (principal payment)	$1,000
Return on shareholders' equity	7%		
Rating	B (low)		
	Dyer Pastries		
Debt to total assets	35%	Bond price	$1,060
Times interest earned	6.0X	Annual interest	10.30%
Fixed charge coverage	3.6X	Maturity	20 years
Current ratio	2.8X	Par value (principal payment)	$1,000
Return on shareholders' equity	19%		
Rating	AA (low)		
	Nolan Bread		
Debt to total assets	47%	Bond price	$950
Times interest earned	4.9X	Annual interest	10.30%
Fixed charge coverage	3.8X	Maturity	25 years
Current ratio	2.1X	Par value (principal payment)	$1,000
Return on shareholders' equity	15%		
Rating	A (medium)		
	Leland Industries*		
Debt to total assets	44%		
Times interest earned	5.7X		
Fixed charge coverage	3.7X		
Current ratio	2.0X		
Return on shareholders' equity	16.8%		
Rating: To be determined			

*The first three ratios for Leland Industries assume the impact of the new bond issue. Of course, these are approximations. The bond rating agencies require such information.

"Normally the risk of changes in yield to maturity is a burden or opportunity that bondholders must consider. If yields go up, bond prices of existing bonds go down, and the opposite is true if rates decline. There is a risk, and many investors do not like this risk. With a floating-rate bond the interest rate that the investor directly receives changes with market conditions and therefore the bond tends to trade at its initial par value. For example, if a bond were issued at 9 percent interest for 20 years and market rates went to 13 percent, a floating-rate bond would adjust its

> payment up to 13 percent, and the market value would remain at $1,000. On a straight bond issue the interest rate would remain at 9 percent, and because it is 4 percent below the market, the bond price would drop to the $700 range."

Al Oliver quickly perceived that with a floating-rate bond he could pay 1¼ percent lower interest than with a fixed-rate bond, but that in future years he could not predict what his interest rates would be. He was pretty turned off by the whole idea until his investment dealer suggested that the futures and options experts at Gilbert, Rollins, and Ross could hedge this risk at a probable aftertax cost of about $120,000 per year. While he was making this point, Ben Gilbert gave Al Oliver a copy of *Foundations of Financial Management* by Block, Hirt, and Short and suggested that he review the material on hedging at the end of Chapter 8 and in Chapter 19. Al Oliver knew that he must make a decision about the benefits and costs of floating-rate bonds.

Before the discussion was over, Al Oliver was presented with one last option. It was possible the firm might wish to issue zero-coupon rate bonds. Because no interest was paid on an annual basis and the only gain to the investor came in the form of capital appreciation, Al Oliver initially liked the idea. However, he remembered the no free lunch argument and asked Ben Gilbert what drawbacks there might be to this type of issue. Ben responded:

> "Well, Al, since you are not paying annual interest or retiring any part of the issue during its life, there can be greater risk, which may mean there is a lower rating on the issue. You, of course, know what that means in terms of a higher required yield on the bond issue."

Al Oliver thought he would need to put some numbers to zero-coupon bonds as well as many of the other items that Ben Gilbert brought up. He called his young assistant in for some help.

a. Compute the yield to maturity and the aftertax cost of debt for the bonds of the other firms. Assume a tax rate of 35 percent for the firms.

b. Based on the data in Table 1, which rating and cost of debt do you think is most likely for Leland Industries?

c. If the bonds of Leland Industries carried a requirement that 5 percent of the bonds outstanding be retired each year, what would be the total amount of bonds outstanding after the third year? What would be the aftertax dollar cost of interest payments on this sum?

d. From a strictly dollars and cents viewpoint, does the floating-rate bond with the hedging approach appear to be viable?

e. Assume the zero-coupon rate bonds would be issued at a yield of ¾ of 1 percent above a regular bond issue for 20 years. What will be the initial price of a $1,000 bond? How many bonds must be issued to raise $20 million? What is the danger in issuing the zero-coupon rate bonds?

30. Gina Thomas was concerned about the effect that high interest expenses were having on the bottom-line reported profits of Warner Motor Oil Co. Since joining the company three years ago as vice president of finance, she noticed that operating profits appeared to be improving each year, but that earnings after interest and taxes were declining because of high interest charges.

Because interest rates had finally started declining after a steady increase, she thought it was time to consider the possibility of refunding a bond issue. As she explained to her boss, Al Rosen, refunding meant calling in a bond that had been issued at a high interest rate and replacing it with a new bond that was similar in most respects, but carried a lower interest rate. Bond refunding was only feasible in a period of declining interest rates. Al Rosen, who had been the CEO of the company for the last seven years, understood the general concept, but he still had some questions.

He said to Gina, "If interest rates are going down, bond prices are certain to be going up. Won't that make it quite expensive to buy in outstanding issues so that we can replace them with new issues?" Gina had a quick and direct answer. "No, and the reason is that the old issues have a call provision associated with them." A call provision allows the firm to call in bonds at slightly over par (usually 8 to 10 percent above par) regardless of what the market price is.

Gina thought if she could present a specific example to Al he would have a better feel for the bond refunding process. She proposed to call in an 11.50 percent $30 million issue that was scheduled to mature in the year 2017. The bonds had been issued in 1997, and since it was now 2002, the bonds have 15 years remaining to maturity. It was Gina's intent to replace the bonds with a new $30 million issue that would have the same maturity date 15 years into the future as that of the original 1997 issue. Based on advice from the firm's investment firm, Walston and Sons, the bonds could be issued at a rate of 10 percent. Joe Walston, a senior partner in the investment firm, further indicated that the underwriting cost on the new issue would be 2.8 percent of the $30 million amount involved.

Before she could do her analysis, Gina needed to accumulate information on the old 11.50 percent bond issue that she was proposing to refund. The original bond indenture indicated that the bonds had an 8 percent call premium, and that the bonds could be called anytime after five years. Gina explained to Al Rosen that the bondholders were protected from having their bonds called in for the first five years after issue, but that the bonds were fair game after that. Furthermore, from the sixth through the 13th year, the call premium went down by 1 percent per year. By the 14th year after issue, there was no call premium and the corporation could merely call in the bonds at par. Since in this case five years had passed, the call premium would be exactly 8 percent.

Gina checked with the chief accountant and found out that the underwriting cost on the old issue had initially been $400,000. The firm was currently paying taxes at a rate of 30 percent.

Outline the considerations in whether or not to refund this bond issue. What must Gina present to Al Rosen? Will Gina achieve her original objective?

Selected References

Altman, Edward. "Revisiting the High Yield Debt Market: Mature but Never Dull." *Journal of Applied Corporate Finance* 13 (Spring 2000), pp. 64-74.

Barclay, Michael J., and Clifford W. Smith, Jr. "The Maturity Structure of Corporate Debt." *Journal of Finance* 50 (June 1995), pp. 609-31.

Chang, Soo-Kim, David C. Mauer, and Mark Hoven Stohs. "Corporate Debt Maturity Policy and Investor Tax-Timing Options: Theory and Evidence." *Financial Management* 24 (Spring 1995), pp. 33-45.

Chen, Yehning, J. Fred Weston, and Edward I. Altman. "Financial Distress and Restructuring Models." *Financial Management* 24 (Summer 1995), pp. 57-75.

Datta, Sudip, Mai Iskandar-Dattaaa, and Ajay Patel. "Do bank relationships matter in public debt offerings?" *Journal of Applied Corporate Finance* 12 (Winter 1999), pp. 120-27.

Dichev, Illa D. "Is the Risk of Bankruptcy a Systematic Risk?" *Journal of Finance* 53 (June 1998), pp. 1131-47.

Graham, John R., Michael L. Lemmon, and James S. Schallheim. "Debt, Leases, Taxes and Endogeneity of Corporate Tax Status," *Journal of Finance* 53 (February 1998), pp. 99-129.

Hong, Gwangheon, and Arthur Wagna. "An Empirical Study of Bond Market Transactions." *Financial Analysts Journal* 56 (March-April 2000), pp. 32-46.

Leland, Hayne E. "Corporate Debt Value, Bond Covenants, and Optimal Capital Structure." *Journal of Finance* 49 (September 1994), pp. 1213-52.

Schall, Lawrence D. "Analytic Issues in Lease vs. Purchase Decisions." *Financial Management* 16 (Summer 1987), pp. 17-22.

APPENDIX 16A

Financial Alternatives for Distressed Firms

Although we have consistently considered businesses as going concerns throughout this book, we have also spoken of the risks (and securities premiums for such risks) associated with failure. For example, we stated that during uncertain economic times, a large, financially secure firm might be able to raise debt capital as much as 3 percentage points more cheaply than a medium-sized firm, even if the latter is well managed. Such a differential recognizes the fact that the smaller firm may more quickly find itself in financial distress under adverse market circumstances.

Bankruptcy and Insolvency Act http://laws.justice.gc.ca/en/B-3/index.html

A firm may be in financial distress because of **technical insolvency or bankruptcy**. Insolvency refers to a firm's inability to generate enough cash to pay its bills as they come due. Thus, a firm may be technically insolvent even though it has a positive net worth; there simply may not be sufficient liquid assets to meet current obligations. In other circumstances the fair market value of a firm's assets are less than its total liabilities—in other words, the firm has a negative net worth. In such a case either management or the creditors may judge that the best remedy possible is liquidation of the firm. Under the Bankruptcy and Insolvency Act then, either management or creditors can initiate legal action to have the firm declared bankrupt and have the firm's assets liquidated. Generally, the term *financial failure* covers the gamut of circumstances from technical insolvency to the declaration of legal bankruptcy.

There are firms that do not fit into either of these categories, but are still suffering from extreme financial difficulties. Perhaps they are rapidly approaching a situation in which they cannot pay their bills or where concerns over net worth deterioration may lead to bankruptcy proceedings.

Firms suffering from technical insolvency or negative net worth may participate in out-of-court settlements or in-court formal bankruptcy proceedings. Out-of-court settlements, where possible, allow the firm and its creditors to bypass certain lengthy and expensive legal proceedings. It follows, however, that if an agreement cannot be reached on a voluntary basis between a firm and its creditors, in-court procedures are necessary.

Out-of-Court Settlement

Out-of-court settlements may take many forms. Four alternatives are examined. The first is an **extension** in which creditors agree to allow the firm more time to meet its financial obligations. A new repayment schedule is developed subject to the acceptance of the creditors.

A second alternative is a **composition**, under which creditors agree to accept a fractional settlement of their original claim. They may be willing to do this because they believe the firm is unable to meet its total obligations, and they wish to avoid formal bankruptcy procedures. In the case of either a proposed extension or a composition, some creditors may not agree to go along with the arrangements. If their claims are relatively small, major creditors may allow them to be paid off immediately and in full to hold the agreement together. If their claims are large, no out-of-court settlement may be possible and formal bankruptcy proceedings may be necessary.

A third out-of-court settlement may take the form of a **creditor committee** established to run the business. Here, the parties involved judge that management can no longer effectively conduct the affairs of the firm. Once the creditors' claims have been partially or fully settled, a new management

FINANCE IN ACTION

Loewen Group Avoids the Grave of Bankruptcy

Loewen Group Inc. of Canada was once the second largest funeral home operator in North America. It had been expanding at an annual growth rate of about 30 percent through the early 1990s by acquiring traditional, family-run funeral homes across the continent. Its operation brought cost economies of scale to the industry.

However, in January 1996 it paid $175 million in cash and stock to a small competitor from Biloxi, Mississippi, to avoid bankruptcy proceedings in the United States. In a deal for about $8 million that had gone sour, the courts in Mississippi had awarded Jerry O'Keefe, the small-town funeral operator, $500 million in damages for breach of contract, massive fraud, and violation of antitrust rules. The "good old local boy" would not be "done wrong by a Canadian carpetbagger."

To appeal the "unjust" decision, Loewen would have had to post a bail bond of $625 million. Financing was proving difficult, and a real alternative appeared to be bankruptcy. Loewen felt that an out-of-court settlement was the path of least resistance and would allow it to continue on its expansion path. Share prices increased $12.25 to $40.00 on the day of the settlement. Standard and Poor's increased Loewen's debt rating from CCC to BB on the same day.

In 1998 Loewen was again on the verge of bankruptcy, but now it was because it had expanded too fast and acquired funeral homes at too high a price. Loewen had financed $1.65 billion of acquisitions mostly with debt and by the end of 1998 was unable to meet its obligations under its debt covenants. Its share price dropped from $45.00 per share to almost $1.00 as it incurred a loss of $600 million in 1998.

In 1999 as part of an agreement with its lenders Loewen attempted to restructure, dividend payments were suspended and a sale of assets was initiated. The lenders in response agreed not to declare Loewen in default under the financial covenants in its debt agreements. Nevertheless by mid-1999, Loewen sought bankruptcy protection.

In January of 2002, Loewen emerged from the bankruptcy protection of Chapter 11 (U.S.) and the Companies Creditors Arrangement Act (Canada) as Alderwoods Group. After the sale of several properties U.S.$2.4 billion in debt had been reduced to U.S.$835 million in debt and U.S.$700 million in equity accepted by creditors and bondholders. The original shareholders got nothing.

www.loewen.ca/

Symbol: AWGI (NASDAQ)

team may be brought in to replace the creditor committee. The outgoing management may be willing to accept the imposition of a creditor committee only when formal bankruptcy proceedings appear likely and they wish to avoid that stigma. There are also circumstances in which creditors are unwilling to form such a committee because they fear lawsuits from other dissatisfied creditors or from common or preferred shareholders.

A fourth out-of-court settlement is an **assignment**, in which liquidation of assets occurs without going through formal court action. To effect an assignment, creditors must agree on liquidation values and the relative priority of claims. This is not easy.

In actuality, there may be combinations of two or more of the just described out-of-court procedures. For example, there may be an extension as well as a composition, or a creditor committee may help to establish one or more of the alternatives.

In-Court Settlements

Proposal for an Arrangement under the Bankruptcy and Insolvency Act

In November 1992 the revision of the Bankruptcy Act of 1949 came into law as the Bankruptcy and Insolvency Act. The most significant revisions concerned the source of proposals for reorganizing a firm in order to save the firm and jobs. In recent years, larger corporations, unlike smaller firms, were able to escape bankruptcy under the Companies Creditors Arrangement Act, which dated from the 1930s. The revised Bankruptcy and Insolvency Act tries to legislate and simplify the provisions that restrict the secured creditors' rights in order to save the firm.

Proposals to reorganize the firm can now come from the bankrupt, the trustee in bankruptcy, the liquidator, or the receiver, but not the creditors. This is significant because under the previous legislation, the proposal had to come from the bankrupt or insolvent firm. In recent memory, Westar Mining could not put forward a proposal to save the company because the directors resigned, fearing certain liabilities. Under the new legislation, a proposal could now come from another source.

A proposal begins with a notice of intention, which allows a stay of proceedings against all creditors, including the secured creditors, for 30 days while a proposal for reorganization is prepared. Extensions of 45 days at a time are possible if the courts believe progress is being made. Because no one wins in a bankruptcy, a proposal allows a firm time to submit a plan to creditors.

The key to the revised legislation is that the secured creditors can now be part of the restructuring. The company in difficulty must keep the creditors informed of such issues as cash flow while attempting to develop a proposal in everyone's interest. Creditors are organized into classes based on their similarity of claims; and two-thirds of the creditors by value in each class, as well as a majority of the creditors voting, must accept the proposal. When Olympia & York sought to satisfy creditors, there were over 30 creditor classes. If accepted by the creditors, the proposal must then be ratified by the court. Ratification depends on a judgment that the plan is fair, equitable, and feasible.

An **internal reorganization** calls for an evaluation of current management and its operating policies. If current management is shown to be incompetent, it will probably be discharged and replaced by new management. An evaluation and possible redesign of the current capital structure is also necessary. If the firm is top heavy with debt (as is normally the case), alternate securities such as preferred or common stock may replace part of the debt.[1] Any restructuring must be fair to all parties involved.

Therefore, under a recapitalization, each of the old security holders must swap its old securities for new ones, the amount of which is determined by a current market valuation of the firm. Under what is called the **absolute priority rule**, all senior claims on asset value must be settled in full before any value can be given to a junior claimant. Thus, a bondholder must be awarded the full face value of his or her bond in a new security before preferred or common shareholders can receive any new securities. A simple example might clarify this a bit (see Table 16A–1).

TABLE 16A–1
Debt restructuring

Company A capital structure (book value) before reorganization:	
Bonds	$20 million
Subordinated debentures	12 million
Preferred stock	4 million
Common stock	25 million
Total capital	$61 million
Company A capital structure after reorganization:	
Bonds	$10 million
Income bonds	10 million
Common stock	20 million
Total capital	$40 million*

*$40 million would be the estimated market evaluation of these securities.

Under this example, the former bondholders and preferred shareholders would receive new securities covering the full value of their former holdings for a total of $36 million, while the shareholders would receive only the residual, or $4 million worth of securities. The bondholders and preferred

[1]Another possibility is the income bond on which interest is payable only if the firm makes money.

Algoma Survives

Algoma Steel of Sault Ste. Marie, Ontario (www.algoma.ca) sought protection under the Companies Creditors Arrangement Act (CCAA) in October 2001. Bondholders with a first mortgage, employees, and unsecured creditors all had significant interests in the rearrangement of the company's capital structure and its survival. So did the City of Sault Ste. Marie where Algoma is an important employer.

In February of 2002 Algoma came out of bankruptcy protection as a restructured company.

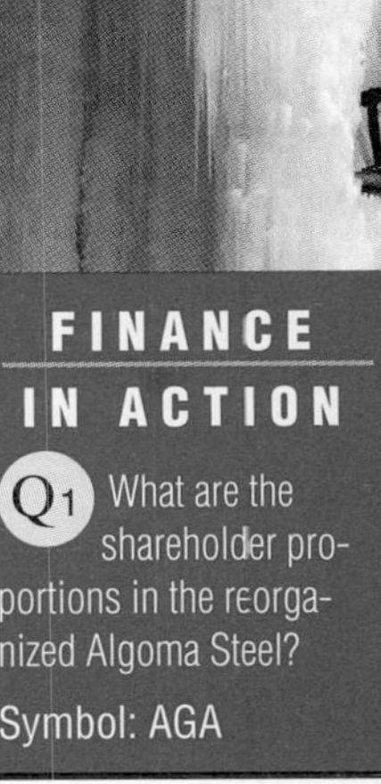

FINANCE IN ACTION

Q1 What are the shareholder proportions in the reorganized Algoma Steel?

Symbol: AGA

shareholders, however, would receive different securities than held previously. This is because the former bonds and debentures were a regular commitment of funds, helping to create a cash flow strain on the corporation. Now there is a smaller commitment to interest payments, but a promise of dividends if the company can improve its profits and cash flow. In the example, the former shareholders would have only 25 percent of the outstanding common shares in the restructured company. It is easy to imagine a corporate reorganization where there would be no residual value left for the common shareholders (such would happen in this case if the market value of the securities at the time of reorganization were pegged at $36 million or less).

An **external reorganization** in which a merger partner is found for the firm may also be considered. The surviving firm must be deemed strong enough to carry out the financial and management obligations of the joint entities. Old creditors and shareholders may be asked to make concessions to ensure that a feasible arrangement is established. Their motivation to do so would be that they hope to come out further ahead than if such a reorganization were not undertaken. Ideally, the firm should be merged with a strong firm in its own industry, although this is not always possible. The Canadian banking industry found such a need to merge weaker firms with stronger firms within the industry in the mid-1980s. As a result of the concerns aroused by the failure of two Alberta-based banks, the Canadian Commercial Bank and the Northland Bank, three other smaller banks (Continental, Mercantile, and Bank of British Columbia) merged with stronger banks. In the 1990s Royal Trust merged with Royal Bank, Guaranty Trust merged with T. D. Bank, First City Trust merged with North America Assurance Company, and General Trust merged with National Trust. All were experiencing severe financial pressures.

Liquidation

A **liquidation**, or sell-off, of assets may be recommended when an internal or external reorganization does not appear possible or when it is determined that the assets of the firm are worth more in liquidation than through a reorganization. Priority of claims becomes extremely important in a liquidation because it is unlikely that all parties will be fully satisfied in their demands.

Secured creditors generally seize the assets on which they have a lien. If, on liquidation, the secured creditors realize less than their secured claims, they become normal unsecured creditors for the unsettled balance remaining.

After the claims of secured creditors are settled, the priority of claims in a bankruptcy liquidation is as follows:

1. Cost of administering the bankruptcy procedures (lawyers get in line first).
2. Wages and salaries due employees up to a maximum of $2,000 per worker.
3. Outstanding source deductions.
4. Rent in arrears within certain proscribed limits.

5. Claims for prior judgements lodged against the bankrupt.
6. Certain other claims of the Crown.
7. General or unsecured creditors are next in line. Examples of claims in this category are those held by debenture (unsecured bond) holders, trade creditors, bankers who have made unsecured loans, and the Crown. There may be senior and subordinated positions within category 7, indicating that subordinated debtholders must turn over their claims to senior debtholders until complete restitution is made to the higher-ranked category. Subordinated debenture holders may keep the balance if anything is left after that payment.
8. Preferred shareholders.
9. Common shareholders.

Under the revised Bankruptcy and Insolvency Act, creditors that have supplied goods to a bankrupt company can repossess those goods for up to 30 days. The 30 days do not include when a stay of proceedings is in force.

Let us examine a typical situation to determine "who" should receive "what" under a liquidation in bankruptcy. Assume the Mitchell Corporation has a book value and liquidation value as shown in Table 16A–2. Liabilities and shareholders' claims are also presented.

TABLE 16A–2
Financial data for the Mitchell Corporation

Assets	Book Value	Liquidation Value
Accounts receivable	$ 200,000	$160,000
Inventory	410,000	240,000
Machinery and equipment	240,000	100,000
Building and plant	450,000	200,000
	$1,300,000	$700,000

Liabilities and Shareholders' Claims	
Liabilities:	
Accounts payable	$ 300,000
First lien, secured by machinery and equipment*	200,000
Senior unsecured debt	400,000
Subordinated debentures	200,000
Total liabilities	1,100,000
Shareholders' claims:	
Preferred stock	50,000
Common stock	150,000
Total shareholders' claims	200,000
Total liabilities and shareholders' claims	$1,300,000

*A lien represents a potential claim against property. The lien holder has a secured interest in the property.

We see that the liquidation value of the assets is far less than the book value ($700,000 versus $1,300,000). Also, the liquidation value of the assets will not cover the total value of liabilities ($700,000 compared to $1,100,000). Since all liability claims will be met, it is evident that lower-ranked preferred shareholders and common shareholders will receive nothing.

Before a specific allocation is made to the creditors (those with liability claims), the three highest priority levels in bankruptcy must first be covered. That would include the cost of administering the proceedings, allowable past wages due to workers, and overdue taxes. For the Mitchell Corporation, we shall assume these total $100,000. Since the liquidation value of assets was $700,000, that would leave $600,000 to cover creditor demands, as indicated in the left-hand column of Table 16A–3.

TABLE 16A–3
Asset values and claims

Balance Sheet		Creditor Claims	
Asset values in liquidation	$ 700,000	Accounts payable	$ 300,000
Administrative costs, wages, and taxes	−100,000	First lien, secured by machinery and equipment	200,000
Remaining asset values	$ 600,000	Senior unsecured debt	400,000
		Subordinated debentures	200,000
		Total liabilities	$1,000,000

Before we attempt to allocate the values in the left-hand column of Table 16A–3 to the right-hand column, we must first identify any creditor claims that are secured by the pledge of a specific asset. In the present case, there is a first lien on the machinery and equipment of $200,000. Referring back to Table 16A–2, we observe that the machinery and equipment has a liquidation value of only $100,000. The secured debtholders will receive $100,000, with the balance of their claim placed in the same category as the unsecured debtholders. In Table 16A–4 we show asset values available for unsatisfied secured claims and unsecured debt (top portion) and the extent of the remaining claims (bottom portion).

TABLE 16A–4
Asset values available for unsatisfied secured claims and unsecured debtholders—and their remaining claims

Asset values:	
Asset values in liquidation	$ 700,000
Administrative costs, wages, and taxes	100,000
Remaining asset values	600,000
Payment to secured creditors	−100,000
Amount available to unsatisfied secured claims and unsecured debt	$ 500,000
Remaining claims of unsatisfied secured debt and unsecured debt:	
Secured debt (unsatisfied first lien)	$ 100,000
Accounts payable	300,000
Senior unsecured debt	400,000
Subordinated debentures	200,000
	$1,000,000

In comparing the available asset values and claims in Table 16A–4, it appears that the settlement on the remaining claims should be at a 50 percent rate ($500,000/$1,000,000). The allocation will occur in the manner presented in Table 16A–5.

Each category receives 50 percent as its initial allocation. However, the subordinated debenture holders must transfer their $100,000 initial allocation to the senior debtholders in recognition of their preferential position. The secured debtholders and those having accounts payable claims are not part of the senior-subordinated arrangement and thus hold their initial positions.

Finally, in Table 16A–6, we show the total amounts of claims, the amount received, and the percent of the claim that was satisfied.

The $150,000 in column (3) for secured debt represents the $100,000 from the sale of machinery and $50,000 from the allocation process in Table 16A–5. The secured debtholders and senior unse-

TABLE 16A–5

Allocation procedures for unsatisfied secured claims and unsecured debt

(1) Category	(2) Amount of Claim	(3) Initial Allocation (50%)	(4) Amount Received
Secured debt (unsatisfied 1st lien)	$ 100,000	$ 50,000	$ 50,000
Accounts payable	300,000	150,000	150,000
Senior unsecured debt	400,000	200,000	300,000
Subordinated debentures	200,000	100,000	0
	$1,000,000	$500,000	$500,000

cured debtholders come out on top in terms of percent of claim satisfied (it is coincidental that they are equal). Furthermore, the subordinated debtholders and, as previously mentioned, the preferred and common shareholders receive nothing. Naturally, allocations in bankruptcy will vary from circumstance to circumstance. Working problem 16A–1 will help to reinforce many of the liquidation procedure concepts discussed in this section.

TABLE 16A–6

Payments and percent of claims

(1) Category	(2) Total Amount of Claim	(3) Amount Received	(4) Percent of Claim Satisfied
Secured debt (1st lien)	$200,000	$150,000	75%
Accounts payable	300,000	150,000	50
Senior unsecured debt	400,000	300,000	75
Subordinated debentures	200,000	0	0

List of Terms

technical insolvency 600
bankruptcy 600
extension 600
composition 600
creditor committee 600
assignment 601
internal reorganization 602
absolute priority rule 602
external reorganization 603
liquidation 603

Discussion Questions

16A–1. What is the difference between technical insolvency and bankruptcy?

16A–2. What are four out-of-court settlements? Briefly describe each.

16A–3. What is the difference between an internal reorganization and an external reorganization under formal bankruptcy procedures?

16A–4. What are the first three priority items under liquidation in bankruptcy?

Problems

16A–1. The trustee in the bankruptcy settlement for Immobile Homes lists the following book values and liquidation values for the assets of the corporation. Liabilities and shareholders' claims are also shown.

Assets	Book Value	Liquidation Value
Accounts receivable	$1,000,000	$ 700,000
Inventory	1,100,000	600,000
Machinery and equipment	800,000	400,000
Building and plant	3,000,000	1,800,000
Total assets	$5,900,000	$3,500,000
Liabilities and Shareholders' Claims		
Liabilities:		
Accounts payable	$2,000,000	
First lien, secured by machinery and equipment	650,000	
Senior unsecured debt	1,300,000	
Subordinated debentures	1,450,000	
Total liabilities	5,400,000	
Shareholders' claims:		
Preferred stock	100,000	
Common stock	400,000	
Total shareholders' claims	500,000	
Total liabilities and shareholders' claims	$5,900,000	

a. Compute the difference between the liquidation value of the assets and the liabilities.

b. Based on the answer to part *a,* will preferred stock or common stock participate in the distribution?

c. Given that the administrative costs of bankruptcy, workers' allowable wages, and unpaid taxes add up to $300,000, what is the total of remaining asset value available to cover secured and unsecured claims? (Wages and taxes owed totalled $50,000.)

d. After the machinery and equipment is sold to partially cover the first lien secured claim, how much will be available from the remaining asset liquidation values to cover unsatisfied secured claims and unsecured debt?

e. List the remaining asset claims of unsatisfied secured debtholders and unsecured debtholders in a manner similar to that shown at the bottom portion of Table 16A–4.

f. Compute a ratio of your answers in part *d* and part *e.* This will indicate the initial allocation ratio.

g. List the remaining claims (unsatisfied secured and unsecured) and make an initial allocation and final allocation similar to that shown in Table 16A–5. Subordinated debenture holders may keep the balance after full payment is made to senior debtholders.

h. Show the relationship of amount received to total amount of claim in a similar fashion to that of Table 16A–6. [Remember to use the sales (liquidation) value for machinery and equipment plus the allocation amount in part *g* to arrive at the total received on secured debt.]

CHAPTER | SEVENTEEN

17 Common and Preferred Stock Financing

LEARNING | OBJECTIVES

1. Outline the rights of shareholders as owners of the corporation.
2. Briefly describe cumulative voting as a method to potentially give minority shareholders representation on the board of directors. Calculate the number of shares required to elect a director.
3. Describe a rights offering as a method used to raise funds for the firm and calculate values of rights, shares, and shareholder wealth during the rights-offering process.
4. Describe poison pills and other provisions that make it difficult for outsiders to gain control of the corporation against management wishes.
5. Describe preferred shares as a type of security somewhere between debt and common stock.
6. Calculate the different tax treatment and resulting aftertax income from preferred dividends as compared to bond interest.
7. Describe the features of various securities in a risk-return framework.

Equity financing is as significant as debt financing for Canadian firms as we observed in Chapter 14, Figure 14–4. During the 1990s, for the first time, the book value of the outstanding equity of Canadian firms exceeded the total outstanding debt by all Canadian entities, including governments. Common and preferred equity are very important components of capital formation in our country.

The ultimate ownership of the firm resides in common stock, whether it is in the form of all outstanding shares of a closely held corporation or one share out of the over 800 million shares of BCE Inc. In terms of legal distinctions, it is the **common shareholder** alone who directly controls the business. While control of the company is legally in the shareholders' hands, it is practically wielded by management on an everyday basis. Even though they have no power to elect board members, at times large creditors may also exert tremendous pressure on a firm to meet certain standards of performance. Furthermore, recent court decisions in Canada have emphasized the fair treatment of all shareholders, including preferred shareholders.

A 2000 TSX survey revealed that 49 percent of Canadians own shares directly or indirectly through mutual funds. Only homeownership has greater participation among Canadians, at over 60 percent, as an investment. This significant participation among Canadians in the stock market can be attributed to rising stock prices, growing investment in mutual funds (not unrelated to the first reason), a more sophisticated investing public, and increased investment by women. This spreading investment activity will likely be tested by the next sustained downturn in market prices. Meanwhile, lower interest rates in the 1990s have encouraged investors to seek the higher returns promised from equity investments in Canada and abroad.

Despite the fact that most adult Canadians do not own common stock directly, the increasingly large stock portfolios held by mutual funds and pension funds, as noted in Figure 14–8, mean that many more millions of Canadians also have a stake in the share price performance of Canadian and foreign firms. As would also be expected, the management of corporations with publicly traded shares has become increasingly sensitive to these large institutional shareholders.

Institutional investors have a significant impact on the market by executing the majority of daily trading volume. Some investment dealers specialize in dealing exclusively with institutional accounts, particularly those dealers that have a foreign parent company. Institutional investors have become the major shareholders in many Canadian companies, supplanting a select group of Canadian families as the dominant players in the financial markets.

Preferred stock represents a hybrid security, combining the fixed payment (dividend) feature of debt with a limited claim on earnings, similar to common stock. The preferred shareholder does not have the same ownership interest in the firm as the common shareholder, but he or she does have a priority claim to dividends superior to that of the common shareholder. On the other hand, the fact that preferred shareholders rank behind debtholders in the event of liquidation makes the presence of preferred shares, rather than more debt, of great value to the corporate lenders.

As was discussed in Chapter 14, preferred stock has been a minor but significant method by which Canadian corporations have raised funds to balance their capital structure. Preferred stock deserves more than the passing mention it is sometimes accorded.

As with bonds, our interest in common and preferred shares extends to their claim on the expected income streams that might be generated by the firm. This is ultimately the source of the value that investors will place on these shares in the marketplace.

Common Shareholders' Claim to Income

All income that is not paid out to creditors or preferred shareholders automatically belongs to common shareholders. They have a residual claim to income, regardless of whether these funds are paid out in dividends or retained in the corporation. Take, for example, a firm that earns $10 million before capital costs and pays $1 million in interest to bondholders and a like amount in dividends to preferred shareholders. Ignoring tax savings on interest payments for the moment, the firm will then have $8 million available for common shareholders. Perhaps half of these funds will be paid out as

FINANCE IN ACTION

Q1 How has Amazon and Ballard performed lately: on the income statement; on the stock market?

Q2 What accounted for Ballard's 1997 and 1998 profits?

Symbol: AMZN BLDP (Nasdaq)

www.nasdaq.com

A Claim to Income?

The shares of Amazon.com, (www.amazon.com) the company that sells books and now a broad range of products online, had a tremendous run up in market value in the late 1990s. In May 1998, Amazon was trading at $7.50 (adjusted), and in late April 1999 it was trading above $105.00 (adjusted). Its equity value of over $17 billion made it worth more than the Royal Bank of Canada. Amazon had only been founded in 1994 and had yet to earn a profit. Nevertheless, investors were willing to pay a substantial price for Amazon in 1999, although the price fell through 2000-2001 and in early 2002 shares traded at about $16.00.

Why were investors willing to pay so much for Amazon? Was it the hysteria surrounding Internet stocks in general at the end of the 1990s, or was there real value in this company? In May 1999, Amazon reported annual sales revenue of $300 million, but it also reported an earnings loss of $60 million, its largest ever. Sales had increased tremendously from the previous year, but so had its earnings loss.

Shareholders have a claim on future income, but the question at Amazon was when investors would see the earnings. Apparently many believed in the late 1990s that the earnings would eventually come, based on their willingness to buy Amazon shares. In the last quarter of 2001, Amazon reported its first ever quarterly profit of $5 million on quarterly sales of over $1 billion. This amounted to $0.01 per share. Predictions for 2002 called for negative earnings until perhaps the last quarter.

Ballard Power (www.ballard.com), developer of a pollution free fuel cell, has had a similar history of rapid share price escalation without positive earnings although it reported small profits in 1997 and 1998. The share price exceeded $125.00 in recent memory but in early 2002 traded at about $30.00 while recording a loss per share of $1.06 for 2001.

All figures in U.S. dollars

common stock dividends. The balance will be reinvested in the business for the benefit of shareholders, with the hope of providing even greater income, dividends, and price appreciation in the future.

Realize, though, that the common shareholder does not have a legal or enforceable claim to dividends. Whereas a bondholder may force the corporation into bankruptcy for failure to make interest payments, common shareholders must accept circumstances as they are or attempt to change management if they desire a new dividend policy.

Occasionally a company has more than one class of common stock outstanding, carrying different rights and privileges. A somewhat recent innovation has come in the form of the targeted share. The Inco VBN share, recently redeemed, was issued in 1996 as part of the payment for a nickel deposit in Voisey's Bay, Labrador. Dividends would be 80 percent of Inco's regular dividend or a "target" of 25 percent of the income generated from the nickel deposit.

The Voting Right

Because common shareholders are the owners of the firm, they are accorded the right to vote for the board of directors and on all other major issues. Common shareholders may cast their ballots as they see fit on a given issue, or they may assign, by way of **proxy,** the power to cast their ballots to management or to some other group interested in assembling a block of votes.

Although voting would seem to be a fundamental right of common share ownership approximately 150 firms listed on the Toronto Stock Exchange have a second class of common share with unusual voting rights. Bombardier Class B common shares have the same dividend as the Class A shares, but the Class A shares have 10 votes for each share, allowing the founding family to maintain ownership control. As the Class A shares have greater voting power they tend to trade at a premium to the Class B shares, although the dividend payment is the same.

There may also be **nonvoting stock.** Telus Corporation has Class A nonvoting shares to access equity capital from non-residents. However, because Telus is in the communications business, Canadians must hold over 70 percent of the voting power. Canadian Tire became a well-publicized example of the potential dangers of nonvoting shares. In 1986 a play was made by the franchised dealers to gain control of Canadian Tire by tendering an offer to purchase a significant number of the voting shares. The voting shares soared in value to over $160.00 per share as compared to the nonvoting shares that traded at about $13.00, as no offer was made for the nonvoting shares.

Telus
www.telus.com/investors

A provision of the Class A Canadian Tire nonvoting shares, supposedly in place to protect the rights of the nonvoting shareholders was circumvented with the tender offer. However the Ontario Securities Commission (OSC) in a decision later backed by the Supreme Court of Ontario, declared that the deal was abusive because it was artificial in form, contrived only to circumvent a *coattail provision* and confound the justifiable expectations of investors. The coattail provision was there to provide that the nonvoting shareholders would become equal voting shareholders and receive the same share price as voting shareholders if there was to be an effective change in controlling ownership of Canadian Tire. The Toronto Stock Exchange shortly after this case adopted new regulations to protect nonvoting shareholders in corporate takeovers.

While the different classes of common stock may at times have different voting rights, they do have a vote. Bondholders and preferred shareholders, on the other hand, may vote only when a violation of their corporate agreements exists. The most common case of this is when a specified number (often two years' worth) of periodic dividends have been omitted on preferred shares. In that situation, the preferred shareholders often acquire voting privileges.

Cumulative Voting

The most important voting matter is the election of the board of directors. As indicated in Chapter 1, the board has primary responsibility for the stewardship of the corporation. If illegal or imprudent decisions are made, the board members can be held legally liable to injured parties. Additionally, corporate directors serve on important subcommittees of the company and, in this manner, have a direct effect on corporate affairs. Examples of board committees include the audit committee, the long-range financial planning committee, and the compensation committee. Selection of a new chief executive officer, sometimes following a decision to prematurely remove the old one, is probably the board's single most important duty.

Election of the members of the board of directors may occur through the familiar **majority voting** system or by a **cumulative voting** method. Under majority voting, any group of shareholders owning more than 50 percent of the common stock may elect all of the directors. Under cumulative voting, it is possible for those who hold less than a 50 percent interest to elect board members. The provision for some minority interest representation on the board is important to those who wish to reserve the right to challenge the prerogatives of the management.

In the cumulative voting process, a shareholder gets one vote for each share of stock he or she owns times one vote for each director to be elected. The shareholder may then accumulate votes in favour of a specified number of directors.

Take, as an example, a situation in which 10,000 shares are outstanding, you own 1,001 shares, and nine directors are to be elected. Your total number of votes under a cumulative system would be:

Number of shares owned	1,001
Number of directors to be elected	9
Number of votes	9,009

Now let us consider the situation where you cast all of your ballots for only one director of your choice. With nine directors to be elected, there is no way you can be stopped from creating one of the nine highest vote-getters. Since you own 1,001 shares, the maximum number of shares a majority interest could control would be 8,999. This would entitle that group to 80,991 votes.

Number of shares owned (majority)	8,999
Number of directors to be elected	9
Number of votes (majority)	80,991

These 80,991 votes cannot be spread thinly enough over nine candidates to stop you from electing your one director. For example, if they are spread evenly over nine choices, each of the majority's directoral picks will receive 8,999 votes, while your choice will receive 9,009 votes. Because the top nine vote-getters are elected, your candidate will claim a director position.

To determine the number of shares needed to elect a given number of directors under cumulative voting, the following formula is used:

$$\text{Shares required} = \frac{\text{Number of directors desired} \times \text{Total number of shares outstanding}}{\text{Total number of directors to be elected} + 1} + 1 \tag{17–1}$$

The formula reaffirms that in the previous instance, 1,001 shares would elect one director.

$$\frac{1 \times 10{,}000}{9 + 1} + 1 = \frac{10{,}000}{10} + 1 = 1{,}001$$

If three director positions out of nine were desired, 3,001 shares would be necessary.

$$\frac{3 \times 10{,}000}{9 + 1} + 1 = \frac{30{,}000}{10} + 1 = 3{,}001$$

It thus turns out that with approximately 30 percent of the outstanding shares, a minority interest can control one-third of the board. If a majority rule instead of a cumulative voting system were used, a minority interest would be able to elect no one. A group controlling 5,001 out of 10,000 outstanding shares could elect each and every director.

The following is a restatement of the proposition: If the number of minority shares outstanding under cumulative voting is known, we can determine how many directors those minority shares can elect by use of the formula:

$$\text{Number of directors that can be elected} = \frac{(\text{Shares owned} - 1) \times (\text{Total number of directors to be elected} + 1)}{(\text{Total number of shares outstanding})} \quad (17\text{–}2)$$

Plugging 3,001 into the formula yields:

$$\frac{(3{,}001 - 1)(9 + 1)}{10{,}000} = \frac{3{,}000(10)}{10{,}000} = 3$$

If the formula yields an uneven result, such as 3.1 or 3.7, the fractional amount is irrelevant. This means all results between 3 and 4 from the application of the formula indicate that three directors can be elected.

Although cumulative voting may give minority interests an opportunity to elect a representative to the board of directors, there is no requirement in Canada that directors must be chosen by cumulative voting, although federal and some provincial statutes provide for it. In the United States, 22 states require cumulative voting in preference to majority rule, 18 consider it permissible as part of the corporate charter, with only 10 states making no judgment on the advisability of its use.

A common method of thwarting the ambitions of the minority is to stagger the terms of directors so only a few are elected each year. If the nine directors referred to earlier were elected three per year, a minority interest would then require 2,501 shares to elect a single board member.

$$\frac{1 \times 10{,}000}{3 + 1} + 1 = 2{,}501$$

In such a case, a minority holder controlling 25 percent of the shares could be denied board representation.

The Right to Purchase New Shares

In addition to a claim to residual income and the right to choose the directors, the common shareholders may also enjoy a privileged position in the offering of new securities. If the corporate charter contains a **preemptive right** provision, holders of common stock must be given the first option to purchase new shares. Even when the corporate charter does not provide a preemptive right clause, new issues of common shares are usually offered first to existing shareholders.

The preemptive right provision ensures that management cannot subvert the position of present shareholders by selling shares to outside interests without first offering them to current shareholders. If such protection were not afforded, a 20 percent shareholder might find his or her interest reduced to 10 percent by a major distribution of new shares to outsiders. Not only would voting rights be diluted, but proportionate claims to corporate earnings would also be similarly reduced.

The Use of Rights in Financing

In Canada, corporations frequently engage in **rights offerings** to tap this built-in market for new securities—the current shareholders. In Figure 15-4 from an earlier chapter, we can see that of new equity financing on the TSX over the 10-year period to 2001, rights offerings raised 3 percent of the total. In 1992 approximately $2.5 billion

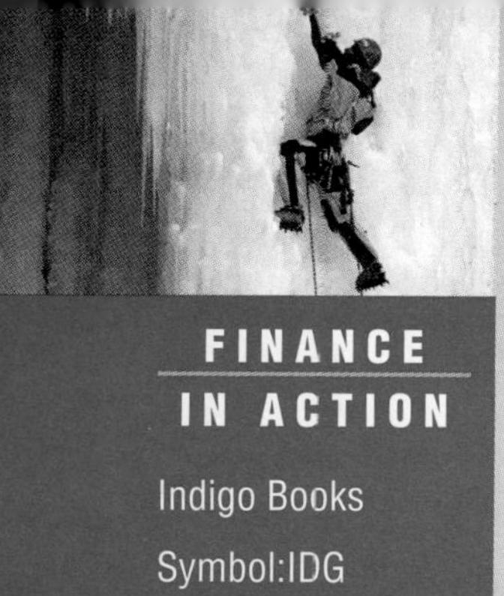

FINANCE IN ACTION

Indigo Books

Symbol:IDG

A Rights Offering! Another Chapter for Indigo

In early 2002, Indigo Books (www.chapters.indigo.ca) sought capital in excess of $14 million for its operations by way of a rights offering. One right was issued for each of the over 16 million common shares outstanding. Terms of the rights offering allowed for the purchase of a new common share for $3.50 plus 4 rights. At the time Indigo shares were trading at about $5.45 per share.

A prospectus was filed in February 2002 at SEDAR (www.sedar.com). A rights offering should cost less than an underwriting through an investment dealer. Costs are expressed as a percentage of the net proceeds to the firm.

1. What was the cost of this offering?
2. Why was the capital raised?

was raised through rights offerings, but in the last three years covered rights offerings were nil.

Let us examine how a rights offering would work for the mythical Walton Corporation, which is in need of some capital funding.

Walton Corporation	
Market share price	$40
Shares outstanding	9 million
Equity market value	$360 million
Required capital funds	$30 million
Subscription price (discounted)	$30
New shares required	1 million

Each old shareholder receives one right for each share of stock owned and may combine a specified number of rights plus $30.00 cash to buy a new share of stock. The discounted subscription price is meant to encourage the success of the rights offering. A share issue through the markets would have a much smaller discount. In a rights offering the following questions must be considered:

1. How many rights should be necessary to purchase one new share of stock?
2. What is the monetary value of these rights?

Rights Required Since 9 million shares are currently outstanding and 1 million new shares are to be issued, the ratio of old to new shares is 9 to 1. On this basis, the old shareholder is able to combine nine rights plus $30.00 cash to purchase one new share of stock.

This means that a shareholder with 90 shares of stock would receive an equivalent number of rights that could be applied toward the purchase of 10 new shares of stock at $30.00 apiece. As is discussed later in this chapter, shareholders may choose to sell their rights rather than exercise them by purchasing new shares.

Monetary Value of a Right Anything that contributes to the privilege of purchasing a higher-priced stock for $30.00 per share obviously has a market value. The following two-step analysis aids in determining that value.

Nine old shares, previously worth $40.00 per share, bestow the capability of buying one new share for $30.00. This means we end up with a total market value of $390.00

FIGURE 17–1
Time line during rights offering

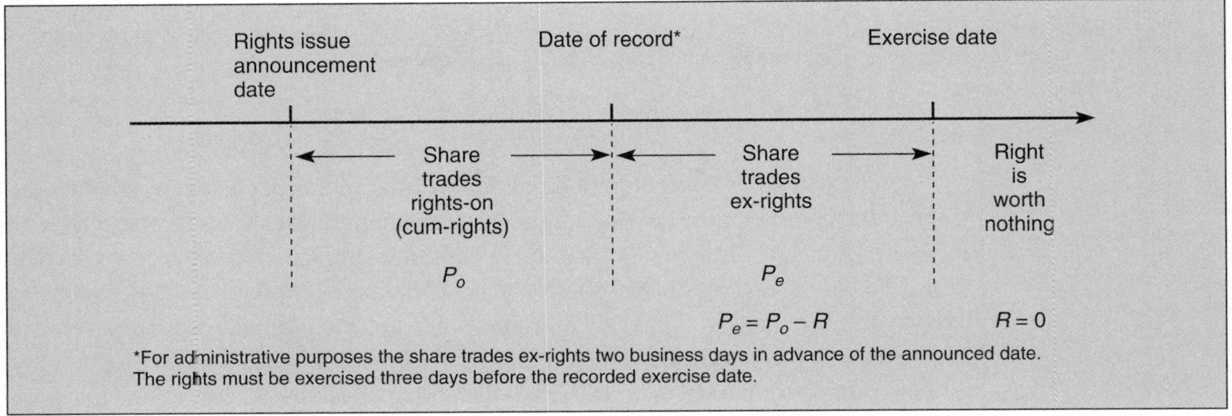

spread over 10 shares. Therefore, on completion of the rights offering, the value of a share would theoretically equal $39.00, if all else remains the same and all rights are utilized.

Nine old shares sold at $40 each	$360
One new share to sell at $30	30
Total value of 10 shares	$390
Average value of one share	$ 39

Thus, the rights offering entitles the holder to buy for $30.00 a share that should carry a value of $39.00. With a differential between the anticipated price and the subscription price of $9.00 and nine rights required to participate in the purchase of one share, the value of a right becomes $1.00.

Average value per share	$39
Subscription price	30
Differential	$ 9
Rights required to buy one share	9
Value of a right ($9/9 shares)	$ 1

The period during which rights may be bought, sold, or exercised is usually four to six weeks after what is termed the **ex-rights date.** This date, along with the other dates during the offering process, is outlined in Figure 17–1. The rights are issued in the same way dividends are paid. On what is called the *record date*, the company's books of record are closed, and all common shareholders listed on that date receive rights. Shares go ex-rights two business days prior to the record date. Investors buying the shares on or after the ex-rights date receive no rights. Between the date of the rights issue announcement and the ex-rights date, the stock is referred to as **cum-rights** or **rights-on,** bestowing on any purchaser of the stock the right to subscribe to the new issue. The following example summarizes the timing:

	Value of Stock	Value of Right
March 1-30: Stock trades cum-rights	$40	$1 (of the $40)
April 3: Stock trades ex-rights	39	1
April 5: Date of record	39	1
April 30: End of subscription period	39	—

Upon reaching the ex-right period, the price of the shares decreases by the theoretical **intrinsic value** of the detached right. The remaining value ($39.00) is the value of the share ex-rights. Though there is a time period remaining between the ex-rights date (April 3) and the end of the subscription period, the market immediately discounts the expected future dilution. Thus, the ex-rights value precisely reflects the same value as can be expected when the new, underpriced $30.00 stock issue is sold.

The formula for the value of the right when the stock is trading cum-rights or rights-on is:

$$R = \frac{P_o - S}{N + 1} \qquad (17\text{–}3)$$

where

P_o = Market value-cum-rights
S = Subscription price
N = Number of rights required to purchase a new share of stock

In the above example:

$$R = \frac{\$40 - \$30}{9 + 1} = \frac{\$10}{10} = 1$$

Using Formula 17–3 we determined that the value of a right in the Walton Corporation offering was $1.00. An alternative formula giving precisely the same answer is:

$$R = \frac{P_e - S}{N} \qquad (17\text{–}4)$$

The only new term is P_e, the market value of the stock when shares are trading ex-rights. The calculation becomes:

$$R = \frac{\$39 - \$30}{9} = \frac{\$9}{9} = 1$$

It is important to realize that rights seldom sell at their theoretical, intrinsic value, due to buying and selling costs and also because imbalances in demand and supply may develop. For example, there may be great enthusiasm for the new issue, causing the market value of the right to exceed the initial theoretical value (perhaps the right will trade for $1.75).

Effect of Rights on Shareholder's Position

At first glance, a rights offering appears to bring great benefits to shareholders. But is this really the case? Does a shareholder really benefit from being able to buy a stock that is initially $40.00 (and later $39.00) for $30.00? Don't answer too quickly!

Think of it this way. Assume 100 people own shares of stock in a corporation and they decide to have the corporation sell new shares to themselves at 25 percent below current value. It cannot really make sense that they can enhance their wealth by selling their own product more cheaply to themselves. What is gained by purchasing inexpensive new shares has to be lost by diluting the value of existing outstanding shares.

Take the case of Shareholder A, who owns nine shares of Walton Corporation before the rights offering and also has $30.00 in cash. His holdings would appear as follows:

Nine old shares at $40	$360
Cash	30
Total value	$390

If he receives and exercises nine rights to buy one new share at $30.00, his portfolio contains:

Ten shares at $39 (diluted value)	$390
Cash	0
Total value	$390

He is no better off. A second alternative would be for him to sell his rights in the market and stay with his position of owning only nine shares and holding cash.

Nine shares at $39 (diluted value)	$351
Proceeds from sale of rights	9
Cash	30
Total value	$390

As indicated, whether he chooses to exercise his rights or not, the stock still goes down to a lower value (others are still diluting). Once again, his overall value remains constant. The value received for the rights ($9.00) exactly equals the extent of dilution in the value of the original nine shares.

It would be foolish for the shareholder to throw away the rights as worthless securities. He would then suffer the pains of dilution without the offsetting gain from the sale of the rights.

Nine shares at $39 (diluted value)	$351
Cash	30
Total value	$381

Empirical evidence indicates that this careless activity occurs 1 to 2 percent of the time.

Desirable Features of Rights Offerings

The student may ask, "If the shareholder is no better off in terms of total valuation, why undertake a rights offering?" There are a number of possible advantages.

As previously indicated, by giving current shareholders a first option to purchase new shares, we protect their current position in regard to voting rights and claims to earnings. Of equal importance, the use of a rights offering gives the firm a built-in

Funds for a Small Business

FINANCE IN ACTION

Q1 What was the cost of the rights offering versus the share offering?

Q2 What was the discount to the original common share price of each offering?

SB Fintech Solutions Limited (www.sylogist.com), a computer systems design firm of Calgary, in early 2002 required additional capital and decided to approach its existing shareholders through a rights offering. At the time its common shares were trading on the TSX Venture Exchange (www.tse-cdnx.com) at about $0.15 each and the rights began trading at about $0.03 each. Fintech (or Sylogist) hoped to raise a little over $550,000 for its operations. We should observe the length of time between the record date and the expiry (subscription) date for this issue.

At about the same time Burntsand Inc. (www.burnstand.com), a firm providing e-business solutions sought to raise approximately $15 million by way of a common share offering on the Toronto Stock Exchange (www.tsx.ca). It was to be underwritten by 4 investment dealers with an issue price of $2.35 per share. At the time of the announcement Burnstand's common shares were trading at $2.70. Besides out of pocket expenses Burnstand would incur underwriting commissions.

A prospectus was filed with SEDAR (www.sedar.com) by both firms.

Symbols: BRT
FSL
FSL.RT

market for new security issues. Because of this built-in base, distribution costs are likely to be considerably lower than under a straight public issue in which investment dealers must underwrite the full risk of distribution. Investment dealers may assist in a rights offering but with a lower expected fee.

Additionally, a rights offering may generate more interest in the market than would a straight public issue. There is a market not only for the stock, but also for the rights. Because the subscription price is normally set 15 to 25 percent below current value, there is the false appearance of a bargain, creating further interest in the offering.

Figure 15-4 in Chapter 15 exhibited the significance of rights offerings in raising new share capital. Although its significance varied greatly from year to year, rights offerings contributed an average of 3 percent of all equity raised during the 10-year period. This compares with the 16 percent raised through private offerings.

American Depository Receipts (ADRs)

NYSE
www.nyse.com/international

American depository receipts (ADRs) are certificates that have a legal claim on an ownership interest in a foreign company's common stock. The shares of the foreign company are purchased and put in trust in a foreign branch of a New York bank. The bank, in turn, receives and can issue depository receipts to the American shareholders of the foreign firm. These ADRs (depository receipts) allow foreign shares to be traded in the United States much like a common stock. ADRs have been around for a long time, and they are sometimes referred to as American Depository Shares (ADSs).

Since foreign companies want to tap into the world's largest capital market, the United States, they need to offer securities for sale in the United States that can be traded by investors and have the same liquidity features of U.S. securities. Dividends are paid in dollars and are more easily collected than if the actual shares of the foreign stock were owned. ADRs are considered to be more liquid, less expensive, and easier to trade than buying a foreign company's stock directly on that country's exchange.

Poison Pills

During the 1980s a new wrinkle was added to the meaning of rights when firms began receiving merger and acquisition proposals from companies interested in acquiring

ADRs or Shares?

There are over 450 foreign companies listed on the New York Stock Exchange (NYSE) in order to access the world's largest and most liquid capital market. The vast majority of these foreign companies are traded as American Depository Receipts (ADRs) or Global Depository Receipts (GDRs). The ADR is a U.S. registered receipt for foreign shares held in the vaults of American banks. The receipts, which have a U.S. dollar value, must be converted to shares before they are sold by investors, which can be a somewhat inconvenient process.

More companies are forgoing the ADR process and listing their shares directly on the exchange. Generally the shares of Canadian companies have been directly listed because the capital markets of Canada and of the United States are quite similar, allowing for seamless trading between the exchanges. Trading across other exchanges has not been as easily accommodated because of different regulations and the exchange rate question. However, as the international financial markets integrate, this is changing. With the amalgamation of Daimler-Benz AG and Chrysler Corporation, the new company DaimlerChrysler has its shares trade in New York the same as in Germany. There is no conversion of shares required, as a share trading in Germany is the same as one in the United States.

FINANCE IN ACTION

Q1 What are seven Canadian companies that trade on the NYSE?

Q2 What are three well-known companies that trade as ADRs on the NYSE?

www.nyse.com

voting control of the firm. Many firms' managements did not want to give up control of their companies, and so they devised a method of making their firms unattractive to potential acquisition-minded companies. A company using majority voting needs to control only over 50 percent of the voting shares to exercise total control. Management of companies considered potential takeover targets began to develop defensive tactics in fending off these unwanted mergers. One widely used strategy was called the **poison pill.**

A poison pill is a rights offer made to existing shareholders of Company X with the sole purpose of making it more difficult for another firm to acquire Company X. Most poison pills have a trigger point. When a potential buyer accumulates a given percentage of the common stock (for example, 20 percent), the other shareholders receive rights to purchase additional shares from the company, generally at very low prices. These new shares may have special privileges not available to shareholders that have acquired a large block of shares. If the rights are exercised by shareholders, this increases the total shares outstanding and dilutes the potential buyer's ownership percentage.

Poison pill strategies often are put in place without a shareholders' vote. In 1988, Inco Ltd. was the first Canadian corporation to introduce a poison pill. Inco's poison pill gave its directors the ability to initiate a rights offering when a hostile buyer acquired more than 20 percent of the company's stock. The rights offering allowed shareholders other than the shareholder with the large share holding to purchase additional shares at half price. Many suggest that poison pills lower the potential for maximizing shareholder value by discouraging potential high takeover bids. Attempts by other companies to introduce poison pills have sometimes been overridden by disgruntled shareholders.

Inco Ltd.
www.inco.com

Preferred Stock Financings

Between bonds and common stock is an intermediate, or hybrid, form of security known as preferred stock. You may question the validity of the term *preferred*, for preferred stock does not possess any of the most desirable characteristics of debt or

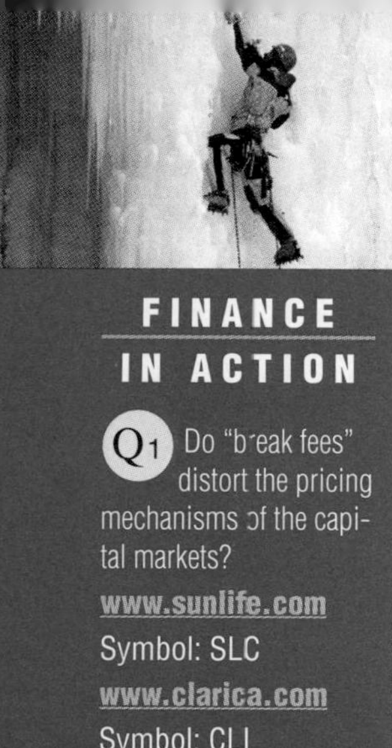

FINANCE IN ACTION

Q1 Do "break fees" distort the pricing mechanisms of the capital markets?

www.sunlife.com

Symbol: SLC

www.clarica.com

Symbol: CLI

An Expensive Pill to Swallow

In 2001, Sun Life Financial made an offer to purchase the outstanding shares of Clarica Life Insurance for $6.9 billion by way of a share exchange or merger. This was part of the consolidation process taking place in the financial services industry in Canada.

Although the price for the shares of Clarica seemed reasonable, many objected to the deal based on the terms of Sun Life's offer. The offer had been arranged on friendly terms between the two companies and contained a "break fee" of $310 million payable to Sun Life if another company bid for Clarica and succeeded in acquiring it. In addition Sun Life could match any competing bid.

The break fee represented 4 percent of the total value of the deal and was supposed to cover out of pocket expenses of Sun Life for investigating the merger and as compensation for the risk of pursuing Clarica. However many suggested the break fee was in effect a poison pill as it would discourage competing bids because the competing bidders would have to absorb this fee, while Sun Life would not have to absorb it.

As we explored in Chapter 13 the capital markets are expected to contain risks and as identified in Chapter 14 the markets operate most efficiently in a freely competitive environment.

common stock. In the case of debt, bondholders have a contractual claim against the corporation for the payment of interest and may force the corporation into bankruptcy if payment is not forthcoming. Common shareholders are the owners of the firm and have a residual claim to all income not paid out to others.

Preferred shareholders are merely entitled to receive a stipulated dividend and generally must receive the dividend before the payment of dividends to common shareholders. However, their right to annual dividends is not compelling to the corporation as interest on debt is, and the corporation may forgo preferred dividends when this is deemed necessary.

For example, XYZ Corporation might receive $100.00 per share for a new issue of preferred stock on which it specifies $6.00 as the annual dividend. Under normal circumstances, the corporation would pay the $6.00 per share dividend. Let us assume it also has $1,000 bonds carrying 7 percent interest and shares of common stock with a market value of $50.00, normally paying a $1.00 cash dividend. The 7 percent interest must be paid on the bonds. The $6.00 preferred dividend has to be paid before the $1.00 dividend on common, but both may be waived without threat of bankruptcy. Common shareholders are the last in line to receive payment, but their potential participation in earnings is unlimited. They may not receive the $1 dividend this year but may receive much larger dividends in the future. On the other hand, the preferred shareholder's dividend remains at $6.00.

Justification for Preferred Stock

Because preferred stock has few unique characteristics, why might the corporation choose to issue it, and equally important, why are investors willing to purchase the security?

One reason corporations issue preferred stock is to achieve a balance in their capital structures. It is a means of expanding the capital base of the firm without diluting the common stock ownership position or incurring contractual debt obligations. Firms that are heavy users of debt, such as public utilities and capital goods producers, may go to preferred stock to balance their sources of financing. Canadian commercial banks have become more frequent issuers of preferreds because perpetual preferred shares are counted as part of the capital in tests of the banks' capital adequacy under the Bank Act as revised in 1980.

Even in these cases there may be a drawback. While interest payments on debt are tax deductible, preferred stock dividends are not. The interest cost on 8 percent debt may be only 4.5 to 6 percent on an aftertax cost basis, while the aftertax cost on 8 percent preferred stock would be the stated amount. A firm issuing the preferred stock may be willing to pay the higher aftertax cost to assure investors that it has a balanced capital structure, thereby lowering the costs of the other sources of funds in the capital structure.

Some dividend yields on preferreds can be quite attractive. In May 2002, when interest rates were low, the Bank of Nova Scotia E preferreds offered a 6.9 percent dividend yield. Royal Bank's J preferreds had an 6.8 percent yield.

Investor Interest Primary purchasers of preferred stock are corporate investors, insurance companies, and pension funds. To the corporate investor, preferred stock offers a very attractive advantage over bonds. In many cases the tax law provides that any corporation that receives either preferred or common dividends from another corporation may receive those dividends tax-free. In 1987, the government no longer allowed the tax-free status on term preferred shares for specified financial corporations if early redemption was possible. This government legislative change, along with a decrease in the relative attractiveness of the dividend tax credit, severely reduced the market for preferred shares. However, new features added to preferred shares through the 1990s have allowed for the continued popularity of preferreds. For the individual investor, the preferred dividend offers the advantage of the **dividend tax credit,** which reduces the amount of tax payable on dividend income. By contrast, the interest on bonds is usually taxable to the recipient.

Because of this tax consideration, it is not surprising that corporations are able to issue preferred stock at a slightly lower pretax yield than debt. For example, let us examine the yields of two financial securities of the Bank of Montreal that were outstanding as of March 2002.

Bank of Montreal
www.bmo.com

Bank of Montreal	
Debenture	
Due	December 31, 2011
Coupon payment	6.685%
Price	100.79
Yield	6.57%
Preferred	
Due	Redeemable (February 2013) Non convertible
Dividend	$1.325
Price	$24.80
Yield	5.34%

On a before-tax basis, the bond offers the higher yield, and yet it is a less risky investment. Let us examine the aftertax yields.

Assuming the investor is in the top tax bracket in the Province of Alberta we will use the top marginal tax rates as identified in Table 2-13. Examining aftertax yields:

Before-tax **debenture** yield	6.57 percent
Combined marginal tax rate (39%)	(2.56)
Aftertax debenture yield	4.01 percent
Before-tax **preferred** yield	5.34 percent
Combined marginal tax rate (24.08%)	(1.29)
Aftertax preferred yield	4.05 percent

Thus, on an aftertax basis, the investor in a top marginal tax bracket achieves a higher yield with the preferreds. You may wish to examine the aftertax yields in your province at the top marginal rate or the lower tax rates given in Table 2-13.

Summary of Tax Considerations Tax considerations work in two opposite directions. First, they make the aftertax cost of debt cheaper than preferred stock to the issuing corporation because interest is tax deductible to the payer. (This is true even though the quoted rate may be higher.) Second, tax considerations generally make the receipt of preferred dividends more valuable than corporate bond interest to the (corporate) recipient because the dividend is exempt from taxation in most instances. For the individual taxpayer, the dividend tax credit reduces the amount of tax payable as compared to that payable on interest income.

Some of the large holding companies that are such important players in Canadian capital markets quite naturally make extensive use of preferred share offerings because of the tax and capital structure effects combined. Some analysts have believed that the intricate use of preferred financings has allowed holding companies to report extra large profits and minimize taxes, all while financing expansion. For example, a company with pretax profit of $10 million would pay about $5 million in tax. The company, it is claimed, could do much better by borrowing substantial sums to buy preferred shares. It could, for example, borrow $100 million at 10 percent. That would create an annual expense of $10 million, reducing the ordinary income to zero. Using the borrowed money to buy $100 million of preferred shares yielding about $7.5 million in dividends would increase the company's end profit by a whopping 50 percent.

Provisions Associated with Preferred Stock

A preferred stock issue contains a number of stipulations and provisions that define the shareholder's claim to income and assets.

1. *Cumulative Dividends.* Most preferred stock issues have a cumulative claim to dividends. That is, if preferred stock dividends are not paid in any one year, they accumulate and must be paid in total before common shareholders can receive dividends. If preferred stock carries a $2.00 cash dividend and the company does not pay dividends for three years, preferred shareholders must receive the full $6.00 before common shareholders can receive anything.

   The **cumulative dividend** feature makes a corporation very cognizant of its obligation to preferred shareholders. When a financially troubled corporation has missed a number of dividend payments under a cumulative arrangement, there may be a financial recapitalization of the corporation in which preferred shareholders receive new securities in place of the dividend arrearage. Assume the corporation has now missed five years of dividends under a $2.00-per-year obligation and still remains in a poor cash position. Preferred shareholders may be offered $10.00 or more in new common stock for forgiveness of the missed dividend payments. Preferred shareholders may be willing to cooperate to keep the corporation financially viable.

2. *Conversion Feature.* Similar to certain forms of debt, preferred stock may be convertible into common shares. Thus, $25.00 in preferred stock may be convertible into x number of shares of common stock at the option of the holder. One new wrinkle on convertible preferreds is the use of **convertible exchangeable preferreds** that allow the company to force conversion from convertible preferred stock into convertible debt. This can be used to allow the company to change preferred dividends into tax-deductible interest payments when it is to the company's advantage to do so.

   Convertibility is discussed at length in Chapter 19. In Canada 25 percent of preferred share issues carry a **conversion feature,** versus about 40 percent in U.S. markets.

3. *Call Feature.* Preferred stock, like debt, may be callable or "redeemable". That is, the corporation may retire the security before maturity at some small premium over par. This, of course, accrues to the advantage of the corporation and to the disadvantage of the preferred shareholder. A preferred issue carrying a **call feature** is accorded a slightly higher yield than a similar issue without this provision. Preferred shares with a call feature are said to be redeemable. The same type of refunding decision applied to debt obligations in Chapter 16 could also be applied to preferred stock.

4. *Retractable Feature.* A preferred share containing a provision that allows redemption of the shares at the option of the shareholder has a **retractable feature.** This provision creates advantages and disadvantages for the company and shareholder in just the opposite direction as does the call provision.

5. *Participation Provision.* A small percentage of preferred stock issues are participating; that is, they may participate over and above the quoted yield when the corporation is enjoying a particularly good year. For example, the **participation provision** may provide that once the common stock dividend equals the preferred stock dividend, the two classes of securities may share equally in additional payouts.

6. *Floating Rate.* Beginning in the early 1980s, some preferred stock issuers made the dividend floating in nature. Usually, the dividend is changed on a monthly or quarterly basis, based on current market conditions. Because the dividend rate changes monthly or quarterly and has a **floating rate,** there is still some small price change possibility between dividend adjustment dates. Nevertheless, it is less than the price change for regular preferred stock. Often, preferred shares paying a fixed return are set to convert to a floating-rate return in the near future. Thus, the issuing firms have protected themselves from being locked into a fixed-rate security in perpetuity-as have the investors.

   Floating rate preferreds are often set based on a common money market rate such as the prime or an average bankers' acceptance rate. Thus the preferred rate is plus or minus a percentage from the selected money market rate.

FINANCE IN ACTION

Do You Trust COPrS, BOaTS, or Teenburgers?

In March 1999, as part of Suncor's ongoing expansion of its oilsands plant in Fort McMurray, Northern Alberta, a long-term power agreement was reached with TransAlta Utilities. TransAlta would build a $315 million facility to supply power to the Suncor plant. For both companies the expansion in capital assets required funding from the capital markets.

Through its investment dealer Merrill Lynch, Suncor announced the sale of Canadian Originated Preferred Securities (COPrS), raising $240 million. In its prospectus, Suncor labelled these securities as junior, subordinated debentures. The securities were to pay interest at 9.05 percent a year for 49 years, almost forever. They were, however, redeemable after 5 years at par.

These newly named securities had features similar to bonds and to preferred shares. The features were set to appeal to the demands of the investment community, and a clever name would assist in their sale. Since that initial offering "income trusts" secured by the revenue streams of various businesses have become all the rage.

In late 2001 A&W issued Revenue Royalties Income Fund units which were to pay out 3 percent of annual sales from A&W outlets to unit holders of the trust. Annual income on these units would initially exceed 10 percent. The Bank of Montreal for the last couple of years has issued BMO BOaTS secured by first mortgages to satisfy its Tier 1 capital requirements. The BOaTS are redeemable and convertible into preferred shares while offering healthy income return to investors. In early 2002 TimberWest Forest introduced an income trust fund based on the cash flow from its lumber and timberland.

These income trust securities are listed on the TSX and a prospectus of the offerings is available at SEDAR.

www.tsx.ca

www.sedar.com
Symbol: A&W.UN
Symbol: TWF.UN

7. *Par Value.* As with common shares, federally incorporated companies issue no-par value preferreds. However, many balance sheets still show **par value** preferred shares issued before the Canada Business Corporations Act was amended to disallow their issue.

   Despite preferreds no longer having a par value, corporations still may use a similar term. They may refer to the "stated value" per share in establishing the redeemable and dividend features.
8. *Dutch Auction Preferred Stock.* **Dutch auction preferred stock** is similar to floating-rate preferred stock, but it is a short-term instrument. The security matures every seven weeks and is sold (reauctioned) at a subsequent bidding. The concept of Dutch auction means the stock is issued to the bidder willing to accept the lowest yield and then to the next lowest bidder, and so on until all the preferred stock is sold. This is much like the Treasury bill auctions held by the Bank of Canada. This auction process at short-term intervals allows investors to keep up with the changing interest rates in the short-term market. Some corporate investors like Dutch auction preferred stock because it allows them to invest at short-term rates and take advantage of the tax benefits available to them with preferred stock investments. Chartered banks have been big buyers of auction preferreds.

Comparing Features of Common and Preferred Stock and Debt

Table 17–1 compares the characteristics of common stock, preferred stock, and bonds. Consider carefully the comparative advantages and disadvantages of each.

In terms of the risk-return relationships embodied in these three classes of securities (as well as in the other investments discussed in Chapter 7), we might expect the risk-return pattern depicted in Figure 17–2. The lowest return is obtained from savings accounts, and the highest return and risk are generally associated with common stock. In between, we note that short-term instruments generally, though not always, provide

TABLE 17–1
Features of alternative security issues

	Common Stock	Preferred Stock	Bonds
1. Ownership and control of the firm	Belongs to common shareholders through voting rights and residual claim to income	Limited rights when dividends are missed	Limited rights under default in interest payments
2. Obligation to provide return	None	Must receive payment before common shareholder	Contractual obligation
3. Claim to assets in bankruptcy	Lowest claim of any security holder	Bondholders and creditors must be satisfied first	Highest claim
4. Cost of distribution	Highest	Moderate	Lowest
5. Risk-return trade-off	Highest risk, highest return (at least in theory)	Moderate risk, moderate return	Lowest risk, moderate return
6. Tax status of payment by corporation	Not deductible	Not deductible	Tax deductible Cost = Interest payment × (1 − tax rate)
7. Tax status of payment to recipient	Dividend to other corporation usually tax exempt Special tax treatment with dividend tax credit	Same as common stock	Interest usually fully taxable

FIGURE 17–2
Risk and expected return for various security classes

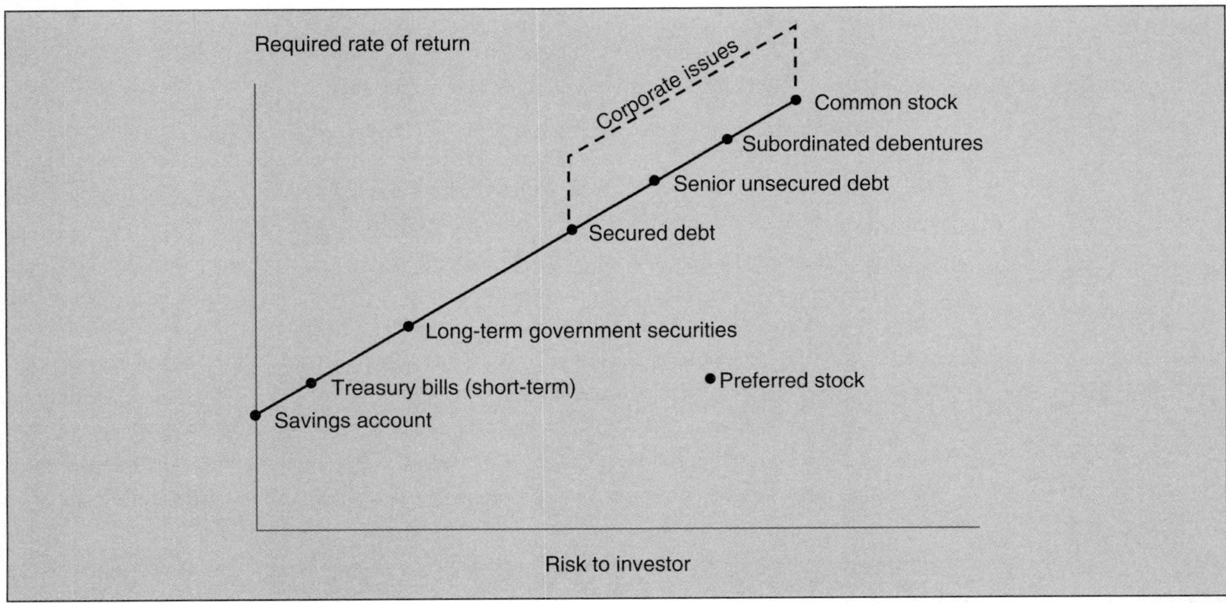

lower returns than longer-term instruments. We also observe that government securities pay lower returns than issues originated by corporations because of the lower risk involved. Next on the scale after government issues is preferred stock. As previously mentioned, this hybrid form of security may pay a lower return than even long-term Government of Canada debt instruments because of the tax-exempt status of preferred stock dividends to corporate purchasers and because of the dividend tax credit available to individual investors. Thus, the risk-return trade-off on preferred stock does not fall on the straight line because of the importance of the tax treatment. If the risk return relationship was expressed on an aftertax basis we would expect to see preferreds somewhere between debentures and common stock.

Next we observe increasingly high return requirements on debt, based on the presence or absence of security provisions and the priority of claims on unsecured debt. At the top of the scale is common stock. Because of its lowest priority of claim in the corporation and its volatile price movement, it has the highest demanded return.

While extensive research studies have tended to validate these general patterns, short-term or even intermediate-term reversals have occurred, in which investments with lower risk have outperformed investments at the higher end of the risk scale.[1]

Summary

1. Common stock ownership carries three primary rights or privileges. First, there is a residual claim to income. All funds not paid out to other classes of securities automatically belong to the common shareholder; the firm may then choose to pay out these residual funds in dividends or to reinvest them for the benefit of common shareholders. Different classes of shares may carry the right to differing dividend amounts. There can also be cases where dividends on a particular class of stock are tied to the performance of a subsidiary company.

   Because common shareholders are the ultimate owners of the firm, they alone have the privilege of voting (except under default or other unusual conditions). The major voting choice for the shareholders is in electing the members of the firm's board of directors. There may be more than one class of stock whose voting rights differ. In Canada there are many examples of stock with different voting rights. The general purpose of such stock is to allow a company to raise additional equity capital without diluting the controlling ownership of a current group of shareholders. Many of the nonvoting issues contain a so-called coattail clause allowing for the participation of their holders in any premium paid by an acquirer for the voting shares.
2. To expand the role of minority shareholders, corporations may use a system of cumulative voting in which each shareholder has voting power equal to the number of shares owned times the number of directors to be elected. By cumulating votes for a small number of selected directors, minority shareholders are sometimes able to have representation on the board.
3. Common shareholders may also enjoy a first option to purchase new shares. This privilege is extended through the procedure known as a rights offering. A shareholder receives one right for each share of stock owned and may combine a certain number of rights, plus cash, to purchase a new share. While the cash or subscription price is usually somewhat below the current market price, the shareholder neither gains nor loses through the process.
4. Poison pills are provisions established by a firm to prevent a hostile takeover. They usually provide for an extensive dilution in ownership if shares are acquired by an unwelcome firm in an attempt to take over the company. A poison pill makes it very expensive for the unwelcome firm

www.mcgrawhill.ca/college/block

[1]Ibbotson Associates, *Stocks, Bonds, Bills and Inflation:* 2000 *Yearbook* (Chicago: Ibbotson Associates Capital Management Research Center, 2000).

to complete the takeover unless the unwelcome firm is prepared to negotiate with the management of a firm being pursued.

5. A hybrid, or intermediate, security falling between debt and common stock is preferred stock. Preferred shareholders are entitled to receive a stipulated dividend and must receive this dividend before any payment is made to common shareholders. Preferred dividends usually accumulate if they are not paid in a given year. Preferred shareholders cannot, however, initiate bankruptcy proceedings or seek legal redress if nonpayment occurs. Recent court decisions have strengthened the position of preferred shareholders during corporate reorganizations.
6. Preferred shares pay dividends that are subject to special provisions under the Income Tax Act. The effect is to make dividends more attractive than interest to the investor, other things being equal. Therefore, when comparing returns offered on preferreds and bonds, it is appropriate to look at aftertax yields.
7. Common stock, preferred stock, bonds, and other securities tend to receive returns over the long run in accordance with risk, with corporate issues generally paying a higher return than government securities

Review of Formulas

1. Shares required

$$\text{Shares Required} = \frac{\text{Number of directors desired} \times \text{Total number of shares outstanding}}{\text{Total number of directors to be elected} + 1} + 1 \quad (17\text{–}1)$$

2. Number of directors

$$\text{Number of directors that can be elected} = \frac{(\text{Shares owned} - 1) \times (\text{Total number of directors to be elected} + 1)}{(\text{Total number of shares outstanding})} \quad (17\text{–}2)$$

3. $R = \dfrac{P_o - S}{N + 1}$ (17–3)

R = value of a right
P_o = market value of the stock-rights-on (stock carries a right)
S = subscription price
N = number of rights required to purchase a new share of stock

4. $R = \dfrac{P_e - S}{N}$ (17–4)

P_e is the market value of stock-ex-rights (stock no longer carries a right)

List of Terms

common shareholder 608
preferred stock 609
proxy 610
nonvoting stock 611
majority voting 511
cumulative voting 611
preemptive right 613
rights offering 613
ex-rights date 615
cum-rights or rights-on 615
intrinsic value 616
poison pill 619
dividend tax credit 621
cumulative dividend 622
convertible exchangeable preferreds 623
conversion feature 623
call feature 623
retractable feature 623
participation provision 623
floating rate 623
par value 624
dutch auction preferred stock 624

Discussion Questions

1. Why has corporate management become increasingly sensitive to the desires of large institutional investors?
2. What is the difference in dividend payments between Bombardier and Telus nonvoting shares and its voting common shares? How do you explain the difference in their trading values?
3. Why do corporations use special categories in issuing common stock?
4. What are the possible disadvantages, from an investor's point of view, of being able to buy only nonvoting shares in a given company? What do you think of the increased tendency among Canadian companies to issue large amounts of nonvoting shares?
5. What is the purpose of cumulative voting? Are there any disadvantages to management?
6. Why has preferred stock been a much more popular source of funds for corporations in Canada than in the United States?
7. How does the preemptive right protect shareholders from dilution?
8. If common shareholders are the owners of the company, why do they have only the last claim on assets and only a residual claim on income?
9. During a rights offering the underlying stock is said to sell rights-on and ex-rights. Explain the meaning of these terms and their significance to current shareholders and potential shareholders.
10. Why might management use a poison pill strategy?
11. Preferred stock is often referred to as a hybrid security. Why?
12. If preferred stock is riskier than bonds, why has preferred stock had lower yields than bonds in recent years?
13. Why is the cumulative feature of preferred stock particularly important to preferred shareholders?
14. A small amount of preferred stock is participating. What would your reaction be if someone said common stock is also participating?
15. What is an advantage of floating-rate preferred stock for the risk-averse investor? What is an advantage for the issuing corporation?
16. Speculate on whether it would be easier to buy control, in general, of a company listed on the TSX or one listed on the NYSE. Which situation strikes you as being better in this regard?
17. Put an X by the security that has the feature best related to the following considerations. You may wish to refer to Table 17–1.

	Common Stock	Preferred Stock	Bonds
a. Ownership and control of the firm			
b. Obligation to provide return			
c. Claims to assets in bankruptcy			
d. High cost of distribution			
e. Highest return			
f. Highest risk			

INTERNET RESOURCES AND QUESTIONS

Web sites for researching preferred and common stocks are numerous. Many sites are free, but the best information is available only for a fee.

Canadian companies file news releases, financial statements, and other relevant information with SEDAR (System for Electronic Document Analysis and Retrieval):
www.sedar.com

The TSX Toronto Stock Exchange site will connect to a company's web site, which often has annual reports available:
www.tsx.ca

Research on Canadian companies is available at Quicken, Investcom (gets you to Zacks), Globe-Investor and Nasdaq-Canada:
www.quicken.ca
www.moneysense.ca/eng/investing/stocks/index.jsp
www.investcom.com
www.globeinvestor.com
www.nasdaq-canada.com

Canadian companies listed on U.S. exchanges are likely to have research available at the U.S. Quicken site:
www.quicken.com/investments/stocks

Big Charts permits the graphing of Canadian stocks and market indexes shown with a ca: prefix:
www.bigcharts.com

1. The major banks, BCE, and TransCanada Pipelines usually have several outstanding preferred share issues.
   a. Identify for two preferred issues: the current price, yield, and any special features. A visit to the company's web site and annual report will likely be required to identify any special features.
   b. Compare the above yields to the yield on corporate bonds.
2. Identify the latest filings at SEDAR. What are the features of any preferred offerings? Are there many trust offerings?

Problems

1. Laura Secord owns 918 shares in the Niagara Candy Company. There are 13 directors to be elected. Thirty-one thousand shares are outstanding. The firm has adopted cumulative voting.
   a. How many total votes can be cast?
   b. How many votes does Laura control?
   c. What percentage of the total votes does she control?
2. Russell Stover wishes to know how many shares are necessary to elect four directors out of the eleven directors up for election in the Tasty Beverage Company. There are 75,000 shares outstanding and cumulative voting is used.
3. Mr. Thomas owns 6,001 shares of the Piston Corp. There are 12 seats on the company board of directors, and the company has a total of 78,000 shares outstanding. The Piston Corp. utilizes cumulative voting.

   Can Mr. Thomas elect himself to the board when the vote to elect 12 directors is held next week?

4. Boston Fishery has been experiencing declining earnings but has just announced a 50 percent salary increase for its top executives. A dissident group of shareholders wants to oust the existing board of directors. There are currently 11 directors and 60,000 shares of stock outstanding. Mr. Bass, the president of the company, has the full support of the existing board. The dissident shareholders control proxies for 20,001 shares. Mr. Bass is worried about losing his job.
   a. Under cumulative voting procedures, how many directors can the dissident shareholders elect with the proxies they now hold? How many directors could they elect under majority rule with these proxies?
   b. How many shares (or proxies) are needed to elect six directors under cumulative voting?
5. Galaxy Corporation is holding a shareholders meeting next month. Mr. Starr is the president of the company and has the support of the existing board of directors. All nine members of the board are up for reelection. Mr. Kramer is a dissident shareholder. He controls proxies for 30,001 shares. Mr. Starr and his friends on the board control 50,001 shares. Other shareholders, whose loyalties are unknown, will be voting the remaining 19,998 shares. The company uses cumulative voting.
   a. How many directors can Mr. Kramer be sure of electing?
   b. How many directors can Mr. Starr and his friends be sure of electing?
   c. How many directors could Mr. Kramer elect if he obtains all the proxies for the uncommitted votes? Will he control the board?
6. In the previous problem, if 12 directors were to be elected, and Mr. Starr and his friends had 50,001 shares and Mr. Kramer had 30,001 shares plus half the uncommitted votes, how many directors could Mr. Kramer elect?
7. Mr. Day controls proxies for 38,000 of the 70,000 outstanding shares of Northern Airlines. Mr. Harper heads a dissident group that controls the remaining 32,000 shares. There are 7 board members to be elected and cumulative voting applies. Day does not understand the cumulative voting and plans to cast 100,000 of his 266,000 (38,000 $\times$ 7) votes for his brother-in-law, Scott. His remaining votes will be spread evenly for three other candidates.

   How many directors can Harper elect if Day acts as described above? Use logical numerical analysis rather than a set formula to answer the question.
8. Higgins Metal Company was established in 1986. Four years later, the company went public. At that time, Henry Higgins, the original owner, decided to establish two classes of stock. The first represents Class A founders' stock and is entitled to 10 votes per share. The normally traded common stock, designated as Class B, is entitled to one vote per share. In late 2002, Mr. Andrews was considering purchasing shares in Higgins Metal Company. While he knew founders' shares were not present in many companies, he decided to buy the shares anyway because of a new high-technology melting process the company had developed.

   Of the 1.4 million total shares currently outstanding, the original founder's family owns 52,525 shares. What is the percentage of the founder's family votes compared to the Class B votes?
9. Grandland Rice Co. has issued rights to its shareholders. The subscription price is $45.00, and four rights are needed along with the subscription price to buy one of the new shares. The stock is selling for $55.00 rights-on.
   a. What would be the value of one right?
   b. If the stock goes ex-rights, what would the new stock price be?
10. Prime Direct Corporation has issued rights to its shareholders. The subscription price is $20.00, and three rights are needed along with the subscription price to buy one of the new shares. The stock is selling for $25.00 rights-on.

  a. What would be the value of one right?
  b. If the stock goes ex-rights, what would the new stock price be?

11. Harmon Candy Co. has announced a rights offering for its shareholders. Cindy Barr owns 500 shares of Harmon Candy Co. stock. Five rights plus $62.00 cash are needed to buy one of the new shares. The stock is currently selling for $70.00 rights-on.
  a. What is the value of a right?
  b. How many of the new shares could Cindy buy if she exercised all her rights? How much cash would this require?
  c. Cindy doesn't know if she wants to exercise her rights or sell them. What alternative would have the most beneficial effect on her wealth?

12. Roy Randall has $9,000 to invest. He has been looking at Barton Petroleum common stock. Barton has issued a rights offering to its common shareholders. Six rights plus $51.00 cash will buy one new share. Barton's stock is selling for $60.00 ex-rights.

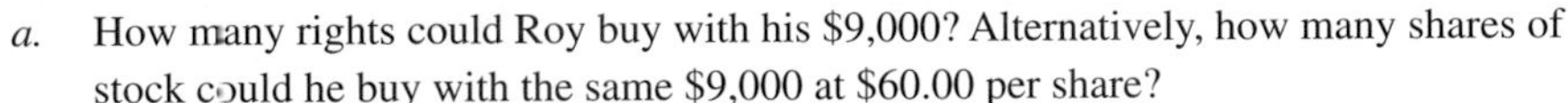

  a. How many rights could Roy buy with his $9,000? Alternatively, how many shares of stock could he buy with the same $9,000 at $60.00 per share?
  b. If Roy invests his $9,000 in Barton rights and the price of Barton stock rises to $72.00 per share ex-rights, what would his dollar profit on the rights be? (First compute profits per right.)
  c. If Roy invests his $9,000 in Barton stock and the price of the stock rises to $72.00 per share ex-rights, what would his total dollar profit be?
  d. What would be the answer to part *b* if the price of Barton's stock falls to $45.00 per share ex-rights instead of rising to $72.00?
  e. What would the answer be to part *c* if the price of Barton's stock falls to $45.00 per share ex-rights?

13. Mr. and Mrs. Anderson own five shares of Magic Tricks Corporation common stock. The market value of the stock is $60.00. They also have $48.00 in cash. They have just received word of a rights offering. One new share of stock can be purchased at $48.00 for each five shares currently owned (based on five rights).
  a. What is the value of a right?
  b. What is the value of the Andersons' portfolio before the rights offering? (Portfolio in this question represents stock plus cash.)
  c. If the Andersons participate in the rights offering, what will be the value of their portfolio, based on the diluted value (ex-rights) of the stock?
  d. If they sell their five rights but keep their stock at its diluted value and hold on to their cash, what will be the value of their portfolio?

14. Smelly Kat Industries, a public company, wishes to raise $25 million for product line expansion. Because the existing shareholders are excited by the company's prospects, a rights offering will be used to raise the necessary capital. Each of the 5 million shareholders will receive one right. The subscription price is $25.00 per share, and the market price of the existing shares is currently $30.00. Calculate the value of a right at the present time.

15. Lost Seas Salvage Limited wants to raise $20 million for additional boats. A rights offering will be used to raise the necessary capital from existing shareholders. Each of the 6 million shareholders will receive one right. The subscription price is $10.00 per share, and the market price of the existing shares is currently $12.00. Calculate the value of a right at the present time.

16. Kristy Fashions, Inc. has 4.5 million shares of common stock outstanding. The current market price of Kristy Fashions common stock is $60.00 per share rights-on. The company's net

income this year is $18 million. A rights offering has been announced in which 450,000 new shares will be sold at $55.00 per share. The subscription price of $55.00 plus 10 rights is needed to buy one of the new shares.

a. What are the earnings per share and price-earnings ratio before the new shares are sold via the rights offering?

b. What would the earnings per share be immediately after the rights offering? What would the price-earnings ratio be immediately after the rights offering? (Assume there is no change in the market value of the common stock, except for the change that occurs when the stock begins trading ex-rights.) Round all answers to two places to the right of the decimal point.

17. The Shelton Corporation has some excess cash that it would like to invest in marketable securities for a long-term hold. Its vice president of finance is considering three investments (Shelton Corporation is in a 36 percent tax bracket). Which one should he select based on aftertax return: (*a*) Government bonds at a 7 percent yield; (*b*) corporate bonds at a 10 percent yield; or (*c*) preferred stock at an 8 percent yield?

18. Silicon Industries has a cumulative preferred stock issue outstanding, which has a stated annual dividend of $8.00 per share. The company has been losing money and has not paid preferred dividends for the last four years. There are 260,000 shares of preferred stock outstanding and 500,000 shares of common stock.

a. How much is the company behind in preferred dividends?

b. If Silicon Industries earns $7.5 million in the coming year after taxes and before dividends, and this is all paid out to the preferred shareholders, how much will the company be in arrears (behind in payments)? Keep in mind that the coming year would represent the fifth year.

c. How much, if any, would be available in common stock dividends in the coming year if $7.5 million is earned as explained in part *b*?

19. Industrial Gas Company is four years in arrears on cumulative preferred stock dividends. There are 650,000 preferred shares outstanding, and the annual dividend is $7.00 per share. The vice president of finance sees no real hope of paying the dividends in arrears. He is devising a plan to compensate the preferred shareholders for 90 percent of the dividends in arrears.

a. How much should the compensation be?

b. Industrial Gas Company will compensate the preferred shareholders in the form of bonds paying 12 percent interest in a market environment in which the going rate of interest is 14 percent. The bonds will have a 25-year maturity. Indicate the market value of a $1,000 par value bond.

c. Based on market value, how many bonds must be issued to provide the compensation determined in part *a*? (Round to the nearest whole number.)

20. The treasurer of Garcia Mexican Food Restaurants (a corporation) currently has $100,000 invested in preferred stock yielding 7.5 percent. He appreciates the tax advantages of preferred stock and is considering buying $100,000 more with borrowed funds. The cost of the borrowed funds is 9.5 percent. He suggests this proposal to his board of directors. The directors are somewhat concerned by the fact that the treasurer is paying 2 percent more for funds than he is earning. The firm is in a 34 percent tax bracket.

a. Compute the amount of the aftertax income from the additional preferred stock if it is purchased.

b. Compute the aftertax borrowing cost to purchase the additional preferred stock. That is, multiply the interest cost times (1 – t).

c. Should the treasurer proceed with his proposal?

d. If interest rates and dividend yields in the market go up six months after a decision to purchase is made, what impact will this have on the outcome?

21. Referring back to the original information in the previous problem, if the yield on the $100,000 of preferred stock is still 7.5 percent and the borrowing cost remains 9.5 percent, but the tax rate is only 20 percent, is this a feasible investment?

22. Hailey Transmission has two classes of preferred stock: floating-rate preferred stock and straight (normal) preferred stock. Both issues have a par value of $100.00. The floating-rate preferred stock pays an annual dividend yield of 7 percent, and the straight preferred stock pays 8 percent. Since the issuance of the two securities, interest rates have gone up by 3 percent for each issue. Both securities will pay their year-end dividend today.

a. What is the price of the floating-rate preferred stock likely to be?

b. What is the price of the straight preferred stock likely to be?

COMPREHENSIVE PROBLEMS

23. The Crandall Corporation currently has 100,000 shares outstanding that are selling at $50.00 per share. It needs to raise $900,000. Net income after taxes is $500,000. Its vice president of finance and its investment dealer have decided on a rights offering, but they are not sure how much to discount the subscription price from the current market value. Discounts of 10 percent, 20 percent, and 40 percent have been suggested. Common stock is the sole means of financing for the Crandall Corporation.

a. For each discount, determine the subscription price, the number of shares to be issued, and the number of rights required to purchase one share. (Round to one place after the decimal point where necessary.)

b. Determine the value of one right under each of the plans. (Round to two places after the decimal point.)

c. Compute the earnings per share before and immediately after the rights offering under a 10 percent discount from the subscription price.

d. By what percentage has the number of shares outstanding increased?

e. Shareholder X had 100 shares before the rights offering and participated by buying 20 new shares. Compute his total claim to earnings both before and after the rights offering (that is, multiply shares by the earnings per share figures computed in part *c*).

f. Should shareholder X be satisfied with this claim over a longer period of time?

24. Snyder Meat Packing Co. is a small firm that has been very profitable over the past five years and has also exhibited a strong earnings growth trend. Mr. Snyder owns 35 percent of the 3 million shares of common stock outstanding, but he is nevertheless worried about being taken over by a larger firm in the future. He has read some articles in the *Financial Post* about techniques used to discourage forced mergers and takeovers. The firm currently uses majority voting for nine directors. Mr. Snyder wonders which of the following proposals would make it easier for him to reject a takeover bid.

a. What would be the effect of cumulative voting?

b. What would be accomplished if shareholders could vote for only one-third of the directors every year (staggered terms)?

c. Should Mr. Snyder reduce or increase the number of directors? Does the answer to this question depend on majority rule or cumulative voting?

25. Dr. Robert Grossman founded Electro Cardio Systems, Inc. (ECS), in 1993. The principal purpose of the firm was to engage in research and development of heart pump devices. Although the firm did not show a profit until 1998, by 2002 it reported aftertax earnings of $1.2 million. The company had gone public in 1996 at $10.00 a share. Investors were initially interested in buying the stock because of its future prospects. By year-end 2002, the stock was trading at $42.00 per share because the firm had made good on its promise to produce life-saving heart pumps and, in the process, was now making reasonable earnings. With 850,000 shares outstanding, earnings per share were $1.41.

Dr. Grossman and the members of the board of directors were initially pleased when another firm, Parker Medical Products, began buying their stock. John Parker, the chairman and CEO of Parker Medical Products, was thought to be a shrewd investor, and the fact that his firm bought 50,000 shares of ECS was taken as an affirmation of the success of the heart pump research firm.

However, when Parker bought the next 50,000 shares, Dr. Grossman and members of the board of directors of ECS became concerned that John Parker and his firm might be trying to take over ECS.

Upon talking to his attorney, Dr. Grossman was reminded that ECS had a poison pill provision that took effect when any outside investor accumulated 25 percent or more of the shares outstanding. Current shareholders, excluding the potential takeover company, were given the privilege of buying up to 500,000 new shares of ECS at 80 percent of current market value. Thus, new shares were restricted to friendly interests.

The attorney also found that Dr. Grossman and "friendly" members of the board of directors currently owned 175,000 shares of ECS.

a. How many more shares would Parker Medical Products need to purchase before the poison pill provision went into effect? Given the current price of ECS stock of $42.00, what would be the cost to Parker to get up to that level?

b. ECS's ultimate fear was that Parker Medical Products would gain over a 50 percent interest in its shares outstanding. What would be the additional cost to Parker to get to 50 percent (plus 1 share) of the stock outstanding of ECS at the current market price of ECS stock? In answering this question, assume Parker had previously accumulated the 25 percent position discussed in question (*a*).

c. Now assume that Parker exceeds the number of shares you computed in part *b* and gets all the way up to accumulating 625,000 shares of ECS. Under the poison pill provision, how many shares must "friendly" shareholders purchase to thwart a takeover attempt by Parker? What will be the total cost? Keep in mind that friendly interests already own 175,000 shares of ECS and that, to maintain control, they must own one more share than Parker.

d. Would you say the poison pill is an effective deterrent in this case? Is the poison pill in the best interest of the general shareholders (those not associated with the company)?

26. Alpha Biogenetics was founded in 1989 by Steve Menger, Ph.D., M.D. At the time, the company consisted of little more than a one-room laboratory, Dr. Menger, and a lab assistant. However, Dr. Menger's outstanding research attracted the attention of the Scientific Venture Capital Fund, and by 1998 the venture capital fund had contributed $4 million in so-called "risk capital" funding. The financial support of the fund along with the work of Dr. Menger and other scientists who joined the company allowed Alpha Biogenetics to develop potential leading-edge drugs in the areas of growth hormones, microgenes, and glycosylation inhibitors.

In the year 1998, the company achieved its first profit of $1.6 million and made a public offering of two million new shares at a price of $9.60 per share. At the same time, the

Scientific Venture Capital Fund sold the 1.2 million shares it had received for its capital contributions, also at $9.60 per share. In the parlance of investment banking, the venture capitalist "cashed in its position."

Between the two million new shares sold by the firm and the 1.2 million old shares sold by the venture capitalist, 3.2 million shares were put in the hands of the public. At the same time, Dr. Menger held one million shares, three other Ph.D.'s working for the company had 600,000 shares in total, and Ami Barnes, the chief financial officer, owned 200,000 shares. Altogether the insiders owned 1.8 million shares or 36 percent of the total of 5 million shares outstanding.

Outside shares	3.2 million	(64%)
Insider shares	1.8 million	(36%)
Shares outstanding	5.0 million	(100%)

By 2002, total earnings had increased to $4.8 million, and the stock price was $33.60. Also, many of the firm's products were well received in the biotech community.

However, there was one problem that troubled Dr. Menger and the other inside investors. They only had control of a minority interest of 36 percent of the shares outstanding. If an unfriendly takeover offer were to be made, they could be voted out of control of the company. In the early stages of the company's development, this was an unlikely event, but such was no longer the case. The company now had products that others in the biotech industry such as Biogen, Cygnus, and Genentech might wish to acquire through a takeover. Most of these firms had their own high-quality scientists who could quickly relate to the products being developed by Dr. Menger and Alpha Biogenetics.

Dr. Menger was particularly concerned because the year 2003 was not likely to be as good as prior ones and could make the company's shareholders a little less happy with its performance. Management was about to settle a lawsuit against the firm that could have adverse consequences in the year 2003. Also, two of the firm's major clients were encountering severe financial difficulties and certain write-offs related to this were inevitable in the year 2003.

Dr. Menger expressed his concern to Bill Larson, who was a partner in the investment banking firm of Caruthers, Larson, and Rosen. Larson had been heavily involved in the initial public offering in 1998 of Alpha Biogenetics when his firm was the lead underwriter.

In response to Dr. Menger's concerns about an unfriendly takeover, Larson suggested the possibility of a poison pill. He said that poison pill provisions were used by many public corporations to thwart potentially unfriendly takeovers.

Poison pills could take many different forms, but Larson suggested that the controlling inside shareholders be allowed to purchase up to 1.5 million new shares in the firm at 70 percent of current market value if an outside group acquired 25 percent or more of the current shares outstanding. This provision could discourage a potential takeover offer, as we shall see. Furthermore, Larson explained that poison pills do not require the approval of shareholders to implement as is true of other forms of anti-takeover amendments.

At the firm's 2002 annual meeting held in the second week of March 2003, Dr. Menger discussed the firm's financial performance for 2002, as well as seven other items on the agenda, including the election of members of the board of directors, the approval of the firm's auditors from Deloitte & Touche, and the announcement of the poison pill provision that the firm planned to implement in the next two months.

Dr. Menger was somewhat surprised at the strong reaction that he got on the latter item. An institutional shareholder that represented the Ontario Public Employees Retirement

System (OPERS) said her multibillion-dollar pension fund was really turned off by poison pill provisions, and that other large institutional investors felt the same way. She said that the role of corporate management was to maximize shareholder wealth and anti-takeover provisions, such as poison pills, tended to discourage tender offers to purchase firms at premiums over current market value.

She further stated that poison pills tended to protect current management against the threat of being displaced and therefore gave them a feeling of security that sometimes led to poor decisions, encouraged unusually high compensation packages, and even potential laziness.

There was a hush in the room after she finished her remarks. Dr. Menger felt compelled to answer her charges and stated that the poison pill provision was not intended to protect poor performance, but was being put into place to provide a sense of permanency to the current management. He said that if management became overly concerned with job security and short-term quarter to quarter performance, they would not take a long-term perspective that was essential to building a company for the future. As an example, he suggested that R&D expenditures might be cut back to beef up a quarterly earnings report.

He also said that a sense of security and permanency allowed the company to compete for top-notch scientists and managers who otherwise would be hesitant to give up their current positions to go to a company that was a takeover target.

Bill Larson, the firm's investment banker, also got into the discussion. He said that while in certain instances poison pills thwarted potential shareholder value maximizing offers, in other cases they had the opposite effect. Because the company was protected against capricious or minimal takeover offers, companies that wanted to acquire firms with poison pill provisions tended to offer a premium price well above the average offer. This was necessary because the firm could easily deflect a normal offer.

As Dr. Menger took all these comments in, he decided to have one last meeting with his executive committee on the topic of implementing a poison pill provision.

a. What were the earnings per share and the P/E ratio in the year that the firm went public (1998)?

b. Assuming a 5 percent underwriting spread, and $120,000 in out-of-pocket costs, what were the net proceeds to the corporation?

c. What rate of return did the Scientific Venture Capital Fund earn on its $4 million investment? Does this appear to be reasonable?

d. What were earnings per share in 2002? Based on the share price of $33.60, what was the P/E ratio?

e. Under the poison pill provision, how much would it cost an unfriendly outside party to acquire 25 percent of the shares outstanding at the 2002 share price?

f. Now assume an unfriendly outside party acquired all the shares not owned by the inside control group. How many shares must the inside control group buy from the corporation to maintain its majority position? What would the total dollar cost be?

g. Based on the pro and con arguments made at the annual meeting, do you think that poison pills are in the best interest of shareholders?

Selected References

Cook, Douglas O., and John C. Easterwood. "Poison Put Bonds: An Analysis of Their Economic Role." *Journal of Finance* 49 (December 1994), pp. 1905–20.

D'Souza, Julie, and John Jacob. "Why Firms Issue Target Stock." *Journal of Financial Economics* 56 (June 2000), pp. 459–83.

Francis, Jack, and Rekesh Bali. "Innovation in Partitioning a Share of Stock." *The Journal of Applied Corporate Finance* 13 (Spring 2000), pp. 128–36.

Kester, W. Carl, and Timothy A. Luehrman. "Rehabilitating the Leveraged Buyout." *Harvard Business Review* 95 (May–June 1995), pp. 119–30.

Lee, Inmoo. "Do Firms Knowingly Sell Overvalued Equity?" *Journal of Finance* 52 (September 1997), pp. 1439–66.

Logue, Dennis E., and James K. Seward. "The Time Warner Rights Offering and the Destruction of Stockholder Value." *Financial Analysts Journal* 48 (March–April 1992), pp. 37–45.

Moyer, R. Charles, Ramesh Rao, and Phillip M. Sisneros. "Substitutes for Voting Rights: Evidence from Dual Class Recapitalizations." *Financial Management* 21 (Autumn 1992), pp. 35–47.

Narayanan, Ranga. "Insider Trading and the Voluntary Disclosure of Information by Firms." *Journal of Banking and Finance* 224 (March 2000), pp. 395–425.

Pare, Terence P. "How to Know When to Buy Stocks." *Fortune* 126 (Fall 1992), pp. 79–83.

Shum, Connie M., Wallace N. Davidson, III, and John L. Glasscock. "Voting Rights and Market Reaction to Dual Class Common Stock Issues." *Financial Review* 30 (May 1995), pp. 275–87.

CHAPTER | EIGHTEEN

18

Dividend Policy and Retained Earnings

LEARNING | OBJECTIVES

1 Discuss management's decision criteria as to whether internally generated funds should be reinvested or paid out as dividends.

2 Describe a dividend payment as a passive or active decision based on investor preference and the informational content of dividends. Calculate dividend payout ratios and dividend yields.

3 Outline the many factors to be considered in dividend policy. Calculate aftertax income from dividends and calculate share prices based on earnings multiples.

4 Outline dividend payment procedures.

5 Describe the impact of stock splits and stock dividends on the position of the shareholders. Calculate the changes in the balance sheet that result.

6 Discuss the reasons for a share repurchase.

7 Explain a dividend reinvestment plan.

SB Owners of successful small businesses must continually decide what to do with the profits their firms have generated. One option is to reinvest in the business—purchasing new plant and equipment, expanding inventory, and perhaps hiring new employees. Another alternative is to withdraw the funds from the business and invest them elsewhere. Prospective uses might include buying other stocks and bonds, purchasing a second business, or perhaps spending a lost weekend in Las Vegas.

A corporation and its shareholders must face exactly the same type of decision. Should funds associated with profits of the corporation be reinvested in assets of the business or be paid to shareholders in the form of dividends?

The Marginal Principle of Retained Earnings

In theory, corporate directors should ask, "How can we make the best use of company funds?" The rate of return the corporation can achieve on retained earnings for the benefit of shareholders must be compared to what shareholders could earn if the funds were paid to them in dividends. This is known as the **marginal principle of retained earnings.** Each potential project to be financed by internally generated funds must provide a higher rate of return than the shareholder could achieve alone. We speak of this as the opportunity cost of using shareholder funds. The return on shareholder funds will be obtained by capital appreciation of the share price. If the firm cannot

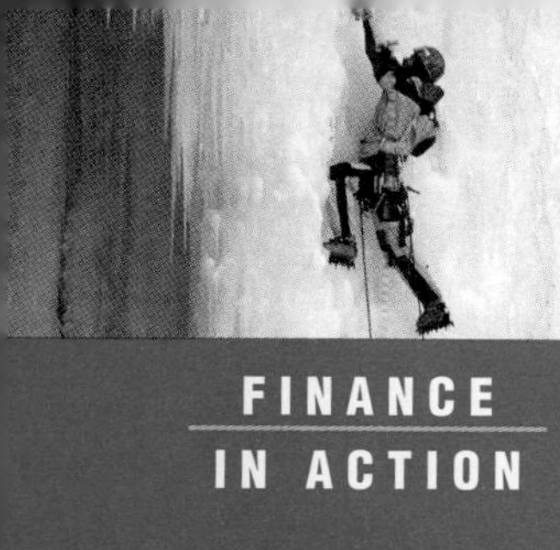

FINANCE IN ACTION

Dividends or Reinvestment at Inco

Q1 Has Inco begun to pay a dividend again?

Q2 Has Voisey's Bay begun development?

www.inco.com

Symbol: N

www.lme.co.uk

On January 9, 1989, Inco Ltd. paid a special dividend of U.S.$10.00 per share, for a total cash payout of U.S.$1.1 billion. As of December 31, 1988, the special common dividend payable represented 25 percent of Inco's balance sheet. To pay the dividend, Inco would use $650 million in cash and marketable securities and would borrow $500 million from its bank line of credit. It anticipated being able to pay off the bank line of credit quickly from anticipated operating cash flows. The large dividend was not a regular occurrence, although extra dividends had been paid in the early 1980s. The regular dividend over the previous six years had been $0.20 annually

Inco had a terrific year in 1988. Net earnings were $735 million, up from $125 million in 1987. Its cash surplus before financing activities was $887 million. The reason for the large increase in earnings and cash flow was a rise in nickel prices. The average realized nickel price for Inco was $4.81 a pound. Nickel prices had gone to a high of $8.55 in 1988 from below $2.00 only two years previously.

Inco management decided not to reinvest the large profits in expanded capital assets or by diversifying into other industries. After surveying the world economy, Inco's analysis suggested that it could not achieve the returns expected by shareholders if it substantially increased capital investment. It was best to pay the profits out to shareholders. The shareholders and the market responded well to the dividend payment.

Ten years later in 1998, Inco was short of cash. In 1996 it had gone heavily into debt to finance its $4.3 billion acquisition of a large nickel deposit at Voisey's Bay, Labrador and was planning capital expenditures on the project that exceeded $1.4 billion. However, by December 1998 nickel prices had plunged below $1.70 per pound from the $3.27 per pound at the time of the Voisey's Bay acquisition. Inco experienced cash flow problems, layoffs, and the delay in the Voisey's Bay project.

Where had all the cash gone? From a special dividend of U.S.$10.00 per share regular dividend payments had been reduced from $0.40 to $0.00 by 1999. Nickel prices had risen to about $3.00 by 2002 and Voisey's Bay development was again a possibility. Reinvestment was the strategy at this time.

All prices and figures in U.S. dollars.

achieve the required rate of return on accumulated funds, they should be paid out to shareholders, usually as dividends.

Dividends as a Passive Variable

The marginal principle of retained earnings suggests that dividends are a passive decision variable. They are to be paid out only if the corporation cannot make better use of the funds for the benefit of shareholders. The active decision variable is retained earnings. Management decides how much retained earnings will be spent for internal corporate needs, and the residual (the amount left after internal expenditures) is paid out to the shareholders in cash dividends.

An Incomplete Theory

The only problem with the **residual theory of dividends** is that we have not given recognition to how shareholders feel about receiving dividends. If the shareholders' only concern is with achieving the highest return on their investment, either in the form of *corporate retained earnings remaining in the business* or as *current dividends paid out*, then there is no issue. But if shareholders have a preference for current funds, for example, over retained earnings, then our theory is incomplete. The issue is not only whether investment of retained earnings or dividends provides the highest return, but also how shareholders react to the two alternatives.

While some researchers maintain that shareholders are indifferent to the division of funds between retained earnings and dividends[1] (holding investment opportunities constant), others disagree.[2] Though there is no conclusive proof one way or the other, the judgment of most researchers is that investors have some preference between dividends and retained earnings. Certainly most financial managers believe investors have a preference.

Argument for the Irrelevance of Dividends

It might seem unreasonable to suggest that dividend policy is irrelevant to the valuation of the firm. In early chapters we discounted future dividends to the present to determine the current price of the shares. However, our choice of annual dividend payments in the model was arbitrary. Would we not get the same result if dividends were delayed to a future time?

Let us examine Figure 18–1 (on the next page), in which a shareholder establishes **homemade dividends.** The shareholder owns 100 shares in a firm expected to pay a dividend of $5.00 per share in each of the next two years. The second dividend is expected to be the last, as there would be no value left in the firm. It would be a **liquidating dividend,** as it would close down the company. If shareholders expect a 16.25 percent return on their investment, the current value of one share in the company should be $8.00.

At the last moment the firm decides to omit the dividend in the first year and reinvest the $5.00 at the 16.25 percent expected by shareholders. The firm will now expect the original liquidating dividend of $5.00 and another $5.81 ($5 × 1.1625), for a total of $10.81 to be paid out as a dividend at the end of the second year. The present value of $10.81 two years from the present at 16.25 percent is $8.00, the same value derived with the annual dividend payments. The value of $10.81 at the time the first dividend is omitted and there is still one year to the receipt of the $10.81 is equal to $9.30.

However, the shareholder with 100 shares might desire an annual cash flow of $500 ($5.00 × 100) and might not want the dividend at Year 1 delayed. If the dividend is not paid in one year, the shares at that time will be worth $930 ($9.30 × 100) on the basis of the present worth of their liquidating value of $1,081 ($10.81 × 100). By selling 53.75 shares, the shareholder can realize $500 ($9.30 × 53.75), which is the same as would have been received if the $5.00 dividend had been paid.

In the second year, the investor will also receive $500 ($10.81 × 46.25) from the dividend of $10.81 on the remaining 46.25 shares that are still held. Figure 18–1 shows the effect of selling some shares in year one and receiving the liquidating dividend on the remaining shares. Cash flow received from an equity investment by selling shares is referred to as a "homemade dividend." Dividend policy doesn't seem relevant to valuation in this illustration.

---

[1]Merton H. Miller and Franco Modigliani, "Dividend Policy, Growth and Valuation of Shares," *Journal of Business* 34 (October 1961), pp. 411–33. Under conditions of perfect capital markets with an absence of taxes and flotation costs, it is argued that the sum of discounted value per share after dividend payments equals the total valuation before dividend payments.

[2]Myron J. Gordon, "Optimum Investment and Financing Policy," *Journal of Finance* 18 (May 1963), pp. 264–77; and John Lintmer, "Dividends, Earnings, Leverage, Stock Prices, and the Supply of Capital to the Corporation," Review of Economics and Statistics 44 (August 1962), pp. 243–69.

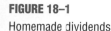

FIGURE 18–1
Homemade dividends

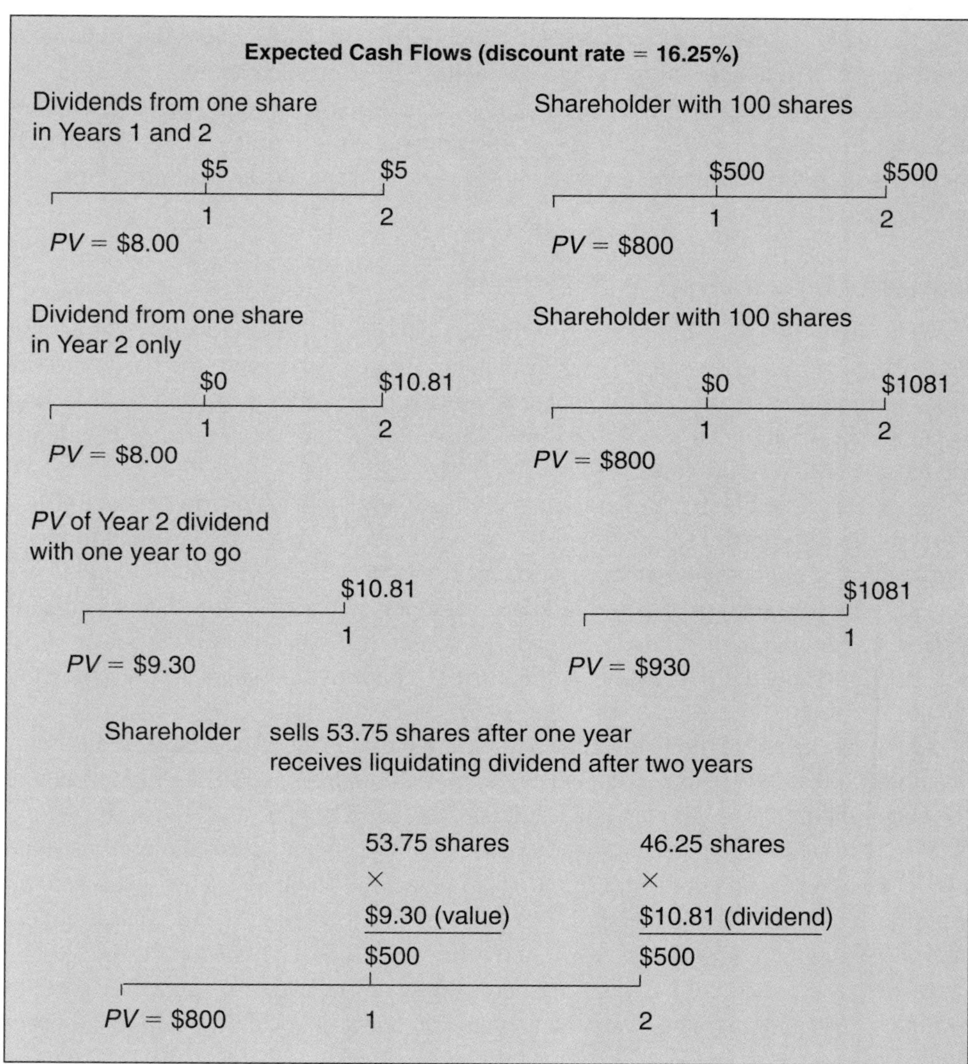

Arguments for the Relevance of Dividends

A strong case can be made for the relevance of dividends because they *resolve uncertainty* in the minds of investors. Though earnings reinvested in the business theoretically belong to common shareholders, there is still an air of uncertainty about their eventual translation into dividends. Thus, it can be hypothesized that shareholders apply a higher discount rate (*Ke*) to yield a lower valuation to funds retained in the business as opposed to those that are paid out.[3]

It is also argued that dividends may be viewed more favourably than retained earnings because of the **information content** of dividends. In essence, the corporation is telling the shareholder, "We are having a good year, and we wish to share the benefits with you." If the dividend per share is raised, then the information content of the dividend increase is quite positive, while a reduction in the dividend generally has negative

[3]See Note 2.

Pay Those Dividends!

In late 2001, Norske Skog Canada and Nortel cut their dividend payments to zero, while Ipsco, Quebecor, and Sheritt International cut their dividend payments. The market reacted badly and dropped the share prices of these companies. The reaction however was not as severe as it has been with TransCanada Pipelines two years earlier when it cut its dividend. The share price dropped significantly even though management maintained that the dividend was cut to refocus the corporate strategy and to reinvest the money in worthy capital projects. Investors didn't buy it at the time, but as management demonstrated effective capital decisions the share price responded well throughout 2001 and into 2002 despite a generally weak market.

Interestingly, Telus also cut their dividend in late 2001 to redeploy the monies into its capital projects and the market responded favourably to the news. In this case, the market saw the wisdom of reinvested the capital. Charts of a firm's performance can be viewed through the TSX web site (www.tsx.ca).

The 1990s could be considered a time when companies reinvested in capital projects because of the strong economy and dividend payouts declined. However in the first decade of the new millennium, companies may revert to higher dividend payouts. Many consider it is time for Microsoft to begin paying dividends. Its share price had stagnated for the three years leading up to 2002 and it had $38 billion in cash. There are those that suggest that a dividend payout prevents management from investing in marginal projects.

FINANCE IN ACTION

Q1 How has the share price of Telus (2001) and TransCanada Pipelines (1999) performed since the dividend was cut?

www.telus.com
Symbol: T

www.transcanada.com
Symbol: TRP

informational content. Even though the corporation may be able to generate the same or higher returns with the fund than the shareholder and perhaps provide even greater dividends in the future, some researchers find that "in an uncertain world in which verbal statements can be ignored or misinterpreted, dividend action does provide a clear-cut means of making a statement that speaks louder than a thousand words."[4]

The primary contention in arguing for the relevance of dividend policy is that shareholders' needs and preferences go beyond the *marginal principle of retained earnings*. The issue is not only who can best utilize the funds (the corporation or the shareholders), but also what are shareholders' preferences. In practice it appears that most corporations adhere to the following logic. First investment opportunities relative to a required return (marginal analysis) are determined. This is then tempered by some subjective notion of shareholders' desires. Corporations with unusual growth prospects and high rates of return on internal investments generally pay a relatively low dividend (perhaps for its informational content). For the more mature firm, an analysis of both investment opportunities and shareholder preferences may indicate a higher rate of payout is necessary.

Dividend Payouts

Dividend policies of selected major Canadian corporations are presented in Table 18–1, over a recent 10-year period. The **payout ratio** is the dividend as a percentage of earnings. The Bank of Montreal, which has maintained an uninterrupted dividend since 1829, had an average payout ratio of 38 percent over the period. Its dividend policy appears to be a fairly consistent percentage of earnings. Canadian Tire on the other hand has maintained the same dividend over the period despite increasing earnings.

Bank of Montreal
www.bmo.com

[4]Ezra Solomon, *The Theory of Financial Management* (New York: Columbia University Press, 1963), p. 142.

TABLE 18–1
Earnings and dividends of selected Canadian corporations

	Ten Year Average	2001	2000	1999	1998	1997	1996	1995	1994	1993	1992
Bank of Montreal											
earnings	$20.45	$2.66	$3.25	$2.34	$2.29	$2.28	$2.06	$1.62	$1.49	$1.28	$1.18
dividends	$7.85	$1.12	$1.00	$0.94	$0.88	$0.82	$0.74	$0.66	$0.60	$0.56	$0.53
payout ratio	**38%**	42%	31%	40%	38%	36%	36%	41%	40%	44%	45%
Canadian Tire											
earnings	$16.17	$2.25	$1.89	$1.89	$2.09	$1.79	$1.51	$1.38	$1.30	$1.11	$0.96
dividends	$4.00	$0.40	$0.40	$0.40	$0.40	$0.40	$0.40	$0.40	$0.40	$0.40	$0.40
payout ratio	**25%**	18%	21%	21%	19%	22%	26%	29%	31%	36%	42%
Dofasco											
earnings	$14.99	$0.35	$2.46	$3.16	$2.02	$2.12	$2.12	$1.98	$2.33	$1.41	($2.96)
dividends	$5.67	$1.06	$1.06	$1.00	$1.00	$0.80	$0.30	$0.00	$0.30	$0.00	$0.15
payout ratio	**38%**	303%	43%	32%	50%	38%	14%	0%	13%	0%	n.a.
Inco											
earnings	$6.43	$1.52	$2.06	$0.08	($0.63)	$0.25	$1.17	$1.82	$0.15	$0.22	($0.21)
dividends	$2.95	$0.00	$0.00	$0.00	$0.10	$0.40	$0.40	$0.40	$0.40	$0.40	$0.85
payout ratio	**46%**	0%	0%	0%	n.a.	160%	34%	22%	267%	182%	n.a.
Noranda											
earnings	$9.47	($0.47)	$1.14	$0.70	$2.68	$1.00	$1.02	$2.26	$1.45	($0.41)	$0.10
dividends	$9.40	$0.80	$0.80	$0.80	$1.00	$1.00	$1.00	$1.00	$1.00	$1.00	$1.00
payout ratio	**99%**	n.a.	70%	114%	37%	100%	98%	44%	69%	−244%	1000%
BCE Inc											
earnings	$28.06	$0.56	$7.43	$8.35	$2.50	$2.00	$1.54	$1.12	$1.43	$1.03	$2.10
dividends	$13.21	$1.20	$1.24	$1.36	$1.36	$1.36	$1.36	$1.36	$1.34	$1.33	$1.30
payout ratio	**47%**	214%	17%	16%	54%	68%	88%	121%	94%	129%	62%
Cognos											
earnings	$3.17	$0.70	$0.67	$0.66	$0.36	$0.40	$0.20	$0.10	$0.04	($0.08)	$0.04
dividends	$0.00	$0.00	$0.00	$0.00	$0.00	$0.00	$0.00	$0.00	$0.00	$0.00	$0.00
payout ratio	**0%**	0%	0%	0%	0%	0%	0%	0%	0%	0%	0%

Note that where earnings per share have declined, the continuance of historical dividend patterns is important. Dofasco had paid a dividend every year since 1937 and continued that practice as long as possible until losses in the early 1990s caused it to miss its 1993 dividend. They have been reinstated and grew significantly through the 1990s.

Inco and Noranda reveal a pattern typical of companies in cyclical industries such as the resource sector. Both tried to maintain a steady dividend despite financial difficulties but eventually they reduced their dividends and Inco's was suspended. Noranda paid out 99 percent of its earnings over this period. BCE, on the other hand, had increased its dividend each year for 20 years until 1995. BCE has not increased its dividend in recent years because changing technology had increased the company's capital expenditure requirements. The dividend dropped after it spun off Nortel in 2000. At the other end of the spectrum, Cognos, a supplier of business intelligence software, with strong growth through the 1990s, paid no dividends. Cognos required large amounts of capital to fund its expanding business.

Inco Ltd.
www.inco.ca

Dividend Yields

At the beginning of 2002, fifty-seven companies on the Toronto Stock Exchange had maintained dividends for over 25 years, down from almost 100 in 1980. Of the over 1,300 companies listed on the exchange, almost half paid a dividend. The **dividend yield** (dividends/market share price) of 1.6 percent for the TSX top 300 companies in 2002 was low by historical standards. With the high earnings for the period, this suggested that companies were reinvesting earnings in company projects for long-run benefits.

Table 18–2 displays the dividend yields for selected Canadian companies in March 2002. These are healthy returns for the period given that savings rates on bank deposits were less than 1 percent at the time. Furthermore, dividends are not taxed as heavily as interest income. Holding companies, utilities, and banks offer the highest dividend yields.

TABLE 18–2
Dividend yields on selected common shares, March 2002

Company	Yield
Rothmans	5.0%
Hollinger	4.9
Noranda	4.6
TransCanada Pipelines	4.5
TransAlta Utilities	4.4
Trilon Financial	3.8
Dofasco	3.9
BCE	3.5

Dividend Stability

In considering shareholders' desires in dividend policy, a primary factor is the maintenance of stability in dividend payments. Thus, corporate management must not only ask, "How many profitable investments do we have this year?" It must also ask, "What has been the pattern of dividend payments in the last few years?" Though earnings may change from year to year, the dollar amount of cash dividends tends to be much more stable, increasing in value only as new permanent levels of income are achieved while resisting any downward adjustment. Note in Figure 18–2 the stable dividends and the considerably greater volatility of earnings for Canadian corporations. During the early 1990s and again in late 2001 as earnings dipped, dividends were greater than earnings.

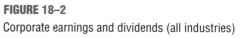

FIGURE 18–2
Corporate earnings and dividends (all industries)

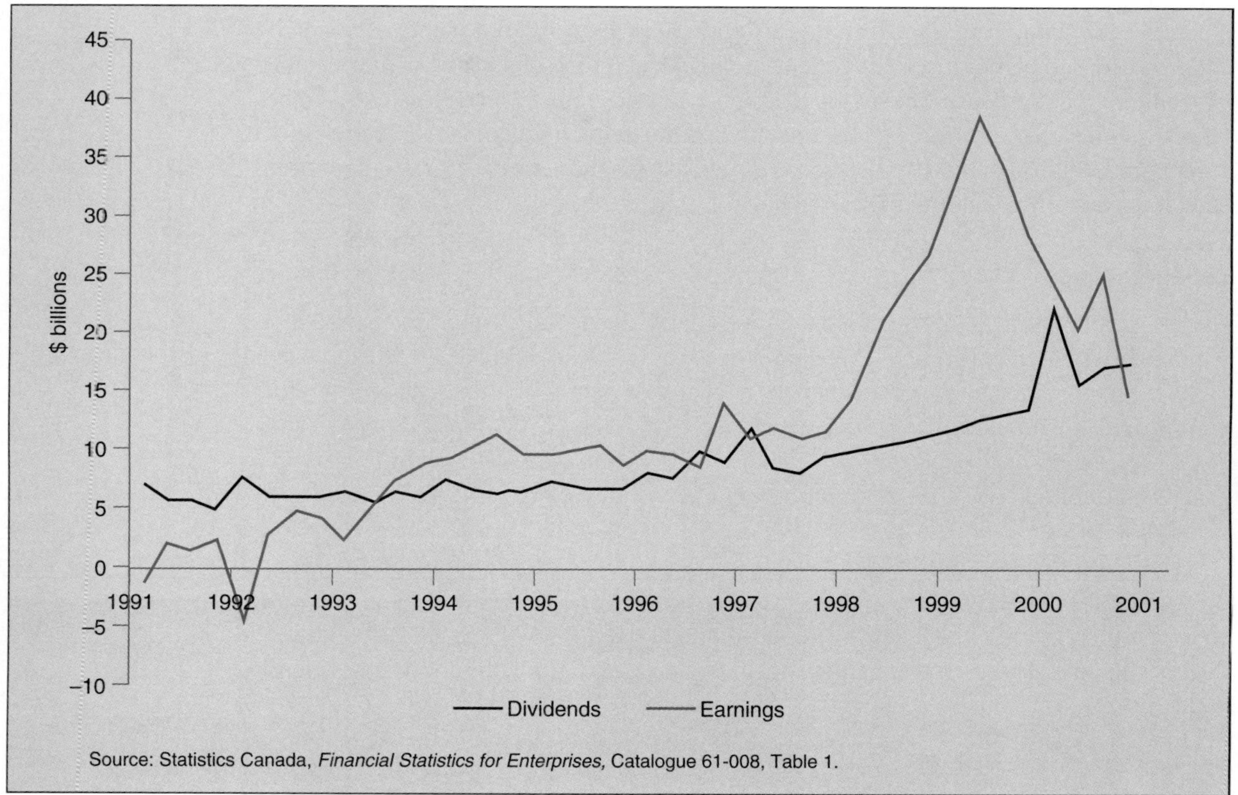

By maintaining a record of relatively stable dividends, corporate management hopes to lower the discount rate (*Ke*) applied to future dividends of the firm. The operative assumption appears to be that a shareholder would much prefer to receive $1.00 per year for three years rather than 75 cents for the first year, $1.50 for the second year, and 75 cents for the third year—for the same $3.00 total. Once again we temper our policy of marginal analysis of retained earnings to include a notion of shareholder preference, with the emphasis on dividend stability. The dividend payout patterns in Table 18–1 seem to demonstrate this consideration.

Other Factors Influencing Dividend Policy

Corporate management must also consider the legal basis of dividends, the cash flow position of the firm, and the corporation's access to capital markets. Other factors that must be considered include management's desire for control and the tax and financial position of shareholders. Each is briefly discussed.

Legal Rules

Canadian firms are not permitted to pay dividends that would impair the initial capital contributions to the firm. For this reason, dividends may be distributed only from past and current earnings. To pay dividends in excess of this amount would mean the corporation is returning to investors their original capital contributions (raiding the capital). If the ABC Company has the following statement of net worth, the maximum dividend payment possible would be $20 million.

Common stock (1 million shares)	$10,000,000
Retained earnings	20,000,000
Net worth	$30,000,000

Why all the concern about impairing permanent capital? Since the firm is going to pay dividends only to those who contributed capital in the first place, what is the problem? There is no abuse to the shareholders, but what about the creditors? They have extended credit on the assumption that a given capital base would remain intact throughout the life of the loan. While they may not object to the payment of dividends from past and current earnings, they must have the protection of keeping contributed capital in place.[5]

Even the laws against having dividends exceed the total of past and current earnings (retained earnings) may be inadequate to protect creditors. Because retained earnings is merely an accounting concept and in no way certifies the current liquidity of the firm, a company paying dividends equal to retained earnings may, in certain cases, jeopardize the operation of the firm. Let us examine Table 18–3.

TABLE 18–3 Dividend policy considerations

Cash	$ 1,000,000	Debt	$10,000,000
Accounts receivable	4,000,000	Common stock	10,000,000
Inventory	15,000,000	Retained earnings	15,000,000
Plant and equipment	15,000,000		$35,000,000
	$35,000,000		

Current earnings	$ 1,500,000
Potential dividends	15,000,000

Theoretically, management could pay up to $15 million in dividends by selling assets even though current earnings are only $1.5 million. In most cases such frivolous action would not be taken, but the mere possibility encourages creditors to closely watch the balance sheets of corporate debtors and, at times, to impose additional limits on dividend payments as a condition for the granting of credit.

Company directors are also prohibited from declaring dividends when the company is insolvent or when the payment of dividends would make the company insolvent. Both legal insolvency (liabilities exceeding assets) and technical insolvency (inability

[5]Of course, on liquidation of the corporation, the contributed capital to the firm may be returned to common shareholders after creditor obligations are met. Normally, shareholders who need to recoup all or part of their contributed capital sell their shares to someone else.

to pay creditors) are included. This restriction is meant to prevent troubled firms from acting to the advantage of shareholders at the obvious expense of creditors. Furthermore, a corporation may be prevented from paying dividends if the conditions under bond indentures or loan provisions are not fulfilled. Debtholders are not eager to see their security position weakened by cash payouts if the corporation doesn't perform to certain expectations.

Cash Position of the Firm

Not only do retained earnings fail to portray the liquidity position of the firm, but there are also limitations to the use of current earnings to indicate liquidity. As described in Chapter 4, a growth firm producing the greatest gains in earnings may be in the poorest cash position. As sales and earnings expand rapidly, there is an accompanying buildup in receivables and inventory that may far outstrip cash flow generated through earnings. Note that the cash balance in Table 18–3 represents only two-thirds of current earnings of $1.5 million. A firm must do a complete analysis of funds available before establishing a dividend policy.

Access to Capital Markets

The medium- to large-size firm with a good record of performance may have relatively easy access to the financial markets. A company in such a position may be willing to pay dividends now, knowing it can sell new stocks or bonds in the future if funds are needed. Some corporations may even issue debt or stock now and use part of the proceeds to ensure the maintenance of current dividends. Though this policy seems at variance with the concept of a dividend as a reward, management may justify its action on the basis of maintaining stable dividends. It should be clear that larger firms have sufficient ease of entry to the capital markets to modify their dividend policy in this regard. Many firms may actually defer the payment of dividends because they know they will have difficulty in going to the capital markets for more funds.

Desire for Control

Management must also consider the effect of the dividend policy on its collective ability to maintain control. The directors and officers of a small, closely held firm may be hesitant to pay any dividends for fear of diluting the cash position of the firm and forcing the owners to look to outside investors for financing. The funds may be available through venture capital sources that wish to have a large say in corporate operations.

A larger firm with a broad base of shareholders may face a different type of threat in regard to dividend policy. Shareholders, spoiled by a past record of dividend payments, may demand the ouster of management if dividends are withheld.

Tax Position of Shareholders

The tax rates applicable to dividend income have been subject to change over the years, and this trend will likely continue. However, the payment of a cash dividend is generally taxable to the recipient, with some feeling the burden more heavily than others. To the wealthy individual, dividend income in 2002 could have attracted a net tax of up to 24 to 33 percent. The average taxpayer, making $30,000 to $50,000, would have paid 15 to 23 percent on dividend income. In the case of the corporate recipient, such as Brascan owning a controlling interest in Noranda, the dividend payment would probably have been tax exempt. In addition, dividends to the many large institutional investors that own so much of the common equity in the market are also usually tax exempt.

The **dividend tax credit** is meant to adjust for the fact that the corporation has already paid tax on the income on which the dividend was based. To adjust for this double taxation, the dividend paid is grossed up and taxes are calculated and then reduced by a dividend tax credit. Provincial taxes are calculated in a similar manner to federal taxes. Overall, the effect on the investor is to have dividend income preferable to interest income, other things being equal. This was identified in Table 2-13 of Chapter 2. Take, for example, a case where taxes must be computed on a $1,000 dividend payment to an individual, living in Alberta, whose combined federal and provincial marginal tax bracket is 2001's top rate of 24.08 percent (for dividends).

Sample Calculation of Tax on Individual Dividend Receipt

Dividend received	$1,000
Gross-up	250
Taxable amount	1,250
Federal tax (at 29%)	363
Less: Federal tax credit (13⅓% of $1,250)	167
Federal tax payable	$ 196
Provincial tax payable (10% of $1,250)	125
Provincial tax credit (32% of $250)	80
Provincial tax payable	45
Total taxes payable ($196 + $45)	241
Net dividend ($1,000 − $241)	$ 759

The preceding is merely meant to show the nature of the dividend tax credit. Each taxpayer must make his or her own calculation in relation to the rules that exist for the year in question. Table 2-13 shows the top and middle combined marginal tax rates in all provinces.

For the individual, the Income Tax Act taxes capital gains at an effective rate of one-half of the individual's normal tax rate. Thus, an individual in a top tax bracket in Alberta would pay $195 tax on $1,000 of capital gains and $390 on interest income (based on Table 2–13).

Because of differences among investors' tax rates, certain investor preferences for dividends versus capital gains have been observed in the market. This investor behaviour is called the **clientele effect.** Investors in high marginal tax brackets usually prefer companies that reinvest most of their earnings, thus creating more growth in earnings and stock prices. The returns from such investments will be in the form of capital gains, which are taxed at low rates or not at all. Investors in lower tax brackets have traditionally had a preference for dividends since the tax penalty is small at lower marginal tax rates and they also receive regular returns on their investment. The clientele effect then can be used to explain the advantages of a stable dividend policy that makes investors more certain about the type and timing of their returns.

Life Cycle Growth and Dividends

One of the major influences on dividends is the corporate growth rate in sales and the subsequent return on assets. Figure 18–3 shows a **corporate life cycle** and the corresponding dividend policy that is most likely to be found at each stage.

FIGURE 18–3

Life cycle growth and dividend policy

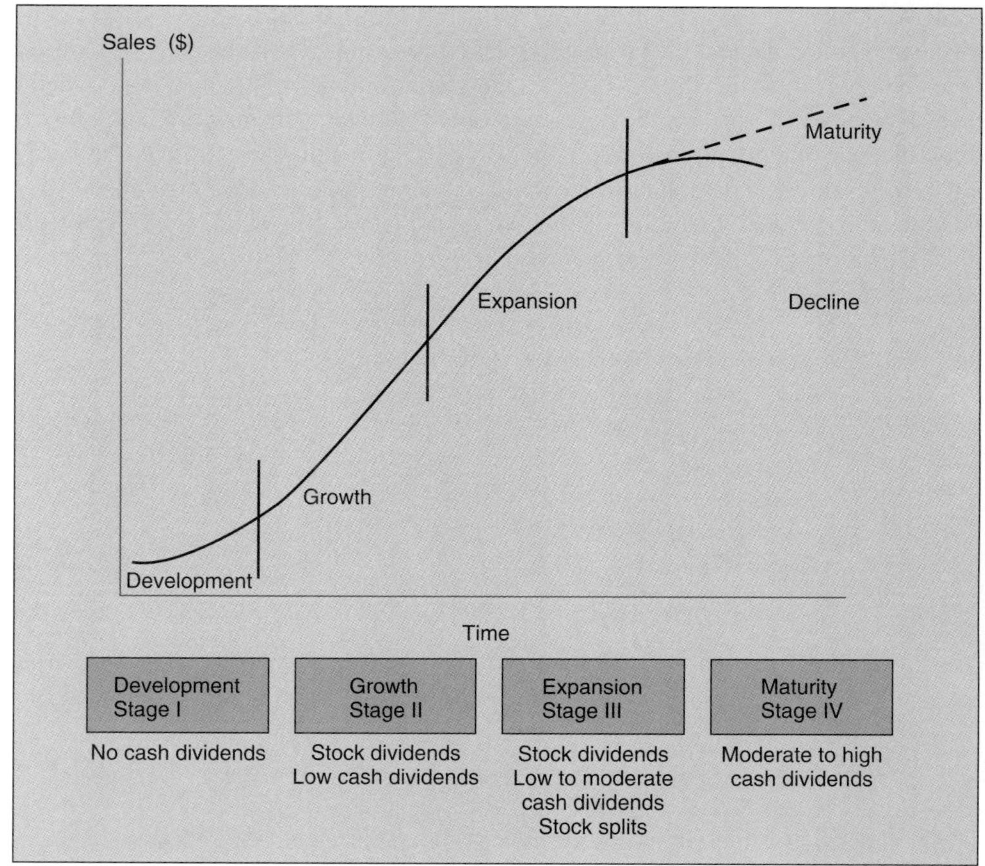

A small firm in the initial stages of development (Stage I) pays no dividends because it needs all of its profits (if there are any) for reinvestment in new productive assets. If the firm is successful in the marketplace, the demand for its products will create growth in sales, earnings, and assets, and the firm will move into Stage II.

In the growth stage, Stage II, the firm has numerous projects that add value. The projects have positive NPVs (Chapter 12), and the returns on the projects exceed shareholder expected rates of return (opportunity costs). Sales and returns on assets will be growing at an increasing rate, and earnings will still be reinvested. In the early part of Stage II, stock dividends (distribution of additional shares) may be instituted, and in the latter part of Stage II, low cash dividends may be started to inform investors that the firm is profitable but cash is needed for internal acquisition. At this stage careful financial forecasting (Chapter 4) is required. The large demand for funds will likely send the firm to the capital markets (Chapter 14) as internal funds are not usually sufficient to meet the growth demands.

After the growth period, the firm enters Stage III. The expansion of sales continues, but at a decreasing rate, and returns on investment may decline as more competition enters the market and tries to take away the firm's market share. During this period the firm is more and more capable of paying cash dividends, as the asset expansion rate slows and external funds become more readily available. Stock dividends and stock splits are still common in the expansion phase, and the dividend payout ratio usually increases from a low level of 5 to 15 percent of earnings to a moderate level of 25 to 40 percent of earnings.

Finally, at Stage IV, maturity, the firm maintains a stable growth rate in sales similar to that of the economy as a whole, and when risk premiums are considered, its return on assets level out to those of the industry and the economy. In unfortunate cases firms suffer declines in sales if product innovation and diversification have not occurred over the years. In Stage IV, assuming maturity rather than decline, dividends might range from 40 to 60 percent of earnings. These percentages differ from industry to industry depending on the individual characteristics of the company, such as operating and financial leverage and the volatility of sales and earnings over the business cycle.

In a general sense, the life cycle of the firm relates to the theory and practice of dividend policy. When opportunities are good the marginal principle of retained earnings applies, but as growth slows and dividends begin, investors expect the dividends to continue for various reasons. Management at this point tries to stabilize the dividend payout.

Dividend Payment Procedures

Now that we have examined the many factors that influence dividend policy, let us track the actual procedures for announcing and paying a dividend. Though dividends are quoted on an annual basis, the payments actually occur quarterly throughout the year.

Dofasco
www.dofasco.com

For example, on March 6, 2002, Dofasco declared quarterly cash dividends on its common shares. The common dividend of $0.27 meant shareholders could expect to receive $1.08 per year in dividends. Because the stock was selling at $28.20 on March 6, we calculate the annual dividend yield to be 3.8 percent ($1.08/$28.20).

As illustrated in Figure 18–4, three key dates are associated with the declaration of a quarterly dividend: the ex-dividend date, the dividend record date, and the dividend payment date.

FIGURE 18–4
Dividend payment time line (Dofasco example)

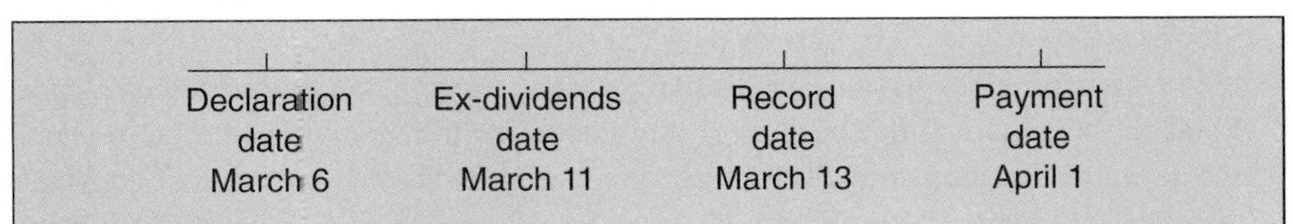

On the **dividend record date** the firm examines its books to determine who is entitled to a cash dividend. To have your name included on the corporate books on the dividend record date, you must have bought or owned the stock before the **ex-dividend date,** which is set at the second business day before the dividend record date. If you bought the stock on the ex-dividend date or later, your name eventually is transferred to the corporate books, but you have bought the stock without the right to receive the quarterly dividend. Thus, we say you have bought the stock ex-dividend. The previous shareholder would receive the dividend payment.

In the Dofasco example, a March 13, 2002, dividend record date resulted in an ex-dividend date of March 11, for the quarterly dividend payable April 1. Therefore, you would have had to have bought the stock before March 11, 2002, to be eligible to receive the April 1, 2002, dividend. Investors are very conscious of the date on which the stock goes ex-dividend, and the value of the stock should go down by exactly the value of the dividend on the ex-dividend date (all other things being equal). Finally, in the Dofasco example, cheques would be sent out to the entitled shareholders on or about the **dividend payment date** of April 1, 2002.

On the ex-dividend date we would expect to see the price of Dofasco shares drop in value by the amount of the dividend, other things being equal. This is because the dividend represents cash that will leave the firm. Studies have shown, however, that the price of the shares does not quite drop by the amount of the dividend. The reason has been attributed to tax considerations. If investors are indifferent between dividends and retention of earnings for capital gains, the share price should drop by the aftertax value of the dividend.

Stock Dividend

A stock dividend represents a distribution of additional shares to common shareholders. The typical size of such a dividend is 10 percent or less of the current amount of stock outstanding. In the case of a 10 percent stock dividend, a shareholder with 100 shares would receive 10 new shares in the form of a stock dividend. Larger distributions of 20 to 25 percent or more are usually considered to be stock splits, which are discussed later in this chapter.

Accounting Considerations for a Stock Dividend

Assume that before the declaration of a stock dividend, the XYZ Corporation has the net worth position indicated in Table 18–4.

TABLE 18–4
XYZ Corporation's financial position before stock dividend

Capital accounts	Common stock (1 million shares issued)	$15,000,000
	Retained earnings	15,000,000
	Net worth	$30,000,000

If a 10 percent stock dividend is declared, the shares outstanding will increase by 100,000 (10 percent of 1 million shares). An accounting transfer will occur between retained earnings and the common stock account based on the market value of the stock dividend. If the stock is selling for $15 per share, we assign $1.5 million to common stock. The net worth position of XYZ after the transfer is shown in Table 18–5. In effect, retained earnings are capitalized.

TABLE 18–5
XYZ Corporation's financial position after stock dividend

Capital accounts	Common stock (1.1 million shares issued)	$16,500,000
	Retained earnings	13,500,000
	Net worth	$30,000,000

Value to the Investor

Is a stock dividend of real value to the investor? When a stock dividend is declared, the asset base of the company remains the same, and the investor's proportionate ownership in the business is unchanged. The investor merely has more paper.

The same is true in the corporate setting. In the case of the XYZ Corporation, shown in Tables 18–4 and 18–5, we assumed that 1 million shares were outstanding before the stock dividend and that 1.1 million shares were outstanding afterward. Now let us assume the corporation had aftertax earnings of \$6.6 million. Without the stock dividend, earnings per share would be \$6.60, and with the dividend, would be \$6.00.

$$\text{Earnings per share} = \frac{\text{Earnings aftertax}}{\text{Shares outstanding}}$$

Without stock dividend:

$$= \frac{\$6.6 \text{ million}}{1 \text{ million shares}} = \$6.60$$

With stock dividend:

$$= \frac{\$6.6 \text{ million}}{1.1 \text{ million shares}} = \$6.00 \text{ (10\% decline)}$$

Earnings per share have gone down by exactly the same percentage that shares outstanding increased. For further illustration, assuming Shareholder A had 10 shares before the stock dividend and 11 afterward, what is the total claim to earnings? As expected, they remain the same at \$66.

$$\text{Claims to earnings} \times \text{Shares} = \text{Earnings per share}$$

Without stock dividend:

$$10 \times \$6.60 = \$66$$

With stock dividend:

$$11 \times \$6.00 = \$66$$

Taking the analogy one step further, assuming the stock sold at 20 times earnings before and after the stock dividend, what is the total market value of the portfolio in each case?

$$\text{Total market value} = \text{Shares} \times \left(\begin{matrix}\text{Price/earnings} \\ \text{ratio}\end{matrix} \times \begin{matrix}\text{Earnings} \\ \text{per share}\end{matrix}\right)$$

Without stock dividend:

$$\begin{aligned} & 10 \times (20 \times \$6.60) \\ & = 10 \times \$132 = \$1{,}320 \end{aligned}$$

With stock dividend:

$$\begin{aligned} & 11 \times (20 \times \$6.00) \\ & = 11 \times \$120 = \$1{,}320 \end{aligned}$$

The total market value is unchanged. Note that if the shareholder sells the 11th share to acquire cash, his stock portfolio is worth $120 less than it was worth before the stock dividend.

Under the federal income tax legislation that became effective May 23, 1985, stock dividends declared and paid after that date are treated as regular dividends. Previously, no tax was payable on stock dividends. This change in the tax law makes stock dividends less attractive to some shareholders than previously and has had a negative effect on the number of stock dividends declared.

Possible Value of Stock Dividends

There are limited circumstances under which a stock dividend may be of value. If at the time a stock dividend is declared the cash dividend per share remains constant, the shareholder receives greater total cash dividends. Assume the annual cash dividend for the XYZ Corporation remains $1.00 per share even though earnings per share decline from $6.60 to $6.00. In this instance a shareholder moving from 10 to 11 shares as the result of a stock dividend has a $1.00 increase in total dividends. The overall value of his portfolio may then increase in response to larger dividends.

Use of Stock Dividends

Stock dividends are most frequently used by growth companies as a form of informational content in explaining the retention of funds for reinvestment purposes. This was indicated in the discussion of the life cycle of the firm earlier in the chapter. A corporation president may state, "Instead of doing more in the way of cash dividends, we are providing a stock dividend. The funds remaining in the corporation will be used for highly profitable investment opportunities." The market reaction to such an approach may be neutral or slightly positive.

A second use of stock dividends may be to camouflage the inability of the corporation to pay cash dividends and to try to cover up the ineffectiveness of the firm's operations in generating cash flow. The president may proclaim, "Though we are unable to pay cash dividends, we wish to reward you with a 15 percent stock dividend." Well-informed investors are likely to think little of a management that uses such a strategy.

Stock Splits

A **stock split** is similar to a stock dividend, only more shares are distributed. For example, a two-for-one stock split would double the number of shares outstanding. In general, distributions increasing the number of shares outstanding by more than 20 to 25 percent are handled as stock splits.

The accounting treatment for a stock split is somewhat different from that for a stock dividend in that there is no transfer of funds from retained earnings to the capital accounts. There is, instead, a proportionate increase in the number of shares outstanding. For example, a two-for-one stock split for the XYZ Corporation would necessitate the statement adjustments shown in Table 18–6.

In this case, all adjustments are in the common stock account. Because the number of shares is doubled, the market price of the stock should drop by half. The financial literature contains much discussion about the impact of a split on overall stock value.

Microsoft and Stock Splits

Bill Gates is one of the most familiar names in the world, and he is the world's wealthiest individual with a net worth of almost U.S.$60 billion. Most of this wealth comes from his ownership of somewhat less than 20 percent of Microsoft. On March 6, 2002, Microsoft common stock closed at U.S.$62.00 per share and had a total market capitalization of U.S.$338 billion dollars. You might wonder how the small investor in Microsoft has fared. If an investor had bought 100 shares of common stock in Microsoft on September 1, 1987, at the market price of $1.58 per share, the investor would have spent $158 plus broker commissions.

When a stock splits, its share price is adjusted accordingly. For example, if an investor has 100 shares of a $20.00 stock and the company splits the stock 2 for 1, the investor now has 200 shares selling at $10.00 per share. In the case of Microsoft, the shares have split 8 times since September 1987. The table below illustrates how stock splits have worked for Microsoft. If you had purchased 100 shares of Microsoft in September 1987 for $158 you would now have 14,400 shares worth $892,800. The interesting question is how many people that bought and owned Microsoft shares in 1987 held on to their shares to reap the full benefits.

Stock Split	Amount	Number of Shares	Share Price	Value
3/06/02	Value	14,400	$62.00	$892,800
3/12/99	2 for 1	14,400		
2/20/98	2 for 1	7,200		
12/6/96	2 for 1	3,600		
5/20/94	2 for 1	1,800		
6/12/92	3 for 2	900		
6/26/91	3 for 2	600		
4/13/90	2 for 1	400		
9/18/87	2 for 1	200		
	Purchase	100	$1.58	$158

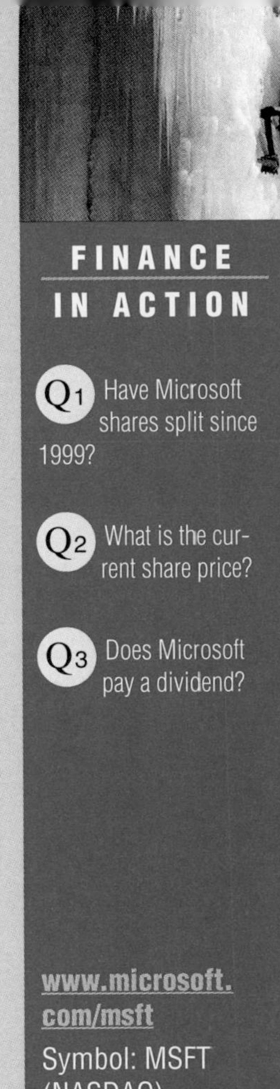

FINANCE IN ACTION

Q1 Have Microsoft shares split since 1999?

Q2 What is the current share price?

Q3 Does Microsoft pay a dividend?

www.microsoft.com/msft

Symbol: MSFT (NASDAQ)

TABLE 18–6

XYZ Corporation before and after stock split

Before	
Common stock (1 million shares issued)	$15,000,000
Retained earnings	15,000,000
Total owners' equity	$30,000,000
After	
Common stock (2 million shares issued)	$15,000,000
Retained earnings	15,000,000
Total owners' equity	$30,000,000

The consensus seems to be that stock splits do not seem to add any real value to share prices.

The primary purpose of a stock split is to lower the price of a security into a more popular trading range. A stock selling for over $50.00 per share may be excluded from consideration by many small investors because they generally must purchase shares in lots of 100. Stronger companies that have witnessed substantial growth in market share price usually initiate splits. Once again, the evidence suggests that the price of a stock is no hindrance to its popularity, and a stock split does not add value to the company's shares.

Berkshire Hathaway
www.berkshirehathaway.com

For example, one share of Berkshire Hathaway (BRK), controlled by Warren Buffett, one of the world's wealthiest individuals, traded on the New York Exchange at a price of almost of $70,000 in March 2002. It is the large institutional investors that drive market prices, and share price does not appear to matter to these investors. Buffett maintained that share splits do not add value and were only attractive to speculators. However, in 1996, he decided to split some of the original Class A shares into 30 Class B shares. Each Class B share, at about $2,300 in 2002, would, however, only have 1/200th the vote of a Class A share. He did this to counter unit investment trusts that had been set up to offer smaller investors a "piece" of Berkshire Hathaway. Buffett was concerned that investors would have to incur fees and commissions when investing in these unit trusts.

Repurchase of Stock as an Alternate to Dividends

A firm with excess cash and inadequate investment opportunities may choose to repurchase its own shares in the market rather than pay a cash dividend. For this reason, the **stock repurchase** decision may be thought of as an alternative to the payment of cash dividends.

We show that the benefits to the shareholder are equal under either alternative, at least in theory. For purposes of study, assume the Morgan Corporation's financial position may be described by the data in Table 18–7.

TABLE 18–7
Financial data of Morgan Corporation

Earnings aftertaxes	$3,000,000
Shares	1,000,000
Earnings per share	$3
Price-earnings ratio	10
Market price per share	$30
Excess cash	$2,000,000

The firm has $2 million in excess cash, and it wishes to compare the value to shareholders of a $2.00 cash dividend (on the million shares outstanding) as opposed to spending the funds to repurchase shares in the market. If the cash dividend is paid, the shareholder would have $30.00 in stock and the $2.00 cash dividend. On the other hand, the $2 million may be used to repurchase shares at slightly over market value (to induce sale).[6] The overall benefit to shareholders is that earnings per share go up as the number of shares outstanding is decreased. If the price-earnings ratio of the stock remains constant, then the price of the stock should also go up. If a purchase price of $32.00 is used to induce sale, then 62,500 shares would be purchased.

$$\frac{\text{Excess funds}}{\text{Purchase price per share}} = \frac{\$2{,}000{,}000}{\$32} = 62{,}500 \text{ shares}$$

[6]To derive the desired equality between the two alternatives, the purchase price for the new shares should equal the current market price plus the proposed cash dividend under the first alternative ($30.00 + $2.00 = $32.00).

Total shares outstanding are reduced to 937,500 (1,000,000 − 62,500). Revised earnings per share for the Morgan Corporation become:

$$\frac{\text{Earnings aftertaxes}}{\text{Shares}} = \frac{\$3{,}000{,}000}{937{,}500} = \$3.20$$

Since the price-earnings ratio for the stock is 10, the market value of the stock should go to $32.00. Thus, we see that the consequences of the two alternatives are presumed to be the same.

(1) Funds Used for Cash Dividend		(2) Funds Used to Repurchase Stock	
Market value per share	$30	Market value per share	$32
Cash dividend per share	2		
	$32		

In either instance the total value is presumed to be $32.00. Theoretically, the shareholder would be indifferent with respect to the two alternatives. This changes somewhat, however, when taxes and transaction costs are brought into the decision-making process. Let us first look at taxes. While the cash dividend is immediately taxed in Alternative 1, the gain in Alternative 2 may be untaxed as a capital gain. Furthermore, if there is to be a capital gains tax incurred, it is delayed until the stock is sold. From a tax viewpoint, the repurchase of shares may provide maximum benefits. On the other hand, one can argue that dividends put cash in the shareholders' hands without any transaction costs. If the company is buying back significant amounts of its shares, it has to pay some premium above $30.00 to induce enough shareholders to sell. Also, there will be transaction costs in managing and executing the buybacks. Finally, the remaining shareholders have to incur transaction costs if they want to realize the equivalent of the cash dividend in cash.

Other Reasons for Repurchase

In addition to using the repurchase decision as an alternative to cash dividends, corporate management may acquire its own shares in the market because it believes they are selling at bargain basement prices. A corporation president, seeing the firm's stock price decline by 50 to 60 percent over a six-month period, may determine that its own stock is the best investment available to the corporation. In other words, he or she is not convinced that the current share price is a best estimate of the present value of the firm's future prospects.

By repurchasing shares the corporation is able to maintain a constant demand for its own securities and to perhaps stave off further price erosion, at least temporarily. This appears to be the logic in a number of share repurchase announcements. Corporate management believes that the announcement of a repurchase reassures investors of the value of their investment. It is hoped that prices will rise on this reassurance, or on the demand created by the buyback. Often firms to not complete a buyback of all the shares announced as their target. The buyback of some shares seems to satisfy the market of their intentions.

FINANCE IN ACTION

Q1 Can you find a recent buyback announcement and what are the details of the offer?

www.tdbank.ca
Symbol: TD

www.methanex.com
Symbol: MX

Timing the Buyback

In June 1999, TD Bank sold some of its interest in TD Waterhouse to the public at $24.00 per share to raise $1 billion during a strong stock market. In late 2001, during a much weaker market, TD Bank decided to buy back all outstanding shares at a premium of 45 percent over the market share price at the time of the offer. However this offer, with the premium, was only $9.00 and would cost TD only $360 million. Some shareholders objected.

Methanex, a producer of methanol for fuel cells, in late 2001 had lots of cash generated from amortization charges on their large capital expenditures of the late 1990s. An announcement was made of its intention to buyback 18 percent of its outstanding shares to boost earnings per share and hopefully its depressed share price. Through a "modified dutch auction" shareholders would select a price between $6.00 and $7.50 to tender their shares. Methanex would then select the price that would achieve their buyback target. The firm agreed to stay in the market after the auction to buyback up to 10 percent more shares, in order to maintain the market price. Share prices have been known to slide after a buyback.

The buyback activity in late 2001 was one way these companies could return cash to their investors at a time when investment alternatives weren't as attractive due to a slowing economy. Information on buybacks can be found at the SEDAR web site (www.sedar.com) with an "issuer bid circular" search, or perhaps a "press release" search.

Reacquired shares may also be useful for employee stock options or as part of a tender offer in a merger or acquisition. Firms also often reacquire part of their shares as a protective device against being taken over by others. As the equity value of a firm decreases relative to the value of its physical assets, outsiders may attempt to gain control of the firm by using the value of the physical assets to finance the purchase of the equity. To reduce the availability of their companies to these highly leveraged buyouts, the managements of potential takeover targets often take on debt to buy back some of their stock.

There is one caveat for firms that continually repurchase their own shares. Some analysts may view the action as a noncreative use of funds. The analysts may ask, "Why aren't the funds being used to develop new products or to modernize plant and equipment?" Thus, it is important that management carefully communicates the reasons for the repurchase decision to analysts and shareholders-such as the fact that the stock is a great bargain at its current price.

Some evidence exists for superior returns on shares after repurchase. It is suggested that management is conveying new information about future expected earnings when a repurchase announcement is made. With improved results in the following months, the share price shows increasing value.

Dividend Reinvestment Plans

During the 1970s many companies started **dividend reinvestment plans (DRIPs)** for their shareholders. These plans take various forms, but basically they provide the investor with an opportunity to buy additional shares of stock with the cash dividend paid by the company. Over 100 companies listed on the Toronto Stock Exchange offer dividend reinvestment plans on their capital stock. Participation in these plans is voluntary.

Some firms permit discounts to share value on dividend reinvestment plans but apparently these are becoming less common. Nevertheless, the shareholder that participates in a DRIP even at the market price benefits by saving on brokerage commissions and administrative costs. Furthermore, this disciplined method for reinvesting the returns from the share investment utilizes the compounding principle of earning returns on returns over time. A shareholder may also be allowed to add cash payments of up to $1,000 per quarter to his or her dividend payments to buy more shares at the reduced rate. With a dividend reinvestment plan, the company is the beneficiary of increased cash flow since dividends paid are returned to it for reinvestment.

Summary

1. The first consideration in establishing a dividend policy is the firm's ability to reinvest the funds generated by the business versus the shareholder's ability to invest those funds elsewhere. The firm's need for earnings retention and growth is represented in the life cycle growth curve.
2. The theory of highest return for internally generated funds must be tempered by a consideration of shareholders' preferences. Shareholders may be given a greater payout than the optimum determined by rational analysis to resolve their uncertainty about the future (that is, for informational purposes). This would seem to be supported by the evidence of firms continuing to pay dividends despite the fact that earnings have declined dramatically. Dividend increases appear to have a positive impact on share value.
3. Shareholders may prefer a greater than normal retention to defer the income tax obligation associated with cash dividends. Another important consideration in establishing a dividend policy may be the shareholders' desire for steady dividend payments. Lesser factors influencing dividend policy are legal rules relating to maximum payment, the cash position of the firm, and the firm's access to capital markets. One must also consider the desire for control by corporate management and shareholders.
4. After a dividend is declared, the ex-dividend date, the record date, and the payment date are of importance.
5. An alternative (or a supplement) to cash dividends may be the use of stock dividends and stock splits. While neither of these financing devices directly changes the intrinsic value of the shareholder position, they may provide communication to shareholders and bring the share price into a more acceptable trading range. A stock dividend may take on some actual value when total cash dividends are allowed to increase. Nevertheless, the alert investor watches for abuses of stock dividends-situations in which the corporation indicates that something of great value is occurring when, in fact, the new shares created merely represent the same proportionate interest for each shareholder.
6. The decision to repurchase shares may be thought of as an alternative to the payment of a cash dividend. Decreasing shares outstanding causes earnings per share, and perhaps the market price, to go up. The increase in the market price may be equated to the size of the cash dividend forgone.
7. Many firms are now offering shareholders the option of reinvesting cash dividends in the company's common stock. Cash-short companies have been using dividend reinvestment plans to raise external funds. Other companies simply provide a service to shareholders by allowing them to purchase shares in the market for low transaction costs.

List of Terms

Discussion Questions

1. How does the marginal principle of retained earnings relate to the returns a shareholder may make in other investments?
2. Discuss the difference between a passive and an active dividend policy.
3. In general, how does the shareholder feel about the relevance of dividends?
4. Explain the relationship between a company's growth possibilities and its dividend policy.
5. Discuss the major factors that may influence the firm's willingness and ability to pay dividends.
6. If you buy a stock on the ex-dividend date, will you receive the upcoming quarterly dividend?
7. Describe the importance of shareholder tax rates in setting dividend policy.
8. How is a stock split versus a stock dividend treated on the financial statements of a corporation?
9. Why might a stock dividend or a stock split be of limited value to an investor?
10. Does it make sense for a corporation to repurchase its own stock? Explain.
11. How does the life cycle curve explain the relationship between corporate growth and residual dividend theory?
12. Why might an investor prefer capital gains to dividends?
13. What advantages to the corporation and the shareholder do dividend reinvestment plans offer?
14. Discuss a corporate repurchase announcement on the basis of market efficiency (Chapter 14).
15. What impact does a repurchase have on a firm's capital structure? Will it increase the value of the shares in the firm?
16. In early 1989, Inco Ltd. paid a special dividend of U.S.$10.00 a share. What was the purpose? By returning over $1 billion in total to shareholders, what was management saying to the investment community?
17. Why do corporate executives consider a stable dividend policy important?
18. If a company, in which you hold shares, decided to increase its dividend, would that increase your expected returns from this investment?

INTERNET RESOURCES AND QUESTIONS

The Toronto Stock Exchange site provides common and preferred share prices, P/E ratios, latest earnings, and dividend yields, under quotes:
www.tsx.ca

Recent filings under securities legislation, including dividend payment announcements, are available from the System for Electronic Document Analysis and Retrieval (SEDAR), owned by the Canadian Depository for Securities (CDS):
www.sedar.com

The Quebecor Media web site provides share pricing, P/E ratios, eps, and dividend yields:
www.webfin.com/en/

1. Update the selected dividend yields from Table 18–2. Comment on any changes and possible reasons for the increase or decrease in yields.
2. Determine earnings and dividends for the last five years for Royal Bank, TransCanada Pipelines, Alcan, and TeckCominco in a manner similar to Table 18–1. Comment on the dividend patterns and the possible reasons for these patterns.
3. Compare the dividend yields on the common and preferred shares of the Toronto Dominion Bank and TransAlta Utilities. Why is there a difference in yields?

Problems

1. Omni Telecom is trying to decide whether to increase its cash dividend or use the funds to increase its future growth rate. It will use the dividend valuation model (Chapter 10) for purposes of analysis. The current values are the following:

   $D_0 = \$1.50$ $K_e = 10\%$

   $g = 4\%$

   Under Plan A, the dividend (D_1) will be increased to \$1.80 with K_e and g unchanged.

   Under Plan B, the dividend (D_1) will remain at \$1.50, K_e will remain unchanged, but g will increase to 6%.

   a. Compute the current price under plan A.

   b. Compute the current price under Plan B.

   c. Which plan produced the higher value, and suggest a reason why?
2. Roget's Search Engine Limited plans to pay dividends of \$2.00, \$3.50, and then a liquidating dividend of \$20.25 over the next three years. If investors expect a 10 percent return on their investment, what is the value of the company today?
3. Suppose Roget's Search Engine, from the previous problem, decides to forgo the dividend payments in years 1 and 2 and instead reinvest the funds in additional projects available to the firm. Demonstrate whether or not the suspension of dividends is appropriate under the following assumptions:

   a. Reinvested funds earn 8 percent.

   b. Reinvested funds earn 10 percent.

   c. Reinvested funds earn 12 percent.
4. Neil Diamond Brokers, Inc. reported earnings per share of \$4.00 and paid \$0.90 in dividends. What is the payout ratio?
5. Moon and Sons, Inc., earned \$120 million last year and retained \$72 million. What is the payout ratio?
6. Swank Clothiers earned \$640 million last year and had a 30 percent payout ratio. How much did the firm add to its retained earnings?
7. The stock of the Pills Berry Corporation is currently selling at \$60.00 per share. The firm pays a dividend of \$1.80 per share.

   a. What is the annual dividend yield?

   b. If the firm has a payout rate of 50 percent, what is the firm's P/E ratio?
8. The stock of Raptor BB Ranch is currently selling at \$25.00 per share. The firm pays a dividend of \$1.25 per share.

   a. What is the annual dividend yield?

   b. If the firm has a payout ratio of 50 percent, what is the firm's P/E ratio?

9. The shares of Dyer Drilling Co. sell for $60.00. The firm has a P/E ratio of 15 and 40 percent of earnings are paid out in dividends. What is the dividend yield?
10. The shares of Chretien Golf Links Limited sell for $50.00. The firm has a P/E ratio of 20 and 30 percent of earnings are paid out in dividends. What is the dividend yield?
11. The Resolute Bay Shipping News is selling for $65.00 the day before the stock goes ex-dividend. The annual dividend yield is 5.5 percent, and the dividends are paid quarterly. Based solely on the impact of the cash dividend, by how much should the share price change on the ex-dividend date? What is the suggested new price of a share?
12. Peabody Mining Company's common stock is selling for $50.00 the day before the stock goes ex-dividend. The annual dividend yield is 5.6 percent, and dividends are distributed quarterly. Based solely on the impact of the cash dividend, by how much should the stock go down on the ex-dividend date? What is the suggested new price of the stock?
13. In doing a five-year analysis of future dividends, Newell Labs, Inc., is considering the following two plans. The values represent dividends per share.

Year	Plan A	Plan B
1	$2.50	$ .80
2	2.55	3.30
3	2.50	0.35
4	2.65	2.80
5	2.65	6.60

a. How much, in total dividends per share, will be paid under each plan over the five years?

b. Ms. Carter, the vice president of finance, suggests that shareholders often prefer a stable dividend policy to a highly variable one. She will assume shareholders apply a lower discount rate to dividends that are stable. The discount rate to be used for Plan A is 10 percent; the discount rate for Plan B is 12 percent. Which plan will provide the higher present value for the future dividends?

14. The following companies have different financial statistics. What dividend policies would you recommend for them? Explain your reasons.

	Mathews Co.	Aaron Corp.
Growth rate in sales and earnings	5%	20%
Cash as a percentage of total assets	15%	2%

15. Goren Bridge Construction Co. has two important shareholders: Ms. Queen and the Ace Corporation. Ms. Queen is in a 31 percent combined marginal tax bracket, while the Ace Corporation is in a 36 percent combined marginal bracket.

a. If Ms. Queen receives $3.80 in cash dividends, how much in taxes (per share) will she pay?

b. If the Ace Corporation receives $3.80 in cash dividends, how much in taxes (per share) will it pay?

16. Below are the earnings per share and the dividends per share of three companies.

Alpha Co.		Beta Co.		Delta Co.	
EPS	DPS	EPS	DPS	EPS	DPS
$4.00	$2.00	$4.00	$2.00	$4.00	$2.00
4.20	2.10	4.20	2.00	4.20	1.50
4.80	2.40	4.80	2.00	4.80	2.00
5.60	2.80	5.60	2.00	5.60	3.00
6.00	3.00	6.00	2.30	6.00	2.00

a. What are the payout ratios for each company on an annual basis?

b. Can you explain some of the reasons for such differences in payout patterns?

c. Which company would you prefer to own as a shareholder? (Assume the bottom row is the most recent years data.) Why? What other kinds of information would you want before you invested your money?

17. A financial analyst is attempting to assess the future dividend policy of Environmental Systems by examining its life cycle. She anticipates no payout of earnings in the form of cash dividends during the developmental stage (I). During the growth stage (II), she anticipates 10 percent of earnings will be distributed as dividends. As the firm progresses to the expansion stage (III), the payout will go up to 30 percent, and eventually reach 50 percent during the maturity stage (IV).

a. Assuming earnings per share will be as follows during each of the four stages, indicate the cash dividend per share (if any) during each stage.

Stage I	$0.15
Stage II	1.80
Stage III	2.60
Stage IV	3.10

b. Assume in Stage IV that an investor owns 275 shares and is in a 31 percent marginal combined tax bracket. What will be the investors aftertax income from the cash dividend?

c. In what two stages is the firm most likely to utilize stock dividends or stock splits?

18. Sun Energy Company has the following capital section in its balance sheet. Its stock is currently selling for $5.00 per share.

Common stock (100,000 shares)	$200,000
Retained earnings	200,000
	$400,000

The firm intends to first declare a 10 percent stock dividend and then pay a $0.30 cash dividend (which also causes a reduction of retained earnings). Show the capital section of the balance sheet after the first transaction and then after the second transaction.

19. Rolex Discount Jewellers is trying to determine the maximum amount of cash dividends it can pay this year. Assume its balance sheet is as follows:

Assets	
Cash	$ 350,000
Accounts receivable	900,000
Capital assets	1,150,000
Total assets	$2,400,000
Liabilities and Shareholders' Equity	
Accounts payable	$ 395,000
Long-term notes payable	330,000
Common stock (250,000 shares)	750,000
Retained earnings	925,000
Total liabilities and shareholders' equity	$2,400,000

a. From a legal perspective, what is the maximum amount of dividends per share the firm could pay? Is this realistic?

b. In terms of cash availability, what is the maximum amount of dividends per share the firm could pay?

c. Assume the firm earned an 18 percent return on shareholders' equity. If the board wishes to pay out 50 percent of earnings in the form of dividends, how much will dividends per share be?

20. The Vinson Corporation has earnings of $500,000, with 250,000 shares outstanding. Its P/E ratio is 20. The firm is holding $300,000 of funds to invest or pay out in dividends. If the funds are retained, the aftertax return on investment will be 15 percent, and this will add to present earnings. The 15 percent is the normal return anticipated for the corporation, and the P/E ratio would remain unchanged. If the funds are paid out in the form of dividends, the P/E ratio will increase by 10 percent, because the shareholders in this corporation have a preference for dividends over retained earnings. Which plan will maximize the market value of the stock?

21. The Wallace Corporation has done very well in the stock market during the last three years. Its stock has risen from $18.00 per share to $44.00 per share. Its current statement of net worth is:

Common stock (3 million shares issued; 9 million shares authorized)	$45,000,000
Retained earnings	45,000,000
Net worth	$90,000,000

a. What changes would occur in the statement of net worth after a two-for-one stock split?

b. What would the statement of net worth look like after a three-for-one stock split?

c. Assume Wallace Corporation earned $6 million. What would its earnings per share be before and after the two-for-one stock split?

d. What would the price per share be before and after the two-for-one and the three-for-one stock splits? (Assume the price-earnings ratio of 22 stays the same.)

e. Should a stock split change the price-earnings ratio for Wallace?

22. Slick Products sells marked playing cards to blackjack dealers. It has not paid a dividend in many years but is currently contemplating some kind of dividend. The capital accounts for the firm are:

Common stock (150,000 shares)	$300,000
Retained earnings	400,000
Net worth	$700,000

The company's stock is selling for $6.00 per share, and it earned $0.60 per share this year, indicating a P/E ratio of 10.

a. What adjustments would have to be made to the capital accounts for a 10 percent stock dividend?

b. What adjustments would be made to EPS and the share price? (Assume the P/E ratio remains constant.)

c. How many shares would an investor end up with if he or she originally had 100 shares?

d. What is the investor's total investment worth before and after the stock dividend if the P/E ratio remains constant? (There may be a small difference due to rounding.)

e. Has Slick Products pulled a magic trick, or has it given the investor something of value? Explain.

23. The Lomax Corporation has $4 million in earnings aftertaxes and 1 million shares outstanding. The stock trades at a P/E of 10. The firm has $3 million in excess cash.

a. Compute the current price of the stock.

b. If the $3 million is used to pay dividends, how much will dividends per share be?

c. If the $3 million is used to repurchase shares in the market at a premium price of $43.00 per share, how many shares will be reacquired? (Round to the nearest share.)

d. What will the new earnings per share be? (Round to the nearest cent.)

e. If the P/E remains constant, what will the new price of the securities be? By how much, in terms of dollars, did the repurchase increase the share price?

f. Has the shareholder's total wealth changed as a result of the stock repurchase as opposed to the cash dividend?

g. Given the passage of recent tax legislation, from the shareholder's perspective, is there any major tax advantage to tendering one's shares versus the receipt of cash dividends?

h. What are some other reasons a corporation may wish to repurchase its own shares in the market?

24. This problem compares the aftertax income on a $35,000 investment for the following two investors resident in Ontario and two possible investments. Table 2–13 will be of assistance. Rudy Hill earns $40,000 a year. This is his only investment. Grace Valley is in the top marginal tax bracket. This is her only investment. Investment A provides $2,800 in dividends and no capital gains. Investment B provides no dividends but $2,800 of capital gains.

a. Calculate the aftertax return for Hill in Investment A and Investment B.

b. Calculate the aftertax return for Valley in Investment A and Investment B.

c. Indicate the difference in aftertax income between the two investors in Investment A.

d. Indicate the difference in aftertax income between the two investors in Investment B.

e. In the answers to parts *c* and *d*, why is there a smaller difference between the answers for one investment than for the other?

25. The Majestic Corporation has the following pattern of net income each year and associated capital expenditure projects for which the firm can earn a higher return than the shareholders could earn if the funds were paid out in the form of dividends.

Year	Net Income	Profitable Capital Expenditure
1	$ 5 million	$4 million
2	8 million	6 million
3	10 million	8 million
4	7 million	7 million
5	12 million	5 million

The Majestic Corporation has 1 million shares outstanding. (Note: The following questions are separate from each other.)

a. If the marginal principle of retained earnings is applied, how much in total cash dividends will be paid over the five years?

b. If the firm simply uses a payout ratio of 40 percent of net income, how much in total cash dividends will be paid?

c. If the firm pays a 10 percent stock dividend in years 2 through 5 and also pays a cash dividend of $2.50 per share for each of the five years, how much in total dividends will be paid?

d. Assume that the payout ratio in each year is to be 30 percent of net income and that the firm will pay a 20 percent stock dividend in years 2 through 5. How much will dividends per share for each year be?

COMPREHENSIVE PROBLEM

26. In January, the board of directors of the Montgomery Corporation, one of Canada's largest retail store chains, was having its regularly scheduled meeting to establish and declare the next quarterly dividend. (Statements for the firm and industry are shown in Tables 1 and 2 on pages 668 and 669.) However, this meeting wasn't so regular. One of the directors, Sidney Mobler, who was also a vice president in the company and chief financial officer, had brought a guest: Don Jackson, a financial analyst. Don had spent a considerable amount of time in the finance department and more than a few hours in Mr. Mobler's office developing a proposal concerning the company's dividend policy. He had finally persuaded Mr. Mobler to allow him to present his idea to the board.

"Ladies and gentlemen," Mr. Jackson began, after being introduced by Mr. Mobler, "I'll skip the preliminaries and get right to the point. I think that Montgomery's dividend policy is not in the best interest of our shareholders."

Observing the rather chilly stares from around the room, he hastened on: "Now, I don't mean we have a bad policy, or anything like that; it's just that I think we could do an even better job of increasing our shareholders' wealth with a few small changes." He paused for effect. "Let me explain. Up to now our policy has been to pay a constant dividend every year, increasing it occasionally to reflect the company's growth in sales and income. The problem is, that policy takes no account of the investment opportunities that the company has from year to year. In other words, this year we will use most of our net income to pay the same, or a greater, dividend than last year, even though there might be company investments available that would pay a much greater return if we committed the funds to the firm's investments instead. In effect, our shareholders are being short-changed: They will realize perhaps a 6 percent yield on their investment as a result of receiving the dividend, when they could realize a 12 percent or higher return as a result of the company's return on its investments. I see this as a serious shortcoming in our management of the shareholders' funds.

"Now, fortunately, correcting this situation is not difficult. All we have to do is adopt what is called a *residual* dividend policy. That is, each year we would allocate money from income to those capital spending projects for which the return—that is, IRR—is greater than our cost of capital. Any money that is not so used in the capital budget would be paid out to the shareholders in the form of dividends. In this way we would ensure that the shareholders' money is working the hardest way it can for them."

Mr. Clarence Autry, who was also on the board of directors of the Canadian Pacific and no stranger to the world of corporate finance, broke in. "Young man," he said dryly, "your proposal ignores reality. It's not whether the shareholders are theoretically better off that counts; it's what they want that counts. You cannot tell the shareholders you're doing what's best for them by cutting the dividend; the dividend is what they want. Not only is that dividend sure money in their pockets now, but the fact that it's the same size as last time, or even higher, is a signal to them that their company is doing well and will continue to do so in the future. These decisions can't always be made on the basis of good-looking formulas from the back room, you know."

Ms. Barbara Reynolds, who was the head of the directors' auditing committee, and somewhat of an accounting expert, agreed with Mr. Autry. "That's a good point, Clarence, and one that's well recognized by our competitors too. If you check, I don't think you'll find a single one of them that's cut their dividend in the last six years, even though their net income may have declined significantly. Furthermore the whole argument is meaningless anyway, because the dividend is not really competing with the capital budget for funds. We don't turn away profitable projects in favor of paying the dividend. If there are worthy projects in which we want to invest, and we would rather use our available cash to pay the dividend, then we seek financing for the investments from outside sources. In a way, we can have our cake and eat it too." She chuckled, pleased at the analogy.

Don Jackson, however, was not to be intimidated so easily. "Yes, ma'am, what you say is true," he replied, "and I would respond that our competitors are not treating their shareholders fairly, either. Furthermore, we do seek outside financing occasionally for large projects, but there are two problems associated with doing it routinely, as you suggest. First, it might be viewed as borrowing, or issuing stock, to pay the dividend, which would cast the company in a very poor light. Second, it's more expensive to finance from outside sources than from inside due to the fees charged by the investment dealers. Therefore, I believe we should exhaust our inside sources of financing before turning to the outside."

Ms. Reynolds held her ground. "That's all very well, but it's still not necessary to cut the dividend in order to fund the capital budget. As a last resort, if the company's cash balances were about to be drawn down too low, we could always declare a stock dividend instead of a cash dividend."

"Ladies, gentlemen," Mr. Edward Asking, the chairman, intervened, "your comments are all very perceptive, but we must move on to the business at hand. All those in favour of changing to a residual dividend policy please raise your hand."

a. Refer to Figure 1. Would you say that Montgomery's policy up to now has been to pay a constant dividend, with occasional increases as the company grows?

b. Refer to Figure 2. What type of dividend policies would you say are being practiced by Montgomery's competitors in the retailing industry? Do you think that any firms are following a residual dividend policy?

c. Calculate the expected return to the common shareholders under the firm's present policy, given an expected dividend next year of $2.10 and a growth rate of 7.1 percent. Montgomery's stock currently sells for $35.00.

TABLE 1

Selected financial data, Montgomery Corporation (in $ millions, except per share data)

	1996	1997	1998	1999	2000	2001	2002
Sales	$27,357.4	$30,019.8	$ 35,882.9	$38,828.0	$40,715.3	$44,281.5	$48,000.0
Net income	$ 650.1	$ 861.2	$ 1,342.2	$ 1,454.8	$ 1,303.3	$ 1,351.3	$ 1,700.0
Amount to preferred dividends	—	—	—	$ 16.7	$ 21.5	$ 16.8	$ 22.6
Amount to common dividends	$ 429.1	$ 476.3	$ 537.0	$ 630.8	$ 639.0	$ 648.3	$ 725.4
Amount to retained earnings	$ 221.0	$ 384.9	$ 805.2	$ 807.3	$ 642.8	$ 686.2	$ 952.0
Common shares outstanding	347.9	351.4	354.6	361.6	363.1	376.6	378.0
Earnings per share (on average common shares	$ 1.96	$ 2.46	$ 3.80	$ 4.06	$ 3.60	$ 3.65	$ 4.51
DPS (on average common shares	$ 1.36	$ 1.36	$ 1.48	$ 1.70	$ 1.76	$ 1.76	$ 1.96
Payout ratio (DPS/EPS)*	69.4%	55.3%	38.9%	41.8%	48.9%	48.2%	43.5%
Total retained earnings	$ 7,041.2	$ 7,426.1	$ 8,231.3	$ 9,038.6	$ 9,681.4	$10,367.6	$11,319.6
Cash balance	$ 1,170.7	$ 1,307.6	$ 1,502.5	$ 1,765.0	$ 2,357.2	$ 2,984.4	$ 3,235.0

*DPS (dividends per share)/EPS (earnings per share).

d. Assume that if Mr. Jackson's proposal were adopted, next year's dividend would be zero but earning growth would rise to 14 percent. What will be the expected return to the shareholders (assuming the other factors are held constant)?

e. Is the size of the capital budget limited by the amount of net income, as Mr. Jackson implies? What is the maximum size that the capital budget can be in 2002 without selling assets or seeking outside financing?

f. Mr. Jackson says the cost of the outside financing is more expensive than the cost of internal financing due to the flotation costs charged by investment dealers. Given the data you have, what would you say is the firm's cost of internal equity financing?

g. Assume Montgomery can sell bonds priced to yield 13 percent. What is the firm's after-tax cost of debt? (The tax rate is 25 percent.)

h. Given the cost of debt and the cost of internal equity financing, why doesn't Montgomery just borrow the total amount needed to fund the capital budget and the dividend as well?

i. Do you go along with Mr. Autry's comment that it's what the shareholders want not their total rate of return, that counts? Why or why not?

j. Barbara Reynolds suggests that if cash is needed for the capital budget, a stock dividend could be substituted for the cash dividend. Do you agree? How do you think the shareholders would react? Regardless of their reaction, is the stock dividend an equivalent substitute for the cash dividend?

k. After all is said and done, do you think the firm's dividend policy matters? If so, what do you think Montgomery's policy should be?

TABLE 2

Selected financial data, other retain chains

	1996	1997	1998	1999	2000	2001	2002
Ears Department Stores:							
EPS	$ 0.69	$ 0.93	$ 1.38	$ 1.82	$ 2.29	$ 2.35	$ 2.50
DPS	$ 0.05	$ 0.05	$ 0.08	$ 0.09	$ 0.10	$ 0.12	$ 0.13
Payout ratio	7.2%	5.4%	5.8%	4.9%	4.4%	5.1%	5.2%
The Lake:							
EPS	$ 0.38	$ 0.61	$ 0.81	$ 1.10	$ 0.95	$ 0.23	$ 0.30
DPS	$ 0.09	$ 0.11	$ 0.13	$ 0.17	$ 0.20	$ 0.20	$ 0.20
Payout ratio	23.7%	18.0%	16.0%	15%	21.1%	87.0%	66.7%
Price One Inc.:							
EPS	$ 0.10	$ 0.19	$ 0.37	$ 0.51	$ 0.80	$ 1.21	$ 1.40
DPS	$ 0.01	$ 0.02	$ 0.04	$ 0.08	$ 0.11	$ 0.16	$ 0.24
Payout ratio	10.0%	10.5%	10.8%	15.7%	13.8%	13.2%	17.1%
Ureka:							
EPS	$ 0.35	$ 0.38	$ 0.54	$ 0.55	$ 0.66	$ 0.91	$ 1.10
DPS	$ 0.06	$ 0.06	$ 0.07	$ 0.10	$ 0.11	$ 0.13	$ 0.18
Payout ratio	17.1%	15.8%	13.0%	18.2%	16.7%	14.3%	16.4%
Sporty:							
EPS	$ 2.75	$ 2.94	$ 3.13	$ 2.91	$ 2.66	$ 3.53	$ 4.70
DPS	$ 0.92	$ 1.00	$ 1.08	$ 1.18	$ 1.18	$ 1.24	$ 1.48
Payout ratio	33.5%	34.0%	34.5%	40.5%	44.4%	35.1%	31.5%
National Wheels:							
EPS	$ 0.16	$ 0.23	$ 0.35	$ 0.48	$ 0.58	$ 0.80	$ 1.10
DPS	$ 0.02	$ 0.02	$ 0.04	$ 0.05	$ 0.07	$ 0.09	$ 0.12
Payout ratio	12.5%	8.7%	11.4%	10.4%	12.1%	11.3%	10.9%

Note: DPS (refers to dividends per share; EPS refers to earnings per share.

Selected References

Carroll, Thomas J. "The Information Content of Quarterly Dividend Changes." *Journal of Accounting, Auditing and Finance* 10 (Spring 1995), pp. 293–317.

Conroy, Robert M., and Robert S. Harris. "Stock Splits and Information: The Role of Share Price." *Financial Management* 28 (Autumn 1999), pp. 28–40.

De Angelo, Harry, Linda De Angelo, and Douglas J. Skinner. "Dividends and Losses." *Journal of Finance* 47 (December 1992), pp. 1837–63.

Denwenter, Kathryn, and Vincent Warther. "Dividends, Asymmetric Information, and Agency Conflicts: Evidence from a Comparison of the Dividend Policies of Japanese and U.S. Firms." *Journal of Finance* 53 (June 1998), pp. 879–904.

Dhillon, Upinder S., and Herb Johnson. "The Effect of Dividend Changes on Stock and Bond Prices." *Journal of Finance* 49 (March 1994), pp. 281–89.

Grullon, Gustavo, and David Ikenberry. "What Do We Know about Stock Repurchases." *Journal of Applied Corporate Finance* 13 (Spring 2000), pp. 31–51.

Lintner, John. "Distribution of Income of Corporations among Dividends, Retained Earnings, and Taxes." *American Economic Review* 46 (May 1956), pp. 97–113.

Michaely, Roni, Richard H. Thaler, and Kent L. Womack. "Price Reactions to Dividend Initiations and Omissions: Overreaction or Drift?" *Journal of Finance* 50 (June 1995), pp. 573–608.

Moh'd, Mahmoud A., Larry G. Perry, and James N. Rimbey. "An Investigation of the Dynamic Relationship between Agency Theory and Dividend Policy." *Financial Review* 30 (May 1995), pp. 367–85.

Rozeff, Michael S. "Stock Splits: Evidence from Mutual Funds." *Journal of Finance* 53 (February 1998), pp. 335–49.

Wu, Chunci, and Xu-Ming Wang. "The Predictive Ability of Dividend and Earnings Yields for Long-Term Stock Returns." *Financial Review* 36 (May 2000), pp. 97–124.

CHAPTER | NINETEEN

19

Derivatives, Convertibles, and Warrants

LEARNING | OBJECTIVES

1. Distinguish between and outline the uses of forwards, futures, and options.
2. Calculate the hedge on futures and the value of call and put options.
3. Describe the securities offered by a corporation that are convertible into common shares at the option of the investor and are a means of raising funds.
4. Outline the benefits of a convertible security, including a fixed rate of return and the potential for capital appreciation.
5. Calculate the conversion value of a convertible security.
6. Describe warrants and compare them to convertible securities.
7. Calculate the intrinsic value and the speculative premium on a warrant.
8. Demonstrate how convertible securities and warrants affect earnings per share as reported on the income statement.

Finance is the study of value. The expected cash flows and the risks associated with those cash flows determine the value of an asset. Throughout the history of trade and commerce there have been attempts to control the cash flows and the risks faced by an enterprise in an uncertain world. Often contracts, establishing the price of commodities before their future exchange, were used to better facilitate the trading of goods and services. These contracts were the beginning of what we today call derivatives. **Derivatives** give the holder the right to buy or sell a particular commodity or asset, at an established price, at some time in the future. The price is guaranteed.

Prices of commodities, foreign exchange, and interest rates have been particularly volatile in recent history. Changing prices lead to a great deal of uncertainty in the trading of goods and services. Derivatives can help to lessen the uncertainty in a trade relationship. Hedging or risk reduction occurs because a derivative allows a purchaser to lock in a price before the actual transaction takes place. The benefit of risk reduction is that it will likely encourage increased trade.

The ultimate value of these financial assets, securities, or contracts comes from or is "derived" from the particular asset to which they lay claim. The right to buy or sell a particular asset (a derivative) becomes more or less valuable as the asset changes in price. Derivatives, which have a limited life, vary in price to a far greater extent than the particular asset from which they derive their value. In recent years derivatives have been one of the most highly publicized areas of finance because of the spectacular losses experienced by some speculators. These speculators in their use of derivatives have increased their expected return (loss), but also the risk of their investments. Many, however, do not use derivatives to increase risks and potential rewards. If deployed properly, derivatives can be used to reduce the risk and the pattern of cash flows that companies experience from changes in exchange rates, interest rates, commodity prices, and other assets.

Today there are numerous financial markets that offer for sale a wide variety of contracts to purchase or sell various assets at a predetermined and fixed price at some time in the future. The contracts sold in these financial markets are forwards, futures, and options. These contracts convey the right to purchase or sell such things as currencies, Treasury bills, market indexes, crude oil, orange juice, and shares in corporations. Financial managers have always looked for ways to control their risks. The market has been able to respond with new financial instruments to meet the needs of financial managers.

In the inflation/disinflation, volatile interest-rate and exchange-rate period of the last few decades, investors have also looked for investment options providing downside protection as well as capital appreciation potential. Corporations, to satisfy investor demands, have issued derivatives, usually options, to raise money for corporate endeavors. Convertible securities, warrants, and rights (studied in Chapter 17) are options that offer the investor in these securities the ability to purchase, or to convert to, common shares of the corporation. These innovative securities give the investor the right to obtain common shares at a fixed (exercise) price, and this right becomes valuable when the market price of the shares exceeds the fixed price. Convertibles, rights, and warrants trade in organized auction and over-the-counter markets.

Convertibles, warrants, and rights take on many of the same characteristics as these derivatives, as they are valued similarly, and they also trade in financial markets. Options issued by corporations are different from derivatives because their purpose is to raise funds for the corporation in an innovative way. The other derivatives are offered in financial markets as side bets on the future price direction of certain assets and have no direct influence on the valuation of a corporation. These derivatives, known as forwards, futures, and options, are not issued by the corporation, but by the market itself to facilitate the altering of the cash flows and risks faced in business transactions.

In this chapter we will very briefly explore derivatives for risk reduction purposes, and then examine convertible securities and warrants issued by corporations.

Forwards

The most basic of derivative contracts are forwards, which have been around since Greek and Roman times. **Forwards** are customized contracts that fix the price of some commodity for delivery at a specified place and a specified time in the future. These contracts are customized because the amount of the contract and the date of delivery (known as the settlement date) are negotiated between the two parties to the contract. These derivatives are not liquid and are not traded on exchanges because of their specific nature.

The Derivatives Market

The Bank of International Settlements reports on the world derivatives market in the OTC (over-the-counter) market and on organized exchanges from the G-10 countries. For 2001, the turnover of derivatives contracts through organized exchanges totalled almost U.S.$600 trillion, with derivative contracts outstanding in June 2001 reaching a value of about U.S.$24 trillion. The over-the-counter market at the same time had outstanding derivatives approaching U.S.$100 trillion. The market is huge! The market is dominated by interest rate contracts, although currency contracts are quite significant in the over-the-counter market.

Organized exchanges (24%)	Futures 40%	Interest rate contracts		92%
	Options 60%	Currency contracts		1%
		Index contracts		7%
OTC markets (76%)	Interest rate contracts	68%	(34% U.S.$, 33% euros)	
	Currency contracts	17%	(90% in U.S.$)	
	Equities contracts	2%		
	Commodities contracts	1%		
	Other	12%		

Some spectacular losses have occurred in the derivatives markets resulting from the speculation by "rogue" traders on the direction of various markets. On behalf of Barings Bank, which eventually failed, Nick Leeson lost $1.4 billion on options and futures derived from the value of the Nikkei (Tokyo Stock Exchange) index. Sumitomo Corporation lost at least $2.4 billion, acknowledged in mid-1996, from purchases of derivatives in the copper market. Orange County, California, had to declare bankruptcy when its treasurer speculated in interest rate derivatives and lost over $1 billion. The treasurer had bet that interest rates would go down. The irony is that if the same strategy had been employed only one year later, Orange County would have made a fortune and the treasurer would be a "genius."

In 1998, Long-Term Capital Management LP was bailed out by The Federal Reserve Bank. that feared its failure might destabilize the world's financial markets. Long-Term Capital was known as a hedge fund, although it apparently did not "hedge" because it took aggressive positions in derivative instruments based on the bond markets. On a capital base of about $4 billion, Long-Term Capital had apparently borrowed well over $100 billion to speculate in interest rate derivatives. The fund's speculation was proved wrong. The banks invested over $3.5 billion for 90 percent of the fund. It is interesting that one of the directors of Long-Term Capital was Myron Scholes, the Nobel laureate, who developed the famous option-pricing model.

Apparently the collapse of Enron in late 2001 was partially due to its speculation in the derivatives market for energy and weather futures.

In Canada, our largest noteworthy loss on derivatives has been that of the Ukrainian (Fort William) Credit Union of Thunder Bay. The credit union suffered $2 million in losses on Government of Canada bond derivatives, forcing its closure.

Again, these are dramatic stories and should not override the value that derivatives can bring in risk reduction if deployed properly. It is worth remembering that derivatives are a zero-sum game. On the other side of the ledger from those who have suffered large losses are those who have gained the same large amounts.

FINANCE IN ACTION

Q1 Why would you think the $U.S. dominates foreign exchange contracts, while interest rate contracts are equally split between euros and the U.S. dollar?

www.bis.org

The advantage of forward contracts to the two parties involved is that by fixing the price and date for future delivery of a commodity they have removed a large portion of the uncertainty surrounding a future transaction. With forwards, no payment is due until the future agreed-upon date. In some cases a good-faith deposit, or other similar security, is required at the time the contract is written.

FINANCE IN ACTION

Derivatives for Bob's Farming Operation

Bob farms in Southern Alberta, growing about 500,000 bushels of corn each year. Most of his crop is sold to the distilleries in Lethbridge to produce liquor. With a little bit of flavouring, distilled corn can produce rum, rye, gin, and all our favourite drinks. There are many risks in farming besides the weather. Bob knows fairly closely his costs of growing the corn, but with the volatile grain markets he is unsure what his crop will earn when sold for cash in the fall.

An average acre in Southern Alberta with heavy irrigation produces about 85 bushels of corn per acre compared to over 200 in Iowa, where little irrigation or fertilization is required. It's tough competition! Iowa, of course, sets the standard, and corn is bought and sold based on U.S. dollars. Corn also is the basis for the pricing of the other grains. Bob may employ one of several techniques to reduce the risk he faces on the price of his corn crop. He may employ forwards, futures, options, and/or insurance programs.

Today's derivative markets trace their beginnings to Chicago. In the middle of the 18th century the produce from the American Midwest passed through Chicago on its way to the rest of the world. In the fall, vast amounts of grain and other produce arrived at the port for shipment all at once. Prices fell drastically with the huge supply, and later jumped when the supply was minimal. The volatility in prices was unsettling to both the producers and users of the produce. An opportunity was presented to the merchants of Chicago to develop the city as an important centre. By introducing forward contracts, they could fix the price that farmers would receive for their produce and the price users of the produce would be required to pay. Increased trade would be encouraged when both parties could reliably predict their revenues and costs based on a fixed price. The merchants of Chicago would gain from introducing the forwards, guaranteeing the contracts, and by building storage facilities. Chicago has since evolved into the world's largest exchange for futures and options.

Perhaps the most common forward market in Canada is the market for currencies provided by banks. Over 40 percent of Canada's GDP is based on foreign trade, and therefore dealing in foreign currencies is a major factor in many businesses. Foreign currency hedging with forwards, futures, and options is illustrated in Chapter 21.

To illustrate the use of a forward we will employ the Finance in Action box entitled "Derivatives for Bob's Farming Operation." A forward will be used to hedge Bob's risk of price fluctuations on his corn crop. In early May, as Bob sows his crop, he agrees to sell his corn to a Lethbridge distiller, at an agreed price and for September delivery. The agreed price is \$2.29 a bushel to be paid by the distillery on delivery in September. Bob could wait until September, but is exposed to a fair amount of uncertainty (or risk) as to the price of corn at that time. Based on corn prices over the last year, corn could sell for \$2.90 a bushel, which would be fortunate, or it could sell for \$2.00, which would be unfortunate. In May corn sells for \$2.25 in the cash market.

	Corn price (\$U.S.)	Cash received
Forward		
Agreed delivery of 500,000 bushels	\$2.29	U.S.\$1,145,000 guaranteed
Could be	2.90	U.S.\$1,450,000 possible
or	2.00	U.S.\$1,000,000 possible

FINANCE IN ACTION

A Brief History of Derivatives

Ancient Greece, Rome, and medieval trade fairs
These early periods showed evidence of forward contracting for the delivery of commodities, but lacked standardization of contracts and an active marketplace.

15th century — London, Bruges, Antwerp, Amsterdam trading centres
Forward contracts in use.

1571 — Royal Exchange of London (London International Financial Futures and Options Exchange)
Designated as a commodity exchange.

1634–38 — Tulip Bulb Craze
Call options were available on tulip bulbs. For a premium at about 20 percent of current prices, an option holder had the right to purchase next year's bulbs at today's prices.

1848 — Chicago Board of Trade/Chicago Board Option Exchange
Formed by local grain merchants, this was a marketplace to sell commodities and reduce the volatility of commodity prices. This prompted investment in storage facilities and transportation networks. Performance bonds (margins) with third parties were established to overcome defaults on forward contracts. Warehouse receipts were issued for the delivery of commodities by a clearing office to satisfy forward contracts. Thereafter, forward contracts could be settled through the clearing office by buying and selling contracts for the same month.

1869 — Royal Exchange of London
The Suez Canal was completed, reducing the shipping and delivery times from Malaya and Chile to three months. The forward contract on tin was set at three months.

1887 — Winnipeg Grain and Produce Exchange (Winnipeg Commodity Exchange, WCE)
Futures contracts for farm produce made available.

1971 — International Money Market (IMM) (part of CME)
Foreign currency futures introduced in response to freely floating exchange rates.

1973 — Black-Scholes model for European call and put options introduced.

1973 — Chicago Board Options Exchange (CBOE)
Standardized listed options on stocks. World's largest options exchange; options on over 1,200 widely traded stocks.

1974 — Montreal Stock Exchange (ME)
Introduces stock options to Canada; introduces interest rate futures in 1979.

1975 — Chicago Board of Trade (CBOT)
Interest rate futures introduced in response to volatile interest rates.

1980 — Toronto Futures Exchange
Opened as division of the Toronto Stock Exchange (TSX).

1981 — Chicago Board of Trade (CBOT)
Eurodollar future introduced as first cash settled contract, with offset based on the market value of an index or spot commodity.

1982 — Kansas City Board of Trade
Stock index futures introduced on Value Line Index.

1983 — New York Mercantile Exchange (NYMEX)
Stock index futures introduced.

1984 — Chicago Board Options Exchange (CBOE)
Options available on stock indexes, followed by interest rate options in 1989, LEAPS (long-term options) in 1990, and FLEX available (Flexible exchange options on indices) in 1993.

1999 — Chicago Mercantile Exchange (CME)
Temperature-related futures (HDD, CDD) are announced.

2000 — CME demutualizes

www.cboe.com

www.tsx.ca

www.me.org

www.cme.com

www.wce.mb.ca

www.liffe.com

By entering into a forward contract with the distillery, Bob has the responsibility to deliver 500,000 bushels of corn in September and in return will receive U.S.$1,145,000 regardless of the price of corn at that time. The advantage of entering into the forward contract is that Bob knows exactly what his revenues will be and can determine if it is worth planting his crop. By waiting to sell the corn in September, Bob is exposed to a great deal of uncertainty. Forward contracts are often customized as to the exact amount and exact date required by the two parties. This exact matching of Bob's crop commodity (asset) with a forward contract (liability) is known as hedging. Perfect hedges are possible in the forward market, but are difficult to achieve in future markets.

Forward contracts can be executed on any commodity, but the most common are foreign exchange or interest rate contracts. Usually these are contracted with financial institutions, which act as brokers. The financial institution enters into a forward contract with one party to buy, let us say, a given amount of foreign currency at an agreed future date. Simultaneously the financial institution enters into another forward contract to sell a similar amount of foreign currency to another party, also at that future date. The financial institution has little risk and is hedged. Moreover, it likely makes a profit by buying at one price and selling at a higher price.

Futures

Chicago Mercantile Exchange
www.cme.com

Futures are similar to forward contracts, except that they are available through financial markets. **Futures** are standardized contracts that fix the price of some commodity for delivery at a specified place and a specified time in the future. Futures are generally available on commodities, interest rates, market indexes, and currencies. They allow for flexibility in delivery, as the underlying asset can be delivered any time during the month of expiry. The standardization of the contract produces contracts that are available only in set amounts or multiples thereof, only for certain months, and may require delivery of a specific quality of asset. For example, on the Chicago Mercantile Exchange the Canadian dollar is available only in multiples of $100,000 and only for the months of March, June, September, and December. In dealing in commodities such as wheat, only a specified grade of wheat is acceptable for delivery. With bond futures, the specified underlying asset is a bond of a minimum given maturity.

Futures exchanges trace their modern development to the middle of the 19th century. The forward markets at the Royal Exchange of London and the Chicago Board of Trade began to develop standardized contracts. These became known as futures. The three-month contract, standard on all futures exchanges today, was instituted at the Royal Exchange in 1869. The reason for the three-month period was the result of the opening of the Suez Canal. Shipping times from suppliers throughout the British Empire now became reliable and achievable in less than three months.

The Chicago Board of Trade established performance bonds (margins), held by third parties, to overcome the defaults that often occurred on forward contracts. To satisfy contract deliveries, a seller had to deliver the underlying asset to a warehouse, and a receipt was issued by a clearing office. When this practice was well established, contracts could be settled through the clearing office by buying and selling contracts for the same month. An actual physical exchange of the asset did not have to take place! Today over 90 percent of futures contracts are satisfied with no actual delivery of the asset to the futures exchange. The contract is closed out in Chicago and the actual delivery of the underlying asset occurs locally. The standardization of contracts and the establishment of procedures have ensured reliable markets with liquidity where traders can establish future prices for assets.

To examine how a futures contract works, let us return to our example of Bob, the farmer in Southern Alberta, who sells his corn crop of 500,000 bushels each fall. Bob sold his corn crop to a Lethbridge distiller by way of a forward contract. However, let us suppose that Bob does not have a firm contract and needs to sell his corn crop to the general market.

With standardized futures contracts, there is unlikely to be one that exactly covers the amount of the underlying asset required or is deliverable on the exact date the asset is required or available. Futures expire on the third Friday of a given month, and it is usually best to select the future with the closest expiry date after the asset is required or available.

In our example, outlined below, a standardized contract happens to cover the underlying asset and delivery date completely, but that is rarely the case. The forward contract results are noted for comparison.

	Corn price ($U.S.)	Cash received
Forward (from previous section)		
Agreed delivery of 500,000 bushels	$2.29	U.S.$1,145,000 guaranteed
In September		
Sell corn at		
Cash (spot) rate	2.00	U.S.$1,000,000
Close out future		
Future (Sept. expiry)		
Sold at	2.28	U.S.$1,140,000
Purchase at	2.02	U.S.$1,010,000
Gain (loss) on future	0.26	U.S.$ 130,000
Total revenues with cash market and future		**U.S.$1,130,000**

In May, through the Chicago Board of Trade Futures Exchange, Bob purchases a contract to sell corn at an agreed price of U.S.$2.28 a bushel for 500,000 bushels. The futures market allows a participant to buy (go long) or to sell (go short) at the quoted future price. Bob has gone short and is obligated to deliver 500,000 bushels of corn by September or close out his contract. With the forward contract Bob is locked in, but the future allows Bob to sell the contract back to the market before it expires.

Chicago Board of Trade
www.cbot.com

In September Bob will deliver his corn to a local buyer, as he does not want to deliver his corn to Chicago. He will receive the September cash price, which in our example is U.S.$2.00 a bushel. This is less than his expectation of $2.28 based on the futures contract that he purchased in May. However, the September futures contract is trading at U.S.$2.02 in Chicago when it is September. Since Bob already has a future contract to sell at $2.28, he now purchases a contract to buy at $2.02. The contracts now offset each other, and the market credits Bob with the gain or loss. In this example, Bob has earned $130,000, which can be added to monies received in the cash market for total revenues of U.S.$1,130,000.

Bob hasn't done as well as in the forward market, because of transportation cost considerations between Chicago and Southern Alberta. This is why the future contract price in Chicago and the cash price in Alberta are slightly different in September. The key to the future contract is that the price of corn is locked in close to a predicted price and there will be no large surprises. The futures market also gives participants the liquidity to move out of a contractual position at their convenience, at prices that are competitively determined. If corn had moved in the opposite direction in this example, the cash market would have presented a gain to Bob, but he would have suffered a loss on the future contract.

When a futures contract is purchased, a small margin deposit is required. This is a small percentage of the overall contract amount such as 5 percent. Each day, as the future contract moves in price, the profit or loss is marked to market. This means that the margin deposit is debited or credited. If the margin deposit begins to be depleted, a further margin deposit may be required. In Bob's case he contracted to sell at U.S.$2.28 a bushel. If the September contract moved to $2.30, Bob is out some money and $10,000 ($0.02 × 500,000) will be debited from his margin account.

This futures example does not identify an important risk to Bob. What would happen in a bad crop year if Bob is only able to produce 167,000 bushels of corn, a worst-case scenario? Bob will have to purchase 333,000 bushels of corn in the market to deliver under his contract or close out the contract. It is likely that if Bob has had a crop failure there has been a general failure, and corn prices will be sky high. Purchasing the corn in the cash market will be very expensive, or alternatively closing out the futures contract, by purchasing a contract to buy, will incur a large loss. How can Bob protect against this possible outcome? In May Bob could have purchased options to buy 333,000 bushels of corn. This would act as insurance.

Options

Although options have been in existence for a long time, their modern development on financial exchanges can also be traced to the middle of the 19th century. Options are similar to futures. **Options** are standardized contracts that fix the price of some commodity for delivery at a specified place and a specified time in the future. Unlike futures and forwards, options can expire. The holder of an option can exercise the option, sell it, or let it expire. In 1973 the Black-Scholes model for pricing European call and put options was introduced, and the Chicago Board Options Exchange (CBOE) listed standardized options on stocks. Today there are options available on stocks, market indexes, currencies, interest rates, and numerous commodities.

Chicago Board of Options Exchange www.cboe.com

There are some key terms to understanding options:

- *Call option* gives the holder the right to *buy* an underlying asset at a preset price.
- *Put option* gives the holder the right to *sell* an underlying asset.
- *Underlying asset* is the commodity, currency, bond, stock, or other asset that is deliverable under the option contract.
- *Exercise or strike price* is the preset price at which the underlying security can be bought or sold, based on the price contracted for under the option. The exercise price is not the same as the current market price of the underlying asset.
- *Premium* is the price at which an option is bought or sold in the market. If you purchase an option, the price you pay is called a premium.
- *Intrinsic value* is the minimum value of an option.

- *Speculative (time value) premium* is the difference between the market price of an option (premium) and its intrinsic value.

As an example, we might purchase a call (put) option, which gives us the right to buy (sell) 5,000 bushels of corn (the underlying asset) at a fixed price of U.S.$2.30 (the exercise price) any time until the third Friday in September. This price would be set even if corn fell to U.S.$1.60 or rose to U.S.$3.00 in the cash markets. For this option we might pay $0.14 a bushel or U.S.$700 ($0.14 × 5,000 bushels). The U.S.$700 is called the premium. When we purchase an option, another party sells it. The seller of an option is called the writer and is under an obligation, if the option is exercised.

- *Call option writer* is obligated to *sell* the underlying asset, at the preset price, to the option holder if the option is exercised.
- *Put option writer* is obligated to *buy* the underlying asset, at the preset price, from the option holder if the option is exercised.

Call Option

Let us examine a **call option** on the shares of a company. In February shares in Walter P. Company trade at $25.00. Call options are available on organized exchanges independent of the company shares. On one such exchange, a May call option on Walter P. Company is being sold, with an exercise price of $24.00. This gives the holder the right to *buy* Walter P. Company shares at the exercise price of $24.00 per share up to May. One call option gives the right to buy one share, but options are usually purchased in multiples of one hundred. There is no obligation to buy.

This call option would have a minimum or intrinsic value of $1.00 ($25.00 − $24.00), because at a minimum we can exercise the option to buy shares worth $25.00 for only $24.00. Experience tells us that options almost always trade above the intrinsic value by a speculative premium. Therefore, in our example the option's market price or premium is $2.50 (picked arbitrarily for this example). The speculative premium is $1.50 ($2.50 − $1.00). For $2.50 the purchaser of the call option can purchase a share of Walter P. Company for $24.00 until May.

The call option pricing relationships are illustrated in Figure 19–1 on the next page. The illustration shows that the actual market price of the option (the premium) is greater than the intrinsic value at all values. Also, the intrinsic value is zero until the market price of the underlying share rises above the exercise price of $24.00.

		Share Price Increases to	Gain
Share price	$25.00	$50.00	$\frac{\$50.00 - \$25.00}{\$25.00}$ = 100%
Call option @ $24.00 for May			
Intrinsic value of the option	$25.00 − $24.00 = $ 1.00	$50.00 − $24.00 = $26.00	
Speculative premium	$ 1.50	$ 0.75 (arbitrary pick)	
Premium (market price of call)	$ 2.50	$26.75	$\frac{\$26.75 - \$2.50}{\$2.50}$ = 970%

		Share Price Decreases to	Loss
Shares	$25.00	$12.50	$\frac{\$12.50 - \$25.00}{\$25.00}$ = −50%
Call option @ $24.00 for May		$12.50 − $24.00 = $ 0.00	
Speculative premium		$ 0.25 (arbitrary pick)	
Premium (market price of call)	$ 2.50	$ 0.25	$\frac{\$0.25 - \$2.50}{\$2.50}$ = −90%

In the illustration above, we see what can happen as the underlying share price moves up or down. If the share price moves up to $50.00, the call option on the share at the fixed price of $24.00 will be worth $26.75, including the speculative premium. However, if the share price moves down, the option almost becomes worthless. The potential gain or loss on the call option is much greater than the gain or loss on the shares by themselves. Figure 19–1 also illustrates the relationships in this example.

The size of a speculative premium in the markets will be determined by:

1. *The time to expiry of the option.* A longer time to expiry gives a greater time for the underlying asset to rise in price.
2. *The volatility of the underlying share (asset).* An asset that has larger price changes stands a greater chance of having a significant price increase. This has value to the option investor.

FIGURE 19–1

Market price relationships for a call option

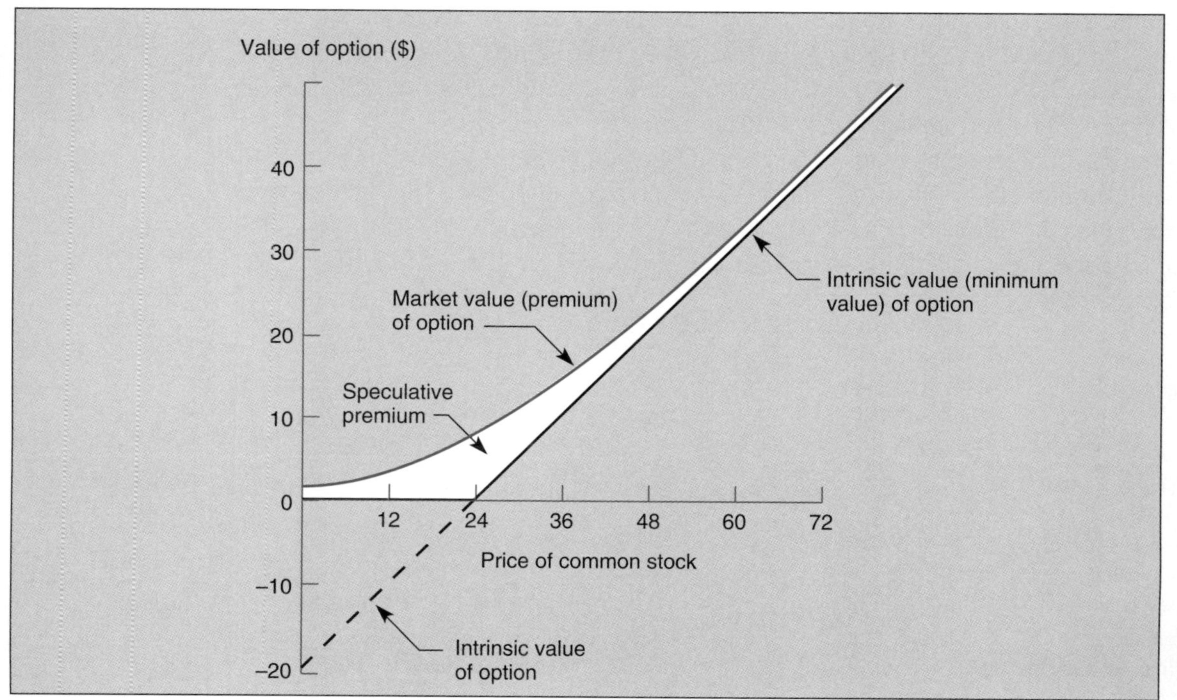

3. *The opportunity cost of funds.* At a higher opportunity cost of funds it is more advantageous for an investor to be holding the option, at a lower cash outlay, than the actual share. This has value to the option investor.

When an investor sees value in a characteristic of an option, the speculative premium will increase. The relationships between intrinsic value, market value of an option, and the underlying share (asset) value are illustrated in Figure 19–1. The actual market price of an option is always greater than the intrinsic value. The intrinsic value is zero until the market price of the underlying shares rises above the exercise price of $24.00.

Put Option

Now let us examine a **put option** on the stock of Walter P. Company. Shares in Walter P. Company in February trade at $25.00. On organized exchanges independent of the company shares, a May put option is available at the exercise price of $27.00. This gives the holder the right to *sell* Walter P. Company shares at an exercise price of $27.00 per share up to May. There is no obligation to sell.

This put option would have a minimum or intrinsic value of $2.00 ($27.00 − $25.00), because we can exercise the option to sell shares at $27.00 that are only worth $25.00. Experience again tells us that options almost always trade above the intrinsic value by a speculative premium. Therefore, in our example the option's market price is $3.00 (picked arbitrarily for this example). The speculative premium is $1.00. For $3.00 the purchaser of the put option can sell a share of Walter P. Company for $27.00 until May.

The put option pricing relationships are illustrated in Figure 19–2. The illustration shows that the actual market price of the option (the premium) is greater than its intrinsic value at all values. Also, the intrinsic value is zero until the market price of the underlying share falls below the exercise price of $27.00.

FIGURE 19–2
Market price relationships for a put option

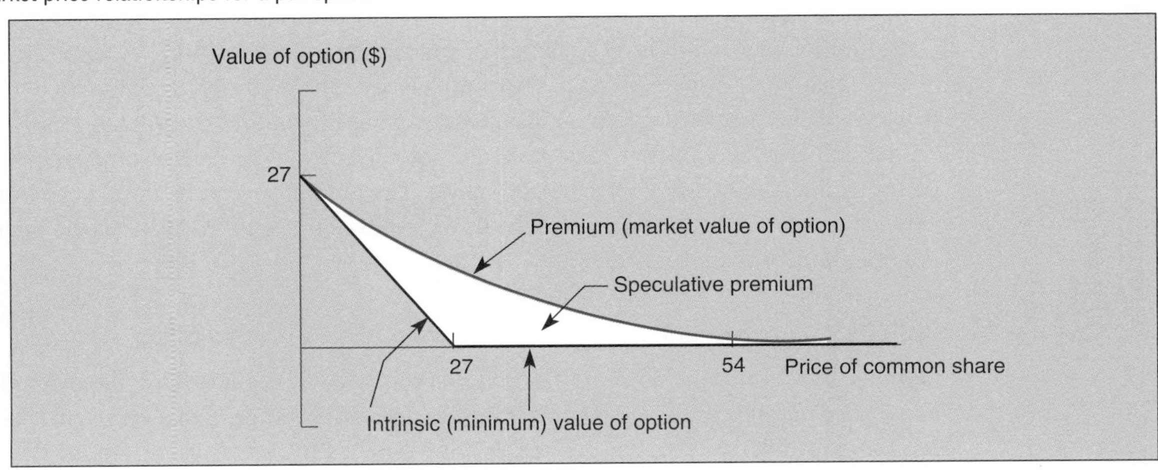

		Share Price Increases to	Gain
Share price	$25.00	$50.00	($50.00 − $25.00) / $25.00 = 100%
Put option @ $27.00 for May			
Intrinsic value of the option	$27.00 − $25.00 = $ 2.00	$27.00 − $50.00 = $ 0.00	
Speculative premium	$ 1.00	$ 0.25 (arbitrary pick)	
Premium (market price of put)	$ 3.00	$ 0.25	($0.25 − $3.00) / $3.00 = −92%
		Share Price Decreases to	**Loss**
Share	$25.00	$12.50	($12.50 − $25.00) / $25.00 = −50%
Put option @ $27.00 for May		$27.00 − $12.50 = $14.50	
Speculative premium		$ 0.50 (arbitrary pick)	
Premium (market price of put)	$ 3.00	$15.00	($15.00 − $3.00) / $3.00 = 400%

In the illustration, we see what can happen as the underlying share price moves up or down. If the share price moves down to $12.50, the put option on the share at the fixed price of $27.00 will be worth $15.00, including the speculative premium. However, if the share price moves up to $50.00, the option almost becomes worthless because of the put option holder's right to sell a $50.00 share at $27.00.

The size of a speculative premium will be determined, as it was for call options, by the time to expiry of the option, the volatility of the underlying share (asset), and the opportunity cost of funds. As the first two factors increase, so will the speculative premium on a put option. The speculative premium of a put option will fall as the opportunity cost increases.

Put options are often used to hedge or reduce the risk of holding an asset. In the above example, if a share of Walter P. Company were held as well as put, notice what happens. If the share price goes up, the investor gains big on the shares, but loses $2.75 on the put. However, if the share price goes down, the loss of $12.50 on the share is offset by the gain of $12.00 on the put option. The put option can be thought of as insurance protecting against a drop in the price of the stock, with the price of the option the premium on the insurance.

Options versus Futures

Options and futures are sold in financial markets and, as suggested by the examples above, can produce spectacular gains or losses through leverage. However, we can also see that these derivatives can reduce the risk one has to face if used properly. Both

Weather Derivatives

Bombardier, the manufacturer of snowmobiles, purchases snowfall options each winter season from one of several companies that offer these options. The option pays off if the snowfall in a designated area falls below an agreed level. Bombardier in turn can offer rebates to its buyers of Ski-Doos if the snowfall in their city falls below some average of the last several years. Bombardier can then sell more snowmobiles.

In 1999 the Chicago Mercantile Exchange began offering temperature-related futures based on the temperature being above or below a given value. Details on weather futures can be found at the CME web site: www.cme.com/products/index/weather/products_index_weather.cfm

Warm temperatures, for example, can have an effect on ski areas, the revenues generated by utility companies, or if the temperatures are quite warm, the costs of running air conditioners. Likewise, cool temperatures can have an effect on business costs. Weather options and futures can reduce the risks companies face if weather conditions are different from the expected. These derivatives can compensate for losses incurred that result from the abnormal weather.

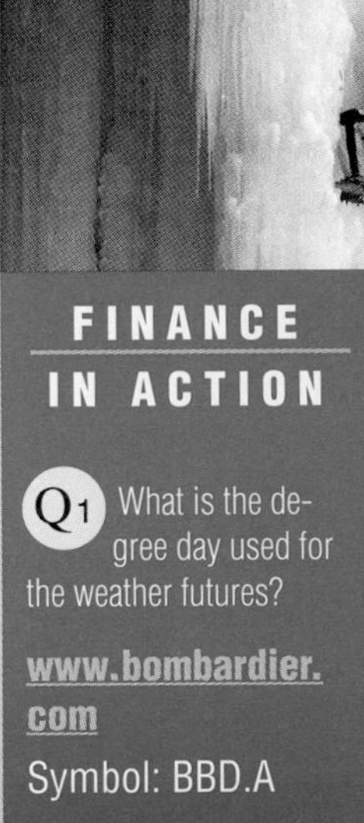

FINANCE IN ACTION

Q1 What is the degree day used for the weather futures?

www.bombardier.com

Symbol: BBD.A

these derivatives have a limited life, are standardized, and are guaranteed by the market acting as a clearinghouse. Differences relate to the pattern of cash flows experienced. Options require a larger up-front payment, with no further payments unless the option is exercised. Futures require a small margin deposit, which is credited or debited (marked to market) daily as the current futures price moves up or down from the original contracted future price. Futures can have delivery only in the delivery month, but options can have delivery anytime. Options are probably most useful when used in conjunction with a potential business contract. If the contract falls through, the option does not have to be exercised. For example, a corporation might be bidding on a contract in France. If the contract is awarded, the corporation may require Euros to pay for wages, supplies, and equipment. A currency option gives the corporation the ability to lock in an exchange rate, without the obligation in case it is not successful in winning the contract.

Options Issued by Corporations

To raise capital for the corporation, options are sometimes issued, as they may better meet the investment objectives of securities investors. Rights, convertible securities, and warrants are types of options issued by corporations, and they confer on the holder the right to acquire shares in the corporation for a preset price and up to a preset date. Once these corporate options are issued they usually trade on organized or over-the-counter exchanges until their expiry. Their value is determined in much the same way as call options.

Convertible Securities

A **convertible security** is a bond or share of preferred stock that can be converted, at the option of the holder, into common stock. Thus, the owner has a fixed-income security that can be transferred to a common stock interest if and when the affairs of the firm indicate that such a conversion is desirable. For purposes of discussion we refer to convertible bonds (debentures), although the same principles apply to convertible preferred stock. These securities are sold by corporations to raise capital.

When a convertible debenture is initially issued, a **conversion ratio** to common stock is specified. The ratio indicates the number of shares of common stock to which the debenture may be converted. The conversion ratio may also be expressed as a **conversion price.** To arrive at the conversion price, we divide the face value of the bond by the conversion ratio.

$$\text{Face value} = \text{Conversion price} \times \text{Conversion ratio} \qquad (19\text{–}1)$$

The Williams Company

$10 million of convertible debentures
Maturity in 25 years
Coupon rate 6%
Current yield on pure bond (no conversion features) of similar risk is 8%.
Each $1,000 bond is convertible into 20 shares (conversion ratio) of common stock.
The conversion ratio is 20 and the conversion price is $50.

$1,000	=	20 × $50 (with Formula 19–1)	
Common share price	=	$45.00	
Conversion value	=	$45 × 20	= $900
Convertible debenture market price	=	$1,010	
Conversion premium	=	$1,010 − $900	= $110

Value of the Convertible Bond

As a first consideration in evaluating a convertible bond, we must examine the value of the conversion privilege. For the Williams Company with the common stock selling at $45.00 per share, the conversion value is $900. The bond will initially sell for close to par or face value ($1,000) in anticipation of future developments in the common stock and because interest payments are being received on the bonds. If the bond sells for $1,010 and a $900 conversion value, there is a $110 **conversion premium**, representing the dollar difference between market value and conversion value. The conversion premium generally is influenced by the expectations of future performance of the common stock. If investors are optimistic about the prospects of the common stock, the premium may be large.

If the price of the common stock really takes off and goes to $60.00 per share, the conversion privilege becomes quite valuable. The bonds, which are convertible into 20 shares, will go up to at least $1,200 and perhaps more. Note that you do not have to convert to common stock immediately, but may enjoy the movement of the convertible in concert with the common.

What happens if the common stock goes in the opposite direction? Assume that instead of going from $45.00 to $60.00, the common stock simply drops from $45.00 to $25.00. What will happen to the value of the convertible debenture? We know the value of a convertible bond will go down in response to the drop in the common stock, but will it fall all the way down to $500 (20 × $25.00 per share)? The answer is no, because the debenture still has value as an interest-bearing security. A pure or straight debt issue of similar maturity (25 years) and quality with an 8 percent yield has a

pure bond value of $785.18.[1] Thus, a convertible bond has a **floor value** but no upside limitations.[2] The price pattern for the convertible bond is depicted in Figure 19–3.

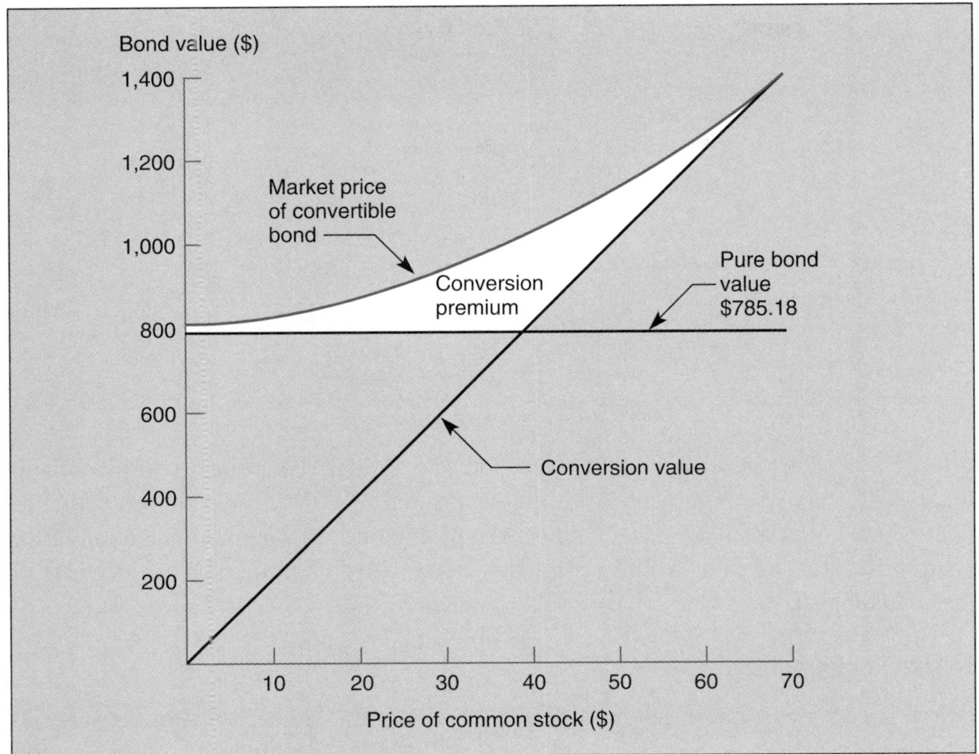

FIGURE 19–3
Price movement pattern for a convertible bond

We see the effect on the convertible bond price as the common stock price, shown along the horizontal axis, is assumed to change. Note that the floor value for the convertible is well above the conversion value when the common stock price is very low. As the common stock price moves to higher levels, the convertible bond moves in concert with the conversion value. Representative information on outstanding convertible debentures is presented in Table 19–1 on the next page.

Notice the variance in value among the convertible issues. The Inco and Noranda debentures are trading primarily as debentures with semiannual coupon payments. Their yield to maturity approximates the yield to maturity of similar-risk debentures that did not have the conversion feature. Inco's low share price produced a value of $499.30 if the debenture was converted to shares, and yet investors were willing to pay $1,000.00 for the convertible debenture because the issue had a coupon rate of 7.75 percent. Its value was primarily as a fixed-income security, as was the Noranda debenture.

George Weston
www.weston.ca

On the other hand, the George Weston issue was trading primarily as an equity security. If converted to shares, the bond would be worth $1,713.60. It traded in the market at $1,739.00. As a bond without the conversion feature, the Weston debenture

[1]Based on the discounting procedures of Chapter 10, with semiannual coupon payments.

[2]The floor value can change if interest rates in the market change. For now we assume they are constant.

TABLE 19–1

Pricing patterns for convertible debentures outstanding, March 2002

Issue; Coupon; Maturity	Rating	Conversion Value	Market Value	Yield to Maturity	Yield to Maturity on Bonds of Similar Risk and Maturity
George Weston					
3%					
June 2023	A	$1,713.60	$1,739.00	n.a.	6.93
Inco					
7.75%					
March 2016	BBB(low)	499.30	1,000.00	7.75	8.68
Noranda					
5%					
April 2007	BBB(high)	631.62	930.00	6.63	6.35

offered a negative yield to maturity, compared to similar-risk nonconvertible debentures that offered 6.93 percent. An investor also enjoyed the downside protection of contractual coupon payments and the benefit of any further capital appreciation in the share price. The investor would be unlikely to convert to common shares because of these dual benefits.

Is This Fool's Gold?

Have we repealed the old risk-return trade-off principle—the idea that to get superior returns we must take larger than normal risks? With convertible bonds, we appear to limit our risk while maximizing our return potential.

Although there is some truth to this statement, there are many qualifications. For example, once convertible debentures begin going up in value, say to $1,100 or $1,200, the downside protection becomes pretty meaningless. In the case of the Williams Company in our earlier example, the floor is at $785.18. An investor who bought the convertible bond at $1,200 would be exposed to $414.82 in potential losses (hardly adequate protection for a true risk averter). Also, if interest rates in the market rise, the floor price, or pure bond value, could fall, creating more downside risk.

A second drawback with convertible bonds is that the purchaser is invariably asked to accept below-market rates of interest on the debt instrument. The interest rate on convertibles is generally one-third below that for instruments in a similar risk class at time of issue. In the sophisticated environment of the bond and stock markets, one seldom gets an additional benefit without having to suffer a corresponding disadvantage.

Recall that the purchaser of a convertible bond pays a premium over the conversion value. For example, if a $1,000 bond were convertible into 20 shares of common at $45.00 per share, a $100 conversion premium might be involved initially. If the same $1,000 were invested directly in common stock at $45.00 per share, 22.2 shares could be purchased. If the shares go up in value we have 2.2 more shares on which to garner a profit.

Last, convertibles may suffer from the attachment of a call provision giving the corporation the option of redeeming the bonds at a specified price above par ($1,000) in the future. In a subsequent section we see how the corporation can use this device to force the conversion of the bonds.

None of these negatives is meant to detract from the fact that convertibles carry some inherently attractive features if they are purchased with investor objectives in mind. If the investor wants downside protection, he or she should search out convertible bonds trading below par, perhaps within 10 to 15 percent of the floor value. Though a fairly large move in the stock may be necessary to generate upside profit, the investor has the desired protection and some hope for capital appreciation.

Advantages and Disadvantages to the Corporation

Having established the fundamental characteristics of the convertible security from the investor's viewpoint, let us now turn the coin over and examine the factors a corporate financial officer must consider in weighing the advisability of a convertible offer for the firm.

Not only has it been established that the interest paid on convertible issues is lower than that paid on a straight debt instrument, but also the convertible feature may be the only device for allowing smaller corporations access to the bond market. In this day of debt-ridden corporate balance sheets, investor acceptance of new debt may be contingent on a special sweetener such as the ability to convert to common.

Convertible debentures are also attractive to a corporation that believes its stock is currently undervalued. Recall that in the case of the Williams Company, $1,000 bonds were convertible into 20 shares of common stock at a conversion price of $50.00. Since the common stock had a current price of $45.00 and new shares of stock might be sold at only $44.00, the corporation effectively received $6.00 over current market price, assuming future conversion.[3] However, conversion would probably occur only if the stock price rises past $50.00. One can then plausibly argue that if the firm had delayed the issuance of common stock or convertibles for a year or two, the stock might have gone up from $45.00 to $60.00, and new common stock might have been sold at this lofty price.

To translate this to overall numbers for the firm, if a corporation needs $10 million in funds and offers straight stock now at a net price of $44.00, it must issue 227,272 shares ($10 million/$44.00 per share). With convertibles, the number of shares potentially issued is only 200,000 shares ($10 million/$50.00). Finally, if no stock or convertible bonds are issued now and the stock goes up to a level at which new shares can be offered at a net price of $60.00, only 166,667 will be required ($10 million/$60.00).

According to Value Line Convertibles, the typical convertible bond issued in U.S. markets has a 20 percent conversion premium at issue. Although comprehensive data are not compiled on Canadian convertible securities that level of premium seems close to the norm. Small companies with less than a top-grade credit rating are obvious users of the convertible bond vehicle, although top-grade borrowers sometimes use them as well.

Value Line
www.valueline.com

Corporations must consider the accounting treatment accorded to convertibles. Proper procedure ensures that there is a dilution effect on earnings per share when convertible securities are issued. In addition management should consider the potential reduction in voting power after conversion occurs.

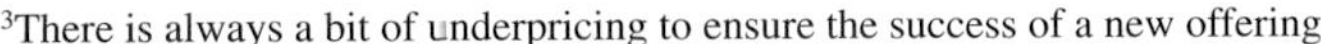

[3]There is always a bit of underpricing to ensure the success of a new offering.

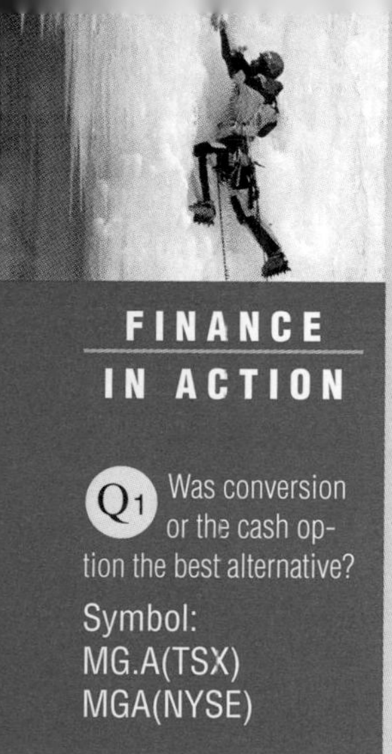

FINANCE IN ACTION

Q1 Was conversion or the cash option the best alternative?

Symbol:
MG.A(TSX)
MGA(NYSE)

To Convert or Not to Convert?

In August 2001, Magna International (www.magna.com) called its convertible debentures due in 2002. The debentures were priced in $U.S. and were redeemable at $1,021.67. Alternatively to accepting the call price bondholders could convert to 18.85 Class A subordinate voting share at a then market share price of $68.15 on the New York Stock Exchange (www.nyse.com), for an equivalent price of $1,285.00. The call was set for September 18, 2001.

Then September 11th happened and the equity markets fell in value. Magna traded at $55.49 on September 10th, which was still an attractive price but by redemption day the share price was at $47.57, for an equivalent price of $897.00. By October 15th the share price of Magna was back up to $55.04, for an equivalent price of $1,038.00

It turns out 65 percent converted and the rest of the bondholders accepted the cash.

Important to the success of a convertible issue is the presumed ability of the corporation to force the security holder to convert the present instrument to common stock. We examine this process.

Forcing Conversion

How does a corporation, desirous of shifting outstanding debt to common stock, force conversion? The principal device is the call provision, as discussed in Chapter 16. We know that when the value of the common stock goes up, the convertible security moves in a similar fashion. Table 19–1 indicates that convertible debentures may go up substantially in value. Some particularly successful convertibles have doubled in price. For this reason the holder of a convertible bond has no immediate incentive to convert to common unless the company calls the bond.

At the time of issue a corporation establishes a future privilege for calling in the bond at some percent above par value. Thus, the $1,000 debenture is redeemable at an amount greater than $1,000. Most bonds have a 5 to 10 percent call premium, often declining as the bond gets closer to maturity. If a corporation wishes to force conversion when the conversion value rises above the call price, it merely announces that it will call the issue at the call price. Bondholders have the choice between converting to shares of stock or accepting the call price. All rational bondholders take the shares if they have a higher value. The term **forced conversion** is derived from the fact that in such a situation, the bondholder has no choice but to convert.

Conversion may also be encouraged through a **step-up in the conversion price** over time. At the end of specified time periods the bond is convertible into a decreasing number of shares. Thus there is a strong inducement to convert rather than accept an adjustment to a higher conversion price and a lower conversion ratio. The effectiveness of this step-up provision in forcing conversion depends on positive share price performance.

Accounting Considerations with Convertibles

Before 1970 the full impact of the conversion privilege as it applied to convertible securities, warrants (long-term options to buy stock), and other dilutive securities was not adequately reflected in reported earnings per share. Because all of these securities may generate additional common stock in the future, the potential effect of the **fully diluted earnings per share** should be considered. Let us examine the unadjusted (for conversion) financial statements of the XYZ Corporation in Table 19–2.

TABLE 19–2
XYZ Corporation

1. *Condensed balance sheet:*	
4.5% convertible debentures (10,000 debentures of $1,000 convertible into 40 shares per bond, or a total of 400,000 shares)	$10,000,000
Shareholders' equity	
Common stock (1 million shares)	10,000,000
Retained earnings	20,000,000
Liabilities and shareholders' equity	$40,000,000
2. *Condensed income statement:*	
Earnings before interest and taxes	$ 2,450,000
Interest (4.5% of $10 million)	450,000
Earnings before taxes	2,000,000
Taxes (50%)	1,000,000
Earnings aftertaxes	$ 1,000,000

3. *Earnings per share:*

$$\frac{\text{Earnings aftertaxes}}{\text{Shares of common outstanding}} = \frac{\$1{,}000{,}000}{1{,}000{,}000} = \$1 \text{ (Basic)}$$

4. *Fully diluted earnings per share:*

$$\frac{\text{Adjusted aftertax earnings}}{\text{Fully diluted shares}} = \frac{\$1{,}225{,}000}{1{,}400{,}00} = .88$$

An analyst would hardly be satisfied in accepting the unadjusted earnings per share figure of $1.00 for the XYZ Corporation. In computing earnings per share, we have not accounted for the 400,000 additional shares of common stock that could be created by converting the bonds.

How then do we make this full disclosure? According to the Canadian Institute of Chartered Accountants we need to compute earnings per share as if the common shares related to conversions had actually been issued at the beginning of the accounting period.

Canadian Institute of Chartered Accountants
www.cica.ca

$$\text{Fully diluted earnings per share} = \frac{\text{Adjusted aftertax earnings}}{\text{Fully diluted shares}} \quad (19\text{–}2)$$

Earnings must be redefined to add the costs related to the convertible securities to the numerator of the EPS ratio. Thus, the adjustment would include adding dividends paid on convertible preferred shares, interest (aftertax) on convertible debt, and appropriate adjustments on the cash that would have been received had warrants, rights, and options been exercised. The denominator in the ratio includes common shares outstanding, the common share equivalent of all convertible preferred shares and bonds, the common shares that would be issued if all outstanding rights to purchase common shares were exercised, and the common shares that would be issued if all outstanding warrants and other options were exercised. Cash received from the potential exercises of a warrant or option is used to reduce the number of shares outstanding. Conversions that result in a higher earnings per share or lower loss per share (that is, antidilutive) are ignored.

We get new earnings per share for the XYZ Corporation by assuming that 400,000 new shares would have been created from potential conversion while, at the same time, allowing for the reduction in interest payments that would have occurred as a result of the conversion of the debt to common stock. Since before-tax interest payments on the convertibles are $450,000 annually for the XYZ Corporation, the aftertax cost is about $225,000. The assumption is that had conversion occurred at the beginning of the year, this aftertax interest cost would have been saved, augmenting the reported income by $225,000. Thus, fully diluted earnings per share for XYZ Corporation become $0.88.

$$\text{Fully diluted earnings per share} = \frac{\text{Adjusted aftertax earnings}}{\text{Fully diluted shares}}$$

$$= \frac{\overset{\text{Reported earnings}}{\$1{,}000{,}000} + \overset{\text{Interest savings}}{\$225{,}000}}{1{,}000{,}000 + 400{,}000} = \frac{\$1{,}225{,}000}{1{,}400{,}000} = \$0.88/\text{share}$$

The result of calculating the fully diluted earnings per share amount is a reduction of 12 percent from the basic earnings per share. The new figure is the one that would be used by a sophisticated investor in analyzing the value of a common share of XYZ Corporation.

Some Final Comments on Convertible Securities

While convertible debentures in the U.S. market are of such importance that they encourage much investor activity and research, in Canada they account for a small percentage of capital market activity. A review of the industrial bond price listings compiled by the Financial Post Information Service reveals that less than 100 industrial bond issues listed as outstanding were convertibles.[4]

Table 19–3 shows some information on a sample of convertible preferred shares outstanding in 2002. The banks dominate as issuers of convertible preferred shares. Notice the healthy yields on the preferred shares as compared to the dividend yields on the common shares. These yields are quite impressive when compared to yields on bonds that do not benefit from the investment tax credit. The Bank of Nova Scotia preferred trades primarily on the basis of the preferred dividend yield. The Bank of Nova Scotia preferreds, like many bank preferreds, have a convertible and redeemable feature that keeps the price fairly close to the issue value, which in this case is $25.00. The conversion value of the Bank of Nova Scotia preferreds is not a factor at this time because conversion cannot take place until the year 2005. Furthermore the Bank can redeem the preferreds for $25.00 after April of 2003. The Westcoast Energy preferreds have the same privileges and this is why the preferreds trade primarily as a fixed income security.

West Coast Energy
www.westcoastenergy.com

Financing through Warrants

A **warrant** is an option to buy a stated number of shares of stock at a specified price over a given time period. There were seven warrants issued on the Toronto Stock Exchange (TSX) in 2001 and 21 issues expired. Warrants are more favoured by small

[4]FP Bonds: Corporate (Toronto 2001)

TABLE 19–3
Convertible preferred shares, March 2002

Issue; Dividend	Rating	Conversion Value	Market Value	Preferred Yield	Common Yield
Bank of Nova Scotia $1.687	Pfd-1	n.a.	$27.50	6.1%	2.9%
Westcoast Energy $1.375	Pfd-2	n.a.	24.15	5.7	3.1

Note: The Bank of Nova Scotia preferred is not convertible until after October 2005 and is redeemable after April 2003 at 95% of value of a common share. Westcoast is only convertible after January 15, 2005, but can be redeemed at $25.00 after October 2004.

businesses and are issued more frequently on the TSX Venture Exchange. The warrants issued on the Venture Exchange tend to expire in a shorter time.

Table 19–4 shows an issue from the TSX and two from the Venture Exchange. The Inco warrants entitled the holder to buy one share of common stock for $30.00 any time until August, 2006. As Inco's common shares already trade above the exercise price there is a positive intrinsic (or minimum) value for these warrants. The two warrants from the Venture Exchange at this point have no intrinsic value, but still trade at a positive value as there is a possibility that the common shares will rise in value.

TABLE 19–4
Relationships determining warrant prices, March 2002

(1) Firm	(2) Warrant Price	(3) Share Price	(4) Exercise Price	(5) Intrinsic Value (3) − (4)	(6) Speculative Premium (2) − (5)	(7) Expiry Date
Inco (N.WT)	$8.45	$30.53	$30.00	$0.53	$7.92	Aug. 2006
Toxin Alert (YTX.WT.A)	0.20	1.35	4.50	0.00	0.20	Mar. 2003
Tech. of Sterilization (TOS.WT)	0.20	$ 2.40	2.50	0.00	0.20	Dec. 2002

www.tse-cdnx.com
www.tsx.ca

Traditionally, warrants were issued as a **sweetener** in a bond offering, making the issue of the debt feasible when it might not otherwise be so. More recently, warrants have been issued in conjunction with preferred share issues, common share issues, and even as a stand-alone fund-raising issue. When warrants are attached to another security issue, such as a bond, the combination of bond and attached warrants is called a unit. Warrants are usually detachable from the other security in the unit and often trade on the Toronto Stock Exchange. After warrants are exercised, the other security to which they were attached remains in existence.

Because a warrant is dependent on the market movement of the underlying common stock and has no "security value" as such, it is highly speculative. If the common stock of the firm is volatile, the value of the warrants may change dramatically. There is a high degree of risk entailed in investing in warrants. Warrants are popular with companies that are young and growing, with companies in some financial difficulty, and with the Canadian chartered banks.

Valuation of Warrants

Because the value of a warrant is closely tied to the underlying stock price, we can develop a formula for the **intrinsic value** of a warrant.

$$I=(M-E)\times N \tag{19–3}$$

where

I = Intrinsic value of a warrant
M = Market value of common stock
E = Exercise price (or strike price) of a warrant
N = Number of shares each warrant entitles the holder to purchase

Using the data from Table 19–4, we see that Inco's common shares were trading at \$30.53 in March 2002. Each warrant carried with it the right to purchase one share of Inco's common stock at the **exercise price,** or strike price, of \$30.00 per share until August 2006. Using Formula 19–3, the intrinsic (or minimum) value was \$0.53, or (\$30.53 − \$30.00) × 1. Since the warrant had several years to run and was an effective vehicle for speculative trading, it was selling at \$8.45 per warrant. This was \$7.92 more than its intrinsic value. Investors were willing to pay a premium because a small percentage gain in the share price could generate large percentage increases in the warrant price. Formula 19–4 demonstrates the calculation of the **speculative premium.**

$$S = W - I \tag{19–4}$$

where

S = Speculative premium
W = Warrant price
I = Intrinsic value

For Inco, we use the formula to show the indicated speculative premium of \$7.92.

$$\$7.92 = \$8.45 - \$0.53$$

Even if Inco were trading at less than the \$30.00 exercise price, the warrant might still have some value in the market. Speculators might purchase the warrant in the hope that the common stock would increase sufficiently in the future to make the option provision valuable.

Toxin Alert
www.toxinalert.com

As an example, the warrant of Toxin Alert in Table 19–4 was selling at \$0.20 even though the share price was \$3.15 below the exercise price. Notice that the intrinsic (minimum) value of the Toxin warrant is zero and is not negative when the market price is less than the exercise price. A warrant cannot have a negative intrinsic (minimum) value. If the share price of Toxin should surpass a price of \$4.50 before March 2003, then the warrant would command a positive intrinsic value.

Since a lot can happen in the time before the warrant expires, investors are prepared to pay a speculative premium for Toxin. This is also the case with Technologies of Sterilization, which has a share price just below the exercise price. Although the expiry date of the warrant is reasonably close at hand, investors are willing to pay a small amount for the warrant, even if its intrinsic value is zero.

The typical relationship between the warrant price and the intrinsic value of a warrant is depicted in Figure 19–4. We assume that the warrant entitles the holder to purchase one new share of common at $20.00. Note that although the intrinsic value of the warrant is negative at a common stock price between $0 and $20.00, the warrant still carries some value in the market. Also observe that the difference between the market price of the warrant and its intrinsic value is diminished at the upper ranges of value. Two reasons may be offered for the declining premium.

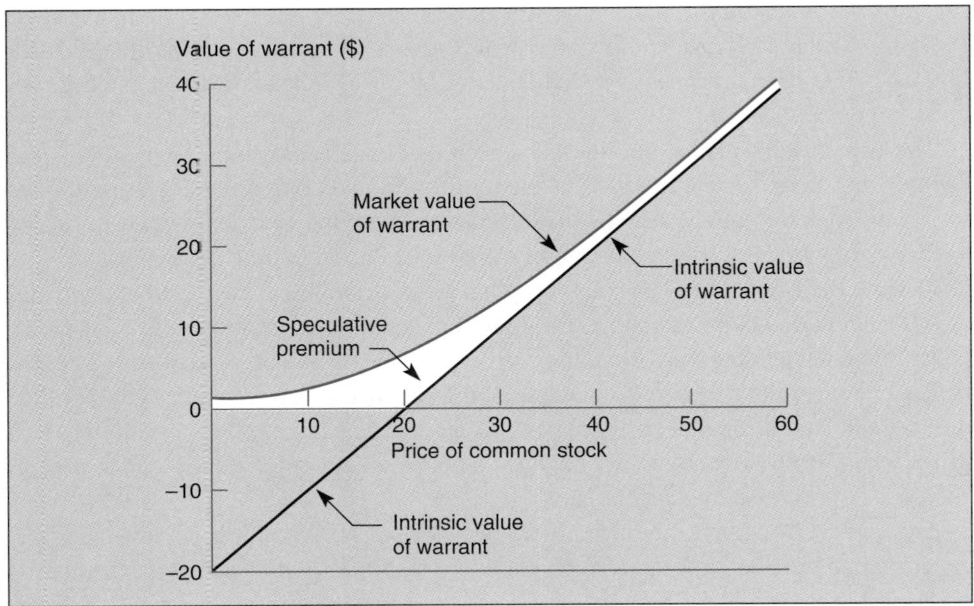

FIGURE 19–4
Market price relationships for a warrant

First, the speculator loses the ability to use **leverage** to generate high returns as the price of the stock goes up. When the price of the stock is relatively low, say $25.00, and the warrant is in the $5.00 range, a $10.00 movement in stock could mean a 200 percent gain in the value of the warrants, as indicated in the left-hand panel of Table 19–5.

TABLE 19–5
Leverage in valuing warrants

Low Stock Price	**High Stock Price**
Stock price, $25; warrant price, $5* + $10 movement in stock price	Stock price, $50; warrant price, $30 + $10 movement in stock price
New warrant price $15 ($10 gain)	New warrant price, $40 ($10 gain)
Percentage gain in warrant $= \frac{\$10}{\$5} \times 100 = 200\%$	Percentage gain in warrant $= \frac{\$10}{\$30} \times 100 = 33\%$

*The warrant price would be greater than $5 because of the speculative premium. Nevertheless, we use $5 for ease of computation.

At the upper levels of stock value, much of this leverage is lost. At a stock value of $50.00 and a warrant value of approximately $30.00, a $10.00 movement in the stock would produce only a 33 percent gain in the warrant, as indicated in the right panel of Table 19–5.

Another reason speculators pay a very low premium at higher stock prices is that there is less downside protection. A warrant selling at $30.00 when the stock price is $50.00 is more vulnerable to downside movement than is a $5.00 to $10.00 warrant when the stock is in the $20.00 range.

Use of Warrants in Corporate Finance

Let us consider for a moment the suitability of warrants for corporate financing purposes. As previously discussed, warrants may allow for the issuance of debt under difficult circumstances. While a straight debt issue may not be acceptable or may be accepted only at very high interest rates, the same security may be well received because of the inclusion of detachable warrants. Warrants may also be included as an add-on in a merger or acquisition agreement. For example, a firm might offer $20 million cash plus 10,000 warrants in exchange for all of the outstanding shares of the acquisition target.

The use of warrants has traditionally been associated with such aggressive high-flying firms as real estate investment trusts, airlines, and conglomerates. A perusal of the daily stock quotations reveals that warrants are a popular investment security issued by firms ranging from chartered banks to speculative mining companies.

Despite their popularity, warrants may not be as desirable as convertible securities as a financing device for creating new common stock. A corporation with convertible debentures outstanding may force the conversion of debt to common stock through a call, while no similar device is available to the firm with warrants. The only possible inducement for causing an early exercise of the warrant might be a step-up in option price, whereby the warrant holder may pay a progressively higher option price if he or she does not exercise by a given date.

The capital structure of the firm after the exercise of a warrant is somewhat different from that created after the conversion of a debenture. In the case of a warrant, the original debt outstanding remains in existence after the detachable warrant is exercised, whereas the conversion of a debenture extinguishes the former debt obligation.

Accounting Considerations with Warrants

As with convertible securities, the potential dilutive effect of warrants must be considered. All warrants are included in computing fully diluted earnings per share through the treasury stock method (CICA Handbook, section 3500). In the fully diluted earnings per share calculation the accountant must recognize the weighted average number of common shares that would result from the exercise of all warrants at the beginning of the period and the proceeds used to buyback common shares at the average market price for the period. The basic and fully diluted earnings per share calculations are now similar to U.S. and International GAAP.

Summary

1. Forwards, futures, and options are derivatives that can be used for speculative investment or more importantly to hedge a transaction. Derivatives increase or decrease risk.
2. Convertible securities are options issued by the corporation as an alternative way to raise funds. Bonds and preferred shares may have a feature that allows conversion to common shares. The option to convert to common shares rests with the investor up to a certain date.
3. Each security offers downside protection and upside potential. The holder has a fixed-income security that will not go below a minimum amount because of the interest or dividend payment feature, and at the same time he or she has a security that is potentially convertible to common stock.

If the common stock goes up in value, the convertible security appreciates as well. From a corporate viewpoint the firm may force conversion to common stock through a call feature and thus achieve a balanced capital structure. Interest rates on convertibles are usually lower than those on straight debt issues. The same is true for dividends on convertible preferred shares.

4. A convertible security has value as a debt instrument and as equity.
5. A warrant is an option to buy a stated number of shares of stock at a specified price over a given time period. The warrant has a large potential for appreciation if the stock goes up in value. Traditionally, warrants have been used primarily as sweeteners for debt instruments or as add-ons in merger tender offers. Their use as investment vehicles in recent years has become quite extensive. When warrants are exercised, the basic debt instrument to which they may have been attached is not eliminated, as is the case for a convertible debenture.
6. A warrant has an intrinsic value, but trades above that value until the exercise date. This is known as the speculative premium.
7. The potential dilutive effect of warrants and convertible securities is an important consideration in computing earnings per share.

Review of Formulas

1. Face value = Conversion price × Conversion ratio (19–1)

2. $$\text{Fully diluted earnings per share} = \frac{\text{Adjusted aftertax earnings}}{\text{Fully diluted shares}} \quad (19\text{–}2)$$

3. Intrinsic value of a warrant

$$I = (M - E) \times N \quad (19\text{–}3)$$

where

I = Intrinsic value of a warrant
M = Market value of common stock
E = Exercise price of a warrant
N = Number of shares each warrant entitles the holder to purchase

4. Speculative premium of a warrant

$$S = W - I \quad (19\text{–}4)$$

where

S = Speculative premium
W = Warrant price
I = Intrinsic value

List of Terms

derivatives 671
forwards 672
futures 676
options 678
call option 679
put option 681
convertible security 683
conversion ratio 684
conversion price 684
conversion value 684
conversion premium 684
pure bond value 685
floor value 685
forced conversion 688
step-up in the conversion price 688
fully diluted earnings per share 689
warrant 690
sweetener 691
intrinsic value 692
exercise price 692
speculative premium 692
leverage 693

Discussion Questions

1. What is the difference between forwards, futures, and options?
2. How can a company force conversion of a convertible bond?
3. What are the basic advantages to the corporation of issuing convertible securities?
4. Explain the difference between basic earnings per share and fully diluted earnings per share.
5. Why, in the case of a convertible preferred share, are investors willing to pay a premium over the theoretical value (pure preferred value or conversion value)?
6. Why is it said that convertible securities have a floor price?
7. Find the price of two convertible securities in a newspaper.
   a. Explain what factors cause their prices to be different from their par values.
   b. What will happen to their value if long-term interest rates decline?
8. What is meant by a step-up in the conversion price?
9. Which adjustments to aftertax earnings are necessary to compute earnings per share when convertible preferred shares are outstanding? When warrants are outstanding?
10. Explain how convertible bonds and warrants are similar and different.
11. Explain why warrants generally are issued and why they are used in corporate finance.
12. Why do warrants sell above their intrinsic values?
13. Which factors determine the size of the speculative premium on a warrant?
14. Investigate and explain put warrants.

INTERNET RESOURCES AND QUESTIONS

Links to U.S. and international futures and options exchanges can be found at:
www.usfederal.com/futures/exchanges.htm

The Globe and Mail (print site), under money and markets, and then foreign exchange, provides forward exchange rates for major currencies:
www.globeandmail.com

The various futures and options exchanges have informative web sites. The sites explain derivatives, list the types of contracts available, and in some cases provide pricing on the derivatives:

Key U.S. sites:	Canadian sites:	International sites:
www.cboe.com	www.tsx.ca	www.liffe.com
www.cme.com	www.me.org	www.lme.co.uk
	www.wce.mb.ca	

The Chicago Board of Trade (CBOT) provides quotes for cash prices, futures settlement prices, and option settlement prices at:
www.cbot.com

The New York Mercantile Exchange (NYMEX) provides charts and quotes for futures, options, and the daily settlement prices at:
www.nymex.com

The Toronto Stock Exchange provides quotes for shares and warrants:
www.tsx.ca

1. Global Surf and Turf has purchased software from a European manufacturer, with payment due three months from today. The payment due is 265,000 euros. Hedge this liability with a

forward contract. How much will Surf and Turf pay in three months in Canadian dollars? How much would they have to pay today?

2. You expect to have 25,000 bushels of wheat for sale in the fall and you would like to hedge your risk of price fluctuations through the CBOT.
   a. Identify today's date and find the cash price for Chicago #2 hard winter wheat.
   b. Identify the settle price on a futures contract to sell your wheat in the fall. Assume you enter into a futures contract for 25,000 bushels of wheat.
   c. Assume the price of wheat in the cash market, in your region of the country, in the fall is U.S.$4.00 a bushel. Without delivering your wheat to Chicago, close out the futures contract and calculate your gains, losses, and net receipts on the 25,000 bushels of wheat.
   d. Assume the price of wheat in the cash market, in your region of the country, in the fall is U.S.$1.75 a bushel. Without delivering your wheat to Chicago, close out the futures contract and calculate your gains, losses, and net receipts on the 25,000 bushels of wheat.
3. You manufacture silver jewellery for sale to local retail outlets. This upcoming spring you will require 2,000 ounces of silver and you would like to hedge your risk of price fluctuations through the CBOT.
   a. Identify today's date and find the cash price for New York spot silver.
   b. Identify the settle price on a futures contract to buy your silver in the spring. Assume you enter into a futures contract for 2,000 ounces of silver.
   c. Assume the price of silver in the cash market, in your region of the country, in the fall is U.S.$8.00 an ounce. Without taking delivery of your silver through the Chicago Exchange, close out the futures contract and calculate your gains, losses, and net receipts on the 2,000 ounces of silver.
   d. Assume the price of silver in the cash market, in your region of the country in the fall, is U.S.$3.00 an ounce. Without taking delivery of your silver through the Chicago Exchange, close out the futures contract and calculate your gains, losses, and net receipts on the 2,000 ounces of silver.
4. You provide light sweet crude oil for several refineries in eastern Canada. This upcoming summer you will require 30,000 barrels and you would like to hedge your risk of price fluctuations through the NYMEX.
   a. Identify today's date and find the cash price for light sweet crude oil.
   b. Identify the settle price on a futures contract to buy your oil in the summer. Assume you enter into a futures contract for 30,000 barrels of crude oil.
   c. Assume the price of crude oil in the cash market in the summer is U.S.$30.00 a barrel. Without taking delivery of your sweet crude oil through the New York Exchange, close out the futures contract and calculate your gains, losses, and net receipts on the 30,000 barrels of oil.
   d. Assume the price of crude oil in the cash market in the summer is U.S.$14.00 a barrel. Without taking delivery of your sweet crude oil through the New York Exchange, close out the futures contract and calculate your gains, losses, and net receipts on the 30,000 barrels of oil.
5. The following companies are listed on the Toronto Stock Exchange (TSX): Alcan, Inco, Nortel, and Suncor. All four companies also have listed call options through the ME.
   a. Identify today's date and the current share price for each company.
   b. Identify the price of the call option that expires in two months for each company, at the first strike price above the current market price of the common shares.
   c. Calculate the intrinsic value and the speculative premium of each call option.

6. Alcan, Inco, Nortel, and Suncor also have listed put options available through the ME.
   a. Identify today's date and the current share price for each company.
   b. Identify the price of the put option that expires in three months for each company, at the first strike price below the current market price of the common shares.
   c. Calculate the intrinsic value and the speculative premium of each put option.

Problems

1. Giffen Forest Products has sold lumber to the British company Bulldog Builders, with payment due six months from today. The payment due is £155,000. The Canadian dollar and British pound rate is 2.2562 and the six-month \$Can/£ forward rate is 2.2356. Hedge this liability with a forward contract. How much will Giffen Forest Products receive in six months in Canadian dollars? How much would they have to pay today?
2. You farm in Alberta and expect to have 1,000 tonnes of canola for sale in the fall. You would like to hedge your risk of price fluctuations through the Winnipeg Commodity Exchange. Today is early March, and the cash price for canola is Can\$347 per tonne. The settle price on a futures contract to sell your canola in November is Can\$334 per tonne. Assume you enter into a futures contract to deliver 1,000 tonnes of canola.
   a. Assume the price of canola in the cash market, in Alberta, in November is Can\$370 per tonne. Without delivering your canola to Winnipeg, close out the futures contract and calculate your gains, losses, and net receipts on the 1,000 tonnes of canola.
   b. Assume the price of canola in the cash market, in Alberta, in November is Can\$300 per tonne. Without delivering your canola to Winnipeg, close out the futures contract and calculate your gains, losses, and net receipts on the 1,000 tonnes of canola.
3. You manufacture gold jewellery for sale to local retail outlets. This upcoming fall you will require 500 troy ounces of gold and you would like to hedge your risk of price fluctuations through NYMEX/COMEX. Today's (March) price of gold is U.S.\$290 per ounce. The settle price on a futures contract to buy gold in August is U.S.\$292 per ounce. Assume you enter into a futures contract for 500 troy ounces of gold.
   a. Assume the price of gold in the cash market, in your region of the country, in August is U.S.\$350 an ounce. Without taking delivery of your gold through the New York Exchange, close out the futures contract and calculate your gains, losses, and net receipts on the 500 ounces of gold.
   b. Assume the price of gold in the cash market, in your region of the country, in April is U.S.\$250 an ounce. Without taking delivery of your gold through the New York Exchange, close out the futures contract and calculate your gains, losses, and net receipts on the 500 ounces of gold.

4. The following companies' shares and options in March (2002) trade at the identified prices. The options have a July expiry and the identified strike prices.

	Share Price	Call Option Price	Put Option Price	
Celestica	\$58.85	\$13.30	\$2.95	Strike at \$50.00
iUnits 60	45.10	2.40	2.30	Strike at \$45.00
Nortel	8.01	1.70	1.50	Strike at \$ 8.00
PetroCanada	39.87	2.85	2.70	Strike at \$40.00

a. Calculate the intrinsic (minimum) value and the speculative premium on the call option of each company.

b. Calculate the intrinsic (minimum) value and the speculative premium on the put option of each company.

c. If the share price of Celestica goes to $70.00, calculate the price of the call and put options if both have a speculative premium of $0.50.

d. If the share price of Celestica goes to $45.00, calculate the price of the call and put options if both have a speculative premium of $1.25.

5. Plunkett Gym Equipment, Inc., has a $1,000 par value convertible bond outstanding that can be converted into 25 shares of common stock. The common stock is currently selling for $34.75 a share, and the convertible bond is selling for $960.

   a. What is the conversion value of the bond?

   b. What is the conversion premium?

   c. What is the conversion price?

6. The bonds of Goldman Sack Company, with $1,000 par value, have a conversion premium of $55.00. Their conversion price is $40.00. The common stock price is $42.00. What is the price of the convertible bonds?

7. Red Deer Meat Packers, Inc., has a convertible bond quoted in the bond market at 85. (Bond quotes represent percentage of par value. Thus, 70 represents $700, 80 represents $800, and so on.) It matures in 15 years and carries a coupon rate of 6 percent. The conversion price is $20.00, and the common stock is currently selling for $12.00 per share on the TSX Venture Exchange.

   a. Compute the conversion premium.

   b. At what price does the common stock need to sell for the conversion value to be equal to the current bond price?

8. Hughes Technology has a convertible bond outstanding, trading in the marketplace at $835. The par value is $1,000, the coupon rate is 5 percent, and the bond matures in 25 years. The conversion ratio is 20, and the company's common stock is selling for $41.00 per share. Interest is paid semiannually.

   a. What is the conversion value?

   b. If similar bonds, which are not convertible, are currently yielding 7 percent, what is the pure bond value of this convertible bond? (Use semiannual analysis as described in Chapter 10.)

9. In the previous problem, if the interest rates on similar bonds, which are not convertible, go up from 7 to 9 percent, what will the new pure bond value be for Hughes Technology? Assume semiannual payments and the same 25 years to maturity.

10. Western Pipeline, Inc., has been very successful in the last five years. Its $1,000 par value convertible bonds have a conversion ratio of 28. The bonds have a quoted interest rate of 5 percent a year, paid semi-annually. The firm's common stock is currently selling for $43.50 per share. The current bond price has a conversion premium of $10.00 over the conversion value.

   a. What is the current price of the bond?

   b. What is the current yield on the bond?

   c. What is the yield to maturity on the bond if it has seven years to maturity?

   d. If the common stock price goes down to $22.50 and the conversion premium goes up to $100, what will be the new yield to maturity on the bond?

11. Eastern Digital Corp. has a convertible bond outstanding with a coupon rate of 9 percent, a par value of $1,000 and a maturity date of 20 years. It is rated A, and competitive, nonconvertible bonds of the same risk class carry a 10 percent return. The conversion ratio is 40. Currently the common stock is selling for $18.25 per share on the Toronto Stock Exchange.
    a. What is the conversion price?
    b. What is the conversion value?
    c. Compute the pure bond value. (Use semiannual analysis.)
    d. Draw a graph that includes the floor price and the conversion value but not the convertible bond price. For the stock price on the horizontal axis, use 10, 20, 30, 40, and 50.
    e. Which will influence the bond price more—the pure bond value (floor value) or the conversion value?
12. Defence Systems, Inc., has convertible bonds outstanding that are callable at $1,070. The bonds are convertible into 33 shares of common stock. The stock is currently selling for $39.25 per share.
    a. If the firm announces that it is going to call the bonds at $1,070, what action are bondholders likely to take and why?
    b. Assume that instead of the call feature, the firm has the right to drop the conversion ratio from 33 down to 30 after 5 years and down to 27 after 10 years. If the bonds have been outstanding for 4 years and 11 months, what will the price of the bonds be if the stock price is $40.00? Assume the bonds carry no conversion premium.
    c. Further assume that you anticipate in two months that the common stock price will be up to $42.50. Considering the conversion feature, should you convert now or continue to hold the bond for at least two more months?
13. Red Cliff Glass Company has $15 million in 8 percent convertible bonds outstanding. The conversion ratio is 125, the share price is $7.00, and the bond matures in 10 years. The bonds are currently selling at a conversion premium of $75.00 over their conversion value.

    If the price of the common shares rises to $10.00 on this date next year, what would your rate of return be if you bought a convertible bond today and sold it in one year. Assume that in one year the conversion premium has shrunk to $20.00.
14. B.C. Fisheries Ltd. has convertible preferred shares outstanding currently trading at $31.00. The preferreds pay an annual dividend of $2.00 and have a redeemable feature effective in two years. It is rated pfd-2, and competitive, nonconvertible preferreds of the same risk class carry an 8 percent return. The conversion ratio is 1.25. The common stock is selling for $24.00 per share on the TSX Venture Exchange and pays an annual dividend of $0.60.
    a. What is the conversion value of the preferreds?
    b. What is the dividend yield on the preferreds?
    c. What is the dividend yield on the common shares?
    d. Why would an investor not switch to another higher yielding preferred share?
    e. Why would an investor not convert to common shares?
15. Wilton Cheese Co. has warrants outstanding that allow the holder to purchase 1.5 shares of stock per warrant at $10.00 per share (option price). The common stock is currently selling for $13.00, while the warrant is selling for $8.25 per share.
    a. What is the intrinsic (minimum) value of this warrant?
    b. What is the speculative premium on this warrant?
    c. What should happen to the speculative premium as the expiration date approaches?

16. Labrador Fields has warrants outstanding that allow the holder to purchase one common share at $15.00 per share (option price). The common stock is currently selling for $25.00. The warrant is selling for $12.00.
    a. What is the intrinsic (minimum) value of this warrant?
    b. What is the speculative premium on this warrant?
17. Sleepless Night Company's warrant is priced at a speculative premium of $3.00 to its intrinsic (minimum) value. Each warrant entitles the holder to purchase one share in Sleepless Night Ltd. for a total cost of $10.00. Sleepless Night shares currently trade in the market for $16.25 each. What is the current price of a Sleepless Night warrant?
18. You can buy a warrant for $3.25 that gives you the option to buy one share of common stock at $12.50 per share. The stock is currently selling at $10.00 per share.
    a. What is the intrinsic (minimum) value of the warrant?
    b. What is the speculative premium on the warrant?
    c. If the stock rises to $22.50 per share and the warrant sells at its intrinsic value plus a speculative premium of $0.75, what will be the percentage increase in the stock price and the warrant price if you bought the stock and the warrant at the prices stated above, $10.00 and $3.25?
19. Assume you can buy a warrant for $5.00 that gives you the option to buy one share of common stock at $14.00 per share. The stock is currently selling at $16.00 per share.
    a. What is the intrinsic (minimum) value of the warrant?
    b. What is the speculative premium on the warrant?
    c. If the stock rises to $24.00 per share and the warrant sells at its theoretical value without a premium, what will be the percentage increase in the stock price and the warrant price if you bought the stock and the warrant at the prices stated above? Explain this relationship.
20. The Redford Investment Company bought 100 Cinema Corp. warrants one year ago and would like to exercise them today. The warrants were purchased for $24.00 each, and they expire when trading ends today (assume there is no speculative premium left). Cinema Corp. common stock is selling today for $50.00 per share. The option price is $30.00, and each warrant entitles the holder to purchase two shares of stock, each at the option price.
    a. If the warrants are exercised today, what would the Redford Investment Company's dollar profit or loss be?
    b. What is the Redford Investment Company's percentage rate of return?

21. Assume in the previous problem that Cinema Corp. common stock was selling for $40.00 per share when the Redford Investment Company bought the warrants.
    a. What was the intrinsic (minimum) value of a warrant at that time?
    b. What was the speculative premium per warrant when the warrants were purchased?
    c. What would the Redford Investment Company's total dollar profit or loss have been had it invested the $2,400 directly in Cinema Corp.'s common stock one year ago at $40.00 per share and sold it today at $50.00 per share?
    d. What would the percentage rate of return be on this common stock investment? Compare this to the rate of return on the warrant investment computed in the previous problem, part *b*.
22. Harvey Cunningham has $1,200 to invest in the market. He is considering buying 48 shares of the Eagle Corporation at $25.00 per share. His broker suggests that he may wish to

consider purchasing warrants instead. The warrants are selling for $6.00, and each warrant allows him to purchase one share of Eagle Corporation common stock at $23.00 per share.

a. How many warrants can Mr. Cunningham purchase for the same $1,200?

b. If the price of the stock goes to $35.00, what would be his total dollar and percentage return on the stock?

c. At the time the stock goes to $35.00, the speculative premium on the warrant goes to zero (though the intrinsic value of the warrant goes up). What would be Mr. Cunningham's total dollar and percentage return on the warrant?

d. Assuming the speculative premium remains $4.00 over the intrinsic value, how far would the price of the stock have to fall before the warrant has no value?

23. Hughes Technology has net income of $450,000 in the current fiscal year. There are 100,000 shares of common stock outstanding along with convertible bonds, which have a total face value of $1,200,000. The $1,200,000 is represented by 1,200 different $1,000 bonds. Each $1,000 bond pays 6 percent interest and was issued when the average A bond yield was 10 percent. The conversion ratio is 20. The firm is in a 34 percent tax bracket. Calculate Hughes' earnings per share.

24. Using information from the previous problem, assume the average A bond yield was 8 percent instead of 10 percent at the time the convertible bonds were issued. All other facts are the same.

a. What are the basic earnings per share for Hughes Technology?

b. Indicate the value for fully diluted earnings per share.

25. Meyers Business Systems has 2 million shares of stock outstanding. It also has two convertible bond issues outstanding with terms as follows:

1. 9 percent convertible, 2000	$12,000,000
2. 10 percent convertible, 2008	$15,000,000

The issue with the 9 percent coupon rate was first sold when average A bonds were yielding 12 percent, and it is convertible into 300,000 shares. The issue with the 10 percent coupon rate was first sold when average A bonds were yielding 15.5 percent, and it is convertible into 400,000 shares. Earnings aftertaxes are $4 million and the tax rate is 50 percent.

a. Compute both basic and fully diluted earnings per share for Meyers.

b. Now assume Meyers also has warrants outstanding, which allow the holder to buy 100,000 shares of stock at $20.00 per share. The stock is currently selling for $40.00 per share. Compute basic earnings per share considering the possible impact of both the warrants and convertibles. The firm's rate of return is 20 percent.

COMPREHENSIVE PROBLEMS

26. M. Stern, Inc., (IMS) has $30 million of convertible bonds outstanding (30,000 bonds at $1,000 par value) with a coupon rate of 10 percent. Interest rates are currently 8 percent for bonds of equal risk. The bonds were originally sold when the average BBB rate was 12 percent, and they have 25 years left to maturity. The bonds may be called at a 10 percent premium over par as well as be converted into 25 shares of common stock. The tax rate for the company is 40 percent.

The firm's common stock is currently selling for $49.00 per share, and it pays a dividend of $4.00. The expected income for the company is $42 million, with 5 million shares of common stock currently outstanding.

Thoroughly analyze this bond and determine whether IMS should call the bond at the 10 percent call premium. In your analysis, consider the following:

a. The impact of the call on basic and fully diluted earnings per share and the common stock price (assume the call forces conversion).

b. The consequences of your decision on financing flexibility.

c. The net change in cash outflows to the company.

d. If the bond is called, will the shareholders take the call price or the 30 shares of common stock?

e. Assuming the bondholders could have converted the bond into common stock whenever they desired, would you as a bondholder have waited for the company to call your bond and thereby force a decision on your part? Explain.

27. Andre Weatherby, an aspiring artist, had just sold his fifth painting of the year and now had $5,000 in cash to invest. His first inclination was to place his money in a CDIC insured savings account, but he was disappointed to find out that his annual return would be less than 2 percent.

Knowing little about investment alternatives, Andre knew he must seek advice from a pro. He recalled that at his 10-year high school reunion he had run into Carol Upshaw, a University of Saskatchewan finance major, who was now a stockbroker with Dominion Securities.

Early Monday morning Andre called Carol and she said she would be able to provide him with help. During the course of their conversation, Andre indicated that he wanted to invest his funds in a stock or bond that provided a good annual return and also had the potential to increase in value. Beyond that, he was able to stipulate little else.

Carol considered a number of alternatives, but decided on Hamilton Products. She was particularly interested in the firm's convertible securities, which paid 6.5 percent annual interest and were also convertible in 27 shares of common stock. The bonds had a maturity date 20 years in the future. She explained to Andre that not only would he receive a good annual return, but he could enjoy appreciation in value if the common stock did well.

The bonds were to be issued at a par value of $1,000 on the day that Andre called. The common stock of Hamilton Products was currently selling for $32.75 per share. Straight, nonconvertible bonds of equal risk and maturity to those of Hamilton Products were currently yielding 8 percent. Carol said that because the bonds paid 6.5 percent interest, they should hold up well in value even if the stock did poorly. The initial pure bond price value was $853.17.

Hamilton Products produced hot asphalt and ready-mixed concrete and was located in Vancouver, British Columbia. Plans called for $12 billion for highway and mass transit projects over the next six years. Although the design and approval of new projects was taking longer than expected, by late 2003 competitive bidding on projects was starting and Hamilton Products stood to be a major winner in the process. For this reason Carol thought the firm's share price could well increase in the future.

Andre decided to buy the convertible bonds. Since his expertise was in painting and not investing, he wanted to get back to his main endeavor as quickly as possible.

Fortunately the stock did well over the next two years, increasing in value to $45.50. The bonds also increased in value to $1,250.

It was at this point that Carol called Andre and warned him that a major provincial investigation into highway construction contracts might be undertaken by a subcommittee of the B.C. legislature. She thought Hamilton Products could be a target of the investigation and suggested that he take his profits and look elsewhere for an investment.

However, Andre was now intrigued by his high returns and decided to hold on to his bonds (somewhat to Carol's disappointment). As it turned out, Hamilton Products was found in violation of provincial regulations on a number of major contracts and the share price plummeted to $29.75 per share in the next year. During the same time period, a combination of a downgrading of the firm's credit rating and an increase in interest rates caused the yield on straight, nonconvertible bonds of those of equal risk and maturity to Hamilton Products to go to 10 percent. Hamilton Product's bonds had 17 years remaining to maturity.

Although Andre was disappointed in the drop in the firm's common stock price, he thought he could take some comfort in the fact that the convertible bonds were an interest-paying security, which gave them a basic value below which they normally would not fall.

a. At the time that Andre purchased the bonds, what was the conversion value? What was the conversion premium?

b. When the bonds got up to $1,250, what was the conversion premium?

c. Assume there is a conversion premium of $98.00 when the common stock price fell to $29.75. What is the price of the convertible bond?

d. What is the pure bond value after interest rates have gone up to 10 percent? You will need to determine the pure bond value based on the annual valuation technique presented in Chapter 10 of the textbook under the "Valuation of Bonds" section. The yield to maturity (required rate of return) is 10 percent and there are 17 years left to maturity. The bonds are continuing to make annual interest payments of 6.5 percent ($65.00). The principal payment at maturity is $1,000.

e. How much comfort should Andre take in the pure bond value computed in part d?

Selected References

Asquith, Paul. "Convertible Bonds Are Not Called Late." *Journal of Finance* 50 (September 1995), pp. 1275-89.

Cowan, Arnold R., Nandkumar Nayar, and Ajai K. Singh. "Underwriting Calls of Convertible Securities." *Journal of Financial Economics* 31 (April 1992), pp. 269-78.

Dunbar, Craig G. "The Use of Warrants as Underwriter Compensation in Initial Public Offerings." *Journal of Financial Economics* 38 (May 1995), pp. 59-78.

Fields, L. Paige, and William T. Moore. "Equity Valuation Effect of Forced Warrant Exercise." *Journal of Financial Research* 18 (Summer 1995), pp. 157-70.

Ganshaw, Trevor, and Deick Dillon. "Convertible Securities: A Toolbox of Flexible Financial Instruments for Corporate Issuers." *Journal of Applied Corporate Finance* 13 (Spring 2000), pp. 22-30.

Jen, Frank C., Dosoung Choi, and Seong-Hyro Lee. "Some New Evidence Why Companies Use Convertible Bonds." *Journal of Applied Corporate Finance* 10 (Spring 1997), pp. 44-53.

Lewis, Craig M.; Richard Rogalski; and James K, Seward. "Is Convertible Debt a Substitute for Straight or Common Stock Equity?" *Financial Management* 28 (Autumn 1999), pp. 5-27.

Mayers, David. "Why Firms Issue Convertible Bonds: The Matching of Financial and Real Investment Options." *Journal of Financial Economics* 47 (January 1998), pp. 83-102.

Stein, Jeremy C. "Convertible Securities as Backdoor Equity Financing." *Journal of Financial Economics* 32 (August 1992), pp. 3-21.

PART | SIX

EXPANDING THE PERSPECTIVE OF CORPORATE FINANCE

The risks and opportunities of mergers, divestitures, and international investment are increasingly important in our competitive and interconnected business world. We can reinforce the valuation techniques and risk considerations learned in earlier chapters as we examine these topics.

CHAPTER | TWENTY

20 External Growth through Mergers

LEARNING | OBJECTIVES

1 Outline some defensive measures taken to avoid an unfriendly takeover.

2 Identify the motives for mergers and divestitures, including financial considerations and the desire to increase operating efficiency. Also, perform an NPV analysis for a merger proposal.

3 Explain acquisition through cash purchases or by one company exchanging its shares for another company's shares.

4 Evaluate the impact of the merger on earnings per share and share value.

5 Discuss the diversification benefits of a merger.

6 Outline the reasons for using a holding company.

Many of the previously discussed points regarding financial planning, risk-return analysis, valuation, capital budgeting, and portfolio management can be examined in the very meaningful context of mergers and acquisitions. To this extent, Chapter 20 may be thought of as an integrative chapter for much of the material discussed throughout the text.

The International and Canadian Merger Environment

The merger movement became popular again at the turn of the millennium after a slowdown in the early 1990s. The impetus for the increased activity could be found in low interest rates, changing regulations, intense competition, evolving technology, and many other factors. Companies were positioning themselves for the twenty-first century.

The mergers of the 1960s and 1970s were motivated by the desire to create conglomerates that would benefit from diversification, and the mergers of the 1980s, as leveraged buyouts, were attempts to achieve financing gains. The mergers of the 1990s and 2000s seemed to focus on strategic positioning to obtain worldwide, or at least trading block, dominance. The communications, entertainment, financial services, pharmaceuticals, consumer goods, and transportation industries were experiencing major structural changes as we passed the year 2000 and convergence was the focus of business associations. This can be seen in Table 20–1. The telecommunications industry received more attention than any other in the late 1990s. The convergence of voice, electronic, and visual mediums was driving these mergers.

Before 1998 the largest deal was the merger of the Mitsubishi Bank with the Bank of Tokyo in 1996,

TABLE 20–1
Largest mergers and acquisitions

	Buyer	Acquired Company	Value ($ U.S. billions)	Year
1.	America Online	Time Warner	$183	2000
2.	Vodaphone Airtouch	Mannesmann	149	2000
3.	Bell Atlantic	GTE	85	2000
4.	SBC Communications	Ameritech	81	1999
5.	Exxon	Mobil	79	1998
6.	Vodaphone	Airtouch	74	1999
7.	Pfizer	Warner-Lambert	73	2000
8.	Travelers Inc.	Citicorp	71	1998
9.	AT&T	MediaOne Group	63	2000
10.	NationsBank	BankAmerica	60	1998

which was valued at $34 billion. The merger wave that ended in 1989 saw RJR Nabisco acquired for $30 billion. The deals of Table 20–1, which took place around the globe, occurred as markets, particularly in the United States, reached historical highs on the strength of solid earnings and low interest rates. Worldwide merger activity, which topped U.S.$3.5 trillion in 2000, dropped to U.S.$1.7 trillion in 2001 with the economic slowdown. The largest deal in 2001 was Comcast's U.S.$57 billion deal for AT&T Cable, while General Electric's U.S.$42 billion bid for Honeywell was blocked by the European Community on competition concerns. Canada was no exception in the late 1990s to the global trends, with proposed mergers in the financial services industry as well as accomplished mergers in the entertainment, telecommunications, and resources sectors.

RJR Nabisco
www.rjrnabisco.com

Corporate divestitures are a significant component of merger activities. A divestiture is the sale or the spin-off of a subsidiary or a division. Divestiture activity is attributed to different reasons: corporate strategies refocusing on core businesses, companies rationalizing their business to take advantage of the global marketplace, and perceptions that valuations of some assets are high. The global trend of merger activity recently has been to solidify market share in a company's core business.

During the late 1970s and early 1980s, the divestiture thrust of many large foreign-based companies had led to a number of leveraged buyouts of Canadian operations. The 1980 implementation of the National Energy Policy, the provisions of which favoured Canadian-owned energy companies, also led to the sale of Canadian oil and gas operations by foreign companies. For example, Dome Petroleum's purchase of Hudson's Bay Oil and Gas from U.S.-based Conoco was a key ingredient in one of the most interesting and nearly disastrous sagas in Canadian corporate history. Additionally, PetroCanada, created as a federal crown corporation in 1976, bought five oil companies for $6.5 billion. However, by 1995 majority ownership of PetroCanada was in private hands as the federal government sold off its interest.

The thrust of the late 1980s merger movement was that it was cheaper to acquire other companies than to expand through new product development or the purchase of new plant and equipment. In the mid-1990s the federal government played a large part in the acquisitions and divestitures market, with the sale of CN Rail, PetroCanada, and Canada's air traffic control system to Nav Canada. Table 20–2 (on the next page) highlights the largest Canadian mergers and acquisitions.

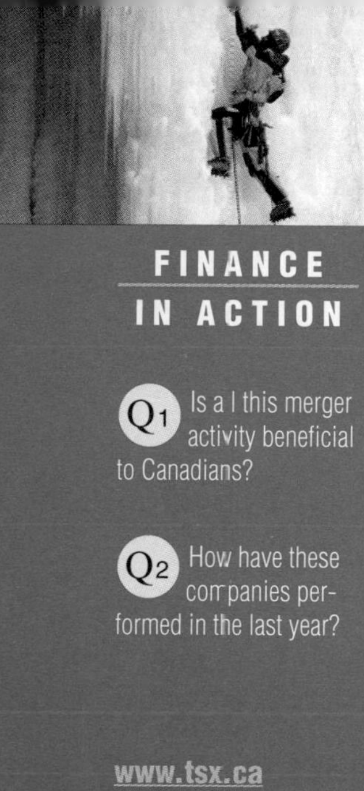

FINANCE IN ACTION

Canada! Part of the Action

By the end of March, the largest announced global merger of 2002 was the purchase of Alberta Energy (AEC) by PanCanadian Energy (PCE) for $10.6 billion. This would create the largest independent oil and gas producer in the world. For Canadians it was a relief to see a made-in-Canada merger. Throughout 2001, U.S. companies had acquired Andersen Energy ($5.3 B), Westcoast Energy ($5.2 B), Canadian Hunter ($3.3 B), Gulf Resources ($6.7 B) and several other Canadian companies in the energy business.

In March 2002 Sun Life Financial (SLC) completed the acquisition of Clarica Life Insurance (CLI) for $7 billion. The insurance business has recently gone through the demutualization process and now was consolidating to compete with the banks. Meanwhile the banks that had been prevented from merging in the late 1990s had expanded rapidly through acquisitions in the United States and in the case of the Bank of Nova Scotia (unfortunately) in Argentina.

In late 2001, we also saw Future Shop bought by Best Buy Company out of the United States. In early 2002, Molson (MOL.A) bought Kaiser, Brazil's second largest brewer, as it pursued its goal of becoming a world scale brewery.

All this activity was rationalizing the marketplace with a global and North American focus. Canadian firms were there to compete. Although we lost many Canadian firms, Canadian firms grew into the United States. With mergers in the oil and gas business we are likely to see asset sales from the merged firms and this should present opportunities for junior companies within Canada.

Q1 Is a l this merger activity beneficial to Canadians?

Q2 How have these companies performed in the last year?

www.tsx.ca

TABLE 20–2
Largest mergers and acquisitions in Canada

	Merger Partners		Value (Cdn. $ billions)
1.	Seagram	Polygram	15.6
2.	TransCanada Pipelines	Nova	15.0
3.	Northern Telecom	Bay Networks	13.4
4.	PanCanadian	Alberta Energy	10.6
5.	Sun Life	Clarica	7.0

Negotiated versus Tendered Offers

Traditionally, mergers have been negotiated in a friendly atmosphere between officers and directors of the participating corporations. Product lines, quality of assets, and future growth prospects were discussed, and eventually an exchange ratio was hammered out and presented to the investment community and the financial press. This was the general case of mergers in the late 1990s and early 2000s, but in the previous decade unfriendly takeover attempts were often a common occurrence.

If the potential buyer cannot come to agreement on merger terms with the potential seller's management and board of directors, there are still two alternatives open. First, it can ask the seller's shareholders for the right to vote their shares at the company's next annual meeting. This gives rise to what is known as a proxy fight, as management and the potential buyers vie for the right to vote a majority of the shareholders' shares. This right to vote the shares of another shareholder is called a proxy.

Second, rather than engage in a lengthy and expensive proxy fight, the potential buyer can elect to make a **tender offer** through a stock exchange directly to the target company's shareholders. If the tender offer is lucrative enough to attract over 50 percent of the voting stock, the buyer gains control and can conclude the merger.

The merger wave of the late 1970s and early 1980s has helped to create a whole new atmosphere. The takeover tender offer, in which a company attempts to acquire a target firm against its will, came into vogue. Takeover targets and their investment advisors developed anti-takeover manoeuvres to avoid being acquired.

Though a tender offer may please the company's shareholders, its management faces the dangers of seeing the company going down the wrong path in a merger and perhaps of their being personally ousted. To avoid an unfriendly takeover, management may institute one or more of several takeover defenses. These defensive tactics are sometimes referred to as applying shark repellent. In many cases the tactics only serve to increase the cost of the takeover without preventing it. These tactics include:

1. Turn to a **white knight.** A white knight is the term for a friendly company that agrees to bid a higher price for the targeted company and cooperate with the existing management in achieving a takeover that management feels is in the firm's (and management's) best interests.
2. Selling **crown jewels.** The targeted company may sell a prized division or asset of the company, making the takeover less attractive to the buyer.
3. A **targeted repurchase** of shares. The targeted company agrees to pay a premium to the acquiring company for the shares already purchased to have them discontinue the acquisition. This is sometimes referred to as *greenmail.*
4. Voting in **golden parachutes.** These are contracts that pay existing management rather large sums of money if the company is taken over and they lose their jobs. Although golden parachutes may make the takeover more expensive, they probably best serve management.
5. Taking on more debt. By going to the capital markets and raising additional debt and perhaps buying back shares, paying large dividends, or purchasing new assets, the targeted firm becomes more expensive to acquire and thus less attractive.
6. Adopting **poison pills.** These are also known as **shareholders' rights plans.** Inco adopted the first Canadian company protection plan, and its plan serves to illustrate this point. If a potential acquirer buys 20 percent or more of Inco's equity and can not reach an agreement with the board of directors, the plan would allow other Inco shareholders, but not the potential acquirer, to buy newly issued shares at half price. This makes the takeover very expensive. Proponents of this practice claim such protection against creeping takeovers is justified because management should be spending its time running the company rather than watching over its shoulder for whoever might be planning to try to take over the company. These plans have drawn criticism from some large investment managers.

While a given takeover bid may not appeal to management, it may still entice shareholders. The bidding may get so high that shareholders demand action. The desire of management to maintain the status quo and institute defensive tactics can come into conflict with the objective of shareholder wealth maximization, as was discussed in Chapter 1.

The proliferation of nonvoting shares in Canada may complicate a given takeover situation. In many cases there are clauses in the corporation's by-laws that attempt to include the nonvoting equity holders in the premium stock pricing generated by a takeover bid. This is generally done by stipulating that a tender offer, aimed at securing voting control, must include an offer to purchase the nonvoting shares as well as the voting. As we noted in Chapter 17 in the Canadian Tire case, these clauses are sometimes

FINANCE IN ACTION

Let's Make a Deal

In early 2002, Open Text (OTC) made a hostile takeover bid for all the common shares of Accelio Corporation (LIO) at $2.75 per share. Accelio (www.accelio.com) sought out Abode Systems as a "white knight" and received a more attractive offer. Takeover bid circulars detailing takeover offers such as this are posted at the SEDAR web site (www.sedar.com).

Canadian Tire (CTR) made a friendly takeover for Mark's Work Wearhouse in February 2002. Sun Life when it completed its takeover of Clarica was accused of employing a "poison pill" by implementing a "break fee." If Clarica received a competing bid for its shares that bettered the Sun Life offer there was to be a somewhat substantial payment to Sun Life for its efforts in making the bid. Any company trying to buy Clarica would in effect be paying this fee to Sun Life. The break fee would make it difficult for any other company to justify the purchase of Clarica and thus the fee became a defensive move.

Q1 What was Accelio's takeover price?

open to varying interpretation. In the situations where there are no provisions for inclusion of the nonvoting shareholders in a control takeover bid, the nonvoting shareholder loses the opportunity to make substantial gains if the firm is taken over.

The Domino Effect of Merger Activity

An attempt by one company to buy control of another often leads to a series of mergers. Two of the most common reasons for this are so: (1) the target company can avoid being taken over or (2) the acquirer can pay for what it has bought. Because so many of Canada's industrial corporations are subsidiaries of foreign multinationals, the chain of merger activity often begins with a transaction in another country. The merger movement has also seen the development of the unfriendly buyout.

The interwoven nature of Canadian and U.S. merger activity and the unfriendly takeover was classically illustrated in the 1980s with an attempted takeover of Gulf Oil. To fend off T. Boone Pickens's unfriendly takeover attempt, Gulf's management arranged to have the company bought by *white knight* Chevron (formerly Standard Oil of California) for a record (at the time) of U.S.$13.3 billion. To reduce the financial strain imposed by the large purchase price, Chevron had Gulf Oil sell its shares of Gulf Canada for $2.8 billion (Canadian) to the Olympia & York Corporation of Canada.

However, the chain of interrelated mergers did not stop there. To raise the financing for the deal, Olympia & York sold to Gulf Canada its stake in Abitibi-Price, one of Canada's largest forest products companies, for $1.2 billion. To raise the capital for the Abitibi-Price acquisition, Gulf Canada sold a portion of its assets to PetroCanada for $890 million, to Ultramar for $120 million, and to Norcen Energy for $300 million. Declining oil prices led Gulf Canada, to make a successful unsolicited takeover bid for Hiram Walker Resources in an attempt to diversify away from an overdependence on oil and gas. The price tag on that takeover was $3.3 billion. After being taken over by Gulf, Walker then sold its ownership of Home Oil to Interprovincial Pipeline for $1.1 billion. This one chain of interrelated events demonstrates not only the linked nature of the U.S. and Canadian merger markets, but also the intricacies of the financial arrangements of large merger transactions.

Although hostile takeovers in Canada are much less prevalent than in the United States because of less widely held companies, they still occur. By swallowing a so-called *poison pill*, a takeover target contrives to have more debt and/or less liquid assets to become less attractive to the would-be acquirer. In the Hiram Walker situation, the acquisition target made a deal to sell its *crown jewel*—its liquor distilling operations—to Allied-Lyons of Britain for $2.6 billion. Allied-Lyons at the time was fending off an unfriendly takeover attempt by Elders Ltd. of Australia. The shark repellent strategy adopted by Hiram Walker did not fend off Gulf Oil, but it did increase the overall costs of the transaction and make the final prize less valuable to the buyer.

One rule for avoiding being targeted as a takeover candidate is to never get caught with a large cash position. A firm with large cash balances serves as an ideal target for a leveraged buyout. The acquiring company is able to negotiate a bank loan based on the target company's assets and then go into the marketplace to make a cash tender offer. Firms with strong asset or market positions and low earnings are also prime takeover targets.

The early 2000s saw a host of takeovers and mergers in the Canadian oil industry with a lot of control of senior producers passing to U.S. control.

Foreign Acquisitions

A relatively recent phenomenon has been the increased tendency of firms from Canada and other countries to purchase major U.S. firms.

An infamous example occurred in 1986 when Robert Campeau of Toronto executed a successful $4.9 billion bid to take over Allied Stores of New York. Campeau's stated objective was to diversify his company's dependence on the Canadian real estate market. Purchases of retail chains had been popular in the late 1980s because of the so-called hidden assets on the balance sheet in terms of real estate worth more than its stated book value. In 1988, Campeau purchased another U.S.-based retailer, Federated Department Stores, for U.S.$6.6 billion. However, in 1989 Allied and Federated filed for Chapter 11 bankruptcy in the United States, and in 1990 Campeau Corporation failed in Canada. Campeau had expanded too fast with merger candidates that were too expensive.

In 1995 Seagram, a Canadian company, sold an interest in DuPont for over $12 billion and bought its interest in MCA for almost $8 billion from a Japanese firm. Both DuPont and MCA were U.S. firms. In 1998 Seagram purchased the record producer Polygram, a British firm, for $15.6 billion and then in 2000 agreed to merge with the French media and entertainment corporation Vivendi.

Vivendi Universal
www.vivendiuniversal.com

Government Regulation of Takeovers

Who knows which company will be a takeover target by the time you read this chapter? The absolute size of the recent merger deals listed in Tables 20–1 and 20–2 and the corporate concentration they imply has caused concern. Unlike in the United States, where fears of undue corporate concentration have been entrenched in antitrust laws since the beginning of the 20th century, Canadians have generally been unconcerned about high concentration levels of corporate power. However, on June 19, 1986, the Competition Act came into force, replacing the toothless Combines Investigation Act. In 75 years there hadn't been one successful prosecution under the Combines Act of a contested merger.

The **competition law** makes a merger or acquisition illegal if it "lessens competition substantially in a given market." Charges under the new act are civil rather than

FINANCE IN ACTION

Q1 What percentage of the Royal and Bank of Montreal's revenue and profit is derived from its U.S. operations?

www.bmo.com

www.rbc.com

NO to Banking Mergers (in Canada)!

In 1998 the Royal Bank of Canada and the Bank of Montreal announced their intentions to merge operations. Shortly thereafter the Toronto Dominion Bank and the CIBC announced their plans to merge as well. These mergers in the financial services industry would concentrate the banking industry within Canada to an unprecedented degree. Each bank claimed the merger was necessary to compete in the financial services industry worldwide. International banking as the millennium approached apparently needed huge economies of scale to adopt new technologies and services. Banking mergers of unprecedented scale were taking place globally to secure a large capital base to compete effectively.

The federal government, with jurisdiction over banking, vetoed the bank mergers, fearing too much concentration of the financial services industry within Canada. The initial response of the banks to the vetoed mergers was disappointment but they have since expanded their operations quickly into the large American market through acquisitions, funded to some extent by raising equity in the capital markets. The federal government has since relaxed its objections to the Bank mergers but at this time there is no longer the urgent need to merge. The expansion into the United States seems to be occupying the banks at present.

criminal, which increases the chances of a conviction if, in fact, competition will be seriously impaired by a merger. The Bureau of Competition Policy, which reviews mergers in relation to the act, has the power to prohibit an acquisition, order sale of certain assets as part of its approval, or even unwind a completed deal. To the surprise of many, the bureau has caused some would-be acquirers to abandon deals, while forcing a number of others to restructure the terms of their proposed takeovers.

If Canadians have been generally unconcerned about corporate concentration, the same cannot be said about foreign ownership. Canadian nationalists made this a major political issue during the 1960s, which led to the establishment of the **Foreign Investment Review Agency** (FIRA) under the Foreign Investment Review Act by the early 1970s. Under the watchful eye of FIRA, virtually no large takeovers of Canadian firms by foreigners occurred. FIRA was replaced by the Investment Canada Act (ICA) in 1985, however, in an attempt to make Canada a more hospitable place for foreign capital.

Since that time there have been a significant takeovers of Canadian firms, particularly in the resource industries. **Investment Canada** does however require some evidence that the takeover of a Canadian company by a foreign entity will result in a net gain for Canada as a whole. The last decade has seen a greater willingness to allow foreign investment in Canada. Also in the late 1990s, we saw the federal government prevent merger activity in the banking industry, on fears of decreased competition and increasing concentration of power.

Motives for Business Combinations

In Canada there is no specific definition of what constitutes a **merger**. In contrast, the term merger in the United States denotes the acquisition of one company by another followed by the liquidation of the acquired company into the acquiring company. Such rarely happens in Canada. Instead, the acquirer usually buys a majority, sometimes all, of the voting shares of the selling company, but both remain as separate legal entities after the acquisition. This normal situation in Canada is commonly referred to by both the merger and acquisition labels.

The term **amalgamation** does, however, have a precise legal definition in Canada. An amalgamation is a statutory combination under one of the provincial corporations or companies acts, the Canada Corporations Act, or the Canada Business Corporations Act. In this chapter we use the term merger to connote any transaction by which two or more companies are combined, either under a statutory amalgamation or just by ownership.

Financial Motives

The financial motives for mergers are a key consideration. As discussed in Chapter 13, a merger allows the acquiring firm to enjoy a potentially desirable **portfolio effect** by achieving risk reduction while perhaps maintaining the firm's rate of return. If two firms that benefit from opposite phases of the business cycle combine, their variability in performance may be reduced. Risk-averse investors may then discount the future expected performance of the merged firm at a lower rate and thus assign it a higher valuation than was assigned to the separate firms. The same point can be made in regard to multinational mergers. Through merger, a firm that has holdings in diverse economic and political climates can enjoy some reduction in the risks that derive from foreign exchange translation, government politics, military takeovers, and localized recessions.

While the portfolio diversification effect of a merger is intellectually appealing, with each firm becoming a mini-internal capital market unto itself; the practicalities of the situation can become quite complicated. One of the major forces of merger activity in the mid- to late-1960s was the desire for diversification. A lesson learned from the frenzied takeover strategies of many conglomerates of that time is that too much diversification can strain the managerial capabilities of a firm, even one with excellent management talent.

Evidence of the lack of success of some mergers is the fact that many of the acquisitions we see involve the sale of a previously acquired subsidiary by one company to another. For example, after undertaking a diversification strategy for decades, Canadian Pacific initiated a divestiture program that eventually resulted in its split into five separate companies (FIA in Chapter 3). Divestiture programs are usually undertaken either to reduce the debt incurred under the old acquisition strategies or to redeploy assets consistent with new corporate strategies. This seemed to be the case in the early 1990s as corporations attempted to deal with the more competitive and demanding conditions of the international marketplace. The stock market reaction to divestitures may actually be positive when it can be shown that management is freeing itself from an unwanted or unprofitable division.[1]

A second financial motive is the *improved financing posture* that a merger can create as a result of expansion in size. Larger firms may enjoy greater access to financial markets and thus be in a better position to raise debt and equity capital. Such firms may also be able to attract larger and more prestigious investment bankers to handle future financing.

[1] J. Fred Weston, "Divestitures: Mistakes or Learning," *Journal of Applied Corporate Finance* 4 (Summer 1989), pp. 68–76.

Greater financing capability may also be inherent in the merger itself. This is likely to be the case if the acquired firm has a strong cash position or a low debt-equity ratio that can be used to expand borrowing by the acquiring company.

One of the popular acquisition devices in the 1980s and to some extent since has been the leveraged buyout. As discussed in Chapter 15, the **leveraged buyout** results when either existing management or an outsider makes an offer to go private by retiring all the shares of the company. The buying group borrows the necessary money, using the assets of the acquired firm as collateral. The buying group then repurchases all of the shares and expects to retire the debt over time with the cash flow from operations or the sale of corporate assets.

Another financial motive is the **tax loss carry-forward** that might be available in a merger if one of the firms has previously sustained a tax loss. An operating loss may be carried forward up to seven years, but not back by the acquiring company. In any event, a tax loss carry-forward must be used up as quickly as possible when there are offsetting profits. In situations such as the Dome Petroleum merger with Amoco in the 1980s, where Dome had incurred substantial losses, the tax loss carry-forward provided significant value to the acquiring company, Amoco. Tax losses approximated $2 billion.

As an example of tax loss benefits, assume Firm A acquires Firm B, which has a $220,000 tax loss carry-forward. We look at Firm A's financial position before and after the merger. Based on the carry-forward, the company can reduce its total taxes from $120,000 to $32,000, and thus it could pay $88,000 for the carry-forward alone (this is on a nondiscounted basis). The tax shield value of a carry-forward is equal to the loss involved times the tax rate ($220,000 × 40% = $88,000).

	2000	2001	2002	Total Values
Firm A (without merger)				
Before-tax income	$100,000	$100,000	$100,000	$300,000
Taxes (40%)	40,000	40,000	40,000	120,000
Income available to shareholders	$ 60,000	$ 60,000	$ 60,000	$180,000
Firm A (with merger and associated tax benefits)				
Before-tax income	$100,000	$100,000	$100,000	$300,000
Tax loss carry-forward	100,000	100,000	20,000	220,000
Net taxable income	0	0	80,000	80,000
Taxes (40%)	0	0	32,000	32,000
Income available to shareholders	$100,000	$100,000	$ 68,000	$268,000

As would be expected, income available to shareholders has gone up by a like amount ($268,000 − $180,000 = $88,000). Of course, Firm B's anticipated operating gains and losses for future years must also be considered in arriving at a purchase price.

Perhaps the greatest management motive for a merger is the possible synergistic effect. **Synergy** is said to occur when the whole is greater than the sum of the parts. This "2 + 2 = 5" effect may be the result of eliminating overlapping functions in production and marketing as well as meshing various engineering and administrative capabilities. The increased cash flows from greater efficiencies are suggested will add value. In planning mergers, however, there is often a tendency to overestimate the possible synergistic benefits that might accrue.

Nonfinancial Motives

The nonfinancial motives for mergers and consolidations include the desire to expand management and marketing capabilities as well as the acquisition of new products. Companies that are in traditional lines of business may attempt to expand into more dynamic industries to upgrade their image. Edgar Bronfman Jr. of Seagram thought the entertainment business more dynamic than chemicals, but eventually sold to the even bigger Vivendi of France.

This also suggests that the desire of management for size and influence may influence decision making when mergers are considered. This may conflict with what is best for the shareholder, which is the topic of agency theory identified in Chapter 1.

Although mergers may be directed toward either horizontal integration (the acquisition of competitors), or vertical integration (the acquisition of buyers or sellers of goods and services to the company), the new competition laws should preclude the substantial elimination of competition. For this reason, mergers may become more directed toward companies in allied but not directly related fields. The pure conglomerate merger of firms with totally unrelated firms is still undertaken, but after more careful deliberation than in the past. The trend in the new millennium seems to be towards convergence or the focusing of the corporation on related businesses on a global scale. Mergers seem to be creating corporations with substantial international operations.

Motives of Selling Shareholders

Most of our discussion has revolved around the motives of the acquiring firm that initiates a merger. Likewise, the selling shareholders' motives are important. They may be motivated by a desire to receive the acquiring company's shares, which may have greater acceptability or activity in the marketplace than the stock they hold. Also, when cash is offered instead of shares, the selling shareholders gain an opportunity to diversify their holdings into many new investments. As we discuss later in the chapter, the selling shareholders generally receive an attractive price for their stock that may well exceed its current market or book value. An exchange offer may represent an opportunity to get a value approaching the replacement costs for their assets in an inflationary environment.

To encourage the support of officers of the selling company, who may also be shareholders, the officers may receive attractive postmerger management contracts as well as directorships in the acquiring firm. In some circumstances they may be allowed to operate the company as a highly autonomous subsidiary after the merger (though this is probably the exception). This is most likely to happen when the acquiring firm is in a different business and is not likely to try to integrate the acquired company into the operating system of its new parent.

A final motive of the selling shareholders may simply be the bias against smaller businesses that has developed in this country and around the world. Real clout in the financial markets may dictate being part of a larger organization. These motives should not be taken as evidence that all or even most officers or directors of smaller firms wish to sell—a matter that we examine further when we discuss negotiated offers versus takeover attempts.

Terms of Exchange

In determining the price to be paid for a potential acquisition, a number of factors are considered, including earnings, dividends, and growth potential. We divide our analysis of merger **terms of exchange** between cash purchases and stock-for-stock exchanges, in which the acquiring company trades stock rather than paying cash for the acquired firm. A good merger is beneficial to both firms. The terms of exchange allow us to re-examine the valuation models of Chapter 10, the cost of capital of Chapter 11, and capital budgeting from Chapter 12.

Cash Purchases

The cash purchase of another company can be viewed within the context of a capital budgeting decision. Instead of purchasing new plant or machinery, the purchaser has opted to acquire a *going concern*. For example, assume the Invest Corporation is analyzing the acquisition of the Sell Corporation for $1 million. The Sell Corporation has expected cash flow (aftertax earnings plus amortization) of $100,000 per year for the next 5 years and $150,000 per year for the 6th through the 20th years. Furthermore, the synergistic benefit of the merger (in this case, combining production facilities) should reduce operating costs by $10,000 per year. Finally, the Sell Corporation has a $50,000 tax loss carry-forward that can be used immediately by the Invest Corporation. Assuming a 40 percent tax rate, the $50,000 loss carry-forward will generate $20,000 extra in aftertax profits immediately. The Invest Corporation has a 10 percent cost of capital, and this is assumed to remain stable with the merger. Our analysis would be as follows:

Cash outflow:	
Purchase price	$1,000,000
Less: tax shield benefit from tax loss carry-forward ($50,000 × 40%)	20,000
Net cash outflow	$ 980,000
Cash inflows:	
Years 1–5: $100,000 operating cash inflow	
10,000 synergistic benefit	
$110,000 annual cash inflow	
Present value of $110,000	$ 416,987
Years 6–20: $150,000 operating cash flow	
10,000 synergistic benefit	
$160,000 annual cash inflow	
Present value of $160,000	755,644
Total present value of cash inflows	$1,172,631

The present value for the first five years is based on n = 5, i = 10 percent. For the 6th through the 20th years, we determine the present value n = 15, i = 10 percent, and then present value the lump sum five years with n = 5, i = 10 percent.

The net present value of the investment is:

Total present value of inflows	$1,172,631
Net cash outflow	980,000
Net present value	$ 192,631

The IRR is 12.51 percent, which exceeds the 10 percent cost of capital.

The acquisition appears to represent a desirable alternative for the expenditure of cash with a positive net present value of $192,631. The market environment of the late 1990s presented opportunities in which firms could be purchased at a value below the replacement costs of their assets and thus represented a potentially desirable capital investment.

Stock-for-Stock Exchange

On a stock-for-stock exchange, we use a somewhat different analytical approach, emphasizing the earnings per share impact of exchanging securities (and ultimately the market valuation of those earnings). The analysis is primarily from the viewpoint of the acquiring firm. The shareholders of the acquired firm are concerned mainly about the initial price they are paid for their shares and about the outlook for the acquiring firm.

Assume Expand Corporation is considering the acquisition of Small Corporation. Significant financial information on the firms before the merger is provided in Table 20–3.

TABLE 20–3
Financial data on potential merging firms

	Small Corporation	Expand Corporation
Total earnings	$200,000	$500,000
Shares of stock outstanding	50,000	200,000
Earnings per share	$ 4.00	$ 2.50
Price-earnings ratio (P/E)	7.5 ×	12 ×
Market price per share	$ 30.00	$ 30.00

We begin our analysis with the assumption that one share of Expand Corporation ($30.00) will be traded for one share of Small Corporation ($30.00). In actuality, Small Corporation will probably demand more than $30.00 per share because the acquired firm usually gets some premium over the current market value. Later we consider the impact of paying such a premium.

If 50,000 new shares of Expand Corporation are traded in exchange for all the old shares of Small Corporation, Expand Corporation then has 250,000 shares outstanding. At the same time, its claim to earnings will go to $700,000 when the two firms are combined. Postmerger earnings per share will be $2.80 for the Expand Corporation, as indicated in Table 20–4.

TABLE 20–4
Postmerger earnings per share

Total earnings: Small ($200,000) + Expand ($500,000)	$700,000
Shares outstanding in surviving corporation:	
Old (200,000) + New (50,000)	250,000

$$\text{New earnings per share for Expand Corporation} = \frac{\$700{,}000}{250{,}000} = \$2.80$$

A number of observations are worthy of note. First, the earnings per share of Expand Corporation have increased as a result of the merger, rising from $2.50 to $2.80.

This has occurred because Expand Corporation's P/E ratio was higher than that of Small Corporation at the time of the merger (12 versus 7.5). *Whenever a firm acquires another entity whose P/E ratio is lower than its own, there is an immediate increase in earnings per share.* The P/E ratio comparison is an important variable to be considered.

However, it is unlikely that Small Corporation will give up its shares at the current market value of $30.00 per share. If we assume Expand Corporation is willing to pay the shareholders of Small Corporation $48.00 worth of stock for each share of its stock outstanding, things will change. Expand will now be paying 12 times Small Corporation's earnings ($48.00/ $4.00), which is equal to the current P/E ratio of Expand Corporation. Under these circumstances there will be no change in postmerger earnings per share for Expand Corporation.

Endless possibilities can occur in mergers based on stock-for-stock exchanges. Even if the acquiring company increases its immediate earnings per share as a result of the merger, the impact on long-term growth should be examined. Furthermore the increased number of shareholders and the possible dilution effects should also be considered.

Shareholders may be concerned about trading or maintaining parity in dividends per share, than with the impact on earnings per share. The acquiring company may offer fixed-income securities as well as common stock to satisfy the shareholders of the acquired company.

Market Value Maximization

The ultimate test of a merger lies in the concept of **market value maximization.** We must try to assess how shareholders (present and potential) will view the merger and how they will price the merged firm's share price in the marketplace. Thus, we must consider not only the immediate impact on earnings per share, but also the effect on the surviving firm's postmerger P/E ratio. Although a merger with Small Corporation, as suggested, increases Expand Corporation's earnings per share from $2.50 to $2.80, there may be a decrease in Expand Corporation's postmerger P/E ratio because of a slowing of the expected growth rate and/or an increase in its risk of the new firm. All the financial factors must be brought together to determine the potential impact on shareholder values in the new firm. The techniques of Chapter 12 should be of assistance in determining the value that may be created.

Portfolio Effect

Inherent in all of our discussions is the importance of the merger's portfolio effect on the risk-return posture of the firm. This is an extension of the Chapter 13 discussion. The reduction or increase in risk may influence the P/E ratio as much as the change in the growth rate. To the extent that we are diminishing the overall risk of the firm in a merger, the P/E ratio may increase even if the potential earnings growth is unchanged. Business risk reduction may be achieved by acquiring another firm that is influenced by business cycle conditions in opposite ways from their influence on our own firm, while financial risk reduction may be achieved by restructuring our postmerger financial arrangements to include less debt.

Perhaps Expand Corporation is diversifying from a heavy manufacturing industry into the real estate/housing industry. While heavy manufacturing industries move with the general business cycle, the real estate/housing industry tends to be countercyclical. Even though the expected value of earnings per share may remain relatively constant as a result of the merger, the standard deviation of possible outcomes may decline as a result of risk reduction through diversification, as is indicated in Figure 20–1.

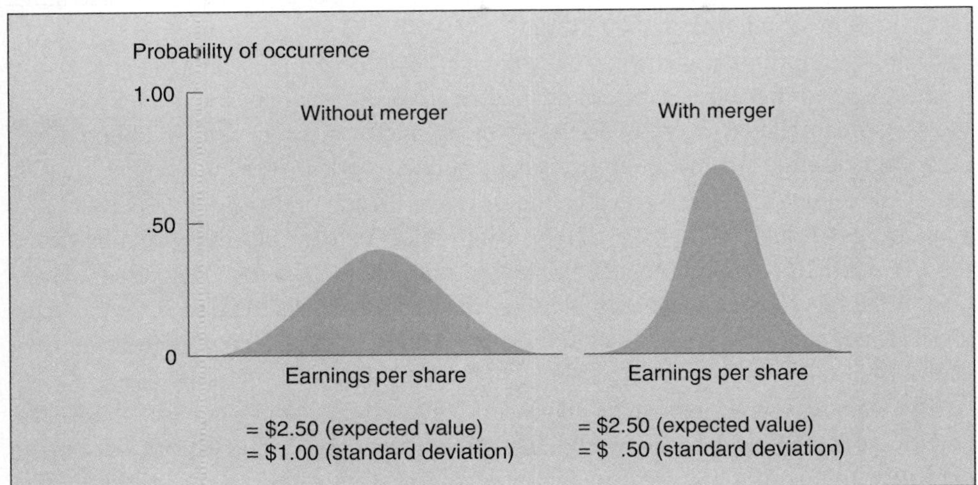

FIGURE 20–1
Risk reduction portfolio benefits

We see that the expected value of the earnings per share has remained constant in this instance, but the standard deviation has gone down. Because there is less risk in the corporation, the investor may be willing to assign a higher valuation, thus increasing the price-earnings ratio.

Like synergy, however, countercyclical effects are hard to capture, as the relationships of different businesses to the general business cycle change somewhat over time. In addition, some have argued persuasively that it is more efficient for the shareholder to diversify his or her portfolio than it is for an individual firm to do so. An associated irony is that, because diversified companies are so difficult for analysts to understand in their totality, they often command a lower P/E than the average of those that would have been assigned to the individual parts. This is one of the reasons that diversified companies, such as Canadian Pacific, in the late 1980s and again in 2001, went through divestment of its numerous businesses.

Accounting Considerations in Mergers and Acquisitions

The role of financial accounting has probably had no greater significance than in the area of mergers and acquisitions. When a price substantially above book value is paid for a potential acquisition, goodwill may be created on the balance sheet of the acquiring firm, and expensing this goodwill over time may reduce earnings per share. Thus, most firms would like to avoid the creation of goodwill if possible. Let's see what the issues and the options are.

A merger can be treated on the books of the acquiring firm as either a **pooling of interests** or a **purchase of assets.** Business combinations in which the ownership interests of two or more companies are joined through an exchange of shares and in which none of the parties involved can be identified as an acquirer can be considered pooling of interests. The key criterion is that one company can own no more than 55 percent of the mergered company. The financial statements of the firms are combined, subject to some minor adjustments, and no goodwill is created.[2] Reported earnings will therefore not suffer from amortized goodwill costs. Pooling of interest accounting treatment is rare since the adoption of the foregoing definition by the accounting profession in the early 1970s. Its widespread use until that time, however, does make an understanding of the pooling of interest method useful.

Goodwill may be created when the second type of merger recording—a purchase of assets—is used. Because of the criteria described for a pooling of interests, a purchase of assets treatment is generally necessary in all current mergers. Under a purchase of assets accounting treatment, any excess of purchase price over book value must be recorded as goodwill. Until recently, the firm amortized goodwill over a period of 40 years or less, which could have a significant impact on earnings. New regulations in the *CICA Handbook,* section 3062, do not permit the amortization of goodwill. However, if the fair value of the goodwill drops, the loss in value is to be recognized on the income statement. Those assets classified as intangible are to be amortized over their useful life.

The main reason we look at the pooling of interests versus the purchase of assets accounting treatment is to recognize the potentially beneficial effect, historically but not currently, to a corporation of exchanging common stock rather than nonequity compensation (cash, bonds, preferred stock, and so on), and thus perhaps qualifying as a pooling of interests. Although merely issuing common stock no longer qualifies for a pooling treatment, a share exchange more readily qualifies a merger for a tax-free exchange under Sections 85(1) or 87(4) of the Income Tax Act. Under a tax-free exchange, the shareholders of the acquired firm may defer any capital gains taxes until the newly acquired shares have been sold. Thus, there would be no immediate tax for trading a share of stock in a corporation that was purchased 10 years ago at $5.00 for $100.00 in an acquiring corporation stock. When the stock is sold, the tax is recognized. If the tender offer were for cash, there would be an immediate tax obligation.

In analyzing accounting and tax considerations, we see that, until the early 1970s, the acquiring corporation had some inducement to offer common stock to qualify as a pooling of interests when the exchange offer exceeded book value. Also, the shareholders of the acquired firm still have some incentive to receive common stock when the exchange offer exceeds their initial cost basis, to avoid immediate taxes. During the 1960s and part of the 1970s, common stock, often supplemented by convertible securities and warrants, was a frequently used mode of exchange.[3] In the merger movement of the late 1970s and in the 1980s, cash offers became popular. The 1990s once again saw a movement toward seeking share issues to finance takeovers.

Why was cash popular? First, shareholders of acquired firms became disenchanted with the performance of acquiring companies' stock and, at times, the stock market in general. For this reason they wanted to take cash, pay tax, and invest in a new,

---

[2]See Section 1580.10 of the *CICA Handbook.*

[3]The popularity of the last two items was reduced somewhat in January 1970 by the introduction of tough new accounting standards for the dilutive effects of convertibles and warrants, as described in Chapter 19.

diversified set of investments. Acquiring corporations went along with the cash tender offer pattern, to satisfy the demands of selling shareholders. The strong stock markets of the 1990s allowed for the return to share issues. However, once again, the bust in the technology market at the turn of the millennium has shown the dangers in accepting stock instead of cash in mergers.

By using cash instead of stock, a corporation may diminish the perceived dilutive effect of a merger. If Small Corporation had been acquired for straight cash by Expand Corporation, no new shares are issued and earnings per share go up proportionately by the amount of new aftertax earnings. This latter argument tends to be weakened by recognition of the fact that cash tendered in a merger has a substantial capital cost associated with it and, furthermore, that new shares of stock may later have to be authorized and sold to finance the cash drain.

Premium Offers and Stock Price Movements

Although premiums of 15 to 20 percent over market value in a merger or acquisition are seen, very high premiums in the 40 to 60 percent range are frequent. These high **merger premiums** may be related to market values for securities in general. To the extent that replacement value exceeds market value, a high premium over market value may be justified. In addition, the motivation of the acquiring company in making the purchase was sometimes not to turn around a poor performer, but to take advantage of the superior market or product position of the acquired company.

Researchers into takeover activity have found that acquirees have superior price performance on a risk-adjusted basis. It is not surprising that a company that is offered a large premium over its current market value has a major upside movement. A related problem for the investor, however, is that much of this activity may occur before the public announcement of the merger offer. If a firm is selling at $25.00 per share when informal negotiations begin, it may be $34.00 by the time an announced offer of $40.00 is made. Still, good profits can be made by investing at $34.00 if the merger goes through.

A group of investors who specialize in merger situations came into high visibility in the late 1970s and the 1980s. Known as **ARBs (arbitrageurs),** their strategy is to purchase the stock of the acquisition candidate in the hope of being bought out at the tender offer price. In the prior example, they would accumulate stock at between $34.00 and $38.00 in the hope of selling at $40.00. The ARBs often become allies of acquiring companies because their profits (and their avoidance of losses) are dependent on the merger's actual completion.

In a stock-for-stock exchange, an arbitrageur may attempt to protect his or her profit position by buying the stock of the acquisition candidate and, at the same time, short-selling the stock of the acquirer. A short sell is a current sale of stock that is not owned, with the intention of acquiring the stock in the future to close out the position. The arbitrageur buys the acquiree's stock at $34.00 and simultaneously short-sells the acquiring company's stock at $40.00. When the merger has been consummated, the arbitrageur will trade the acquiree's stock for a share of the acquiring company's stock and use the stock to cover the $40.00 short position. Thus, the selling price is preestablished at $40.00, and the buy price is preestablished at $34.00. Even if the acquiring company's stock goes up or down from $40.00 after the merger has been announced, the sale price and profit spread have been established.

The only problem with this strategy or of any merger-related investment strategy is that the merger may be called off. In that case the merger candidate's stock, which shot up from $25.00 to $34.00, may fall back to $25.00, and the Johnny-come-lately investor would lose $9.00 per share. The arbitrageur also would not have new stock of the acquiring company to cover his or her short position, since there would be no exchange of shares.

All this information on price movement patterns has significance to corporate financial managers, who must understand and react to the motivations of investors. For example, once the ARBs have established their investment position, these arbitrageurs will do everything possible to see that the merger goes through. This, at a minimum, will include voting all their shares in favour of a merger. On a more active basis, it may encompass a strategy of influencing other large shareholders, and it could ultimately include an attempt to discredit the management of a target company in the eyes of the shareholders.

Mergers and Market for Corporate Control

The high level of corporate merger activity is sometimes justified by the proposition that a competitive **market for corporate control** is an effective brake on any tendency for agent managers to diverge from striving to maximize shareholder wealth. However, to the extent that activity in this so-called market for corporate control creates financial value for shareholders, there have been studies where results suggest that all of the excess value is transferred to the selling shareholders.

Although the evidence seems to support the general conclusion that the shareholders of acquired companies realize substantial excess returns when a merger occurs, studies suggest that the shareholders of bidder firms realize negligible excess returns on takeovers. Because the bidding firms in the U.S. situation are generally much larger than the acquired firms and because the bidding firms' corporate strategies are often based on active acquisition programs, however, those research results are at least partially muddied by measurement problems. In effect, the expectation of its making attractive acquisitions may be already discounted in the company's normal share price.

A study of Canadian merger activity between 1964 and 1983 came to what may be a significantly different conclusion in regard to the sharing of the abnormal returns between buyer and seller.[4] As Figure 20–2 shows, the data from that study revealed that, consistent with U.S.-based studies, target firms received higher abnormal returns on average than did the bidder firms. Unlike the U.S. studies, however, the bidder firms did receive significant abnormal returns on average. In addition, Figure 20–2 indicates that there were generally higher abnormal returns in cases where the mergers were related, especially for the acquirees.

Thus, the evidence to this point seems to infer there may be some overall benefit to merger activity. In many cases, if value is actually created, it can be attributed to a new management team changing the status quo. This may be particularly appropriate in a company where the previous management had become too wedded to investing in the traditional industry regardless of whether or not the cost of capital was higher than the

[4]B. Espen Eckbo, "Mergers and the Market for Corporate Control: The Canadian Evidence," *Canadian Journal of Economics* 19, no. 2 (May 1986), pp. 236–60.

Refocusing Strategies

Diversification at one time had been a key goal of many large corporations and they expanded into many varied lines of business. Many found the experience less than successful. Some have suggested that there is little need for the firm to diversify if its shareholders already own a diversified share portfolio. Instead the firm should concentrate on what it knows best, perhaps on a global scale.

We see a new trend as business and government attempt to direct their energies on a simpler and more focused line of business. In Canada the federal government has shed PetroCanada and CN Rail. Ontario has sold off the Skydome and in 2002 hopes to sell off HydroOne. Alberta sold off Telus in the mid-1990s.

For corporations we have seen BCE spin off Nortel (what a great move) and Canadian Pacific split into five separate companies (see Chapter 3). As for companies like Brascan, they have tried to simplify their vast holdings along three lines of business even though they continue to hold many firms. Quebecor is another vast empire with numerous interwoven firms but whether they are in printing, TV, magazine publishing, the Internet (www.canoe.ca) or newspapers the common theme is communications. These various mediums are converging and this is the focus of Quebecor's operations.

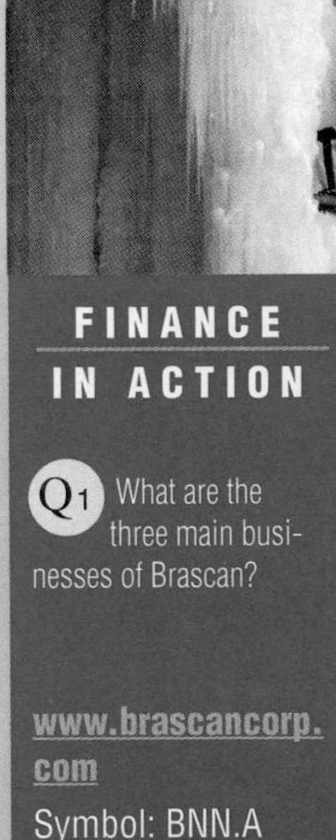

FINANCE IN ACTION

Q1 What are the three main businesses of Brascan?

www.brascancorp.com

Symbol: BNN.A

FIGURE 20–2

Abnormal returns relative to merger announcements

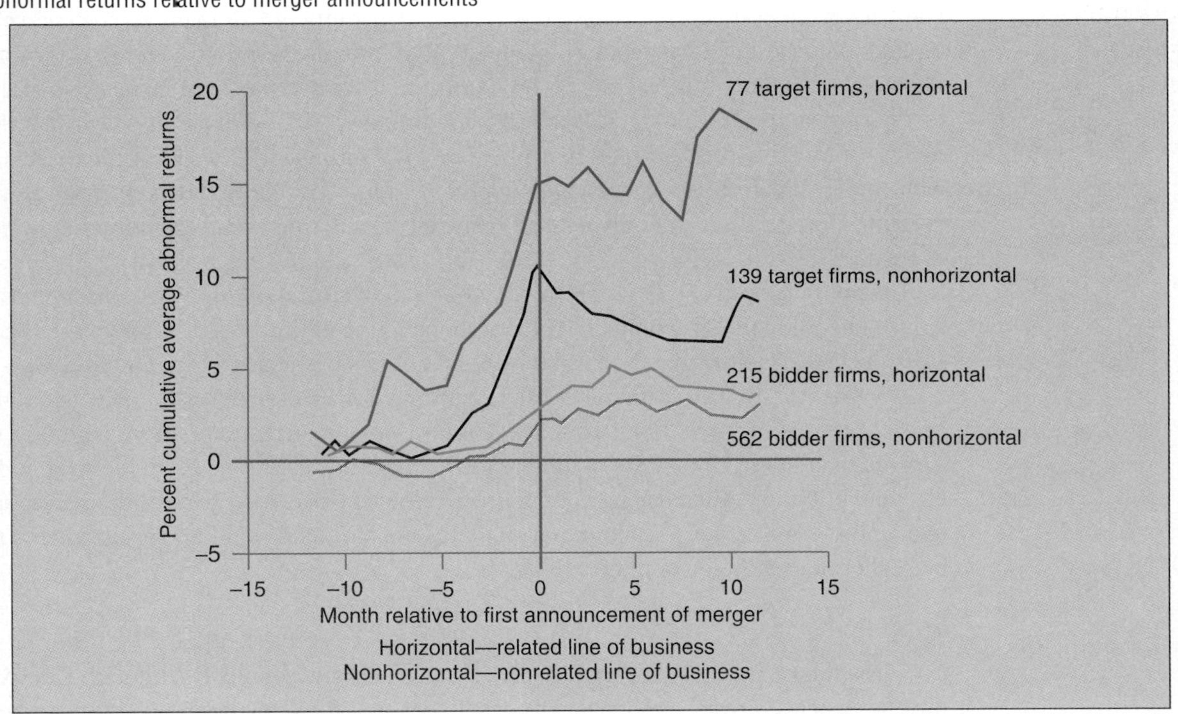

potential returns. Whether or not the buyer gets some of the value created by the merger is still a question requiring further research.

Holding Companies

Although the holding company has been declining in prominence in the United States as a corporate entity since the early 20th century, it is still a very important part of the ownership and control structure of the Canadian economy. A **holding company** is one that has control over one or more other firms. Power Corporation (POW), Onex (OCX), and Brascan (BNN.A) are significant Canadian holding companies. To establish voting control, the holding company may sometimes own less than a majority interest, but it is still able to determine policy as a result of widely spread minority interests among the other shareholders. Brascan in 2002, was controlling shareholder of Great Lakes Power, Trilon Financial, Noranda (and thus Falconbridge), Nexfor (pulp and paper), Brookfield Properties, and until October 2001, Canadian Hunter (Oil and Gas). There was a trend as we entered the 2000s to focus the businesses of the holding company. Brascan targeted real estate, financial services, and power generation. Power Corporation targeted financial services, communications, and in Europe, the energy/power sector. Onex took a broader view with firms in entertainment, automotives, building products, technology, and any other business that it felt could generate value.

Onex
www.onex.com

The primary advantage of the holding company is that it affords unusual opportunities for leverage. It also allows effective corporate control with minimal equity investments. Assume Giant Holding Corporation (GHC) has the investment interests in Companies A, B, and C shown in Table 20–5. Assume also that GHC has effective voting control of the three companies because of the widely dispersed interests of these companies' other owners. It owns 20 percent of the equity of Company A, 37.5 percent of Company B, and 25 percent of Company C. Through these interlocking positions, Giant Holding Corporation controls \$420 million in assets (the combined assets of the three companies), with only \$20 million of common stock equity in its own firm. Its equity-to-assets controlled ratio is 4.8 percent (\$20 million/\$420 million). If we really want to get creative, we can assume another holding company has control of Giant Holding Corporation with only a small investment in it, thus creating additional levels of ownership.

The holding company device also benefits from the isolation of the legal risks of the firms. Theoretically, if Company C loses money, this will not legally affect the other firms, because Company C is a separate legal entity with separate shareholders.

The fact that dividends paid from one Canadian corporation to another are generally free of tax makes the holding company form of organization much more common in Canada than in the United States, where those dividends would be partially taxable. In Canada, holding companies have often placed their investments in subsidiary companies in preferred rather than common shares as the dividends paid on preferred tend to be higher than those on common stock.

Drawbacks

The drawbacks are those inherent in any pyramiding arrangement. Although Companies A, B, and C are separate legal entities that cannot force the bankruptcy of another, there can still be a disastrous indirect chain effect. For example, if Company A has a bad year, it may be unable to pay dividends to the holding company, which in turn may be unable to pay interest on the \$15 million it has in long-term debt. The more complicated the arrangement, the more vulnerable the operation is to reversals.

The complicated administrative policies and procedures of a holding company are also worthy of note. With multiple managements, boards of directors, dividend policies, and reporting systems, the expenses are high and the opportunities for problems are substantial.

TABLE 20–5
Assets, liabilities, and owners' equity of Giant Holding Corporation and related companies (in $ millions)

GIANT HOLDING CORPORATION

Assets		Liabilities and Shareholders' Equity	
Common shareholdings:			
Company A	$ 10	Long-term debt	$ 15
Company B	15	Preferred stock	10
Company C	20	Common stock equity	20
	$ 45		$ 45

COMPANY A

Assets		Liabilities and Shareholders' Equity	
Current assets	$ 50	Current liabilities	$ 20
Plant and equipment	50	Long-term debt	30
	$100	Common stock equity	50
			$100

COMPANY B

Assets		Liabilities and Shareholders' Equity	
Current assets	$ 60	Current liabilities	$ 10
Plant and equipment	60	Long-term debt	70
	$120	Common stock equity	40
			$120

COMPANY C

Assets		Liabilities and Shareholders' Equity	
Current assets	$ 80	Current liabilities	$ 20
Plant and equipment	120	Long-term debt	100
	$200	Common stock equity	80
			$200

The Hees-Edper empire of the Bronfman family is a good example of these potential problems. In 1993 the entire structure, controlled through Brascan, was under severe strain as a result of cash flow deficiencies brought on by the recession of the early 1990s. It was thought the Hees-Edper structure was recession proof, but that was not the case. Extreme cash shortages were felt in several companies. The cash flow difficulties brought on by the slump in economic activity were pushed up the Hees-Edper structure as these companies could no longer afford to continue payment of their substantial dividends. The structure was dependent on these dividend payments to service debt. The continued high dividend payouts worsened the situation in several companies.

As a result of these painful cash flow problems, prize holdings were sold and the structure of the large conglomerate was greatly simplified. The Bronfman family's dominance was reduced significantly. Leverage is a two-edged sword. Poor returns are magnified in a corporate structure with heavy debt commitments. Furthermore, investors do not easily understand the structure of holding companies and this tends to depress the share price. This is part of the reason we have seen the breakup of large conglomerates at the turn of the millennium.

Summary

1. During the 1980s, the unsolicited tender offer for a target company gained in popularity. Offers were often made at values well in excess of the current market price, and management of the target company became trapped in the agency dilemma of maintaining its current position versus agreeing to the wishes of the acquiring company, and even the target company's own shareholders. To prevent takeovers, defensive measures include poison pills, shareholders' rights plans, targeted repurchase of shares, selling of crown jewels, and welcoming white knights.
2. Corporations may seek external growth through mergers to achieve risk reduction, to improve access to the financial markets through increased size, or to obtain tax loss carry-forward benefits. A merger may also expand the marketing and management capabilities of the firm and allow for new product development. While some mergers promise synergistic benefits (the 2 + 2 = 5 effect), these can be elusive, with initial expectations exceeding subsequent realities. Recently, as the economic environment has become more competitive and demanding, we have seen corporations refocus on their core business. Furthermore, many corporations may not realize the expected benefits of diversification.
3. The cash purchase of another corporation takes on many of the characteristics of a classic capital budgeting decision. In a stock-for-stock exchange, there is often a trade-off between an immediate increase in earnings per share and current dilution to achieve faster growth. If a firm buys another firm with a P/E ratio lower than its own, there is an immediate increase in earnings per share. However, long-term earnings growth prospects must also be considered. The ultimate objective of a merger, as is true of any financial decision, is shareholder wealth maximization, and the immediate and delayed effects of the merger must be evaluated in this context.
4. The accounting considerations in a merger are also important. Where the purchase price exceeds the book value of the acquired firm (after postmerger asset value adjustments), goodwill may be created. To avoid goodwill creation, many earlier mergers were treated as pooling of interests rather than purchases of assets. Virtually all current mergers, however, must be accounted for as purchases of assets with the attendant possibility of creating goodwill.
5. Diversification by combining entities with different patterns of cash flows reduces the variability of the overall cash flows. This should reduce risk and the attractiveness of the combined entity. Unfortunately for corporations, diversification has not always added the expected benefits, and in some cases, it has added unexpected management problems brought on by unfamiliarity with the new business. The benefits of diversification may be best achieved at the investor level.
6. The holding company is viewed as a means of accumulating large asset control with a minimum equity investment through leveraging the investment. The holding company is an important participant in the Canadian industrial and financial infrastructure. Surprisingly, there has been little research into the administrative problems inherent in this important form of organization. The drawbacks of holding companies have been seen in the difficulties of the Edper group in the early 1990s.

List of Terms

tender offer 708
white knight 709
crown jewels 709
targeted repurchase 709
golden parachutes 709
poison pills 709

shareholders' rights plans 709
competition law 711
Foreign Investment Review Agency 712
Investment Canada 712
merger 712
amalgamation 713
portfolio effect 713
leveraged buyout 714
tax loss carry-forward 714
synergy 714
terms of exchange 716
market value maximization 718
pooling of interests 719
purchase of assets 719
goodwill 720
merger premiums 721
ARBs (arbitrageurs) 721
market for corporate control 722
holding company 723

Discussion Questions

1. Briefly discuss three significant features of the merger movement of the past few decades.
2. Is risk reduction in the firm's portfolio of undertakings likely to be best achieved through horizontal integration, vertical integration, or conglomerate-type acquisitions?
3. If a firm wishes to achieve immediate appreciation in earnings per share as a result of a merger, how can this be best accomplished in terms of exchange variables? What is a possible drawback to this approach in terms of long-range considerations?
4. What is the essential difference between the pooling of interests and the purchase of assets accounting treatments of a merger? What is the effect of including goodwill?
5. Suggest synergy that might occur in mergers in the financial services or in the energy sectors.
6. Generally, a shareholder of the selling corporation demands a higher price if cash consideration is tendered. Explain why this might be the case.
7. Explain how the weak stock market of the late 1970s served as an impetus to the merger wave of the late 1970s and 1980s.
8. It is possible for the postmerger P/E ratio to move in a direction opposite to that of the immediate postmerger earnings per share. Explain why this could happen.
9. Explain why unusually high premiums have sometimes been paid in the latest merger movement.
10. Suggest some ways firms have tried to avoid being takeover targets.
11. Why do management and shareholders often have divergent viewpoints about the desirability of a takeover?
12. How can the ordinary investor benefit from a possible merger? What is the danger of investing in a proposed merger target? Explain.
13. How does a merger arbitrageur benefit from a possible merger? What is the danger in being a merger arbitrageur? Explain.
14. Compare the use of leverage in a holding company to the concept of operating and financial leverage explained in Chapter 5. Does a holding company have any tax complications related to dividends?
15. Why has the United States been traditionally concerned about corporate concentration arising from merger activity, while Canada's concern has been much more with foreign ownership?

INTERNET RESOURCES AND QUESTIONS

Mergers, acquisitions, and divestitures occur with increasing frequency in the financial markets. News services, public filings, company web sites, and share price activity are the best sources for this information.

News services:	www.canoe.ca
	www.globeandmail.com
	www.newswire.ca
Public securities filings:	www.sedar.com
Company web sites through:	www.tsx.ca
Share price charting:	www.bigcharts.com

1. Using recent news items, identify a potential or accomplished merger or acquisition.
   a. Comment on why the merger was proposed?
   b. Was the merger a friendly or hostile takeover?
   c. What share price was set on each company for the proposed takeover? Was the merger an exchange of shares or was it a cash offer?
   d. What relevant information was filed with the securities commission?
   e. Chart the price performance of both parties to the merger, for a reasonable period before and after the announcement date of the proposed merger. Comment on how the shares in each company performed over this period.
   f. Do you believe the merger is positive for the shareholders of the companies involved? Was the takeover positive for other stakeholders?

Problems

1. The Clark Corporation desires to expand. It is considering a cash purchase of Kent Enterprises for $3 million. Kent has a $700,000 tax loss carry-forward that could be used immediately by the Clark Corporation, which is paying taxes at the rate of 30 percent. Kent will provide $420,000 per year in cash flow (aftertax income plus CCA) for the next 20 years. If the Clark Corporation has a cost of capital of 13 percent, should the merger be undertaken?
2. The Wayne Corporation desires to expand. It is considering a cash purchase of the Gretz Corporation, a company in a similar business, for $3 million. The Gretz Corporation has a $600,000 tax loss carry-forward that could be used immediately by the Wayne Corporation, which is paying taxes at the rate of 40 percent. The Gretz Corporation is projected to provide $380,000 per year in available cash flows for the next 20 years. If the Wayne Corporation considers its cost of capital as 11 percent should it pursue the Gretz merger?

3. Assume the Citrus Corporation is considering the acquisition of Orange Juice, Inc. The latter has a $500,000 tax loss carry-forward. Projected earnings for the Citrus Corporation are as follows:

	2003	2004	2005	Total
Before-tax income	$200,000	$250,000	$380,000	$830,000
Taxes (40%)	80,000	100,000	152,000	332,000
Income available to shareholders	$120,000	$150,000	$228,000	$498,000

   a. How much will the total taxes of Citrus Corporation be reduced as a result of the tax loss carry-forward?
   b. How much will the total income available to shareholders be for the three years if the acquisition occurs?
4. Border Investments, Inc., is considering a cash acquisition of Bubba Brewing Co. for $2.2 million. Bubba Brewing will provide the following pattern of cash inflows and synergistic benefits for the next 20 years. There is no tax loss carry-forward.

	Years		
	1–5	6–15	16–20
Cash inflow (aftertax)	$220,000	$240,000	$280,000
Synergistic benefits (aftertax)	$20,000	$22,000	$40,000

The cost of capital for the acquiring firm is 12 percent. Should the merger be undertaken?

5. Assume the following financial data for the Barker Corporation and Howell Enterprises.

	Barker Corporation	Howell Enterprises
Total earnings	$400,000	$1,200,000
Number of shares of stock outstanding	200,000	1,000,000
Earnings per share	$2.00	$1.20
Price-earnings ratio (P/E)	12×	20×
Market price per share	$24.00	$24.00

a. If all the shares of the Barker Corporation are exchanged for shares of the Howell Enterprises on a share-for-share basis, what will postmerger earnings per share be for Howell Enterprises? Use an approach similar to Table 20–4.

b. Explain why the earnings per share of Howell Enterprises changed.

c. Can we necessarily assume that Howell Enterprises is better or worse off?

6. Gil Whitaker helped start Marshall Engineering Company in 1962. At the time, he purchased 200,000 shares of stock at one dollar per share. In 2003 he has the opportunity to sell his interest in the company to Beta Technology for $40.00 a share. His tax rate would be 28 percent.

a. If he sells his interest, what will be the value for before-tax profit, taxes, and aftertax profit?

b. Assume, instead of cash, he accepts stock valued at $40.00 per share. He holds the stock for five years and then sells it for $72.50 (the stock pays no cash dividends). What will be the value for before-tax profit, taxes, and aftertax profit?

c. Using an 11 percent discount rate, compare the aftertax profit figure in part *b* to part *a*.

7. Winnipeg Athletics Corporation is planning to make an offer for Halifax Sporting Goods Ltd. The shares of Halifax Sporting Goods are currently selling for $40.00 per share.

a. If the tender offer is planned at a premium of 60 percent over market price, what will be the offered share price for Halifax Sporting Goods?

b. Suppose before the offer is actually announced the share price of Halifax rises to $56.00 because of strong merger rumors. If you buy the shares at that price and the merger goes through at the price computed in part *a*, calculate your percentage gain?

c. There is always the possibility that the merger will be called off after it is announced and the share will fall to their original price Calculate your percentage loss if this occurs and you bought at $56.00?

d. If there is an 80 percent probability that the merger will go proceed and only a 20 percent chance that it will be called off, does this appear to be a good investment? Assume your purchase price was $56.00.

8. A merger between Pica Corporation and Elite Corporation is under consideration. The financial information for these firms is as follows:

www.mcgrawhill.ca/college/block

	Elite Corporation	Pica Corporation
Total earnings	$300,000	$600,000
Number of shares of stock outstanding	100,000	300,000
Earnings per share	$3	$2
Price-earnings ratio (P/E)	8×	12×
Market price per share	$24	$24

a. On a share-for-share exchange basis, what will the postmerger earnings per share be?

b. If Pica Corporation pays a 25 percent premium over the market value of Elite Corporation, how many shares will be issued?

c. With the 25 percent premium, what will the postmerger earnings per share be? (Round to the nearest cent.)

d. With a 50 percent premium, how many shares will be issued and what will be the postmerger earnings per share?

e. With a 75 percent premium, how many shares will be issued and what will be the postmerger earnings per share?

f. Explain what has happened in parts *a, c, d*, and *e* in terms of relative P/E ratios and the earnings per share impact of the acquisition.

9. In the case of the Pica and Elite merger described in the previous problem, assume a 100 percent premium will be paid, but there is a 20 percent synergistic benefit to total earnings from the merger. Will the postmerger earnings go up or down based on your calculations?

10. Assume the Knight Corporation is considering the acquisition of Day Inc. The expected earnings per share for the Knight Corporation will be $4.00 with or without the merger. However, the standard deviation of the earnings will go from $2.40 to $1.60 with the merger because the two firms are negatively correlated.

a. Compute the coefficient of variation for the Knight Corporation before and after the merger (consult Chapter 13 to review statistical concepts if necessary).

b. Discuss the possible impact on Knight's postmerger P/E ratio, assuming investors are risk-averse.

11. Bork Construction Company is considering two mergers. The first is with Firm A in its own volatile industry; the second is a merger with Firm B in an industry that moves in the opposite direction (and will tend to level out performance due to negative correlation).

Bork Construction Merger with Firm A		Bork Construction Merger with Firm B	
Possible Earnings ($ in millions)	Probability	Possible Earnings ($ in millions)	Probability
$10	.30	$30	.25
40	.40	40	.50
70	.30	50	.25

a. Compute the mean, standard deviation, and coefficient of variation for both investments. (Consult Chapter 13 to review statistical concepts if necessary.)

a. Assume investors are risk-averse, which alternatives can be expected to bring the higher valuation?

12. Wright Aerospace is considering the acquisition of Columbus Shipping Corporation. The book value of the Columbus Shipping Corporation is $30 million, and Wright Aerospace is

willing to pay $90 million in cash and preferred stock. No upward adjustment of asset values is anticipated. Wright Aerospace Corporation has 2 million shares outstanding. A purchase of assets financial recording will be used.

a. How much will the annual amortization be?

b. Is any tax benefit involved?

c. Explain how the recording of goodwill could have been avoided.

13. The Montreal Power Corporation, a holding company, has investments in three other firms. Values are expressed in millions of dollars.

MORENZ CORPORATION

Assets		Liabilities and Shareholders' Equity	
Current assets	$100	Current liabilities	$ 50
Plant and equipment	200	Long-term debt	150
		Common equity	100
	$300		$300

RICHARD CORPORATION

Assets		Liabilities and Shareholders' Equity	
Current assets	$150	Current liabilities	$150
Plant and equipment	250	Long-term debt	100
		Common equity	150
	$400		$400

LAFLEUR CORPORATION

Assets		Liabilities and Shareholders' Equity	
Current assets	$175	Current liabilities	$ 50
Plant and equipment	275	Long-term debt	200
		Common equity	200
	$450		$450

The Montreal Power Corporation has voting control of the three other corporations with the following investment interests in each: 20 percent of the equity in Morenz Corporation, 30 percent of the equity in Richard Corporation, and 25 percent of the equity in the Lafleur Corporation.

Montreal Power Corporation's long-term debt is equal to 30 percent of its assets; its preferred stock is equal to 20 percent; and its common stock is equal to 50 percent.

a. Fill in the following table for Montreal Power Corporation:

Assets		Liabilities and Shareholders' Equity	
Common shareholdings:			
Morenz Corporation	______	Long-term debt	______
Richard Corporation	______	Preferred stock	______
Lafleur Corporation	______	Common equity	______
Total	______	Total	______

b. Compute the percentage of Montreal Power Corporation's common equity to the total holding company assets in the three corporations.

COMPREHENSIVE PROBLEM

14. It was 5:30 Friday afternoon, January 22, 2003. Bill Hall, the chairman and CEO of National Brands, Inc., was clearing up the last of the papers on his desk and was looking forward to a relaxing weekend. It had been a good week. The company's annual results were in, and they showed that 2002 had been the best year in the company's history. Sales and net income were up over 8 percent from last year, and there was over $1.1 billion in the cash and equivalents account to invest in the coming year.

The phone rang. It was Maria Ortiz, his secretary. "Did you hear the latest on the newswire?" Maria asked.

"No, what's up?" Bill replied, with a suspicious feeling that his evening wasn't going to be so relaxing after all.

"Kelly O'Brien, head of A-1 Holdings, just announced that he's bought 5 percent of our outstanding shares, and now he's making a tender offer for all of the rest at $55.00."

"I knew it!" Bill spat out. "He was in here just a few weeks ago, talking about whether we would sell the company to him. We turned down his offer because we want to stay independent, and he left after implying that we weren't looking out for our shareholders. He's got some plan to restructure the company around a six-member board of directors instead of the 15 we have now. Now he's trying to do it anyway, whether we like it or not!"

"Looks like it," Maria agreed. "So what do you think we should do?"

"OK, contact Tom Straw, the chief operating officer and Doris Faraday in finance, and tell them to get up here for a meeting right away," Bill directed. "Oh, and have Stan Lindner from public relations come, too; we're sure to have a press release about this, and—oh, wait—call my wife and tell her I won't be home until late tonight."

After about half an hour, those that Bill had called for began arriving, armed with pencils, papers, and calculators in anticipation of the coming session. Bill, in the meantime, had managed to compile some financial data about A-1 Holdings, which he had summarized on a sheet of paper along with like data about his own company, National Brands, for comparison as shown in Table 1. He passed the sheet around among the others.

"OK, let's start with what we know," Bill led off. "A-1 already has 5 percent of our outstanding shares, and it is making a bid for the rest at $55.00, or 7.875 over market."

"I hate to be the devil's advocate," Stan said, thinking of the 1,000 shares he owned personally, "but that sounds like a pretty fair offer. What will happen if he succeeds?"

"Most of us will be out of a job, and this company will become just another card in Kelly O'Brien's poker hand," Bill said acidly. "Our employees deserve better than that, so let's talk about what we can do to keep it from happening."

"What about a poison pill?" Tom suggested. "We could take out a fair-sized loan based on our heavy cash position, and A-1 would have a tough time absorbing it—just look at the amount of debt they're carrying now!

"That would probably work, but it's not very good for us, either," Stan agreed. He was still thinking about the $7.00 per share profit to be made in a buyout. "So how about someone else? You know, a white knight who would top A-1's offer but would keep the structure of the company substantially the same as it is now."

TABLE 1
Selected financial data

	National Brands	A-1 Holdings
Total earnings expected in the coming year	$ 500,000,000	$ 192,000,000
Number of shares outstanding	113,640,000	61,800,000
Earnings per share	$ 4.40	$ 3.11
Price-earnings ratio	10.9	4.2
Market price	$ 47.88	$ 13.00
Book value per share	$ 26.84	$ 6.39
Growth rate before merger	8.53%	19.61%
Liquid assets (cash and equivalent)	$1,153,000,000	$1,736,800,000
Total assets	$5,160,300,000	$2,294,500,000
Total debt	$2,110,300,000	$1,899,500,000
Total equity	$3,050,000,000	$ 395,000,000
Dividend-payout ratio	48.0%	0.0%

"I don't know who we could ask," Bill said, "and besides that, the basic problem would probably still occur—we would lose our status as an independent entity."

Doris had been working on some figures on her pad, and she spoke up now. "There's another alternative," she said, "that I'm surprised you all haven't mentioned, given the financial status of the two companies."

"What, what!" Bill said. "Don't keep us in suspense!"

"It's the Pacman defence," she continued, unruffled. "What we do is launch a tender offer of our own for all of A-1's outstanding stock. If it's successful, we not only thwart the takeover attempt but we gain a new business in the bargain."

"Didn't Martin Marietta try that with Bendix back in 1982?" Bill asked. "As I recall, it didn't turn out very well for them."

"You're right; it didn't," Doris agreed, "and no one else has tried it since. But just comparing the numbers here between National and A-1, I think it might work out quite well for us. I've been doing some calculating here, and I think an offer to A-1's shareholders of $17.00 a share would be accepted, and we could conclude the whole affair rather quickly."

"I'm interested." Bill said. "Tell you what: Put your finance staff on it over the weekend and have them work up the proposal formally. Get the legal and accounting people to help you too. In the meantime, Stan, tip off the news media that we will have an announcement of our own shortly and draft up a public notice for A-1's shares at $17.00 each. Don't release it yet, but be ready to on Monday. Oh, and be sure to include in it that I said the deal will not cause any dilution of National's earnings per share. One last thing, Doris, draft an open letter to our shareholders for my signature, explaining what's happening and reassuring them that we will keep their company intact and prosperous.

"Any questions? If not, let's get on it. Mr. O'Brien is about to get a surprise!"

a. (1) A-1 is offering $55.00 per share for National's stock. How much total cash will it have to raise to buy the company? (The remaining 95 percent?)

(2) Assume A-1 plans to borrow the money needed to make the purchase. If A-1 uses the amount of liquid assets presently on hand at National to offset the amount it needs to borrow, what is the net amount it will have to borrow?

(3) Assuming A-1 does borrow the amount you determined in (2) above, what will A-1's total debt be after the purchase is completed? In making your calculation, consider all forms of debt that the combined firm will have. Now compute A-1's debt-to-equity ratio (A-1's equity will not increase). Given this ratio, do you think it is likely that A-1 will be able to obtain the necessary debt financing?

(4) Suppose instead that A-1 decides to issue stock to raise the money needed for the purchase (i.e., the amount you computed in (2) above will be raised through a stock issue instead of by borrowing). How many shares of A-1 stock will have to be issued? (Assume the price at which it will be issued is $13.00 and disregard flotation costs.)

(5) If A-1 raises the money by issuing new shares of its stock, what will A-1's EPS be after the purchase is complete and the earnings are combined?

(6) Do you think A-1's shareholders will be happy if this deal goes through? What about the old National shareholders?

b. (1) If National employs the Pacman defence and tries to buy A-1 for $17.00 per share, how much will the total dollar price be?

(2) If National wants to finance the purchase by issuing stock, and it plans to use the amount of liquid assets on hand at A-1 to offset the amount of stock that needs to be issued, what will the total dollar price be? (Assume they will be issued at $47.88 and disregard flotation costs.)

(3) What will be National's debt-to-equity ratio after the purchase is complete? (Assume it was completed per your calculations in (2) above.) Note that National's total equity will not increase since no new shares are issued.

(4) Suppose instead that National decides to first use A-1's liquid assets to pay down most of A-1's debt. How many shares of National at $47.88 will have to be issued? Use the cost figure from your answer to (1).

(5) What will the new National's EPS be, assuming the deal is completed per your calculations in (4) above?

(6) Is Bill Hall correct in his statement that National's EPS will not be diluted as a result of the purchase of A-1?

c. If National's P/E does not change following the purchase of A-1, what will its stock price be? Is it likely that National's P/E will remain at 10.9? Or do you think it will rise or fall?

d. (1) Do you think National's Pacman defence will be successful? Or do you think A-1 will succeed in buying out National?

(2) Do you think that National's shareholders are better off as a result of A-1's attack and National's Pacman defence (assuming it succeeds)?

(3) Do you think Kelly O'Brien, head of A-1, should be viewed as a "good guy," whose action will produce more efficient companies, or a "bad guy," who is a destroyer of traditional values and employees' careers?

Selected References

Boswell, Stewart. "Buying and Selling Companies in the New Millennium." *Journal of Applied Corporate Finance* 12 (Winter 2000), pp. 70–80.

Dewenter, Kathryn L. "Does the Market React Differently to Domestic and Foreign Takeover Announcements? Evidence from the U.S. Retail and Chemical Industries." *Journal of Financial Economics* 37 (March 1995), pp. 421–41.

Ghosh, Aloke, and William Ruland. "Managerial Ownership, the Methods of Payment for Acquisitions, and Executive Job Retention." *Journal of Finance* 53 (April 1998), pp. 785–98.

Golbe, Debra L., and Mary L. Schanz. "Bidder Incentives for Informed Trading before Hostile Offer Announcements." *Financial Management* 23 (Winter 1994), pp. 57–68.

Kohers, Ninon, and Theodor Kohers. "The Value Creation Potential of High-Tech Mergers." *Financial Analysts Journal* 56 (May-June 2000), pp. 40–50.

Loughran, Tim, and Anand M. Vijh. "Do Long-term Shareholders Benefit from Corporate Acquisitions?" *Journal of Finance* 52 (December 1997) pp. 1765–90.

Song, Moon H., and Ralph A. Walking. "Abnormal Returns to Rivals of Acquisition Targets: A Test of the Acquisition Probability Hypothesis." *Journal of Financial Economics* 55 (February 2000), pp. 143–171.

Sridharan, Uma V., and Marc R. Reinganum. "Determinants of the Choice of the Hostile Takeover Mechanism: An Empirical Analysis of Tender Offers and Proxy Contests." *Financial Management* (Spring 1995), pp. 57–67.

Stulz, Rene M., Ralph A. Walkling, and Moon H. Song. "The Distribution of Target Ownership and the Division of Gains in Successful Takeovers." *Journal of Finance* 45 (July 1990), pp. 817–33.

Vijh, Anand M. "The Spinoff and Merger Ex-Date Effects." *Journal of Finance* 49 (June 1994), pp. 581–609.

CHAPTER | TWENTY-ONE

21 International Financial Management

LEARNING | OBJECTIVES

1. Describe the purposes and nature of the multinational operations of the corporation.
2. Discuss the effects of exchange rates on the firm's profitability and cash flow.
3. Outline the factors influencing exchange rates.
4. Define spot and forward exchange rates and compute forward premiums and discounts.
5. Evaluate techniques to hedge or reduce foreign exchange risk.
6. Discuss the impact of political risk on the foreign investment decision.
7. Analyze a foreign investment decision.
8. Outline potential ways to finance international operations.

Introduction

By the turn of the new millennium, world exports had reached $10 trillion in merchandise and commercial services. The political systems that emerged from World War II contributed to the establishment of trade relations between nations and the sustained growth of the world economy. During the 1950s and 1960s, the United States became the dominant player in the world economy, with the U.S. dollar used as the reserve currency. Meanwhile, the European nations formed the European Common Market in an effort to promote better trade relations among themselves, and today the EC Market rivals the might of the U.S. market. In the East, the rise of Japan and other Asian countries has added significant players to the world economy. Today the U.S. economy is not as dominant as after World War II. In recent years the United States has incurred enormous trade deficits and external debt, which has necessitated large capital flows and placed great demands on the world financial markets. Enormous capital investments around the globe have followed the increased trade.

Nations today are dependent on one another for many valuable and scarce resources. Just as Canada is dependent on Japan for a large portion of the automobiles used here, Japan is dependent on Canada for the coal it uses in making the steel that is incorporated in those cars. Russia, once dependent on Canada and the United States for agricultural commodities and high-technology goods, now seems dependent on capital. This growing interdependence necessitates the development of sound international business relations. It is virtually impossible for any country to isolate itself from the impact of international developments in an integrated world economy, and today capitalism seems part of every economy, including the Chinese economy.

To a greater extent than any other industrialized economy, Canada is truly open to the forces of world trade. The significance of international business operations becomes more apparent if we look at the importance of foreign trade relative to the size of the Canadian economy. Figures 21–1 and 21–2 (on the next page) show the world's top merchandise exporters and importers in 2000. Canada exported \$479 billion worth of goods out of a total production of \$1.1 trillion in 2001, or almost 45 percent of Canada's annual production of goods and services. In comparison, the United States, a major player in international trade by any absolute measure, exports just over 10 percent of its domestic production.

The importance of access to U.S. markets for Canadian economic success is demonstrated by Figure 21–3 (on the next page). In exports and imports, trade with the United States dwarfs our trade with other regions of the world. Canada's strong trade ties with the United States combined with Canada's physically large but economically small domestic market, led to the implementation of the Free Trade Agreement (FTA) between Canada and the United States in 1989. This agreement opens more opportunities for truly competitive Canadian enterprises, on the one hand, while threatening the viability of others not able to match international levels of efficiency. This agreement was followed in the 1990s by the North American Free Trade Agreement (NAFTA).

Alcan
www.alcan.com

In such a trade-oriented economy, it is natural that many of our Canadian corporations would be heavily involved in international operations. Alcan, the large aluminum company, generated 95 percent of its revenue outside of Canada in 2000, although 32

FIGURE 21–1

World's leading merchandise exporters, 2000

$ billions
1,400
1,200
1,000
800
600
400
200
0
United States
Germany
Japan
France
Britain
Canada
China
Italy
Netherlands
Hong Kong

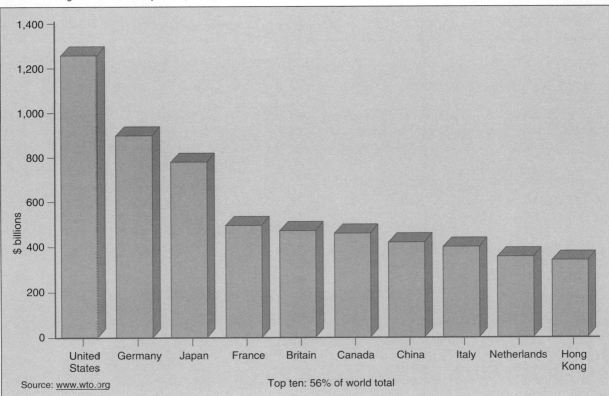

Source: www.wto.org

Top ten: 56% of world total

FIGURE 21–2

World's leading merchandise importers, 2000

$ billions

2,000
1,800
1,600
1,400
1,200
1,000
800
600
400
200
0

United States
Germany
Japan
Britain
France
Canada
Italy
China
Hong Kong
Netherlands

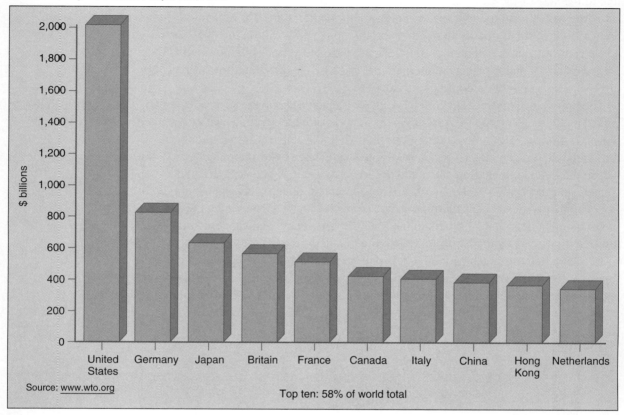

Source: www.wto.org

Top ten: 58% of world total

FIGURE 21–3

Canada's 2001 merchandise exports and imports by region

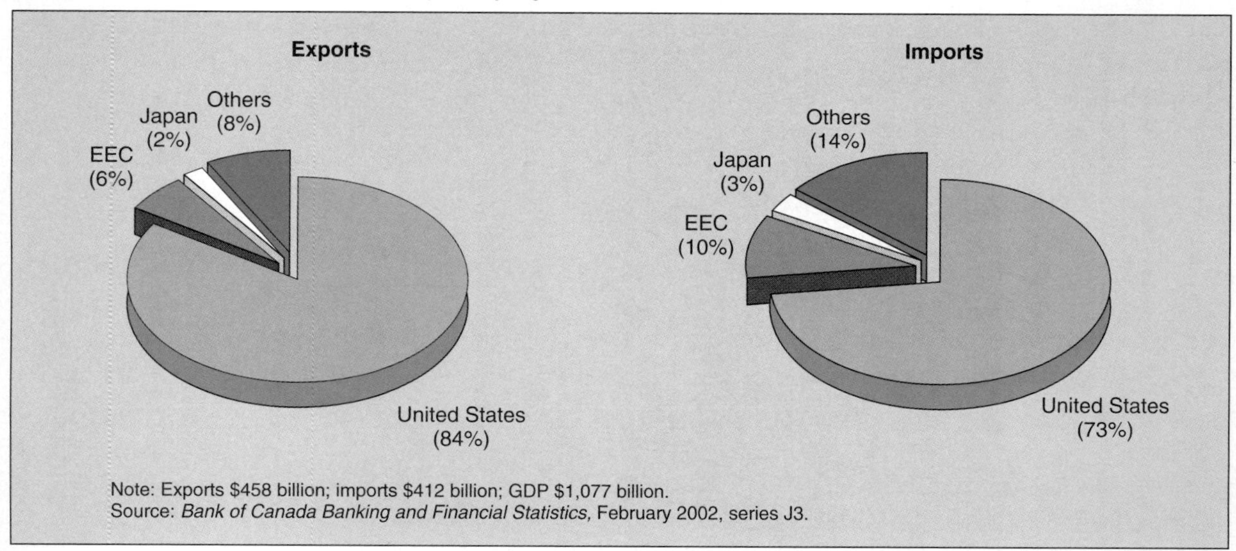

Note: Exports $458 billion; imports $412 billion; GDP $1,077 billion.

percent of its assets were in Canada. Bombardier, a world leader in transportation equipment, produced only 7 percent of its revenues in Canada. Historically, the country's major Canadian banks have derived a significant percentage of their earnings from foreign operations. International operations represent over 40 percent of the assets of Canadian banks.

Just as foreign operations affect the performance of Canadian business firms, developments in international financial markets also affect our lifestyles. In early 2000, if you had vacationed in Buenos Aires, $3,000 Canadian dollars could have been exchanged for $1,875 Argentinean pesos, but one year later you would have received $5,000 pesos. On the other side of the ledger, if you have gone to Disneyland lately, you would have noticed a tremendous price increase compared to its cost only a few years earlier. The much lower value of the Canadian dollar in relation to the U.S. dollar is one of the reasons for the significant increase in American visits to Canada in recent years. Fluctuations in currency values affect Canadians in one way or another, as about 45 percent of our purchases are for products and services from other countries.

Travel to Argentina or Disneyland highlights another aspect of Canada's dealings with the rest of the world, besides merchandise trade. International trade and financial transactions are identified in the current account of Canada's international balance of payments, as shown in Figure 21–4 (on the next page). The international balance of payments attempts to record all the transactions that occur between Canada and the rest of the world over one year. Included in the current account are merchandise exports and imports, travel, other services (i.e., business), payments on capital investments by way of interest and dividends, and other transfers such as inheritances or personal remittances. The other portion of the balance of payments, the capital account, records direct investment and investment in financial securities. From Figure 21–4 we note the substantial flows on merchandise trade and that in 2001 Canada had a surplus (exports exceeded imports). Despite deficit in other accounts the balance of payments had an overall surplus in 2001 of approximately $22 billion. Interest on the debts of Canadians is in a significant deficit position. Fortunately the capital account will show a deficit indicating increased foreign investment by Canadians, which balances the current and capital accounts. The current account surplus should have a positive influence on our dollar although there are other factors that come into play in determining exchange rates.

This chapter deals with the international dimensions of corporate finance. We believe this chapter provides a basis for understanding the complexities of international financial decisions. Such an understanding is important whether you work for a multinational manufacturing firm, a large commercial bank, a major brokerage firm, or any firm involved in international transactions or are just involved in managing your own personal financial affairs.

International business operations, by their very nature, are often complex, risky, and require special understanding. Many major Canadian banks have had to learn the lessons of international finance through painful experience. During recessionary periods, many less developed countries have had trouble repaying their bank debt obligations due to declining exports. The inability of these countries to make payments on mammoth debts owed to the commercial banking system severely tests the ingenuity of world financial institutions. As we enter the next millennium, the risks of international lending are again being relearned as Argentina initiates the world's biggest debt default.

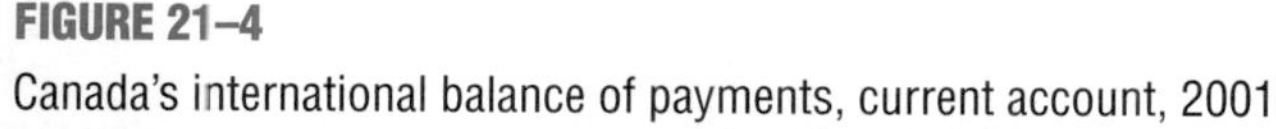

FIGURE 21–4

Canada's international balance of payments, current account, 2001

$ billions

450
400
350
300
250
200
150
100
50
0
–50

Merchandise | Travel | Other services | Interest income | Dividends & R.E. | Transfers

Receipts | Payments | Net (+$22,104)

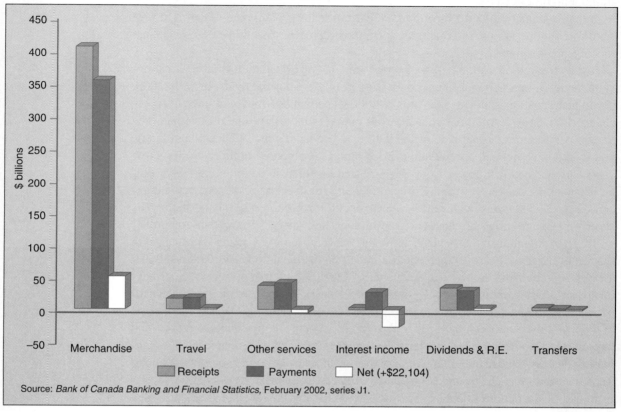

Source: *Bank of Canada Banking and Financial Statistics,* February 2002, series J1.

The following section describes the international business firm and its environment. Then, foreign exchange rates and the factors influencing these rates are explained, followed by strategies for dealing with foreign exchange risk. Briefly, political risk is described, and the reasons for foreign investment are examined. Finally, international financing sources, including the Eurodollar market, the Eurobond market, and foreign equity markets, are discussed.

The Multinational Corporation: Nature and Environment

The focus of international financial management has been the multinational corporation (MNC). One might ask, just what is a multinational corporation? Some definitions of a **multinational corporation** require that a minimum percentage (often 30 percent or more) of a firm's business activities be carried on outside its national borders. For purposes of our discussion, however, a firm doing business across its national borders is considered a multinational enterprise. Four of the several forms that such multinational corporations can take are briefly examined.

Exporter An MNC could produce a product domestically and export some of that production to one or more foreign markets. This is generally considered the least risky method of going international—reaping the benefits of foreign demand without committing any long-term investment to a foreign country.

Licensing Agreement A firm with exporting operations may get into trouble when a foreign government imposes or substantially raises an import tariff to a level at which the exporter cannot compete effectively with the local domestic manufacturers. The foreign government may even ban all imports into the country at times. When this happens, the exporting firm may grant a license to an independent local producer to use the firm's technology in return for a license fee or a royalty. In essence, then, the MNC exports technology rather than the product to that foreign country. Another advantage of licensing over straight export arises when some adaptation of the product for local preference is desirable.

Joint Venture As an alternative to licensing, the MNC may establish a joint venture with a local foreign manufacturer. The legal, political, and economic environments around the globe are more conducive to the joint venture arrangement than any of the other modes of operations. Many countries permit foreign multinationals to carry out business in their countries only if they have a local partner with a substantial ownership interest. Such regulations explain why Ford did not set up operations in China in the 1950s, or Coca-Cola in India. Historical evidence also suggests that a joint venture with a local entrepreneur exposes the firm to the least amount of political risk. Consequently, this form of business is preferred by many business firms and by foreign governments as well.

Fully Owned Foreign Subsidiary Although the joint venture form is desirable for many reasons, it may be hard to find a willing and cooperative local entrepreneur with sufficient capital to participate. In addition, as mentioned earlier, some multinationals have had policies prohibiting joint ventures. Under these conditions the MNC may have to set up foreign operations alone. For political reasons, however, a wholly owned foreign subsidiary is becoming more of a rarity. During the remainder of this chapter, we use the term foreign affiliate to refer to either a joint venture or a fully owned subsidiary.

The environment faced by the MNC is riskier and more complex than that of the domestic economy. Differences in rates of taxation, financial market structure, local administrative practices, social customs, and cultural mores must all be dealt with by the MNC. The attraction of international finance is that with increased risk comes the possibility of increased returns. The major risks that the firm must contend with are foreign exchange fluctuations and political interference.

Foreign Exchange Rates

Suppose you are planning to spend a semester in Paris studying French culture and you have been granted a $4,000 scholarship to support you while you are there. To put your plan into operation, you will no longer need French currency (i.e., French francs-FF), but euros, the common currency of Europe, to pay for your expenses during your stay in France. How many euros you obtain for $2,000 depends on the exchange rate at the particular time you offer your Canadian dollars for sale in exchange for the euros. The relationship between the values of two currencies is known as the **foreign exchange rate.** The exchange rate between Canadian dollars and euros can be stated as dollars per euros or euros per dollar. For example, the quotation of $1.3805 per euro is the same as 0.7244 euros per dollar (1/1.3805 = 0.7244). At this exchange rate you can purchase 1,449 euros with $2,000.

FINANCE IN ACTION

Q1 What is the current exchange rate of the Euro to the $ Canadian, £ British, and $ U.S.?

www.ecb.int

The Birth of a New Currency—The Euro!

The dream of a united Europe with one currency has existed since the 1950s. On January 4, 1999, the dream of a single currency became a reality as the European Monetary Union (EMU) came into effect. A new common currency, the euro, became the legal currency for eleven countries (Germany, France, Italy, Austria, the Netherlands, Spain, Portugal, Finland, Belgium, Ireland, and Luxembourg). These countries used their traditional currencies such as the German deutsche mark, Italian lira, and French franc alongside the euro until 2002. Then the euro became the only legal currency in the countries of the European Monetary Union, with currency notes and coins available. Greece came into the Union by 2002. All electronic payments, bank transactions, and stock and bond market trades are recorded in euros. If you travel to Europe and use a credit card, it will be recorded in euros and translated to Canadian dollars.

Over the weekend before its debut, the banks of Europe reprogrammed their computers to handle all future transactions in euros. On opening day the euro jumped from U.S.$1.17 to U.S.$1.18, and all European stock markets, except Britain's, were up about 5 percent. Britain chose not to join the EMU. The initial euphoria created by the new currency waned in the period after its introduction, and by the time the euro became the official currency with coins and bills in circulation in 2002, its value had drifted downward to about U.S.$0.90. This was likely the result of the U.S. economy's strong performance compared to Europe's, over the following years.

This monetary union exerts pressure for common monetary policy through the European Central Bank and will create more uniform economic policy across the region. In fact, to join the EMU, individual countries had to achieve targeted goals on budget deficits and inflation rates. The new currency should reduce the cost of doing business in many ways. One very tangible way is the elimination of exchange rates between these currencies. Hedging activities between the German mark and French franc will no longer be necessary. A German company buying French products will no longer have to buy forward contracts to deliver French francs in payment of those French goods. Of course, foreign trading between Canada and the other members of the European Monetary Union will still require hedging the Canadian dollar against the euro.

In terms of trading goods between countries, the eleven EMU countries are being referred to as the Euro Zone or Euroland. The Euro Zone represents a larger exporting presence than the United States. The union is as much political as economic, and for it to be abandoned at some time in the future, there would have to be a breakdown in free trade and a political decision among the participants. It will get harder and harder for the EMU to collapse the longer it exists. Many experts predict that the euro will eventually rival the U.S. dollar as a world reserve currency.

Exchange Rates
pacific.commerce.ubc.ca/xr/data.html

The Globe and Mail and the *Financial Post* publish exchange rates for the major currencies daily. A good web site for quotes is available at (pacific.commerce.ubc.ca/xr/data.html). Table 21–1 illustrates the currencies of a number of countries and their exchange rates relative to the Canadian dollar. This table lists the number of units (or fractions thereof) of a foreign currency that one could purchase with one Canadian dollar (foreign currency units/$) on a particular day in the month indicated. Foreign exchange rates change from minute to minute and from day to day.

The changes in the exchange rates can be readily noticed from this table. By comparing exchange rates in September 1985 with those of March 2002, you observe that $1.00 would buy less of many European foreign currencies as time went on, but now those currencies are gone. In other words, the value of the Canadian dollar—its exchange rate—had fallen against many of these currencies between 1985 and 2002. For example, one dollar would have bought 1.76 Swiss francs in September 1985, but only

TABLE 21–1
Selected currencies and exchange rates (number of foreign currency units you can purchase with one Canadian dollar)

		Exchange Rate (per Canadian $1)			
Country	**Currency Unit**	**Sept. 1985**	**April 1996**	**Feb. 1999**	**March 2002**
Austria	schilling	15.0277	7.7598	8.1967	**euro**
Brazil	cruzeiro	5.2544	changed to real		
	real			1.2367	1.4719
China	renminbi	2.1561	6.1200	5.5648	5.1894
Denmark	krone	7.7475	4.2735	4.4287	5.3821
France	franc	6.5008	3.7538	3.9078	**euro**
Germany	deutsche mark	2.1390	1.1068	1.1651	**euro**
India	rupee	8.9137	25.1572	28.4981	30.5064
Italy	lira	1,417.00	1,152.07	1,153.40	**euro**
Jamaica	dollar	–	27.8200	24.734	29.7177
Japan	yen	177.2300	78.6782	76.0456	83.6120
Mexico	peso	254.5167	changed to new peso		
	n. peso			6.7705	5.6948
Netherlands	guilder	2.3956	1.2370	1.3127	**euro**
Portugal	escudo	127.02	113.37	119.47	**euro**
South Africa	rand	1.8839	3.1348	3.9984	7.0572
Spain	peseta	125.52	91.99	99.11	**euro**
Sudan	dinars	–	110.000	143.280	162.075
Sweden	krona	6.2673	4.9261	5.2770	6.5789
Switzerland	franc	1.7655	0.8984	0.9530	1.0693
Thailand	baht	–	18.6518	24.8016	27.3673
United Kingdom	pound	0.5506	0.4842	0.4106	0.4418
United States	dollar	0.7300	0.7346	0.6721	0.6269
Venezuela	bolivar	–	213.9999	386.8472	630.120
Europe	euro	–	–	0.5957	0.7244

1.07 Swiss francs in March 2002. This means that the purchasing power of the dollar against the Swiss franc fell almost 40 percent over this period. By taking the reciprocal of these two values, we could also say the Swiss franc was worth 0.5664 (1/1.7655) dollars in September 1985 and 0.9352 (1/1.0693) dollars in March 2002. Thus, had you received your $4,000 scholarship in 1985 and gone to Switzerland, it would have bought you SF7,062 and higher standard of living during a stay in Zurich than if you received it in 2002.

Over the most recent period from 1996 to 2002, the Canadian dollar strengthened against most currencies, with the notable exceptions of the U.S. dollar, the British pound, the Mexican N. peso and the Chinese renminbi. Too often the Canadian dollar is judged only against the U.S. dollar, perhaps because of how closely our economy is tied to the U.S. economy. Notice that the Brazilian and Mexican currencies had such severe devaluation, due to high inflation rates in the late 1980s that they had to rename their currencies and start over again.

Factors Influencing Exchange Rates

The present international monetary system consists of a mixture of freely floating exchange rates and fixed rates. The currencies of Canada's major trading partners are traded in free markets. In such a market, the supply of, and the demand for, those currencies determine the exchange rate between two currencies. This activity, however, is subject to intervention by many countries' central banks. Factors that tend to increase the supply or decrease the demand schedule for a given currency bring down the value of that currency in foreign exchange markets. Similarly, the factors that tend to decrease the supply or increase the demand for a currency raise the value of that currency. Since fluctuations in currency values result in foreign exchange risk, the financial executive must understand the factors causing these changes in currency values. Although the value of a currency is determined by the aggregate supply and demand for that currency, this alone does not help our financial manager understand or predict the changes in exchange rates. Fundamental factors such as inflation, interest rates, foreign trade balances, and government policies are important in explaining both the short-term and long-term fluctuations of a currency value.

Inflation Parity between the purchasing powers of two currencies establishes the rate of exchange between the two currencies. Suppose apples are the commodity of value in Canada and China. It takes $1.00 to buy one dozen apples in Toronto and 5.1894 renminbi to buy the same apples in Shanghai. Then, the rate of exchange between the Canadian dollar and renminbi is renminbi 5.19/$1.00 or $0.1927/renminbi. If the price of apples doubles in Toronto while the price in Shanghai remains the same, the purchasing power of a dollar in Toronto drops 50 percent. Consequently, you can exchange $1.00 for only 2.5947 renminbi in foreign currency markets (or now receive $0.3854, or double the previous rate, per renminbi). This means currency exchange rates tend to vary inversely with their respective purchasing powers to provide the same or similar purchasing power in each country. This is called the **purchasing power parity theory**. When the inflation rate between two countries is different, the exchange rate adjusts to correspond to the relative purchasing powers of the countries. Purchasing power parity is based on the "law of one price." Identical goods should be priced the same, after adjusting for the exchange rate differential. Otherwise there is an incentive to buy in one country and sell in another at a profit. Such action will drive the price of the identical goods toward each other.

Interest Rates Another economic variable that has a significant influence on the exchange rate is interest rates. As a student of finance, you readily recognize that investment capital flows in the direction of higher yield for a given level of risk. This flow of short-term capital between money markets occurs because investors seek equilibrium through arbitrage buying and selling. If investors could earn 3 percent interest per year in Canada and 5 percent per year in Britain, they would prefer to invest in Britain, provided the inflation rate and perceived risk is the same in both countries. As investors sell Canadian dollars to buy British pounds, the value of the pound appreciates relative to the dollar. At the same time, the increased demand for British securities also tends to reduce the interest rate differential between the United Kingdom and Canada. Thus, interest rates and exchange rates adjust until the foreign exchange market and

Interest Rates in Other Countries: Are They Any Better?

On February 12, 1999, an investor could have earned 4.85 percent in Canada or 0.21 percent in Japan for 90 days with the purchase of a deposit through a major bank. Suppose a Japanese firm had 100,000,000 yen in excess funds for 90 days and was looking to achieve a return on its monies. One could suggest that a draft backed by a Canadian bank would have comparable risk to a draft guaranteed by a Japanese bank. And besides, the Canadian bank's deposit rate does look more attractive!

To invest in a Canadian deposit, the Japanese firm would have to convert its funds to Canadian dollars at the spot rate (1Cdn/114.10 yen). This would allow an investment of Can$876,424 ($100,000,000/114.10). Over 90 days this investment would earn Can$10,481 ($876,424 × .0485 × 90/365). The firm now has Can$886,905. The 90 days are now up, and the Japanese firm requires the funds for its operation, so these funds must be converted back into Japanese yen.

The firm could wait until the 90 days are up and then convert the Canadian dollars back into Japanese yen, but that would expose the firm to uncertainty as to what the exchange rate would be in 90 days. To remove this foreign exchange risk, the Japanese firm could lock in the exchange rate it would receive in 90 days with a forward contract. The forward rate on February 12, 1999, was 112.81 yen to the Canadian dollar. This would give the Japanese firm 100,051,753 yen.

The Japanese firm would therefore achieve a return of 0.21 percent on its funds (51,753 yen/100,000,000 yen × 365/90). This return is identical to what the Japanese firm could have earned by investing in the Japanese deposit. This example was constructed using rates that are found daily in major business newspapers. It demonstrates interest rate parity and the connection among spot rates, forward rates, and interest rates between countries. If we found that the return achieved in Canada on a similar risk investment was different from what was available in Japan, the return difference would not last for long. Investors would move their money to take advantage of the better return, and the movement of large sums of money would cause the exchange rates and available interest rates on deposits to adjust. This would ensure the relationship found in our example remains close.

Interest rate parity should always make this example work. You can use forward rates available through the print edition of the Globe and Mail and the rates on government bonds available through Bloomberg to reconstruct this example with current rates.

FINANCE IN ACTION

Q1 Demonstrate at this time, interest rate parity through the forward rate between Canada and Britain. Canada/ U.S.

www.bloomberg.com

www.globeandmail.com

the money market reach equilibrium. This interplay between interest rate differentials and exchange rates is called the **interest rate parity theory**. Interest rate parity suggests that the interest rate paid (charged) on similar-risk financial instruments should be the same through the forward exchange rate. The forward exchange rate is the exchange rate at which monies can be exchanged when the financial instrument matures. This is demonstrated in the Finance in Action box above.

Balance of Payments The term balance of payments refers to a system of government accounts that catalogues the flow of economic transactions between the residents of a given country and the residents of all other countries. The **balance of payments** statement for Canada is prepared by Statistics Canada. Figure 21–4 shows Canada's balance of payments in 2001. It resembles the funds flow statement presented in Chapter 2 and keeps track of the country's exports and imports as well as the flow of capital and gifts. When a country sells (exports) more goods and services to foreign countries than it purchases (imports) from abroad, it has a surplus in its balance of trade. Japan, for example, through its aggressive competition in world markets, exports far more goods than it imports and has been enjoying large trade surpluses for many years. Since the foreigners who buy Japanese goods are expected to pay their bills in yen, the demand for yen and its value has increased in foreign currency markets. On the other hand, continuous deficits in the balance of payments depress the value of a currency because such deficits would increase the supply of that currency relative to the demand.

Government Policies A national government may, through its central bank, intervene in the foreign exchange market, buying and selling currencies as it sees fit to support the value of its currency relative to others. Sometimes a given country may deliberately pursue a policy of maintaining an undervalued currency to promote cheap exports. In communist countries the currency values are set by government decree. Even in some free market countries, the central banks fix the exchange rates subject to periodic review and adjustment. At times, some nations affect the foreign exchange rate indirectly by restricting the flow of funds into and out of the country. Monetary and fiscal policies also affect the currency value in foreign exchange markets. For example, expansionary monetary policy and excessive government spending are primary causes of inflation; continual use of such policies eventually reduces the value of the country's currency. In the Canadian example, a rapid expansion of the money supply in the late 1970s and increasingly large government deficits caused a substantial decline in our foreign exchange rate from U.S.$1.05 in 1976 to a low of U.S.$0.69 in 1986. As discussed earlier, a policy of high interest rates in early 1990 strengthened the foreign exchange value of the Canadian currency by lowering inflation. Although the Canadian dollar has increased in value against most currencies since the mid 1990s it had fallen against the U.S. dollar to an all-time low of just under $0.62 in early 2002.

Other Factors Other factors may also affect the demand for a country's currency and its exchange rate. A pronounced and extended stock market rally in a country attracts investment capital from other countries, thus creating a huge demand by foreigners for that country's currency. This increased demand tends to increase the value of that currency. The huge capital flows into the United States, which has been seen as the best place to invest over the last decade, have contributed to the rise in its currency's value against most world currencies. Similarly, a significant drop in demand for a country's principal exports worldwide is expected to result in a corresponding decline in the value of its currency. A precipitous drop in gold prices caused the South African rand to drop in value during the early 1980s.

Political turmoil within a country has often been responsible for driving capital out of a country into more stable countries. A mass exodus of capital, due to the fear of political risk, undermines the value of a country's currency in the foreign exchange market. This has been in evidence in Canada when the separatist movement in Quebec appears to be gathering strength. If widespread labour strikes appear to weaken the nation's economy, they also have a depressing influence on its currency value.

The Canadian dollar also seems to be perceived as a play on commodity prices because of the influence natural resources have on our economy. As the world economy slows and/or the demand for commodities declines, with declines in their prices, the Canadian dollar falls in value against the U.S. dollar. The U.S. dollar is considered a currency more broadly based on a manufacturing/service economy.

Although a wide variety of factors influencing exchange rates have been discussed, a few words of caution are in order. All of these variables do not necessarily influence all currencies to the same degree. Some factors may have an overriding influence on one currency's value, while their influence on another currency may be negligible at that time. In other words, exchange rates are partially measures of our confidence in the future performance of a particular economy. An event that may destroy our confidence in one economy's future may not do so in another.

Spot Rates and Forward Rates

When you look into a major financial newspaper, you discover that two exchange rates exist simultaneously for most major currencies—the spot rate and the forward rate. The **spot rate** for a currency is the exchange rate at which the currency is traded for immediate delivery. For example, you might walk into the local branch of the Toronto Dominion Bank and ask for euros. The banker will indicate the rate at which the euro is selling, say euro 0.7244/$. If you are satisfied with the rate, you buy 724.40 euros with $1,000 and walk out the door. This is a spot market transaction at the retail level.

The trading of currencies for future delivery is called a forward market transaction. Suppose EnCana oil expects to receive 20 million euros from a French customer 90 days from now. Given the recent volatility in foreign exchange markets, it is not certain what these euros will be worth in dollars 90 days from today. To eliminate this uncertainty, the treasurer at EnCana oil calls a bank and offers to sell 20 million euros for Canadian dollars 90 days from now. In their negotiation, the two parties may agree on an exchange rate of euro 0.7267/$. Because the exchange rate is established for future delivery, it is a **forward rate.** After 90 days, EnCana oil delivers 20 million euros to the bank and receives $27.52 million. The difference between spot and forward exchange rates, expressed in dollars per unit of foreign currency, may be seen in the following values quoted in March 2002.

EnCana
www.encana.com

Rates	Japanese Yen (yen) ($/yen)	British Pound (£) ($/£)
Spot	0.011960	2.2633
30-day forward	0.011981	2.2596
90-day forward	0.012023	2.2525
180-day forward	0.012095	2.2418

The forward exchange rate of a currency is generally slightly different from the spot rate prevailing at that time. Since the forward rate deals with a future time, the expectations regarding the future value of that currency are reflected in the forward rate. Forward rates may be greater than the current spot rate (trade at a premium) or less than the current spot rate (trade at a discount). In March 2002, forward rates on the Japanese yen were at a premium in relation to the spot rate, while the forward rates for the British pound were at a discount from the spot rate. This means on that day the participants in the foreign exchange market expected the yen to appreciate relative to the Canadian dollar in the near-term future, while they expected the British pound to depreciate against the dollar. The size of the premium or discount gives a hint as to the degree to which market participants expect the currency to appreciate (depreciate). The premium or discount also reflects the time value of money and the degree to which interest rates in each country differ. In this example interest rates are lower in Japan and higher in Britain.

It is very common to express the discount or premium as an annualized percentage deviation from the spot rate. The percentage discount or premium is computed with the following formula:

$$\textit{Forward premium (discount)} = \frac{\textit{Forward} - \textit{spot}}{\textit{spot}} \times \frac{12}{\textit{contract length (months)}} \quad (21\text{–}1)$$

For example, in March 2002, the 90-day forward contract in yen was selling at a 2.11 percent premium:

$$\frac{0.012023 - 0.011960}{0.011960} \times \frac{12}{3} = 0.0211 = 2.11\%$$

while the 90-day forward contract in pounds was trading at a 0.34 percent discount:

$$\frac{2.2525 - 2.2633}{2.2633} \times \frac{12}{3} = -0.0191 = -1.91\%$$

The spot and forward transactions occur in what is called the over-the-counter market. Foreign currency dealers (usually large commercial banks or investment dealers) and their customers (importers, exporters, investors, multinational firms, etc.) negotiate the exchange rate, the length of the forward contract, and the commission in a mutually agreeable fashion. Although the length of a typical forward contract may generally vary between one month and six months, contracts for longer maturities are not uncommon. The dealers, however, may require higher returns for longer contracts.

Cross Rates

Quite often, exchange rates for different currencies are expressed only in terms of a dominant currency, such as the U.S. dollar. In Canada, exchange rates are likely to be expressed only in terms of the Canadian dollar. If currency quotations were in Canadian dollars only, we would have to make some further calculations if we were interested in the exchange rate between currencies that did not involve the Canadian dollar. This exchange rate is achieved by calculating a cross rate, an exchange rate calculated for two currencies by relating each currency to a common currency.

For example, in March, the Japanese yen was selling for $0.011960 and the British pound was selling for $2.2633. The cross rate between the yen and the pound was then 189.24 yen/£. In determining this value, we know that $1.00 Canadian will buy 83.612 yen (1/0.011960), and a pound will purchase 2.2633 dollars. Thus, 83.612 yen per 1 dollar times 2.2633 dollars per pound equals 189.24 yen for 1 pound (2.2633/0.011960).

	Canadian dollar	Japanese yen	British pound
Canadian dollar	–	0.011960	2.2633
Japanese yen	83.612	–	189.24
British pound	0.4418	0.005284	–

Cross currency rates are available daily in the *Financial Post* and *The Globe and Mail*.

Managing Foreign Exchange Risk

When conducting business internationally, corporations or investors inevitably must deal with more than one currency. The international monetary system, to accommodate the free-trading, Western nations, established a freely floating rate system to replace the rigid fixed exchange rate system. For the most part, the new system proved its agility and resilience during the most turbulent years of oil price hikes and hyperinflation of the 1970s and 1980s. The free market exchange rates responded and adjusted well to these adverse conditions. Consequently, exchange rates fluctuated over a much wider range than they had in the past. The increased volatility of exchange markets forced many multinational firms, importers, and exporters to pay more attention to the function of foreign exchange risk management.

Since most foreign currency values fluctuate from time to time, the monetary value of an international transaction or investment, measured in either the seller's or the buyer's currency, is likely to change over time. As a result, the value of an investment or the expected receipt (payment) of funds from a commercial transaction will be more or less than the value originally established. Exposure refers to the amount by which the value of assets and liabilities may vary due to fluctuations in the exchange rate. This exposure to a change in value may actually be realized or it may not. As shareholders and financial managers, our concern should be how exposure to exchange rate fluctuations affects the value of shareholders' equity.

Economic exposure identifies the market value of assets and liabilities, denominated in foreign currencies, that is subject to change in economic value because of fluctuations in exchange rates. Expressed another way, it is the amount of possible change in the market value of equity resulting from exchange rate fluctuations. This economic exposure is a measure of concern to financial practitioners, but it is sometimes difficult to measure. **Foreign exchange risk** refers to the possible change in value of foreign exchange rates. Importers, exporters, investors, and multinational corporations (MNC) are all exposed to foreign exchange risk. The foreign exchange risk impacts on the economic exposure of a multinational company in foreign countries. We identify foreign exchange risk as accounting or translation exposure and as transaction exposure. Although transaction exposure certainly represents economic exposure, it is unclear as to whether or not translation exposure properly captures economic exposure.

Accounting or **translation exposure** is the amount of loss or gain resulting from the treatment of foreign investments in the parent company's books, based on the accounting rules established by the parent company's government. In Canada, these rules are spelled out in the *CICA Accounting Recommendations*, Section 1650, which identifies the foreign operation as integrated or self-sustaining. To some extent, translation exposure attempts to identify economic gain or loss on foreign investments. However, in practice the accounting rules may not achieve this desired result. Gains or losses based on translation exposure for the most part are not realized at the time they are accounted for on the books of the parent company.

The CICA recommendations for an integrated operation's exposure suggest its transactions be captured as if they had been performed by the parent company. Under the recommended temporal method, the value of capital assets and liabilities normally carried at historical cost would not be retranslated each time a balance sheet is prepared. Monetary items are translated at the rate of exchange in effect on the balance sheet date. This translation of monetary items at the current exchange rate will show up in net income immediately, although under certain circumstances there is provision to amortize the gain or loss. The temporal method best approximates economic exposure and value change.

A self-sustaining operation's exposure, it is suggested, is best captured by its net investment or equity position. Under the current rate method, all assets and liabilities denominated in foreign currency are converted at the rate of exchange in effect on the date of balance sheet preparation. A gain or loss should be reported in a separate category of shareholders' equity. The effect of this method is to restate equity based on changes in the exchange rate. However, this may not represent economic exposure. For example, a declining exchange rate may not make a foreign capital asset less valuable because the prices of products produced with the asset can be increased in step with the exchange rate, particularly if the product is sold on the world market. The exception to reporting a self-sustaining operation with the current rate method is when there is extreme inflation in a foreign country and therefore devaluation of its currency. In this case, the reported value of an equity investment would quickly disappear, although that is not likely the true situation. Overall, the impact of the accounting exposure on reported earnings of multinational firms resulting from the translation of a foreign subsidiary's balance sheet may be substantial. However, it is often an unrealized gain or loss.

Transaction exposure is identified as the foreign exchange gains and losses resulting from international transactions that are realized when foreign funds are converted to Canadian dollars. These gains or losses, because they are realized, will be reflected in the corporation's income statement and do represent a real loss or gain in economic value. As a consequence of these transactional gains and losses, the volatility of reported earnings per share increases. There are several different strategies that can be used to minimize this transaction exposure. Strategies for reducing the foreign exchange risk of transaction exposure are known as hedging techniques. The advantage of a hedging technique is that it allows the firm to lock in its profit margin because it fixes the value for the foreign currency transaction. There is no or little foreign exchange risk. We identify four hedging techniques.

1. Hedging in the forward exchange market.
2. Hedging in the money market.
3. Hedging in the currency futures market.
4. Hedging in the options market.

Nortel
www.nortelnetworks.com

To see how to employ the hedging or covering techniques, we can identify a transaction where a firm is exposed to foreign exchange risk. Suppose British Telephone purchases a large telephone switching station from Nortel of Canada for £1.5 million in March 2002 (at last), and Nortel is promised the payment in British pounds in 90 days. Nortel is now exposed to foreign exchange risk by agreeing to receive the payment in a foreign currency in the future. It is up to Nortel to find a way to hedge or reduce this exposure, if it so desires. An alternative transaction could be where British Telephone agrees to pay $3,394,950 Canadian in 90 days. British Telephone in this situation has the transaction exposure, and that can also be hedged.

Forward Exchange Market Hedge One simple method to hedge the exposure is in the forward exchange market. The forward exchange market is controlled in Canada by six of the major banks. Forward exchange traders are prepared to guarantee today, by contract, an exchange rate (buy or sell) for many currencies, based on settlement on some future date. No matter what the actual exchange rate is on that future date, the forward traders will live up to their contract.

To establish forward cover, Nortel would sell a forward contract in March 2002 to deliver the £1.5 million, 90 days from then, in exchange for Can$3,378,750 million (based on a 90-day forward rate of 2.2525). In June, Nortel receives payment from British Telephone and delivers the £1.5 million to the bank that signed the contract. In return, the bank delivers Can$3,378,750 million to Nortel. Regardless of what happened to the value of the British pound in the interim, Nortel is guaranteed the funds. Nortel has hedged and eliminated its foreign exchange risk. In contrast, if the sale had been invoiced in Canadian dollars, British Telephone, not Nortel, would have been exposed to the exchange risk.

Money Market Hedge A second way to eliminate transaction exposure in this example is to borrow money in British pounds, converting them to Canadian dollars immediately. When the accounts receivable from the sale are collected three months later, the loan is cleared with the proceeds. This strategy consists of taking the following steps in March 2002:

1. Borrow £1,485,930 (£1,500,000/ 1.00946849 = £1,485,930) at the British rate of 3.84 percent per year for three months. You borrow less than the full amount of £1,500,000 in recognition of the fact that interest must be paid on the loan. The annual rate of 3.84 percent interest translates into 0.946849 percent for 90 days. To arrive at the size of the loan required today, the £1,500,000 is divided by 1.00946849.
2. Convert the British pounds into Canadian dollars in the spot market (2.2633). Receipt is Can$3,363,105 (1,485,930 × 2.2633).
3. Invest the Can$3,363,105 in Canada for the 90 days. Canadian interest rates at 2.09 percent annually or 0.51534 percent quarterly are lower than British rates. The investment available in 90 days, to compare with the forward, is $3,380,436 (3,363,105 × 1.0051534).

Then, in June 2002 (90 days later):

4. Receive the payment, £1,500,000, from British Telephone.
5. Clear the loan with the proceeds from that payment.

The money market hedge basically calls for matching the exposed asset (accounts receivable) with a liability (loan payable) in the same currency. Some firms prefer this money market hedge because of the earlier availability of funds this method provides.

Currency Futures Market Hedge Transaction exposure associated with a foreign currency can also be covered in the currency futures market. The International Monetary Market (IMM) of the Chicago Mercantile Exchange began trading futures contracts in foreign currencies on May 16, 1972, and today it is the world's largest **currency futures** exchange. Although the futures market and forward market are similar in concept, they differ in their operations.

Chicago Mercantile Exchange
www.cme.com

To keep our example simple we will assume that there is a currency futures contract between Canadian dollars and British pounds. In reality Nortel would have to complete two futures contracts on the Chicago exchange first by selling pounds for U.S. dollars, and second by buying Canadian dollars with the U.S. dollars. Furthermore, as examined in Chapter 19, the futures market has standardized contracts, as to date and amount, which makes it difficult to hedge a position completely. Currency futures usually expire in March, June, September, and December. A hedge may be able to cover most of the exposure, but would not be perfect. The advantage of the currency hedge would be the liquidity of a market, which gives the flexibility of closing out the contracts early if it suits Nortel.

For Nortel, an expectation must be set for what the exchange rate will be in June. A good choice is the rate at which the pound (or dollar) is currently trading in the forward or futures market. This becomes the target rate to be hedged. Nortel then enters into a futures contract to sell £1.5 million in June. When June comes around and Nortel receives the £1.5 million, it will convert to Canadian dollars in the cash (spot) market and close out the future contract by buying pounds. In the futures market, contracts are generally closed out for cash and delivery is not taken of the underlying commodity, in this case a currency.

Date		Futures Market
March	Expectation £1.5 m. at $2.2581/£ = $3.387 m.	Sells £1.5 m. for May delivery at $2.2581/£ = $3.387 m.
	Spot Market	
June	Sells £1.5 m. at $2.2075/£ = $3.311 m. Loss = $0.076 m.	Buys £1.5 m. at $2.2075/£ = $3.311 m. Gain = $0.076 m.

While Nortel was waiting for its receivable, the pound dropped in value relative to the Canadian dollar. Had Nortel remained unhedged, it would have lost $76,000 based on its expectation for the exchange rate in June. By hedging in the futures market, Nortel reduced the loss to nil. A $76,000 gain in the futures market cancelled out the $76,000 loss in the spot market. In an actual situation, there would be some small gain or loss because of the inability to hedge the full exposure due to the standardization of contracts as to the amount and date of expiry. It is unlikely that the spot and future markets would quote the same rate when there is still time to expiry.

Options Market Hedge The options market for currencies is primarily available on the Chicago Mercantile Exchange. An option on currencies gives the purchaser the right to buy (call) or to sell (put) the foreign currency at an agreed exchange rate up to a predetermined date, if the purchaser is so inclined. An option gives a right but not an obligation to the purchaser. For this right, the purchaser pays a fee called a premium.

Again, to keep our example simple we will assume that there is a currency options contract between Canadian dollars and British pounds. Furthermore, we will assume that an option is available for the size of the contract (£1.5) (nonstandard amounts are unavailable), a nonstandard option price (£2.2581, the expected rate), and for the month of June.

Devaluation and Deflation

In 2002, two equally troubling concerns were raised in the world's financial and foreign exchange markets. Both were putting downward pressure on the value of certain currencies.

In Japan interest rates hovered around zero percent in the short term. The Japanese economy had stagnated during the 1990s and for many years had shown little or no growth. Declining values in the stock and real estate markets had put downward pressure on prices. The banks were struggling with numerous bad loans. Combined these factors suggested that holding cash was not so bad an idea. The aging population, with fixed capital resources, was happy to see declining prices. The result was that Japan was forced to deal with deflationary pressures that were placing severe strain on the economy. Furthermore with deflationary pressures the value of the yen was declining, which was a concern to many trading nations.

In Argentina, three years of recession and government excesses lead to the biggest default on debt in history. The government was forced to devalue the peso by 40 percent overnight. Tough economic measures were called for in an economy that already had unemployment rates nearing 20 percent. Cash was unavailable to many and some of the Argentina's major cities took to issuing their own currencies to provide the means for the exchange of goods and services to occur. The Bank of Nova Scotia was one of many foreign firms that suffered significant losses in Argentina as a result of the devaluation.

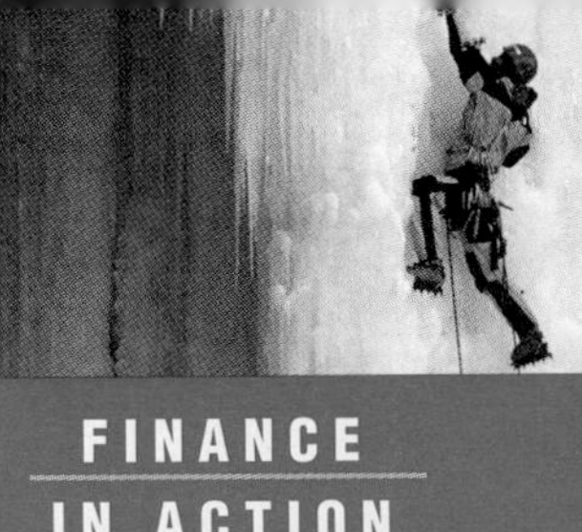

FINANCE IN ACTION

Q1 How have these two currencies performed since late 2001?

http://pacific.commerce.ubc.ca/xr

Nortel would purchase an option (put) to sell £1.5 million in June at a fixed price of (£2.2581/$). For a price (the premium) of perhaps $0.015 per pound, Nortel could purchase the option, for a total cost of $22,500. The option would give Nortel protection if the pound dropped in value, but would also allow Nortel to gain if the pound appreciated in value. If the pound appreciated, Nortel would sell the pounds in the cash (spot) market and let the option expire, receiving more on the transaction than expected. If the pound dropped in value, Nortel would also sell pounds in the cash (spot) market, losing money based on its expectation, but selling the option would offset this, which would have increased in value. In the latter case Nortel has hedged its exposure for a price.

Hedging is not the only means companies have for protecting themselves against foreign exchange risk. Over the years multinational companies have developed elaborate foreign asset management programs that involve such strategies as switching cash and other current assets into strong currencies, while piling up debt and other liabilities in depreciating currencies. Companies also encourage the quick collection of bills in weak currencies by offering sizable discounts, while extending liberal credit in strong currencies.

Foreign Investment Decisions

Foreign investments by Canadians are significant. As seen in Figure 21–5 on the next page, Canadians held $778 billion in assets outside of Canada in 2000. Direct investment in foreign enterprises, at $301 billion, accounted for the bulk of this investment, although there is a significant portfolio investment of $212 billion held directly in stocks and bonds. This portfolio investment has become larger as individual Canadians seek to diversify their holdings internationally. Of some concern was the $1,023 billion (37 percent by bonds, 28 percent by direct investment) of Canadian liabilities held by foreigners. Government and government enterprise bonds represented 61 percent of the bond total held by foreigners.

Direct foreign investment by Canadians is undertaken after considering the expected cash flows from the investment and the possible risks. Foreign investment is therefore a special case of the capital budgeting decision discussed in Chapters 12 and 13. However, the expected cash flows from foreign investments are more volatile than in Canada due to political and foreign exchange risks. Host countries, particularly the less developed countries (LDCs), have at times charged that foreign affiliates subverted their governments, caused instability in their currencies' exchange rates, and exploited their labour with low wages. This often makes it difficult to conduct business in these countries, and the expected cash flows from investments become more uncertain. The instability of a host country government also tends to increase the volatility of the exchange rate. Despite these increased risks, Canadians continue to invest abroad.

One reason for foreign investment is that the average rate of return is often higher than the rate of return on domestic investments. This is perhaps the major reason Canadian firms expand their operations outside of Canada's borders. Foreign investments offer higher rates of return for several reasons. Resources may be more readily available and more easily exploited, which lowers the costs of production. Production costs will also be lower overseas because of significantly lower wages. Firms in labour-intensive industries, such as textiles and electronics, find this quite attractive. Furthermore, the tax burden on foreign investments may be substantially less than in

FIGURE 21–5

Canada's international investment position, 2000.

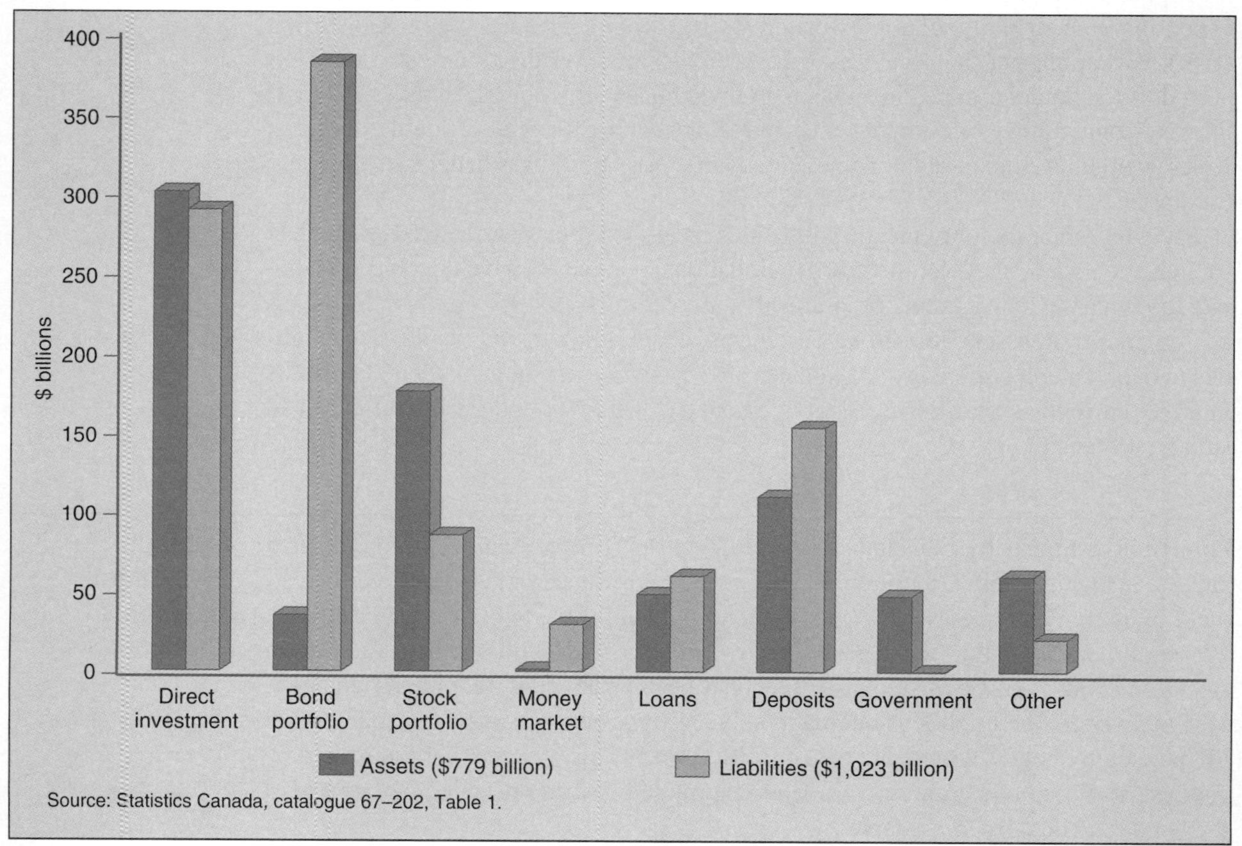

Source: Statistics Canada, catalogue 67–202, Table 1.

Canada, which increases the cash flows from investments. Canadian-based multinational firms can postpone the payment of Canadian taxes on income earned abroad until such income is actually repatriated (forwarded) to the parent company. Also, the corporate income tax rates elsewhere are often lower than in Canada. Countries such as Israel, Ireland, and South Africa offer special tax incentives for foreign firms that establish operations there (just as Canada does for designated geographic regions). Finally, because technology is easily transferred around the globe, today MNCs can readily relocate to many countries.

Canadian MNCs have invested in foreign countries for strategic reasons. With the emergence of trading blocs such as the Common Market in Europe, North American firms feared their goods might face import tariffs in those countries. To avoid such trade barriers, firms started manufacturing in foreign countries. Figure 21–6 shows that the primary recipient of Canadian investment abroad is the United States, our largest trading partner. One of the major driving forces has been to locate production facilities close to the large U.S. market. Political stability, large market size, access to advanced technology, and continued economic growth have also been prime motivating factors for Canadian firms to establish their operations in the United States. The decision to invest in a foreign country by a firm operating in an oligopolistic industry is also motivated by strategic considerations. When a competitor undertakes a direct foreign investment, other companies quickly follow with defensive investments in the same foreign country. Foreign investments undertaken by U.S. tire and rubber companies were classic examples of this competitive reaction, at least historically. Wherever you found a Firestone subsidiary in a foreign country, you were likely to see a Goodyear affiliate also operating in that country.

FIGURE 21–6

Canada's investment abroad by region, 2000 (assets)

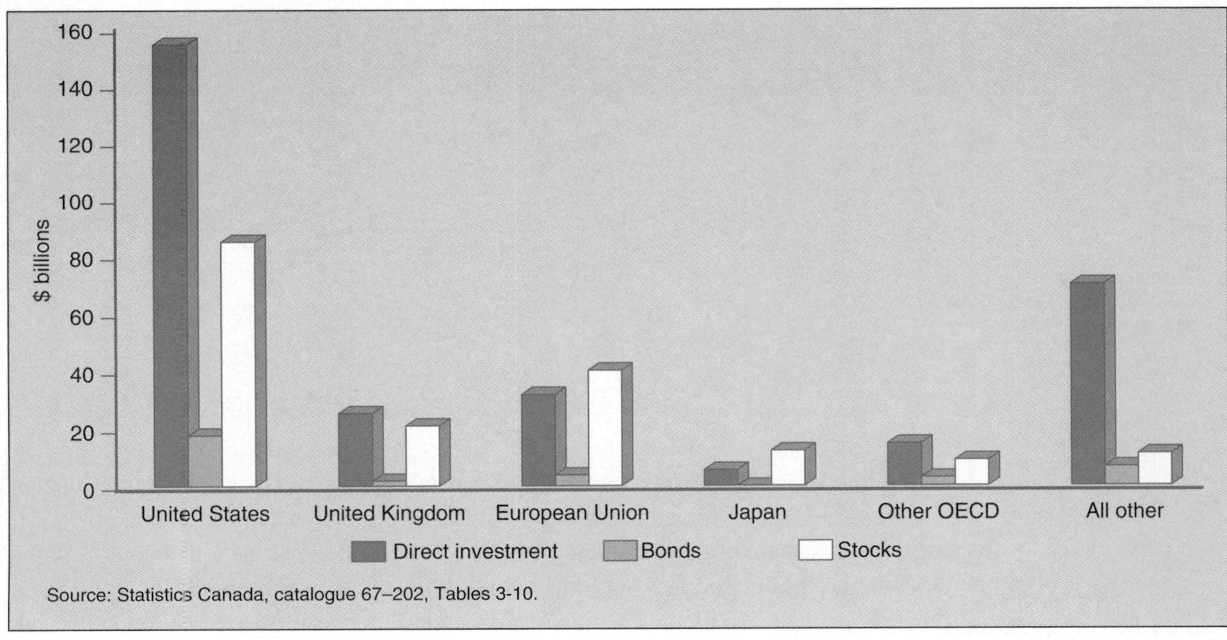

Source: Statistics Canada, catalogue 67–202, Tables 3-10.

Many academicians believe international diversification of risks is also an important motivation for direct foreign investment. The basic premise of portfolio theory in finance is that an investor can reduce the risk level of a portfolio by combining those investments whose returns are less than perfectly positively correlated. Figure 21–7, comparing single-country versus multicountry investment portfolios, implies that further reduction in investment risk can be achieved by diversifying across national boundaries. International stocks in Figure 21–7 show a consistently lower percentage of risk compared to any given number of Canadian stocks in a portfolio. It is argued, however, that institutional and political constraints, language barriers, and lack of adequate information on foreign investments prevent investors from diversifying across nations. However, multinational firms, through their unique position around the world, can derive the benefits of international diversification. This is due, at least partially, to their ability to operate as an efficient internal capital market, bypassing the many frictions that exist among and within nation-based capital, managerial, and technology markets.

FIGURE 21–7
Risk reduction from international diversification

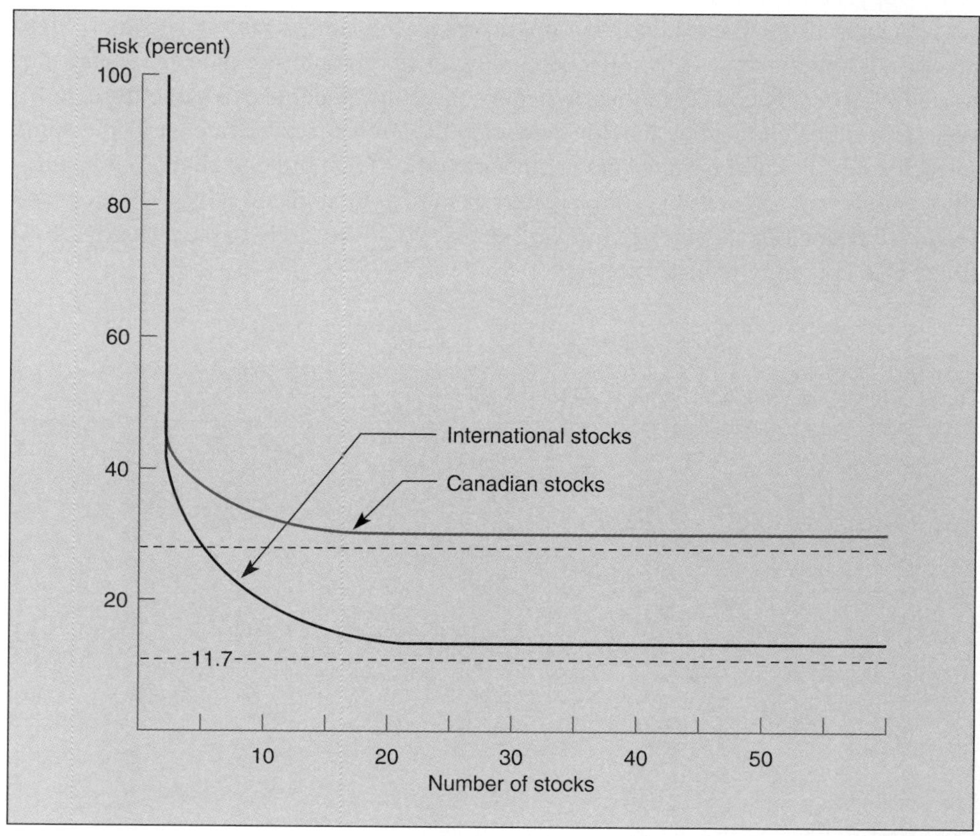

While the U.S.-based firms took the lead in establishing overseas subsidiaries during the 1950s and 1960s, European and Japanese firms started this activity in the 1970s. Although Japan's share of the documented totals is low about 6 percent, investments in the Canadian automobile industry and Japan's holdings of Canadian bonds are significant. From 1985 to 1990, the Japanese rate of investment increased 17 percent annually, but dropped significantly during the 1990s Nevertheless, as Figure 21–8 documents, the United States dominates foreign direct investment in Canada with about 62 percent. Much of this investment is a legacy of the establishment of American branch plants in Canada following World War II. This foreign domination of ownership of important sectors of the Canadian economy has been blamed for many ills, not the least of which is the failure of our firms to invest heavily in new product research and development.

FIGURE 21–8

Foreign investment in Canada by region, 2000 (liabilities)

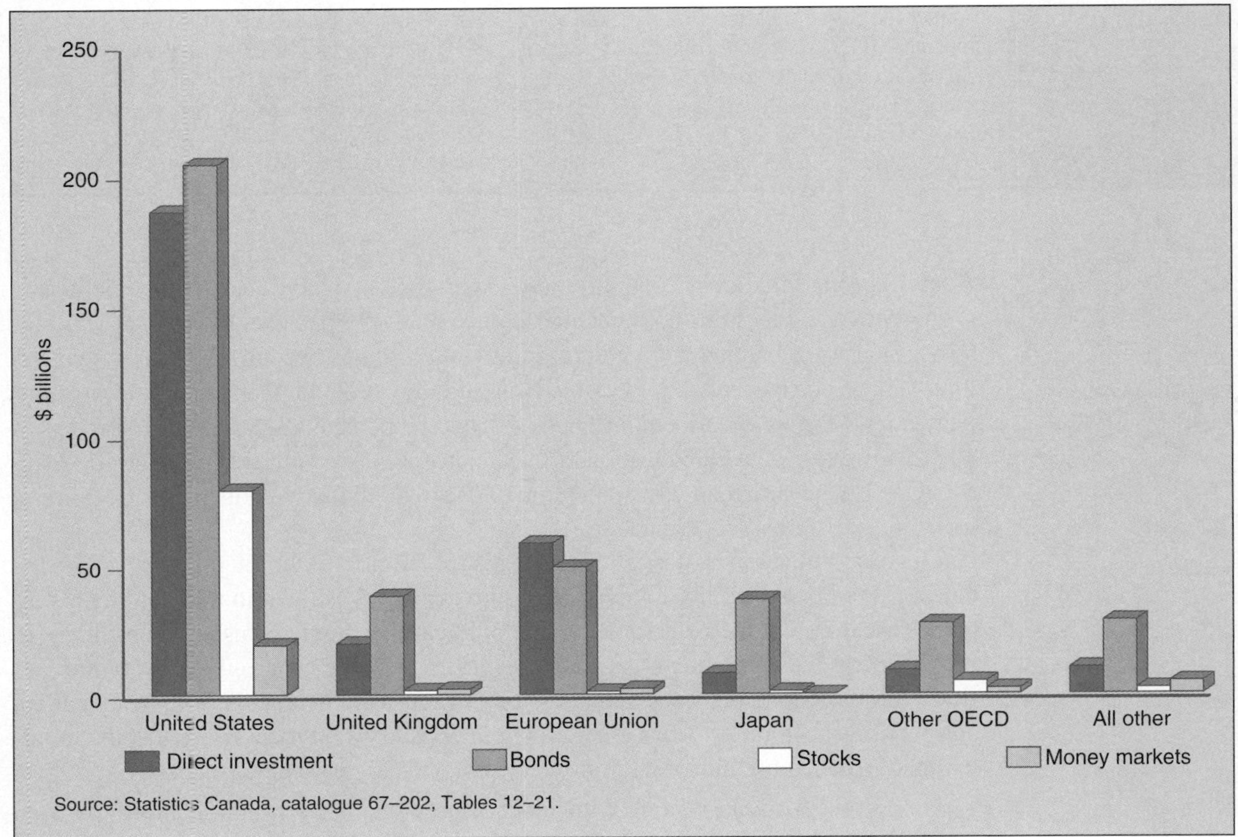

Source: Statistics Canada, catalogue 67–202, Tables 12–21.

Analysis of Political Risk

Decisions by business firms to make direct investments in foreign countries are taken with a relatively long-time horizon in view. This is natural because of the time period necessary to recover the initial investment on large capital projects. The government may change several times during the foreign firm's tenure in that country, and the new government may not be as friendly or as cooperative as the previous administration. An unfriendly government can interfere with the foreign affiliates in many ways. It may impose foreign exchange restrictions, or the foreign ownership share may be limited to a set percentage of the total. **Repatriation** (transfer) of a subsidiary's profit to the parent company may be blocked, at least temporarily. In the most extreme cases of interference, the government may even **expropriate** (take over) the foreign subsidiary's

FINANCE IN ACTION

Whiskey Is Risky!

India decided to open its market to foreign distillers in the mid-1990s. Fifteen million drinkers and $5 billion in annual sales with tremendous growth potential, was a wonderful investment opportunity for worldwide distillery companies such as Seagram of Canada.

However, Seagram was not fully prepared for the differences of the Indian market. Although they bottled their scotch whiskey in India, they were still subject to a 400 percent duty on the product. Furthermore, the local product that used molasses rather than grain sold for $7.00, compared to Seagram's price of $40.00 a bottle. To prevent tampering with their bottles, which was a widespread Indian practice, Seagram had to use special caps on their bottles. The bottles themselves were superior and therefore more expensive than locally used bottles. Complicating Seagram's cash flow considerations was the evaporation rate in India due to the high heat, which took 8 percent of the whiskey annually versus 2 percent in Canada.

India is a federation of states, many with different laws. Seagram was required to produce different labels in eighteen states, four states had announced prohibition, and there was a nationwide ban on advertising.

The subcontinent of India presents many varied cultural and political risks to Seagram. Fortunately, a little "dram" might put things in a better perspective.

Sherritt International
www.sherritt.com

assets. The multinational company may experience a sizable loss of income and/or property as a result of this political interference. In the 1990s, executives of Sherritt International were banned from entering the United States because American senators didn't like Sherritt investing in Cuba. Brascan, the dominant Canadian holding company conglomerate described in Chapter 20, had 89 percent of its assets in Brazil as of 1977. However, the nationalization of its 83 percent interest in Light-Servicos de Electricidade by the Brazilian government in 1978 provided the impetus for Brascan to refocus its investments on Canada.

The best protection against political risk is for the firm to thoroughly investigate the country's political stability long before it makes any investment in that country. Companies use different methods for assessing political risk. Some firms hire consultants to provide them with a political risk analysis. Others form their own advisory committees (little foreign affairs departments) consisting of top-level managers from headquarters and foreign subsidiaries. After ascertaining the country's political risk level, the multinational firm can use one of the following strategies to guard against such risk:

1. Establish a joint venture with a local entrepreneur. By bringing a local partner into the deal, the MNC not only limits its financial exposure, but also minimizes anti-foreign feelings. It may also enhance its chances of commercial success by including a partner who knows the culture intimately.
2. Enter into a joint venture, preferably with firms from other countries. For example, Gulf Canada may pursue its oil production operation in Zaire in association with Royal Dutch Petroleum and Nigerian National Petroleum as partners. A foreign government is more hesitant to antagonize partner-firms of many nationalities at the same time.
3. Obtain insurance in advance against such risks when the perceived political risk level is high. **Export Development Corporation (EDC)**, a federal government agency, sells insurance policies to qualified firms. This agency can insure against losses due to expropriation, war, revolution, or any resulting impossibility of repatriating revenues or capital. Many firms have used this service over the years. Private insurance companies such as Lloyds of

London, American International Group Inc., CIGNA, and others issue similar policies to cover political risk. Political-risk umbrella policies do not come cheaply. Coverage for projects in fairly safe countries can cost anywhere from 0.3 percent to 12 percent of the insured values per year. They are more expensive or unavailable in troubled countries. EDC's rates are lower than those of private insurers, and its policies extend for 20 years, compared to 3 years or less for private insurance policies.

Financing International Business Operations

When the parties to an international transaction are well known to each other and the countries involved are politically stable, sales are generally made on credit, as is customary in domestic business operations. If the foreign importer is relatively new and/or the political environment is volatile, the possibility of nonpayment by the importer is worrisome for the exporter. To reduce the risk of nonpayment, an exporter generally requests that the importer furnish a **letter of credit.** The importer's bank normally issues the letter of credit in which the bank promises to subsequently pay the money for the merchandise.

For example, assume Canadian Western Farms (CWF) is negotiating with a South Korean trading company to export soybean meal. The two parties agree on price, method of shipment, timing of shipment, destination point, and so forth. Once the basic terms of sale have been agreed to, the South Korean trading company (importer) applies for a letter of credit from its commercial bank in Seoul. The Korean bank, if it so desires, issues such a letter of credit, which specifies in detail all of the steps that must be completed by the Canadian exporter before payment is made. If CWF complies with all specifications in the letter of credit and submits to the Korean bank the proper documentation to prove it has done so, the Korean bank guarantees the payment on the due date. On that date, the Canadian firm is paid by the Korean bank, not by the buyer of the goods. All of the credit risk to the exporter is absorbed by the importer's bank, which is in a good position to evaluate the creditworthiness of the importing firm.

The exporter that requires cash payment or a letter of credit from foreign buyers of marginal credit standing is likely to lose orders to competitors. Instead of risking the loss of business, Canadian firms can find an alternative way to reduce the risk of nonpayment by foreign customers. This alternative method consists of obtaining export credit insurance. The insurance policy provides assurance to the exporter that should the foreign customer default on payment, the insurance company will pay for the shipment. The Export Development Corporation, an agency of the Canadian federal government, provides this kind of insurance to exporting firms.

Export Development Corporation
www.edc.ca/e-services

Funding of Transactions

Assistance in the funding of foreign transactions may take many forms.

Export Development Corporation (EDC) This agency of the federal government facilitates the financing of Canadian exports through its miscellaneous programs. In its credit insurance, EDC protects the exporter by insuring 90 percent of the value of export sales. The EDC also guarantees loans made by financial institutions to foreign purchasers of Canadian products. In addition, EDC can make projects possible by financing them when no commercial credit is available. In these cases the Canadian supplier receives payment from the proceeds of the loan to the foreign buyer. Such capital goods might include communications equipment, heavy machinery especially for use in energy-related projects, radar systems, and the like.

Loans from the Parent Company or a Sister Affiliate An apparent source of funds for a foreign affiliate is its parent company or its sister affiliates. In addition to contributing equity capital, the parent company often provides loans of varying maturities to its foreign affiliate. Although the simplest arrangement is a direct loan from the parent to the foreign subsidiary, such a loan is rarely extended because of foreign exchange risk, political risk, and tax treatment. Instead, the loans are often channeled through an intermediary to a foreign affiliate. Parallel loans and fronting loans are two examples of such indirect loan arrangements between a parent company and its foreign affiliate. Figure 21–9 depicts a typical **parallel loan** arrangement.

FIGURE 21–9
A parallel loan arrangement

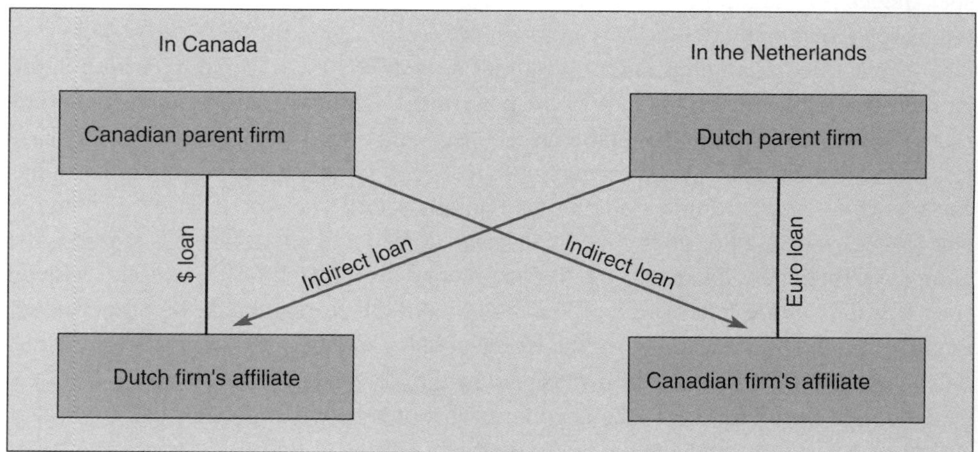

In this illustration, a Canadian firm wanting to lend funds to its Dutch affiliate locates a Dutch parent firm that wants to transfer funds to its Canadian affiliate. Avoiding the exchange markets, the Canadian parent lends dollars to the Dutch affiliate in Canada, while the Dutch parent lends euros to the Canadian affiliate in the Netherlands. At maturity, the two loans would be repaid to the original lenders. Notice that neither loan carries any foreign exchange risk. In essence, both parent firms are providing indirect loans to their affiliates.

A **fronting loan** is simply a parent's loan to its foreign subsidiary channeled through a financial intermediary, usually a large international bank. A schematic of a fronting loan is shown in Figure 21–10.

In the example, the Canadian parent company deposits funds in an Amsterdam bank, and that bank in turn lends the same amount to its affiliate in the Netherlands. In this manner, the bank fronts for the parent by extending a risk-free (fully collateralized) loan to the foreign affiliate. In the event of political turmoil, the foreign government is more likely to allow the Canadian subsidiary to repay the loan to a large international bank than to allow the same affiliate to repay the loan to its parent company. Thus, the

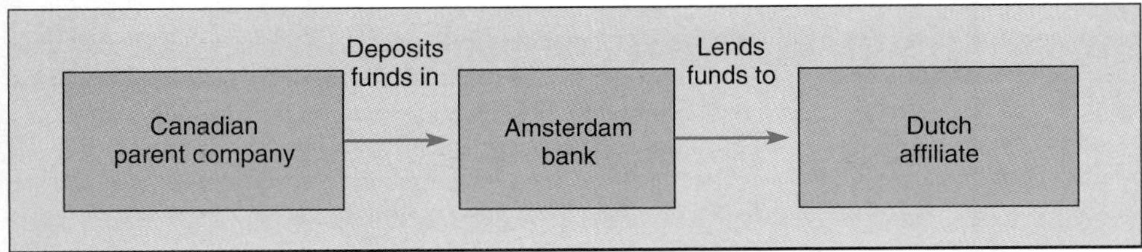

FIGURE 21–10
A fronting loan arrangement

parent company reduces its political risk substantially by using a fronting loan instead of transferring funds directly to its foreign affiliate.

Even though the parent company would prefer that its foreign subsidiary maintain its own financial arrangements, many banks are apprehensive about lending to a foreign affiliate without a parent guarantee. A large portion of bank lending to foreign affiliates is based on some sort of a guarantee by the parent firm. Usually, because of its multinational reputation, the parent company has a better credit rating than its foreign affiliates. The lender advances funds on the basis of the parent's creditworthiness even though the affiliate is expected to pay back the loan. The terms of a parent guarantee may vary greatly, depending on the closeness of the parent-affiliate ties, the parent-lender relations, and the home country's legal jurisdiction.

Eurocurrency Loans The Eurocurrency market is an important source of short-term loans for many multinational firms and their foreign affiliates. A **Eurocurrency** is a unit of currency held on deposit in a bank outside of the country issuing the currency. The origins of the Eurocurrency market date back to the 1960s, when interest rate ceilings in the United States provided a disincentive for American corporations to repatriate revenues generated abroad. Thus, American companies desired to deposit U.S. dollar funds with banks outside of the United States.

Since the early 1960s, the Eurocurrency market has established itself as a significant part of world credit markets. Hundreds of corporations and banks, mostly from the United States, Canada, Western Europe, and Japan, are regular borrowers and depositors in this market.

The Eurocurrency market became an increasingly important source of short-term financing for the multinational company throughout the 1970s and 1980s. The lower costs and greater credit availability of the Eurocurrency market continue to attract borrowers. The lower borrowing costs in the Eurocurrency market are attributed to the smaller overhead costs for lending banks given the huge size of transactions, the creditworthiness of borrowing corporations and nations, and the absence of reserve or capital requirements on the part of the lending institution. These currency transactions are outside the regulatory control of the domestic financial regulators. The lending rate for borrowers in the Eurocurrency market is based on the **London Interbank Offered Rate (LIBOR),** which is the benchmark interest rate for large deposits. Interest rates on loans are calculated by adding premiums to this basic rate. These premiums are usually between 0.25 percent to 0.50 percent depending on the customer, length of the loan period, and size of the loan. Although the rates in the Eurocurrency market tend to be cheaper than domestic rates in either Canada or the United States, the LIBOR rate

FINANCE IN ACTION

Rating the Countries

Most governments of the world issue debt securities to fund the projects and programs they deem appropriate for their country. Buyers of these debt securities will require a yield that reflects the risk investors perceive for each country's ability to meet its payment obligations. Considerations will be given to how well the government manages the economy and the overall financial wealth of the country. Inflation rates, unemployment, total government debt, and the annual deficit will all be factors in rating the debt securities of each government. Moody's Bond rating service out of New York rates the bond issues of many sovereign governments.

A sampling follows:

United States	Aaa	Indonesia	Baa1
Canada	Aa1	Dominion Republic	Ba2
China	A3	Brazil	B1
Turkey	A2	Argentina	Ca

These ratings give us an idea of the risk faced in the countries rated. A rating of Aaa is of exceptional quality, Aa is excellent, A is good, Baa is adequate, Ba is questionable, B is poor, and Caa is very poor as an investment. Therefore, the ratings may suggest a discount rate appropriate for the risk of an investment in that particular country. Of course, these are government ratings. Any corporate ratings within a country would in all likelihood be lower due to higher risk, suggesting a higher discount rate.

Q1 What is the current rating of these countries?

www.moodys.com

www.standardandpoors.com

tends to be more volatile than the banks' prime rates because of the volatility of supply and demand in the Eurocurrency market.

Lending in the Eurocurrency market is almost exclusively done by commercial banks. Large Eurocurrency loans, especially if they are for any extended time period, are often syndicated by a group of participating banks. Eurocurrency loans with maturities greater than one year are known as Eurocredits. The loan agreement is put together by a lead bank known as the manager, which historically has usually been one of the largest U.S., European, or Canadian banks. Until recently, subsidiaries of Canadian banks such as the Royal and the Bank of Montreal were major participants in Eurocurrency lending. The manager charges the borrower a once-and-for-all fee or commission of 0.25 percent to 1 percent of the loan value. A portion of this fee is kept by the lead bank, and the remainder is shared by all the participating banks. The aim of forming a syndicate is to diversify the risk, which would be too large for any single bank to handle by itself. Multicurrency loans and revolving credit arrangements can also be negotiated in the Eurocurrency market to suit borrowers' needs.

Eurobond Market When long-term funds are needed, borrowing in the Eurobond market has become an important alternative for leading multinational corporations. **Eurobond** issues are sold simultaneously in several different national capital markets, but they are denominated in a currency different from that of the nation in which the bonds are issued. Although the U.S. dollar dominates this market, the Euro is expected to become a significant rival currency. Eurobond issues are underwritten by an international syndicate of banks and securities firms. Eurobonds of longer than seven years in maturity generally have a sinking-fund provision.

Disclosure requirements in the Eurobond market are much less stringent than those required by the securities commissions in Canada and the United States. Furthermore, the registration costs in the Eurobond market are generally lower than those charged in

Canada and the United States. The Eurobond market offers tax flexibility for borrowers and investors alike. Because most Eurobonds are issued by a fully owned offshore finance subsidiary in a tax-haven country such as Luxembourg, no withholding taxes on interest are paid. Historically, many wealthy investors bought Eurobonds through Swiss bank accounts so that their interest income could be kept anonymous. All these advantages of Eurobonds enable the borrowers to raise funds at a lower cost.

Nevertheless, a caveat may be in order with respect to the effective cost of borrowing in the Eurobond market. When a multinational firm borrows by floating a foreign currency-denominated debt issue on a long-term basis, it creates transaction exposure, a kind of foreign exchange risk. If the foreign currency appreciates in value during the bond's life, the cost of servicing the debt could be prohibitively high. For example, many Canadian multinational firms borrowed at an approximately 7 percent coupon interest by selling Eurobonds denominated in deutsche marks and Swiss francs in the late 1960s and early 1970s. However, these firms experienced an average debt service cost of approximately 13 percent, or almost twice the coupon rate. This extra cost resulted from the declining Canadian dollar exchange rate vis-à-vis these two strong currencies. Thus, currency selection for denominating Eurobond issues must be made with extreme care and foresight. To lessen the impact of foreign exchange risk, some recently issued Eurobond issues were denominated in multicurrency units.

International Equity Markets The entire amount of equity capital comes from the parent company for a wholly owned foreign subsidiary, but a majority of foreign affiliates are not owned completely by their parent corporations. For example, in India and Malaysia the local citizens must hold majority ownership of a foreign affiliate. In some other countries, the parent corporations are allowed to own their affiliates completely in the initial stages, but they are required to relinquish partial ownership to local citizens after five or seven years. To avoid nationalistic reactions to wholly owned foreign subsidiaries, multinational firms such as Unilever, DaimlerChrysler, General Motors, Nortel, and IBM sell shares to worldwide shareholders. It is also believed that widespread foreign ownership of the firm's common stock encourages the loyalty of foreign shareholders and employees toward the firm. Thus, selling common stock to residents of foreign countries is not only an important financing strategy, but it is also a risk-minimizing strategy for many multinational corporations.

New York Stock Exchange
www.nyse.com

As you learned in Chapter 14, a well-functioning secondary market is essential to entice investors into owning shares. To attract investors from all over the world, reputable multinational firms list their shares on major stock exchanges around the world. Many Canadian companies are listed on the New York Stock Exchange and on Nasdaq. Even more foreign firms would sell stock issues in the United States and list on the NYSE were it not for the tough and costly disclosure rules in effect in that country and enforced by the Securities and Exchange Commission. Many foreign corporations such as Hoechst, Honda, Hitachi, Sony, Magnet Metals Ltd., DeBeers, and the like accommodate American investors by issuing **American Depository Receipts (ADRs).** All of the American-owned shares of a foreign company are placed in trust in a New York bank. In turn, the bank issues its depository receipts to the American shareholders and maintains a shareholder ledger on these receipts, thus enabling the holders of ADRs to sell or otherwise transfer them as easily as they transfer any American company shares. Most ADRs trade in the over-the-counter market, although a few are listed on the New York Stock Exchange. ADR prices tend to move parallel with the prices of the underlying securities in their home markets.

Looking elsewhere around the world, approximately 50 international firms have listed their shares on the Toronto Stock Exchange and there are many on the TSX Venture Exchange. The New York Stock Exchange, the world's largest, lists over 400 foreign firms, the London Stock Exchange also over 400, and the Tokyo Stock Exchange about 50, including such names as McDonalds and Toronto Dominion Bank. To obtain exposure in an international financial community, listing securities on world stock exchanges is a step in the right direction for a multinational firm. Table 21–2 indicates the size of major world stock markets.

TABLE 21–2
International equity markets by capitalization, 2001

New York	$11.0 trillion
NASDAQ	2.9
Tokyo	2.3
London	2.1
Euronext	1.8
Deutsche Bourse	1.1
Toronto	0.6

This international exposure also brings an additional responsibility for the MNC to understand the preferences and needs of heterogeneous groups of investors of various nationalities. The MNC may have to print and circulate its annual financial statements in many languages. Some foreign investors are more risk averse than their counterparts in North America, preferring dividend income to less certain capital gains. Common stock ownership among individuals in countries such as Japan and Norway is insignificant, with financial institutions holding substantial amounts of common stock issues.

Institutional practices around the globe also vary significantly when it comes to issuing new securities. Unlike the Canadian situation, commercial banks in many European countries have long played a dominant role in the securities business. They underwrite stock issues, manage portfolios, vote the stock they hold in trust accounts, and hold directorships on company boards. In Germany, the banks also run an over-the-counter market in many stocks. Canadian banks have recently been allowed to own securities subsidiaries that underwrite stock issues and manage portfolios.

The International Finance Corporation Whenever a multinational company has difficulty raising equity capital due to lack of adequate private risk capital in a foreign country, the firm may explore the possibility of selling partial ownership to the International Finance Corporation (IFC). The International Finance Corporation, a unit of the World Bank Group, was established in 1956 and is owned by 119 member countries of the World Bank. Its objective is to further economic development by promoting private enterprises in these countries. The profitability of a project and its potential benefit to the host country's economy are the two criteria the IFC uses to decide whether or not to assist a venture. The IFC participates in private enterprise through either buying equity shares of a business or providing long-term loans, or a combination of the two, for up to 25 percent of the total capital. The IFC expects the other partners to assume managerial responsibility, and it does not exercise its voting rights as a

International Finance Corporation
www.ifc.org

shareholder. The IFC helps finance new ventures as well as the expansion of existing ones in a variety of industries. Once the venture is well established, the IFC sells its investment position to private investors to free up its capital.

Global Cash Management

The issues discussed in this chapter directly affect how the multinational corporation would organize its finance function and how it should manage its funds globally. The multinational finance function can be organized with (1) each subsidiary completely decentralized, (2) all finance functions centralized at parent headquarters, or (3) a mix of centralization/decentralization. Because of government restrictions of funds flows, differing rates of inflation, and volatile exchange rates, global cash management involves a number of trade-offs and explicit decisions. The considerations in any such system include a method for:

1. Estimating the levels of local and corporate cash needs at given times.
2. Creating the ability to withdraw cash from the subsidiary and centralize it.
3. Deciding how to reallocate cash once it has been centralized.

Although any such system is highly dependent on a good information system, it is easy to underestimate the difficulties in language problems, technical problems in operating in many countries, local resistance to losing resources, and government regulations restricting multinational cash flows.

Once local needs have been allowed for, a decision is made as to whether or not to have the local manager invest excess funds or have them remitted to the parent's central cash pool. To centralize cash, a dividend paid from the subsidiary to the parent is often the most straightforward method. Outright government restrictions on dividends, exchange controls, capital investment requirements, withholding taxes, or other problems, however, usually complicate the decision. Given high rates of inflation and devaluations that occur in some countries, the parent must often develop approaches such as revaluing capital assets because foreign governments restrict the amount of cash that can be taken out as dividends to some percentage of invested capital.

When dividends are not the best way to move cash from the subsidiary to the parent, other ways include management fees, sales commissions, royalties, and repayment of principal and interest on loans. In addition, transfer pricing of components and finished products moving from the parent to subsidiary or among subsidiaries from different countries can be used to manage the flows of cash internationally. However, the setting of transfer prices is affected by so many other company and environmental considerations, such as performance measures of subsidiary managements or country taxation rates that cash management considerations tend often not to be major determinants of transfer pricing policy. The obvious attractiveness of using transfer pricing is that, unlike dividends, transfer prices are not subject to withholding taxes or many other restrictions.

Some Unsettled Issues in International Finance

As firms become multinational in scope, the nature of their financial decisions also becomes more complex. A multinational firm has access to more sources of funds than a purely domestic corporation. Interest rates and market conditions vary between the alternative sources of funds, and corporate financial practices may differ significantly between countries. For example, the debt ratios in many foreign countries are higher than those used by Canadian firms, which are, in turn, higher than those used by U.S. firms. A foreign affiliate of a Canadian firm faces a dilemma in its financing decision: Should it follow the parent firm's norm or that of the host country? Who must decide this? Will it be decided at the corporate headquarters in Toronto or by the foreign affiliate? This matter of control over financial decisions has important strategic overtones for the multinational firm.

Dividend policy is another area of debate. Should the parent company dictate the dividends the foreign affiliate must distribute or should it be left to the discretion of the foreign affiliate? Foreign government regulations also often influence this decision.

Questions such as these do not have clear-cut answers. The complex environment in which the MNCs operate does not permit simple, clear-cut solutions. Each situation has to be evaluated individually, and specific guidelines for decision making must be established. Such coordination, it is to be hoped, will result in cohesive policies in the areas of working capital arrangement, capital structure optimization, and dividend payouts throughout the MNC network.

Summary

1. When a domestic business firm crosses its national borders to do business in other countries, it enters a riskier and more complex environment. A multinational firm is exposed to foreign exchange risk and political risk in addition to the usual business and financial risks. In general, international business operations have been more profitable than domestic operations, and this higher profitability is one factor that motivates business firms to go overseas. International operations account for a significant proportion of the earnings for many North American firms. Multinational firms have played a major role in promoting economic development and international trade for several decades. Canada has been the site of large multinational investments. Canadian firms are investing significant sums in other countries, most notably in the United States. The multinational firm can operate in a foreign jurisdiction as an exporter, through a licensing agreement, a joint venture, or by way of a fully owned subsidiary.
2. International business transactions are denominated in foreign currencies. The rate at which one currency unit is converted into another is called the exchange rate. In today's global monetary system, the exchange rates of major currencies are fluctuating rather freely. These freely floating exchange rates expose multinational business firms to foreign exchange risk. To deal with this foreign currency exposure effectively, the financial executive of an MNC must understand foreign exchange rates and how they are determined.
3. Foreign exchange rates are influenced by differences in inflation rates among countries, by differences in interest rates, by governmental policies, and by the expectations of the participants in the foreign exchange markets.
4. A spot rate is the exchange rate one receives for immediate delivery of the foreign currency. A forward exchange rate is the exchange rate fixed today by contract for the delivery of the foreign currency at a fixed date in the future.
5. The international financial manager can reduce the firm's foreign currency exposure by hedging in the forward exchange market, in the money markets, in the currency futures market, or in the options market.
6. Multinational companies have made billions of dollars worth of direct investments in foreign countries over the years. Lower production costs overseas, tax deferral provisions, strategic advantages, and benefits of international diversification are some of the motivational factors behind

the flow of direct investment between nations. Foreign direct investments are usually quite large, and many of them are exposed to political risk.

7. Although discounted cash flow analysis is applied to screen the projects in the initial stages, strategic considerations and political risk are often the overriding factors in reaching the final decision. One of the most important differences between domestic and international investments is that the information on foreign investments is generally less complete and often less accurate. Therefore, analyzing a foreign investment proposal is more difficult than analyzing a domestic investment project.
8. Financing international trade and investment is another important area of international finance that one must understand in order to raise funds at the lowest cost possible. The multinational firm has access to both the domestic and foreign capital markets. The Export Development Corporation aids in financing Canadian exports to foreign countries. Borrowing in the Eurobond markets may appear less expensive at times, but the effect of foreign exchange risk on debt-servicing cost must be weighed carefully before borrowing in these markets. Floating common stock in foreign capital markets is another viable financing alternative for many multinational companies. The International Finance Corporation, which is a subsidiary of the World Bank, also provides debt capital and equity capital to qualified firms. These alternative sources of financing may significantly differ with respect to cost, terms, and conditions. Therefore, the financial executive must carefully locate and use the proper means to finance international business operations.

Review of Formulas

1. $$\textit{Forward premium (discount)} = \frac{\textit{Forward} - \textit{spot}}{\textit{spot}} \times \frac{12}{\textit{contract length (months)}} \qquad (21\text{–}1)$$

List of Terms

multinational corporation 740
foreign exchange rate 741
purchasing power parity theory 744
interest rate parity theory 745
balance of payments 745
spot rate 747
forward rate 747
economic exposure 749
foreign exchange risk 749
translation exposure 749
transaction exposure 750
currency futures 751
repatriation 757
expropriate 757
Export Development Corporation (EDC) 758
letter of credit 759
parallel loan 760
fronting loan 760
eurocurrency 761
London Interbank Offered Rate (LIBOR) 761
eurobond 762
American Depository Receipts (ADRs) 763

Discussion Questions

1. What risks do foreign affiliates of a multinational firm face in today's business world?
2. What are some allegations sometimes made against foreign affiliates of multinational firms and against the multinational firms themselves?
3. List the factors that affect the value of a currency in foreign exchange markets.
4. Explain how exports and imports tend to influence the value of a currency.
5. Differentiate between the spot exchange rate and the forward exchange rate.
6. What is meant by translation exposure in terms of foreign exchange risk?

7. Which factors influence a Canadian business firm to look into expanding in international markets?
8. Which procedures would you recommend for a multinational company in studying exposure to political risk? Which actual strategies can be used to guard against such risk?
9. What factors beyond the normal domestic analysis go into a financial feasibility study for a multinational firm?
10. What is a letter of credit?
11. What are the differences between a parallel loan and a fronting loan?
12. What is LIBOR? How does it compare to the Canadian banks' domestic prime rates?
13. What is the danger or concern in floating a Eurobond issue?
14. What are ADRs?
15. Comment on any dilemmas that multinational firms and their foreign affiliates may face in regard to debt ratio limits and dividend payouts.

INTERNET RESOURCES AND QUESTIONS

Daily foreign exchange rates on over 200 currencies and historical rates on over 60 currencies, including the ability to plot historical price trends, are available at this University of British Columbia site:
pacific.commerce.ubc.ca/xr

The Globe and Mail site has forward rates in its money and markets section on the U.S. dollar, British pound, euro, and Japanese yen:
www.globeandmail.com

Daily settlement prices on currency futures and options for several currencies are available at the Chicago Mercantile Exchange site. There is also a free hookup to live quotes:
www.cme.com

Bond ratings on the debt of numerous governments are available at two sites:
www.moodys.com
www.standardandpoors.com

1. Explain the functions of the Export Development Corporation (EDC) and the International Finance Corporation (IFC). Further information is available at www.edc.ca and www.ifc.org.
2. Find the current exchange rate, the rate one year ago, and the rate three years ago in relation to:
   a. The Canadian dollar on the following currencies: Bahamian dollar, Belgian franc, Czech koruna, Chilean peso, Egyptian pound, and Indian rupee. Which currencies have appreciated?
   b. The British pound on the following currencies: Bahamian dollar, Belgian franc, Czech koruna, Chilean peso, Egyptian pound, and Indian rupee. Which currencies have appreciated?
   c. Plot the exchange rate movement of the British pound against the Egyptian pound over the last year.
3. Find the forward rate to the Canadian dollar of the euro, British pound, Japanese yen, and U.S. dollar for three, six, and twelve months.
   a. Which currencies are trading at a premium and which ones are at a discount?
   b. What does this suggest about the expected future spot rates for these currencies?
   c. What does this suggest about the inflation rates for these countries in relation to Canada?

4. For yesterday's date find the settle price for a currency future on the Chicago Mercantile Exchange for the next three traded months for the following currencies: Canadian dollar, euro, British pound, Brazilian real, and Russian ruble. Which currencies are expected to depreciate in value in relation to the U.S. dollar?
5. For yesterday's date find the last price for a currency call option and put option on the Chicago Mercantile Exchange for the next traded month, with an option price slightly above the current spot price for the following currencies: Canadian dollar, euro, British pound, Brazilian real, and Russian ruble. Which currencies are expected to depreciate in value in relation to the U.S. dollar?

Problems

1. Using the foreign exchange rates for March 2002 presented in Table 21–1, determine the number of Canadian dollars required to buy the following amounts of foreign currencies:
   a. 10,000 euros
   b. 2,000 rupees
   c. 100,000 yen
   d. 5,000 Swiss francs
   e. 20,000 krona
   f. 50,000 baht
2. Obtain and recalculate the currency exchanges of problem 1 at today's rates. How do these figures compare to those obtained in that problem? Has the dollar strengthened or weakened against these securities?
   a. Use a recent edition of *The Globe and Mail—Report on Business.*
   b. Use pacific.commerce.ubc.ca/xr/data.html
3. *The Globe and Mail* reported the following spot and forward rates for the euro ($/euro) as of March 2002:

Spot	1.3805
30-day forward	1.3790
90-day forward	1.3761
180-day forward	1.3723

   a. Was the euro selling at a discount or premium in the forward market in March 2002?
   b. What was the 30-day forward premium (or discount)?
   c. What was the 90-day forward premium (or discount)?
   d. Suppose you executed a 90-day forward contract to exchange 100,000 euros into Canadian dollars. How many dollars would you get 90 days hence?
   e. Assume a Swiss bank entered into a 180-day forward contract with TD Bank to buy $100,000. How many euros will the Swiss bank deliver in six months to get the Canadian dollars?
4. Suppose an Egyptian pound is selling for $0.3432 and a Jordanian dinar is selling for $2.2396. What is the exchange rate (cross rate) of the Egyptian pound to the Jordanian dinar? That is, how many Egyptian pounds are equal to a Jordanian dinar?
5. Suppose a Mexican N. peso is selling for $0.1744 and a Maltese lira is selling for $3.4674. What is the exchange rate (cross rate) of the Mexican N. peso to the Maltese lira? That is, how many Mexican N. pesos are equal to a Maltese lira?

6. Suppose a Thai baht is selling for $0.0366 and a Panamanian balboa is selling for $1.5855. What is the exchange rate (cross rate) of the Thai baht to the Panamanian balboa? That is, how many Thai baht are equal to the Panamanian balboa?
7. From the base price level of 100 in 1974, Swiss and Canadian price levels in 2002 stood at 200 and 472, respectively. If the 1974 $/Sf exchange rate was $0.40/Sf, what should the exchange rate be in 2002?
8. In the previous problem, if Canada had somehow managed no inflation since 1974, what should the exchange rate be in 2002, using the purchasing power parity theory?
9. An investor in Canada bought a one-year New Zealand security valued at 146,263 New Zealand dollars. The Canadian dollar equivalent was $100,000. The New Zealand security earned 8 percent during the year, but the New Zealand dollar depreciated 3 cents against the Canadian dollar during the time period ($0.6837/NZD to $0.6520/NZD). After transferring the funds back to Canada, what was the investor's return on her $100,000?
10. A French investor buys 100 shares of Alcan for $2,600 ($26.00 per share). Over the course of a year, Alcan goes up by $5.00.
    a. If there is a 10 percent gain in the value of the dollar versus the French franc, what will be the total percentage return to the French investor?
    b. Now assume the stock increases by $6.00, but the dollar decreases by 10 percent versus the French franc. What will be the total percentage return to the French investor?
11. A Canadian investor buys 200 shares of Microsoft for $12,200 ($61.00 per share). Over the course of a year, Microsoft shares decline by $3.00.
    c. If there is a 4 percent gain in the value of the U.S. dollar versus the Canadian dollar, what will be the total percentage return to the Canadian investor?
    d. Now assume the stock declines by $6.00, but the U.S. dollar decreases by 2 percent versus the Canadian dollar. What will be the total percentage return to the Canadian investor?
12. Saturn Industries sells its products under a licensing agreement to many parts of the globe. Under the terms of an agreement reached with a German company, a payment for Saturn's services is due in one year for 1 million euros. There is some concern over the value of the Euro in one year, as the Canadian dollar has been strengthening.

    The spot rate is 1.3805 Canadian dollars for one euro, but the one-year forward rate is 1.3676 Canadian dollars for one euro. Currently, interest rates are 3 percent in Canada and 4 percent in Germany for one year. There is also a belief within the firm that the spot rate in one year will be 1.3825 because the euro is due to get stronger.

    a. Outline the various options available to Saturn Industries to handle its foreign exchange exposure.
    b. Make a recommendation.
13. Fox Silver Products has purchased 20,000 ounces of silver from Royal Minty of Britain at U.S.$6.25, payable in 180 days. The current spot rate is 1.4188 ($U.S. / £) and the 180-day forward is 1.4039. The CEO at Fox Silver suggests that the spot rate in six months time will be 1.4125.

    Interest rates in Britain are currently 4.33 percent for 180 days and 2.11 percent in the United States.

    a. Outline the various options available to Fox Silver to handle its foreign exchange exposure.
    b. Make a recommendation.

14. Nickel Plains of Canada has purchased 500,000 pounds of nickel from Coin Ltd. at U.S.$2.95, payable in 90 days. The current spot rate is 1.5823 ($Can / $U.S.) and the 90-day forward is 1.5831. The vice president of finance at Nickel Plains suggests that the spot rate in three months time will be 1.5625.

Interest rates in Canada are currently 2.27 percent for 90 days and 1.89 percent in the United States.

a. Outline the various options available to Nickel Plains to handle its foreign exchange exposure.

b. Make a recommendation.

15. Weese R. Grains of Canada has sold 5,000 tonnes of wheat to Pete's Apasta Company of Italy at 110 euros per tonne and payable in 1 year. The current spot rate is 1.3805 ($Can/ euro) and the 1 year forward is 1.3676. The financial analyst at Weese R. suggests that the spot rate in one year will be 1.3485.

Interest rates in Canada are currently 3.40 percent for 1 year and 3.77 percent in Italy.

a. Outline the various options available to Weese R. Grains to handle its foreign exchange exposure.

b. Make a recommendation.

16. You are the vice president of finance for Exploratory Resources, headquartered in Calgary. In January 2002, your firm's American subsidiary obtained a six-month loan of $1 million (U.S.) from a bank in Calgary to finance the acquisition of an oil-producing property in Oklahoma. The loan will also be repaid in U.S. dollars. At the time of the loan, the spot exchange rate was U.S.$0.6322/Canadian dollar and the U.S. currency was selling at a premium in the forward market. The June 2002 futures contract (face value = $100,000 per contract) was quoted at U.S.$0.6315.

a. Explain how the Calgary bank could lose on this transaction.

b. How much is the bank expected to lose/gain due to foreign exchange risk?

c. If there is a $100 total brokerage commission per contract, would you still recommend that the bank hedge in the currency futures market?

17. Campbell Electronics Corporation has a wholly owned foreign subsidiary in Jamaica. The subsidiary earns $5 million per year before taxes in Jamaica. The foreign income tax rate is 20 percent. Campbell's subsidiary repatriates the entire aftertax profit in the form of dividends to the parent corporation. The Canadian corporate tax rate is 38 percent of foreign earnings before taxes. Disregard any problems associated with exchange rates.

a. Complete the following table:

Before-tax earnings	
Foreign income tax @ 20%	
Earnings after foreign income taxes	
Dividends repatriated	
Gross Canadian taxes	
Foreign tax credit	
Net Canadian taxes payable	
Aftertax cash flow	

b. Now assume there is a 10 percent withholding tax on dividends in Jamaica. Recompute the answer to part *a* by again completing the above table:

APPENDIX 21A

Cash Flow Analysis and the Foreign Investment Decision

Direct foreign investments are often relatively large. As we mentioned previously, these investments are exposed to some extraordinary risks, such as foreign exchange fluctuations and political interference, which are nonexistent for domestic investments. Therefore, the final decision is often made by the board of directors after considering the financial feasibility and the strategic importance of the proposed investment. Financial feasibility analysis for foreign investments is basically conducted in the same manner as it is for domestic capital budgets. Certain important differences exist, however, in the treatment of foreign tax credits, foreign exchange risk, and remittance of cash flows. To see how these are handled in foreign investment analysis, let us consider a hypothetical illustration.

Q Systems Inc., a Quebec-based manufacturer of word processing equipment, is considering the establishment of a manufacturing plant in Salaysia, a country in Southeast Asia. The Salaysian plant will be a wholly owned subsidiary of Q Systems, and its estimated cost is 90 million ringgits (2 ringgits = $1.00). Based on the exchange rate between ringgits and dollars, the cost of dollars is $45 million. In addition to selling in the local Salaysian market, the proposed subsidiary is expected to export its word processors to the neighboring markets in Singapore, Hong Kong, and Thailand. Table 21A–1 shows expected revenues and operating costs. The country's investment climate, which reflects the foreign exchange and political risks, is rated BBB (considered fairly safe) by a leading Asian business journal.

After considering the investment climate and the nature of the industry, Q Systems has set a target rate of return of 20 percent for this foreign investment. Salaysia has a 25 percent corporate income tax rate and has waived the withholding tax on dividends repatriated (forwarded) to the parent company. A dividend payout ratio of 100 percent is intended for the foreign subsidiary. Q Systems' marginal tax rate is 30 percent. It was agreed by Q Systems and the Salaysian government that the subsidiary will be sold to a Salaysian entrepreneur after six years for an estimated 30 million ringgits. The plant will be amortized over a period of six years using the straight-line method. The cash flows generated through amortization cannot be remitted to the parent company until the subsidiary is sold to the local private entrepreneur six years from now. The Salaysian government requires the subsidiary to invest the amortization-generated cash flows in local government bonds yielding an after-tax rate of 15 percent. The amortization cash flows thus compounded and accumulated can be returned to Q Systems when the project is terminated. Although the value of ringgits in the foreign exchange market has remained fairly stable for the past three years, the projected budget deficits and trade deficits of Salaysia are likely—according to a consultant hired by Q Systems—to result in a gradual devaluation of ringgits against the Canadian dollar at the rate of 2 percent per year for the next six years.

Note that the analysis in Table 21A–1 is primarily done in terms of ringgits. Expenses (operating, amortization, and Salaysian income taxes) are subtracted from revenues to arrive at earnings after foreign income taxes. These earnings are then repatriated (forwarded) to Q Systems in the form of dividends. Dividends repatriated thus begin at 5.25 ringgits (in millions) in Year 1 and increase to 18.75 ringgits in Year 6. The next item, gross Canadian taxes, refers to the unadjusted Canadian tax obligation. Dividends received from a foreign subsidiary, unlike those received from a Canadian subsidiary, are fully taxable. In the case of Q Systems, this rate is equal to 46 percent of foreign earnings before taxes (earnings before Salaysian taxes).[1] For example, gross Canadian taxes in the first year are equal to:

[1]If foreign earnings had not been repatriated, there is a possibility that this tax obligation would not be due.

TABLE 21A–1

Cash flow analysis of a foreign investment

	Projected Cash Flows (millions ringgits unless otherwise stated)					
	Year 1	Year 2	Year 3	Year 4	Year 5	Year 6
Revenues	45.00	50.00	55.00	60.00	65.00	70.00
– Operating expenses	28.00	30.00	30.00	32.00	35.00	35.00
– Amortization	10.00	10.00	10.00	10.00	10.00	10.00
Earnings before Salaysian taxes	7.00	10.00	15.00	18.00	20.00	25.00
– Salaysian income tax (25%)	1.75	2.50	3.75	4.50	5.00	6.25
Earnings after foreign income taxes	5.25	7.50	11.25	13.50	15.00	18.75
= Dividends repatriated	5.25	7.50	11.25	13.50	15.00	18.75
Gross Canadian taxes (46% of foreign earnings before taxes)	3.22	4.60	6.90	8.28	9.20	11.50
– Foreign tax credit	1.75	2.50	3.75	4.50	5.00	6.25
Net Canadian taxes payable	1.47	2.10	3.15	3.78	4.20	5.25
Aftertax dividend received by Q Systems	3.78	5.40	8.10	9.72	10.80	13.50
Exchange rate (ringgits/$)	2.00	2.04	2.08	2.12	2.16	2.21
Aftertax dividend (Can. $)	1.89	2.65	3.89	4.58	5.00	6.11
PV of dividends ($) (at 20%)	1.58 +	1.84 +	2.25 +	2.21 +	2.01 +	2.05 = $11.94

Earnings before Salaysian taxes	$7.00
46% of foreign pretax earnings	46%
Gross Canadian taxes	$3.22

From gross Canadian taxes, Q Systems may take a foreign tax credit equal to the amount of Salaysian income tax paid. Gross Canadian taxes minus this foreign tax credit are equal to net Canadian taxes payable. Finally, aftertax dividends received by Q Systems are equal to dividends repatriated minus Canadian taxes payable. In the first year, the values are:

Dividends repatriated	$5.25
Less: net Canadian taxes payable	1.47
Aftertax dividends received by Q	$3.78

The figures for aftertax dividends received by Q Systems are all stated in ringgits. These ringgits are now converted into dollars. The initial exchange rate is 2.00 ringgits per dollar, and this will go up by 2 percent per year.[2] For the first year, 3.78 million ringgits will be translated into $1.89 million. Aftertax dividends in Canadian dollars grow from $1.89 million in Year 1 to $6.11 million in Year 6. The last row of Table 21A–1 shows the present value of these dividends at a 20 percent discount rate. The *total* present value of estimated aftertax dividends to be received by Q Systems adds up to $11.94 million. We know that repatriated dividends will be just one part of the cash flow. The second part consists of amortization-generated cash flow accumulated and reinvested in Salaysian government

[2]The 2 percent appreciation means the dollar is equal to an increasing amount of ringgits each year. The dollar is appreciating relative to ringgits, and ringgits are depreciating relative to the dollar. Since Q Systems' earnings are in ringgits, they are being converted at a less desirable rate each year. Q Systems may eventually decide to hedge its foreign exchange risk exposure.

bonds at 15 percent per year. The compound value of reinvested amortization cash flows (10 million ringgits per year) is:

$$10 \text{ million ringgits} = 87.54 \text{ million ringgits after six years}$$
$$n = 6\ i = 15\%$$

These 87.54 million ringgits must next be translated into dollars and then discounted back to the present. Since the exchange rate is forecast at 2.21 ringgits per dollar in the sixth year (third line from the bottom in Table 21A–1), the dollar equivalent of 87.54 million ringgits becomes:

$$87.54 \text{ million ringgits} \div 2.21 = \$39.61 \text{ million}$$

The $39.61 million can now be discounted back to the present for six years at 20 percent.

$39.61 million	$n = 6$, $i = 20\%$
= $13.27 million	

The final benefit to be received is the 30 million ringgits when the plant is sold six years from now. We first convert this to dollars and then take the present value.

$$30 \text{ million ringgits} \div 2.21 = \$13.57 \text{ million}$$

The present value of $13.57 million after six years at 20 percent is:

$13.57 million	$n = 6$, $i = 20\%$
= $ 4.55 million	

The present value of all cash inflows in dollars is equal to:

Present value of dividends	$11.94 million
Present value of repatriated amortization	13.27
Present value of plant sale	4.55
Total value of inflows	$29.76 million

The cost of the project was initially specified as 90 million ringgits, or $45 million. Thus, we see the total present value of inflows in dollars is less than the cost, and the project has a negative net present value.

Total present value of inflows	$29.76 million
Cost	45.00
Net present value	$−15.24 million

The project is not acceptable on the basis of net present value criteria. However, before such a recommendation is made to the board of directors, the financial analyst must reconsider the project and assess its strategic importance for the firm. One must debate whether or not the specific foreign project is consistent with the firm's overall long-term goals. If the firm wants to use this foreign project as a base for its future marketing of small computers in this part of the world, then the negative net present value should not be the only factor in making the decision. As a next step, the analyst considers any special circumstances of a nonroutine nature that may have led the firm to consider this foreign investment. For example, if Q Systems' North American domestic market share is eroding, a new market penetration like the one under consideration may be part of a much larger decision that is crucial for the firm's future.[3]

[3]The impact of the 20 percent discount rate should also be considered. At discount rates commonly applied to conventional domestic investments, often closer to 10 percent, the project would be accepted on a net present value basis.

Problems

21A–1. The Office Automation Corporation is considering a foreign investment. The initial cash outlay will be $10 million. The current foreign exchange rate is 2 francs = $1.00. Thus, the investment in foreign currency will be 20 million francs. The assets have a useful life of five years and no expected salvage value. The firm is allowed a straight-line method of amortization. Sales are expected to be 20 million francs and operating cash expenses 10 million francs every year for five years. The foreign income tax rate is 25 percent. The foreign subsidiary will repatriate all aftertax profits to Office Automation in the form of dividends. Furthermore, the amortized cash flows (equal to each year's amortization) will be repatriated during the same year they accrue to the foreign subsidiary. The applicable cost of capital that reflects the riskiness of the cash flows is 16 percent. The Canadian tax rate is 40 percent of foreign earnings before taxes.

a. Should the Office Automation Corporation undertake the investment, if the foreign exchange rate is expected to remain constant during the five-year period?

b. Should Office Automation undertake the investment if the foreign exchange rate is expected to be as follows?

Year 0	$1 = 2.0 francs
Year 1	$1 = 2.2 francs
Year 2	$1 = 2.4 francs
Year 3	$1 = 2.7 francs
Year 4	$1 = 2.9 francs
Year 5	$1 = 3.2 francs

APPENDIXES

APPENDIX A

Future Value of \$1, FV_{IF}

APPENDIX B

Present Value of \$1, PV_{IF}

APPENDIX C

Future Value of an Annuity of \$1, FV_{IFA}

APPENDIX D

Present Value of an Annuity of \$1, PV_{IFA}

APPENDIX E

Using Calculators for Financial Analysis

Appendix A

Future Value of $1, FV_{IF} $FV = PV(1 + i)^n$

	Percent										
Period	1%	2%	3%	4%	5%	6%	7%	8%	9%	10%	11%
1	1.010	1.020	1.030	1.040	1.050	1.060	1.070	1.080	1.090	1.100	1.110
2	1.020	1.040	1.061	1.082	1.103	1.124	1.145	1.166	1.188	1.210	1.232
3	1.030	1.061	1.093	1.125	1.158	1.191	1.225	1.260	1.295	1.331	1.368
4	1.041	1.082	1.126	1.170	1.216	1.262	1.311	1.360	1.412	1.464	1.518
5	1.051	1.104	1.159	1.217	1.276	1.338	1.403	1.469	1.539	1.611	1.685
6	1.062	1.126	1.194	1.265	1.340	1.419	1.501	1.587	1.677	1.772	1.870
7	1.072	1.149	1.230	1.316	1.407	1.504	1.606	1.714	1.828	1.949	2.076
8	1.083	1.172	1.267	1.369	1.477	1.594	1.718	1.851	1.993	2.144	2.305
9	1.094	1.195	1.305	1.423	1.551	1.689	1.838	1.999	2.172	2.358	2.558
10	1.105	1.219	1.344	1.480	1.629	1.791	1.967	2.159	2.367	2.594	2.839
11	1.116	1.243	1.384	1.539	1.710	1.898	2.105	2.332	2.580	2.853	3.152
12	1.127	1.268	1.426	1.601	1.796	2.012	2.252	2.518	2.813	3.138	3.498
13	1.138	1.294	1.469	1.665	1.886	2.133	2.410	2.720	3.066	3.452	3.883
14	1.149	1.319	1.513	1.732	1.980	2.261	2.579	2.937	3.342	3.797	4.310
15	1.161	1.346	1.558	1.801	2.079	2.397	2.759	3.172	3.642	4.177	4.785
16	1.173	1.373	1.605	1.873	2.183	2.540	2.952	3.426	3.970	4.595	5.311
17	1.184	1.400	1.653	1.948	2.292	2.693	3.159	3.700	4.328	5.054	5.895
18	1.196	1.428	1.702	2.026	2.407	2.854	3.380	3.996	4.717	5.560	6.544
19	1.208	1.457	1.754	2.107	2.527	3.026	3.617	4.316	5.142	6.116	7.263
20	1.220	1.486	1.806	2.191	2.653	3.207	3.870	4.661	5.604	6.727	8.062
25	1.282	1.641	2.094	2.666	3.386	4.292	5.427	6.848	8.623	10.835	13.585
30	1.348	1.811	2.427	3.243	4.322	5.743	7.612	10.063	13.268	17.449	22.892
40	1.489	2.208	3.262	4.801	7.040	10.286	14.974	21.725	31.409	45.259	65.001
50	1.645	2.692	4.384	7.107	11.467	18.420	29.457	46.902	74.358	117.39	184.57

Note: Factor calculation with calculator.
Set $PV = 1$ Set $PMT = 0$
Select n = number of required periods
Select $\%i$ = required interest reate
$CPT\ FV = ?$

Excel Spreadsheet
FV (i, n, 0, PV, 0)
i = decimal or %
1 = for beginning of period (5th spot)

Appendix A (concluded)

Future Value of $1

Period	12%	13%	14%	15%	16%	17%	18%	19%	20%	25%	30%
1	1.120	1.130	1.140	1.150	1.160	1.170	1.180	1.190	1.200	1.250	1.300
2	1.254	1.277	1.300	1.323	1.346	1.369	1.392	1.416	1.440	1.563	1.690
3	1.405	1.443	1.482	1.521	1.561	1.602	1.643	1.685	1.728	1.953	2.197
4	1.574	1.630	1.689	1.749	1.811	1.874	1.939	2.005	2.074	2.441	2.856
5	1.762	1.842	1.925	2.011	2.100	2.192	2.288	2.386	2.488	3.052	3.713
6	1.974	2.082	2.195	2.313	2.436	2.565	2.700	2.840	2.986	3.815	4.827
7	2.211	2.353	2.502	2.660	2.826	3.001	3.185	3.379	3.583	4.768	6.276
8	2.476	2.658	2.853	3.059	3.278	3.511	3.759	4.021	4.300	5.960	8.157
9	2.773	3.004	3.252	3.518	3.803	4.108	4.435	4.785	5.160	7.451	10.604
10	3.106	3.395	3.707	4.046	4.411	4.807	5.234	5.696	6.192	9.313	13.786
11	3.479	3.836	4.226	4.652	5.117	5.624	6.176	6.777	7.430	11.642	17.922
12	3.896	4.335	4.818	5.350	5.936	6.580	7.288	8.064	8.916	14.552	23.298
13	4.363	4.898	5.492	6.153	6.886	7.699	8.599	9.596	10.699	18.190	30.288
14	4.887	5.535	6.261	7.076	7.988	9.007	10.147	11.420	12.839	22.737	39.374
15	5.474	6.254	7.138	8.137	9.266	10.539	11.974	13.590	15.407	28.422	51.186
16	6.130	7.067	8.137	9.358	10.748	12.330	14.129	16.172	18.488	35.527	66.542
17	6.866	7.986	9.276	10.761	12.468	14.426	16.672	19.244	22.186	44.409	86.504
18	7.690	9.024	10.575	12.375	14.463	16.879	19.673	22.091	26.623	55.511	112.46
19	8.613	10.197	12.056	14.232	16.777	19.748	23.214	27.252	31.948	69.389	146.19
20	9.646	11.523	13.743	16.367	19.461	23.106	27.393	32.429	38.338	86.736	190.05
25	17.000	21.231	26.462	32.919	40.874	50.658	62.669	77.388	95.396	264.70	705.64
30	29.960	39.116	50.950	66.212	85.850	111.07	143.37	184.68	237.38	807.79	2,620.0
40	93.051	132.78	188.88	267.86	378.72	533.87	750.38	1,051.7	1,469.8	7,523.2	36,119.
50	289.00	450.74	700.23	1,083.7	1,670.7	2,566.2	3,927.4	5,988.9	9,100.4	70,065.	497,929.

Appendix B

Present Value of $1, PV_{IF} $PV = FV\left[\frac{1}{(1+i)^n}\right]$

Period	1%	2%	3%	4%	5%	6%	7%	8%	9%	10%	11%	12%
	Percent											
1	0.990	0.980	0.971	0.962	0.952	0.943	0.935	0.926	0.917	0.909	0.901	0.893
2	0.980	0.961	0.943	0.925	0.907	0.890	0.873	0.857	0.842	0.826	0.812	0.797
3	0.971	0.942	0.915	0.889	0.864	0.840	0.816	0.794	0.772	0.751	0.731	0.712
4	0.961	0.924	0.885	0.855	0.823	0.792	0.763	0.735	0.708	0.683	0.659	0.636
5	0.951	0.906	0.863	0.822	0.784	0.747	0.713	0.681	0.650	0.621	0.593	0.567
6	0.942	0.888	0.837	0.790	0.746	0.705	0.666	0.630	0.596	0.564	0.535	0.507
7	0.933	0.871	0.813	0.760	0.711	0.665	0.623	0.583	0.547	0.513	0.482	0.452
8	0.923	0.853	0.789	0.731	0.677	0.627	0.582	0.540	0.502	0.467	0.434	0.404
9	0.914	0.837	0.766	0.703	0.645	0.592	0.544	0.500	0.460	0.424	0.391	0.361
10	0.905	0.820	0.744	0.676	0.614	0.558	0.508	0.463	0.422	0.386	0.352	0.322
11	0.896	0.804	0.722	0.650	0.585	0.527	0.475	0.429	0.388	0.350	0.317	0.287
12	0.887	0.788	0.701	0.625	0.557	0.497	0.444	0.397	0.356	0.319	0.286	0.257
13	0.879	0.773	0.681	0.601	0.530	0.469	0.415	0.368	0.326	0.290	0.258	0.229
14	0.870	0.758	0.661	0.577	0.505	0.442	0.388	0.340	0.299	0.263	0.232	0.205
15	0.861	0.743	0.642	0.555	0.481	0.417	0.362	0.315	0.275	0.239	0.209	0.183
16	0.853	0.728	0.623	0.534	0.458	0.394	0.339	0.292	0.252	0.218	0.188	0.163
17	0.844	0.714	0.605	0.513	0.436	0.371	0.317	0.270	0.231	0.198	0.170	0.146
18	0.836	0.700	0.587	0.494	0.416	0.350	0.296	0.250	0.212	0.180	0.153	0.130
19	0.828	0.686	0.570	0.475	0.396	0.331	0.277	0.232	0.194	0.164	0.138	0.116
20	0.820	0.673	0.554	0.456	0.377	0.312	0.258	0.215	0.178	0.149	0.124	0.104
25	0.780	0.610	0.478	0.375	0.295	0.233	0.184	0.146	0.116	0.092	0.074	0.059
30	0.742	0.552	0.412	0.308	0.231	0.174	0.131	0.099	0.075	0.057	0.044	0.033
40	0.672	0.453	0.307	0.208	0.142	0.097	0.067	0.046	0.032	0.022	0.015	0.011
50	0.608	0.372	0.228	0.141	0.087	0.054	0.034	0.021	0.013	0.009	0.005	0.003

Note: Factor calculation with calculator.
Set $FV = 1$ Set $PMT = 0$
Select n = number of required periods
Select $\%i$ = required interest reate
$CPT\ PV = ?$

Excel Spreadsheet
PV (i, n, 0, FV, 0)
i = decimal or %
1 = for beginning of period (5th spot)

Appendix B (concluded)

Present Value of $1

Period	Percent												
	13%	14%	15%	16%	17%	18%	19%	20%	25%	30%	35%	40%	50%
1	0.885	0.877	0.870	0.862	0.855	0.847	0.840	0.833	0.800	0.769	0.741	0.714	0.667
2	0.783	0.769	0.756	0.743	0.731	0.718	0.706	0.694	0.640	0.592	0.549	0.510	0.444
3	0.693	0.675	0.658	0.641	0.624	0.609	0.593	0.579	0.512	0.455	0.406	0.364	0.296
4	0.613	0.592	0.572	0.552	0.534	0.515	0.499	0.482	0.410	0.350	0.301	0.260	0.198
5	0.543	0.519	0.497	0.476	0.456	0.437	0.419	0.402	0.320	0.269	0.223	0.186	0.132
6	0.480	0.456	0.432	0.410	0.390	0.370	0.352	0.335	0.262	0.207	0.165	0.133	0.088
7	0.425	0.400	0.376	0.354	0.333	0.314	0.296	0.279	0.210	0.159	0.122	0.095	0.059
8	0.376	0.351	0.327	0.305	0.285	0.266	0.249	0.233	0.168	0.123	0.091	0.068	0.039
9	0.333	0.300	0.284	0.263	0.243	0.225	0.209	0.194	0.134	0.094	0.067	0.048	0.026
10	0.295	0.270	0.247	0.227	0.208	0.191	0.176	0.162	0.107	0.073	0.050	0.035	0.017
11	0.261	0.237	0.215	0.195	0.178	0.162	0.148	0.135	0.086	0.056	0.037	0.025	0.012
12	0.231	0.208	0.187	0.168	0.152	0.137	0.124	0.112	0.069	0.043	0.027	0.018	0.008
13	0.204	0.182	0.163	0.145	0.130	0.116	0.104	0.093	0.055	0.033	0.020	0.013	0.005
14	0.181	0.160	0.141	0.125	0.111	0.099	0.088	0.078	0.044	0.025	0.015	0.009	0.003
15	0.160	0.140	0.123	0.108	0.095	0.084	0.074	0.065	0.035	0.020	0.011	0.006	0.002
16	0.141	0.123	0.107	0.093	0.081	0.071	0.062	0.054	0.028	0.015	0.008	0.005	0.002
17	0.125	0.108	0.093	0.080	0.069	0.060	0.052	0.045	0.023	0.012	0.006	0.003	0.001
18	0.111	0.095	0.081	0.069	0.059	0.051	0.044	0.038	0.018	0.009	0.005	0.002	0.001
19	0.098	0.083	0.070	0.060	0.051	0.043	0.037	0.031	0.014	0.007	0.003	0.002	0
20	0.087	0.073	0.061	0.051	0.043	0.037	0.031	0.026	0.012	0.005	0.002	0.001	0
25	0.047	0.038	0.030	0.024	0.020	0.016	0.013	0.010	0.004	0.001	0.001	0	0
30	0.026	0.020	0.015	0.012	0.009	0.007	0.005	0.004	0.001	0	0	0	0
40	0.008	0.005	0.004	0.003	0.002	0.001	0.001	0.001	0	0	0	0	0
50	0.002	0.001	0.001	0.001	0	0	0	0	0	0	0	0	0

Appendix C

Future Value of an Annuity of $1, FV_{IFA} $FV_A = A\left[\frac{(1+i)^n - 1}{i}\right]$

Period	Percent 1%	2%	3%	4%	5%	6%	7%	8%	9%	10%	11%
1	1.000	1.000	1.000	1.000	1.000	1.000	1.000	1.000	1.000	1.000	1.000
2	2.010	2.020	2.030	2.040	2.050	2.060	2.070	2.080	2.090	2.100	2.110
3	3.030	3.060	3.091	3.122	3.153	3.184	3.215	3.246	3.278	3.310	3.342
4	4.060	4.122	4.184	4.246	4.310	4.375	4.440	4.506	4.573	4.641	4.710
5	5.101	5.204	5.309	5.416	5.526	5.637	5.751	5.867	5.985	6.105	6.228
6	6.152	6.308	6.468	6.633	6.802	6.975	7.153	7.336	7.523	7.716	7.913
7	7.214	7.434	7.662	7.898	8.142	8.394	8.654	8.923	9.200	9.487	9.783
8	8.286	8.583	8.892	9.214	9.549	9.897	10.260	10.637	11.028	11.436	11.859
9	9.369	9.755	10.159	10.583	11.027	11.491	11.978	12.488	13.021	13.579	14.164
10	10.462	10.950	11.464	12.006	12.578	13.181	13.816	14.487	15.193	15.937	16.722
11	11.567	12.169	12.808	13.486	14.207	14.972	15.784	16.645	17.560	18.531	19.561
12	12.683	13.412	14.192	15.026	15.917	16.870	17.888	18.977	20.141	21.384	22.713
13	13.809	14.680	15.618	16.627	17.713	18.882	20.141	21.495	22.953	24.523	26.212
14	14.947	15.974	17.086	18.292	19.599	21.015	22.550	24.215	26.019	27.975	30.095
15	16.097	17.293	18.599	20.024	21.579	23.276	25.129	27.152	29.361	31.772	34.405
16	17.258	18.639	20.157	21.825	23.657	25.673	27.888	30.324	33.003	35.950	39.190
17	18.430	20.012	21.762	23.698	25.840	28.213	30.840	33.750	36.974	40.545	44.501
18	19.615	21.412	23.414	25.645	28.132	30.906	33.999	37.450	41.301	45.599	50.396
19	20.811	22.841	25.117	27.671	30.539	33.760	37.379	41.446	46.018	51.159	56.939
20	22.019	24.297	26.870	29.778	33.066	36.786	40.995	45.762	51.160	57.275	64.203
25	28.243	32.030	36.459	41.646	47.727	54.865	63.249	73.106	84.701	98.347	114.41
30	34.785	40.588	47.575	56.085	66.439	79.058	94.461	113.28	136.31	164.49	199.02
40	48.886	60.402	75.401	95.026	120.80	154.76	199.64	259.06	337.89	442.59	581.83
50	64.463	84.579	112.80	152.67	209.35	290.34	406.53	573.77	815.08	1,163.9	1,668.8

Note: Factor calculation with calculator.
Set $PMT = 1$ Set $PV = 0$
Select n = number of required periods
Select $\%i$ = required interest reate
$CPT\ FV = ?$

If annuity in advance calculate factor with BGN set on calculator.

Excel Spreadsheet
FV (i, n, 0, PMT, 0)
i = decimal or %
1 = for beginning of period (5th spot)

Appendix C (concluded)

Future Value of an Annuity of $1

Period	Percent										
	12%	13%	14%	15%	16%	17%	18%	19%	20%	25%	30%
1	1.000	1.000	1.000	1.000	1.000	1.000	1.000	1.000	1.000	1.000	1.000
2	2.120	2.130	2.140	2.150	2.160	2.170	2.180	2.190	2.200	2.250	2.300
3	3.374	3.407	3.440	3.473	3.506	3.539	3.572	3.606	3.640	3.813	3.990
4	4.779	4.850	4.921	4.993	5.066	5.141	5.215	5.291	5.368	5.766	6.187
5	6.353	6.480	6.610	6.742	6.877	7.014	7.154	7.297	7.442	8.207	9.043
6	8.115	8.323	8.536	8.754	8.977	9.207	9.442	9.683	9.930	11.259	12.756
7	10.089	10.405	10.730	11.067	11.414	11.772	12.142	12.523	12.916	15.073	17.583
8	12.300	12.757	13.233	13.727	14.240	14.773	15.327	15.902	16.499	19.842	23.858
9	14.776	15.416	16.085	16.786	17.519	18.285	19.086	19.923	20.799	25.802	32.015
10	17.549	18.420	19.337	20.304	21.321	22.393	23.521	24.701	25.959	33.253	42.619
11	20.655	21.814	23.045	24.349	25.733	27.200	28.755	30.404	32.150	42.566	56.405
12	24.133	25.650	27.271	29.002	30.850	32.824	34.931	37.180	39.581	54.208	74.327
13	28.029	29.985	32.089	34.352	36.786	39.404	42.219	45.244	48.497	68.760	97.625
14	32.393	34.883	37.581	40.505	43.672	47.103	50.818	54.841	59.196	86.949	127.91
15	37.280	40.417	43.842	47.580	51.660	56.110	60.965	66.261	72.035	109.69	167.29
16	42.753	46.672	50.980	55.717	60.925	66.649	72.939	79.850	87.442	138.11	218.47
17	48.884	53.739	59.118	65.075	71.673	78.979	87.068	96.022	105.93	173.64	285.01
18	55.750	61.725	68.394	75.836	84.141	93.406	103.74	115.27	128.12	218.05	371.52
19	63.440	70.749	78.969	88.212	98.603	110.29	123.41	138.17	154.74	273.56	483.97
20	72.052	80.947	91.025	102.44	115.38	130.03	146.63	165.42	186.69	342.95	630.17
25	133.33	155.62	181.87	212.79	249.21	292.11	342.60	402.04	471.98	1,054.8	2,348.80
30	241.33	293.20	356.79	434.75	530.31	647.44	790.95	966.7	1,181.9	3,227.2	8,730.0
40	767.09	1,013.7	1,342.0	1,779.1	2,360.8	3,134.5	4,163.21	5,529.8	7,343.9	30,089.	120,393.
50	2,400.0	3,459.5	4,994.5	7,217.7	10,436.	15,090.	21,813.	31,515.	45,497.	280,256.	165,976.

Appendix D

Present Value of an Annuity of $1, PV_{IFA} $PV_A = A\left[\dfrac{1 - \dfrac{1}{(1+i)^n}}{i}\right]$

Period	1%	2%	3%	4%	5%	6%	7%	8%	9%	10%	11%	12%
1	0.990	0.980	0.971	0.962	0.952	0.943	0.935	0.926	0.917	0.909	0.901	0.893
2	1.970	1.942	1.913	1.886	1.859	1.833	1.808	1.783	1.759	1.736	1.713	1.690
3	2.941	2.884	2.829	2.775	2.723	2.673	2.624	2.577	2.531	2.487	2.444	2.402
4	3.902	3.808	3.717	3.630	3.546	3.465	3.387	3.312	3.240	3.170	3.102	3.037
5	4.853	4.713	4.580	4.452	4.329	4.212	4.100	3.993	3.890	3.791	3.696	3.605
6	5.795	5.601	5.417	5.242	5.076	4.917	4.767	4.623	4.486	4.355	4.231	4.111
7	6.728	6.472	6.230	6.002	5.786	5.582	5.389	5.206	5.033	4.868	4.712	4.564
8	7.652	7.325	7.020	6.733	6.463	6.210	5.971	5.747	5.535	5.335	5.146	4.968
9	8.566	8.162	7.786	7.435	7.108	6.802	6.515	6.247	5.995	5.759	5.537	5.328
10	9.471	8.983	8.530	8.111	7.722	7.360	7.024	6.710	6.418	6.145	5.889	5.650
11	10.368	9.787	9.253	8.760	8.306	7.887	7.499	7.139	6.805	6.495	6.207	5.938
12	11.255	10.575	9.954	9.385	8.863	8.384	7.943	7.536	7.161	6.814	6.492	6.194
13	12.134	11.348	10.635	9.986	9.394	8.853	8.358	7.904	7.487	7.103	6.750	6.424
14	13.004	12.106	11.296	10.563	9.899	9.295	8.745	8.244	7.786	7.367	6.982	6.628
15	13.865	12.849	11.938	11.118	10.380	9.712	9.108	8.559	8.061	7.606	7.191	6.811
16	14.718	13.578	12.561	11.652	10.838	10.106	9.447	8.851	8.313	7.824	7.379	6.974
17	15.562	14.292	13.166	12.166	11.274	10.477	9.763	9.122	8.544	8.022	7.549	7.102
18	16.398	14.992	13.754	12.659	11.690	10.828	10.059	9.372	8.756	8.201	7.702	7.250
19	17.226	15.678	14.324	13.134	12.085	11.158	10.336	9.604	8.950	8.365	7.839	7.366
20	18.046	16.351	14.877	13.590	12.462	11.470	10.594	9.818	9.129	8.514	7.963	7.469
25	22.023	19.523	17.413	15.622	14.094	12.783	11.654	10.675	9.823	9.077	8.422	7.843
30	25.808	22.396	19.600	17.292	15.372	13.765	12.409	11.258	10.274	9.427	8.694	8.055
40	32.835	27.355	23.115	19.793	17.159	15.046	13.332	11.925	10.757	9.779	8.951	8.244
50	39.196	31.424	25.730	21.482	18.256	15.762	13.801	12.233	10.962	9.915	9.042	8.304

Note: Factor calculation with calculator.
Set $PMT = 1$ Set $FV = 0$
Select n = number of required periods
Select $\%i$ = required interest reate
$CPT\ PV = ?$

If annuity in advance calculate factor with BGN set on calculator.

Excel Spreadsheet
PV (i, n, 0, PMT, 0)
i = decimal or %
1 = for beginning of period (5th spot)

Appendix D (concluded)

Present Value of an Annuity of $1

Period	Percent												
	13%	14%	15%	16%	17%	18%	19%	20%	25%	30%	35%	40%	50%
1	0.885	0.877	0.870	0.862	0.855	0.847	0.840	0.833	0.800	0.769	0.741	0.714	0.667
2	1.668	1.647	1.626	1.605	1.585	1.566	1.547	1.528	1.440	1.361	1.289	1.224	1.111
3	2.361	2.322	2.283	2.246	2.210	2.174	2.140	2.106	1.952	1.816	1.696	1.589	1.407
4	2.974	2.914	2.855	2.798	2.743	2.690	2.639	2.589	2.362	2.166	1.997	1.849	1.605
5	3.517	3.433	3.352	3.274	3.199	3.127	3.058	2.991	2.689	2.436	2.220	2.035	1.737
6	3.998	3.889	3.784	3.685	3.589	3.498	3.410	3.326	2.951	2.643	2.385	2.168	1.824
7	4.423	4.288	4.160	4.039	3.922	3.812	3.706	3.605	3.161	2.802	2.508	2.263	1.883
8	4.799	4.639	4.487	4.344	4.207	4.078	3.954	3.837	3.329	2.925	2.598	2.331	1.922
9	5.132	4.946	4.772	4.607	4.451	4.303	4.163	4.031	3.463	3.019	2.665	2.379	1.948
10	5.426	5.216	5.019	4.833	4.659	4.494	4.339	4.192	3.571	3.092	2.715	2.414	1.965
11	5.687	5.453	5.234	5.029	4.836	4.656	4.486	4.327	3.656	3.147	2.752	2.438	1.977
12	5.918	5.660	5.421	5.197	4.988	4.793	4.611	4.439	3.725	3.190	2.779	2.456	1.985
13	6.122	5.842	5.583	5.342	5.118	4.910	4.715	4.533	3.780	3.223	2.799	2.469	1.990
14	6.302	6.002	5.724	5.468	5.229	5.008	4.802	4.611	3.824	3.249	2.814	2.478	1.993
15	6.462	6.142	5.847	5.575	5.324	5.092	4.876	4.675	3.859	3.268	2.825	2.484	1.995
16	6.604	6.265	5.954	5.668	5.405	5.162	4.938	4.730	3.887	3.283	2.834	2.489	1.997
17	6.729	6.373	6.047	5.749	5.475	5.222	4.988	4.775	3.910	3.295	2.840	2.492	1.998
18	6.840	6.467	6.128	5.818	5.534	5.273	5.033	4.812	3.928	3.304	2.844	2.494	1.999
19	6.938	6.550	6.198	5.877	5.584	5.316	5.070	4.843	3.942	3.311	2.848	2.496	1.999
20	7.025	6.623	6.259	5.929	5.628	5.353	5.101	4.870	3.954	3.316	2.850	2.497	1.999
25	7.330	6.873	6.464	6.097	5.766	5.467	5.195	4.948	3.985	3.329	2.856	2.499	2.000
30	7.496	7.003	6.566	6.177	5.829	5.517	5.235	4.979	3.995	3.332	2.857	2.500	2.000
40	7.634	7.105	6.642	6.233	5.871	5.548	5.258	4.997	3.999	3.333	2.857	2.500	2.000
50	7.675	7.133	6.661	6.246	5.880	5.554	5.262	4.999	4.000	3.333	2.857	2.500	2.000

APPENDIX E Using Calculators for Financial Analysis

This appendix is designed to help you use the Texas Instruments (BA-35 Solar), the Hewlett-Packard Financial Calculator, or Sharp's Business/Financial Calculator. We realize that most calculators come with comprehensive instructions, and this appendix is only meant to provide basic instructions for commonly used financial calculations.

There are always three things to do before starting your calculations as indicated in the first table: clear the calculator, set the decimal point, and set the mode. If you do not want to lose data stored in memory, do not perform steps 2 and 3 in the first box below.

Each step is listed vertically as a number followed by a decimal point. After each step you will find either a number or a calculator function denoted by a box [ ]. Entering the number on your calculator is one step, and entering the function is another.

Notice that the Hewlett-Packard is color coded. When two boxes are found one after another, you may have an [f] or a [g] in the first box. An [f] is orange coded and refers to the orange functions above the keys. After typing the [f] function, automatically look for an orange-coded key to punch. For example, after [f] in the first Hewlett-Packard box (middle panel), you punch in the orange color coded [REG]. If the [f] function is not followed by another box, you merely type in [f] and the value indicated.

The [g] is coded blue and refers to the functions on the bottom of the function keys. After the [g] function key, automatically look for blue-coded keys.

Familiarize yourself with the keyboard before you start. In the more complicated calculations, keystrokes will be combined into one step.

In the first four calculations we simply instruct you on how to get the interest factors for Appendixes A, B, C, and D. We use examples as our method of instruction.

Texas Instruments (BA-II Plus)

When changing variables with Ba II Plus: end with [2nd] [Quit]
[I/Y] Interest/year (nominal
[P/Y] Payments/year [C/Y] Compounding/year

BA II and Hewlett-Packard must set theses above keys appropriately.
For [I/Y] to be equivalent to [%i] used in text illustrations:
Set [P/Y] = [I/Y] = 1

BA II Plus: [2nd] [P/Y] 1 [ENTER] [2nd] [Quit]
HP: 1 [ ] [P/Y]

	Texas Instruments	Hewlett-Packard	Sharp
Clear the calculator: TI BA II Plus 'ready to go'	1. [AC/ON] [ON/C] 2. 0 3. [Fix] Clears Memory	1. [CLX] Clears screen 2. [f] 3. [REG] Clears Memory	1. [C CE] 2. [2nd F] 3. [CA] 4. [X→M] Clears Memory
Set the decimal point: For floating decimal point: (•) BA II Plus: Format = Fix HP: DISP = f	1. [2nd] 2. [Fix]	1. [f] 2. 4 (# of decimals)	1. [2nd F] 2. [TAB] 3. 4 (# of decimals)
Set the mode: TI BA II Plus 'ready to go'	1. [2nd F] 2. [FIN]	'ready to go'	1. [2nd F] 2. [MODE] 3. Keep repeating until [FIN] appears on screen

Verify these calculations (A, B, C, D) to appendixes (A, B, C, D). Tables are rounded.

		Texas Instruments	Hewlett-Packard	Sharp
A	Appendix A Compound Sum of $1 i = 9% or .09; n = 5 years $IF_S = (1 + i)^n$ Sum = Present Value $\times IF_S$ $S = P \times IF_S$	To Find Interest Factor 1. 1 2. + 3. .09 (interest rate) 4. [=] 5. [y^x] 6. 5 (# of periods) 7. = answer 1.538624	To Find Interest Factor 1. 1 2. [enter] 3. .09 (interest rate) 4. + 5. 5 (# of periods) 6. [y^x] answer 1.5386	To Find Interest Factor 1. 1 2. [+] 3. .09 (interest rate) 4. [=] 5. [y^x] 6. 5 (# of periods) 7. [=] answer 1.5386

		Texas Instruments	Hewlett-Packard	Sharp
B	Appendix B Present Value of $1 i = 9% or .09; n = 5 years $IF_{pv} = 1/(1 + i)^n$ Present Value = Sum $\times IF_{pv}$ $p = S \times IF_{pv}$	To Find Interest Factor Repeat steps 1 through 7 above. Continue with step 8. 8. [1/x] answer .6499314	To Find Interest Factor Repeat steps 1 through 6 above. Continue with step 7. 7. [1/x] answer .6499	To Find Interest Factor Repeat steps 1 through 7 above. Continue with step 8. 8. [1/x] answer .6499314

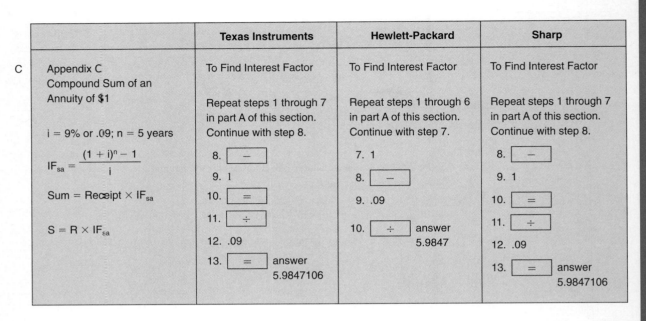

	Texas Instruments	**Hewlett-Packard**	**Sharp**
C			
Appendix C Compound Sum of an Annuity of $1 i = 9% or .09; n = 5 years $IF_{sa} = \frac{(1 + i)^n - 1}{i}$ Sum = Receipt × IF_{sa} $S = R \times IF_{sa}$	To Find Interest Factor Repeat steps 1 through 7 in part A of this section. Continue with step 8. 8. [−] 9. 1 10. [=] 11. [÷] 12. .09 13. [=] answer 5.9847106	To Find Interest Factor Repeat steps 1 through 6 in part A of this section. Continue with step 7. 7. 1 8. [−] 9. .09 10. [÷] answer 5.9847	To Find Interest Factor Repeat steps 1 through 7 in part A of this section. Continue with step 8. 8. [−] 9. 1 10. [=] 11. [÷] 12. .09 13. [=] answer 5.9847106

	Texas Instruments	**Hewlett-Packard**	**Sharp**
D			
Appendix D Present Value of an Annuity of $1 i = 9% or .09; n = 5 years $IF_{pva} = \frac{1 - [1/(1 + i)^n]}{i}$ Annuity = Receipt × IF_s $A = R \times IF_s$	To Find Interest Factor Repeat steps 1 through 8 in parts A & B. Continue with step 9. 9. [−] 10. 1 11. [=] 12. [+/−] 13. [÷] 14. .09 15. [=] answer 3.8896513	To Find Interest Factor Repeat steps 1 through 7 in parts A & B. Continue with step 8. 8. 1 9. [−] 10. [CHS] 11. .09 12. [÷] answer 3.8897	To Find Interest Factor Repeat steps 1 through 8 in parts A & B. Continue with step 9. 9. [−] 10. 1 11. [=] 12. [+/−] 13. [÷] 14. .09 15. [=] answer 3.8896513

On the following pages, you can determine bond valuation, yield to maturity, net present value of an annuity, net present value of an uneven cash flow, internal rate of return for an annuity, and internal rate of return for an uneven cash flow.

Bond Valuation

Solve for P_b = Price of the bond
Given:

I_t = \$80 annual coupon payments or 8% coupon (\$40 semiannually)
P_n = \$1,000 principal (par value)
n = 10 years to maturity (20 periods semiannually)
Y = 9.0% yield to maturity or required rate of return (4.5% semiannually)

You may choose to refer to Chapter 10 in the textbook for a complete discussion of bond valuation.

Yield to Maturity

Solve for Y = Yield to maturity
Given:

P_b = 895.50 price of bond
I_t = \$80 annual coupon payments or 8% coupon (\$40 semiannually)
P_n = \$1,000 principal (par value)
n = 10 years to maturity (20 periods semiannually)

You may choose to refer to Chapters 10 and 11 in the textbook for a complete discussion of yield to maturity.

Net Present Value of an Annuity

Solve for PV = Present value of annuity
Given:

n = 10 years (number of years cash flow will continue)
PMT = \$5,000 per year (amount of the annuity)
i = 12% (cost of capital K_a)
Cost = \$20,000

You may choose to refer to Chapter 12 in the textbook for a complete discussion of net present value.

	Texas Instruments	Hewlett-Packard	Sharp
BOND VALUATION All steps begin with number 1. Numbers following each step are keystrokes followed by a box [ ]. Each box represents a keystroke and indicates which calculator function is performed. The Texas Instrument and Sharp calculators require that data be adjusted for semiannual compounding, otherwise they assume annual compounding. The Hewlett-Packard internally assumes that semiannual compounding is used and requires annual data to be entered. The HP is more detailed in that it requires the actual day, month, and year. If you want an answer for a problem that requires a given number of years (e.g., 10 years), simply start on a date of your choice and end on the same date 10 years later, as in the example.	Set Finance Mode [2nd] [FIN] Set decimal to 2 places [2nd] Decimal [Fix] 1. 40 (semiannual coupon) 2. [PMT] 3. 4.5 (yield to maturity) semiannual basis 4. [% i] 5. 1000 (principal) 6. [FV] 7. 20 (semiannual periods to maturity) 8. [N] 9. [CPT] 10. [PV] answer 934.96 Answer is given in dollars, rather than % of par value.	Clear memory [f] [REG] Set decimal to 3 places [f] 3 1. 9.0 (yield to maturity) 2. [i] 3. 8.0 (coupon in percent) 4. [PMT] 5. 1.091999 (today's date month-day-year)* 6. [enter] 7. 1.092009 (maturity date month-day-year)* 8. [f] 9. [Price] answer 93.496 Answer is given as % of par value and equals $934.96. If Error message occurs, clear memory and start over. *See instructions in the third paragraph of the first column.	Set Finance Mode [2nd] [MODE] Set decimal to 2 places [2nd] [TAB] 2 1. 40 (semiannual coupon) 2. [PMT] 3. 4.5 (yield to maturity) semiannual basis 4. [i] 5. 1000 (principal) 6. [FV] 7. 20 (semiannual periods to maturity) 8. [n] 9. [COMP] 10. [PV] answer −934.96 Answer is negative to indicate outflow today to receive future inflows (principal and semiannual coupon).

www.mcgrawhill.ca/college/block

	Texas Instruments	Hewlett-Packard	Sharp
YIELD TO MATURITY All steps are numbered. All numbers following each step are keystrokes followed by a box ☐. Each box represents a keystroke and indicates which calculator function is performed. Texas Instruments and Sharp do not internally compute a semiannual rate, so the data must be adjusted to reflect semiannual payments and periods. The answer received in step 10 is a semiannual rate, which must be multiplied by 2 to reflect an annual yield. The Hewlett-Packard internally assumes that semiannual payments are made and, therefore, the answer in step 9 is the annual yield to maturity based on semiannual coupons. If you want an answer on the HP for a given number of years (e.g., 10 years), simply start on a date of your choice and end on the same date 10 years later, as in the example.	Set Finance Mode 2nd FIN Set decimal to 2 places Decimal 2nd Fix 1. 20 (semiannual periods) 2. N 3. 1000 (par value) 4. FV 5. 40 (semiannual coupon) 6. PMT 7. 895.50 (bond price) 8. PV 9. CPT 10. %i answer 4.83% 11. x 12. 2 13. = answer 9.65% (annual nominal rate)	Clear memory f REG Set decimal f 2 1. 89.95 (bond price as a percent of par) 2. PV 3. 8.0 (annual coupon in %) 4. PMT 5. 1.091999 (today's date)* 6. enter 7. 1.092009 (maturity date)* 8. f 9. YTM answer 9.65% In case you receive an Error message, you have probably made a keystroke error. Clear the memory f REG and start over *See instructions in the third paragraph of the first column.	Set Finance Mode 2nd MODE Set decimal to 2 places 2ndF TAB 2 1. 20 (semiannual periods) 2. n 3. 1000 (par value) 4. FV 5. 40 (semiannual coupon) 6. PMT 7. 895.50 (bond price) 8. +/− 9. PV 10. COMP 11. i answer 4.83 12. x 13. 2 14. = answer 9.65 (annual nominal rate)

	Texas Instruments	Hewlett-Packard	Sharp
NET PRESENT VALUE OF AN ANNUITY All steps are numbered and some steps include several keystrokes. All numbers following each step are keystrokes followed by a box [ ]. Each box represents a keystroke and indicates which calculator function is performed on that number. The calculation for the present value of an annuity on the TI requires that the project cost be subtracted from the present value of the cash inflows. The HP 12C could solve the problem exactly with the same keystrokes as the TI. However, since the HP uses a similar method to solve uneven cash flows, we elected to use the method that requires more keystrokes but which includes a negative cash outflow for the cost of the capital budgeting project. To conserve space, several keystrokes have been put into one step.	Set Finance Mode [2nd] [FIN] Set decimal to 2 places [2nd] [Fix] Decimal 1. 10 (years of cash flow) 2. [N] 3. 5000 (annual payments) 4. [PMT] 5. 12 (cost of capital) 6. [%i] 7. [CPT] 8. [PV] 9. [–] 10. 20000 11. [=] answer $8,251.12	Set decimal to 2 places [f] 2 [f] [REG] clears memory 1. 20000 (cash outflow) 2. [CHS] changes sign 3. [g] 4. [CFo] 5. 5000 (annual payments) 6. [g] [CFi] 7. 10 [g] [Nj] (years) 8. 12 [i] (cost of capital) 9. [f] [NPV] answer $8,251.12 If an Error message appears, start over by clearing the memory with [f] [REG].	Set Finance Mode [2ndF] [MODE] Set decimal to 2 places [2ndF] TAB 2 1. 10 (years of cash flow) 2. [n] 3. 5000 (annual payments) 4. [PMT] 5. 12 (cost of capital) 6. [i] 7. [COMP] 8. [PV] 9. [+/–] 10. [–] 11. 20000 12. [=] answer $8,251.12

Net Present Value of an Uneven Cash Flow

Solve for NPV = Net present value
Given:

n = 5 years (number of years cash flow will continue)
PMT = \$5,000 (yr. 1); 6,000 (yr. 2); 7,000 (yr. 3); 8,000 (yr. 4); 9,000 (yr. 5)
i = 12% (cost of capital K_a)
Cost = \$25,000

You may choose to refer to Chapter 12 for a complete discussion of net present value concepts.

Internal Rate of Return for an Annuity

Solve for IRR = Internal rate of return
Given:

n = 10 years (number of years cash flow will continue)
PMT = \$10,000 per year (amount of the annuity)
Cost = \$50,000 (this is the present value of the annuity)

You may choose to refer to Chapter 12 in the textbook for a complete discussion of internal rate of return.

Internal Rate of Return with an Uneven Cash Flow

Solve for IRR = Internal rate of return (return that causes present value of outflows to equal present value of the inflows)
Given:

n = 5 years (number of years cash flow will continue)
PMT = \$5,000 (yr. 1); 6,000 (yr. 2); 7,000 (yr. 3); 8,000 (yr. 4); 9,000 (yr. 5)
Cost = \$25,000

You may choose to refer to Chapter 12 for a complete discussion of internal rate of return.

	Texas Instruments	Hewlett-Packard	Sharp
NET PRESENT VALUE OF AN UNEVEN CASH FLOW All steps are numbered and some steps include several keystrokes. All numbers following each step are keystrokes followed by a box . Each box represents a keystroke and indicates which calculator function is performed on that number. Because we are dealing with uneven cash flows, each number must be entered. The TI requires that you make sure of the memory. In step 2, you enter the future cash inflow in year 1 and, in step 3, you determine its present value, which is stored in memory. After the first year 1-year calculation, following year present values are calculated in the same way and added to the stored value using the SUM key. Finally, the recall key RCL is used to recall the present value of the total cash inflows. The HP requires each cash flow to be entered in order. The CFo key represents the cash flow in time period 0. The CFj key automatically counts the year of the cash flow in the order entered and so no years need be entered. Finally, the cost of capital of 12% is entered and the f key and NPV key are used to complete the problem.	Clear memory AC/ON 0 STO Set decimal to 2 places Decimal 2nd Fix Set finance mode 2nd FIN 1. 12 %i 2. 5000 FV 3. 1 N CPT PV SUM 4. 6000 FV 5. 2 N CPT PV SUM 6. 7000 FV 7. 3 N CPT PV SUM 8. 8000 FV 9. 4 N CPT PV SUM 10. 9000 FV 11. 5 N CPT PV SUM 12. RCL (answer 24420.90) 13. – 14. 25000 (cash outflow) 15. = answer –$579.10 Negative Net Present Value	Set decimal to 2 places f 2 f REG clears memory 1. 25000 (cash outflow) 2. CHS changes sign 3. g CFo 4. 5000 g CFj 5. 6000 g CFj 6. 7000 g CFj 7. 8000 g CFj 8. 9000 g CFj 9. 12 i 10. g NPV answer –$579.10 Negative Net Present Value If you receive an Error message, you have probably made a keystroke error. Clear memory with f REG and start over with Step 1.	Clear memory 2ndF CA Set decimal to 2 places 2ndF TAB 2 Set finance mode 2ndF MODE 1. 12 2. i 3. 25000 4. +/– 5. 5000 CFi 6. 6000 CFi 7. 7000 CFi 8. 8000 CFi 9. 9000 CFi 10. NPV answer –$579.10 Negative Net Present Value

	Texas Instruments	Hewlett-Packard	Sharp
INTERNAL RATE OF RETURN ON AN ANNUITY All steps are numbered and some steps include several keystrokes. All numbers following each step are keystrokes followed by a box [ ]. Each box represents a keystroke and indicates which calculator function is performed on that number. The calculation for the internal rate of return on an annuity on the TI and Sharp require relatively few keystrokes. The HP requires more keystrokes than the TI or Sharp, because it needs to use the function keys [f] and [g] to enter data into the internal programs. The HP and Sharp methods require that the cash outflow be expressed as a negative, while the TI uses a positive number for the cash outflow. To conserve space, several keystrokes have been put into one step.	Clear memory [AC/ON] 0 [STO] Set Finance Mode [2nd] [FIN] Set decimal to 2 places [2nd] Decimal [Fix] 1. 10 (years of cash flow) 2. [N] 3. 10000 (annual payments) 4. [ANN] 5. 50000 (present value) 6. [PV] 7. [CPT] 8. [%i] answer is 15.10% At an internal rate of return of 15.10%, the present value of the $50,000 outflow is equal to the present value of $10,000 cash inflows over the next 10 years.	Set decimal to 2 places [f] 2 [f] [REG] clears memory 1. 50000 (cash outflow) 2. [CHS] changes sign 3. [g] 4. [CFo] 5. 10000 (annual payments) 6. [g] [CFi] 7. 10 [g] [Nj] (years) 8. [f] [IRR] answer is 15.10% If an Error message appears, start over by clearing the memory with [f] [REG].	Clear memory [2ndF] [CA] Set Finance Mode [2ndF] [MODE] Set decimal to 2 places [2ndF] [TAB] 2 1. 10 (years of cash flow) 2. [n] 3. 10000 (annual payments) 4. [PMT] 5. 50000 (present value) 6. [+/−] 7. [PV] 8. [COMP] 9. [i] answer is 15.10%. At an internal rate of return of 15.10%, the present value of the $50,000 outflow is equal to the present value of $10,000 cash inflows over the next 10 years.

	Texas Instruments	Hewlett-Packard	Sharp
INTERNAL RATE OF RETURN ON UNEVEN CASH FLOW All steps are numbered and some steps include several keystrokes. All numbers following each step are keystrokes followed by a box . Each box represents a keystroke and indicates which calculator function is performed on that number. Because we are dealing with uneven cash flows, the mathematics of solving this problem with the TI is not possible. A more advanced algebraic calculator would be required. However, students willing to use trial and error can use the NPV method and try different discount rates until the NPV equals zero. Check Chapter 12 on methods for approximating the IRR. This will provide a start. The HP 12C requires each cash flow to be entered in order. The CFO key represents the cash flow in time period 0. The CFO key automatically counts the year of the cash flow in the order entered and so no years need be entered. To find the internal rate of return, use the f IRR keys and complete the problem.	Clear memory AC/ON 0 STO Set decimal to 2 places 2nd Decimal Fix Set finance mode 2nd FIN 1. 12 %i (your IRR est.) 2. 5000 FV 3. 1 N CPT PV STO 4. 6000 FV 5. 2 N CPT PV SUM 6. 7000 FV 7. 3 N CPT PV SUM 8. 8000 FV 9. 4 N CPT PV SUM 10. 9000 FV 11. 5 N CPT PV SUM 12. RCL (answer 24,420.90) 13. − 14. 25000 (cash outflow) 15. = Answer −$579.10 Negative NPV. Start over with a lower discount rate (try 11.15). Answer is 24999.75. With a cash outflow of $25,000, the IRR would be 11.15%.	Set decimal to 2 places f 2 f REG clears memory 1. 25000 (cash outflow) 2. CHS changes sign 3. g CFo 4. 5000 g CFj 5. 6000 g CFj 6. 7000 g CFj 7. 8000 g CFj 8. 9000 g CFj 9. f IRR answer 11.15% If you receive an Error message, you have probably made a keystroke error. Clear memory with f REG and start over with Step 1.	Repeat steps given for Net Present Value of an Uneven Cash Flow and add 11. IRR answer 11.15

Glossary

A

abnormal return A gain or loss above what should be expected, given the degree of risk inherent in an investment.

absolute priority rule Under the bankruptcy act, all senior claims on asset value must be settled in full before any value can be given to a junior claimant.

accounts receivable Claims against customers for monies, goods, or services.

after-acquired property clause Property purchased is placed under the original mortgage if purchased after the mortgage is executed.

aftermarket The market for a new security offering immediately after it is sold to the public.

agency theory This theory examines the relationship between the owners of the firm and their agents, the managers of the firm. Does management act in the best interests of shareholders?

agent One who sells, or "places," an asset for another party. An agent works on a commission or fee basis. Investment dealers sometimes act as agents for their clients.

aging of accounts receivable Analyzing accounts by the amount of time they have been on the books.

amalgamation A statutory combination of companies under one of the provincial or federal acts.

American Depository Receipts (ADR) These receipts represent the ownership interest in a foreign company's common shares that are held in trust in a New York bank. The depository receipts are in U.S. dollars while the shares are not. Many ADRs are listed on the NYSE and many more are traded in the over-the-counter market.

amortization Expensing of a cost (usually includes interest if a debt) over a number of periods. Generic term to include depreciation and depletion.

annuity A series of consecutive payments or receipts of equal amount.

annuity in advance A series of equal payments at the beginning of each period.

ARBS (arbitrageurs) Specialists in merger investments who attempt to capitalize on the difference between the value offered and the current market price of the acquisition candidate.

asset-based securities Public offerings backed by receivables as collateral. Essentially, a firm factors (sells) its receivables in the securities markets.

asset utilization ratios A group of ratios that measures the speed at which the firm is turning over or utilizing its assets. We measure inventory turnover, capital asset turnover, total asset turnover, and the average time it takes to collect accounts receivable.

assignment The liquidation of assets without going through formal court procedures. To effect an assignment, creditors must agree on liquidation values and the relative priority of claims.

average accounting return (AAR) This profitability measure is calculated as average earnings after tax divided by average book value.

average collection period The average amount of time accounts receivable have been on the books. It may be computed by dividing accounts receivable by average daily credit sales.

B

balance of payments The term refers to a system of government accounts that catalogues the flow of economic transactions between countries.

balance sheet A financial statement that indicates what assets the firm owns and how those assets are financed in the form of liabilities or ownership interest.

bankers' acceptance Short-term securities that frequently arise from foreign trade. The acceptance is a draft drawn on a bank for approval for future payment and is subsequently presented to the payer.

bank rate The rate of interest the Bank of Canada charges on loans to the chartered banks. It is a monetary tool used for management of the money supply.

bankruptcy The market value of a firm's assets are less than its liabilities, and the firm has a negative net worth. The term is also used to describe in-court procedures associated with the reorganization or liquidation of a firm.

basic earnings per share Earnings per share unadjusted for dilution.

basis point One basis point equals 1/100 of 1 percent.

bearer deposit notes Short-term notes that are negotiable and issued by chartered banks.

bear market A falling or lethargic stock market. The opposite of a bull market.

best efforts A distribution, also referred to as a marketed effort, in which the investment dealer agrees to work for a commission rather than actually underwriting (buying) the issue for resale. It is a procedure often used by smaller investment dealers with relatively unknown companies. The investment dealer is not directly taking the risk for distribution.

beta A measure of the volatility of returns on an individual stock relative to the market. Stocks with a beta of 1.0 are said to have risk equal to that of the market (equal volatility). Stocks with betas greater than 1.0 have more risk than the market, while those with betas of less than 1.0 have less risk than the market.

blanket inventory liens A secured borrowing arrangement in which the lender has a general claim against the inventory of the borrower.

bond indenture (See indenture.)

bond ratings Bonds are rated according to risk by Dominion Bond Rating Services and Standard and Poor's Rating Service. A bond that is rated AAA has the lowest risk, while a bond with a C rating has the highest risk. Coupon rates are greatly influenced by a corporation's bond rating.

book-entry transaction A transaction in which no actual paper or certificate is created. All transactions simply take place on the books via computer entries.

book value (See net worth.)

bought deals An issue of securities that has been prepurchased by an investment dealer. The investment dealer has thus guaranteed proceeds to the issuing corporation, and the investment dealer bears the risk of holding or selling the security issue.

break-even analysis A numerical and graphical technique that is used to determine at what point the firm will break even (Revenue = Cost). To compute the break-even point, we divide fixed costs by price minus variable cost per unit.

brokers Members of organized stock exchanges who have the ability to buy and sell securities on the floor of their respective exchanges. Brokers act as agents between buyers and sellers.

bull market A rising stock market. For our purposes, a bull market exists when stock prices are strong and rising and investors are optimistic about future market performance.

Bureau of Competition Policy Federal agency set up to review mergers in relation to the Competition Act to determine if they lessen competition substantially in given markets.

business risk The risk related to the inability of the firm to hold its competitive position and maintain stability and growth in earnings.

C

call feature Used for bonds and some preferred stock. A call or redemption feature, written into a bond indenture, allows the corporation to retire securities before maturity by forcing the bondholders to sell bonds back to it at a set price.

call option A call option gives the holder the right to buy an underlying asset at a preset price.

call option writer A call option writer sells a contract giving the purchaser the right to buy an underlying asset at a preset price. The writer has an obligation to sell the underlying asset at the preset price.

call premium The premium paid by a corporation to call in a bond issue before the maturity date.

call provision Used for bonds and some preferred stock. A call allows the corporation to retire the securities before maturity by forcing the bondholders to sell bonds back to it at a set price. The call provisions are included in the bond indenture.

Canadian Dealing Network (CDN) This is Canada's over-the-counter equity market for smaller firms.

Canadian Depository for Securities (CDS) An on-line, real-time national clearinghouse for money market, bond, and equity transactions. CDS is owned by the banks, investment dealers, and trust companies.

capital Sources of long-term financing that are available to the business firm.

capital asset pricing model (CAPM) A model that relates the risk-return trade-offs of individual assets to market returns. A security is presumed to receive a risk-free rate of return plus a premium for risk.

capital cost allowance (CCA) Declining balance method of amortization allowed by the Income Tax Act as a tax-deductible expense.

capital gains taxes Taxes on gains from holding assets. Currently, only 75 percent of the gain is taxable.

capital (or financing) lease A long-term, noncancellable lease that has many of the characteristics of debt. Under CICA guidelines, the lease obligation must be shown directly on the balance sheet.

capital markets Competitive markets for equity securities or debt securities with maturities of more than one year. The best examples of capital market securities are common stock, bonds, and preferred stock.

capital rationing Occurs when a corporation has more dollars of capital budgeting projects with positive net present values than it has money to invest in them. Therefore, some projects that should be accepted are excluded because financial capital is rationed.

capital structure The combination or weightings of the different liabilities and equities used to finance a corporation.

capital structure theory The study of the relative importance of debt and equity in financing a firm. Early development of this theory was by Modigliani and Miller.

carrying costs The cost to hold an asset, usually inventory. For inventory, carrying costs include such items as interest, warehousing costs, insurance, and material-handling expenses.

cash budget A series of monthly or quarterly budgets that indicate cash receipts, cash payments, and the borrowing requirements for meeting financial requirements. It is constructed from the pro forma income statement and other supportive schedules.

cash conversion cycle The time between the initial outlay of funds for materials and the final collection of funds from clients.

cash discount A reduction in the invoice price if payment is made within a specified time period. An example would be 2/10, net 30.

cash flow A value equal to income after taxes plus noncash expenses. In capital budgeting decisions, the usual noncash expense is amortization.

cash flow cycle The pattern in which cash moves in and out of the firm. The primary consideration in managing the cash flow cycle is to ensure that inflows and outflows of cash are properly synchronized for transaction purposes.

cash flows from financing activities Cash flow that is generated (or reduced) from the sale or repurchase of securities or the payment of cash dividends. It is the third section presented in the statement of cash flows.

cash flows from investing activities Cash flow that is generated (or reduced) from the sale or purchase of long-term securities or plant and equipment. It is the second section presented in the statement of cash flows.

cash flows from operating activities Cash flow information that is determined by adjusting net income for such factors as amortization expense, changes in current assets and liabilities, and other items. It is the first section presented in the statement of cash flows.

CCA tax shield The reduction of taxes otherwise payable because the corporation can expense capital costs and therefore reduce taxable income.

certainty equivalents The adjustment of uncertain cash flows as represented by a probability distribution to a value that is considered equal and certain.

certificate of deposit A certificate offered by a bank, trust company, or other financial institutions for the deposit of funds at a given interest rate over a specified time period.

CICA Handbook This manual outlines the requirements for financial statements prepared by chartered accountants.

clientele effect The effect of investor preferences for dividends or capital gains. Investors tend to purchase securities that meet their needs.

coefficient of correlation The degree of associated movement between two or more variables. Variables that move in the same direction are said to be positively correlated, while negatively correlated variables move in opposite directions.

coefficient of variation A measure of risk determination that is computed by dividing the standard deviation for a series of numbers by the expected value. Generally, the larger the coefficient of variation, the greater the risk.

combined leverage The total or combined impact of operating and financial leverage.

commercial paper An unsecured promissory note that large corporations issue to investors. The minimum amount is usually $25,000.

common equity The common stock or ownership capital of the firm. Common equity may be supplied through retained earnings or the sale of new common stock.

common shareholder Holders of common shares are the owners of the company. They have a residual claim to the earnings.

common stock Represents the ownership interest of the firm. Common shareholders have the ultimate right to control the business.

common stock equity Shareholder ownership interest in the firm, represented by new shares and retained earnings. Also referred to as net worth.

common stock equivalent Warrants, options, and any securities convertible into common shares.

compensating balances A bank requirement that business customers maintain a minimum average balance. The required amount is usually computed as a percentage of customer loans outstanding or as a percentage of the future loans to which the bank has committed itself.

competition law A federal law that makes a merger or acquisition illegal if it "lessens competition substantially in a given market."

composition An out-of-court settlement in which creditors agree to accept a fractional settlement on their original claim.

compounded semiannually A compounding period of every six months. For example, a five-year investment in which interest is compounded semiannually would indicate an n value equal to 10 and an i value at one-half the annual rate.

compound sum The future value of a single amount or an annuity when compounded at a given interest rate for a specified time period.

Computer Assisted Trading System (CATS) Buy or sell orders for securities can be executed electronically on the TSX, without the use of floor traders.

conglomerate A corporation that is made up of many diverse, often unrelated divisions. This form of organization is thought to reduce risk, but it may create problems of coordination.

consolidation The combination of two or more firms, generally of equal size and market power, to form a new entity.

consumer price index An economic indicator published monthly by Statistics Canada. It measures the rate of inflation for consumer goods.

contribution margin The contribution to fixed costs from each unit of sales. The margin may be computed as price minus variable cost per unit.

conversion The process of swapping one security for common shares in a corporation.

conversion feature A provision of a security that allows the swapping of that security for common shares under specified conditions.

conversion premium The market price of a convertible bond or preferred stock minus the security's conversion value.

conversion price The conversion ratio divided into the par value. This is the price of the common stock, at which the security is convertible into shares. An investor would usually not convert the security into common stock unless the market price is greater than the conversion price.

conversion ratio The number of shares of common stock an investor receives if he or she exchanges a convertible bond or convertible preferred stock for common stock.

conversion value The conversion ratio multiplied by the market price per share of common stock.

convertible exchangeable preferred A form of preferred stock that allows the company to force conversion from convertible preferred stock into convertible debt. This can be used to allow the company to take advantage of falling interest rates or to allow the company to change aftertax preferred dividends into tax-deductible interest payments.

convertible security A security that may be traded into the company for a different form or type of security. Convertible securities are usually bonds or preferred stock that may be exchanged for common stock.

corporate financial markets Markets in which corporations, in contrast to governmental units, raise funds.

corporate life cycle (See life cycle curve.)

corporate stock repurchase A corporation may purchase its issued shares in the market as an alternative to paying a cash dividend. Earnings per share will go up, and if the price-earnings ratio remains the same, the shareholder receives the same dollar benefit as through a cash dividend. Reacquired shares may be used for employee options, as part of a tender offer in a merger or acquisition, or as a protective device against being taken over as a merger candidate.

corporation A form of ownership in which a separate legal entity is created. A corporation may sue or be sued, engage in contracts, and acquire property. It has a continual life and is not dependent on any one shareholder for maintaining its legal existence. A corporation is owned by shareholders who enjoy the privilege of limited liability. There is, however, the potential for double taxation in the corporate form of organization, the first time at the corporate level in the form of profits, and again at the shareholder level in the form of dividends.

cost-benefit analysis A study of the incremental costs and benefits that can be derived from a given course of action.

cost of capital The cost of alternative sources of financing to the firm. (See also weighted average cost of capital.)

cost of goods sold The cost specifically associated with units sold during the time period under study.

cost of ordering Those costs incurred in placing an order for goods, receiving those goods, and placing them into inventory.

coupon rate The actual interest rate on the bond, usually payable in semiannual installments. The coupon rate normally stays constant during the life of the bond and indicates what the bondholder's annual dollar income will be.

crash of 1987 The market decline on October 19, 1987, in which the Dow Jones Industrial Average declined by 22.6 percent. In the great crash of 1929, the decline was only 12.9 percent. The Toronto Stock Exchange (TSX) declined 17.2 percent over October 19 and 20, 1987.

creditor committee A group of creditors established to run a business to avoid bankruptcy.

credit terms The repayment provisions that are part of a credit arrangement. An example would be a 2/10, net 30 arrangement in which the customer may deduct 2 percent from the invoice price if payment occurs in the first 10 days. Otherwise, the full amount is due.

cross rates The relationship between two foreign currencies expressed in terms of a third currency (the dollar).

crown jewels A targeted company in a takeover may sell a prized division or asset (crown jewel), making the takeover less attractive to the buyer.

cum-rights The situation in which the purchase of a share of common stock includes a right attached to the stock. Also rights-on.

cumulative dividends (See cumulative preferred stock.)

cumulative preferred stock If dividends from one period are not paid to the preferred shareholders, they are said to be in arrears and are then added to the next period's dividends. When dividends on preferred stock are in arrears, no dividends can legally be paid to the common shareholders.

cumulative voting Allows shareholders more than one vote per share. They are allowed to multiply their total shares by the number of directors being elected to determine their total number of votes. This system enables minority shareholders to elect directors even though they do not have 51 percent of the vote.

currency futures contract A futures contract that may be used for hedging or speculation in foreign exchange.

current cost accounting A method of inflation-adjusted accounting. Financial statements are adjusted to reflect changing price levels using specific price indexes related to the specific types of goods being adjusted. This is shown as supplemental information in the firm's annual report.

current yield The yearly dollar interest payment divided by the current market price.

D

Data Universal Number System (D-U-N-S) A unique, nine-digit code assigned by Dun & Bradstreet to each business in its information base.

dealer paper A form of commercial paper that is distributed to lenders through an intermediate dealer network. It is normally sold by industrial companies, utility firms, or financial companies too small to have their own selling network.

dealers Participants in the market who transact security trades over the counter from their own inventory of stocks and bonds. They are often referred to as market makers, since they stand ready to buy and sell their securities at quoted prices.

debenture A long-term unsecured corporate bond. Debentures are usually issued by large, prestigious firms having excellent credit ratings in the financial community.

debt utilization ratios A group of ratios that indicates to what extent debt is being used and the prudence with which it is being managed. Calculations include debt to total assets, times interest earned, and fixed charge coverage.

decision tree A tabular or graphical analysis that lays out the sequence of decisions that are to be made and highlights the differences between choices. The presentation resembles branches on a tree.

declaration date The day on which the board of directors officially states a dividend will be paid.

decremental cash flows The cash flows that are subtracted as a result of an investment decision.

deferred annuity An annuity that will not begin until some time in the future.

deflation Actual declining prices.

degree of combined leverage (DCL) A measure of the total combined effect of operating and financial leverage on earnings per share. The percentage change in earnings per share is divided by the percentage change in sales at a given level of operation. Other algebraic statements are also used (see Formulas 5-8a and 5-8b in Chapter 5).

degree of financial leverage (DFL) A measure of the impact of debt on the earnings capability of the firm. The percentage change in earnings per share is divided by the percentage change in earnings before interest and taxes at a given level of operation. Other algebraic statements are also used, such as Formula 5-5.

degree of operating leverage (DOL) A measure of the impact of fixed costs on the operating earnings of the firm. The percentage change in operating income is divided by the percentage change in volume at a given level of operation. Other algebraic statements are also used, such as Formulas 5-3a and 5-3b.

derivatives These financial contracts give the holder the right to buy or sell a particular commodity or asset at an established price at some time in the future.

diluted earnings per share EPS adjusted for all potential dilution from the issuance of any new shares of common stock arising from convertible bonds, convertible preferred stock, warrants, or any other options outstanding.

dilution of earnings This occurs when additional shares of stock are sold without creating an immediate increase in income. The result is a decline in earnings per share until earnings can be generated from the funds raised.

dilutive effect on shares The potential reduction in market share value as additional shares are issued.

direct paper A form of commercial paper that is sold directly by the lender to the finance company. It is also referred to as finance paper.

discount brokers Buyers and sellers of securities that provide no research to clients; therefore, commissions are generally less expensive than through a full-service broker.

discounted loan A loan in which the calculated interest payment is subtracted or discounted in advance. Because this lowers the amount of available funds, the effective interest rate is increased.

discount rate The interest rate at which future sums or annuities are discounted back to the present.

disinflation A levelling off or slowing down of price increases.

diversification Placing monies in a variety of investments that are somewhat unrelated (less than perfect positive correlation). Variability of returns, or risk, will be reduced.

divestiture A divestiture is the sale or spin-off of a subsidiary or a division of a company.

dividend information content This theory of dividends assumes that dividends provide information about the financial health and economic expectations of the company. If this is true, corporations must actively manage their dividends to provide the market with information.

dividend payment date The day on which a shareholder of record will receive his or her dividend.

dividend payout The percentage of dividends to earnings after taxes. It can be computed by dividing dividends per share by earnings per share.

dividend record date Shareholders owning the stock on the holder-of-record date are entitled to receive a dividend. To be listed as an owner on the corporate books, the investor must have bought the stock before it went ex-dividend.

dividend reinvestment plans Plans that provide the investor with an opportunity to buy additional shares of stock with the cash dividends paid by the company.

dividend tax credit Tax credit accorded to individuals receiving corporate dividends. Its purpose is to compensate for the fact that corporate earnings are taxed in the hands of the corporation and possibly again in the hands of the shareholder.

dividend valuation model A model for determining the value of a share of stock by taking the present value of an expected stream of future dividends.

dividend yield Dividends per share divided by market price per share. Dividend yield indicates the percentage return that a shareholder will receive on dividends alone.

dual trading Exists when one security, such as Alcan common stock, is traded on more than one stock exchange. This practice is common for larger corporations that list on the TSX, the Montreal Exchange, and international exchanges such as New York.

Dun & Bradstreet A credit-rating agency that publishes information on over 30 million business establishments through its Reference Book.

DuPont system of financial analysis An analysis of profitability that breaks down return on assets between the profit margin and asset turnover. The second, or modified, version shows how return on assets is translated into return on equity through the amount of the firm's debt.

Dutch auction preferred stock A preferred stock security that matures every several weeks and is sold (reauctioned) at a subsequent bidding. The concept of Dutch auction means that the stock is issued to the bidder willing to accept the lowest yield, and then to the next lowest bidder, and so on until all of the preferred stock is sold.

E

earnings per share The earnings available to common shareholders divided by the number of common stock shares outstanding.

EBIT/EPS indifference point The amount of operating earnings required for one financing plan to equal an alternative financing plan with respect to the impact on earnings per share.

economic exposure This measure identifies the market value of assets and liabilities, denominated in a foreign currency, that is subject to possible change in market value because of fluctuations in exchange rates.

economic indicators Hundreds of indicators exist, each of which is a specialized series of data. The data are analyzed for their relationship to economic activity, and the indicator is classified as either a lagging indicator, a leading indicator, or a coincident economic indicator.

economic ordering quantity (EOQ) The most efficient ordering quantity for the firm. The EOQ allows the firm to minimize the total ordering and carrying costs associated with inventory.

effective rate of interest Yield that includes compounding effects over a given time period.

efficient frontier A line drawn through the optimum point selections in a risk-return trade-off diagram. Each point represents the best possible trade-off between risk and return (the highest return at a given risk level or the lowest risk at a given return level).

efficient market hypothesis Hypothesis that suggests that markets adjust very quickly to new information and that it is very difficult for investors to select portfolios of securities that outperform the market. The efficient market hypothesis may be stated in many different forms, as indicated in Chapter 14.

electronic communications network (ECNU) Electronic trading systems that automatically match buy and sell orders at specific prices.

electronic funds transfer A system in which funds are moved between computer terminals without the use of written cheques.

EMU The European Monetary Union is the eleven European countries that share a common currency and common interest rates.

euro The common currency shared by the eleven members of the European Monetary Union.

Eurobonds Bonds payable or denominated in the borrower's currency but sold outside the country of the borrower, usually by an international syndicate.

Eurocurrency deposit A unit of currency held on deposit in a bank outside of the country issuing the currency.

Eurodollar certificate of deposit A certificate of deposit in U.S. or Canadian dollars held in a foreign bank.

Eurodollar loan A loan from a foreign bank denominated in dollars.

Eurodollars Dollars held on deposit by foreign banks and loaned out by those banks to anyone seeking dollars.

European Monetary Union (EMU) A group of eleven European countries that will share a common currency (euro) and common interest rate.

EVA The economic value added (EVA) is equal to the formula: net operating profit after taxes minus capital times the cost of capital.

exchange rate The relationship between the value of two or more currencies. For example, the exchange rate between Canadian dollars and French francs is stated as dollars per francs or francs per dollar.

ex-dividend date Two business days before the holder-of-record date. On the ex-dividend date the purchase of the stock no longer carries with it the right to receive the dividend previously declared.

exercise price The price at which a warrant (or other similar security) allows the investor to purchase common stock.

expectations hypothesis The hypothesis maintains that the yields on long-term securities are a function of short-term rates. The result of the hypothesis is that, when long-term rates are much higher than short-term rates, the market is saying it expects short-term rates to rise. Conversely when long-term rates are lower than short-term rates, the market is expecting short-term rates to fall.

expected value A representative value from a probability distribution arrived at by multiplying each outcome by the associated probability and summing up the values.

Export Development Corporation (EDC) Agency of the federal government whose role is to facilitate the financing of Canadian exports through credit insurance, loan guarantees, special loans, and so forth.

expropriate The action of a country in taking away or modifying the property rights of a corporation or individual.

ex-rights The situation in which the purchase of common stock during a rights offering no longer includes rights to purchase additional shares of common stock.

ex-rights date The date after which common shares no longer include rights. Trading of shares, ex-rights, occurs two business days before the actual ex-rights date.

extension An out-of-court settlement in which creditors agree to allow the firm more time to meet its financial obligations. A new repayment schedule is developed, subject to the acceptance of creditors.

externally generated corporate funds Corporate financing raised through sources outside of the firm. Bonds, common stock, and preferred stock fall in this category.

external reorganization A reorganization under the formal bankruptcy laws in which a merger partner is found for the distressed firm. Ideally, the distressed firm should be merged with a strong firm in its own industry, although this is not always possible.

F

factoring receivables Selling accounts receivable to a finance company or a bank.

FASB (Financial Accounting Standards Board) A privately supported rule-making body for the U.S. accounting profession.

federal deficit Government expenditures are greater than government tax revenues, and the government must borrow to balance revenues and expenditures. These deficits act as an economic stimulus.

federal surplus Government tax receipts are greater than government expenditures. A rarity during the past 20 years. These surpluses have a dampening effect on the economy.

Federal Reserve discount rate The rate of interest charged by the U.S. Federal Reserve Bank, as lender of last resort, to the banking system to manage the money supply

field warehousing An inventory financing arrangement in which collateralized inventory is stored on the premises of the borrower but is controlled by an independent warehousing company.

FIFO A system of writing off inventory into cost of goods sold in which the items purchased first are written off first. Referred to as first-in, first-out.

finance paper A form of commercial paper that is sold directly to the lender by the finance company. It is also referred to as direct paper.

financial capital Common stock, preferred stock, bonds, and retained earnings. Financial capital appears on the corporate balance sheet under long-term liabilities and equity.

financial disclosure Presentation of financial information to the investment community.

financial futures market A market that allows for the trading of financial instruments related to a future time. A purchase or sale occurs in the present, with a reversal necessitated in the future to close out the position. If a purchase (sale) occurs initially, then a sale (purchase) will be necessary in the future.

financial intermediary A financial institution, such as a bank or a life insurance company, that directs other people's money into such investments as government and corporate securities.

financial lease A long-term, noncancellable lease. The financial lease has all the characteristics of long-term debt.

financial leverage A measure of the amount of debt used in the capital structure of the firm.

financial markets The place of interaction for people, corporations, and institutions that either need money or have money to lend or invest.

financial risk The risk related to the inability of the firm to meet its debt obligations as they come due.

financial sweetener Usually refers to equity options, such as warrants or conversion privileges, attached to a debt security. The sweetener lowers the interest cost to the corporation.

fiscal deficit (See federal deficit.)

fiscal policy The tax policies of the federal government and the spending associated with its tax revenues.

fixed costs Costs that remain relatively constant regardless of the volume of operations. Examples are rent, amortization, property taxes, and executive salaries.

float The difference between the corporation's recorded cash balance on its books and the amount credited to the corporation by the bank.

floating rate bond The interest payment on the bond that changes with market conditions, rather than the price of the bond.

floating-rate preferred stock The quarterly dividend on the preferred stock changes with market rates. The market price is considerably less volatile than it is with regular preferred stock.

floor value Usually equal to the pure bond value. A convertible bond will not sell at less than its pure bond value even when its conversion value is below the pure bond value.

flotation cost The distribution cost of selling securities to the public. The cost includes the underwriter's spread and any associated fees.

forced conversion Occurs when a company calls a convertible security that has a conversion value greater than the call price. Investors will take the higher of the two values and convert the security to common stock rather than take a lower cash call price.

foreign exchange rate The relationship between the value of two or more currencies. For example, the exchange rate between Canadian dollars and French francs is stated as dollars per francs or francs per dollar.

foreign exchange risk A form of risk that results from a change in value of foreign exchange rates. This risk impacts on economic exposure.

Foreign Investment Review Agency A federal agency established in the early 1970s to review takeovers of large Canadian firms by foreigners. It was disbanded in 1985.

foreign trade deficit A deficit that occurs because Canadians buy more foreign goods than Canadian companies sell to foreigners.

forward rate A rate that reflects the future value of a currency based on expectations. Forward rates may be greater than the current spot rate (premium) or less than the current spot rate (discount). One can contract at this rate.

forwards Forwards are customized contracts that fix the price of some commodity for delivery at a specified price, at a specified amount, and at a specified time in the future. Forwards generally cannot be resold.

founders' shares Stock owned by the original founders of a company. It often carries special voting rights that allow the founders to maintain voting privileges in excess of their proportionate ownership.

four Cs of credit These are used by bankers and others to determine whether a loan will be repaid on time. The four Cs are character, capital, capacity, and conditions.

four pillars of finance Traditional separation of financial institution roles in Canada among chartered banks, trusts, insurance companies, and securities dealers.

fourth market A market of stocks and bonds in which there is direct dealing between financial institutions, such as investment dealers, insurance companies, pension funds, and mutual funds.

free cash flow Cash flow from operating activities, minus expenditures required to maintain the productive capacity of the firm, minus dividend payouts.

fronting loan A parent company's loan to a foreign subsidiary is channelled through a financial intermediary, usually a large international bank. The bank fronts for the parent in extending the loan to the foreign affiliate.

fully diluted earnings per share Equals adjusted earnings after taxes divided by shares outstanding, plus common stock equivalents, plus all convertible securities.

futures Futures are standardized contracts that fix the price of some commodity for delivery at a specified place, at a specified price, and at a specified time in the future. Futures generally trade through a market and can be resold.

futures contract A contract to buy or sell a commodity at some specified price in the future.

future value The value that a current amount grows to at a given interest rate over a given time period.

future value of an annuity The sum of the future value of a series of consecutive equal payments.

G

general partnership A partnership in which all partners have unlimited liability for the debts of the firm.

going private The process by which all publicly owned shares of common stock are repurchased or retired, thereby eliminating listing fees, annual reports, and other expenses involved with publicly owned companies.

golden parachute Highly attractive termination payments made to current management in the event of a takeover of the company.

goodwill An intangible asset that reflects value above that generally recognized in the tangible assets of the firm. It arises when one firm acquires another for an amount greater than the acquired firm's book value.

H

half rate rule In the year of acquisition capital assets are entitled to only half of their designated capital cost allowance.

hedging To engage in a transaction that partially or fully reduces a prior risk exposure by taking a position that is the opposite of your initial position. As an example, you buy some copper now but also engage in a contract to sell copper in the future at a set price.

historical or original cost basis The traditional method of accounting, in which financial statements are developed based on original cost minus depreciation.

holder-of-record date Shareholders owning the stock on the holder-of-record date are entitled to receive a dividend. In order to be listed as an owner on the corporate books, the investor must have bought the stock before it went ex-dividend.

holding company A company that has voting control of one or more other companies. It often has less than a 50 percent interest in each of these other companies.

homemade dividend Cash-payment-like dividend determined by an investor by selling a portion of the investor's share holdings.

homemade leverage The use of leverage directly by investors in place of corporate leverage. It allows investors to bring into balance the value of unlevered and levered firms by providing the missing leverage themselves. Homemade leverage is part of the initial Modigliani and Miller approach.

horizontal integration The acquisition of a competitor.

hurdle rate The minimum acceptable rate of return in a capital budgeting decision.

I

income statement A financial statement that measures the profitability of the firm over a time period. All expenses are subtracted from sales to arrive at net income.

incremental cash flows The identification of only those cash flows that are added as the result of an action or decision.

indenture A legal contract between the borrower and the lender that covers every detail regarding a bond issue.

indexing An adjustment for inflation incorporated into the operation of an economy. Indexing may be used to revalue assets on the balance sheet and to automatically adjust wages, tax deductions, interest payments, and a wide variety of other categories to account for inflation.

inflation The phenomenon of price increase with the passage of time.

inflation premium A premium to compensate the investor for the eroding effect of inflation on the value of the dollar. In the 1980s the inflation premium was 3 to 4 percent. In the late 1970s it was in excess of 10 percent.

information content (See dividend information content.)

initial public offering (IPO) The first time a corporation or government raises capital through the public markets.

insider trading Occurs when someone has information that is not available to the public and then uses this information to profit from trading in a company's common stock.

installment loan A borrowing arrangement in which a series of equal payments are used to pay off the loan.

institutional investors Large investors such as pension funds and mutual funds.

interest factor The tabular value to insert into the various formulas. It is based on the number of periods (n) and the interest rate (i).

interest rate hedging Reduction of the risk of what interest rate one will pay (receive) at some time in the future. Financial futures can be employed.

interest rate parity theory A theory based on the interplay between interest rate differentials and exchange rates. If one country has a higher interest rate than another country after adjustments for inflation, interest rates and foreign exchange rates will adjust until the foreign exchange rates and money market rates reach equilibrium (are properly balanced between the two countries).

internally generated funds Funds generated through the operations of the firm. The principal sources are retained earnings and cash flow added back from depreciation and other noncash deductions.

internal rate of return (IRR) A discounted cash flow method for evaluating capital budgeting projects. The IRR is a discount rate that makes the present value of the cash inflows equal to the present value of the cash outflows.

internal reorganization A reorganization under the formal bankruptcy laws. New management may be brought in and a redesign of the capital structure may be implemented.

international diversification Achieving diversification through many different foreign investments that are influenced by a variety of factors.

International Finance Corporation (IFC) An affiliate of the World Bank established with the sole purpose of providing partial seed capital for private ventures around the world. Whenever a multinational company has difficulty raising equity capital due to lack of adequate private risk capital, the firm may explore the possibility of selling equity or debt (totalling up to 25 percent) to the International Finance Corporation.

intrinsic value The true or inherent worth.

inventory profits Profits generated as a result of an inflationary economy, in which old inventory is sold at large profits because of increasing prices. This is particularly prevalent under FIFO accounting.

inverted yield curve A downward-sloping yield curve. Short-term rates are higher than long-term rates.

Investment Canada The replacement for the Foreign Investment Review Agency. It has a mandate to make Canada a more hospitable place for foreign investment.

investment dealer A financial organization that specializes in selling primary offerings of securities. Investment dealers can also perform other financial functions, such as advising clients, negotiating mergers and takeovers, and selling secondary offerings.

Investment Dealers Association The self-regulatory organization of the Canadian securities industry.

investment tax credit (ITC) For capital investments in certain industries or regions of the country, a specified percentage of the capital cost can be deducted from income taxes payable.

J

junk bond A bond that is not in default, but one that is of questionable quality and speculative in nature.

just-in-time (JIT) inventory management The production process credited to the Japanese whereby parts required on the assembly line arrive at the appropriate station at the exact moment they are required. This cuts down on inventories and requires high quality control.

L

leading indicators Selected statistics that, on average, indicate changes in the business cycle ahead of the economy as a whole. These relate to capital investment, business starts and failures, employment, profits, stock prices, inventory adjustment, housing starts, and the prices of some commodities.

lease A contractual arrangement between the owner of equipment (lessor) and the user of equipment (lessee) that calls for the lessee to pay the lessor an established lease payment. There are two kinds of leases: financial leases and operating leases.

letter of credit A credit letter, normally issued by the importer's bank, in which the bank promises to pay out the money for the merchandise when delivered.

level production Equal monthly production used to smooth out production schedules and employ labour and equipment more efficiently and at a lower cost.

leverage The use of fixed-charge items with the intent of magnifying the potential returns to the firm.

leveraged buyout Existing management or an outsider makes an offer to "go private" by retiring all the shares of the company. The buying group borrows the necessary money, using the assets of the acquired firm as collateral. The buying group then repurchases all the shares and expects to retire the debt over time with the cash flow from operations or the sale of corporate assets.

leveraged lease The lessor for a large capital item may finance a portion with a loan from a financial institution.

LIBOR (See London Interbank Offered Rate.)

life cycle curve A curve illustrating the growth phases of a firm. The dividend policy most likely to be employed during each phase is often illustrated.

LIFO A system of writing off inventory into cost of goods sold in which the items purchased last are written off first. Referred to as last-in, first-out.

limited partnership A special form of partnership to limit liability for most of the partners. Under this arrangement, one or more partners are designated as general partners and have unlimited liability for the debts of the firm, while the other partners are designated as limited partners and are liable only for their initial contribution.

line of credit An established limit up to which a financial institution will lend funds if appropriate security is in place. Although generally available to the borrowing client at any time, the financial institution makes no formal guarantees.

liquidating dividend A final payment made to shareholders when a corporation is wound up or liquidated.

liquidation A procedure that may be carried out under the formal bankruptcy laws when an internal or external reorganization does not appear to be feasible and it appears that the assets are worth more in liquidation than through a reorganization. Priority of claims becomes extremely important in liquidation because it is unlikely that all parties will be fully satisfied in their demands.

liquidity The relative convertibility of short-term assets to cash. Thus, marketable securities are highly liquid assets, while inventory may not be.

liquidity premium theory This theory indicates that long-term rates should be higher than short-term rates. The premium of long-term rates over short-term rates exists because short-term securities have greater liquidity, and therefore higher rates have to be offered to potential long-term bond buyers to entice them to hold these less liquid and more price-sensitive securities.

liquidity ratios A group of ratios that allows one to measure the firm's ability to pay off short-term obligations as they come due. Primary attention is directed to the current ratio and the quick ratio.

listing requirements Financial standards that corporations must meet before their common stock can be traded on a stock exchange. Listing requirements are not standard; instead, they are set by each exchange.

lockbox system A procedure used to expedite cash inflows to a business. Customers are requested to forward their cheques to a post-office box in their geographic region, and a local bank picks up the cheques and processes them for rapid collection. Funds are then wired to the corporate home office for immediate use.

London Interbank Offered Rate (LIBOR) An interbank rate applicable for large deposits in the London market. It is a benchmark rate, just like the prime interest rate in Canada. Interest rates on Eurodollar loans are determined by adding premiums to this basic rate. Most often, LIBOR is lower than the Canadian prime rate.

M

majority voting All directors must be elected by a vote of more than 50 percent. Minority shareholders are unable to achieve any representation on the board of directors.

managing investment dealer An investment dealer who is responsible for the pricing, prospectus development, and legal work involved in the sale of a new issue of securities.

margin The amount paid by a client who uses credit to buy a security, the balance being loaned by the investment dealer. The margin requirement depends on the exchange and the price level of the security being bought on margin.

marginal cost of capital The cost of the last dollar of funds raised. It is assumed that each dollar is financed in proportion to the firm's optimum capital structure.

marginal principle of retained earnings The corporation must be able to earn a higher return on its retained earnings than a shareholder would receive after paying taxes on the distributed dividends.

marginal tax rate The rate that applies to the last dollar of taxable income.

market efficiency Markets are considered to be efficient when (1) prices adjust rapidly to new information; (2) there is a continuous market, in which each successive trade is made at a price close to the previous price (the faster the price responds to new information and the smaller the differences in price changes, the more efficient the market); and (3) the market can absorb large dollar amounts of securities without destabilizing the prices.

market for corporate control The possibility of leveraged buyouts, takeovers, and mergers is suggested as a control on management's tendencies to diverge from the goal of maximization of shareholder wealth.

market maker (See dealers.)

market risk premium A premium over and above the risk-free rate. It is represented by the difference between the market return (Km) and the risk-free rate (Rf), and it may be multiplied by the beta coefficient to determine the additional risk-adjusted return on a security.

market stabilization Intervention in the secondary markets by an investment dealer to stabilize the price of a new security offering during the offering period. The purpose of market stabilization is to provide an orderly market for the distribution of the new issue.

market value maximization The concept of maximizing the wealth of shareholders. This calls for recognition, not only of earnings per share, but also how they will be valued in the marketplace.

market value per share The price of a share traded on a public exchange by open auction.

maturity date The date on which the bond is retired and the principal (par value) is repaid to the lender.

medium-term notes These debt instruments are like bonds but of a shorter time to maturity and are issued in a quicker manner through a POP prospectus.

merger The combination of two or more companies, in which the resulting firms maintain the identity of the acquiring company.

merger arbitrageur A specialist in merger investments who attempts to capitalize on the difference between the value offered and the current market value of the acquisition candidate.

merger premium The part of a buyout or exchange offer that represents a value over and above the market value of the acquired firm.

monetary policy Management by the Bank of Canada of the money supply and the resultant interest rates.

money market accounts Accounts at banks, trust companies, and credit unions in which the depositor receives competitive money market rates on a typical minimum deposit of $1,000.

money market funds A fund in which investors may purchase units for as little as $500 or $1,000. The fund then reinvests the proceeds in high-yielding money market securities. Investors receive their pro rata portion of the interest proceeds daily as a credit to their units.

money markets Competitive markets for securities with maturities of one year or less. The best examples of money market instruments would be treasury bills, commercial paper, and bankers' acceptances.

mortgage agreement A loan that requires real property (plant and equipment) as collateral.

multinational corporation (MNC) A firm doing business across its national borders is considered a multinational enterprise. Some definitions require a minimum percentage (often 30 percent or more) of a firm's business activities to be carried on outside its national borders.

mutually exclusive The selection of one choice precludes the selection of any competitive choice. For example, several machines can do an identical job in capital budgeting. After one machine is selected, the other machines are not used.

N

Nasdaq Market The U.S. computer-based over-the-counter market; it has less stringent listing requirements.

National Association of Securities Dealers (NASD) An industry association that supervises the U.S. over-the-counter securities market.

net income (NI) approach Under the net income approach, it is assumed that the firm can raise all the funds it desires at a constant cost of debt and equity. Since debt tends to have a lower cost than equity, the more debt utilized, the lower the overall cost of capital and the higher the valuation of the firm.

net operating income (NOI) approach Under this approach, the cost of capital and valuation do not change with the increased utilization of debt. Under this proposition, the low cost of debt is assumed to remain constant with greater debt utilization, but the cost of equity increases to such an extent that the cost of capital remains unchanged.

net present value (NPV) The NPV equals the present value of the cash inflows minus the present value of the cash outflows, with the cost of capital used as a discount rate. This method is used to evaluate capital budgeting projects. If the NPV is positive, a project should be accepted.

net present value profile A graphic presentation of the potential net present values of a project at different discount rates. It is very helpful in comparing the characteristics of two or more investments.

net trade credit A measure of the relationship between the firm's accounts receivable and accounts payable. If accounts receivable exceed accounts payable, the firm is a net provider of trade credit; otherwise, it is a net user.

net worth or book value Shareholders' equity minus preferred share ownership. Basically, net worth is the common shareholders' interest as represented by common stock par value, contributed surplus, and retained earnings. If you take all of the assets of the firm and subtract its liabilities and preferred stock, you arrive at net worth.

New York Stock Exchange (NYSE) The largest organized security exchange in the United States. It also has the most stringent listing requirements.

nominal GDP GDP (gross domestic product) in current dollars without any adjustments for inflation.

nominal interest rate Yield expressed without compounding effects over a given time period. Includes real return, inflation premium, and risk premium.

nominal yield A return equal to the coupon rate.

nonfinancial corporation A firm not in the banking or financial services industry. The term would primarily apply to manufacturing, mining, wholesaling, and retail firms.

nonlinear break-even analysis Break-even analysis based on the assumption that cost and revenue relationships to quantity may vary at different levels of operation. Most of our analysis is based on linear break-even analysis.

nonvoting stock Stock that entitles the holder to an equal or greater dividend than voting stock, but not to a vote on company business. Often issued to allow one party to maintain control of the company.

normal yield curve An upward-sloping yield curve. Long-term interest rates are higher than short-term rates.

O

Ontario Securities Commission (OSC) The regulatory body that oversees securities-related activities in Ontario. The OSC sets the standards for other provincial commissions because the majority of dollar volume of securities trading occurs in Toronto.

open-market operations The purchase and sale of government securities in the open market by the Bank of Canada for its own account. The most common method for managing the money supply, it works by increasing or decreasing the cash reserves in the banking system.

operating lease A short-term, nonbinding obligation that is easily cancellable.

operating leverage A reflection of the extent to which capital assets and fixed costs are utilized in the business firm.

options Contract that gives the holder the right but not the obligation to buy or sell an underlying security at a set price for a given time period.

optimum capital structure A capital structure that has the best possible mix of debt, preferred stock, and common equity. The optimum mix should provide the lowest possible cost of capital to the firm.

overnight (call) money The interest rate at which financial institutions lend money to each other for a short period is called the overnight rate.

over-the-counter markets Markets for securities (both bonds and stock) in which market makers, or dealers, transact purchases and sales of securities by trading from their own inventory of securities.

P

parallel loan A Canadian firm that wishes to lend funds to a foreign affiliate (such as a Dutch affiliate) locates a foreign parent firm (such as a Dutch parent firm) that wishes to loan money to a Canadian affiliate. Avoiding the foreign exchange markets entirely, the Canadian parent lends dollars to the Dutch affiliate in Canada, while the Dutch parent lends euros to the Canadian affiliate in the Netherlands. At maturity, the two loans would each be repaid to the original lender. Notice that neither loan carries any foreign exchange risk in this arrangement.

participation provision A small number of preferred stock issues are participating with regard to corporate earnings. For such issues, once the common stock dividend equals the preferred stock dividend, the two classes of securities may share equally (or in some ratio) in additional dividend payments.

partnership A form of ownership in which two or more partners are involved. Like the sole proprietorship, a partnership arrangement carries unlimited liability for the owners. However, there is only single taxation for the partners, an advantage over the corporate form of ownership.

par value Sometimes referred to as the face value or the principal value of the bond. Most bond issues have a par value of $1,000 per bond. Older issues of common and preferred stock may also have an assigned par value.

payback period A value that indicates the time period required to recoup an initial investment. The payback does not include the time-value-of-money concept.

payout ratio (See dividend payout.)

percent-of-sales method A method of determining future financial needs that is an alternative to the development of pro forma financial statements. We first determine the percentage relationship of various asset and liability accounts to sales, and then we show how that relationship changes as our volume of sales changes.

permanent current assets Current assets that will not be reduced or converted to cash within the normal operating cycle of the firm. Though from a strict accounting standpoint the assets should be removed from the current assets category, they generally are not.

perpetuity An investment without a maturity date.

planning horizon The length of time it takes to conceive, develop, and complete a project and to recover the cost of the project on a discounted cash-flow basis.

pledging receivables Using accounts receivable as collateral for a loan. The firm usually may borrow 60 to 80 percent of the value of acceptable collateral.

point-of-sales terminals Computer terminals in retail stores that either allow digital input or use optical scanners. The terminals may be used for inventory control or other purposes.

poison pill A strategy that makes a firm unattractive as a potential takeover candidate. Poison pills may take many different forms.

pooling of interests A method of financial recording for mergers in which the financial statements of the firms are combined, subject to minor adjustments, and goodwill is not created. The use of this method is rarely allowed anymore.

portfolio effect The impact of a given investment on the overall risk-return composition of the firm. A firm must consider not only the individual investment characteristics of a project, but also how the project relates to the entire portfolio of undertakings.

precautionary balances Cash balances held for emergency purposes. Precautionary cash balances are more likely to be important in seasonal or cyclical industries, where cash inflows are more uncertain.

preemptive right The right of current common shareholders to maintain their ownership percentage on new issues of common stock.

preferred stock A hybrid security combining some of the characteristics of common stock and debt. The dividends paid are not tax-deductible expenses of the corporation, as is true of the interest paid on debt.

premium Premium is the price paid for an option contract.

present value The current or discounted value of a future sum or annuity. The value is discounted back at a given interest rate for a specified time period.

present value of an annuity The sum of the present value of a series of consecutive equal payments.

price-earnings ratio The multiplier applied to earnings per share to determine current value. The P/E ratio is influenced by the earnings and sales growth of the firm, the risk or volatility of its performance, the debt-equity structure, and other factors.

primary market Initial sale of corporate securities to investors when a corporation raises capital.

prime rate The rate a bank charges its most creditworthy customers.

private placement The sale of securities directly to a financial institution by a corporation. This eliminates the middleperson and reduces the cost of issue to the corporation.

privatization A process in which investment dealers take companies that were previously owned by the government to the public markets.

profitability index This measure is the ratio of cash inflows to cash outflows in present value terms.

profitability ratios A group of ratios that indicates the return on sales, total assets, and invested capital. Specifically, we compute the profit margin (net income to sales), return on assets, and return on equity.

pro forma balance sheet A projection of future asset, liability, and shareholders' equity levels. Notes payable or cash is used as a plug, or balancing figure, for the statement.

pro forma financial statements A series of projected financial statements. Of major importance are the pro forma income statement, the pro forma balance sheet, and the cash budget.

pro forma income statement A projection of anticipated sales, expenses, and income.

program trading Computer-based trigger points in the market are established for unusually big orders to buy or sell securities by institutional investors.

prospectus A document describing securities offered for sale to the public that includes the important information that has been filed with the appropriate provincial securities commission. It contains the list of officers and directors, financial reports, potential users of funds, and the like. It is for distribution to investors.

proxy Written authorization given by a shareholder to someone else to represent him or her and to vote his or her shares at a shareholders' meeting.

public financial markets Markets in which federal, provincial, and municipal governments raise money for public activities.

public placement The sale of securities to the public through the investment dealer-underwriter process. Public placements must be registered with the provincial securities commission.

public warehousing An inventory financing arrangement in which inventory, used as collateral, is stored with and controlled by an independent warehousing company.

purchase of assets A method of financial recording for mergers in which the difference between the purchase price and the adjusted book value is recognized as goodwill and is amortized over a maximum time period of 40 years.

purchasing power parity theory A theory based on the interplay between inflation and exchange rates. A parity between the purchasing powers of two countries establishes the rate of exchange between the two currencies. Currency exchange rates therefore tend to vary inversely with their respective purchasing powers to provide the same or similar purchasing power.

pure bond value The value of the convertible bond if its present value is computed at a discount rate equal to interest rates on straight bonds of equal risk, without conversion privileges.

put option A put option gives the holder the right to sell an underlying asset at a preset price.

put option writer A put option writer sells a contract giving the purchaser the right to sell an underlying asset at a preset price. The writer has an obligation to buy the underlying asset at the preset price.

R

ratio of bad debts to credit sales Bad debts as a percentage of credit sales. An indication of an aggressive or restrictive credit policy.

real capital Long-term productive assets (plant and equipment).

real GDP GDP (gross domestic product) in current dollars adjusted for inflation.

real rate of return The rate of return an investor demands for giving up the current use of his or her funds on a noninflation-adjusted basis. It is payment for forgoing current consumption. Historically, the real rate of return demanded by investors has been of the magnitude of 2 to 3 percent. However, throughout the 1980s the real rate of return was higher at 5 to 7 percent.

real return bond A financial obligation that promises a coupon payment at a fixed yield above the inflation rate.

recapture The inclusion in income of the capital cost allowance previously taken, when an asset pool closes and the last asset is sold for more than the undepreciated capital cost (UCC). Provided no capital gains occur, the difference between the sale price and the UCC is added to income.

refunding decision The process of retiring an old bond issue before maturity and replacing it with a new issue. Refunding occurs when interest rates have fallen and new bonds may be sold at lower interest rates.

reinvestment assumption An assumption must be made concerning the rate of return that can be earned on the cash flows generated by capital budgeting projects. The NPV method assumes the rate of reinvestment to be the cost of capital, while the IRR method assumes the rate to be the actual internal rate of return.

repatriation of earnings Returning earnings to the multinational parent company in the form of dividends.

replacement cost The cost of replacing the existing asset base at current prices as opposed to original cost.

replacement cost accounting Financial statements based on the present cost of replacing assets.

replacement decision The capital budgeting decision on whether to replace an old asset with a new one. An advance in technology is often involved.

required new funds (RNF) The amount of additional financing needed as a result of sales expansion.

required rate of return That rate of return investors demand from an investment (securities) to compensate them for the amount of risk involved.

reserve requirements The amount of funds chartered banks at one time were required to hold in reserve for each dollar of deposits, as set by the Bank Act.

residual claim to income The basic claim that common shareholders have to income that is not paid out to creditors or preferred shareholders. This is true regardless of whether these residual funds are paid out in dividends or retained in the corporation.

residual theory of dividends This theory of dividend payout states a corporation will retain as much earnings as it may profitably invest. If any income is left after investments, the firm will pay dividends. This theory assumes that dividends are a passive decision variable.

restructuring This can take many forms in a corporation, such as changes in the capital structure (liability and equity on the balance sheet). It can also result in the selling of low-profit-margin divisions, with the proceeds being reinvested in better investment opportunities. Restructuring can result in the removal of the current management team and/or large reductions in the work force.

resultant cash flows These are the cash flows that stem from a possible investment decision.

retractable feature A provision available with a security that entitles the holder to offer the security back to the issuer at a predetermined price at certain future dates.

revolving credit A formal line of credit.

rights offering A sale of new common stock through a preemptive rights offering. Usually, one right will be issued for every share held. A certain number of rights may be used to buy shares of common stock from the company at a set price lower than the market price.

rights-on The situation in which the purchase of a share of common stock includes a right attached to the stock. Also come rights.

risk A measure of uncertainty about the outcome from a given event. The greater the variability of possible outcomes, on both the high side and the low side, the greater the risk.

risk-adjusted discount rate A discount rate used in the capital budgeting process that has been adjusted upward or downward from the basic cost of capital to reflect the risk dimension of a given project.

risk averse An aversion or dislike for risk. To induce most people to take larger risks, there must be increased potential for return.

risk-free rate of interest A return on an investment that has no volatility and hence no risk. It is also the market price for the rent of money with no risk. Treasury bills are for practical purposes considered to be the risk-free rate of interest.

risk-free rate of return Rate of return on an asset that carries no risk. Treasury bills are often used to represent this measure, although longer-term government securities have also proved appropriate in some studies.

risk premium A premium associated with the special risks of an investment. Of primary interest are two types of risk, business risk and financial risk. Business risk relates to the inability of the firm to maintain its competitive position and sustain stability and growth in earnings. Financial risk relates to the inability of the firm to meet its debt obligations as they come due. The risk premium also differs (is greater or less) for different types of investments (bonds, stocks).

S

safety stock Inventory that is held in addition to regular needs to protect against being out of an item.

sale and leaseback An arrangement whereby a capital item is sold to a financial institution and then leased back from that financial institution. The arrangement may free monies and may allow for more effective use of the tax laws.

Saturday night special A merger tender offer that is made just before the market closes for the weekend and takes the target company's officers by surprise.

screen-based market A market for securities with no physical location that facilitates trading on computers and other communications mediums.

seasoned offering The sale of securities that add to the stock of similar securities already outstanding for a corporation or government.

secondary market The market for securities that have already been issued. It is a market in which investors trade back and forth with each other.

secondary offering The sale of a large block of stock in a publicly traded company, usually by estates, foundations, or large individual shareholders.

secondary trading The buying and selling of publicly owned securities in secondary markets, such as the Toronto Stock Exchange and the over-the-counter markets.

secured debt (claim) A general category of debt, which indicates that the loan was obtained by pledging assets as collateral. Secured debt has many forms and usually offers some protective features to a given class of bondholders.

securities Evidence of financial obligation.

Securities and Exchange Commission (SEC) The primary regulatory body for security offerings in the United States.

securitization of assets The issuance of a security that is specifically backed by the pledge of an asset.

security market line A line or formula that depicts the risk-related return of a security based on a risk-free rate plus a market premium related to the beta coefficient of the security.

segmentation theory A theory that government securities are divided into market segments by various financial institutions investing in the market. The changing needs, desires, and strategies of these investors tend to strongly influence the nature and relationship of short-term and long-term interest rates.

self-liquidating assets Assets that are converted to cash within the normal operating cycle of the firm. An example is the purchase and sale of seasonal inventory.

self-liquidating loan A loan expected to be repaid as assets are converted to cash within the normal operating cycle of the firm.

semiannual compounding A compounding period of every six months. For example, a five-year investment in which interest is compounded semiannually would indicate an n value equal to 10 and an i value at one-half the annual rate.

semivariable costs Costs that are partially fixed but still change somewhat as volume changes. Examples are utilities and repairs and maintenance.

sensitivity analysis The altering of one variable at a time within an analysis to determine that variable's impact on the results of the analysis.

serial bond A bond issued by one company or municipality with a series of different maturity dates and interest rates that correspond to rates on competitive bonds with the same maturity and risk.

serial payments A bond may be paid off in installments over the life of the issue.

shareholders' equity The total ownership position of preferred and common shareholders.

shareholders' rights plan A protection plan against a creeping takeover whereby existing shareholders are allowed to buy newly issued shares at a substantial discount from market. This right is activated if a single investor acquires more than a stated percentage (often around 20 percent) of the company's outstanding shares without having reached any agreement with the company's board of directors.

shareholder wealth maximization Maximizing the wealth of the firm's shareholders through achieving the highest possible value for the firm in the marketplace. It is the overriding objective of the firm and should influence all decisions.

simulation A method of dealing with uncertainty in which future outcomes are anticipated. The model may use random variables for inputs. By programming the computer to randomly select inputs from probability distributions, the outcomes generated by a simulation are distributed about a mean; instead of generating one return or net present value, a range of outcomes with standard deviations is provided.

sinking-fund provision A method for retiring bonds in an orderly process over the life of a bond. Each year or semiannually, a corporation sets aside a sum of money equal to a certain percentage of the total issue. These funds are then used by a trustee to purchase the bonds in the open market and retire them. This method prevents the corporation from being forced to raise a large amount of capital at maturity to retire the total bond issue.

sole proprietorship A form of organization that represents single-person ownership and offers the advantages of simplicity of decision making and low organizational and operating costs.

speculative premium The market price of the warrant (or option) minus the warrant's intrinsic value.

spontaneous sources of funds Funds arising through the normal course of business, such as accounts payable generated from the purchase of goods for resale.

spot rate The rate at which the currency is traded for immediate delivery. It is the existing cash price.

standard deviation A measure of the spread or dispersion of a series of numbers around the expected value. The standard deviation tells us how well the expected value represents a series of values.

statement of cash flows (SCF) A required financial statement that outlines a company's cash flows over the course of a specified period.

step-up in the conversion price A feature that is sometimes written into the contract that allows the conversion ratio to decline in steps over time. This feature encourages early conversion when the conversion value is greater than the call price.

stock dividend A dividend paid in stock, rather than cash. A book transfer equal to the market value of the stock dividend is made from retained earnings to the capital stock. The stock dividend may be symbolic of corporate growth, but it does not increase the total value of the shareholders' wealth.

stock repurchase A corporate initiative to buy back its own shares. This decreases the number of shares outstanding.

stock split A division of shares by a ratio set by the board of directors. The par value is divided by the ratio set, and the new shares are issued to the current shareholders of record to increase their shares to the stated level. For example, a two-for-one split would increase your holdings from one share to two shares.

straight-line amortization A method of amortization, which takes the cost of an asset and divides it by the asset's useful life to determine the annual amortization expense. Straight-line amortization creates uniform amortization expenses for each of the years in which an asset is amortized.

strip bond A bond in which the investor only receives the maturity or face value with all coupons removed.

subordinated debenture An unsecured bond in which payment to the holder occurs only after designated senior debenture holders are satisfied.

supernormal growth A rate of corporate growth that cannot be maintained indefinitely.

sustainable growth rate That level of growth in sales that can be maintained by a corporation without seeking additional debt or equity financing to support the increasing investment in assets.

swapped deposit A short-term security offered by chartered banks that involves a foreign currency spot transaction, a foreign currency time deposit, and a forward contract. In effect, the purchaser lends money to the financial institution for investment in a foreign jurisdiction for a specified period. At maturity of the investment, the exchange rate is guaranteed.

sweep account A banking account that allows companies to maintain zero balances with all excess monies swept into an interest earning account.

sweetener (See financial sweetener.)

synergy The recognition that the whole may be equal to more than the sum of the parts. The "2+2=5" effect.

T

takeover tender offer An unfriendly acquisition that is not initially negotiated with the management of the target firm. A tender offer is usually made directly to the shareholders of the target firm.

targeted repurchase A targeted company in a takeover agrees to pay a premium to the acquiring company for the shares already purchased to have them discontinue the acquisition. This is sometimes referred to as greenmail.

tax loss carry-forward A loss that can be carried forward for a number of years to offset future taxable income and perhaps be utilized by another firm in a merger or an acquisition.

tax savings or tax shield The reduction of taxes otherwise payable by the ability to lower taxable income. This takes the form of a deduction to which the taxpayer is entitled.

technical insolvency When a firm is unable to pay its bills as they come due.

temporary current assets Current assets that will be reduced or converted to cash within the normal operating cycle of the firm.

term deposit The lending of money to a financial institution for a specified time period and at a specified rate of interest.

terminal loss A deduction from income occurring when the last item in a CCA pool is sold and the sale price is less than the undepreciated capital cost (UCC). The difference is the amount of the deduction.

term loan An intermediate-length loan in which credit is generally extended from one to seven years. The loan is usually repaid in monthly or quarterly installments over its life, rather than with one single payment.

terms of exchange The buyout ratio or terms of trade in a merger or an acquisition.

term structure of interest rates The term structure shows the relative level of short-term and long-term interest rates at a point in time for securities of equal risk.

third market An over-the-counter market in listed securities. This market was created by traders attempting to buy and sell listed securities at lower commissions than could be obtained on the exchanges.

three-sector economy Households, business, and government are the three sectors in the Canadian economy.

tight money A term to indicate time periods in which financing may be difficult to find and interest rates may be quite high by normal standards.

Toronto Stock Exchange (TSX) The largest organized security exchange in Canada.

trade credit Credit provided by sellers or suppliers in the normal course of business.

traditional approach to cost of capital Under the traditional approach, the cost of capital initially declines with the increased use of low-cost debt, but it eventually goes up due to the greater risk associated with increasing debt.

transaction exposure Foreign exchange gains and losses resulting from actual international transactions when the foreign funds are converted to Canadian dollars. These may be hedged through the foreign exchange market, the money market, or the currency futures market.

transactions balances Cash balances held to pay for planned corporate expenditures such as supplies, payrolls, and taxes, as well as the infrequent acquisitions of long-term capital assets.

translation exposure The foreign-located assets and liabilities of a multinational corporation, which are denominated in foreign currency units and are exposed to losses and gains resulting from their treatment in the parent company's books, based on accounting rules and due to changing exchange rates. This is called accounting or translation exposure.

treasury bills Short-term obligations of the federal government with maturities of up to one year.

treasury shares Corporate stock that has been reacquired by the corporation.

trend analysis An analysis of performance that is made over a number of years to ascertain significant patterns.

trust receipt An instrument acknowledging that the borrower holds the inventory and proceeds for sale in trust for the lender.

S&P/TSX Composite Index The value-weighted index established by Standard and Poor's to represent the capital market value of the Toronto Stock Exchange companies.

two-step buyout An acquisition plan in which the acquiring company attempts to gain control by offering a very high cash price for 51 percent of the shares of the target company. At the same time, the acquiring company announces a second lower price that will be paid, either in cash, stocks, or bonds, at a subsequent point in time.

U

undepreciated capital cost (UCC) The amount within a given CCA class (or pool) of assets available for tax-deductible amortization. The maximum amount of CCA that can be expensed in a given year in relation to a particular CCA class is the UCC multiplied by the applicable CCA rate. Special adjustments have to be made for in-year purchases and sales of assets in the class.

underpricing When new or additional shares of stock are to be sold, investment dealers will generally set the price at slightly below the current market value to ensure a receptive market for the securities.

underwriting The process of selling securities and, at the same time, assuring the seller a specified price. Underwriting is done by investment dealers and represents a form of risk taking.

underwriting spread The difference between the price that a selling corporation receives for an issue of securities and the price at which the issue is sold to the public. The spread is the fee that investment dealers and others receive for selling securities.

underwriting syndicate A group of investment dealers formed to share the risk of a security offering and also to facilitate the distribution of the securities.

unsecured debt A loan that requires no assets as collateral, but allows the bondholder a general claim against the corporation, rather than a lien against specific assets.

V

variable costs Costs that move directly with a change in volume. Examples are raw materials, factory labour, and sales commissions.

vertical integration The acquisition of customers or suppliers by the company.

W

warrant An option to buy securities at a set price for a given time period. Warrants commonly have a life of one to five years or longer, and a few are perpetual.

weighted average cost of capital The computed cost of capital determined by multiplying the cost of each item in the optimal capital structure by its weighted representation in the overall capital structure and summing up the results.

white knight A firm that management calls on to help it avoid an unwanted takeover offer. It is an invited suitor.

working capital management The financing and management of the current assets of the firm. The financial manager determines the mix between temporary and permanent current assets and the nature of the financing arrangement.

write-offs Corporations may choose to expense an asset all in one year, rather than amortize it over several more years, when the corporation believes the asset has declined significantly in value.

Y

yield The interest rate that equates a future value or an annuity to a given present value.

yield curve A curve that shows interest rates at a specific point for all securities having equal risk but different maturity dates. Government securities are usually used to construct such curves. The yield curve is also referred to as the term structure of interest rates.

yield to maturity The required rate of return on a bond issue. It is the discount rate used in present-valuing future interest payments and the principal payment at maturity. The term is used interchangeably with market rate of interest.

Z

zero-coupon rate bond A bond that is sold at a deep discount from face value. The return to the investor is the difference between the investor's cost and the face value received at the end of the life of the bond.

Index

(bolded blue terms are key terms; bolded blue company names indicate that web sites are provided in the text)

A

C

D

E

F

N

O

P

Q

R

S